Research and Innovations in Industrial and Marine Biotechnology: A Circular Economy 2024

The conference proceedings book *Research & Innovations in Industrial & Marine Biotechnology: A Circular Economy 2024* encapsulates the key outcomes of the National Seminar cum Industrial Meet (RIIMBCE-2024), held to advance sustainable practices in biotechnology. Centered on the integration of circular economy principles, this volume brings together pioneering research, expert insights, and case studies that highlight innovative approaches in industrial and marine biotechnology. It presents a unique confluence of academic and industrial perspectives, showcasing developments aimed at addressing environmental challenges and promoting resource efficiency. Through contributions from researchers, industry professionals, and policymakers, the book emphasizes real-world applications, strategic collaborations, and interdisciplinary solutions. Topics covered span biotechnological innovations, sustainable marine practices, industrial bioprocess optimization, and the development of eco-friendly technologies. Distinguished by its dual thematic focus, this proceedings volume serves as a vital resource for those aiming to reshape biotechnology through sustainable and circular models. It offers readers not only current scientific advancements but also a vision for building resilient, green bio-industries. Ideal for academicians, practitioners, and decision-makers, this book bridges research and application, reflecting the transformative potential of biotechnology in a circular economy.

Research and Innovations in Industrial and Marine Biotechnology: A Circular Economy 2024

Editors

Prof. Hrudayanath Thatoi

Dr. Amrita Banerjee

Dr. Sourav Chattaraj

CRC Press
Taylor & Francis Group
Boca Raton London New York

CRC Press is an imprint of the
Taylor & Francis Group, an **informa** business

First edition published 2026
by CRC Press
4 Park Square, Milton Park, Abingdon, Oxon, OX14 4RN

and by CRC Press
2385 NW Executive Center Drive, Suite 320, Boca Raton FL 33431

CRC Press is an imprint of Informa UK Limited

British Library Cataloguing-in-Publication Data
A catalogue record for this book is available from the British Library

ISBN: 978-1-041-28352-2 (hbk)
ISBN: 978-1-041-28285-3 (pbk)
ISBN: 978-1-003-75900-3 (ebk)

DOI: 10.1201/9781003759003

Typeset in Times New Roman
by Aditiinfosystems

Contents

Research and Innovations in Industrial and Marine Biotechnology: A Circular Economy 2024 – Prof. Hrudayanath Thatoi et al. (eds)
© 2026 Taylor & Francis Group, London, ISBN 978-1-041-28285-3

List of Figures

Research and Innovations in Industrial and Marine Biotechnology: A Circular Economy 2024 – Prof. Hrudayanath Thatoi et al. (eds)
© 2026 Taylor & Francis Group, London, ISBN 978-1-041-28285-3

List of Tables

Research and Innovations in Industrial and Marine Biotechnology: A Circular Economy 2024 – Prof. Hrudayanath Thatoi et al. (eds)
© 2026 Taylor & Francis Group, London, ISBN 978-1-041-28285-3

Preface

The National Seminar "Research & Innovations in Industrial & Marine Biotechnology: A Circular Economy (RIIMBCE-2024)" was organized by the Centre for Industrial Biotechnology Research (CIBR), Siksha 'O' Anusandhan Deemed to be University (SOA DU), Bhubaneswar, during 4th and 5th November, 2024. Sponsored by the Department of Science and Technology's Science and Engineering Research Board (DST-SERB), Government of India, and organized in collaboration with the National Research Development Corporation (NRDC) and the Biotechnology Research Society of India (BRSI), this event served as a platform to bridge the knowledge gap between academia and industry. The seminar focused on the critical roles of industrial and marine biotechnology in addressing global challenges such as resource scarcity, environmental degradation, and climate change. Industrial biotechnology emphasizes sustainable alternatives to conventional methods through biological processes, while marine biotechnology harnesses marine resources for applications in food security, pharmaceuticals, and biofuels. The event highlighted the importance of a circular economy, which promotes resource reuse and recycling, minimizing waste and enhancing sustainability. Distinguished dignitaries, including Prof. Pravat Kumar Roul, Vice-Chancellor of Odisha University of Agriculture & Technology, and Prof. Pradipta Kumar Nanda, Vice Chancellor of SOA DU, emphasized the need for innovation-driven solutions. Keynote addresses by renowned experts Prof. Ashok Pandey and Prof. N. Thajuddin provided profound insights into the future of industrial and marine biotechnology. Over 30 professors, researchers, and industry professionals presented their work, enriching the seminar with cutting-edge discussions on topics such as microbial, plant, and animal biotechnology, enzymology and bioprocessing, marine biotechnology, industrial applications in agriculture, medicine, pharmacy, bioresource utilization for rural development, and circular economy. The proceedings "Research and Innovations in Industrial and Marine Biotechnology: A Circular Economy 2024" serve as a comprehensive record of the seminar's knowledge exchange. Around 62 carefully reviewed papers have been submitted for publication, reflecting the high scientific value and relevance of the research presented. These papers cover a diverse range of themes, providing a valuable resource for researchers, educators, and industry practitioners exploring sustainable biotechnology within a circular economy framework. Over 100 authors from various universities, institutes, and companies contributed their research, showcasing a wide range of innovative approaches. Special appreciation is extended to the Academic Committee, Organizing Committee, and supporting staff for their dedication. We extend our sincere gratitude to all the authors whose research contributions enriched the conference and played a vital role in its success. This volume brings together a curated selection of papers presented during the event, featuring insights from both academic and industry researchers. These contributions offer a comprehensive view of advancements in applied biotechnology worldwide. The high scientific quality of these papers serves as a valuable resource for researchers, enabling them to achieve more meaningful outcomes in their work.

Acknowledgement

We express our heartfelt gratitude to all those whose support and contributions made the successful organization of the National Seminar cum Industrial Meet and the compilation of this conference proceedings, *"Research and Innovations in Industrial and Marine Biotechnology: A Circular Economy 2024"*, possible. We are deeply indebted to Prof. (Dr.) Manojranjan Nayak, Hon'ble Founder President, Siksha 'O' Anusandhan (SOA), for his visionary leadership, constant encouragement, and unwavering support in promoting research and innovation across the University. We extend our sincere thanks to Prof. (Dr.) Pradipta Kumar Nanda, Hon'ble Vice Chancellor, SOA Deemed to be University, for his inspiring guidance and administrative support in making this event a success. Our special appreciation goes to all the eminent resource persons, whose valuable insights and expert deliberations enriched the sessions and added immense academic value to the seminar. Our sincere thanks are due to the Deans of all the Schools of SOA Deemed to be University for their continued support, cooperation, and encouragement throughout the planning and execution of this event. We also wish to thank all the faculty members, administrative staff, and technical teams of SOA Deemed to be University whose behind-the-scenes efforts ensured smooth coordination and successful execution of the seminar. We gratefully acknowledge the Science and Engineering Research Board (SERB) of the Department of Science and Technology (DST), Government of India, for their support, and extend our sincere thanks to our collaborators, the National Research Development Corporation (NRDC) and the Biotechnology Research Society of India (BRSI), for their valuable partnership. We gratefully acknowledge the dedicated efforts of all the reviewers who critically evaluated the submissions and helped maintain the academic rigor and quality of the conference proceedings. Finally, we acknowledge all the participants and contributors for their active engagement and scholarly input, which have significantly enriched the scope and relevance of this conference.

Editors

Research and Innovations in Industrial and Marine Biotechnology: A Circular Economy 2024 – Prof. Hrudayanath Thatoi et al. (eds)
© 2026 Taylor & Francis Group, London, ISBN 978-1-041-28285-3

About the Editors

Prof. Hrudayanath Thatoi

Prof. Hrudayanath Thatoi, Director at Centre for Industrial Biotechnology Research, Siksha O Anusandhan Deemed to be University, Bhubaneswar, is a distinguished biotechnologist and former Head of Department, Biotechnology, Maharaja Sriram Chandra Bhanja Deo University, Baripada with over 370 publications, 28 Ph.D. scholars guided, and notable roles in academia and research. His impactful contributions to environmental biotechnology are widely recognized, with over 11000 citations, an h-index of 50, and extensive leadership experience. He is the recipient of the prestigious Samanta Chandra Sekhar award by DST, Govt. of Odisha and the Lifetime Devotion Award by Microbiologist Society, India 2025 among other awards.

Dr. Amrita Banerjee

Dr. Amrita Banerjee, Assistant Professor at Siksha O Anusandhan Deemed to be University, Bhubaneswar, holds a Ph.D. in Microbiology with 15 years of research and 7 years of teaching experience. She has 45 publications and 5 book chapters, with notable COVID-19 research contributions in immunoinformatics, enzyme technology, vaccine development, and cancer biology diagnostics.

Dr. Sourav Chattaraj

Dr. Sourav Chattaraj, Assistant Professor at Siksha O Anusandhan Deemed to be University, Bhubaneswar, specializes in Aquaculture Biotechnology. Holding a Ph.D. in Microbiology, he has published extensively in reputed journals, contributed books and chapters, and serves as editor and reviewer. His research spans aquaculture, nanotechnology, probiotics, immunology, and fermentation and feed technology.

Research and Innovations in Industrial and Marine Biotechnology: A Circular Economy 2024 – Prof. Hrudayanath Thatoi et al. (eds)

1 DNA Barcode based Cultivar Authentication in Allamanda L. Using rbcL Conserve Regions

Subhadarshani Dhall,
Mahima Patra, Laxmikanta Acharya*
Molecular Biology and Genetic Engineering Lab,
Centre for Biotechnology, School of Pharmaceutical Sciences,
Siksha 'O' Anusandhan (Deemed to be University),
Bhubaneswar, Odisha, India

Abstract: *Allamanda* L. is a perennial plant that belongs to the family Apocynaceae and has a cosmopolitan distribution. The plant is also known as the golden trumpet flower. This plant can withstand heat and several poisonous substances; it can also stimulate blood circulation and diuresis. It is effective against snake bites. It is used in traditional medicine to treat skin infections, and different inflammations. Flavonoids, polyphenols, tannins, and alkaloids are among the secondary metabolite chemicals found in this plant. Some pharmacological research determined that this plant has remarkable bioactivities such as wound healing, anti-inflammatory, anti-microbial, and so on. In the present investigation, five cultivars were identified utilising globally accepted conserved DNA sequences or DNA barcodes. DNA barcoding depends on genetic marker technology, mostly employed for diversity assessment or species identification. We examined five unique taxa of *Allamanda* L. (*Allamanda cathartica* yellow single large whorl, *Allamanda cathartica* yellow double whorl, *Allamanda blanchetti* purple single whorl, *Allamanda violacea* sandal single whorl, *Allamanda schottii* yellow small whorl) has been collected from Bhubaneswar, Odisha. Employing nine conserved barcode loci: psbK-psbL, trnH-psbA, rpoB, matK, rpoC, atpF-atpH, and rbcL. The amplified portions of the rbcL barcode primers showed insertion and deletion based on phylogenetic analysis and sequencing, resulting in consistent separation of all five cultivars. As a result, these markers may be used to differentiate among different cultivars of *Allamanda* L. The focus is on investigating DNA barcoding is used to verify the authenticity and dependability of herbal and plant-based medicinal products. This helps to minimize potential health risks associated with substitute products and contamination.

Keyword: *Allamanda*, DNA barcode, In/del, rbcL, SNPs, Genetic marker

1. INTRODUCTION

DNA barcodes are standardised sequences that are ideally distinct, whether they encode proteins or not, and are extracted from the genetic material of the organism or from its cellular organelles. Species richness is a key element of biodiversity, while intraspecific genetic variation is the primary driver of evolutionary change. The species constitutes the essential unit of biodiversity, whereas the variety of intra-specific genetic variation underpins the foundation of biodiversity. Biodiversity encompasses the complex variety of life, including species distinctions and genetic diversity, which enhance the endurance and adaptation of ecosystems [1]. The traditional taxonomy system has inherent drawbacks, especially since it relies heavily on morphological standards. Variability and ambiguity are introduced into the identification process by vegetative features, which are subject to environmental effects [2]. Taxonomists are increasingly employing DNA barcoding, a genetic technique that uses short DNA sequences from specific genomic loci within an organism's genome to classify it as a species. This method

*Corresponding author: laxmikantaacharya@soa.ac.in

DOI: 10.1201/9781003759003-1

involves aligning a DNA sequence from an unidentified specimen with a reference database of DNA barcodes established. *Allamanda* Linn. is a tropical flowering plant genus belonging to the Apocynaceae family. *Allamanda* L. is native to Central and South America, particularly Brazil, and is often grown as an ornamental plant due to its vibrant and eye-catching flowers, which are typically bright yellow but can also be pink or purple depending on the species. It's distinguished by its whorled leaf structure, infundibuliform corolla, hairs within and the plant has pollen sacs, a stigma with a basal ring-shaped structure, dry, splitting fruits with a spiny outer surface, and winged seeds [3; 4]. The plant blooms year-round, with fruit production occurring from April to July and in October. *Allamanda* L. is documented in botanical literature as having extensive global distribution in warm areas [5]. The genus *Allamanda* L. is an evergreen plant family that has a cosmopolitan distribution in tropical and subtropical zones. It has fifteen recognised species, including *A. puberula, A. blanchetti, A. cathartica, A. doniana, A. weberbaueri , A. laevis, A. martii, A. nobilis, A. oenotherifolia, A. calcicola , A. polyantha, , A. setulosa, A. thevetifolia, A. augustifolia*, and *A. schottii* [6]. It is not only appreciated for its beauty but also has some traditional medicinal applications. This plant is useful for medicine because it has many phytochemicals in it, including phenols, tannins, flavonoids, anthocyanins, glycosides, plumieride saponins, terpenoids, alkaloids, steroids, iridoids, lignins, etc. This plant can withstand heat and several poisonous substances. It is used in traditional medicine to treat skin infections and various inflammations, stimulates blood circulation and diuresis, and is effective against snake bites [7]. The plant contains bioactive compounds that can act as antibacterial, antioxidant, and anti-inflammatory properties [5]. Genomic DNA barcoding helps for the undisputed identification of species variation in complicated biological ecosystems by comparing the sequence of standardised gene sections. This method utilizes standardised, short DNA sequences from specific genomic loci (between four hundred and eight hundred base pairs) as "barcodes" to identify known species and assess species richness and community composition . One popular method for identifying species or variants is DNA barcoding based on molecular markers. It has been shown to be a successful technique for species identification and is currently frequently utilised in the assessment and documentation of biological resources. Conserved chloroplast regions like psbK-psbI, rpoB, matK, trnH-psbA, rpoC, atpF-atpH, and rbcL for plant and mitochondrial COI region are needed for the animal DNA barcoding . The capacity to reliably identify a significant difference between the average genetic distances within a species and conserved DNA barcodes across species is essential for successful species identification. DNA barcoding, which usually requires a small and recoverable DNA fragment, has recently attracted a lot of interest from the fields of bio-conservation, systematics, forensic investigation, and ecology The preservation of this significant and endangered ethnomedical plant bioresource, the identification of species with precision, the finding of traditional knowledge regarding the use of these plants, and the enhancement of these plants through biological prospecting. Five distinct *Allamanda* varieties that were gathered from Bhubaneswar, Odisha, were examined in this study. Nine conserved locus barcode sections (psbK-psbI, rpoB, matK, trnH-psbA, rpoC, atpF-atpH, and rbcL) were the target of the analytical investigation. The discovery of appropriate In/Del and any SNPs that might be specifically linked to a particular variety.

2. Materials and Methods

2.1 Collection of Leaf Sample

Early leaf developmental stages from each of the five Allamanda species were gathered in Bhubaneswar, Odisha. Fresh, disease-free plants were collected with local consent from the Regional Plant Research Centre in Odisha (20.188 N, 85.622 E). The department (SOAU/CBT/2024/ER/11) kept a voucher specimen in an ecologically controlled greenhouse for future use. Experimental plant research complies with institutional, national, and international rules and laws.

2.2 Isolation of DNA

The modified Doyle & Doyle DNA isolation process was used to recover genomic DNA from fresh leaf tissue [8]. In comparison the normal uncut lambda DNA band intensity in an Agarose Gel of 0.8% stained with EtBr, the amount of pure DNA was determined. DNA samples were diluted to a working concentration of 25 ng/μL with nuclease-free water. The BOLD Systems database provided the barcode primer sequences. These primers were used in PCR amplification to create DNA barcodes.

2.3 Amplification of PCR

In this amplication, Applied Bio Systems' Veriti 96 well and GeneAmp 9700 thermal cyclers are utilised. A 25 μl reaction mixture was prepared for the experiment, which was then performed 35 times under various heat settings. Five minutes of initial denaturation at 96 °C, one minute of denaturation at 92 °C, one minute of annealing at a temperature that varied based on the primer set, and two minutes of extension at 72 °C were among the temperatures used. The last extension stage was carried out for seven minutes at 72 °C. 1.5% agarose gel electrophoresis was used for the analysis of the PCR-amplified products [9].

2.4 PCR Product Purification and Sequencing

The visible bands were extracted using the PCR results from a pair of primer sets (LKB 15-16), which produced the Silica Bead DNA Gel Extraction Kit. The Silica Bead

DNA Extraction Kit from Thermo-Fisher Scientific was used to extract only amplified genes with expected band sizes from gels using the technique described below. The separated DNA fragments that were present in the agarose gel were cut into the desired DNA pieces using a scalpel blade. The isolated DNA segments were then illuminated by the UV illuminator. The DNA fragments from the gel bits were immediately transferred into numerous microcentrifuge tubes. Weights of eluted gel fragments were recorded. The gel fragments were then placed in numerous micro-centrifuge tubes, and high concentrated gel melting solution was added in an amount three times the weight of the gel slice. The gel was then completely melted by immersing these centrifuge tubes in a water bath at 55 °C for an additional 10-15 minutes. After being removed from the water bath, the tubes were filled with 10µl of silica gel and centrifuged at ambient temperature for one minute at 10,000 rpm. Following centrifugation, the supernatants were removed from each micro-centrifuge tube holding the pellets, and 1ml of an ultra-clean solution was added. The samples were centrifuged again at 10,000 rpm for 1 minute at room temperature to pellet cellular debris. The supernatant was carefully removed, and the pellet was washed twice with ultraclean solution. The samples were then centrifuged again to remove residual contaminants. After discarding the supernatants, to each micro-centrifuge tube 50µl of nuclease-free water was added and was gently mixed by tapping. They were allowed to incubate for 5-10 minutes at room temperature. The pellets were discarded after a second centrifugation at 10,000 rpm for 1 minute. After collecting the final supernatants, they were transferred to new micro-centrifuge tubes. After purification, the Sanger sequencing method was used to sequence the PCR results on an ABI3730XL platform. Using the appropriate primers, both forward and backward sequencing were carried out.

2.5 Sequence Analysis

CAP3 Sequence Assembly Program (PRABI-Doua) (https://doua.prabi.fr/software/cap3) clipped acquired sequences to create consensus sequences. The sequences identified for rbcL (LKB 15-16) were around 550 bp, respectively. The open reading frames (ORFs) within the nucleotide sequences were identified (https://www.ncbi.nlm.nih.gov/orffinder), and the corresponding amino acid sequences were determined using the Expasy Translate Tool (https://web.expasy.org/translate). The Clustal X tool was used for sequence alignment or individual rbcL and rpoB sequences for the combined dataset. The CLUSTAL multiple sequence alignment approach was used with the MUSCLE (3.8) technique to compute both intra- and inter-species divergence [11; 12].

2.6 Phylogenetic Analysis

MUSCLE (3.8) was used to perform multiple sequence alignment of the nucleotide sequences based on pairwise nucleotide sequence comparisons, and MEGA 11's distance matrices were used to analyse the evolutionary relationships among the five cultivars of the *Allamanda* species taken for the present study.

3. Results and Discussion

In the present study, five species of *Allamanda* had been collected (Fig. 1.1. & Table 1.1). The five DNA barcodes, rpoB, atpF-atpH rpoC, trnH-psbA, psbK-psbL, matK, and rbcL were effectively amplified; therefore, in Fig. 1.2. a sharp DNA band was seen in agarose gel electrophoresis, which, after purification, yielded good sequencing

Fig. 1.1 Different *Allamanda* L. cultivars collected from different parts of Odisha

Table 1.1 The exterior features of several cultivars of *Allamanda* L.

Name of the cultivar, morphological description	Allamanda cathartica yellow single large whorl	Allamanda cathartica yellow double whorl	Allamanda blanchetti purple single whorl	Allamanda violacea sandal single whorl,	Allamanda schottii yellow small whorl
Flower Colour	Yellow	Golden yellow	Purple	Deep purple (violaceous)	Bright yellow
Average Leaf Length(cm)	5-17 cm long	5-10 cm	10-20 cm	10-20 cm	6-12 cm
Petal Arrangement	Quincuncial	Quincuncial	Quincuncial (over-lapping, twisted)	Quincuncial (over-lapping, twisted)	Quincuncial (over-lapping, twisted)
Seed Number	2-4 seeds	6-10 seeds.	6-10 seeds	4-6 seeds	6-8 seeds
Seed size (cm)	1.2-1.5 cm	1.2-1.5cm	1-2 cm	1.5-2.5cm	1-2 cm
Flower Symmetry	Radial (Actinomorphic)	Radial (Actinomorphic)	Radial (Actinomorphic)	Radial (Actinomorphic)	Radial (Actinomorphic)

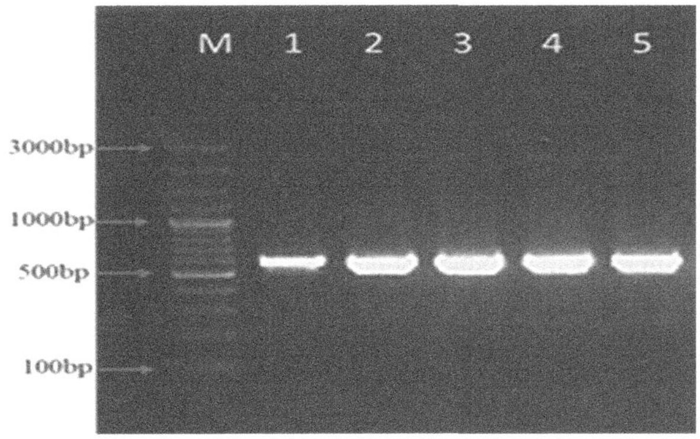

Fig. 1.2 The gel picture shows unique bands (~550 bp) for the rbcL barcode primer in five cultivars of *Allamanda* L

Table 1.2 The SNPs and In/Dels found in rbcL in the five cultivars of Allamanda were determined to be as follows following multiple sequence alignment

SL No.	Code	Cultivar Name	SNPs	In/Del
1	MP7	*Allamanda cathartica* yellow single large whorl	7	3
2	MP8	*Allamanda cathartica* yellow double whorl	9	3
3	MP9	*Allamanda blanchetti* purple single whorl	1	4
4	MP11	*Allamanda violacea* sandal single whorl	7	1
5	MP12	*Allamanda schottii* yellow small whorl	1	3

findings. After distance and phylogenetic analysis, all DNA markers yielded distinct base-pair lengths with insertions or deletions (Fig. 1.3.). The lack of traditional taxonomists and differences in obvious characteristics have made species identification difficult. Sequencing amplified segments from conserved areas rbcL a showed many variants, transitions, transversions, and In/Dels [12]. Unique SNPs and In /Del have been discovered to be useful for precise species identification. Incase of *Allamanda cathartica* yellow double whorl the unique SNP higher, which is different from other species of *allamanda* and similarly *Allamanda blanchetti* purple single whorl has been shown higher number of In/Del. According to the analysis given earlier [13]. Genetic variation within each cultivar was indicated by the identification of five different rbcL barcode sequences for each of the five cultivars. By doing multiple sequence alignment analysis, we were able to determine the frequency of insertions and deletions (In/Dels) and single nucleotide polymorphisms (SNPs) in the sequences. Table 1.2 provides a list of all the insertions and deletions (In/Dels) and single nucleotide polymorphisms (SNPs) found in the rbcL barcode. In rbcL, single nucleotide polymorphisms (SNPs) are present in all sequences, in contrast to the other sequences, and they include both insertion and deletions. Total Unique single nucleotide polymorphism and In/Del has been 25 and 14 respectively. The highest number of SNPs ad In/Del are present in *Allamanda cathartica* yellow double whorl. Comparing *Allamanda cathartica* yellow single large whorl and *Allamanda cathartica* yellow double whorl, The position of SNPs and In/Dels has caught our attention as an interesting feature. However, *Allamanda schottii* and *Allamanda violacea* sandal single whorl has been somehow similar to each other. We observed an exclusive In/Dels for *Allamanda blanchetti* purple single whorl. It has been possessing highest number of SNPs and also In/Dels as compare to all other cultivar. The analysis identifies conserved areas in *Allamanda* L. cultivars, which can be used to authenticate taxons at varietal level. It is possible to develop distinct primers for cultivar identification using these sequence-specific areas. The cultivars are highly diverse, forming unique groups (Fig. 1.3). Comparative chloroplast DNA, intergenic spacers, and SNPs in rbcL barcode regions can serve as molecular markers for distinguishing between and within cultivars, enabling further genetic diversity studies.

4. Conclusion

In order to authenticate five species of *Allamanda* L. cultivars, we have examined the usage of DNA barcode markers in this work. The exclusive gaps, In/Dels and

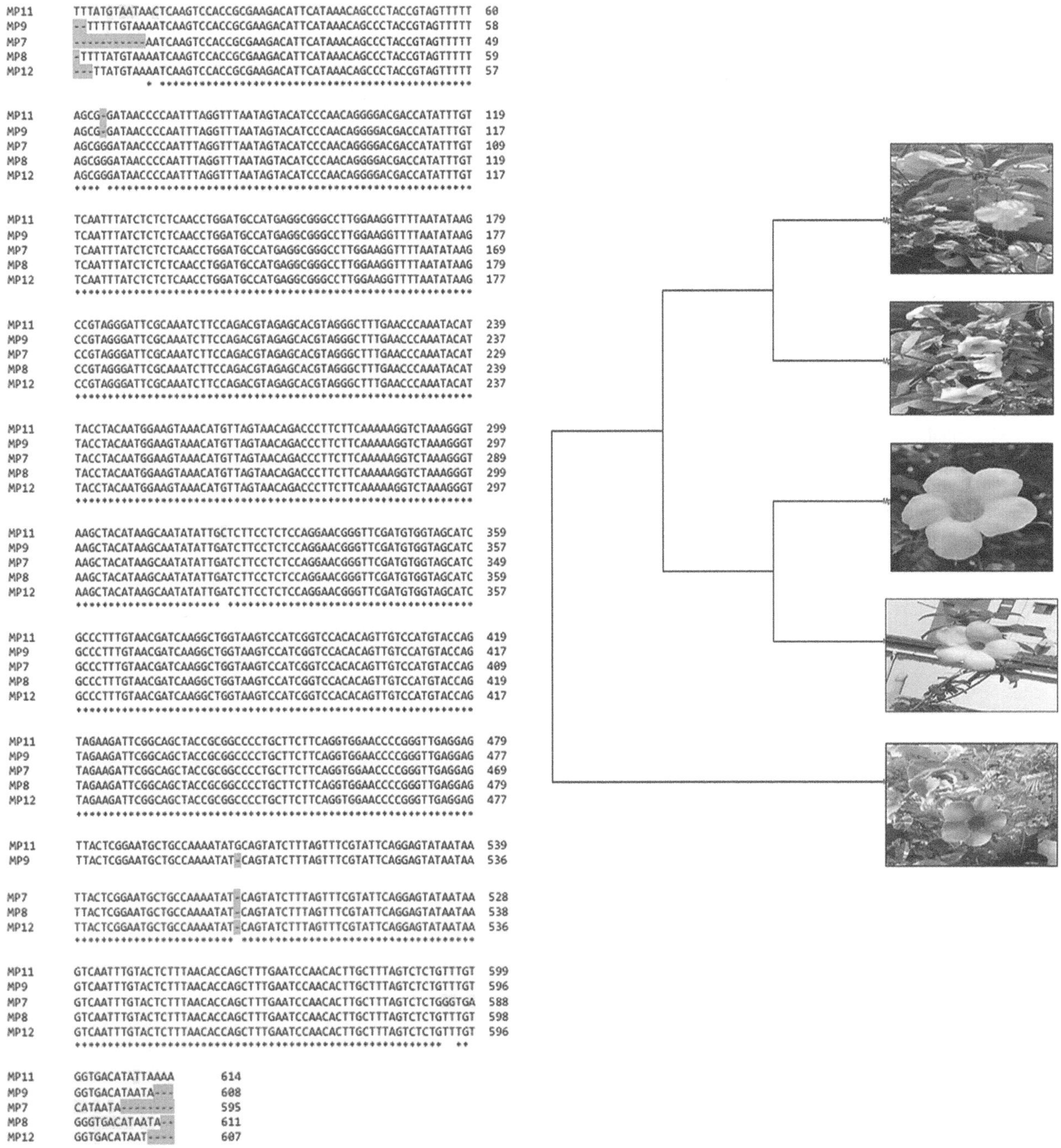

Fig. 1.3 Multiple sequence alignment and phylogenetic analysis of five *Allamanda* L. rbcL sequences

SNPs detected in intra-genetic distance and inter-species distance make it easier to identify the aforementioned taxa. Although we have only considered a tiny percentage of the conserved parts, we will be able to remark on the outcome further if we sequence the entire rbcL and additional genes associated to barcoding. Therefore, the DNA barcode marker technology is a viable choice for settling taxonomy disputes, detecting illegally trafficked species, and figuring out whether herbal products are contaminated. It may also be useful in determining the genetic connections among the varied species. Therefore, determining the genetic relationships between the many species in the tribe may be aided by the DNA barcode marker technique.

ACKNOWLEDGMENTS

All authors thank Prof. (Dr.) Manojranjan Nayak, Founder, and President, Siksha 'O' Anusandhan (Deemed to be University), Bhubaneswar, Odisha, India for providing the required infrastructure for the study. The authors are grateful to the Head, Centre for Biotechnology and Dean, School of Pharmaceutical Sciences, Siksha O Anusandhan (Deemed to be University) for the support.

References

1. Mora, Camilo et al. 2011. "How Many Species Are There on Earth and in the Ocean?" *PLoS Biology* 9(8): 1–8.
2. Sawarkar, Ankush D. et al. 2021. "Traditional System Versus DNA Barcoding in Identification of Bamboo Species: A Systematic Review." *Molecular Biotechnology* 63(8): 651–75. https://doi.org/10.1007/s12033-021-00337-4.
3. Apocynaceae, L Species, Nesamony Memorial, Christian College, and Tamil Nadu. 2023. "The Comparative Morphology Study of Three Allamanda." 6(11): 473–78.
4. Chaveerach, Arunrat et al. 2010. "Genetic Verification and Chemical Contents Identification of Allamanda Species (Apocynaceae)." 1: 417–24.
5. Petricevich, Vera L, and Rodolfo Abarca-vargas. 2019. "Allamanda Cathartica : A Review."
6. Balkrishna, Acharya et al. 2022. "Phytochemical, Medicinal, and Green Approaches of Allamanda Cathartica L.: A Mini Review." *Current Indian Science* 1.
7. Implications, Clinical. 2022. "Inflammation and Oxidative Stress in Snakebite Envenomation :" : 1–13.
8. Aras, Sümer, Ahmet Duran, and Gülay Yenilmez. 2003. "Isolation of DNA for RAPD Analysis from Dry Leaf Material of Some Hesperis L. Specimens." *Plant Molecular Biology Reporter* 21(4).
9. Gupta, Shweta et al. 2008. "Analogy of ISSR and RAPD Markers for Comparative Analysis of Genetic Diversity among Different Jatropha Curcas Genotypes." *African Journal of Biotechnology* 7(23): 4230–43.
10. Chenna, Ramu et al. 2003. "Multiple Sequence Alignment with the Clustal Series of Programs." 31(13): 3497–3500.
11. Karlsen, Christian R, and Nils P Willassen. 2021. "Phylogenetic Revision of the Genus Aliivibrio : Intra- and Inter-Species Variance Among Clusters Suggest a Wider Diversity of Species." 12(February).
12. Ferri, Emanuele et al. 2009. "Integrated Taxonomy: Traditional Approach and DNA Barcoding for the Identification of Filarioid Worms and Related Parasites (Nematoda)." *Frontiers in Zoology* 6(1): 1–12.
13. Taranto, F. et al. 2016. "Genome-Wide SNP Discovery and Population Structure Analysis in Pepper (Capsicum Annuum) Using Genotyping by Sequencing." *BMC Genomics* 17(1): 1–13. http://dx.doi.org/10.1186/s12864-016-3297-7.

Note: All the figures and tables in this chapter were made by the authors.

Research and Innovations in Industrial and Marine Biotechnology: A Circular Economy 2024 – Prof. Hrudayanath Thatoi et al. (eds)

2 Isolation, Assessment, Identification and Characterization of the Phyto-Compounds for the Control of Beetles Infesting Stored Groundnut (*Arachis hypogaea L.*)

Lalit Chowdhury*,
Manoja Dash, Sarada Mohapatra
GIET University, India
Debasis Mohanty,
Prakash Kumar Sahoo
Department of Chemistry, BJB Autonomous College, India
Sushree Chowdhury
Gwinnett Technical College, Georgia, USA

Abstract: The efficacy of many plants was tested against the major pests of groundnuts, under artificial conditions, in the Lab for 365 days. Aromatic Oils obtained by Clevengers instrument, @1% (v/w) of *Pongamia glabra*, *Azadirachta indica*, *Brassica campestris*, Crown oil (Resin of *Shorea robusta*), *Cymbopogon nardus, Dalbergia sisso, Oryza sativa*, *Helianthus annus*, *Ricinus communis*, *Aegle marmelos*, *Sesamum indicum* etc were tested for their bioefficacy against the major pests, of shelled groundnuts, *Trogoderma granarium*, and *Rhyzopertha dominica* for 365 days. Out of all these plant products *Cymbopogon nardus* (Citronella) oil and Crown oil (Resin of *Shorea robusta*) gave total protection. The LD50 parameter was estimated as - 0.5% v/w . Spectroscopic GC MS analysis of Citronella oil (*Cymbopogon nardus*), lead to the identification of D-Limonene, Neral, Citral as major constituents. Spectroscopic GC MS analysis of Crown oil (Resin of *Shorea robusta*) are identified as 2-Ethyl-oxetane (RT 2.223), as the major products.

Keywords: Clevengers apparatus, *Trogoderma granarium*, *Rhyzopertha dominica* and LD_{50}

1. Introduction

Groundnut, *Arachis hypogaea* (L.) is an oilseed crop of India and popularly known as peanut or earthnut. *Trogoderma granarium* and *Rhyzopertha dominica* are main pests of stored groundnuts under hot dry conditions. India has a rich flora of economic importance especially higher plants having pesticidal properties [1]. About 2000 species of botanicals were reported having biopesticidal bio-active components [6]. The existing information on insecticidal, repellant and feeding deterrent properties of plant components was reviewed by McIndoo [7]. Jacobson [8]. Botanical insecticides tend to have a wide activity[9]. They are safe and specific in their mode of action, easy to process and use [10,11]. There is a need to explore these plant products for their biopesticidal properties against the beetles *Trogoderma granarium* and *Rhyzopertha dominica*

Hence the experiment was set up to find out the bioefficacy of certain phyto products against beetles *Trogodermagranarium* and *Rhyzopertha dominica* for their use in control of the losses caused by these insects on shelled groundnuts.

*Corresponding author: lalitchowdhuryoes@gmail.com

DOI: 10.1201/9781003759003-2

2. Materials and Methods

First the promising plants were screened against the beetles *Trogoderma granarium* and *Rhyzopertha dominica* their bioefficacy was tested. The effectiveness of certain plant products (table) were tested under artificial infestation in laboratory conditions for nine months. Hundred grams of groundnut pods/Kernels were taken in glass bottles in three replicated sets for each test plant products.

Oil formulations extracted by **Clevenger's apparatus** (Hydro distillation method) were applied @ 0.1% v/w to the pods/Kernels. The cut leaves of the plants were inserted into the 5000 ml Flask of the Clevenger's Apparatus for extraction of volatile essential oils.

Ten pairs of freshly emerged live beetles of equal number of both sexes were released into each bottle 24 hours after treatment. The adult male & female population of the test insect was counted and recorded at intervals of 24h, 48h, 72h, 96h, and 3 months of release. The final adult male and female population of test was recorded after 270 days of release.

Fig. 2.1 Samples of plant extracts

Fig. 2.2 Clevengers apparatus

The percent reduction of beetle population over control has been calculated using the formula as follows –

The % Population Decrease

$$= \frac{\textbf{Insects in control} - \textbf{Insects in treatment}}{\textbf{Insects in control}} \times 100$$

The values were analyzed statistically for presentation in the tables. That active ingredients of the most effective oil formulations were further analysed by Gas chromatography mass spectroscopy to find out the chemical structure of the active components.

2.1 GCMS Analysis

Both Citronella oil and crown oil proved efficacious against the beetles *Trogoderma granarium* and *Rhyzopertha dominica.*

The major compounds identified in the GC MS study of the isolated Citronella oil (*Cymbopogon nardus*) are as follows-

Table 2.1 Comparative study of efficacy of essential oils against the test insects

Sr. No	Treatment	Concentration of Treatment	Beetle population after 270 days			Mean Beetle population	% Reduction of beetle population over Control
			R1	R2	R3		
1.	*Arachis hypogea* (Groundnut Oil)	0.1% v/w	21	30	23	24.66	64.77
2.	*Menthaspicata* (Mint Oil)	0.1% v/w	27	17	19	21.0	70.00
3.	*Pongamiaglabra* (Karanja Oil)	0.1% v/w	21	30	23	22.66	68.57
4.	*Brassica campestris* (Mustard Oil)	0.1% v/w	41	37	38	36.67	47.61
5.	*Azadirachtaindica* (Neem Oil)	0.1% v/w	11	10	21	19.67	71.9
6.	*Aeglemarmelos* (Bael Oil)	0.1% v/w	27	34	21	28	60.0
7.	*Sesamumindicum* (Til Oil)	0.1% v/w	28	17	13	20.34	70.94
8.	Crown oil (*Shorea robusta*)	0.1% v/w	**NIL**	**NIL**	**NIL**	**NIL**	**100.00**
9.	*Oryza sativa* (Rice bran oil)	0.1% v/w	24	22	26	24	65.71
10.	*Helianthus annus* (Sunflower Oil)	0.1% v/w	45	47	41	40.34	42.37
11.	*Ricinuscommunis* (Castor Oil)	0.1% v/w	31	41	45	34.34	50.94
12.	*Dalbergiasisso* (Sisso Oil)	0.1% v/w	36	42	41	32.67	53.32
13.	*Linumusitatissamum* (Linseed Oil)	0.1% v/w	42	44	38	45.67	34.75
14.	Citronella oil (*Cymbopogon nardus*)	0.1% v/w	**NIL**	**NIL**	**NIL**	**NIL**	**100.00**
	Control		**72**	**68**	**70**	**70**	

Table 2.2 Characteristics of active components of efficacious essential oils (citronella and crown oils)

Sl. No.	Name of the Oil	Major component	Structure	Remark
1	Citronella oil (*Cymbopogon nardus*)	D-Limonene	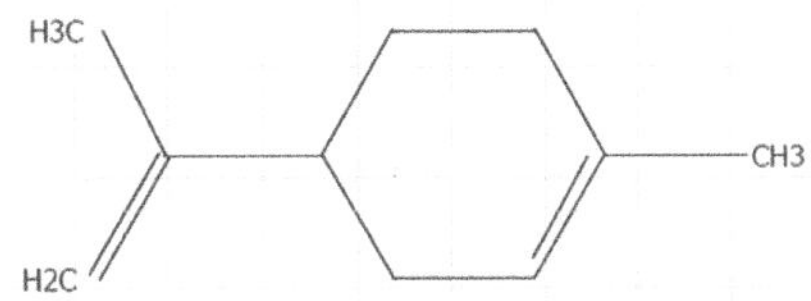	Pleasant citrus aroma, Insect Repellents, Deodorizing Properties
2		Neral	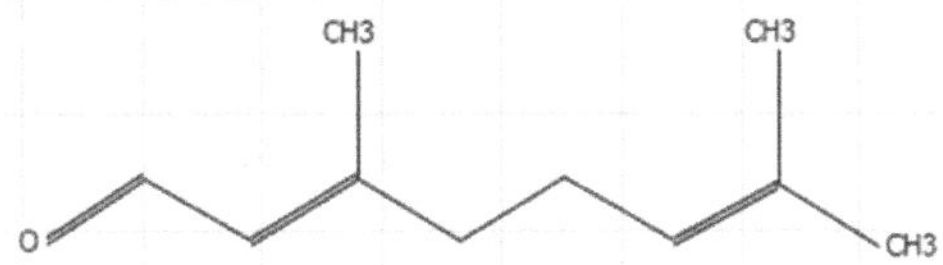	Aromatic Deterrence, antimicrobial, antifungal, and anti-inflammatory.
3		Citral	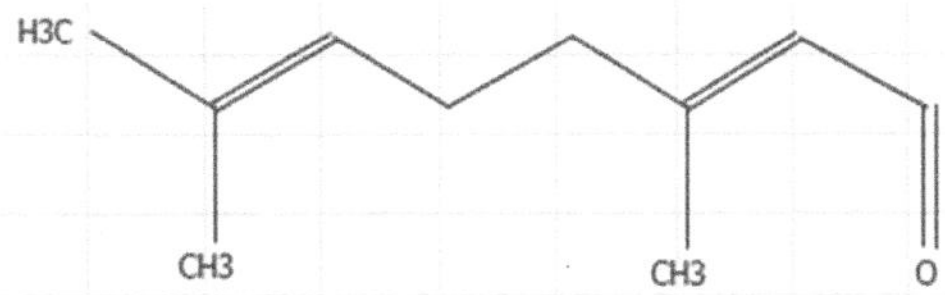	Fresh, lemony aroma.
4		2,6-octadien-1-ol,3,7-dimethyl acetate (Z)	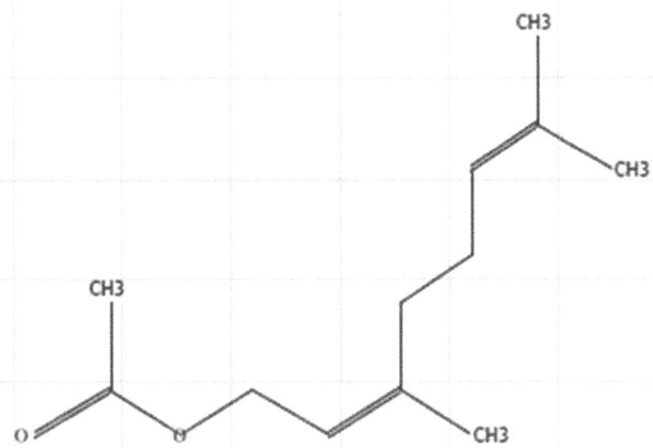	Found in essential oils : Lavender (Lavandula spp.) Bergamot (*Citrus bergamia*) Clary sage (*Salvia sclarea*)
5	Crown oil	2-Ethyl-oxetane	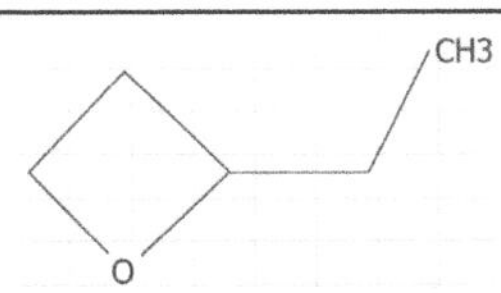	Ether-like smell.

Table 2.3 D-Limonene is one of the major products (RT 4.007)

Compound Label	Name	RT	Algorithm
Cpd 7: D-Limonene; C10H16; 4.007	D-Limonene	4.007	Find by Integration

Table 2.4 MS spectrum peak list

m/z	z	Abund
67.1		1998696.25
68.1		227947.75
77.1		1262120.13
79.1		1811141.13
91.1		1735272.88
92.1		1326500.88
93.1		3366274.25
94.1		1263497.13
121.1	1	1390161
136.2	1	1270134.5

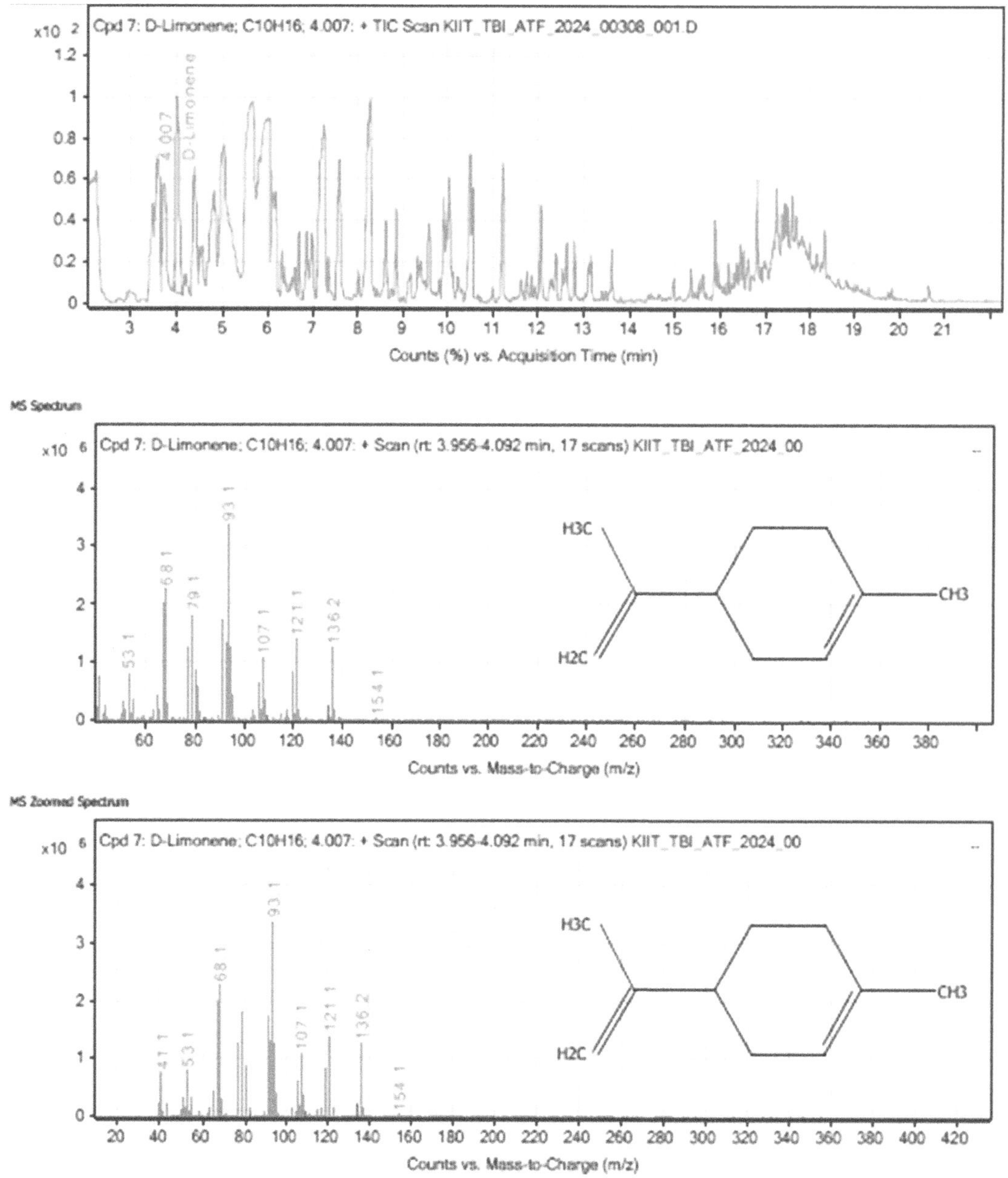

Fig. 2.3 GC MS spectra of limonene

Table 2.5 Neral is one of the major products (RT 5.672)

Compound Label	Name	RT	Algorithm
Cpd 14: Neral; C10H16O; 5.672	Neral	5.672	Find by Integration

Table 2.6 MS spectrum peak list

m/z	Calc *m/z*	Diff (ppm)	z	Abund	Formula	Ion
41.1				3141769.75		
67.1				1386761.25		
69.1				4079399.75		
81.1				1244124		
82.1				1143467.13		

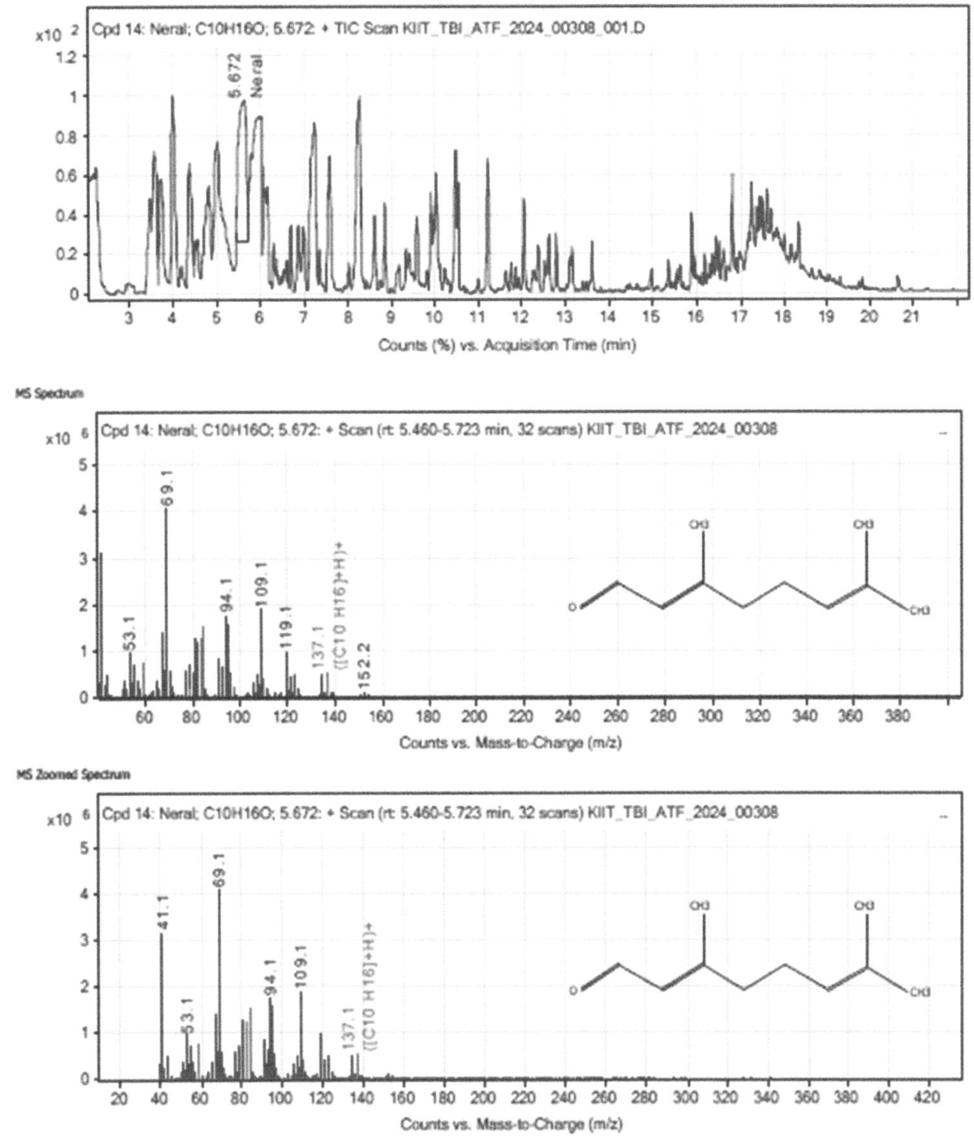

Fig. 2.4 GC MS Spectrum of neral

Table 2.7 Citral is one of the major products

Compound Label	Name	RT	Algorithm
Cpd 14: Citral; C10H16O; 5.995	Citral	5.995	Find by Integration

Table 2.8 MS spectrum peak list

m/z	Calc *m/z*	Diff (ppm)	z	Abund	Formula	Ion
41.1				4188797.25		
53.1				1169810.38		
67.1				1096767.63		
69.2				5946461		
83.1				1372431.75		
84.1			1	2754443.25		
94.1				1971483		
109.1				1383663.88		
123.2				1341724.75		
137.1	136.1	-7331.35	1	1537158.63	C10 H16	(M+H)+

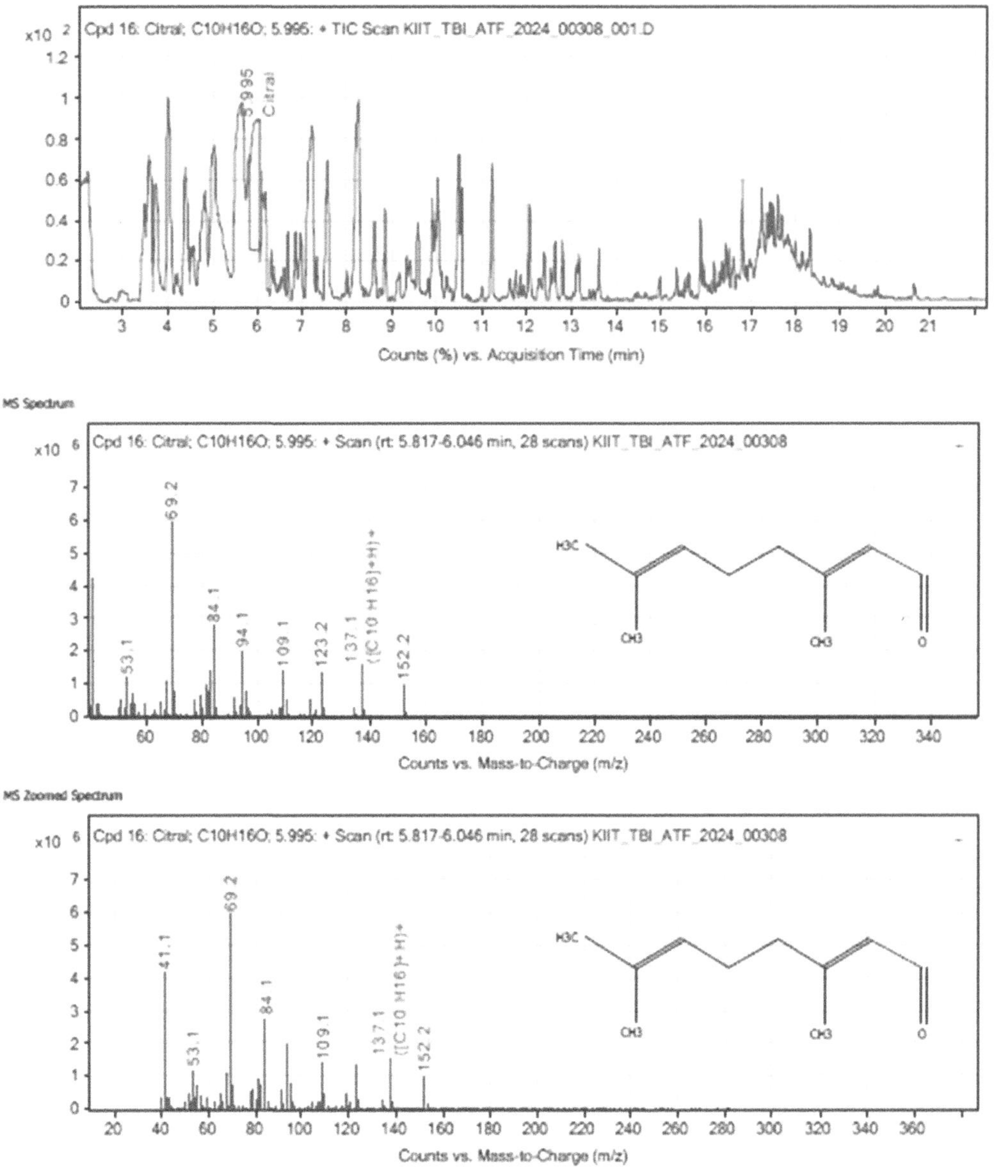

Fig. 2.5 GC MS spectrum of citral

Table 2.9 Isolated active component of citronella oil

Compound Label	Name	RT	Algorithm
Cpd 28: 2,6-Octadien-1-ol, 3,7-dimethyl-, acetate, (Z)-; C12H2002; 7.244	2,6-Octadien-1-ol, 3,7-dimethyl-, acetate, (Z)-	7.244	Find by Integration

Table 2.10 MS spectrum peak list

m/z	Calc *m/z*	Diff (ppm)	z	Abund	Formula	Ion
41.1				1854846.75		
43.1			1	1853784.5		
53.1				533093.38		
67.1				995897.19		
68.1				1780784		
69.1				3690500.25		
80.1	80.1	7.56		734706.19	C2 H6 O2	(M+NH4)+
93.1	93.1	10.81		1798012.38	C4 H12 O2	(M+H)+
121.1	103.1	-148911.27	1	1419201.13	C5 H11 O2	(M+NH4)+
136.1				1230713.88	C6 H14 O2	(M+NH4)+

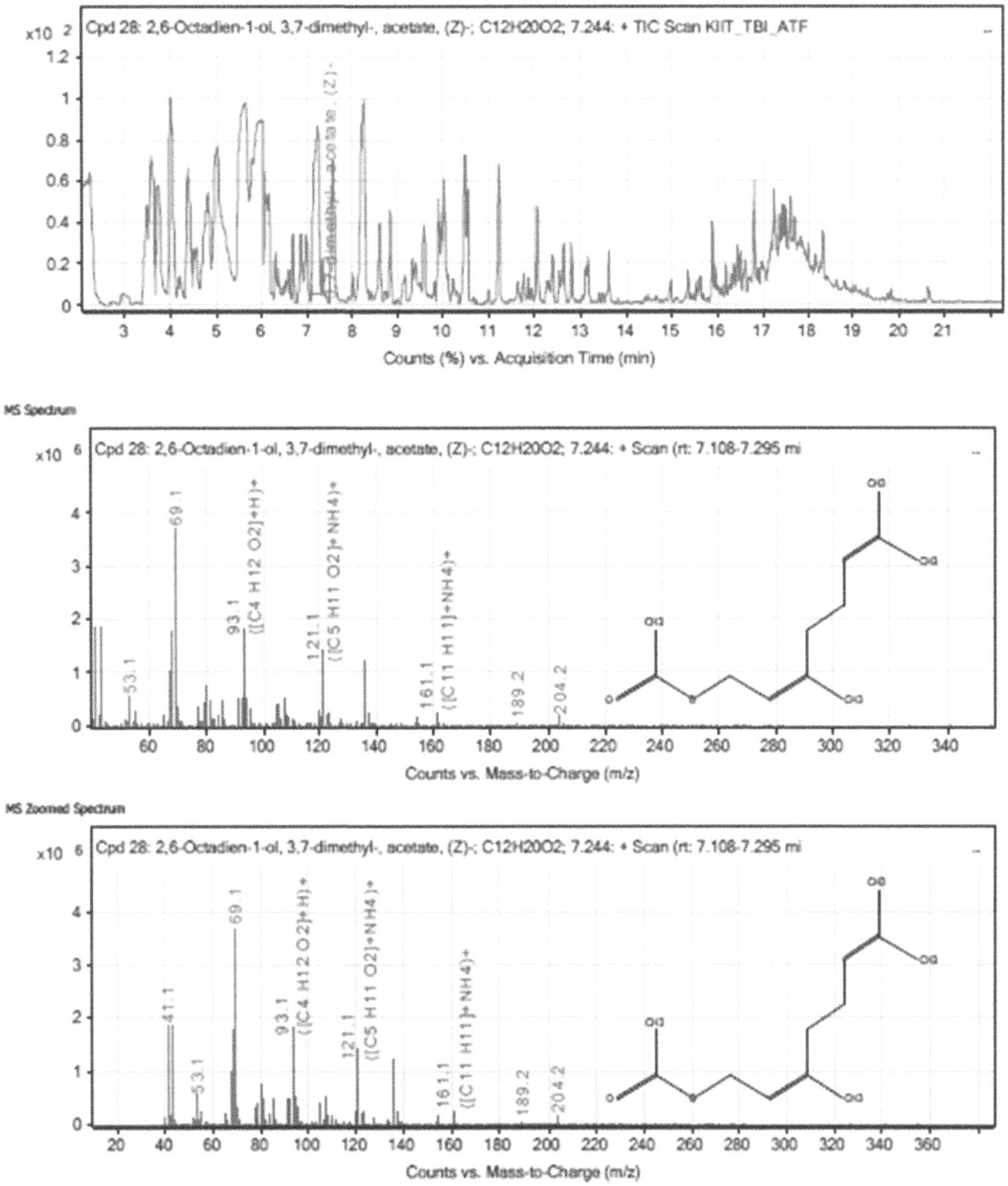

Fig. 2.6 GC MS spectrum of 2,6-octadien-1-ol, 3,7-dimethyl-, acetate, (Z)-

The major compound identified in the GC-MS study of the isolated Crown oil are as follows-

Table 2.11 MS spectrum peak list

m/z	Calc *m/z*	Diff (ppm)	z	Abund	Formula	Ion
41.1				2635557.5		
42.1				1352945.38		
43.1			1	2163007		
55.1				613889.56		
56.1				2641819.75		
57.1			1	2926010.25		
69.1	69.1	-1.79		489190.5	C5 H8	(M+H)+
71.1				358559.94		
84.1	84.1	9.23		261556.2	C5 H6	(M+NH4)+
86.1			1	944073.5		

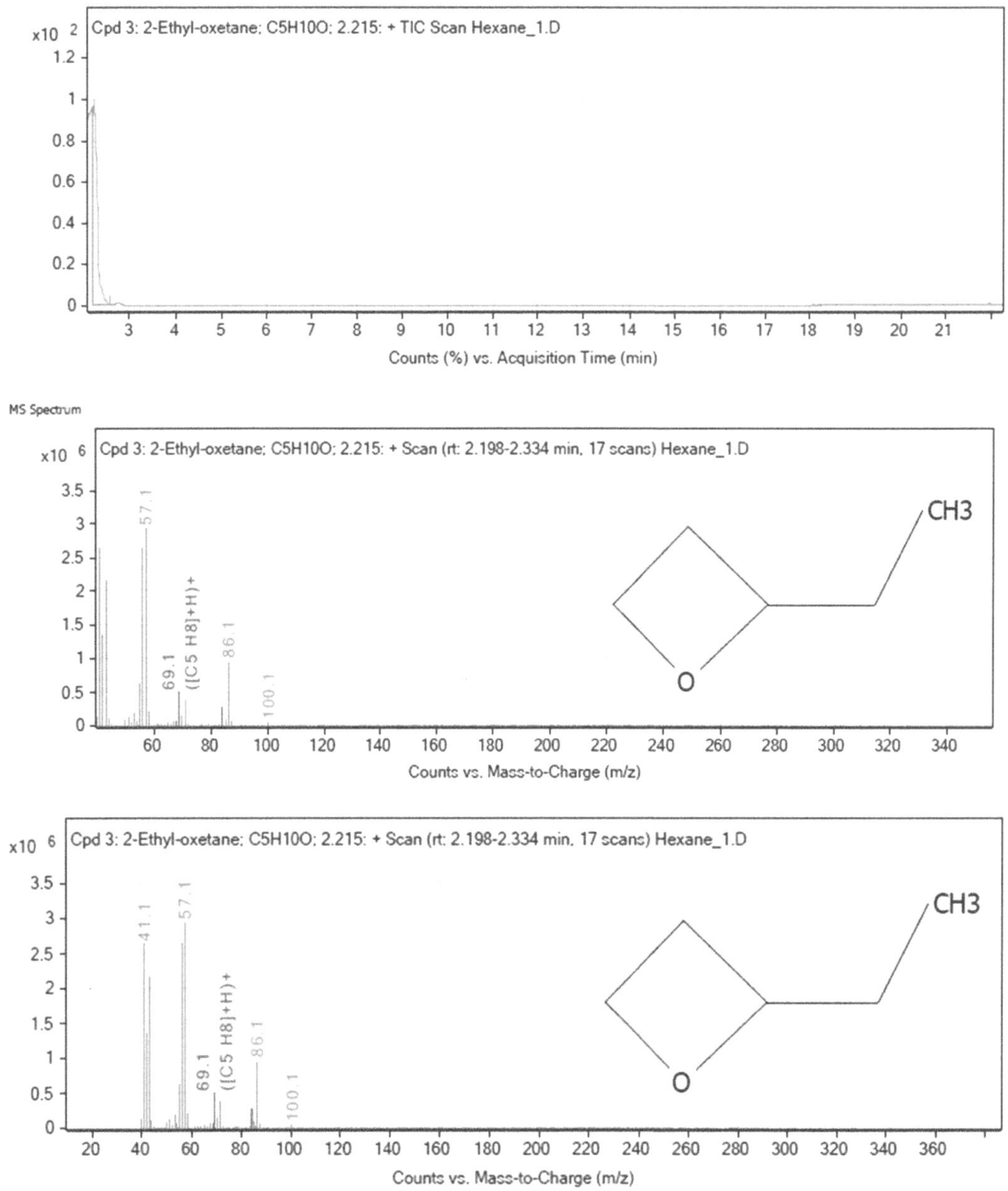

Fig. 2.7 GC MS spectrum of 2-ethyl oxetane

Table 2.12 MS spectrum peak list

m/z	Calc *m/z*	Diff (ppm)	z	Abund	Formula	Ion
41.1				2635557.5		
42.1				1352945.38		
43.1			1	2163007		
55.1				613889.56		
56.1				2641819.75		
57.1			1	2926010.25		
69.1	69.1	-1.79		489190.5	C5 H8	(M+H)+
71.1				358559.94		
84.1	84.1	9.23		261556.2	C5 H6	(M+NH4)+
86.1			1	944073.5		

3. Results and Discussion

Spectroscopic GC-MS analysis of Citronella oil (*Cymbopogon nardus*), lead to the identification of D-Limonene, Neral, Citral as major constituents. Spectroscopic GC-MS analysis of active component of Crown oil (*Shorea robusta*) are identified as 2-Ethyl-oxetane as the major component. The experiment revealed that the extracts have potent pesticidal effects on the groundnut seed beetles. The extract reduced egg-hatching rates and induced mortality among adult beetles, according to the laboratory's present investigation. The extract worked better at higher concentrations, indicating a dose-dependent response. To create commercial formulations, the ideal concentration for optimum performance without phytotoxicity was determined as 0.1% v/w. The protective capability of treated seeds was demonstrated by their reduced degrees of damage as compared to untreated controls. This suggests that it could be used as a natural substitute for artificial insecticides.Citronella oil (*Cymbopogon nardus*) and Crown oil leaf extracts are an eco-friendly choice because they are plant-based. The presence of bioactive substances in both plant leaves, such as D-Limonene, Neral, Citral, 2-Ethyl-oxetane, Carene, which cause pesticide effect. These substances probably cause death and decreased reproduction by interfering with the beetle's neurological system, breathing system, or eating habits. Its application lessens chemical pesticides' risks to our health and the ecosystem. Because the extract is economical, biodegradable, and unlikely to cause the bugs to develop resistance, it is consistent with sustainable pest management techniques. The plant extracts are affordable for farmers with low resources because it is widely accessible and its extraction procedure is not too complicated. The leaf extract is a safer option for ecological and agricultural systems because it may present less danger to non-target creatures. This finding encourages more research and development for practical application while highlighting the potential of the studied leaf extract as a green insecticide.

Hence these phytoproducts may be used as fumigants or insect repellants against the beetles *Trogoderma granarium* and *Rhyzopertha dominica*, (Coleoptera).

4. Conclusion

The study successfully isolated and characterized bioactive phyto-compounds from natural sources that demonstrate effective pesticidal properties against groundnut beetles, a significant pest in stored groundnuts. Using GC-MS, the compounds were identified and assessed for their bioactivity. The following conclusions can be drawn:

1. **Effective Phyto-Compounds:** Several plant-derived compounds were identified with potent insecticidal and repellant properties. Among these, compounds such as **limonene, neral, citronellal, and other monoterpenes** exhibited strong pesticidal activity against groundnut beetles.
2. **Mechanism of Action:** The efficacy of these compounds was attributed to their ability to interfere with the beetles' sensory perception, causing deterrence or mortality. Their aromatic nature also plays a role in creating an unfavorable environment for pest infestation.
3. **Eco-Friendly Alternative:** These natural phyto-compounds provide an environmentally sustainable alternative to synthetic chemical pesticides, reducing harmful residues in food storage systems and contributing to safer agricultural practices.
4. **Economic Viability:** The study highlights the cost-effectiveness of using plant-derived pesticides, especially in rural and agrarian settings where groundnuts are a staple crop.
5. **Future Scope:** Further research and formulation studies are required to develop these phyto-compounds into commercial pesticidal products with enhanced stability and prolonged efficacy. Exploring synergistic combinations of these compounds may yield even better results in pest management.

In summary, the study underscores the potential of natural phyto-compounds as a sustainable and effective solution for managing groundnut beetles, ensuring the safety and quality of stored groundnuts while promoting eco-friendly pest control practices.

References——

1. Prakash,A. and J.Rao. 1997. Botanical Pesticides in Agriculture, 1st Edn. CRC Pess Inc., Baton Rouge, Florida Pages: 461.
2. Isman, M. (2006). Botanical insecticides, deterrents, and repellents in modern agriculture and an increasingly regulated world. Annu. Rev. Entomol. 51, 45–66.
3. Peter, D.S. (1985): An introduction of insect pest and their control. Macmillan press Ltd pp1–73.
4. Golob, P., & Hodges, R. (1982). Study of an outbreak of *Prostephanustruncatus* (Horn) in Tanzania. Report of the Tropical Products Institute (G164).C
5. Delobel A. and P. Malonga (1987) Insecticidal properties of six plantmaterials against *Caryedonsreratus* (01.). J. stored Prod. Res. 23, 173–176.
6. Ahmed, S., M. Grainge, J. W. Hylin, W. C. Mitchell and J. A. Litsinger. 1984. Some promising plant species for use as pest control agents under traditional farming system, pp. 565–580. /n.' H. Schmutterer and K. R. S. Ascher (eds.). Proc. 2nd Int. Neem Conf. (Rauischholzhausen, Germany, 1983). GTZ, Eschborn, Germany
7. Mclndoo, N.E.1945. Plants of possible insecticidal value: A review of literature up to 1941. E-661. Agricultural Research Administration, Bureau of Entomology and Plant Quarantine, US Department of Agriculture, Washington DC, USA.
8. Jacobson, M(1958). Insecticides from plants. A review of literature. USDA Agric. Hand, govt. Printing office, Washington, DC, p-219.
9. Talukder, F. A., & Howse, P. E. (2000). Isolation of secondary plant compounds from Aphanamixispolystachya as feeding deterrents against adult Tribolium castaneum (Coleoptera: Tenebrionidae)/Isolierungsekundärer Pflanzeninhaltsst offeaus Aphanamixispolystachiamitfraßabschreckender Wirkunggegenadulte Tribolium castaneum (Coleoptera: Tenebrionidae). *Zeitschrift für Pflanzenkrankheiten und Pflanzenschutz/Journal of Plant Diseases and Protection*, 498–504.
10. Sighamony, S., Anees, I., Chandrakala, T. S., & Osmani, Z. (1984). Natural products as repellents for Tribolium castaneum Herbst.
11. Rajapakse, R., & Van Emden, H. F. (1997). Potential of four vegetable oils and ten botanical powders for reducing infestation of cowpeas by Callosobruchus maculatus, C. chinesis and C. rhodesianus. *Journal of Stored Products Research*, *33*(1), 59–68.
12. Prakash, A., Pasalu IC and mathur KC (1982). Evaluation of plant products as grain protectants in paddy storage. International Journal of Entomology1(1), 75–77.

Note: All the figures and tables in this chapter were made by the authors.

Research and Innovations in Industrial and Marine Biotechnology: A Circular Economy 2024 – Prof. Hrudayanath Thatoi et al. (eds)
 ISBN 978-1-041-28285-3

3 Effect of LED Light Treatments and Photoperiod on Growth and Morphological Traits of Coriander (*Coriandrum Sativum* L.) at Seedling Stage

Debasmita Dash, Ashish Panigrahi
Department of Botany, School of Applied Sciences (SoAS),
Centurion University of Technology and Management (CUTM),
Ramchandrapur, Jatni, Odisha, India

Shibani Mohapatra
Center for Industrial Biotechnology Research,
Siksha O Anusandhan University

Srimay Pradhan and Madhusmita Barik*
Department of Botany, School of Applied Sciences (SoAS),
Centurion University of Technology and Management (CUTM),
Ramchandrapur, Jatni, Odisha, India

Abstract: Coriander (*Coriandrum sativum* L.) is highly recognised due to its pharmaceutical characteristics, and its fragrance is utilized extensively in cookery and culinary sector. Its morphological growth is significantly impacted by light treatment and photoperiod. Plant factories based on artificial light are increasing in popularity because of the development of light-emitting diodes (LEDs). The use of LEDs on facility cultivation systems can measure the lighting conditions with precision, resulting in better energy efficiency in coriander cultivation. This current study, investigated 4 lights- white (400 nanometre), yellow (580 nanometre), red (640 nanometre) and blue (480 nanometre), and 3 photoperiods (6 Light/18 Dark, 12 Light/12 Dark, and 24 Light) to wholly determine their impacts on corianders morphological growth and development at seedling stage under NFT condition. This investigation aimed to find a combined effect of light treatment and photoperiod to examine the coriander growth by recording various morphological characteristics such as plant height (PH), leaf area, chlorophyll content, stem, root, leaf fresh weight and yield. Findings revealed that across the light treatments used, blue and yellow light exposed plants with cont. 24-hour light decrease the height of coriander plants, area of leaf, root, stem, leaf fresh weight, and its yield, whereas 24 hours of constant red light can increase 6.91% of yield substantially in comparison to 6 hours. Twelve hours of red light, established favourable conditions for the height of plant, chlorophyll content, and yield in contrast to others.

Keywords: Coriander, Yield, Chlorophyll content, Photoperiod, Seedling stage

1. Introduction

Coriander (*Coriandrum sativum* L.) is an edible micro vegetable that is entirely edible (the whole plant from seed to foliage) and has a fresh, unique aromatic flavour. It belongs to the family Apiaceae and is a common ingredient in world cuisines [1]. It represents an important source of carotenoids, vitamin C, dietary fiber, and other nutrient component-rich foods [2]. In different dishes, its leaves, stems and the roots are used to flavor and warm

*Corresponding author: meetali.barik@gmail.com

DOI: 10.1201/9781003759003-3

broth [3]. Coriander presents a multifaceted character as a functional food ingredient that combines significant therapeutic potential with great economic significance. Though coriander is a global valued crop, its quality and yield are susceptible to several challenges, such as weather conditions, phenotypic variability, biotic stress, agricultural practices, and genotypic effects. Specifically, poor weather conditions, like cold and excessive rainfall occurring in the flowering period, are likely to hinder its growth and encourage the disease spread such as flower blight that causes high yield loss [4]. Coriander through the small farm procedures is typically cultivated outside, which makes it highly susceptible to bacteria. Consequently, coriander production might fail to meet consumer requirements for food safety. Increased consumer demand for farm fresh, free from chemical and safe to consume, production has driven interest in best-quality agricultural products.

In the growth and developmental process of plants, light is a vital resource that affects anatomy, physiology, morphology, and accumulation of bioactive compounds [5]. Optimal light intensity is crucial as inadequate light restricts mesophyll photosynthesis, while excessive light causes damage to cellular membranes and photosynthetic tissues. Literature shows that increased photoperiod enhances photosynthesis, stimulates growth and enhances the secondary metabolite content of vegetables [6, 7, 8]. Therefore, to maximize crop yields, photoperiod, and light need to be properly balanced. For these requirements to be fulfilled, plant factories are employing artificial illumination, for example, LEDs (light-emitting diodes), which provides controlled growing conditions precisely and minimizes reliance on variable natural conditions. In the cultivation of coriander within a hydroponic solution, the optimal interaction of photoperiods, and efficient LED lighting is important for improving cultivation productivity as these conditions relate strongly. Our research utilized 4 different light sources (White-400nm, Yellow-580, Blue-480, and Red-640) and 3 photoperiod levels (6 Light/18 Dark, 12 Light/12 Dark, and 24 Light) to investigate their effects on morphological development and total chlorophyll content of coriander, with the objective of identifying efficient and energy-saving combinations suitable for hydroponic cultivation.

2. Materials and Methods

2.1 Plant Material and Growth Condition

The coriander seeds were purchased from the local market. The seeds were pre-germinated by wrapping them in a clean cloth, soaking at 50°C for 20 minutes. After soaking, the seeds were subjected to a six-day dark period at 4°C for germination. Germinated seeds were transplanted into net pots with 50 mm (height) × 55 mm (top diameter) × 38 mm (bottom diameter) packed with coco beads, and placed in a NFT hydroponic system. The relative humidity (RH) at 48% and 25° C was maintained throughout the growing period. A hydroponic solution was made with city green powder nutrients (A, B, C) at half-strength adjusted to a pH of 6.4 and an electrical conductivity of 1.2 ds/m and in every 4days it was recycled.

2.2 Experimental Setup

The research work was performed inside the polyhouse during the dry season at Centurion University, Ramchandrapur, India (20° 17′ 40″ N, 85° 70′ 52″ E). A pair of NFT hydroponics systems with A- frame slopes were employed for the experiment. The systems were comprised of six parallel tubes, each for ten pots. The tubes were designed to ensure that plant roots remained continuously immersed in water. The system has a total area of 20 square feet and hydroponic tank of 100 litres. This study employed 4 wavelengths of light- white (400 nanometer), yellow (580 nanometer), red (640 nanometer) and blue (480 nanometer), and 3 photoperiods (6 Light/18 Dark, 12 Light/12 Dark, and 24 Light) which were controlled by Arduino Uno and Real-time Clock (RTC) system.

2.3 Growth Measurement

Observations were assessed during the seedling stage. The height of coriander (centimetres) was measured from base to apex of plant using a Vernier caliper. Fresh biomass of shoots, roots and leaves (grams) were determined using a digital weighing balance. Leaf area (cm^2) was estimated with the grid counting technique.

Yield = Fresh weight of (Shoot + Root+ Leaf)

2.4 Estimation of Total Chlorophyll

The total chlorophyll content of leaf was estimated according to [9]. A coriander leaf of 0.02 g was homogenized with 5 millilitres of 80% acetone solution (v/v) in a motor-pestle, and at 4 °C it was incubated overnight, then it was centrifuged at 2,500 rpm for 12 mins. In an eppendorf tube the supernatant was transferred using pipette and the absorbance of Chlorophyll a and Chlorophyll b in acetone at 646 and 663 nanometre was analysed through spectrophotometer (Thermo Scientific, Evolution 201, USA).

The following equations were used to determine the chlorophyll content

Chlorophyll a = $(12.25 \times A_{663} - 2.55 \times A_{646}) \times$ volume of supernatant (millilitre)/ weight of sample (gram),

Chlorophyll b = $(20.31 \times A_{646} - 4.91 \times A_{663}) \times$ volume of supernatant (millilitre)/weight of sample (gram),

Total chlorophyll content = $[(17.76 \times A_{646} + 7.34 \times A_{663})] \times$ volume of supernatant (millilitre)/ weight of sample (gram).

Absorbance at 663 and 646 nm were termed as A_{663} and A_{646} respectively.

2.5 Statistical Analysis

This investigation was conducted by using completely randomized design (CRD) which consist of 5 replications of each treatment. The standard deviation (SD), standard error, mean and ANOVA (analysis of variance) estimates were obtained using GraphPad Prism 5 software. One-way ANOVA followed by Tukey's test was performed to evaluate the significance of variations among the light treatments.

3. Results and Discussions

Light, as a form of electromagnetic radiation, is one of the most significant signals influencing plant growth, regulating their responses, growth habits and chemical composition. Coriander morphology traits and growth are greatly influenced by LED light with plants exhibiting varied responses under diverse light conditions and photoperiods. To evaluate the effects of the 4 light treatments and 3 photoperiods of coriander, we recorded changes in morphological and yield-related traits (plant height, leaf area, stem, leaf, and root fresh weight, and yield) which exhibited clear growth responses (Fig. 3.1). We investigated the effects of LED lights on coriander growth, and observed significant variations across the measured traits.

The total chlorophyll content accumulations in coriander leaves were different. Plants modify their physiological and morphological functions to enhance their photosynthetic capacity and adapt to various light conditions [10]. Plant response to light and its modification can be unique for every species and sometimes cultivars [11]. In this present research, we have examined the influence of four treatments of different photoperiods of light.

Chlorophyll is the most important pigment in green plants' photosynthetic apparatus, and it has a direct influence on crop yield and photosynthetic ability. The total chlorophyll content significantly under 6 and 24 hours of photoperiods by 3.91 and 9.02% respectively, against 12 hours treatment. The 24 hours treatment exhibited the reduced chlorophyll content compared to all photoperiods. In red-light, the content of total chlorophyll in 12 hours photoperiod increased considerably by 2.61 and 14.16% compared to 6 and 24-hours treatments, whereas in white light, the content dropped considerably by 5.03 and 4.82% in the 6-hours and 24-hours photoperiods relative to the 12-hours photoperiod.

Light composition influences the production and accumulation of photosynthetic pigments in leaves, modulates gene expression by photoreceptor-mediated signal cascades and drives morphological changes in plants under the same light spectrum when exposed for different durations. Light of the same spectrum but with varying exposure durations are responsible for inducing morphological changes in plants [9]. The growth and quality of coriander are directly influenced by light treatments and photoperiods. It was also found that all the growth characteristics were much greater in red light compared to other light treatments. Previous studies have reported that red LEDs often promote stem elongation, leaf area expansion and biomass accumulation. This aligns partially with our findings, where leaf area was highest under blue light followed by red. Notably blue LEDs play a greater role in photosynthesis, stomata opening and chlorophyll synthesis [12]. Under 24 hours of red light treatment, stem and leaf fresh weight was greater; likewise, under 12 hours, plant height, total content of chlorophyll, fresh weight of root, and the yield showed greatest increases, with red light exerting the most significant effects overall (Fig. 3.1).

The experiment determined that plants grown under the red-light treatment for 24 hrs photoperiod were observed

Table 3.1 Influence of four light treatments (colour) and three photoperiods on multiple traits

Srl. No.	Light treatments (colour)	Photoperiod	Plant Height (centimeters)	Leaf surface area (centimeter^2)	Total chlorophyll (milligrams per gram)	Yield (gram)
1	Y	6	5.01 ± 0.292c	1.35 ± 0.154c	0.92 ± 0.037c	4.37 ± 0.161b
2	Y	12	5.37 ± 0.281c	1.62 ± 0.155c	0.96 ± 0.038b	4.95 ± 0.134b
3	Y	24	5.05 ± 0.211c	0.54 ± 0.264d	0.94 ± 0.040b	4.70 ± 0.156b
4	W	6	4.47 ± 0.194d	2.61 ± 0.162b	0.90 ± 0.033bc	4.21 ± 0.083b
5	W	12	6.16 ± 0.303b	3.23 ± 0.332a	0.96 ± 0.015b	4.57 ± 0.096b
6	W	24	5.63 ± 0.261c	1.21 ± 0.312cd	0.92 ± 0.035bc	4.44 ± 0.097b
7	R	6	6.15 ± 0.231b	2.31 ± 0.163b	1.18 ± 0.024a	5.63 ± 0.102ab
8	R	12	7.07 ± 0.190a	3.06 ± 0.142a	1.22 ± 0.023a	5.91 ± 0.104a
9	R	24	6.51 ± 0.191b	1.64 ± 0.091c	1.07 ± 0.034b	6.07 ± 0.092a
10	B	6	5.21 ± 0.330c	3.31 ± 0.262a	1.13 ± 0.039a	3.62 ± 0.064d
11	B	12	6.21 ± 0.163b	3.16 ± 0.102a	1.14 ± 0.033a	4.09 ±0.097bc
12	B	24	6.07 ± 0.193b	1.62 ± 0.311c	1.02 ± 0.034ab	3.82 ± 0.078c

*Y (Yellow); W (White); R (Red), B (Blue)
*Significant differences were marked statistically by different letters.

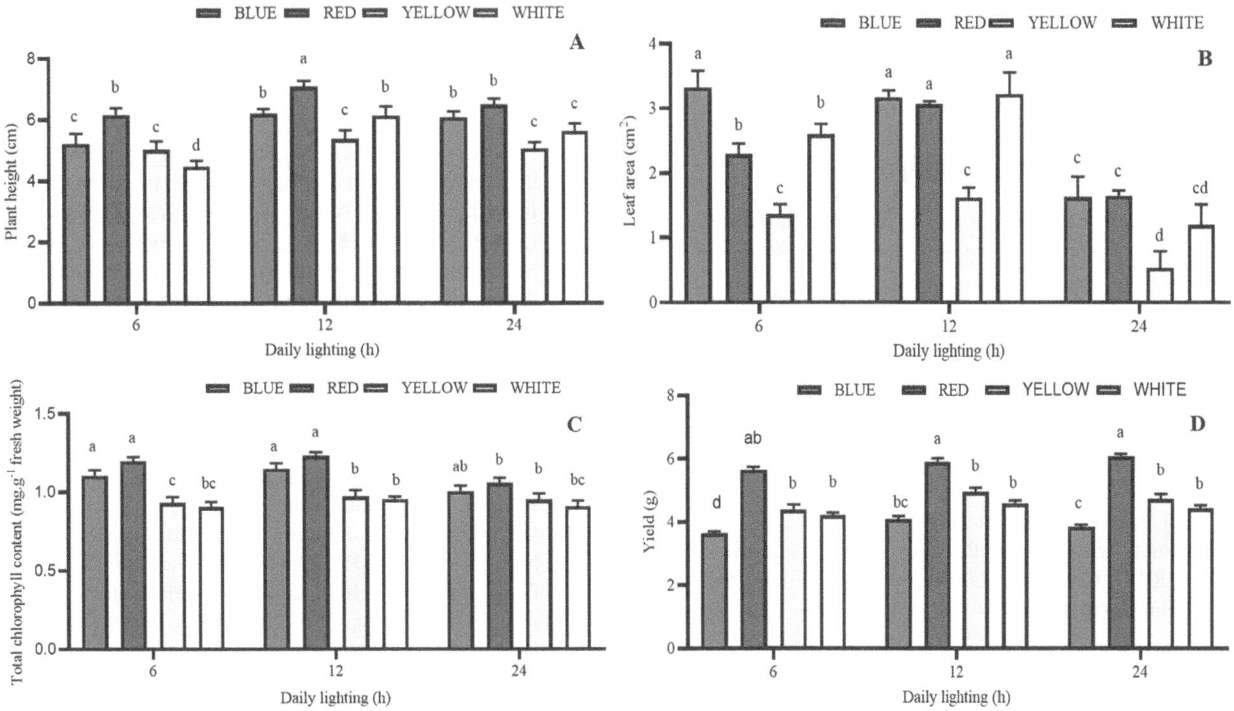

Fig. 3.1 (A) Plant height (B) Leaf area (C) Chlorophyll content (D) Yield. The X-axis shows different photoperiodic condition, each day lightning is 6 (6 hours light/18 hours dark), 12 (12 hours light/12 hours dark), and 24 (24 hours of uninterrupted light period). The different letters above the bar represents significant variations across treatments

with slender and tall, however plants exposed to white light were shorter, whereas those under blue light exhibited reduced fresh weights of roots, stems, leaves and yield. During the 12-hour photoperiod treatment, coriander exhibited the maximum plant height (increased by 15.80 % and 6.22 %), leaf area (13.56 % and 54.82 %), root fresh weight (10.79 % and 7.13 %), and yield (8.50% and 2.43%) than the 6 and 24 hours treatment. Furthermore, coriander grown under 24 hours photoperiod, showed the highest leaf (increased by 9.50 and 3.70%) and stem fresh weight (increased by 7.89 and 3.60%) than 6 and 12 hours treatment. Also, for the 24 hours photoperiod, the stem fresh weight was significantly lower in blue and yellow lights (0.79 ± 0.031 and 0.80 ± 0.052 g) than all other treatments (0.96 ± 0.021 ~ 0.86 ± 0.025 g) which suggests that the fresh weight of coriander stems was reduced in the absence of blue and yellow light.

The minimum yield was observed in blue light with a 6 hours photoperiod. In contrast with the trend observed in leaf and stem fresh weight, 24 hours red light treatment significantly increased the aboveground dry matter accumulation of coriander plants. Comparatively, during light treatments under red light, the fresh weight of roots increased with an increase in photoperiod. There was no statistical difference found in the fresh weight of root during the 6 and 12 hours photoperiods, but it was significantly higher in 24 hours. The coriander exhibited slow growth under blue light, whereas red light promoted robust growth and higher yield. In addition, a 12 hours photoperiod was found to be most favourable for coriander growth.

The photosynthetic pigments involved in photosynthesis are essential in the transport and absorption of light energy [13]. Previous studies, have found that both the red and blue light increased the expression of important genes which encode carotenoid and chlorophyll pigment-type enzymes, increase in pigment accumulation, increases light absorption and photosynthesis [14], which coincides with our study. In both red, and blue lights the chlorophyll content was higher compared to others.

4. Conclusion

The current study examined the morphological characteristics and chlorophyll accumulation in coriander seedlings under different of light treatments (light sources) and photoperiods. Results indicated that red-light (640nm) had an optimistic influence on coriander height, chlorophyll pigment accumulation, yield, fresh weight of root, leaf, and stem. Even though the increase in leaf area was quite pronounced under blue light (480nm). The 12-hour photoperiod showed poor effect on plant height, total chlorophyll content, leaf area, root biomass (fresh weight) and yield, despite seeing increases in parameters of 6.21, 9.01, 54.81, 7.12 and 2.44%, respectively, relative to the 24-hour photoperiod. Of the all four light treatments, coriander exhibited the minimum yield under blue light, whereas red light promoted robust growth and higher yield. Notably, the combination of red light with a 12 hour photoperiod created the most favourable conditions for plant height, chlorophyll accumulation and yield compared to others.

Acknowledgement

The authors are thankful to the Botany Department, for providing laboratory and polyhouse facilities and Vice Chancellor of the Centurion University for their constant cooperation and support.

References

1. Wang, F., Gao, Q., Ji, G., Wang, J., Ding, Y., and Wang, S. (2024). Effects of light intensity and photoperiod on morphological development and photosynthetic characteristics of coriander. Horticulturae. 10(3): 215.
2. Bhat, S., Kaushal, P., Kaur, M., and Sharma, H. K. (2014). Coriander (*Coriandrum sativum* L.): Processing, nutritional and functional aspects. Afr. J. Plant Sci. 8(1): 25–33.
3. Punetha, D., Tewari, G., and Pande, C. (2018). Compositional variability in inflorescence essential oil of Coriandrum sativum from North India. J. Essent. Oil Res. 30(2): 113–119.
4. Khare, M. N., Tiwari, S. P., and Sharma, Y. K. (2017). Disease problems in the cultivation of coriander (*Coriandrum sativum* L.) and their management leading to production of high quality pathogen free seed. Int. J. Seed Spices. 7(1):1–7.
5. Ilić, Z. S., and Fallik, E. (2017). Light quality manipulation improves vegetable quality at harvest and postharvest: A review. Environ. Exp. Bot. 139:79–90.
6. Li, X., Liang, T., & Liu, H. (2022). How plants coordinate their development in response to light and temperature signals. The Plant Cell. 34(3): 955–966.
7. Shibaeva, T. G., Sherudilo, E. G., Rubaeva, A. A., and Titov, A. F. (2022). Continuous LED lighting enhances yield and nutritional value of four genotypes of Brassicaceae microgreens. Plants. 11(2): 176.
8. Zhang, X., He, D., Niu, G., Yan, Z., and Song, J. (2018). Effects of environment lighting on the growth, photosynthesis, and quality of hydroponic lettuce in a plant factory. International, Int. J. Agric. Biol. Eng. 11(2): 33–40.
9. Chen, C. C., Huang, M. Y., Lin, K. H., Wong, S. L., Huang, W. D., and Yang, C. M. (2014). Effects of light quality on the growth, development and metabolism of rice seedlings (*Oryza sativa* L.). Res. J. Biotechnol. 9(4): 15–24.
10. Pan, T., Ding, J., Qin, G., Wang, Y., Xi, L., Yang, J., and Zou, Z. (2019). Interaction of supplementary light and CO2 enrichment improves growth, photosynthesis, yield, and quality of tomato in autumn through spring greenhouse production. HortScience. 54(2): 246–252.
11. Kulchin, Y. N., Nakonechnaya, O. V., Gafitskaya, I. V., Grishchenko, O. V., Epifanova, T. Y., Orlovskaya, I. Y., and Subbotin, E. P. (2018, November). Plant morphogenesis under different light intensity. In Defect and diffusion forum (Vol. 386, pp. 201–206). Trans Tech Publications Ltd.
12. Miao, Y. X., Wang, X. Z., Gao, L. H., Chen, Q. Y., & Qu, M. (2016). Blue light is more essential than red light for maintaining the activities of photosystem II and I and photosynthetic electron transport capacity in cucumber leaves. J. Integr. Agric. 15 (1): 87–100.
13. Simkin, A. J., Kapoor, L., Doss, C. G. P., Hofmann, T. A., Lawson, T., and Ramamoorthy, S. (2022). The role of photosynthesis related pigments in light harvesting, photoprotection and enhancement of photosynthetic yield in planta. Photosynth. Res. 152(1):23–42.
14. Ma, G., Zhang, L., Kato, M., Yamawaki, K., Kiriiwa, Y., Yahata, M., and Matsumoto, H. (2012). Effect of blue and red LED light irradiation on β-cryptoxanthin accumulation in the flavedo of citrus fruits. J. Agric. Food Chem. 60(1): 197–201.

Note: The figure and the table in this chapter were made by the authors.

Research and Innovations in Industrial and Marine Biotechnology: A Circular Economy 2024 – Prof. Hrudayanath Thatoi et al. (eds)
© 2026 Taylor & Francis Group, London, ISBN 978-1-041-28285-3

4 Exploring the PGPR Potential of Rhizosphere Bacteria for Enhanced Plant Growth and Soil Health

Basundhara Lenka[1]
School of Biotechnology, Kalinga Institute of Industrial Technology (KIIT)
Deemed to be University, Bhubaneswar,
Odisha, India

Raklami Anas[2]
Cadi Ayyad University (UCA),
Faculty of Sciences Semlalia, Laboratory of Water Sciences,
Microbial Biotechnologies, and Natural Resources Sustainability (AQUABIOTECH),
Unit of Microbial Biotechnologies, Agrosciences, and Environment (BIOMAGE),
Labeled Research Unit-CNRST N°4,
Marrakesh, Morocco

Snehasish Mishra
School of Biotechnology, Kalinga Institute of Industrial Technology (KIIT)
Deemed to be University, Bhubaneswar,
Odisha, India

Abstract: Rhizosphere is the microhabitat of numerous microbial communities, most of which exhibit plant growth promoting (PGP) activity. These tiny creatures can enhance plant development, improve soil texture and increase crop wellbeing through several direct and indirect processes and known as plant beneficial microorganisms. This study investigated the PGP activity of isolated bacterial strains (KCP15, KCP17 and KCP18) from the garden rhizosphere of KIIT University, Bhubaneswar, India. The strains were screened for PGP attributes like synthesis of siderophores, HCN (hydrogen cyanide) and IAA (indole acetic acid), production of hydrolytic enzymes, phosphorus solubilization, N_2-fixation, and tolerance to high salt concentrations. Additionally, effect of isolates was tested on mung bean plants in hydroponic system. Growth parameters of mung bean plants such as shoot and root length, chlorophyll content, plant fresh and dry biomass, and hypocotyl length were evaluated. Notably, KCP15 and KCP17 exhibited the highest salt tolerance and significantly enhanced plant biomass. Thus, KCP15 and KCP17 would be considered as crucial PGPR (plant growth promoting rhizobacteria) and can serve as effective biofertilizers under saline stress condition.

Keywords: Iaa, pgpr, Plant growth, Rhizosphere, 16S rRNA

1. Introduction

Mung bean (moong or green gram) is a staple and economically important crop in India, cultivated across ~7 million acres globally with a yield of ~5 million tons [1]. India alone contributes ~54% of global production, accounting for 65% of its total pulse output [2]. It is grown seasonally across various Indian regions, covering ~5.13 million hectares and yielding ~3.08 million tons with an average productivity of ~600 kg/ha [3]. Mung bean production in the country has significantly enhanced from 0.70 million tonnes in 1970–1971 to 3.08 million tonnes in 2020–2021. Over this period, the cultivation area expanded from 2.06 million hectares to 5.13 million hectares, and productivity nearly doubled, rising from 339 kg/ha to 601 kg/ha. This growth is likely attributed to the availability of

Corresponding author: [1]lenkabasundhara95@gmail.com, [2]a.raklami@uca.ac.ma

DOI: 10.1201/9781003759003-4

high-yielding varieties and improved irrigation facilities [3]. Despite significant efforts to enhance mung bean yield, productivity remains relatively low.

Biofertilizers have emerged as sustainable alternatives to synthetic agrochemicals, promoting plant growth and reducing environmental harm. These formulations, often composed of PGPR, colonize the rhizosphere and enhance nutrient uptake and stress resistance [4]. Although only 2–5% of rhizobacteria act as effective PGPR, they significantly influence soil and plant health by suppressing pathogens and mitigating abiotic stress [5]. Genera such as *Pseudomonas, Proteus, Ensifer,* and *Amycolatopsis* have been widely studied for these traits [4]. PGPR enhance nitrogen fixation, solubilize nutrients, produce phytohormones, and degrade organic matter making them valuable tools for sustainable agriculture [6].

In this context, this study aims to isolate bacterial strains, characterize their PGP attributes, and their potential to improve mung bean growth in hydroponic system.

2. Material and Methods

2.1 Collection of Soil and Isolation of Bacteria

Soil samples were collected from garden of KIIT University, Bhubaneswar, India. Soil sampling was done by collecting soil from the upper 20 cm layer, using stainless-steel corer and kept into the plastic bags and immediately stored at 4 °C. Bacterial isolation was done through serial dilution-spreading technique on Luria -Bertani (LB) agar. Bacterial colonies with distinct morphological characters (size, color, and shape) were isolated and pure cultured on LB.

2.2 Molecular Identification of Isolated Strains

Genomic DNA was isolated through the Quick-DNA Bacterial Miniprep Kit (Zymo Research, Irvine, CA). 16S rRNA encoding DNA sequence was amplified through PCR by employing universal primers 27F (5' GAGTTTGATCATGGCTCAG3') and 1492R (5'TACGGTTACCTTGTTACGACTT3'). Sequencing of purified DNA was done by Heredity Biosciences (Odisha, India). Sequences were aligned using ClustalW within the MEGA software (v5.0), developed for molecular evolutionary genetic analysis [7]. A phylogenetic tree was generated using maximum likelihood approach, applying the Tamura-Nei model with 1,500 bootstrap replicates [8]. Sequences were deposited to NCBI database (accession numbers: PQ675774-PQ675776).

2.3 *In Vitro* Characterization of Isolated Bacterial Strains

Screening for Salt Tolerance

Salt tolerance of isolated strains was evaluated at different salt concentrations (0.09 M to 2 M) in LB broth, followed by incubation at 30 °C for 24 h [4]. Absorbance was measured at 600 nm.

Evaluation of Plant Growth Promoting Activity

Phosphorus solubilization was evaluated through spot inoculation of isolates on Pikovskaya's agar and incubated at 30 °C for five days [9]. IAA synthesis was quantified by using LB broth added with L-Trp (0.1%), incubated at 28 °C for 24 h. Following centrifugation, 4 mL of Salkowski reagent and 2 mL of supernatant were mixed, and the mixture was incubated for 30 minutes at 37 °C [10]. Absorbance was recorded at 530 nm to estimate IAA concentration via standard curve. Siderophore production was assessed by streaking isolates on CAS (Chrome Azurol S) agar, incubating at 30 °C for 3 days [10]. Nitrogen fixation ability was analyzed by streaking the strains on Jensen's medium and incubating at 37 °C for 24 h [11].

Screening for HCN, Catalase and Hydrolytic Enzyme Production Activity

HCN production test was done by streaking the bacteria on LB agar added with 4.4 g/L of glycine. The petri plate lid was sealed over filter paper saturated in alkaline picrate solution, which was then incubated for four days at 30 °C [12]. Catalase assay was performed by adding 2-3 drops of 3% H_2O_2 to clean glass slides containing 48-h old bacterial cultures [9]. Hydrolytic enzyme activities such as amylase [13], cellulase [14], pectinase [15], and chitinase [16] of bacterial strains were evaluated by spot inoculation on solid medium containing different substrates, followed by incubation at 30 °C for 24 h.

2.4 Biological Material, Experimental Design, and Plant Bioassay

After surface sterilization, mung bean (*Vigna radiata* L. Wilczek) seeds were immersed in bacterial suspensions (10^6 CFU/mL) and placed in perforated sponges soaked with same suspensions. This study employed the randomized complete block design with 4 treatments: one uninoculated control and three inoculated groups (KCP15, KCP17, KCP18), each with three replicates of 5–6 seeds. In a greenhouse, plants were cultivated in a regulated environment (16/8 h photoperiod, 28 ± 2 °C, 60 ± 2% humidity). After 14 days, growth metrics like shoot and root length, hypocotyl length, dry and fresh biomass, and chlorophyll content [17] were assessed.

2.5 Statistical Data Analysis

Statistical data analysis was done by accessing software PRISM 8. One-way ANOVA was executed to analyze significant differences among plants with different bacterial inoculations. Mean ± SD values differing at $p \leq 0.05$ were separated using the LSD test.

3. Results and Discussions

3.1 Molecular Identification of Isolated Strains

BLAST analysis has revealed that the strains KCP15 and KCP17 belong to *Staphylococcus* genus, showing

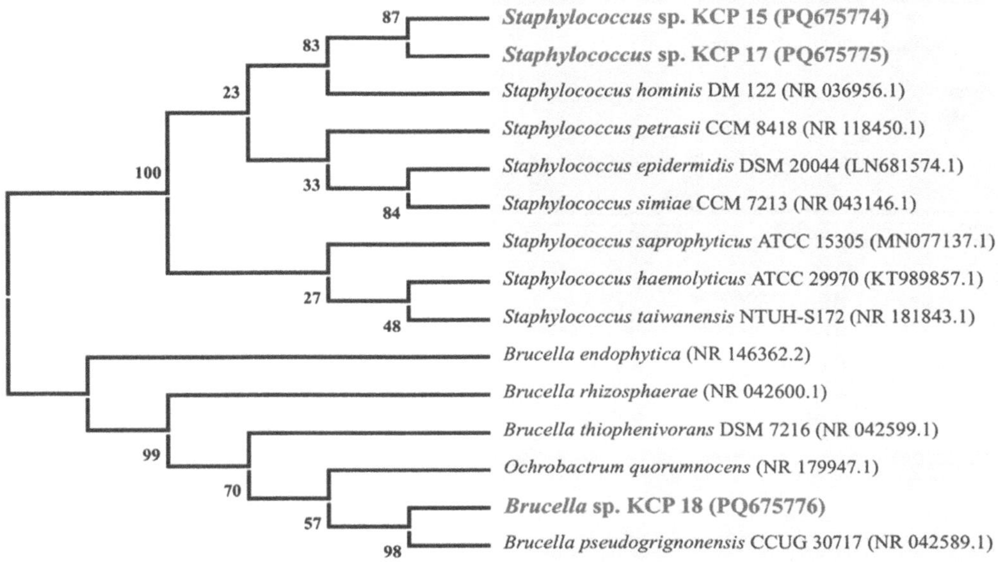

Fig. 4.1 Phylogenetic tree designed on the basis of 16S rRNA gene sequences of bacterial isolates showing relations with other bacteria obtained from GenBank database

99.77%, and 89.65% similarity to *Staphylococcus hominis* DM 122, respectively, while KCP18 aligned with *Brucella* genus, showing 99.66% similarity to *Brucella pseudogrignonensis* CCUG 30717 (Fig. 4.1). Unlike other pathogenic staphylococci, such as *S. aureus*, *S. hominis* is coagulase-negative and generally considered non-pathogenic [18]. It is commonly found in human microbiota, though its virulence remains poorly understood [19]. Recent findings by Aktar et al. [20] revealed the PGP potential of *S. hominis,* which enhanced biomass and induced phytohormone gene expression in jute plants. However, some studies suggest that it may possess pathogenic potential [21]. Similarly, the pathogenicity of *B. pseudogrignonensis,* unlike classical *Brucella* species, has not been documented.

3.2 *In vitro* Evaluation of Bacterial Isolates

Screening for Salt Tolerance

All the bacterial strains demonstrated salt tolerance however, their growth declined with increasing NaCl concentrations. KCP15 tolerated up to 2 M, KCP17 up to 1 M, while KCP18 survived up to 0.5 M NaCl. Aligned to this result, Bakhtiyarifar et al. [22] reported that *S. hominis* tolerated a high salt concentration (4 M). Similarly, Feigl et al. [23] observed that *B. pseudogrignonensis* could alleviate 5% saline stress.

Screening for Plant Growth Promoting Activity

Phosphorus solubilization was assessed by halo zone formation on Pikovskaya's medium. All of the strains except KCP18 did not show clear zone (Fig. 4.2). KCP18 likely solubilizes P by secreting organic acids that can chelate phosphate-bound cations, enhancing P availability to plants [24]. Similar mechanisms have been reported in *Pseudomonas*, *Proteus, Ensifer,* and *Streptomyces* [4]. Interestingly, although *S. hominis* was previously reported to solubilize up to 506.3 mg/L of P [25], no activity was observed in our isolates. IAA production, a key phytohormone, was observed in all isolates. KCP18 produced the highest amount (31.42 μg/ml), followed by KCP17 (18.69 μg/ml) and KCP15 (9.30 μg/ml) (Table 4.1; Fig. 4.2). This aligns with Bakhtiyarifar et al. [22] findings, though *S. hominis* strains have shown variable IAA production capacity. Siderophore production was observed in KCP17 and KCP18, as indicated by yellow-orange halos on CAS medium, supporting findings by Moturu et al. [26] and Khanna et al. [27]. In contrast, KCP15 did not produce siderophores. For nitrogen fixation, only KCP18 showed growth on nitrogen-free medium, indicating its N_2-fixation potential (Table 4.1; Fig. 4.2), consistent with

Table 4.1 PGP characteristics of isolated strains

Bacterial Isolates	*Staphylo-coccus* sp. (KCP15)	*Staphylo-coccus* sp. (KCP17)	*Brucella* sp. (KCP18)
Accession number	PQ675774	PQ675775	PQ675776
Salt tolerance (M)	2	1	0.5
P solubilization	-	-	+
IAA production (μg/ml)	9.30	18.69	31.42
Siderophore production	-	+	+
Nitrogen fixation	-	-	+
HCN production	+	+	-
Catalase production	+	+	+
Amylase production	-	-	-
Cellulase production	-	-	-
Pectinase production	-	-	-
Chitinase production	-	-	-

+: presence; -: absence of the activity

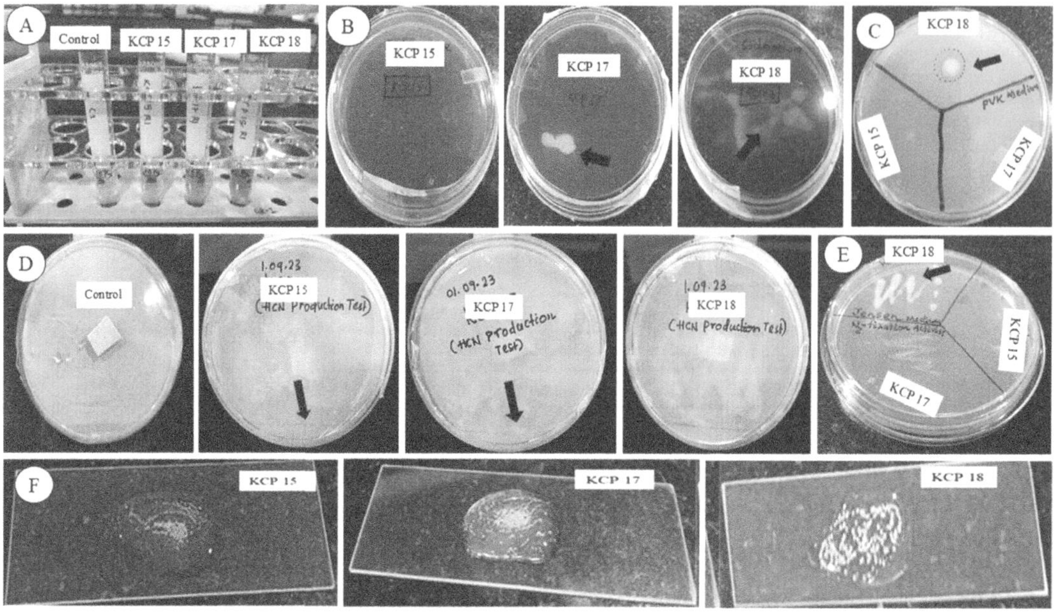

Fig. 4.2 PGP attributes of isolated strains [IAA (A); Siderophore (B); Phosphate solubilization (C); HCN (D); Nitrogen fixation (E); Catalase (F)]

Hussain et al. [28]. *Staphylococcus* isolates showed no such activity, in agreement with Bakhtiyarifar et al. [22].

Screening for HCN, Catalase and Hydrolytic Enzyme Production

Beyond primary PGP traits, strains exhibited HCN and catalase activity. KCP15 and KCP17 tested positive for HCN production, while KCP18 showed no color change, indicating the absence of HCN synthesis (Table 4.1; Fig. 4.2). All strains produced catalase, as evidenced by effervescence upon exposure to H_2O_2 (Table 4.1; Fig. 4.2). HCN production by *S. hominis* has been previously reported and is known to suppress phytopathogens, contributing to plant growth [26]. Similarly, catalase activity has been observed in *B. pseudogrignonensis* and is associated with enhanced bacterial resilience against environmental and oxidative stress [29]. Isolated bacterial strains did not exhibit any clear zone around their colonies (Table 4.1), confirming that they lack the ability of hydrolytic enzyme production.

3.3 The Growth Promotion Effect of Strains on Mung Bean Plant

The *in-vitro* PGP potential of the isolates was assessed using a hydroponic mung bean system. All strains enhanced growth after 14 days (Fig. 4.3), with KCP15

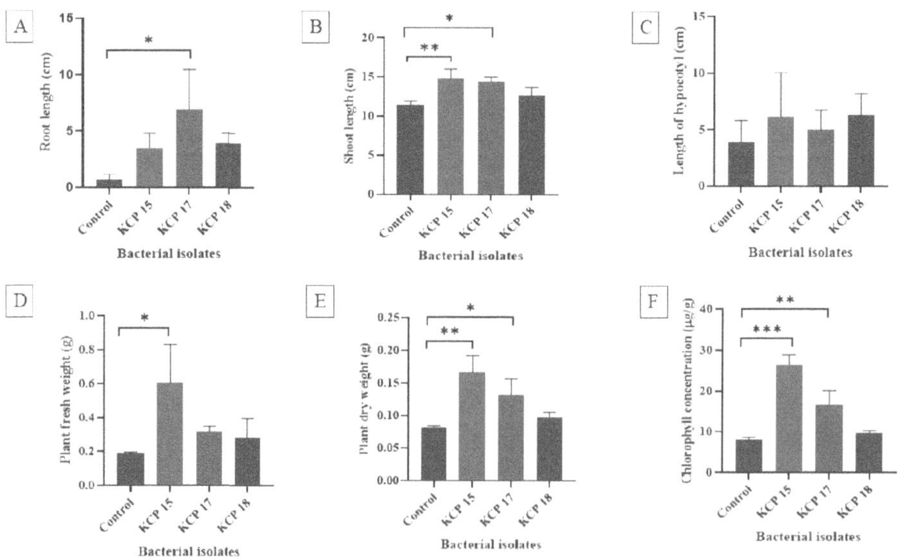

Fig. 4.3 Evaluation of different plant growth parameters [Root length (A); Shoot length (B); Length of hypocotyl (C); Plant fresh weight (D); Plant dry weight (E); Leaf chlorophyll concentration (F)] upon inoculation of different treatments. Under the same parameter, mean ± SD values with various asterisks differ considerably ($P < 0.05$)

showing the most notable effects. Inoculation with KCP15 led to significant increase in shoot length (14.83 cm), fresh weight (0.603 g), and dry weight (0.166 g) of plant, representing 29% and 105% improvement in shoot length and dry biomass, respectively. This strain also enhanced chlorophyll content (26.38 µg/g), supporting its positive impact on plant growth. KCP17-treated plants displayed the longest roots (6.9 cm). These outcomes are corroborated by Cheng et al. [25], who found that improved fresh weight and chlorophyll content in white clover upon inoculation with *S. hominis*. Similarly, Vijay and Kavitha [30] observed enhanced sugars, proteins, and chlorophyll in groundnut inoculated with *S. hominis*. Overall, the tested strains especially KCP15 demonstrated strong potential as biofertilizers for mung bean cultivation.

4. Conclusion

This study was designed to emphasize the potency of isolated bacteria and their effect on mung bean growth through hydroponic system. The isolates were classified as PGPR from the genera *Staphylococcus* and *Brucella*. Characterization of these strains revealed their PGP traits, including siderophore production, phosphorus solubilization and IAA synthesis. The results demonstrated the potential of KCP15, KCP17, and KCP18 to enhance plant growth in a hydroponic system. These isolates are considered as promising PGP bacteria with potential applications in the development of biofertilizer inoculants. Nonetheless, additional research is required to verify the non-pathogenic properties of these strains, thereby ensuring their safety for broad application. Additionally, subsequent investigations should focus on validating the efficacy of these strains in promoting mung bean growth under diverse conditions, including greenhouse and field experiments. Investigating the interactions between rhizospheric bacteria and rhizobia nodulating mung bean, as well as their combined effects on plant growth and yield, should also be prioritized to develop effective and sustainable inoculants.

Acknowledgment

Authors would like to express gratitude to B.L. for data analysis; R.A. for MS writing, editing and proofreading and S.M. contributed special remarking in MS.

References

1. Nair, R. M., Pandey, A. K., War, A. R., Hanumantharao, B., Shwe, T., Alam, A. K. M. M., Pratap, A., Malik, S.R., Karimi, R., Mbeyagala, E. K., Douglas, C. A., Rane, J., and Schafleitner, R. (2019). Biotic and abiotic constraints in mung bean production—progress in genetic improvement. *Front. Plant Sci.*, 10, 1340.
2. Rahevar, P. M., Chauhan, R. M., Patel, P. T., Solanki, S. D., and Gami, R. A. (2023). Delineation of selection criterion using pearson correlation and path coefficient analysis in mutant mung bean (*Vigna radiata*) lines. *Indian J. Agric. Sci.*, 93(7), 738–742.
3. Kumari, N., and Malik, D. (2024). Growth and instability in mung bean production in India. *J. Food Legumes*, 37(2), 224–231.
4. Raklami, A., Babalola, O. O., Jemo, M., and Nafis, A. (2024). Unlocking the plant growth-promoting potential of yeast spp.: exploring species from the Moroccan extremophilic environment for enhanced plant growth and sustainable farming. *FEMS Microbiol. Lett.*, 371, fnae015
5. Santoyo, G., Urtis-Flores, C. A., Loeza-Lara, P. D., Orozco-Mosqueda, M. D. C., and Glick, B. R. (2021). Rhizosphere colonization determinants by plant growth-promoting rhizobacteria (PGPR). *Biology*, 10(6), 475.
6. He, Y., Pantigoso, H. A., Wu, Z., and Vivanco, J. M. (2019). Co-inoculation of *Bacillus* sp. and *Pseudomonas putida* at different development stages acts as a biostimulant to promote growth, yield and nutrient uptake of tomato. *J. Appl. Microbiol.*, 127(1), 196–207.
7. Kumar, S., Stecher, G., Li, M., Knyaz, C., and Tamura, K. (2018). MEGA X: Molecular evolutionary genetics analysis across computing platforms. *Mol. Biol. Evol.*, 35(6), 1547–1549.
8. Tamura, K., Nei, M., and Kumar, S. (2004). Prospects for inferring very large phylogenies by using the neighbor-joining method. *PNAS*, 101(30), 11030–11035.
9. Kumar, A., Kumar, A., Devi, S., Patil, S., Payal, C., and Negi, S. (2012). Isolation, screening and characterization of bacteria from Rhizospheric soils for different plant growth promotion (PGP) activities: an in vitro study. *Recent Res. Sci. Technol.*, 4(1), 1–5.
10. Raklami, A., Slimani, A., Oufdou, K., Jemo, M., Bechtaoui, N., Imziln, B., and Pajuelo, E. (2024). The potential of plant growth-promoting bacteria isolated from arid heavy metal contaminated environments in alleviating salt and water stresses in alfalfa. *Lett. Appl. Microbiol.*, 77(8), ovae075.
11. Ding, Y., Wang, J., Liu, Y., and Chen, S. (2005). Isolation and identification of nitrogen-fixing bacilli from plant rhizospheres in Beijing region. *J. Appl. Microbiol.*, 99(5), 1271–1281.
12. Ahmad, F., Ahmad, I., and Khan, M. S. (2008). Screening of free-living rhizospheric bacteria for their multiple plant growth promoting activities. *Microbiol. Res.*, 163(2), 173–181.
13. Saleem, A., and Ebrahim, M. K. (2014). Production of amylase by fungi isolated from legume seeds collected in Almadinah Almunawwarah, Saudi Arabia. *J. Taibah Univ. Sci.*, 8(2), 90–97.
14. Islam, F., and Roy, N. (2018). Screening, purification and characterization of cellulase from cellulase producing bacteria in molasses. *BMC Res. Notes*, 11, 1–6.
15. Jabeen, A., Hanif, Q. A., Hussain, M., Munawar, A., Farooq, N., and Bano, S. (2015). Screening, isolation and identification of pectinase producing bacterial strains from rotting fruits and determination of their pectinolytic activity. *Sci. Lett.*, 3(2), 42–45.
16. Jenifer, S., Jeyasree, J., Laveena, D. K., and Manikandan, K. (2014). Purification and characterization of chitinase from *Trichoderma viride* N9 and its antifungal activity against phytopathogenic fungi. *World J. Pharm. Pharm. Sci.*, 3(2), 1604–1611.

17. Gu, D. D., Wang, W. Z., Hu, J. D., Zhang, X. M., Wang, J. B., and Wang, B. S. (2016). Nondestructive determination of total chlorophyll content in maize using three-wavelength diffuse reflectance. *J. Appl. Spectrosc.*, 83, 541–547.
18. Becker, K., Heilmann, C., and Peters, G. (2014). Coagulase-negative staphylococci. *Clin. microbiol. Rev.*, 27(4), 870–926.
19. Gautam, V., Sethuraman, N., Kaur, R., Sachdev, S., Marwaha, N., and Ray, P. (2017). Changing epidemiology of coagulase-negative staphylococci in normal flora of skin. *Indian J. Med. Microbiol.*, 35(2), 277–278.
20. Aktar, N., Hossain, M. S., Amin, M. R., Ahmed, R., Ahmed, B., Ullah, M. W., ... and Islam, M. S. (2023). Endophytic bacteria improve jute growth through induction of phytohormones-related gene expression. *Physiol. Mol. Plant Pathol.*, 127, 102115.
21. Szczuka, E., Krzymińska, S., Bogucka, N., and Kaznowski, A. (2018). Multifactorial mechanisms of the pathogenesis of methicillin-resistant *Staphylococcus hominis* isolated from bloodstream infections. *Antonie Van Leeuwenhoek*, 111, 1259–1265.
22. Bakhtiyarifar, M., Enayatizamir, N., and Mehdi Khanlou, K. (2021). Biochemical and molecular investigation of non-rhizobial endophytic bacteria as potential biofertilisers. *Arch. Microbiol.*, 203(2), 513–521
23. Feigl, V., Medgyes-Horváth, A., Kari, A., Török, Á., Bombolya, N., Berkl, Z., Farkas, E., and Fekete-Kertész, I. (2024). The potential of Hungarian bauxite residue isolates for biotechnological applications. *Biotechnol. Rep.*, 41, e00825.
24. Bhattacharyya, P. N., and Jha, D. K. (2012). Plant growth-promoting rhizobacteria (PGPR): emergence in agriculture. *World J. Microbiol. Biotechnol.*, 28, 1327–1350.
25. Cheng, Y., Luo, J., Wang, Y., Ge, J., Zhou, S., Yang, W., and Kou, J. (2021). *Staphylococcus hominis* YJILJH and *Staphylococcus epidermidis* YJ101 promote the growth of white clover (*Trifolium repens* L.) by increasing available phosphorus. *Symbiosis*, 83, 103–114.
26. Moturu, U. S., Nunna, T., Avula, V. G., Jagarlamudi, V. R., Gutha, R. R., and Tamminana, S. (2023). Investigating the diversity of bacterial endophytes in maize and their plant growth-promoting attributes. *Folia Microbiol.*, 68(3), 369–379.
27. Khanna, A., Raj, K., Kumar, P., and Wati, L. (2022). Antagonistic and growth-promoting potential of multifarious bacterial endophytes against *Fusarium* wilt of chickpea. *Egypt. J. Biol. Pest Control*, 32(1), 17.
28. Hussain, M. Z., Suman, S., Kashyap, S., Verma, R., and Rani, L. (2022). Molecular identification of stress tolerant diazotrophic endophytic bacteria from Kaladani rice of Jharkhand. *Eur. Chem. Bull.*, 11, 1570–1577.
29. Ahmad, S., Chaudhary, H. J., and Damalas, C. A. (2022). Microbial detoxification of dimethoate through mediated hydrolysis by *Brucella* sp. PS4: molecular profiling and plant growth-promoting traits. *Environ. Sci. Pollut. Res.*, 29(2), 2420–2431.
30. Vijay, K., and Kavitha, T. (2022). Inoculation of Medicinal Plant Resident *Staphylococcus hominis* subsp. *novobiosepticus* Strain KE6 for Improved Plant Growth and Antagonism to *Pithomyces atro-olivaceous* in Groundnuts. *Asian J. Biosci.*, 2022(4), 12–25.

Note: All the figures and tables in this chapter were made by the authors.

Research and Innovations in Industrial and Marine Biotechnology: A Circular Economy 2024 – Prof. Hrudayanath Thatoi et al. (eds)
© 2026 Taylor & Francis Group, London, ISBN 978-1-041-28285-3

5 Harnessing Nature's Power: Weed-Based Bioformulations in the Management of Sustainable Pest Control in Tea Cultivation

Sandipan Ghosh
Department of Botany, University of North Bengal, Raja Rammohanpur, Siliguri, West Bengal, India

Gargi Sen
Bioinformatics Facility Center, University of North Bengal, Raja Rammohanpur, Siliguri, West Bengal, India

Abisekh Karki
Department of Botany, University of North Bengal, Raja Rammohanpur, Siliguri, West Bengal, India

Arnab Sen*
Department of Botany, University of North Bengal, Raja Rammohanpur, Siliguri, West Bengal, India
Bioinformatics Facility Center, University of North Bengal, Raja Rammohanpur, Siliguri, West Bengal, India
Biswa Bangla Genome Center, University of North Bengal, Raja Rammohanpur, Siliguri

Abstract: The tea industry faces significant annual crop losses due to pests, and traditional chemical pesticides have detrimental environmental and health impacts. Bioformulations made from weed plants have become a viable substitute for environmentally friendly and sustainable pest control methods. Rich in secondary metabolites with strong insecticidal effects, these formulations are made of aqueous solutions that have been isolated from a variety of weed species. Upon use on infected plants, the bioformulation initiates a chain of biochemical reactions that results in the production of reactive oxygen species (ROS), that cause oxidative stress on pests and eventually kill them. Extensive field trials were conducted in the Terai and Dooars regions, renowned for their tea production. The results showed that plants treated with the bioformulation exhibit significantly elevated levels of ROS and antioxidant enzymes compared to untreated and chemically treated controls. The fermentation process introduced a diverse microbial community, some of which possess well-documented pesticidal properties, which can colonize the plant surface and surrounding soil, forming a protective barrier against pests and producing secondary metabolites that further enhance pest control. Our metagenomic investigation successfully unveiled the microbial population in the sample. Reverse ecology studies provided valuable insights into their intricate interactions, illuminating new pathways for effective pest control strategies. The integration of bioformulations and microbial communities offers a holistic approach to pest management, harnessing the power of nature and providing a sustainable and environmentally friendly solution to agricultural challenges.

Keywords: Biofomulation, Metagenomics, Reverse ecology, Weed plants, Microflora

*Corresponding author: arnab.nbu@gmail.com

DOI: 10.1201/9781003759003-5

1. Introduction

Globally, tea ranks among the most widely consumed beverages, with billions of cups prepared every day across more than sixty nations [1-2]. The hill tribes of Northeast India used tea in several traditional methods, and it was initially used as a medicinal beverage in China before becoming popular [3]. Following China, India stands as the second-largest producer of tea globally [4]. In India, tea cultivation supports the employment of over a million workers. Within North Bengal, the three main producing zones—Darjeeling, Terai, and Dooars—span areas of about eighteen, twenty-two, and seventy-five thousand hectares, respectively.In terms of productivity, tea estates in Dooars and Terai record averages close to 1.7–1.8 tonnes per hectare, whereas Darjeeling plantations yield considerably less, around half a tonne per hectare.

The most popular methods for managing plant diseases and reducing pests and pathogens include using chemical pesticides, the removal of infected plants, and the management of weed hosts. Conventional methods, such as resistant cultivars, expensive agrochemicals, and alteration of cultural practices, have reportedly been linked to dangerous outcomes and present risk to people and other living forms [5].

It has been observed that products originating from plants represent a valuable reservoir of diverse bioactive compounds capable of efficiently managing agricultural pests, all the while mitigating the development of pest tolerance. This underscores the preference for employing "Botanicals" crafted from raw extracts of higher plants [6]. Weed plants produce important secondary metabolites that help protect against pests, and they have long been utilized in bioformulations for pest control in the tea industry. However, the intricate microbial interactions underlying their pesticidal activity remain largely unstudied [7-9]. Tea cultivation is threatened by a wide range of insect pests, including thrips, jassids, red slugs, red spider mites, and mosquito bugs. Among these, the mosquito bug and the red spider mite are particularly destructive in North Bengal, leading to substantial annual yield losses.

This study is conducted to evaluate the effectiveness of bioformulations obtained from weed plants in managing tea pests while taking microbial populations and their interactions into account. The goal of the study is to enhance environmentally friendly pest control practices in the tea industry.

2. Materials and Methods

2.1 Preparation of Bioformulation Sample

A bioformulation was created using Indigenous knowledge and cultural practices from tea gardens in West Bengal. Young stem and leaves, 400 gm for 10 L each of *Melia azedarach* (Ghora neem), *Clerodendrom viscosum* (Ghato), *Vitex negundo* (Nishinda), *Justicia adhatoda* (Basak), *Polygonum hydropiper* (Sukurpota), *Tithonia diversifolia* (Hemsl.) (Gray Wild sunflower), *Moringa oleifera* (Sajna), *Murraya koenigii* (Kari patta), *Artemisia vulgaris* L. (Tetepati) were cut into small pieces, dried under the shade, and then soaked in water. As an enhancer, 500 mL of cow urine was added to this mixture and kept for 10-12 days at room temperature. After the incubation period, the mixture was sieved through muslin cloth and the filtrate was ready to use as a foliar spray in the field [10].

2.2 Field Evaluation of Bioactivity of Our Botanical Bioformulation Against Red Spider Mites

Our bioformulation, developed locally, comprises an aqueous mixture of weed plants at concentrations of 10%, 5%, and 2%, which was evaluated in a field trial across two tea estates, Merry View and Ellenbari, during April and May 2023. Positive controls included Etoxazole 10 SC and Cyflumetofen 20 SC. Following plot selection, a calibrated knapsack sprayer was used to sprayed twice with a one-day gap between applications. Mite populations were measured on the adaxial and abaxial surfaces of ten randomly chosen adult leaves from thirty bushes in each plot, and post-treatment observations were documented every day [11]. The given formula was used to find the mean population decrease of mites for each treatment:

$$Mites\ population = \frac{Pretreatment\ population\ count - Posttreatment\ population\ count}{Pretreatment\ population\ count} \times 100$$

Then, the mortality percentage was calculated by subtracting the mite population reduction value from 100.

2.3 Analysis of Changes in Different Non-Enzymatic after Pest Attack and Amelioration Through Bioformulation

2.4 MDA Determination

Mortar and pestle were employed to blend 5 mL of 0.25% TBA with 10% TCA with 250 mg fresh tissue. The mixture was incubated for thirty minutes at 95 °C before centrifuging it for ten minutes at 13,500 rpm. The reading of the supernatant was taken at 532 nm, and then the reading value was subtracted from the absorbance at 600 nm. For determining the MDA concentration, a 155 mM cm-1 extinction coefficient was employed [12].

2.5 Proline Content Determination

A centrifuge was used for 15 minutes at 10,000 rpm with 500 mg of fresh tissue and 5 mL of 3% sulfosalicylic acid. An hour was spent at 100°C incubating one millilitre of the supernatant with one millilitre of glacial acetic acid and one millilitre of acid ninhydrin reagent. After stopping the reaction with an ice bath for fifteen minutes, the tube was vortexed and two millilitres of toluene were added. The top chromophore was used to take its absorbance at 520 nm using toluene as a blank in order to determine the proline concentration [13].

2.6 Reduced Glutathione (GSH) Determination

Upon homogenizing 500 mg of fresh tissue in 5 mL of phosphoric acid, it was centrifuged at 15000 rpm for 15 minutes at 4 °C to analyze the quantity of GSH that is present. From the clear supernatant, 1 mL was reacted with phosphate buffer (3 mL, 0.1 M, pH 6.8) and 0.5 mL of Ellman's reagent (10 mM). The absorbance of the colored complex was then measured at 412 nm as described by Meister and Anderson (1983) [14].

2.7 The Antioxidant Enzymes Activity Under Biotic Stress and Amelioration by Botanicals

Fresh tissue of the plant was homogenized using chilled 0.1 M potassium phosphate buffer (pH 6.8), 0.1 mM EDTA, and 1% PVP in a chilled pestle and mortar to isolate the enzymes. At 4 °C and 15000 rpm for 20 minutes, the homogenate was centrifuged. SOD, CAT, and APX measurements were carried out using the obtained supernatant solution as the enzyme extract.

2.8 *Superoxide Dismutase Activity Assay* (SOD) (EC 1.15.1.1)

SOD was measured at 560 nm following a modification of the method described by Wang et al. (2003), which minimizes photochemical breakdown of nitro blue tetrazolium (NBT). The reaction mixture consisted of 1 mL of 50 mM sodium carbonate, 0.4 mL of 25 μM NBT, 0.2 mL of 0.1 mM freshly prepared hydroxylamine hydrochloride, and the enzyme extract. After mixing, the tubes were exposed to strong light for 15 minutes, and the change in absorbance was recorded at 560 nm. [15].

2.9 *Catalase Activity Assay* (CAT) (EC 1.11.1.6)

There were 2 mL of phosphate buffer and 1 mL of H_2O_2 (19 mM) in the CAT (Catalase) reaction mixture. Subsequently, 500μL of enzyme extract was added. Absorption was finally seen at 240 nm [16].

2.10 *Ascorbate peroxidase Activity Assay (APX)* (EC 1.11.1.11)

Ascorbate peroxidase activity was measured with a substrate solution of ascorbate and H_2O_2 in phosphate buffer, and enzyme activity was measured spectrophotometrically at about 290 nm, according to Nakano & Asada (1987) [17].

2.11 *Peroxidase Assay Activity Assay (POX)* (EC 1.11.1.7)

In the reaction mixture for POX, there were 2 mL of 0.1 M phosphate buffer, 300 μL of 1% Guaiacol, 300 μL of 1% H_2O_2, and 300μL of enzyme extract. At 470 nm, absorbance was measured following a 5-minute incubation period [18].

2.12 Metagenomics Analysis of the Bioformulation

The liquid bioformulation sample was created by filtering the liquid and extracting the DNA using a kit. The mixture was vortexed, lysis buffer was added, protein and RNA removed, and centrifuged. A buffer solution was added, and the DNA was bound. The sample was then mixed with the supernatant, centrifuged, washed, and elution buffer added. The DNA was stored at low temperature for later use.

The study used 16S Metagenomic amplicon sequencing based on the V3–V4 region, and the IlluminaTM Nextseq platform was used for analysis. The primer sequences were 5′ AGAGTTTGATGMTGGCTCAG3′ and 5′TTACCGCGGCMGCSGGCAC3′, and eight PCR cycles were run.

Using a Qubit dsDNA High Sensitivity test kit with ampere beads, libraries were measured and purified. Illumina Miseq and a 2 300PE v3 kit were used for sequencing, along with TRIMGALORE for trimming adapters.

For raw data QC, FASTQC and MULTIQC were employed, followed by QIIME/MOTHUR/KRAKEN/BRACKEN protocols for an accurate genus-level study. NCBI, SILVA, and Green Genes databases were used [19].

2.13 Reverse Ecology

Reverse ecology analysis was employed to examine microbial interactions in bioformulation, focusing on competition and complementarity, using accessible full genome sequences and KEGG Ontology data. To demonstrate the microbial interaction with a person, we have also used the pest two-spotted red spider mite *Tetranychus urticae*'s KO data. To explore microbial interactions, we employed the RevEcoR tool (R-based), which was modified to utilize KEGG Orthology information for calculating indices of competition and complementarity. Utilizing competition and complementation indices, the investigation offers comprehensive insights into the ecological dynamics and interdependencies among the bacterial type strains under study [20].

3. Results and Discussion

3.1 Field Evaluation of Bioactivity of Our Botanical Bioformulation Against Red Spider Mites

The bioefficacy of aqueous extracts from our bioformulation was assessed in two different plots during

Table 5.1 Bio-efficacy of aqueous extract of bioformulation against red spider mite (*Oligonychus coffeae*) in field condition; Merry view tea estate

Treatment	Concentration	Pre-treatment (average)	Post treatment											
Bioformulation (aqueous solution)			Mite population reduction (MPR)											
			Day 1		Day 2		Day 3		Day 4		Day 5		Day 6	
			Pop.	MPR	Pop.	MPR	Pop.	MPR	Pop	MPR	Pop	MPR	Pop.	MPR
	10 %													
		60.9	14.8	75.69	9.4	84.5	6.1	89.9	4	93.4	3.2	94.7	2.5	95.8
		39.8	27.1	31.9	23.7	40.4	18.2	54.2	13.5	66	9.5	76.1	6.8	82.9
	5 %													
		30.8	27	12.3	25.4	17.5	23.7	23	21.9	28.8	37.8	19.9	17.5	43.1
	2 %													
Positive control		27.8	11.6	58.2	6.2	77.6	4	85.6	2.9	89.5	1.7	93.8	1.2	95.6
Control		32.7	31.9	2.3	31.3	3	30.4	6.72	28	12.1	27.4	16	24.8	24.0

field experiments in April and May 2023. During the seven-day trial, a paired t-test was used to evaluate the findings (p-value = 0.01). (Fig. 5.1). The mite population reduction was evaluated for both the positive control group and the control group (Table 5.1). The bioformulation dramatically decreased the mite population at higher doses (10% mortality) in comparison to lower concentrations (2% mortality), much like chemical acaricides as Etoxazole 10 SC and Cyflumetofen 20 SC (Table 5.2).

3.2 Analysis of Changes in Different Non-Enzymatic After Pest Attack and Amelioration Through Bioformulation

The aim of the field experiment was to understand better the stress and coping mechanisms of stressed and control plants by examining their biochemical responses through a range of tests.

3.3 MDA Analysis of Plants

The MDA concentration indicates damage to plant membranes [23]. Our study found that the application

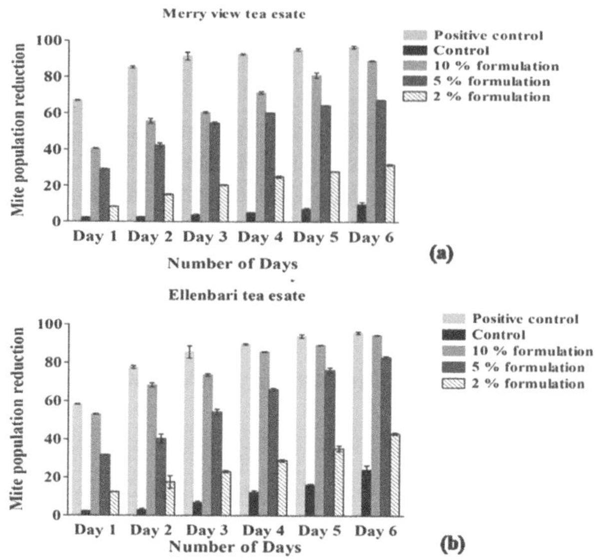

Fig. 5.1 Mite population reduction graph after field trail application; (a) Meery view tea esate; (b) Ellenbari tea esate

Table 5.2 Bio-efficacy of aqueous extract of bioformulation against red spider mite (*Oligonychus coffeae*) in field condition; Ellenbari tea estate

Treatment	Concentration	Pre-treatment (average)	Post treatment											
Bioformulation (aqueous solution)			Mite population reduction (MPR)											
			Day 1		Day 2		Day 3		Day 4		Day 5		Day 6	
			Pop.	MPR	Pop.	MPR	Pop.	MPR	Pop	MPR	Pop	MPR	Pop.	MPR
	10 %													
		64.7	34.8	46.2	30	53.6	26.3	59.3	19.2	70.3	11.4	82.3	7	89.1
		33.7	26.2	22.2	21.8	35.3	19	43.6	17.8	47.1	16.3	51.63	14	58.4
	5 %													
		49.9	45.7	8.41	42.9	14	40.7	18.4	39	21.8	37.8	24.24	36.7	6.45
	2 %													
Positive control		22.1	9.9	55.2	3.1	85.9	2.3	89.5	1.4	93.6	0.5	97.7	0.3	98.6
Control		31.7	30.2	4.73	29.3	7.5	28.4	10.4	28	11.6	27.2	15.62	25.1	20.8

of the bioformulation resulted in a decrease in the MDA content at greater concentrations compared to lower quantities. However, as shown in (Fig. 5.2.) (a), it is noteworthy that the positive control, which contained the chemical acaricide, had a more notable drop than even our highest bioformulation concentration [21].

3.4 Proline and GSH Content Determination

When different concentrations of the bioformulation were applied, there was a notable decline observed in both proline and GSH content, indicating a reduction in plant stress. What's intriguing is that the positive control showed superior outcomes when compared to the highest concentration of bioformulation per gram of fresh tissue, as depicted in Fig. 5.2 (b-c). This suggests that the positive control, possibly containing a chemical acaricide, exerted a more pronounced influence in alleviating plant stress markers [21].

3.5 Antioxidant Enzyme Activity Under Biotic Stress and Its Amelioration by Plants

There is a noticeable increase from day 1 to day 3 following the application of the bioformulation to the diseased bushes. However, when we compare the enzyme activity of APX with the positive control, it is evident that the increase in the highest concentration of bioformulation is not as significant. However, following the application of the bioformulation, Fig. 5.2 (d-g) demonstrates a considerable increase in the activity levels of other enzymes, such as catalase, peroxidase (POX), and superoxide dismutase (SOD) activity assay. This suggests that the system's antioxidant defence mechanisms may have been strengthened [22].

3.6 Enzymatic Assay

This study presents a cost-effective bioformulation using plants with pesticidal properties for tea pest control. The bioformulation uses reactive oxygen species to enhance its effectiveness, which are generated in response to biotic stresses like insect attacks. These stresses induce the activation of hormonal pathways, such as the jasmonic acid signaling pathway. After bioformulation, enzymes like SOD, catalase, and POX showed elevated activity levels, suggesting strengthened antioxidant defence mechanisms. The bioformulation's diverse capabilities suggest its potential in addressing oxidative stress and

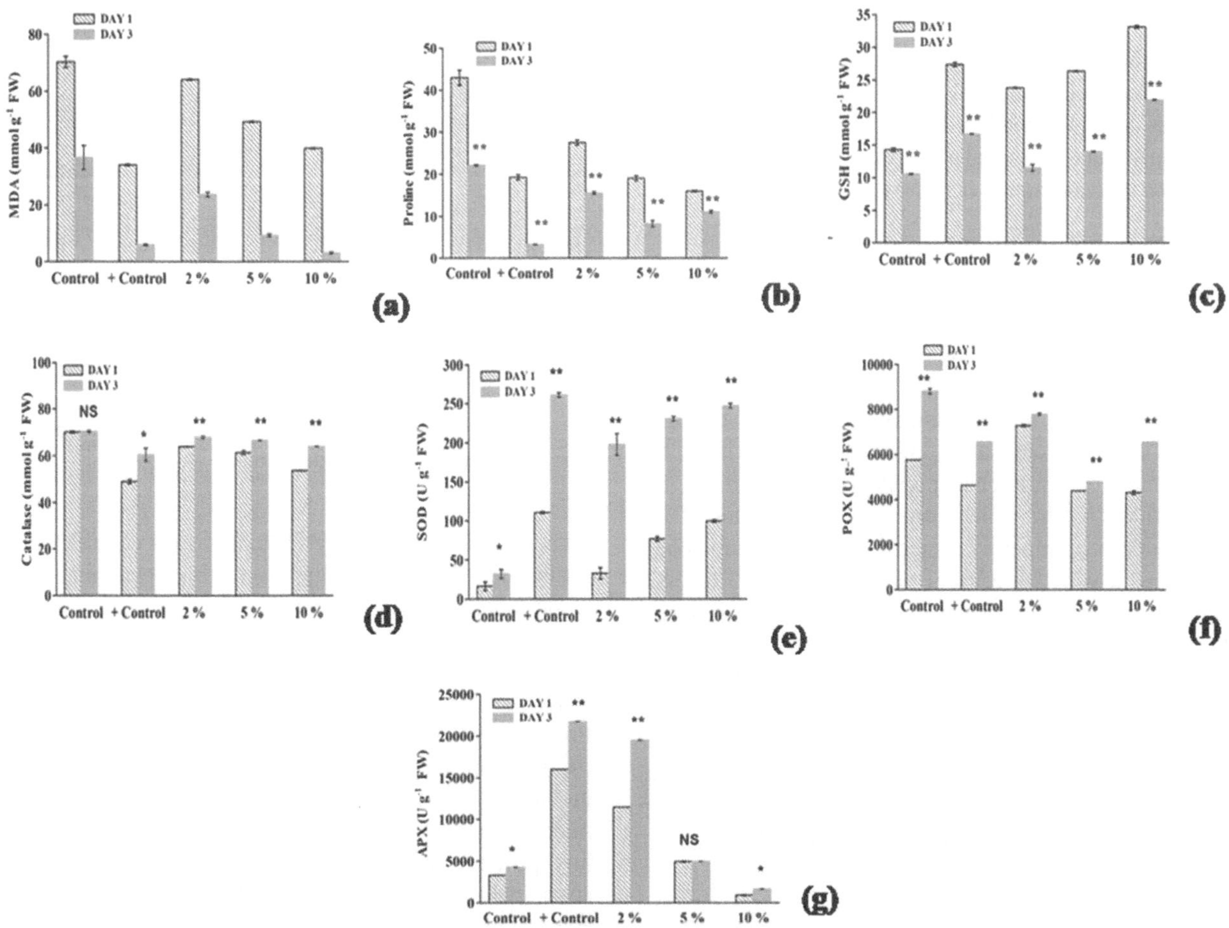

Fig. 5.2 Non enzymatic assay and enzymatic assay of the leaf sample of pest infected plant: (a) MDA content ; (b) Proline content ; (c) GSH content; (d) Catalase; (e) SOD; (f) POX (g) APX

fortifying plant resistance. Glutathione in plants primarily functions in defence metabolism, and the study found a lower activity of the GSH enzyme on day 3 compared to day 1, suggesting a reduction in biotic stress within the plant. Superoxide dismutase (SOD) and peroxidase (POX) play crucial roles in eliminating excess H_2O_2 under stress conditions, and the bioformulation aided in mitigating stress in plants [23-26].

3.7 Metagenomic Profiling of Bioformulation

The bacterial composition of the bioformulation was identified down to the genus level from the phylum. The bioformulation found several major taxa, including Planctomycetes, Spirochaetes, Fusobacteria, Tenericutes, Firmicutes, Proteobacteria, and Bacteroidetes (Fig. 5.3 a-b). Interestingly, the profiling primarily includes unclassified Enterobacteria that have been shown to have nematicidal and acaricidal properties [27]. Biopesticides are also reported to be used by bacteria like Pseudomonas to combat *Tetranychus urticae*. *Streptomyces*, *Rubrobacter*, and *Brevundimonas* have nematicidal action against a variety of pests, whilst *Arcobacter*, *Enterococcus*, *Delftia*, and *Pantoea* have antibacterial qualities and may be used as biocontrol agents against various plant diseases. *Leuconostoc* and *Pseudomesenteroides* are Gram-positive bacteria that have insecticidal effects against aphid and drosophilid pests, while *Bacillus* and *Bifidobacterium* are known for their acaricidal activities. When it comes to diseases and red spider mites, actinomycetes have both antagonistic and acaricidal properties in tea. It is also known that *Methylobacterium* is harmful to *Oligonychus ununguis*.

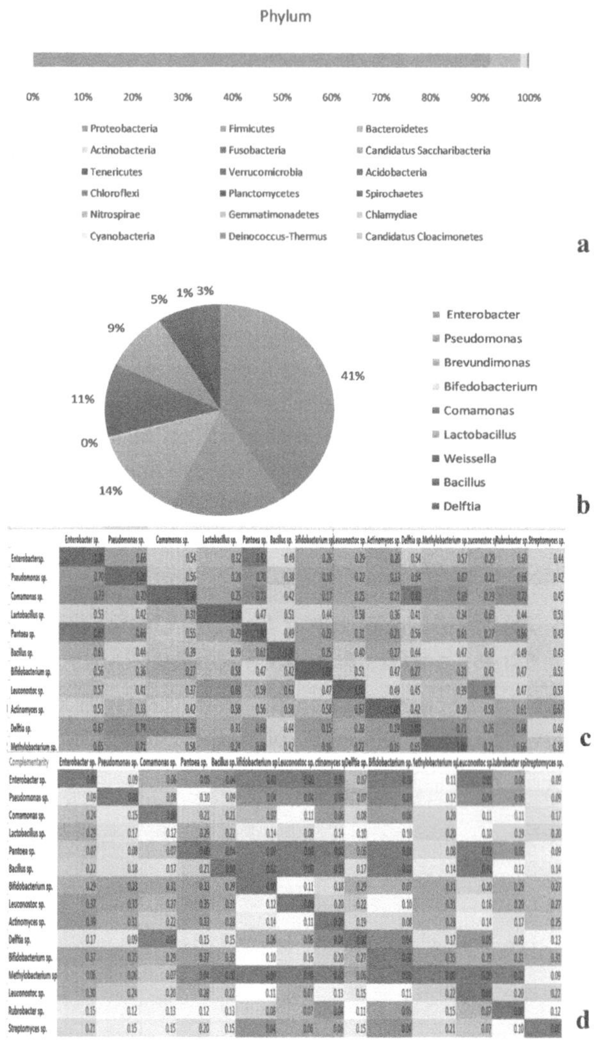

Fig. 5.3 Metagenomics and reverse ecology study (a) Major phylum present found in bioformulation; (b) Major genera found in bioformulation; (c) Heatmap of competition index of different bacteria that have pesticidal activity; (d) Heatmap of complementation index of different bacteria that have pesticidal activity

3.8 Reverse Ecology Study

Uncovering the complex relationships between microbial communities and the red spider mite *Tetranychus urticae* required the use of a reverse ecology methodology. As seen in Fig. 5.3 c-d, the investigation revealed a complementation index ranging from 0.09 to 0.39, suggesting a strong anti-pesticidal effect within the bioformulation's microbial population. Furthermore, the competition index, which serves as an indicator of the magnitude of competitive interactions among microbes, displayed a varied spectrum, ranging from 0.13 to 0.83. We were especially interested in studying how different things interact with the two-spotted red spider mite *Tetranychus urticae*, a pest that affects plants worldwide. The competitiveness score of 0.50 in this case suggested a highly competitive connection [20]. These results offer important new information on the intricate microbial dynamics in the bioformulation, which may help develop more focused and efficient pest management techniques.

4. Conclusion

The study reveals the efficacy of a bioformulation derived from readily available plants that have established anti-mite and pesticidal qualities. Strong results were obtained against tea red spider mites using this economical and environmentally safe approach. In accordance with the study, the jasmonic acid signalling pathway controls the generation of ROS, that cause oxidative damage, which in turn controls plant biotic stress, such as attacks by insects. Proline levels and membrane damage were decreased by the bioformulation, indicating that it was successful in lowering oxidative stress. The study investigates the microbiological composition of bioformulations using metagenomic analysis to identify microorganisms with acaricidal and pesticidal qualities. Reverse ecology studies show both complementary and competing interactions between these bacteria and the red spider mite pest. The findings highlight the significance of the microbial population's poor pest control as well as the potential of organic, microbe-driven approaches.

ACKNOWLEDGMENT

AS acknowledges Biswa Bangla Genome Center, University of North Bengal.

References

1. Khan, N., Mukhtar, H. (2013). Tea and health: studies in humans. *Curr. Pharm. Des.*, 19(34), 6141–6147.
2. Pan, S.Y., Nie, Q., Tai, H.C., Song, X.L., Tong, Y.F., Zhang, L.J.F., Liang, C. (2022). Tea and tea drinking: China's outstanding contributions to the mankind. *Chin. Med. J.*, **17**(1), 1–40.
3. Das, S., Choudhury, P.R., Saha, P., Choudhury, M.D., Bhattacharjee, S., Nath, D., Talukdar, A.D. (2019). Management of Plant-Derived Beverages of North-East India: A Traditional Approach. In: Production and Management of Beverages (pp. 123–150). Woodhead Publishing.
4. Hajra, N.G. (2021). Indian Tea: Robust Growth Amid Rising Challenges. *J. Tea Sci. Res.*, **11**, 1–7.
5. Shahrajabian, M.H., Petropoulos, S.A., Sun, W. (2023). Survey of the influences of microbial biostimulants on horticultural crops: Case studies and successful paradigms. *Horticulturae*, **9**(2), 193.
6. Feng, R., Isman, M.B. (1995). Selection for resistance to azadirachtin in the green peach aphid, *Myzus persicae*. *Experientia*, **51**, 831–833.
7. Saha, T., Modi, S. (2024). Extracts from weed plants: a better resource for biopesticides formulation – a review. *Agric. Sci. Dig.*, **4**(2), 1–8.
8. Rao, K.V.B., Karthik, L., Elumalai, E.K., Srinivasan, K., Kumar, G. (2010). Antibacterial and antifungal activity of *Euphorbia hirta* L. leaves: A comparative study. *J. Pharm. Res.*, **3**(3), 548–551.
9. Şin, B., Öztürk, L. (2021). Nematicidal weeds in the control of plant parasitic nematodes. *J. Agric. Biotechnol.*, **2**(2), 19–28.
10. Ghosh, S., Sen, G., Sengupta, S., Ghosh, C., Sen, A. (2023). Survey on indigenous botanicals used by tea planters for control of pests and diseases of tea (*Camellia sinensis* (L.) O. Kuntze) in the North. *Science and Culture*, **89**, 436–442.
11. Roy, S., Mukhopadhyay, A., Gurusubramanian, G. (2010). Baseline susceptibility of *Oligonychus coffeae* (Acarina: Tetranychidae) to acaricides in North Bengal tea plantations, India. *Int. J. Acarol.*, **36**(5), 357–362.
12. Zhang, K., Khan, Z., Wu, H., Khan, M.N., Hu, L. (2022). Gibberellic acid priming improved rapeseed drought tolerance by modulating root morphology, ROS homeostasis, and chloroplast autophagy. *J. Plant Growth Regul.*, 1–14.
13. Faizan, M., Bhat, J.A., Chen, C., Alyemeni, M.N., Wijaya, L., Ahmad, P., Yu, F. (2021). Zinc oxide nanoparticles (ZnO-NPs) induce salt tolerance by improving the antioxidant system and photosynthetic machinery in tomato. *Int. J. Plant Physiol. Biochem.*, **161**, 122–130.
14. Meister, A., Anderson, M.E. (1983). Glutathione. *Annu. Rev. Biochem.*, **52**(1), 711–760.
15. Wang, W., Vinocur, B., Altman, A. (2003). Plant responses to drought, salinity and extreme temperatures: Towards genetic engineering for stress tolerance. *Planta*, **218**, 1–14.
16. Aebi, H. (1974). Catalase. In: Methods of enzymatic analysis (pp. 673–684). Academic Press.
17. Nakano, Y., Asada, K. (1987). Purification of ascorbate peroxidase in spinach chloroplasts; its inactivation in ascorbate-depleted medium and reactivation by monodehydroascorbate radical. *Plant Cell Physiol.*, **28**(1), 131–140.
18. Rao, M.V., Paliyath, G., Ormrod, D.P., Murr, D.P., Watkins, C.B. (1997). Influence of salicylic acid on H_2O_2 production, oxidative stress, and H_2O_2-metabolizing enzymes (salicylic acid-mediated oxidative damage requires H_2O_2). *Plant Physiol.*, **115**(1), 137–149.
19. Sarkar, I., Kar, P., Sen, G., Chhetri, S., Bhattacharya, M., Bhattacharyya, S., Sen, A. (2022). Metagenomic outlooks of microbial dynamics influenced by organic manure in tea garden soils of North Bengal, India. *Arch. Microbiol.*, **204**, 1–9.
20. Bhattacharjee, S., Sarkar, I., Sen, G., Ghosh, C., Sen, A. (2023). Biochemical and metagenomic sketching of microbial populations in the starter culture of 'Chokot', a rice-based fermented liquor of Rabha Tribe in North Bengal, India. *Ecol. Genet. Genom.*, **29**, 100193.
21. Banerjee, S., Islam, J., Mondal, S., Saha, A., Saha, B., Sen, A. (2023). Proactive attenuation of arsenic stress by nano-priming: Zinc oxide nanoparticles in *Vigna mungo* (L.) Hepper trigger antioxidant defense response and reduce root–shoot arsenic translocation. *J. Hazard. Mater.*, **446**, 130735.
22. Liu, J.X., Feng, K., Duan, A.Q., Li, H., Yang, Q.Q., Xu, Z.S., Xiong, A.S. (2019). Isolation, purification and characterization of an ascorbate peroxidase from celery and overexpression of the *AgAPX1* gene enhanced ascorbate content and drought tolerance in *Arabidopsis*. *BMC Plant Biol.*, **19**(1), 1–13.
23. Morales, M., Munné-Bosch, S. (2019). Malondialdehyde: Facts and artifacts. *Plant Physiol.*, **180**(3), 1246–1250.
24. Nakano, Y., Asada, K. (1987). Purification of ascorbate peroxidase in spinach chloroplasts; its inactivation in ascorbate-depleted medium and reactivation by monodehydroascorbate radical. *Plant Cell Physiol.*, **28**(1), 131–140.
25. Noctor, G., Mhamdi, A., Chaouch, S., Han, Y.I., Neukermans, J., Marquez-Garcia, B., Foyer, C.H. (2012). Glutathione in plants: An integrated overview. *Plant Cell Environ.*, **35**(2), 454–484.
26. Rajput, V.D., Harish, Singh, R.K., Verma, K.K., Sharma, L., Quiroz-Figueroa, F.R., Mandzhieva, S. (2021). Recent developments in enzymatic antioxidant defence mechanism in plants with special reference to abiotic stress. *Biology*, **10**(4), 267.
27. Ruiz-May, E., Álvarez-Sánchez, M.E., Aguilar-Tipacamú, G., Elizalde-Contreras, J.M., Bojórquez-Velázquez, E., Zamora-Briseño, J.A., López-Esparza, A. (2022). Comparative proteome analysis of the midgut of *Rhipicephalus microplus* (Acari: Ixodidae) strains with contrasting resistance to ivermectin reveals the activation of proteins involved in the detoxification metabolism. *J. Proteomics*, **263**, 104618.

Note: All the figures and tables in this chapter were made by the authors.

Research and Innovations in Industrial and Marine Biotechnology: A Circular Economy 2024 – Prof. Hrudayanath Thatoi et al. (eds)

6 Diversity of Honey Bees in Odisha, India: A Review

Rajkishore Swain
Department of Wildlife and Biodiversity Conservation,
Maharaja Sriram Chandra Bhanja Deo University,
Baripada, Odisha

Sandesh Behera
Centre for Industrial Biotechnology Research,
Siksha 'O' Anusandhan University, Deemed to be University,
Bhubaneswar, Odisha

Subhani Rath*
Department of Wildlife and Biodiversity Conservation,
Maharaja Sriram Chandra Bhanja Deo University,
Baripada, Odisha

Abstract: Odisha, characterized by its diverse topography and abundant biodiversity, provides an ideal habitat for a variety of honey bee species. These bees are significant in pollination processes, agriculture, and forest ecosystem dynamics. This review synthesizes findings from numerous studies to illuminate the diversity, ecological functions, and conservation challenges faced by honey bees in Odisha. It emphasizes the necessity for targeted conservation strategies to protect these vital pollinators.

Keywords: Diversity, Ecosystem, Forest, Honey bee, Pollination

1. Introduction

Odisha, with its diverse climatic conditions, provides an ideal habitat for thriving honeybee populations. Honeybees skilfully collect pollen and nectar from flowers, assisting in the pollination process that makes other flowers fertile [1]. The extensive floral diversity in Odisha not only sustains native honeybee species but also attracts introduced species, all of which play crucial roles in maintaining ecological balance and enhancing local economies. Honeybees are particularly recognized for their significant contribution to increasing the yields of various crops and wild plants. In the Dhenkanal district of Odisha, three honeybee species—*Apis cerana indica, Apis florea, Apis dorsata,* and —often forage for nectar and pollen from both crop and wild plant flowers, primarily in the early afternoon. In Bhubaneswar, the predominant pollinators include Apidae species *(Apis mellifera and Apis cerana indica*) and members of the Andrenidae and Syrphidae families (such as *Eristalis tenax*). Apidae accounts for 73.1% of the pollinators in ornamental crops, while Andrenidae comprises 9.5% [2]. Additionally, other animal species are closely associated with different geomorphic types. Odisha's forests host a diverse range of bird species, including the bee-eater species, honey buzzard, and other birds [3], all of which rely on honey and honeybees for survival sustenance.

1.1 Honey Bee Species Diversity in Odisha

Honeybees mainly pollinate many crops. Currently, seven Apis species are identified, with five in India. Two of these are domesticated: *Apis cerana indica*, vital for beekeeping,

*Corresponding author: subhani.rath@gmail.com

DOI: 10.1201/9781003759003-6

and found nationally. This species thrives at altitudes up to 2,500 meters and possesses significant biological and economic value. *A. cerana indica* naturally inhabits various climatic regions, from tropical rainforests to dry grasslands [4]. Pollen grains, high in protein, are essential for honey bee colony growth and tissue repair [5]. The colony's diet mainly consists of carbohydrates for healthy larvae and adults. Major sources of carbohydrates for honeybees are nectar and honey, which support brood rearing and colony development in adverse conditions. While pollen is crucial for brood rearing, nectar is the primary food for larvae and adult bees. Pollen provides protein, and nectar supplies carbohydrates, together meeting bees' nutritional needs [6]. This study investigates the foraging behavior of A*pis cerana indica, Apis dorsata,* and *Apis florea* on cereals, oilseeds, pulses, vegetables, fruits, and forest flora in Angul and Subarnapur districts [7]. These species visiting oilseed crops like mustard, sesame, sunflower, safflower, and niger in Phulbani district. Jena (2021) mentions five prevalent honey bee species in Odisha: *Apis cerana indica* (Indian hive bee), *Trigona iridipennis* (stingless bee), *Apis mellifera* (Italian bee), *Apis dorsata* (rock bee), and *Apis florea* (little bee).

Apis Dorsata (Giant Honey Bee)

In Odisha's forests, *Apis dorsata* builds large combs on tall trees and cliffs. This species plays a significant role in pollination and honey production. It is native to South and Southeast Asia, including India. *Apis dorsata* (Fig. 6.2.A) is widespread throughout South and Southeast Asia and inhabits India's sub-mountainous regions at altitudes up to 2,000 meters. This species migrates locally in response to floral changes. Known for its aggressive defence, *Apis dorsata* is among the most dangerous animals in Southeast Asia, more defensive than the African honey bee. It ranges from 17 to 20 mm in body length and builds exposed combs on tall structures, often in colonies of thousands. Additionally, it can migrate for nectar and pollen resources. As a vital pollinator, it supports biodiversity and ecosystem sustainability. In India, particularly in Odisha, it enhances forest ecology and agriculture through pollination and provides wild honey with medicinal properties to tribal communities. However, it faces threats from habitat destruction, pesticide exposure, climate change, and unsustainable honey harvesting. Conservation initiatives on sustainable honey collection, habitat preservation, and community education are crucial for safeguarding *Apis dorsata* populations and their ecological roles.

Apis Cerana Indica (Asian Hive Bee)

Widely domesticated in Odisha, *Apis cerana indica* adapts well to the state's climatic conditions. It is an important species for small-scale apiculture, especially in rural and tribal regions (Fig. 6.2.B). It is a medium-sized honey bee that builds multi-comb nests in natural cavities such as tree hollows, rock crevices, and human-made beekeeping boxes. This species is a key pollinator for a variety of crops, including fruits, oilseeds, and vegetables, playing a crucial role in agriculture and biodiversity conservation. However, its honey yield is comparatively lower, making it less popular for large-scale commercial beekeeping. *Apis cerana indica* faces threats from habitat destruction, pesticide exposure, and competition from *Apis mellifera*. Conservation strategies, such as sustainable apiculture practices and habitat enhancement, are essential for preserving this ecologically and economically important species [8].

Apis Florea (Dwarf Honey Bee)

Apis florea, commonly referred to as the dwarf honey bee, is one of the smallest honey bee species native to South and Southeast Asia. This species builds its nests on shrubs and small trees. *Apis florea* (Fig. 6.2.C) plays a significant role in pollinating local plants and maintaining biodiversity. It is widely distributed across India, thriving in warm tropical and subtropical regions. This species constructs

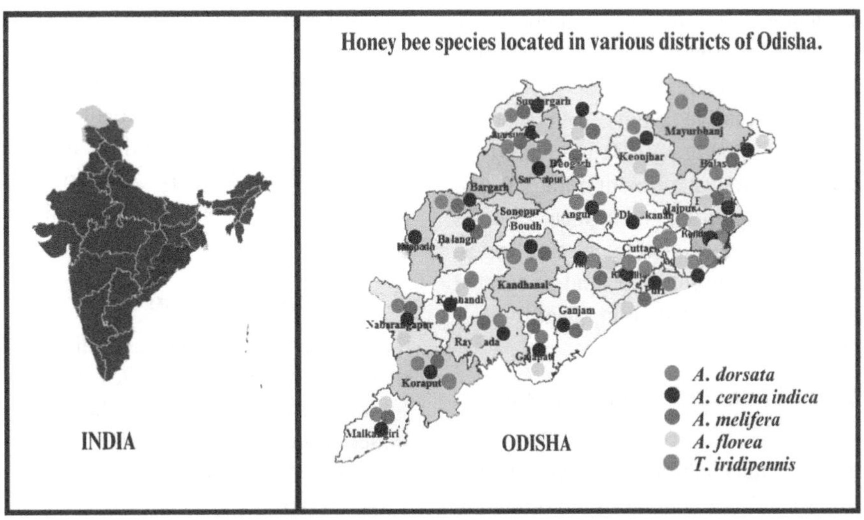

Fig. 6.1 Honey bee species are located in various districts of Odisha

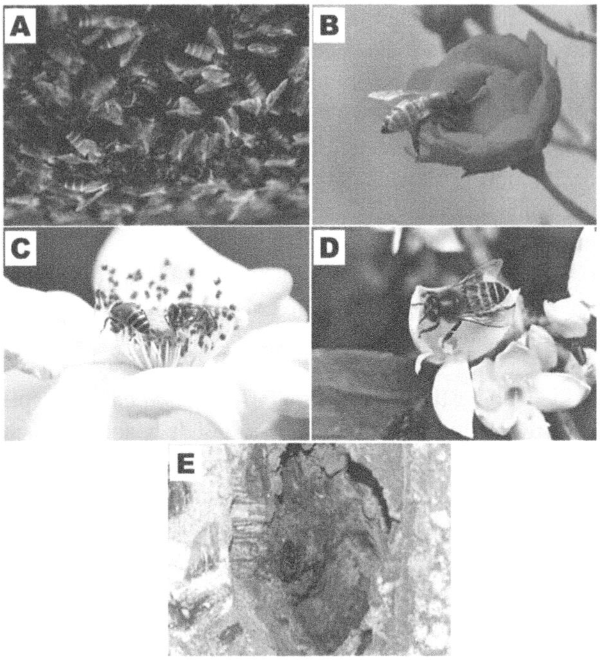

Fig. 6.2 The picture shows the different honey bee species found in Odisha

single, exposed combs on shrubs, small trees, or other low vegetation. *Apis florea* is non-aggressive. The honey of *Apis florea* is highly valued for its medicinal properties. This species plays a vital ecological role by pollinating wild plants and crops. *Apis florea* encounters several challenges, including habitat loss, exposure to pesticides, and the impacts of climate change. Conservation efforts, such as preserving floral resources and raising awareness about their ecological significance, are essential for maintaining their population and pollination services.

Apis Mellifera (Western Honey Bee)

This species is cultivated in select regions for large-scale honey production. Known as the Western honey bee, this species is native to Europe, Africa, and Asia, impacting ecosystems as a pollinator and resource competitor [9]. It has also established feral populations [10]. Despite these issues, feral honey bees are vital for pollinating important crops [11] and native plants. Managed in artificial hives, *Apis mellifera* (Fig. 6.2.D) is favored for large-scale beekeeping due to its efficient foraging and easy management. Its competition with local species like *Apis cerana indica* may pose ecological challenges. Sustainable practices, regular monitoring, and integrated pest management are crucial for maintaining healthy *Apis mellifera* populations.

Tetragonula Iridipennis (Indian Stingless Bee or Dammar Bee)

Stingless bees, found in various habitats, produce valuable medicinal honey. Their small size enables the pollination of various plants. *Tetragonula iridipennis*, known as stingless bees (Fig. 6.2.E), are small, highly social insects from the Apidae family, distributed across tropical and subtropical regions, including India. They can't sting and defend themselves by biting. These bees build hives in old tree trunks, rock crevices, and man-made structures using plant resin, wax, and sticky mud. They are crucial pollinators, aiding the reproduction of wild plants and crops with flowers. Conservation efforts, including habitat protection and awareness programs, are essential for survival.

2. Ecological Significance

The honey bee populations in Odisha contribute significantly to pollination services for agricultural and forest ecosystems. Crops like mustard, sunflower, pulses, and various fruit species depend heavily on these pollinators. Forests in Odisha, such as Mayurbhanj and Kandhamal, Koraput, Keojhar, Angul, and Kahandi, benefit greatly from the pollination of native plants by bees, which supports biodiversity and forest regeneration.

3. Challenges and Threats

3.1 Deforestation and Habitat Loss

The expansion of agriculture, mining activities, and urbanization has significantly reduced the natural habitats of honey bees, especially in forested areas like Similipal, Satkosia, and various other forests in Odisha. Honey bees play a crucial role in pollination and maintaining ecosystem health, making their conservation and habitat restoration essential for preserving biodiversity and supporting agriculture. Various anthropogenic threats—habitat loss, pesticide exposure, climate change, and invasive species pose significant challenges to honey bee ecology. One effective strategy is to restore and create habitats by planting diverse native flowers and vegetation.

3.2 Pesticide Use

The excessive use of chemical pesticides in agriculture negatively impacts bee populations, diminishing their foraging efficiency and overall colony health. Pesticides, along with a decrease in available floral resources, can increase bees' susceptibility to diseases and reduce their tolerance [12,13]. Additionally, the global trade of managed pollinators has contributed to the spread of diseases to new areas and hosts [14,15]

3.3 Climate Change

Temperature fluctuations and rainfall variations in Odisha disrupt honey bee life cycles. Weather factors influence honey bee flight patterns, showing behavioral changes under different conditions [16]. Air temperature, humidity, precipitation, and wind speed significantly impact their foraging activities. A worker bee's activity level is also affected [17]. Climate change threatens pollination

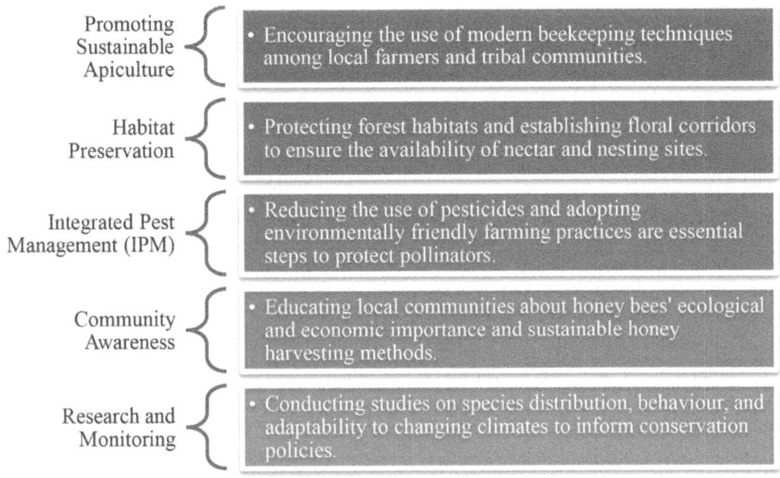

Fig. 6.3 Conservation and management strategies

services, as the honey bee population jeopardizes food security due to changes in foraging rates.

3.4 Diseases and Parasites

In Odisha, bee populations face threats from pests like Varroa mites and diseases. Unsustainable honey hunting practices in tribal regions harm bee colonies and affect population dynamics. The bacterium *Paenibacillus larvae* causes American Foulbrood, the most destructive bacterial disease affecting honey bees. While the *A. cerana* can be infected by *P. larvae*, clinical symptoms are rarely seen in *A. cerana* colonies, making AFB insignificant for beekeeping with this species [18]. *Melissococcus plutonius* also causes European Foulbrood (EFB) in larvae. The Western honey bee (*A. mellifera*) and, Eastern honey bee (*A. cerana*) are all susceptible to this disease [19].

4. Future Research Directions

Research on honey bees has identified several critical gaps that require further exploration. Notably, the exact causes of colony collapse disorder (CCD) remain unclear, including pesticide exposure, pathogens, poor nutrition, and stressors. The effects of pesticides, especially neonicotinoids, and their sublethal impacts on bee health need continued investigation to inform sustainable practices in the agricultural field. Additionally. Studying genetics for disease resistance, alongside developing monitoring programs for population dynamics and health [20]. Research is underway on sustainable farming methods promoting honey bee health, including habitat restoration and crop diversification.

5. Field of Interdisciplinary Research

Interdisciplinary research is essential for a comprehensive understanding of honeybee ecology, as it enables scientists from various fields. Collaboration among entomologists, ecologists, physiologists, and vital for understanding their functioning and adaptation. Research involving ecologists and toxicologists can reveal how environmental factors like pesticides and climate change affect honeybee populations, informing effective conservation strategies [21]. Additionally, partnerships between agronomists and economists highlight the economic value of honeybee pollination, promoting sustainable practices.

6. Conclusion

The diversity of honey bees in Odisha is vital for the health of our agricultural and forest ecosystems. Yet, these invaluable pollinators face growing threats from human activities. Adopting effective conservation strategies that prioritize habitat preservation, sustainable practices, and enhanced public awareness is imperative to safeguard honey bee populations and maintain ecological balance. Moreover, investing in research is critical to better understand how different bee species can adapt and thrive amidst the environmental changes occurring in Odisha. Protecting our honey bees is not just an ecological necessity; it's a commitment to the future of our environment and agriculture.

References

1. Dalio, J. S. (2015). Foraging behaviour of Apis mellifera on Trianthema portulacastrum. *Journal of Entomology and Zoology studies*, *3*(2), 105–108.
2. Patnaik, H. P., Satapathy, C. R., & Panda, N. N. (2012). Prevalence, species richness and diversity of flower visiting insects at Bhubaneswar (Odisha).
3. Swain, R., & Samantarai, R. (2024). A study on the avifaunal diversity of Dhaltangarh Reserve Forest in Jagatsinghpur district, Odisha, India. e-planet, 22(2), 200–209.
4. Koetz, A., (2013). The Asian honey bee (Apis cerana) and its strains-with special focus on Apis cerana Java genotype. Department of Agriculture, Fisheries, and Forestry, State of Queensland, Australia. 58 pp.

5. Somerville, D. (2000). Honey bee nutrition and supplementary feeding. *Agnote DAI/178. NSW Agriculture*, 1034–6848.
6. Seeley, T.D., Seeley, R.H. and Akratanakul, P., 1982. Colony defense strategies of the honeybees in Thailand. Ecological monographs, 52(1), pp.43–63.
7. Panigrahi, D. (2013). Diversity of bee flora and its availability in Subarnapur District of Orissa.
8. Sharma, D., & Gupta, R. K. (2014). Management of Asian honeybees. In *Beekeeping for Poverty Alleviation and Livelihood Security* (pp. 205–245). Springer, Dordrecht.
9. Geslin, B., Gauzens, B., Baude, M., Dajoz, I., Fontaine, C., Henry, M., ... & Vereecken, N. J. (2017). Massively introduced managed species and their consequences for plant–pollinator interactions. In *Advances in ecological research* (Vol. 57, pp. 147–199). Academic Press.
10. Muñoz, I., & De la Rúa, P. (2021). Wide genetic diversity in Old World honey bees threaten by introgression. *Apidologie*, *52*(1), 200–217.
11. Williams, I. H. (1994). The dependence of crop production within the European Union on pollination by honey bees. *Agricultural Science Reviews*, *6*, 229–257.
12. Alaux, C., Ducloz, F., Crauser, D., & Le Conte, Y. (2010). Diet effects on honeybee immunocompetence. *Biology letters*, *6*(4), 562–565.
13. Di Prisco, G., Cavaliere, V., Annoscia, D., Varricchio, P., Caprio, E., Nazzi, F., ... & Pennacchio, F. (2013). Neonicotinoid clothianidin adversely affects insect immunity and promotes replication of a viral pathogen in honey bees. *Proceedings of the National Academy of Sciences*, *110*(46), 18466–18471.
14. Potts, S. G., Imperatriz-Fonseca, V., Ngo, H. T., Aizen, M. A., Biesmeijer, J. C., Breeze, T. D., ... & Vanbergen, A. J. (2016). Safeguarding pollinators and their values to human well-being. *Nature*, *540*(7632), 220–229.
15. Wilfert, L., Long, G., Leggett, H. C., Schmid-Hempel, P., Butlin, R., Martin, S. J. M., & Boots, M. (2016). Deformed wing virus is a recent global epidemic in honeybees driven by Varroa mites. *Science*, *351*(6273), 594–597.
16. Clarke, D., & Robert, D. (2018). Predictive modelling of honey bee foraging activity using local weather conditions. *Apidologie*, *49*(3), 386–396.
17. Page, R. E., & Robinson, G. E. (1991). The genetics of division of labour in honey bee colonies. In *Advances in insect physiology* (Vol. 23, pp. 117–169). Academic Press
18. Chen, Y. W., Wang, C. H., An, J., & Kai-Kuang, H. (2000). Susceptibility of the Asian honey bee, Apis cerana, to American foulbrood, Paenibacillus larvae larvae. *Journal of Apicultural Research*, *39*(3-4), 169–175.
19. Allen, M. F., Ball, B. V., & Underwood, B. A. (1990). An isolate of Melissococcus pluton from Apis laboriosa.
20. Rundlöf, M., Andersson, G. K., Bommarco, R., Fries, I., Hederström, V., Herbertsson, L., ... & Smith, H. G. (2015). Seed coating with a neonicotinoid insecticide negatively affects wild bees. *Nature*, *521*(7550), 77–80.
21. Seeley, T. D., Seeley, R. H., & Akratanakul, P. (1982). Colony defense strategies of the honeybees in Thailand. *Ecological monographs*, *52*(1), 43–63.

Note: All the figures in this chapter were made by the authors.

Research and Innovations in Industrial and Marine Biotechnology: A Circular Economy 2024 – Prof. Hrudayanath Thatoi et al. (eds)

7 Regulation of Risks in Biotech Crops: Evaluating Aspects of Public Health and Intellectual Property Rights

Amruta Das*
SOA National Institute of Law,
Siksha 'O' Anusandhan Deemed to be University,
Bhubaneswar, India

Abstract: Biotech crops and their necessity is well-known theoretical experiment for countries of the world. Innovations in Biotechnology being successfully implemented in agriculture sector has empowered fragments of stakeholders and brought ease to farming as well as farmers' economic well-being. The impact however, is assessed on varying parameters and considerations. Increased resilience, resistance to environmental stress and pests in crops boost productivity and profitability, influencing market preference for various crop types and varieties. Amidst scientific assessment and reliability, there are underlying socio-economic and ethical issues on acceptance of biotech crops among public. The debate over the impact on nutritional health is further fueled by poor standards of Biosafety research across domestic laws. These aspects of regulation are coupled with political and economic factors alongside cultural values in a given legal system which ultimately impact scope of commercialization of such crops. Internationally, many countries have trade restrictions banning export-import of biotech crops, resulting in imbalance in trade negotiations. International food safety standards and guidelines for GM foods are also welcoming, subject to preparedness of national regulatory framework. In this background, the author intends to understand the ethical concerns around the genetically modified crops involving regulatory challenges. Additionally, there is an effort to assess response of judiciary on the extent of intellectual property rights granted in these innovations. The paper suggests scope and limitations on adopting sustainable methodologies to synergize biotechnology with agricultural health.

Keywords: Biotech, Crops, Ethics, Intellectual property rights, Regulatory

1. Introduction

Biotechnology in agriculture has driven a significant increase in production capacity, comparable to the remarkable growth experienced during the Green Revolution of the early 1970s [1]. In the 21st century technological revolution offered genetically modified (GM) crops as a promising approach to achieve sustainable agriculture, however, the adoption of these biotech crops sparked intricate concerns regarding their safety and long-term viability. Since 1994 i.e. the advent of Flavr Savr tomato, the biotech industry rapidly expanded globally [2]. It increased from modest 1.7 million ha in 2016 to 190.4 million ha (by 112 fold) in 2018. Subsequently, these crops got commercialized at an elevated rate. In the 2023 survey, about 190 million hectares areas were cultivated by farmers for GM crops which subsequently increased at an inflated rate in the history of modern agriculture [3]. Also, the trend of approval is also witnessing a steady rise. Since January 2022, about 44 countries secured regulatory clearance for 40 GM crops and around 509 instances of genetic modification [4]. But, as early as 1946, when scientists discovered that DNA of a species is transferable, China emerged to be first country to allow commercialization of transgenic virus resistant tobacco in 1983 [5].

*Corresponding author: amrutadas@soa.ac.in

DOI: 10.1201/9781003759003-7

2. International Regulatory Commitments

With rising concerns over biotech crops and their impact, the Cartagena Protocol on Biosafety (2003) mandated countries to regulate their safe use and cross-border movements. It upholds the precautionary principle from the Rio Declaration. Further, global food safety standards, including for GM foods, are guided by the *Codex Alimentarius Commission*. Cross-border travel of GM goods further carries risk of contamination. Also, the SPS Agreement of the WTO in its effort towards protecting human health, animals and plant life, Incorporates key principles of transparency, risk assessment, equivalence, harmonization, appropriate level of protection (ALOP) along with region-specific conditions [6].

Globally, the Communities adhered to regulations have strived to adhere to the "*precautionary principle*" so as to minimize any potential injury resulting from scientific uncertainty of GMOs. There is a transatlantic conflict over regulation of GM crops. While the United States support exemption of "gene editing" technologies from regulations in case of no plant pest risk, the European Union under the **Directive 2001/18/EC** strives to take strict safety measures over GM foods. Even under the legal regime of the EU (i.e. Article 191(2) of the Treaty on the Functioning of the European Union), the Court has somewhat compromised on its strict stance over biotech crops as witnessed in cases of *Monsanto Italy, and France Monsanto and Fidenato* [7]. The series of precedents especially *Fidenato's* criminal prosecution focused on demonstration of higher "standards of proof" in order to impose ban on cultivation of biotech crops. So, any safeguard issued under Article 34 of the "Food and Feed Regulation" need to be validly based upon scientific evidence and not any hypothetical stance to 'risk' [8]. While the EU is transitioning through shifting ideologies, most of the countries opted to declare "GM free zones" restricting planting of biotech crops.

The dilemma over protecting biodiversity and using it for innovation, triggers diverse ethical conflicts involving breeders, farmers and consumers. The TRIPS, 1995 although promotes patenting rights for innovations, it squarely controls patenting of "life forms" under Article 27.2 by allowing member countries the choice to refuse grant of patents to inventions which pose environmental risk.

3. Regulatory Framework in India

In India, the erstwhile Environment Protection Act, 1986 has limited application with respect to biotech crops. But, it was instrumental to give rise to subordinate legislations in the form of "***Rules for the Manufacture/Use/Import/ Export and Storage of Hazardous Microorganisms, Genetically Engineered Organisms or Cells, 1989.***" Initiatives were undertaken as early as 2004 and in 2012 asserting an urgency to draft overarching regulation governing biosafety issues.

Each GM Crop being different, evaluation for each crop is to be done on a case to case basis on grounds of environment, health, food and feed safety. Having been regimented such framework; it failed to categorize a specific code for biosafety laws. But, it is in 2008 only, protocols were devised under the 1989 Rules to examine validity of GE crops, following which series of guidelines on GMOs e.g. 1998 Research Guidelines on Transgenic Plants were adopted. In the meantime, the Food Safety & Standards Act, 2006 too enthusiastically incorporated few specific provisions on regulation of GE food products, including processed foods.

Subsequently, law transitioned and matured with protocols in 2008 and regulations over environmental harm and in 2016 i.e. "*Guide for Environmental Risk Assessment of Genetically Engineered Plants.*" Additionally, there were committees set up under the rules; like Committee on Institutional Biosafety, Review-Committee on Genetic Manipulation (RCGM) etc. out of which the GEAC (Genetic Engineering Appraisal Committee) acts as the designated authority for conducting evaluation of "*biotech food and agricultural products*", as well as products

Table 7.1 Timeline of events vis-a- vis court's intervention in biotech crops

1.	01.05.2006	: Court directed Field Trial of GMO with approval of GEAC
2.	22.09.2006	: GEAC's Approval for GM crops until further orders
3.	13.10.2006	: Court permitted to plant newly developed DMH-II in identified fields for experimental purpose.
4.	08.05.2007	: The UOI asked for modification of order dated 22.09.2006 which halted further approvals.
	GEAC was allowed to consider Applications filed for use of Bt Cotton varieties for Commercial use.	
5.	08.04.2008	: Modification of order dated 08.05.2007 was sought by Petitioners.
6.	10.05.2012	: A Technical Expert Committee(TEC) was appointed
7.	07.10.2012	: Interim Report submitted by the TEC
8.	23.08.2015	: Final Report submitted with the Court
9.	07.10.2016	: The Central Government assured it wouldn't release any new GM crops or GMOs before 17.10.2016 without public feedback.
10.	22.11.2017	: UOI apprised that Consensus of all stake-holders to be taken on plantation of GM Mustard
11.	18.10.2022	: GEAC granted conditional Approval of transgenic mustard hybrid DMH-11

Source: Compilation

resulting from biotech plants and even animals. Further, the NBPGR controls importing of GM plants for research purpose and the Department of Biotechnology (DBT) certifies quarantine facilities post entry into the Indian territory.

4. Judicial Approach

India's legal and ethical struggle with GM crops and approval for commercialization has compelled judicial activism since 2002 and years subsequent to it.

On aspects of Public health, history of cases in GM crops dates back to almost two decades. The PIL in ***Gene Campaign v. Union of India., W.P. (C) No. 115/2004*** also sought the GEAC to ensure rigorous biosafety protocols before approving clearance to GMOs. It raised the concern; *whether Union Government's order granting environmental release of GM mustard was as per law?* While its approval was challenged being violative of Article 14, 19 and 21 of the Constitution, controversies piled up from environmental activities questioning the threats of field trials and impact on health. The year following it, the Centre faced bold opposition in the petition ***Aruna Rodrigues*** v. ***Union of India & Others, W.P.(C)No.260 of 2005*** which unraveled the reasons and genesis of such anti-GM idea.

The case of Bt Cotton is the landmark decision which summarizes the dialogue and controversies around ownership rights of stakeholders in Bt Crop and its appropriate regime of IP protection. In the case of ***Monsanto Technology LLC and Ors v. Nuziveedu Seeds Ltd. and Ors AIR 2019 SC 559*** Monsanto filed for trademark violation against Nuziveedu [9]. Under the provisions of contractual obligation, Nuziveedu and others agreed with Monsanto to develop GM planning seeds for 'hybrid cotton' utilizing patented invention of Monsanto and thereby, to commercially exploit the developed seeds against payment of license fee to Monsanto. While refusing to pay any amount more than the "trait value" mandated by different States, Nuziveedu argued invalidity of Monsanto's patent praying for its cancellation by virtue of Section 3 (j) of the Patent Law. The Hon'ble Apex Court criticized the summary adjudication of technical suits by Division Bench and remanded back the counterclaim field by Nuziveedu to revoke "***patent invalidity***" (u/section 64(1)(d)) to the single judge.

Meanwhile, in 2022 the government gave green signal to the GM mustard for its environmental release so as to reduce dependency on import of mustard oil from outside. But, trials halted after activists filed complaint with the Supreme Court. Deciding upon the issue; *whether GEAC's approval and subsequent decision (dated 25-10-2022) for the field release of DMH-11 was violative of the precautionary principle*? Justice Nagarathna observed that GM crops can't be allowed to adversely affect sustainable farming, rural livelihoods and health. Strict directions were issued emphasizing upon the 'precautionary principle' and government was urged to draft robust national policy on GM crops, their research, use, and trade.

5. Results and Discussion

Issues in Biotech crops not only invite socio-political and legal debates, but there are ethical concerns as well. Pertinent issues are; *a) whether biotech crops are the only solution to impending dangers of food security? and; b) whether biotech crops ensure sustainability amidst challenges of depleting resources?*

1. **Impact on Public Health:** Concerns of diminishing nutritional value, increased allergies, toxicity and antibiotic-resistance often raise issue of sustainability [10]. While the "*Codex Alimentarius*" sufficiently assess allergenic potential of Biotech crops (inserted proteins in GM crops) and claim to be as safe as conventionally bred varieties, however, there are studies that claim counterclaim when conducted across animals and their feeds [11, 12].
2. **Environmental Injury:** GM crops are believed to show signs of positive impact on soil health in terms of herbicide tolerant crops that encourage no tilling in order to get rid of weeds. Careless planting of biotech crops can create super weeds resistant to herbicides, risking future public health. Gene flow to wild plants, non-GM, and organic crops adds to the concern. But simultaneously, evidence of excessive use of "glyphosate" (herbicide) across Canada since 1994 to 2021 signals potential hazard in future [13].
3. **Sustainability:** Irresponsible and unregulated experimentation of biotech crops threat possibilities of eradication of other species or variety. Events like; a) destruction of ecosystem for "monarch butterfly" in North America due to herbicide-tolerant GM corn and soy and; b) controversial "Séralini" research suggestive of potential toxicity of liver and kidney when exposed to herbicide Roundup' in rats spiral up debates over sustainability [14].
4. **Public Acceptance:** Public acceptance of biotechnology in food crops depends on how people weigh risks versus benefits. Perceptions vary widely across different demographics and contexts. The case of "GM Rice" in China (fends off pests by toxin from Bt), although witnessed low acceptance, yet it reflected participation of consumers via Social media campaigns [15]. Moreover, recent effort of the "Ministry of Agriculture and Rural Affairs (MARA)" in December 2023 to get approval of 37 biotech corn and 14 soybean varieties with a pilot study clearly indicates significance of public perception in shaping GM friendly environment to foster internal food security and independence.

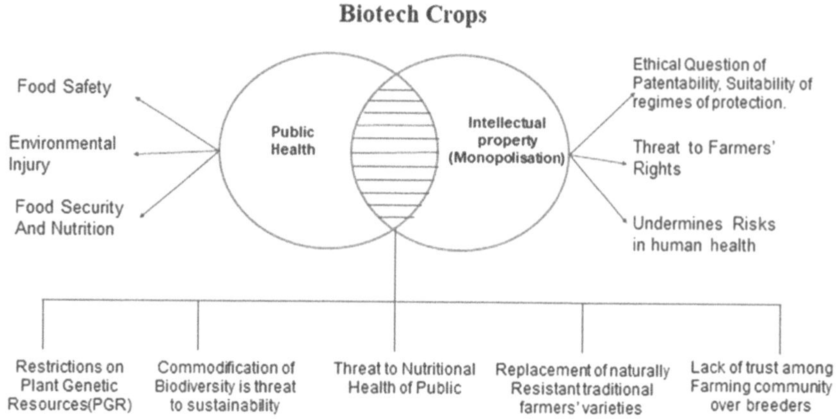

Fig. 7.1 Intersection of public health with IP aspects of biotech crops

Source: Author's Own.

5. **Impact on Export-Import:** Cross border transfer of GM products is regulated under the GEAC equipped with norms of "declaration." Corporations like Bayer Monsanto, Syngenta etc. are exploring opportunities of commercialization of GE crop-products outside India including Philippines and Bangladesh because India's indefinite moratoriums on Biotech crops since 2010 has substantially slowed down trade in India [16].
6. **Agrarian Distress:** Biotech crops, with their high and shifting prices, deepened farmers' financial struggles as they tried to stay competitive. This widened the gap, favoring wealthy, industrial farmers while sidelining small and marginal ones.
7. **Weak Regulatory Environment:** Inadequate clear guidelines and a proper biosafety law in India hinder biotech research. Delays and restrictive policies push seed companies to look abroad, causing economic setbacks at home.
8. **Lack of Transparency:** Absence of disclosures from Government about Biosafety data (environmental contamination etc.) over field experiments of BM Crops creates doubts towards public acceptance. Lack of consultative process with farmer's representatives over commercialization of Bt Crops does not infuse sense of trust.

The intersection between IP and public health in biotech crops remains unclear. Innovations in crops often overlap with pharmaceutical and food sectors. In India, there were no special (*sui generis)* law to recognize "new" plant varieties until 2001 i.e. the Protection of Plant Varieties and Farmers' Rights Act which too invited ethical contentions over suitability of plant breeders' rights (PBR) or 'plant patents' over crops; be it new variety, seed or technology. Material Transfer Agreements (MTAs) controlling access to genetic materials (including unprotected genes, either uncharacterized, or identified with markers) too could be put in place between importing and exporting countries or agencies while promoting breeding of biotech crops. But, there is need for disclosures on its source or origin so as to facilitate benefit sharing schemes.

India recognized the limitations on GM plants under section 3(j) of the Patent (Amendment) Act, 2002, wherein non-patentable inventions are listed out and included *"plants and animals in whole or any part thereof other than microorganisms but including seeds, varieties and species and essentially biological processes for production or propagation of plants and animals."* While, the *"product of nature"* theory still holds ground, the landmark verdict of ***Diamond v. Chakrabarty*, 447 US 303 [1980]** remains the guiding precedent for major jurisdictions which had earlier settled the position that, bacterium "(which can digest multiple components of crude oil) is patentable as it was undiscovered in nature and was never exhibited in any/other naturally occurring bacteria. It is the landmark verdict of 1948 in ***Funk Brothers's*** case that guides patent laws on transgenic crops till today, ruling that natural discoveries alone can't be patented and innovation lies in how we apply nature to create something 'new' and 'useful'.

6. Conclusion

Genetically engineered crops are potential solution to food security, but are opposed over unnatural methods of intervention. In India, weak alignment between science, law, and stakeholder consensus fuels ongoing debate. Poor coordination between lawmakers and the government deepens the deadlock. So far, only Bt cotton could be cultivated commercially and only Bt Brinjal is the only food crop which has come closer to commercialization in India. Other crops including GM mustard; chickpea, corn, pigeon pea, sugarcane etc. are in different stages of such approval. Surprisingly, farmers demand technological up-gradation in the "Bt cotton technology" in India stating declining effectiveness in the older "BG-II variety" against new pests and weeds, especially in changing climate conditions. The recent split verdict of July 23rd 2024 reflects uncertainty within judiciary too while it tried to navigate through the dilemma of allowing GM mustard in farmer's fields. It further testifies the negative environment around risks and safety over environmental release of GM Mustard. While each crop is unique in its traits, it demands separate and sui generis protocol for testing, release etc.

The public sentiment and the regulatory environment in India are yet to accept biotech crops amidst regulatory laxity, pending litigations and socio-cultural barriers. The recently proposed policy on liability standards, defining final and appellate jurisdiction to GEAC, seem hopeful. Aspect of "labeling" on GM products signaling use of GM ingredients would facilitate informed choices among consumers and would ensure healthy regulatory environment. Additionally, the premises of sustainable agriculture with respect to biotech crops can thrive only with mutual exchange of benefits and "common but differentiated responsibility (CBDR)" of stakeholders.

Acknowledgment

The author acknowledges the valuable contribution of the editor as well as reviewers for their recommendations in enhancing the visibility of the paper.

References

1. Raman, R. (2017). The impact of genetically modified (GM) crops in modern agriculture: A review. *GM Crops Food*, 8(4), 195–208. doi: 10.1080/21645698.2017.1413522.
2. Bruening, G., and Lyons, J. (2000). The case of the FLAVR SAVR tomato. *California Agriculture*, 54(4), 6–7.
3. Tome K. G. N. (2024, December 4). What is the Impact of GM Crops on the Environment?. *Science Speaks*.
4. Hamdan, M. F., Mohd Noor, S. N., Abd-Aziz, N., Pua, T. L., and Tan, B. C. (2022). Green revolution to gene revolution: Technological advances in agriculture to feed the world. *Plants (Basel)*, 11(10), 1297. doi: 10.3390/plants11101297.
5. James, C. (2008). *Global status of commercialized biotech crops in 2008*.
6. WTO. The WTO Agreements Series Sanitary and Phytosanitary Measures.
7. Guida, A. (2021). The precautionary principle and genetically modified organisms: A bone of contention between European institutions and member states. *Journal of Law and the Biosciences*, 8(1). doi: 10.1093/jlb/lsab012.
8. Corcione, E. (2018, March 19). Emergency Measures Against GMOs Between Harmonizing and De-harmonizing Trends: The Case Fidenato et al., *European Papers*.
9. Kanaujia, A., and Bhattacharya, S. (2021). Genetically Modified Crops and Indian Agriculture: Issues Relating to Governance and Regulation. In Sudesh Ratna, R., Sharma, S.K., Kumar, and R., Dobhal, A. (Eds.), *Indian Agriculture Under the Shadows of WTO and FTAs: Issues and Concerns* (pp. 215–233). Springer, Singapore. doi: https://doi.org/10.1007/978-981-33-6854-5_11.
10. Benbrook, C. M. (2012). Impacts of Genetically Engineered Crops on Pesticides Use in the U.S.—The First Sixteen Years. *Environmental Science Europe,* 24. doi: https://doi.org/10.1186/2190-4715-24-24.
11. Joint FAO/WHO Codex Alimentarius Commission, Joint FAO/WHO Food Standards Programme, & World Health Organization. (2004). *Codex Alimentarius: Foods derived from biotechnology*. Food and Agriculture Org.
12. Shen, C., Yin, XC., Jiao, BY. *et al.* (2022). Evaluation of adverse effects/events of genetically modified food consumption: a systematic review of animal and human studies. *Environmental Science Europe,* 34. doi: https://doi.org/10.1186/s12302-021-00578-9.
13. Benbrook, C. M. (2016). Trends in glyphosate herbicide use in the United States and globally. *Environmental Sciences Europe*, *28*. doi: https://doi.org/10.1186/s12302-016-0070-0.
14. Casassus, B. (2014). Paper claiming GM link with tumours republished. *Nature*.
15. Huo, L., and Liu, Y. (2022). Genetically modified rice: do Chinese consumers support or go against it? Based on the perspectives of perceived risk and trust. *Frontiers in Psychology,* 13. doi: 10.3389/fpsyg.2022.813862.
16. Aga, A. (2023, September 21) Genetically modified crops: Twenty years of debate in India. *HEINRICH BOLL STIFTUNG*.

Research and Innovations in Industrial and Marine Biotechnology: A Circular Economy 2024 – Prof. Hrudayanath Thatoi et al. (eds)
 ISBN 978-1-041-28285-3

8 Exploring the Impact of Local Bioresource Utilization on Guest Preferences for Healthy Food in Odisha's Restaurant

Aakash Dash and Susanta Ranjan Chaini*
School of Hotel Management Faculty of Hospitality and Tourism Management,
Siksha 'O' Anusandhan (Deemed to be University),
Bhubaneswar, Odisha

Abstract: This study examines the impact of using local bioresources on guest preferences for healthy food in restaurants across Odisha's cities—Bhubaneswar, Puri, Konark, and Sambalpur. The aim is to connect sustainable restaurant practices with guest behaviour by exploring how locally sourced ingredients influence dining choices within a circular economy framework.A mixed-method approach was used, combining structured surveys with group interviews to gain insights into guest preferences. Respondents were grouped based on age, income, and health awareness. Thematic analysis was applied to qualitative interview data, while quantitative survey data were analysed statistically to find patterns between bioresource usage and guest preferences.The study found a strong guest preference for restaurants using local bioresources. Health-conscious guests especially valued the traceability and quality of ingredients. Younger guests (15-35) preferred innovative, health-focused options, middle-aged guests (35-55) valued traditional yet health-centric food, while older guests (55+) preferred traditional, nutrient-dense meals. Income also influenced preferences, with higher-income groups showing greater interest in bioresource-based meals. Restaurants integrating fresh, locally sourced ingredients—such as seasonal vegetables, organic dairy, and farm-raised meats—showed enhanced guest satisfaction and brand loyalty. These practices support environmental sustainability and local economies.Incorporating local bioresources in restaurant offerings aligns with guest preferences and supports rural development and sustainable food systems within a circular economy, helping communities and businesses alike.

Keywords: Local bioresources, Guest preferences, Healthy dining, Circular economy, Odisha, Sustainable restaurant practices, Health awareness

1. Introduction

Healthy food means the food that hasbeen generated from organic compost or natural compost without using of excessive pesticides or harmful fertilizers that degrade the quality and nature of food [1]. Nowadays, guest is becoming more conscious about own health. So, even when they are visiting restaurants, they prefer healthy or organic food that satisfy their requirement of being healthy [2]. In recent times a huge turn takes place from the guest preference in choosing food while visiting restaurants in Odisha. As Odisha is considered as an eastern coastal state of India which is popular for its culture and traditions apart from thenative food [3]. The soil of Odisha is rich in local-bioresource which helps in producing the organic food materials withoutexcessive use of pesticides, fertilizers that degrade the quality and growth of ingredients that are produced. Bioresource means natural raw materials that are obtained from local sources, besides, manyother ingredients such as plants, fresh-vegetables, fruits (seasonal), herbs, spices and dairy products, obtaining meats from the organic meat farming

*Corresponding author: susanta_chaini@yahoo.co.in

DOI: 10.1201/9781003759003-8

[4]. All these ingredients are produced from local source withouttransporting from long distance by minimizing the environmental impacts. While understanding the bioresource it is necessary to know about the organic food materials. Organic food materialsmean the agriculture ingredients and other food products that are produced without using pesticides, chemicals, artificial fertilizers. These products are the foundation of the organic food systems which supports the health as well as environmental development by using soil fertility and sustainable practices. Organic food materials performsignificant rolein the food market that sustain the health and the environment [5]. The food materials must be generated in their natural habitat with natural compost and biological pest control which does not harm the agricultural process of generating organic food materials [6].According to the sustainability, these food materials focused on proper crop rotation from time to time in order toenhance the quality of the mixture of natural compost in order tomaintain the life span of the soil, in this way it not only produced quality products but it also helps in balancing the ecosystem. Thus, organic practicing helps in preventing soil from degradation and preserving the water from contamination. In Odisha there are some places where organic food materials are generated topractices sustainability and balancing the ecosystem for keeping the environment safe and healthy. These places are Koraput, Balangir, Kalahandi and Keonjhar where organic food materials are produced [7]. Koraput district is found at southern part of the Odisha in the eastern ghats known for its culture and traditions along with the finegrowth of organic food materials because of its soil fertility and using of natural composed for enhancing the quality and standard of the products.Koraput region is the home traditional farming communities that uses sustainable and natural methods for growing organic food product as well as for their generations to generations. Koraput region has agro-climate region that supports multiple diverse agriculture practices that helps in growthof multiple organic food materials in their natural habitat without using excessive number of pesticides and fertilizers.The cultivation product in Koraput is coffee [8]. Apart from coffee, rice, millets, spices and fruits & vegetables are also cultivated organic way to support the local communities as well as keeping the biodegradable process for supporting the ecosystem of the surroundings. Balangir district is another place where organic farming practices slowly growing contributing towards sustainable agriculture practices. Rice, millets, pulses, vegetables etc, are cultivated for fulfilling the demand of local people as well as market demand with promoting the sustainable farming [9]. There are more places in Odisha where these organic farming by using of local bioresource are performing for setting up the organic farming in Odisha. The study examines the impact of local bioresourceuse for guest preference towards healthy food [10].

1.1 Impact of Local Bioresource on Selecting the Healthy Food According to the Guets Choices

Nutritional Based

The most important impact of local bioresource is nutritional based on supporting the taste and health of the guest. The food or ingredients that has been sourced from local bioresource is rich in nutritional value because it is cultivated by using natural compost and other natural fertilizers without using excessive of pesticides which damage the fertility of the soil as well as degrade the quality and standards of the food or ingredients materials. According to the suitable climate and environment the food must be grown in their favourable conditions by using local bioresource which enhance their quality and standards of the products that is cultivated [11]. For example, rice, paddy, millets are grown in Odisha at huge volume because it supports the favourable environment conditions. The second most important thoughts come under the nutritional based is to cultivate seasonal vegetables and fruits for getting better nutritional value as well as it supports the quality and standards of the products [12].The seasonal vegetables and fruits have certain benefits like - environmental, health, economic, soil & water,sustainability and circular economy. These benefits will discuss further in the study.

Environmental Benefits

Seasonal vegetables and fruits are grown naturally without needed much of pesticides, fertilizers and other chemicals. So, the seasonal vegetables and fruits are rich-in nutrients and food value. The purpose of growing seasonal vegetables & fruits also helps in balancing the ecosystem through the process of crop rotation by using natural compost and fertilizers which strengthen the fertility of the soil resulting in growth of the vegetables and fruits in their natural habitats [13]. The process of cultivating seasonal vegetables and fruits by using local bioresource gives a diverse range of agriculture systems which helps in preserving other species, soil's health and plants that contributes to supporting biodiversityin the ecosystem [14].

Health Benefits

As these seasonal vegetables and fruits are produced from natural process including friendly environment conditionswithout using of artificial fertilizers and pesticides that helps in enhancing their nutrients value and supporting their quality which gives proper value to the health of guest. Consumption of seasonal vegetables and fruits that grown by using local bioresource are full of nutritious which gives proper vitamins and minerals to thebody as well as it helps in clearing the digestion problems [15]. While consuming these naturally using local bioresource products increase immunity level in human body by detoxifying the germs in the form of sweat and urine. It makes the blood smooth that helps to flow easily and rich to every part of the body that provide strength and energy to each &parts of the body to perform different activities irrespective of body parts.

Cost Benefits

The economic advantage of seasonal vegetables and fruits by using of local bioresource for the local farmers as well as in the local economies by following the sustainable and cost-effective practices [16]. Expenditure of farming is reduced due to the use of local bioresource. Seasonal vegetables and fruits are naturally adapting the environment conditions as well as it needednatural compost without many needs of artificial fertilizers and pesticides that degrade in the growth of products. It requires less rotation process, irrigation, usage of water and other cost for the quality and standards of the vegetables and fruits.As these are grown under favourable conditions yield higher-quality produce [17]. Thus,this might be increases the price of these crops or these crops might be at the premium level in the market but those who wants the organic and fresh crops they may willing to pay more which results profitable for the farmers who engaged in practicing sustainable or organic farming. These profitable income from the seasonal crops boast the agricultural economy in local areas and communities, which gives empowerment to the local farmersby generating the employment opportunities [18]. It develops the channels of farm-to-consumers where, consumers directly buy the crops from the local farmersthat generates revenue from small-scale local farmers which helps in setup the farmers' market. These channels support the marginal farmers of local area by the help of the communities for keeping the profits earned without much relay on the mechanism. While cultivating the seasonal crops in the local areashelps in reducing the imports charges or relay on off-seasonal vegetables and fruits. It not only helps in be self-sufficient, but it also reduces the transportation costincluding the fuel expenses and storage costs.These selling of crops locally reduce the percentage of both spoilage and food-waste by enhance the margin of profit [19].

Local bioresource helps in increasing the circular economy by reducing the agriculture waste that reuse in farming. This reducing of production cost by setting up the use of resource through sustainable cycle processto preserve the environmental impact and balance the ecosystem [20]. Allthese processesof making use of local bioresource fully leads to promote sustainable tourism where the local resource must be used by preserving it for their future needs and the next generation [21].

1.2 Sustainable Impact

The use local bioresource is an example of practicing sustainability in restaurant industries. If the crops both seasonal & off-seasonal are produce by using local bioresource is known to be sustainable farming.According tosustainable impact, nowadays restaurants are sourcing their ingredients from the local areas tosetting up sustainable practices [22]. This sustainable practice helps in reducing environmental impact and contributes to rising the local economy positively [23]. The main purpose of the restaurants is to do sustainable sourcing tofulfil the guest preferenceto provide healthy food using local bioresource [24].

There are some points on which sustainable restaurants can takes place: -

- Avoid products not to be consider such imported exotic ingredients or overfished sea food because its harmful impact on biodiversity [25].
- Restaurant can save energy by implementing the renewable energy sources like solar panels. Thus, applying of solar panels helps in reducing the energy consumption [26].
- Water conservation is another valuable point to be discuss about the sustainable practices in restaurant industries. Now there are many ways to control the water supply as well as several waysof using water economical manner to support environment. Restaurants can apply low-flow faucets and dishwashing systems that manage the water consumption. These helps in saving water from extra expenses and from environment impact by practicing the sustainability in the restaurants. Another way of saving water by reusing of wastewaterfor gardening and cleaning the other parts of the restaurants. Rainwater harvesting is the better options for water conservation in restaurants.In restaurants staff training will be held for economically water use in several ways for water conservation process [27].
- The main purpose of control waste management is to reduce the waste by reusing of resources as well as recycling the materials that helps in reducing the environmental degradation by implementing efficient operations [28].For better sustainable practices and follow eco-friendly dinning trends the effective waste management must be set up.Waste management can be focused on various parts of the restaurants [29].

1.3 Cultural and Authentic Dinning Experience

The main purpose of restaurants to preserve these culture and authentic dining experience by using local bioresource toreduce waste as well as fulfil the preference of guests towards healthy food [30]. The culture can be preserved through the food by serving at the restaurants which gives some cultural aspects of that area to the guests.Sustainable restaurants focus on reducingenvironmental impact along with following cultural and their local identities [31]. While discussing on cultural and dining experience along with the use of local bioresource that gives a new dimension to the restaurants for fulfilling the guest choices towards healthy food served at restaurants [32].

Here, restaurants are sourcingfrom local bioresource for getting fresh and natural ingredients along with seasonal vegetables and fruits that naturally grown without using ofpesticides and artificial fertilizers to enhance their quality and standards. These seasonal vegetable and fruits or other crops giveunique tastes that express the authenticity.

The culture and authentic can be express through the food by its cooking method.So, the most important thing for the restaurants is to know the traditional way of cooking of dishes tokeep their culture and enhance the authentic flavours into the food. While following the traditional method of cooking it expresses about the origin of ingredients and traditional method of cooking whichconnects the guest with their local heritage [33]. There are some local culinary techniques that each and all restaurants are following in a way to preserve the culture and authenticity of the dish, such as clay-pot cooking, hand-grinding spices. These local culinary methods arepracticing sustainable cooking methods by using local bioresource for reducing waste and carbon that gives environmental impact [34].

So, the traditional method of cooking is not only for preserving the culture or authenticity of heritage, but it also preserves environmental impact along with the practicing of sustainability by using of local bioresource. Thus, this is a way to acknowledge the guest about the culture and authentic dining experience.The main goal of practicing sustainable restaurants is to introduce the local bioresourcein the restaurants for their source of gathering organic ingredients as well as crops for satisfying the guest preferences [35].

So, local bioresource means the source of collecting the raw food material locally which are grown natural waywithout using of pesticides, fertilizers or any harmful chemicals that enhance the quality of the ingredients. It is a process of placing the crops or ingredients that are freshly sourced from local areas directly through the local farmers or producers for getting seasonal and authentic taste of the products [36]. Utilization of local bioresource is ultimately the source of promoting sustainable practices in the restaurants because once the organic ingredients or other raw food materials are introducing into the restaurants, it genuinely protecting the environmental impact of degradation as well as it reduces the waste of the restaurants which drives the economic benefit for the restaurant as well as local surroundings.While reducing the waste it is necessary to use plates, cutlery or packaging materials made from banana leaves, or bamboo for both supporting biodiversity as well askeeping authenticity [37].

Thus, use of local bioresource helps in supporting to the local farmers as well as local communities economically and it also helps in rising the local economy.Under the culture and authentic dining experience, the interior of the restaurants can also be made-up of with natural materials like bamboo or wood that supports the sustainability and promoting green practices.

1.4 Guests Preference on Local Bioresource Used in Restaurants

Guest is the most important person for any restaurants. According to the guest preference the food is serve at the restaurants.Guest choices are drastically changes from fried, oily and spicy food to organic healthy food at the restaurants as well [38]. So, restaurants are sourcing their ingredients from local areas by using local bioresource that gives natural crops, vegetables, fruits and even organic meat are also available at the market which are grow at the natural conditions by not using of pesticides, harmful fertilizers and other chemicals [39].These preferences Sof guests are standing on three pillars mentioned at below: - Guest satisfaction, Guest Loyalty & Unique Engagement.

1.5 Guest-Satisfaction

Guest satisfaction means how a restaurant meets the customers expectationabout the quality, service and experience. Guest measures their needs according to the freshness of the product. Restaurant must use fresh ingredients as well as products to meet the preferences of guest have fresh food. The fresh food hashigh nutrients values as well as it is less harmful to the health of the guest [40].

As guest preference towards healthy food of using local bioresource means consider the local natural ingredients or crops that are produce naturally without pesticides, artificial fertilizers or chemicals that are harm to the soil. The taste, quality and from nutritional point these crops & ingredients are having high values and good for the health. So, as guest preferring these organicfood productsthat source from local bioresource, restaurants are also sourcing from local areas for getting fresh and quality crops and ingredients to satisfy the guest preference for getting healthy food at the restaurants [41].

The theme of many restaurants isbasedon local bioresource for havingnew dining experience with regional identity, connecting with the culture of local communities to know their values and ethics about the society and life [42].

Nowadays, guest prefer more sustainable practicing restaurants for getting better healthy food with zero spicy, oily and fried items that usually harmfulfor the health. Sustainable practices have transparency image of healthy food which is getting prepared from local sourced natural ingredients, crops or other raw food material from the local bioresources [43].

1.6 Guest-loyalty

Guest prefers to visit same restaurant more often because for its positive response. It shows the restaurants keep their quality and standard on the food that serve to the guest. Restaurants are sourcing from local farmers of the areas in order of getting better organic raw foodmaterial which are grow naturally through local bioresource [44]. Thus, it differentiates the restaurants from other restaurantsby serving organic healthy food that is prefer by the guest. Once, the guest satisfied then the guest often recommended the restaurants to others. This recommendation gives indirectly attraction to new guests as well as it works as positive promotion for the restaurants [45].

1.7 Unique Engagement

Unique engagement means having good memory of service, food quality and hospitality by the guests towards the restaurants that creates good impression as well as positive promoting of the restaurants by referring others new guest [46].Uniqueness is having a history or story of using local bioresource into the restaurants for providing organic food on the guest tables from the local farms [47]. The narration of restaurants history or story of using local bioresource attracts the guest as well as made them believe that the ingredients or crops that are used in restaurant are naturally grown from local source [48]. Restaurants have their warehouse where these crops and ingredients are use in the cooking process to prove their loyalty with the quality and standards [49].

This made capitalised dinners into the restaurants. Furthermore, restaurants must have created QR code choice in the menu which helps to know the stories oflocal producer and their hard work of bringing the organic food into the restaurants industry. During the seasonal time restaurants must display different bioresources that helps in promotion of local bioresource use in restaurants for providing the healthy food to the guest [50].Restaurants are planning of having theme-based plan setup where ambience, menu and overall atmosphere that reflect the heritage, traditions and local communities connecting with the local organic ingredients and crops [51]. So, for using local bioresource the restaurants must keep the connection with local community as well as local farmers & producers for getting pure and natural crops and ingredients regarding of shared purpose [52].

2. Hypothesis

2.1 Local Bioresource Use in Restaurant Menus Significantly Influences Guest Preferences for Healthy Food Options in Odisha's Restaurants

It explains the relation between the use of Local Bioresource and Guest Preference. Local bioresource is the food that is grow in the natural environment of Odisha without use of pesticides and harmful chemicals & fertilizers which are become sources of Odisha's restaurants collected from local areas or purchase from local farmers and producers.

Restaurants are more focused on healthy food because of guest's awareness towards the health. The menu planned at the restaurants according to the organic ingredients and raw food materials that are more nutritious, fresh and keep the quality and standard.

Key Components: - Organic Food, Guest Demand, Local Source, Sustainable-Practices, Odisha's Restaurants.

The impact of local bioresource results in guests' choices towards the healthy food items in the menu which is prepared from organic raw food materials and organic ingredients to fulfil the guests' preferences. Local bioresource associates with sustainable practices which means the items in the menu are not only prepared with organic ingredients and raw food materials, but the theme of the restaurant also belongs to the local communities and supports heritage of the areas to practices sustainability. The study aims whether the local bioresource fulfil the guest's satisfaction by implementing the organic ingredients and raw food materials sourced from local areas, whether it meets the expectation of the guest or they survive in the market competition.

2.2 Demographic Factors Such as Age, Income, and Health Awareness Significantly Moderate the Relationship Between Local Bioresource use and Guest Preferences for Healthy Food in Odisha's Restaurants

The relation between the local bioresource utilisation and guest preference effects on the demographic factors.

Key Components: - Local Bioresource, Healthy Food, Guest Preference, Demographic factor (age, income and health).

Understand the relation between local bioresource and guest preference it is necessary to study the three demographical elements about the guest's age, income and health, because the organic food is at quite expenses side so it difficult to afford by some people. Secondly, the guest preference towards food is different according to the guest's age. Youngsters or youth side choose the food based on taste, while the middle-aged group of people's choices of food based on both taste and health. Now the third group is for old aged which prefer only healthy food.

2.3 The use of Local Bioresources in Restaurant Menus Positively Affects Guests' Feelings of Nutritional Quality and Authenticity of the Food

There is certain key attributes of the food offered at the restaurant by the influence of local bioresource on the guest preferences.

Local bioresource: - Organic food that is produced in the natural environment without the use of pesticides and fertilizers. Organic food rich in nutrients and quality and standards. These ingredients are fresh, and they directly come from the farms to the guests' plate.

Nutritional Value – organic food that grow under the natural compost without using of pesticides and fertilizers.

Authenticity – food relate with the culture and traditional values of local areas and local-communities that shows the local heritage and culinary practices.

3. Objectives

3.1 To Analyze how Guest Preferences for Healthy Food Options Vary with Demographic Characteristics, Particularly Age, Income, and Health Awareness

Guest preference for healthy food options varies with different demographic groups (age, income and health awareness), because as we take age then there are three age groups. The first group belongs to youth 15-35 who choose tasty and innovative food which is generally available at the restaurants. The second group is from 35-55 i.e. middle-aged group who choose tasty as well as healthy food. Here for healthy restaurants are sourcing from local areas for getting natural and organic raw food materials. The third group belongs to seniors i.e. 55 & + who select only healthy food due to the considering the health. Income is the main factor in choosing healthy food. Every individual cannot afford healthy food due to its expensiveness. Thus, the price of organic ingredients or raw food materials must be reduced by using local bioresource of the area that helps directly to the local farmers and producers. On the other hand, restaurants are offering their customized menu and developing their strategies for marketing considering the diverse demographic of guests.

3.2 To Evaluate the Influence of Local Bioresource use on Guest Preferences for Sustainable and Healthy Dining Choices in Odisha's Restaurant Industry

Guest is preferring the healthy food which are produce through the local areas by using local bioresource in order of getting fresh and natural raw food materials which rich in nutrients and of high quality that enhance the taste of culture and heritage. It satisfies the guest demand of having healthy food at restaurants by receiving of food made up of organic raw food materials which are grow naturally without use of pesticides and harmful fertilizers. It not only fulfils the demand of guest but it also helps in increasing of circular economy by reducing waste, raw food materials directly receiving from the local farmers or producers, by using of sustainable practices in the restaurants as well as use of as much of sustainable thing which can be further reuse, that benefits to the local economy and communities of the areas.

3.3 To Assess Guest Beliefs of Menu Choice, Focusing on Preferences for Locally Sourced, Bioresource-Based Ingredients

Restaurants are sourcing from local areas to get natural and pure raw food material that offers proper menu planning for fulfilling the preference of guests. Restaurants must follow the sustainable theme for attracting the guest using local bioresource for making an impact of practicing sustainability in the restaurant's ambience. Thus, if the restaurant being loyal to their quality and taste then it gains the trust of the guest and the positive promotion of the restaurants in returned.

4. Material Method

4.1 Literature Review

During the recent time Organic food has become environmentally friendly products due to the increased awareness of health among the guest as well as food safety and environmental concerns [53]. The growth of organic food markets has risen leads to show the change in the attitude and behaviour of consumersby having critical awareness and knowledgeabout the healthy food [54]. The positive attitudes of the guest towards the organic food and organic food products shows the healthy behaviour of the guest [55]. In developing countries like India, South Korea, and Southeast Asia the guests demand for healthy food is at peak [56].By seen this rise and peak demand of organic healthy food several businesses & restaurants have started buying locally grown food to fulfil the guest choices as well as it rise the revenue [57]. Sustainable practices in restaurants by offering the sustainable food that associates with green restaurants to promote environmentally friendly nature [58]. The most vital thing in food industry is the food through which services are provided to the customers. Organic, local, and sustainable food belonged to the green food practices. Thus, while using of local bioresource by restaurants for their sourcing raw food materials from the local areas [59].

5. Result and Discussion

5.1 Guest Preferences Towards Local Bioresources

The quantitative data from the structured surveys revealed a strong overall preference among guests for restaurants incorporating local bioresources into their offerings. Approximately 78% of respondents indicated that they were more likely to choose a restaurant that advertised the use of fresh, local, and seasonal ingredients. These preferences were especially pronounced among health-conscious individuals and those familiar with the concept of sustainable eating [1].The thematic analysis of group interviews supported these findings. Guests consistently expressed positive attitudes towards traceable and organic ingredients, associating them with better health outcomes, freshness, and higher quality [60]. The demographic variables influenced based on age-based preferences and income-based preferences.

Age-Based Preferences

Guest preferences varied significantly by age group:

Young guests (15–35 years) showed enthusiasm for innovative and health-focused menus, such as millet-based dishes, cold-pressed juices, and vegan options. They also valued social media visibility and branding around sustainability.Middle-aged guests (35–55 years) preferred traditional dishes made healthier with local, nutrient-rich ingredients. This group responded well to traditional Odia recipes reimagined using organic produce.Older guests (55+ years) expressed a strong affinity for nutrient-dense, home-style meals with minimal processing, preferring dishes rooted in Odia culture and local farming practices.

Income-Based Preferences

The marked correlation between the income levels and preference for bioresource-based meals divided into three categories - Higher-income groups (>₹50,000/month) displayed heightened interest in premium, health-oriented meals and were more aware of sustainability issues. Middle-income groups showed moderate interest but were price-sensitive and preferred value-based offerings. Lower-income groups appreciated affordability and taste over health claims, though still showed interest when traditional foods were emphasized.

5.2 Health Awareness and Ingredient Traceability

Health awareness emerged as a crucial factor influencing guest decisions. Participants with higher levels of nutritional awareness consistently preferred restaurants that highlighted ingredient sourcing and traceability [61]. These guests were more likely to ask about food origins, preparation methods, and nutritional value.Restaurants promoting the use of organic dairy, farm-raised meats, and seasonal vegetables were seen as trustworthy and transparent, leading to increased customer loyalty and satisfaction [62].

5.3 Operational and Branding Impacts on Restaurants

Restaurants that integrated local bioresources reported improved guest retention, positive word-of-mouth, and a distinct brand identity tied to sustainability and local culture [63]. This not only benefitted customer satisfaction but also supported rural farmers and producers, thereby contributing to rural economic development [64].The use of local ingredients also reduced transportation costs and carbon footprint, aligning with circular economy principles. These practices enabled restaurants to simultaneously meet guest expectations and environmental goals, bridging commercial success with social responsibility [65].

6. Conclusion

The study shows the significant relationship link between local bioresources and preferences of guest towards healthy food in restaurants across cities of Odisha. Circular economy approach helps restaurants to collect the fresh ingredients from local source not only use for the mindset of guest towards health-conscious but also it contributes in the environmental sustainability and rural development. The findings reveal preferences of guest based on age, income, and health awareness, with a appreciation for the quality ingredients. Restaurants which are successful in integrate the traditional as well as healthy dishes by using local bioresources are enjoying the satisfaction and loyalty of the guest. This research supports the value of restaurants practices along with both consumer expectations and sustainable development goals – which is a strong valuable point regarding the expanding of bioresources utilization as a strategic approach in the hospitality sector.

References

1. Thakur, N. (2017). Organic farming, food quality, and human health: A trisection of sustainability and a move from pesticides to eco-friendly biofertilizers. *Probiotics in agroecosystem*, 491–515.
2. Azlie, W. E., Zahari, M. S. M., Majid, H. N. A., &Hanafiah, M. H. (2023). To what extent does consumers' perceived health consciousness regarding organic food influence their dining choices at organic restaurants? An empirical investigation. *International Journal of Gastronomy and Food Science*, *34*, 100843.
3. Mohapatra, P., & Biswas, S. N. (2017). Gastronomy and its impact on tourism: a case study on regional cuisine of coastal Odisha, India. *International Journal of Research in Social Sciences*, *7*(6), 154–168..
4. Shirhatti, V. R., Marathe, S. J., Shah, N. N., & Singhal, R. S. (2023). Traditional food systems: Going backwards to move forward towards finding solutions to nutritional problems. In *Nutrition science, marketing nutrition, health claims, and public policy* (pp. 95–117). Academic Press.
5. Reeve, J. R., Hoagland, L. A., Villalba, J. J., Carr, P. M., Atucha, A., Cambardella, C., ... & Delate, K. (2016). Organic farming, soil health, and food quality: considering possible links. *Advances in agronomy*, *137*, 319–367.
6. Singh, S., Singh, P., Sharma, A., & Choudhury, M. (Eds.). (2022). *Agriculture waste management and bioresource: the circular economy perspective*. John Wiley & Sons.
7. Rath, S., Sahoo, P., Sarangi, K. K., &Kareemulla, K. (2022). Environmental implications of agricultural development in Odisha State. *J. Financ. Econ*, *3*, 2–25.
8. Gantait, S., Arisdason, W., Kumar, V. S., & Bandyopadhyay, S. BIBLIOGRAPHY AND ABSTRACTS OF PAPERS ON FLORA OF ODISHA.

9. Sati, V. P. (2024). Farming Systems and Sustainable Agriculture. In *Farming Systems and Sustainable Agriculture in the Himalaya* (pp. 49–62). Cham: Springer Nature Switzerland.
10. Roy, S., Singh, A., & Prakash, A. (2024). Unlocking the Potential of Organic Farming: Balancing Health, Sustainability, and Affordability in India. *Sustainable Food Systems (Volume I) SFS: Framework, Sustainable Diets, Traditional Food Culture & Food Production*, 247–274.
11. Sharma, N., Bohra, B., Pragya, N., Ciannella, R., Dobie, P., & Lehmann, S. (2016). Bioenergy from agroforestry can lead to improved food security, climate change, soil quality, and rural development. *Food and Energy Security*, *5*(3), 165–183.
12. Rubatzky, V. E., & Yamaguchi, M. (2012). *World vegetables: principles, production, and nutritive values*. Springer Science & Business Media.
13. Ouma, G., & Jeruto, P. (2010). Sustainable horticultural crop production through intercropping: The case of fruits and vegetable crops: A review. *Agriculture and Biology Journal of North America*, *1*(5), 1098–1105.
14. Kareem, A., Farooqi, Z. U. R., Kalsom, A., Mohy-Ud-Din, W., Hussain, M. M., Raza, M., & Khursheed, M. M. (2022). Organic farming for sustainable soil use, management, food production and climate change mitigation. *Sustainable agriculture: technical progressions and transitions*, 39–59.
15. Wadhwa, M., & Bakshi, M. P. S. (2013). Utilization of fruit and vegetable wastes as livestock feed and as substrates for generation of other value-added products. *RAP publication*, *4*(2013), 67.
16. Ogwu, M. C. (2023). Local food crops in Africa: sustainable utilization, threats, and traditional storage strategies. In *Sustainable utilization and conservation of Africa's biological resources and environment* (pp. 353–374). Singapore: Springer Nature Singapore.
17. Qadir, M., Wichelns, D., Raschid-Sally, L., Minhas, P. S., Drechsel, P., Bahri, A., ... & van der Hoek, W. (2013). Agricultural use of marginal-quality water–opportunities and challenges. *Water for Food Water for Life*, 425–458.
18. Altieri, M. A., Funes-Monzote, F. R., & Petersen, P. (2012). Agroecologically efficient agricultural systems for smallholder farmers: contributions to food sovereignty. *Agronomy for sustainable development*, *32*(1), 1–13.
19. Reijntjes, C., Haverkort, B., & Waters-Bayer, A. (1992). *Farming for the Future*. Macmillan Educ..
20. Ghisellini, P., Cialani, C., &Ulgiati, S. (2016). A review on circular economy: the expected transition to a balanced interplay of environmental and economic systems. *Journal of Cleaner production*, *114*, 11–32.
21. Muhanna, E. (2006). Sustainable tourism development and environmental management for developing countries. *Problems and Perspectives in Management*, *4*(2), 14–30.
22. Karagiannis, D., &Andrinos, M. (2021). The role of sustainable restaurant practices in city branding: The case of Athens. *Sustainability*, *13*(4), 2271.
23. Kholijah, S. (2024). Analysis of economic and environmental benefits of green business practices in the hospitality and tourism sector. *Involvement International Journal of Business*, *1*(1), 60–74.
24. Yoon, B., Chung, Y., & Jun, K. (2020). Restaurant industry practices to promote healthy sustainable eating: A content analysis of restaurant websites using the value chain approach. *Sustainability*, *12*(17), 7127.
25. De Silva, S. S. (2012). Aquaculture: a newly emergent food production sector—and perspectives of its impacts on biodiversity and conservation. *Biodiversity and conservation*, *21*, 3187–3220.
26. Mekhilef, S., Saidur, R., & Safari, A. (2011). A review on solar energy use in industries. *Renewable and sustainable energy reviews*, *15*(4), 1777–1790.
27. Kasim, A., Gursoy, D., Okumus, F., & Wong, A. (2014). The importance of water management in hotels: A framework for sustainability through innovation. *Journal of Sustainable Tourism*, *22*(7), 1090–1107.
28. Gupta, M. C. (1995). Environmental management and its impact on the operations function. *International Journal of Operations & Production Management*, *15*(8), 34–51.
29. Della Corte, V., Amin, M., Sepe, F., Luongo, S., & Cobanoglu, C. (2025). Exploring the impact of environmental management on sustainable concerns in restaurants. *British Food Journal*, *127*(6), 2147–2168.
30. Masieri, L. F. (2021). Customers Perception of Sustainable Restaurants Case: Hyper-local Restaurant Bucco and Dumlegården Farm.
31. Reynolds, P. C. (1993). Food and tourism: towards an understanding of sustainable culture. *Journal of Sustainable Tourism*, *1*(1), 48–54.
32. Karagiannis, D., &Andrinos, M. (2021). The role of sustainable restaurant practices in city branding: The case of Athens. *Sustainability*, *13*(4), 2271.
33. Bessière, J. (1998). Local development and heritage: traditional food and cuisine as tourist attractions in rural areas. *Sociologiaruralis*, *38*(1), 21–34.
34. Bhatia, L., Jha, H., Sarkar, T., & Sarangi, P. K. (2023). Food waste utilization for reducing carbon footprints towards sustainable and cleaner environment: a review. *International journal of environmental research and public health*, *20*(3), 2318.
35. Masieri, L. F. (2021). Customers Perception of Sustainable Restaurants Case: Hyper-local Restaurant Bucco and Dumlegården Farm.
36. It is a process of placing the crops or ingredients that are freshly sourced from local areas directly through the local farmers or producers for getting seasonal and authentic taste of the products.
37. Kora, A. J. (2019). Leaves as dining plates, food wraps and food packing material: Importance of renewable resources in Indian culture. *Bulletin of the National Research Centre*, *43*, 1–15.
38. Filimonau, V., &Krivcova, M. (2017). Restaurant menu design and more responsible consumer food choice: An exploratory study of managerial perceptions. *Journal of cleaner production*, *143*, 516–527.
39. Duram, L. A. (2009). Encyclopedia of organic, sustainable, and local food.
40. Sazdova, J., Janevski, L., &Conić, M. (2022). QUALITY OF SERVICES AND GUESTS SATISFACTION IN THE RESTAURANT. *Horizons-International Scientific Journal*, *31*(2), 313–327.
41. Poulston, J., &Yiu, A. Y. K. (2011). Profit or principles: Why do restaurants serve organic food?. *International Journal of Hospitality Management*, *30*(1), 184–191.

42. Fanfani, D., & Rovai, M. (2022). The role of sense of place in the recovery of Local Food Systems in bioregional contexts. Challenges and opportunities. *Preserving and constructing place attachment in Europe*, 201–217.
43. Smith, B. G. (2008). Developing sustainable food supply chains. *Philosophical Transactions of the Royal Society B: Biological Sciences*, *363*(1492), 849–861.
44. Duram, L., & Oberholtzer, L. (2010). A geographic approach to place and natural resource use in local food systems. *Renewable Agriculture and Food Systems*, *25*(2), 99–108.
45. Poulston, J., &Yiu, A. Y. K. (2011). Profit or principles: Why do restaurants serve organic food?. *International Journal of Hospitality Management*, *30*(1), 184–191.
46. Bowden, J. (2009). Customer engagement: A framework for assessing customer-brand relationships: The case of the restaurant industry. *Journal of Hospitality Marketing & Management*, *18*(6), 574–596.
47. Ljunggren, E., Markowska, M., Mynttinen, S., Samuelsen, R., Sæmundsson, R., & Virtanen and Johan Wiklund, M. (2010). *Explore-experiencing local food resources in the Nordic countries*. Nordic Council of Ministers.
48. Ljunggren, E., Markowska, M., Mynttinen, S., Samuelsen, R., Sæmundsson, R., & Virtanen and Johan Wiklund, M. (2010). *Explore-experiencing local food resources in the Nordic countries*. Nordic Council of Ministers.
49. Inwood, S. M., Sharp, J. S., Moore, R. H., & Stinner, D. H. (2009). Restaurants, chefs and local foods: insights drawn from application of a diffusion of innovation framework. *Agriculture and human values*, *26*, 177–191.
50. Ljunggren, E., Markowska, M., Mynttinen, S., Samuelsen, R., Sæmundsson, R., & Virtanen and Johan Wiklund, M. (2010). *Explore-experiencing local food resources in the Nordic countries*. Nordic Council of Ministers.
51. Markwick, M. (2009). *Eating as a cultural performance in early 21st century New Zealand: an exploration of the relationships between food and place: a thesis presented in partial fulfilment of the requirements for the degree of Master of Arts in Social Anthropology at Massey University, Auckland, New Zealand* (Doctoral dissertation, Massey University).
52. Norberg-Hodge, H., Merrifield, T., & Gorelick, S. (2002). *Bringing the food economy home: Local alternatives to global agribusiness*. Zed Books.
53. Kumar, S., & Ali, J. (2011, June). Analyzing the factors affecting consumer awareness on organic foods in India. In *21st annual IFAMA world forum and symposium on the road to* (Vol. 2050, pp. 1–12).
54. Dash, M., Samantaray, A., & Dash, M. (2014). Consumer's Perception towards Organic Food Products. *International Journal of Engineering and Management Research (IJEMR)*, *4*(3), 110–113.
55. Tsakiridou, E., Boutsouki, C., Zotos, Y., & Mattas, K. (2008). Attitudes and behaviour towards organic products: an exploratory study. *International Journal of Retail & Distribution Management*, *36*(2), 158–175.
56. Gupta, V., Roy, H., &Promsivapallop, P. (2021). Local cuisine image dimensions and its impact on foreign tourist's perceived food contentment in Delhi. *Tourism Recreation Research*, *46*(4), 487–499.
57. Pršić, M., Pivarski, B. K., Šmugović, S., & Ivanović, V. (2024). PROCENA SPREMNOSTI MENADŽMENTA UGOSTITELJSKIH OBJEKATA VRNJAČKE BANJE DA PONUDE LOKALNU HRANU. *Turističkoposlovanje*, (34).
58. Namkung, Y., & Jang, S. S. (2013). Effects of restaurant green practices on brand equity formation: Do green practices really matter?. *International Journal of Hospitality Management*, *33*, 85–95.
59. Lavecchia, G., Ferrarini, F., Brozzetti, F., De Nardis, R., Boncio, P., &Chiaraluce, L. (2012). From surface geology to aftershock analysis: Constraints on the geometry of the L'Aquila 2009 seismogenic fault system. *Italian Journal of Geosciences*, *131*(3), 330–347.
60].Saulais, L. Natural and healthy? Consumers' knowledge, understanding and preferences regarding processing, naturalness, and healthiness of food products. *MENU*, 45.
61. Filimonau, V., &Krivcova, M. (2017). Restaurant menu design and more responsible consumer food choice: An exploratory study of managerial perceptions. *Journal of cleaner production*, *143*, 516–527.
62. Garner, B. (2014). *Believe Me!': An ethnography of persuasive interaction at the farmers' market* (Doctoral dissertation).
63. Madanaguli, A., Dhir, A., Kaur, P., Srivastava, S., & Singh, G. (2022). Environmental sustainability in restaurants. A systematic review and future research agenda on restaurant adoption of green practices. *Scandinavian Journal of Hospitality and Tourism*, *22*(4-5), 303–330.
64. Verma, S., & Chaudhuri, R. (2008). Creating Customer Satisfaction And Profitable Value Chain With E-commerce In Rural India: A case based approach. *International Journal of Business Insights & Transformation*, *2*(1).
65. Sharma, S. (2014). Sustainable Culinary Practices. *2014). Managing Sustainability in The Hospitality and Tourism Industry: Paradigms and Directions for the Future*, 303–334.

Research and Innovations in Industrial and Marine Biotechnology: A Circular Economy 2024 – Prof. Hrudayanath Thatoi et al. (eds)
 ISBN 978-1-041-28285-3

9 Bridging The Gap: Integrating Social and Economic Dimensions for Sustainable Business Models in Circular Economy

Sasmita Mohanty*,
John Festus Vandy, Elisha Sheriff
Institute of Business and Computer Studies,
Siksha O Anusandhan University (Deemed to be a University),
Kalnga Nagar, Bhubaneswar India
Aravind Agrawal
Department of Higher Education, Government of Odisha,
India
Suresh Sivanandan[3]
Commissioner Income Tax (TDS), Cochin,
Kerala, India

Abstract: The transition from the traditional linear model of production and consumption to the Circular Economy (CE) has gained significant traction among scholars and policymakers, promising significant economic and environmental benefits. However, while prior studies highlight CE's economic and environmental contributions, they overlook social equity, inclusivity, and employment dynamics in CE strategies. Thus, balancing the social dimensions with economic and environmental goals in CE adoption remains largely underexplored. Therefore, this conceptual paper seeks to fill this gap by examining how social and economic considerations interact in shaping sustainable business models. Building on extant literature that emphasizes "closing the loop" and circularity, the study identifies critical trade-offs, synergies, and enablers between profitability and social justice. Using a micro-level analysis, this study develops a conceptual framework that identifies key conditions, constraints, and compromises in integrating social and economic objectives. The findings emphasize the necessity of collaborative approaches and legislative support in overcoming barriers to CE adoption. Academically, the research contributes to the literature by integrating social aspects into CE models, offering a holistic perspective. Practically, it provides actionable insights for policymakers and businesses to design inclusive CE strategies that align economic performance with social sustainability.

Keywords: Circular economy, Sustainability, Social impact, Economic impact, Conceptual framework, Business model

1. Introduction

The circular economy (CE) has emerged as a transformative economic framework for addressing the limitations and environmental threats posed by the traditional linear model of production [1,2] which has been heavily criticized for its emphasis on resources extraction, production and disposal viz-a-viz take-make-dispose [1]. thus resulting in waste , resource depletion , obsolesce , scarcity, environmental degradation and climate change challenges through environmental pollution and heavy industrial emission [4,2,3]. Alternatively, CE has received

*Corresponding author: sasmitamohanty@soa.ac.in

DOI: 10.1201/9781003759003-9

significant tractions among scholars, practitioners and policy makers in recent years for its sustainable and economic principles such as waste minimization[1]. resources efficiency [4], material recovery[5]. through recycling, reusing, refurbishing and remanufacturing[4,6] (Jabbour et al 2020, Korhonen 2018), and environmental sensitivity [4,7,6]., and Korhonen et al., 2018). It's argued that CE practices has the potential to not just contribute to waste minimization and material recovery but economic growth and environmental sustainability [9,10]. A practice that could contribute to the realization of the United Nations' Sustainable Development Goals (SDG 12) which advocates for a sustainable and responsible production and consumption of the earth's natural resources for economic advancement and environmental sustainability[10,9,11].

The theory, principles and practices CE is heavily influenced by ecological economics and industrial ecology, which strongly emphasize the concepts of 'closing the loop' and 'circularity' in the production process to ensure zero-wastage and infinite material usage through reuse, recycling and remanufacturing[12,6,1]. These principles advocate for strategic innovations in processes and business models to establish circular material and product flows There are a number of empirical studies confirming the economic and environmental benefits of adopting CE practices across various economies , sectors and industry around the world[2,4]. For instance, the extant literature in Sustainability and CE has justified that CE principles such as material recovery, waste reduction, recycling and remanufacturing and product lifecycle extension in manufacturing, built and agricultural sector contribute significantly to financial performance and environmental sustainability in Europe [4,13,14].

The profitability of Circular Economy principles is significantly attributed to its cost savings and operational efficiencies[15]. However, it is argued that implementing the circular business models necessarily require an upfront investment on technology, infrastructure and collaborations across the value chains[16]. While it is expected that such investments would improve and enhance the ability for long term returns, this expectation may clash with short term targets especially for small and medium sized enterprises (SME) [17]. In addition, the focus on economic and social development tends to contradict as companies try to balance strong expectations about performance with respect for social justice[18]. For example, despite the socio-economic policy constraints that may accompany the more widespread adoption of circular practices in supply chains, which can deliver a number of ecological and economic benefits, their implementers can envisage addressing such constraints [18,9].

Hence the sustainable adoption of CE requires addressing these tensions through the adoption of stakeholders' perspectives on CE as both facilitators or hinderers of its implementation [19]. Collaboration amongst stakeholders is emphasized as an important enabler, which helps instil confidence and alignment of various actors such as, businesses, consumers, the state, etc.[9]. With strategic engagements of these stakeholders, and inclusive social approaches in the planning of the CE initiatives, businesses can not only enhance CE acceptance and adaptability but also facilitate the success of its implementation [9,19]. Furthermore, the regulatory framework helps in facilitating these transitions by providing legal guidance for better business behaviour, for example tax deductions and penalties for non-compliance, but ensuring that businesses are held responsible[20]. The increasing concern regarding climate change, resources scarcity, and the dynamic consumer's preferences makes this research especially relevant. By examining these nexus, trade-offs, synergies, and enablers of CE adoption, this study contributes to the current discussions on sustainable development and informs further empirical research. Further testing of the proposed conceptual model within different industries and geographical boundaries will help to clarify how CE contributes to welfare-oriented sustainable business models.

2. Literature Review

2.1 Integrating Economic Efficiency and Social Equity in Circular Economy: Opportunities, Challenges and Gap

Transitioning to CE comes with several challenges too. Small and medium enterprises (SMEs) for instance are faced with the challenge in enhancing CE infrastructures and application including high capital investment requirement [9]. intersectoral collaboration[21]. and a lack of technical know-how on how to successfully transition from linear mode to CE framework[22,17]

The extant literature is quite robust on the environmental impact and the economically induced opportunities created by the adoption and application of the CE concept, principles and initiatives [4,22,15]. And it is generally believed among scholars that this framework is gaining widespread importance because of its focus on sustainability and economic development through waste reduction, efficient use of resources and environmental sensitivity[23,24] However, while scholars agree that CE principles and practices present obvious economic gains, such as lowering costs and having a competitive edge[25]. (Bocken et al., 2021) while ensure environmental preservation [2]. (Akhilesh & Arora 2024), its social aspects remain neglected and unexamined. There is a gap on the social impacts associated with CE adoption and application, this includes matters of social justice as well as inclusion[26,27]. This void in literature necessitates the integration of the economic profitability and social equity within the CE framework – a paradox that is yet to receive attention among scholars and practitioners[18].

2.2 Sectoral Application and Socio-Economics Dynamics in Circular Economy: Opportunities, Barriers and the Need for Integrative Models

Since its emergence as a preferred alternative to the traditional linear model of production which is widely known for waste mis-handling, resources obsolesce and scarcity, CE has been explored across various sectors and Industries of global economic[4]. and has shown promising socioeconomic potentials (COM 2014; COM 2015; Akhilesh & Arora 2024). However, the Waste Management sector is at the centre of the empirical proof of CE prospects[25]. .Recycling, waste reduction through reuse or remanufacturing, or refurbishing have been of great economic benefit through raw material cost savings, greater product life, and lower waste disposal costs. [24,26]. It is statistically observed that CE approaches in Europe can save around 600 billion euros each year and reduce greenhouse gas emissions about 48 percent by 2030 emphasizing on environmental and economic integration[25].

Socially, the CE provides potential for job creation and community advancement. The recycling industry and remanufacturing plants have created hundreds of thousands of jobs throughout the world especially in developing countries where informal waste systems have been transformed into formal structures[26]. However, despite these documented benefits, critics have outlined outline structural problems that could hinder the development of CE within the frame of sustainable business models such as employment substitution in traditional sectors and the inability of certain sections of society to access CE related technologies. For example, it is often the case that recycling projects in developed nations do not successfully assimilate informal workers into formal employment systems, which leads to income inequality [27].

3. Methodology

This conceptual paper uses a synthesis methodology, following Lucy and Caren (2015) and Whetten's 1989 Framework for conceptual development. It aims to bridge the gap between economic and social impact in Circular Economy (CE) frameworks for a sustainable business model. The review approach analyses complex relationships between economic and social impact dimensions, enhancing descriptive strength and advancing current discourse in Circular Economy and Sustainability

4. Findings

4.1 Conceptual Framework

The objective of this paper is to bridge the gap between the economic objectives and social aspirations within the CE framework with the aim of enhancing a sustainable business model. In order to achieve this a framework that logically links the two constructs is hereunder proposed thereafter called "S-E Integrative Framework".

This framework is grounded on a number of theories including the Stakeholder Theory (Freeman, 1984) which highlighted the need to balance the interests of all stakeholders including employees, consumers, suppliers and the society, not just the shareholders in order to deliver sustainable financial and competitive organizational performance [28]. (Donald & Preston 1995; Harrison & Wick 2013). When businesses consider the interests of their employees, consumers, suppliers, and society, they are able to practice such an approach that meets both the economic and social aspects of the business. Another useful perspective towards this conceptual framework comes from the Institutional Theory [29]. (Scott, 1995), which posits that business organizations are reactive to the pressures from their institutional setting composed of policies, culture and market structure. The framework is sustained by the Triple Bottom Line concept [30]. (Elkington, 1997) which argues that business success should not only be reflected in profit but also in social justice and care for the environment. Integrating these three dimensions - economic, social, and environmental - would allow the companies to ensure that the CE strategies result in certain values that are beneficial to society as well as the firm's bottom line.

This framework argues that businesses should always examine their strategies critically and ensure they make decisions that balances the profitability objective with its social value or impact in order to contribute towards sustainability. Additionally, it highlights the need for cooperation of various stakeholders: governments, businesses, and consumers, to ensure equitable distribution of benefits arising from CE and that the adoption of circular practices furthers the long-term social and economic development (Bocken et al., , 2018). In order to advance this discourse, we advise that future research focuses on the implementation of the proposed framework across different industries and geographical contexts. This will help determine in what contexts, and for what-competitive and social ends-CE may be used so as to fill gap concerning the inclusivity and the scalability of these models (Sassanelli et al, 2022).

The diagram Fig. 9.1 and 9.2 presents a graphical representation of the Integrative framework for the Integration Social and Economy impact of CE for a sustainable business mode. It lays the theoretical background regarding the balance of Social Impact and Profitability in Circular Economy (CE) for Sustainable Business Models as it incorporates CE Strategies, Business Performance, Stakeholder Engagement, Regulatory Framework, Product Life Cycle, and Innovation in it. We shall explain these frameworks and propose research

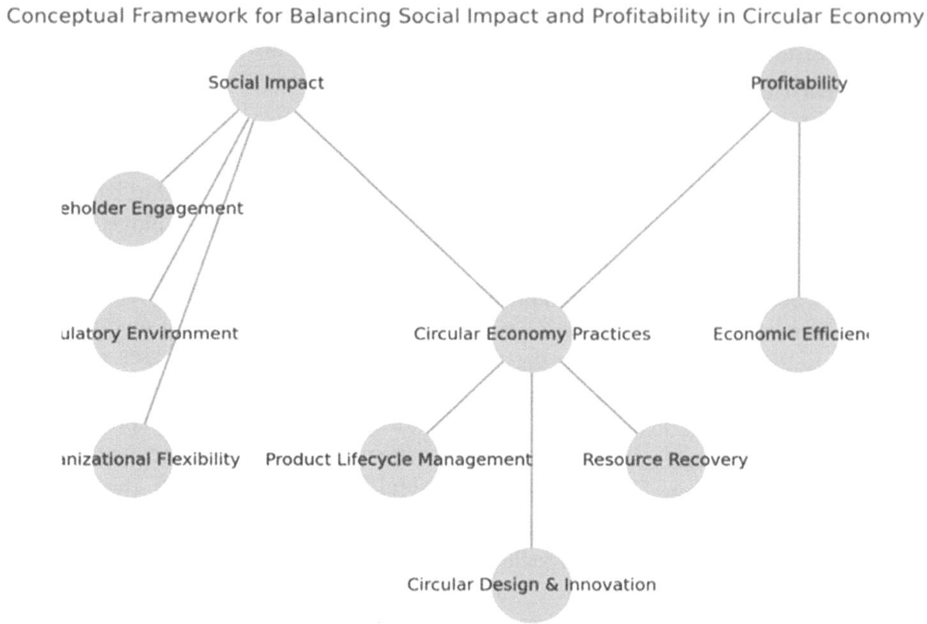

Fig. 9.1 Showing the conceptual framework for balancing social impact and profitability in CE business model

Source: Author Created

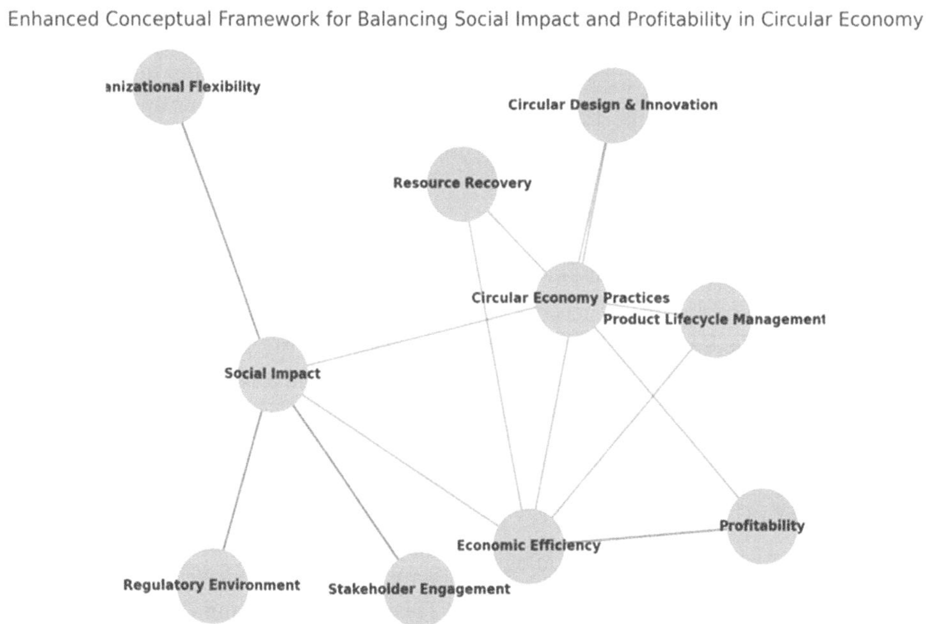

Fig. 9.2 Showing the expanded conceptual framework for balancing social impact and profitability in CE business model

Source: Author Created

propositions on the basis of the variables mentioned in these frameworks:

- Circular Economy Strategies (CE Strategies): At the centre of the framework is the CE strategies which aims to close the loop in to minimize waste while increasing material reuse, recovery recycling. These strategies comprise resource recovery, product life cycle management, circular economy design, and circular design innovation.
- Profitability: In the domain of CE, profitability is achieved as a result of cost savings, energy-efficient practices, less dependence on raw materials usage and waste minimization. It also includes possibilities for generating revenue by creating goods and services that satisfy the increasing demand for eco-friendly solutions.
- Social Impact: The social impact of the S-E Integrative framework argues that CE strategies should as well add

social values and should be aimed at meeting social needs. These impacts can be reflected in employment opportunities, better health and wellbeing of the society and level of fairness in the communities on where the circular practices are conducted. Social value is often embedded in stakeholder relations and includes employees, customers, communities, and suppliers.

- Stakeholder Engagement and Regulatory Framework: The engagement of all relevant stakeholders—businesses, employees, consumers and regulators—will contribute positively to both the economic and social aspects of the Society. In addition, the existence of a regulatory framework is required for clarifying mechanisms for getting firms to embrace sustainable business models and be accountable. Existence of policies, tax incentives, social penalties and norms of social responsibility have the potential to influence greatly the success of implementation of CE.
- Product life cycle management and creation: The product life cycle management stage entails re-designing products to extend life span thereby enhancing reuse and recycling. In the design and production stages, this element must not be overlooked. The lifecycle management practices are enabled by the businesses commitment to innovations, which shapes more sustainable technology and business models to closes the loop of production and consumption.
- Business Performance as An Output: Within the confines of this framework, the term business performance is understood as a composite indicator based on the economic benefit (with some measure of profitability growth) and social profit (or some measure of socially useful impact). Both of these considerations are of equal weight and great significance towards the realization of the long term stability of the organization and achievement of competitive position.

5. Discussion

This research furthers the ongoing discourse in circular economy (CE) by exploring how CE practices can be socially responsible, thereby addressing the critical gap in balancing the profitability and social impact in CE application across various sectors and industries. This disparity is adequately addressed in the framework proposed in this study. The finding unveils why CE principles adoption in business has the potential of yielding economic and environmental benefits; its impact on society needs to be addressed in a manner that avoids exclusionary and inequitable practices.

Another important contribution of this study is highlighting the significance of stakeholder engagement and regulatory framework as one of the key resources for operationalizing CE. This paper argues that societies with active stakeholder engagement, inclusivity, and participation in strategizing and implementing policies are more likely to balance their pursuit of profits with societal gains. Such complementary understanding is also critical in nurturing trust and consumer loyalty, and thus guaranteeing service or utility provision in the long run.

From the academic standpoint, this study integrates both social equity and business case profitability within CE. The interdisciplinary perspective offers a fresh perspective in understanding what makes CE transformational. It also provides a conceptual framework which forms the basis for future empirical research aimed at testing and improving the framework, thus enhancing the prospects for inter-disciplinary research. For practitioners, the framework elaborates on how CE tactics can be used to build sustainable business models while noting that shareholders' short-term interests should not be overvalued against social objectives in the long run. In addition, we have proposed the following recommendation:

- Policy Development and regulation mechanisms designed to ensure that CE practices are uniform across the various sectors of the economy to ensure fairness.
- Engagement with Stakeholders
- Forward looking Investment in Technology

The article further extends the existing literature on sustainability by offering one more framework that helps not only achieve economic and social returns but also offers the basis for the implementation of country wide sustainable development strategies.

6. Conclusion

This study has made a novel contribution to the CE literature by bridging the gap between profitability and social impact. It further recognizes important trade-offs, synergies, and enablers such as stakeholder engagement, regulatory frameworks, and product lifecycle management. The proposed conceptual framework provides a holistic approach to CE adoption by interlinking economic and social perspective dimensions. This framework should be tested empirically for scalability and inclusivity across industries and regions in future research. These findings help add to the emerging academic literature on CE, as well as providing researched insights for businesses and policy makers who want economic performance to meet societal needs.

Acknowledgement

The authors would like to acknowledge the immense support received from the Institute of Business and Computer Studies, Siksha O Anusandhan University in writing this paper.

References

1. Meyer, B., et al. (2018). Transitioning to circular production models. Journal of Sustainable Economics, 7(2), 98–112. https://doi.org/10.1016/j.jse.2018.1024
2. Akhilesh, K. B., & Arora, M. (2024). Circular Economy Principles and Practices. Wiley.
3. Arruda, L. R., et al. (2022). Material recovery and circular strategies in emerging economies. Journal of Environmental Economics, 45(2), 123–136. https://doi.org/10.1016/j.jenvman.2022.12345
4. Jabbour, C. J. C., de Sousa Jabbour, A. B. L., Sarkis, J., & Godinho Filho, M. (2017). Unlocking the circular economy through new business models: An integrative framework. Journal of Cleaner Production, 144, 546–552. https://doi.org/10.1016/j.jclepro.2019.03.038
5. Arruda, E. H., et al. (2020). Circular Economy: A brief literature review (2015–2020). Sustainable Operations and Sustainability. https://doi.org/10.1016/j.susoc.2021.05.001
6. Korhonen, J., Honkasalo, A., & Seppälä, J. (2018). Circular economy: The concept and its limitations. Ecological Economics, 143, 37–46.
9. Manea, F., et al. (2021). Enablers and barriers of circular practices: A multi-sector analysis. CE Management Review, 12(1), 56–72. https://doi.org/10.1016/j.cemr.2021.12.004
10. Geissdoerfer, M., Savaget, P., Bocken, N. M. P., & Hultink, E. J. (2020). The circular economy – A new sustainability paradigm? Journal of Cleaner Production, 143, 757–768. https://doi.org/10.1016/j.jclepro.2019.10.124
11. UNEP. (2022). Achieving SDG 12: A guide to responsible consumption and production. United Nations Environment Programme
12. Stahel, W. R. (2020). The circular economy: A user's guide. The Atlantic.
13. Bocken, N. M. P., Short, S. W., Rana, P., & Evans, S. (2021). A literature and practice review to develop sustainable business models. Journal of Cleaner Production, 1(7), 1–16. https://doi.org/10.1016/j.jclepro.2020.123456
14. Ghisellini, P., Ripa, M., & Ulgiati, S. (2022). Exploring environmental and social benefits of CE in agriculture. Journal of Environmental Management, 307, 114521
15. Arruda, E. H., et al. (2020). Circular Economy: A brief literature review (2015–2020). Sustainable Operations and Sustainability. https://doi.org/10.1016/j.susoc.2021.05.001
16. Ellen MacArthur Foundation. (2021). Completing the picture: How the circular economy tackles climate change. https://ellenmacarthurfoundation.org
17. Sassanelli, C., Rosa, P., Rocca, R., & Terzi, S. (2022). Exploring CE scalability through regulatory and technological synergies. Sustainable Operations Journal, 14(2), 89–102. https://doi.org/10.1016/j.sust.2022.08.012
18. Mestre, A., & Oliveira, J. (2021). Policy and societal challenges in CE adoption. Environmental Policy Review, 29(3), 435–455. https://doi.org/10.1016/j.epr.2021.03.004
19. Brennan, G., et al. (2020). Engaging stakeholders in CE initiatives: A framework for inclusive transitions. Sustainability, 12(15), 6312. https://doi.org/10.3390/su12156312
20. Ranta, V., Aarikka-Stenroos, L., Ritala, P., & Mäkinen, S. J. (2021). Exploring institutional drivers and barriers of the circular economy: A cross-regional comparison of China, the US, and Europe. Resources, Conservation and Recycling, 145, 70–81.
21. Gregson, N., et al. (2021). The societal impacts of CE: A qualitative exploration of equity concerns. Circular Economy and Society Journal, 8(3), 145–166. https://doi.org/10.1016/j.cesj.2021.08.002
24. Kirchherr, J., Reike, D., & Hekkert, M. (2021). Conceptualizing the circular economy: An analysis of 114 definitions. Resources, Conservation and Recycling, 127, 221–232.
25. Bocken, N. M. P., et al. (2018). Business model experimentation for sustainability: A CE perspective. Journal of Cleaner Production, 198, 285–298.
27. Kouhizadeh, M., Sarkis, J., & Searcy, C. (2021). Sustainability in the circular economy: A review of business models. Business Strategy and the Environment, 30(4), 2112–2126. https://doi.org/10.1002/bse.2912
28. Donaldson, T., & Preston, L. E. (1995). The stakeholder theory of the corporation: Concepts, evidence, and implications. Academy of Management Review, 20(1), 65–91.
29. Scott, W. R. (1995). Institutions and organizations. Sage.
30. Elkington, J. (1997). Cannibals with forks: The triple bottom line of 21st century business. Capstone.

Freeman, R. E. (1984). Strategic management: A stakeholder approach. Pitman

Research and Innovations in Industrial and Marine Biotechnology: A Circular Economy 2024 – Prof. Hrudayanath Thatoi et al. (eds)
© 2026 Taylor & Francis Group, London, ISBN 978-1-041-28285-3

10 Circular Economy and Sustainable Infrastructure Financing: Analysis of Sustainable Strategies

Elisha Sheriff, Sasmita Mohanty*
Institute of Business and Computer Studies,
Siksha O Anusandhan (Deemed to be) University,
Kalnga Nagar, Bhubaneswar Odisha

John Festus Vandy
Institute of Public Administration and Management,
University of Sierra Leone, AJ Momoh Street Tower Hill – Freetown,
Sierra Leone

Commissioner Income Tax (TDS),
Cochin, Kerala, India

Aravind Agrawal
Department of Higher Education, Government of Odisha,
India

Suresh Sivanandan[5]
Institute of Public Administration and Management,
University of Sierra Leone, AJ Momoh Street, Tower Hill Freetown,
Sierra Leone

Abstract: The transition to a circular economy (CE) is crucial for sustainable development in the face of climate change and resource depletion. This document explores how sustainable infrastructure financing can support CE adoption, emphasizing tools such as green bonds, green financing, and public-private partnerships. It highlights barriers like greenwashing, limited sustainability-linked bonds, and regional funding gaps. A key contribution is the introduction of the "CIRCLES" model, which aligns CE principles with infrastructure financing by promoting circularity, innovation, resilience, collaboration, leverage, evaluation, and scalability. Effective CE implementation requires robust financial frameworks, supportive policies, and cross-sector collaboration to realize significant economic, environmental, and social benefits.

Keywords: Circular economy, Sustainable infrastructure, Green finance, Public-private partnerships, Green bonds, Lifecycle cost reduction, Resource efficiency

1. INTRODUCTION

The global economy faces major issues like resource depletion, climate change, and environmental degradation, increasing interest in the circular economy – a system where products are reused, repaired, or repurposed (European Investment Bank's Circular Economy Overview, 224). Circular practices could address 45% of global GHG emissions not covered by renewable energy alone (Global Infrastructure Hub, 2023 update). Businesses are adopting circular models to save costs, optimize revenue, and mitigate risks, driven by resource scarcity, digitalization, and demographic shifts [1]. Effective financial mobilization is critical for the circular

*Corresponding author: sasmitamhanty@soa.ac.in

DOI: 10.1201/9781003759003-10

economy's success. Green finance and logistics, integrated into organizational strategies, promote sustainable production and economic inclusivity but face challenges around data and legitimacy [2,3]. Financial institutions, alongside governments, central banks, and regulators, must champion this transition by investing and adjusting risk frameworks to embed circular economy principles [4].

2. LITERATURE REVIEW

2.1 Green Finance and Sustainable Infrastructure Development

Green Finance (GF) is crucial for promoting sustainable infrastructure and technological progress in line with the Sustainable Development Goals (SDGs). Mahmood et al. [5] reveal a strong link between environmental innovation and economic, social, and environmental sustainability. Digital finance boosts green finance and technological innovation, enhancing sustainable total factor eco-efficiency (STFEcE), especially where financial regulations are more relaxed [6]. The need for strong green banking systems and targeted funding is highlighted by Xiaofei [7], they find that co-financing arrangements lead to better environmental outcomes, fewer project cancellations, and higher completion rates. Green finance supports circular practices and sustainable production in sectors like tourism and logistics. Jinru et al. [2] stress the importance of operational green integration and stakeholder engagement. They highlight governance, nature-based solutions, and data as enablers for water infrastructure finance in Asia. For sustainable infrastructure financing, government funding, concessional loans, bonds and private equity, with green bonds gaining importance. Equity ratios, interest rates, and consumer behaviour influence circular pricing and profitability [8]. Portfolio theory supports optimized resource-user combinations for mitigating macro-level resource use [9], and Public Private Partnership (PPP) require governance to balance investor and public interests [11]. Standardized financial policies and fuzzy-AHP methods are recommended for assessing green infrastructure risk [10]. Portillo-Tarragona et al. [12] reveal that CE buildings lower emissions despite higher initial costs. Stakeholder alignment, supported by National Development Banks, is crucial for CE success [13], and AI-based risk models aid CE forecasting [14]

3. RESEARCH METHODOLOGY

The study explores sustainable practices related to the circular economy and infrastructure finance. It aims to identify financial mechanisms driving the transition and assess how circular economy principles can be integrated into infrastructure funding models. A mixed-methods approach combining qualitative insights with quantitative data provides a comprehensive understanding of sustainable plans and financial processes. The study is grounded in a critical review of scholarly literature, industry reports, and case studies. It identifies knowledge gaps in financial integration, circular models, and the role of sustainable finance in infrastructure development. The study analyses infrastructure projects that have adopted circular economy principles, focusing on regions like the EU, Asia, Africa, the US, and Japan. Data is sourced from development bank frameworks, government reports, and corporate sustainability-linked bonds, and green bonds, in advancing circular infrastructure is demonstrated. The report assesses how circular economy finance supports the UN Sustainable Development Goals (SDGs), considering environmental, social, and economic aspects.

A paradigm for funding infrastructure projects in the circular economy is suggested in light of the results. The "CIRCLES" framework, as it is known, incorporates the concepts of circularity, innovation, resilience, teamwork, leverage, assessment, and scalability. This framework is designed to guide future infrastructure projects towards sustainability, leveraging diverse financing mechanisms to support the transition to a circular economy.

4. RESULTS AND DISCUSSION

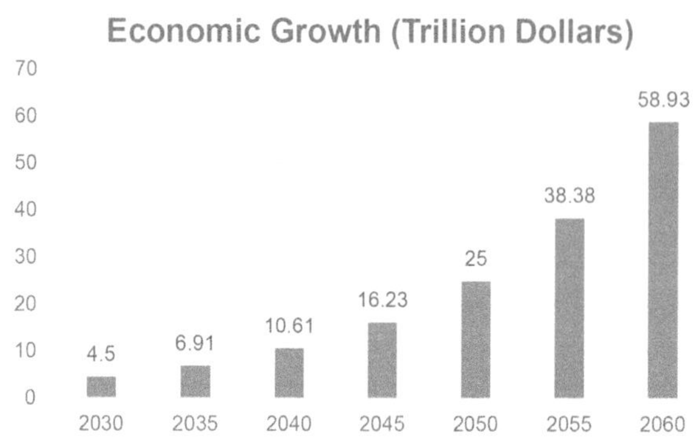

Fig. 10.1 Projected economic growth by 2060

Source: Accenture Strategy Publication, Waste to Wealth - 2015

4.1 The Capital Market Union Dynamics

The European Commission promotes sustainable infrastructure by eliminating investment barriers and encouraging long-term investments through the Capital Market Union. Key actions include enhancing ELTIFs, revising CRR, and unifying prudential standards to improve EU financial integration. In line with the Green Deal, it also seeks legal reforms to attract institutional investors and align markets with environmental and economic goals.

4.2 Global Investment Report

The sustainable finance market continues to grow, with total investment products surpassing $7 trillion in 2023, a 20% increase from 2022. Sustainable bonds primarily drove this growth, reaching over $4 trillion in market value. however, net inflows to sustainable funds dropped significantly, from $161 billion in 2022 to $63 billion in

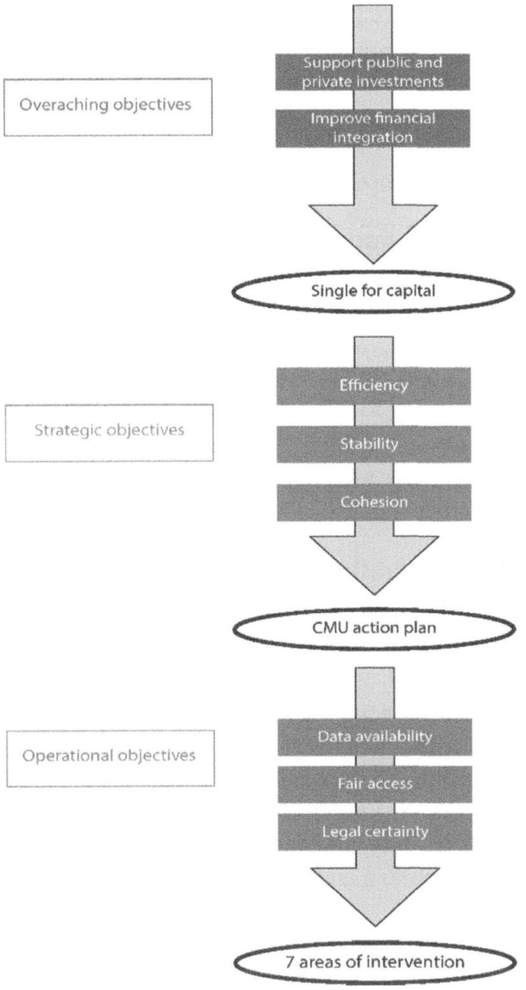

Fig. 10.2 Showing mid-term review

Source: CMU 2017 Mid-term Review

Table 10.1 World investment report

World Investment Report	Value (in Billion Dollars)
Sustainable Bond Market Global Issuance (2023)	872
Sustainable Bond Cumulative Issuance (Since 2018)	4000
Green Bonds Issuance (2023)	587
Social Bonds Issuance (2023)	153
Sustainability Bonds Issuance (2023)	109
Sustainability-Linked Bonds Issuance (2023)	22
Sustainable Fund Market Value (2023)	3000
Net Inflows to Sustainable Funds (2023)	63
Sustainable Fund Market Value in Europe (2023)	2492
Sustainable Fund Market Value in the United States (2023)	324

Source: World Investment Report

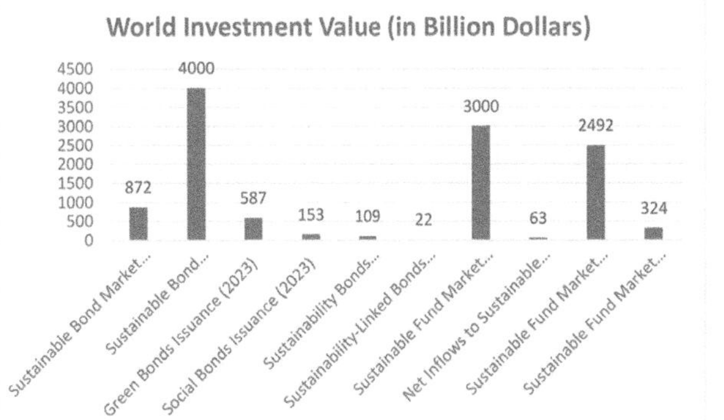

Fig. 10.3 World investment values

Source: Author's own analysis

2023. Greenwashing remains the main obstacle to market expansion.

4.3 Sustainable Funds - Scaling Green Finance

There is a $3 trillion global market value in 2023, led by Europe at $2.49 trillion and the U.S. at $324 billion. Net inflows of $63 billion indicate rising investor preference for sustainable portfolios. Green finance ensures capital for green technologies and circular business models, with Europe's leadership highlighting the impact of policy initiatives like the EU Green Deal. This encourages other regions, such as the US, to pursue similar incentives and regulations.

4.4 Strategic Recommendations

Enhanced Policy Frameworks

To strengthen the role of sustainable finance in the development of the circular economy, countries may benefit by imitating Europe's coordinated regulatory approach, including taxonomical alignment.

Instruments Diversification

Tailored funding avenues for circular innovations could be created by expanding sustainability-linked instruments. The data does not disaggregate by sectors, but strategically aligning bond and fund issuance with critical economy sectors (i.e., recycling, bioeconomy, or e-waste management) would eventually yield tremendous positive outcomes.

Collaborative Stakeholder Engagement

It is also worthwhile to take advantage of the strategic partnership between the public and commercial sectors to jointly develop financial products that take into account the changing environment of the circular economy.

4.5 The CIRCLES Model for Circularity and Sustainable Financing

The CIRCLES model is a six-step framework developed to properly match sustainable infrastructure funding with the concepts of a circular economy. "Circularity, Innovation, Resilience, Collaboration, Leverage, Evaluation, and Scaling" is what the acronym stands for.

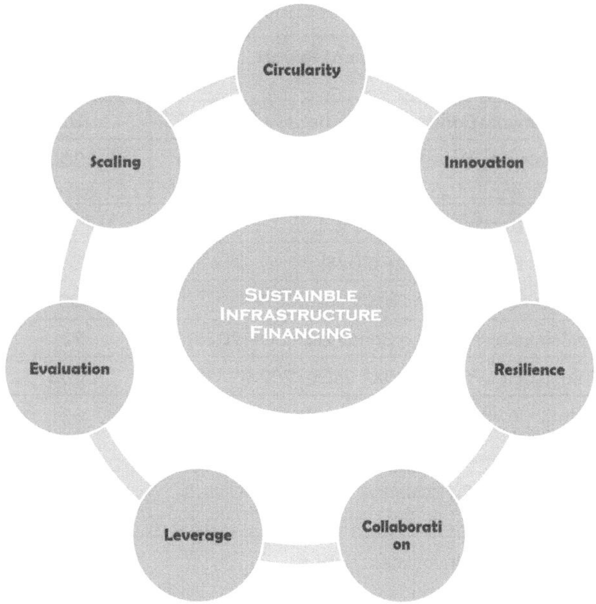

Fig. 10.4 Framework indicating how sustainable financing influences CE growth and effectiveness

Source: Author's own Framework

4.6 C - Circularity Integration

This aims to incorporate the concepts of the circular economy into the planning and funding of infrastructure projects. This can be achieved by encouraging projects to maintain a focus on renewable resources, material efficiency, and end-of-life recyclability. It also requires life cycle assessments in project evaluations to prioritize circular design, while introducing "green premiums' for projects with high circularity indexes.

4.7 I - Innovation Financing

This dimension of the framework enhances the development and adoption of circular technologies and business models in the circular economy. For this objective to be achieved, establishing innovation funds aimed at SMEs and startups focused on circular solutions. While promoting fintech solutions like blockchain transparency in resource monitoring, another strategic emphasis may be creating channels for funding public-private partnerships (PPPs) that include state-of-the-art sustainable technology.

4.8 R - Resilience Building

This is to guarantee that the infrastructure is adapted to economic uncertainty and climatic change. Strategies for achieving such could be: compulsory climate risk assessment for financed projects; aligning financing rates to resilience metrics, rewarding projects with higher adaptive capacities; leveraging catastrophe bonds and insurance-related bonds for mitigating potential risks.

4.9 C - Collaborative Stakeholder Engagement

This is meant to promote cooperation among private, public, and civil society stakeholders by creating regional circular economy coalitions to align objectives and share resources on a common ground. Employing participatory finance mechanisms, such as green bonds issued in partnership with local investors, is another way to do this. establishing collaborations with banks, local governments, and global organizations to finance extensive projects.

4.10 L - Leverage Blended Finance

By combining grants, equity, and debt in financing models to draw in a variety of investors, the goal is to maximize the use of public and private money for circular infrastructure. A smart way to use blended finance and international guarantees to de-risk hazardous ventures and draw in private capital would be to prioritize concessional financing for high-impact projects in developing economies.

4.11 E - Evaluation Metrics and KPIs

Impact measurement and strategic alignment with sustainability objectives are the aims of this. The implementation of key performance indicators (KPIs) such as social equality, resource efficiency, and carbon reduction may help accomplish this. While consistent impact reporting based on ESG and SDG alignment frameworks is necessary, the usage of AI-driven technologies may also be utilized to monitor real-time project effects as a major tactic.

4.12 S - Scaling Sustainable Strategies

Replicating and extending successful models across industries and geographical areas is the ultimate objective here. This might be accomplished by creating standardized resource kits for funding circular infrastructure, pushing regional development banks to use scalable tactics, and fostering knowledge-sharing platforms to spread best practices throughout the world.

5. Conclusion

Transitioning to a circular economy promotes long-term sustainability. Efficient financial resource use, sustainable infrastructure funding, and aligning finance with circular principles are essential. Challenges like greenwashing and uneven financial access require strategic solutions. The CIRCLES model advocates creativity, collaboration, and adaptability. Key actions include improving partnerships, assessment methods, and policy alignment. Ultimately, circular finance drives innovation and ensures a resilient, eco-conscious future.

Acknowledgement

The authors would like to acknowledge the immense support received from the Institute of Business and Computer Studies, Siksha O Anusandhan University in writing this paper.

Authors' contribution: ES Conceptualized and wrote the entire manuscript. SM provided the necessary supervision and editing of the work. JFV edited the work while AA and SS also helped to read through and confirm the manuscript.

References——

1. Raes, J. (2020). *Financing circularity: Demystifying finance for circular economies.*
2. JinRu, L., Qamruzzaman, M., Hangyu, W., & Kler, R. (2022). Do environmental quality, financial inclusion, and good governance ensure the FDI sustainably in Belt and Road countries? Evidence from an application of CS-ARDL and NARDL. *Frontiers in Environmental Science*, 10, 936216.
3. Van Niekerk, A. J. (2024). Economic Inclusion: Green Finance and the SDGs. *Sustainability (Switzerland)*, **16**(3).
4. Ellen MacArthur Foundation. (2020). *Financing the circular economy: Capturing the opportunity.*
5. Mahmood, S., Sun, H., Iqbal, A., Alhussan, A. A., & El-Kenawy, E. S. M. (2024). Green finance, sustainable infrastructure, and green technology innovation: pathways to achieving sustainable development goals in the belt and road initiative. *Environmental Research Communications*, **6**(10).
6. Shen, J., Ren, X., Feng, Z., & Nie, J. (2025). The impact of public environmental concerns on port sustainability: evidence from 44 port cities in China. *Frontiers in Marine Science*, *11*, 1454242.
7. Xiaofei, Y. (2021). Research on the action mechanism of circular economy development and green finance based on entropy method and big data. *Journal of Enterprise Information Management*, 35(4/5), 988-1010.
8. Zhou, Q., & Yuen, K. F. (2020). Analyzing the effect of government subsidy on the development of the remanufacturing industry. *International Journal of Environmental Research and Public Health*, **17**(10).
9. Figge, F., Thorpe, A. S., & Manzhynski, S. (2021). Between you and I: A portfolio theory of the circular economy. *Ecological Economics*, **190**.
10. Dai, J., & Solangi, Y. A. (2023). Standardized financial policies and fuzzy-AHP methods for assessing green infrastructure risk. *(Publication details not specified in reference list—assumed from text context).*
11. Bayliss, K., Romero, M. J., & Waeyenberge, E. van. (2021). Uneven outcomes from private infrastructure finance: evidence from two case studies. *Development in Practice*, **31**(7), 934–945.
12. Portillo-Tarragona, P., Scarpellini, S., & Marín-Vinuesa, L. M. (2024). 'Circular patents' and dynamic capabilities: new insights for patenting in a circular economy. *Technology Analysis and Strategic Management*, **36**(7), 1571–1586.
13. Tessitore, S., Corsini, F., & Iraldo, F. (2023). Exploring the alignment and misalignment in the transition to a circular economy within private companies and public organizations. *Journal of Cleaner Production*, **430**.
14. Toxopeus, H., Achterberg, E., & Polzin, F. (2021). How can firms access bank finance for circular business model innovation? *Business Strategy and the Environment*, **30**(6).

Research and Innovations in Industrial and Marine Biotechnology: A Circular Economy 2024 – Prof. Hrudayanath Thatoi et al. (eds)
 ISBN 978-1-041-28285-3

11 Transition to Circular Economy in India: Conceptualizing the Contribution of GHRM

John Festus Vandy,
Sasmita Mohanty*, Elisha Sheriff, Aravind Agrawal
Institute of Business and Computer Studies,
Siksha O Anusandhan University (Deemed to be a University),
Kalnga Nagar, Bhubaneswar India
Suresh Sivanandan[2]
[3]Commissioner Income Tax (TDS), Cochin,
Kerala, India

Abstract: Transition to circular economy (CE) has become essential for achieving sustainable development, especially in countries such as India that face acute challenges in resource utilization and waste management. Green Human Resource Management (GHRM) is crucial in conceptualizing and facilitating this transition by embedding sustainability principles into organizational practices. This paper explores the intersection of GHRM and CE, emphasizing how green HR functions as eco-centric recruitment, sustainability-driven training, green performance appraisal, resilience and engagement of employees can foster circular business models. Drawing on institutional and resource-based perspectives, the study conceptualizes GHRM as a key enabler of circular strategies, aligning workforce capabilities with sustainability goals. Despite its potential, challenges such as policy gaps, organizational inertia, and skill mismatches hinder the seamless integration of GHRM into CE transitions. This paper contributes to the discourse on sustainable business practices by outlining a framework for leveraging GHRM in driving India's shift toward a circular economy.

Keywords: Circular economy, Green human resource management, Conceptual framework, Sustainability

1. Introduction

Adopting circular economy (CE) principles is recognized as a vital route toward sustainable development, notably in emerging nations such as India, where accelerated industrial growth and heavy resource dependence generate major environmental pressures.[1].The circular economy stresses on reducing waste, using resources efficiently, and establishing regenerative systems, in line with international sustainability commitments like the UN SDGs [3], linking with sustainability targets of Sustainable Development Goals [4]. While policy frameworks and technological innovations have been widely discussed as enablers of CE, the role of human capital particularly through Green Human Resource Management (GHRM) remains underexplored in both academic and practical discourse [2].

Green HRM promotes sustainability by employing eco-conscious employees, expanding capacity, and delivering performance ratings based on outcomes.[5]. Given that human capital is central to organizational transformation, conceptualizing GHRM as a strategic enabler of CE could provide new insights into how businesses embed circular principles into their workforce strategies. However, current literature largely focuses on the technical and policy dimensions of CE, with limited attention to how HRM can drive this transition [6]. This gap underscores the need to conceptualize how GHRM facilitates CE adoption in India's organizational landscape. This defines

*Corresponding author: sasmitamohanty@soa.ac.in

DOI: 10.1201/9781003759003-11

the objective of this study. By using the Whetten [7] Model, we conceptualize GHRM's role in CE transition in India while highlighting its contribution across various Industries.

2. Literature Review

2.1 Circular Economy: Progress, Prospects and Plights

The concept circular economy (CE) has evolved in response to environmental degradation, resource scarcity, and the need for sustainable development. Traditionally, India's economic trajectory has followed a linear model of production, consumption, and disposal, which has substantially added to pollution and waste accumulation. [8]. However, policy interventions such as the Swachh Bharat Abhiyan and the Extended Producer Responsibility (EPR) have provided impetus to circular economy [9].

India's transition to Circular Economy (CE) offers immense benefits, including GDP growth, job creation, resource efficiency, and carbon footprint reduction. Projections indicate that adopting CE practices could add approximately $624 billion (INR 40 lakh crore) to India's economy by 2050 and create millions of employment opportunities in sectors like recycling, renewable energy, and remanufacturing. By adopting circular practices in key industries such as agriculture, textiles, and manufacturing, India can significantly reduce waste, optimize resource use, and cut emissions by 44% by 2050 [10,11]. However, regulatory gaps, infrastructure limitations, and financial constraints remain key challenges, requiring stronger policies, investment in CE infrastructure, and consumer awareness programs [12,13]. If effectively implemented, CE will enhance India's industrial resilience, global trade competitiveness, and sustainability leadership, positioning it as a pioneer in circular economic development.

The theoretical foundation for HRM's integration into CE organizations is twofold. First, the Stakeholder Theory [14] suggests that successful CE initiatives depend on organizations recognizing and addressing the diverse expectations of internal groups (employees, managers, investors) as well as external stakeholders such as customers and society. Meanwhile, RBV [15] suggests that organizations gain a competitive advantage by leveraging unique, valuable, and inimitable resources, where HRM has critical functions to play in growth of human capital that meets these criteria. Guest [16] and Armstrong and Taylor [17] reinforce the applicability of these theories in HRM research, justifying their adoption in understanding HRM's role in CE organizations.

To address this gap, several scholars have explored the intersection of HRM and CE. Obeidat et al. [18] conducted a study in the service sector firms in Qatar, revealing that green HRM steers the development of circular economy initiatives within organizations. Priya et al. [19] conducted an investigation into the potential of HRM to assist India in this regard highlighting the importance of HRM in bridging the divide between organizational sustainability objectives and workforce capabilities. HRM can facilitate this transformation by cultivating a workforce that is qualified to assist CE initiatives through sustainable resource practices, environmental awareness, and creativity, as per their research.

This research seeks to contribute to this growing field by critically examining and conceptualizing HRM and GHRM's role and in fostering sustainable business models within CE organizations, particularly from an Indian perspective.

2.2 Conceptualizing GHRM Integration in CE Framework: A Sustainable Business Model

Green recruitment plays a key role in ensuring employee skills are consistent with organizational sustainability goals [20]. For example, selecting individuals with strong environmental values and a pro-sustainability orientation enables firms to foster a workforce supportive of circular innovation[20]. This proactive hiring approach ensures that employees possess the necessary skills to drive CE principles, such as resource efficiency and waste minimization, from the outset [21]. Within GHRM, training initiatives are designed to build employee competence in sustainable practices such as reducing waste, conserving resources, and adopting eco-conscious methods. [6].

Despite these advancements, the direct integration of GHRM in CE strategies is scant. Only a few studies explicitly highlight the important contribution of human resources to CE initiatives. This reinforces the critique that CE frameworks often overlook the "human side" of sustainability [22]. However, after reviewing the papers from GHRM obtained from Scopus it was observed that Practices like eco-focused hiring, sustainability-oriented training, incentive systems, performance appraisals, and pro-environmental citizenship behaviour among employees indirectly but significantly support CE objectives. Thus, agreeing with the ReSOLVE framework in Jabbour et al. [2], we agree with the current argument in literature for an Integration of CE principles in GHRM as proposed by Jabbour et al.[23]. In addition, we hereunder propose an Outcome-based Approach to CE integration in GHRM for organizational wide application in Indian Industries as in the figure below.

3. Materials and Methods

3.1 Study Approach

This study follows Lucien and Caren's [24] methodology, which prioritizes conceptual work's coherence, clarity, and contextual relevance in order to meet its goals. Using Whitten's [7] model, the study ensures a theoretically sound

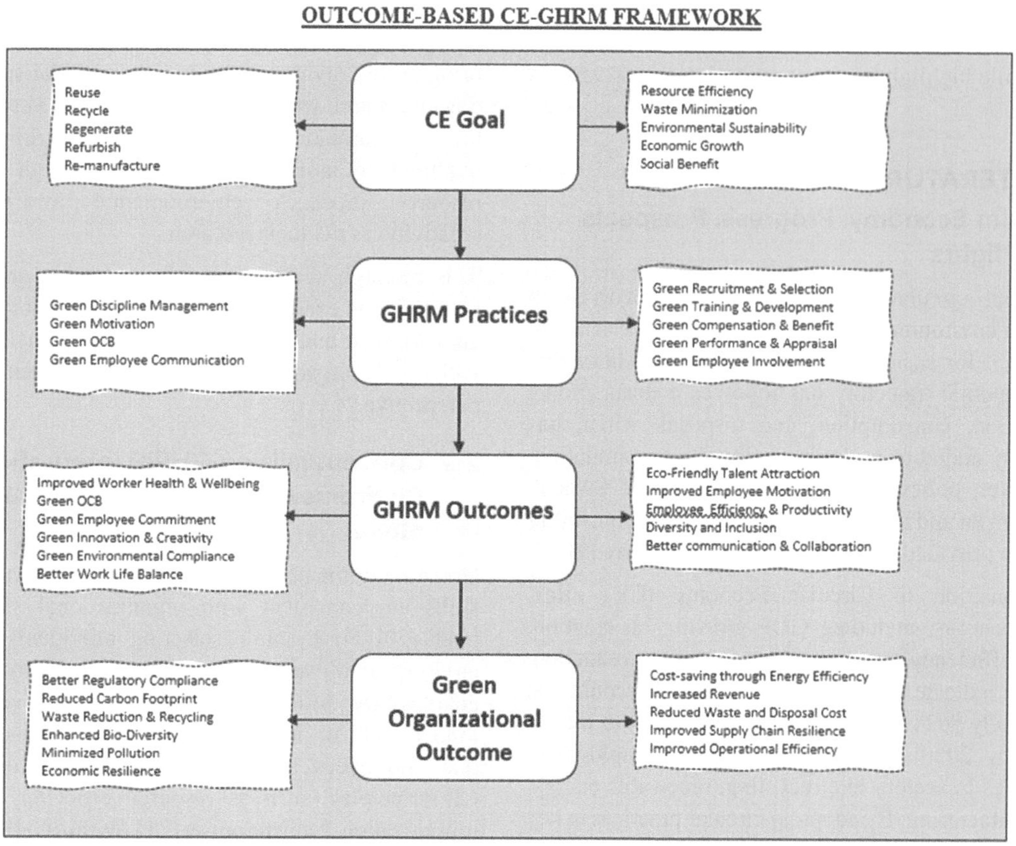

Fig. 11.1 Conceptual framework for integrating circular economy into green human resource management for sustainable business models

Source: Authors

and contextually grounded framework by identifying key concepts (what), their interrelationships (how), their significance (why), and their scope (who/where/when). This was done through a systematic examination and critical analysis of the existing discourse in GHRM and Ce, while standing on the existing Framework advanced by Jabbour et al. [2] etc.

4. Findings and Discussions

4.1 Contribution of GHRM Practices to Circular Economy Adoption in India

These studies reveals that GHRM practices ranging from Green job analysis, green recruitment and selection, green training and development, green employee involvement, green performance appraisal, green reward and benefit, green employee involvement, green psychological contract lead to enhancing green employee commitment, green organizational citizenship behaviour, green and green employee performance which encompasses but not limited to green organization, organizational efficiency, environmental-sensitive organization, happy and green work environment, waste reduction. These Green Organizational Outcome will ultimately lead to the achievement of the CE Goal.

4.2 Practical Implications and Challenges for Sustainable Business Models

The Outcome-based GHRM-CE framework (Fig. 11.1) above illustrates how CE should be Integrated to GHRM. GHRM and CE are established to have similar objectives, we therefore propose GHRM Practices or policies such as Green recruitment and selection, training and development etc., should be informed by or pre-defined or should integrate key CE principles of resources re-use, recycle, refurbish and regenerate for the achievement of the CE goals. This could ultimately result in GHRM outcomes that are CE-influenced and hence Green Organizational outcomes which will ultimately lead to the realization of CE goals. The measurement and scaling of the variables of this frameworks outside the scope of this paper. The integration of GHRM within the CE framework has practical implications for developing sustainable business models. Strategic HR initiatives that integrate environmental values enhance organizational capacity for innovation, promote efficient resource management, and contribute to waste minimization. This cultural shift is essential for the successful implementation of circular strategies, as it ensures that employees at all levels are committed to and capable of driving sustainability initiatives. Despite the promising frameworks, challenges

Table 11.1 Contribution of GHRM to CE adoption in India

SN	Name of Author and year	Year	Green HRM Practices observed in the Study	How this paper links with and/or Contributes to the realization of CE Goals
1	Katta &Padhy [25]	2024	Green HR Practices, employee engagement, employee behavior	It contributed in terms of the realization of goals of circular economy through promotion of eco-friendly and sustainable business and human resource management practices.
2	Arun Kumar et al. [26]	2024	Green HRM Practices (recruitment, employee development, employee engagement)	By linking GHRM Practices to happiness at work, this study promotes and motivates Green employee behaviour which indirectly contributes to CE environmental, sustainability and resource efficiency goal.
3	Pathak and Agarwal [27]	2024	Green recruitment, involvement, performance	The study mainly promotes green HR Practices, sustainability consciousness and practices. All three contributes to the realization of the key CE goals (environmental sensitivity, resource efficiency and sustainability)
4	Agarwal et al. [28]	2024	Green HRM, Employee Performance and OCBE	By linking GHRM to Employee Performance (EP) a specific focus on Organizational Citizenship behaviour of the Environment, this study aligns with the CE goals by promoting an eco-friendly behaviour and citizenship among employees GHRM to EP indirectly links employee's performance to CE goals
5	Kranti P et al. [29]	2024	SHRM and Green HRM Practices- acquisition and retention of employee, employee development & engagement, performance management etc)	This paper attempts to align GHRM to SHRM seeking for an overall organizational integration. This will ultimately support a eco-friendly culture thus directly supporting CE goal for environmental consciousness, waste reduction, efficiency and sustainability.
6	Jnaneswar, K [30]	2023	GHRM, Green Employee behaviour, mediated by employees' commitment at a psychological level	Undoubtedly, the realization of CE goals demands a green commitment. This paper advances this goal by exploring the influence of GHRM on employee green behaviour.
7	Yadav and Mathew [31]	2023	Green Training/Development & Green Organizational Citizenship Behaviour	contributes in the realization of CE goals by promoting the need for employee green skill acquisition which adds efficiency and effectiveness in the realization of CE objectives.
8	Agarwal and Bansal [32]	2022	Green Recruitment & Selection, Training & Development, Compensation and benefits, Employee Engagement	This paper supports the realization of CE goals by promoting Greenbehaviour, commitment and results.
9	Khaton et al. [33]	2020	GHRM Practices (recruitment and selection, compensation and benefits, involvement etc)	GHRM and their role in making the organization eco-sensitive through an adoption of GHR Practices, promotes the achievement of CE goals.
10	Poddar and Samanta [34]	2019	Green Recruitment & Selection, Green IT, Green Training and Development	Integrating Green IT into GHRM foster sustainable organizational practices results in the realization of CE sustainability objective

Source: Author's Literature Analysis

persist in operationalizing GHRM within CE contexts. Barriers include a lack of standardized metrics to assess the impact of GHRM on circular outcomes and the need for comprehensive training programs that equip employees with the necessary skills for CE practices. Future research should focus on empirical studies that validate proposed frameworks, develop standardized assessment tools, and explore sector-specific applications of GHRM in promoting circularity.

5. Conclusion

This paper examines the role of GHRM in India's circular economy (CE) adoption and development across various sectors. It found that CE and GHRM are still in their nascent stage, with promising developments in sectors like agriculture, bio-tech, energy, healthcare, mining, and construction. However, other sectors like manufacturing, banking, retail, fashion, insurance, and finance remain underexplored. The study also found that most papers focused on CE from a micro perspective, indicating a need for a more micro-organizational approach. The paper proposes an outcome-based framework to integrate GHRM into sustainable business models, but emphasizes the need for empowering and enforcing policies.

Acknowledgement

The authors acknowledge the immense support received from the Institute of Business and Computer Studies, Siksha O Anusandhan, (Deemed to be) University in writing this paper.

References

1. Ellen MacArthur Foundation. (2017). Towards a circular economy: Business rationale for an accelerated transition.
2. Jabbour, C. J. C., Fiorini, P. D. C., Wong, C. W. Y., Jugend, D., & Lopes de Sousa Jabbour, A. B. (2017). First-mover firms in the transition towards the circular economy: A case study-based analysis on key drivers and barriers. Journal of Cleaner Production, 160, 198–209. https://doi.org/10.1016/j.jclepro.2017.09.209
3. Korhonen, J., Honkasalo, A., & Seppälä, J. (2018). Circular economy: The concept and its limitations. Ecological Economics, 143, 37–46. https://doi.org/10.1016/j.ecolecon.2017.06.041
4. Geissdoerfer, M., Savaget, P., Bocken, N. M. P., &Hultink, E. J. (2017). The Circular Economy–A new sustainability paradigm? Journal of Cleaner Production, 143, 757–768. https://doi.org/10.1016/j.jclepro.2016.12.048
5. Ren, S., Tang, G., & Jackson, S. E. (2018). Green human resource management research in emergence: A review and future directions. Asia Pacific Journal of Management, 35(3), 769–803. https://doi.org/10.1007/s10490-017-9532-1
6. Jabbour, C. J. C., & de Sousa Jabbour, A. B. L. (2016). Green human resource management and green supply chain management: Linking two emerging agendas. Journal of Cleaner Production, 112, 1824–1833. https://doi.org/10.1016/j.jclepro.2015.01.052
7. Whetten, D. A. (1989). What constitutes a theoretical contribution? Academy of Management Review, 14(4), 490–495. https://doi.org/10.5465/amr.1989.4308371
8. Singh, S. K., Chen, J., Del Giudice, M., & El-Kassar, A. N. (2020). Environmental ethics, environmental performance, and competitive advantage: Role of environmental training. Technological Forecasting and Social Change, 160, 120239. https://doi.org/10.1016/j.techfore.2020.120239
9. NITI Aayog. (2021). Strategy on resource efficiency.
10. International Energy Agency. (2022). India energy outlook 2022.
11. Ellen MacArthur Foundation. (2020). Completing the picture: How the circular economy tackles climate change.
12. Chaturvedi, R., Prakash, S., & Sharma, M. (2022). Policy frameworks for circular economy transition in India. Journal of Sustainable Development, 15(3), 205–223.
13. Patel, A., Verma, P., & Gaur, V. (2023). Challenges and prospects of circular economy in India: Policy analysis and framework. Environmental Economics and Policy Studies, 25, 523–538. https://doi.org/10.1007/s10018-023-00368-w
14. Freeman, R. E. (1984). Strategic management: A stakeholder approach. Pitman.
15. Barney, J. (1991). Firm resources and sustained competitive advantage. Journal of Management, 17(1), 99–120. https://doi.org/10.1177/014920639101700108
16. Guest, D. E. (1987). Human resource management and industrial relations. Journal of Management Studies, 24(5), 503–521. https://doi.org/10.1111/j.1467-6486.1987.tb00460.x
17. Armstrong, M., & Taylor, S. (2017). Armstrong's handbook of human resource management practice (14th ed.). Kogan Page.
18. Obeidat, S. M., Abdalla, S., & Al Bakri, A. A. K. (2023). Integrating green human resource management and circular economy to enhance sustainable performance: An empirical study from the Qatari service sector. Employee Relations, 45(2), 535–563. https://doi.org/10.1108/ER-04-2022-0219
19. Priya, M., Singh, N., & Kumar, R. (2024). HRM for sustainable development: The role of circular economy in shaping India's workforce. Journal of Sustainable Human Resource Management, 12(1), 34–50.
20. Tang, G., Chen, Y., Jiang, Y., Paillé, P., & Jia, J. (2018). Green human resource management practices: Scale development and validity. Asia Pacific Journal of Human Resources, 56(1), 31–55.
21. Ahmad, S. (2015). Green human resource management: Policies and practices. Cogent Business & Management, 2(1), 1030817. https://doi.org/10.1080/23311975.2015.1030817
22. Sharma, M., & Gupta, R. (2023). Human factor in sustainability: Linking employee engagement and circular economy in Indian organizations. Indian Journal of Human Resources and Sustainability, 5(2), 75–89.
23. Jabbour, C. J. C., Sarkis, J., de Sousa Jabbour, A. B. L., Renwick, D. W. S., Singh, S. K., Grebinevych, O., & Godinho Filho, M. (2019). Who is in charge? A review and a research agenda on the 'human side' of the circular economy. Journal of Cleaner Production, 222, 793–801.
24. Lucien, L., & Caren, N. (2015). The structure of theory and the theory of structure: A new approach to guiding conceptual work in the social sciences. Sociological Theory, 33(3), 205–227. https://doi.org/10.1177/0735275115603430
25. Katta, V., & Padhy, P. C. (2024). Examining the role of green human resource management practices on environmental behavior with the environmental knowledge mediation effect. International Journal of Human Capital in Urban Management, 9(2), 317–330. https://doi.org/10.22034/IJHCUM.2024.02.09
26. Arun Kumar, P., Nivethitha, S., &Vilvanathan, L. (2024). Empowering employees, empowering the environment: Green HRM's journey to happiness, resilience and feedback seeking. Journal of Hospitality and Tourism Insights, 7(2), 1130–1147. https://doi.org/10.1108/JHTI-11-2023-0800
27. Pathak, R. K., & Agarwal, S. (2024). Sustainability in human resources: Evaluating competencies and overcoming challenges in India's service sector. Library Progress International, 44(3), Article 1780.
28. Agarwal, P., Upadhyay, R. K., Anuj, A., Ahalawat, K., Kukreti, R., & Akhtar, A. (2024). Environmental performance in higher education and green HRM: The mediating role of organisational citizenship behaviour. International Journal of Management Practice, 17(6), 713–734.
29. Kranthi, P., Thoti, K. K., Bhakar, S., Arun, R., & Mishra, B. R. (2024). The relationship between sustainable human resource management and green human resource management-a case of medical sector in Hyderabad, India. South Eastern European Journal of Public Health, 6, Article 1190. https://doi.org/10.70135/seejph.vi.1190
30. K., Jnaneswar (2023). Green HRM and employee green behavior in the manufacturing firms: Do psychological

green climate and employee green commitment matter? Social Responsibility Journal, 19(10), 1852–1869. https://doi.org/10.1108/SRJ-11-2022-0477

31. Yadav, P., & Mathew, J. (2023). Improving organizational sustainable performance of organizations through green training. International Journal of Social Ecology and Sustainable Development, 14(1), Article 1–11. https://doi.org/10.4018/IJSESD.321166
32. Agrawal, N., & Bansal, R. (2022). Green HRM: A medium of social responsibility and sustainable development. International Journal of Innovation and Sustainable Development, 16(2), 172–185. https://doi.org/10.1504/IJISD.2022.121781
33. Khatoon, A., Khan, N. A., Parvin, F., Wahid, M. S., Jamal, M. T., & Azhar, S. (2022). Green HRM: pathway towards environmental sustainability using AHP and FAHP in a nascent parsimony. International Journal of Manpower, 43(3), 805–826. https://doi.org/10.1108/IJM-04-2020-0164
34. Podder, S. K., & Samanta, D. (2019, February). Level of green computing-based management practices for digital revolution and new India. International Journal of Engineering and Advanced Technology (IJEAT), 8(3S), 133–136.

Research and Innovations in Industrial and Marine Biotechnology: A Circular Economy 2024 – Prof. Hrudayanath Thatoi et al. (eds)

12 Practice of Waste Management in Star Category Hotels: A Study based on Kolkata

Mou Roy, Susanta Ranjan Chaini
School of Hotel Mgmt., Siksha 'O' Anusandhan Deemed to be University,
Bhubaneswar, India

Bireswar Pradhan*
School of Tourism & Hospitality Services Management,
Indira Gandhi National Open University,
New Delhi, India

Abstract: Hospitality is the fastest growing industry in the world, but at the same time it is a majorcontributorand a great challenge to global environmental issues, concerning waste management issues. Sustainable waste management is now an increasing pressure to apply in the world for survival. The application of sustainable waste management in metropolitan cities is necessary for future conservation, but in Kolkata, the application of the technique is not gained momentum, which is unclear. The focus of the study is to analyse luxury hotels' environmental efforts in Kolkata, India in context of global sustainability standard as well as local waste management regulations. In context of the focus, the objectives of the study are to explore technologies, which are related innovative waste management. The applied technologies in Kolkata's luxury hotels enable to minimize environmental impact and maximize resource allocation. Sustainable waste management practices in five stars hotels in Kolkata were studied by using in-dept interviews and focus group discussions with supervisory staff from renowned hotel chain. The result showed that Kolkata's hotel industry faces challenges in sustainable waste management due to financial constraints, technological limitations, infrastructure gaps, and guest behaviour. Progress has been made through waste segregation, plastic reduction, and digital tools. Overcoming these challenges requires government support, technological advancements, community engagement, and behavioural change programs. By integrating waste reduction, recycling, and resource recovery, hotels can establish a sustainable circular economy model. Continuous monitoring, innovation, and collaboration are circular for long-term success.

Keywords: Hospitality industry, Sustainable waste management, Environmental impact, Kolkata metropolitan

1. Introduction

The hospitality sector significantly contributes to environmental issues through waste generation and carbon emissions [1]. While sustainability is increasingly embraced worldwide, implementing such practices in developing urban centres like Kolkata remains challenging [2]. This study explores how innovative waste management technologies and sustainable practices can be effectively integrated into the operational frameworks of Kolkata's star-rated hotels to reduce environmental impact and improve resource recovery. It addresses key barriers such as financial constraints, inadequate infrastructure, limited technical expertise, and regulatory gaps. By examining current practices and challenges, the research aims to recommend context-specific, strategic measures to promote the adoption of sustainable solutions in Kolkata's hospitality industry. Ultimately, the study supports the advancement of environmentally conscious practices aligned with global standards. It is fostering operational

*Corresponding author: bpradhan1232013@gmail.com

DOI: 10.1201/9781003759003-12

efficiency and long-term sustainability in urban hotel waste management. Collaborative engagement with stakeholders is essential for this transformation [3].

2. Literature Review

The hospitality industry plays a significant role in environmental degradation due to its high level of waste generation,including food waste, plastics, packaging, and hazardous materials, all of which can harm ecosystems. As the industry increasingly acknowledges its responsibility to the environment, sustainable waste management practices are becoming essential [1]. However, luxury hotels often lag due to high implementation costs and limited awareness. In urban areas, hospitality establishments are adopting practices like recycling, composting, and waste-to-energy initiatives [4], through infrastructural weaknesses remain, especially in emerging economies such as India. Indian hotels show inconsistent application of basic waste management techniques [5]. Policy frameworks play a critical role in shaping sustainable practices [6]. Growing eco-consciousness among touristspressures hotels to improve their sustainability efforts [7]. Key barriers to adoption include financial limitations, lack of training, and knowledge gaps, which require capacity-building and tech-driven solutions [8]. Mixed-method research has been valuable in capturing the complexity of sustainable waste management [9]. Success stories, such as hotels in Southeast Asia that utilize advanced technologies and collaborate with communities, offer valuable insights [10]. While awareness is increasing, critical knowledge gaps persist, underscoring the need for further research and systematic reforms. The industry is beginning to recognize that sustainability is not only ethical but also essential for long-term success.

3. Research Gap

Lack of research on technologies related to waste management in Kolkata luxury hotels. There is also limited research on integration with existing operation related waste management in star hotels.

4. Methodology

This study adopts a qualitative research design to explore sustainable waste management practices in five-star hotels within Kolkata Metropolitan area. It investigates the attitudes, experiences, and challenges faced by supervisory-level staff, who play a key role in the daily waste operations. Data were gathered from 30 participants using semi-structured interviews and focus group discussion. Thematic and content analyse were applied to identify patterns and specific practices. Thematic and content analyse were applied to identify patterns and specific practices. A purposive sample included five hotels from major chains- two each from the Taj and J.W. Marriott groups, and one from ITC- ensuring diverse insights. Focusing on Kolkata, a hub of luxury hospitality, the study offers an in-depth look at environmental sustainability in urban hotel management through staff directly engaged in operational practices.

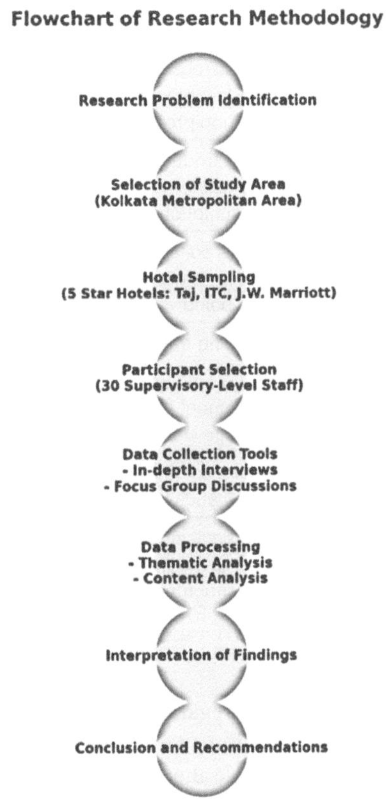

Fig. 12.1 Flowchart of research methodology

Source: Researchers' plot

5. Results

This study categorized hotel waste management into themes. These themes are: segregation at sources with colour-coded bins, partnerships for recycling, plastic reduction via bamboo straws and dispensers, paperless digital solutions, food redistribution through NGOs, and sustainability training. These practices ensure compliance, promote circularity, and foster a culture of environmental responsibility in hospitality operations.

The study identifies nine key themes shaping sustainable waste management in Kolkata's hospitality sector. These include financial, technological, regulatory barriers, as well as cultural resistance and guests' perception. It also outlines benefits, limitations, and plans (future), offering insights into the sector's struggles and strategies for environmental responsibility and innovation.

6. Discussion

Table 12.1 highlights key themes in sustainable waste management within hotels, emphasizing strategies like

Table 12.1 Key themes, content descriptions, and corresponding research questions on hotel waste management

Theme	Content Description	Research Question
Waste Segregation at source	Hotels implement colour-coded bin system (e.g., green for biodegradable, blue for recyclable, red for hazardous waste) and train staff to ensure compliance	In what ways are waste segregation methods and staff training executed in hotel operations?
Recycling Initiatives	Materials such as plastic, glass, and paper are recycled through collaborations with certified centres or environmental NGOs.	What approaches are most effective in enhancing material recycling in hotels?
Reduction of single-Use-Plastic	Hotels reduce reliance on single-use plastic items by adopting eco-friendly alternatives such as reusable dispenser and bamboo products.	What practices are implemented to eliminate single-use plastics?
Digital solutions to reduce paper	The introduction of digital systems- e.g., QR codes, e-receipts, and online communication- significantly cuts down paper consumption.	How have digital tools contributed to a reduction in paper waste in hotel settings?
Food waste management programs	Hotels collaborate with food rescue platforms and NGOs to donate excess food, reducing waste and supporting community well-being.	In what ways do food redistribution efforts contribute to waste reduction and social impact?
Staff training and awareness	Ongoing training for employees and educational efforts for guests strengthen sustainable practices within the organization.	How do employee and guest education initiatives foster a culture of sustainability?
On-site waste processing facilities	Equipment like bio-digesters,compactors,andbalers are used to manage waste volume efficiently within the premises.	What technologies support on-site waste processing in the hospitality industry?
Monitoring and reporting system	Hotels keep comprehensive records and conduct regular waste audits to ensure transparency and track progress.	How do monitoring and reporting systems support accountability in waste management?
Sustainability challenges	Barriers include high implementation costs, inadequate guest participation in segregation, and insufficient recycling infrastructure.	What are the major barriers faced by hotels in achieving sustainable waste management practices?

Source: Primary data collected on sustainable waste management practices in hospitality sector

colour-coded waste segregation, staff training, and regulatory compliance. Efforts to reduce single-use plastic include adopting sustainable alternatives [11], while digital tools such as e-bills and QR codes minimize paper waste. Partnerships with NGOs and food redistribution programs contribute to social responsibility [12]. Regulation training and awareness campaigns promote a sustainability-oriented culture. Additionally, on-site waste processing and robust monitoring systems improve efficiency. While hotels show strong commitment, addressing financial, behavioural, and infrastructural barriers remains critical to advancing sustainability goals.

Table 12.2 outlines challenges and opportunities in Kolkata's hotel sector regarding sustainable waste management. Key barriers include high initial costs and uncertain ROI [14], limited technology access and skilled manpower, and inadequate regulatory support. Operational constraints, unclear guest communication, and luxury perception issues further hinder adoption, despite emerging opportunities for integrated, sustainable practices.Current waste management in Kolkata hotels yields some benefits but faces challenges like high cost, limited space, and weak participation. Innovative approaches-food redistribution, composting, and guest engagement- help improve sustainability. A multi-pronged strategy involving investment, technology, policy support, and cultural change is vital to reduce environmental impact and enhance hotel brand reputation. Table 12.3 highlights how AI, IoT, and sustainable innovations enhance waste management efficiency in hospitality [15]. Supportive regulations and rising public awareness can drive adoption, promote behavioural change, and accelerate the shift towards environmentally responsible practices across the sector.Scalability and affordability are vital for adopting sustainable technologies in regions like Kolkata facing financial and infrastructural challenges [16]. Innovations in food waste reduction, energy recovery, plastic management, and data-driven strategies offer strong environmental and economic potential when supported by ongoing research and collaboration. Table 12.4 outlines a strategic framework combining technology, behavioural change, and engagement to reduce waste in hospitality. Integrating water-saving and recycling technologies fosters sustainable cycles and reduce environmental impact [17]. It is supporting SDG12 while enhancing brand reputation and guest satisfaction. Table 12.5 reveals that sustainable waste management in hospitality faces financial, cultural, and operational barriers [18]. Addressing them requires internal measures like training and optimization, and external support such as subsidies and streamlined regulations [19], balancing sustainability goals with short-term operational demand. This study highlights that engaging communities and stakeholders are vital for sustainable waste management, turning challenges into opportunities for long-term environmental and economic gains [20].

Table 12.2 Themes contextual insights, and research questions related to sustainable waste management in the hospitality sector

Theme	Content Description	Guiding Research Question
Financial Constraints	The high initial investment, uncertain financial returns, and limited budgets present obstacles, especially in cost-sensitive market like Kolkata.	What funding mechanisms can support the adoption of sustainable waste practices in hotels?
Technological accessibility	Hotels struggle with limited availability of modern waste management technologies and lack skilled personnel for operation.	How can technology interventions enhance waste handling in Kolkata's hotel industry?
Regulatory barriers	Inadequate governmental support and complex regulations restrict the implementation of innovative waste system.	What policy framework can incentivize and facilitate sustainable waste practices in hospitality?
Operational challenges	Constraints such as limited physical space, integration issues with existing systems, and the need for retraining staff impede adoption.	How can urban hotels overcome operational limitations to improve waste management?
Cultural and behavioural factors	Resistance to change among both staff and guests, coupled with low awareness, affects participation in sustainability efforts.	What strategies can improve stakeholder engagement in waste reduction initiatives within hotels?
Guest perception and participation	Efforts may conflict with luxury branding, and lack of communication can deter guest involvement in waste segregation or recycling.	How can hotels encourage guest cooperation in sustainability without affecting service quality?
Existingbenefits	Responsible waste practices help minimize environmental impact and offer potential economic advantages through efficiency and branding.	What measurable gains have hotels achieved through current waste management efforts?
Present limitations	Persistent issues include high cost, erratic waste collection, weak participation, inadequate space, and poor infrastructure for local recycling.	What major constraints hinder the widespread and consistentimplementation of sustainable initiatives?
Future strategies	Hotels are exploring solutions such as composting, food donation networks, and interactive sustainability programs for guests	What emerging innovations are shaping the future of waste management in the hospitality sector?

Source: Primary data

Table 12.3 Themes, descriptions, and inquiry prompts related to innovative technologies and practices

Theme	Description of Theme-Related Practices	Example Question
Food waste management	Utilization of food digesters that convert biodegradable leftovers into compost; OWCs handle mixed organic waste to produce nutrient-rich manure.	How do digesters impact composting efficiency? What is the scalability of OWCs in urban environments?
Waste Segregation	Deployment of AI-based smart sensors for automated sorting and IoT-enabled bins that signal optimized collection schedules.	Can smart bins reduce operational costs? How reliable is AI in mixed-waste segregation?
Energy Recovery	Use of biodigesters to process organic matter and wastewater, producing biogas for clean energy applications.	What is the net energy yield from biodigesters? What are the emission reduction observed?
Water treatment	Implementation of Membrane Bioreactor (MBR) systems to treat wastewater for non-potable uses like landscaping and surface cleaning.	How effective are MBR systems compared to traditional methods?
Plastic waste management	Application of plastic shredders to break down waste materials, enabling recycling into reusable forms.	How cost-effective are shredders in plastic reuse?
Data-driven Practices	Use od digital platforms to monitor food waste trends and inform smarter procurement and inventory decisions.	What insights can waste tracking systems offer to reduce overproduction?
Collaborative Efforts	Strategic partnerships with municipal waste agencies to promote safe disposal and increase recycling rates.	How do partnerships influence compliance and policy implementation?
Sustainability Outcomes	Outcomes include a 30% decline in landfill waste and 15% monthly saving onenergy through biogas adoption.	What are the long-term environmental and economic effects?

Source: Primary data

Table 12.4 Themes, descriptions, and inquiry prompts on innovative waste reduction strategies

Theme	Theme-related Content	
Water-saving Technologies	Advanced dishwashers recycle rinse water and adjust consumption based on load type. Conservation programs such as towel/linen reuse are implemented in rooms and public areas.	How do load-sensing technologies contribute to water saving? What is the guest response to reuse programs?
Sustainable Packaging	Initiatives include reusing glass water bottles, utilizing compostable containers for meals, and eliminating single-use plastic packaging.	What are the cost implications of switching to compostable materials?
Food waste Management	Food waste is addressed through on-site composting, food donation, reuse in staff meals, and optimizing meal preparation practices.	What are the benefits of food donations in reducing organic waste? How effective is staff meal repurposing?
Recycling and Upcycling	Recycling stations are used for sorting paper, glass, and plastics. Local artisans are engaged to convert discarded materials into decorative items.	How does collaboration with artisans enhance circular economy goals?
Waste water recycling	Wastewater from kitchen and laundries is treated on-site and reused in colling systems to reduce fresh water consumption.	What are the operational costs and ROI of wastewater reuse systems?
Digitalization for paper reduction	Paper usage is reduced via electronic check-inns, digital billing, and QR code menus. These solutions replace traditional printed materials.	How much paper waste is saved through digital guest interaction?
Energy efficient practices	Strategic include LED lighting, staff training in energy conservation, and sustainable operational protocols to enhance efficiency.	How do energy-saving programs impact hotel operational costs?
Staff and guest awareness	Staff are trained in sustainability principles, while guests are educated via in-room literature and participatory events.	What role does education play in changing guest behaviour toward sustainability?

Source: Primary data gathered from sustainability stakeholders in hospitality settings

Table 12.5 Themes, contents-barriers and challenges

Theme	Theme-related Content
Cost Constraints	High Initial cost: Implementing technologies like anaerobic digesters, composting units, and advanced recycling systems requires significant upfront investments. Ongoing operational Costs: These systems also incur ongoing expenses for maintenance energy consumption, and labour.
Lack of Technical Expertise	Technical expertise may be limited in-house, requiring external consultants. Training staff across departments is complex and costly.
Awareness and Attitudinal Challenges	Resistance to change may arise from a lack of awareness of potential benefits. The perception of waste as a low-priority issue hinders proactive waste reduction efforts.
Regulatory and Policy Issues	Policy Vacuum: Lack of clear government policies and incentives. Regulatory Burden: Overwhelming regulations without adequate support.
Space and Infrastructure Limitations	Space Limitations; Urban hotels often lack the space for on-site waste processing. Infrastructure Deficiencies: External waste processing systems are unreliable.
Customer and stake holder Expectations	Guest Awareness: Guests may lack understanding of sustainable practices. Vender Alignment: Suppliers may not fully align with sustainability goals.
Integration with Existing Practices	Transition challenges: Shifting to innovative waste management requires significant operational changes, leading to disruptions.

Source: Primary data collected from hospitality managers and sustainability coordinators

This model requires further empirical investigation for conclusion and application. It serves as a framework for future research.

7. Conclusion

The pursuit of sustainable waste management in Kolkata's hotel industry presents a complex challenge. It also includes significant potential for positive environmental and economic impacts. Progress has been made through initiatives. These are waste segregation, plastic reduction, and digital tools, sustainable persist. Financial constraints, technological limitations, inadequate infrastructure, and guest behaviour pose significant hurdles. It leads to widespread adoption of sustainable practices.To overcome those challenges, Amultifaceted approach is necessary to

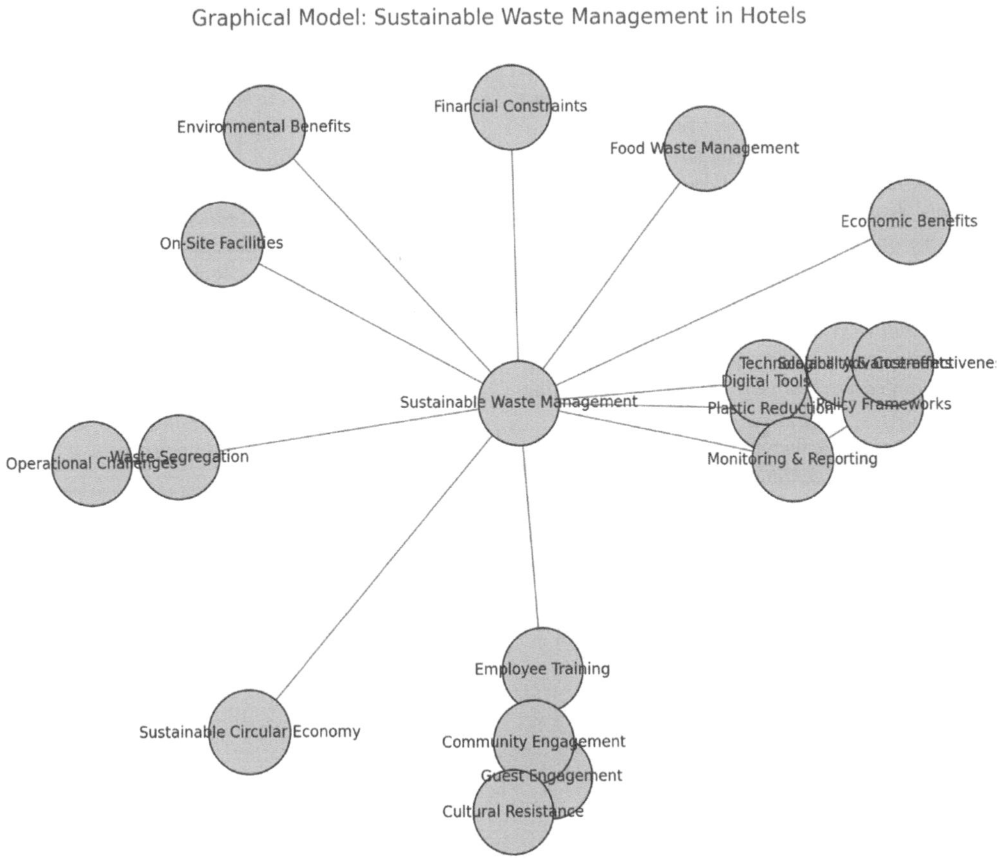

Fig. 12.2 Proposed model (sustainable waste management in hotel)-researchers' model

Source: Authors

overcome those challenges. Itneeds synergic support of government, technological advancements, community engagement, and behavioural change programs. By mixing waste reduction, recycling and resource recovery with broader sustainability initiatives, hotels can establish a sustainable circular economy model.

Continuous monitoring, innovations, and collaboration among policy makers, industry stakeholders, and the community are essential. It aids to ensure the long-term success of sustainable waste management in the hospitality industry. By addressing the issues of cost, infrastructure, and guest behaviour, hotels can transform waste management into a cornerstone.

Acknowledgment

We acknowledge the responses and time of the respondents

References

1. Jones, P., Hillier, D., & Comfort, D. (2016). Sustainability in the hospitality industry: Some personal reflections on corporate challenges and research agendas. *International Journal of Contemporary Hospitality Management*, *28*(1), 36–67.
2. Kumar, H., & Gupta, A. K. (2024). Himalayan fruit and circular economy: nutraceutical potential, traditional uses, challenges and opportunities.
3. Ouro-Salim, O., & Guarnieri, P. (2025). Sustainable food waste management: comparative study of NGO and restaurant practices in Brazil and Togo. *Review of Agricultural, Food and Environmental Studies*, 1–38.
4. Tang, Y., & Law, J. (2020). "Urban Hotel Waste Management: Trends and Challenges." *Asia Pacific Journal of Tourism Research*, 25(3), 297–309.
5. Singh, P., &Chandel, S. (2017). "Waste Management Practices in Indian Urban Hotels." *Indian Journal of Environmental Studies*, 24(1), 59–74.
6. Hobson, K., & Essex, S. (2018). "Regulations and Urban Waste Management." *Waste Management & Research*, 36(6), 548–558.
7. Chen, H., Tang, J., & Law, R. (2021). "Green Certifications and Consumer Preferences in Hospitality."*Journal of Sustainable Tourism*, 29(5), 753–768
8. Okumus, B., Altinay, L., &Chathoth, P. (2019). "Capacity-Building in Hospitality Waste Management."*Tourism and Hospitality Research*, 19(4), 367–382.
9. He, W., Zhao, Q., & Smith, M. (2020). "Mixed-Method Research in Sustainability Studies."*Sustainability Science*, 15(3), 345–360.
10. Jalil, S. A., Rahman, A., & Kamal, N. (2022). "Best Practices in Sustainable Hotel Waste Management." *Sustainability Advances*, 3(2), 121–133.
11. Pérez López, M.C., & Plata Díaz, A.M. (2024).*A machine learning approach to classifying sustainability practices in hotel management*. Journal of Sustainable Tourism.
12. Bekele, H., Raj, S., Singh, A., Joshi, M., & Kajla, T. (2024). *Digital transformation and environmental sustainability*

in the hospitality industry: A three-wave time-lagged examination. Journal of Cleaner Production.

13. Maheshwari, A., Chhabra, D., &Atal, N. (2024). *Sustainable Development and Resilience of Tourism: Wellbeing and Quality of Life Perspectives*. Springer.
14. Das, K.K., & Roy, S. (2024). *Perception Study on the Effect of Sivok-Rangpo Railway Project on the Geo-environmental Issues of Darjeeling Himalaya*. In *Climate Change and Mitigation Strategy for Sustainable Management* (pp. 109–120). Springer.
15. Gursoy, D., Başer, G., & Chi, C.G. (2025). *Corporate digital responsibility: Navigating ethical, societal, and environmental challenges in the digital age and exploring future research directions*. Journal of Hospitality Marketing & Management.
16. Ndhlovu, E., Dube, K., &Shereni, N.C. (2024). *Tourism and Hospitality for Sustainable Development: Volume Three – Implications for Customers and Employees of Tourism Businesses*. Springer.
17. Leal Filho, W., Dinis, M.A.P., Liakh, O., et al. (2024). *Reducing the carbon footprint of the textile sector: an overview of impacts and solutions.Textile Research Journal*, SAGE.
18. Cardenas, M., Schivinski, B., & Brennan, L. (2024). *Circular practices in the hospitality sector regarding food waste. Journal of Cleaner Production.*
19. Filimonau, V., & Tochukwu, C.O. (2020). *Exploring managerial approaches to mitigating solid waste in hotels of Lagos, Nigeria.Journal of Cleaner Production.*
20. Guarnieri, P., &Ouro-Salim, O. (2025). *Sustainable food waste management: Comparative study of NGO and restaurant practices in Brazil and Togo. Journal of Agricultural, Food and Environmental Sciences.*

Research and Innovations in Industrial and Marine Biotechnology: A Circular Economy 2024 – Prof. Hrudayanath Thatoi et al. (eds)

13 Bioprospecting of Cd(II), Pb(II), and As(III)-Tolerant Marine Bacteria from the Bay of Bengal and Assessment of their Metal Removal Efficacy: A Sustainable Bioremediation Strategy

Ranjan Kumar Mohapatra[1]
Department of Environmental & IT Convergence Engineering,
Chungnam National University,
Daejeon, South Korea
Environment and Sustainability Department,
CSIR-Institute of Minerals and Materials Technology,
Bhubaneswar, India

Subhashree Rath
Centre for Industrial Biotechnology Research,
Siksha 'O' Anusandhan, Deemed to be University,
Bhubaneswar, India

Chitta Ranjan Panda
Environment and Sustainability Department,
CSIR-Institute of Minerals and Materials Technology,
Bhubaneswar, India

Hrudayanath Thatoi[2]
Centre for Industrial Biotechnology Research,
Siksha 'O' Anusandhan, Deemed to be University,
Bhubaneswar, India

Abstract: The contamination of heavy metals in the environment has become a major global issue due to its toxicity and carcinogenic qualities. Marine bacteria possess promise for environmental remediation due to their unique adaptation mechanisms and biochemical features compared to non-saline bacteria. This research investigated metal-resistant bacteria from the Paradip harbor region of the Bay of Bengal. A total of 212, 106, and 110 strains of lead (Pb), cadmium (Cd), and arsenic (As) resistant bacteria were found and assessed for their enhanced resistance to the respective metals. After screening, four metal-resistant marine bacteria were identified: one lead-resistant strain (PbRESW01), one cadmium-resistant strain (CdRPSW48), and two arsenic-resistant strains (AsRPSD20 and AsRPSD83), determined by their metal tolerance capacity. The tolerance capacity was evaluated by examining the minimal inhibitory concentration. PbRESW01 demonstrated resistance to Pb (II) concentrations of up to 1800 mg/L, CdRPSW48 tolerated Cd (II) levels of up to 800 mg/L, whereas AsRPSD20 and AsRPSD83 revealed maximum resistance of 800 mg/L and 1700 mg/L for As (III) heavy metal. The heavy metal-resistant bacteria were identified as *Brevibacillus halotolerance* PbRPSW01, *Staphylococcus aureus* CdRPSW48, *Bacillus clausii* AsRPSD20, and *Leucobacter chromireducens* AsRPSD83, using morphological, biochemical, and 16S rRNA gene sequencing methods. The metal removal efficiency and probable growth impacts of the specified bacteria in the presence of respective metals (200 mg/L) and NaCl (2%) were evaluated, indicating that all strains displayed vigorous growth and achieved substantial metal removal efficiency (~90%).

Keywords: Marine bacteria, Halotolerant, Toxic metal, Biosorption, Phylogenetic analysis

Corresponding author: [1]mranjankumar.biotech@gmail.com, [2]director.cibr@soa.ac.in
DOI: 10.1201/9781003759003-13

1. Introduction

Heavy metals from mining by-product, metal plating, coal-based waste, chemical, nuclear, and pesticide industrial wastes, mineral leaching, paper production, battery and gasoline burning, etc. pollute soil, water, and air [1,2]. Growing population, fast urbanization, and heavy industrialization in India have increased hazardous heavy metals to the environment and affected the natural ecology [3]. Heavy metals, inorganic contaminants, penetrate the food chain and bioaccumulate in living tissues because they cannot be destroyed by chemical or biological processes [4]. Some heavy metals are needed for physiochemical processes at low concentrations, while others are very poisonous and mutagenic, carcinogenic, teratogenic, and neurotoxic [5]. These hazardous heavy metals threaten the biological ecology and humans by causing cardiovascular disease, kidney tubular malfunction, and nervous diseases [5]. Thus, sustained hazardous metal removal or neutralization in soil, sediment, and water systems is crucial [4]. Precipitation, filtration using membrane, ion exchange, packed-bed metal treatment, and electro-coagulation processes are uneconomical, generate secondary waste, are inefficient, and require disposal [6,7]. For its ease of use, non-generation of secondary pollutants, and high removal efficiency at low metal concentration, bioremediation of heavy metals using bacteria having heavy metal tolerance activity is a promising alternative [8]. Metal bioremediation employing native metal-tolerant bacteria is a promising method for developing green metal detoxification technologies through oxidation, reduction, bio-sorption, precipitation, and sequestration [9]. Genetically modified plasmids help metal-polluted bacteria survive and withstand hazardous heavy metals [4]. Thus, exploring native bacterial strains in high-heavy metal pollution environments is vital for harmful heavy metal detoxification [5,10]. Bacterial metal detoxification is attracting growing interest among biotechnologists, owing to their metal and antibiotic tolerance and the presence of functional groups such as amino, carboxyl, sulphate, and phosphate in their extracellular polysaccharides and lipoprotein layers having metal-binding ability [2]. It has been discovered that both live and inactivated bacteria can bioremove metal ions through two well-defined mechanisms: biosorption (an energy-independent binding mechanism) and bioaccumulation (an energy-dependent metal uptake mechanism) [1,2,11].

Environments contaminated with metals typically exhibit either high or low temperatures, an alkaline or acidic pH, and elevated salt concentrations. High salt-tolerant marine bacteria have superior abilities for metal bioremediation compared to non-marine bacteria, owing to their capacity to adapt to various marine conditions such as pH, temperature, salinity, water currents, and conductance [12]. Marine bacteria have complicated adaptability and several anionic and cationic cell surface functional groups to enhance metal adsorption and accumulation [13]. Thus, marine microorganisms are effective heavy metal remediators in saline conditions.

Many researchers have found metal-resistant halo-tolerant bacteria from various maritime environments those bioremediate heavy metals. These include *Lysinibacillus sphaericus* strain AsRPSD99 [2], *Bacillus altitudinis* strain CdRPSD103 [1], *Bacillus xiamenesis* PBRPSD202 [11], *Exiguobacterium indicum* MW1 [12], *Brevibacillus laterosporus* CrRPSD40 [14], *Bacillus* sp. Pb15 [15], *Bacillus* sp. KM02 [16], *Acinetobacter* sp. THKPS16 [17], *Alcaligens* sp. [18], and *Halomonas* sp. [19]. However, efficient marine bacteria for toxic metal bioremediation in metal-contaminated saline environments are being studied. Thus, bioprospecting metal-resistant and salt-tolerant microorganisms is crucial for better bioremediation.

This study uses marine samples from Paradip port in Bay of Bengal. The goal is to isolate, screen, characterise, and identify highly metal-resistant indigenous marine bacteria from Paradip harbour and test their bioremediation capabilities against three hazardous metals (Cd, Pb, and As). This investigation would help identify marine metal-resistant saline bacterial species that may detoxify heavy metals in metal-contaminated saline environments.

2. Materials and Methods

2.1 Chemicals and Reagents

Separate stock solutions (1 g/L) of Pb(II), Cd(II), As(III), Cr(VI), Zn(II), Ni(II), and Cu(II) were prepared. Metal compounds like lead nitrate, cadmium nitrate, sodium arsenite, potassium dichromate, zinc sulphate, nickel nitrate, and copper sulphate (Merck India Pvt. Ltd.) of analytical grade are dissolved in ultrapure Millipore water. The media used for bacterial culture, biochemical tests and carbohydrate utilization test (KB009A, KB009B1, and KB009C) were procured from HiMedia Laboratories Pvt. Ltd. Before the start of each experiment, all the glasswares were made free from metal by washing these with nitric acid and then rinsing three times with distilled water.

2.2 Sampling Location and Collection of Marine Samples

Paradip port, on the East Coast of India in Odisha on the Bay of Bengal, is a major ship port and a hub for national and international marine trade [20]. Exporting ores and minerals through this port caused heavy metal contamination in the harbour [21]. The harbour bacteria are tolerant of several metals and good candidates for metal bioremediation. Thus, Port harbour water and sediment samples may include metal-tolerant bacteria that can be used for heavy metal detoxification (Fig. 13.1). A total of thirty water and sediment samples were collected from these ten major jetties within the harbor. Samples

Fig. 13.1 Location map showing the ten sampling points of sample collection for bacteria isolation

of surface water, bottom water (from depths greater than 10 m), and sediment were gathered from each jetty of the harbor using a bucket, Niskin water sampler, and Van Veen Grab sampler. These samples were placed in sterilized sampling bottles and transported to the lab while kept frozen.

2.3 Bacterial Isolation and Screening

The isolation of Pb(II), Cd(II), and As(III) resistant bacteria from collected surface and bottom layer marine water and sediments. Both water samples and sediments were diluted upto 10^{-3} dilution factor and spread on nutrient agar plates containing 50 mg/L of respective heavy metals. All the plates were incubated at 37 °C for 24 h to 48 h. Bacterial colonies grown on 50 mg/L metal ion containing plates were subsequently tested against higher concentrations (200, 500, 700, and 1000 mg/L) of the respective metals. This was achieved through a stepwise streaking method on nutrient agar medium containing increasing metal concentrations [21]. Bacterial strains capable of growth in 1000 mg/L metal concentrations exhibited high metal resistance and underwent strain purification through two successive quadrant streaks on nutrient agar plates.

2.4 Multiple Metal Tolerance Test

The minimum inhibitory concentrations (MIC) for Pb (II), Cd (II), and As (III) heavy metals were assessed for all selected bacterial strains in nutrient broth using the broth dilution method as outlined by Mohapatra et al. [21] and Jain et al. [22]. The growth of the strains was verified by visual observation and taking absorbance at 600 nm. The lack of bacterial growth at a specified metal concentration is defined as the minimum inhibitory concentration (MIC) for that metal. The highest MIC values for lead, cadmium, and arsenic heavy metal tolerant bacteria underwent multi-metal tolerance testing to evaluate their resistance to additional toxic metals beyond those for which they were initially screened

2.5 Characterisation and Identification of Bacterial Isolates

Phenotypic Characterisation

All selected metal-resistant bacteria were phenotypically characterized using morphological and biochemical observations, outlined by Bergey's Manual of Systematic Bacteriology [23]. Morphological observations, including colony morphology (shape, surface, opacity, texture, elevation, and pigmentation) and Gram staining of the selected bacteria, were recorded through both visual and microscopic examination using a light compound microscope. Utilization tests for 35 carbohydrates were conducted using the KB009A, KB009B1, and KB009C Himedia carbohydrate test kits. A study on antibiotic resistance for all selected bacteria was conducted against fifteen antibiotics using Muller Hinton agar medium (Himedia) in accordance with the Kirby-Bauer disc diffusion method [21]. The antibiotic resistance of each bacterium to the tested antibiotics was assessed by comparing the measured inhibition zone diameters with the interpretative chart of antimicrobial zone sizes from Himedia Laboratories.

Genotypic Identification

The selected metal-resistant bacteria were undertaken 16S rRNA sequencing and phylogenetic analyses. The DNA from metal-resisrant bacteria was isolated and assessed for quality using electrophoresis. The 16S rRNA gene present in genomic DNA was amplified employing polymerase chain reaction (PCR) using universal 27F (5'-GATCCTGGCTCAG-3') and 1492R (5'-TACGGYTACCTTGTTACGACTT-3') primers. Basic Local Alignment Search Tool (BLAST) was used for the phylogenetic analysis of the isolated bacteria by retrieving similar sequences of the respective bacterial 16S rRNA gene sequences from the GenBank database of NCBI. The multiple sequence alignment was undertaken using the Clustal_X program [24] and MEGA 8.0 software was utilized to construct the phylogenetic tree [25].

Field Emission Scanning Electron Microscope (FESEM)

The FESEM was employed to capture cellular morphology images of all selected highly metal-resistant marine bacteria. For FESEM analysis, 72 hours old bacterial culture was centrifuged at 10,000 rpm for 10 min at 4°C. The pellets were washed thrice using phosphate-buffered saline (1X PBS, pH 7.2), then 3 ml of glutaraldehyde (2.5%) was used to fix bacterial cell, followed by washing with PBS buffer [20]. Then the obtained fixed cells were progressively dehydrated using increasing concentrations of ethanol (20% to 100% (v/v)), air dried and placed within a desiccator [26]. Before being examined with a FESEM (Carl Zeiss, SUPRA GEMINI55), the specimens were placed in the sample holder and then covered in gold.

2.6 Growth and Metal Removal Study in the Presence of Pb (II), Cd (II) and As (III)

The growth pattern of isolated metal-resistant bacteria under heavy metal stress, as well as their concomitant metal sorption efficiency, was evaluated by employing a 200 mg/L concentration of heavy metals. In this investigation, new bacterial isolates were inoculated in 200 mg/L metal ions (Pb (II), Cd (II), and As (III)) supplemented nutritional broth medium (pH ~7.0; NaCl 2% w/v). The experiment was carried out at 37°C with an agitation speed of 120 rotations per minute for 120 hours. The rate of growth of bacteria was measured using Ultraviolet-visible spectrophotometer (VARIAN Cary 50 Bio), taking absorbance at 600 nm from 0 and 120 hours of incubation. The concentration of metal in the culture supernatant was measured employing atomic absorption spectrophotometer (AAS, SHIMADZU AA7000) coupled with a hydride vapor production device after centrifugation of culture at 10,000 rpm for 10 minutes and filtering through Whatman filter paper (0.22 μm). All experiments were executed in triplicate, and the mean values and standard errors were calculated. The biosorption capacity (%) of heavy metal removal was calculated following the formula presented in Equation (1).

$$Biosorption(\%) = \frac{(C_i - C_f)}{C_i} \times 100 \qquad (1)$$

Where, C_i = the concentration of metal at 0 h treatment with bacteria (initial) and C_f = the concentration of metal after 120 h (final) treatment with bacteria.

3. Results and Discussion

3.1 Isolation, Screening and Metal Tolerance of Bacteria

A total of 212 Pb(II), 106 Cd(II), and 110 As(III) resistant bacteria were isolated from Paradip port harbour water and sediment samples at a metal concentration of 50 mg/L. Following further screening with escalating metal ion concentrations (100 to 1000 mg/L), only 18, 7, and 13 bacterial strains demonstrated tolerance and growth at 1000 mg/L of Pb(II), Cd(II), and As(III), respectively (data not shown). The metal tolerance test regarding the minimum inhibitory concentration (MIC) of the selected strains against Pb(II), Cd(II), and As(III) indicated that the bacterium PbRPSW01 tolerated up to 1800 mg/L of Pb(II). Strain CdRPSW48 exhibited a tolerance capacity against Cd(II) with a MIC of 800 mg/L. Additionally, strains AsRPSD20 and AsRPSD83 demonstrated maximum resistance to As(III) with MIC values of 800 and 1700 mg/L, respectively (Fig. 13.2). The selected highly metal-resistant bacteria demonstrated multiple metal tolerance capacities against heavy metals such as Pb(II), Cd(II), As(III), Cr(VI), Zn(II), Ni(II), and Cu(II), as illustrated in Fig. 13.2.

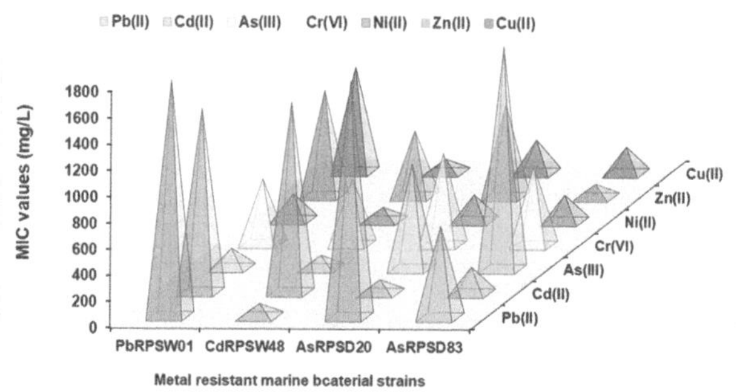

Fig. 13.2 Evaluation of MIC values against six metals and one metalloid for selected multiple metal resistant marine bacterial strains

Isolated lead-resistant PbRPSW01 bacteria demonstrate enhanced tolerance, with a maximum MIC of Pb(II) exceeding that of previously studied Pb(II) resistant bacteria including *Halomonas* sp. strain D/NA-7 (5 mM ~1036 mg/L) (Amoozegar et al., 2012), *Delftia tsuruhatensis* (6 mM~1243 mg/L) (Bautista-Hernandez et al., 2012), *Bacillus* sp. Pb-15 (4.82 mM~995 mg/L) (Pepi et al., 2016), *Halomonas* BVR1 (200 mg/L) (Manasi et al., 2016),, *Pseudomonas aeruginosa* BC15 (800 mg/L), *Bacillus cereus* and *Alcaligenes* sp. (1000 mg/L) (Ansari et al., 2016). Isolated Cd(II) resistant marine bacteria CdRPSW48 exhibited superior tolerance and MIC values compared to previously documented saline and non-saline Cd-resistant bacteria. For instance, *Halomonas* sp. demonstrated resistance at 5 Mm [19], while *Alcaligens* sp. and *Staphylococcus* sp. showed resistance in the range of 0.05–4.0 mM [18]. Other bacteria such as *Pseudoalteromonas* sp. SCSE709 had a resistance level of 100 mg/L [27], *Alteromonas macleodii* ASC1 at 150 mg/L [28], and *Bacillus* sp. NT-1 and Pseudomonas sp. TT-10 at 400 mg/L and 500 mg/L, respectively [29]. Additionally, *Pseudomonas aeruginosa* BC15 had resistance levels of 500 mg/L, while Bacillus cereus and *Alcaligenes* sp. showed resistance at 1000 mg/L [8]. Likewise, isolated As(III) tolerant bacteria (AsRPSD20 and AsRPSD83) exhibited greater tolerance and MIC compared to several previously reported strains, including *Bacillus* sp. KM02 at 500 mg/L [16]. As a result, the strains indicated above can be used to bioremediate a variety of metal-contaminated environments.

3.2 Bacterial Characterisation and Identification

The mthe bacteria PbRPSW01, CdRPSW48, AsRPSD20, and AsRPSD83 were undertaken morphological and biochemical characterization, and the results were presented in Tables (13.1, 13.2, and 13.3). The scanning microscopic analysis presented in Fig. 13.3 confirmed the cellular morphology of the bacteria. The strain PbRPSW01 is a Gram-negative, rod-shaped, motile, γ-haemolytic bacterium that utilizes dextrose, fructose, mannitol, and

Table 13.1 Assessment of morphological and biochemical characterisation of isolated heavy metal tolerant bacteria

Morphological and Biochemical Characterisation				
Tests	**PbRPSW01**	**CdRPSW48**	**AsRPSD20**	**AsRPSD83**
Gram's stain	Gram-ve	Gram+ve	Gram-ve	Gram+ve
Shape	Rod	Cocci	Rod	Rod
Motility	Motile	Non motile	Motile	Non motile
Triple sugar iron	+	NA	NA	-
H_2S/ Gas production	NA	-	NA	NA
Simmon's Citrate utilisation	-	+	-	NA
Methyl red	-	Present	Present	-
Voges-Proskaur	-	-	-	-
Indole production	-	+	-	-
Oxidative/ Fermentative reaction	Oxidative	Neither O nor F	Fermentative	NA
Alkaline reaction	NA	Present	NA	NA
Carbohydrate Utilization Test				
Tests	**PbRPSW01**	**CdRPSW48**	**AsRPSD20**	**AsRPSD83**
Adenitol	-	-	-	-
Arabinose	NA	-	+	NA
Arabitol	-	-	-	NA
Cellobiose	-	-	-	-
D-arabinose	-	-	-	-
Dextrose	+	+	+	NA
Dolcitol	-	-	+	NA
Erythritol	-	-	-	+
Esculin hydrolysis	-	NA	-	NA
Fructose	+	+	+	+
Galactose	-	-	-	-
Glucose	NA	+	NA	NA
Glycerol	-	-	+	+
Inositol	-	-	-	-
Inulin	-	-	+	+*
Lactose	-	+	-	NA
L-Arabinose	-	-	+	-
Malonet utilization	-	-	-	NA
Maltose	-	-	+	-
Mannitol	+	-	+	NA
Mannose	-	-	+	-
Melezitose	-	-	-	-
Melibiose	-	-	-	NA
ONPG	NA	-	+	NA
Ornithine utilization	NA	-	NA	NA
Raffinose	-	-	+	+*
Rhamnose	-	-	+	+
Salicin	-	-	+	NA
Sodium gluconate	-	-	-	NA
Sorbitol	-	-	+	+*
Sorbose	-	-	-	-
Sucrose	+	+	+	+*
Trehalose	-	-	+	+*
Xylitol	-	-	-	NA
Xylose	-	-	+	NA
α –methyl-D-mannoside	-	-	-	-
α –methyle-D glucoside	-	-	-	-

Note: NA- not available, * partial
- Negative + Positive

Table 13.2 Enzyme production by the isolated metal resistant bacteria

	Enzyme production			
Enzymes	**CdRPSW01**	**CdRPSW48**	**AsRPSD20**	**AsRPSD83**
Alkaline phosphatise	+	+	+	+
Amylase	+	-	-	-
Casein Hydrolase	-	+	+	-
Catalase	+	+	+	+
Gelatin Hydrolase	+	+	-	-
Lipase	-	-	-	-
Oxidase	+	+	+	-
Urease	+	+	-	-
Nitrate reductase	-	+	-	-
Haemolytic hydrolase	γ-haemolytic	β-haemolytic	α-haemolytic	γ-haemolytic

- Negative + Positive

Table 13.3 Antibiotic resistance test

Antibiotics (Conc. in μg)	CdRPSW01	CdRPSW48	AsRPSD20	AsRPSD83
Ampicillin (10)	Intermediate	AR	AR	AR
Azithromycin (15)	AS	AS	AS	AS
Cefixime (5)	AR	AR	NT	AS
Cholomphenicol (30)	AS	Intermediate	Intermediate	Intermediate
Ciprofloxacin (5)	AS	Intermediate	AS	AS
Erythromycin (15)	AS	Intermediate	AS	NT
Gentamicin (10)	AS	AS	AS	AS
Kanamycin (30)	AR	Intermediate	AS	AR
Nalidixic acid (30)	AS	Intermediate	AS	AS
Neomycin (30)	AS	AS	Intermediate	NT
Norfloxacin (10)	AS	AS	AS	AS
Penicillin-G (10)	AR	AR	AR	AR
Rifampicin (5)	AS	AR	AS	AR
Streptomycin (10)	AS	AS	AS	AR
Tetracycline (30)	AS	Intermediate	NT	AR

Note: NT- Not tested
AR - Antibiotic resistant
AS- Antibiotic sensitive

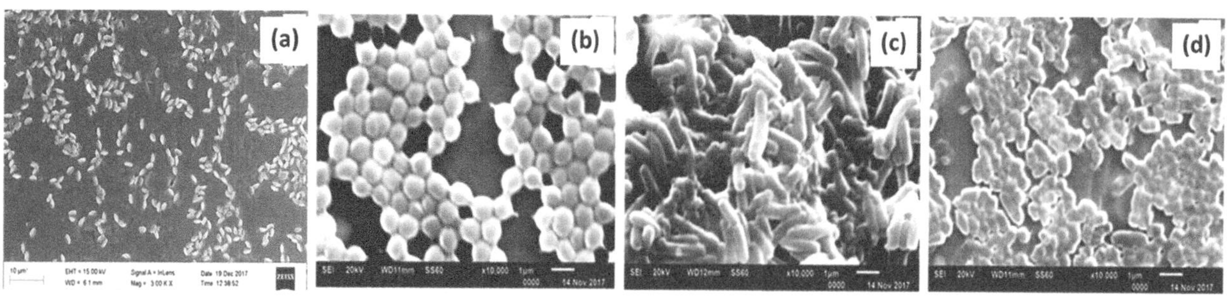

Fig. 13.3 Scanning electron micrographs of the isolated four metal resistant marine bacteria (a) *Brevibacillus halotolerance* PbRPSW01, (b) *Staphylococcus aureus* CdRPSW48, (c) *Bacillus clausii* AsRPSD20, (d) *Leucobacter chromiireducens* AsRPSD83

sucrose as carbohydrate sources and exhibits a positive Voges-Proskauer test. This bacterium also showed resistance to penicillin, cefixime, gatifloxacin, and kanamycin antibiotics. The bacterium CdRPSW48 was characterized as a Gram-positive coccus, non-motile, and γ-haemolytic bacterium and utilized glucose, dextrose, fructose, lactose, sucrose, and citrate as carbohydrate sources. Additionally, it exhibits methyl red and indole positive, and an alkaline reaction in the triple sugar iron test. The strain AsRPSD20 is characterized as a Gram-negative, rod-shaped, motile, γ-haemolytic bacterium. It utilizes various carbohydrates, including arabinose, dextrose, dulcitol, galactose, glycerol, inulin, maltose, mannitol, mannose, sucrose, trehalose, and xylose. Additionally, it exhibits a positive methyl red reaction and a fermentative response in the triple sugar iron test. It also showed resistance to penicillin and ampicillin antibiotics. The strain AsRPSD83 is characterized as a Gram-positive, rod-shaped, non-motile, non-sporulating, γ-haemolytic bacterium that utilizes fructose, rhamnose, sorbitol, and sucrose as carbohydrate sources. All four strains showed the generation of several hydrolytic enzymes. The bacterium exhibited resistance to several antibiotics, including penicillin, kanamycin, rifampicin, streptomycin, tetracycline, and ampicillin.

Phylogenetic analyses (Fig. 13.4) of PbRPSW01, CdRPSW48, AsRPSD20, and AsRPSD83 demonstrated 99% similarity with *Brevibacillus halotolerans* LAM0312 (KJ627768), *Staphylococcus aureus* (D83357), *Bacillus clausii* DSM 8716 (X76440), and *Leucobacter chromiireducens* subsp. *chromiireducens* L-1 (AJ781046), respectively (Fig. 13.4). Consequently, through the integration of morphological and biochemical characteristics alongside genetic analysis, the above bacterial strains were classified as *Brevibacillus halotolerans* sp. PbRPSW01, *Staphylococcus aureus* sp. CdRPSW48, *Bacillus clausii* sp. AsRPSD20, and *Leucobacter chromiireducens* sp. AsRPSD83, respectively.

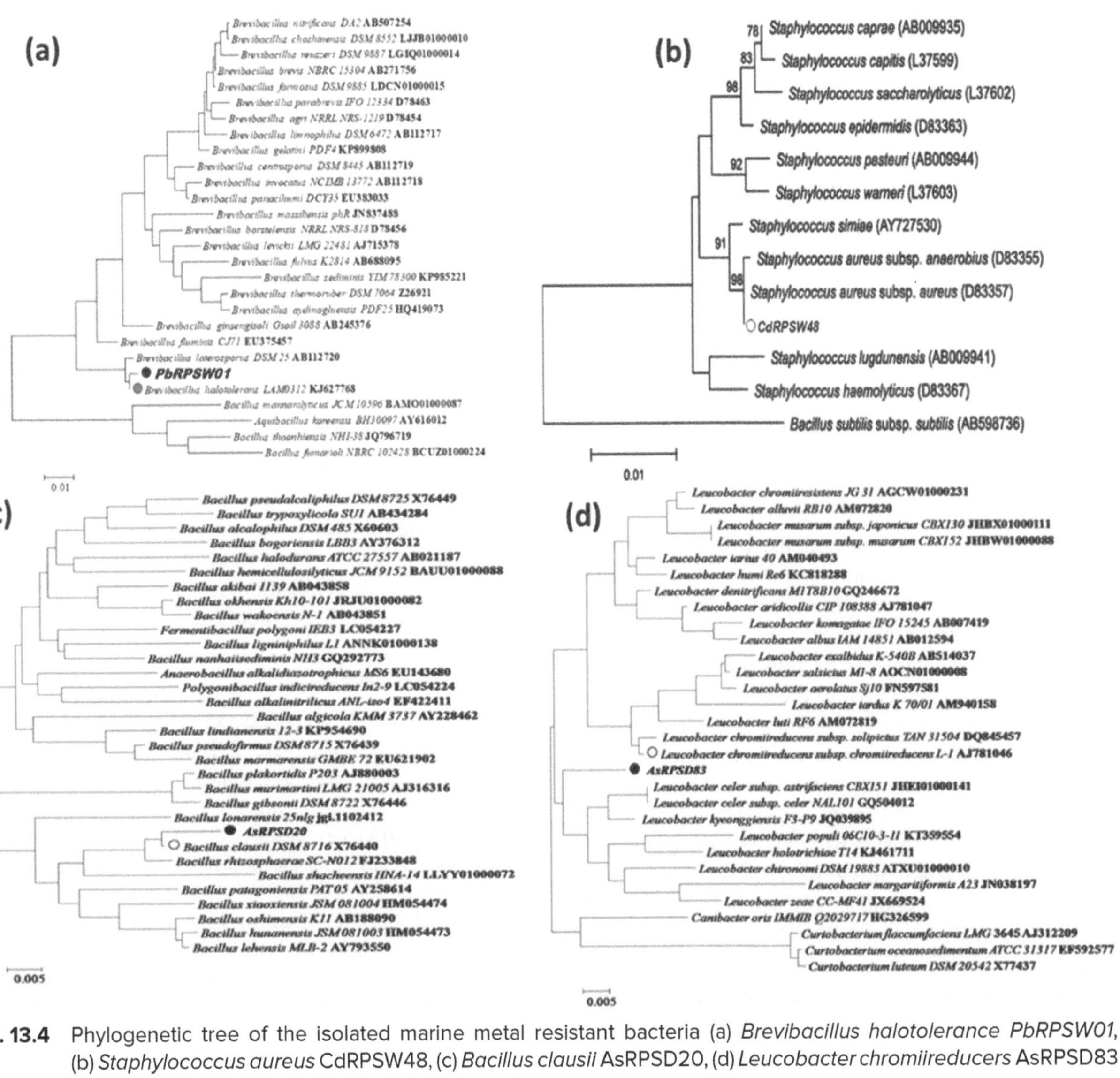

Fig. 13.4 Phylogenetic tree of the isolated marine metal resistant bacteria (a) *Brevibacillus halotolerance PbRPSW01*, (b) *Staphylococcus aureus* CdRPSW48, (c) *Bacillus clausii* AsRPSD20, (d) *Leucobacter chromiireducers* AsRPSD83

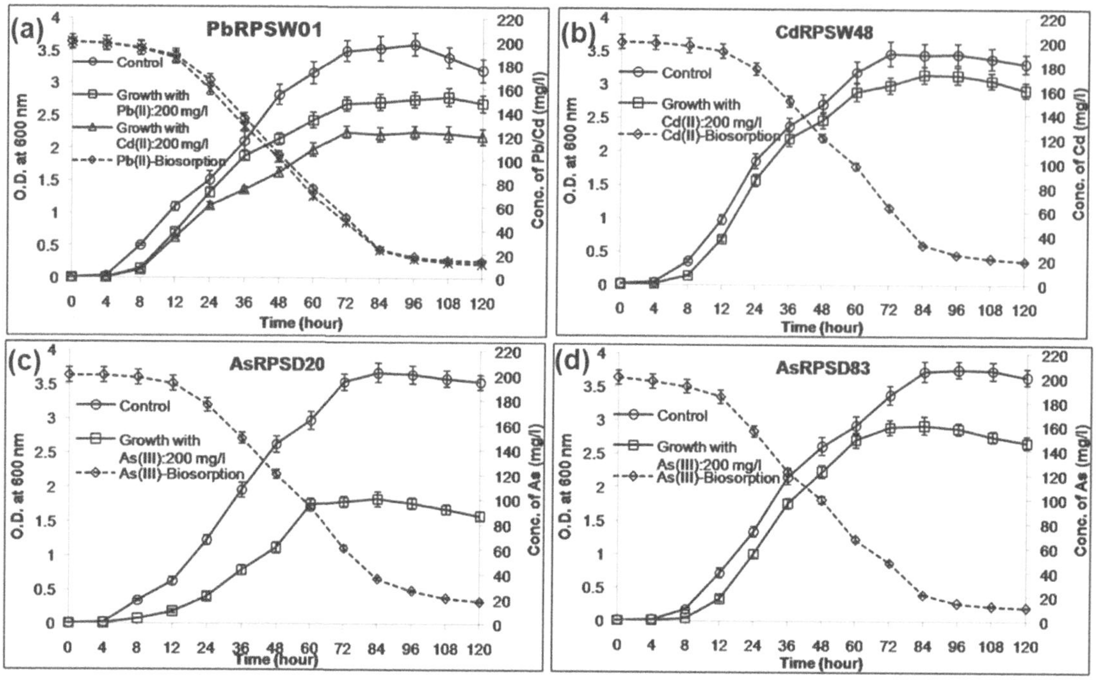

Fig. 13.5 Growth and metal removal efficiency of the selected metal-resistant marine bacteria

3.3 Evaluation of Bacterial Growth and Metal Biosorption

The study of bacterial growth and concurrent metal sorption capacity in the presence of respective heavy metals (200 mg/L) is illustrated in Fig. 13.5. In the control condition without metals, a lag phase in bacterial growth was noted for 4 h to 8 h, log phase lasting from 72 h to 96 h and from 72 h to 108 h. Subsequently, growth slowed, reaching stationary phases after 96 h to 108 h of incubation (Fig. 13.5a-d). In the presence of metal ions, bacterial growth exhibited slight inhibition due to metal toxicity, resulting in a reduced growth pattern compared to the control group. Subsequently, growth stabilized and began to decline after 108 h to 120 h of incubation. The growth pattern of the isolated metal-resistant bacteria shows no significant deviation in the presence or absence of various metal ions, confirming their capacity for metal tolerance. The bacterial growth in metal-supplemented nutrient medium demonstrated a decrease in initial metal concentration relative to the bacterial growth rate, indicating that simultaneous growth and metal removal via a sorption mechanism occurred within the bacterial cells. Approximately 90% of metal ion removal was achieved after 120 h of bacterial treatment at 2% w/v NaCl and pH 7.0 for all four isolated bacterial strains. Comparable biosorption efficiency was observed in various marine isolates, including *Bacillus xiamenensis* PbRPSD202, *Bacillus altitudinis* CdRPSD103, and *Lysinibacillus sphaericus* AsRPSD99, as reported by Mohapatra et al. [1,2,11]. Consequently, the bacterial strain identified in this study may serve as a potential agent for the bioremoval of various toxic metals from contaminated environments.

4. Conclusions

The isolated marine bacteria (*B. halotolerance* PbRPSW01, *S. aureus* CdRPSW48, *B. clausii* AsRPSD20, and *L. chromiireducers* AsRPSD83) exhibit enhanced metal tolerance capacity against various metals and metalloids. Bacterial biomass can grow in hazardous metal ions containing plates and eliminate them through the process of biosorption. The biosorption process primarily entails various cell surface functional ligands, including hydroxyl, carboxyl, phosphate, and amine, located in the outer cell membrane. The outcomes of this work indicate that these marine bacterial strains may be exploited for effective metal removal from contaminated saline environments in a cost-efficient and sustainable manner. The results of this study may be beneficial for the future large-scale application of this strain, promoting the generation of significant biomass.

References

1. Mohapatra, R. K., Nayak, M., Parhi, P. K., Pandey, S., Thatoi, H., Panda, C. R., & Choi, Y. (2024). Biosorption performance and mechanism insights of live and dead biomass of halophilic Bacillus altitudinis strain CdRPSD103 for removal of Cd (II) from aqueous solution. *International Biodeterioration & Biodegradation*, 191, 105811.
2. Mohapatra, R. K., Rath, S., Nayak, M., Parhi, P. K., Pandey, S., Panda, C. R., & Choi, Y. (2025). Arsenite biosorption from contaminated water using live and dead biomass of marine Lysinibacillus sphaericus strain AsRPSD99: A modeling-based approach. *Journal of Water Process Engineering*, 75, 107905.

3. Marzan, L. W., Hossain, M., Mina, S. A., Akter, Y., & Chowdhury, A. M. A. (2017). Isolation and biochemical characterization of heavy-metal resistant bacteria from tannery effluent in Chittagong city, Bangladesh: Bioremediation viewpoint. *The Egyptian Journal of Aquatic Research*, *43*(1), 65–74.
4. Mihdhir, A. A., Assaeedi, A. S. A., Abulreesh, H. H., & Osman, G. E. H. (2016). Detection, Identification and Characterization of Some Heavy Metals Tolerant Bacteria. *Journal of Microbial and Biochemical Technology*, *8*, 226–230.
5. Gupta, K., Chatterjee, C., & Gupta, B. (2012). Isolation and characterization of heavy metal tolerant Gram-positive bacteria with bioremedial properties from municipal waste rich soil of Kestopur canal (Kolkata), West Bengal, India. *Biologia*, *67*(5), 827–836.
6. Inyang, M., Gao, B., Yao, Y., Xue, Y., Zimmerman, A. R., Pullammanappallil, P., & Cao, X. (2012). Removal of heavy metals from aqueous solution by biochars derived from anaerobically digested biomass. *Bioresource technology*, *110*, 50–56.
7. François, F., Lombard, C., Guigner, J. M., Soreau, P., Brian-Jaisson, F., Martino, G., ... & Peduzzi, J. (2012). Isolation and characterization of environmental bacteria capable of extracellular biosorption of mercury. *Applied Environmental Microbiology*, *78*(4), 1097–1106.
8. Ansari, R. A., Qureshi, A. A., & Ramteke, D. S. (2016). Isolation and characterization of heavy-metal resistant microbes from Industrial soil. *International journal of environmental sciences*, *6*(5), 670–680.
9. Mohapatra, R. K., Parhi, P. K., Patra, J. K., Panda, C. R., & Thatoi, H. N. (2017a). Biodetoxification of toxic heavy metals by marine metal resistant bacteria-a novel approach for bioremediation of the polluted saline environment. Microbial Biotechnology:. *Applications in Agriculture and Environment*, 1, 343–376.
10. Sherameti, I., & Varma, A. (Eds.). (2011). *Detoxification of heavy metals* (Vol. 30). Springer Science & Business Media.
11. Mohapatra, R. K., Parhi, P. K., Pandey, S., Bindhani, B. K., Thatoi, H., Panda, C. R. (2019). Active and passive biosorption of Pb (II) using live and dead biomass of marine bacterium Bacillus xiamenensis PbRPSD202: Kinetics and isotherm studies. *Journal of environmental management*, 247, 121–134.
12. Mohapatra, R. K., Parhi, P. K., Thatoi, H., & Panda, C. R. (2017b). Bioreduction of hexavalent chromium by Exiguobacterium indicum strain MW1 isolated from marine water of Paradip Port, Odisha, India. *Chemistry and Ecology*, 33(2), 114–130.
13. Kumar, M. (2016). Understanding the remobilization of copper, zinc, cadmium and lead due to ageing through sequential extraction and isotopic exchangeability. *Environmental monitoring and assessment*, *188*, 1–10.
14. Mohapatra, R. K., Pandey, S., Thatoi, H., & Panda, C. R. (2017c). Reduction of chromium (VI) by marine bacterium *Brevibacillus laterosporus* under varying saline and pH conditions. *Environmental Engineering Science*, 34(9), 617–626.
15. Pepi M, Borra M, Tamburrino S, Saggiomo M, Viola A, Biffali E, Balestra C, Sprovieri M, Casotti R (2016) A bacillus sp. isolated from sediments of the Sarno River mouth, gulf of Naples (Italy) produces a biofilm biosorbingPb (II). *Science of Total Environment*, 562, 588–595.
16. Dey U, Chatterjee S, Mondal NK (2016) Isolation and characterization of arsenic-resistant bacteria and possible application in bioremediation. *Biotechnology Reports*, 10, 1–7.
17. Ma, Y., Wang, P., Wang, C., Zhang, S. H., & Cheng, S. (2015). Isolation and characterization of Pb-resistant strains and the removal of Pb (II). *Fresenius Environ. Bull*, *24*(3B), 1150–1157.
18. Sowmya, M., Rejula, M. P., Rejith, P. G., Mohan, M., Karuppiah, M., & Hatha, A. M. (2014). Heavy metal tolerant halophilic bacteria from Vembanad Lake as possible source for bioremediation of lead and cadmium. *Journal of Environmental Biology*, *35*(4), 655.
19. Amoozegar, M. A., Ghazanfari, N., & Didari, M. (2012). Lead and cadmium bioremoval by Halomonas sp., an exopolysaccharide-producing halophilic bacterium. *Progress in Biological Sciences*, *2*(1), 1–11.
20. Mohapatra, R. K., & Panda, C. R. (2017). Spatiotemporal variation of water quality and assessment of pollution potential in Paradip port due to port activities. *Indian Journal of Geo Marine Sciences*, 46(07), 1274–1286
21. Mohapatra, R. K., Pandey, S., Thatoi, H. N., & Panda, C. R. (2016). Screening and evaluation of multi-metal tolerance of chromate resistant marine bacteria isolated from water and sediment samples of Paradip port, Odisha coast. *Journal of Advanced Microbiology*, *2*(3), 135–147.
22. Jain, A., Sharma, V. K., & Mbuya, O. S. (2009). Removal of arsenite by Fe (VI), Fe (VI)/Fe (III), and Fe (VI)/Al (III) salts: Effect of pH and anions. *Journal of hazardous materials*, 169(1-3), 339–344.
23. Bergey, D. H. (1994). Bergey's manual of determinative bacteriology. Lippincott Williams & Wilkins.
24. Thompson, J. D., Gibson, T. J., Plewniak, F., Jeanmougin, F., & Higgins, D. G. (1997). The CLUSTAL_X windows interface: flexible strategies for multiple sequence alignment aided by quality analysis tools. *Nucleic acids research*, 25(24), 4876–4882.
25. Tamura, K., Peterson, D., Peterson, N., Stecher, G., Nei, M., & Kumar, S. (2011). MEGA5: molecular evolutionary genetics analysis using maximum likelihood, evolutionary distance, and maximum parsimony methods. *Molecular biology and evolution*, 28(10), 2731–2739.
26. Mangaiyarkarasi, M. M., Vincent, S., Janarthanan, S., Rao, T. S., & Tata, B. V. R. (2011). Bioreduction of Cr (VI) by alkaliphilic Bacillus subtilis and interaction of the membrane groups. *Saudi journal of biological sciences*, *18*(2), 157–167.
27. Zhou, W., Zhang, H. O., Ma, Y., Zhou, J., & Zhang, Y. (2013). Bio-removal of cadmium by growing deep-sea bacterium Pseudoalteromonas sp. SCSE709-6. *Extremophiles*, *17*, 723–731.
28. El-Moselhy, K. M., Shaaban, M. T., Ibrahim, H. A., & Abdel-Mongy, A. S. (2013). Biosorption of cadmium by the multiple-metal resistant marine bacterium Alteromonas macleodii ASC1 isolated from Hurghada harbour, Red Sea. *Arch Sci*, *66*(2), 259–272.
29. Mathivanan, K., & Rajaram, R. (2014). Isolation and characterisation of cadmium-resistant bacteria from an industrially polluted coastal ecosystem on the southeast coast of India. *Chemistry and Ecology*, *30*(7), 622–635.

Note: All the figures and tables in this chapter were made by the authors.

Research and Innovations in Industrial and Marine Biotechnology: A Circular Economy 2024 – Prof. Hrudayanath Thatoi et al. (eds)
© 2026 Taylor & Francis Group, London, ISBN 978-1-041-28285-3

14 Application of Ginger (*Zingiber Officinale*) for Removal of Heavy Metals from Environment

Swapnashree Satapathy
Centre for Biotechnology,
Siksha O Anusandhan University, Kalinga Nagar, Ghatikia,
Bhubaneswar, Odisha, India

Dattatreya Kar
Department of Medical Research,
Health Science, IMS & SUM Hospital, Siksha O Anusandhan University,
Bhubaneswar, Odisha, India

Ananya Kuanar*
Centre for Biotechnology,
Siksha O Anusandhan University, Kalinga Nagar, Ghatikia,
Bhubaneswar, Odisha, India

Abstract: Heavy metals and toxic chemicals are serious, persistent threats to human health and the environment because of their accumulation in the body and ecosystem. Cadmium and lead are highly carcinogenic heavy metals often found in industrial effluents from mining, metallurgy, petrochemicals, and manufacturing. Thus, effective removal methods are essential. Research indicates that ginger can help relieve sore throats, cold symptoms, nausea, vomiting, and muscle pain, and may also inhibit cancer growth. Regular consumption of soft drinks increases the risk of obesity, type II diabetes, and dental erosion, prompting a shift toward healthier natural options like ginger root beverages. Previous studies have utilized ginger root to eliminate harmful metal cations. This research examines the potential of *Zingiber officinale* to remove heavy metals effectively.

Keywords: Environmental risks, Ginger root, Heavy metals, Human health, *Zingiber officinale*

1. Introduction

In the last 20 years, bioremediation has progressed as a cost-effective method for cleaning up pollution resulting from chemical production, storage, and transport. By utilizing bacteria, plants, and fungi, it can break down, eliminate, or detoxify environmental pollutants. Toxic heavy metals such as cadmium (Cd), arsenic (As), mercury (Hg), chromium (Cr) others, contaminate the environment and pose serious health risks to humans. While they are essential in small amounts, an excess has impacted 75% of India's population, leading to significant health challenges [1]. Statistics show that 80% of illnesses and infections in the world are caused by contaminated water, and if nothing is done soon, that percentage might double [2]. To prevent toxicity, these metals must be eliminated as they are harmful to humans, animals, and plants. Lead (Pb) is recognized by the Environmental Protection Agency (EPA) as a major heavy metal pollutant [3].

Ginger has traditionally been grown in many tropical and subtropical nations, including India, Malaysia, China, and Korea *(Zingiber officinale).* According to health professionals, natural items like ginger drink are extremely beneficial to the human body [4]. Recent research showed that it helps soothe sore throats, reduce colds, prevent nausea and vomiting, and relieve muscle

*Corresponding author: ananyakuanar@gmail.com

DOI: 10.1201/9781003759003-14

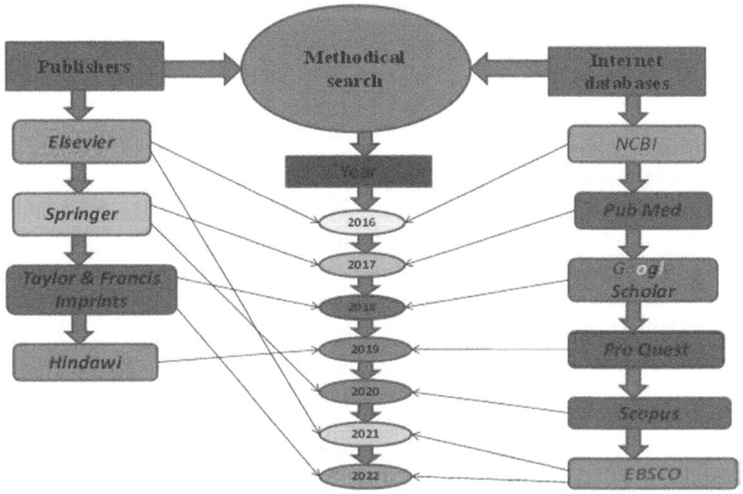

Fig. 14.1 Review strategy flowchart

Source: Biorender.com

discomfort and cancer growth. The concentrations of As, Hg, Pb and Cd in ginger rhizomes were measured using an atomic absorption spectrophotometer (AAS). The rhizome is the edible part of ginger. It grows directly in the soil and is very susceptible to heavy metal contamination. The "Lai Wu Da Jiang" ginger variety was grown at the experimental station of Shandong Agricultural University in Taian, Shandong Province, China (36° 09′ N, 117° 09′ E). The toxicity of 80% of heavy metals poses a major risk to human health and the environment in various parts of India, including Gujarat, Andhra Pradesh, and Maharashtra [5]. Several treatment methods are used to remove these carcinogenic heavy metals, including reverse osmosis, physicochemical processes, membrane filtration, ion exchange, phytoremediation, precipitation, adsorption, and biological processes with activated sludge [6]. As a result, further research should be done on using edible and non-edible plants to cure various pollutants. Future research should focus on eliminating ginger-based.

2. Review Methodology

A comprehensive review of the literature up to 2024 was conducted to explore the removal of heavy metals using ginger (*Zingiber officinale*). Various online and offline databases were used, with key sources including research papers from reputable publishers such as Taylor & Francis, Springer, Elsevier and Hindawi. Several online databases, including ProQuest, NCBI, Google Scholar, PubMed, Scopus, and EBSCO were searched using terms related to data mining. Paid articles were accessed through the Centre Library of Siksha O Anusandhan University. I also gathered information on current challenges, research progress, and potential applications from various sources, including conference proceedings, magazines, websites, and book chapters. This review discusses several studies on using ginger (*Zingiber officinale*) for heavy metal removal. This study highlights recent advancements in utilizing ginger for this purpose, offering researchers insight into current progress and future directions in phytoremediation. The search incorporated various sources and methods, including publishers and online databases, are shown in (Fig. 14.1.).

3. Impacts of Heavy Metals on Human Health and Environment

Metallic resistance decreases with rising absolute temperature because metals are highly conductive. In environmental science, "heavy metals" are defined in different ways, often based on properties like density, atomic mass, atomic number, or chemical behaviour. The following sections discuss various heavy metals that are significant to the environment and human health.

3.1 Lead

It was among the earliest heavy metals used in products like pesticides, ceramic glazes, and hair dyes. This is a naturally occurring bluish-gray metal that is soft, flexible, and shiny when freshly cut. Lead has a specific gravity of 11.35. Its atomic weight is 207.2 grams per mole (g/mol) [5].

3.2 Cadmium

Cadmium is a soft, bluish-white metal. Its atomic mass is 112.4 g/mol, and it has a melting point of 594 K. This rare element is often found in its pure form in nature, typically associated with zinc. It can also be present in natural phosphates, such as those found in Tunisia (40 ppm) and Morocco (26 ppm), as well as in lead and copper ores [6].

3.3 Mercury

Mercury (Hg) is a heavy metal with an atomic mass of 200.6 g/mol and a density of 13.6 g/cm^3. It occurs as a rare mineral in various ore forms within the Earth's crust.

A significant factor in mercury poisoning is mitochondrial damage, which results in an increased production of free radicals [5].

3.4 Chromium

This heavy metal naturally exists in the Earth's crust and oceans. It is used in industrial processes. The most common stable forms of chromium are trivalent and hexavalent. A recent meta-analysis found that human cancers of the thyroid, larynx, kidney, bladder, testicles, and bladder may have higher mortality and incidence rates when people are exposed to Cr (VI) [4].

3.5 Arsenic

Arsenic, a harmful heavy metal, poses one of the greatest hazards to the general public's health. The "king of poisons" is a well-known mark for it. Possible mechanisms of action for as induced carcinogenesis include oxidative damage, chromosomal abnormalities, and altered growth factor expression [6].

3.6 Iron

The oxidation states (+2) and (+3) of iron are found in nature. It is widely acknowledged that a key mechanism supporting the development of some chronic diseases is tissue damage caused by free radicals [6].

3.7 Copper

In living organisms, copper mainly exists in two oxidation states: Cu(II) and Cu(I). Cu(I) is the more common form. Copper is an essential trace element that acts as a cofactor in several important enzymes, including cytochrome c oxidase, ascorbate oxidase, and superoxide dismutase. Besides its role in enzymes, copper also helps transport electrons in biological systems [4].

3.8 Iodine

Iodine is vital for making thyroid hormones. These hormones help control growth, development, and metabolism. If there is not enough iodine during the early development of the brain and nervous system, it can cause cretinism, which is a lasting condition. Foods that are rich in iodine include shellfish and marine fish [4].

3.9 Manganese

Manganese is one of the most common harmful heavy metals, and it occurs in different oxidation states in nature. Combustion of the gasoline additive methyl cyclopentadienyl manganese tri carbonyl (MMT) releases manganese oxides into the atmosphere. While manganese is essential for many physiological functions, excessive intake can cause serious harm [6].

3.10 Zinc

Zinc is an essential and widely distributed metal that acts as a cofactor in many enzymatic activities. It is primarily obtained through mining and smelting. However, mineral processing releases significant amounts of zinc into the environment, impacting ecosystems and living organisms [7].

3.11 Nickel

Nickel is a naturally abundant element that is widely utilized across various industries. It comes from both natural and human-made sources and is released into the atmosphere. Inhaling air contaminated with nickel can be harmful to humans, potentially causing allergies, nasal and lung cancer, kidney damage, and cardiovascular diseases [6].

3.12 Selenium

Selenocysteine, an amino acid, is essential for the function of selenium-dependent enzymes, which are crucial for cellular processes. A lack of selenium can lead to "Keshan disease," a type of heart disease that mainly affects children and women who can become pregnant. Selenium is particularly abundant in the liver, kidney, and shellfish [6]. In Fig. 14.2., there are several types of heavy metals which affect both human health and environment. Table 14.1 lists different types of heavy metals and their sources. Table 14.2 outlines the heavy metals that are extremely harmful to both the environment and human health, which are described below.

Table 14.1 Types of different heavy metals and their sources [1]

S.l. no.	Heavy metals	Sources of metals
1	Lead	Paint, Pesticides, Batteries, Automobile emission, Mining
2	Cadmium	Welding, Electroplating, Pesticides, Fertilizer, Batteries
3	Mercury	Paper industries, Pesticides, Batteries
4	Chromium	Mining, Electroplating, Textiles, Tannery industries
5	Arsenic	Pesticides, Fungicides, Metal smelters

4. Accumulation of Heavy Metals in Ginger Plant

We discuss the most recent information on metal accumulating mechanisms in plants in this review. Some plants tolerate or accumulate hazardous metals by binding them to cell walls in roots and leaves, isolating them from sensitive cellular areas, or storing them in vacuoles. Accumulator plants have been reported for metals such as iron, manganese, copper, nickel, cobalt, cadmium, zinc, lead, and selenium [6]. The use of effective technology for removing heavy metals from plants involves phytoremediation, which utilizes plants to eliminate elemental contaminants. Phytostabilization

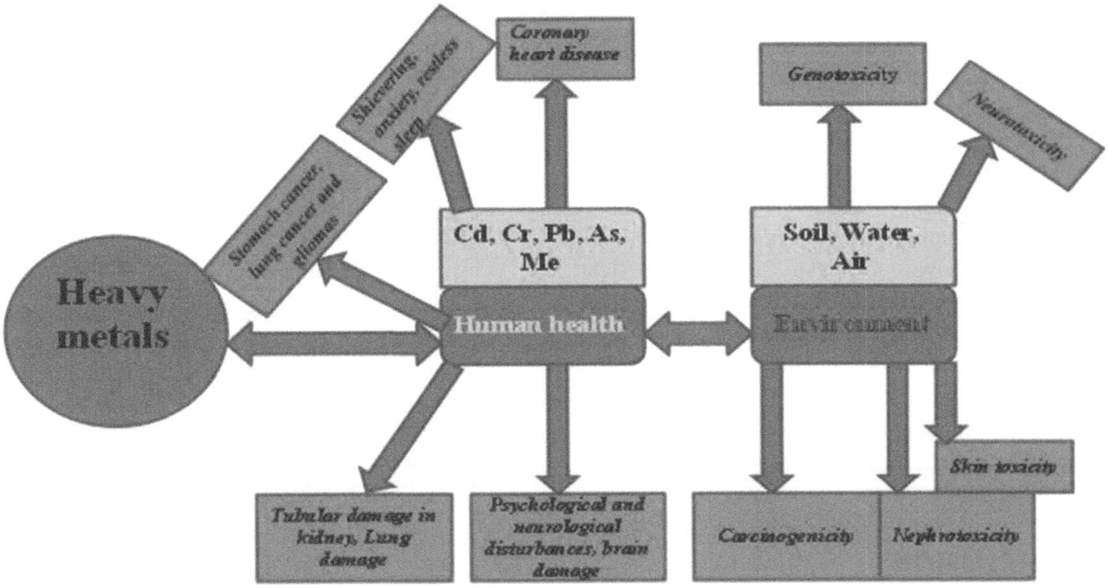

Fig. 14.2 Cyclic process of heavy metals removal effects on environment and human health

Source: Biorender.com

Table 14.2 Different heavy metals effect on human health and environment [6]

Heavy metals	Effect on human health	Limits	Effect on environment	Limits
Lead	Liver, Kidney, Gastrointestinal damage, Mental retardation in children	0.1mg/l	Increased total and differential WBC count, increased inflammatory disorders, Chromatid exchange	0.01mg/l
Cadmium	Gastrointestinal disorder, Bronchitis, Cancer, Kidney damage, Bone marrow	5.0ppb	Carcinogenic, causes lung destruction, Vomiting, Kidney and bone damage	5.0ppb
Mercury	Protoplasm poisoning, Damage to nervous system	0.01mg/l	Vomiting, Carcinogenic	0.5mg/l
Chromium	Gastrointestinal disorder, Dermatitis	0.05mg/l	Carcinogenic, causes heart disease, lung and kidney damage	0.01mg/l
Arsenic	Bronchitis, Dermatitis	0.01ppm	Carcinogenic can cause skin, lung, liver, Leukocyte decrement	0.01ppm

uses plants to lower the availability of heavy metals in the soil. Phytoextraction and phytovolatilization describe processes where plants take up heavy metals from the soil and then release them as gases into the air. Phytofiltration is a process that uses hydroponically grown plants to absorb or collect heavy metal ions from groundwater and wastewater. The effectiveness of this process is measured using the Bioconcentration Factor (BCF) or Biological Accumulation Coefficient (BAC) of *Zingiber officinale*, a plant known for its ability to accumulate heavy metals. This factor is calculated by dividing the concentration of heavy metals found in the plant's shoots by their concentration in the soil. Cadmium (Cd) accumulation was highest in the roots of potatoes and ginger, with levels of 44 μg/g and 35 μg/g dry weight, respectively. This was followed by the stems and leaves of potatoes, the roots and leaves of ginger, as well as the roots of fenugreek and the leaves of mustard. Ginger roots also contained the highest levels of nickel (Ni) at 27 μg/g dry weight, followed by the stems at 23 μg/g, the leaves at 20 μg/g, and the fruits. However, ginger roots had the lowest copper (Cu) concentration at 13 μg/g dry weight, which was the same as the copper content in carrot roots (13 μg/g) and lower than that in cabbage heads (17 μg/g). The range of accumulation for lead ranged from 3 to 43 μ g/g dry weight, with ginger having the lowest accumulation and potato tubers having the highest accumulation. Different tuber crops examined for heavy metal deposition exhibited varying levels of accumulation.

5. Removal of Heavy Metals Using Ginger

To prevent toxicity, heavy metals must be removed because they are poisonous to human health, environment, animals and plants. Potential health risks will be decreased by lowering the heavy metal content in crops. One of the most well-known members of the ginger family is

Zingiber officinale, whose rhizome is used to manufacture ginger (Zingiberaceae). Hence, it is the spice that is most commonly used globally. It contains more than 60 different active compounds, including various minerals, vitamins, enzymes, hydrocarbons, sesquiterpenes, and non-volatile substances like gingerols, shogaols, paradols and zingerone [8]. Ginger contains over 20 phenolic phytochemicals, including gingerols and diarylheptanoids [9]. Ginger is known to have several beneficial pharmacological properties, including gastroprotective, antiviral, and anti-diabetic effects [10]. This paper gives an overview and a detailed look at what we currently know about the harmful effects of heavy metals. The buildup of these metals can be dangerous. Adding ginger to your diet might help reduce its harmful effects, which is good for both your humanhealth and the environment.

6. Conclusion

A previous study found that toxic heavy metals can cause serious harm. Researchers have also used ginger to help eliminate both vital and non-vital heavy metals. Despite the fact that humans and the environment were constantly exposed to heavy metals, some researchers have reported an initial large increase in accumulated heavy metals that eventually declined. According to reports, *Zingiber officinale* has strong antioxidant qualities that also contribute to its free radical scavenging properties, making it an effective antitoxic agent. The results of the present investigation indicate that this is useful for usage as a nutritional supplement in the management of heavy metal toxicity because of its antioxidant characteristics. Research has shown that metals often bind selectively to certain macromolecules. The highest levels of heavy metal accumulation were observed in the roots, followed by the leaves, while the stems exhibited the lowest levels of accumulation (root > leaf > stem). Thus, Ginger could be used effectively in terms of heavy metals accumulation and this plant will be used for further purposes. A significant advancement in the field will be the creation of particular biomarkers for heavy metal monitoring. The evaluation of new targets for heavy metal elimination using ginger will be beneficial for future study.

Acknowledgment

The authors are grateful to Prof (Dr.) S.C. Si, Dean, Centre of Biotechnology and Prof (Dr.) M.R. Nayak, President, Siksha 'O' Anusandhan University for providing facilities and encouraging throughout the research work.

References

1. Abbaspour, N., Hurrell, R., & Kelishadi, R. (2014). Review on iron and its importance for human health. *Journal of research in medical sciences: the official journal of Isfahan University of Medical Sciences*, *19*(2), 164.
2. Ahmad, B., Rehman, M. U., Amin, I., Arif, A., Rasool, S., Bhat, S. A., ... & Mir, M. U. R. (2015). A review on pharmacological properties of zingerone (4-(4-Hydroxy-3-methoxyphenyl)-2-butanone). *The scientific world journal*, *2015*(1), 816364.
3. Briffa, J., Sinagra, E., & Blundell, R. (2020). Heavy metal pollution in the environment and their toxicological effects on humans. *Heliyon*, *6*(9).
4. Chen, Z., Xu, J., Xu, Y., Wang, K., Cao, B., & Xu, K. (2019). Alleviating effects of silicate, selenium, and microorganism fertilization on lead toxicity in ginger (Zingiber officinale Roscoe). *Plant Physiology and Biochemistry*, *145*, 153–163.
5. Genchi, G., Carocci, A., Lauria, G., Sinicropi, M. S., & Catalano, A. (2020). Nickel: Human health and environmental toxicology. *International journal of environmental research and public health*, *17*(3), 679.
6. Gsupta, D. K., Tiwari, S., Razafindrabe, B. H. N., & Chatterjee, S. (2017). Arsenic contamination from historical aspects to the present. *Arsenic contamination in the environment: the issues and solutions*, 1–12.
7. Khan, A. M., Shahzad, M., Raza Asim, M. B., Imran, M., & Shabbir, A. (2015). Zingiber officinale ameliorates allergic asthma via suppression of Th2-mediated immune response. *Pharmaceutical biology*, *53*(3), 359–367.
8. Levin, R., Vieira, C. L. Z., Mordarski, D. C., & Rosenbaum, M. H. (2020). Lead seasonality in humans, animals, and the natural environment. *Environmental research*, *180*, 108797.
9. Kuanar, A., Kabi, S. K., Rath, M., Dhal, N. K., Bhuyan, R., Das, S., & Kar, D. (2022). A comparative review on bioremediation of chromium by bacterial, fungal, algal and microbial consortia. *Geomicrobiology Journal*, *39*(6), 515–530.
10. Park, J. D., & Zheng, W. (2012). Human exposure and health effects of inorganic and elemental mercury. *Journal of preventive medicine and public health*, *45*(6), 344.

Research and Innovations in Industrial and Marine Biotechnology: A Circular Economy 2024 – Prof. Hrudayanath Thatoi et al. (eds)
© 2026 Taylor & Francis Group, London, ISBN 978-1-041-28285-3

15 Biodegradation of Low-Density Polyethylene by *Bacillus* sp. Isolated from Plastic Dumping Site, Baripada, Odisha

Bikash Ranjan Giri, Subhashree Rath, Sourav Chattaraj, Hrudayanath Thatoi*
Centre for Industrial Biotechnology Research,
Siksha 'O' Anusandhan Deemed to be University,
Bhubanseswar, Odisha, India

Abstract: Plastic waste accumulation has become a global issue and a significant environmental threat. Chemically, plastics have high molecular weight and long hydrocarbon chain polymers, which are non-biodegradable. This study isolated ten polyethylene-degrading ligninolytic bacteria from the plastic dumping site. Bacterial isolates, PEB1 and PEB9, have been isolated from the soil samples. The capacity of isolates to degrade polyethylene was evaluated separately in a synthetic medium that contains polyethylene as a carbon source. Morphological, biochemical tests, and molecular identification confirmed that the possible isolate PEB1 relates to the genus *Bacillus*. Current investigations show that *Bacillus* sp. generates ligninolytic enzymes in the medium and degrades low-density polyethylene efficiently.

Keywords: Thermoplastics, Ligninolytic bacteria, Low-density polyethylene, Ligninolytic enzyme, FTIR

1. Introduction

One of the most vital materials utilized in daily life is plastic. It is produced in large quantities, and its demand is increasing worldwide. Chemically, plastic is a polymer with a long hydrocarbon chain with a large molecular weight [1]. The elements that make up plastics are carbon, hydrogen, silicon, oxygen, nitrogen, and chloride [2]. Plastics are divided into two groups such as biodegradable and non-biodegradable plastics. Biodegradable plastics are eco-friendly due to their sustainable approach. Whereas, nonbiodegradable materials cause environmental pollution, enter the food chain, and disrupt the ecology. Moreover, these plastics are considered the most dangerous environmental pollutants due to their higher persistence, cancer-causing effects, lack of biodegradability, and pose a health risk to humans [3]. In addition, the presence of microscopic plastic particles in soils emits hazardous chemicals and greenhouse gas emissions and degrades the surroundings [4]. Polymer consumption in India is currently growing at a pace of 16 % annually, which is significantly greater than the annual growth rate of China and other important Asian countries [5]. Based on this, it is predicted that between 2000 and 2030, the global consumption of plastic will increase by a factor of six. India presently recycles 47% of the total plastic trash produced, a percentage higher than that of the majority of other nations. Over the next three decades, the share of recycling will drop to 35% because of the growing amount of extended-life items in the economy and the increase in the volume of garbage production[6]. Thermal deterioration (Specifically pyrolysis), landfill storage, or environmental disposal are the three methods now available for disposing of plastic trash [7,8]. According toWilcox et al. [9], polythene is recycled using a process called pyrolysis, which converts it into biofuel. However, the procedure is costly and time-consuming. However, microbes exhibit remarkable metabolic flexibility and are capable of decomposing a broad variety of chemicals, including certain plastics. Microorganisms such as *Arthrobacter, Aspergillus, Micrococcus, Penicillium, Pseudomonas, and Rhodococcus* have the ability to

*Corresponding author: director.cibr@soa.ac.in

DOI: 10.1201/9781003759003-15

degrade plastics found in a variety of environments. PE biodegradation involves a few enzymes, such as laccase and manganese peroxidase (MnP) [10,11]. According to the above considerations, the main objectives of the present study were to isolate lignocellulolytic bacteria from the soil samples of the plastic waste dumping site, Baripada, and to evaluate their ligninase production potential was evaluated. Further, the most efficient bacterium was used for the degradation of low-density polyethylene. Moreover, the cell surface hydrophobicity of the isolates was characterized to evaluate their maximum polyethylene degrading efficiency.

2. Materials and Methods

2.1 Collection of Samples

Soils were taken from five distinct locations of Dargadhi, Baripada, Mayurbhanj, Odisha (Fig. 15.1.). They were stored in a sterile bag for future studies following the procedure followed by Rath et al., [12].

2.2 Isolation of Microorganisms by the Enrichment Method

One gram of soil samples was added to the flasks that hold 100 ml of sterile synthetic media (SM) (Ammonium nitrate: 1.0 g; Magnesium sulphate: 0.2 g; Potassium hydrogen phosphate: 10.0 g; Calcium chloride: 0.1 g; Potassium chloride: 0.15 g; and yeast extract: 0.1g; and 1.0 mg; micro-elements: iron sulphate: 1.0 mg, Zinc sulphate:1.0 mg and manganese sulphate:1.0 mg; mix with 1 litre distilled water) supplement with 300 mg of sterile polyethene as carbon source and incubate at 30°C for 7 days in a shaker incubator at 150 rpm (Revolutions per minute). Standard protocol was followed for the isolation of polyethylene-degrading bacteria [13].

2.3 Screening of Bacteria for Ligninolytic Activity

Quantitative screening for ligninase activity of ligninolytic bacteria was performed to screen lignin peroxidase (LiP), manganese peroxidase (MnP), and Dye decolorising peroxidase (DyP) activity, following the protocol by Kameshwar et al., Kumar et al., and Yu et al. [14,15,16]

2.4 Characterisation and Identification of Efficient Ligninolytic Bacteria

Morphological characterization and the shape of isolates were examined using a microscope. Gram stains of the lignin-degrading bacteria were checked by following standard microbial methods [17,18]. Bergey's manual was followed for performing several biochemical tests [19] to identify the bacterial isolates. The DNA of an efficient bacterium was extracted using the standard DNA extraction procedure. Universal primers were used to amplify the 5' ends of the 16S rDNA. MEGA version 6 was used to build the phylogenetic tree using the neighbor-joining strategy [20].

2.5 Evaluation of Polyethylene Degradation using an Efficient Lignolytic Bacterium

Polyethylene is the sole carbon source in synthetic media (SM), where the identified bacterial strains were inoculated and cultured for 30 days at 30°C to evaluate their capacity to degrade polyethylene. The LDPE (Low Density Polyethene) films were removed from the fluid

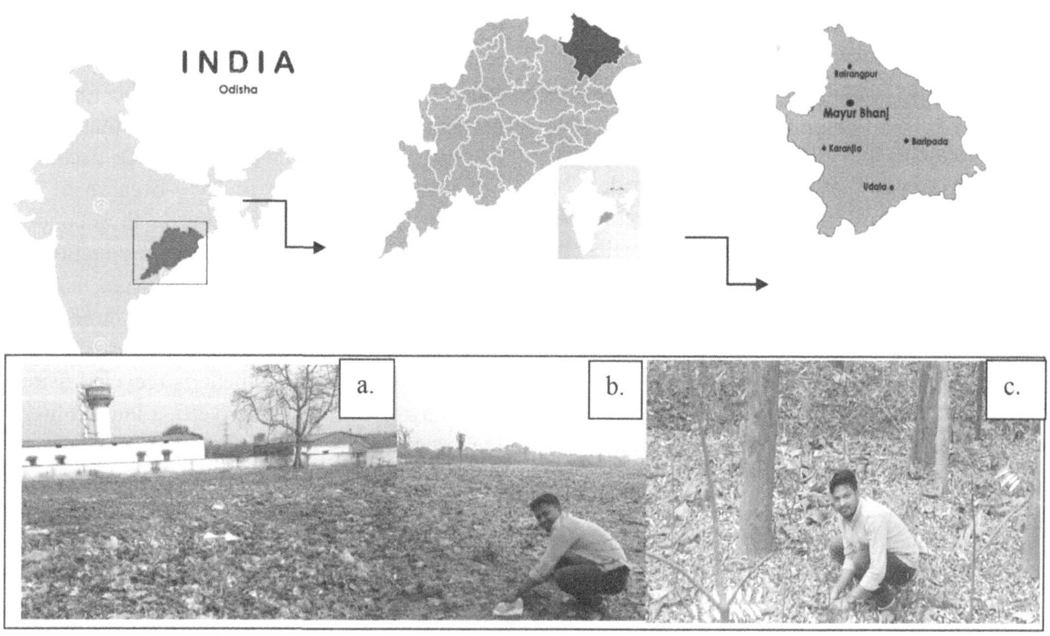

Fig. 15.1 (A) Map showing collection site, Soil sample collection site (a) Municipal solid waste dumping site, (b) Collection of soil sample from dumping site, (c) Collection of soil sample from forest area

Table 15.1 Morphological characteristics of isolated bacteria

Isolates name	Shape	Margin	Elevation	Texture	Colour	Opacity
PEB1	Punctiform	Entire	Flat	Rough	White	Opaque
PEB2	Dot like	Entire	Raised	Smooth	White	Opaque
PEB3	Irregular	Undulate	Flat	Rough	White	Opaque
PEB4	Circular	Entire	Convex	Wrinkled	White	Opaque
PEB5	Irregular	Lobate	Light flat	Dry	White	Transparency
PEB6	Rhizoid	Lobate	Light flat	Rough	Yellowish	Opaque
PEB7	Small out	Entire	Raised	Dry	White	Transparency
PEB8	Circular	Entire	Flat	Smooth	Yellowish	Opaque
PEB9	Irregular	Curled	Flat	Smooth	Yellowish	Opaque
PEB10	Circular	Entire	Raised	Glistening	Yellowish	Transparency

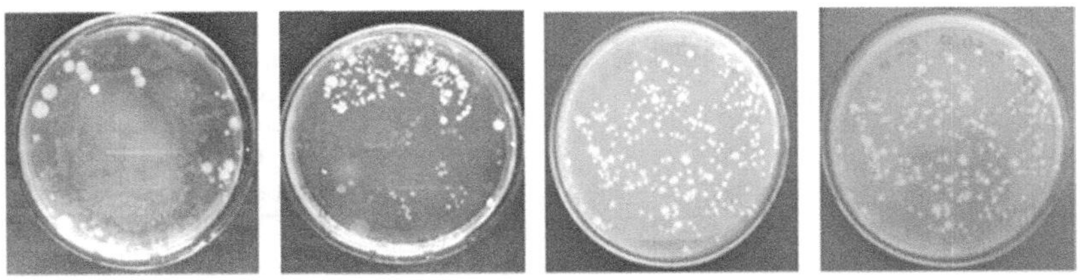

Fig. 15.2 The colony growth of plastic-degrading bacterial strains in the MS medium agar plates after 24 hours of incubation

and examined physicochemically using FTIR and SEM (Scanning Electron Microscope) [21]. The low density polyethene film samples were then measured and dried for a whole night at 60°C. The subsequent formula was employed to calculate the loss of weight:

Weight loss (%) = (Initial weight – final weight/ initial weight) × 100

2.6 Assessment of the Isolates' Hydrophobicity on the Cell Surface

The BATH test (bacterial adhesion to hydrocarbon) was used by following the procedure followed by [22,23] to measure the hydrophobicity of the bacterial isolates to the cell surface to ascertain how they interacted with polyethylene.

3. Results and Discussion

A total of 10 polyethylene-degrading bacterial strains were isolated from various soil samples contaminated with waste polyethylene plastic bags using Minimal salt medium added with low-density polyethylene films as a carbon source. Most of the isolated strains were white in colour and irregularly circular. These bacterial strains were named as Polyethene degrading bacteria PEB (Table 15.1.; Fig. 15.2.). These bacteria were selected for further Ligninolytic activity assay.

3.1 Screening for Ligninolytic Enzymes Involved in Polythene Degradation

Out of the total 10 bacteria isolated strains from the soil samples, 8 bacterial isolates showed manganese peroxidase activity, whose H:C value (H-hydrolysing zone, C-colony diameter) were given in Table 15.2. Based on their comparative H:C (H-C) values, the isolate PEB1 showed the maximum decolourization zone and was considered as efficient MnP producing bacteria with a H:C value of 7.7 ± 0.666, followed by values of respectively (Table 15.2.; Fig. 15.3.). Eight out of ten bacterial strains showed DyP activity in terms of the halogen formation using the azure B plate assay method. The enzyme activity was measured as H:C value (H-hydrolysing zone, C-colony diameter) and is given in Table 15.3 and Fig. 15.4. The bacterium PEB1 showed 2.6 ± 0.057 hydrolyzing zone. Screening of DyP activity of ligninolytic bacteria capable of metabolizing Azure B dye as an indicator was carried out as reported by Yu et al., [24] is a basic procedure for inspecting the DyP activity of bacteria, which was undertaken in the current experiment. Furthermore, seven out of 10 bacterial

Table 15.2 Manganese peroxidase (MnP) screening activity of bacterial isolate daragadhi, baripada

Isolate name	Colony diameter (cm)	Hydrolyzing zone (cm)	MnP activity (H:C) (cm)
PEB1	0.4	3.1	7.7 ± 0.666
PEB5	0.4	1.8	4.5 ± 0.057
PEB9	0.5	2.9	5.8 ± 0.057
PEB8	0.5	1.2	2.4 ± 0.033
PEB11	0.4	2.2	5.5 ± 0.057
PEB12	0.5	2	4.0 ± 0.666
PEB13	0.5	1.9	3.8 ± 0.088
PEB14	0.4	2.2	5.5 ± 0.033

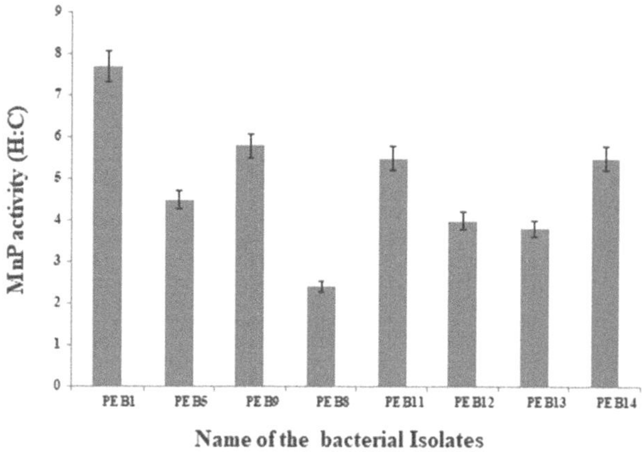

Fig. 15.3 The graph showing the MnP activity of isolated ligninolytic bacteria

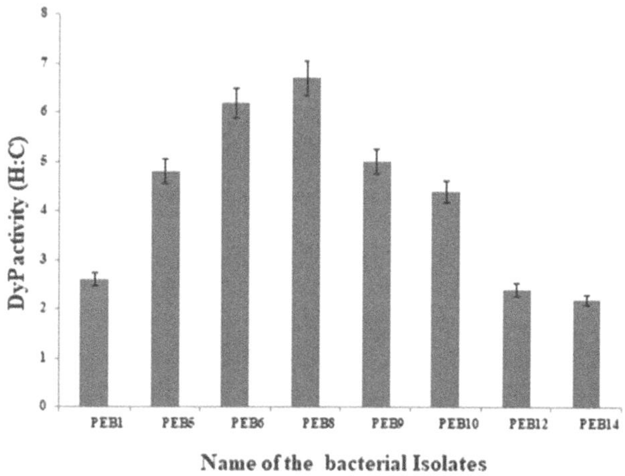

Fig. 15.4 The graph showing the DyP activity of isolated ligninolytic bacteria

isolates showed lignin peroxidase (LiP) activity using methylene blue dye as an indicator Fig. 15.5. Only seven isolates showed LiP activity, which was measured as per the H:C value (H-hydrolysing zone, C-colony diameter) and are given in Table 15.4 and Figs. 15.5 & 15.6.

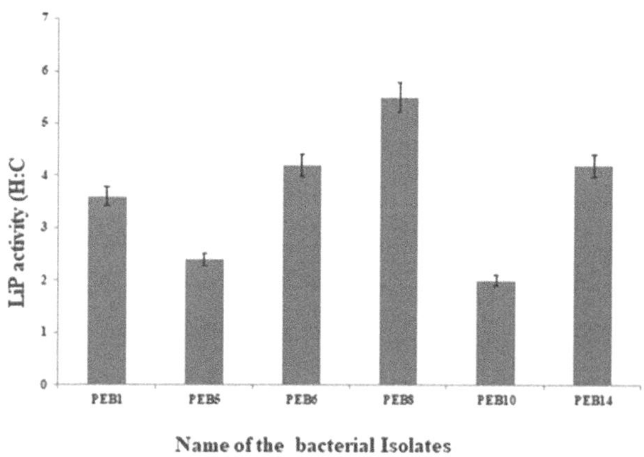

Fig. 15.5 The graph showing the LiP activity of isolated ligninolytic bacteria

Table 15.3 Dye-decolorizing peroxidase (DyP) screening activity of bacterial isolate from daragadhi, baripada

Isolates name	Colony diameter (cm)	Hyrolysing zone (cm)	DyP activity (H:C) (cm)
PEB1	0.5	1.3	2.6 ± 0.057
PEB5	0.5	2.4	4.8 ± 0.057
PEB6	0.4	2.5	6.2 ± 0.088
PEB8	0.4	2.7	6.7 ± 0.088
PEB9	0.4	2	5.0 ± 0.057
PEB10	0.5	2.2	4.4 ± 0.033
PEB12	0.5	1.2	2.4 ± 0.033
PEB14	0.4	0.9	2.2 ± 0.057

Table 15.4 Lignin peroxidase (LiP) screening activity of bacterial isolate from daragadhi, baripada

Isolate name	Colony Diameter (cm)	Hydrolyzing zone (cm)	LiP activity H:C (cm)
PEB6	0.4	1.7	4.2 ± 0.08
PEB10	0.5	1.0	2.0 ± 0.08
PEB5	0.5	1.2	2.4 ± 0.08
PEB9	0.4	0.8	2.0 ± 0.12
PEB8	0.4	2.2	5.5 ± 0.27
PEB1	0.5	1.8	3.6 ± 0.05
PEB14	0.4	1.7	4.2 ± 0.05

3.2 Comparative Analysis for Morphological, Biochemical, and 16S rRNA Identification by Gene Sequencing

Gram staining of 4 bacteria that have been represented in Fig. 15.7 and Table 15.5 for morphological characterization, the ligninolytic strains were studied for their shape and the pattern of gram staining. The phenotype characterisation and results obtained revealed that bacterium PEB1 was gram positive, and all the bacteria were Gram-negative.

Table 15.5 Gram staining result of isolated bacteria

Bacterial strains	PEB9	PEB14	PEB12	PEB1
Gram (+ve)	-	-	-	+
Gram (-ve)	+	+	+	-

Biochemical characterizations were also performed to identify the isolated bacteria PEB1, PEB9, PEB12, and PEB14. The bacterium PEB1 exhibited a positive result to methyl red test, starch hydrolysis test, and a negative result inthe oxidase, Simon citrate, Voges-Proskauer test, sugar utilization, and triple sugar iron (TSI) test, respectively (Table 15.6.). The results of the biochemical test for the other three bacteria were presented in Table 15.6. For the identification of genus of the potent isolate (PEB1), 16S rRNA was sequenced and subjected to BLAST analysis

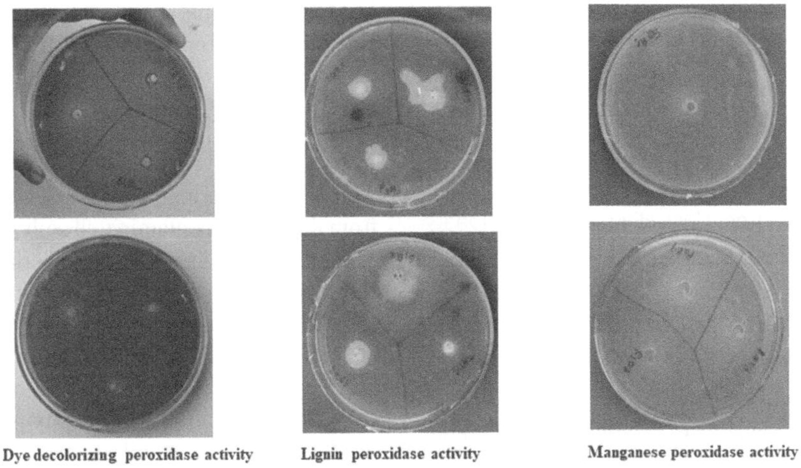

Fig. 15.6 Screening of ligninolytic enzymeactivity showing bacteria

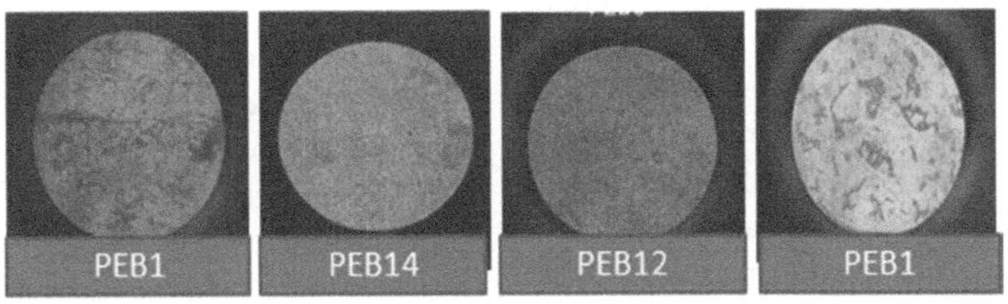

Fig. 15.7 Microscopic view of isolates bacteria PEB1, PEB9, PEB12, and PEB14

Table 15.6 Biochemical tests of four polyethylene degrading bacterial isolates, PEB1, PEB9, PEB12, and PEB14

Bacterial isolates	Oxidase	Catalase	Methyl red	Voges proskauer	Simmon citrate	TSI	Sugar utilization	Starch hydrolysis
PEB1	-	+	+	-	-	-	-	+
PEB9	-	-	+	-	+	-	-	-
PEB12	+	-	+	-	+	-	-	+
PEB14	+	+	+	-	-	-	-	+

to find the best homologous sequences. From the results, the isolate PEB1 was identified as the genus *Bacillus*. The details molecular phylogenetic analysis weregiven in Fig. 15.9. Evolutionary analyses were conducted in MEGA X [25].

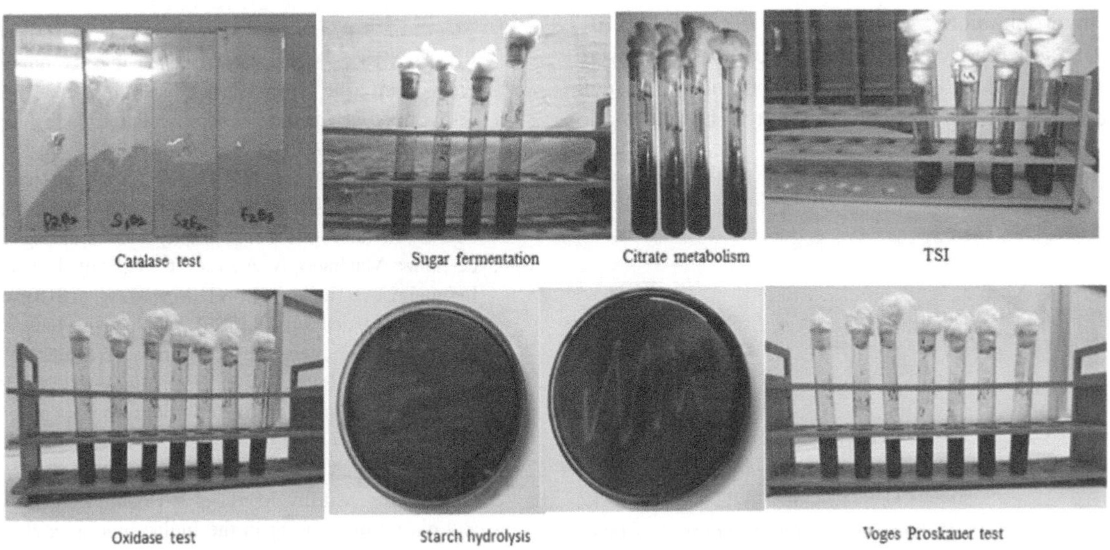

Fig. 15.8 Biochemical characterization of isolated ligninolytic bacteria

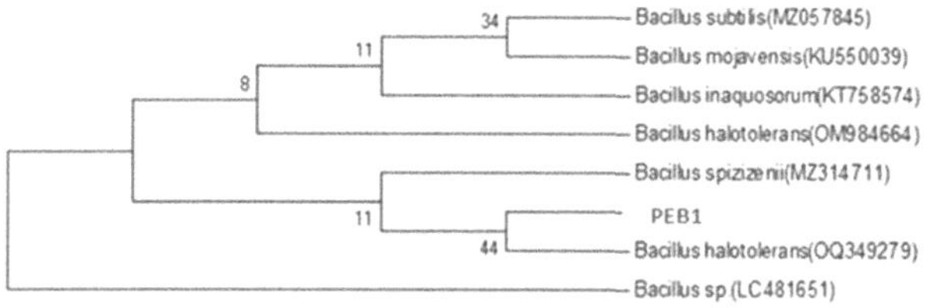

Fig. 15.9 Phylogenetic tree illustrating the evolutionary relationships among *Bacillus* sp

3.3 Evaluation of the Most Effective Isolate's Capacity to Degrade Polyethylene

Two bacterial strains with the highest ligninolytic activity were tested for their capacity to degrade polyethylene. The decrease of weight of the low-density polyethylene film was evaluated following the incubation time. The PEB1 showed the greatest drop in polyethylene weight (7.68 ± 0.76%) as compared to PEB9 showed (3.48 ± 0.42%). According to earlier research, when low-density polyethylene has been incubated in soil for ten years, the weight loss varied from 3.5 to 8.4% [26]. After one month of treatment with *Rhodococcusruber*, the UV-treated HDPE exhibited a decrease in weight of around 8%. After one month of treatment of UV-treated LDPE with *Brevibacillusborstelensis*, adecrease in weight of 11.0 ± 1.1 % was observed [27]. After one month of incubation with bacteria such as *K. Palustris* M16, *B. pumilus* M27, and *B. subtilis* H1584, the decrease in weight of polyethylene was observed around 1 ± 0.033%, 1.5 ± 0.038%, and 1.75 ± 0.06%, respectively[28].

3.4 Assessment of the Isolate's Cell Surface Hydrophobicity

The degree of attachment on the polymer substrate will depend on the relationship between the hydrophobicity of the microorganism and its surface.PEB1 showed a decrease of 34.41% turbidity at the lowest dose of hexadecane (0.04 ml). The bacterial strain PEB1 has significant cell-surface hydrophobicity, according to the data (Fig. 15.10). Bacterial adherence and biofilm development were substantially induced by the hydrophobicity of cell surfaces [29]. Strong biofilms, difficult to break up and last for a long time, were produced as a result of increased cell surface hydrophobicity [30].

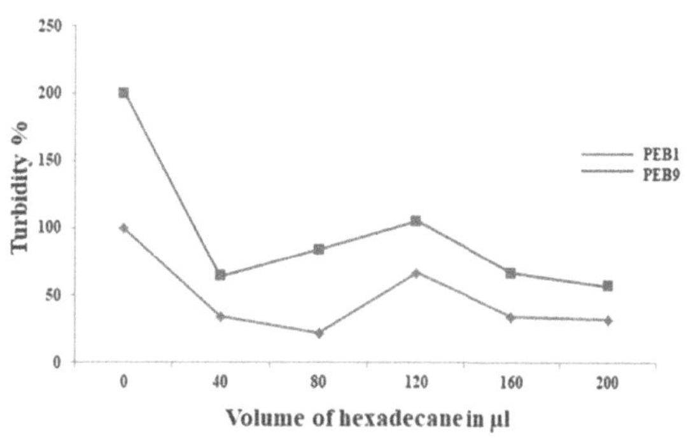

Fig. 15.10 Cell surface hydrophobicity of bacterial isolates PEB1 and PEB9

4. Conclusion

In the current experiment, low-density polyethylene-degrading bacterium PEB1 (*Bacillus sp.*) was isolated from the plastic-contaminated soils of Dargadhi, Baripada, Mayurbhanj, Odisha. This bacterium also showed LiP, MnP, and DyP activity, which are useful for various industrial applications, including biodegradation. This bacterium efficiently showed the reduction in weight of LDPE and, therefore, could be a potential bacterium for the biodegradation of low-density polyethylene present in plastic-contaminated soil.

Authors' Contributions

BRG and SR conducted the major part of the experiments, investigated the results, analysed data, validated the results with related prior research, and contributed to writing the original manuscript and formatting. SC and HNT supervised the whole work, conceptualized the research, and guided the writing and editing of the manuscript. All authors have read and approved the manuscript.

Acknowledgments

Authors are grateful to the HOD of the Department of Biotechnology, Maharaja Sriram Chandra Bhanja Deo University, Baripada, Odisha, India, for providing infrastructure facilities to conduct the experimental works. The authors are also thankful to the Director, CIBR, SOA, and SOA University for providing the facility to contribute a chapter to the Conference proceedings RIIMBCE-2024.

References

1. Shimao, M. (2001). Biodegradation of plastics. Current opinion in biotechnology, 12(3), 242–247.
2. Bhardwaj, R., Mohanty, A. K., Drzal, L. T., Pourboghrat, F., & Misra, M. (2006). Renewable resource-based green composites from recycled cellulose fiber and poly (3-hydroxybutyrate-co-3-hydroxyvalerate) bioplastic. *Biomacromolecules*, *7*(6), 2044–2051.
3. Quero, G. M., & Luna, G. M. (2017). Surfing and dining on the "plastisphere": microbial life on plastic marine debris. Advances in Oceanography and Limnology, 8(2).
4. de Souza Machado, A. A., Lau, C. W., Till, J., Kloas, W., Lehmann, A., Becker, R., &Rillig, M. C. (2018). Impacts of microplastics on the soil biophysical environment. *Environmental science & technology*, *52*(17), 9656–9665.
5. Mutha, N. H., Patel, M., &Premnath, V. (2006). Plastics materials flow analysis for India. *Resources, conservation and recycling*, *47*(3), 222–244.
6. Sivadas, S. K., Mishra, P., Kaviarasan, T., Sambandam, M., Dhineka, K., Murthy, M. R., ... & Hoehn, D. (2022). Litter and plastic monitoring in the Indian marine environment: A review of current research, policies, waste management,

and a roadmap for multidisciplinary action. *Marine Pollution Bulletin*, *176*, 113424.

7. Peng, B. Y., Li, Y., Fan, R., Chen, Z., Chen, J., Brandon, A. M., ... & Wu, W. M. (2020). Biodegradation of low-density polyethylene and polystyrene in superworms, larvae of Zophobas atratus (Coleoptera: Tenebrionidae): Broad and limited extent depolymerization. *Environmental Pollution*, *266*, 115206.
8. Ru, J., Huo, Y., & Yang, Y. (2020). Microbial degradation and valorization of plastic wastes. *Frontiers in Microbiology*, *11*, 442.
9. Wilcox, C., Van Sebille, E., & Hardesty, B. D. (2015). Threat of plastic pollution to seabirds is global, pervasive, and increasing. *Proceedings of the national academy of sciences*, *112*(38), 11899–11904.
10. Sowmya, H. V., Ramalingappa, Krishnappa, M., & Thippeswamy, B. (2015). Degradation of polyethylene by Penicillium simplicissimum isolated from local dumpsite of Shivamogga district. *Environment, development and sustainability*, *17*, 731–745.
11. Ehara, K., Iiyoshi, Y., Tsutsumi, Y., & Nishida, T. (2000). Polyethylene degradation by manganese peroxidase in the absence of hydrogen peroxide. *Journal of wood science*, *46*, 180–183.
12. Rath, S., Paul, M., Behera, H. K., & Thatoi, H. (2022). Response surface methodology mediated optimization of Lignin peroxidase from Bacillus mycoides isolated from Simlipal Biosphere Reserve, Odisha, India. *Journal of Genetic Engineering and Biotechnology*, *20*(1), 2.
13. Bhatia, M., Girdhar, A., Tiwari, A., &Nayarisseri, A. (2014). Implications of a novel Pseudomonas species on low density polyethylene biodegradation: an in vitro to in silico approach. *SpringerPlus*, *3*, 1–10.
14. Kameshwar, A. K. S., and Qin, W. (2017). Qualitative and quantitative methods for isolation and characterization of lignin-modifying enzymes secreted by microorganisms. BioEnergy Research, 10(1), 248–266.
15. Kumar, A., Samadder, S. R., Kumar, N., & Singh, C. (2018). Estimation of the generation rate of different types of plastic wastes and possible revenue recovery from informal recycling. *Waste Management*, *79*, 781–790.
16. Yu, J., Sundqvist, B., Tonpheng, B., & Andersson, O. (2014). Thermal conductivity of highly crystallized polyethylene. *Polymer*, *55*(1), 195–200.
17. Society of American Bacteriologists. Committee on Bacteriological Technic, Pelczar, M. J., Bard, R. C., & Burnett, G. W. (1957). *Manual of microbiological methods*. McGraw-Hill Book Company.
18. Vestlund, A. T., Al-Ashaab, R., Tyrrel, S. F., Longhurst, P. J., Pollard, S. J., & Drew, G. H. (2014). Morphological classification of bioaerosols from composting using scanning electron microscopy. *Waste management*, *34*(7), 1101–1108.
19. Holt, R. D., & Lawton, J. H. (1994). The ecological consequences of shared natural enemies. *Annual review of Ecology and Systematics*, 495–520.
20. Tamura, K., Stecher, G., Peterson, D., Filipski, A., & Kumar, S. (2013). MEGA6: molecular evolutionary genetics analysis version 6.0. *Molecular biology and evolution*, *30*(12), 2725–2729.
21. Hadad, D., Geresh, S., & Sivan, A. (2005). Biodegradation of polyethylene by the thermophilic bacterium Brevibacillusborstelensis. *Journal of applied microbiology*, *98*(5), 1093–1100.
22. Rosenberg, E., & Mitchell, R. (1985). Microbial surfactants. *Critical Reviews in Biotechnology*, *3*(2), 109–132.
23. Hadad, D., Geresh, S., & Sivan, A. (2005). Biodegradation of polyethylene by the thermophilic bacterium Brevibacillusborstelensis. *Journal of applied microbiology*, *98*(5), 1093–1100.
24. Yu, J., Sundqvist, B., Tonpheng, B., & Andersson, O. (2014). Thermal conductivity of highly crystallized polyethylene. Polymer, 55(1), 195–200.
25. Kumar, A., Samadder, S. R., Kumar, N., & Singh, C. (2018). Estimation of the generation rate of different types of plastic wastes and possible revenue recovery from informal recycling. *Waste Management*, *79*, 781–790.
26. Albertsson, A. C., & Karlsson, S. (1990). The influence of biotic and abiotic environments on the degradation of polyethylene. *Progress in Polymer science*, *15*(2), 177–192.
27. Hadad, D., Geresh, S., & Sivan, A. (2005). Biodegradation of polyethylene by the thermophilic bacterium Brevibacillusborstelensis. *Journal of applied microbiology*, *98*(5), 1093–1100.
28. Harshvardhan, K., & Jha, B. (2013). Biodegradation of low-density polyethylene by marine bacteria from pelagic waters, Arabian Sea, India. *Marine pollution bulletin*, *77*(1-2), 100–106.
29. Krasowska, A., & Sigler, K. (2014). How microorganisms use hydrophobicity and what does this mean for human needs?. *Frontiers in cellular and infection microbiology*, *4*, 112.
30. Mirani, Z. A., Naz, S., Khan, F., Aziz, M., Khan, M. N., & Khan, S. I. (2017). Antibacterial fatty acids destabilize hydrophobic and multicellular aggregates of biofilm in S. aureus. *The Journal of Antibiotics*, *70*(2), 115–121.

Note: All the figures and tables in this chapter were made by the authors.

Research and Innovations in Industrial and Marine Biotechnology: A Circular Economy 2024 – Prof. Hrudayanath Thatoi et al. (eds)
© 2026 Taylor & Francis Group, London, ISBN 978-1-041-28285-3

16 Assessment and Prevalence of Faunal Diversity in Niyamgiri Hill Range of Eastern Ghats, Odisha: A Cohort Study

Punyasloka Sahu[1]
Department of Life Science, GIET University,
Gunupur, Rayagada, Odisha

Diptikanta Acharya[2]
Department of Biotechnology, GIET University,
Gunupur, Rayagada, Odisha

Ram Prasad Panda*
Department of Zoology, Gopalpur College,
Ganjam, Odisha

Abstract: Niyamgiri is located in the Eastern Ghats of Rayagada district of Odisha, which is rich with highest biodiversity. It is lying between 19° 26' to 19° 43' North latitude and the 83°-18' to 83°-28' East longitude. It is containing a large number of endemic, threatened, endangered and vulnerable species of flora and fauna. The hill forest hosts a large number of conservation dependent or endangered species as listed in schedule I of Wildlife Protection Act (WPA1972) such as elephant, wild dog, Golden Gecko etc. Proper conservation strategy must be adopted for the endangered and vulnerable species and detailed inventories and proper assessment needs to be done in the forest as it may reveal some of rare and previously undiscovered species. In the current study we have investigated the faunal diversity in Niyamgiri hill range with respect to their diversified topography, favourable climatic conditions and perennial river streams. A detailed checklist of animals such as Pisces, Amphibians, Reptiles, Aves and Mammals were reported with their scientific names, common names and IUCN status.

Keywords: Wildlife, Niyamgiri, Rayagada district, Biodiversity, Faunal assessment

1. Introduction

The diversity of life on our planet is one of its most striking features. Our planet is home to millions of species, with roughly 86 percent of life occurring on land, 13 percent in the deep subsurface and only 1 percent in the ocean. Species discovery and classification into their systematic hierarchy, with documentation notes on ecosystem series, biological sources, and social benefits are important features in biology [1]. Wildlife is a part and parcel of the environment constitutes the wealth of the nation. In terms of species diversity, all plants and animals follow an intriguing pattern, namely, latitudinal and longitudinal gradients with greater diversity near the equator and decreasing towards the poles [2]. The wildlife in Odisha is grouped under the Indian peninsular sub-region which forms a part of the Zoo-geographical scope of the world. The biodiversity of Odisha consists of 479 birds, 110 reptiles, 86 mammals and 19 amphibians. According to ZSI Report 2022, there are a total of 1,03,920 faunal species consisting of 436 mammals, 1,346 birds, 738 reptiles, 450 amphibians and 3,532 Pisces [3]. The Eastern Ghats stretching from Mahanadi valley in north to Nilgiris hill in south forms the major mountain system of Odisha stretching over 1.5 lakh sq km area. It is about 4.24% of the total landmass of the Odisha state,

*Corresponding author: dr.rampanda@gmail.com

DOI: 10.1201/9781003759003-16

basing on geographical and tectonic considerations. The Eastern Ghats has a rich aggregation of flora, fauna and many endangered and endemic species. It harbours many species of fauna including 376 species of birds, 81species of mammals, nearly 100 species of reptiles and 14 species of amphibians [4, 5, 11].The Niyamgiri is a significant bio diversified hill range of the Eastern Ghats situated in the districts of Rayagada and Kalahandi in Odisha. It is also known as "Land of Dongrias" as one of the most PVGTs tribes of state, 'DongriaKondhs', resides there in harmony and with nature. The mountains system consists of irregular and undulating lofty hills ranging from 400m to 1516m. The highest peak is considered as "Niyam Raja Penu", which is worshipped during Dusshera and Jura Parab. The Dongrias claim to be descendants of Niyam Raja and have a very distinguished heritage [6, 7, 8, 11].

2. Materials and Methods

2.1 Study Area

The faunal assessment was conducted in the biodiversity rich Niyamgiri hill range of the Eastern Ghats belonging to Rayagada district ranging between 19° 26' to 19° 43' North latitude and 83° 18' to 83 ° 28' East longitudes. The mountain system consists of irregular hills ranging from 400m to 1516m. The climate is sub- tropical, while hot and dry in summer and cold in winter, humid and moisture in rainy season. The forest covers about 250 squares Km and inhabits specimens of unique richness of wild flora and fauna. The soil of the district is of three different types; red, black cotton and lateritic soils [9, 10, 11].

2.2 Field Work and Collection of Data

The assessment involved intensive explorations, critical study and documentation of specimens to explore the biodiversity and ecological significance of fauna in Niyamgiri. Fieldtrips were organized to cover maximum areasoftheforestby trekking nearby villages as Lakhpadar, Dangamati, Gumma, Khambesi, Chatikona, Kurli etc. in the hill forest at regular intervals in the years 2022 and 2023. The main aim of survey to collect and analysing evidence on presence or absence data of mammals, birds, reptiles, amphibians and Pisces [9].

2.3 Survey and Monitoring of Fishes

The fish diversity was studied by collecting them from water body using locally available fishing nets along different streams. They were identified on the basis of their morphological characters as shape, size, colour etc. Visual survey and netting was done along with photo-documentation for surveying the fishes.

2.4 Survey and Monitoring of Amphibians

Amphibians were surveyed and sampled in aquatic and terrestrial ecosystems during dusk and night in all cool damp places as under stones and logs, in litter and soil, in tree hollows, in short bushes, under fallen barks and water catchments. The amphibians were monitored using traditional methods as visual and auditory observations and capture study with the help of local tribal during night visits to the area. The pitfall trap method was adopted for terrestrial frogs [16].

2.5 Survey and Monitoring of Reptiles

Reptiles were surveyed by visual encounter surveys, and standard walk transect in all habitats of study area. Species were identified from their morphology since shape and size of scales are unique to each individual. Photographs were taken for all species and identified by computer aided identification procedures. Molted skins of snakes were collected for species identification.

2.6 Survey and Monitoring of Birds

Birds were surveyed in the early morning hours after sunrise at around 6-7am by using point count method, line-transect method and opportunistic bird sightings and were viewed with the help of 8×30 binoculars. The species were identified visually and by their calls with the help of local tribes who are closely associated with the nature. Birds were tracked by assessing their habitat range and behaviour. Indirect evidences like pellets, dropped feathers were collected.

2.7 Survey and Identification of Mammals

The mammals were surveyed by transect method for all major habitats. Direct observation method was followed for small mammals as squirrels, mongoose, hare, langur, porcupine, sambar deer, barking deer etc. Indirect observations as pug-marks, scats, pellets, molted skins, foot-prints etc. were recorded on these transects. While walking, alarm calls of sambar deer, langur, hare, and squirrels were listened and their possible causes investigated. This helped to get more information on predators and their prey species. The tribals closely associated with animals provided a lot of information about behaviour of the wild animals [12]. Different ethological aspects like their social behaviour, communication, breeding and interaction with fellow mates, were all studied. Photographs were taken for species identification.

3. Results and Discussion

The Niyamgiri hill forest is a habitat for many endangered, endemic and threatened faunal species. Eight distinct types of vegetation found in Niyamgiri make it home to a large number of animals and birds.

According to EIA report, "The study area being mainly a forest area shows wide faunal diversity. The area exhibits a well-balanced ecosystem with a poised prey-predator relationship with a variety of faunal species under categories like endangered and vulnerable as per the Zoological Survey of India's Red Data Book [13]."

Table 16.1 List of major pisces of niyamgiri hill forest

Sl. No.	Zoological name	Common name	Family	IUCN status
1.	*Notopterusnotopterus*	Bronze featherback	Notopteridae	LC
2.	*Catlacatla*	Catla	Cyprinidae	LC
3.	*Cirrhinusmirigila*	Mirikali	Cyprinidae	LC
4.	*Wallagoattu*	Freshwater shark	Siluridae	VU
5.	*Puntiusambassis*	Indian barbell	Cyprinidae	DD
6.	*Amblypharyngodonmola*	Molacarplet	Cyprinidae	LC
7.	*Labeorohita*	Rohu	Cyprinidae	LC
8.	*Channapunctatus*	Spotted snakehead	Channidae	LC
9.	*Clariasbatrachus*	Walking catfish	Clariidae	LC
10.	*Ophiosephalusstriatus*	Snakehead murrel	Channidae	LC

The perennial streams provide habitat for a large number of fishes and a unique micro-climatic niches where rare species like Golden Gecko, termite hill gecko, blue keelback snakes and many other undiscovered and unrecorded species flourish. These micro niches and open spaces on the top having profound grass growth also provide feed for herbivores as barking deer, mouse deer, sambar deer etc. Other animals as leopard, jackal, and jungle cat etc. The profusion of perennial drinking water sources in the Niyamgiri is one of the key reasons for the concentration of mammalian and other fauna [9].

3.1 Pisces

The Niyamgiri hosts almost 10 species of fishes as Mirikali, Catla, walking catfish, snakehead murrel etc. and vulnerable species as freshwater shark distributed across 05 families. Cyprinidae family being the most dominant of all having 04 members. Most of the fishes found in the forest are edible as catla, rohu, molacarplet, bronze featherback etc.

3.2 Amphibians

The forest hosts large number of amphibians of which in the present assessment 09 species as Tree frog, Indian bull frog, Balloon frog and Common toad distributed across 04 families were reported. Ranidae family being the most dominant family having 04 members. All the amphibians discovered are abundant in nature being the least concerned species of IUCN Red Data Book.

3.3 Reptiles

Almost 25 species of reptiles were identified distributed across 10 families. Colubridae family being the most dominant family having 07 members. The hill forest also hosts near threatened species as Common Indian monitor, Indian rock python; vulnerable species as King Cobra; endangered species as Golden gecko along with other species as Indian rat snake, Golden skink, banded krait, common trinket snake and Red Necked keelback etc. The rarest species of India, Golden gecko is endemic to Eastern Ghats [15].

3.4 Aves

The Niyamgiri forest hosts almost 22 species of birds as peafowl, common mynah, spotted dove, rock pigeon, house sparrow, house crow all of which are found abundantly in nature being the least concerned species of IUCN Red Data Book. The forest is home to rare birds like myna and pied hornbill. The birds are distributed across 13 families of which Phasianidae family is the most dominant [14].

3.5 Mammals

Availability of dense forests, perennial streams, balanced ecosystem, favourable macro and micro climatic requirements makes Niyamgiri home to a variety of mammals including leopard, chital, sambar, barking deer, Indian pangolin, wolf and Indian boar along with the endangered species as elephant, wild dog and vulnerable species as sloth bear and chousingha. The survey recorded about 24 species of mammals spread across 15 families. Most number of mammals was recorded from the families' canidae, felidae and cervidae.

Table 16.2 Family wise species distribution (Pisces)

Sl. No.	Family name	Total number of species
1.	Channidae	02
2.	Clariidae	01
3.	Cyprinidae	05
4.	Notopteridae	01
5.	Siluridae	01
	Total	10

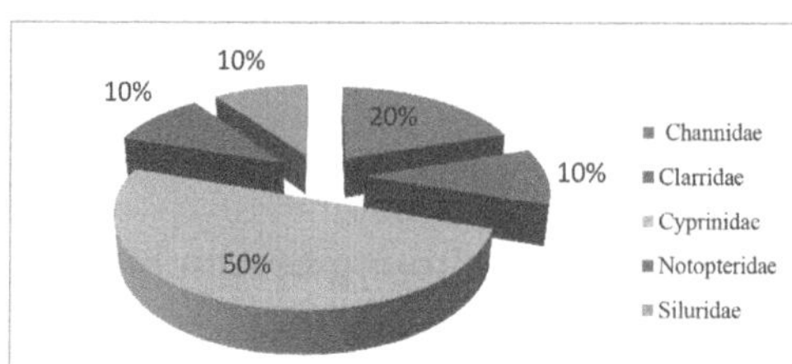

Fig. 16.1 Family wise species distribution of pisces

Table 16.3 List of amphibians

Sl.no	Scientific Name	Common Name	Family	IUCN status
1	*Bufomelanostictus*	Commontoad	Bufonidae	LC
2	*Bufofergusonii*	Dwarf toad	Bufonidae	LC
3	*Fejervaryalimnocharis*	Asian grass frog	Ranidae	LC
4	*Hoplobatracustigerinus*	Indianbullfrog	Ranidae	LC
5	*Euphlyctiscyanophlyctis*	Skipperfrog	Ranidae	LC
6	*Spaerothecabreviceps*	Burrowingfrog	Ranidae	LC
7	*Uparodonglobulosum*	Balloonfrog	Microhylidae	LC
8	*Polypedatesmaculates*	Treefrog	Rachophoridae	LC
9	*Philautustectus*	Bush frog	Rachophoridae	LC

Table 16.4 Family wise species distribution of amphibians

Sl. No.	Family name	Total no. of species
1.	Bufonidae	02
2.	Ranidae	04
3.	Microhylidae	01
4.	Rachophoridae	02
	Total	09

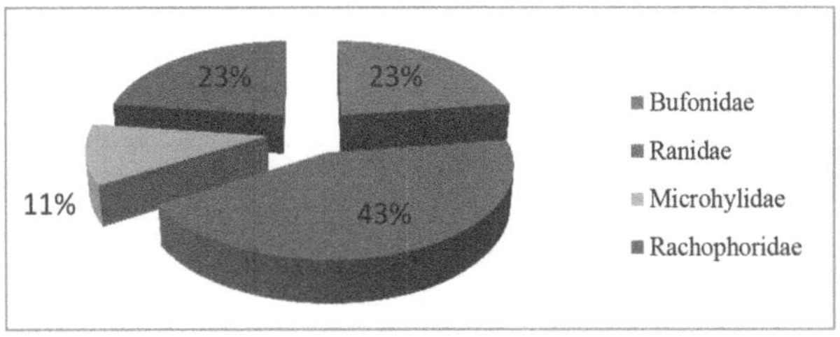

Fig. 16.2 Family wise species distribution of amphibians

Table 16.5 List of reptiles

Sl. No	ScientificName	CommonName	Family	IUCN STATUS
1	*Calotesversicolor*	GardenLizard	Agamidae	LC
2	*Chamaeleonzeylanicus*	IndianChameleon	Chamaeleonidae	LC
3	*Eutropismacularia*	LittleSkink	Scincidae	LC
4	*Eutropiscarinata*	GoldenSkink	Scincidae	LC
5	*Calotesrouxi*	ForestCalotes	Agamidae	LC
6	*Psamophilusblanfordanus*	Rocklizard	Agamidae	LC
7	*Varanusbengalensis*	CommonIndian Monitor	Varanidae	NT
8	*Calodactylusaureus*	Goldengecko	Gekkonidae	EN
9	*Ptyasmucosus*	IndianRatSnake	Colubridae	LC
10	*Craspedocephalusgramineus*	Bamboo pit viper	Viperidae	LC
11	*Python molurus*	IndianRockPython	Pythonidae	NT
12	*Russell's viper*	Chandanboda	Viperidae	LC
13	*Ahaetullanasuta*	Laudankasapa	Colubridae	LC
14	*Eryxconicus*	CommonSandBoa	Boidae	LC
15	*Najanaja*	Cobra	Elapidae	LC
16	*Ophiophagus Hannah*	King cobra	Elapidae	VU
17	*Lycodonaulicus*	CommonWolfSnake	Colubridae	LC
18	*Bungaruscaeruleus*	Common krait	Elapidae	LC
19	*Bungarusfasciatus*	Banded krait	Elapidae	LC
20	*Rhabdophissubminiatus*	Red Necked keelback	Colubridae	LC
21	*Echiscarinatus*	Saw scaled viper	Viperidae	LC
22	*Xenocrophispiscator*	CheckeredKeelback	Colubridae	LC
23	*Amphiesmastolatum*	Striped keelback	Colubridae	LC
24	*Coelognathus Helena*	Common trinket Snake	Colubridae	LC
25	*TrimeresurusGramineus*	Indian green tree viper	Viperidae	LC

Table 16.6 Family wise species distribution of reptiles

Sl. No.	Family name	Total no. of species
1.	Viperidae	04
2.	Colubridae	07
3.	Elapidae	04
4.	Boidae	01
5.	Pythonidae	01
6.	Gekkonidae	01
7.	Varanidae	01
8.	Agamidae	03
9.	Scincidae	02
10.	Chamaeleonidae	01
	Total	25

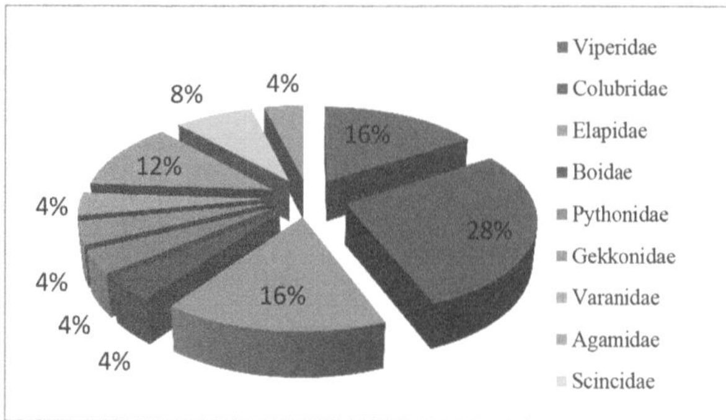

Fig. 16.3 Family wise species distribution of reptiles

Table 16.7 Aves in Niyamgiri

Sl. No.	Common name	Scientific name	Family	IUCN Status
1	Indiangrayhornbill	*Ocycerosbirostris*	Bucerotidae	LC
2	IndianPeafowl	*Pavocristatus*	Phasianidae	LC
3	Indianroller	*Coraciasbengalensis*	Coraciidae	LC
4	Asiankoel	*Eudynamysscolopacea*	Cuculidae	LC
5	Houseswift	*Apusaffinis*	Apodidae	LC
6	Barnowl	*Tytoalba*	Tytonidae	LC
7	Rockpigeon	*Columbalivia*	Columbidae	LC
8	Collared Scopsowl	*Otusbakkamoena*	Strigidae	LC
9	Commonkingfisher	*Alcedoatthis*	Alcedininae	LC
10	Spottedowlet	*Athenebrama*	Strigidae	LC
11	IndianNightjar	*Caprimulgusasiaticus*	Caprimulgidae	LC
12	Spotteddove	*Streptopeliachinensis*	Columbidae	LC
13	Blackkite	*Milvusmigrans*	Acciptridae	LC
14	Shikra	*Accipiterbadius*	Acciptridae	LC
15	Indian pondheron	*Ardeolagrayii*	Ardeidae	LC
16	Housecrow	*Corvussplendens*	Corvidae	LC
17	Cattleegret	*Bubulcusibis*	Ardeidae	LC
18	Redjunglefowl	*Gallusgallus*	Phasianidae	LC
19	Bayaweaver	*Ploceusphilippinus*	Ploceidae	LC
20	Housesparrow	*Passerdomesticus*	Passeridae	LC
21	CommonQuail	*Coturnixcoturnix*	Phasianidae	LC
22	Commonmynah	*Acridotherestristis*	Sturnidae	LC

Table 16.8 Family wise species distribution of Aves

Sl. No.	Family name	No. of species
01	Sturnidae	01
02	Phasianidae	05
03	Ploceidae	01
04	Passeridae	01
05	Corvidae	01
06	Ardeidae	02
07	Acciptridae	02

Sl. No.	Family name	No. of species
08	Caprimulgidae	01
09	Columbidae	02
10	Strigidae	02
11	Tytonidae	01
12	Apodidae	01
13	Coraciidae	01
	TOTAL	22

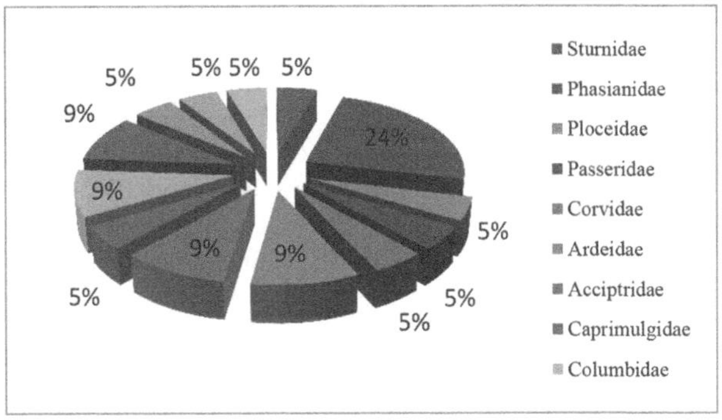

Fig. 16.4 Family wise species distribution of aves

Table 16.9 List of mammals of niyamgiri

Sl.no.	Scientificname	Commonname	Family	IUCNstatus
1	*Pantherapardus*	Leopard	Felidae	LC
2	*Prionailurusbengalensis*	Leopardcat	Felidae	LC
3	*Felischaus*	Junglecat	Felidae	LC
4	*Elephasmaximus*	Elephant	Elephantidae	EN
5	*Melursusursinus*	SlothBear	Ursidae	VU
6	*Cervusunicolor*	Sambar	Cervidae	LC
7	*Axisaxis*	Chital	Cervidae	LC
8	*Muntiacusmuntjak*	BarkingDeer	Cervidae	LC
9	*Moschiolameminna*	MouseDeer	Tragulidae	LC
10	*Lepusnigricollis*	Hare	Leporidae	LC
11	*Hystrixindica*	Porcupine	Erethizontidae	LC
12	*Maniscrassicaudata*	IndianPangolin	Manidae	LC
13	*Cuonalpines*	WildDog	Canidae	EN
14	*Canislupus*	Wolf	Canidae	LC
15	*Canisaureus*	Jackal	Canidae	LC
16	*Herpestesedwardsii*	Greymongoose	Herpestidae	LC
17	*Herpestessmithii*	Ruddymongoose	Herpestidae	LC
18	*Susscrofa*	Wildpig	Suidae	LC
19	*Semnopithecusentellus*	Hanumanlangur	Cercopithecidae	LC
20	*Macacamulatta*	Rhesusmonkey	Cercopithecidae	LC
21	*Viverriculaindica*	Small Indian civet	Viverridae	LC
22	*Sus scrofacristatus*	Indian boar	Suidae	LC
23	*Bandicotabengalensis*	Indian mole	Talpidae	LC
24	*Tetracerusquadricornis*	Chousingha	Bovidae	VU

Table 16.10 Family wise species distribution of mammals

Sl. No.	Family name	No. of Species
1.	Bovidae	1
2.	Talpidae	1
3.	Suidae	2
4.	Viverridae	1
5.	Cercopithecidae	2
6.	Herpestidae	2
7.	Canidae	3
8.	Erethizontidae	1

Sl. No.	Family name	No. of Species
9.	Manidae	1
10.	Leporidae	1
11.	Tragulidae	1
12.	Cervidae	3
13.	Ursidae	1
14.	Elephantidae	1
15.	Felidae	3
	Total	24

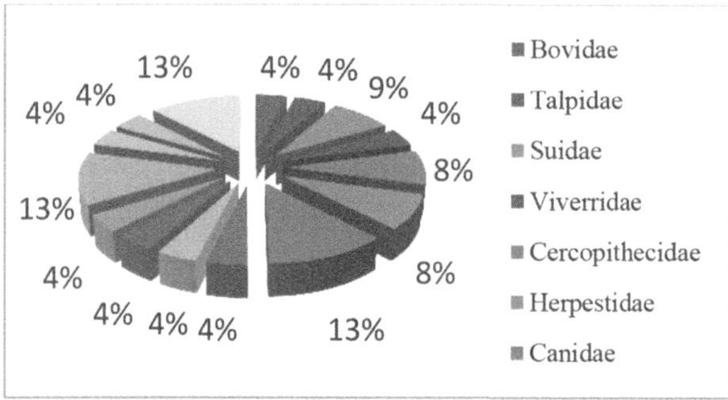

Fig. 16.5 Family wise spices distribution of mammals

4. Conclusion

The irregular and undulating hills of Niyamgiriis home to a lots of mammalian species, many rare and exotic birds, variety of herpetofaunal species, and many fishes. The forest hosts a large number of endemic species as well whose identification and ecological significance must be assessed before the species become endangered or extinct. Proper taxonomical identification and maintenance of inventories should be done. The forest species as giant squirrel indicates the density of forest. The presence of keystone species of animals indicates a healthy ecosystem prevailing in the forest. Proper conservation strategy needs to be adopted for the preservation of vulnerable and endangered species found in the area. The biodiversity in many parts of Niyamgiri hill range is still undiscovered to resolve their full potential. A detailed biodiversity study and conservation strategy must be a part of broad plan to ensure the viability of these valuable resources.

References

1. Mora C, Tittensor DP, Adl S, Simpson AG, Worm B. How many species are there on Earth and in the ocean? PLoS Biol. 2011 Aug;9(8):e1001127. doi: 10.1371/journal.pbio.1001127. Epub 2011 Aug 23. PMID: 21886479; PMCID: PMC3160336.
2. Sanders, Nathan & Moss, Jarrod & Wagner, Diane. (2003). Pattern of ant species richness along elevational gradients in an arid ecosystem. Global Ecology and Biogeography. 12. 93–102. 10.1046/j.1466-822X.2003.00324.x.
3. Naik, A., Narayanan, S.P., Palita, S.K., Thomas, A. &Paliwal, R. (2024) Two new species of the genus *Megascolex* Templeton, 1844 (Clitellata, Megascolecidae) from the Eastern Ghats of Odisha state, India. *Zootaxa*, 5424 (5), 569–580. https://doi.org/10.11646/zootaxa.5424.5.5
4. Karyamsetty, Henry. (2007). Threats to biodiversity of Eastern Ghats: the need for conservation and management measures. EPTRI-ENVIS Newletter. 13. 9–10.
5. Sharat Kumar Palita, Ashis Kumar Das, AnirbanMahata. "Diversity and Distribution Pattern of Herpetofauna in Tropical Forest Microhabitats of Eastern Ghats, Odisha", Proceedings of the Zoological Society, 2023.
6. Knowledge of Tribals in Biodiversity Conservation in the Eastern Ghats Forests Dr. A. J. Solomon Raju and K. Henry Jonathan.
7. Environmental Protection Group, Orissa (2007). *Niyamgiri Hills: Abode of the DongriaKondh*. The Tribal Tribune, Vol. 3, issue 2.
8. Tatpati, Meenal& Kothari, Ashish& Mishra, Rashi. (2018). The Niyamgir Story: Challenging the idea of Growth without Limits?. In N. Singh, S. Kulkarni, & N. Pathak Broome (Eds.) *Ecologies of hope and transformation, post development alternatives from India*. Kalpavriksh and SOPPECOM.
9. NH RANGES, Biodiversity and Ecological Significance of Niyamgiri Hill ranges, Indian environment Portal
10. SudamCharanSahu, Nabin Kumar Dhal, BrijLal, Rama Chandra Mohanty. "Differences in tree species diversity and soil nutrient status in a tropical sacred forest ecosystem on Niyamgiri hill range, Eastern Ghats, India", Journal of Mountain Science, 2012.
11. Kanyana, S., 2008. Biodiversity of Eastern Ghats (www.nbaindia.org/docs/semi_conservationeasternghats.pdf)
12. Glennie R, Buckland ST, Thomas L. The effect of animal movement on line transect estimates of abundance. PLoS One. 2015 Mar 23;10(3):e0121333. doi: 10.1371/journal.pone.0121333. PMID: 25799206; PMCID: PMC4370374.
13. Casazza, Michael & Overton, Cory & Bui, Thuy-Vy& Hull, Joshua & Albertson, Joy & Bloom, Valary&Bobzien, Steven & McBroom, Jennifer &Latta, Marilyn &Olofson, Peggy & Rohmer, Tobias &Schwarzbach, Steven & Strong, Donald &Grijalva, Erik & Wood, Julian &Skalos, Shannon &Takekawa, John. (2016). Endangered species management and ecosystem restoration: Finding the common ground. Ecology and Society. 21. 10.5751/ES-08134-210119.
14. SantoshSuradkar, MilindShirbhate, Purushottam Ingle, MilindSawdekar, AmolSawant, Amrita Shirbhate, Samish Ravi Dhongle (2023). "Study on avifauna and species richness in Karanja-Sohol wildlife sanctuary, (MS) India", Environment Conservation Journal, 24 (4).
15. Patankar, Pratyush. "Community structure of reptiles in selected habitats of Gujarat with major emphasis on the distribution and ecobiology of lizards.", Maharaja Sayajirao University of Baroda (India).
16. Knapp, Michal; KnappovÃ¡, Jana; Jakubec, Pavel; VoniÄ ka, Pavel; Moravec, Pavel (2020). Incomplete species lists produced by pitfall trapping: How many carabid species and which functional traits are missing?. Biological Conservation, 245(), 108545–. doi:10.1016/j.biocon.2020.108545

Note: All the figures and tables in this chapter were made by the authors.

Research and Innovations in Industrial and Marine Biotechnology: A Circular Economy 2024 – Prof. Hrudayanath Thatoi et al. (eds)

17 Multivariate Assessment of Surface Water Quality and Health Risks in a Vital Hydrological Structure in Odisha, India

Narmada Dalai,
Swayam Siddha, B. Anjan Kumar Prusty*
Department of Environmental Science, Berhampur University,
Berhampur, Odisha, India
Bhabani Shankar Panda and
Sarada Srinivas Pati
Coastal Monitoring Cell, State Pollution Control Board,
Bhubaneswar, Odisha, India

Abstract: This study presents a comprehensive assessment of the surface water quality of the Taladanda Canal in Cuttack, a critical hydrological structure in Odisha. It emphasises identifying dominant pollution sources and evaluating potential human health risks. Water samples were collected from ten strategically selected locations along the canal during the pre-monsoon season of 2024 and analysed for eighteen physico-chemical and biological parameters. The Water Quality Index (WQI) was computed to classify the water into categories of potability, and Multivariate statistical analysis was applied to discern the underlying structure of the dataset as well as key influencing variables. The WQI values ranged from 159 to 704, classifying several sites as "unsuitable for drinking" due to elevated levels of turbidity, total dissolved solids (TDS), nitrate, and biochemical oxygen demand (BOD). The first two principal components, accounting for 68.01% of the total variance, represented pollution from ionic and nutrient sources (PC1), and those associated with organic and microbial contamination (PC2). Health risk assessment revealed that ingestion could be a significant pathway for inducing non-carcinogenic risk as compared with dermal exposure, particularly amongst children. The findings necessitate the need for urgent intervention through targeted pollution control, periodic monitoring, and community-engaged canal management strategies.

Keywords: Health risk assessment, Pollution load, Principal component analysis, Surface water, Water quality index

1. Introduction

The ongoing degradation of freshwater ecosystems because of increasing anthropogenic pressures has emerged as a significant issue in global environmental management. Within numerous freshwater sources, surface waters, particularly rivers, lakes, and canals, are highly susceptible to contamination owing to their direct interface with industrial, agricultural, and domestic discharge pathways [1]. In contrast to relatively protected groundwater systems, surface water bodies exhibit greater spatial and temporal variability in physicochemical parameters, driven by land-use patterns, hydrological connectivity, and pollutant loading regimes. Surface water pollution is typically characterized by elevated concentrations of suspended solids, nutrients (e.g., nitrate, phosphate), toxic metals, and organic matter, all of which exert deleterious effects on aquatic ecosystems and compromise their functional integrity [2].

The influx of allochthonous nutrients contributes to eutrophication, while organic pollutants elevate

*Corresponding author: anjaneia@gmail.com

DOI: 10.1201/9781003759003-17

biochemical oxygen demand (BOD) and diminish dissolved oxygen (DO), inducing hypoxic or anoxic conditions. Moreover, unchecked contaminant transport into fluvial systems leads to downstream propagation of pollutants, affecting estuarine and coastal zones through altered biogeochemical cycles, habitat degradation, and trophic disruptions [3]. In the context of water quality assessment, the application of integrative tools such as the Water Quality Index (WQI) and multivariate statistical methods (e.g., Principal Component Analysis, PCA) has gained prominence. The WQI provides a dimensionless score derived from weighted aggregation of standardized water quality parameters, facilitating comparative assessment across space and time [4]. PCA, on the other hand, enables the decomposition of multivariate datasets to identify orthogonal axes (principal components) that represent latent pollution gradients or source-specific contributions [5]. The integration of these approaches allows for robust classification of water bodies and identification of critical pollution drivers.

In India, the canal irrigation network constitutes a major component of water resource infrastructure, especially in agrarian economies such as Odisha. Canals function not only as water conveyance systems for irrigation but also as sources for industrial and municipal supply in peri-urban and urban regions [6]. However, these systems are increasingly compromised by unregulated effluent discharge, sediment accumulation, and informal waste dumping, which significantly alter the hydrochemical regime and reduce hydraulic efficiency. The Taladanda Canal, a critical hydrological structure in Odisha, was constructed in the mid- 19th century to divert water from the Mahanadi River for multipurpose use, including irrigation, navigation, and domestic supply. With a stretch of 82.3 km, the canal traverses major urban agglomerations in Cuttack and Jagatsinghpur districts before draining into the Bay of Bengal near Paradip [7]. Over the years, the canal has been subjected to severe anthropogenic stress from industrial effluents, biomedical waste, and untreated sewage originating from densely populated catchments and institutions such as the SCB Medical College [7]. Seasonal activities, such as immersion of idols and religious offerings, further contribute to episodic spikes in pollution load, particularly during the pre- and post-monsoon periods [8]. Preliminary assessments indicate a progressive decline in water quality and sediment transport capacity, potentially linked to chronic pollutant input and reduced flow velocities due to channel clogging. These changes not only undermine the canal's ecological functioning but also pose significant public health risks to the user community utilizing untreated water for domestic purposes [9][10]. The interplay of climatic variability, anthropogenic pollution, and unplanned urban development has made the Taladanda Canal highly vulnerable to degradation. Understanding these environmental and social drivers is essential for the formulation of targeted water management and remediation strategies in the region.

In view of these specifics, this study was aims to (i) quantitatively assess the surface water quality of the Taladanda Canal using eighteen physico-chemical and biological indicators, (ii) compute the WQI to classify water quality status and determine its suitability for human use, (iii) identify the dominant variables contributing to spatial variation and infer potential sources of pollution using multivariate tools, e.g., PCA, and (iv) evaluate non-carcinogenic health risks associated with exposure to key contaminants via ingestion and dermal contact amongst different demographic groups, including children, adult females, and adult males.

2. Materials and Methods

2.1 Study Area

The Taladanda Canal, a distributary of the Mahanadi River, originates at Jobra Barrage in Cuttack and traverses the study region along a west-to-east gradient. It functions as a critical surface water conduit, fulfilling multiple sectoral demands including agricultural irrigation, municipal supply, and industrial usage. Systematic water sampling was conducted at selected sites along the canal's course to evaluate spatial variability in water quality. During field investigations, the canal was also observed to support various anthropogenic activities, such as fishing, bathing, laundering, and domestic cleaning, indicating direct human-water interaction and potential pathways for contamination [11]. Water samples were collected from various locations along the Taladanda canal, where residents engage in fishing, bathing, washing, and cleaning. With a stretch of 82.3 km, it is the longest canal in Odisha. The present study covers about a 16km stretch of the Canal in Cuttack, i.e. from Jobra Aniket to Bidyadharpur (20.446161°N to 20.479515°N and 85.939638°E to 85.939638°E, Fig. 17.1).

The study area falls under a tropical monsoon climate regime, characterized by three distinct seasons: summer (March–June), monsoon (July–October), and winter (November–February). The region experiences average annual rainfall of approximately 1,450–1,600 mm, with a major proportion (~75%) received through the southwest monsoon. This seasonal rainfall pattern significantly influences surface water dynamics, runoff generation, and pollutant transport into fluvial and canal systems. The region experiences pronounced seasonal thermal variability, with maximum ambient air temperatures during the summer months ranging between 30°C and 43°C, while winter minima can decline to approximately 12°C. Such temperature fluctuations influence hydrological and biogeochemical processes, including the solubility of gases, microbial activity, and rates of organic matter decomposition in surface water systems. Such

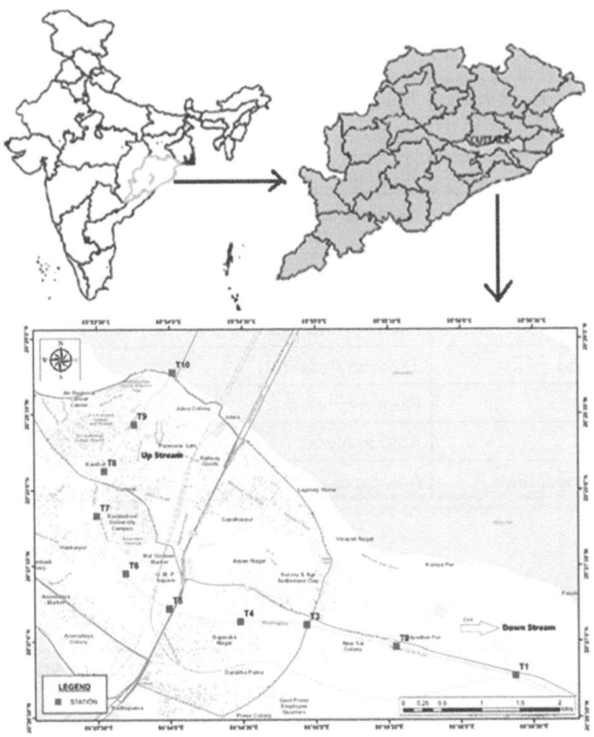

Fig. 17.1 Study area of taladanda canal showing sampling location points

thermal gradients influence water chemistry, particularly parameters like DO, BOD, and nutrient solubility. High temperatures during the pre-monsoon season also promote the proliferation of microbial activity, thereby enhancing the degradation of organic pollutants [12].

The city of Cuttack, through which the Taladanda Canal flows, is one of the oldest and most densely populated urban centres in eastern India. Rapid and largely unregulated urban expansion, coupled with infrastructural limitations in waste management, has exacerbated environmental pressures on adjacent water bodies. Solid waste disposal, illegal sewer connections, and untreated effluent discharge into natural and artificial drainage systems are prevalent across the city [12].The Taladanda Canal, off-taking from the right bank of the Mahanadi River at Jobra Barrage, serves as a critical water conveyance structure for municipal supply, industrial usage, and agricultural irrigation across Cuttack and parts of Jagatsinghpur district. Despite its original design for irrigation and navigation, the canal has evolved into a multipurpose water resource over the decades, underpinning the region's drinking water security, agriculture, and economic activity. However, this increasing dependence has also led to unsustainable exploitation [12]. Several communities continue to depend on the untreated canal water for domestic activities, including bathing, washing, and even consumption, particularly in peri-urban and rural stretches. The combination of hydrological stress, urban encroachment, and institutional inefficiencies has led to the deterioration of both water quality and ecosystem services provided by the canal and its parent river, the Mahanadi.

2.2 Water Sample Collection

Surface water samples were systematically collected from ten georeferenced stations (Fig. 17.1) along the Taladanda Canal during the pre-monsoon season, selected to represent diverse hydro-environmental conditions and potential pollution sources. Sampling and preservation protocols were followed in accordance with APHA standard procedures [13].

Key field parameters—temperature, pH, and electrical conductivity (EC)—were measured in situ with a calibrated YSI Professional Plus (Model YSI-556) multiparameter probe before each sampling. Total Suspended Solids (TSS) and Total Dissolved Solids (TDS) were quantified using gravimetric methods, employing 47 mm diameter GF/C glass microfiber filters (Whatman, pore size 1.2 µm) and subsequent desiccation to constant weight in a hot air oven at 103–105°C for TSS and 180°C for TDS determination [14].

Dissolved oxygen (DO) concentrations were determined using the classical iodometric titration technique, following Winkler's modified method, as prescribed by APHA [12]. Biochemical oxygen demand (BOD_5) was measured by incubating water samples in the dark at 27 ± 1 °C for a duration of three days, after which the residual DO was quantified using the same titrimetric approach. The concentrations of ammonia (NH_3-N), phosphate (PO_4^{3-}), nitrate (NO_3^-), and nitrite (NO_2^-) were analysed calorimetrically using a continuous flow autoanalyzer (Model: San++, Manufacturer: Scalar, Netherlands) with appropriate calibration and QA/QC protocols.

Microbial contamination was assessed through the enumeration of Total Coliforms (TC) and Faecal Coliforms (FC) by the Most Probable Number (MPN) technique in accordance with standard protocols detailed in the APHA 22nd Edition [13]. A total of 18 physicochemical and microbiological indicators (listed in Table 17.1), including temperature, pH, conductivity, alkalinity, turbidity, DO, BOD, TSS, TDS, total hardness, ammonia, nitrate, nitrite, phosphate, potassium, chloride, fluoride, TC, and FC, were evaluated against their respective guideline values to assess compliance with regulatory standards. The overall water quality status at each sampling location was synthesized employing the WQI. The WQI computation followed the weighted arithmetic mean method, applying standard classification thresholds based on the Coastal Water Quality Criteria of the Central Pollution Control Board [12], the Australian and New Zealand Environment and Conservation Council [15], and the Canadian Council of Ministers of the Environment [16] methodology.

2.3 Water Quality Index (WQI)

The Water Quality Index (WQI) was computed to derive a single, composite value representing the overall status

Table 17.1 Methodsused in the analysis of water samples

Sl. No	Parameter	Methods	Instrument
1	Temperature	Potentiometric/ electrode methods	Thermometer
2	pH, EC	Metal electrode methods	pH meter, conductivity meter
3	DO, BOD, Alkalinity & Total Hardness	Iodometric titration method	Titration Assembly
4	Turbidity	Nephelometric Method	Nephele turbidity meter
5	Nitrate, Nitrite & Phosphate	Spectrophotometric Method	Spectrophotometer
6	TDS, TSS	Gravimetric method	Electrochemical meter – Analytical balance
7	Potassium	Flame photometric method	Flame Photometer
8	Chloride	Argentometric Method	Titration Assembly
9	Fluoride	Ion selective Method	Fluoride meter
10	Ammonia	Phenate Method	Auto analyser
11	TC/FC	Most probable method (MPM)	Autoclave and Laminar Air Flow

Source: APHA (13)

of water quality at each sampling site. This integrative index facilitates spatial comparison and simplifies the interpretation of complex water quality datasets. The methodology employed follows the weighted arithmetic mean approach, as outlined in APHA. To determine the WQI for each surface water sample, a three-step procedure was implemented using four governing equations. Initially, an individual weight (w_i) was attributed to each of the twenty evaluated parameters, representing their respective importance to overall water quality and public health [17]. These weights ranged from 1 to 5 and were established based on prior literature and expert judgement. Parameters with significant health implications—such as nitrate (NO_3^-)—were assigned the maximum weight ($w_i = 5$) due to their acute and chronic toxicity potential, particularly from anthropogenic sources such as agricultural runoff and sewage infiltration [18]. Elevated nitrate levels in surface water are often indicative of intensive anthropogenic influence. Conversely, parameters such as calcium (Ca^{2+}), magnesium (Mg^{2+}), and total hardness, which have relatively minimal direct health implications in the concentrations typically observed, were assigned a lower weight ($w_i = 2$). These parameters primarily influence aesthetic and operational aspects (e.g., scaling) rather than posing substantial health risks. In step two, each parameter's relative weight (W_i) was calculated as follows [19]:

$$WQIi = \frac{\mathbf{wqi}}{\sum_{i=1}^{n} \mathbf{wqi}}$$

where,

WQIi = relative weight,

wqi = weight of each parameter,

n = the no. of parameters,

Table 17.1 presents the respective weighting of each parameter.

Table 17.2 Physiochemical parameters with a statistical outline

Parameters	Range	Mean ± SD
Temperature	1.6 - 32.4	30.4 ± 1.59
pH	0.3 - 7.4	7.057 ± 0.32
EC (μS/cm)	31.6 – 302.1	260 ± 31.63
DO (mg/l)	2.1 – 10.5	7.71 ± 2.05
BOD (mg/l)	1.2 – 6.7	4.025 ± 1.23
Hardness(mg/l)	10.8 – 136.0	118.80 ± 10.84
Alkalinity(mg/l)	9.2 – 108.0	93.2 ± 9.25
Nitrate(mg/l)	0.2 – 2.0	0.63 ± 0.55
Nitrite(mg/l)	0.2 – 2.0	0.06 ± 0.10
Phosphate(mg/l)	0.0 – 0.1	0.04 ± 0.03
TDS (mg/l)	21.2 – 202.4	174.1135 ± 21.23
TSS (mg/l)	2.8 – 40.0	14.6 ± 11.34
Potassium (mg/l)	0.9 – 5.3	4.15 ± 0.91
Chloride (mg/l)	0.9 – 6.0	4.2 ± 0.88
Fluoride(mg/l)	0.31 – 0.56	0.44 ± 0.08
Ammonia (mg/l)	0.5 – 2.2	1.90 ± 0.47
Turbidity (NTU)	4.1- 58.6	23.06 ± 17.05

The third stage assigns a quality rating (qi) to each parameter by dividing its concentration in each groundwater sample by its respective standard from IS 10500:2012, then multiplying the result by 100.

$$\mathrm{r}_i = \left(\frac{C_i}{S_i}\right) \times \mathbf{100}$$

where,

ri = the rating built on the conc. of ith parameter,

Ci = the conc. of Individual chemical parameters in distinct surface water samples in mg/l

Si = the Indian standard for drinking water of disctict parameters in mg/l as stated by the rules of the IS 10500:2012.

To calculate the WQI according to the following equations [19]:

$$SIi = W_i = q_i$$

$$WQI = \sum SI_i$$

where,

SIi = the sub-index of the ith parameter,

WQI = Water Quality Index

2.4 Principal Component Analysis (PCA)

To explore latent relationships among water quality variables and identify dominant pollution sources, Principal Component Analysis (PCA) was employed to the standardized dataset (z-scores) using Origin 2025[20]. The analysis was based on the correlation matrix to minimize the influence of differing units. Eigenvalues >1.0 were retained as per the Kaiser criterion, and factor loadings ≥ ± 0.5 were considered significant. The first two components (PC1 and PC2) were used to construct a biplot, enabling visualization of variable clustering and site-group differentiation.

2.5 Assessment of Human Health Risk

The non-carcinogenic human health risks associated with exposure to nitrate (NO_3^-) and fluoride (F^-) via contaminated surface water were evaluated in accordance with the risk assessment framework established by the United States Environmental Protection Agency [21]. The assessment considered two primary exposure pathways: oral ingestion and dermal absorption during water use activities. To capture the variability in physiological sensitivity and water use patterns, the risk calculations were stratified across three demographic groups: children, adult females, and adult males, as per established risk modeling conventions [22]. The non-carcinogenic risk was quantified by calculating the Average Daily Dose (ADD) for each exposure route using the following equations:

$$ADD_{Oral} = \left(\frac{A \times B \times C \times D}{W \times T}\right)$$

where,

ADD_{Oral} = the exposure dose over the oral route expressed as [mg/(kg × day)],

A = Concentration of Pollutant in water (mg/L),

B = Rate of Ingestion (L/day)

C = Frequency of exposure (days/year)

D = Duration of Exposure (years)

W = Individual weight of the body (kg)

T = Time (Average) (days) [22]

$$HQ_{Oral} = \frac{I_{Oral}}{RfD}$$

where,

HQ = Hazard Quotient,

RfD = reference dose expressed as [mg/(kg × day)],

At present, RfD_{oral} measured for NO^{3-}, F^-, are 1.6, 0.06 mg/ (kg × day), respectively [23].

$$ADD_{Dermal} = \frac{C \times SA \times K_p \times ET \times EF \times ED}{BW \times AT}$$

where,

ADD_{Dermal} = Dermal exposure [mg/(kg × day)],

SA = skin surface area exposed (cm²)

K_p = dermal permeability coefficient (cm/h)

ET = exposure time (hours/day) [23]

To calculate the surface area of skin, following formula wasemployed:

$$Kp = 239 \times H^{0.417} \times \beta^{0.517}$$

where,

H = Accepted universal height of the inhabitants expressed in cm, (children H = 99.4 cm, females 153.4 cm and males 165.3 cm)

$$HQ_{dermal} = \frac{ADD_{dermal}}{RfD_{dermal}}$$

$$RfD_{dermal} = RfD_{Oral} \times ABS_{gi}$$

ABSgi = factor for gastrointestinal absorption[23].

$$HI_i = HQ_{oral} + HQ_{dermal}$$

$$HI_{total} = \sum_{i=1}^{n} HI_i$$

where,

HI = Hazard index,

HIi = Hazard index of contaminant not classified as carcinogens in the evaluation of the risk,

HI > 1 = a potential health risk.

3. Results and Discussion

The analytical results revealed spatial variability in water quality parameters, indicative of localized anthropogenic influences and hydrological conditions. Temperature across the sampling sites ranged from 28.0 °C to 32.4 °C, with the highest values recorded at P10. The pH values varied from 6.44 to 7.38, indicating near-neutral to slightly alkaline conditions. pH levels close to neutral may facilitate the solubility and mobilization of various pollutants, thereby increasing their bioavailability and potential toxicity [24]. Electrical conductivity (EC) vary between 209 µS/cm and 302.1 µS/cm, with the highest measurements at P2, suggesting a higher ionic concentration and possible contamination from domestic or industrial sources [25]. Elevated turbidity levels were also recorded at P2 (58.6 NTU), in contrast to the lowest levels observed at P10 (4.54 NTU), reflecting significant sediment and particulate matter loads at downstream locations. Total Dissolved Solids (TDS) concentrations exhibited relatively consistent values across most sampling locations; however, notable elevations were observed at stations P1, P2, and P4, suggesting localized inputs of dissolved ionic constituents, potentially from domestic or industrial discharges. In contrast, Total Suspended Solids (TSS) levels demonstrated wider spatial variability, ranging from 2.8 mg/L at P10 to a maximum of 29.5 mg/L at P2. The elevated TSS concentrations, particularly at P2, indicate a significant particulate load, corroborating enhanced sediment transport and surface runoff influence, likely from downstream anthropogenic activities or erosional processes within the canal catchment [26]. Chloride concentrations exhibited minimum values at P7 and P8 (03 mg/L), with elevated concentrations at other sites likely due to inputs from urban runoff, sewage, and industrial discharges [27]. The DO levels fluctuated between 3.06 and 10.49 mg/L. Sites with lower DO levels may reflect increased organic loading and microbial activity, leading to oxygen depletion [28]. Biochemical Oxygen Demand (BOD) concentrations varied between 2.15 mg/L at station P6 and 6.68 mg/L at station P8, reflecting spatial heterogeneity in organic pollution levels along the canal. Elevated BOD values are indicative of enhanced microbial oxidation of biodegradable organic matter, which leads to increased oxygen consumption in the water column and may result in hypoxic conditions detrimental to aquatic biota [27]. Total alkalinity exhibited a pronounced elevation at station P9, indicating enhanced buffering capacity, likely due to elevated concentrations of bicarbonate and carbonate ions. Such a condition may result from anthropogenic influences, particularly the influx of alkaline substances from domestic detergents or agricultural runoff rich in lime-based soil amendments [29]. Conversely, the highest concentrations of nitrate and nitrite were recorded at station P1, suggestive of localized nitrogenous contamination arising from either agricultural fertilizers or untreated domestic sewage. However, it is important to note that buffering capacity and nitrogen enrichment are often co-associated in systems receiving diffuse pollution inputs, such as agricultural runoff. Therefore, the spatial disjunction observed in this study—where total alkalinity peaked at P9 while nitrate/nitrite were elevated at P1—suggests that the underlying pollution sources and hydrochemical conditions differ between these sites. This spatial heterogeneity implies that P1 may be predominantly influenced by nitrogen-rich effluents with limited carbonate buffering, while P9 is more impacted by alkaline inputs that do not necessarily coincide with high nitrogen loads [30]. Such decoupling of alkalinity and nitrogen concentrations emphasizes the site-specific nature of pollutant inputs and the complex interactions between chemical constituents, particularly in a canal system subject to variable anthropogenic pressures [31].

Ammonia levels varied significantly across sites, supporting the hypothesis of localized wastewater intrusion. Phosphate concentrations peaked at P7 (0.131 mg/L), and potassium levels were highest at P3 (5.33 mg/L), both suggestive of nutrient enrichment from fertilizers and/or detergents. Total hardness values ranged from 104 mg/L at station P10 to a maximum of 136 mg/L at station P2, with elevated hardness levels primarily attributed to increased concentrations of divalent cations, particularly calcium (Ca^{2+}) and magnesium (Mg^{2+}). Fluoride (F^{-}) concentrations exhibited spatial variation, ranging from 0.31 mg/L at P1 to 0.56 mg/L at P7. Although these values remain within the permissible limits prescribed for potable water, continued monitoring is essential, as chronic exposure to elevated fluoride levels can pose public health risks, including dental and skeletal fluorosis [28].

3.1 Drinking Water Quality Assessment (WQI)

Based on the analytical results, the Water Quality Index (WQI) was computed for the investigated canal segment. The classification of drinking water potability, derived from the WQI values, is presented in (Table 17.3.). The calculated WQI values exhibited a substantial range, from a minimum of 159 (P10) to a maximum of 704. These values were systematically categorized into four distinct classifications: 'good,' 'medium,' 'bad,' and 'unsuitable for drinking' water quality. Notably, only one sampling location, designated as P10, demonstrated water quality deemed suitable for human consumption.

Table 17.3 WQI values of each sampling locations

Water Types	Range	Locations
Good	50-150	1 (P10)
Medium	150-300	4 (P5, P6, P8, P9)
Bad	300-450	2 (P3, P4)
Unsuitable for drinking	>450	3 (P1, P2, P7)

3.2 Health Risk Assessment

The assessment of predicted health hazards from non-carcinogenic pollutants, specifically nitrate (NO_3^{-}) and fluoride (F^{-}), revealed a graded risk profile across different demographic groups within the study area. These groups included children, adult females, and adult males. The primary exposure pathway considered in this analysis was the oral intake of potable water. The complete findings of this assessment are presented in (Table 17.4.).

Table 17.4 Overview of non-carcinogenic health risk assessment

Site	HQ_{Oral}			HQ_{Dermal}			HI_{Total}		
	Children	Females	Males	Children	Females	Males	Children	Females	Males
Minimum	0.29	0.17	0.13	0.0011	0.0007	0.0006	0.29	0.17	0.13
Maximum	0.45	0.27	0.19	0.0017	0.0011	0.0010	0.45	0.27	0.19
Mean	0.36	0.21	0.15	0.0014	0.0009	0.0008	0.36	0.21	0.15
SD	0.06	0.03	0.02	0.0002	0.0001	0.0001	0.06	0.03	0.02

The Oral Exposure (HQ_{oral}) is the dominant pathway contributing to overall risk, with mean HQ values for children, females, and males computed to be 0.36, 0.21 and 0.15, respectively. The Dermal Exposure (HQ_{Dermal}) exhibited substantially lower mean values across all groups ($\leq$0.0014), indicating a minimal contribution to total non-carcinogenic risk. Consequently, the Hazard Index (HI) values mirror the HQ_{oral} values due to the negligible magnitude of HQ_{Dermal}. All the calculated mean HI values, remained below the acceptable threshold of 1.0, are suggestive of no significant non-carcinogenic health risk under the current exposure scenarios [19]. Amongst the three population groups, children exhibited the highest HQ and HI values, indicating their increased susceptibility to environmental contaminants, likely due to higher intake rates relative to body weight, and immature metabolic and detoxification systems. The standard deviation (SD) values indicate a moderate variability in risk, particularly for children (SD = 0.06 for HQ_{oral} and HI), which is notably higher than that for adults.

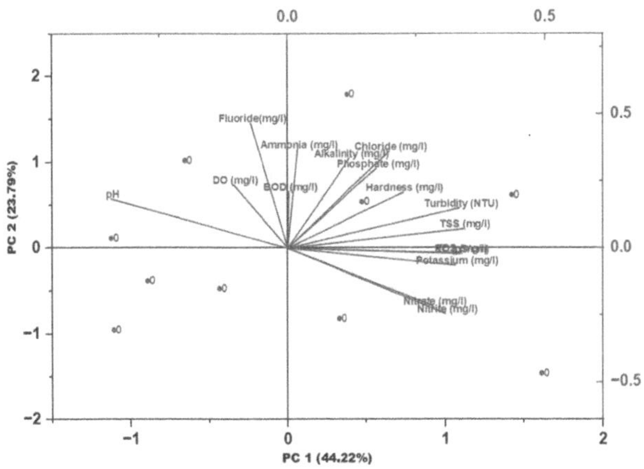

Fig. 17.2 PCA biplot of the principal components and associated parameters

Table 17.5 Eigen values of the correlation matrix

Eigenvalues of the Correlation Matrix		
Eigenvalue	Percentage of Variance	Cumulative
7.07582	44.22%	44.22%
3.80616	23.79%	68.01%
1.66128	10.38%	78.40%
1.1322	7.08%	85.47%
0.77526	4.85%	90.32%
0.75273	4.70%	95.02%
0.43846	2.74%	97.76%
0.29106	1.82%	99.58%
0.06704	0.42%	100.00%

3.3 Multivariate Statistical Implications

Principal Component Analysis (PCA) was utilized to achieve two primary objectives regarding the multivariate water quality dataset. Firstly, it served to reduce the dimensionality of the dataset, thereby simplifying its complexity. Secondly, PCA was employed to identify the most significant parameters that contribute to the observed variability in water quality across the various sampling sites situated along the canal. The eigenvalue decomposition of the correlation matrix (Table 17.5) revealed that the first two principal components (PC1 and PC2) accounted for a cumulative 68.01% of the total variance in the dataset. Specifically, PC1 explained 44.22% of the variance, while PC2 contributed 23.79%, indicating that these two components sufficiently capture the dominant patterns and gradients present in the water quality data. The PCA biplot (Fig. 17.2.) provides a visual summary of the relationship between the sampling sites and the physico-chemical parameters. Each vector represents a water quality parameter, while the red dots denote individual sampling locations projected onto the PC1–PC2 plane.

PC1, the primary axis of variation, is predominantly influenced by pollution-associated parameters such as turbidity, TSS, potassium, nitrate, nitrite, phosphate, chloride, and total hardness. The strong loading of these parameters along the positive direction of PC1 suggested that it primarily represents a pollution gradient, likely driven by anthropogenic activities such as urban runoff, industrial discharges, and agricultural effluents[30]. PC2 captures secondary variation in the dataset and is strongly associated with fluoride, ammonia, total alkalinity, BOD, and DO. This component likely reflects biochemical processes and buffering capacity within the aquatic system, including microbial decomposition, nitrification, and the presence of organic waste[20]. Interestingly, pH exhibited a high negative loading on PC1 and was oriented in a direction opposite to most other parameters, indicating an inverse relationship with pollution indicators. This suggests that increased pollutant concentrations may destabilize pH values or reflect acidic/alkaline shifts resulting from specific contaminants [32].

4. Conclusion

The present investigation revealed that the water quality of the Taladanda Canal is significantly degraded at multiple locations due to anthropogenic pressures including industrial discharge, agricultural runoff, and municipal effluents. The WQI values indicated that a substantial proportion of sampling sites are unfit for direct human consumption without adequate treatment. The PCA highlighted those parameters (e.g., turbidity, nitrate, TSS, phosphate, and BOD) as the primary contributors to water quality deterioration, representing a complex mixture of physical, chemical, and biological contamination. Furthermore, the health risk assessment substantiates that children exhibit a heightened susceptibility to the adverse effects of non-carcinogenic pollutants. This increased vulnerability is primarily attributed to their exposure through oral pathways. Thus, to mitigate the degradation of this vital water resource, it is recommended that systematic remediation measures - including sediment removal, pollution source regulation, and microbiological surveillance - be urgently implemented. Additionally, strengthening the existing water quality monitoring network and promoting community-based awareness and stewardship programs will be critical in restoring the ecological integrity, and safe and wise use of the Taladanda Canal.

References

1. Prusty R, Biswal T. Assessment of Pollution Load in Terms of Water Quality Index and Modelling of Taladanda Canal and Mahanadi River in Paradip Area, Odisha, India. Asian J. Water Environ. Pollut. 2020 Oct 31;17(4); 59–72.
2. Wu Z, Lai X, Li K. Water quality assessment of rivers in Lake Chaohu Basin (China) using water quality index. Ecol. Indic. 2021 Feb;121:107021.
3. HasanMdF, Nur-E-AlamMd, Salam MA, Rahman H, Paul SC, Rak AE, et al. Health Risk and Water Quality Assessment of Surface Water in an Urban River of Bangladesh. Sustainability. 2021 Jun 17;13(12):6832.
4. Huang J, Zhang Y, Bing H, Peng J, Dong F, Gao J, et al. Characterizing the river water quality in China: Recent progress and on-going challenges. Water Res. 2021 Aug;201:117309.
5. Yan T, Shen SL, Zhou A. Indices and models of surface water quality assessment: Review and perspectives. Environ. Pollut. 2022 Sep;308:119611.
6. Chen SS, Kimirei IA, Yu C, Shen Q, Gao Q. Assessment of urban river water pollution with urbanization in East Africa. Environ. Sci. Pollut. Res. 2022 Jun 27;29(27); 40812–25.
7. Pany R, Rath A, Swain PC. Water quality assessment for River Mahanadi of Odisha, India using statistical techniques and Artificial Neural Networks. J Clean Prod. 2023 Sep;417:137713.
8. Das A, Goya A, Soni A. Use of water quality indices and its evaluation to verify the impact of Mahanadi river basin, Odisha. In 2023. Innov. Infrastr. Solut. 9(12):484p. 040003.
9. Das A. Surface water quality evaluation of Mahanadi and its Tributary Katha Jodi River, Cuttack District, Odisha, using WQI, PLSR, SRI, and geospatial techniques. Appl. Water Sci. 2025 Feb 23;15(2):26.
10. Das A. An innovative approach for quality assessment and its contamination on surface water for drinking purpose in Mahanadi River Basin, Odisha of India, with the integration of BA-WQI, AHP-TOPSIS, FL-DWQI, MOORA, and RF methodology. Appl Water Sci. 2024 Dec 25;14(12):263.
11. Das A. Identification of Surface Water Contamination Zones and its Sources on Mahanadi River, Odisha Using Entropy-Based WQI and MCDM Techniques. In: Optimization and Computational Case Studies in Civil Engineering. Grinrey Publishing; 2023. p. 67–92.
12. CGWB. Ground water quality in shallow aquifers of India. New Delhi; 2010; p. 87.
13. APHA Standard methods for the examination of water and wastewater. 22nd Edn. Washington DC; 2012.
14. Wu J, Zhou H, He S, Zhang Y. Comprehensive understanding of groundwater quality for domestic and agricultural purposes in terms of health risks in a coal mine area of the Ordos basin, north of the Chinese Loess Plateau. Environ Earth Sci. 2019 Aug 1;78(15).
15. ANZECC. Australian water quality guidelines for fresh and marine waters. Canberra; 1992. p. 171.
16. CCME. Canadian water quality guidelines for the protection of aquatic life: Summary tables. Winnipeg; 2001. p.13
17. Owamah HI. A comprehensive assessment of groundwater quality for drinking purpose in a Nigerian rural Niger delta community. Groundw. Sustain. Dev. 2020 Apr 1; p.10.
18. Sarath Prasanth S V., Magesh NS, Jitheshlal K V., Chandrasekar N, Gangadhar K. Evaluation of groundwater quality and its suitability for drinking and agricultural use in the coastal stretch of Alappuzha District, Kerala, India. Appl. Water Sci. 2012;2(3); 165–75.
19. Siddha S, Sahu P. Assessment of Groundwater Quality and Associated Human Health Risk of Central Gujarat, India. Clean–Soil, Air, Water. 2020 Dec 2;48(12).
20. Siddha S, Sahu P. A. Statistical Approach to Study the Evolution of Groundwater of Vishwamitri River Basin (VRB), Gujarat. J. Geol. Soc. India. 2020 May 1;95(5); 503–6.
21. USEPA. Risk Assessment Guidance for Superfund, Volume I: Human Health Evaluation Manual (Part E, Supplemental Guidance for Dermal Risk Assessment). Washington, DC; 2004. p. 156.
22. He S, Wu J. Hydrogeochemical Characteristics, Groundwater Quality, and Health Risks from Hexavalent Chromium and Nitrate in Groundwater of Huanhe Formation in Wuqi County, Northwest China. Exp. Health. 2019 Jun 15;11(2); 125–37.
23. Li P, Feng W, Xue C, Tian R, Wang S. Spatiotemporal Variability of Contaminants in Lake Water and Their Risks to Human Health: A Case Study of the Shahu Lake Tourist

Area, Northwest China. Exp. Health. 2017 Sep 1;9(3); 213–25.

24. Das A. Assessment of potability of surface water and its health implication in Mahanadi Basin, Odisha. Mater. Today: Proc. 2023 May; Mater. Today: Proc.; https://doi.org/10.1016/j.matpr.2023.05.367.
25. Das A. Evaluation and downstream effects of household and industrial effluents discharge on some physicochemical parameters and surface Water Quality Index of River Mahanadi, Odisha, India. Discov. Water. 2025 Apr 21;5(1):30.
26. Das A. Anthropogenic Effects on Surface Water Quality Assessment in Baitarani River Basin, Odisha Using GIS and MCDM Techniques. In: Integrated Water Resources Management for Quality Enhancement (Eds. Rao KJ, Khuntia JR and Nemade PD). Grinrey Publishing; 2023. p. 37–64.
27. Das A. Applying the water quality indices, geographical information system, and advanced decision-making techniques to assess the suitability of surface water for drinking purposes in Brahmani River Basin (BRB), Odisha. Environ. Sci. Pollut. Res. 2025 Mar 31; doi: 10.1007/s11356-025-36329-z.
28. Das A. Evaluation of surface water quality in Brahmani River Basin, Odisha (India), for drinking purposes using GIS-based WQIs, multivariate statistical techniques and semi-variogram models. Innov. Infrastruct. Solut. 2024 Dec 23;9(12):484.
29. Panda BP, Mohanta YK, Paul R, Prusty BAK, Parida SP, Pradhan A, et al. Assessment of environmental and carcinogenic health hazards from heavy metal contamination in sediments of wetlands. Sci. Rep. 2023 Sep 28;13(1):16314.
30. Prusty BAK, Azeez PA, Jagadeesh EP. Alkali and Transition Metals in Macrophytes of a Wetland System. Bull. Environ.Contam.Toxicol. 2007 Jul 27;78(5):405–10.
31. Bhatti NB, Siyal AA, Qureshi AL, Solangi GS, Memon NA, Bhatti IA. Impact of small dam's construction on groundwater quality and level using water quality index (WQI) and GIS: Nagarparkar area of Sindh, Pakistan. Hum. Ecol. Risk Assess. 2020 Nov 25;26(10); 2586–607.
32. Azeez PA, Prusty BAK, Jagadeesh EP. Alkali and alkaline earth metals in decomposing macrophytes in a wetland system. Acta Ecol. Sin. 2009 Jun;29(1); 13–9.

Note: All the figures and tables in this chapter were made by the authors.

Research and Innovations in Industrial and Marine Biotechnology: A Circular Economy 2024 – Prof. Hrudayanath Thatoi et al. (eds)

18 Exploring Microbial Diversity in Spring Water: A Key to Sustainable Development

Harekrishna Hembram, Payal Garai
Department of Microbiology, Bankura Sammilani College,
Bankura, West Bengal, India

Manasi Chattaraj
Department of Geography, Bankura University,
Bankura, West Bengal, India

Mousumi Ganguly
Department of Nutrition, Bankura Sammilani College,
Bankura, West Bengal, India

Sourav Chattaraj, Subhashree Rath
Centre for Industrial Biotechnology Research,
School of Pharmaceutical Sciences, Siksha 'O' Anusandhan,
Deemed to be University, Kalinga Nagar,
Bhubaneswar, Odisha, India

Arindam Ganguly*
Department of Microbiology, Bankura Sammilani College,
Bankura, West Bengal, India

Abstract: Spring water ecosystems, rich in minerals and distinct physicochemical properties, support diverse microbial communities with vast biotechnological potential. These microbes are valuable for applications in agriculture, ocean farming, bioremediation, food production, and pharmaceuticals. Advanced tools like 16S rRNAamplicon sequencing and metagenomics enable detailed analysis of microbial diversity and functions in spring water. Notable microbial products include Taq polymerase from *Thermus aquaticus*, protease and lipase from *Bacillus* sp., polymyxin from *Bacillus polymyxa*, and erythromycin from *Saccharopolyspora erythraea*. Exopolysaccharides from *Pseudomonas* sp. also hold pharmaceutical and cosmetic relevance. This study focuses on identifying economically significant microorganisms from spring water sources and understanding their roles, despite challenges from seasonal variations in water parameters. Exploring these microbiomes offers opportunities for sustainable innovations across various industries and emphasizes the need for continued investigation into spring water microbial ecosystems for novel bioactive compounds and enzymes with commercial and therapeutic applications.

Keywords: Spring water, Microbiome, Biotechnology, Metagenomic analysis, Sustainable development

1. Introduction

Natural springs are critical freshwater sources that emerge from aquifers, offering mineral-rich habitats supporting diverse flora, fauna, and microbial life. Their economic value lies in providing hydration, supporting ecotourism, cultural heritage, and health benefits. Globally, various spring types—gravity, artesian, filtration, lava, karst, thermal, cold, fracture, and mineral springsharbor unique microbial ecosystems contributing to nutrient cycling,

*Corresponding author: arindam.microbiology@gmail.com

DOI: 10.1201/9781003759003-18

organic matter degradation, and ecological balance [1,2]. These springs offer specific physicochemical conditions that foster microbial communities adapted to their environment [3]. Microbes have evolved to produce industrially significant enzymes [4,5] and bioactive compounds [6-8], benefiting pharmaceuticals, agriculture [9], food, aquaculture [10], cosmetics, and environmental conservation. Their applications drive growth in the blue economysupporting marine biotechnology, bioremediation, and sustainable aquaculture and the white economy, which includes antibiotic and enzyme production [11,12]. Integrating biotechnology with sustainable practices boosts economic advancement while preserving aquatic ecosystems and ensuring the long-term availability and health of these valuable natural resources [13-16].

2. Methodology

This comprehensive review discusses the diversity of microbial phyla inhabiting spring ecosystems, their adaptations to physicochemical conditions and the pivotal role of microbes in the growth of economy. A literature review was conducted to investigate the potential of microorganisms as bioresources. Furthermore, a systematic review was performed to evaluate the applications of microorganisms and their byproducts in blue and white economy sectors, alongside a detailed analysis on the growing market trends and broader economic impact of microbial byproducts.

2.1 Microbial Diversity in Springs

Microbial communities in springs, including bacteria, fungi, and algae, play significant ecological roles. Common bacterial phyla include Proteobacteria, Firmicutes, Acidobacteriota, and Actinobacteriota, while fungal phyla include Ascomycota and Basidiomycota[17] and algae phyla like Chlorophyta and Cyanobacteria [18]. Microbes from springs also serve as valuable bioresources, such as Taq polymerase from *Thermusaquaticus* for PCR [19], polymyxin from *Paenibacilluspolymyxa* for antibiotic resistance [20] and exopolysaccharides from *Pseudomonas putida* for bioremediation (Song et al., 2024).

2.2 Factors Inducing Microbial Adaptation

The environmental factors provided by springs influence microbial life and induce adaptation and evolution, allowing only surviving species to thrive in their extreme environments. The factors are summarized in the Table 18.1.

Table 18.1 Microbial adaptation to environmental conditions

Factors	Impact on microbes	References
Temperature	High temperature in hot springs promotes the evolution of thermophiles with heat-resistant enzymes. Cold temperatures lead to development of psycrophiles with specialized protein.	[22]
pH	Acidophiles and alkaliphiles evolved to survive in extreme pH.	[23]
Mineral content	Microorganisms develop metabolic pathways to utilize specific minerals such as iron, phosphate, and silicate etc.	[24]
Oxygen levels	Fluctuating oxygen levels of springs promote the evolution of facultative anaerobes and obligate aerobes.	[25]
Water clarity	Phototrophic microbes may adapt to varying light conditions.	[26]
Organic matter	High organic content promotes the evolution of heterotrophs. Low organic matter encourages autotrophic microbes.	[27]

3. Contributions of Microorganisms in Blue Economy Sectors

The blue economy aims to harness oceanic and freshwater resources to drive economic growth while ensuring their sustainable conservation [28]. Springs, as mineral-rich aquatic ecosystems, support bottled water industries and harbor diverse microbial communities with unique metabolic traits. These microbes offer vast potential for advancing the blue and white economies. In biotechnology, extremophiles from springs produce enzymes and bioactive compounds; for example, *Acidithiobacillusferrooxidans* aids in bioleaching [26]. In bioremediation, spring-dwelling microbes like *Pseudomonas sp.* break down pollutants, cleaning contaminated aquatic areas [21]. In sustainable aquaculture, *Bacillus sp.* acts as a probiotic, improving fish health and nutrient cycling [29,30]. For renewable energy, microbes such as *Thermotogamaritima* generate biohydrogen from biomass [31]. In carbon sequestration, microalgae and diatoms help mitigate climate change by capturing CO_2 [32]. In the white economy, spring microbes contribute to biopharmaceuticals with antimicrobial, anti-inflammatory, and anti-cancer agents [33,34], nutraceuticals with antioxidant-rich probiotics like *Lactobacillus sp.*[35], and cosmetics, offering anti-aging and skin-soothing compounds [36].

3.1 Limitations

Sampling of spring water ecosystems is challenging due to seasonal variations and fluctuating microbial populations, particularly during monsoon and summer [37]. Contamination from human activities and climate change further complicates microbial assessments, promoting pollutant-tolerant and thermophilic species. Technological limitations, such as conventional methods failing to detect rare species, require advanced, costly tools like metagenomics and bioinformatics, which are inaccessible to many researchers [38]. Regular environmental monitoring is crucial for assessing the impacts of anthropogenic activities and climate change on microbial diversity.

4. Market Trends of Microbial Byproducts

4.1 Rising Demand

As the preference for sustainable, eco-friendly products and green technologies increases, there is a burgeoning need for microbial-based products and services. Consequently, microbial technologies are being employed across various fields such as industries, agriculture and foods sectors [39], and providing opportunities for entrepreneurs to initiate startups and generate wealth. The global market for microbial byproducts is currently worth USD 160 billion in 2022 which is estimated to have a value of USD 286.53 billion by 2033 (Fig. 18.1), growing at a Compound annual growth rate of 6% [40].

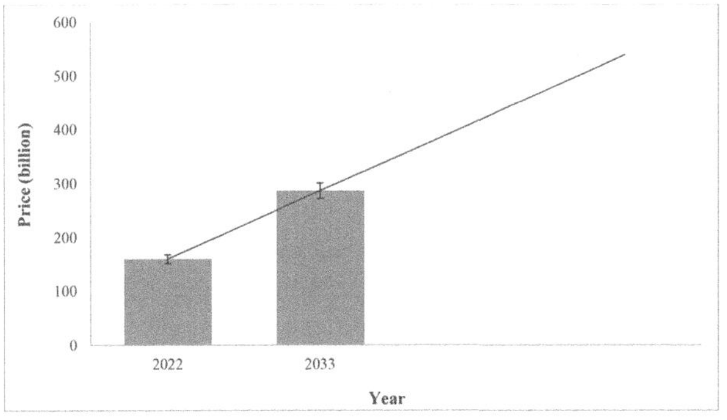

Fig. 18.1 Expected growth of global market value of microbial byproducts

4.2 Research and Innovations in Applications

There is a growing interest on leveraging microbial inherent capabilities to produce cutting-edge products. Recent developments include biofertilizers, biopolymers, microbial enzymes and proteins [40]. Microbial derivatives are at the forefront of biotechnology, showcasing a broad range of applications in the field of agriculture, healthcare, food production and industrial processes[41]. Many countries are seeking to adopt microbe-based technologies due to low costs of raw materials, high profits and creation of eco-friendly solutions. There are ongoing developments in countries like India, China, Japan, United Kingdom, USA, European Union, and Asian countries [42]. According to bioeconomy report provided by the Biotechnology Industry Research Assistance Council (2024), The Indian bioeconomy has gained around $151 billion in 2023. In the United States, the bioeconomy has experienced significant growth, reaching a substantial value of USD 952.2 billion [43]. The world's bio-economy is expected to rise from $4 trillion to $30 trillion by 2050 [44].

4.3 Economic Impacts of Microbial Byproducts

The integration of microbial biotechnology across industries and commercialization of bio-based products have paved the way for multiple job opportunities. Rural areas, with the establishment of microbe-based industries, can overcome the challenge of limited availability of jobs and outmigration of local people in urban areas. Microbial biotechnology presents benefits in long-term production and management of resources as it reduces cost and increases efficiency of bio-based products [9]. Bio-based industries often utilize agricultural residues, waste products and other leftover materials to produce sustainable goods, thereby cutting waste management costs. This also aids in sustainable management of resources, for example, removal of agricultural wastes leads to enhanced soil fertility and crop yield.

5. Conclusion

This study emphasizes the importance of microbial diversity in springs for ecological balance, waste management, and sustainable energy production. Microbes offer eco-friendly alternatives to traditional energy, supporting circular economies and enhancing water quality. Metagenomics helps discover economically important microorganisms that support industries, benefiting the blue economy. These microbes aid in bioremediation, improving water quality and biodiversity. The discovery of new strains drives advancements in biotechnology and pharmaceuticals, fostering economic growth and ensuring sustainable development for future generations.

References

1. Nerantzaki, S.D. and Nikolaidis, N.P. (2020). The response of three Mediterranean karst springs to drought and the impact of climate change. *J. Hydrol.*, 591, 125296.
2. Wang, F., Bai, Y., Yang, F., Zhu, Q., Zhao, Q., Zhang, X., ... Liao, H. (2021). Degradation of nitrogen, phosphorus, and organic matter in urban river sediments by adding microorganisms. Sustainability, 13(5), 2580.
3. Ganguly, A., Mandal, A., Khan, M.A., Dutta, T.K., Raha, S. and Das Mohapatra, P.K. (2017). Study of physico-chemical parameters, planktonic diversity, and bacterial load of *Clariasbatrachus* cultivation pond at Bankura, WB, India. *Int. Res. J. Biol. Sci.*, **6**(12), 23–34.
4. Nad, S., Konar, U., Chattaraj, S. and Ganguly, A. (2024). Valorization of feather waste by microbial enzymatic activity: Bioconversion, production, and application. In *Agro-waste to Microbe Assisted Value Added Product: Challenges and Future Prospects* (pp. 337–363). Springer Nature. https://doi.org/10.1007/978-3-031-58025-3_15
5. Bhattacharjee, M., Banerjee, M., Mitra, P. and Ganguly, A. (2018). Investigation of alkaline phosphatase enzyme of a novel Bacillus species isolated from rhizospheric soil of potato field. Res. J. Life Sci. Bioinf. Pharm. Chem. Sci., 4(2), 129–144.

6. Chattaraj, S., Mitra, D., Chattaraj, A., Chattaraj, M., Kundu, M., Ganguly, A. and Das Mohapatra, P.K. (2023b). Anti-oncogenic potential of probiotics: Challenges and future prospects. Indian J. Microbiol. Res., 10(1), 1–10. https://doi.org/10.18231/j.ijmr.2023.001
7. Chattaraj, S., Mitra, D., Ganguly, A., Das Mohapatra, P.K. and Thatoi, H. (2024a). 16S amplicon sequencing of the gastrointestinal microbiota of Cirrhinusreba and isolation of an autochthonous probiotic using culture-based approaches. Syst. Microbiol. Biomanuf., https://doi.org/10.1007/s43393-024-00285-5
8. Chattaraj, S. and Das Mohapatra, P.K. (2024). Immunostimulatory and antagonistic potential of the methanolic extract of *Oedogoniumintermedium* SCB in *Cirrhinusreba* challenged with *Aeromonashydrophila. Aquac. Int.*, 32(3), 2523–2548.
9. Samantaray, A., Chattaraj, S., Mitra, D., Ganguly, A., Kumar, R., Gaur, A., Das Mohapatra, P.K., de los Santos-Villalobos, S., Rani, A. and Thatoi, H. (2024). Advances in microbial-based bio-inoculum for amelioration of soil health and sustainable crop production. *Curr. Res. Microb. Sci.*, https://doi.org/10.1016/j.crmicr.2024.100251
10. Chattaraj, S., Ganguly, A. and Das Mohapatra, P.K. (2023a). Study of intestinal bacteria of Cirrhinusreba and characterization of a new probiotic bacterium: An initiative to save the threatened species of Cirrhinus. Appl. Biochem. Microbiol., 59(6), 833–849. https://doi.org/10.1134/S0003683823060248
11. Chattaraj, S., Mitra, D., Chattaraj, M., Ganguly, A., Thatoi, H. and Das Mohapatra, P.K. (2024b). Brewers' spent grain as fish feed ingredient: Evaluation of bio-safety and analysis of its impact on gut bacteria of Cirrhinusreba by 16S metagenomic sequencing. Curr. Res. Microb. Sci., https://doi.org/10.1016/j.crmicr.2024.100286
12. Ganguly, A. and Mandal, A. (2024). Production and optimization of xylanase enzyme from *Bacillus cereus* BSA1 by submerged fermentation. *Int. Res. J. Basic Appl. Sci.*, **9**(1), 13–20.
13. Ganguly, A., Banerjee, A., Mandal, A., Khan, M.A. and Das Mohapatra, P.K. (2019). Isolation and characterization of bacteria from the intestine of *Clariasbatrachus* for probiotic organism. *Proc. Zool. Soc.*, **72**(4), 411–419. https://doi.org/10.1007/s12595-018-0283-x
14. Chattaraj, S., Ganguly, A., Mandal, A. and Das Mohapatra, P.K. (2022). A review of the role of probiotics for the control of viral diseases in aquaculture. Aquac. Int., https://doi.org/10.1007/s10499-022-00915-6
15. Chattaraj, S., Das, S., Ganguly, A., Thatoi, H. and Das Mohapatra, P.K. (2024c). Valorization of wastewater by the application of probiotic, nitrifying, and denitrifying bacterial consortium. In: Application of Microbial Technology in Wastewater Treatment and Bioenergy Recovery, Springer Nature, 133–156. https://doi.org/10.1007/978-981-97-3458-0_6
16. Chattaraj, S., Behera, B.K. and Das Mohapatra, P.K. (2024d). Effective valorization of Chlorella biomass and brewers' spent grain substituting fish meal and soybean meal in the diet of herbivorous fish Cirrhinusreba for higher growth, digestibility and sustainable cultivation. J. Appl. Phycol., 36(1), 217–232.
17. Oza, Y., Karande, M., Ghosh, R., Rawat, J.M., Purohit, S., Rawat, B., ... Sharma, A. (2024). Microbial diversity associated with the natural spring water of Western Himalayas. *Vegetos*, 1–9.
18. Fecteau, K.M., Boyd, E.S., Lindsay, M.R., Amenabar, M.J., Robinson, K.J., Debes, R.V. and Shock, E.L. (2022). Cyanobacteria and algae meet at the limits of their habitat ranges in moderately acidic hot springs. *J. Geophys. Res. Biogeosci.*, 127(1), e2021JG006446.
19. Rowe, L., Dowd, S.E., Davidson, K., Kovarik, C., VanAken, M., Jarabek, A. and Taylor, C. (2024). Comparing microbial populations from diverse hydrothermal features in Yellowstone National Park: hot springs and mud volcanoes. *Front. Microbiol.*,15, 1409664.
20. Pandey, A.K., Barbetti, M.J. and Lamichhane, J.R. (2023). *Paenibacilluspolymyxa. Trends Microbiol.*, **31**(6), 657–659.
21. Song, Y.J., Zhao, N.L., Dai, D.R. and Bao, R. (2024). Prospects of Pseudomonas in microbial fuel, bioremediation, and sustainability. ChemSusChem, e202401324.
22. Bhatia, R.K., Ullah, S., Hoque, M.Z., Ahmad, I., Yang, Y.H., Bhatt, A.K. and Bhatia, S.K. (2021). Psychrophiles: a source of cold-adapted enzymes for energy efficient biotechnological industrial processes. J. Environ. Chem. Eng., 9(1), 104607.
23. Aliyu, G.O., Ezugworie, F.N., Onwosi, C.O., Nnamchi, C.I., Ekwealor, C.C., Igbokwe, V.C. and Sani, R.K. (2024). Multi-stress adaptive lifestyle of acidophiles enhances their robustness for biotechnological and environmental applications. Sci. Total Environ., 176190.
24. Sharma, N., Kumar, J., Abedin, M.M., Sahoo, D., Pandey, A., Rai, A.K. and Singh, S.P. (2020). Metagenomics revealing molecular profiling of community structure and metabolic pathways in natural hot springs of the Sikkim Himalaya. BMC Microbiol., 20, 1–17.
25. Zhang, Y., Liu, T., Li, M.M., Hua, Z.S., Evans, P., Qu, Y., ...Guo, J. (2023). Hot spring distribution and survival mechanisms of thermophiliccomammoxNitrospira. ISME J., 17(7), 993–1003.
26. Zhang, S., Yang, J., Dong, B., Yang, J., Pan, H., Wang, W., ...Gu, J.D. (2022). An Fe(II)-oxidizing consortium from Wudalianchi volcano spring in Northeast China for bioleaching of Cu and Ni from printed circuit boards (PCBs) with the dominance of Acidithiobacillus spp. Int. Biodeterior. Biodegrad., 167, 105355.
27. Fernandes-Martins, M.C., Keller, L.M., Munro-Ehrlich, M., Zimlich, K.R., Mettler, M.K., England, A.M., ... Boyd, E.S. (2021). Ecological dichotomies arise in microbial communities due to mixing of deep hydrothermal waters and atmospheric gas in a circumneutral hot spring. *Appl. Environ. Microbiol.*,**87**(23), e01598-21.
28. Ganguly, A., Banerjee, A., Mandal, A. and Das Mohapatra, P.K. (2018b). Study of indigenous freshwater fish diversity of Bankura (West Bengal), India with special reference to *Clariasbatrachus. J. Appl. Nat. Sci.*, **10**, 1162–1172. https://doi.org/10.31018/jans.v10i4.1892
29. Ganguly, A., Banerjee, A., Mandal, A. and Das Mohapatra, P.K. (2018a). Probiotic-based cultivation of *Clariasbatrachus*: Importance and future perspective. *Acta Biol. Szeged.*, **62**(2), 158–168. https://doi.org/10.14232/abs.2018.2.158-168
30. Ganguly, A., Kirtania, D. K., Chhetri, M., &Chattaraj, S. (2025a). Sustainable development through probiotics: A scientometric analysis of Indian research and innovation.

Discover Sustainability, 6, Article 455. https://doi.org/10.1007/s43621-025-01263-0

31. Shao, W., Wang, Q., Rupani, P.F., Krishnan, S., Ahmad, F., Rezania, S., ... Din, M.F.M. (2020). Biohydrogen production via thermophilic fermentation: A prospective application of Thermotoga species. Energy, 197, 117199.
32. Sarwer, A., Hamed, S.M., Osman, A.I., Jamil, F., Al-Muhtaseb, A.A.H., Alhajeri, N.S. and Rooney, D.W. (2022). Algal biomass valorization for biofuel production and carbon sequestration: a review. Environ. Chem. Lett., 20(5), 2797–2851.
33. Pal, S., Mitra, P., Dey, S., Ganguly, A. and Mandal, A. (2024). Appraisal of ethno-veterinary practices used for different livestock ailments in rural and periurban areas of PurbaBardhaman, West Bengal, India. *Ethnobot. Res. Appl.*, 27, 30. https://doi.org/10.32859/era.27.30.1-21
34. Ganguly, A., Nad, S., Singha, K., Pathak, R., Hazra, P., Singha, P., Dhua, P., Mahapatra, P.K. and Mandal, A. (2021). Diversity and distribution of wild mushrooms in different forest areas of Bankura district, WB, India. *Acta Biol. Szeged.*, 65(2), 185–198. https://doi.org/10.14232/abs.2021.2
35. Ganguly, A., Chattaraj, S., Ganguly, M., Chattaraj, M., Banerjee, A., Mandal, A., Khan, M.A., Sen, S.K. and Das Mohapatra, P.K. (2024). Effect of three probiotic *Bacillus* strains supplemented feeds on growth, carcass composition and blood parameters of *Clariasmagur* (Hamilton). *J. Appl. Aquacult.*, https://doi.org/10.1080/10454438.2024.2330499
36. Tyagi, U. and Sarma, A.K. (2024). Bioactive compounds from algae: Extraction, purification, and applications. In Value Added Products From Bioalgae Based Biorefineries: Opportunities and Challenges (pp. 259–288). Singapore: Springer Nature Singapore.
37. Sajib, M.S.I., Brunker, K., Oravcova, K., Everest, P., Murphy, M.E. and Forde, T. (2024). Advances in host depletion and pathogen enrichment methods for rapid sequencing–based diagnosis of bloodstream infection. *J. Mol. Diagn.*, 26(9), 741–753.
38. Mitra, D., Nachhmin, B., Ganguly, A. and Das Mohapatra, P.K. (2022). Computational approach to assess mucormycosis: A systematic review. In *Computational Intelligence in Healthcare Applications* (pp. 71–85). Academic Press. https://doi.org/10.1016/B9x78-0-323-99031-8.00004-1
39. Ganguly, A., Konar, R., Karuppiah, P., Eswaranpillai, U., Ganguly, M., Chattaraj, M., Mitra, D., &Chattaraj, S. (2025b). Sustainable valorization of food waste through bacterial biofilm: A pathway towards environmental safety and economic viability. In T. Sarkar, D. Lahiri, M. Nag, & D. Bhattacharya (Eds.), *Biofilm applications to revolutionize food technology*. Springer. https://doi.org/10.1007/978-3-031-85205-3_13
40. Chukwuka, G.E. and Chukwuka, E.J. (2024). Entrepreneurial Microbiology: A Perspective of Microbiology for Wealth Creation. *Afr. J. Environ. Nat. Sci. Res.*, 7(4), 10–19.
41. Ganguly, A., Kaibarta, R., Das, S., Kundu, R., Paramanik, S., Mohapatra, S., Mukherjee, S. K., Mitra, D., &Chattaraj, S. (2025c). Biodegradation and valorisation of plastic-based food packets: A microbial solution for sustainability and circular economy. *Discover Sustainability, 6*, Article 447. https://doi.org/10.1007/s43621-025-01257-y
42. Khandekar, P. and Ghosh, P.K. (2023). Bioeconomy: Different Countries, Different Strategies, Multiple Benefits. *Asian Biotechnol. Dev. Rev.*, 25(3).
43. Aworunse, O.S., Olorunsola, H.A., Ahuekwe, E.F. and Obembe, O.O. (2023). Towards a sustainable bioeconomy in a post-oil era Nigeria. Resour. Environ. Sustain., 11, 100094
44. Biotechnology Industry Research Assistance Council (BIRAC). (2024). Innovation and Biotechnology Entrepreneurship Research (IBER) Report 2024. Retrieved from https://birac.nic.in/webcontent/IBER_2024.pdf

Note: The figures and tables have been prepared by the authors based on the analyzed data and findings of the present study.

Research and Innovations in Industrial and Marine Biotechnology: A Circular Economy 2024 – Prof. Hrudayanath Thatoi et al. (eds)

19 Analyzing the Impacts of Environmental Degradation on Coleoptera and Proposing its Geospatial Conservation Strategies: A Study on Barjora Forest Range, Bankura District, West Bengal, India

Manasi Chattaraj, Aditi Goswami
Department of Geography, Bankura University,
Bankura, W.B, India

Druheen Chakrabortty
Department of Geography, Bankura Christian College,
Bankura,W.B, India

Arindam Ganguly
Department of Microbiology, BankuraSammilani College,
Bankura, W.B, India

Subhashree Rath, Sourav Chattaraj*
Centre for Industrial Biotechnology Research,
School of Pharmaceutical Sciences,
Siksha 'O' Anusandhan, Deemed to be University,
Bhubaneswar, Odisha, India

Abstract: Alteration of physical and behavioral properties of all zoological species is noticed in Anthropocene. This study is based on the anthropogenicity induced changes in characteristics of Coleoptera in Barjora forest range in recent past based on Primary Survey. Maps and Satellite imageries are consulted for determining anthropogenic changes in geographical aspects that affects the Coleoptera. Index basedzoo-geographical variation was computed and Remote Sensing Ecological Index and Land Use Land Cover Change analyzed. The change in the form of habitat alteration and adapted modifications is noteworthy. In the end some bio-geospatial technology-based action strategies have been suggested for conservation.

Keywords: Biodiversity, Conservation, Diversity indices, LULC, RSEI

1. Introduction

Man-environment interactions started sinceorigin of species. With the advent of Anthropocene, humansare getting detached from nature and affecting the biosphere. Biodiversity loss, primarily driven by human activities, is posing a global concern.Investigations on species richness and species diversity in geoenvironmental perspectives[1] and behavioral patterns[2] have been previously attempted in relation to changing landscape dynamics.Insects dominate the biosphere and are essential to ecosystem functions. Coleoptera, the largest insect order, comprises 40% of all insect species and 30% of all animal species [3], occurring across nearly all zoogeographical zones. The term

*Corresponding author: souravchattaraj@soa.ac.in

DOI: 10.1201/9781003759003-19

"Coleoptera" ['koleon'(sheath)+'pteron'(wing)], refers to hardened forewings (elytra) protecting the hind wings, eg. marsh beetles, lady beetles, glowworms, etc. Coleoptera play crucial role due to their abundance, diversity, and ecological significance. Research on Coleoptera phylogeny and adaptability in human-modified environments [4], and their roles in agriculture as pests and beneficial predators [5,6] highlight their ecological versatility. Coleopteras are bio-indicators for determining habitat quality and entropy levels [7], contribute to pollination, nutrient cycling, reduce methane emissions, and help to control invasive species [8]. Additionally, they have forensic applications in criminology [9]. Despite their obvious relevance, insects are underrepresented in conservation literature. Effective conservation demands detailed knowledge of species' morphological, ecological, and genetic traits, necessitating a biosystematic and geospatial approach. Different coefficients (Simple Matching, Jaccard, and Sorensen-Dice) as measures of co-occurrence of species were compared by scientists and implementation of Shannon's diversity, Simpson's diversity, Simpson's dominance, Simpson's evenness, and Berger–Parker dominance is noteworthy [10, 11]. [12,13] evaluated the importance of α and β diversity in assessing species richness and [14] implemented Fischer's alpha index for determining species abundance and richness and Sorensen index for sampling similarity checking. [15] emphasized on geographical scale for biodiversity assessment and conservation. Land Use-Land Cover (LULC) changes, largely anthropogenic, are major threats to biodiversity [16]. Remote Sensing Ecological Index (RSEI) emerged as a strong tool for evaluating ecological health [17]. The anthropologically influenced Barjora Forest Range, rich in biodiversity, offers a critical study area. This research uses indices to assess Coleoptera diversity, alongside RSEI and LULC analysis (2013-2022) to point out anthropogenicity induced environmental degradation. The findings aim to illuminate anthropogenic impacts on Coleoptera and inform conservation strategies through geo-biosystematics for protecting these ecologically vital organisms.

1.1 Study Area

The present studyon Barjora Forest Range (Bankura North Division) isbounded by 23°15'N-23°30'N latitude and 87°10'E-87°24'E longitude (Fig. 19.1), covering 393.23 Km^2, comprising 38.47% forested area including Barjora, Shitla, Sangrampur, Barjora C.P. and Barjora beet office.

1.2 Objectives

The present study aims to:

a. analyzespatio-temporal changes in Coleoptera count and behavior.
b. assesslevel of ecological degradation of the area that triggers Coleoptera disruption.
c. proposebio-geospatial technology-based strategies for Coleoptera conservation.

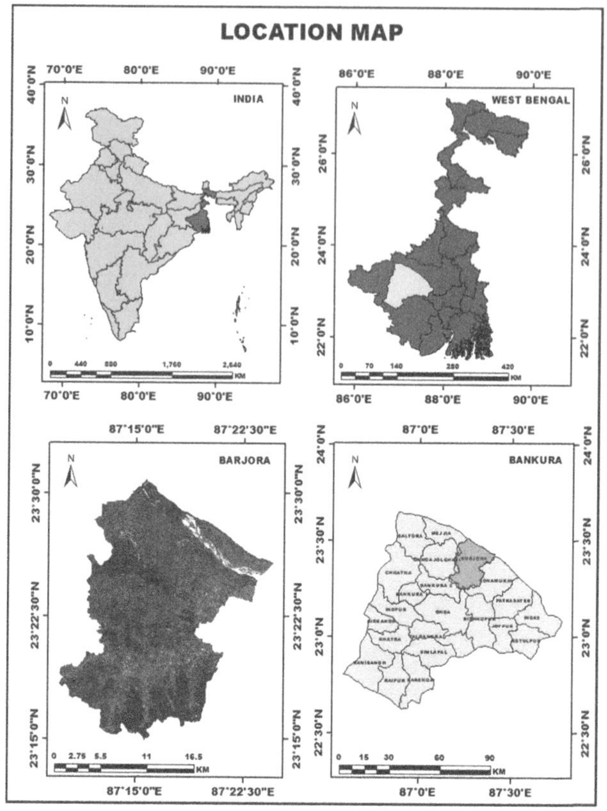

Fig. 19.1 Location of the study area

Source: Prepared by Authors in ArcGIS

2. Database and Methodology

2.1 Database

The study uses primary fielddata and secondary data from reports, articles etc. RSEI and LULCmaps prepared by geoprocessingLandsat data (2013,2022) in Arc GIS(10.2.2).

2.2 Methodology

The Zoological species are identified and counted taking two sites: a) Near locality(Periphery) b)Less interrupted zone(Core). Samples collected by Hand Picking and Fly trapping techniques during Pre and post-Monsoon.The study compares 2013 and 2022 data to assess changes in species count and individual identification.

Sorensen- Dice Coefficient: Used for comparing similarity between two samples [18,19].

$$SSD = [2a/(2a + b + c)] * 100\%$$

Where, a = number of individuals in both sites; b=number of individuals in second site ; c = number in the first site.

Fischer's Diversity Index: A parametric index of species diversity following logarithmic series for finding species abundance [20]:

$$S/N = (1 - x)/x\,(-ln\,(1 - x));\ \alpha = N(1 - x)/x$$

Where, S = Number of Species; N = Total number of Individuals

Table 19.1 Numerical details

Year	Core			Periphery			Average		
	Species	Individual	Coleoptera	Species	Individual	Coleoptera	Species	Individual	Coleoptera
2013	12	237	71	8	198	58	10	218	65
2022	10	226	66	7	177	53	9	202	60

Source: Primary Survey

Simpson's Diversity Index: Used to determinecommunity diversity. 0 = less diverse, 1 = more diverse.

$$D = 1 - \frac{\sum n(n-1)}{N(N-1)};$$

Where, n = number of individuals of each species; N = total number of individuals of all species.

2.3 For RSEI

Calculated following the formula:

1st Indicator (Wetness): LSM (Land Surface Moisture) [21]:

a. **LSM for TM** = 0.0135 * B_{Blue} + 0.2021 * B_{Green} + 0.3102 * B_{Red} + 0.1595 * B_{NIR} – 0.6806 * B_{SWIR1} – 0.6109 * B_{SWIR2}

b. **LSM for OLI** = 0.1511 * B_{Blue} + 0.1972 * B_{Green} + 0.3283 * B_{Red} + 0.3407 * B_{NIR} – 0.7117 * B_{SWIR1} – 0.4559 * B_{SWIR2}

2nd Indicator (Temperature): LST (Land Surface Temperature):

LST = BT/{1 + [λ * BT/P) * ln * ελ]}

Where, LST - Land surface Temperature; BT - Raster at Sensor (°C); λ - Wavelength of emitted radiance; ελ- Emissivity; ln-Raster calculation operation; P- (1.4388)

3rd Indicator (Greenness): NDVI(Normalized Difference Vegetation Index):

NDVI = (NIR – RED)/(NIR + RED)(0 = bare soils ; > 0 – 1 = different types of vegetation condition)

4th Indicator (Dryness): NDBSI(Normalized Difference Building and Bare Soil Index):

NDBSI = (IBI + SI)/2 [Soil Index (SI), Built-up Index (IBI)]

Combining Indicators: To generate RSEI, all aforementioned variables are standardized between 0 and 1 using the equation:

XI = [xi – min(xi)] / [max(xi) – min(xi)]

Where, X_I is the standardized value of factor I, and x_i is the initial value of factor I.

Principal Component Analysis: RSEI generated in ArcGIS, weighting four indicators based on their PC1 loadings.

RSEI = f (Greenness, Heat, Wetness, Dryness). So, RSEI = PC1 [f (NDVI, LST, LSM, NDBSI)]

RSEI was inverted and standardized between 0 (poor) to 1 (excellent).

RSEI = (1 – RSEI0) [RSEI0 = formerly generated RSEI raster]

RSEI values categorized according to **Equal Interval method.**

Laboratory works, Mapping, Cartographic tools and ***Statistical methods,*** have been used to portray the variability of associated factors and resultants.

3. Results and Discussions

60% of the Earth faces moderate to severe anthropogenic effects, with species extinction surpassing natural levels due to agriculture, changing climate, habitat fragmentation, pollution, etc. [22].

3.1 Numerical Details of Identified Insects, Especially Coleoptera

Surveyduring pre and post-monsoon clubbed to normalize seasonal variability and reduction of 1.05 % is noticed (Table 19.1).

3.2 Sorensen-Dice Coefficient (SDC)

Similarity of 67% and dissimilarity of 33% noticed, indicating similarityin sample collection (Table 19.2).

Table 19.2 Level of similarity

Zone↓ Year →	2013	2022	Total	SDC
Core	71	66	137	67%
Periphery	58	53	111	67%
Total	129	119	248	67%
SDC	67%	67%	67%	

Source: Primary Survey

3.3 Fischer's Diversity Index (FDI)

Intra-order diversity and abundance value of the core is more than the periphery regions both in 2013 and 2022 and the overall abundance reduced (Table 19.3).

3.4 Simpson's Diversity Index (SDI)

Inter-order diversity is more incorethan Periphery (Table 19.4).

Table 19.3 Fischer's alpha index values

Year	FDI		Differential Values
	Core	Periphery	
2013	4.1397	2.515	1.6247
2022	3.277	2.158	1.119
Differential Values	0.8627	0.357	

Source: Primary Survey

Table 19.4 Intra-order diversity, 2013-2022

	Core			Periphery		
	Cole-optera	Indi-viduals	SDI	Cole-optera	Indi-viduals	SDI
Total	129	435	0.045	119	403	0.042

Source: Primary Survey

Table 19.5 RSEI change, 2013-2022

Category	Area (Km^2)		Change	Category	Area (Km^2)		Change
	2013	2022			2013	2022	
Very Poor	1.73	14.54	12.81	**Good**	139.92	71.32	-68.6
Poor	34.75	74.01	39.26	**Natural**	16.24	5.88	-10.36
Acceptable	200.04	226.93	26.89	**Total**	393.23	393.23	---

Source: Computed by Author(s)

3.5 Changes in Geospatial Parameters

RSEI assesses ecological health by integrating environmental indicators for spatio-temporal comparisons [23]. In the study area, RSEI shows a sharp increase in poor ecological zones from 2013 to 2022, with degradation of natural landscapes. Comparison of RSEI (Table 19.5, Fig. 19.2) and LULC (Table 19.6, Fig. 19.3) reveals rapid settlement expansion in the northeast and conversion of a central river into agricultural land, placing it in the critical zone. Forest cover has declined significantly, while settlement areas have surged. Resulting forest fragmentation has severely disrupted Coleoptera habitats, restricting their movement within core zones.

LULC analysis is vital for assessing ecological health by revealing natural-to-cultural landscape conversion [24]. In this study, LULC change shows a notable decline in forest cover, especially south of the Damodar River (Fig. 19.3, Table 19.6). Fallow lands converted into settlements, and widespread patch and channel fragmentation has contributed significantly to biodiversity loss.

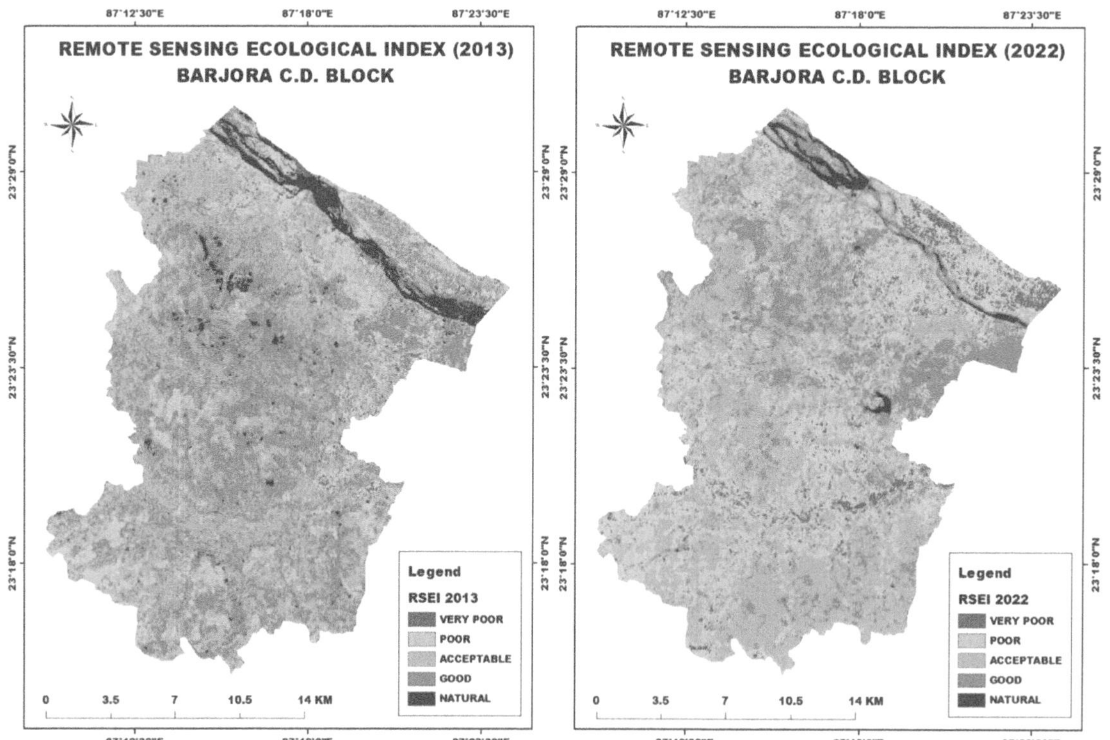

Fig. 19.2 Level of ecological degradation (2013-2022)

Table 19.6 LULC change, 2013-2022

Category	Area (Km^2)		Change	Category	Area (Km^2)		Change
	2013	2022			2013	2022	
Forest	194.81	104.84	-89.97	Agricultural Land	8.38	17.57	9.19
River	9.46	9.07	-0.39	Settlement	20.40	96.85	76.45
Waterbody	5.53	4.95	-0.58	Culturable Fallow	132.45	122.91	-9.54
Sand	4.26	5.16	0.9	Transportation	4.26	10.33	6.07
Stony Waste	13.14	21.01	7.87	Total	393.23	393.23	---

Source: Computed by Author(s)

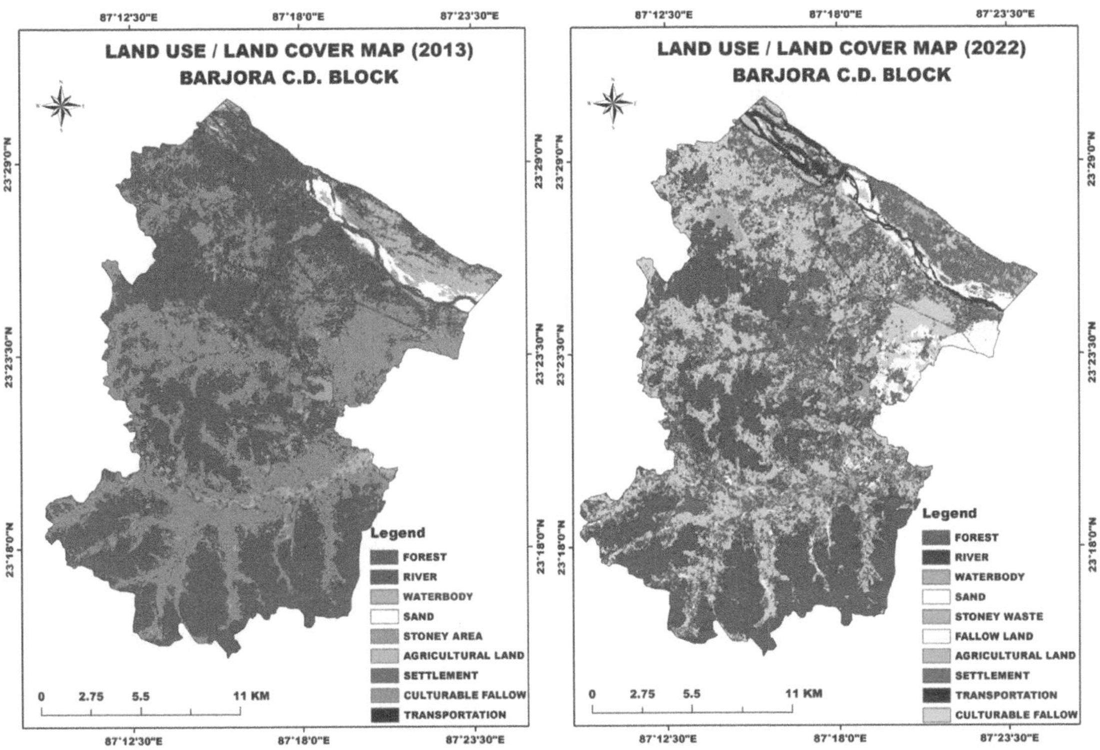

Fig. 19.3 LULC 2013-2022

Sources: Prepared by Authors in ArcGIS

3.6 Anthropogenic Causes that Accelerated the Diversity Loss of the Coleoptera

Analysis of inter/intra-species diversity reveals that anthropogenically influenced peripheral areas exhibit lower Coleoptera diversity (2013-2022). Key drivers of this decline include:

Deforestation

Nearly 10% forest cover lost due to lumbering, urban encroachment, industrial expansion, and infrastructure development. Forest fragmentation resulted habitat stress.

Urbanization

Urban growth negatively impacts biodiversity via pollution, landdegradation, and habitat disruption [25]. Roads and transportation create barriers, further limiting habitat of Coleoptera[26] (Fig. 19.4).

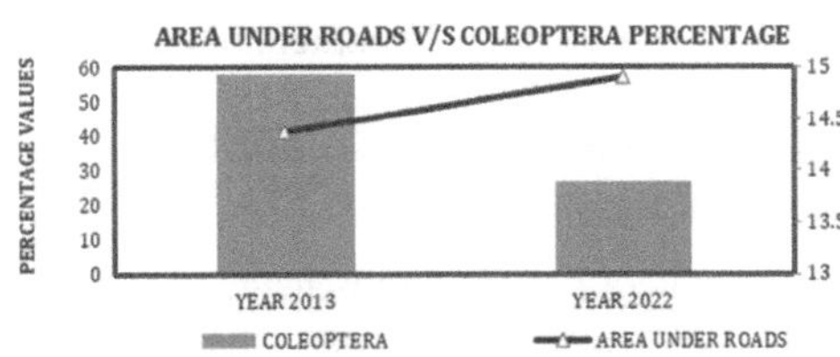

Fig. 19.4 Road expansion and coleoptera availability

Source: Primary survey and district regional transport office data

Economic Activities

Forest resource extraction (lumbering, twig gathering) causes regular disturbances. Frequent burning of forested tracts has led to a notable decline in species richness.

Agricultural Practices

Intensified agriculture, excessive pesticide and fertilizer use and unsustainable groundwater extraction—reduces

Coleopteradiversity and disrupts their ecological roles [27]. Increased pesticide use correlates with a sharp decline in Coleoptera population (Fig. 19.5).

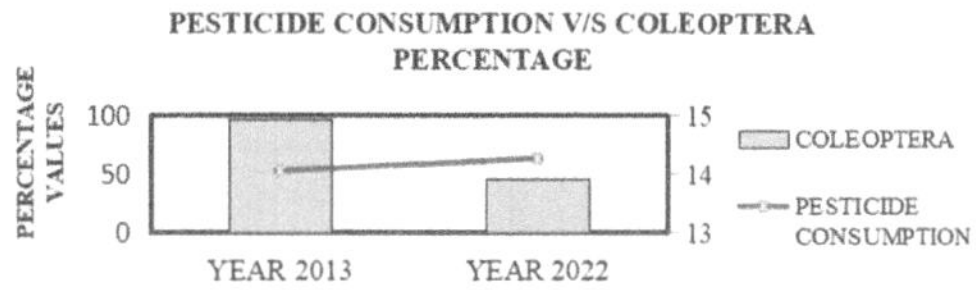

Fig. 19.5 Pesticide consumption and coleopteran availability

Source: Primary survey and district agricultural office data

Overall, anthropogenic pressures, deforestation, urban expansion, forest resource exploitation, and unsustainable agricultural practices pose a substantial threat to Coleoptera diversity, emphasizing the urgent need for conservation.

3.7 Impact of Anthropogenic Activities on Coleoptera

The anthropogenic activities largely impact the Coleoptera in terms of both physical and biological characteristics. The impacts include:

Habitat Alteration

Increased habitat destruction in peripheral areas reduced Coleoptera availability over the study period.

Decline in Number and Frequency

Coleoptera presence declined by 7.04% in core and 8.62% in periphery zones; the periphery had 18.98% fewer individuals than the core.

Altered Phenology

Reproductive cycles, including egg-laying, have shifted from natural patterns.

Behavioral and Feeding Pattern Change

Seasonal availability and feeding habits are altered due to pesticide and herbicide use, reducing food sources. Parasitic, stem-sap-feeding Coleoptera have become rare.

3.8 Action Strategies for Coleoptera Conservation

OngoingColeoptera decline and behavioral changes raise global concerns, demanding immediate conservation actions at micro levels. Strategies that can help to reduce anthropogenic impacts on Coleoptera (Fig. 19.6) are:

a. Survey, identification and geospatial inventorization for species listing.
b. DNA bar-coding, molecular techniques, and imaging technologies toaid traditional methods.
c. Implement species census, even for minor taxa.
d. Implementing Geo-spatial techniques like Cluster analysis, Overlay Analysis, Proximity study, and decision support for bio-geo-monitoring.
e. Conservation through habitat maintenance, sustainable landuse practice and habitat restoration.
f. Establishing protected corridors to safeguard critical habitats and facilitate movement.
g. Integrating Indigenous knowledge system and mass awareness for in-situ conservation.

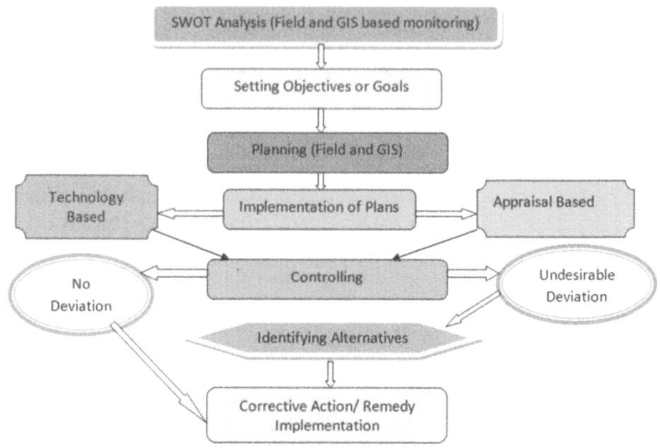

Fig. 19.6 Action strategy for coleoptera conservation

Source: Prepared by Authors

4. Conclusion

Coleoptera, the largest order of Insecta, showed a decline of 7.02% in the core and 8.62% in the periphery between 2013–2022—highlighting significant anthropogenic impact. Urbanization, deforestation, forest-based economic activities, and intensified agriculture have negatively affected their diversity and behavior. The altered physico-behavioral traits, along with a 1.05% overall decline in this dominant group, in 10-year micro-temporal scaleraise serious biodiversity concerns.Geospatial and biosystematic strategies such as cluster analysis, overlay analysis, and transformation models will definitely offer effective tools for conservation and decision-making. Systematic data collection and Coleoptera census can further aid conservation. This study paves way for future research and conservation in the Barjora Forest Range and similar areas. Understanding anthropogenic impacts and applying targeted strategies approach will support global biodiversity conservation and promote sustainable landscape management.

References

1. Ganguly, A., Banerjee, A., Mandal, A., Dutta, T. K., &Mohapatra, P. K. D. (2018). Study of indigenous freshwater fish diversity of Bankura (West Bengal), India with special reference to Clariasbatrachus. Journal of Applied and Natural Science, 10(4), 1162–1172.
2. Banerjee, M. (2014). Diversity and composition of beetles (order: Coleoptera) of Durgapur, West Bengal, India. *Psyche: A Journal of Entomology, 2014.*
3. Meyer, J.R. (2020). https://projects.ncsu.edu/cals/course/ent425/library/compendium/coleoptera.html.

4. Deppe, F., & Fischer, K. (2023). Landscape type affects the functional diversity of carabid beetles in agricultural landscapes. Insect Conservation and Diversity.
5. Allen R.T.(1979). The Occurrence and Importance of Ground Beetles in Agricultural and Surrounding Habitats. In: Carabid Beetles. Springer, Dordrecht. 485–505.
6. Kim, T. N., Bukhman, Y. V., Jusino, M. A., Scully, E. D., Spiesman, B. J., &Gratton, C. (2022). Using high-throughput amplicon sequencing to determine diet of generalist lady beetles in agricultural landscapes. Biological Control, 170, 104920.
7. Das, J., &Maity, J. (2025). Assessing the health of freshwater ecosystems: the role of biomonitoring scores and diversity indices in evaluating aquatic insect populations. Journal of Applied Entomologist, 5(2), 01–10.
8. Farrell, B. D., Sequeira, A. S., O'Meara, B. C., Normark, B. B., Chung, J. H., &Jordal, B. H. (2001). The evolution of agriculture in beetles (Curculionidae: Scolytinae and Platypodinae). Evolution, 55(10), 2011–2027.
9. Gruszka, J. and Matuszewski, S.(2022). Temperature models of development for Necrodeslittoralis L.(Coleoptera: Silphidae), a carrion beetle of forensic importance in the Palearctic region. Scientific Reports, 12(1), 1–11.
10. Dalirsefat, S. B., da Silva Meyer, A., &Mirhoseini, S. Z. (2009). Comparison of similarity coefficients used for cluster analysis with amplified fragment length polymorphism markers in the silkworm, Bombyxmori. Journal of Insect Science, 9(1), 71.
11. Morris, E. K., Caruso, T., Buscot, F., Fischer, M., Hancock, C., Maier, T. S., ...&Rillig, M. C. (2014). Choosing and using diversity indices: insights for ecological applications from the German Biodiversity Exploratories. Ecology and evolution, 4(18), 3514–3524.
12. Flohre, A., Fischer, C., Aavik, T., Bengtsson, J., Berendse, F., Bommarco, R., ...& Tscharntke, T. (2011). Agricultural intensification and biodiversity partitioning in European landscapes comparing plants, carabids, and birds. Ecological Applications, 21(5), 1772–1781.
13. Sharma, K., Acharya, B. K., Sharma, G., Valente, D., Pasimeni, M. R., Petrosillo, I., & Selvan, T. (2020). Land use effect on butterfly alpha and beta diversity in the Eastern Himalaya, India. Ecological Indicators, 110, 105605.
14. Uwimbabazi, M., &Eilu, G.(2014). Avian frugivore assemblages on Celtisgomphophylla, Baker, in B udongo F Forest Reserve, Uganda. African journal of ecology, 52(1), 97–102.
15. Le Provost, G., Schenk, N. V., Penone, C., Thiele, J., Westphal, C., Allan, E., ...& Manning, P. (2023). The supply of multiple ecosystem services requires biodiversity across spatial scales. Nature ecology & evolution, 7(2), 236–249.
16. Roy, A., &Srivastava, V. K.(2012). Geospatial approach to identification of potential hotspots of land-use and land-cover change for biodiversity conservation. Current science, 102(8), 1174–1180.
17. Zhu, D., Chen, T., Wang, Z., &Niu, R.(2021). Detecting ecological spatial-temporal changes by Remote Sensing Ecological Index with local adaptability. Journal of Environmental Management, 299, 113655.
18. Sorensen, T. A. J. B. S. (1948). Videnski Selskab Biologiske Skrifter. A method of establishing groups of equal amplitude in plant sociology based on similarity of species content and its application to analyses of the vegetation on Danish commons, 5, 1–34.
19. Dice, L.R. (1945) Measures of the amount of ecologic association between species. Ecology 26, 297–302.
20. Fisher, R. A., Corbet, A. S., Williams, C. B., (1943) "The relation between the number of species and the number of individuals in a random sample of an animal population." Journal of Animal Ecology, 12, 42–58.
21. Liu, Y., Xu, W., Hong, Z., Wang, L., Ou, G., Lu, N., & Dai, Q.(2023). Integrating three-dimensional greenness into RSEI improved the scientificity of ecological environment quality assessment for forest. Ecological Indicators, 156, 111092.
22. Chowdhury, S., Jennions, M. D., Zalucki, M. P., Maron, M., Watson, J. E., & Fuller, R. A. (2023). Protected areas and the future of insect conservation. *Trends in Ecology & Evolution*, *38*(1), 85–95.
23. Zhang, X., Jia, W., Lu, S., & He, J.(2024). Ecological assessment and driver analysis of high vegetation cover areas based on new remote sensing index. Ecological Informatics, 82, 102786.
24. Zhao, H., & Deng, X. (2024). Spatiotemporal variation in ecosystem health caused by land use and land cover changes in Pakistan. Ecosystem Health and Sustainability, 10, 0161.
25. Sarkar, A., Chattaraj, S., Chattaraj, M., Maity, S., Ganguly, A., Nandi, B., ...& Das Mohapatra, P. K. (2022). Ichthyodiversity and water quality parameters of Uttar Dinajpur, West Bengal, India. North-Western Journal of Zoology, 18(2).
26. Da Silva, P. M., Aguiar, C. A., Niemelä, J., Sousa, J. P., & Serrano, A. R. (2008). Diversity patterns of ground-beetles (Coleoptera: Carabidae) along a gradient of land-use disturbance. Agriculture, ecosystems & environment, 124(3-4), 270–274.
27. Cheli, G. H., Bosco, T., & Flores, G. E.(2022). The role of Nycteliadorsata Fairmaire, 1905 (Coleoptera: Tenebrionidae) on litter fragmentation processes and soil biogeochemical cycles in arid Patagonia. In Annales Zoologici, 72(1), 129–134.

Research and Innovations in Industrial and Marine Biotechnology: A Circular Economy 2024 – Prof. Hrudayanath Thatoi et al. (eds)

20 Biodegradation of Plastics: A Microbial Solution for a Sustainable Future

Riyan Kaibarta, Suman Das, Raina Kundu
Department of Microbiology, Bankura Sammilani College,
Bankura, W.B., India
Subhashree Rath, Sourav Chattaraj
Centre for Industrial Biotechnology Research,
School of Pharmaceutical Science, Siksha 'O' Anusandhan University, Kalinga Nagar,
Bhubaneswar, Odisha, India
Arindam Ganguly*
Department of Microbiology, Bankura Sammilani College,
Bankura, W.B., India

Abstract: Plastics, made from synthetic or semi-synthetic organic and inorganic materials, have emerged as a major global environmental issue. While they offer benefits like affordability and long-lasting performance, their large-scale production has resulted in serious environmental problems. Current waste management methods, including incineration, landfilling, and recycling, are insufficient and create additional environmental hazards, such as air and water pollution. Improper disposal of plastics also impacts tourism, nutrient production, and human health. They are often the root cause of the deadliest diseases. Current research has explored the utilization of beneficial microorganisms to degrade plastics into valuable products. This study highlights the potential of microbial degradation of plastic as a cost-effective and eco-friendly sustainable solution for waste management.

Keywords: Plastics, Waste management, Sustainable solution, Bio-degradation

1. Introduction

Plastic, a highly durable and often essential material in modern times, has become a foundational component across numerous industries. Its versatility makes it suitable for a wide range of applications in today's world [1,2]. Polymer or plastic materials are polyethylene terephthalate (PET), polystyrene (PS), polyethylene (PE), polyhydroxyalkanoate (PHA), polypropylene (PP), polycaprolactone (PCL), polybutylene succinate (PBS), polyurethane (PUR), polylactic acid or polylactide (PLA), polyvinyl chloride (PVC) and polyhydroxybutyrate (PHB). But the steady rise in the production of plastics has created serious and immediate environmental concerns. Indeed, over 70 years of plastic production, worldwide output has amounted to 359 million metric tons (Mt) in 2018, from 1.5 million metric tons in the 1950s [3,4]. Such recent plastic waste management practices continue to have a significant environmental threat [5]. Most of the chemicals employed in the lobar of plastic items have been proven to be carcinogenic and endocrine disruptors responsible for reproductive, developmental, immunological, and neurological disorders in human and wildlife [4]. The ability of some microorganisms such as bacteria and fungi to degrade both bio-based and fossil-based biodegradable polymers at an incredible rate has been documented in most stressful environments [5,6]. Microbes break down complex polymers either by directly using plastic pieces as a source of energy or by the combined action of different microbial enzymes. *Pseudomonas fluorescens,*

*Corresponding author: arindam_ganguly@yahoo.com

DOI: 10.1201/9781003759003-20

Table 20.1 Plastic degrading microorganisms

SL. No.	Source	Microorganisms	Plastic type	Degradation efficiency (%)	Duration	Reference
1.	Soil contaminated with plastics	*Pseudomonas alcaligenes*	PE	16.2	1 month	[9]
2.	Textile Wastewater Drainage Site	*Pseudomonassp.*	PE	39.70	8 weeks	[10]
3.	Sediment from Mangroves	*Sporosacrinaglobispora*	PP	11	40 days	[11]
4.	Marine Plastic Sediments	*Alcanivoraxborkumensis*	LDPE	3.5	80 days	[12]
5.	Plastic contaminated soil	*Desulfotomaculumnigrifans*	PE	16.2	1 month	[9]
6.	Garbage soil	*Pseudomonas fluorescens*	LDPE	22	1 month	[13]
7.	Soil	*Streptomyces SSP4*	PE	11	1 month	[14]
8.	Soil contaminated with oil	*Streptomyces coelicoflavus*	LDPE	30	4 weeks	[15]
9.	Landfill soil	*Ochrobacterumanthropi*	HDPE	20	45 days	[16]
10.	Forest soil	*Micrococcus luteus*	Plastic cups	38	45 days	[17]
11.	Digester Sludge	*Bacillus weihenstephanensis*	LDPE	35.64	6 months	[18]
12.	Forest soil	*Masoniella sp.*	Plastic cups	27.40	45 days	[17]

Penicillium simplicissimum and *Pseudomonas aeruginosa* are the most widely used employed bacterial and fungal species in polymer biodegradation [7]. Proteases, lipases, and chitinases are significant microbial enzymes involved in the polymer biodegradation [8]. This review is centered on microbial degradation mechanisms of polymers.

2. Types of Plastics

There are six main categories of plastics: High-density polyethylene (HDPE), Polystyrene (PS), Low-density polyethylene (LDPE), Polyvinyl chloride (PVC), Polyethylene terephthalate (PET) and Polypropylene (PP). Polyethylene terephthalate (PET) is a flexible thermoplastic, strong and clear.

3. Degradation of Plastic

Plastic waste degradation consists of different treatments of physical, chemical and biological factors. Photo-oxidation, thermal degradation, ozone degradation and mechano-chemical degradation are some examples of the processes involved in the degradation of polymers [19].

3.1 Biodegradation

Biodegradation is a cost-effective, economic and efficient way of processing plastics waste. This ability of most microorganisms including fungi, actinomycetes and bacteria to break down plastic polymers is a beneficial factor that can be utilized in the direction of addressing plastic waste management challenges associated with increased loads of plastics waste produced daily. Different types of enzymes from microorganisms synthesized extracellularly and intracellularly catalyze the degradation of plastic polymers into their smaller nontoxic pieces. As enzymes are much substrate specific, a wide range of enzymes are utilized for depolymerization of various types of plastics. Proteases, esterases, ureases and lipases are the hydrolytic enzyme families which hydrolyse the polymers by breaking the ester linkages [5]. Biodegradation process is of two types: aerobic biodegrading and anaerobic biodegradation. Aerobic microorganisms utilize oxygen as an electron acceptor to break down the large organic molecules into small ones.

3.2 Microorganisms' Role on Biodegradation of Plastic

The degradation of synthetic plastics and natural plastics are carried out by microorganisms such as bacteria, actinomycetes, and fungi.

Bacteria

The majority of plastics found in landfills include plastic bags (69.13%) that consist of low-density polyethylene (LDPE). Some newly discovered isolates include *Bacillus pumilus*, *Aacidovorax delafieldii*, *Azotobacter sp* and *Pseudomonas aeruginosa*[20]. Five bacteria utilized were *Pseudomonas putida*, *Bacillus subtilis*, *Bacillus amylolyticus*, *Pseudomonas fluroscence* and *Bacillus firmus*. *Bacillus* genus of bacteria is very versatile, providing a green alternative to petrochemical-based production processes [21]. These hardy microorganisms have the capacity to grow in varied environments, such as agro-industrial wastes [22,23,24] to produce a vast array of valuable and environmentally friendly products [25], such as feeds [25,26], foods [27,28], probiotics [29,30,31], plant growth regulators [32], enzymes [33], biocides [34], and bioactive chemicals [35].

Fungi

As for the fungal species, numerous studies on the degradation of plastic have been reported, e.g., the species of *Fusariummoniliforme*, *Tritirachium album*, *Aspergillusaavus*[36], *Purpureocilliumlilacinus*[37], *Thermoas-*

cusaurantiacus[38]. It was also found that different fungal genera degrade PVC, polyesters and polyhydroxybutyrates (PHBs). Examples include *Debaryomyces, Mucor, Cladosporium, Paecilomyces, Fusarium, Penicillium, Rhodosporidium* and *Emericellopsis*.

Actinomycetes

There are various actinomycetes including *Amycolatopsis sp.*[39], *Streptomyces bangladeshensis*[40], *Saccharothrix*, which can degrade polybutylene succinate (PBS), polycaprolactone and polylactic acid. Degradation of PLA was detected by actinobacteria.

4. Mechanism of Biodegradation

Microbial degradation occurs on the principle of four main phases, colonization, bio-fragmentation, assimilation, and mineralization [41]. Microbial adhesion on the surface of plastic can be aided by the formation of various polysaccharides [42]. These compounds are capable of penetrating and adjusting the pore size of the polymer as well as altering the morphological character of the plastic surface [43]. These slimes, present in the extracellular environment, were seen to encourage the buildup of pollutants that can be used as a source of nutrients, thus enhancing microbial generation and metabolic processes that result in an increase in the biodeteriogenic process. Polymer materials go through biofragmentation in this stage, wherein the polymeric molecular structure will degrade due to the action of certain enzymes including depolymerases, hydrolases, oxidases, oxidoreductases, peroxidases and free radicals. At this phase, the microbial cell employs these synthesized monomers as their carbon and energy source that led to the microbial growth. Certain molecules or big monomers are not readily assimilated because of the permeability of the cell membrane. But by employing biotransformation the enzyme-catalyzed to convert of one chemical compound into other products or smaller monomers that can be assimilated by the same or different microorganism, by this process microbial cell can utilize those un-assimilated monomers[44]. The final phase mineralization, those small monomers that really diffused in to the cells are oxidized and utilized for the production of energy (Fig. 20.1). The energy then utilized for biomass production [45].

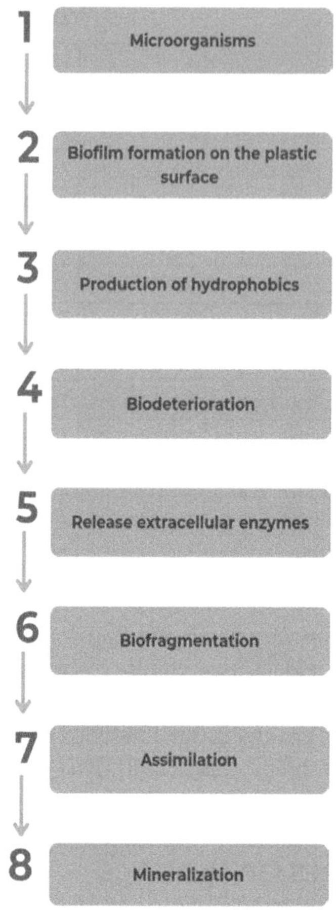

Fig. 20.1 Schematic diagram for microbial biodegradation of plastics

5. Conclusion

So versatile and long-lasting, plastics became a key part of numerous contemporary industries, yet their presence in the world as a whole can pose hazardous threats to ecosystems and human health. Global plastic production boomed and poor disposal ended up contaminating the environment on a large scale. The application of conventional practices in plastic waste management, including landfilling and incineration, contributes to pollutant generation, necessitating more environmentally friendly alternatives. In fact, microbial degradation has emerged as a promising method of remediating plastic pollution, and bacterial, fungal and actinomycetal enzymatic degradation of polymers has immense potential. Microbial degradation is a complex multi-step process which encompasses colonization, bio-fragmentation, assimilation and mineralization. Microbial organisms like *Pseudomonas aeruginosa*, *Bacillus subtilis*, *Aspergillus niger*, and *Amycolatopsis sp.* have exhibited significant capability towards the degradation of plastic. The major enzymes responsible for breaking down polymer chains into smaller, utilizable units are hydrolases, oxidoreductases, and depolymerases. Plastic contamination does not only affect our physical space but also human health through harmful endocrine disruptors such as phthalates, which are introduced into plastic products. Moreover, the use and dumping of plastics are major sources of greenhouse gas emissions and particulate matter pollution, and developing nations share disproportionately high burdens. Though biodegradation is potentially a cleaner way of handling waste, enhancing its viability for use at scales larger than small pilot plants has not been easy. Polymers are inherently stable. It may be centuries before they degrade and looks doubtful in isolation that microbial degradation is the solution for plastic pollution.

References

1. Ganguly, A., Kaibarta, R., Das, S., Kundu, R., Paramanik, S., Mohapatra, S., ...& Chattaraj, S. (2025). Biodegradation and valorisation of plastic based food packets: a microbial solution for sustainability and circular economy. *Discover Sustainability*, *6*(1), 1–17.
2. Muthukumar, A., &Veerappapillai, S. (2015). Biodegradation of plastics–a brief review. *Int. J. Pharm. Sci. Rev. Res*, *31*(2), 204–209.
3. Statista. (2020). Production of plastics worldwide from 1950 to 2018.
4. Rochman, C. M., Browne, M. A., Halpern, B. S., Hentschel, B. T., Hoh, E., Karapanagioti, H. K., ...& Thompson, R. C. (2013). Classify plastic waste as hazardous. *Nature*, *494*(7436), 169–171.
5. Ghosh, S. K., Pal, S., & Ray, S. (2013). Study of microbes having potentiality for biodegradation of plastics. *Environmental Science and Pollution Research*, *20*, 4339–4355.
6. Ganguly, A., Konar, R., Karuppiah, P., Eswaranpillai, U., Ganguly, M., Chattaraj, M., ... & Chattaraj, S. (2025). Sustainable valorization of food waste through bacterial biofilm: a pathway towards environmental safety and economic viability. In *Biofilm applications to revolutionize food technology* (pp. 293–307). Springer, Cham.
7. Singh, B., & Sharma, N. (2008). Mechanistic implications of plastic degradation. *Polymer degradation and stability*, *93*(3), 561–584.
8. Tokiwa, Y., Calabia, B. P., Ugwu, C. U., &Aiba, S. (2009). Biodegradability of plastics. *International journal of molecular sciences*, *10*(9), 3722–3742.
9. Begum, M. A., Varalakshmi, B., &Umamagheswari, K. (2015). Biodegradation of polythene bag using bacteria isolated from soil. *Int J CurrMicrobiol App Sci*, *4*(11), 674–680.
10. Nanda, S., Sahu, S., & Abraham, J. (2010). Studies on the biodegradation of natural and synthetic polyethylene by Pseudomonas spp. *Journal of Applied Sciences and Environmental Management*, *14*(2).
11. Auta, H. S., Emenike, C. U., &Fauziah, S. H. (2017). Screening of Bacillus strains isolated from mangrove ecosystems in Peninsular Malaysia for microplastic degradation. *Environmental Pollution*, *231*, 1552–1559.
12. Delacuvellerie, A., Cyriaque, V., Gobert, S., Benali, S., &Wattiez, R. (2019). The plastisphere in marine ecosystem hosts potential specific microbial degraders including Alcanivoraxborkumensis as a key player for the low-density polyethylene degradation. *Journal of hazardous materials*, *380*, 120899.
13. Patil, R. C. (2018). Screening and characterization of plastic degrading bacteria from garbage soil. *Br J Environ Sci*, *6*(4), 33–40.
14. Soud, S. A. (2019). Biodegradation of Polyethylene LDPE plastic waste using Locally Isolated Streptomyces sp. *Journal of Pharmaceutical Sciences and Research*, *11*(4), 1333–1339.
15. Duddu, M. K., Tripura, K. L., Guntuku, G., &Divya, D. S. (2015). Biodegradation of low density polyethylene (LDPE) by a new biosurfactant-producing thermophilic Streptomyces coelicoflavus NBRC 15399T. *African Journal of Biotechnology*, *14*(4), 327–340.
16. Riandi, M. I., Kawuri, R., & Sudirga, S. K. (2017). Potensibakteri Pseudomonas sp. dan Ochrobactrum sp. yang di isolasidariberbagaisampeltanahdalammendegradasilim bahpolimerplastikberbahandasar high density polyethylene (hdpe) dan low density polyethylene (ldpe). *Jurnal Simbiosis*, *5*(2), 58–63.
17. Sivasankari, S., &Vinotha, T. (2014). In vitro degradation of plastics (plastic cup) using Micrococcus luteus and Masoniella Sp. *Sch. Acad. J. Biosci*, *2*(2), 85–89.
18. Mukherjee, S., & Chatterjee, S. (2014). A comparative study of commercially available plastic carry bag biodegradation by microorganisms isolated from hydrocarbon effluent enriched soil. *International Journal of Current Microbiology and Applied Sciences*, *3*(5), 318–325.
19. Elahi, A., Bukhari, D. A., Shamim, S., &Rehman, A. (2021). Plastics degradation by microbes: A sustainable approach. *Journal of King Saud University-Science*, *33*(6), 101538.
20. Lee, S. H., & Kim, M. N. (2010). Isolation of bacteria degrading poly (butylene succinate-co-butylene adipate) and their lip A gene. *International Biodeterioration& Biodegradation*, *64*(3), 184–190.
21. Ganguly, A., Banerjee, A., Mandal, A., Khan, M. A., &Mohapatra, P. K. D. (2019, December). Isolation and characterization of bacteria from the intestine of *Clarias batrachus* for probiotic organism. *Proceedings of the Zoological Society* (Vol. 72, pp. 411–419). Springer India.
22. Chattaraj, S., Mitra, D., Ganguly, A., Thatoi, H., &Mohapatra, P. K. D. (2024). A critical review on the biotechnological potential of Brewers' waste: Challenges and future alternatives. *Current Research in Microbial Sciences*, 100228.
23. Chattaraj, S., Mitra, D., Chattaraj, M., Ganguly, A., Thatoi, H., & Mohapatra, P. K. D. (2024). Brewers' spent grain as fish feed ingredient: evaluation of bio-safety and analysis of its impact on gut bacteria of Cirrhinusreba by 16S Metagenomic sequencing. *Current Research in Microbial Sciences*, *7*, 100286.
24. Chattaraj, S., Behera, B. K., & Das Mohapatra, P. K. (2024). Effective valorization of Chlorella biomass and Brewers spent grain substituting fish meal and soybean meal in the diet of herbivorous fish Cirrhinusreba for higher growth, digestibility and sustainable cultivation. *Journal of Applied Phycology*, *36*(1), 217–232.
25. Ganguly, A., Chattaraj, S., Ganguly, M., Chattaraj, M., Banerjee, A., Mandal, A., ...& Das Mohapatra, P. K. (2025). Effect of three probiotic *Bacillus* strains supplemented feeds on growth, carcass composition and blood parameters of *Clarias magur* (Hamilton). *Journal of Applied Aquaculture*, *37*(1), 19–44.
26. Ganguly, A., Banerjee, A., Mandal, A., & Das Mohapatra, P. K. (2018). Optimization of effective dose of a newly isolated probiotic bacteria for growth and disease resistance of *Clarias batrachus* (Linn.). *Res J Life SciBioinform Pharm ChemSci*, *4*(4), 344–354.
27. Ganguly, A., Banerjee, A., Mandal, A., &Mohapatra, P. K. D. (2018). Probiotic-based cultivation of *Clarias batrachus*: importance and future perspective. *ActaBiologicaSzegediensis*, *62*(2), 158–168.

28 Ganguly, A., Banerjee, A., Mandal, A., Dutta, T. K., & Mohapatra, P. K. D. (2018). Study of indigenous freshwater fish diversity of Bankura (West Bengal), India with special

reference to Clariasbatrachus. *Journal of Applied and Natural Science*, *10*(4), 1162.
29. Ganguly, A., Kirtania, D. K., Chhetri, M., &Chattaraj, S. (2025). Sustainable development through probiotics: a scientometric analysis of Indian research and innovation. *Discover Sustainability*, *6*(1), 1–15.
30. Ganguly, A., Konar, R., Kirtania, D. K., Ganguly, M., Chattaraj, M., Mitra, D., & Chattaraj, S. (2025). *Employing technological innovation for eco-friendly waste disposal at a global scale*. In *AI technologies for enhancing recycling processes* (pp. 135–152). IGI Global. https://doi.org/10.4018/979-8-3693-7282-1.ch008
31. Chattaraj, S., Ganguly, A., Mitra, D., Mitra, D., & Das Mohapatra, P. K. (2023). Study of intestinal bacteria of Cirrhinusreba and characterization of a new probiotic bacteria: an initiative to save the threatened species of Cirrhinus. *Applied Biochemistry and Microbiology*, *59*(6), 833–849.
32. Samantaray, A., Chattaraj, S., Mitra, D., Ganguly, A., Kumar, R., Gaur, A., ...& Thatoi, H. (2024). Advances in microbial based bio-inoculum for amelioration of soil health and sustainable crop production. *Current Research in Microbial Sciences*, 100251.
33. Nad, S., Konar, U., Chattaraj, S., &Ganguly, A. (2024). Valorization of feather waste by microbial enzymatic activity: bioconversion, production and application. In *Agro-waste to Microbe Assisted Value Added Product: Challenges and Future Prospects: Recent Developments in Agro-waste Valorization Research* (pp. 337–363). Cham: Springer Nature Switzerland.
34. Chattaraj, S., Ganguly, A., Mandal, A., & Das Mohapatra, P. K. (2022). A review of the role of probiotics for the control of viral diseases in aquaculture. *Aquaculture International*, *30*(5), 2513–2539.
35. Chattaraj, S., Mitra, D., Chattaraj, A., Chattaraj, M., Kundu, M., Ganguly, A., &Mohapatra, P. K. D. (2023). Antioncogenic potential of probiotics: challenges and future prospective. *Indian J Microbiol Res*, *10*(1), 1–10.
36. Benedict, C. V., Cook, W. J., Jarrett, P., Cameron, J. A., Huang, S. J., & Bell, J. P. (1983). Fungal degradation of polycaprolactones. *Journal of Applied Polymer Science*, *28*(1), 327–334.
37. Oda, Y., Asari, H., Urakami, T., &Tonomura, K. (1995). Microbial degradation of poly (3-hydroxybutyrate) and polycaprolactone by filamentous fungi. *Journal of fermentation and bioengineering*, *80*(3), 265–269.
38. Sanchez, J. G., Tsuchii, A., &Tokiwa, Y. (2000). Degradation of polycaprolactone at 50° C by a thermotolerantAspergillus sp. *Biotechnology Letters*, *22*, 849–853.
39. Pranamuda, H., &Tokiwa, Y. (1999). Degradation of poly (L-lactide) by strains belonging to genus Amycolatopsis. *Biotechnology letters*, *21*, 901–905.
40. Hsu, K. J., Tseng, M., Don, T. M., & Yang, M. K. (2012). Biodegradation of poly (β-hydroxybutyrate) by a novel isolate of Streptomyces bangladeshensis 77T-4. *Botanical studies*, *53*(3).
41. Chattaraj, M., Goswami, A., Ganguly, A., & Chattaraj, S. (2025). *Considerations of policy and morality in waste management*. In *AI technologies for enhancing recycling processes* (pp. 233–266). IGI Global. https://doi.org/10.4018/979-8-3693-7282-1.ch012
42. Sarmah, P., & Rout, J. (2018). Algal colonization on polythene carry bags in a domestic solid waste dumping site of Silchar town in Assam. *Phykos*, *48*(67), e77.
43. Hakkarainen, K., Ilomäki, L., Lipponen, L., Muukkonen, H., Rahikainen, M., Tuominen, T., ...&Lehtinen, E. (2000). Students' skills and practices of using ICT: Results of a national assessment in Finland. *Computers & Education*, *34*(2), 103–117.
44. Al-Tohamy, R., Sun, J., Fareed, M. F., Kenawy, E. R., & Ali, S. S. (2020). Ecofriendly biodegradation of Reactive Black 5 by newly isolated Sterigmatomyceshalophilus SSA1575, valued for textile azo dye wastewater processing and detoxification. *Scientific reports*, *10*(1), 12370.
45. Lucas, N., Bienaime, C., Belloy, C., Queneudec, M., Silvestre, F., & Nava-Saucedo, J. E. (2008). Polymer biodegradation: Mechanisms and estimation techniques–A review. *Chemosphere*, *73*(4), 429–442.

Note: The figure and the table in this chapter were made by the authors.

Research and Innovations in Industrial and Marine Biotechnology: A Circular Economy 2024 – Prof. Hrudayanath Thatoi et al. (eds)

21 Lignin-Based Adsorbent for Removal of Heavy Metal from Contaminated Water

Sandesh Behera
Department of Biotechnology, Maharaja Sriram Chandra Bhanja Deo University, Baripada, Odisha, India
Centre for Industrial Biotechnology Research, Siksha 'O' Anusandhan, Deemed to be University, Bhubaneswar, Odisha, India

Sangram Basudev Mallik, Hrudayanath Thatoi*
Centre for Industrial Biotechnology Research, Siksha 'O' Anusandhan, Deemed to be University, Bhubaneswar, Odisha, India

Abstract: Heavy metal ion contamination of water is a major problem nowadays. In recent years, affordable adsorbents produced from biomass have been made. Heavy metals have caused significant impacts on aquatic ecosystems and human health, as well as increased pollution incidents. Therefore, there is a need for efficient and successful methods to get rid of heavy metal ions. There is great promise for using lignin, a naturally occurring amorphous polymer, as a raw material for developing biodegradable products. It is possible to create new hybrid nanoparticles. Because of its distinct polyphenol structure, physicochemical characteristics, and accessibility, lignin can create a wide range of heavy metal ion sorbents. Thus, the purpose of this chapter is to look over the many modification forms that have been documented for turning lignin into heavy metal adsorbents. Most significantly, because lignin is abundant in plants and stable and biocompatible, lignin-derived adsorbents can positively impact the environment. Producing novel lignin-based adsorbents with improved adsorbent quality for heavy metal ions may be possible.

Keywords: Adsorption, Composite, Heavy metal, Lignin nanoparticle, Wastewater

1. General Aspects of Heavy Metal Ions

A class of metals identified as heavy metals those with atomic numbers greater than 20. Some heavy metals have biological purposes, but practically all are harmful to human beings, even in small amounts. Heavy metals can be described as metal and metalloid species which are typically bio-accumulative, non-biodegradable, and carcinogenic, such as manganese, lead, iron, copper, cobalt, chromium, cadmium, arsenic, mercury, nickel, silver, and zinc in terms of environmental hazards. The major global threats to agricultural, industrial, aquatic, and drinking water sources are the environment and water pollution. One significant class of harmful substances found in water sources and often produced by human industrial activity on earth are heavy metals. Therefore, efforts are being made globally to treat and manage the removal of heavy metals. Heavy metals are only considered hazardous to living things when they reach a specific concentration. For example, all Zn, Ni, Se, Si, Cr, Mo, Mn, Fe, Cu, and Co are essential metals. However, if threshold values are exceeded, they may become hazardous. Other elements like Hg, Cd, Pb, and As are unnecessary for plants and animals, and at any amount of exposure, they are hazardous to all biological processes. Because of this consequence,

*Corresponding author: hnthatoi@gmail.com

DOI: 10.1201/9781003759003-21

Table 21.1 The benefits and drawbacks of the adsorption method

Benefits	Drawbacks
Flexibility, ease of use, cheap cost, and excellent effectiveness against heavy metal contaminants	With the help of precipitation, it removed heavy metals from water.
It produces excellent wastewater and effluent treatment.	The discharge of precipitated hydroxide into the environment is a major drawback.
Adsorbents can be regenerated and utilized again using appropriate desorption techniques.	During adsorption, it is bit reversible properties
Heavy metals with low concentrations are removed from the wastewater solution using the adsorption technique.	Adsorption does not effectively remove heavy metal ions from inorganic effluents; hence chemical precipitation is used alternatively.

Source: Authors

even in extremely low quantities, they may be harmful to species. Various heavy metal cleaning methods, including chemical, physical, electrical, and biological methods, have been proposed. To remove heavy metals, several methods have been contrasted to show their drawbacks and potential, and their combination has been emphasized as a possible method to create effective technologies (Table 21.1).

2. Lignin Potential as Heavy Metal Absorber

Due to the specific surface area and strong chemical stability, carbonaceous materials have found wide applications as adsorbents in the treatment of water. However, producing and renewing activated carbon is an expensive and energy-intensive process. To replace the expensive activated carbons, a renewable, low-cost material containing a significant amount of carbon could potentially be used [1]. Most lignin, cellulose, and hemicellulose, consisting of several surface functional groups, i.e., -COOH, -C=O, and -OH groups, are found in biosorbents derived from plant wastes [2]. These biosorbents have A wide variety of adsorbates, such as inorganic heavy metal ions. Due to the presence of monomeric units (Table 21.2) in the lignin, and lower affinity to heavy metal ions, it typically has a poor capacity for adsorption. Lignin is functionalized to increase the removal of heavy metals using amine and sulfonic groups an it also can be modified with various materials, including lignin-grafted nanocomposites, chitosan-lignin composites, ion-exchange resins, lignin-based hydrogels, chitin-lignin hybrids, and lignin-based nano traps [3].

Table 21.2 Monomeric unit content is derived from several pulp sources [4]

Source of lignin	Monomeric unit (%)		
	p-coumaryl alcohol (H)	Coniferyl alcohol (G)	Sinapyl alcohol (S)
Softwood	0.5-3.5	90-95	0-1
Hardwood	-	25-50	50-75
Pulp	10-25	25-50	25-50

3. Development of Functional Lignin-Based Materials

Chemical alterations have to be made, nevertheless, to use biomaterials in complex functional products. Although certain products made of lignin are used to remove hazardous metal ions. To further adapt lignin-based materials for heavy metals removal, and hybridization, copolymerization, grafting, and cross-linking should be used as modification techniques. Some lignin-based adsorbents are present in Fig. 21.1.

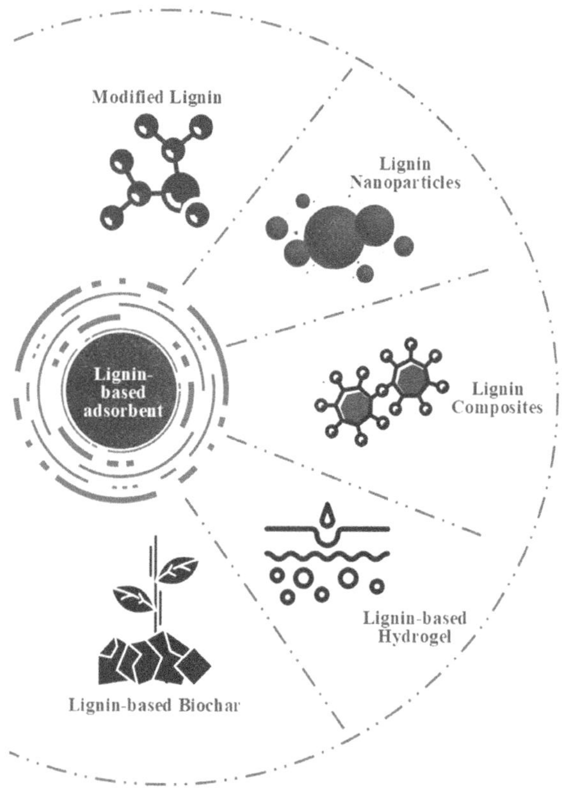

Fig. 21.1 Lignin-based materials for the adsorption of heavy metals
Source: Authors

3.1 Modified Lignin

Lignin may be modified to create a polymer that can adsorb metals through sulfur- nitrogen-, oxygen-, functional groups, and grafting. NMR spectra may be used to determine the active chemical sites in order to optimize the circumstances for the ensuing change. Carboxylic and hydroxyl groups in lignin are oxygenated functional groups that occur naturally. Oxygen-containing groups may act as a reducing agent or provide a free electron pair to chelate metal ions. The adsorption and dispersion properties of lignin can be improved by increasing the number of oxygenated groups [5].

3.2 Lignin Nanoparticles

Due to the large surface area and porosity, LNPs can further boost adsorption capacity. However, it is still challenging to produce nanoparticles with a high yield using an environmentally friendly process. To overcome this difficulty, LNPs can be created using ultrasonic treatment and solvent-shifting methods. The dispersibility, form regularity, and yield of lignin nanoparticles may all be improved by ultrasonic treatment [6]. The modified nanoparticles can efficiently remove the heavy metal ions by chemisorption and physisorption mechanisms. Furthermore, lignin-based absorbent materials may significantly shorten their adsorption time and improve their reusability.

3.3 Lignin Composites

Other potential absorbent materials for removing heavy metals are lignin composites. Hybrid composite materials with lignin and organic or inorganic materialls have better physicochemical qualities than pure materials. These materials are now more appropriate for adsorption in aqueous solution. One form of hybrid composites may be produced hydrothermally by dispersing various amounts of lignosulfonate into a graphene oxide solution [7]. Additionally, lignin-based hydrogels can transport inorganic nanoparticles in an ecologically secure manner. Behera et al. [8] utilized grass biomass lignin to create carboxymethylated tetraethoxysilane lignin nanocomposites. The surface was then changed using carboxymethylation. In CML-T nanocomposites, methyl (-CH_3) and hydroxyl (-OH) groups provide binding sites for the removal of Cr(VI) ions.

3.4 Lignin-Based Hydrogels

Biopolymer hydrogels have emerged as a more ecologically responsible, long-lasting alternative for metal remediation. To generate novel functional adsorbents, lignin-based hydrogels can be combined with natural and synthetic polymers. These novel materials have enhanced reusability and hydrophilic, morphological, and physicochemical characteristics. According to Chandna et al. [9], these adsorbents with a 3D network are generated through the chemical or physical crosslinking of the polymeric chains. According to Thakur et al. [10], hydrogels are usually distinguished by their resistance to compression, flexibility, elasticity, and, most significantly, by the fact that they are highly hydrophilic with high water-absorbing capacity without losing their insolubility. The shape and structure of the hydrogel have a significant role in the diffusion of water and contaminants across the polymer chains.

3.5 Lignin-Based Biochar

Lignin-based biochar is another potential substance for heavy metal treatment. In the absence of oxygen or with minimal oxygen present, biomass is thermally pyrolyzed, hydrothermally carbonized, or gasified to generate biochar [11]. The characteristics of the raw material that makes up this substance, such as municipal solid waste or manure, wood chips, and agricultural leftovers, as well as the thermal decomposition techniques employed to create it, have a significant impact on its efficacy. Additionally, it has been claimed that adding lignin to the biochar production results in friendly biochar adsorbents with good metal removal characteristics. This is because lignin is stable, biocompatible, and abundant [12].

3.6 Lignin-Based Adsorbents for Removal of Single Heavy Metal Ion

The current study's findings demonstrated that grafting amination, esterification, copolymerization, and compounding may create lignin-based adsorbents. The micromorphological properties of these adsorbents will vary depending on the different production techniques and reactants, which will eventually impact the adsorption effect.

Adsorption of Cu^{2+}

The frequent heavy metal contaminant in industrial effluent is Cu^{2+}. Cu^{2+} consistency in the human body can reach certain levels, resulting in severe hemolysis and anemia. Because of this, removing Cu^{2+} is a necessary social issue [13]. Li et al. [14] developed lignin-based nanocapsules which can react with branched polyethyleneimine. The higher adsorption capacity of lignin-based nanocapsules was found at 298K and pH 7, and the adsorption of Cu^{2+} in the batch adsorption process. Using lignin and montmorillonite, Sun et al. [15] created super-adsorbed hydrogels for the adsorption of Cu^{2+}. The convenience of metal ions adsorption was made possible by the interwoven network structure, various pore structures, and large specific surface area. It further demonstrates that lignin had potential uses for eliminating Cu^{2+}. These findings also demonstrate that lignin-based adsorption materials have promising adsorption potential for heavy metal ions.

Adsorption of Pb^{2+}

Pb^{2+} is a typical metal ion that is present in large amounts in soil and that poses a serious threat to industrial effluent [16]. Due to its hazardous nature and difficulty in degrading, even small amounts of lead can be harmful to a human being. According to Liu et al. [17], excessive lead consumption can result in malfunction, organ problems, and even cancer. Therefore, the creation of a system that can efficiently remove lead ions is crucial. Chen et al. [18] utilized Kraft lignin to investigate the adsorption effects on Pb^{2+} and characterized the interaction between adsorbates. Additionally, the Kraft lignin adsorption was a multivalent binding process, allowing for the practical application of the theory. Under neutral circumstances, Kraft lignin with phenolic carboxyl and hydroxyl groups had a Pb^{2+} adsorption capability of 49.8 mg/g.

Adsorption of Cr^{6+}

One trace element required by the human body is chromium (Cr). A modest amount of chromium has a significant impact on healthy growth. It is also beneficial for human development and blood sugar management. The human body will still suffer if it consumes too much chromium [19]. The two most common states of chromium are trivalent and hexavalent. Nearly little harm is caused by Cr^{3+} to the human body. However, Cr^{6+} is highly toxic and readily accumulates in the human body, interfering with the body's normal metabolism. Chemical reactions allow for the transformation of Cr^{6+} and Cr^{3+}. As a result, in addition to adsorption, valence transformation may also be used to remove Cr^{6+} from wastewater.

Adsorption of Hg^{2+}

A non-essential element and hazardous heavy metal for the human body is mercury (Hg). It may enter the human body through the food chain when present in the water and cause harm to the brain, liver, and neurological system. Gong et al. [20] employed modified lignin-bentonite and sodium alginate to create novel green composite microspheres. On Hg^{2+}, it exhibited an adsorption effect. The prepared nanocomposite was porous, 2.8 mm diameter sphere with many internal folds and a smooth plane. Additionally, batch and column adsorption tests were carried out.

Adsorption of Cd^{2+}

A certain quantity of Cd can harm the liver, kidneys, and gastrointestinal tract, soften bones, and induce liver and kidney disease. Therefore, it is crucial to remove Cd^{2+} from wastewater to efficiently avoid the hazard to human. Jin et al. [21] created a 1,2,4-triazole-3-thiol-modified adsorbent using a thiol-alkyne click reaction triggered by UV light. Under conditions of several ions coexisting, this type of adsorbent exhibited adsorption to Cd^{2+}. The most adsorption was found at 298K, 100 rpm, and pH 6. Although the removal of Cd^{2+} is impacted by the lignin-based adsorbent. The adsorption of the adsorbent can continue to function at a certain level even after multiple cycles. According to the studies, lignin-based adsorbents perform less at adsorbing Cd^{2+} than the other metal ions like Pb^{2+} and Cu^{2+}.

4. Conclusions and Perspectives

At present, lignin is used in the development of adsorbents for a number of purposes. The functional groups present increase the adsorbent's active sites and enhance its capacity to adsorb ions. The adsorption capacity is more significantly impacted by the evident variations between different forms of lignin when adsorbents are prepared. Because of the hydroxyl groups present in its macromolecular structure, active adsorption sites are thought to be responsible for this feature. However, altering the lignin's functional groups makes metal adsorption more favorable.

Only a few research have been done on the removal of anionic species, although several publications have described the removal of metal ions. It is vital to look at how effectively sorbent materials can remove certain harmful metal ions from water since they are present in an aqueous solution as anions. To enhance the novel lignin-based adsorbents' adsorption properties, biodegradability, and recyclability, further research should be done on the usage of lignin in the fabrication of hybrid materials. Therefore, streamlining and environmentally friendly adsorbent preparation should be the focus of the forthcoming study. Similarly, adsorbents can be created with high cycling capabilities by taking advantage of the chemical reaction properties between metal ions and adsorbents to increase the recyclability of adsorbents. For instance, the heavy metal ion-loaded adsorbents are recycled, and through the properties of the heavy metal ions, lignin-based supercapacitors, flame-retardant products, and fluorescence-detecting materials are generated. In addition to helping to solve the issue of wastewater pollution and achieve environmental protection, this type of multifunctional study also facilitates the value-added use of lignin resources.

References

1. Li, H., Sun, Z., Zhang, L., Tian, Y., Cui, G., & Yan, S. (2016). A cost-effective porous carbon derived from pomelo peel for the removal of methyl orange from aqueous solution. *Colloids and Surfaces A: Physicochemical and Engineering Aspects*, *489*, 191–199.
2. Ali Redha, A. (2020). Removal of heavy metals from aqueous media by biosorption. *Arab Journal of basic and applied sciences*, *27*(1), 183–193.
3. Behera, S., Bikash, C., &Hrudayanath, T. (2023b). Valorization of Lignin Based Nanoparticle from Grass Biomass: An Overview on Synthesis, Characterization and Application. *Asian J. Biol*, *17*, 34–46.
4. Wang, B., Ran, M., Fang, G., Wu, T., & Ni, Y. (2020). Biochars from lignin-rich residue of furfural manufacturing process for heavy metal ions remediation. *Materials*, *13*(5), 1037.
5. Supanchaiyamat, N., Jetsrisuparb, K., Knijnenburg, J. T., Tsang, D. C., & Hunt, A. J. (2019). Lignin materials for adsorption: Current trend, perspectives and opportunities. *Bioresource Technology*, *272*, 570–581.

6. Chauhan, P. S. (2020). Lignin nanoparticles: Eco-friendly and versatile tool for new era. *Bioresource technology reports*, *9*, 100374.
7. Klapiszewski, Ł., Siwińska-Stefańska, K., &Kołodyńska, D. (2017). Preparation and characterization of novel TiO2/lignin and TiO2-SiO2/lignin hybrids and their use as functional biosorbents for Pb (II). *Chemical Engineering Journal*, *314*, 169–181.
8. Behera, S., Rath, S., Mohapatra, S., Behera, B. C., &Thatoi, H. (2024). Hybrid synthesis of Carboxymethylated-Lignin-Tetra ethoxysilane nanocomposite for adsorption of hexavalent chromium. *Separation and Purification Technology*, 130861.
9. Chandna, S., Bhardwaj, S. K., Paul, S., & Bhaumik, J. (2020). Synthesis and applications of lignin-derived hydrogels. *Lignin: Biosynthesis and Transformation for Industrial Applications*, 231–252.
10. Thakur, S., Govender, P. P., Mamo, M. A., Tamulevicius, S., Mishra, Y. K., & Thakur, V. K. (2017). Progress in lignin hydrogels and nanocomposites for water purification: Future perspectives. *Vacuum*, *146*, 342–355.
11. Wang, J., & Wang, S. (2019). Preparation, modification and environmental application of biochar: A review. *Journal of Cleaner Production*, *227*, 1002–1022.
12. Li, L., Tong, Z., Meng, S., Li, T., Wang, H., & Chen, Y. (2020a). Lignin-based nanocapsules with tunable size for Cu (II) ion absorption. *ACS Applied Nano Materials*, *3*(11), 10835–10843.
13. Si, R., Wu, C., Yu, D., Ding, Q., & Li, R. (2021). Novel TEMPO-oxidized cellulose nanofiber/polyvinyl alcohol/polyethyleneimine nanoparticles for Cu 2+ removal in water. *Cellulose*, *28*, 10999–11011.
14. Li, Y., Wang, F., Miao, Y., Mai, Y., Li, H., Chen, X., & Chen, J. (2020b). A lignin-biochar with high oxygen-containing groups for adsorbing lead ion prepared by simultaneous oxidization and carbonization. *Bioresource technology*, *307*, 123165.
15. Sun, X. F., Hao, Y., Cao, Y., & Zeng, Q. (2019). Superadsorbent hydrogel based on lignin and montmorillonite for Cu (II) ions removal from aqueous solution. *International journal of biological macromolecules*, *127*, 511–519.
16. Li, Q., Yang, F., Zhang, J., & Zhou, C. (2020c). Magnetic Fe 3 O 4/MnO 2 core–shell nano-composite for removal of heavy metals from wastewater. *SN Applied Sciences*, *2*, 1–11.
17. Liu, W. Y., Ju, X. J., Faraj, Y., He, F., Peng, H. Y., Liu, Y. Q., ... & Chu, L. Y. (2020). Capsule membranes encapsulated with smart nanogels for facile detection of trace lead (II) ions in water. *Journal of Membrane Science*, *613*, 118523.
18. Chen, H., Qu, X., Liu, N., Wang, S., Chen, X., & Liu, S. (2018). Study of the adsorption process of heavy metals cations on Kraft lignin. *Chemical Engineering Research and Design*, *139*, 248–258.
19. Shi, X., Qiao, Y., An, X., Tian, Y., & Zhou, H. (2020). High-capacity adsorption of Cr (VI) by lignin-based composite: Characterization, performance and mechanism. *International Journal of Biological Macromolecules*, *159*, 839–849.
20. Gong, L., Kong, Y., Wu, H., Ge, Y., & Li, Z. (2021). Sodium alginate microspheres interspersed with modified lignin and bentonite (SA/ML-BT) as a green and highly effective adsorbent for batch and fixed-bed column adsorption of Hg (II). *Journal of Inorganic and Organometallic Polymers and Materials*, *31*, 659–673.
21. Jin, C., Zhang, X., Xin, J., Liu, G., Wu, G., Kong, Z., & Zhang, J. (2017). Clickable synthesis of 1, 2, 4-triazole modified lignin-based adsorbent for the selective removal of Cd (II). *ACS Sustainable Chemistry & Engineering*, *5*(5), 4086–4093.

Research and Innovations in Industrial and Marine Biotechnology: A Circular Economy 2024 – Prof. Hrudayanath Thatoi et al. (eds)

22 Study of Metal-Microbes Interaction and It's Biotechnological Exploitation

Saqlain Mustaq, Dibyendu Maity,
Soumitra Das, Pradeep K. Das Mohapatra*
Department of Microbiology, Raiganj University, Uttar Dinajpur,
Raiganj, West Bengal, India

Abstract: Over geological time spans, metals including copper (Cu), nickel (Ni), iron (Fe), zinc (Zn), cadmium (Cd), arsenic (As), chromium (Cr), platinum (Pt), silver (Ag), lead (Pb), etc., are found naturally on earth's surface. Among all living beings on earth, microorganisms utilize a variety of metals to meet their requirements of nutrition. Metals are associated with some metabolic or biochemical reactions essential for cell survival. Though some metals are essential for all organisms, others are harmful in a particular concentration. Toxicity effects of metals on microbes include activation of enzymes, disruption of cellular function, destruction of nucleic acids and proteins, hindrances of cell division and transcription, etc. Metal pollution is a common problem and reported worldwide. Several bacterial phyla like Firmicutes, Proteobacteria, Acidobacteria, Actinobacteria, Chloroflexi, etc., are known to tolerate heavy metal stress. Metal-resistant bacteria have been playing a great role regarding the control of environmental pollution through bioremediation and bioleaching. This review provides an idea about the diversity, mechanism, and function of metal-resistant bacteria.

Keywords: Heavy metals, Tannery, Industry, Hot spring, Medicine, Biofilm

1. Introduction

Over geological times pans metals including copper (Cu), nickel (Ni), iron (Fe), zinc (Zn), cadmium (Cd), arsenic (As), chromium(Cr), platinum (Pt), silver (Ag), lead (Pb) etc. are found naturally on earth surface. Metals, like Zn, Fe, Cu, Ni etc., associated with some metabolic or biochemical reactions are essential for the survival of almost all organisms. For example, Fe containing proteins during respiration, nickel or zinc containing enzymes during several metabolic reactions, copper-containing proteins during protection against free radicals are playing important role in nature [1]. In addition to the above roles, metals a real so part of some essential enzymes found in bacterial nitrogenase enzymes in nitrogen-fixing bacteria, which possess cofactors like Mo/Fe (molybdenum-iron) or V/Fe (vanadium-iron) clusters, which are also crucial for their catalytic function in nitrogen reduction. Fe, Mo, Cu,Zn found as cofactors in superoxide dismutase; Mg is found in peptidoglycan, as part of bacteriochlorophylls, or as cofactors of several other enzymes[2]

Though some metals are essential for all organisms, but metals are harmful in a particular concentration. Mercury, silver, cadmium, arsenic etc. do not participate in metabolic pathway of any organism but harmful even in very low concentrations [3].Toxicity effect of metals not only cause environmental hazards but metal toxicity is also associated with living being like bone loss, kidney Damage, neurological damage, skin cancer and lung cancer, other Sevier disease[4].

Some microorganisms resist the toxic effects of metal by changing their valence state, metabolic pathways, producing secondary metabolites. In which "Metal resistant bacteria" characterize a specific mechanism that protect them from toxic effect of metal. Bacteria developed resistant mechanism and metal resistant gene that encoded by chromosome, plasmid or transposons [5].

*Corresponding author: pkdmvu@gmail.com

DOI: 10.1201/9781003759003-22

Table 22.1 Represents the different phyla, i.e., *Proteobacteria, Firmicutes, Acidobacteria, Actinobacter, Cyanobacteria,* Chloroflexi, *etc.*, with Proteobacteria as the major phylum. Proteobacteria include a wide variety of different organisms, i.e., *Roseomonas coralli* sp., *Salmonella* sp., *Hafnia* sp., *Geobacter* sp., etc. Here second major phylumis *Firmicutes* they also include several numbers of bacteria like *Bacillus* sp., *Staphylococcus* sp., *Enterococcus* sp., *Gamella*sp. etc.

Table 22.1 Diversity of metal resistant bacteria

Phylum	Order	Representative organisms	Isolate dfrom	Features	Referen ces
Firmicutes	*Caryophanales*	*Bacillus cereus* (BPS-9)	Soil (industri-al waste)	Highest lead Accumulation potential	[18]
		Bacillus sp.	Soil	Biochar-Baciilus combination assured the best Arabidopsisgrow-thon As and Pd polluted soil	[19]
	Eubacteriales	*Acetobacterium* sp.	Paddy fields	Metal resistant gene coexist with antibiotics resistant gene	[20]
	Lactobacillales	*Enterococcushirae Streptococcusmutans*		Cpx type ATPase exporting monovalent Cu and Ag	[21]
Proteobacteria	*Rhodospirillales*	*Roseomonas coralli* sp.	Coral	Cu, Cd, As, Zn	[22]
	Desulfuromonad-ales	*Geobacter* sp.	Paddy fields	Metal resistant gene co Exists with Antibiotics resistant gene	[20]
	Enterobacterales	*Morganella* sp.	Miningsite	Toxic metal Bioremediation potential	[23]
		Salmonella enterica	Animalorigin	Antimicrobial resistant gene associ-ated with Mobile genetic Element	[24]
		Hafniasp.	Tanner yindustry	Resistanttopd, Cr, cd	[25]
	Caulobacterales	*Brevundimonas diminuta*		Enhanced Cu phytoremediation	[26]
	Rhodobacterales	*Rhodobacter capsulatus*		Gold resistant and bio accumula-tion of gold nanoparticles	[27]
		Rhodobacter sphaeroides		Have metal to larencegene	[28]
	Hyphomicrobiales	*Ochrobactrum intermedi- um BPS-20, Ochrobac- trum ciceri BPS-26*		Pd, Nibio accumulation property and have EPS	[18]
		Rhizobium leguminosarum		Intercellular sequestration of cadmiumionbyglutathione	[29]
	Pseudomonadales	*Pseudomonas putida*		Cd tolerantbacteria, Zn ion export-ed from cytoplasm via efflux system	[30]
	Burkholderiales	*Cupriavidus metallidurans BS1*	Au, Cu mine	Biomineralizing	[31]
Actinobacteria	*Solirubrobacte-rales*	*Solirubrobacter* sp	Paddy field	Metal resistant co exists with antibiotics resistantgene	[20]
	Micrococcales	*Micrococcus luteus*	Industri alwater	Arsenic Bioremediation	[32]
		Brevibacterium sp.		Passive absorption of heavy metal	[33]
Acidobacteria	*Acidobacteriales*	*Acidobacteria* sp.	Paddy Field Soil	Antibiotic resistant genepresent with metal resistant gene Secreted EPS Polysaccharide and EPSProtein to detoxifyCr	[20]
Cyanobacteria	*Synechococcales*	*Synechococcus* sp.	soil	Synthesis of metallothionin	[34]
		Synechocystis PCC6803		Zn ion exported from cytoplasm	[34]
Chloroflexi	*Chloroflexales*	*Chloroflexus* sp.	Paddy Field	Metal resistant gene present with antibiotics resistant gene	[20]

2. Genetic Determinants of Metal Resistant Bacteria

Basically metal resistant property associated with genetic determinants like plasmid and transposon [6]. While some bacteria have metal resistant property on their chromosome and *cop* operon of *Pseudomonas*is one of the example[8]. Mer operon is best studied metal to lerance system of mercury. Keygenes in volve with this operon are reductasegene (*mer*A), transport protein gene (*mer*T), extra cellular mercury binding protein gene (*mer*P), regulatory protein gene (*mer*R), gene conferring to resistance to phenyl mercury (*mer*G) and other additional gene like *mer*B, *mer*C, *mer*D, *mer*E, (associated with regulatory and transport protein gene) (Narita Me *et al.,* 2003). Furthermore for Ars operon, 3 to 5 gene are involved for arsenate tolerance (*ars*R, *ars*A, *ars*D, *ars*B and *ars*C).

3. Mechanism of Bacterial Heavy Metal Resistance

Five main mechanisms are associated with metal resistant bacteria. It should be necessary to mentioned that several resistant mechanisms performed by same bacteria. The resistance mechanism are (i) Extra cellular barrier (ii) Efflux (iii) Extracellular sequestration (iii) Intracellular sequestration (iv) Reduction of metal ions.

3.1 Extra Cellular Barrier

Bacterial capsule or plasma membrane have different ionizable group like carboxyl, amino, phosphate and hydroxyl that can absorb metal and prevent the entry of metal ion into the cell. Accumulation of metal ion also have been shown by extracellular biopolymer of *Enterobacter chloaceae, Marinobacter* sp., *klebsiella aerogenes, Actinobacter* sp. Exopolysaccharide (EPS) synthesis also associated with metal tolerance; for example, resistant strain of *Pseudomonas aeruginosa* synthesize twice exopolysaccharide as compare to sensitive strain [9].

3.2 Efflux (Active Transport of Metalion)

Bacteria efflux metal ions from cells by using an active transport system, and it is the most attending resistant system of metal resistance bacteria. ATP -hydrolysis or the utilization of an electrochemical gradient, provides the required energy for the effluxion of metal ions. During transportation of essential nutrients, some metal ions enter into the cell; for example, chromate ions can be transported via sulfate transport systems (Cervantes C *et al.*,1994), Similarly, in *Ralstonia metallidurans*, cadmium (Cd), zinc (Zn), and manganese (Mn) can enter the cell during magnesium transport system [10].

3.3 Extra Cellular Sequestration

It is the accumulation of metal ions in the periplasm or outer membrane by cellular components. Cop A, Cop B (periplasmic protein) and Cop C (outer membrane protein) bind with Cu ions and cause accumulation of metal ions. As a result, colonies turn blue. The strategy is employed by *Pseudomonas syringae.* In this process, the sensitive strain accumulates Cu ions in free ionic form, which are toxic for cells, whereas the Cu-resistant strain accumulates Cu as a complex form and transports it to the cytoplasm. Here, Cu-tolerant *Pseudomonas pickettii* strain accumulates Cu in periplasm or outer membrane [11].

3.4 Inter Cellular Sequestration

The binding of ions or metals in the bacterial cytoplasm with diverse molecules are facilitates their segregation from other constituents of biological systems. Metallothioneins, characterized by a reduced number of cysteine residues, are produced in diverse species, including cyanobacteria. For instance, *Synechococcus sp.* PCC 7942 synthesizes metallothionein, which is determined by two genes, smtA and smtB. These genes are induced by the existence of Cd and Zn, showcasing a biological response to heavy metal stress [12].

3.5 Reduction of Metal Ions

Bacterial metal reduction process is also associated with bacterial energy generation process, in which metal act as an electrondonororan electronacceptor. Basically, anaerobic bacteria are uses metal during respiration. Another aspect of metal reduction is associated with reducing toxicity because they reduced toxic metal to less toxic form [13]. The predominant micro organisms involved in metal reduction process in the environment are represented in (Table 22.2).

Reduction of Hg^{2+} to Hg^{0} is associated with MerA gene and performed by most of the microorganisms. On the other hand, a different approach is MerP/MerT, which is also associated with mercury resistance in marine bacteria[14].

4. Applications

Various technologies and methods are involved in the remediation of heavy metal-contaminated environments, including chemical precipitation, oxidation/reduction, filtration, ion exchange, reverse osmosis, membrane technology, evaporation, electrochemical treatment, etc. Biological methods for controlling metal pollution became more interesting and widespread. Due to resistance mechanism Metal-resistant bacteria are able to neutralize the toxic effects of metal by absorbing metal via changing the valence of metal and making the metal insoluble. The term metal-resistant bacteria in environmental purposes is mainly associated with two terms: bioremediation and bioleaching.

Table 22.2 Example of metalion reduction by metal resistant bacteria

Class	Representative organisms	Reduction of metal	References
Deltaproteobacteria Deltaproteobacteri Bacilli	*Geobacter sp. Geobacter metallireducens Bacillus thermoamylovorans*	Fe^{3+}/Fe^{2+}	[35]
Gammaproteobacteria	*Shewanella putrefaciens*	Mn^{4+}/Mn^{2+}	[36]
Deltaproteobacteria Actinobacteria Alphaproteobactera Actinobacteria	*Desulfomicrobium norvegicum, Microbacteriumsp. Ochrobacterium intermedium, Brevibacterium*	Cr^{6+}/Cr^{3+}	[37]
Gammaproteobacteria	*Pseudomonas* Sp.		[38]
Betaproteobacteria	*Thiobacillus ferrooxidans*	Mo^{6+}/Mo^{5+}	[39]
Gammaproteobacteria	*Stenotrophomonas sp.*	Au^{3+}/Au^{0}	[40]
Betaproteobacteria, Bacilli Gammaproteobacteria	*Ralstoniametallidurans, Bacillus thermoamylovorans, Shewanella oneidensis*	$Se^{6+}/Se^{4+}/Se^{0}$ Se^{4+}/Se^{0}	[38]
Gammaproteobacteria Deltaproteobacteria	*Shewanella oneidensis, Geobacter metallireducens*	V^{5+}/V^{4+}	[36]
Bacilli	*Staphylococcus aureus*	As^{5+}/As^{3+}	[40]
Deltaproteobacteria Gammaproteobacteria Clostridia	*Desulfovibriode sulfuricans, Shewanella putrefaciens, Thermoterrabacterium ferrireducens*	U^{6+}/U^{4+}	[41]
Bacilli Gammaproteobacteria	*Bacilluscereus, Klebsiella pneumoniae*	Hg^{2+}/Hg^{0}	[42]
Gammaproteobacteria	*Pseudomonas stutzeri*		[43]
Bacilli Gammaproteobacteria	*Bacillus thermoamylovoras, Shewanella oneidensis*	Te^{4+}/Te^{0}	[44]
Deltaproteobacteria	*Geobacter sulfurreducens*		[45]
Gammaproteobacteria	*Pseudomonas* Sp.		[38]

4.1 Bioremediation

Bioremediation is a process in which metals are removed from the environment without creating auxiliary metabolites; basically, it's a green-based application. *Rhizobium leguminosarumbv. viciae* has biosorption characteristics of cadmium and cobalt. *Rhizopus stolonifer* is associated with the removal of lead and mercury from aqueous solution. *Aspergillus niger and Penicillium* sp. have biosorption properties for nickel, chromium, and cadmium. *Aspergillus niger is* also responsible for the bioremediation of tannery waste [15].

One recent study highlights the role of the merB gene from *Organomonasaeruginosa*, which encodes organomercuriallyase, a crucial enzyme for mercury resistance. This enzyme is break down the toxic organomercurial compounds into less toxic forms, it plays an essential role in bioremediation. To enhance production and facilitate further study, the merB gene was successfully cloned and expressed in *E. coli* BL21 (DE3).

4.2 Bioleaching

Another approach bioleaching is the extraction of metal from various solid waste. Bioleaching is also a green-based application. *E. coli is*used for bioleaching of heavy metals [16]. Nowadays, the efficacy of bioleaching on a commercial scale for leaching copper and gold is increasing. There are two types of pathways: one is a direct approach, where bacteria attach directly to the metal surface and facilitate the leaching process[17]. Example and reaction shown in (Table 22.3).

Table 22.3 Example and reaction of bioleaching

Metalleaching	Organism involved	Reaction
Cu leaching	*Leptospirillum ferrooxidans Acidithiobacillus ferrooxidans*	a. Oxygen-dependent-$CuS+2O_2—Cu^{2+}+SO_4^{2-}$ b. Oxygen-independent –$CuS + 8 Fe_3+ +4 H_2O—Cu^{2+}+8Fe^{2+}+SO_4^{2-}+8H+$
Gold leaching	*Acidithiobacillus ferrooxidans Acidithiobacillus thiooxidans Leptospirillum ferrooxidans*	$2FeAsS[Au]+7O_2+2H_2O+H_2SO_4—Fe_2(SO_4)_3+2H_3AsO_4+$ [Au]
Uranium leaching	*Acidithiobacillus ferrooxidans*	$UO_2 + Fe_2 (SO_4)_3 — UO_2SO_4+2 FeSO_4$

Thus, copper and iron sulfide ores such as pyrrhotite (FeS) and covellite (CuS) are nowadays readily leached because of their higher solubility and reactivity nature. Whereas, because of low solubility lead and molybdenum ores lesser-used in leaching process.

5. Conclusion and Future Prospects

The widespread use of microorganisms resistant to metals in bioremediation and bioleaching is admirable. Focusing on bioremediation technology and genetic engineering advancements, numerous microorganisms have been designed to exhibit desirable characteristics through overexpression of proteins and peptides that neutralize or chelate metal ions. In summary, this research area is crucial to the leaching and bioremediation of metal-contaminated sites; hence it must be actively explored. Accordingly, the field of study for microbial fuel cells (MFCs) and biofilm-mediated bioremediation has to be expanded in recent years. These would eventually make it easier to create an environment free of metal pollution. Moreover, metal-resistant bacteria should be in agricultural yields because safe food demands for the world are rapidly increasing.

References

1. C. Rensing and G. Grass, "Escherichia coli mechanisms of copper homeostasis in a changing environment," *FEMS Microbiol. Rev.*, vol. 27, no. 2–3, pp. 197–213, Jun. 2003, doi: 10.1016/S0168-6445(03)00049-4.
2. H. L. Ehrlich, "Technical Potential for Bioleaching and Biobeneficiation of Ores to Recover Base Metals (Other than Iron or Copper), Platinum-Group Metals and Silver," in *Biomining*, D. E. Rawlings, Ed., Berlin, Heidelberg: Springer Berlin Heidelberg, 1997, pp. 129–150. doi: 10.1007/978-3-662-06111-4_7.
3. W. Bazzi *et al.*, "Heavy Metal Toxicity in Armed Conflicts Potentiates AMR in A. baumannii by Selecting for Antibiotic and Heavy Metal Co-resistance Mechanisms," *Front. Microbiol.*, vol. 11, p. 68, Feb. 2020, doi: 10.3389/fmicb.2020.00068.
4. H. K. Rokadia and S. Agarwal, "Serum Heavy Metals and Obstructive Lung Disease," *Chest*, vol. 143, no. 2, pp. 388–397, Feb. 2013, doi: 10.1378/chest.12-0595.
5. M. R. Bruins, S. Kapil, and F. W. Oehme, "Microbial Resistance to Metals in the Environment," *Ecotoxicol. Environ. Saf.*, vol. 45, no. 3, pp. 198–207, Mar. 2000, doi: 10.1006/eesa.1999.1860.
6. D. H. Nies, "Microbial heavy-metal resistance," *Appl. Microbiol. Biotechnol.*, vol. 51, no. 6, pp. 730–750, Jun. 1999, doi: 10.1007/s002530051457.
7. R. Mukhopadhyay, B. P. Rosen, L. T. Phung, and S. Silver, "Microbial arsenic: from geocycles to genes and enzymes", Accessed: May 28, 2025. [Online]. Available: https://onlinelibrary.wiley.com/doi/10.1111/j.1574-6976.2002.tb00617.x
8. C. Cervantes *et al.*, "Interactions of chromium with microorganisms and plants," *FEMS Microbiol. Rev.*, vol. 25, no. 3, pp. 335–347, May 2001, doi: 10.1111/j.1574-6976.2001.tb00581.x.
9. F. Malekzadeh, A. Farazmand, H. Ghafourian, M. Shahamat, M. Levin, and R. R. Colwell, "Uranium accumulation by a bacterium isolated from electroplating effluent," *World J. Microbiol. Biotechnol.*, vol. 18, no. 4, pp. 295–302, Jun. 2002, doi: 10.1023/A:1015215718810.
10. L. A. Zacharoff, D. J. Morrone, and D. R. Bond, "Geobacter sulfurreducens Extracellular Multiheme Cytochrome PgcA Facilitates Respiration to Fe(III) Oxides But Not Electrodes," *Front. Microbiol.*, vol. 8, p. 2481, Dec. 2017, doi: 10.3389/fmicb.2017.02481.
11. M. R. Bruins, S. Kapil, and F. W. Oehme, "Pseudomonas pickettii: A Common Soil and Groundwater Aerobic Bacteria with Pathogenic and Biodegradation Properties," *Ecotoxicol. Environ. Saf.*, vol. 47, no. 2, pp. 105–111, Oct. 2000, doi: 10.1006/eesa.2000.1951.
12. E. Pinto, T. C. S. Sigaud-kutner, M. A. S. Leitão, O. K. Okamoto, D. Morse, and P. Colepicolo, "HEAVY METAL–INDUCED OXIDATIVE STRESS IN ALGAE[1]," *J. Phycol.*, vol. 39, no. 6, pp. 1008–1018, Dec. 2003, doi: 10.1111/j.0022-3646.2003.02-193.x.
13. T. Barkay, S. M. Miller, and A. O. Summers, "Bacterial mercury resistance from atoms to ecosystems," *FEMS Microbiol. Rev.*, vol. 27, no. 2–3, pp. 355–384, Jun. 2003, doi: 10.1016/S0168-6445(03)00046-9.
14. Q. Gui, J. Zhang, K. Hu, Q. Ouyang, S. Shi, and X. Chen, "Hydrogen bonding-induced hydrophobic assembly yields strong affinity of an adsorptive membrane for ultrafast removal of trace organic micropollutants from water," *J. Mater. Chem. A*, vol. 8, no. 32, pp. 16487–16496, 2020, doi: 10.1039/D0TA05469K.
15. K. Jyoti, K. Soni, and R. Chandra, "Pharmaceutical industrial wastewater exhibiting the co-occurrence of biofilm-forming genes in the multidrug-resistant bacterial community poses a novel environmental threat," *Aquat. Toxicol.*, vol. 273, p. 107019, Aug. 2024, doi: 10.1016/j.aquatox.2024.107019.
16. S. Vyas and Y.-P. Ting, "Sequential biological process for molybdenum extraction from hydrodesulphurization spent catalyst," *Chemosphere*, vol. 160, pp. 7–12, Oct. 2016, doi: 10.1016/j.chemosphere.2016.06.060.
17. S. K. Sen, S. Raut, T. K. Dora, and P. K. D. Mohapatra, "Contribution of hot spring bacterial consortium in cadmium and lead bioremediation through quadratic programming model," *J. Hazard. Mater.*, vol. 265, pp. 47–60, Jan. 2014, doi: 10.1016/j.jhazmat.2013.11.036.
18. B. Sharma and P. Shukla, "A comparative analysis of heavy metal bioaccumulation and functional gene annotation towards multiple metal resistant potential by Ochrobactrum intermedium BPS-20 and Ochrobactrum

ciceri BPS-26," *Bioresour. Technol.*, vol. 320, p. 124330, Jan. 2021, doi: 10.1016/j.biortech.2020.124330.

19. M. Simiele *et al.*, "In-depth study to decipher mechanisms underlying Arabidopsis thaliana tolerance to metal(loid) soil contamination in association with biochar and/or bacteria," *Environ. Exp. Bot.*, vol. 182, p. 104335, Feb. 2021, doi: 10.1016/j.envexpbot.2020.104335.
20. J. Zhang, Q. Shi, S. Fan, Y. Zhang, M. Zhang, and J. Zhang, "Distinction between Cr and other heavy–metal–resistant bacteria involved in C/N cycling in contaminated soils of copper producing sites," *J. Hazard. Mater.*, vol. 402, p. 123454, Jan. 2021, doi: 10.1016/j.jhazmat.2020.123454.
21. A. Odermatt, H. Suter, R. Krapf, and M. Solioz, "Primary structure of two P-type ATPases involved in copper homeostasis in Enterococcus hirae," *J. Biol. Chem.*, vol. 268, no. 17, pp. 12775–12779, June 1993.
22. F. Li *et al.*, "Roseomonas coralli sp. nov., a heavy metal resistant bacterium isolated from coral," *Int. J. Syst. Evol. Microbiol.*, vol. 71, no. 2, Feb. 2021, doi: 10.1099/ijsem.0.004624.
23. O. U. Orji *et al.*, "Toxic metals bioremediation potentials of *Paenibacillus* sp. strain SEM1 and *Morganella* sp. strain WEM7 isolated from Enyigba Pb–Zn mining site, Ebonyi State Nigeria," *Bioremediation J.*, vol. 25, no. 4, pp. 285–296, Oct. 2021, doi: 10.1080/10889868.2020.1871315.
24. M. H. K. Johansson, V. Bortolaia, S. Tansirichaiya, F. M. Aarestrup, A. P. Roberts, and T. N. Petersen, "Detection of mobile genetic elements associated with antibiotic resistance in Salmonella enterica using a newly developed web tool: MobileElementFinder," *J. Antimicrob. Chemother.*, vol. 76, no. 1, pp. 101–109, Jan. 2021, doi: 10.1093/jac/dkaa390.
25. L. W. Marzan, M. Hossain, S. A. Mina, Y. Akter, and A. M. M. A. Chowdhury, "Isolation and biochemical characterization of heavy-metal resistant bacteria from tannery effluent in Chittagong city, Bangladesh: Bioremediation viewpoint," *Egypt. J. Aquat. Res.*, vol. 43, no. 1, pp. 65–74, Mar. 2017, doi: 10.1016/j.ejar.2016.11.002.
26. M. Rathi and Y. K N, "Brevundimonas diminuta MYS6 associated Helianthus annuus L. for enhanced copper phytoremediation," *Chemosphere*, vol. 263, p. 128195, Jan. 2021, doi: 10.1016/j.chemosphere.2020.128195.
27. D. Maity, P. Kundu, and S. Adhikari (Nee Pramanik), "Bioremediation of 4-chlorophenol and catechol as a mixed compound from pharmaceutical waste water by a microbial consortium and optimization of process parameters by response surface methodology for better performance in bio reactor," *Bioremediation J.*, pp. 1–26, July 2025, doi: 10.1080/10889868.2025.2522821.
28. H. Johnson, H. Cho, and M. Choudhary, "Bacterial Heavy Metal Resistance Genes and Bioremediation Potential," *Comput. Mol. Biosci.*, vol. 09, no. 01, pp. 1–12, 2019, doi: 10.4236/cmb.2019.91001.
29. A. A. D. Lima E Silva *et al.*, "Heavy metal tolerance (Cr, Ag and Hg) in bacteria isolated from sewage," *Braz. J. Microbiol.*, vol. 43, no. 4, pp. 1620–1631, Dec. 2012, doi: 10.1590/S1517-83822012000400047.
30. S.-W. Lee, E. Glickmann, and D. A. Cooksey, "Chromosomal Locus for Cadmium Resistance in *Pseudomonas putida* Consisting of a Cadmium-Transporting ATPase and a MerR Family Response Regulator," *Appl. Environ. Microbiol.*, vol. 67, no. 4, pp. 1437–1444, Apr. 2001, doi: 10.1128/AEM.67.4.1437-1444.2001.
31. S. H. Mazhar *et al.*, "Comparative Insights Into the Complete Genome Sequence of Highly Metal Resistant Cupriavidus metallidurans Strain BS1 Isolated From a Gold–Copper Mine," *Front. Microbiol.*, vol. 11, p. 47, Feb. 2020, doi: 10.3389/fmicb.2020.00047.
32. S. Sher, S. Sultan, and A. Rehman, "Characterization of multiple metal resistant Bacillus licheniformis and its potential use in arsenic contaminated industrial wastewater," *Appl. Water Sci.*, vol. 11, no. 4, p. 69, Apr. 2021, doi: 10.1007/s13201-021-01407-3.
33. J. Taniguchi, H. Hemmi, K. Tanahashi, N. Amano, T. Nakayama, and T. Nishino, "Zinc biosorption by a zinc-resistant bacterium, Brevibacterium sp. strain HZM-1," *Appl. Microbiol. Biotechnol.*, vol. 54, no. 4, pp. 581–588, Oct. 2000, doi: 10.1007/s002530000415.
34. G. R. Ybarra and R. Webb, "Effects of Divalent Metal Cations and Resistance Mechanisms of the Cyanobacterium Synechococcus SP. Strain PCC 7942," *J. Hazard. Subst. Res.*, vol. 2, no. 1, Jan. 1999, doi: 10.4148/1090-7025.1011.
35. O. L. Snoeyenbos-West, K. P. Nevin, R. T. Anderson, and D. R. Lovley, "Enrichment of Geobacter Species in Response to Stimulation of Fe(III) Reduction in Sandy Aquifer Sediments," *Microb. Ecol.*, vol. 39, no. 2, pp. 153–167, Feb. 2000, doi: 10.1007/s002480000018.
36. C. R. Myers and K. H. Nealson, "Bacterial manganese reduction and growth with manganese oxide as the sole electron acceptor," *Science*, vol. 240, no. 4857, pp. 1319–1321, June 1988, doi: 10.1126/science.240.4857.1319.
37. C. Michel, M.-T. Giudici-Orticoni, F. Baymann, and M. Bruschi, "Bioremediation of Chromate by Sulfate-Reducing Bacteria, Cytochromes c3 and hydrogenases," *Water Air Soil Pollut. Focus*, vol. 3, no. 3, pp. 161–169, May 2003, doi: 10.1023/A:1023969415656.
38. M. Faisal and S. Hasnain, "Comparative study of Cr(VI) uptake and reduction in industrial effluent by Ochrobactrum intermedium and Brevibacterium sp," *Biotechnol. Lett.*, vol. 26, no. 21, pp. 1623–1628, Nov. 2004, doi: 10.1007/s10529-004-3184-1.
39. T. Sugio, Y. Tsujita, T. Katagiri, K. Inagaki, and T. Tano, "Reduction of Mo6+ with elemental sulfur by Thiobacillus ferrooxidans," *J. Bacteriol.*, vol. 170, no. 12, pp. 5956–5959, Dec. 1988, doi: 10.1128/jb.170.12.5956-5959.1988.
40. G. Ji and S. Silver, "Reduction of arsenate to arsenite by the ArsC protein of the arsenic resistance operon of Staphylococcus aureus plasmid pI258.," *Proc. Natl. Acad. Sci.*, vol. 89, no. 20, pp. 9474–9478, Oct. 1992, doi: 10.1073/pnas.89.20.9474.

41. D. R. Lovley, E. J. P. Phillips, Y. A. Gorby, and E. R. Landa, "Microbial reduction of uranium," *Nature*, vol. 350, no. 6317, pp. 413–416, Apr. 1991, doi: 10.1038/350413a0.
42. [25] A. Gupta, K. Matsui, J.-F. Lo, and S. Silver, "Molecular basis for resistance to silver cations in Salmonella," *Nat. Med.*, vol. 5, no. 2, pp. 183–188, Feb. 1999, doi: 10.1038/5545.
43. D. Reniero, E. Mozzon, E. Galli, and P. Barbieri, "Two aberrant mercury resistance transposons in the Pseudomonas stutzeri plasmid pPB," *Gene*, vol. 208, no. 1, pp. 37–42, Feb. 1998, doi: 10.1016/s0378-1119(97)00641-0.
44. A. I. Slobodkin, "[Thermophilic microbial metal reduction]," *Mikrobiologiia*, vol. 74, no. 5, pp. 581–595, 2005.
45. J. R. Lloyd, V. A. Sole, C. V. Van Praagh, and D. R. Lovley, "Direct and Fe(II)-mediated reduction of technetium by Fe(III)-reducing bacteria," *Appl. Environ. Microbiol.*, vol. 66, no. 9, pp. 3743–3749, Sept. 2000, doi: 10.1128/AEM.66.9.3743-3749.2000.

Research and Innovations in Industrial and Marine Biotechnology: A Circular Economy 2024 – Prof. Hrudayanath Thatoi et al. (eds)

23 Health Consequences of Biomass Fuel Usage on Women and Children in Rural Low Income Households: A Study from Bankura II C.D. Block, Bankura District, West Bengal

Manasi Chattaraj[1], Aditi Goswami
Department of Geography, Bankura University,
Bankura, West Bengal, India

Abhishek Chattaraj
Department of Allied Health Science, Brainware University,
Kolkata, West Bengal, India

Raja Paramanik
Department of Geography, Calcutta University,
Kolkata, West Bengal, India

Sourav Chattaraj[2]
Centre for Industrial Biotechnology Research,
Siksha 'O' Anusandhan Deemed to be University,
Bhubanseswar, Odisha, India

Abstract: Smoke exposure and indoor air pollution (IAP) from traditional biomass fuel burning is a major cause of morbidity among women and children in rural low-income households. Over 50% of the Indian population still relies on biomass and coal, ranking lowest on energy ladder. Inefficient solid fuel burning release toxic pollutants and increase toxin concentration within a confined area. Women and children are the worst victims facing diseases like pneumonia, obstructive pulmonary disease, asthma, cancer, tuberculosis, infertility, low birth weight, dermatological issues and more. Bankura District, with 43% rural low-income households is particularly vulnerable to IAP. This paper aims to assess the impact of biomass energy use on woman and children of Bankura II Community Development Block and propose geospatial and Artificial Intelligence based mitigation strategies.

Keywords: Biomass fuel, Energy ladder, Energy poverty, Household energy, IAP

1. Introduction

Biomass fuel refers to organic materials used for energy production. Though biomass fuels are renewable and have carbon-neutral potential, but their low energy density causes higher pollution levels than fossil fuels. Despite technological and knowledge advancements, low-income groups in the developing countries continue to rely on biomass fuels like firewood, crop residues, and animal dung for their household energy needs due to their wide availability and affordability [1]. However, their semi-aerobic combustion in poorly ventilated indoor environments leads to severe indoor air pollution (IAP) [2,3]. Exposure to IAP, coupled with limited healthcare access and inadequate awareness, poses significant health risk, particularly for women and children [4,5]. IAP is a shadow killer that accounts for about 7.7% of world's morbidity and morality [6]. Geospatial technology and

Corresponding author: [1]monaverygood@gmail.com, [2]souravchattaraj@soa.ac.in

DOI: 10.1201/9781003759003-23

statistical tool based research across developing countries demonstrated linkage between biomass fuel usage and health issues of women and children [7,8]. Studies by [9,10] highlighted that exposure to both low and high-grade biomass fuel leads to dizziness, chest pains, forgetfulness, shortness of breath, irritation in eyes, night phlegm etc. among rural women and children. World Health Organisation [11] highlighted the health crisis due to Household Air Pollution, noting that 60% of premature fatalities due to IAP occurred in women and children due to more exposure than men. Similar studies in Bangladesh, Kenya and Vietnam [12-14] confirmed that poor Indoor Air Quality (IAQ) correlates with increased respiratory ailments. In India, [15] deviced PAF (Population Attributable Fraction) method to assess disease cases linked to biomass fuel use and [16] further explored impacts of IAP. [17] analyzed annual health survey data to portray the adverse effects of biomass fuel combustion on children's respiratory health in Uttar Pradesh. In West Bengal, [18] investigated how biomass fuel use affects rural women's health in Medinipur and Jhargram. While these researches provide significant insights, further region specific studies are required. Hence this study aims to address this gap by focusing on Bankura II C.D. Block, assessing the impact of IAP on women and children in low-income rural households, prepare AI and Geospatial Technology based model and provide some insightful suggestions aimed at safeguarding public health.

1.1 Objectives

The present study aims to

a. identify the type of biomass fuel used in rural low-income households of Bankura II CD block.
b. assess health impacts of biomass fuel use and associated IAP on women and children of low-income households.
c. suggest some controlling measures.
d. prepare AI and Geospatial Technology-based model for providing sustainable solution.

1.2 Study Area

Bankura II CD block of Bankura District, West Bengal is a part of backward Jangalmahal [19] with latitudinal extension between 23°13'N and 23°23'N and 87°1' East to 87°15' East longitude, engulfing an area of 220.84 km^2 (Fig. 23.1.). The CD block consists of 7-gram panchayats (GP) with 144 inhabited villages and rural background with population of 140,864, out of which 37.63% belonging to low-income group [20]. The villages selected for the study were Agyanandanpur, Bagneja, Bankata, Bhaktabandh, Bheduapurushottampur, Brindabanpur, Chapatora, Chotochaka, Domanbandi, Jarka, Jugsahar, Katapesia, khejurbediya and Telighara.

2. Database and Methodology

Both primary and secondary data has been used. Interview schedule-based survey and group discussions are the primary sources. Secondary data has been collected from Census handbooks, Human development report of Bankura district. Out of total 144 villages across 7GPs, 2 villages from each panchayats were selected on simple random sampling for the survey. 700 samples (7 GPs x 2 villages x 50 respondents) purposively selected, focusing on non-smoking house-wives and children under 5 years. Statistical techniques like Mean, Standard Deviation,

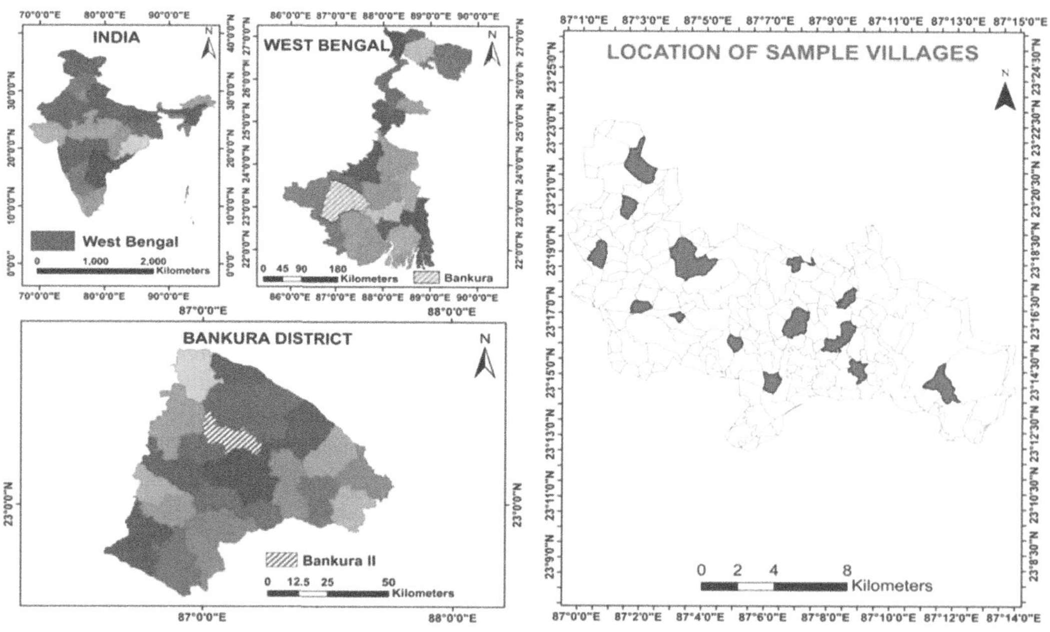

Fig. 23.1 Location of the study area

Source: Prepared by Authors in ArcGIS

Coefficient of variation, Correlation and Regression were used. Cartographic techniques (bar, pie, line) were used. Data processed in SPSS (v22) and geospatial maps prepared in ArcGIS (v10.8).

3. Results and Discussions

In the study area, high cost of LPG/electricity, limited access to alternatives and preference for traditional cooking methods drive widespread biomass fuel use (Fig. 23.2.). Among respondents, 18.1% aged between 13-25 years, 64.6% were 25-45, 12% were 45-60 and rest 5.3% above 60 years, aiding to analysis of exposure duration and IAP-related illnesses. 60.14% had children below five, who, along with women, bear a disproportionate burden of IAP as they spend more time near the cooking places and on fuel collection.

3.1 Pattern of Fuel Usage in the Study Area

Respondents mostly use wood, charcoal, cow dung cake and agricultural waste (Fig. 23.2., Fig. 23.7.), which ranks lowest in energy ladder, with maximum negative impacts (Fig. 23.3.).

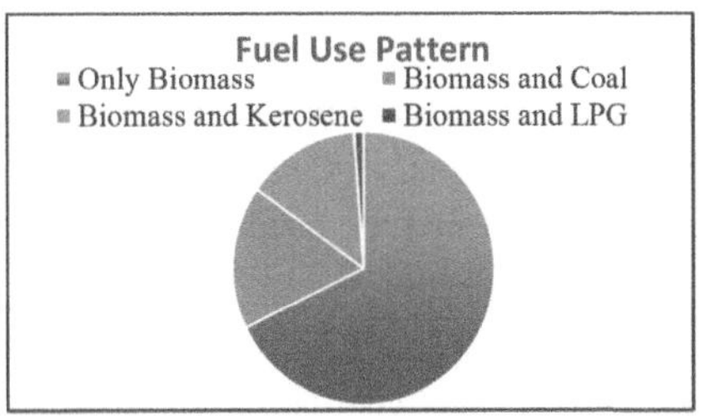

Fig. 23.2 Fuel use pattern of respondents

Source: Primary Survey

Since agriculture is the mainstay [21,22], crop residues are readily available, with 49% of the respondents using it as fuel. Despite the availability of subsidized LPG under Ujjwala Yojana, only 33% of respondents use it (Fig. 23.2.). Bankura, being part of Jangalmahal, provides

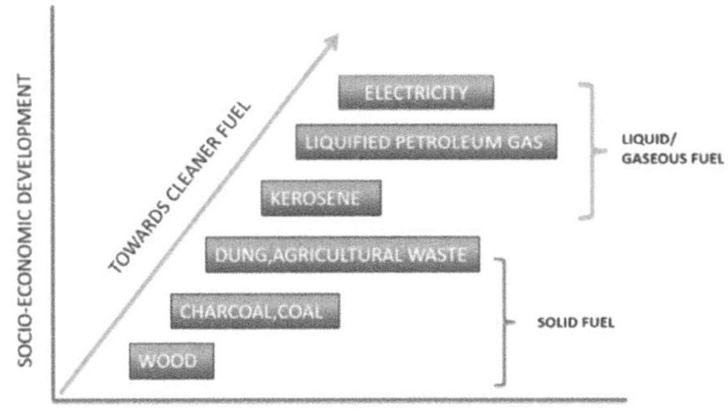

Fig. 23.3 The energy ladder

Source: Primary Survey

lush forests, so respondents use twigs, dried leaves and branches of trees as fuel. The animal husbandry of the area is also notable, owing to 59.57% people using mixture of crop residue, leaves and dung cakes as the major biomass fuel. Kerosene is the least preferred fuel (18%) used mainly for igniting.

3.2 Impacts of IAP on Women and Children

Indoor air pollution from prolonged biomass fuel exposure, heighten the risks of respiratory, cardiovascular, and ocular diseases [23]. The gender gap in socio-economic perspectives in the study area leads to greater IAP related disease incidence among women. The impacts of IAP are direct (health ailments), indirect, and secondary—extending beyond health to socio-economic and cognitive domains, hindering regional development. Respiratory Diseases includes Pneumonia, Acute Lower Respiratory Infections, Chronic Obstructive Pulmonary Disease, Lungs Cancer and Tuberculosis. Obstetrics disfunctionability related issues includes Neonatal and Perinatal Mortality and Low Weight at Birth (Fig. 23.4.). The skin and eye related problems in women above 55 include itchy, dry, red eyes, and cataract. Microbial growth in polluted indoors make the condition more critical. Fuel collection is hazardous due to attack of pests or wild animals. The dung cakes made by women contain

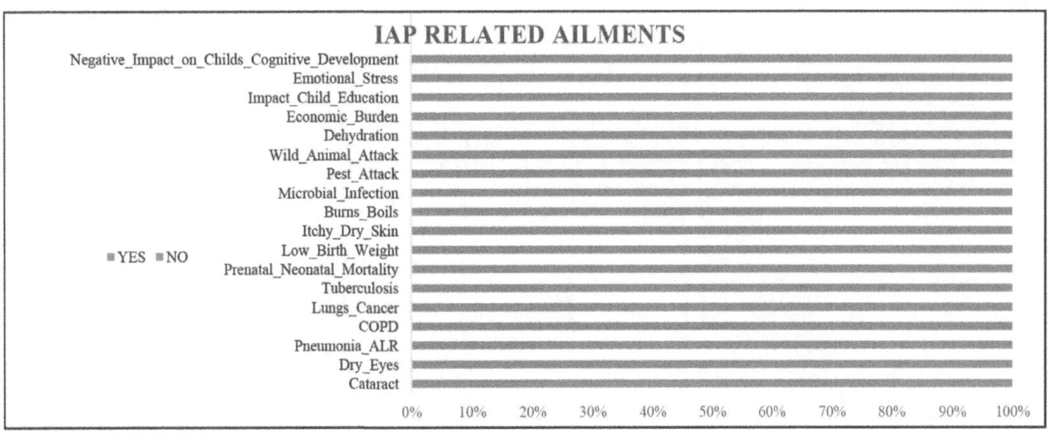

Fig. 23.4 IAP related issues in women and children

Source: Primary Survey

several microbes which causes skin diseases. Continuous heat exposure causes dehydration and fatigue, impacting productivity, strength and cognitive development [24].

The overburden of cost of these diseases adds to the already fragile economy, affecting children's education and increasing school absenteeism [25]. Self-reported symptoms/conditions and supporting medical evidences revealed 13 IAP related ailments. Out of these diseases, Microbial Infections (83%), Itchy dry skin (63.6%), Dehydration (61.4%), Low Birth Weight (61.3%) were more common (Fig. 23.4.). Lungs cancer or similar symptoms (3.7%) were least frequent. Though secondary, but emotional stress of women (94.6%) due to family ailments caused by IAP exposure pose a great mental health issue, which needs urgent attention.

Relation between Exposure to IAP and Diseases Caused

Average number of disease per person was calculated and correlated with exposure hours and exposure years. In both the cases strong positive correlation was observed (R^2 value of 0.9374 and 0.9322 respectively) to the number of diseases ($P<0.05$) (Fig. 23.5., 23.6.).

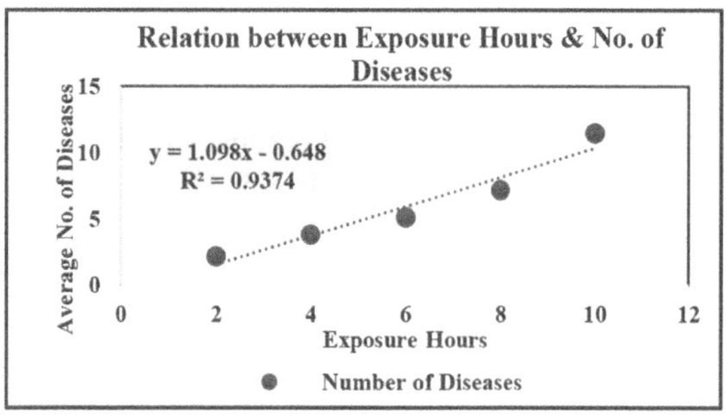

Fig. 23.5 Exposure hours & no. of diseases

Source: Primary Survey

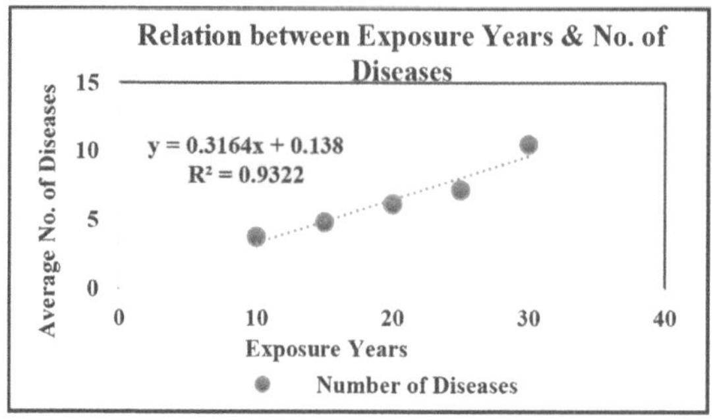

Fig. 23.6 Exposure years & no. of diseases

Source: Primary Survey

3.3 Suggestions and Recommendations

For tackling the issues of IAP on women and children in rural low-income households of Bankura II CD Block and ensure sustainable development, the following suggestions are prescribed-

a. **Changing fuel use pattern and creating awareness:** Promote transition from conventional to non-conventional energy. Conducting awareness campaigns on the harmful side-effects of traditional fuels and benefits of clean alternatives.
b. **Modification in cooking method:** Fuel efficient stoves, ovens should be used. Pressure cookers or closed utensils may be used to reduce the time for cooking, decreasing the exposure to IAP.
c. **Improved Ventilation:** Promote open kitchen or kitchen with cross ventilation for households using low grade biomass fuels.
d. **Leveraging Renewable Energy Solutions:** Facilitating solar cook-stove distribution and making arrangements for small-scale biogas plants.

Fig. 23.7 Survey pictures showing- a) woman using traditional biomass fuel; b) Cow dung cakes; c) wood charcoal; d,e) dung mixed with straw for making dung cakes; f) Dry firewood

Source: Authors

Table 23.1 Diseases caused by IAP and their radiographic impressions

Pollutant	Disease	Receptor Binding	Radiographic Sign
PM 2.5, PM10, NO2, SO2	Tuberculosis	C-type lectin receptors	lungs Consolidation, Mediastinal/hilar adenopathy, Pleural Effusion
Carbon Monoxide (CO), PM 2.5, PM 10, NO2, SO2	COPD	Adenosine receptors	Ground glass opacity/ hyperlucency
Any air pollutant	Cancer	___	Mass lesions, lung volume loss, pleural effusion/collapse

Source: Authors

e. **Covering:** Faces and nose should be covered with masks or piece of cloth during cooking to reduce the intake of pollutants.

f. **Strengthening Healthcare Systems:** Facilitating access to affordable healthcare and arranging continuous Indoor air quality monitoring in most polluted pockets can be an effective solution.

g. **Governmental Support and collaborative community efforts:** Different sectors of the government, local NGOs, women's self-help groups, and community leaders should work together for solving the problems of IAP.

3.4 Role of Radiology in Providing Solutions

Radiology plays a pivotal role in diagnosing, prognosis and managing diseases caused by IAP [26], establishing linkage between specific pollutants to distinct diseases and their radiographic impressions [27,28] (Table 23.1.), making radiology an effective tool for IAP-related health assessment. So regular radiological monitoring of vulnerable populations could be effective in reducing fatality rates.

3.5 AI & Geospatial Technology-Based Model for Reducing the Impacts of IAP

AI and Geospatial integration can yield effective results in identifying, managing and reaching sustainable solutions to IAP. The proposed model (Fig. 23.8.) has a futuristic outlook aiming to solve the problems related to IAP, but it can have some limitations relating to network availability, accuracy and reliability of sensor data in remote areas. Moreover developing cost-effective models for rural low-income households is a challenging task that should be considered by policymakers, and stakeholders should encourage community participation and adoption of recommended interventions to maximize model's benefits.

4. Conclusion

This study has highlighted the severe health consequences of biomass fuel usage on women and children in rural low-income households in Bankura II C.D. Block. The findings reveal that biomass fuels, widely relied upon due to economic constraints, lack of access to clean alternatives and traditional methods of cooking, expose women and young children to high levels of IAP. This exposure is strongly associated with respiratory illnesses, cardiovascular issues, eye problems, and adverse pregnancy outcomes as evident from the radiological perspectives. Children are particularly vulnerable, showing increased rates of respiratory infections and developmental risks due to continuous exposure to harmful pollutants. The study underscores the need for urgent intervention to mitigate these health risks. Transitioning to cleaner fuel sources could significantly reduce IAP. Stakeholders at all levels should collaborate to solve the issues related to IAP. Additionally, raising awareness about the health hazards associated with biomass fuel and improving household ventilation are critical steps in protecting these vulnerable populations. In the end, a model has been prescribed by coupling AI and Geospatial Technologies, which is believed to have the potential to build a framework for justified utilization of biomass without impacting health and environment, which is very much important for sustainable rural development.

References

1. Sibanda, T., & Uzabakiriho, J. D. (2024). Animal Manure as an Alternative Bioenergy Resource in Rural Sub-Saharan Africa: Present Insights, Challenges, and Prospects for Future Advancements. Energies, 17(8), 1839.
2. Poddar, M., & Chakrabarti, S. (2016). Indoor air pollution and women's health in India: an exploratory analysis. Environment, development and sustainability, 18, 669–677.
3. Dwivedi, S., Taushiba, A., Zehra, F., Gupta, S. K., & Lawrence, A. (2023). Revelations to indoor air pollutants and health risk assessment on women: a case study. *Hygiene and Environmental Health Advances*, *5*, 100038. https://doi.org/10.1016/j.heha.2022.100038.
4. Dutta, S., & Banerjee, S. (2014). Exposure to indoor air pollution & women health: the situation in urban India. *Environment and Urbanization ASIA*, *5*(1), 131–145. https://doi.org/10.1177/0975425314521545.
5. Chavan, R. G., Kaur, J., & Charan, G. S. (2024). Unseen crisis: Revealing the hidden health impact of indoor air pollution—A scoping review. Journal of Education and Health Promotion, 13(1), 410.
6. James, B. S., Shetty, R. S., Kamath, A., & Shetty, A. (2020). Household cooking fuel use and its health effects among rural women in southern India—A cross-sectional study. PloS one, 15(4), e0231757. https://doi.org/10.1371/journal.pone.0231757.

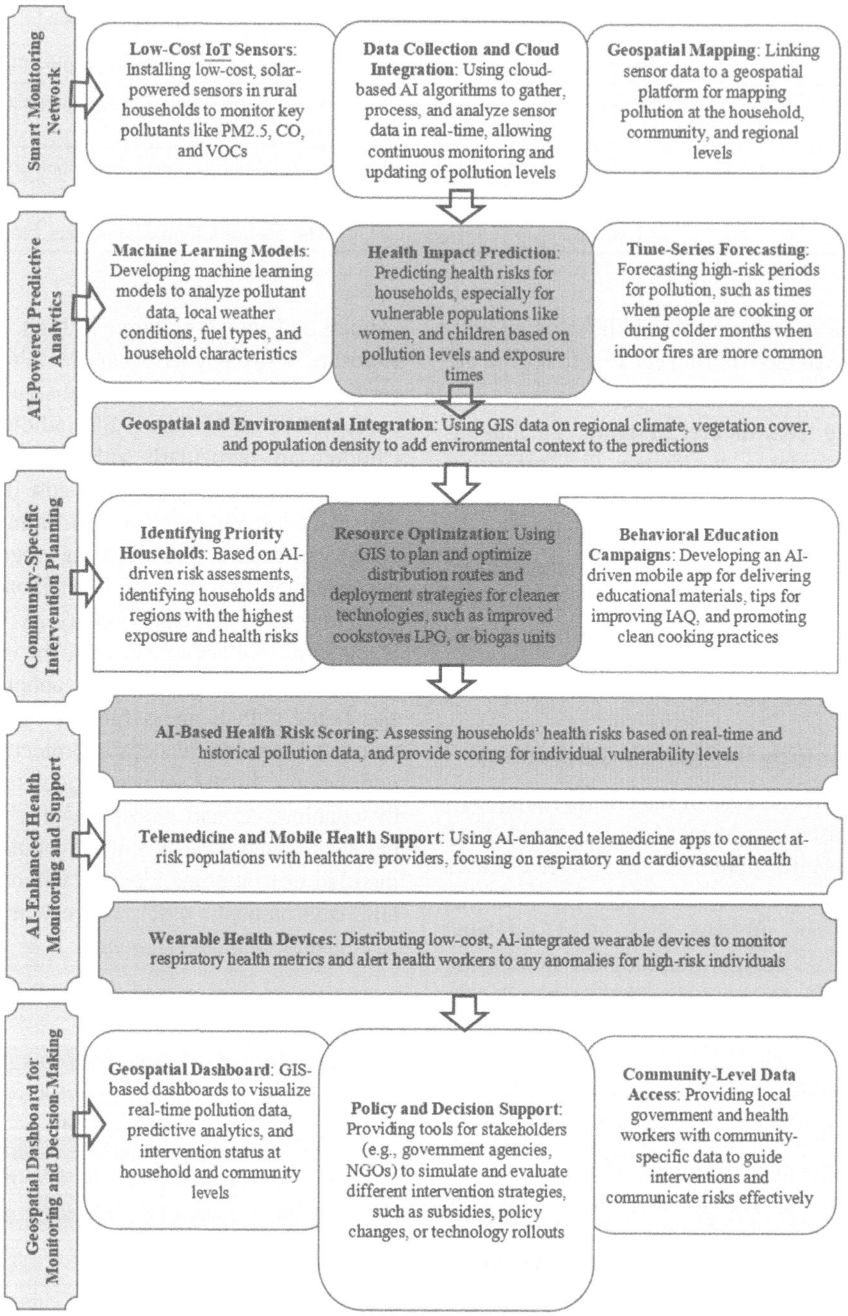

Fig. 23.8 Model for reducing the impact of IAP

Source: Prepared by Authors

7. Oguntoke, O., Adebulehin, A. T., & Annegarn, H. J. (2013). Biomass energy utilisation, air quality and the health of rural women and children in Ido LGA, south-western Nigeria. *Indoor and Built Environment*, *22*(3), 528–534.
8. Kyayesimira, J., & Florence, M. (2021). Health concerns and use of biomass energy in households: Voices of women from rural communities in Western Uganda. *Energy, Sustainability and Society*, *11*, 1–13.
9. Oluwole, O., Otaniyi, O. O., Ana, G. A., & Olopade, C. O. (2012). Indoor air pollution from biomass fuels: a major health hazard in developing countries. *Journal of Public Health*, *20*, 565–575.
10. Das, I., Jagger, P., & Yeatts, K. (2017). Biomass cooking fuels and health outcomes for women in Malawi. *Ecohealth*, *14*, 7–19.
11. World Health Organization. (2016). Burning opportunity: clean household energy for health, sustainable development, and wellbeing of women and children.
12. Po, J. Y., FitzGerald, J. M., & Carlsten, C. (2011). Respiratory disease associated with solid biomass fuel exposure in rural women and children: systematic review and meta-analysis. *Thorax*, *66*(3), 232–239.
13. Dida, G. O., Lutta, P. O., Abuom, P. O., Mestrovic, T., & Anyona, D. N. (2022). Factors predisposing women and

children to indoor air pollution in rural villages, Western Kenya. Archives of Public Health, 80(1), 46.

14. Le, H. H., Ngo, H. K., Hieu, L. S., Sly, P. D., Phung, D., Le An, P., ... & Thai, P. K. (2024). Indoor air pollution is associated with respiratory symptoms in children in urban Vietnam. Science of The Total Environment, 917, 170556.
15. Sehgal, M., Rizwan, S. A., & Krishnan, A. (2014). Disease burden due to biomass cooking-fuel-related household air pollution among women in India. *Global health action, 7*(1), 25326.
16. Pratap, M. (2024, June). Air Pollution: Health and Livelihood Challenges of Women in India. In NDIEAS-2024 International Symposium on New Dimensions and Ideas in Environmental Anthropology-2024 (NDIEAS 2024) (pp. 282–292). Atlantis Press.
17. Patel, S. K., Patel, S., & Kumar, A. (2019). Effects of cooking fuel sources on the respiratory health of children: evidence from the Annual Health Survey, Uttar Pradesh, India. *Public health, 169*, 59–68.
18. Bisui, S., Hasanuzzaman, M., Sing, J., Midya, S., & Shit, P. K. (2024). Exploring the cooking energy biomass and its impact on women's health and quality of life in rural households: a micro-environmental study from West Bengal in India. *Environmental Monitoring and Assessment, 196*(12), 1184.
19. Chattaraj, M., & Chakrabortty, D. (2019). Trend of metamorphosis of traditional agro-based tribal society to non-agricultural society: a case study of Jangalmahal of Bankura district, West Bengal. *research journal of social sciences, 10*(6), 339–350.
20. Chandramouli, C., & General, R. (2011). Census of india. Rural urban distribution of population, provisional population total. New Delhi: Office of the Registrar General and Census Commissioner, India.
21. Sutradhar, A., Chattaraj, M., & Chakrabortty, D. (2019). Identification of agricultural productivity regions and its major determinants: a case study from Bankura district, West Bengal. *International Journal of Research in Social Sciences, 9*(5), 661–678.
22. Modak, S. S., Chattaraj, M., & Chakrabortty, D.(2023). Patterns of Crop and Agricultural Regionalisation: A Case Study From Bankura District, West Bengal. *International Journal of Creative Research Thoughts, 11*(7), g128–g140.
23. Khatun, F., & Begum, M. J.(2024). Impact of Indoor Air Pollution on Women's Health: A Study on Sylhet City. *International Journal of Current Science Research and Review*. 7(10), 7641–7653. https://doi.org/10.47191/ijcsrr/V7-i10-19.
24. Nie, T., Zhang, G., Sun, Y., Wang, W., Wang, T., & Duan, H. (2025). Effects of Indoor Air Quality on Human Physiological Impact: A Review. Buildings, 15(8), 1296.
25. Lahiri, T., & Ray, M. R. (2010). Effects of indoor air pollution from biomass fuel use on women's health in India. *Health and Environmental Impacts, 135*.
26. Gall, E. T., Carter, E. M., Matt Earnest, C., & Stephens, B. (2013). Indoor air pollution in developing countries: research and implementation needs for improvements in global public health. American journal of public health, 103(4), e67–e72.
27. Dimala, C. A., & Kadia, B. M. (2022). A systematic review and meta-analysis on the association between ambient air pollution and pulmonary tuberculosis. Scientific reports, 12(1), 11282.
28. Shetty, B. S. P., D'Souza, G., & Padukudru Anand, M. (2021). Effect of indoor air pollution on chronic obstructive pulmonary disease (COPD) deaths in Southern Asia—a systematic review and meta-analysis. Toxics, 9(4), 85.

Research and Innovations in Industrial and Marine Biotechnology: A Circular Economy 2024 – Prof. Hrudayanath Thatoi et al. (eds)
© 2026 Taylor & Francis Group, London, ISBN 978-1-041-28285-3

24 Exploring the Environmental Impacts of Biodegradable Packaging for Hospitality Amenities in Star Hotels in Bhubaneswar, Odisha

Subhra Pattanaik,
Susanta Ranjan Chaini*
School of Hotel Management,
Faculty of Hospitality and Tourism Management,
Siksha 'O' Anusandhan (Deemed to Be University),
Bhubaneswar, Odisha

Abstract: Hospitality industry is highly depending on plastic disposable amenities, plastic key cards, laundry bags, bathroom plastic amenities etc which create plastic waste. On the other hand, biodegradable Packaging is the most promising option which gives maximum environmental benefits in this industry. The use of biodegradable Packaging for amenities in hospitality industry can improve the sustainability and reduce the environmental harms. This industry is mostly customer-based business sector where the economic activities are directly or indirectly depending on hotels, restaurants, catering, cruise lines, airlines, tours, travels, tourism etc. In this generation the hospitality industry not only rise the sustainability but also moving forward to the eco-friendly practices under the umbrella of traditional practices. This Paper first explores on basic idea about hospitality industry and its impact on environmental condition, mostly considering the star hotels in Bhubaneswar, Odisha. Finally, it focuses on the understanding about biodegradable Packaging for the amenities in the hospitality industry, their benefits, challenges and their need in this industry which provide green planet for everyone in future.

Keywords: Biodegradable packaging, Hospitality amenities, Environmental impact, Sustainable practices, Plastic pollution, Bhubaneswar hotels

1. Introduction

Housekeeping department is a major department in of Hospitality Sector where it includes different types of Hotels, Motels, Chain Hotels, Heritage hotels, Boutique hotels, Conferences and Conventions, Wedding Venues, Resorts Etc.

Food and Beverage outlets are also most maximum revenue giving sector in hospitality industry. In this Sector Guests or Customers can get their food and beverage as per their wish for which they are paying money. This may also include in breakfast café, restaurant, Multicuisine Restaurant, Coffee Shop, Bar, Discotheque Etc. Sometimes this Food and Beverage sector can Provide Food to the People directly by Food Truck Business, own Restaurant Business etc. This Sector also Provide Different types Conference, Meeting Room, Convention Room as per guest Demand in the Hospitality Industry.

Therefore, this Hospitality industry is not only included in Food and Beverage sector but also expand towards to its business to the culinary industry, lodging sector, Food business, indoor and Outdoor recreation etc.

Sustainability and Biodegradable Packaging both are playing a major role in various industry. Hospitality industry is one of them. This utilization of Sustainable product and using biodegradable packaging for theamenities not only for the guest requirement but also to provide a green and toxic free environment. This sustainable applications in hospitality industry not only provide the revenue generated

*Corresponding author: susanta_chaini@yahoo.co.in

DOI: 10.1201/9781003759003-24

business but also make happy and trust worthy customer for future business.

This industry is a large Business Sector. Many people have an idea about the similarity between Travel and Tourism but it is not actually similar. But both this Travel and Tourism are casting the under the same broad Umbrella of Hospitality Industry. Sometimes this Travel and Tourism industry includes in airlines, Railways, Travel agents, etc which help to develop the travel and tourism through visiting different places, know the different culture and giving employment to many interested and qualified people in same field.

The Hospitality industry is basically known for its luxurious Service providing industry in terms of Food, Beverage, Accommodation, Tourism and Travel for its guests or customer Satisfaction. It is a very vast sector which includes the economic growth directly or indirectly through different industry like Food industry, Restaurant business, Tour and operators, Service Sector, Guest houses, lodging businesses, Hotel Industry, Railway Catering, Airlines Catering, Retail Sector, Travel and Tourism industry etc. Hence the amenities are available for guest comfort, immediate available and useful element with free of cost. Biodegradable Supplies and Amenities in hotel and Hospitality industry is the major aspect for guests benefit and comfort with green life. Whereas this biodegradable product can decompose naturally and not create any harmful product in the environment. Different types of products like sugar cane, corn starch, Bamboo etc can reduce the environmental harms without any harmful products or reduces of it. The hospitality industry can operate with these biodegradable toxic free environments by using the ecofriendly product in the restaurant with different cutlery and Crockery, in the guest rooms and bath rooms by using ecofriendly product, supplies and amenities with biodegradable packaging to provide a guest with green experience during their stay at hotel.

The amenity or amenities are the essential and very useful factor for hotel Hospitality Industry. For different star category hotels, the amenities are like Room amenities or washroom amenities. Which may include Mini bar in the room, Complementary breakfast, WIFI Services, Personal care services, Hair dryer, Shaving kit, Dental Kit, Hand towel, Bath towel, Tissue Box, Bath robes, Slippers etc. Sometimes some of the amenities are providing to the guest to give a comfortable and luxurious services and to provide a positive experience during their stay. These amenities are the most main selling point for any hotel.

2. Objective

- To reduce the environmental impact
- To meet the customer demand through eco-friendly practices
- To embracing sustainability in hospitality industry

3. Literature Review

Now a days hospitality industry is more in demand for its service and product for the customers or for guests. This industry influences the entire world for its world economy and for its guests. On the other side it is a threat to the environment by the use of plastic products and non-biodegradable amenities used in hospitality industry. As a greater number of guests are conscious for the sustainability and ecofriendly practices in the hospitality industry that is why the use of biodegradable amenities, product and its packaging is more on demand. Also, it is becoming a standard for hospitality and hotel industry.

In today's world the use of biodegradable packaging is not only make a standard in hospitality industry but also make a responsible platform for making of green world. By these practices the entire world is more sensitive with its daily habits, develop the bio degradable packages, responsible citizen along with satisfactory consumers in future.

The ecofriendly waste product management practices and biodegradable packaging for amenities by the staff or employees for the guest in hospitality industry. The waste generates in the hotel and hospitality industry create the environmental harm. Similarly, the poor waste management and loss of biodiversity is the major part for the poor environment and poor sustainability. The various strategies like reuse of the product along with recycle, recovering of the waste product can enhance the efficiency of the product with the help of technology. This way the product can be used properly, limited amount, develop the brand image, save the costs etc.

The awareness and perception towards the using of eco-friendly product than plastic product is the main limitation in this paper. Similarly, this paper focuses on the use, lifespan, price, limited suppliers, hygiene, impact of people negatively towards eco-friendly product to give a plastic free environment [1] Hotel industry is the guest-oriented industry where each and every department has a role towards guests and their service. This paper explores on the waste management system in this industry and giving importance on IOT, trash monitoring system, develop the operational efficiency on daily basis [2]This paper highlights on sustainable biodegradable packaging on the food and Beverage table ware, different packaging material etc in this same field [3] The hotel industry the primary focus on food safety, sanitization in the whole environment of hotel industry is highlighted in this paper [4] This study examines on the guest perception towards to the eco-friendly practices and awareness about hotel industry. [5] This paper focuses at the tourism literature and the examine the guest experience who are staying in green hotel. [6] This paper highlights on the green practices in the hotel industry as well as guest perceptions towards sustainability [7] This research paper gives importance on the types of domestic tourist and international tourist perception to stay at green certified hotel in Turkey [8] This Paper is examining and encouraging towards to the transportation, Food packaging, Biological Diversity for the guest in the hospitality industry (Jaykumar)On the other hand this paper highlights on different types of environmental performance criteria to provide an Eco-label for hotel compliance [9]This Paper provide the importance on four Ps (Product, Price, Promotion, Place) where it provides the relationship between implementation and awareness of green practise [10]This Study give the importance between hotel employee and customer perception for the green marketing practices [11] This paper concerns about the green washing process and policies in green environment [12]

Ecotourism concept or sustainable environment mostly based on their application and benefits after use by guest and getting a positive response on this. This Eco-friendly Product or sustainable product may be use in different way in the hospitality industry or in the hotel industry. From agriculture to water conservation, Rain water harvesting, less use of plastic, zero waste Product etc. Due to this sustainable use to provide a green experience the hotel industry also provides high-quality, Eco-friendly amenities in the guest room like tooth brush, tooth paste, shampoo, Conditioner, bath gel with biodegradable packaging.

This paper first explores on the Corporate social responsibility towards to the green practices and taken many suggestions, recommendations to make the environmental sustainability in the hotel [13] This study examines and comprises on the different amenities and facilities use in the hotel for the guests for their comfort. Whereas it shows that these green initiatives provide a good rating, guest positive feedback at the end.[14]This Paper shows the path on guest expectation and experience before and after the service through green practices by placing the bathroom and room amenities in the hotel can create a brand image and popularity in the hospitality industry [15]This paper focuses on the guest room amenities, their services through green implementation can create a brand image of the hotel and get the good feedback from the guests [16]This Paper Shows on the path of Eco-Hotel or green hotel concept in the hospitality industry where the guests are feeling happier, relaxed and touched to the nature through the green services [17]The sustainable eco-friendly practices in hospitality industry mostly in hotel industry is a major aspect for guest perception and expectation. Now a days these Eco-Friendly practices in the hospitality industry can reduce the environmental impact through different green initiatives with the services, products, Waste management, reduces the excess amount use of water, electricity, etc and make them in to the RRR (Reduce, Re-use, Recycle) Concept for further use in future to provide a green world to the present and future generation. This Paper highlights on the eco-friendly practices in the Indian hotels and its impact for the future generation [18] This paper explains about the guest's perception and attitude towards to the green marketing management in restaurant operation [19] This Paper indicates the gap between manger's awareness and implementing the services for the guest towards to the green practices [20]The purpose of this paper is adopting green practices for the restaurant business for the future generation growth and awareness in restaurant business in Malaysia [21]This study based on the online food delivery system and its impacts on the society with the green practices to perceive guests on eco-friendly behaviour [22]

4. Environmental Impact

By the adaptation of this biodegradable product in hospitality industry specially in the hotel industry can give huge number of benefits. By minimising the waste can directly reduce the carbon foot print in the hospitality industry. By using these biodegradable products can be reuse as it decomposes in the earth properly and naturally can reduce the maximum use of the plastic. Through these sustainable practices and green environment, the hotels can build a good position for its food, services etc for the guests. Different types of environmental concern factors can be happened through Reducing plastic Pollution, Less Carbon Foot Print, Resources can be conserved, Biodiversity can be Promoted, it also increases and encourage the sustainable practices in hotel industry.

5. Solution and Recommendation

The Hotel industry reflects towards to the biggest responsibility for the guests as well as for us to make a green planet in this present era and for future generation. Though this innovation and adaptation the hospitality industry looks more promising for guests. Therefore, the hospitality industry must encourage the different partnership and packaging supplies with biodegradable product. This sustainable step is not only for guest but also for employees as well. So, each and every employee must be welled trained and understand its utilisation and everyone must be aware not to use plastic, not to create more wastage etc. for green planet.

6. Future Research Direction

The study Highlights on biodegradable product and its packaging in the hospitality or in the hotel industry can give a sustainable environment. The future research based on that the product knowledge along with the sustainable practices can make more successful hospitality industry for the eco conscious guests in the hotel.

7. Conclusion

Transforming traditional product to the biodegradable packaging product can create an initial cost on the challenging aspect but we must focus on its durability and productivity through ecofriendly product. Hence in this hotel and hospitality business must be aware about its biodegradable product use and its packaging for different amenities. Hotel industry must be promoted this through the sustainability.

References——

1. Rachel Mc Caffery, J. H. (2023). Zero plastic in Hotels . In H. K. Willy Legrand, *Critical Questions in Sustainability and Hospitality* (p. 11). London : Taylor & Francis eBooks.
2. Roy, B. K. (2024). Prospective Developments and Advancements in the Hospitality Sector for Eco-Friendly Waste Handling. In A. G. Amrik Singh, *Sustainable Disposal Methods of Food Wastes in Hospitality Operations* (p. 22). Hershey, Pennsylvania: IGI Global .
3. Song, X. Y. (2013). Analysis on Green Hotel Marketing Management under the Background of Circular Economy. In *Advances in Energy Science and Technology* (pp. 1478–1481). Switzerland: Scientific .Net (Trans Tech Publication).
4. Adryansyah Pakpahan, G. A. (2022). Best Practices of Sustainable Development to Make Six Senses Uluwatu a Green Hotel. *JURNAL BALI MEMBANGUN BALI*, 24.
5. Akram Atef RAWASHDEH, M. M.-A. (2021). Hotel Guests' Perceptions of Environmentally Friendly Practices in Jordan. *Journal of Environmental Management and Tourism.*
6. Usman Ali, H. A. (2023). Determinants and Impacts of Quality Attributes on Guest Perceptions in Norwegian Green Hotels. *Sustainable Innovation in Tourism and Hospitality.*
7. Vivek Kumar Verma, B. C. (2016). Hotel Guest's Perception and Choice Dynamics for Green Hotel Attribute: A Mix Method Approach. *Indian Journal of Science and Technology, Vol 9(5)*, 9.
8. Can, A. S. (2014). TOURISTS' PERCEPTION OF GREEN PRACTICES IN ECO-FRIENDLY HOTELS: A CASE STUDY FROM THE ANTALYA REGION OF TURKEY. *Scholarly Journal*, 25.
9. Michele Preziosi, P. T. (2019). The role of environmental practices and communication on guest loyalty: Examining EU-Ecolabel in Portuguese hotels. *Journal of Cleaner Production.*
10. Mat Yusof, N. A. (2014). Customers' expectations of hotel green marketing: a New Zealand quantitative study. Auckland University of Technology.
11. Chan, E. S. (2013). Gap analysis of green hotel marketing. *International Journal of Contemporary Hospitality Management,emerald insight*, 32.
12. Ansh Gupta, S. D. (2019). All that glitters is not green: Creating trustworthy ecofriendly services at green hotels. *Tourism Management, Science direct*, 155–169.
13. Bobbett, E. J. (2010). An Investigation of sustainable environmental practices and consumer attitudes & behaviors toward hotel bathroom amenities. Las Vegas: University of Nevada.
14. Woo Gon Kim, J. (.(2015). The influence of recent hotel amenities and green practices on guests' price premium and revisit intention. *Sage Journal.*
15. Miyoung Jeong, M. K. (2020). Do the brand and packaging matter? The case of hotel bathroom amenities. *Journal of Hospitality and Tourism- Emerald Publishing* , 17.
16. Monsanto, F. H. (2021). "HOTEL GUESTS' PREFERENCES REGARDING IN-ROOM AMENITIES - A WAY FOR HOTELIERS TO IMPROVE CUSTOMER SATISFACTION. *Proquest*, 54.
17. Rakesh Dani, K. T. (2021). Ecological approach towards sustainability in hotel industry. *Science Direct.*
18. Mohinder Chand, S. G. (2017). Eco Friendly Practices in Indian Hotel Industry:An Exploratory Study. *International Journal of Hospitality & Tourism Systems*, 8.
19. EunHa Jeong, S. (. (2014). The impact of eco-friendly practices on green image and customer attitudes: An investigation in a café setting. *The International Journal of Hospitality Management* .
20. Miriam Mbasera, E. D. (2016). Environmentally-friendly practices in hotels : original research. *Sabinet African Journals.*
21. Booi Chen Tan, T. C. (2018). A qualitative study of green practices adoption for restaurants in Malaysia. *SOCIAL RESPONSIBILITY JOURNAL*, 13.
22. Xiaohua Chen, T. J. (2022). Potential effects of green brand legitimacy and the biospheric value of eco-friendly behavior on onlinefood delivery: a mediation approach. *International Journal of Contemporary Hospitality Management -Emerald insights*, 23.

Research and Innovations in Industrial and Marine Biotechnology: A Circular Economy 2024 – Prof. Hrudayanath Thatoi et al. (eds)

25 Anti-Pseudomonal Activities of *Combretum Albidum* in Chronic Supporative Otitis Media in Confirmation with GC-MS and Molecular Docking

Utkalika Mallick[1]
Centre for Biotechnology,
Siksha 'O' Anusandhan Deemed to be University,
Kalinganagar, Bhubaneswar, Odisha, India

Santosh Kumar Swain[2]
Department of Otorhinolaryngology and Head and Neck Surgery,
All India Institute of Medical Sciences,
Bhubaneswar, Odisha, India

Mahesh Chandra Sahu[3,*]
Division of Microbiology,
ICMR-Regional Medical Research Centre,
Chandrasekharpur, Bhubaneswar, Odisha, India

Abstract: Chronic Suppurative Otitis Media (CSOM) is frequently linked to infections caused by *Pseudomonas aeruginosa*, a multidrug-resistant bacterium. This study explores the potential of methanoli leaf extract of *Combretum albidum* in combating *P. aeruginosa* infections. The extract was analyzed for its phytochemical constituents and physical characteristics. To evaluate its antipseudomonal activity, in vitro tests were performed. Phytol, hexadecanoic acid, squalene, heptanoic acid, cyclopropanecarboxamide, and 6,9,12,15-octadecatrienoic acid were among the bioactive substances found by Gas Chromatography-Mass Spectrometry (GC-MS) analysis. These compounds were retrieved from PubChem and subjected to molecular docking using AutoDock 4.1 against the *P. aeruginosa* protein 5b3k (Flavodoxin), obtained from the Protein Data Bank. Docking results showed notable binding affinities ranging from -3.4 to -5.6 kcal/mol. Among the compounds, phytol and 6,9,12,15-octadecatrienoic acid demonstrated strong interactions with amino acid residues such as ALA, VAL, ASP, and TYR, indicating potential interference with bacterial protein function. The findings suggest that the methanolic leaf extract of *C. albidum* contains phytocompounds with promising activity against *P. aeruginosa*, supporting its possible use as an alternative therapy for CSOM and encouraging further pharmacological and clinical investigations.

Keywords: CSOM, *Pseudomonas aeruginosa*, *Combretum albidum*, Molecular docking, Phytocompounds, Protein 5b3k

1. Introduction

Chronic suppurative otitis media (CSOM) is one of the main conditions associated with hearing loss, and it is highly prevalent globally, including in India [1]. In this disease, an infection occurs in the middle ear cavity, affecting more than 300 million people globally. It is documented that 60% of those affected by this condition worldwide suffer from hearing loss. In India, the total frequency is 16 per 1000 people in urban areas and 46

*Corresponding author: mchsahu@gmail.com

DOI: 10.1201/9781003759003-25

per 1000 people in rural areas[2]. A study by Teele et al., 1989 shows that 80% of kids should have gone through at least once by their 3rd birthday [3]. It is of two types one is benign or tubotympanum and dangerous atticoantrum ear. This infection is usually polymicrobial caused by different bacteria like *Staphylococcus aureus, Proteus spp., Fusobacterium spp., Klebsiella spp., Bacteroides spp.* and most common caused by *Pseudomonas aeruginosa* [4, 5]. Resistance of these bacteria isolated from CSOM to various medicines has become a serious concern to global health in recent decades.

Antibiotic resistance is a global health concern that is rapidly expanding among environmental bacteria, animals and human pathogens. When antibiotics are misused, resistant bacteria are more likely to be selected, which increases the likelihood of resistant genotypes arising via spontaneous mutation or horizontal gene transfer. The fight against antibacterial resistance to antibiotics is still developing in modern medicine. Nowadays, bacterial infections are reported involving both old and new pathogens that are resistant to all types of antibiotics[6]. At least 70,000 deaths in Europe and 23,000 in the US are attributed to bacterial infections annually and at least two million infections occur globally[7]. It is estimated that hundreds of thousands of deaths worldwide are attributed to antibiotic resistance each year.[7]. The multidrug resistance strains of *P. aeruginosa* is the most common cause for drug resistance CSOM. Aminoglycosides like amikacin and netilmicin were active against these infected bacteria. Different antibiotics like tobramycin, gentamicin, ciprofloxacin and neomycin are used to treat CSOM. Torbamycin, gentamicin, ciprofloxacin is most commonly used antibiotics and having sensitivity of 83.8%, 78.1% and 75.6% respectively[8]. Neomycin shows less sensitive of 3.5%[9]. In CSOM, the antibiotics ciprofloxacin (Amoxicillin and clavulanic acid), augmentin and gentamicin had a broad spectrum of susceptibility (70–80%) to several gram positive and gram negative bacteria species[10]. Because of the long term treatment of these disease patients' intake antibiotics without drug sensitivity check some bacteria cannot be detected and cause drug resistance.A study by Shoo et al., 2018 revealed the predominant pathogens were *P. aeruginosa* and *S. aureus*, both showing significant levels of multidrug resistance, particularly against commonly used antibiotics such as amoxicillin and ciprofloxacin. However, higher sensitivity was observed with antibiotics like piperacillin-tazobactam and meropenem. This research emphasizes how important it is to continuously check for antibiotic sensitivity to inform treatment protocols and combat rising antimicrobial resistance in CSOM management [11].

Exploring the therapeutic potential of medicinal plants for developing treatments against various diseases is a broad area of research. By investigating the bioactive compounds present in plants, scientists aim to uncover new medicines and treatments. Harnessing the healing properties of nature's pharmacy offers promising avenues for addressing health challenges and improving overall well-being. The development of novel modern drugs against drug-resistant candidasis has been aided by natural products derived from medicinal plants. Cinnamon has a long history of medicinal use, with many cultures using its properties for a variety of health benefits. In 2021, Alhadad and Elmhdwi reported that the *Combretaceae* family exhibits high levels of antimicrobial activity, with stem bark of *Combretum albidum* demonstrating efficacy against *Salmonella typhimurium, E. coli, P. aeruginosa, Proteus mirabilis, B. subtilis*, and *K. pneumonia*, while methanol leaf extract of the plant showed antibacterial activity against multiple drug-resistant (MDR) *P. aeruginosa*. Different bioactive compounds like Phenol, Benzoic acid, 3-Octadecene, Diethyl phthalate, 3-Hexadecanol that present in *Combretaceae* plant and act as antibiotics against different bacterial disease[12].The C101A mutant of Flavodoxin from *P. aeruginosa* is a specific variation of the Flavodoxin protein where the cysteine at position 101 has been replaced with alanine. This mutation is part of experimental studies to understand the role and function of Flavodoxin, which is involved in various electron transfer processes within the cell. The structure of this mutant protein has been determined through X-ray diffraction methods, achieving a resolution of 1.70 Å, indicating detailed structural information is available.This mutant, like its native form, is expressed in an *E. coli* system and has been deposited in the PDB with the identifier 5B3K. Such studies are crucial for elucidating the molecular mechanisms of bacterial resistance and understanding how mutations in key proteins like Flavodoxin might affect bacterial metabolism and pathogenicity.

P. aeruginosa, Staphylococcus aureus, and *Proteus mirabilis* emerged as the predominant bacterial organisms associated with CSOM. Additionally *Aspergillus* and *Candida* species were frequently implicated in cases of otomycosis [13]. Fungal pathogens in otomycosis cases also posed therapeutic challenges, especially with recurrent or chronic infections. The findings underscore the importance of ongoing microbial surveillance to monitor emerging resistance patterns and guide appropriate treatment protocols, ultimately improving patient outcomes in managing CSOM and otomycosis[14].

One important topic of research is the genetic diversity of *P. aeruginosa* isolated from CSOM, especially in light of patterns of antibiotic susceptibility. *P. aeruginosa* strains show high genetic variability, which enhances their resistance mechanisms. Isolates from CSOM cases often exhibit resistance to common antibiotics like aminoglycosides, fluoroquinolones, and beta-lactams. Molecular typing methods, such as PFGE and MLST, have revealed diverse genetic profiles, linked to the emergence of MDR strains[15]. Understanding this diversity is crucial for developing effective treatments and controlling the spread of MDR *P. aeruginosa*. Regular surveillance of genetic and resistance profiles is essential for managing CSOM effectively [16].

As a povidone-iodine solution, Betadine is proficient at a broad spectrum of bacteria, viruses , and fungi, helping to reduce the microbial load in the middle ear, which is critical for controlling infection [17]. Irrigation with Betadine can assist in cleaning the ear canal, promoting *P. aeruginosa* and *S. aureus*. Studies have shown that regular Betadine irrigation, when used as part of an overall treatment regimen including antibiotics, can enhance the resolution of infection and reduce the recurrence of CSOM symptoms. However, its use should be carefully monitored, as excessive or improper application may cause irritation or damage to the ear canal or tympanic membrane[17].

In our previous *in-vitro* study [18] revealed the methanolic extract of *C. albidum* had anti-pseudomonal activity alone and with the antibiotic ceftriaxone. In this study, we evaluated the *in-silico* molecular docking study with compounds found in GC-MS of methanolic extract of *C. albidum*. The purpose of this study is to review the literature on the anti-pseudomonad activity of phytocompounds found in *C. albidum* plants based on results from in vitro and in vivo investigations. It also suggests possible therapeutic uses for compounds derived from *Combretum* against *Pseudomonas*. Additionally, finding the significance of computational approaches in drug discovery by *in- silico* molecular docking study to find the molecular interaction between *C. albidum* and key MDR protein of *P. aeruginosa*. Identifying the limitations of traditional experimental methods in exploring molecular interaction, this study will then transition to the integration of computational techniques, specifically *in-silico* molecular docking. This approach allows for a deeper insight into the binding affinities and structural aspects of the interactions between *C. albidum* phytocompounds and key MDR protein of *P. aeruginosa* targets. By combining experimental evidence with computational predictions, we aim to enhance our understanding of the mechanistic basis underlying the anti-pseudomonal activity of Combretum -derived compounds.

2. Materials and Methods

2.1 Bioassay Guided Fractionation and GC-MS Analysis of *C. Albidum* Leaves

Dried leaf powders of *C. albidum* were treated in a soxhlet apparatus with methanol for a whole day as part of the hot extraction technique. After filtering the resultant extract, the filtrate was vacuum-dried. The extracts' antipseudomonal efficacy was evaluated. The methanol crude extract was dissolved in water and then successively partitioned using solvents such as n-hexane, dichloromethane, ethyl acetate, chloroform, and n-butanol for bioassay-guided fractionation. The final product, known as the methanol fraction, was produced by concentrating each of the acquired fractions at decreased pressure until a black residue was produced [19].

2.2 GC-MS Analysis

The ethyl acetate fraction was analyzed using GC-MS, which was equipped with a VF-5 ms 30-meter-long, 0.25-mm-diameter, fused silica capillary column with a 0.25-µm film thickness. An electron ionization system running at an ionization energy of 70 eV was used for detection. The carrier gas was high-purity helium gas (99.99%), which was kept at a steady flow rate of 1.51 mL/min. The temperatures of the mass transfer line and injector were set to 240 ºC and 200 °C, respectively. The oven temperature was set to rise by 10°C every minute from 70°C to 220°C, then to stay at an isothermal state for one minute before rising once more at the same pace to 300°C.With a split ratio of 1:40, diluted sample aliquots of 2 µL were manually injected in splitless mode while the mass scan range was set to 50–600 amu. It took sixty minutes to conduct the GC-MS analysis[20].

2.3 Identification of Compounds

By contrasting their retention indices and mass spectral fragmentation patterns with reference data from the WILEY8.LIB and NIST08.LIB databases (Stein SE, National Institute of Standards and Technology, Mass Spectral Database and Software, Version 3.02, USA, 1990), (MACLafferly FW, Registry of Mass Spectral Data, 5th edition, Wiley, New York, 1989), as well as with information found in published literature, the phytochemical constituents of the bioactive ethyl acetate fraction were identified.

2.4 Retrieval of Ligand and Target

The protein structure of 5b3k of *P. aeruginosa*was retrieved from PDB(www.rcsb.org). The required protein was downloaded the associated PDBfile containing the three-dimensional coordinates of the protein's atoms. Visualization of this protein structure is done by using such as PyMOL to remove the water molecule and to add hydrogen molecules for proper binding of the ligand[21]. Six chemical compounds i.e phytol, Hexadecanoic acid, Squalene, Heptanoic acid, Cyclopropanecarbroxamide and 6, 9,12,15 octadecatrienoic acid were identified from the methanolic extract of *C. albidum* through GCMS study. These compounds were chosen as ligands due to their potential antipseudomonal activities. To acquire the 3D structures of these isolated ligands, they were retrieved from the PubChem server of NCBI (National Center for Biotechnology Information) with different compound ID i.e 5280435, 92836, 638072, 8094, 80376 and 5282837 respectively. PyMol software was employed to generate the three-dimensional structures of the ligands. PyMol offers a user-friendly interface for molecular visualization and manipulation, allowing for a detailed examination of the ligand structures. These 3D structures will facilitate further molecular docking, to explore the interactions between the ligands and target proteins involved in Pseudomonas infection pathways.

2.5 Protein-Ligand Interaction

Docking analysis was done between the selected protein and six different ligands using AutoDock tools. AutoDock explores the proteins as the receptor and the ligand as drugs. Different parameters were set to default in AutoDock tools, with AutoGrid pre-, calculating grids for the receptor and AutoDcocking ligands to these grids. Molecular dynamics and force field analyses were utilized to evaluate the relative stabilities of the protein-ligand complexes, while free energy simulations were employes to assess binding affinity[22].

3. Results

3.1 Physico-Chemical Properties of C. *Albidum*

Methanol leaf extract of C. albidum was the most successful in reducing the number of isolated MDR pathogenic bacteria, according to the results of plant screening. Further, standardization of crude powders had been done. The moisture content of crude powders was 6.18 %. Total ash of crude powders of *C. albidum* was 18.04%, acid insoluble ash was 1.37 % and water soluble ash was 22.42 %. Pertinent Physicochemical properties of *C. albidum* leaf powdersare summarized (Table 25.1.). There was no microbiological contamination in the extract or crude powders used in this study.

3.2 Phytochemical Analysis by GC-MS Study

The methanol fraction of leaf of *C. albidum* was tested for the existence of glycosides, alkaloids, terpenoids, steroids, tannins and saponins using phytochemical screening. Different chemicals in the methanol fraction were easier to identify thanks to the results of the GC-MS analysis (Fig. 25.1.). The structures of these compounds were determined by examining the fragmentation patterns of the mass spectra and directly comparing the spectral data with previously published mass spectra and the National Institute of Standards' chemical profiles and Technology (NIST) collection. Table 25.2. Gives an overview of the chemical analysis of the compounds found, including retention times, percentage peak areas, molecular weights, molecular formulas, structures, types of compounds, and biological activities that have been documented (Table 25.2.). Research on the bioactive compounds identified through GC-MS analysis of *C. albidum* revealed six notable compounds with their respective percentages: 9,12,15-octadecatrienoic acid, (Z,Z,Z) (1.20%), hexadecanoic acid methyl ester (0.84%), phytol (3.23%), squalene (6.52%), N-(4-fluorophenyl) (22.52%), heptanoic acid anhydride (1.83%), and cyclopropanecarboxamide, (Table 25.2.). Six unique peaks with retention durations of 18.538, 20.336, 20.440, 26.472, 29.169, and 30.031 minutes, respectively, were identified in the GC-MS spectrum and corresponded to various substances (Fig. 25.2.). At these retention durations, the compounds

Table 25.1 Physicochemical properties of *C. albidum* with 2 g leaf powders (w/w)

Parameters	Value for leaves
Loss on drying	6.18
Total ash	18.04
Acid insoluble ash	1.37
Water soluble ash	12.07
Water soluble extractive	25.02
Ethanol soluble extractive	22.42
Methanol soluble extractive	12.15
Petroleum ether soluble Extractive	2.0
pH of methanol extract	5.03

Note: RT, retention time in min; Peak area in microvolt-seconds.

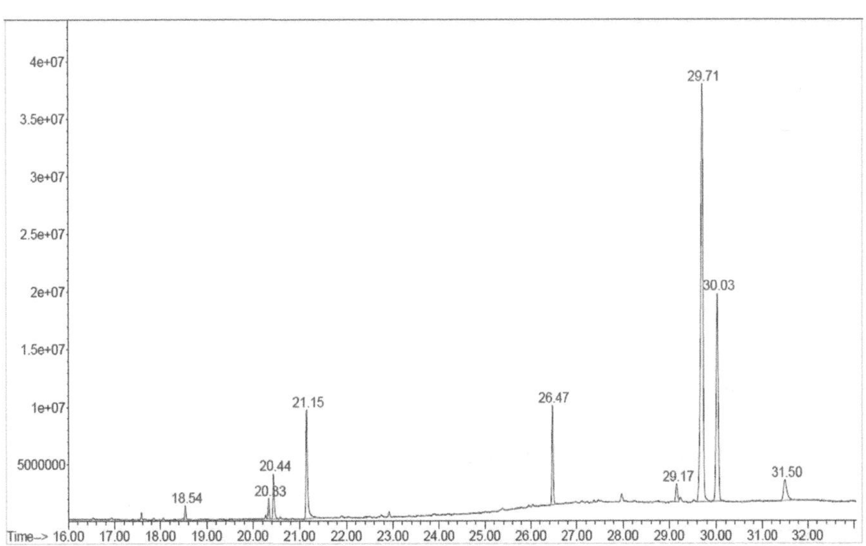

Fig. 25.1 Chromatogram of methanol fraction of *C. albidum*

Table 25.2 Phyto-components identified in the methanol fraction of leavesof *C. albidum*

Sl. No	Phytochemical	RT	MF	MW	Peak area	Structure
1	Hexadecanoic acid methyl ester	18.538	$C_{17}H_{34}O_2$	270.4507	0.84	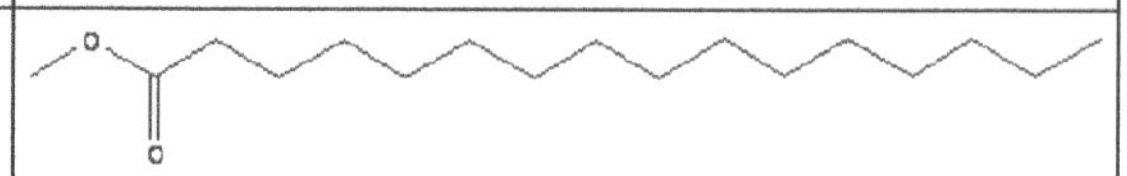
2	9,12,15-Octade-catrienoic acid, (Z,Z,Z)-	20.336	$C_{18}H_{30}O_2$	278.4296	1.20	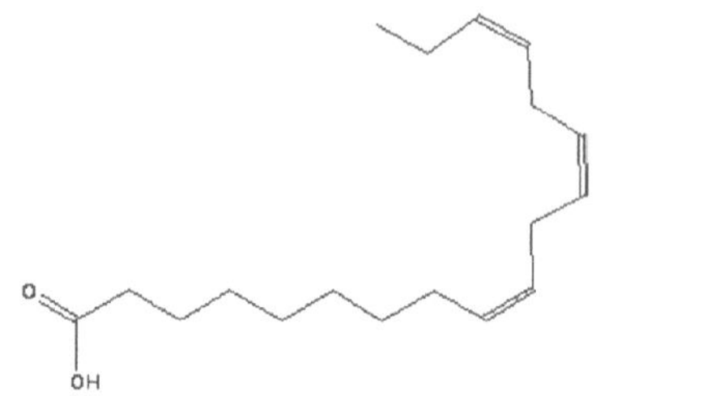
3	Phytol	20.440	$C_{20}H_{40}O$	296.5310	3.23	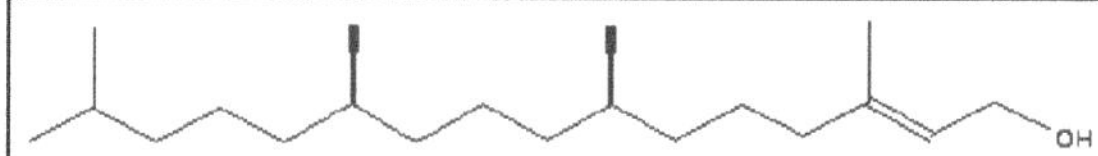
4	Squalene	26.472	$C_{30}H_{50}$	410.7180	6.52	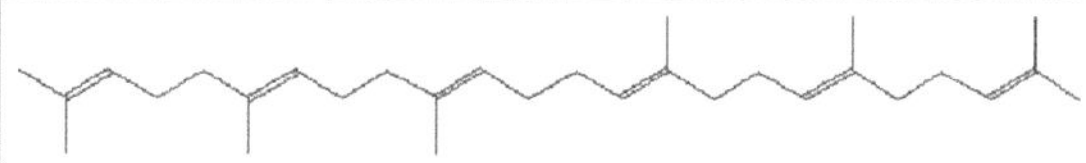
5	Heptanoic acid, anhydride	29.169	$C_{14}H_{26}O_3$	242.3544	1.83	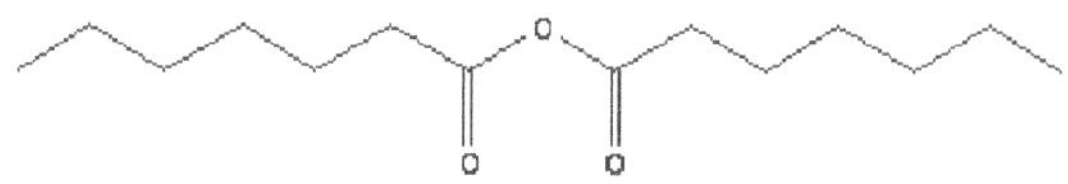
6	Cyclopropan-ecarboxamide, N-(4-fluorophe-nyl)-	30.031	$C_{10}H_{10}FNO$	179.1909	22.52	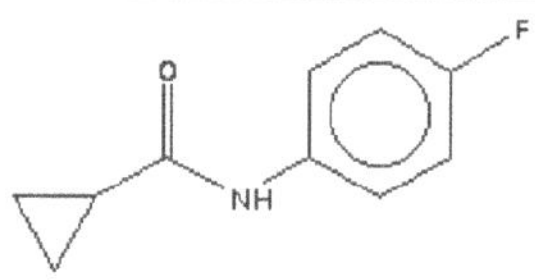

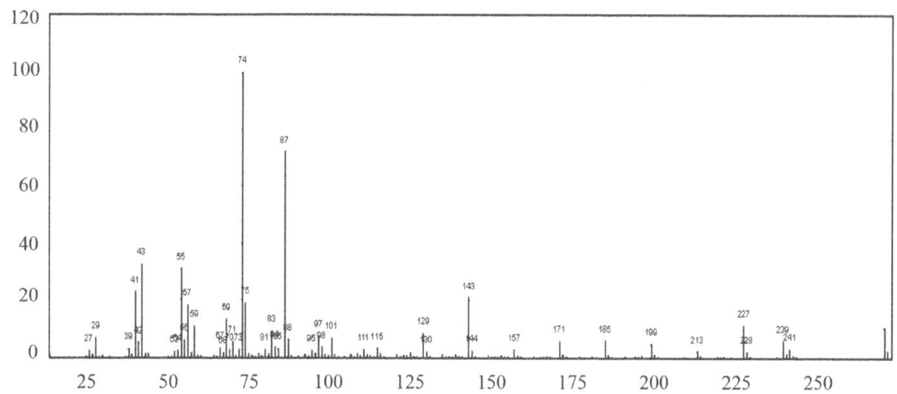

Fig. 25.2 Chromatogram of hexadecanoic acid methyl ester fraction of *C. albidum*

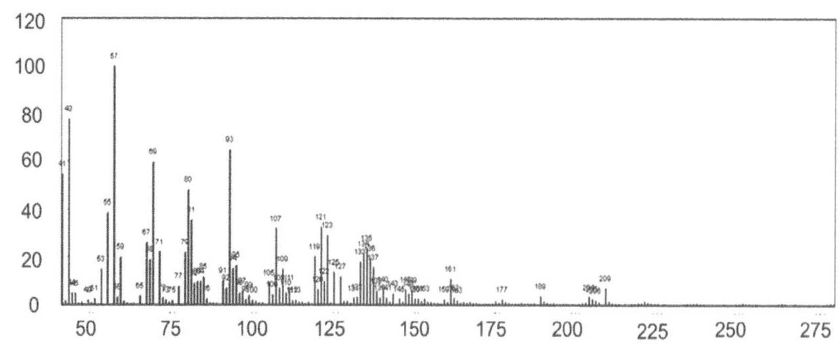

Fig. 25.3 Chromatogram of 9,12,15-Octadecatrienoic acid, (Z,Z,Z) fraction of *C. albidum*

were examined by the mass spectrometer in conjunction with the GC to determine their chemical makeup and structures. Peaks appeared at different microvolt-seconds as a result of larger compounds breaking up into smaller components.

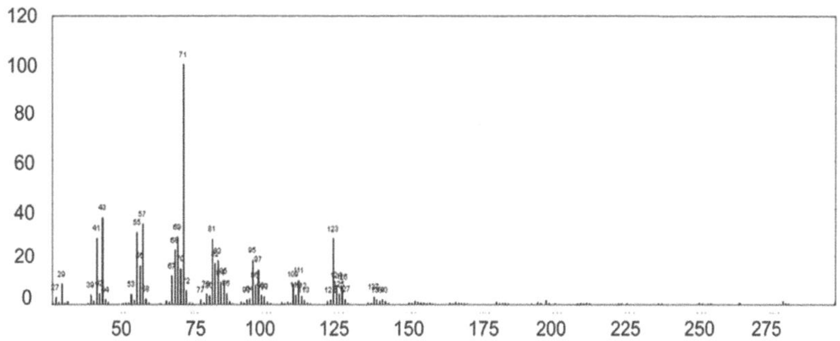

Fig. 25.4 Chromatogram of Phytol fraction of *C. albidum*

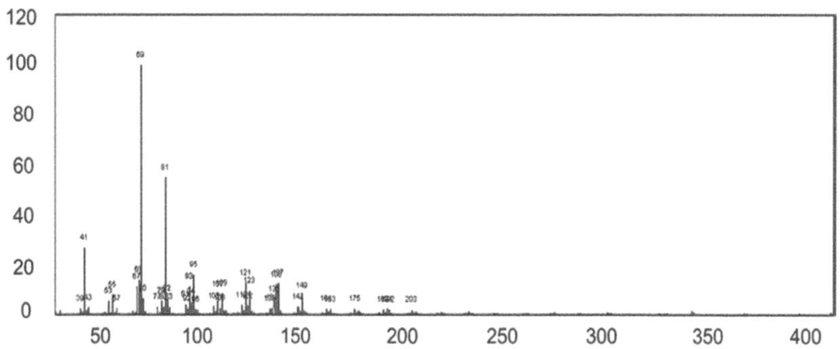

Fig. 25.5 Chromatogram of Squalene fraction of *C. albidum*

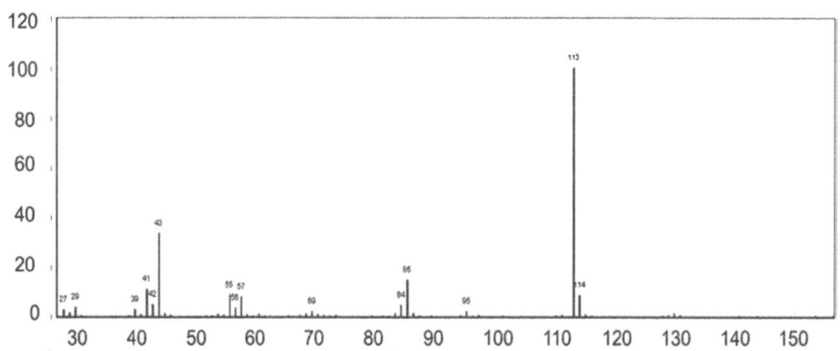

Fig. 25.6 Chromatogram of Heptanoic acid, anhydride fraction of *C. albidum*

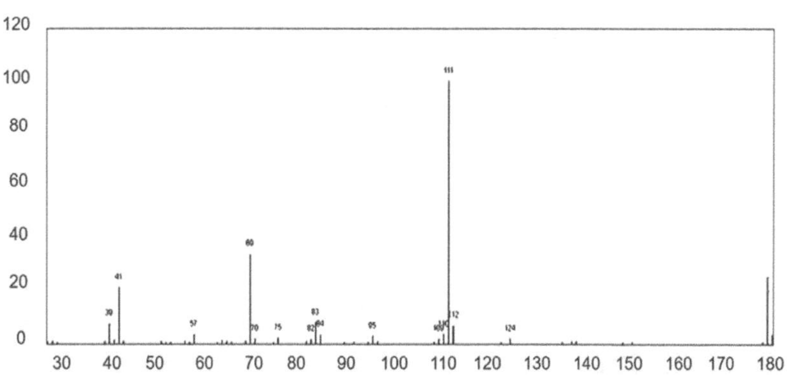

Fig. 25.7 Chromatogram of Cyclopropanecarboxamide, N-(4-fluorophenyl)- μ fraction of *C. albidum*

3.3 Retrieval of Target and Ligand

The flavodoxin protein with PDB ID 5B3K was retrieved in FASTA format from the Protein Data Bank (Fig. 25.3.) and phytocompounds like phytol, Hexadecanoic acid, Squalene, Heptanoic acid, Cyclopropanecarbroxamide and 6,9,12,15 octadecatrienoic acid having Pubchem ID 5280435, 8181, 638072, 69376, 532027 and 5280934 were retrived from pubchemrespectively (Table 25.3.).

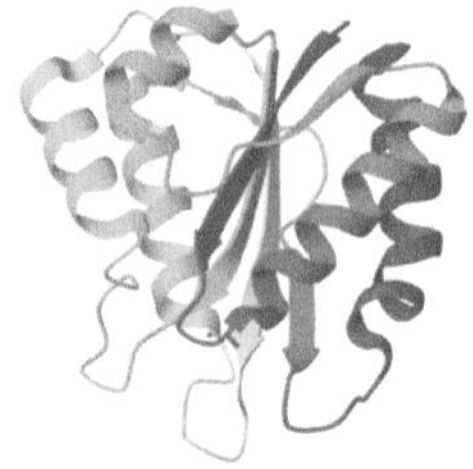

Fig. 25.8 3D structure of the protein flavodoxin (PDB ID:5b3k) present in *pseudomonas aeruginosa*

Table 25.3 The binding energy of each compound of *C. albidum*, H- bond donner and acceptor and protein 5B3K residue interacting with analyzed compounds.

Sl no	Ligand	3D Structure	2D structure	Binding affinity	Amino acid
1	Phytol	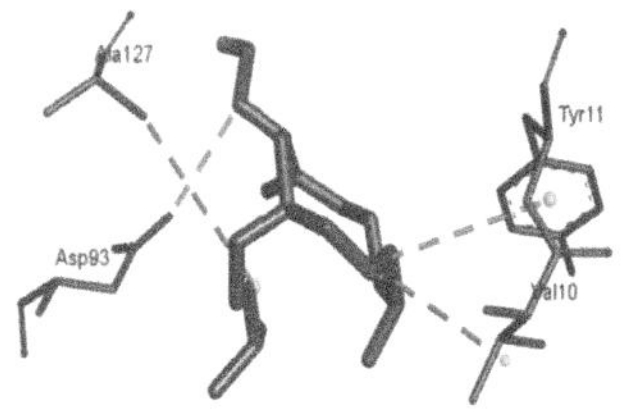	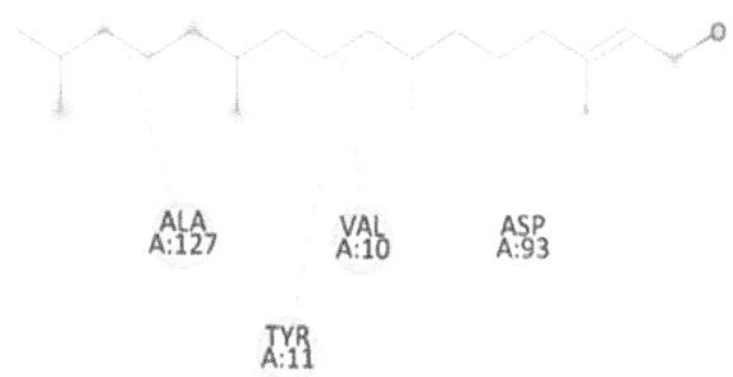	-4.3	ALA, VAL, ASP, TYR
2	Hexadecanoic acid	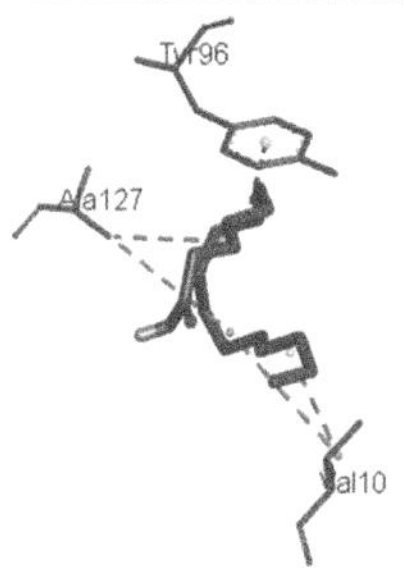	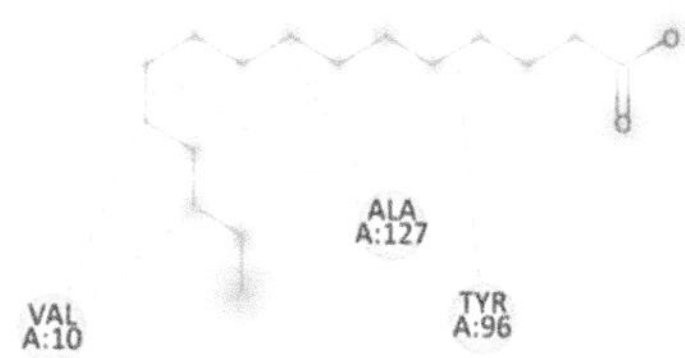	-4.1	VAL, ALA, TYR
3	Squalene	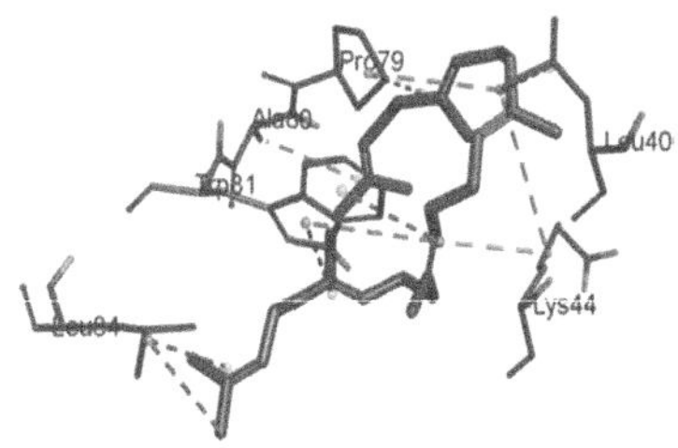	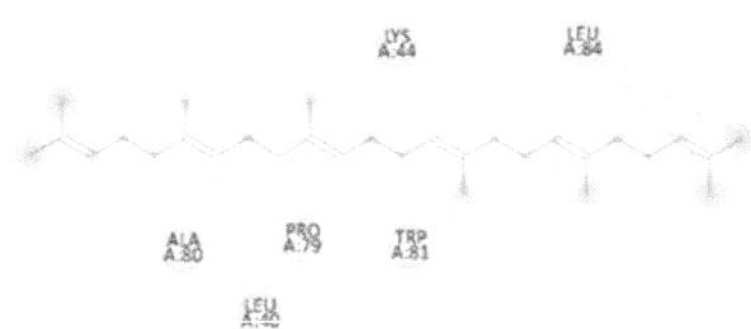	-5.6	LYS, LEU, ALA, LEU, PRO, TRP, TRP
4	Heptanoic acid	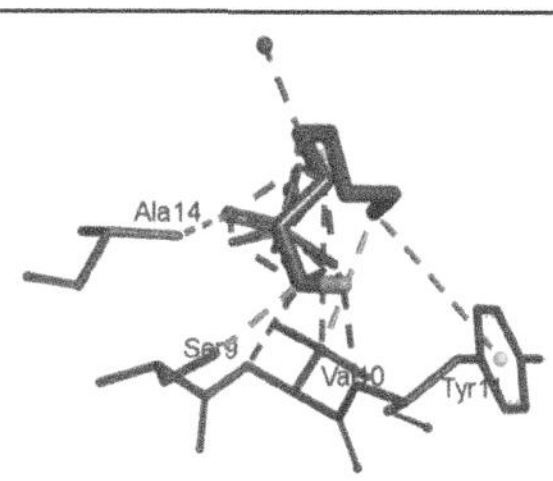	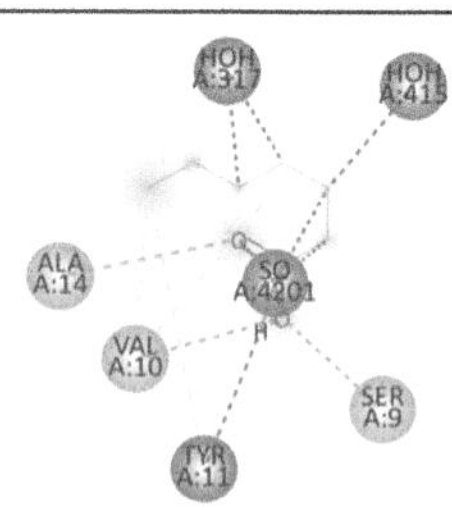	-4.1	HOH, SO, TYR, VAL, ALA, SER
5	6,9,12,15 octadecatrienoic acid	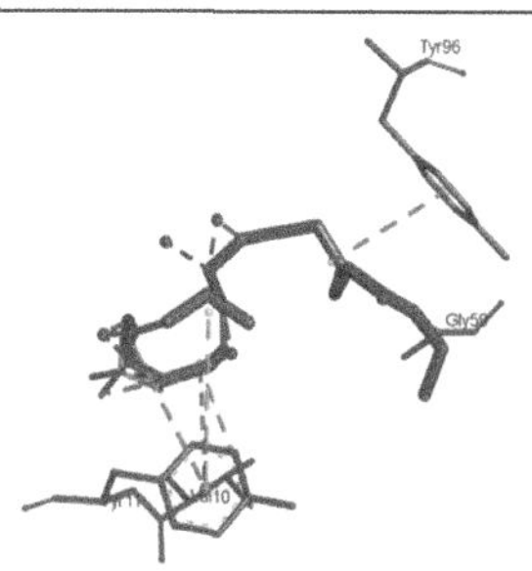	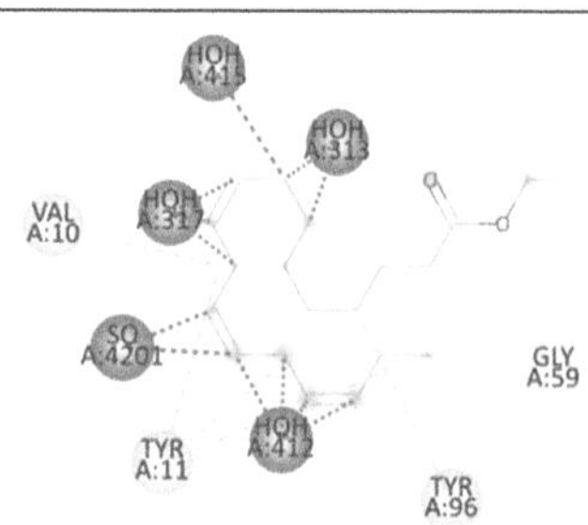	-4.3	VAL, SO, TYR, HOH, GLY

Sl no	Ligand	3D Structure	2D structure	Binding affinity	Amino acid
6	9,12,15-Octa-decatrienoic acid, (Z,Z,Z)	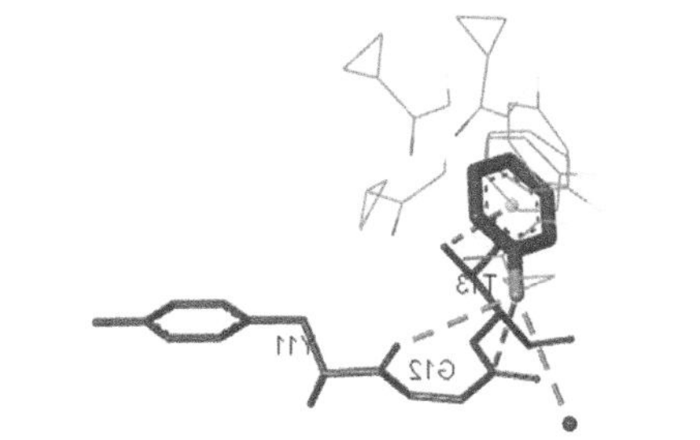	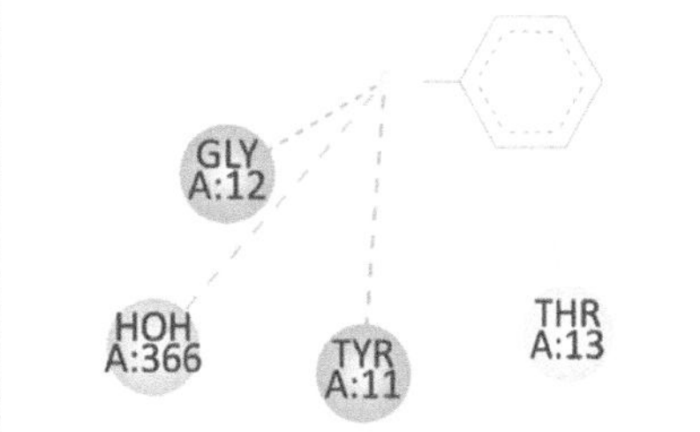	-4.03	GLY, TYR, THR, HOH

3.4 Docking Study using AutoDock

The molecular docking study shows the docking scores along with hydrogen bonding interactions and associated atoms were recorded for each drug.Phytol and 6,9,12,15 octadecatrienoic acid exhibited a docking score of -4.3 and formed bond with ALA, VAL, ASP, TYR in Phytol and VAL, SO,TYR,HOH,GLY in 6,9,12,15 octadecatrienoic acid. Hexadecanoic acid and Heptanoic acid displayed a docking score of -4.1, involved with VAL, ALA,TYR in Hexadecanoic acid and HOH, SO,TYR,VAL, ALA, SER in Heptanoic acid. Squalene shows -5.6 binding affinity. Cyclopropanecarbroxamide exhibited a docking score of -3.4 and formed a hydrogen bond with ALA38:O, with LEU70:HN acting as the atom involved in the interaction. These results provide insights into the binding interactions of these drugs with the target protein, shedding light on their potential efficacy and mechanism of action (Table 25.3.).

4. Discussion

The efficacy of *C. albidum* in addressing *P. aeruginosa* infections in CSOM illustrates the potential of phytochemicals as alternative therapeutic agents. This study utilized GC-MS analysis to identify key compounds within *C. albidum* and molecular docking to explore their interactions with the protein 5b3k, which is implicated in the pathogenicity of *P. aeruginosa*.

Treatment options for drug-resistant CSOM remain case of concern, with limited evidence-based data showing expert guidelines. This dearth of comprehensive information underscores the critical need for further research and development of effective therapies to address this challenging medical condition. For treating *P. aeruginosa* in CSOM, alternatives to standard antibiotics include acetic acid has shown potential in inhibiting and eradicating biofilm complexes formed by *P. aeruginosa*, making it a supplementary option for managing bacterial infections in CSOM where traditional treatments might be less effective due to antimicrobial resistance. In our study, the crude extract of *C. albidum* revealed good antipseudomonal activity alone and with ciprofloxacin [18].

C. albidum Phytocompounds include tannins, flavonoids, saponins, and alkaloids, which are commonly found in many medicinal plants. These substances are known to have antibacterial, anti-inflammatory, and antioxidant qualities. Bioactive substances with known antibacterial properties, such as phytol, hexadecanoic acid, squalene, heptanoic acid, cyclopropanecarboxamide, and 6, 9, 12, 15-octadecatrienoic acid, were confirmed to be present by the GC-MS analysis. [23]. Particularly, phytol and 6, 9, 12, 15-octadecatrienoic acid demonstrated significant interactions with the amino acids of the protein 5b3k, suggesting potential mechanisms through which these compounds may inhibit bacterial function and virulence. Phytol demonstrates antibacterial effects on *P. aeruginosa* by initiating an oxidative stress response within the bacteria. Through the buildup of reactive oxygen species, this mechanism basically interferes with the bacteria's regular cellular processes, causing bacterial damage and inhibition[24].

Hexadecanoic acid, also known as palmitic acid, exhibits anti-Pseudomonal activity, which may be attributed to its ability to disrupt bacterial cell membranes. This fatty acid can integrate into the lipid membrane of bacteria, destabilizing the membrane structure, leading to increased permeability and ultimately, bacterial cell death. This mechanism is significant in the context of treating infections caused by *P. aeruginosa*, a pathogen known for its resilience against many conventional antibiotics[25]. Heptanoic acid, also known as enanthic acid, is a fatty acid that could potentially exhibit antimicrobial properties, including activity against *P. aeruginosa.* Like other fatty acids, it might disrupt bacterial cell membranes, leading to increased permeability and disruption of essential metabolic functions. However, detailed studies specifically addressing the anti-pseudomonal activity of heptanoic acid are less common, and more research would be needed to confirm its effectiveness and mechanism against this particular bacterium. Squalene has been studied for its potential antimicrobial activities, including activity against *P. aeruginosa.* Its mechanism is believed to involve disruption of bacterial cell membranes, similar to other terpenoids. By integrating into the lipid bilayer, squalene can alter the membrane's fluidity and integrity, leading to impaired cellular function and potentially cell death[26].

In our molecular docking study showed significant binding potency, with scores ranging from -3.4 to -5.6. Phytol and 6,9,12,15-octadecatrienoic acid showed notable interactions with amino acids such as ALA, VAL, ASP, and TYR, suggesting strong potential to inhibit the bacterial protein's function. The molecular docking results provide valuable insights into the potential mechanism by which the identified phytocompounds interact with *P. aeruginosa*. The docking scores indicate a strong likelihood of these compounds to effectively bind and possibly inhibit the function of the protein 5b3k, which is crucial for the bacterium's survival and pathogenicity [27]. These findings are promising and suggest that *C. albidum* could be a source of novel anti-pseudomonal agents.

The rising antibiotic resistance among *P. aeruginosa* strains, especially those isolated from CSOM cases poses a significant challenge to current treatment paradigms [7]. The phytocompounds identified in this study offer potential alternatives to traditional antibiotics, which are becoming increasingly ineffective against resistant strains [28]. The study emphasized the existence *C. albidum* exhibits significant anti-pseudomonal activity, with its bioactive compounds effectively targeting critical bacterial proteins and pathways. Compared to other plant-based treatments, *C. albidum* shows superior binding affinities and a broader spectrum of antibacterial action, making it a promising candidate for treating CSOM. To completely determine its therapeutic potential and maximize its use in medical applications of related bioactive chemicals, more comparative research and clinical trials are necessary. On the other hand, *C. albidum* exhibited more diverse bacterial targets and more specific binding affinities [29].

Additionally, the Martini et al. investigation demonstrated that extraction of *C. albidum* contains a more diverse range of phenolic acids, enhancing its antimicrobial spectrum. The anti-pseudomonal efficacy of *C.albidum* is important, as its bioactive components efficiently target essential bacterial proteins and processes. *C.albidum* is a viable option for treating CSOM since it has better binding affinities and a wider spectrum of antibacterial action than other plant-based therapies. In order to completely determine its therapeutic potential and maximize its use in medical applications, more comparative research and clinical trials are necessary [30]. *In vivo* research and To advance these initial findings, clinical trials are necessary to assess the safety and efficacy of these substances in humans. Additionally, exploring synergistic effects with existing antibiotics could enhance their therapeutic potential and help to overcome current resistance issues [31]. The integration of traditional knowledge with contemporary scientific approaches provides a robust framework for the discovery of new drugs. The medicinal properties of *C. albidum*, as demonstrated in this study, highlight the importance of ethno-pharmacological practices in contributing to modern medicine [32]

Although it is aware that *Phyllanthus* species can be used to treat jaundice, the tribes of Chinnar, in Kerala's Idukki District, have been employing *C. albidum* G. Don as an effective treatment for the ailment. Initial plant compound showed a more concentration of triterpenes, tannins and flavonoids, while histochemical analysis showed the existence of starch grain, lignin and tannin. Physicochemical parameters that were evaluated included extractive values for alcohol (6.56%), ethyl acetate (1.85%), water (7.51%), total ash (4.32%), and acid-insoluble ash (0.06%). Additionally evaluated were the sequential extractive values for methanol (6.91%), Moisture content (7.82%), and petroleum ether (0.64%) [33].

Another study looked at C. *albidum*'s antibacterial and antioxidant properties and found that it worked well against eight Gram-negative and Gram-positive bacteria, including strains of methicillin-resistant S. aureus (MRSA), bacteria that produce metallo-beta-lactamase (MBL), and bacteria that are resistant to multiple drugs. The MBL-producing bacteria E. coli had the lowest zone of inhibition (9.3±0.57 mm), while B. subtilis had the highest zone of inhibition (19.8±0.57 mm). GC-MS analysis of the ethanol extract identified 23 chemicals, including phenol, methyl 6-O-[1-methylpropyl]-β-d-galactopyranoside, eicosane, isopropyl myristate, heptadecane, and n-hexadecanoic acid [23].

The essential oil extracted from *C. albidum* G. Don leaves exhibited moderate antibacterial action against a range of pathogens, including *E. faecalis, E. coli, K. pneumoniae, P. aeruginosa*, and *S. aureus*. This broad-spectrum antimicrobial activity suggests potential applications in industries such as pharmaceuticals, cosmetics, and food preservation where natural antimicrobial agents are sought after for their effectiveness against pathogenic bacteria and fungi[34].

According to a previous study, *C. albidum* leaf extract in methanol had a MIC of 0.866 mg/mL and that it had effects when mixed in 5:5 ratios with the antibiotic ceftriaxone. The leaf extract alone had a minimum bactericidal concentration (MBC) of 4.39 mg/mL, whereas ceftriaxone had an MBC of 87.7 mg/mL. The range of the combined MBC values was 0.33 to 3.07 mg/mL. The extract of leaf LC25 was 53.70 mg/mL and 58.88 mg/mL. This study demonstrated that the methanol leaf extract of *C. albidum*, when used with ceftriaxone, exhibited synergistic antibacterial activity against multidrug-resistant *P. aeruginosa*. Additionally, the leaf extract was found to be non-toxic to human lymphocytes at concentrations below 50 mg/mL.[18].

Numerous compounds are present in the leaves of *C. albiduum*, according to a phytochemical analysis. Certain compounds, including linalool (10.69%), caryophyllene (21.58%), phytol (7.02%), and b-phellandrene (8.74%) are identified as the main constituents by GC-MS analysis. These compounds contribute to the medicinal properties and potential therapeutic uses of *C.albidum*[33].

Phytochemical analysis of the *C. albidum* heartwood extract revealed five triterpenoids: arjunolic acid, ursolic acid, betulin.gallic acid, oleanolic acid, betulinic acid, ellagic acid, and beta-sitosterol were also present in the extract. It is noteworthy that this plant yielded the first isolated and published forms of oleanolic acid, betulinic acid, arjunolic acid, betulin, and ellagic acid. Furthermore, spectroscopic methods were used for the first time to describe gallic acid, beta-sitosterol, and ursolic acid. All of these compounds' structures were verified by spectroscopic investigation and comparison with data from the literature[34].

In a study, five plants extracts of *Argemone mexicana, Alangium salviifolium, Butea monosperma, C. albidum,* and *Strychnos nux-vomica*were evaluated for their antibacterial activities against isolated MDR bacteria. The antibacterial properties of the plant extracts were assessed using the agar well diffusion method. The antimicrobial activity of the five plant extracts, which came from various families, against the MDR bacteria varied. Following the isolation of pure phytocompounds and toxicity testing, all five plant extracts demonstrated strong antimicrobial activity, suggesting potential as sources for creating new medications [35].

5. Conclusion

The outcomes of GC-MS and molecular docking studies provide strong support for the use of *C. albidum* in the treatment of *P. aeruginosa* infections, particularly in the case of chronic illnesses like CSOM. The plant's ability to block a range of bacterial targets makes it a potential supplement or substitute for conventional antibiotics. This is particularly crucial given the rise in antibiotic-resistant *P. aeruginosa* strains. To completely determine its therapeutic potential and safety for treating CSOM and other bacterial infections, more research is needed in this subject, including in vivo investigations and clinical trials.

Conflicts of Interest

No conflicts of interest are disclosed by the writers.

Acknowledgements

Miss Utkalika Mallick is pursing PhD from Centre for Biotechnology at SOA University (PhD Reg. No 2381611022). The authors are grateful to Dean Research, SOA University and Director, ICMR-RMRC, Bhubaneswar for the extended facility in research.

References

1. Padhy, R. N. (2014). Incidence of hearing loss, tinnitus and vertigo among diabetes patients. *Siriraj Medical Journal, 66*(5).
2. Dudapaka, S. R., Bhushan, I. P., Kondra, S., & Padmanabhan, K. (2024). A study on influence of chronic sinusitis on mucosal active type of chronic otitis media in a tertiary care hospital, hyderabad. *Journal of Population Therapeutics and Clinical Pharmacology, 31*(1), 439–450.
3. Teele, D. W., Klein, J. O., Rosner, B., & Greater Boston Otitis Media Study Group. (1989). Epidemiology of otitis media during the first seven years of life in children in greater Boston: a prospective, cohort study. *Journal of infectious diseases, 160*(1), 83–94.
4. Nath, S., Mulik, S. S., Ayurved, P., Dhotre, G. A., & Lathwal, N. AN OVERVIEW OF CHRONIC SUPPURATIVE OTITIS EXTERNA (KARANASRAVA) AND TRIPHALA GUGGUL.
5. Song, J. J., Lee, B. D., Lee, K. H., Lee, J. D., Park, Y. J., & Park, M. K. (2016). Changes in antibiotic resistance in recurrent Pseudomonas aeruginosa infections of chronic suppurative otitis media. *Ear, Nose & Throat Journal, 95*(10-11), 446–451.
6. Terreni, M., Taccani, M., & Pregnolato, M. (2021). New antibiotics for multidrug-resistant bacterial strains: latest research developments and future perspectives. *Molecules, 26*(9), 2671.
7. Aguilar, G. R., Swetschinski, L. R., Weaver, N. D., Ikuta, K. S., Mestrovic, T., Gray, A. P., ... & Naghavi, M. (2023). The burden of antimicrobial resistance in the Americas in 2019: a cross-country systematic analysis. *The Lancet Regional Health–Americas, 25*.
8. Goswami, S., Kesarwaani, S., & Basumata, D. K. Saudi Journal of Medical and Pharmaceutical Sciences ISSN 2413–4929 (Print).
9. Swain, S. K., Lenka, S., Dubey, D., & Jena, P. P. (2022). Microbiology of chronic otitis media—a review. *DY Patil Journal of Health Sciences, 10*(2), 67–72.
10. Çetin, Y. S., Mollamehmetoğlu, S. O., Düzenli, U., Turan, M., & Bozan, N. (2022). Treatment of multi-drug resistant microorganisms in chronic suppurative otitis media. *B-ENT, 18*(1), 44–51.
11. Sahu, M. C., & Swain, S. K. (2019). Surveillance of antibiotic sensitivity pattern in chronic suppurative otitis media of an Indian teaching hospital. *World Journal of Otorhinolaryngology-Head and Neck Surgery, 5*(02), 88–94.
12. Alhadad, A. O., Elmhdwi, M. F., Salem, G. S., & Elshareef, S. M. (2021). Evaluation the in vitro antibacterial activity of acetone leaf extracts from Pistacia lentiscus against multi-drug resistant Pseudomonas aeruginosa and Staphylococcus aureus. *Journal of Medicinal Plants, 9*(4), 100–105.
13. Jia, X., Liang, Q., Chi, F., & Cao, W. (2012). Otomycosis in Shanghai: aetiology, clinical features and therapy. *Mycoses, 55*(5), 404–409.
14. Sahoo, S., Swain, S. K., Samal, S., & Sahu, M. C. (2018). Survilance of organisms associated with CSOM and otomycosis at a Tertiary Care Teaching Hospital. *Indian Journal of Public Health Research & Development, 9*(11), 2205–2213.
15. Kumar, S., Anwer, R., & Azzi, A. (2023). Molecular typing methods & resistance mechanisms of MDR Klebsiella pneumoniae. *AIMS microbiology, 9*(1), 112.
16. Sahu, M. C., Swain, S. K., & Kar, S. K. (2019). Genetically diversity of Pseudomonas aeruginosa isolated from chronic suppurative otitis media with respect to their antibiotic

sensitivity pattern. *Indian Journal of Otolaryngology and Head & Neck Surgery*, *71*, 1300–1308.
17. Swain, S. K., Behera, I. C., & Sahu, M. C. (2019). Role of Betadine irrigation in chronic suppurative otitis media: Our experiences in a tertiary care teaching hospital of East India. *Int J Health Allied Sci*, *8*(1), 29–32.
18. Sahu, M. C., Patnaik, R., & Padhy, R. N. (2014). In vitro combinational efficacy of ceftriaxone and leaf extract of Combretum albidum G. Don against multidrug-resistant Pseudomonas aeruginosa and host-toxicity testing with lymphocytes from human cord blood. *Journal of Acute Medicine*, *4*(1), 26–37.
19. Dubey, D., Patnaik, R., Ghosh, G., & Padhy, R. N. (2014). In vitro antibacterial activity, gas chromatography–mass spectrometry analysis of Woodfordia fruticosa Kurz. leaf extract and host toxicity testing with in vitro cultured lymphocytes from human umbilical cord blood. *Osong Public Health and Research Perspectives*, *5*(5), 298–312.
20. Hossain, M. A., AL-Raqmi, K. A. S., AL-Mijizy, Z. H., Weli, A. M., & Al-Riyami, Q. (2013). Study of total phenol, flavonoids contents and phytochemical screening of various leaves crude extracts of locally grown Thymus vulgaris. *Asian Pacific journal of tropical biomedicine*, *3*(9), 705–710.
21. Kozakov, D., Grove, L. E., Hall, D. R., Bohnuud, T., Mottarella, S. E., Luo, L., ... & Vajda, S. (2015). The FTMap family of web servers for determining and characterizing ligand-binding hot spots of proteins. *Nature protocols*, *10*(5), 733–755.
22. Morris, G. M., Huey, R., & Olson, A. J. (2008). Using autodock for ligand-receptor docking. *Current protocols in bioinformatics*, *24*(1), 8–14.
23. CHANDAR, B., & RAMASAMY, M. K. (2016). Evaluation of antioxidant, antibacterial activity of ethanolic extract in the leaves of Combretum albidum and gas chromatography-mass septrometry analysis. *Evaluation*, *9*(4).
24. Lee, W., Woo, E. R., & Lee, D. G. (2016). Phytol has antibacterial property by inducing oxidative stress response in Pseudomonas aeruginosa. *Free radical research*, *50*(12), 1309–1318.
25. Shah, S. D., Vadadoriya, N., & Bajpai, B. (2023). Evaluation of anti-quorum sensing activity of-hexadecanoic acid produced by PSEUDOMONAS stutzeri SJ4–A marine EPIBIOTIC bacterium. *Journal of microbiology, biotechnology and food sciences*, *13*(2), e5644-e5644.
26. Nazemi, M., Motallebi, A., Abbasi, E., Khaledi, M., & Zare, M. (2022). Antibacterial, antifungal, and cytotoxic activity of the fraction contains squalene in the acetone extract of a sea cucumber, Stichopus hermanni. *Iranian Journal of Fisheries Sciences*, *21*(6), 1495–1507.
27. Shoaib, M., Ali, Y., Shen, Y., & Ni, J. (2024). Identification of potential natural products derived from fungus growing termite, inhibiting Pseudomonas aeruginosa quorum sensing protein LasR using molecular docking and molecular dynamics simulation approach. *Journal of Biomolecular Structure and Dynamics*, *42*(3), 1126–1144.
28. Hassmann-Poznańska, E., Dzierżanowska, D., & Poznańska, M. (2014). Ostre rozlane zapalenie ucha zewnętrznego. *Polski Przegląd Otorynolaryngologiczny*, *3*(2), 84–89.
29. Martini, N. D. (2003). *The isolation and characterisation of antibacterial compounds from Combretum erythrophyllum (Burch.) Sond* (Doctoral dissertation, University of Pretoria).
30. Pandey, R., & Mishra, A. (2010). Antibacterial activities of crude extract of Aloe barbadensis to clinically isolated bacterial pathogens. *Applied biochemistry and biotechnology*, *160*, 1356–1361.
31. Khatun, M. R., Alam, K. M. F., Naznin, M., & Salam, M. A. (2021). Microbiology of chronic suppurative otitis media: an update from a tertiary care hospital in Bangladesh. *Pakistan journal of medical sciences*, *37*(3), 821.
32. Bantho, S., Naidoo, Y., Dewir, Y. H., & Singh, M. (2023). A review on the secretory structures, bioactive compounds and biological activities of selected Combretum species. *South African Journal of Botany*, *158*, 18–30.
33. Sreedhar, S., Kumar, U. P., Girija, T. P., & Remashree, A. B. (2013). Pharmacognostic standardisation of Combretum albidum G. Don leaf; a medicinally important liana. *Pharmacognosy Journal*, *5*(6), 247–255.
34. Kumar, U. P., Sreedhar, S., Remashree, A. B., & Purushothaman, E. (2017). Studies on chemical constituents, antioxidant and antimicrobial activity of essential oil from leaves of Combretum albidum G. Don. *Journal of Essential Oil Bearing Plants*, *20*(6), 1570–1578.
35. Sahu, M. C., Sahoo, S., & Samal, S. (2018). Antibacterial Activities of 5 Plants Against MDR Bacteria Isolated from Clinical Samples at a Tertiary Care Teaching Hospital. *Indian Journal of Public Health Research & Development*, *9*(11).

Note: All the tables and figures have been prepared by the author based on the research work

Research and Innovations in Industrial and Marine Biotechnology: A Circular Economy 2024 – Prof. Hrudayanath Thatoi et al. (eds)
© 2026 Taylor & Francis Group, London, ISBN 978-1-041-28285-3

26 Metagenomics: Unlocking Microbial Potential in Bioremediation

Bishwambhar Mishra*, Spoorthi Sada, Rajasri Yadavalli, C. Nagendranatha Reddy, Sanjeeb Kumar Mandal
Department of Biotechnology, Chaitanya Bharathi Institute of Technology, Gandipet, Hyderabad, Telangana, India

Jibanjyoti Panda
Bioresources and Traditional Knowledge Laboratory, Department of Wildlife and Biodiversity Conservation, Maharaja Sriram Chandra Bhanja Deo University, Sriram Chandra Vihar, Baripada, Mayurbhanj, Odisha, India

Amilia Nongbet
Department of Botany, University of Science & Technology Meghalaya, Baridua, Ri-Bhoi, Meghalaya, India

Bibhu Prasad Panda
Environmental Sciences, Department of Chemistry, ITER, Siksha 'O' Anusandhan (Deemed to be University), Bhubaneswar, Odisha, India

Yugal Kishore Mohanta
Nano-biotechnology and Translational Knowledge Laboratory, Department of Applied Biology, University of Science and Technology Meghalaya (USTM), Baridua Meghalaya, India

Abstract: The expanding population is resulting in a significant rise in daily demands, thereby driving industrialization. The application of diverse chemicals in various contexts is resulting in the pollution of our natural resources. This compels us to identify more effective strategies to address this issue. A beneficial technique for restoring a contaminated environment is microbial bioremediation. Numerous more methods, including biopile and bioslurping, are employed in microbial bioremediation. Metagenomics is a reliable technique employed to ascertain the genomes present in an environmental sample, which are subsequently evaluated. Researchers have used a variety of methods, some of which depend on culture and some that don't, to learn about the structure and function of microbial communities in contaminated areas. Recent advancements in metagenomics have facilitated the analysis of millions of genes with reduced time and expense. This degree of efficacy is achieved through the utilization of next-generation sequencing techniques, third-generation sequencing techniques, and other fluorescent in-situ hybridization methods, among others. This chapter aims to provide insights into metagenomic applications and emphasize the effectiveness of these methods in understanding compromised environmental samples to inform optimal solutions for environmental rehabilitation.

Keywords: Metagenome, Gene enrichment, Biodegradative genes, PCR, Microbial communities

*Corresponding author: bishwambhar_biotech@cbit.ac.in

DOI: 10.1201/9781003759003-26

1. INTRODUCTION

The initial decade of the 20th century witnessed the emergence of metagenomics, which introduced the 'omics' methodology and revolutionized the field of microbial ecology. Metagenomics necessitates no prior understanding of the community and involves the comprehensive reassembly of microbial genomes extracted from DNA samples obtained from environmental sources [1]. Metagenomic technology operates on the premise that DNA extracted directly from environmental samples ostensibly represents the complete genome of a community, which can be sequenced and analyzed akin to the entire genome of a pure bacterial culture, thereby enabling microbial ecologists to attain a comprehensive understanding of the community as a whole [2]. Microbial bioremediation denotes the method of employing microorganisms to cleanse or detoxify contaminated environments. These bacteria possess the capability to decompose, modify, or immobilize contaminants, thereby reducing their detrimental effects on the environment. Bioremediation is an environmentally sustainable way for eliminating pollution. Current methodologies encompass qualitative T-RFLP, which generates fingerprinting profiles for comparative analysis but fails to provide information on the specific identities of microbial contaminants, and quantitative real-time PCR (qPCR), which also lacks extensive data on microbial contaminants and microorganisms in biowaste, soil, and wastewater streams [3].

This chapter will present an overview of microbial community extraction, gene library construction, diverse screening methodologies for sample acquisition from contaminated sites, and several applications along with recent case studies involving the bioremediation of environmental contaminants within a contaminated matrix.

1.1 Enrichment of the Genome and Target Genes

A significant difficulty is the low frequency of positive findings in metagenomic library analysis. Numerous techniques have been devised to enhance metagenome libraries with valuable sequences, thereby increasing the representation of genes or pathways of interest [4]. The primary enrichment approach involves incorporating specific chemicals of interest into the medium as the exclusive source of carbon and energy to enhance cell proliferation. A principal enrichment approach entails incorporating a designated target chemical into the culture medium as the exclusive source of carbon and energy to enhance the fraction of the population that metabolizes that molecule [5].

The disparity in density between heavy (isotope-labeled) and light (unlabeled) DNA, SIP DNA, is separated utilizing density gradient ultracentrifugation with cesium chloride or cesium trifluoroacetate. Ethidium bromide causes tagged and unlabeled DNA to create two separate bands observable under UV light [6]. Environmental DNA was extracted using ultracentrifugation to obtain communities with elevated GC content. Enriching target genes before library construction will enhance the likelihood of positive outcomes in subsequent screening processes [7].

Figure 26.1 illustrates the various strategy for bioremediation alongwith metagenomics approach.

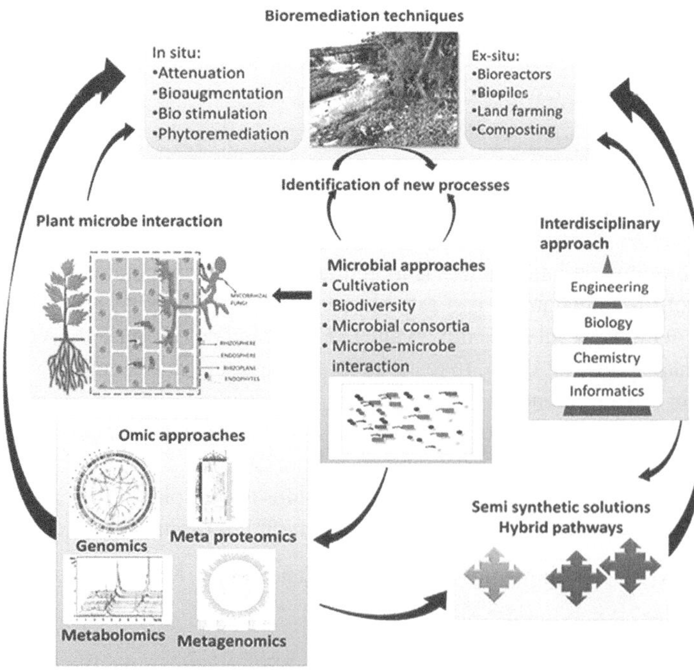

Fig. 26.1 Novel processes in order to improve bioremediation of polluted environments [22]. This figure is used under a creative commons CC BY 4.0 license

1.2 Extraction of Metagenomes and Construction of Libraries from Polluted Locations

Progress in science and technology has resulted in enhancements in research instruments utilized across several domains of scientific inquiry [8]. The predominant number of microorganisms in environmental samples cannot be cultivated using established methods, resulting in a misrepresentation of species diversity and gene functionality. Consequently, the methods employed must be meticulously chosen, as they represent the operator's initial interaction with the sample and can assess the quality of the analysis [9]. Metagenomic DNA can be directly retrieved from contaminated media via a culture-independent technique. To represent all microbial genomes, it is important to harvest metagenomic DNA from polluted locations. Two approaches exist for isolating metagenomic DNA from environmental samples: cell extraction and direct lysis. Typically, metagenomic extraction is conducted by physical or chemical techniques. Mechanical cell destruction via bead beating yields greater diversity than chemical approaches, facilitating the separation of high molecular weight DNA appropriate for the building of extensive intercalated metagenomic DNA libraries [10]. Figure 26.2 representation the metogenomic analysis of microorganisms from contaminated water.

Procedure for isolating and purifying genetic material from soil, water, or enrichment samples obtained from seas or agricultural land to construct metagenomic libraries. A library is established by cloning DNA fragments into designated vectors for incorporation into host cell lines, thereafter screening for genes and/or activities of interest. Extensive DNA fragments (25 to 200 Kb) derived from environmental samples and inserted into designated vectors can be utilized to construct metagenomic libraries [11]. Libraries are categorized into two categories based on insert size: tiny inserts (under 15 Kb) utilize plasmids, whereas large inserts employ vectors such as fosmids, cosmids, and BACs. Small-insert libraries possess a notable

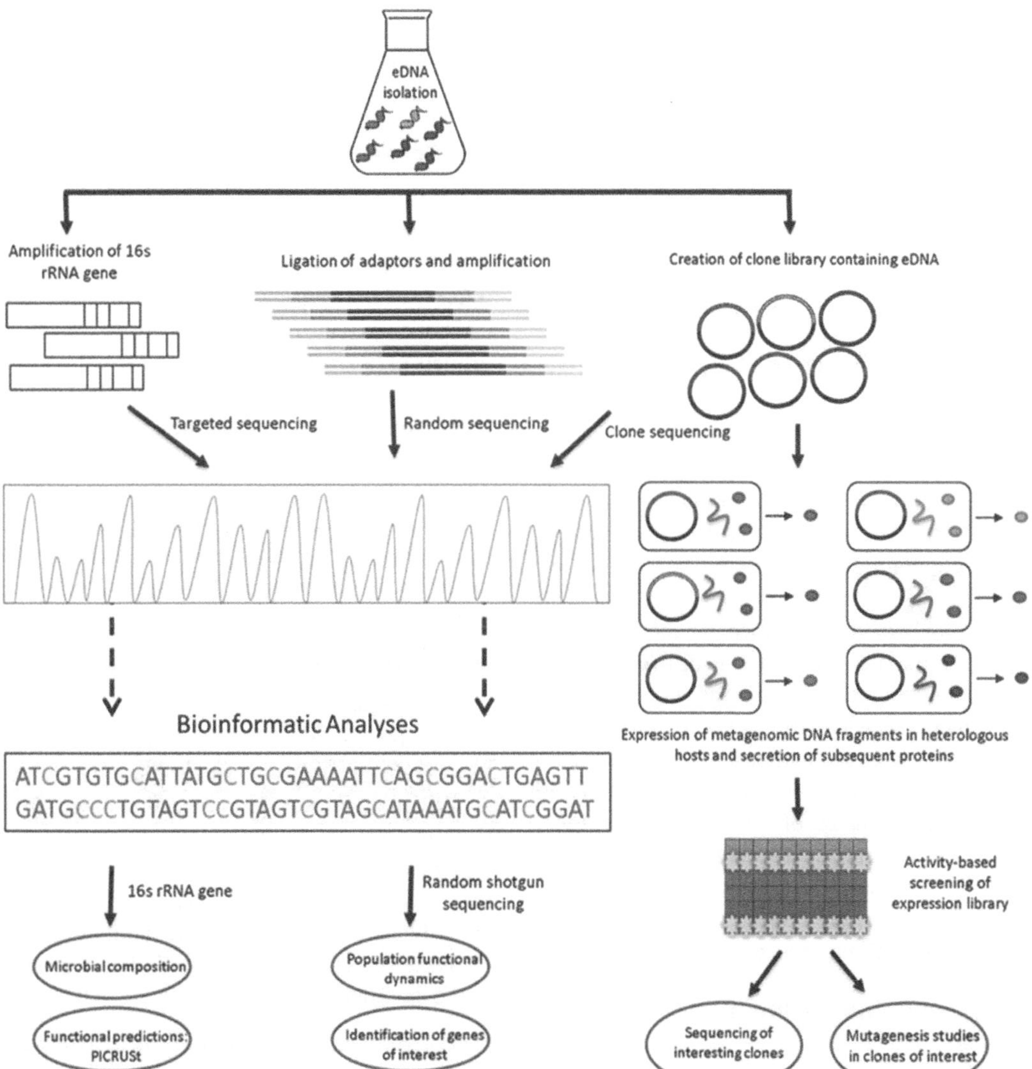

Fig. 26.2 Schematic representation of metogenomic analysis from contaminated samples [23]. This figure is used under a creative commons CC BY 4.0 license

advantage over big-insert libraries, as microorganisms can be lysed using aggressive methods that fragment the DNA of large inserts to yield small inserts [12].

The majority of genes in metagenomic libraries typically cannot be expressed in a singular host organism. An example of a vector with an extensive host range is VECA (Artificial E. coli Chromosome Vectors - Streptomyces). Most actinomycete genes are not expressed in E. coli, which fails to recognize around 80% of actinomycete promoters when utilized as a host due to a substantial disparity in G+C content [13]. These organisms possess numerous intriguing genes that encode enzymes and antibiotics, making metagenomic libraries essential for discovering functional genes of actinomycetes in environmental samples. This should produce a library of subgenomes utilizing Streptomyces as a host. Metagenomic DNA was sorted by G+C content using VECA vectors and ultracentrifugation prior to constructing expression libraries. DNA with elevated G+C content is utilized in Streptomyces libraries, whereas DNA with diminished G+C content is employed for transformation into the E. coli host. Owing to the elevated G+C content of actinomycete DNA, metagenome libraries exhibited a greater quantity of active colonies when Streptomyces served as the host [14].

1.3 Metagenomic Approaches for Obtaining Biodegradative Genes from Contaminated Locations

In open systems or confined habitats, several physicochemical and biological parameters that require periodic assessment and monitoring significantly affect bioremediation strategies and outcomes. Microorganisms are significant, particularly in bioremediation applications, however research into their catabolic capabilities and in situ kinetics is ongoing [4]. Metagenomic approaches for sample classification investigate the correlations between alterations in environmental or host circumstances and microbial populations by detecting or predicting these categories. Metagenomic sequencing data can be categorized into two groups based on the analytical methodologies employed: one group utilizes whole-genome sequencing fragments, while the other employs marker gene sequences such as 16S rRNA [15]. Numerous screening techniques, such as function and sequence-based methods, have been employed to isolate biodegradable genes from the metagenomes of contaminated settings. The remaining four primary screening techniques now employed are feature-based screening, sequence-guided screening, SIGEX (Substrate-Induced Gene Expression) screening, and cross-configuration screening [15].

1.4 Profiling Gene Expression Induced by Substrate

A high-throughput technique known as SIGEX employs operon trap vectors to identify substrate-induced genes. The SIGEX vector (pGFP18) was initially employed to construct a metagenomic DNA library, although self-ligating clones exhibiting GFP fluorescence post-induction with isopropyl-D-1-thiogalactopyranoside (IPTG) were disregarded. Furthermore, IPTG-induced sorting of non-fluorescent DNA-laden cells was employed to identify genes potentially activated by the substrate. This method can be used to find biodegradable genes of interest without using colorimetric tests or traditional coating methods[16]. In contrast to unmodified substrates, which pose risks, incur high costs, and exhibit side effects, colourimetric displays do not necessitate modified substrates. Researchers have recently identified the cup operon (phenol degradation operon), genes associated with the benzoate and catechol pathways, and genes that encode enzymes for aromatic hydrocarbon conversion, including BZO062 (dehydrogenase), BZO135 (tyrosine lyase), BZO0750 (cytochrome P4), BZO032 (decarboxylase), and NAP3 (hydroxylase) [2]. Due to SIGEX's sensitivity to the dimensions and orientation of the genes conferring the desired trait, its utility is limited. Catabolic genes that are continuously expressed were excluded from the screening process. Furthermore, SIGEX could not identify active clones containing the requisite catabolic genes that were cloned in the reverse orientation relative to GFP [4].

1.5 Screening Based on Sequence

Screening using PCR Degenerate Primer

This technique employs conserved nucleotide sequences of established catabolic enzymes to pinpoint regions of interest within genes. Consensus sequences of established catabolic enzymes were utilized to create degenerate primers or hybridization probes for the direct amplification of genes encoding enzymes with analogous activities in environmental metagenomes. The expression of the identified genes in a culturable heterologous expression system will thereafter provide confirmation of their presence. Degenerate primers or probes designed from the sequence of a target gene with a specific function also exclude homologous genes in the development of novel catabolic enzymes, presenting a notable drawback of this approach [4].

Microarray and PCR Based Strategies

Recent progress in microarray technology has made it possible to test large metagenomic libraries for biodegradable genes at the same time. The array has 24,243 oligonucleotide probes that target 10,000 genes that are linked to the breakdown of organic contaminants and the decrease or resistance of metals [17]. The primers and target-specific probes used in the screening program are only made from known gene families or proteins in the database. This makes it hard to find new genes or proteins in the environment. [4].

Next-Generation Sequencing and Third-Generation Sequencing

Utilizing Rosalind Franklin's foundational research in X-ray diffraction and DNA crystallography, Watson and Crick elucidated the structure of DNA in 1953. Robert Holley's 1965 research on tRNA and subsequent investigations on the RNA of bacteriophage MS2 established RNA as the inaugural molecule to be sequenced. The chain-termination method, developed in 1977 by Fredrick Sanger and his associates, was a significant advancement that enabled numerous research organizations to utilize these techniques for DNA sequencing. The foundational method developed in 1986 for automated DNA sequencing. This marked the onset of a golden era for the development of advanced sequencing systems, notably encompassing capillary DNA sequencers. Sanger sequencing, also known as the chain-termination method, employs a DNA sequence of interest as a template for PCR, including modified nucleotides, commonly termed dideoxyribonucleotides (ddNTPs), during the extension phase of strand synthesis [18]. Upon the incorporation of ddNTPs by DNA polymerase, elongation halts, leading to the production of multiple copies of the DNA sequence of varying lengths. The determination of these chain-terminated oligonucleotides is achieved through size differentiation, utilizing either capillary tubes in modern automated capillary sequencers or gel electrophoresis in earlier methodologies [19]. The significant technological advancements led to the completion of the Human Genome Project in 2003. In contrast to Sanger sequencing, the inaugural commercially viable next-generation sequencing (NGS) technique, or second generation (2G), was introduced in 2005 and had the capability to amplify millions of copies of a single DNA sequence in a massively parallel manner.

The next-generation DNA sequencing method, third-generation sequencing (TGS), has gained recognition in biology as a tool to examine genomes, transcriptomes, and metagenomes in previously unheard-of detail [20]. These outcomes, which came from single-molecule sequencing techniques, provide:

- Long reads without amplification.
- Immediate single-molecule sequencing and detection of epigenetic alterations on native DNA.
- Direct sequencing through portions of the genome that are unavailable or difficult to examine using short-read technologies.
- Constant genome coverage because they are less susceptible to GC content than short-read platforms.

The UMGC offers a comprehensive array of advanced sequencing options that can meet any project size, budget, or turnaround time. The UMGC provides long-read sequencing products from PacBio and Oxford Nanopore. As a PacBio Certified Service Provider with five years of experience utilizing the Sequel II system, we routinely undergo PacBio certification to demon-strate our capability to generate high-quality data using the latest workflows [21].

2. Conclusion

Metagenomics is a significant achievement in the emerging area that focuses on microorganisms essential for the functioning of ecosystems. Bioremediation procedures employ the metabolic powers of microorganisms to cleanse polluted environments. Metagenomics is augmenting our comprehension of the variety, ecology, evolution, and functionality of the microbial realm by granting access to the hitherto unattainable genomes of extensive communities of bacteria, viruses, and fungi. Furthermore, it is fostering the advancement of innovative applications across several sectors. Similarly, direct DNA sequencing of environmental samples has enabled the exploration of previously unexamined bacteria. Monitoring bacterial communities associated with humans facilitates the formulation of methods for their regulation to enhance human health.

References

1. Xie, R., Danso, B., Sun, J., Al-Zahrani, M., Dar, M. A., Al-Tohamy, R., & Ali, S. S. (2024). Biorefinery and Bioremediation Strategies for Efficient Management of Recalcitrant Pollutants Using Termites as an Obscure yet Promising Source of Bacterial Gut Symbionts: A Review. Insects, 15(11), 908. https://doi.org/10.3390/insects15110908
2. Zhang, C., Wohlhueter, R., & Zhang, H. (2016). Genetically modified foods: A critical review of their promise and problems. Food Science and Human Wellness, 5(3), 116–123.
3. Zaouri, N., Jumat, M.R., Cheema, T., & Hong, P.Y., (2020) Metagenomics-based evaluation of groundwater microbial profiles in response to treated wastewater discharge, Environ. Res., 180, 108835. doi:10.1016/j.envres.2019.108835.
4. Pushpanathan, M., Jayashree, S., Gunasekaran, P., & Rajendhran, J., (2014). Microbial bioremediation. Microb. Biodegrad. Biorem., 1, 407–419.
5. Dias, R., Silva, L. C., Eller, M. R., Oliveira, V. M., De Paula, S., & Silva, C. C. (2014). Metagenomics: Library construction and screening methods. *V Metagenom. Methods Appl. Perspect*, *5*, 28–34.
6. Kim, J., Hwangbo, M., Shih, C. H., & Chu, K. H. (2023). Advances and perspectives of using stable isotope probing (SIP)-based technologies in contaminant biodegradation. Water Research X, 20, 100187.
7. Bai, X., Li, K., Xu, L., Zhang, G., Zhang, M., & Huang, Y. (2024). Direct evidence for selective microbial enrichment with plastic degradation potential in the plastisphere. Science of The Total Environment, 954, 176576.
8. Satam, H., Joshi, K., Mangrolia, U., Waghoo, S., Zaidi, G., Rawool, S., ... & Malonia, S. K. (2023). Next-generation sequencing technology: current trends and advancements. Biology, 12(7), 997.
9. Sahu, A., Kumar, N., Singh, C. P., & Singh, M. (2023). Environmental DNA (eDNA): Powerful technique for biodiversity conservation. Journal for Nature Conservation, 71, 126325.

10. Bag, S., Saha, B., Mehta, O., Anbumani, D., Kumar, N., Dayal, M., ... & Das, B. (2016). An improved method for high quality metagenomics DNA extraction from human and environmental samples. Scientific reports, 6(1), 26775.
11. Zhang L, Chen F, Zeng Z, Xu M, Sun F, Yang L, Bi X, Lin Y, Gao Y, Hao H, Yi W, Li M and Xie Y (2021) Advances in Metagenomics and Its Application in Environmental Microorganisms. Front. Microbiol. 12:766364. doi: 10.3389/fmicb.2021.766364
12. Fachinetti, D., Masumoto, H., & Kouprina, N. (2020). Artificial chromosomes. Experimental Cell Research, 396(1), 112302.
13. Rebets, Y., Kormanec, J., Luzhetskyy, A., Bernaerts, K., & Anné, J. (2017). Cloning and expression of metagenomic DNA in Streptomyces lividans and subsequent fermentation for optimized production. Metagenomics: Methods and Protocols, 99–144.
14. Wilson, M. C., & Piel, J. (2013). Metagenomic approaches for exploiting uncultivated bacteria as a resource for novel biosynthetic enzymology. Chemistry & biology, 20(5), 636–647.
15. Kumar Awasthi, M., Ravindran, B., Sarsaiya, S., Chen, H., Wainaina, S., Singh, E., Liu, T., Kumar, S., Pandey, A., Singh, L., & Zhang, Z., (2020). Retracted article: Metagenomics for taxonomy profiling: Tools and approaches. Bioeng., 11(1), 356–374. https://doi.org/10.1080/21655979.2020.1736238
16. Uchiyama, T., & Miyazaki, K. (2010). Substrate-induced gene expression screening: a method for high-throughput screening of metagenome libraries. Metagenomics: Methods and Protocols, 153–168.
17. He, Z., Gentry, T.J., Schadt, C.W., Wu, L., Liebich, J., Chong, S.C., et al., 2007. GeoChip: a comprehensive microarray for investigating biogeochemical, ecological and environmental processes. ISME J., 1(1), 6777.
18. Bunaciu, A. A., UdriŞTioiu, E. G., & Aboul-Enein, H. Y. (2015). X-ray diffraction: instrumentation and applications. Critical reviews in analytical chemistry, 45(4), 289–299.
19. Sanger, F., Nicklen, S., & Coulson, A.R., (1977). DNA sequencing with chain-terminating inhibitors. Proceed. Nat. Acad. Sci., 74(12), 5463–5467.
20. Lee, H., Gurtowski, J., Yoo, S., Nattestad, M., Marcus, S., Goodwin, S., ... & Schatz, M. C., (2016). Third-generation sequencing and the future of genomics. BioRxiv, 048603.
21. Rhoads, A., & Au, K.F., (2015). PacBio sequencing and its applications. Genom. Proteom. Bioinform., 13(5), 278–289.
22. Malla, M. A., Dubey, A., Yadav, S., Kumar, A., Hashem, A., & Abd_Allah, E. F. (2018). Understanding and designing the strategies for the microbe-mediated remediation of environmental contaminants using omics approaches. Frontiers in Microbiology, 9, 1132.
23. Coughlan, L. M., Cotter, P. D., Hill, C., & Alvarez-Ordóñez, A. (2015). Biotechnological applications of functional metagenomics in the food and pharmaceutical industries. Frontiers in microbiology, 6, 672.

Research and Innovations in Industrial and Marine Biotechnology: A Circular Economy 2024 – Prof. Hrudayanath Thatoi et al. (eds)
© 2026 Taylor & Francis Group, London, ISBN 978-1-041-28285-3

27 Prevalence and Characterization of Colistin-Resistant Gram-Negative Bacteria in Wastewater: A Geospatial and Microbiological Analysis

Shreya Singh, Alisha Sinha
Centre for Biotechnology,
Siksha 'O' Anusandhan Deemed to be University,
Kalinganagar, Bhubaneswar, Odisha, India
Division of Microbiology,
ICMR-Regional Medical Research Centre, Chandrasekharpur,
Bhubaneswar, Odisha, India

Rajesh Kumar Sahoo
Centre for Biotechnology,
Siksha 'O' Anusandhan Deemed to be University,
Kalinganagar, Bhubaneswar, Odisha, India

Mahesh Chandra Sahu*
Division of Microbiology,
ICMR-Regional Medical Research Centre, Chandrasekharpur,
Bhubaneswar, Odisha, India

Abstract: Colistin is an antibiotic used in the last defence treatment of multidrug-resistant gram-negative infections. But the rise of colistin resistance poses a serious threat to human health, especially in environmental reservoirs like wastewater. Wastewater treatment plants are critical monitoring sites as they receive influent from various sources, including hospitals and agricultural facilities. This study investigates the prevalence of colistin-resistant gram-negative bacteria (GNB) in wastewater samples from multiple wastewater locations. Wastewater samples were collected from 11 different waste waterline located at varying geographic coordinates in Bhubaneswar. Coordinates for each location were recorded, Sai Vihar drain no. 1B, Service drain no. 1 East 1, and so forth. Bacteria were isolated on media like MacConkey agar, followed by biochemical and identification with help of VITEK 2. Antibiotic susceptibility testing (ABST) was conducted to determine resistance profiles for colistin and other relevant antibiotics using the disk diffusion method. A total of 100 GNB isolates were identified, with an overall colistin resistance prevalence of 16 % across all sites. The Sahi Vihar 1B drain had the greatest rate of colistin resistance, where 8% of isolates displayed resistance. The identified colistin-resistant species primarily included *Shigella Sonnei*, *Citrobacter freundii*, *Proteus mirabilis*. ABST results indicated multidrug resistance patterns in 3% of colistin-resistant isolates, with frequent resistance to cephalosporins, carbapenems. The study highlights the significant prevalence of resistance to colistin in GNB isolates from wastewater and emphasizes the role of WWTPs as critical points for monitoring resistance. These findings underscore the need for stringent wastewater management practices and enhanced surveillance of antibiotic resistance in environmental reservoirs to limit the spread of resistance genes. The geographic and microbiological data presented herein provide valuable insights for future monitoring and control strategies targeting colistin-resistant pathogens in wastewater environments.

Keywords: Colistin resistance, Wastewater, Gram-negative bacteria, Antibiotic susceptibility testing, MCR gene, Environmental surveillance, Multidrug resistance

*Corresponding author: mchsahu@gmail.com

DOI: 10.1201/9781003759003-27

1. Introduction

The global rise of antimicrobial resistance (AMR) is one of the significant challenges to public health and environmental sustainability in the modern era [1]. AMR, driven by the overuse and inappropriate use of antibiotics in clinical, agricultural, and industrial settings, has severely undermined the efficacy of many critical antimicrobial treatments [2]. Among the most alarming developments in this context is the incidence and proliferation of colistin insusceptibility in Gram-negative bacteria (GNB). Colistin, considered as treatment for last line defence, is used to treat serious infections caused by multidrug-resistant (MDR) pathogens [3]. However, its increasing ineffectiveness due to resistance threatens its efficacy, leaving limited therapeutic options for managing critical infections. AMR as a globalized issue, exacerbated by interconnected factors such as population growth, urbanization, and inadequate waste management systems. The role of environmental reservoirs in the dissemination of AMR, particularly wastewater, has drawn increasing attention in recent years [1].

Wastewater systems have become recognized as important reservoirs for antibiotic resistance genes (ARGs) [4]. These settings are perfect for the selection and spread of resistance strains due to the high density of microbial communities and enduring presence of antibiotic residues [5]. The horizontal transfer of resistance genes, such as the mobile colistin resistance (mcr) genes, makes the issue worse by facilitating the quick spread of resistance among many bacterial species [6]. The presence of mcr genes in aquatic environments, underscoring their critical role in resistance dissemination further proves this issue. Similarly, untreated or inadequately treated wastewater could serve as a great place for the spread of resistant bacteria into surrounding ecosystems, including agricultural lands and natural water bodies [7, 8].

The occurrence of colistin-resistant GNB in wastewater poses significant risks to both environmental and public health. GNB such as *Klebsiella pneumoniae, Escherichia coli*, and *Pseudomonas aeruginosa* are often associated with colistin resistance. These pathogens not only cause severe infections in humans but also exhibit remarkable adaptability, allowing them to persist in wastewater environments [9]. Recent studies have highlighted the function of wastewater treatment plants (WWTPs) in shaping the dynamics of resistance. While these facilities are designed to mitigate microbial contamination, evidence suggests they may inadvertently select for antimicrobial-resistant bacteria, particularly when treatment processes are insufficient to remove ARGs or residual antibiotics [10, 11]. Untreated wastewater serves as a great spot for MDR and colistin-resistant *K. pneumoniae*. Similarly, Sims and Kasprzyk-Hordern (2020) emphasized the role of wastewater in driving AMR propagation, warning of the significant risks posed by inadequately managed effluents [12, 13].

The implications of wastewater contamination with colistin-resistant bacteria are far-reaching. Pathogens from wastewater can infiltrate agricultural systems via irrigation, enter aquatic environments, and subsequently impact the food chain [14]. The potential risks associated with antibiotic-resistant bacteria and ARGs from municipal solid waste landfills, drawing parallels to wastewater systems. These contaminated environments can lead to direct human exposure or indirect consequences, such as the contamination of drinking water sources and food products. Moreover, the environmental persistence of colistin-resistant bacteria and their genetic determinants complicates efforts to curb their spread [15]. The scarcity of accessible treatments for illnesses brought on by bacteria resistant to colistin highlights the urgent need for efficient monitoring and mitigation techniques [16].

Despite significant risks posed by colistin resistance in wastewater, there remains a lack of comprehensive research addressing this issue. While various studies have explored the occurrence of resistance in wastewater systems, gaps persist in understanding the geospatial and microbiological characteristics of colistin-resistant bacteria [17]. Factors such as population density, urbanization, and environmental variability influence the distribution of resistance, yet the interplay between these factors remains insufficiently studied. The pathogenicity of resistant organisms in various environments are well documented, but few studies have combined microbiological and geospatial analyses to provide a holistic view of resistance dissemination patterns. This gap is particularly significant given the geospatial variability in resistance prevalence, which has implications for designing targeted interventions and policies [17, 18].

By examining the frequency and characteristics of colistin-resistant GNB in wastewater using a combination of microbiological and geospatial analysis, this study seeks to close these gaps. Specifically, the objectives are to determine the occurrence of colistin-insusceptibility bacteria in wastewater samples collected from diverse geographical locations, characterize their resistance profiles and genetic determinants, and analyse their geospatial distribution to identify environmental and anthropogenic factors influencing their spread. By integrating microbiological insights with geospatial analyses, this study provides a comprehensive understanding of how colistin resistance is disseminated through wastewater systems and to identify potential hotspots for targeted monitoring and mitigation efforts. The intersection of AMR, colistin resistance, and environmental reservoirs such as wastewater represents a critical area of concern for public health and ecological safety. This study will contribute to bridging the knowledge gap in this field by addressing the microbiological and geospatial dimensions of colistin-resistant bacteria in wastewater. The findings will provide valuable insights for developing various strategies to curb the dissemination of resistance and safeguard the environmental and human health.

2. Materials and Methods

2.1 Study Sites and Sample Collection

Samples of wastewater were gathered from 11 sites in Bhubaneswar, each geolocated to document potential geospatial patterns in colistin resistance. Sites included the following: Sai Vihar drain no. 1B (Latitude: 20.332253°, Longitude: 85.816754°), Service drain no. 1 East 1 (Latitude: 20.332731°, Longitude: 85.816755°). Coordinates for each site were recorded and plotted for analysis of spatial distribution [19].

2.2 Bacterial Isolation and Identification

The collected sample were serially diluted and 10^{-1}, 10^{-2},10^{-3} times dilution was spread on Nutrient agar and MacConkey agar for different colony forming unit and then the diversity of the gram-negative bacteria was noted according to different location. Using selective medium, like MacConkey agar, collected samples were further processed to extract Gram-negative bacteria. After isolation, VITEK 2 was used to identify the bacteria, allowing for accurate and rapid identification of the species [20].

2.3 Antibiotic Susceptibility Testing (ABST)

ABST was conducted to assess resistance patterns, with colistin susceptibility tested via the disk diffusion method Kirby Baur method according to CLSI guidelines. Additional antibiotics, including cephalosporins, carbapenems, were tested to evaluate the prevalence of multidrug resistance [21].

3. Results

In Bhubaneswar, wastewater samples were collected from 11 different spots (Table 27.1.), each showing different levels of microbes and resistance. The number of microbes, counted as CFUs, depicted variation according to the different location (Fig. 27.1). The highest count observed from Sai Vihar Drain 1B, which had 398 CFUs at a 10^{-1} dilution. On the other hand, Club Town Apartment Service Drain 4 had the lowest count, with just 13 CFUs at a 10^{-3}

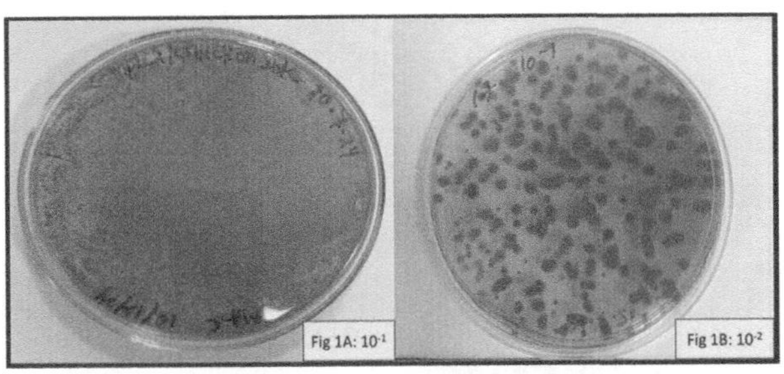

Fig. 27.1 MacConkey agar plate showing colonies (CFU). Figure 1A: Gram negative colonies on MacConkey agar plate from 10^{-1} serial dilution. Figure 1B: Gram negative colonies on MacConkey agar plate from 10^{-2} serial dilution

Table 27.1 Representing colony forming unit with several dilution and from different location of wastewater

S. No.	Waste Water location	(latitude/ longitude)	Dilution Factor	No. of Colony (CFU)
1.	Sai premium apartment Service drain no. 1 East 1	(Lat 20.332253/ long 85.816754)	10^{-1} 10^{-2} 10^{-3}	316 289 158
2.	Pragati Vihar drain no. 1B	(Lat 20.332781/ long 85.816754)	10^{-1} 10^{-2} 10^{-3}	352 298 189
3.	Sai Vihar drain no. 1B	(Lat 20.332253 / long 85.816754)	10^{-1} 10^{-2} 10^{-3}	398 286 149
4.	Vihar Road Service drain 2 East 2	(Lat 20.332781/ long 85.816754)	10^{-1} 10^{-2} 10^{-3}	265 184 98
5.	Kanaka durganagar Service drain 1	(Lat 20.33305/ long 85.816915)	10^{-1} 10^{-2} 10^{-3}	287 134 56
6.	West kanaka durganagar Service drain 3,	(Lat 20.333143/ long 85.817015)	10^{-1} 10^{-2} 10^{-3}	203 127 64
7.	Club town apartment Service drain 4,	(Lat 20.222152/ long 85.82624)	10^{-1} 10^{-2} 10^{-3}	198 97 13
8.	Club town apartment Main drain 3	(Lat 20.221456/ long 85.74264)	10^{-1} 10^{-2} 10^{-3}	346 252 134
9.	Niladri vihar road Supported drain 1, South 1	(lat 20.325034/ long 85.815833)	10^{-1} 10^{-2} 10^{-3}	207 124 78
10.	Prachi enclave Supported drain east 1 care hospital	(lat 20.322214/ long 85.813052)	10^{-1} 10^{-2} 10^{-3}	234 124 72
11.	Kanak Durga Nagar Main drain 1	(Lat 20.335502/ long 85.521283)	10^{-1} 10^{-2} 10^{-3}	356 246 108

dilution. These findings suggest considerable geospatial variability in microbial load, likely influenced by factors such as population density and wastewater composition. The bacterial profile (Table 27.2.) across different drain locations demonstrated the prevalence of both Gram-negative and Gram-positive species (Fig. 27.2.).

We found a total of 100 bacterial samples, mostly from GNB. The most dominant were *C. freundii* at 16% and *E. coli* at 14.10% (Table 27.3.). In comparison, Gram-positive bacteria like *S. aureus* were observed less often, making up only 6.31% (Fig. 27.3.). Certain drains had clear dominant bacteria; for example, *E. coli* was prevalent in Sai Premium Apartment Service Drain 1 East 1, while Vihar Road Service Drain 2 East 2 was mostly home to *S. sonnei*. Notable patterns included higher diversity in drains receiving mixed urban and industrial effluents, further emphasize the role of wastewater as a reservoir for

Table 27.2 Microbiological profile from different drain location

Drain name/location/ Sample number	E. coli	P. mirabilis	P. aeruginosa	S. sonnei	C. freundi	S. typhi	E. aerogenes	P. vulgaris	S. aureus	E. faecalis
Sai premium apartment Service drain no. 1 East 1 (10)	19	14	9	15	19	8	3	6	7	5
Pragati Vihar drain no. 1B (10)	15	13	10	4	11	2	3	2	2	4
Sai Vihar drain no. 1B (10)	18	2	15	5	8	5	5	3	6	7
Vihar Road Service drain 2 East 2 (10)	12	8	12	18	13	6	2	10	5	8
Kanaka durganagar Service drain 1 (10)	6	12	7	16	21	8	5	13	9	7
West kanaka durganagar Service drain 3 (10)	8	15	8	5	15	7	12	8	6	12
Club town apartment Service drain 4 (10)	13	9	14	12	16	4	8	12	8	6
Club town apartment Main drain 3 near (10)	4	12	3	15	10	5	12	4	5	5
Niladri vihar road Supported drain 1, South 1 (10)	12	8	5	16	12	7	7	3	5	3
Prachi enclave Supported drain east 1 care hospital, (10)	15	10	4	13	16	8	9	5	3	7
Kanak Durga Nagar Main drain 1(10)	12	5	5	5	11	5	7	6	4	6

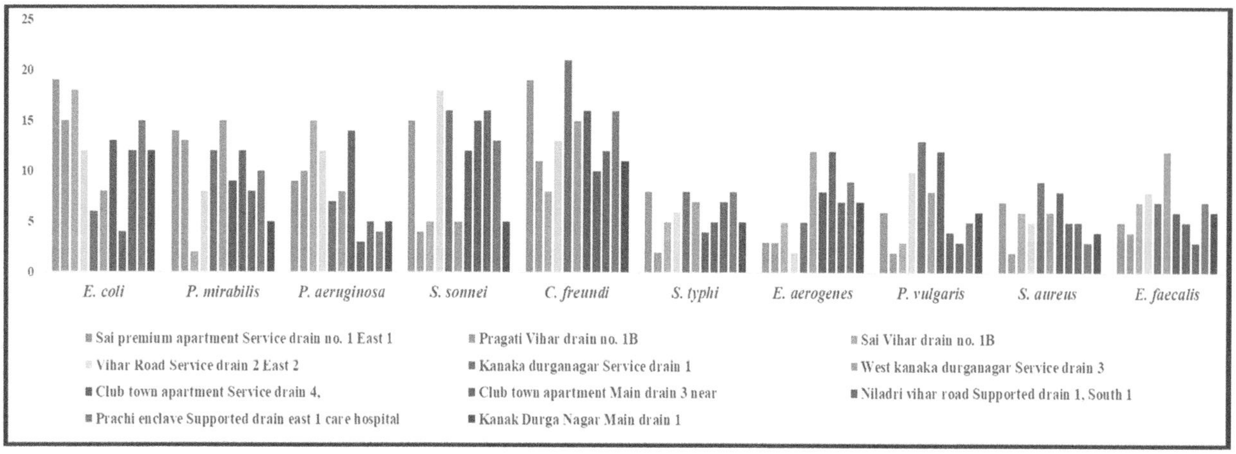

Fig. 27.2 Microbiological profile from different drain location of Bhubaneswar

Table 27.3 Gram negative and gram-positive bacteria prevalence % from wastewater drains

S. No	Organism	Prevalence %
1.	*C. freundi*	16
2.	*P. mirabilis*	11.36
3.	*P. aeruginosa*	9.68
4.	*S. sonnei*	13.05
5.	*E. coli*	14.10
6.	*S. typhi*	6.8
7.	*E. aerogenes*	7.68
8.	*P. vulgaris*	7.57
9.	*S. aureus*	6.31
10.	*E. faecalis*	7.36

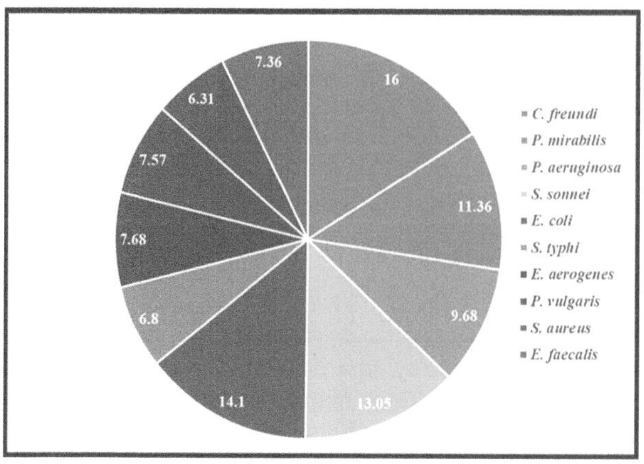

Fig. 27.3 Gram negative and gram-positive bacteria prevalence % from wastewater drains

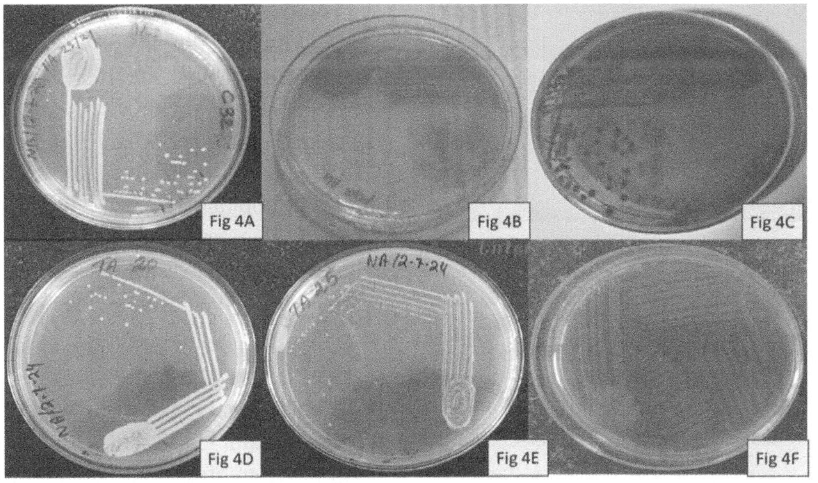

Fig. 27.4 Nutrient agar and MacConkey agar plate showing different gram negative and gram-positive bacteria. Figure 4A: *A. baumannii* on NA, Figure 4B: *P. aeruginosa* on NA, Figure 4C: *K. pneumoniae* on MacConkey agar, Figure 4D: *S. aureus* on NA, Figure 4E: *E. faecalis* on NA, Figure 4F: *S. typhi* on MacConkey agar

diverse microbial communities (Fig. 27.4.). These trends underscore the predominance of Gram-negative organisms in wastewater environments, which pose significant risks due to their potential for multidrug resistance.

Antibiotic susceptibility testing (Table 27.4.) revealed concerning resistance patterns, especially among gram-negative isolates (Fig. 27.5.). *P. aeruginosa* demonstrated 42.39% resistance to gentamicin, and *P. vulgaris* exhibited 58.33% resistance to cefepime. Colistin resistance was observed in 16% of isolates, with the highest prevalence in Sai Vihar Drain 1B, followed by Pragati Vihar Drain 1B and Service Drain 1 East 1. Among colistin-resistant bacteria, resistance levels ranged from 13.15% in *C. freundii* to 24.07% in *P. mirabilis*. Gram-positive isolates (Table 27.5.), such as *S. aureus* and *E. faecalis* (Fig. 27.6.), exhibited significant resistance to penicillin

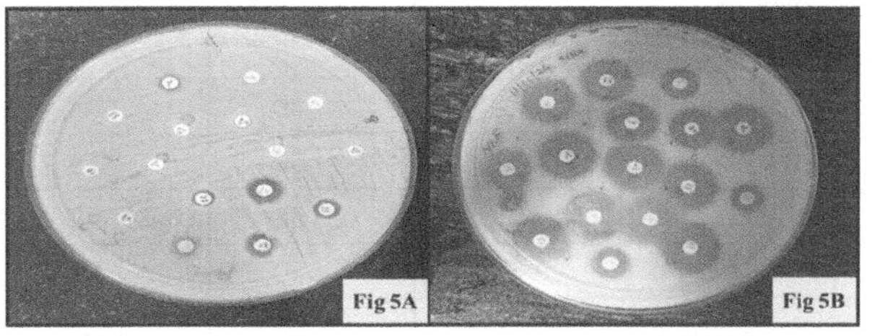

Fig. 27.5 Antibiotic resistance patterns of gram negative bacteria on MHA plate

Table 27.4 Comparison of antibiotic resistance patterns among gram negative bacterial species

Bacteria	C. freundi	P. mirabilis	P. aeruginosa	S. sonnei	E. coli	S. typhi	E. aerogene	P. vulgaris
CPM (Cefepime 30)	23.68	20.37	27.17	28.22	33.58	27.69	35.61	58.33
IPM (Imipenem 10)	27.63	32.40	31.52	31.45	28.35	12.30	43.83	50
AT (Aztreonam 30)	25	23.14	13.04	33.06	18.65	24.61	39.72	43.05
PI (Piperacillin 100)	16.44	36.11	34.78	30.64	11.94	35.38	24.65	36.11
CPZ (Cefoperazone 75)	7.89	26.85	23.91	25.80	9.70	27.69	34.24	48.61
CL (Colistin 10)	13.15	24.07	17.39	16.93	19.40	16.92	20.54	23.61
LE (Levofloxacin 5)	21.05	32.40	14.13	20.96	24.62	18.46	31.50	52.77
OF (Ofloxacin 2)	23.68	11.11	22.82	16.93	21.64	35.38	47.94	19.44
CTR (Ceftriaxone 30)	7.89	28.70	38.04	9.67	19.40	23.07	53.42	25
GEN (Gentamicin 30)	34.21	12.96	42.39	14.51	22.38	24.61	57.53	30.55
CFS (Cefoperazone/Sulbactam 75/30)	12.5	36.11	39.13	12.90	13.43	38.46	52.05	41.66
PIT (Piperacillin/Tazobactam 100/10)	13.81	38.88	33.69	16.93	20.89	32.30	32.87	38.88
CPZ (Cefoperazone 75)	25	29.62	28.26	14.51	32.08	26.15	20.54	25
CAC (Ceftazidime/Clavulanic acid 30/10)	23.68	37.96	30.43	25.80	26.11	40	42.46	31.94
CPT (Cefepime/Tazobactam 30/10)	27.63	31.48	27.17	16.12	29.10	27.69	30.13	48.61
IC (Imipenem/Cilastin 10/10)	25	25.92	34.78	15.32	17.91	30.76	26.02	34.72

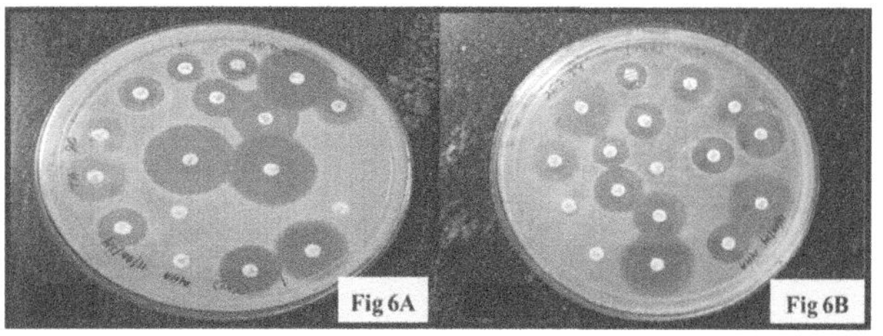

Fig. 27.6 Antibiotic resistance patterns of gram positive bacteria on MHA plate

Table 27.5 Comparison of antibiotic resistance patterns among gram positive bacterial species

Bacteria	S. aureus	E. faecalis
P (Penicillin 10)	80	75.71
MZ (Metronidazole 75)	43.33	21.42
DO (Doxycycline 10)	48.33	45.71
OF (Ofloxacin 2)	25	25.71
R (Rifampicin 5)	58.33	60
CZ (Cefazolin 30)	41.66	47.14
LZ (Linezolid 30)	60	37.14
C (Chloramphenicol 50)	50	11.4
TEI (Teicoplanin 30)	51.66	34.28
OX (Oxacillin 1)	30	27.14
CLR (Clarithromycin 15)	20	45.71
VA (Vancomycin 3)	40	15.71
MO (Moxifloxacin 5)	28.33	14.28
CIP (Ciprofloxacin 5)	21.66	40
TGC (Tigecycline 15)	36.66	51.42
NV (Novobiocin 5)	53.33	41.42

(80% and 75.71%, respectively). These results depict the critical role of wastewater environments in harbouring and disseminating colistin-resistant pathogens.

4. Discussion

This study emphasizes the critical role of wastewater as a reservoir and transmission vector for AMR. With an overall colistin resistance prevalence of 16%, in environmental reservoirs the result was similar to study done by Monte et al., 2024 which highlight the significant prevalence and geospatial distribution of resistant GNB in wastewater environments. The predominance of *C. freundii* and *E. coli* among colistin-resistant isolates aligns with previous studies, which identify these species as common environmental contaminants [3, 9, 22, 23]. The observed multidrug resistance patterns, including resistance to cephalosporins and carbapenems, are consistent with findings from Manaia et al. (2018), indicating the potential for wastewater to harbour multidrug-resistant strains. The role of WWTPs in selecting for bacterial resistance is well-known, with inadequately treated effluents serving as hotspots for resistance dissemination [11-13, 24]. The geospatial variability in colistin resistance, with Sai Vihar Drain 1B showing the highest prevalence, highlights the influence of urbanization and industrial activity on resistance patterns. Studies by Nnadozie and Odume (2019) and Anand et al. (2021) similarly underscore the impact of population density and wastewater composition on resistance prevalence. These findings suggest that targeted interventions in high-risk areas could significantly mitigate the spread of resistance [4, 15, 25].

The contamination of agricultural systems through wastewater irrigation and the subsequent incidence of resistant bacteria into the food chain pose significant risks to public health [14, 8, 26]. The detection of *mcr* genes in wastewater environments, as highlighted by Cherak et al. (2021), reinforces the important function of horizontal gene transfer in accelerating resistance. This study contributes to understanding the environmental persistence of colistin-resistant bacteria, a challenge highlighted in reviews by Harris et al. (2012) and Anyanwu et al. (2020) [5-7]. The integration of advanced monitoring technologies, such as wastewater-based epidemiology, could enhance resistance tracking and control [13, 27, 28]. Policies aimed at reducing antibiotic residues in wastewater, as suggested by Amulele (2022), could further limit the selection pressure driving resistance. The findings also underscore the importance of incorporating geospatial analyses into AMR surveillance, a gap identified in studies by Denissen and Petrosillo et al.[16, 17, 22].

While this study reveals valuable findings into the prevalence and geospatial distribution of colistin resistance, several research gaps remain. The pathogenicity of resistant strains in different environmental contexts require further investigation [17, 29, 30]. Additionally, integrating whole-genome sequencing with geospatial data could offer deeper insights into resistance dissemination pathways [3, 31, 32]. The potential role of wastewater in spreading resistance to rural and peri-urban areas, as discussed by Anand et al. (2021), also warrants closer examination [15]. The differences in resistance levels across different areas show that city growth and industrial activities affect these patterns. Sai Vihar Drain 1B has the highest levels of resistance. Nnadozie and Odume (2019) found similar results, pointing out that population in an area and wastewater content are important factors influencing resistance. Cherak et al. (2021) found mcr genes in wastewater, which shows how resistance can spread between bacteria. This means wastewater could help resistant bacteria move into farms and then into the food supply, which can be a serious risk to public health [7, 32].

This study offers some helpful information, but it does have its limits. For instance, it doesn't include whole-genome sequencing to verify resistance mechanisms, and it lacks long-term data to observe how resistance changes over time. Going forward, research could benefit from using advanced methods like genomic analyses and looking at wastewater to better understand how resistance develops. Also, focusing on specific actions, like enhancing wastewater treatment and creating policies to cut down on antibiotic waste, might help control the spread of resistance. Policymakers should enforce regulations to limit antibiotic discharge and promote wastewater-based epidemiology for real-time AMR monitoring. Public awareness campaigns on proper antibiotic use and pharmaceutical disposal are crucial. These measures can mitigate resistance spread and protect environmental and public health. By merging microbiology with geography, this study creates a strong basis for finding areas most at risk for antibiotic resistance and guiding efforts to protect both the environment and public health.

5. Conclusion

This study focuses on significant function of wastewater environments in the spreading of colistin-resistant GNB and emphasizes the need for robust wastewater management practices. By integrating microbiological and geospatial analyses, the findings contribute to a comprehensive understanding of AMR dynamics in wastewater, paving the way for effective monitoring and mitigation strategies. These results collectively underline the importance of wastewater as both a reservoir and a transmission pathway for colistin-resistant and multidrug-resistant bacteria, with serious implications for environmental and public health. Enhanced focus on wastewater treatment and environmental policies is important to limit the dissemination of resistance genes and safeguard public health.

Conflicts of Interest

The authors declare no conflicts of interest.

Acknowledgement

Miss Shreya Singh, PhD Research Scholar (Reg No: 2381611018) and Alisha Sinha, PhD Research Scholar (Reg No: 2381611006) at Centre for Biotechnology, Siksha 'O' Anusandhan Deemed to be university, Bhubaneswar. Author is thankful to Dean Research, SOA University and Director, ICMR-RMRC, Bhubaneswar for extend facility in research. We are thankful to ChatGPT for improving languae part of our manuscript.

References

1. Aijaz, M., Ahmad, M., Ansari, M. A., & Ahmad, S. (2023). Antimicrobial Resistance in a Globalized World: Current Challenges and Future Perspectives. *International Journal of Pharmaceutical Drug Design*, *1*(1), 7–22.
2. Ahmed, S. K., Hussein, S., Qurbani, K., Ibrahim, R. H., Fareeq, A., Mahmood, K. A., & Mohamed, M. G. (2024). Antimicrobial resistance: impacts, challenges, and future prospects. *Journal of Medicine, Surgery, and Public Health*, *2*, 100081.
3. Mondal, A. H., Khare, K., Saxena, P., Debnath, P., Mukhopadhyay, K., & Yadav, D. (2024). A Review on Colistin Resistance: An Antibiotic of Last Resort. *Microorganisms*, *12*(4), 772.
4. Nnadozie, C. F., & Odume, O. N. (2019). Freshwater environments as reservoirs of antibiotic resistant bacteria and their role in the dissemination of antibiotic resistance genes. *Environmental pollution*, *254*, 113067.
5. Harris, S. J., Cormican, M., & Cummins, E. (2012). Antimicrobial residues and antimicrobial-resistant bacteria: impact on the microbial environment and risk to human health—a review. *Human and Ecological Risk Assessment: An International Journal*, *18*(4), 767–809.
6. Anyanwu, M. U., Jaja, I. F., & Nwobi, O. C. (2020). Occurrence and characteristics of mobile colistin resistance (mcr) gene-containing isolates from the environment: a review. *International journal of environmental research and public health*, *17*(3), 1028.
7. Cherak, Z., Loucif, L., Moussi, A., & Rolain, J. M. (2021). Epidemiology of mobile colistin resistance (mcr) genes in aquatic environments. *Journal of Global Antimicrobial Resistance*, *27*, 51–62.
8. Ibekwe, A. M., Bhattacharjee, A. S., Phan, D., Ashworth, D., Schmidt, M. P., Murinda, S. E., ... & Yang, C. H. (2023). Potential reservoirs of antimicrobial resistance in livestock waste and treated wastewater that can be disseminated to agricultural land. *Science of The Total Environment*, *872*, 162194.
9. Memesh, R., Yasir, M., Ledder, R. G., Zowawi, H., McBain, A. J., & Azhar, E. I. (2024). An update on the prevalence of colistin and carbapenem-resistant Gram-negative bacteria in aquaculture: an emerging threat to public health. *Journal of applied microbiology*, *135*(1), lxad288.
10. Ifedinezi, O. V., Nnaji, N. D., Anumudu, C. K., Ekwueme, C. T., Uhegwu, C. C., Ihenetu, F. C., ... & Onyeaka, H. (2024). Environmental Antimicrobial Resistance: Implications for Food Safety and Public Health. *Antibiotics*, *13*(11), 1087.
11. Manaia, C. M., Rocha, J., Scaccia, N., Marano, R., Radu, E., Biancullo, F., ... & Nunes, O. C. (2018). Antibiotic resistance in wastewater treatment plants: Tackling the black box. *Environment international*, *115*, 312–324.
12. Di Cesare, A., Cornacchia, A., Sbaffi, T., Sabatino, R., Corno, G., Cammà, C., ... & Pomilio, F. (2024). Treated wastewater: A hotspot for multidrug-and colistin-resistant Klebsiella pneumoniae. *Environmental Pollution*, *359*, 124598.
13. Sims, N., & Kasprzyk-Hordern, B. (2020). Future perspectives of wastewater-based epidemiology: monitoring infectious disease spread and resistance to the community level. *Environment international*, *139*, 105689.
14. Sun, Z., Hong, W., Xue, C., & Dong, N. (2024). A comprehensive review of antibiotic resistance gene contamination in agriculture: Challenges and AI-driven solutions. *Science of The Total Environment*, 175971.
15. Anand, U., Reddy, B., Singh, V. K., Singh, A. K., Kesari, K. K., Tripathi, P., ... & Simal-Gandara, J. (2021). Potential environmental and human health risks caused by antibiotic-resistant bacteria (ARB), antibiotic resistance

genes (ARGs) and emerging contaminants (ECs) from municipal solid waste (MSW) landfill. *Antibiotics*, *10*(4), 374.
16. Petrosillo, N., Taglietti, F., & Granata, G. (2019). Treatment options for colistin resistant Klebsiella pneumoniae: present and future. *Journal of clinical medicine*, *8*(7), 934.
17. Amulele, A. V. (2022). *The Effect of Multi-drug Resistance on the Fitness and Pathogenicity of Carbapenem Resistant Organisms (CROs) in the Absence of Selective Pressure* (Doctoral dissertation, The Open University).
18. Denissen, J. K. (2023). *Prevalence and risk assessment of nosocomial associated pathogens in environmental water samples* (Doctoral dissertation, University of Stellenbosch).
19. Jovcic, B., Novovic, K., Dekic, S., & Hrenovic, J. (2021). Colistin resistance in environmental isolates of Acinetobacter baumannii. *Microbial drug resistance*, *27*(3), 328–336.
20. Suranjit S, Singh OS. (2017). Isolation and identification of pathogenic bacteria from sewage waters in imphal city-a community health aspect. *International Journal of Current Research in Life Sciences,*6(8), 710–713.
21. Ghandour, A., Sror, S., Sabet, M., & Rashwan, R. (2021). Detection of colistin resistant E. coli in children at pediatric hospital of Assiut University, using phenotypic and genotypic Methods. *Microbes and Infectious Diseases*, *2*(4), 748–759.
22. Bogoshi, D. (2020). *Molecular epidemiology and mechanisms of colistin and carbapenem resistance in Enterobacteriaceae from clinical isolates, the environment and porcine samples in Pretoria, South Africa* (Master's thesis, University of Pretoria (South Africa).
23. Monte, D. F., Lemos, M. L. P., & de Oliveira, C. J. B. (2024). Emerging threats: global distribution and diversity of carbapenem resistance genes in Kluyvera intermedia. *The Lancet Microbe*, *5*(4), e310–e311.
24. Puljko, A., Milaković, M., Križanović, S., Kosić-Vukšić, J., Babić, I., Petrić, I., ... & Udiković-Kolić, N. (2022). Prevalence of enteric opportunistic pathogens and extended-spectrum cephalosporin-and carbapenem-resistant coliforms and genes in wastewater from municipal wastewater treatment plants in Croatia. *Journal of hazardous materials*, *427*, 128155.
25. Foxman, B., Salzman, E., Gesierich, C., Gardner, S., Ammerman, M., Eisenberg, M., & Wigginton, K. (2024). Wastewater surveillance of antibiotic resistant bacteria for public health action: Potential and Challenges. *American Journal of Epidemiology*, kwae419.
26. Dickin, S. K., Schuster-Wallace, C. J., Qadir, M., & Pizzacalla, K. (2016). A review of health risks and pathways for exposure to wastewater use in agriculture. *Environmental health perspectives*, *124(7)*, 900–909.
27. Struelens, M. J., Ludden, C., Werner, G., Sintchenko, V., Jokelainen, P., & Ip, M. (2024). Real-time genomic surveillance for enhanced control of infectious diseases and antimicrobial resistance. *Frontiers in Science, 2,* 1298248.
28. Cuetero-Martínez, Y., de Los Cobos-Vasconcelos, D., Aguirre-Garrido, J. F., Lopez-Vidal, Y., & Noyola, A. (2023). Next-generation sequencing for surveillance of antimicrobial resistance and pathogenicity in municipal wastewater treatment plants. *Current Medicinal Chemistry*, *30*(1), 5–29.
29. Walther, B. A., & Ewald, P. W. (2004). Pathogen survival in the external environment and the evolution of virulence. *Biological Reviews*, *79*(4), 849–869.
30. Hughes, D., & Andersson, D. I. (2017). Environmental and genetic modulation of the phenotypic expression of antibiotic resistance. *FEMS microbiology reviews*, *41*(3), 374–391.
31. Oniciuc, E. A., Likotrafiti, E., Alvarez-Molina, A., Prieto, M., Santos, J. A., & Alvarez-Ordóñez, A. (2018). The present and future of whole genome sequencing (WGS) and whole metagenome sequencing (WMS) for surveillance of antimicrobial resistant microorganisms and antimicrobial resistance genes across the food chain. *Genes*, *9*(5), 268.
32. Pinilla-Redondo, R., Cyriaque, V., Jacquiod, S., Sørensen, S. J., & Riber, L. (2018). Monitoring plasmid-mediated horizontal gene transfer in microbiomes: recent advances and future perspectives. *Plasmid*, *99*, 56–67.

Note: All the Figures and tables in this chapter have been prepared by the author based on research work.

Research and Innovations in Industrial and Marine Biotechnology: A Circular Economy 2024 – Prof. Hrudayanath Thatoi et al. (eds)

28 Molecular Characterization and Prevalence of Colistin-Resistant Gram-Negative Bacteria in Clinical Samples: Mechanistic Insights and Implications for Therapy

Alisha Sinha, Shreya Singh
Centre for Biotechnology,
Siksha 'O' Anusandhan Deemed to be University,
Kalinganagar, Bhubaneswar, Odisha, India
Microbiology Division,
ICMR-Regional Medical Research Centre, Chandrasekharpur,
Bhubaneswar, Odisha, India

Ambika Sahoo[1]
Centre for Biotechnology,
Siksha 'O' Anusandhan Deemed to be University,
Kalinganagar, Bhubaneswar, Odisha, India

Mahesh Chandra Sahu*
Microbiology Division,
ICMR-Regional Medical Research Centre, Chandrasekharpur,
Bhubaneswar, Odisha, India

Abstract: Colistin, a polymyxin antibiotic of last resort, is confronted with emerging resistance due to mobile colistin resistance (mcr) genes. mcr-1 to mcr-10 genes are identified in this study and colistin resistance in Gram-negative bacteria (GNB) in clinical samples is explored. Primers for their selective detection are designed and established. Clinical samples, including pus, blood, urine, wound swabs, and aspirates, were collected from hospitalized patients in Bhubaneswar. GNB isolates were recovered on the basis of selective media, characterized by biochemical tests, VITEK 2, and molecular techniques. Antibiotic susceptibility testing (ABST) was done on the basis of disk diffusion with 10, 25, and 50 micrograms (mcg) of colistin concentrations. Primers targeting mcr genes were designed using Primer3 software and validated by PCR against positive controls. Out of 500 clinical samples, 7% of GNB were resistant at 10 mcg, decreasing to 1.8% at 25 mcg and 1.4% at 50 mcg colistin concentrations. Blood samples showed the highest resistance (15%), followed by urine (6.4%) and pus (5.6%). The most common colistin-resistant species were *Klebsiella pneumoniae*, *Proteus mirabilis*, *Acinetobacter baumannii*, *Escherichia coli*, and *Pseudomonas aeruginosa*. Among the resistant isolates, 5.8% also showed resistance to carbapenems and cephalosporins. PCR testified to mcr genes, where mcr-2 was most common, followed by mcr-8 and mcr-10. Colistin resistance among GNB is significant, with notable prevalence in blood and urine samples. Successful primer design for mcr-1 to mcr-10 facilitates the specific and sensitive detection of resistance mechanisms. Improved surveillance and rigorous infection control measures are critical in preventing the spread of mcr-mediated colistin resistance and preserving therapeutic options in clinical practice.

Keywords: Colistin resistance, Antibiotic susceptibility testing, Gram-negative bacteria, mcr genes, multidrug resistance, molecular detection

*Corresponding author: mchsahu@gmail.com

DOI: 10.1201/9781003759003-28

1. Introduction

Colistin resistance is one of the most disturbing parts of the rising worldwide health epidemic known as antimicrobial resistance (AMR). When all other treatment fails, colistin is employed as the antibiotic of last resort and is utilized to treat life-threatening infections caused by multidrug-resistant (MDR) Gram-negative bacteria (GNB) [1]. But with increasing prevalence rate of colistin-resistant bacteria nowadays, it has been extremely challenging to treat many infections caused by bacteria and this is creating an enormous threat to public health.

AMR being the rising problem has become a significant hindrance to successful clinical diagnosis and treatment, emphasizing the vital necessity to address it [2]. Specifically, colistin resistance in clinical pathogens increases morbidity and mortality associated with resistant infections by complexing infection control and limiting the therapeutic options available to healthcare practitioners [3].

GNB, which are notable sources of hospital-acquired infections, such as *Klebsiella pneumoniae, Pseudomonas aeruginosa* and *Acinetobacter baumannii*, are frequently associated to antibiotic resistance. Colistin's efficiency is reduced by these bacteria's sophisticated resistance mechanisms [4]. *A. baumannii's* critical role in infections in healthcare settings, where resistance mechanisms result in menial clinical outcomes [5]. Colistin resistance can occur through acquired mechanisms mediated by plasmid-borne mobilized colistin resistance (mcr) genes or intrinsic mechanisms, such as alterations in lipid A that reduce drug binding. Horizontal transmission of resistance among bacterial population largely relies on the mcr genes mcr-1 to mcr-10 [6]. In spite of mounting concern over the prevalence of colistin resistance, especially mcr-mediated resistance [7], the frequency and dissemination of these resistance genes among clinical isolates have not been well elucidated. The mcr gene not only causes colistin resistance but is also associated with the transmission of other resistance traits, potentially complicating treatment planning, but its presence in clinical sample represents a major public health risk. The molecular changes that allow bacteria to evade this important antibiotic are manifested by both innate and acquired mechanism of colistin resistance [8]. Therefore, tracking the frequency and molecular characteristics of colistin-resistant GNB, especially those harbouring mcr genes, is important to assess the extent of the problem and determine treatment in clinical settings [9]. Several factors, including the misuse and overuse of antibiotics, poor infection control practices, and transference of resistance genes between environmental reservoirs, are responsible for the prevalence of colistin-resistant GNB in clinical environments [8,10]. Moreover, this research illustrated how resistance is correlated among human, animal, and environmental reservoirs and emphasized the role of the mcr gene in facilitating resistance across various ecological niches. These results highlight how challenging colistin resistance is to treat, as it impacts environmental and agricultural systems in addition to drug therapy [6, 11]

The impact of colistin resistance is widespread, threatening the efficacy of existing treatment regimens and complicating infection control practices in healthcare settings [12]. Spread of colistin resistance is a major threat to universal healthcare systems, particularly in countries with poor access to other treatments. The ability of colistin-resistant bacteria to persist in clinical environments raises the risk of hospital-acquired infections and increases the vulnerability of susceptible patients. Furthermore, the limited efficacy of current diagnostic tools to rapidly detect colistin resistance further complicates timely interventions [13, 14]. Emerging technologies for detecting antibiotic-resistant bacteria highlights the importance of integrating rapid diagnostic methods to curb the spread of resistant pathogens. Despite advances in diagnostic capabilities, the molecular characteristics and prevalence of colistin-resistant bacteria in clinical samples remain poorly understood, leaving significant gaps in our understanding of the resistance mechanisms and their clinical implications [15].

A major challenge in fighting against colistin resistance is the deficient understanding of its molecular foundation in clinical pathogens [16]. There are limited studies that integrate molecular characterization and epidemiological data to identify high-risk populations and environments that contribute to the prevalence of resistance [17]. Although studies have documented the prevalence of resistance, few studies provide detailed insight into the specific genetic and mechanistic drivers of resistance and the rate of prevalence from different clinical sources like pus, blood, tracheal aspirate, urine etc [18, 19]. It is important to understand these interactions in order to create targeted interventions to reduce the effects of colistin resistance on patient care. Despite this increase in research, considerable holes exist in our knowledge base for understanding molecular mechanisms of colistin resistance in GNB and its occurrence in clinical environments from various sources. Furthermore, the role of genetic determinants such as mcr genes in driving resistance remains incompletely characterized, leaving critical questions about their prevalence, diversity.

The study aims to investigate the molecular characterization and prevalence of colistin-resistant GNB in clinical samples from different sources, focusing on its mechanistic insights by addressing the above gap. The main objectives are to first to determine the prevalence of GNB colistin resistance in clinical isolates and then characterized the genetic factors and mechanisms causing its resistance. By addressing these, this study aims to provide insights into its prevalence rate in clinical practice and develop strategies to combat colistin resistance and improve patient outcomes in clinical practice.

2. Materials and Methods

2.1 Sample Collection

Clinical samples such as blood, wound, pus, swabs, tracheal aspirates, ET aspirates, urine and CBD stents were collected from hospitalized patients at SUM Hospital between January and October 2024. Collected samples were transported to the laboratory immediately after collection under controlled temperature and sterile conditions. A total of 500 bacterial cultures were extracted from different clinical specimens. This observational study was approved by the scientific advisory comity of ICMR- Regional Medical Research Centre (RMRC), Bhubaneswar and subsequently, it was approved by the Human Institutional Ethics Comity, ICMR- RMRC, Bhubaneswar.

2.2 Laboratory Procedures

Bacterial Isolation and Identification

GNB were first stained by gram staining and observed under microscope then isolated on MacConkey agar and identified using different biochemical tests, VITEK 2, and molecular methods like PCR (polymerase chain reaction).

Antibiotic Susceptibility Testing (ABST)

Testing for antibiotic susceptibility was conducted using the Kirby-Bauer disk diffusion technique following CLSI guidelines. This conventional technique assesses the susceptibility of bacteria to a range of different antibiotics, providing vital information for therapeutic intervention. Colistin resistance was further evaluated by Kirby-Bauer disk diffusion method, different colistin concentrations of 10 μg, 25 μg, and 50 μg was taken. The resistance of isolates to carbapenems and cephalosporins was also determined.

Identification of Bacteria

Bacterial Identification performed by isolating pure colonies on MacConkey and then performing VITEK 2 system to ensure species identification accuracy.

Confirmation of Bacterial Identification

To guarantee the accuracy of species identification, all bacterial isolates were first identified using standard techniques and subsequently confirmed by the VITEK 2 system.

Molecular Detection of mcr Genes

Using Primer 3 software, primers for mcr-1 to mcr-10 were created, focusing on distinct areas of each gene. Sequence alignment was used to confirm primer specificity. Colistin-resistant isolates were subjected to PCR amplification using verified primers, including negative controls for every variant of the mcr gene.

3. Results

A total of 500 clinical samples from various sources such as blood, urine, pus, ET aspirates, tracheal aspirates, wound swabs, CBD stents, and so on were examined to identify the prevalence of colistin-resistant GNB. Table 28.1 presents a summary of the prevalence of some of the most important GNB species in clinical environments. *K. pneumoniae* was the most prevalent species (30.6%), followed by *P. aeruginosa* (21.6%) and *A. baumannii* (19%). Other species, such as *Enterobacter cloacae* (9.2%) and *Proteus mirabilis* (4.4%), were detected at lower frequencies as shown in the Fig. 28.1.

Table 28.1 Prevalence percentage of gram-negative bacteria in clinical settings

S. No.	Gram negative bacteria	Total	Prevalence percentage % Total/N*100
1.	*Acinetobacter baumannii*	95	19
2.	*Klebsiella pneumoniae*	153	30.6
3.	*E. coli*	67	13.4
4.	*Pseudomonas aeruginosa*	108	21.6
5.	*Enterobacter cloacae*	46	9.2
6.	*Proteus mirabilis*	22	4.4
7.	*Enterobacter aerogenes*	9	1.8

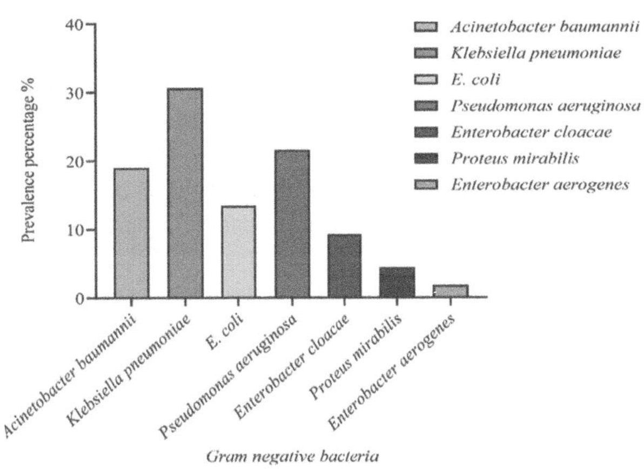

Fig. 28.1 Prevalence percentage of gram-negative bacteria in clinical settings during the study period

The prevalence of MDR GNB across clinical sources is detailed in Table 28.2 and visualized in Fig. 28.2. Blood samples had the highest GNB prevalence (15%), followed by sputum (6.4%), bile (5.6%), and dialysis line tips (8.2%). ET and tracheal aspirates contributed 5% and 4.4%, respectively. Wound swabs and CBD stents showed the lowest prevalence at 0.8% and 0.6%, respectively. The antibiotic resistance profiles of the GNB species were further characterized using a variety of antibiotics, as shown in Table 28.3. Co-resistance to carbapenems and cephalosporins was observed in 5.8% of colistin-resistant isolates, indicating the prevalence of MDR strains and their potential to compromise treatment outcomes. Antibiotic susceptibility testing revealed

Table 28.2 Prevalence of multi drug-resistant gram-negative bacteria from different clinical sources

S. No.	Clinical Sources	GNB	GNB percentage %
1.	Blood	75	15
2.	Urine	32	6.4
3.	Pus	28	5.6
4.	ET aspirate	25	5
5.	Tracheal aspirates	22	4.4
6.	Wound swab	4	0.8
7.	CBD stent	3	0.6
8.	Bile	28	5.6
9.	Sputum	32	6.4
10.	Drain fluid	34	6.8
11.	Dialysis line tip	41	8.2
12.	Throat swab	39	7.8
13.	Bal fluid	45	9
14.	Central line tip	37	7.4
15.	HVS (high vaginal swab)	29	5.8
16.	CSF (cerebrospinal fluid)	26	5.2

colistin resistance in 7% of isolates at 10 µg, decreasing to 1.8% at 25 µg and 1.4% at 50 µg concentrations as shown in the Fig. 28.3 (Table 28.4). Blood samples showed the highest resistance rates (15%), followed by urine (6.4%) and pus (5.6%). Among the isolates, *K. pneumoniae, Escherichia coli, P. mirabilis, P. aeruginosa,* and *A. baumannii* exhibited significant resistance patterns

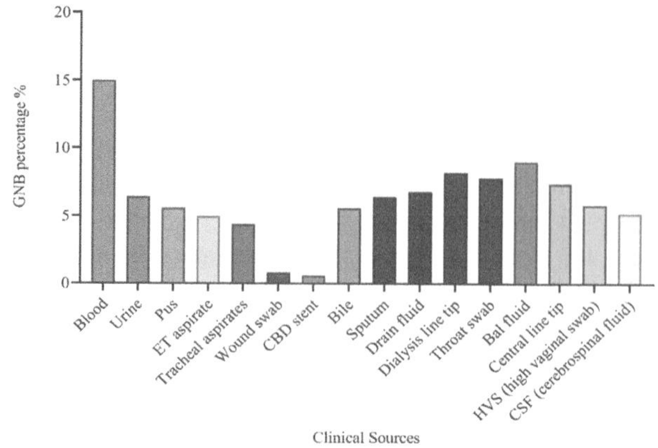

Fig. 28.2 Prevalence of multi drug-resistant gram-negative bacteria from different clinical samples during the study period

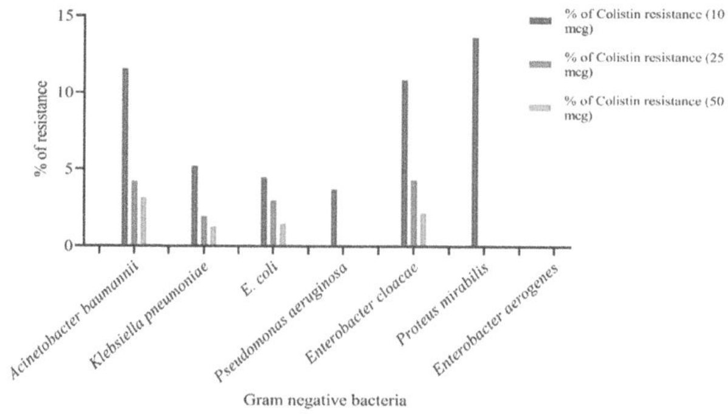

Fig. 28.3 Prevalence percentage of colistin resistance (concertation of colistin with 10, 25, 50 mcg) in different gram-negative bacteria

Table 28.3 Comparison of antibiotic resistance % patterns among bacterial species

Bacteria	E. aerogenes (%)	E. cloacae (%)	P. mirabilis (%)	P. aeruginosa (%)	A. Baumannii (%)	K. pneumoniae (%)	E. Coli (%)
CPM (Cefepime 30)	ND	15.21	40.90	26.85	12.63	19.6	23.88
TE (Tetracycline 10)	22.22	6.5	9.09	11.11	7.36	7.84	ND
IPM (Imipenem 10)	22.22	15.21	NA	5.55	ND	0.65	17.91
PIT (Piperacillin/Tazobactam 100/10)	ND	4.3	18.18	3.7	15.62	5.88	1.49
AT (Aztreonam 30)	11.11	13.04	ND	ND	ND	4.57	8.95
PI (Piperacillin 100)	ND	ND	ND	7.4	2.10	1.30	4.47
CPZ (Cefoperazone 75)	ND	21.73	ND	ND	ND	13.72	ND
CL (Colistin 10)	ND	13.04	9.09	3.70	11.57	4.57	7.46
CFS (Cefoperazone/Sulbactam 75/30)	11.11	ND	ND	ND	ND	0.65	4.47
CPT Ceftaroline (30/10)	ND	10.86	ND	15.74	9.47	1.96	2.98
LE (Levofloxacin 5)	ND	ND	31.81	13.88	1.05	9.80	5.97
NA (Nalidixic acid)	ND	ND	ND	ND	13.68	3.92	1.49
OF (Ofloxacin 2)	22.22	ND	ND	0.92	ND	1.30	ND
TI (Ticarcillin 75)	ND	ND	4.54	10.18	3.15	5.88	2.98
CTR (Ceftriaxone)	11.11	ND	ND	ND	23.15	17.64	17.91
IC (Imipenem/Cilastin 10/10)	ND	ND	ND	0.92	ND	0.65	ND

Table 28.4 Prevalence percentage of colistin resistance (10, 25, 50 mcg) in different gram-negative bacteria

Sl no	Organism	Total number	Total N*100%	Colistin resistance (10 mcg)	% of Colistin resistance (10 mcg)	Colistin (25 mcg)	% of Colistin resistance (25 mcg)	Colistin (50 mcg)	% of Colistin resistance (50 mcg)
1.	*Acinetobacter baumannii*	95	19	11	11.57%	4	4.21%	3	3.15%
2.	*Klebsiella pneumoniae*	153	30.6	8	5.22%	3	1.96%	2	1.30%
3.	*E. coli*	67	13.4	3	4.47%	2	2.98%	1	1.49%
4.	*Pseudomonas aeruginosa*	108	21.6	4	3.70%	0	0	0	0
5.	*Enterobacter cloacae*	46	9.2	5	10.86%	2	4.3%	1	2.17%
6.	*Proteus mirabilis*	22	4.4	3	13.63%	0	0	0	0
7.	*Enterobacter aerogenes*	9	1.8	0	0	0	0	0	0

(Table 28.4). The resistance patterns were confirmed using Mueller-Hinton Agar (MHA) plates, Figure 28.4A states distinct zones of inhibition for sensitive strains and Fig. 28.4B shows absence of inhibition for resistant strains. Whereas Fig. 28.5 Antibiotic Resistance Patterns of gram-negative bacteria on MHA plate. PCR analysis identified the occurrence of mcr genes, validating colistin mechanisms of resistance among Fig. 28.6 isolates (Table 28.5). The mcr-2 gene was the most commonly identified followed by mcr-8 and mcr-10. Distribution of species specificity revealed that *A. baumannii* harbored multiple mcr variants of genes such as mcr-2, mcr-6, mcr-8, and

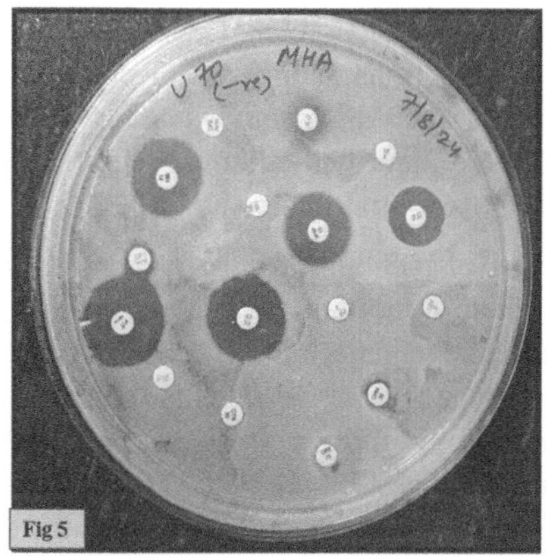

Fig. 28.5 Antibiotic resistance patterns of gram-negative bacteria on MHA plate

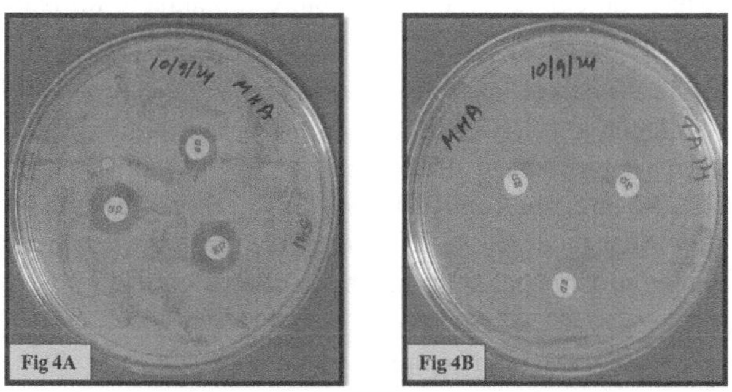

Fig. 28.4 Colistin resistance pattern on MHA plate, 4A showing colistin sensetive whereas 5B showing colistin reistance

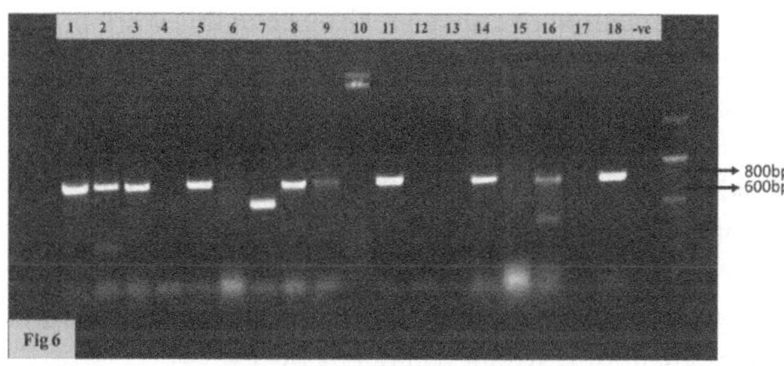

Fig. 28.6 Gel image for MCR genes among different gram-negative bacteria

Table 28.5 Prevalence of mcr genes (mcr-1to mcr-10) among different gram-negative bacteria

Bacteria	mcr-1	mcr-2	mcr-3	mcr-4	mcr-5	mcr-6	mcr-7	mcr-8	mcr-9	mcr-10
Acinetobacter baumannii	0	4	1	0	1	1	0	2	0	1
Klebsiella pneumoniae	1	3	0	0	0	1	0	1	0	1
E. coli	0	1	0	0	2	0	0	1	0	1
Pseudomonas aeruginosa	0	1	0	1	0	0	0	1	1	0
Enterobacter cloacae	1	1	0	1	0	0	0	1	1	1
Proteus mirabilis	0	0	0	0	0	0	0	0	0	2
Enterobacter aerogenes	0	0	0	0	0	0	0	0	0	0

mcr-10 while *K. pneumoniae* generally harbored mcr-2, mcr-8, and mcr-10 (Table 28.5).

These findings illustrate the urgent need for regular monitoring and focused interventions to stem the transmission of colistin-resistant and MDR GNB. This study illustrates the utility of phenotypic and molecular approaches, such as the established PCR-based detection system, in describing the resistance patterns and tracking emerging dangers in clinical settings.

4. Discussion

The increasing prevalence of colistin-resistant GNB represents a significant global health challenge, especially in clinical settings. This research indicates the prevalence of resistance in isolates of all types of clinical samples, with a 15% resistance rate highest among bloodstream infections, followed by urine (6.4%) and pus (5.6%) as reported in study of Deori et al. (2024), which focused on bloodstream infections as an area of concern for AMR. Key pathogens such as *K. pneumoniae*, *E. coli*, and *A. baumannii* were identified, aligning with trends reported globally for nosocomial infections [4, 5, 20].

The presence of *mcr* genes (*mcr-2*, *mcr-8*, and *mcr-10*) highlights their important role in promoting resistance through horizontal gene transfer. Along with the confer colistin resistance these genes also state co-resistance to carbapenems and cephalosporins, complicating therapeutic options [7, 11]. The co-resistance pattern observed in 5.8% of the isolates highlights the emergence of MDR strains and supports the results of Kumar et al. (2024) and Memesh et al. (2024), as they a similar trend in hospital-acquired infections [3, 10].

The identification of colistin resistance in this work points out the need for reliable molecular diagnostics. The PCR-based detection system established presents a sensitive and specific means to detect the mcr genes and can be used in addition to other sophisticated approaches like whole genome sequencing. This answers the need for rapid diagnostic tools, as suggested by Andersson et al. (2020), who emphasized that they allow timely intervention and containment of resistant pathogens [8, 15, 19].

The results also point out the role of environmental reservoirs and inadequate infection control measures in the spread of colistin resistance. Studies by Luo et al. [7] and Memesh et al. [10] have demonstrated the interconnectedness of resistance between humans, animals, and ecological niches [7, 10]. This "One Health" perspective emphasizes the need for comprehensive surveillance beyond clinical environments, as highlighted by Anyanwu et al. (2020). The spread of the mcr gene in the environment, especially in agricultural systems, further exacerbates the resistance problem [12,21].

Recent data suggest that intrinsic mechanisms, such as lipid A modification, and acquired mechanisms mediated by the *mcr* gene are the primary drivers of resistance [6]. This dual mechanism states the complexity of combating colistin resistance, especially in pathogens such as *K. pneumoniae* and *A. baumannii*, which exhibit very complex adaptations to evade antimicrobial agents [4, 5]. The persistence of these pathogens in clinical settings increases the risk of Hospital-acquired infection or it can be called nosocomial outbreaks, disproportionately affecting vulnerable patients [18, 22].

Despite these advances, significant gaps remain in our understanding of the molecular epidemiology of the *mcr* genes. Limited data on the geographic distribution and diversity of *mcr* variants hinder the development of targeted interventions [11, 23]. Furthermore, Leavis et al. (2006) discussed the role of high-risk clonal complexes in the spread of resistance and further investigations to identify potential reservoirs and vectors within hospitals [17].

This study highlights the urgent need to integrate molecular surveillance into antimicrobial stewardship programs to limit the spread of colistin resistance. Incorporation advanced diagnostic techniques such as multiplex PCR and genome-wide association studies may lead to a more comprehensive understanding of resistance mechanisms [16, 24]. Furthermore, innovative approaches such as antimicrobial peptides, offer promising alternatives to conventional treatments for resistant infections [16, 25].

Efforts to combat colistin resistance must also include policies aimed at regulating antibiotic use in the clinical and agricultural sectors. As reported by Mondal et al. (2024) and Navales et al., Indiscriminate use of antibiotics is accelerating the development of resistance, necessitating stricter guidelines and educational campaigns to mitigate misuse [8, 12].

This research points out the emergent danger of colistin resistance in GNB and the need to stress routine surveillance, sophisticated molecular diagnostics, and comprehensive infection control measures. Targeted interventions should be made possible through identifying the genetic and environmental determinants in future studies.

5. Conclusion

This study shows a high incidence of colistin-resistant GNB in clinical samples, with bloodstream infections showing the highest resistance (15%), followed by urine (6.4%) and pus (5.6%). The main causative bacteria include *K. pneumoniae*, *E. coli*, and *A. baumannii*, reflecting the global resistance trend. The finding of mcr genes (mcr-2, mcr-8, mcr-10) highlights their role in horizontal resistance transfer and accelerates its spread. 5.8% of isolates shows co-resistance to carbapenems and cephalosporins complicating the treatment and highlighting the threat posed by MDR bacteria. The developed PCR-based detection system provides an accurate tool for monitoring mcr-mediated resistance and many further improve monitoring with advanced diagnostics such as whole genome sequencing. This research identifies the necessity of routine surveillance, rigorous infection control and judicious use of antibiotics for the preservation of colistin as a last-resort antibiotic and fight the worldwide trend of AMR.

Conflicts of Interest

The authors declare no conflicts of interest.

Acknowledgement

Miss Alisha Sinha, PhD Research Scholar (Reg No: 2381611006) and Shreya Singh, PhD Research Scholar (Reg No: 2381611018) at Centre for Biotechnology, Siksha 'O' Anusandhan Deemed to be university, Bhubaneswar. Author is thankful to Dean Research, SOA University and Director, ICMR-RMRC, Bhubaneswar for extend facility in research.

References

1. Deori, C., Sonowal, T., & Das, M. (2024). Antimicrobial resistance: a looming threat to public health and global well-being. *Indian Journal of Community and Family Medicine*, *10*(1), 18–25.
2. Alara, J. A., & Alara, O. R. (2024). An Overview of the Global Alarming Increase of Multiple Drug Resistant: A Major Challenge in Clinical Diagnosis. *Infectious Disorders-Drug Targets (Formerly Current Drug Targets-Infectious Disorders)*, *24*(3), 26–42.
3. Kumar, N. R., Balraj, T. A., Kempegowda, S. N., & Prashant, A. (2024). Multidrug-resistant sepsis: A critical healthcare challenge. *Antibiotics*, *13*(1), 46.
4. Ah, Y. M., Kim, A. J., & Lee, J. Y. (2014). Colistin resistance in Klebsiella pneumoniae. *International journal of antimicrobial agents*, *44*(1), 8–15.
5. Nguyen, M., & Joshi, S. G. (2021). Carbapenem resistance in Acinetobacter baumannii, and their importance in hospital-acquired infections: a scientific review. *Journal of applied microbiology*, *131*(6), 2715–2738.
6. Gogry, F. A., Siddiqui, M. T., Sultan, I., & Haq, Q. M. R. (2021). Current update on intrinsic and acquired colistin resistance mechanisms in bacteria. *Frontiers in medicine*, *8*, 677720.
7. Luo, Q., Wang, Y., & Xiao, Y. (2020). Prevalence and transmission of mobilized colistin resistance (mcr) gene in bacteria common to animals and humans. *Biosafety and Health*, *2*(2), 71–78.
8. Mondal, A. H., Khare, K., Saxena, P., Debnath, P., Mukhopadhyay, K., & Yadav, D. (2024). A Review on Colistin Resistance: An Antibiotic of Last Resort. *Microorganisms*, *12*(4), 772.
9. Noster, J., Thelen, P., & Hamprecht, A. (2021). Detection of multidrug-resistant Enterobacterales—from ESBLs to carbapenemases. *Antibiotics*, *10*(9), 1140.
10. Memesh, R., Yasir, M., Ledder, R. G., Zowawi, H., McBain, A. J., & Azhar, E. I. (2024). An update on the prevalence of colistin and carbapenem-resistant Gram-negative bacteria in aquaculture: an emerging threat to public health. *Journal of applied microbiology*, *135*(1), lxad288.
11. Hussein, N. H., Al-Kadmy, I. M., Taha, B. M., & Hussein, J. D. (2021). Mobilized colistin resistance (mcr) genes from 1 to 10: a comprehensive review. *Molecular biology reports*, *48*(3), 2897–2907.
12. Navales, I. A. M., Paglas, M. A., Panibon, R., Parcasio, R. D., Parcon, A. B., Pascua, L., ... & Padilla, J. (2023) Novel Strategies for Combating Antimicrobial Resistance: Alternative Agents on the Horizon.
13. Endale, H., Mathewos, M., & Abdeta, D. (2023). Potential causes of spread of antimicrobial resistance and preventive measures in one health perspective-a review. *Infection and Drug Resistance*, 7515–7545.
14. Mentzelopoulos SD, Pratikaki M, Platsouka E, Kraniotaki H, Zervakis D, Koutsoukou A, Nanas S, Paniara O, Roussos C, Giamarellos-Bourboulis E, Routsi C. Prolonged use of carbapenems and colistin predisposes to ventilator-associated pneumonia by pandrug-resistant Pseudomonas aeruginosa. Intensive care medicine. 2007 Sep; 33: 1524–32.
15. Yamin, D., Uskoković, V., Wakil, A. M., Goni, M. D., Shamsuddin, S. H., Mustafa, F. H., ... & Yusof, N. Y. (2023). Current and future technologies for the detection of antibiotic-resistant bacteria. *Diagnostics*, *13*(20), 3246.
16. Moghadam, M. T., Mojtahedi, A., Moghaddam, M. M., Fasihi-Ramandi, M., & Mirnejad, R. (2022). Rescuing humanity by antimicrobial peptides against colistin-resistant bacteria. *Applied microbiology and biotechnology*, *106*(11), 3879–3893.
17. Leavis, H. L., Bonten, M. J., & Willems, R. J. (2006). Identification of high-risk enterococcal clonal complexes: global dispersion and antibiotic resistance. *Current opinion in microbiology*, *9*(5), 454–460
18. Jung, H. (2021). *Genomic epidemiology of carbapenem-and/or colistin-resistant Pseudomonas aeruginosa in the Gauteng region, South Africa* (Doctoral dissertation, University of Pretoria (South Africa)).
19. Andersson, D. I., Balaban, N. Q., Baquero, F., Courvalin, P., Glaser, P., Gophna, U., ... & Tønjum, T. (2020). Antibiotic resistance: turning evolutionary principles into clinical reality. *FEMS microbiology reviews*, *44*(2), 171–188.
20. Ravi, K., & Singh, B. (2024). ESKAPE: Navigating the Global Battlefield for Antimicrobial Resistance and Defense in Hospitals. *Bacteria*, *3*(2), 76–98.
21. Anyanwu, M. U., Jaja, I. F., & Nwobi, O. C. (2020). Occurrence and characteristics of mobile colistin resistance (mcr) gene-containing isolates from the environment: a review. *International journal of environmental research and public health*, *17*(3), 1028.
22. Chia, P. Y., Sengupta, S., Kukreja, A., SL Ponnampalavanar, S., Ng, O. T., & Marimuthu, K. (2020). The role of hospital environment in transmissions of multidrug-resistant gram-negative organisms. *Antimicrobial Resistance & Infection Control*, *9*, 1–11.
23. Hawken, S. E., & Snitkin, E. S. (2019). Genomic epidemiology of multidrug-resistant Gram-negative organisms. *Annals of the New York Academy of Sciences*, *1435*(1), 39–56.
24. Gerace, E., Mancuso, G., Midiri, A., Poidomani, S., Zummo, S., & Biondo, C. (2022). Recent advances in the use of molecular methods for the diagnosis of bacterial infections. *Pathogens*, *11*(6), 663.
25. Ghosh, C., Sarkar, P., Issa, R., & Haldar, J. (2019). Alternatives to conventional antibiotics in the era of antimicrobial resistance. *Trends in microbiology*, *27*(4), 323–338.

Note: All the figures and tables in this chapter were made by the authors.

Research and Innovations in Industrial and Marine Biotechnology: A Circular Economy 2024 – Prof. Hrudayanath Thatoi et al. (eds)

29 Genetic Diversity of *Candida* Species Isolated from Vulvovaginal Candidiasis in Relation to their Antifungal Resistance Patterns

Binaya Krushna Sahu
Centre for Biotechnology,
Siksha 'O' Anusandhan (Deemed to be University),
Kalinganagar, Bhubaneswar, Odisha, India

Utkalika Mallick
Centre for Biotechnology,
Siksha 'O' Anusandhan (Deemed to be University),
Kalinganagar, Bhubaneswar, Odisha, India
Division of Microbiology,
ICMR-Regional Medical Research Centre, Chandrasekharpur,
Bhubaneswar, Odisha, India

Jyotirmayee Turuk, Mahesh Chandra Sahu*
Division of Microbiology,
ICMR-Regional Medical Research Centre, Chandrasekharpur,
Bhubaneswar, Odisha, India

Sujogya Kumar Panda
Centre for Biotechnology,
Siksha 'O' Anusandhan (Deemed to be University),
Kalinganagar, Bhubaneswar, Odisha, India

Abstract: Vulvovaginal candidiasis (VVC), predominantly caused by *Candida* species, remains one of the most common fungal infections among women worldwide. Understanding antifungal resistance patterns and genetic diversity is crucial for effective management and epidemiological surveillance. A total of 170 vaginal swabs from suspected VVC cases were collected from Kalinga Hospitals and IMS SUM Hospital, Bhubaneswar. *Candida* species were identified using culture-based methods on Candida Differential Agar (CDA), germ tube test, and VITEK-2 analysis. The disk diffusion technique was used to measure antifungal susceptibility, and 14 Random Amplified Polymorphic DNA (RAPD) and 19 Inter-Simple Sequence Repeat (ISSR) markers were used to evaluate genetic diversity. Out of 170 samples, 122 (71.76%) were identified as *Candida* species. Prevalence rates included *C. albicans* (28.69%), *C. glabrata* (27.05%), and *C. tropicalis* (14.75%), among others. Antifungal susceptibility varied: *C. albicans* were ketoconazole and voriconazole were resistant (60%), *C. auris* were resistant to every antifungal examined in this study, *C. glabrata* was highly resistant to fluconazole (75.8%) and other species exhibited specific resistances. Based on resistance profiles, 18 isolates were selected for genetic diversity analysis showed wide differences among the isolates, especially in *C. albicans* and other non-*albicans Candida* species, as seen in the correlation matrices, phylogenetic tree, and PCA analyses. These findings highlight the urgent need for precise species identification, routine antifungal susceptibility testing, and molecular surveillance to improve treatment strategies and patient outcomes in VVC.

Keywords: *Candida* species, Clinical isolates, ISSR, Non-*albicans Candida.* RAPD, Vulvovaginal candidiasis

*Corresponding author: mchsahu@gmail.com

DOI: 10.1201/9781003759003-29

1. Introduction

A highly common fungal infection affecting women worldwide that affecting about 75% at least once in their lifetime is vulvovaginal candidiasis (VVC), with 5–10% developing recurrent VVC (RVVC)[1-2]. VVC has the greatest burden in women of reproductive age, but represents an elevated risk for immunocompromised patients, such as, diabetes mellitus, HIV infection, malignancies, long-term use of antibiotics or corticosteroids, are especially vulnerable to severe and recurrent infections[1, 3, 4].

Candida albicans has consistently represented the primary causative agent of VVC and in fact, is the cause of most cases[1]. Non-*albicans Candida* (NAC) species have been increasingly isolated in recent decades that reflecting a change in the epidemiology of *Candida* infections [5, 6]. NAC species represent an increasing clinical concern because of their intrinsic and acquired resistance to the antifungals normally utilized in treatment. For example, *C. glabrata* frequently has reduced susceptibility to the azoles, whereas *C. krusei* is intrinsically resistant to fluconazole. It is fast becoming very difficult to manage these types of infections [7, 8].

The rapid emergence of antifungal resistance in species of *Candida* has created a significant challenge in clinical settings[9]. Resistance to all three classes of antifungals-azoles, echinocandins, and polyenes that making treatment outcomes more challenging, and they may prolong an infection or contribute considerable morbidity and mortality [9, 10]. In addition, inappropriate or empirical use of antifungals without susceptibility testing propels the development of resistance, emphasizing the need for continuous surveillance and species level identification of *Candida* isolates in clinical settings.

Antifungal susceptibility testing (AST) is crucial for determining appropriate treatment for infections but examining resistance through growth patterns in a laboratory (phenotypically testing) does not represent the complex nature of resistance development by *Candida.* As part of this effort, now using the molecular methods to study genetic variation and antifungal resistance in species within the genus *Candida.* Molecular markers, namely Inter-Simple Sequence Repeat (ISSR) and Random Amplified Polymorphic DNA (RAPD) have value in assessing genetic diversity and differentiation at the genetic level. ISSR and RAPD markers provide important evidence of the epidemiology, pathogenicity and resistance mechanisms of *Candida* species[10-12]. To predict the emergence of antifungal-resistant strains, it is important to analyse the genetic variation in susceptible and resistant isolates and this can be effectively achieved using ISSR and RAPD markers[12-14]. Combining AST and molecular approaches will offer a comprehensive strategy for addressing the challenges of VVC management. Identifying the antifungal sensitivity patterns of *Candida* isolates helps clinicians select appropriate therapies, while exploring genetic diversity offers insights into the potential emergence and spread of resistant strains.

The primary objective of this study is to identify *Candida* species from cases of suspected VVC, evaluate their antifungal resistance patterns and examine their genetic diversity using ISSR and RAPD markers. The information gained will provide evidence to help identify patterns of resistance and of genetic differences that can be utilized for better treatment, inform proper antifungal drug use, and assist with infection control in hospitals.

2. Materials and Methods

2.1 Sample Collection and Identification of *Candida* Species

At IMS SUM and Kalinga Hospitals in Bhubaneswar, vaginal swab samples (n=170) were taken from suspected VVC patients and processed sterilely. Sabouraud Dextrose (SD) broth was used for the initial culture, and SD agar (SDA) plates were then incubated at 37 °C for 24 to 48 hours. *Candida* growth was indicated by creamy white colonies. *C. albicans* was presumed to be identified via germ tube testing and Gram staining. As outlined in our earlier study [15], species-level differentiation was carried out using HiCrome™ Candida Differential Agar(HiMedia Laboratories Pvt. Ltd., India), and confirmatory identification was accomplished using the VITEK-2 Compact System [15].

2.2 Antifungal Susceptibility Test

AST of the *Candida* isolates was carried out using the disk diffusion method following the Clinical and Laboratory Standards Institute (CLSI) guidelines.Following the inoculation preparation and uniform distribution on SDA plates antifungal disks were applied. Six azoles, two polyenes, and one echinocandin were among the antifungal drugs that were evaluated [16-18].

2.3 Genomic DNA Extraction and Amplification Using ISSR and RAPD Markers

As per our previous study [15], genomic DNA were extracted from *Candida* isolates using a modified phenol: chloroform: isoamyl alcohol method. The purity and concentration of the extracted DNA were analysed using a 0.8% agarose gel electrophoresis and Nanodrop spectrophotometer. PCR amplification were conducted using 19 ISSR and 14 RAPD under standardized cycling conditionsin 10 µl reactions containing TAKARA master mix (5 µl), primer (1 µl), nuclease-free water (3 µl), and template DNA (1 µl). The annealing temperature for each primer was provided by the manufacturer based on its base composition[10, 14, 19, 20]. The PCR amplicons were analysed by electrophoresis on 1.5% agarose gel in 1x TBE, stained with ethidium bromide and visualized using a gel documentation system. Only primers producing clear and reproducible bands were analysed further[14, 20].

2.4 Genetic Diversity Analysis

The gel image generated from RAPD and ISSR analyses were manually scored for bands presence (1) and absence (0) producing a binary matrix. Bands that differed between isolates were defined as polymorphic. Genetic similarity between isolates was estimated using Jaccard's coefficient [21],and a dendrogram was produced from the distance matrix using the unweighted pair group method with arithmetic mean (UPGMA)[20, 22].Furthermore, to further examine the clustering patterns and relationships among the isolates, Principal Component Analysis (PCA) were performed with the NTSYS-pc Software[20, 23].

3. Results

The study involved 170 clinical samples suspected of VVC, of these, 122 (71.76%) were confirmed as *Candida* species. This high percentage indicates a significant prevalence of *Candida* species in the sampled population. Among the confirmed samples, *C. albicans* was the predominant identified species, accounting for 28.69% of the total, followed closely by *C. glabrata* at 27.05%. Other species included *C. tropicalis* (14.75%), *C. kefyr* (13.11%), *C. utilis* (8.19%), *C. krusei* (7.38%), and a single case of *C. auris*. This demonstrates the diversity of *Candida* species present in the clinical samples.Culture on HiCrome™ CDA provided clear differentiation of *Candida* species based on colony colours. Germ tube formation was observed in *C. albicans* isolates, confirming their identity. The colony colours of various *Candida* species grown on CDA are depicted in Fig. 29.1. Out of the 122 *Candida* isolates, 18 samples were selected for genetic diversity analysis based on their antifungal resistance profiles (resistance to 5 or more tested antifungal). The chosen samples, characterized by their corresponding reference numbers, comprised of *C. glabrata* (204, 216, 227, 241), *C. albicans* (205, 208, 209, 215, 226), *C. tropicalis* (206, 211, 212, 213, 214), *C. krusei* (217, 233, 243), and *C. auris* (210).

3.1 Antifungal Resistance Patterns

The antifungal susceptibility patterns showed varying degrees of resistance and sensitivity among the species. Nystatin exhibited the greatest activity against *C. albicans*(60%), subsequently by miconazole (54.29%). However, it exhibited significant resistance to ketoconazole (60%) and voriconazole (60%). *C. glabrata* showed high resistance to fluconazole (75.8%), and caspofungin, itraconazole, and ketoconazole each (66.7%) but displayed 69.7% sensitivity to nystatin and miconazole. *C. tropicalis* had high resistance to amphotericin B (61.1%) and caspofungin (66.7%) but showed strong sensitivity to nystatin (77.8%). *C. krusei* demonstrated complete sensitivity to nystatin and significant sensitivity to miconazole (77.8%). *C. krusei* showed intrinsic and considerable resistance, including 55.6% to fluconazole, while the single *C. auris* isolate

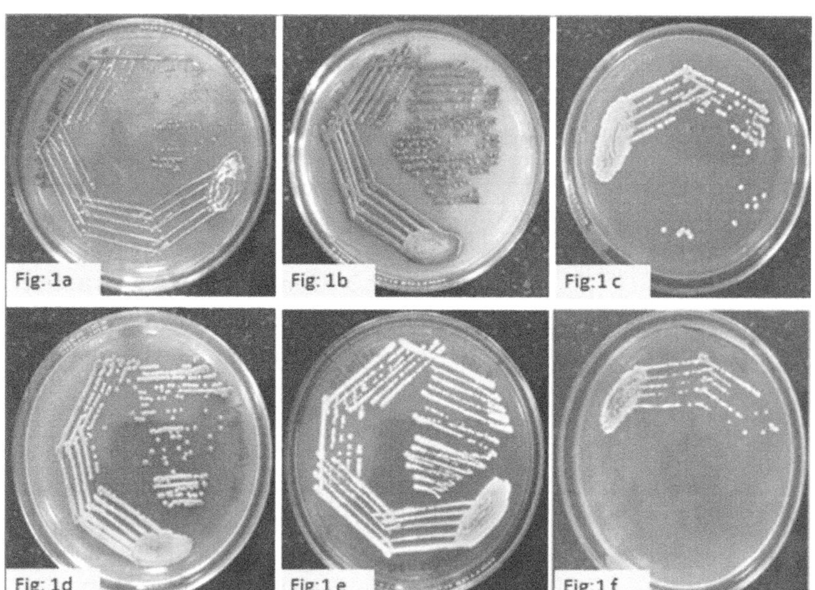

Fig. 29.1 The figure represents the colony colours of various *Candida* species cultured on HiCrome™ Candida Differential Agar (CDA). Each species displays a distinct colony colour, aiding in its identification. (a) *C. albicans* produces light green colonies, (b) while *C. tropicalis* ranges from blue to purple. (c) *C. kefyr* appears cream to white with a slight purple in centre, (d) *C.krusei* exhibits a purple, fuzzy appearance. (e) *C. glabrata* forms cream to white colonies, (f) whereas *C. auris*, shows a pale pink to pinkish coloration

Table 29.1 Percentage resistance of identified *Candida* species against various antifungal agents

Organism Name	Total	Resistance Percentage								
		MIC 30	NS 100	CC 10	KT 10	AP 20	FLC 10	CAS 10	IT 10	VRC 1
C. albicans	35	37.14	17.14	48.57	60	34.29	54.29	48.57	51.43	60
C. glabrata	33	18.2	21.2	45.5	66.7	51.5	75.8	66.7	66.7	57.6
C. tropicalis	18	22.2	11.1	27.8	44.4	61.1	55.6	66.7	38.9	55.6
C. kefyr	16	6.2	6.2	12.5	12.5	75	18.8	62.5	25	6.2
C. utilis	10	0	0	20	10	50	30	80	20	0
C. krusei	9	22.2	0	44.4	33.3	44.4	55.6	44.4	44.4	33.3
C. auris	1	100	100	100	100	100	100	100	100	100

Note: AP 20 = Amphotericin B (20 μg); CAS 10 = Caspofungin (10 μg); CC 10 = Clotrimazole (10 μg); FLC 10 = Fluconazole (10 μg); IT 10 = Itraconazole (10 μg); KT 10 = Ketoconazole (10 μg); MIC 30 = Miconazole (30 μg); NS 100 = Nystatin (100 units); VRC 1 = Voriconazole (1 μg).

that resistance to all antifungal agents tested, highlighting its multidrug-resistant nature. Table 29.1 shows the percentage of resistance of all identified *Candida* species to three different classes of antifungals.

3.2 RAPD and ISSR-PCR Analysis

The RAPD analysis was carried out, using 14 different primers. Out of which 5 were (OPA 01, OPA 03, OPE 04, OPA 07, and OPA 18) revealed varying amplification patterns and levels of genetic diversity. OPA 03 demonstrated the highest efficacy, producing 47 bands across samples with significant polymorphism, a resolving power of 0.65, and a primer index of 0.44, making it highly effective in distinguishing between species. OPA 18, and OPA 04 and OPA 07 also showed moderate discriminatory capacity with 5 and 1 polymorphic bands, respectively, while OPA 01 produced only a single unique band, indicating very low variability.Similarly, in the ISSR analysis, 19 different ISSR primers were used. Out of which 16 were revealed varying amplification patterns and shows levels of genetic diversity. Primer ISSR 14 generated the highest number of bands (73), while ISSR 1 produced only two, reflecting significant variation in the ability of primers to amplify polymorphic genomic regions. The most polymorphic profiles were obtained with ISSR 19 and ISSR 18, which generated 11, and 10 polymorphic bands, respectively. Resolving power values for ISSR primers were generally higher (0.11–0.95) than those of RAPD primers, with ISSR 7 showing the highest value (0.95), followed by ISSR 4 (0.94) and ISSR 5 (0.91). Similarly, the primer index was highest (0.5) for ISSR 4, ISSR 5, ISSR 7, and ISSR 14, indicating their superior efficiency in differentiating *Candida* isolates. These findings highlight the utility of ISSR markers in exploring genetic diversity, with certain primers demonstrating superior discriminatory power among *Candida* samples (Table 29.2).

The genetic diversity of the 18 *Candida* isolates was further analyzed using UPGMA-based dendrograms

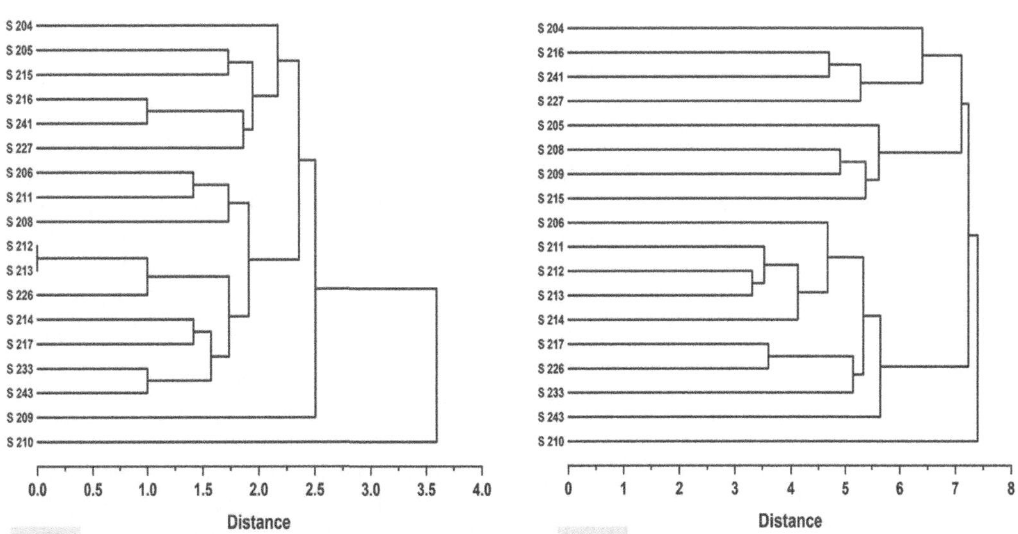

Fig 2a

Fig 2b

Fig. 29.2 Phylogenetic tree analysis depicting the genetic diversity among 18 *Candida* isolates (a) using RAPD marker (b) using ISSR marker

Note: C. glabrata (204, 216, 227, 241), *C. albicans* (205, 208, 209, 215, 226), *C. tropicalis* (206, 211, 212, 213, 214), *C. krusei* (217, 233, 243), and *C. auris* (210)

Table 29.2 Detailed RAPD and ISSR banding pattern, resolving power and primer index of 18 *Candida* samples

Primer Name	Nucleotide Sequencing	Band Present	Resolving Power	Primer Index	Polymorphic Band	Unique Bands
OPA 01	CAGGCCCTTC	1	0.111	0.11	0	1
OPA 03	AGTCAGCCAC	47	0.65	0.44	7	1
OPE 04	GTGACATG CC	2	0.22	0.2	1	0
OPA 07	GAAACGGGTG	7	0.19	0.18	1	3
OPA 18	AGCTGACCGT	15	0.24	0.21	5	3
ISSR 1	(GTGC)4	2	0.111	0.11	0	2
ISSR 2	(GACAC)4	3	0.333	0.28	1	0
ISSR 4	(AG)8	59	0.94	0.5	7	0
ISSR 5	(GTG)5	49	0.91	0.5	5	1
ISSR 6	(GGA)4	64	0.71	0.46	9	1
ISSR 7	(GAC)5	60	0.95	0.5	7	0
ISSR 8	(GACA)4	45	0.63	0.43	7	0
ISSR 9	(GA)9T	40	0.64	0.43	6	1
ISSR 10	(CTGC)4	26	0.36	0.3	6	2
ISSR 11	(GA)8G	53	0.74	0.47	7	1
ISSR 12	A(CT)8	61	0.57	0.41	9	3
ISSR 13	(GCT)8	28	0.52	0.38	5	1
ISSR 14	(AGG)6	73	0.9	0.5	9	0
ISSR 15	T(GA)7GCYAGA	46	0.51	0.38	9	1
ISSR 18	(CCA)5	57	0.576	0.41	10	1
ISSR 19	(CGA)4	70	0.648	0.44	11	1

generated from RAPD and ISSR marker data (Fig. 29.2a, 29.2b). The RAPD dendrogram (Fig. 29.2a) grouped the isolates into distinct clusters, with shorter branch lengths indicating close genetic relatedness. For example, isolates S216 and S241 formed a tight cluster, suggesting minimal genetic divergence, whereas isolates S209 and S210 were placed at relatively longer distances, reflecting higher genetic variation. Several intermediate clusters were observed, such as S206, S211, and S208, which were grouped together, indicating moderate similarity. Interestingly, S210 appeared as an outlier in the RAPD dendrogram, highlighting its distinct genetic profile compared to the rest of the isolates. Similarly, in the ISSR dendrogram (Fig. 29.2b) provided a higher resolution of genetic relationships, producing more defined clusters and wider genetic distances. Closely related isolates, such as S212, S213, and S211, clustered tightly, reflecting their strong genetic similarity. Larger branch distances separated isolates like S210 and S243, suggesting substantial divergence from the main groups. The clustering pattern also showed that ISSR markers were more effective in differentiating isolates that appeared similar in the RAPD analysis, thereby providing a clearer understanding of intra-species variability.

The Principal Component Analysis (PCA) results based on RAPD and ISSR profiles highlight the genetic variation among the *Candida* samples. In Fig. 29.3a, PC1 and PC2 account for 34.05% and 16.11% of the total variation, respectively, with each red dot representing a sample's genetic variation relative to others. Samples clustered together share a similar genetic makeup, while those further apart show greater genetic differentiation, such as S210, which is distinct on the positive side of PC1, indicating significant genetic divergence. Similarly, Figure 29.3b reveals three distinct clusters, with PC1 and PC2 explaining 21.84% and 14.49% of the variance, respectively. The first cluster near the origin includes samples like S212, S213, and S217, showing minimal genetic divergence. The second cluster, in the lower right quadrant, includes S205, S208, S209, and S210, reflecting unique genetic features. The third cluster, in the upper right quadrant, comprises S204, S216, S227, and S241, indicating significant divergence from the other groups.

The genetic similarity matrices present genetic similarity coefficients between pairs of samples, ranging from 0 to 1, where a value of 1.000 indicates complete genetic identity, signifying that the samples are genetically identical. Lower values reflect greater genetic divergence. For instance, in RAPD (Fig. 29.4a), similarity coefficients ranged from 0.5333 to 1.000, indicating both high similarity and substantial genetic divergence within the population. Several isolates showed very close relationships, such as samples 233 and 243 exhibit high similarity (0.9667), indicating close genetic relationships, while samples 204

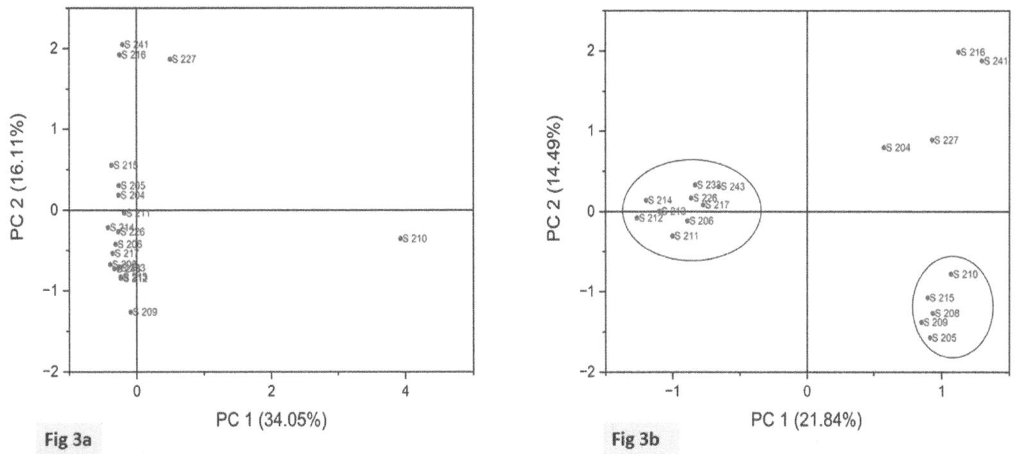

Fig. 29.3 Illustrating the genetic relationships among 18 *Candida* isolates by principal component analysis (PCA) based on (a) using RAPD marker (b) using ISSR marker

Note: C. glabrata (204, 216, 227, 241), *C. albicans* (205, 208, 209, 215, 226), *C. tropicalis* (206, 211, 212, 213, 214), *C. krusei* (217, 233, 243), and *C. auris* (210)

and 210 show a lower similarity (0.5333), reflecting more divergence. Similarly, in ISSR (Fig. 29.4b), provided a broader range of coefficients, spanning from 0.4882 to 1.000, reflecting the higher discriminatory power of ISSR markers. IsolatesS212 and S213 (0.9134) and S211 and S213 (0.9055) demonstrated high similarity, consistent with their clustering in PCA and dendrogram analyses. Conversely, pairs like S210 and S212 (0.5197) and S210 with several other isolates showed lower similarity.

4. Discussion

Antifungal resistance in *Candida* species, as observed in this study, can be attributed to multiple adaptive mechanisms that allow these pathogens to survive antifungal treatment and persist in clinical environments. Many authors have reported various alternation in ERG11, the gene encoding lanosterol 14α-demethylase, which leads significant reduction in azole drug binding affinity, and effectiveness [7, 8]. Additionally, the overexpression

Fig 4a	204	205	206	208	209	210	211	212	213	214	215	216	217	226	227	233	241	243
204	1.0000																	
205	0.9000	1.0000																
206	0.9000	0.8667	1.0000															
208	0.8000	0.9000	0.9000	1.0000														
209	0.8000	0.8333	0.8333	0.8667	1.0000													
210	0.5333	0.5667	0.5667	0.5333	0.5333	1.0000												
211	0.8333	0.8667	0.9333	0.9000	0.8333	0.6333	1.0000											
212	0.8000	0.8333	0.9000	0.8667	0.8000	0.6000	0.9000	1.0000										
213	0.8000	0.8333	0.9000	0.8667	0.8000	0.6000	0.9000	1.0000	1.0000									
214	0.8667	0.9000	0.9000	0.8667	0.8000	0.5333	0.9000	0.9333	0.9333	1.0000								
215	0.8000	0.9000	0.8333	0.8667	0.8000	0.5333	0.9000	0.8667	0.8667	0.9333	1.0000							
216	0.8667	0.9000	0.8333	0.8000	0.7333	0.5333	0.8333	0.7333	0.7333	0.8000	0.8667	1.0000						
217	0.8000	0.8333	0.8333	0.8000	0.7333	0.5333	0.8333	0.8667	0.8667	0.9333	0.8667	0.7333	1.0000					
226	0.7667	0.8000	0.8667	0.8333	0.7667	0.5667	0.8667	0.9667	0.9667	0.9000	0.9000	0.7667	0.8333	1.0000				
227	0.8000	0.8333	0.7667	0.7333	0.6667	0.6667	0.8333	0.7333	0.7333	0.8000	0.8667	0.8667	0.7333	0.7667	1.0000			
233	0.8000	0.8333	0.9000	0.8667	0.8000	0.6000	0.9000	0.9333	0.9333	0.9333	0.8667	0.7333	0.9333	0.9000	0.7333	1.0000		
241	0.8333	0.8667	0.8000	0.7667	0.7000	0.5667	0.8667	0.7667	0.7667	0.8333	0.9000	0.9667	0.7667	0.8000	0.9000	0.7667	1.0000	
243	0.8333	0.8667	0.9333	0.9000	0.8333	0.5667	0.8667	0.9000	0.9000	0.9000	0.8333	0.7667	0.9000	0.8667	0.7000	0.9667	0.7333	1.0000

Fig 4b	204	205	206	208	209	210	211	212	213	214	215	216	217	226	227	233	241	243
204	1.0000																	
205	0.5906	1.0000																
206	0.6614	0.5669	1.0000															
208	0.5827	0.7717	0.5906	1.0000														
209	0.6142	0.7559	0.6378	0.8110	1.0000													
210	0.5433	0.6220	0.5669	0.5984	0.6299	1.0000												
211	0.6220	0.6378	0.8346	0.6457	0.6457	0.5748	1.0000											
212	0.5984	0.5354	0.8425	0.5591	0.5748	0.5197	0.8976	1.0000										
213	0.6063	0.5748	0.8189	0.6142	0.6142	0.5276	0.9055	0.9134	1.0000									
214	0.6220	0.5433	0.8189	0.5827	0.5827	0.5118	0.8740	0.8661	0.8583	1.0000								
215	0.5827	0.7244	0.5906	0.7795	0.7638	0.5354	0.6142	0.5906	0.5984	0.5512	1.0000							
216	0.6693	0.5276	0.5512	0.5984	0.5669	0.5591	0.5591	0.5354	0.5906	0.5433	0.5984	1.0000						
217	0.6220	0.6063	0.7717	0.6142	0.6299	0.5433	0.7480	0.7559	0.7795	0.7795	0.5669	0.5906	1.0000					
226	0.6142	0.5984	0.7953	0.5906	0.6220	0.5827	0.8031	0.7795	0.8189	0.8189	0.5906	0.5984	0.8976	1.0000				
227	0.6772	0.6142	0.6063	0.7008	0.6378	0.5984	0.5984	0.5433	0.5984	0.5984	0.6535	0.7874	0.6299	0.6535	1.0000			
233	0.5984	0.5827	0.7165	0.5591	0.5591	0.5827	0.7559	0.7323	0.7717	0.7874	0.5433	0.5827	0.7874	0.7953	0.5748	1.0000		
241	0.6850	0.5433	0.5512	0.6142	0.5984	0.5591	0.5276	0.4882	0.5433	0.5276	0.5984	0.8268	0.5591	0.5669	0.7717	0.5669	1.0000	
243	0.5906	0.6063	0.7402	0.5827	0.5512	0.6063	0.7638	0.7244	0.7638	0.7165	0.5827	0.6063	0.7165	0.7717	0.6457	0.7874	0.5748	1.0000

Fig. 29.4 Genetic similarity among 18 *Candida* isolates analysed using (a) RAPD markers and (b) ISSR markers

Note: C. glabrata (204, 216, 227, 241), *C. albicans* (205, 208, 209, 215, 226), *C. tropicalis* (206, 211, 212, 213, 214), *C. krusei* (217, 233, 243), and *C. auris* (210)

of efflux pumps has been reported to actively expel antifungal agents from the fungal cell, leading to sub-therapeutic intracellular concentrations [24]. Bilal et al. [25] conducted a systematic analysis of 44,716 *Candida* isolates from mainland China over a ten-year period, revealing *C. albicans* (49.36%) as most dominant species, with *C. tropicalis* (21.89%) and *C. parapsilosis* (13.92%) occurring next in frequency. Their study showed the lowest susceptibility to azoles, with fluconazole resistance most notable in *C. auris* (100%) and *C. tropicalis* (22.05%), while anidulafungin and amphotericin B remained the major effective drugs, aligning with our findings where azole resistance, particularly in NAC species, represents a major therapeutic challenge. Biofilm production has also been implicated as a major factor in antifungal resistance, utilized as a physical and biochemical protective barrier for fungal cells against drug penetration and immune responses [26, 27]. In addition, with respect to antifungal stewardship, there is an augmented dilemma of antifungal resistance found in both hospital and community settings, exacerbated by antifungal avoidance or selective pressure prevent resistant strains from potential extinction[28]. The use and misuse of antifungals both in hospitals and communities have generated a potential for infection to be sustained and multiplied following previous exposure to antifungals. Most hospital settings and medical devices act as reservoirs for multidrug-resistant isolates, and isolations can occur in the hospital setting following exposure to these resistant isolates[29]. Taken together, these findings suggest that antifungal resistance arises not only from genetic mutations but also from adaptive responses driven by clinical practices and environmental factors, highlighting the need for stringent antifungal stewardship and routine surveillance[30].

The current study indicates a marked prevalence of *Candida* species (71.76%) among women suspected to have VVC. Ali et al. [31]observedthe prevalence of VVC is 61.4% among pregnant women in Yemen, with *C. albicans*(59.26%) as the leading speciesand NAC showing high resistance rates, which is congruent with global data indicating that *Candida* is the primary cause of fungal infections of the vagina in reproductive-age women. Our study reflects this global trend, as *C. albicans* (28.69%) represents the highest percentage of our isolates, and is historically the main causative agent of VVC. Particularly *C. glabrata* (27.05%) and *C. tropicalis* (14.75%), indicate a significant epidemiological shiftamong NAC species. This change has been well documented in recent years, as NAC species increasingly replace *C. albicans* in clinical infections due to their enhanced capacity for antifungal resistance and persistence in hostile environments[5, 6, 32].

In particular, we were alarmed with the finding of *C. auris*, which although rare in our cohort, raises serious clinical and epidemiological implications. The isolate in our report exhibited resistance to all antifungal agents tested, consistent with global reports indicating concerning resistance profiles of this species [33]. The isolate in our study displayed resistance to all antifungal agents tested, which is in line with global reports highlighting the alarming resistance profile of this species [34-36]. Its detection, even in a single case, underscores the importance of robust surveillance mechanisms to prevent nosocomial spread and to ensure that diagnostic laboratories are equipped to rapidly identify this species, which can often be misidentified using conventional phenotypic methods[37, 38].

The AST showed some concerning resistance patterns within both *C. albicans* and NAC isolates. Resistance of *C. albicans* to ketoconazole and voriconazole in our study is similar to reports associating azole resistance with *ERG11* mutations, efflux pump utilization, and biofilm formation[7, 8]. The high fluconazole resistance rate among *C. glabrata* is particularly troubling since it is commonly used first-line treatment for VVC. This observation aligns with studies from other regions reporting intrinsic and acquired azole resistance in *C. glabrata*, which significantly limits therapeutic choices [39-41]. *C. tropicalis*, another NAC species with clinical significance, displayed high resistance to amphotericin B and caspofungin, indicating the emergence of strainsresistant to both polyenes and echinocandins, which are often considered alternative treatments in azole-resistant infections[42]. Collectively, these findings highlight the urgent need to reconsider empirical treatment practices and to incorporate species-level identification with AST before initiating therapy.

The genetic similarity, dendrogram, and PCA analyses in this study revealed significant genetic diversity and relatedness among the *Candida* isolates, providing important insights into their evolutionary patterns and resistance mechanisms. In the dendrogram constructed using RAPD or ISSR markers, clustering was evident, some isolates appear in related groups, while outliers, including *C. auris* (S210) distinctly separated by genetic divergence. ISSR markers showed better discrimination than RAPD markers which is consistent [43], and the PCA analysis further supported these results by distinctly separating clusters, with the first two principal components explaining a considerable proportion of the total variation. This genetic heterogeneity reflects ongoing recombination, clonal expansion, and adaptive evolution under antifungal pressure [20]. The clustering of *C. albicans* isolates suggests potential clonal expansion driven by selective antifungal use, while the broader genetic distances observed among NAC species highlight their diverse evolutionary trajectories. Such genetic diversity not only contributes to antifungal resistance but may also influence clinical outcomes by enhancing virulence factors such as biofilm formation, enzyme secretion, and immune evasion, underscoring the importance of integrating genetic diversity analyses into routine surveillance for effective monitoring and control of resistant *Candida* strains.

These findings have important clinical consequences. The increasing predominance of NAC species and the emergence of *C. auris* in VVC cases raises concerns that current treatment regimens could become unsuitable in the near future. Whereas NAC species are known to have poor susceptibility to fluconazole, other agents such as echinocandins and amphotericin B may not even be an option in a given place for patients with VVC because they cannot be obtained in low-resource settings. Thus, there is a need for antifungal stewardship, routine surveillance for resistance patterns, and molecular typing for epidemiological tracking. Consideration of both phenotypic susceptibility testing and analysis of genotypic diversity as in this study will lend to a comprehensive way in which we can describe the trends of antifungal resistance in NAC species and develop tailored treatment strategies. Furthermore, correlating genetic diversity markers with patient outcomes in future research could provide deeper insights into how specific genotypes influence clinical response, persistence, and recurrence.

This study is alarmingly clear about the need for accurate species identification and comprehensive AST to guide the treatment of VVC. The presence of concurrent and multidrug-resistant NAC species with *C. auris* poses an urgent threat to the continued use of antifungal medications within clinical settings. Expanding routine diagnostics to include MIC testing and molecular surveillance will be essential for in developing targeted interventions, limiting the spread of resistance, and improving patient outcomes in *Candida*-associated infections.

5. Conclusion

This research examines antifungal drug resistance in various *Candida* species in VVC patients with genetic diversity using ISSR and RAPD markers. The data shows that the predominant species is *C. albicans* and that NAC species are also common and resistant to various antifungal drugs. These findings highlight the need for accurate species identification and antifungal susceptibility testingto ensure that patients receive the most appropriate antifungal therapy. Future studies should investigate the relationships between markers of genetic diversity and antifungal resistance mechanisms. Overall this research serves as data towards establishing better-targeted treatment options and patient outcomes in candidiasis.

Acknowledgement

The authors sincerely acknowledge the Dean of Research and Development, Siksha 'O' Anusandhan University, and the Director of the Indian Council of Medical Research-Regional Medical Research Centre (ICMR-RMRC), Bhubaneswar, for their invaluable support and for providing the necessary facilities to carry out this research. Author SKP also extends gratitude to Prof. (Dr.) ManojranjanNayak, President of Siksha 'O' Anusandhan (Deemed to be University), Bhubaneswar, India, for providing the required infrastructure facility for this work.

References

1. Mallick U, Sahu BK, Hegde R, Jena P, Turuk J, Sahu MC, Panda SK: Antifungal Resistance in Vaginal Candidiasis Among Reproductive-age Women: A Review. *Current Pharmaceutical Biotechnology*, 2025, Epub ahead of print. https://doi.org/10.2174/0113892010368329250503175104.
2. Gonçalves B, Ferreira C, Alves CT, Henriques M, Azeredo J, Silva S: Vulvovaginal candidiasis: Epidemiology, microbiology and risk factors. *Critical Reviews in Microbiology* 2016, 42(6):905–927.
3. Das S, Mallick U, Sahu BK, Turuk J, Sahu MC: Clinical mycology: understanding pathogenesis, diagnosis, and antifungal strategies for invasive fungal infections: a review. *Microbes and Infectious Diseases* 2024, https://doi.org/10.21608/MID.2024.331599.2319.
4. Jafarzadeh L, Ranjbar M, Nazari T, Naeimi Eshkaleti M, Aghaei Gharehbolagh S, Sobel JD, Mahmoudi S: Vulvovaginal candidiasis: An overview of mycological, clinical, and immunological aspects. *Journal of Obstetrics and Gynaecology Research* 2022, 48(7):1546–1560.
5. Neal CM, Martens MG: Clinical challenges in diagnosis and treatment of recurrent vulvovaginal candidiasis. *SAGE Open Medicine* 2022, 10:20503121221115201.
6. de Cássia Orlandi Sardi J, Silva DR, Anibal PC, de Campos Baldin JJCM, Ramalho SR, Rosalen PL, Macedo MLR, Hofling JF: Vulvovaginal candidiasis: epidemiology and risk factors, pathogenesis, resistance, and new therapeutic options. *Current Fungal Infection Reports* 2021, 15(1): 32–40.
7. Czajka KM, Venkataraman K, Brabant-Kirwan D, Santi SA, Verschoor C, Appanna VD, Singh R, Saunders DP, Tharmalingam S: Molecular mechanisms associated with antifungal resistance in pathogenic *Candida* species. *Cells* 2023, 12(22):2655.
8. Bhattacharya S, Sae-Tia S, Fries BC: Candidiasis and mechanisms of antifungal resistance. *Antibiotics* 2020, 9(6):312.
9. Sanguinetti M, Posteraro B, Lass-Flörl C: Antifungal drug resistance among *Candida* species: mechanisms and clinical impact. *Mycoses* 2015, 58:2–13.
10. Jha V, Giri R, Koli J, Poojari D, Dhamapurkar V, Jhangiani A, Nikumb D, Rumani S, Markam M, Sahu A: RAPD typing, antibiotic resistance profiling and genetic diversity of *Candida* isolates. *Microbiology&Infectious Disease*2022, 6(4):1–8.
11. Boldo XM, Villa-Tanaca L, Zúniga G, Hernández-Rodríguez C: Genetic diversity among clinical isolates of *Candida glabrata* analyzed by randomly amplified polymorphic DNA and multilocus enzyme electrophoresis analyses. *Journal of Clinical Microbiology* 2003, 41(10):4799–4804.

12. Tamai IA, Pakbin B, Fasaei BN: Genetic diversity and antifungal susceptibility of *Candida albicans* isolates from Iranian HIV-infected patients with oral candidiasis. *BMC Research Notes* 2021, 14(1):93.
13. Hammadi SY, Hussein AS, Majeed DM, Dheeb BI, Ismail EN: RAPD and ISSR analyses of *Saccharomyces cerevisiae* isolates from different sources. *Journal of Biotechnology Research Center* 2018, 12(2):40–50.
14. Mishra P, Sinha A, Sahoo D, Sahu MC: Genetically diversity of *Enterobacter cloacae* isolated from clinical samples with respect to their antibiotic sensitivity patten. *Microbes and Infectious Diseases* 2025, https://doi.org/10.21608/MID.2025.349597.2430.
15. Sahu BK, Mallick U, Hegde R, Turuk J, Sahu MC, Panda SK: Genetic diversity and antifungal resistance in *Candida albicans* from VVC cases in Indian women. *BMC Microbiology* 2025, 25;535. https://doi.org/10.1186/s12866-025-04256-1.
16. ElFeky DS, Gohar NM, El-Seidi EA, Ezzat MM, AboElew SH: Species identification and antifungal susceptibility pattern of *Candida* isolates in cases of vulvovaginal candidiasis. *Alexandria Journal of Medicine* 2016, 52(3):269–277-269–277.
17. Bauer AW, Kirby WM, Sherris JC, Turck M: Antibiotic susceptibility testing by a standardized single disk method. *American Journal of Clinical Pathology* 1966, 45(4_ts):493–496.
18. Oz Y, Gokbolat E: Evaluation of direct antifungal susceptibility testing methods of *Candida* spp. from positive blood culture bottles. *Journal of Clinical Laboratory Analysis* 2018, 32(3):e22297.
19. Banerjee R, Chattopadhyay S, Saha A: Genetic diversity and relationship of mulberry genotypes revealed by RAPD and ISSR markers. *Journal of Crop Improvement* 2016, 30(4):478–492.
20. Mishra P, Sahoo D, Sahu MC: Genetic Diversity and Antimicrobial Resistance of Clinical *Klebsiella pneumoniae* Isolates: An ISSR-PCR Analysis. *Journal of Infection and Public Health* 2025:102813.
21. Jaccard P: Nouvelles recherches sur la distribution florale. *Bull Soc Vaud Sci Nat* 1908, 44:223–270.
22. Dangi RS, Lagu MD, Choudhary LB, Ranjekar PK, Gupta VS: Assessment of genetic diversity in *Trigonella foenum-graecum* and *Trigonella caerulea* using ISSR and RAPD markers. *BMC Plant Biology* 2004, 4(1):13.
23. Rohlf FJ: NTSYS-pc: numerical taxonomy and multivariate analysis system: Exeter Publishing; 1988.
24. Pourakbari B, Teymuri M, Mahmoudi S, K Valian S, Movahedi Z, Eshaghi H, Mamishi S: Expression of major efflux pumps in fluconazole-resistant *Candida albicans*. *Infectious Disorders-Drug Targets (Formerly Current Drug Targets-Infectious Disorders)* 2017, 17(3):178–184.
25. Bilal H, Shafiq M, Hou B, Islam R, Khan MN, Khan RU, Zeng Y: Distribution and antifungal susceptibility pattern of *Candida* species from mainland China: a systematic analysis. *Virulence* 2022, 13(1):1573–1589.
26. Fan F, Liu Y, Liu Y, Lv R, Sun W, Ding W, Cai Y, Li W, Liu X, Qu W: *Candida albicans* biofilms: antifungal resistance, immune evasion, and emerging therapeutic strategies. *International Journal of Antimicrobial Agents* 2022, 60(5–6):106673.
27. Kaur J, Nobile CJ: Antifungal drug-resistance mechanisms in *Candida* biofilms. *Current Opinion in Microbiology* 2023, 71:102237.
28. Chakrabarti A, Oladele R, Hermsen E, Novis de Figueiredo ML, Muñoz P, Johnson M: Building upon the core elements of antifungal stewardship: practical recommendations for effective antifungal stewardship in resource-limited settings. *Expert Review of Anti-infective Therapy* 2025: 1–19.
29. Markogiannakis A, Korantanis K, Gamaletsou MN, Samarkos M, Psichogiou M, Daikos G, Sipsas NV: Impact of a non-compulsory antifungal stewardship program on overuse and misuse of antifungal agents in a tertiary care hospital. *International Journal of Antimicrobial Agents* 2021, 57(1):106255.
30. Fisher MC, Alastruey-Izquierdo A, Berman J, Bicanic T, Bignell EM, Bowyer P, Bromley M, Brüggemann R, Garber G, Cornely OA: Tackling the emerging threat of antifungal resistance to human health. *Nature Reviews Microbiology* 2022, 20(9):557–571.
31. Ali M, Edrees WH, Al-Shehari WA, Xue G, Al-Hammadi S, Qasem EA, Chaulagain RP, Lal N: Antifungal susceptibility pattern of *Candida* species isolated from pregnant women. *Frontiers in Cellular and Infection Microbiology* 2024, 14:1434677.
32. Hussen I, Aliyo A, Abbai MK, Dedecha W: Vaginal candidiasis prevalence, associated factors, and antifungal susceptibility patterns among pregnant women attending antenatal care at bule hora university teaching hospital, Southern Ethiopia. *BMC Pregnancy and Childbirth* 2024, 24(1):619.
33. Panda SK, Khan A, Swain SS, Aissa A, Mukazayire MJ, Van Puyvelde L, Luyten W: The anticandidal activity of the diterpenediol 8 (14), 15-sandaracopimaradiene-7alpha, 18-diol from *Tetradenia riparia* against the emerging pathogen *Candida auris*. *Phytotherapy Research* 2023, 37(1):3–6.
34. Krishnasamy L, Senthilganesh J, Saikumar C, Nithyanand P: Biofilm-forming fluconazole-resistant *Candida auris* causing vulvovaginal candidiasis in an immunocompetent patient: a case report. *Asian Pacific Journal of Tropical Medicine* 2021, 14(2):94–96.
35. Arendrup MC, Patterson TF: Multidrug-resistant *Candida*: epidemiology, molecular mechanisms, and treatment. *The Journal of Infectious Diseases* 2017, 216(suppl_3):S445–S451.
36. Carolus H, Sofras D, Boccarella G, Jacobs S, Biriukov V, Goossens L, Chen A, Vantyghem I, Verbeeck T, Pierson S: Collateral sensitivity counteracts the evolution of antifungal drug resistance in Candida auris. *Nature Microbiology* 2024, 9(11):2954–2969.
37. Kordalewska M, Perlin DS: Identification of drug resistant *Candida auris*. *Frontiers in Microbiology* 2019, 10:1918.
38. Mahmoudi S, Afshari SAK, Gharehbolagh SA, Mirhendi H, Makimura K: Methods for identification of *Candida auris*, the yeast of global public health concern: A review. *Journal de Mycologie Medicale* 2019, 29(2):174–179.
39. Cárdenas Parra LY, Rojas Rodríguez AE, Pérez Cárdenas JE, Pérez-Agudelo JM: Molecular evaluation of the mRNA expression of the ERG11, ERG3, CgCDR1, and CgSNQ2 genes linked to fluconazole resistance in *Candida glabrata*

in a Colombian population. *Journal of Fungi* 2024, 10(7):509.

40. Deravi N, Fathi M, Tabatabaeifar SN, Ahmadi B, Shokoohi G, Ansari S: Azole antifungal resistance in *Candida albicans* and *Candida glabrata* isolated from vulvovaginal candidiasis patients. *Archives of Clinical Infectious Diseases* 2021, 16(2).
41. Zarrinfar H, Kord Z, Fata A: High incidence of azole resistance among *Candida albicans* and *C. glabrata* isolates in Northeastern Iran. *Current Medical Mycology* 2021, 7(3):18.
42. Xiong H, Zhao R, Han S, Liu Z, Zhang X, Jia Z, Cui J, Zhang Y, Wang X: Research progress on the drug resistance mechanisms of *Candida tropicalis* and future solutions. *Frontiers in Microbiology* 2025, 16:1594226.
43. Souframanien J, Gopalakrishna T: A comparative analysis of genetic diversity in blackgram genotypes using RAPD and ISSR markers. *Theoretical and Applied Genetics* 2004, 109(8):1687–1693.

Note: All the figures and tables in this chapter were made by the authors.

Research and Innovations in Industrial and Marine Biotechnology: A Circular Economy 2024 – Prof. Hrudayanath Thatoi et al. (eds)
© 2026 Taylor & Francis Group, London, ISBN 978-1-041-28285-3

30 Modernizing and Enhancing the Innovation of Microbial Banks

Dinesh Chand Agrawal
Department of Biotechnology,
School of Life and Basic Science, Jaipur National University,
Jaipur, Rajasthan, India

Rajeev Kumar Jha
School of Health Sciences,
The Neotia University, Diamond Harbour Road,
Kolkata, West Bengal, India

Jibanjyoti Panda
Bioresources and Traditional Knowledge Laboratory,
Department of Wildlife and Biodiversity Conservation,
Maharaja Sriram Chandra Bhanja Deo University, Sriram Chandra Vihar,
Baripada, Mayurbhanj, Odisha, India

B. Sumithra, Kiran Yellappa Vajanthri
Department of Biotechnology,
Chaitanya Bharathi Institute of Technology,
Gandipet, Hyderabad, Telangana, India

Shibani Mohapatra
Centre for Biotechnology,
Siksha 'O' Anusandhan (Deemed to be University),
Bhubaneswar, Odisha, India

Kuno Chuzho
Department of Botany,
University of Science and Technology Meghalaya (USTM),
Baridua, Ri-Bhoi, Meghalaya, India

Bishwambhar Mishra*
Department of Biotechnology,
Chaitanya Bharathi Institute of Technology,
Gandipet, Hyderabad, Telangana, India

Abstract: Microorganisms were the first living organism to appear on the earth. Because of their close relationship with all animal, plant taxa as well as abiotic factors, they are present in almost every ecosystem in the form of biomass. In agriculture, microorganisms facilitate nitrogen fixation, solubilizing phosphate, enhancing soil fertility, producing biofertilization, and the management of diseases and pests. In the environmental sector, they are employed in bioremediation to address pollutants, including heavy metals and oil spills. Microorganisms are crucial to human health, serving both advantageous and detrimental functions. Comprehending their intricate interactions with the human body is essential for progressing medical science, formulating novel treatments, and enhancing overall health and well-being. Microorganisms are essential to our existence and health, whether by aiding digestion, generating antibiotics,

*Corresponding author: bishwambhar_biotech@cbit.ac.in

DOI: 10.1201/9781003759003-30

or inducing diseases. Scientists and researchers have been using microbes as model organisms and living tools in the laboratory to study human genetics, biochemistry and various diseases have revolutionized human understanding of the biological world. Ultimately, microorganisms are responsible for regulating most of the global systems that make Earth hospitable to human habitation. For this purpose, collecting and storing microbes by screening, isolating, and preserving the biotechnologically important microorganisms through various tools like metagenomics, SIGEX method, ichip, co-culture techniques, micro-fluidic approach, micro-manipulation etc. those have been discussed in this chapter.

Keywords: Microbial bank, SIGEX, Ichip, co-culture techniques, Micro-fluidic approach, Micro-manipulation

1. Introduction

Microorganisms are said to be the most diverse of species in the biosphere and are hence subject to various attempts to classify and study their nature and diversity, especially for their utility to humans [1]. For this purpose, collecting and storing microbes serves as a great source to identify and study novel species that aid environmental, biotechnological, energy and other applications. Microbial Banks are forms of ex situ conservation of microbial species that serve as repositories for microbial biodiversity [2]. In essence, microbial banks are large collections of microbes isolated and cultured for storage and future use in research, industry etc. Culture collections are microbial repositories that directly store potential microbial cells that could be activated and grown when needed. They are the most conventional type of microbial banks. Gene banks are collections of whole genomes: the complete set of genes in the microbes. Both culture collections and gene banks are important methods to store microbial diversity [3]. Today, more and more culture collections are becoming endangered due to lack of proper maintenance and faulty preservation protocols. In order for us to preserve the valuable genetic pool of these useful organisms and also to confer researchers with real-time microbial resources and gene pools for study, there is essentially a great need for building Microbial banks. Technical challenges include preservation techniques, loss of viability, contamination risks, and genome stability [4]. Operational challenges include resource limitations, inconsistent data management, and logistical challenges in international sharing [5]. Regulatory and legal challenges include Nagoya Protocol compliance, intellectual property disputes, biosafety protocols, and ethical and societal issues [6]. To address these challenges, microbial banks need increased financing, global cooperation, standardized processes, investments in advanced technologies, transparent regulatory frameworks, and public awareness initiatives. By overcoming these obstacles, microbial banks can facilitate scientific innovation, biodiversity preservation, and global health initiatives.

2. Culture Collections

Culture collections are the most reliable sources of authentic biological material for scientific and industrial use. Due to the high-quality standards usually followed in assembling culture collections, They are heavily depended upon by researchers to obtain superior quality strains. One of world's first culture collections was assembled by Prof. Frantisek Karl of Prague, more than a century ago [7]. The number of culture collections has seen a significant increase throughout the world and there are 647 culture collection in 27 countries, out of then 27 cultures of collections are present in India [8].

2.1 Private Collections

This type of culture collections is maintained by individual institutions or laboratories, small firms etc. The strains in such collections are not open for public access.

2.2 Public Collections

This type of culture collections contains huge number of strains that are established for public use. The Microbial Culture Collection at National Centre for Cell Science in India is an example.

2.3 Specialized Culture Collections

This type of culture collections is established when a specific group of microbes in specialized field are required. For example, collection of yeast strains for brewing industry [3].

3. Isolation and Screening

3.1 Metagenomic Approach

Jo Handelsman first used the term metagenomics in 1998. Metagenomics is the study of genetic material collected from a particular environmental sample. The individual genomes of growing bacteria are actually similar to it. It contains no information about the full genetic potential of a population of microorganisms. It skips over looking at a particular gene (like 16S rRNA) that is present in the environment. A given ecosystem's population dynamics and composition, which are impacted by both spatial and selective pressures, are referred to as the microbial community structure. A thorough grasp of the relationships between the many elements that make up a community may be gained by looking at its structure, which is also essential for clarifying the ecological or biological activities that take place among its members [9]. Thousands of metagenomic clones are included in expression libraries created by the functional metagenomic approach, which then uses activity-based screens to identify genes encoding a particular function [10]. Figure 30.1 illustrates the overview of structural and functional metagenomic approaches as primary strategies for investigating key ecological and biotechnological features in environmental samples. The timeline of major metagenomics breakthroughs is shown in Table 30.1.

3.2 ICHIP

The Ichip (Isolation chip) is a methodology of culturing microorganism. In the conventional techniques, about 99% of microorganisms are not able to be cultivated as they do not grow in optimized conditions made in a laboratory, which is known as "Great Plate Count Anomaly". Generally, in the methodology ichip can cultures the microorganisms within its soil environment. The soil of interest from which the microorganism to be screened is diluted in the

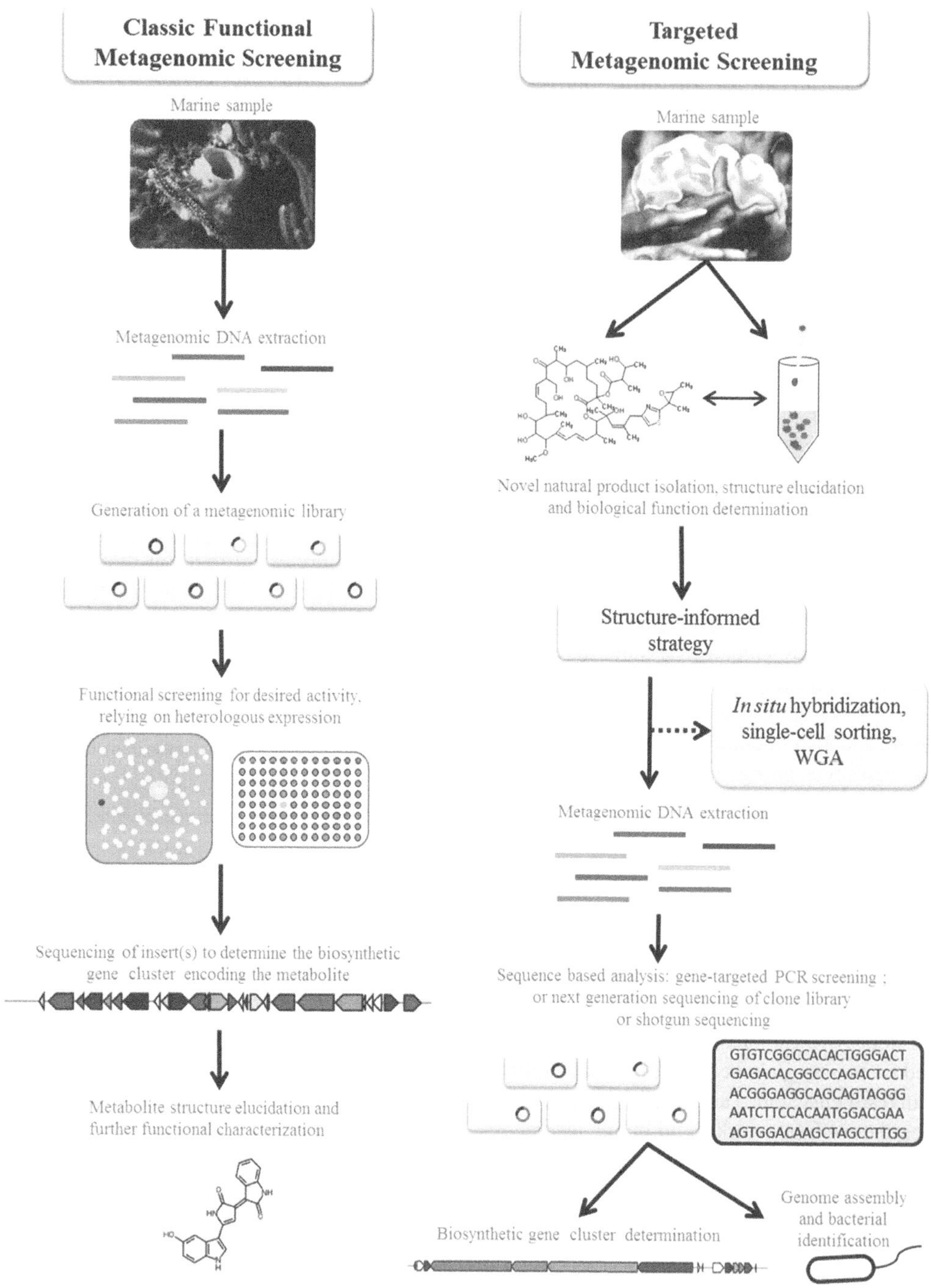

Fig. 30.1 Both structural and functional metagenomic approaches are the main strategies for exploring key ecological and biotechnological features in environmental samples, respectively [11]. This figure is used under a creative commons CC BY 4.0 license

Table 30.1 Timeline of important advancements in metagenomics

Sl. No.	Year	Event	Remarkable points	References
1	2004	Human Microbiome Project Launched	This landmark project explored the microbial communities in the human body, transforming microbiome research.	[15]
2	2007	Metagenomics Standards Established	The development of standardized protocols for DNA extraction, sequencing, and data analysis enhanced global metagenomic research	[16]
3	2010	Next-Generation Sequencing (NGS) Expansion:	NGS technologies revolutionized metagenomics by enabling high-throughput sequencing, making genome analysis faster and more affordable	[17]
4	2012	CRISPR-Cas Discovery:	The CRISPR-Cas system, discovered through metagenomic analysis, advanced genetic editing technologies.	[18]
5	2015	Earth Microbiome Project:	A global effort to catalog microbial diversity in different ecosystems was launched, generating a massive reference database.	[19]
6	2020	Single-Cell Genomics & Long-Read Sequencing:	Advances in single-cell genomics, long-read sequencing, and artificial intelligence improved metagenomic resolution, uncovering previously hidden microbial species.	[20]

molten agar medium and nutrients. The wells in the ichip are designed such a way that only a single cell, on average, grows in the ichip's small wells or compartment. Hence it is called as 'Isolation'Chip or 'ichip'. The chip is then enclosed in a semipermeable membrane and buried back to allow in nutrients not available in the lab [12]. With this technique, 50% to 60% of bacterial species can survive. An antibiotic named as Teixobactin has shown promising target against many drug-resistant strains (Methicillin-resistant Staphylococcus aureus) was produced from Eleftheria terrae. This ichip methodology helped in isolating this Eleftheria terrae strain from the soil in 2015 [13]. With the advancement of technology, important microbial strains can be collected from other deep ocean trenches and even other planets. A schematic diagram for ichip working principles is illustrated in Fig. 30.2.

3.3 SIGEX Methods

SIGEX, or substrate-induced gene expression, is a new method for screening a library of environmental metagenomes. It is employed to acquire catabolic genes, the expression of which is triggered by environmental stimuli, such as the presence of a chemical molecule. An operon-trap gfp vector, known as p18GFP, is created using this technology and is ideal for shotgun cloning. To screen the positive clones in liquid cultures, this p18GFP is used with fluorescence activated cell sorting (FACS). In the presence of the gfp gene, cells that contain stimuli-responsive metagenome fragments and exhibit fluorescence in response to a stimulus can thus be efficiently isolated using FACS. Pathogenic bacterial genes that were expressed in human and plant bodies have been identified using the SIGEX technique [21]. Traditional

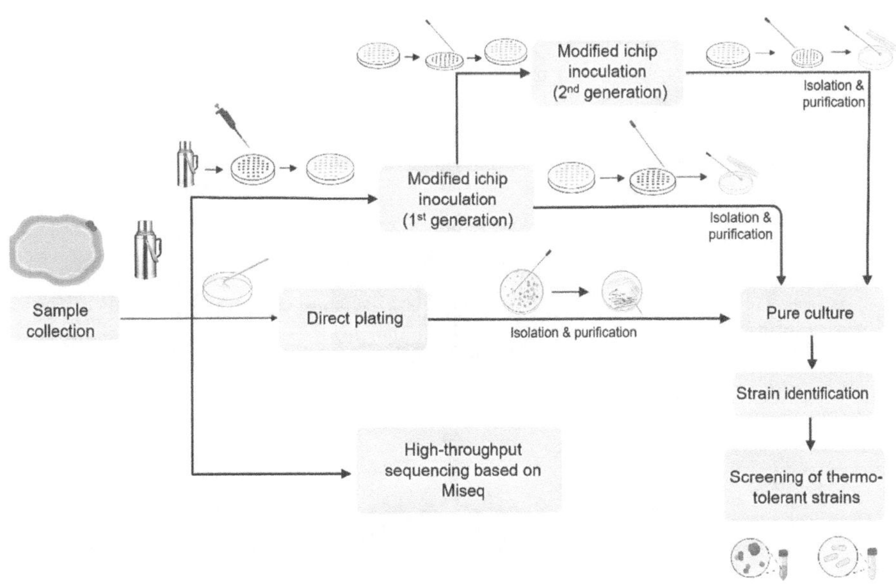

Fig. 30.2 Working principle of ichip in order to isolate a single microorganism from soil sample [14]. This figure is used under a creative commons CC BY 4.0 license

metagenomic library screening methods frequently have poorer sensitivity and relatively low throughput. The SIGEX methodology's high sensitivity, high throughput, and versatility make it an especially appropriate method for screening metagenomic libraries. The ability to access a gene's possible function independent of sequence information is another benefit of the SIGEX approach. This allows it to investigate the unknown function of the metagenome found in the environment [22].

3.4 Coculture Technique

To understand how various cell populations interact, the co-culture technique has been employed. Investigating any type of cell-to-cell interaction is a crucial procedure. These kinds of systems have caught the interest of synthetic biologists, who are now exploring and creating intricate multicellular synthetic systems. A co-culture method is, at its most basic, a system of cell culture where two or more distinct cell populations are grown in some degree of interaction with one another. However, when complexity increases, this benefit may be lost, and the microfluidic device would not work with higher quantities. There is also a growing trend of adapting monoculture procedures, such as "cell migration assays," for co-culture [23]. Figure 30.3 describes the biotechnological applications of the co-culture technique, highlighting its potential to enhance metabolic capabilities, improve product yields, and facilitate complex bioprocesses.

3.5 Microfluidic Approach

Among the most recent methods in microbiology research, microfluidics offers a great platform for analyzing microorganisms and their nucleic acids. This technology uses engineering computing, chemistry, biology, physics, and other transdisciplinary subject applications to control the devices. The technology involves manipulating fluid flow in 10-100μm channels using surface tension and laminar effects. Following this, the field of nanofluidics—which studies and applies fluid flow around nanoscale objects—has emerged [24].

Typically, glass and polymers are used to create microfluidic devices that distribute and transfer precise fluid volumes to the detecting device. It can also be integrated with other procedures, like nucleic acid detection and quantification. In certain experiments, electrical measurements and tests based on cells and molecules were combined with microfluidics. The ability to record measurements using amperometric, impedence, and patch-clamps as electric signals is therefore very advantageous [25]. Electrodes that produce current when molecules are electrochemically active are used in the amperometric device that is connected to microfluidics devices. Three electrode systems (working, reference, and counter electrodes) or two electrode systems (reference and working) are typically utilized [26].

3.6 Micromanipulation

One of the most important aspects of physics and biological study is the manipulation of biological cells or tiny particles. A technique called micromanipulation uses a precise strategy to extract a single cell so that it may be manipulated. In general, micromanipulation can be divided into two categories: mechanical and optical. Using microcapillary glass or tubes, individual cells are identified and separated from a heterogeneous population in the event of mechanical micromanipulation. They are then successively moved to a culture medium or other reaction solution [27]. It is possible to cultivate the separated cells afterward. Culture-independent analysis is sometimes also performed. Through mechanical

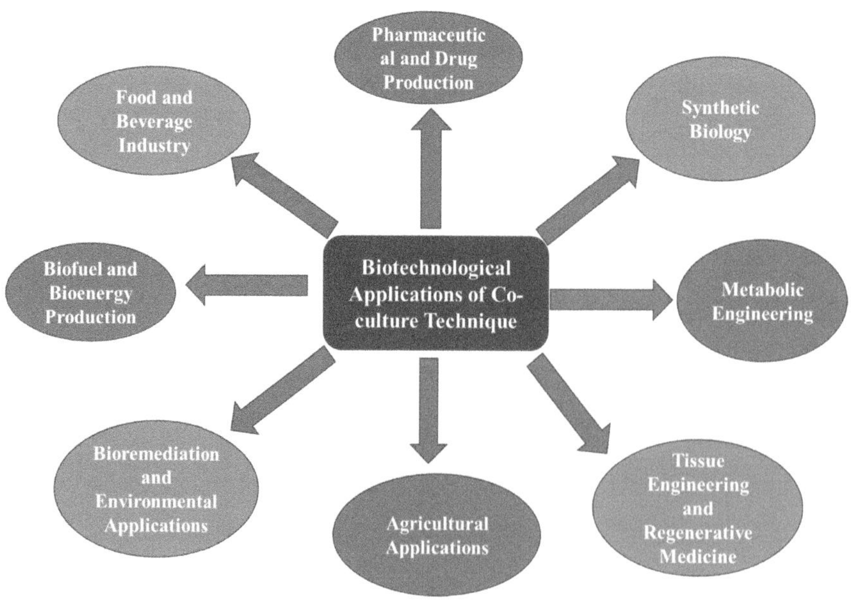

Fig. 30.3 Biotechnological application of co-culture technique

micromanipulation, researchers have identified a variety of possible microorganisms from termite guts, wetland rice soils, hot spring samples, and endosymbiotic protozoans [21].

4. Challenges and Future Scope

For microbiological and biotechnological research, several single-cell isolation methods have been developed and used. Each technique, however, has advantages and disadvantages. Thus, the goal of the study always determines which of these techniques is used. However, the most important things to think about are low-cost, high-throughput, and precise analysis. Of these methods, the use of microfluidics in cell sorting for single-cell separation shows promise for the near future. Many databases are currently requesting more and more metagenomic and other meta-"omics" data (https://www.ebi.ac.uk/metagenomics/). Essential information such as phylogeny, microbial diversity, and their function has been made available by these data. Single-cell isolation may be able to connect phenotypic and metagenomic data. Numerous academics and scientists are delving into the subject of "-omics," but single-cell investigations are just as significant [28].

5. Conclusion

In summary, microbes are essential to life on Earth and crucial to various ecosystems and human enterprises. Their functions encompass agriculture, where they improve soil fertility and control pests, as well as environmental applications like as bioremediation and waste management. Microorganisms play a significant role in the industrial manufacture of enzymes, biodegradable polymers, and vital biomolecules. Furthermore, their importance in human health highlights their dual function in promoting medical advancements and contributing to sickness. Microorganisms function as essential research instruments, transforming our comprehension of genetics, biochemistry, and pathology. Utilizing modern tools, like metagenomics and microfluidic techniques, to preserve and exploit these organisms guarantees their sustainable application and fosters ongoing innovation in science and technology.

References

1. Shu, W.-S. and L.-N. Huang (2022). Microbial diversity in extreme environments. Nature Reviews Microbiology 20(4): 219–235.
2. De Vero, L., M. B. Boniotti, M. Budroni, P. Buzzini, S. Cassanelli, R. Comunian, M. Gullo, A. F. Logrieco, I. Mannazzu and R. Musumeci (2019). Preservation, characterization and exploitation of microbial biodiversity: The perspective of the italian network of culture collections. Microorganisms 7(12): 685.
3. Smith, D., K. McCluskey and E. Stackebrandt (2014). Investment into the future of microbial resources: culture collection funding models and BRC business plans for biological resource centres. Springerplus 3: 1–12.
4. De Paoli, P. (2005). Biobanking in microbiology: from sample collection to epidemiology, diagnosis and research. FEMS microbiology reviews 29(5): 897–910.
5. Bharti, R. and D. G. Grimm (2021). Current challenges and best-practice protocols for microbiome analysis.Briefings in bioinformatics 22(1): 178–193.
6. Hurtado-Ortiz, R., A. Hébreu, E. Bégaud and C. Bizet-Pinson (2019). Implementation of the Nagoya Protocol within the Collection of institut Pasteur. Access Microbiology 1(2): e000008.
7. Malik, K. A. and D. Claus (1987). Bacterial culture collections: their importance to biotechnology and microbiology. Biotechnology and Genetic engineering reviews 5(1): 137–198.
8. Sharma, S. K., S. Saini, A. Verma, P. K. Sharma, R. Lal, M. Roy, U. B. Singh, A. K. Saxena and A. K. Sharma (2019). National agriculturally important microbial culture collection in the global context of microbial culture collection centres. Proceedings of the National Academy of Sciences, India Section B: Biological Sciences 89: 405–418.
9. Singh, S. and S. Shankar (2021). Microbial metagenomics: potential and challenges. Advances in animal genomics, Elsevier: 109–122.
10. Tyagi, B., P. Kumar, S. Takkar and I. S. Thakur (2022). Metagenomics, Microbial Diversity, and Environmental Cleanup. Omics Insights in Environmental Bioremediation, Springer: 47–72.
11. Trindade, M., Van Zyl, L. J., Navarro-Fernández, J., & Abd Elrazak, A. (2015). Targeted metagenomics as a tool to tap into marine natural product diversity for the discovery and production of drug candidates. *Frontiers in microbiology*, *6*, 890.
12. Polrot, A., J. Kirby, F. Olorunniji, J. Birkett and G. Sharples (2022). iChip increases the success of cultivation of TBT-resistant and TBT-degrading bacteria from estuarine sediment. World Journal of Microbiology and Biotechnology 38(10): 180.
13. Wang, J.-C., S.-W. Chi, D.-B. Shieh and H.-S. Chuang (2019).Development of a self-driving bioassay based on diffusion for simple detection of microorganisms Sensors and Actuators B: Chemical 278: 140–146.
14. Zhao, J., Shakir, Y., Deng, Y., & Zhang, Y. (2023). Use of modified ichip for the cultivation of thermo-tolerant microorganisms from the hot spring. *BMC microbiology*, *23*(1), 56.
15. Ley, R. E., Peterson, D. A., & Gordon, J. I. (2006). Ecological and evolutionary forces shaping microbial diversity in the human intestine. Cell, 124(4), 837–848.
16. Turnbaugh, P. J., Ley, R. E., Hamady, M., Fraser-Liggett, C. M., Knight, R., & Gordon, J. I. (2007). The human microbiome project. Nature, 449(7164), 804–810.
17. Mardis, E. R. (2013). Next-generation sequencing platforms. Annual review of analytical chemistry, 6(1), 287–303.
18. Jinek, M., Chylinski, K., Fonfara, I., Hauer, M., Doudna, J. A., & Charpentier, E. (2012). A programmable dual-RNA–

guided DNA endonuclease in adaptive bacterial immunity. science, 337(6096), 816–821.
19. Gilbert, J. A., Jansson, J. K., & Knight, R. (2014). The Earth Microbiome project: successes and aspirations. BMC biology, 12, 1–4.
20. Lawrence, D., Campbell, D. E., Schriefer, L. A., Rodgers, R., Walker, F. C., Turkin, M., ... & Baldridge, M. T. (2022). Single-cell genomics for resolution of conserved bacterial genes and mobile genetic elements of the human intestinal microbiota using flow cytometry. Gut Microbes, 14(1), 2029673.
21. Ngara, T. R. and H. Zhang (2018). "Recent advances in function-based metagenomic screening." Genomics, proteomics & bioinformatics 16(6): 405–415.
22. Sahoo, R. K., M. Gaur and E. Subudhi (2019). Function profiling of microbial community. New and Future Developments in Microbial Biotechnology and Bioengineering, Elsevier: 77–85.
23. Ko, J., D. Park, J. Lee, S. Jung, K. Baek, K. E. Sung, J. Lee and N. L. Jeon (2024). Microfluidic high-throughput 3D cell culture. Nature Reviews Bioengineering 2(6): 453–469.
24. He, Z., H. Wu, X. Yan and W. Liu (2022). Recent advances in droplet microfluidics for microbiology. Chinese Chemical Letters 33(4): 1729–1742.
25. Aralekallu, S., R. Boddula and V. Singh (2023). Development of glass-based microfluidic devices: A review on its fabrication and biologic applications. Materials & Design 225: 111517.
26. Holman, J. B., Z. Shi, A. A. Fadahunsi, C. Li and W. Ding (2023). Advances on microfluidic paper-based electroanalytical devices. Biotechnology Advances 63: 108093.
27. Marshall, W., B. Baum, A. Fairhall, C.-P. Heisenberg, E. Koslover, A. Liu, Y. Mao, A. Mogilner, C. M. Nelson and E. K. Paluch (2024). Where physics and biology meet. Current Biology 34(20): R950–R960.
28. Zhou, X., H. Wu, H. Wen and B. Zheng (2022). "Advances in single-cell printing." Micromachines 13(1): 80.

Note: All the figures and the table in this chapter were made by the authors.

Research and Innovations in Industrial and Marine Biotechnology: A Circular Economy 2024 – Prof. Hrudayanath Thatoi et al. (eds)

31 Effect of Microbiome Dysbiosis on Tannase Producing Gut Bacterial Population and its Subsequent Role in Colorectal Cancer Regulation

Pratikshya Parhi, Amrita Banerjee
Centre for Industrial Biotechnology Research,
Siksha 'O' Anusandhan Deemed to be University, Campus-2,
Kalinganagar, Bhubaneswar, Odisha, India

Pradeep Kumar Das Mohapatra
Department of Microbiology, Raiganj University,
Raiganj, Uttardinajpur, West Bengal, India

Hrudayanath Thatoi*
Centre for Industrial Biotechnology Research,
Siksha 'O' Anusandhan Deemed to be University, Campus-2,
Kalinganagar, Bhubaneswar, Odisha, India

Abstract: Tannic acid, a plant-derived secondary metabolite, undergoes enzymatic hydrolysis resulting in the production of Gallic Acid and Glucose. Gallic acid lowers the threat of Colorectal cancer (CRC) by down-regulating inflammation and controlling oxidative stress through MAPK and NF-κB signaling pathways. As an antioxidant, tannic acid itself protects normal cells from being cancerous cells by lowering oxidative stress. Microbial dysbiosis acts as an indicator of localized tissue abnormalities. CRC metadata analysis also reflects microbial dysbiosis from healthy probiotic protectors to harmful disease-influencing bacterial colonization and crosstalk. Now in both cases, tannase-producing bacterial prevalence was prominent. The risk of CRC is often lower in vegetarians and individuals with diets high in fruits, vegetables, legumes, whole grains, tea, berries, nuts, and legumes due to the increased consumption of foods high in tannins, having anticancer properties. Recent studies have emphasized the significance of tannase-producing gut bacteria with CRC but the actual role is still unclear. As CRC ranks third among the most prevalent cancers globally, with its progression affected by different variables, including the gut microbiota, this review has emphasized understanding the intricate role of Tannase producers in CRC control and induction. The association of tannase-producing bacteria in the presence of abundant dietary tannins in CRC regulation is an important aspect of this study. This review aims to help design further research work, required in gut microbiome transplantation which may improve the overall health status of Colorectal cancer patients.

Keywords: Colorectal cancer, Tannase-producing bacteria, Dietary tannins, Gut microbiota, Dysbiosis

1. Introduction

Colorectal cancer (CRC) ranks as the third most prevalently diagnosed malignancy worldwide, exerting impact on public health and accounting for a significant proportion of cancer-associated mortality [1]. It is predominantly derived from adenomatous polyps, progressing through a well-established pathway characterised by alterations in essential tumour suppressor genes, particularly the Adenomatous polyposis coli (APC) gene, along with triggering of oncogenes like Kirsten Rat Sarcoma Viral Oncogene (KRAS) [2]. Various dietary and lifestyle

*Corresponding author: director.cibr@soa.ac.in

DOI: 10.1201/9781003759003-31

factors have been linked with the CRC progression, potentially via various metabolic and inflammatory pathways. Likewise, it has been determined that the gut microbiota is a significant immunological and metabolic regulator and is also linked to CRC [3]. By 2030, CRC is anticipated to result in 2.2 million newly diagnosed cases and 1.1 million fatalities globally [4]. Furthermore, due to the world's population growth, age, and economic development, the incidence is anticipated to reach around 3.2 million new cases by 2040 [5].

Gut microbial dysbiosis, or disruptions in the gut environment consisting of various factors (Fig. 31.1), is frequently seen in conditions that cause inflammatory conditions of the gut, including food allergies, CRC, infections and inflammatory bowel disease [6]. With over 10^{13} species, the gut microbiota represents the largest symbiotic ecosystem within the human body and is influenced by age, diet, drugs, and lifestyle [7].

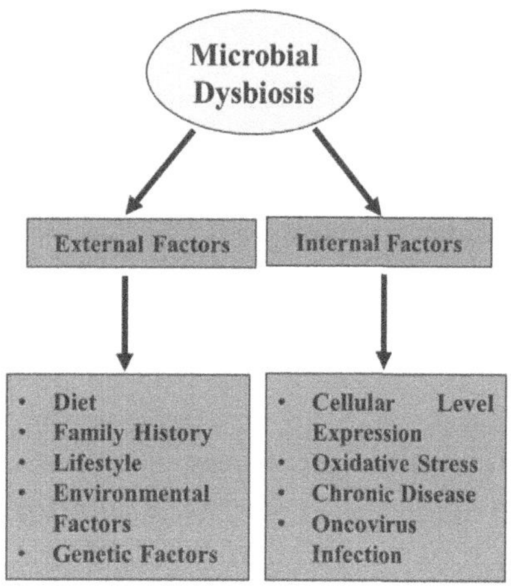

Fig. 31.1 Factors affecting microbial dysbiosis

Numerous investigations demonstrate the biological role of gut microbes in CRC development. Through impaired gut barriers, the symbiotic oral bacterium *Fusobacterium nucleatum* damages colon epithelial cells, leading to gene alterations and carcinogenesis [8]. By changing the production of cholesterol, *Peptostreptococcus anaerobius* affects the CRC development [9]. Various toxins released by *Bacteroides fragilis* lead to inflammation and malignancy [10]. Through its metabolite, biliverdin, *Enterococcus faecalis* accelerates the development of CRC [11].

Tannins are polyphenolic substances present in a diverse array of fruits, vegetables, and nuts as existing specialized products. It has been reported that a variety of tannins have anti-diabetic, anti-microbial, anti-inflammatory and anti-fibrotic other protective qualities [12]. For industrial applications, microbial tannase is chosen over other sources. Hydrolyzable tannins undergo degradation through the cleavage of ester and depside linkages, resulting in the production of Gallic Acid and Glucose [13]. Determining the microbiota that metabolizes tannins is very crucial as it is linked to CRC. Tannins can be converted into gallic acid, which acts as a survival bridge over other gut microorganisms by inhibiting the richness of the species, and improving their adaptability [14]. Some gut microorganisms generate tannase, which converts tannins into beneficial molecules such as gallic acid and pyrogallol, which aids in CRC prevention [15].

This review will help to design further research work, required in gut microbiome transplantation which may improve the quality of life of CRC patients.

2. Diet, Microbiome Composition, and Genetic Factors in CRC

Diet, composition of gut flora, and varied genetic factors affect CRC in different ways. Diet, specifically high-fat and processed meat consumption affects gut flora, thereby enhancing CRC development or altering the outcomes of the treatment [16]. Imbalance in the gut environment leads to dysbiosis leading to inflammation, and cancer metabolite production which further promotes the risk of CRC. CRC development and response to the therapy are also enhanced by various genetic factors, such as acquired genetic traits and gene mutations such as TP53 [17].

While diets high in fiber can alter the gut flora and promote beneficial metabolites having various anticancer properties, diets high in red and processed meat and fats can shift the gut microbiota composition encouraging the risk of CRC development and progression [18]. Different types of food help maintain the microbiome balance as mentioned in (Fig. 31.2)

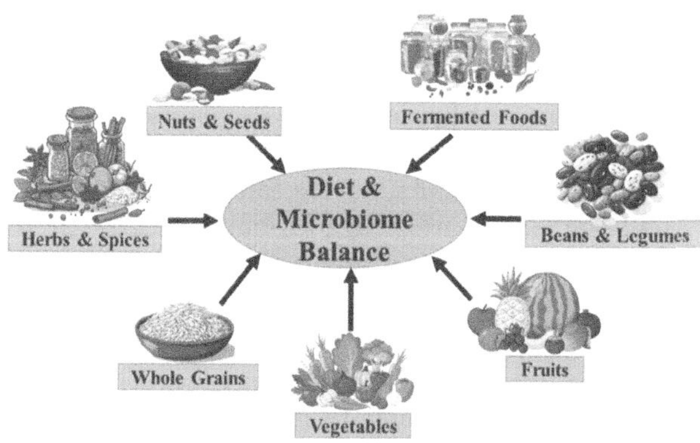

Fig. 31.2 Different types of diet help maintain the microbiome balance

3. Sources and Properties of Dietary Tannins

Tannins, water-soluble polyphenols found in plant diets, are considered to have low nutritional value. However, studies suggest that they decrease nutrient conversion efficiency. The antimutagenic and anticarcinogenic properties of tannins are potentially attributed to their antioxidative activity, which safeguards cells against oxidative stress. Tannins along with other bioactive compounds, have been shown to suppress the generation of superoxide radicals [19]. Tannins come from various plants and shrubs, including quebracho wood, black wattle bark, mangrove wood, oak bark, chestnut wood, and more. These tannin-rich species contain abundant hydrolyzable and condensed tannin structures [20].

4. Role of Tannase and Tannic Acid in the Regulation of Gut Microbiome

Tannin degradation, Tannase, a key enzyme in the microbiota, degrades high molecular weight tannins into gallic acid and glucose [21]. This process can lower toxicity in tannery effluents and control tannin levels in tea and distilleries. Tannic acid has been demonstrated to inhibit activity of α-amylase and modulate gut microbiota composition, which may contribute to delayed metabolism of resistant starch [21]. The tannin metabolism pathway is discussed below (Fig. 31.3).

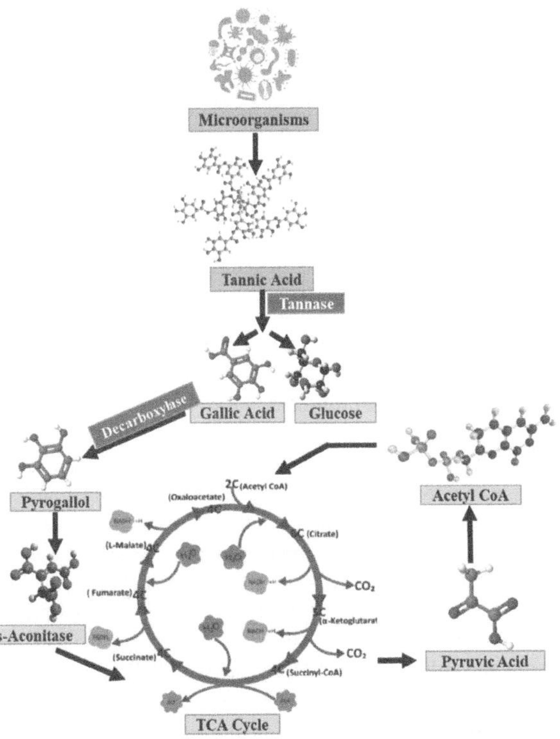

Fig. 31.3 Tannin metabolism pathway

Research revealed that dietary polyphenols may influence gut microbiota health [22]. The inclusion of tannic acid in diet has also been associated with reduced populations of pathogenic gut microbes and enhanced development of beneficial probiotics [23]. Numerous studies have demonstrated that consuming Tannic acid in different forms can improve gut microbiota and its barrier integrity [14]. Different researchers have reported that tannic acid present in the diet has different physiological effects including decreasing cholesterol, blood sugar, and glucose levels, and possesses antioxidant, antibacterial, and anti-inflammatory characteristics [24]. Tannic acid has demonstrated to inhibit the growth of gut pathogenic microorganisms including *Salmonella* an *E. coli* [25]. A study by Jamroz et al., 2009 reported that dietary supplementation along with tannic acid enhanced gut flora efficiency by lowering the colonization of pathogenic bacteria like *Salmonella* and *E. coli* [26].

5. Influence of Dietary Patterns in CRC Regulation

Long-term health is influenced by dietary habits and BMI which is a CRC risk indicator [27]. By triggering signaling pathways that promote carcinogenesis, the Western dietary pattern facilitates the development of chronic illnesses like metabolic syndrome, diabetes and obesity. Diets high in calories, red and processed meats, and a high glycemic index are linked to an increased risk of CRC, whereas diets abundant in dietary fiber and omega-3 fatty acids may reduce the risk [28]. Dietary habits are crucial for CRC prevention, as various nutrients and food combinations can influence cancer risk via metabolic pathways and inflammation [29].

6. Role of Tannase-Producing Bacteria in CRC Prevention

Tannase-producing bacteria are increasingly recognized for their potential role in modulation an its prevention of CRC. One of the key enzymes in the human microbiota, tannase, breaks down TA into downstream metabolites, the most common of which is GA. By changing the gut flora composition, lowering inflammation, and generating compounds with anti-cancer qualities, tannase-producing bacteria contribute significantly to CRC prevention [30]. The ability of gut tannin-degrading bacteria to transform tannic acid is probably crucial in raising the Gallic Acid and Pyrogallol content in the colon and its bioactivity. The accumulation of Gallic Acid and Pyrogallol within the microbial biofilms may represent an additional mechanism that enhances these bioactive chemicals' anti-carcinogenic properties [31].

7. Therapeutic Interventions of CRC

Surgical interventions remain the primary treatment modality for CRC, while non-resectable cases are managed through chemotherapy, radiotherapy, and immunotherapy. However, these treatments can be non-specific and cytotoxic, leading to secondary problems [32]. Combinational therapies can help, but over 50% of patients develop multidrug resistant CRC [33]. Recent treatments include cytokine therapy, T cell receptor mutations, chimeric antigen receptor (CAR) T cell therapy, and immune checkpoint inhibition. Other treatments include probiotic use, natural products, RNA-based therapies, and oncolytic viral treatments [34]. Factors such as patient health, adjuvant therapy, co-medication, patient compliance, comorbidities, psychosocial factors, administration route, prior resection results, logistical support, side effect profiles, tumour biology, primary tumour location, and mutations like RAS and BRAF [35].

Radiotherapy is often combined with chemotherapy or surgery to reduce tumor growth or eradicate remaining cancer cells. In advanced colorectal cancer (CRC), chemotherapy is the primary treatment, often using cytotoxic medications to target and destroy cancer cells. However, chemotherapy can be toxic and cause side effects like thrombocytopenia, leukopenia, stomatitis, and mucositis, impacting the quality of life for patients [36]. Targeted therapies focus on specific molecular markers, enabling the selective elimination of cancer cells while minimizing damage to normal tissues [37]. Emerging therapeutic approaches, such as natural products, probiotics, biomarker-driven therapies, non-coding RNA-based therapeutics, and oncolytic viral medicines tailored immune boosting therapies, are promising to enhance treatment outcomes and overcome traditional medicines' drawbacks [38]. Treatments can be combined based on the stage and course of CRC, but acquired multidrug resistance remains a significant issue [39].

8. Conclusion and Future Perspective

Various genetic, microbiological, and dietary factors influence CRC. The gut bacteria producing tannase is interlinked to its control via reducing inflammation and oxidative stress. Consumption of tannin-rich diet has been associated with a reduced incidence of colorectal cancer (CRC). Various molecular pathways impacted by tannic acid equilibrium can provide information about potential treatment approaches. Long-term dietary intervention studies are crucial for understanding microbial dynamics and outcomes of CRC. Probiotics targeting tannase production and gut microbiome transplantation could restore the microbial population balance in CRC patients. Future research may contribute to understanding the mechanisms by which tannase-producing bacteria influence the prevention of CRC.

Acknowledgments

Authors are grateful to the President and Vice Chancellor for providing infrastructure facilities to conduct the review works. The authors are also thankful to the Director, CIBR, SOA, and SOA University for providing the facility to contribute a chapter to Conference proceedings RIIMBCE-2024.

References

1. Xi, Y., & Xu, P. (2021). Global colorectal cancer burden in 2020 and projections to 2040. Translational oncology, 14(10), 101174.
2. Aghabozorgi, A. S., Bahreyni, A., Soleimani, A., Bahrami, A., Khazaei, M., Ferns, G. A., ... & Hassanian, S. M. (2019). Role of adenomatous polyposis coli (APC) gene mutations in the pathogenesis of colorectal cancer; current status and perspectives. Biochimie, 157, 64–71.
3. Song, M., & Chan, A. T. (2019). Environmental factors, gut microbiota, and colorectal cancer prevention. Clinical Gastroenterology and Hepatology, 17(2), 275–289.
4. Arnold, M., Sierra, M. S., Laversanne, M., Soerjomataram, I., Jemal, A., & Bray, F. (2017). Global patterns and trends in colorectal cancer incidence and mortality. Gut, 66(4), 683–691.
5. Xi, Y., & Xu, P. (2021). Globalcolorectal cancer burden in 2020 and projections to 2040. Translationaloncology, 14(10), 101174..
6. Zeng, M. Y., Inohara, N., & Nuñez, G. (2017). Mechanisms of inflammation-driven bacterial dysbiosis in the gut. Mucosal immunology, 10(1), 18–26.
7. Gill, S. R., Pop, M., DeBoy, R. T., Eckburg, P. B., Turnbaugh, P. J., Samuel, B. S., ... & Nelson, K. E. (2006). Metagenomic analysis of the human distal gut microbiome. science, 312(5778), 1355–1359.
8. Yang, Y., Weng, W., Peng, J., Hong, L., Yang, L., Toiyama, Y., ... & Ma, Y. (2017). Fusobacterium nucleatum increases proliferation of colorectal cancer cells and tumor development in mice by activating toll-like receptor 4 signaling to nuclear factor– κB, and up-regulating expression of microRNA-21. Gastroenterology, 152(4), 851–866.
9. Tsoi, H., Chu, E. S., Zhang, X., Sheng, J., Nakatsu, G., Ng, S. C., ... & Yu, J. (2017). Peptostreptococcus anaerobius induces intracellular cholesterol biosynthesis in colon cells to induce proliferation and causes dysplasia in mice. Gastroenterology, 152(6), 1419–1433.
10. Zhang, W., Zhu, B., Xu, J., Liu, Y., Qiu, E., Li, Z., ... & Zhi, F. (2018). Bacteroides fragilis protects against antibiotic-associated diarrhea in rats by modulating intestinal defenses. Frontiers in immunology, 9, 1040.
11. Zhang, L., Liu, J., Deng, M., Chen, X., Jiang, L., Zhang, J., ... & Qiu, Y. (2023). Enterococcus faecalis promotes the progression of colorectal cancer via its metabolite: biliverdin. Journal of Translational Medicine, 21(1), 72.
12. Rajasekar, N., Sivanantham, A., Ravikumar, V., & Rajasekaran, S. (2021). An overview on the role of plant-derived tannins for the treatment of lung cancer. Phytochemistry, 188, 112799.
13. Kumar, S. S., Sreekumar, R., & Sabu, A. (2019). Tannase and its applications in food processing. Green bio-processes: Enzymes in industrial food processing, 357–381.
14. Reveron, I., Rodriguez, H., Campos, G., Curiel, J. A., Ascaso, C., Carrascosa, A. V., ... & de Felipe, F. L. (2013). Tannic acid-dependent modulation of selected Lactobacillus plantarum traits linked to gastrointestinal survival. PLoS One, 8(6), e66473.

15. López de Felipe F, De Las Rivas B, Muñoz R. Bioactive compounds produced by gut microbial tannase: implications for colorectal cancer development. Frontiers in microbiology. 2014 Dec 5;5:684.
16. Macedo, J. A., Ferreira, L. R., Camara, L. E., Santos, J. C., Gambero, A., Macedo, G. A., & Ribeiro, M. L. (2012). Chemopreventive potential of the tannase-mediated biotransformation of green tea. *Food chemistry*, *133*(2), 358–365.
17. Park, C. H., Eun, C. S., & Han, D. S. (2018). Intestinal microbiota, chronic inflammation, and colorectal cancer. Intestinal research, 16(3), 338.
18. Artemev, A., Naik, S., Pougno, A., Honnavar, P., & Shanbhag, N. M. (2022). The association of microbiome dysbiosis with colorectal cancer. Cureus, 14(2).
19. Chung, K. T., Wong, T. Y., Wei, C. I., Huang, Y. W., & Lin, Y. (1998). Tannins and human health: a review. Critical reviews in food science and nutrition, 38(6), 421–464.
20. Pizzi, A. (2008). Tannins: major sources, properties and applications. In Monomers, polymers and composites from renewable resources (pp. 179–199). Elsevier.
21. Mancheño, J. M., Atondo, E., Tomás-Cortázar, J., Luís Lavín, J., Plaza-Vinuesa, L., Martín-Ruiz, I., ... & Rodríguez, H. (2022). A structurally unique Fusobacterium nucleatum tannase provides detoxicant activity against gallotannins and pathogen resistance. Microbial Biotechnology, 15(2), 648–667.
22. Liu, Z., Luo, S., Liu, C., & Hu, X. (2024). Tannic acid delaying metabolism of resistant starch by gut microbiota during in vitro human fecal fermentation. Food Chemistry, 440, 138261.
23. Ashwin, K., Pattanaik, A. K., & Howarth, G. S. (2021). Polyphenolic bioactives as an emerging group of nutraceuticals for promotion of gut health: A review. Food Bioscience, 44, 101376.
24. Song, Y., Luo, Y., Yu, B., He, J., Zheng, P., Mao, X., ... & Yu, J. (2021). Tannic acid extracted from gallnut prevents post-weaning diarrhea and improves intestinal health of weaned piglets. Animal Nutrition, 7(4), 1078–1086.
25. Bonelli, F., Turini, L., Sarri, G., Serra, A., Buccioni, A., & Mele, M. (2018). Oral administration of chestnut tannins to reduce the duration of neonatal calf diarrhea. BMC Veterinary Research, 14, 1–6.
26. Choi, J., Marshall, B., Ko, H., Shi, H., Singh, A. K., Thippareddi, H., ... & Kim, W. K. (2022). Antimicrobial and immunomodulatory effects of tannic acid supplementation in broilers infected with Salmonella Typhimurium. Poultry Science, 101(11), 102111.
27. Jamroz, D., Wiliczkiewicz, A., Skorupińska, J., Orda, J., Kuryszko, J., & Tschirch, H. (2009). Effect of sweet chestnut tannin (SCT) on the performance, microbial status of intestine and histological characteristics of intestine wall in chickens. British poultry science, 50(6), 687–699.
28. Pietrzyk, L., Torres, A., Maciejewski, R., & Torres, K. (2015). Obesity and obese-related chronic low-grade inflammation in promotion of colorectal cancer development. Asian Pacific Journal of Cancer Prevention, 16(10), 4161–4168.
29. Pietrzyk, Ł. (2017). Food properties and dietary habits in colorectal cancer prevention and development. International Journal of Food Properties, 20(10), 2323–2343.
30. He, Q., Guo, K., Wang, L., Xie, F., Zhao, Q., Jiang, X., ... & Li, C. (2023). Tannins amount determines whether tannase-containing bacteria are probiotic or pathogenic in IBD. Life Science Alliance, 6(5).
31. Tjalsma, H., Boleij, A., Marchesi, J. R., & Dutilh, B. E. (2012). A bacterial driver–passenger model for colorectal cancer: beyond the usual suspects. Nature Reviews Microbiology, 10(8), 575–582.
32. Schuell, B., Gruenberger, T., Kornek, G. V., Dworan, N., Depisch, D., Lang, F., ... & Scheithauer, W. (2005). Side effects during chemotherapy predict tumour response in advanced colorectal cancer. British journal of cancer, 93(7), 744–748.
33. Zhou, J., Ji, Q., & Li, Q. (2021). Resistance to anti-EGFR therapies in metastatic colorectal cancer: underlying mechanisms and reversal strategies. Journal of Experimental & Clinical Cancer Research, 40, 1–17.
34. Ding, S., Hu, C., Fang, J., & Liu, G. (2020). The protective role of probiotics against colorectal cancer. Oxidative Medicine and Cellular Longevity, 2020(1), 8884583.
35. van de Velde, C. J., Boelens, P. G., Borras, J. M., Coebergh, J. W., Cervantes, A., Blomqvist, L., ... & Valentini, V. (2014). EURECCA colorectal: multidisciplinary management: European consensus conference colon & rectum. European journal of cancer, 50(1), 1–e1.
36. Comella, P. (2007). A review of the role of capecitabine in the treatment of colorectal cancer. Therapeutics and clinical risk management, 3(3), 421–431.
37. Moertel, C. G., Fleming, T. R., Macdonald, J. S., Haller, D. G., Laurie, J. A., Goodman, P. J., ... & Mailliard, J. A. (1990). Levamisole and fluorouracil for adjuvant therapy of resected colon carcinoma. New England Journal of Medicine, 322(6), 352–358.
38. Kumar, A., Gautam, V., Sandhu, A., Rawat, K., Sharma, A., & Saha, L. (2023). Current and emerging therapeutic approaches for colorectal cancer: A comprehensive review. World Journal of Gastrointestinal Surgery, 15(4), 495.
39. Siegel, R. L., Miller, K. D., Fuchs, H. E., & Jemal, A. (2022). Cancer statistics, 2022. CA: a cancer journal for clinicians, 72(1), 7–33.

Note: All the figures in this chapter were made by the authors.

Research and Innovations in Industrial and Marine Biotechnology: A Circular Economy 2024 – Prof. Hrudayanath Thatoi et al. (eds)
© 2026 Taylor & Francis Group, London, ISBN 978-1-041-28285-3

32 Bacterial Laccase: Mechanistic Insights and Biotechnological Potential

Subhas Giri, Krishnendu Mondal, Shilpee Pal, Sourav Santra, Tanmoy Jana, Sudipta Samanta, Arijit Jana, Keshab Chandra Mondal*

Department of Microbiology, Vidyasagar University, Midnapore, West Bengal, India

Abstract: Enzymes are becoming a viable alternative to traditional chemical catalysts in industrial processes due to green chemistry advancements. The need for sustainable catalysis has prompted a concentrated emphasis on discovering novel enzymes. Laccase is one of the most essential enzymes, with a wide range of applications and substantial promise for future developments in many industries. The distribution of laccase enzymes across bacterial phyla, revealing their ubiquitous occurrence and functional significance was explored in this study. In addition, we investigated the molecular interactions between laccase and its substrates, lignin and ABTS, to better understand the enzyme's catalytic operations. The numerous applications of laccase in various industries based on bioremediation, textile processing, and biofuel generation, focusing on their potential as sustainable biocatalysts has been addressed here. By consolidating current knowledge on bacterial laccases, this work hopes to inform future research directions and facilitate the development of novel applications that utilize the unique features of these enzymes in biotechnology.

Keywords: Green chemistry, Laccase, Lignin, ABTS and bioremediation

1. Introduction

Enzymes are biological catalysts that are replacing chemical catalysts in multiple industries varying from consumables and pharmaceutical to textiles, biofuels, and in environmental management for their high substrate specificity, low production cost, ability to with stand harsh environment and eco-friendly nature [1]. Laccases (EC 1.10.3.2), also identified as benzenediol: oxygen oxidoreductase, have become of special interest due to their widespread applications including bioremediation of toxic environmental effluents, delignification of pulp and paper, oxidation of synthetic dyes, and stabilization of wine colour. As of 2023, the global laccase market was around $3 billion, with projections indicating it will reach around $4.37 billion with a 4.5% compound annual growth rate (CAGR) by 2032. Laccases are multi-copper oxidase enzymes that catalyze the oxidation of non-phenolic and phenolic compounds using molecular oxygen as an electron acceptor [2]. Lignin, found in the cell wall of woods, is the primary natural substrate of laccase. It is a complex heterogeneous polymer of monolignols such as paracoumaryl alcohol, simply alcohol and coniferyl alcohol. Synthetic aromatics compounds like ABTS (2,2'-azino-bis (3-ethylbenzothiazoline-6-sulfonic acid), guaiacol, and catechol are used in assay for determination of laccase activity [3]. In nature, laccases are globally scattered across numerous organisms, including fungi, bacteria, insects, and plants. Microbial sources are preferred for laccase production in industries due to their higher yields, cost-effectiveness, and efficiency in production times [4]. Till date, most studies have been on fungal laccases as compared to bacterial one due to their extracellular production and diversity. Among fungi, ascomycetes such as *Gaeumannomycesgraminis*, *Magnaporthegrisea*, *Neurosporacrassa*, and basidiomycetes such as *Pycnoporuscinnabarinus*, *Trametesversicolo* have been recorded to produce laccase. However, bacteria possess some unique advantages over fungi in large scale enzyme production, for instant, rapid

*Corresponding author: kcmondal@mail.vidyasagar.ac.in

DOI: 10.1201/9781003759003-32

growth, genetic manipulation using recombinant DNA technology makes the fermentation process more efficient with reduced costs [5]. Moreover, many bacterial laccases are more stable under changing environmental conditions, such as temperature and pH, which makes them highly applicable in various bioremediation and waste treatment applications [6]. Among bacteria, genera of *Bacillus, Streptomyces,* and *Pseudomonas* have found to be effective laccase producers [7]. However, the demand for bacterial laccases with unique characteristics is increasing across various industries, and to identify novel bacterial laccase, it is vital to gain knowledge about distribution of laccase among various bacterial phyla. This review aims to provide an extensive overview of the present concept of bacterial laccase enzymes, focusing on diversity of laccase in various bacterial phyla, the molecular interactions of laccase with both natural and synthetic substrates, specifically lignin and ABTS respectively to better understanding of the molecular interactive between laccase and its substrates, and their potential applications in diverse industrial sectors and waste water treatment.

2. Distribution of Laccase among Bacteria

Bacteria are considered as prime candidates as a source of industrially important enzymes. Laccase, being one of the most crucial enzyme, has gained research interest. Understanding the distribution of laccase across various bacterial phyla are essential for identifying novel laccases with unique characteristics. In the present study, among total 889 bacterial laccase protein sequences (length 21aa – 1968aa) present in Uniprot database (https://www.uniprot.org/uniprotkb) (as on 29.12.2024), 775 laccase sequences (selected in species level) with length > 100aa were selected for phylogenetic analysis. Sequences from uncultured bacteria and unidentified species were not considered for the analysis. Total 775 laccase protein sequences were aligned using ClustalX (v2.1) [8]. Further Neighbor-Joining (NJ) tree was built using PROTGAMMAWAG model in FastTree (v2.1) included in PhyloSuite (v1.2.3), an integrated software platform [9] with 100 bootstrap by taking *Trametesvillosa*as an outgroup. The tree was visualised using iTOL (v7) [10].

All the 775 laccase protein sequences were included in total 23 bacterial phyla i.e., Acidobacteriota, Aquificota, Actinomycetota, Bacteroidota, Bacillota, Bdellovibrionota, Candidatus Muiribacteriota, Campylobacterota, Cyanobacteriota Chloroflexota, Deinococcota, Deferribacterota, Dictyoglomota, Fusobacteriota, Gemmatimonadota, Myxococcota, Pseudomonadota, Planctomycetota, Synergistota, Spirochaetota, Thermosulfidibacterota, Thermodesulfobacteriota, and Verrucomicrobiota. Higher amount of sequence diversity among laccase protein sequences were observed among the phyla Pseudomonadota, Bacillota, and Actinomycetota than others. However, laccase sequences were conserved in Actinomycetota species than Pseudomonadota (Fig. 32.1.).

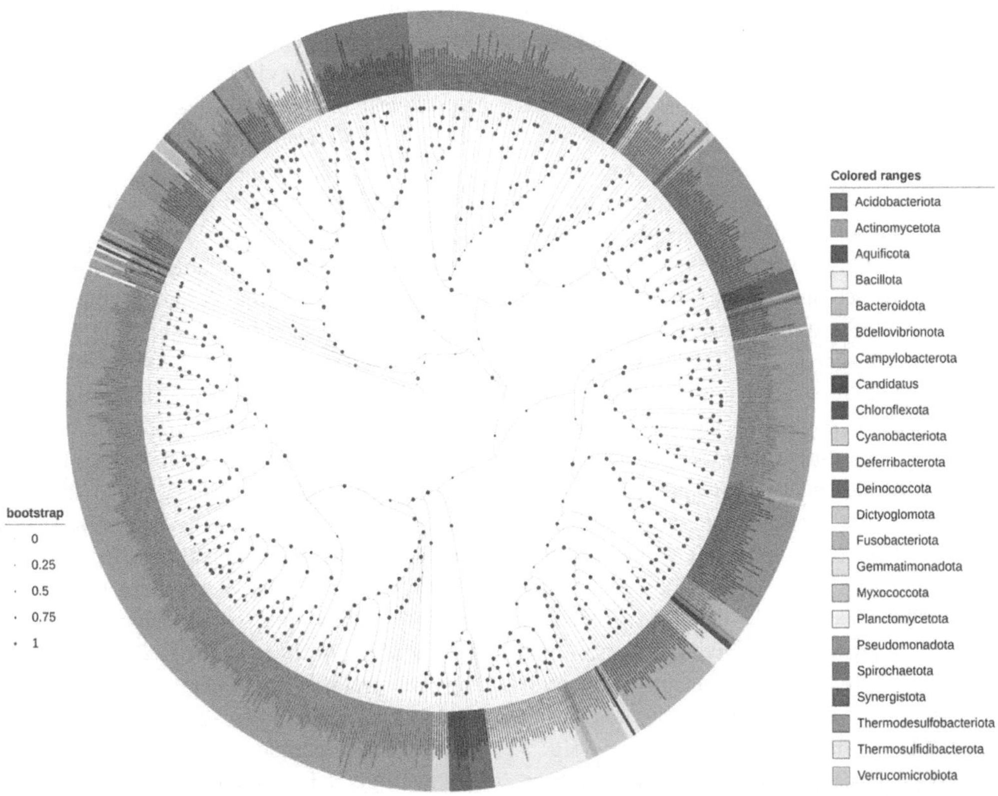

Fig. 32.1 Phylogenetic tree based on bacterial laccase protein shows their diversity among 23 phyla indicated by coloured squares

Both Pseudomonadota and Bacillota generally include a wide variety of metabolically diverse bacteria. They have the capability to adapt to a vast range of environmental factors for instance high temperature, low oxygen, etc. which might be the reason of functional divergence of the laccase enzyme. Most of the Actinomycetota species are soil dwelling and their metabolic specific genes functioning for niche adaptation, complex substrate such as lignin degradation, secondary metabolite synthesis, antibiotic production, etc. are conserved [2] might lead to lower diversification of laccase. Moreover, frequent horizontal gene transfer (HGT) might be the reason of rapid diversification of laccase genes across Pseudomonadota and Actinomycetota species [11]. Further annotation of laccase protein sequences from bacteria across different phyla would elucidate the prominent evolutionary diversity as well as catalytic efficiency which would further help researchers to design novel laccase enzyme with improved properties useful for biotechnological applications.

3. Laccase Production by Bacteria

First reported bacterial laccase was isolated from *Azospirillum lipoferum* [12], sampled from rice rhizosphere. Since then, laccase has been isolated from both gram-positive and also gram-negative bacteria. Bacteria including *Bacillus*, *Geobacillus*, *Streptomyces*,(gram-positive) and *Pseudomonas*, *Enterobacter*, and *Proteobacterium (*gram-negative) were reported to produce laccase [13]. Laccase production is highly impacted by nutritional composition such as C/N ratio, nitrogen source, carbon source, salts, and physical factors like temperature, pH, incubation time etc. Several sugar such as lactose, glucose, maltose, fructose act as carbon source in laccase production. However, presence of lignin and other phenolic compounds enhance laccase production as they act as inducer. Several lignin rich agricultural waste like rice husk, sugarcane bagasse, rice and wheat straw, have been utilised in laccase production [14]. Both inorganic nitrogen sources $(NH_4)_2SO_4$, $NaNO_3$ and organic nitrogen sources like peptone, yeast extract, urea, have been used in media for laccase production. Different divalent cations show distinct effects on laccase yield produced by various bacteria. Each species shows different response to the presence of various divalent cations based on their own metabolic pathways and physiological characteristics. Metal ions including copper (Cu^{2+}), cobalt (Co^{2+}), and calcium (Ca^{2+}), act as cofactors in the enzymatic activity of laccases. For instance, copper salts are proven to be most impactful for amplifying laccase production. Similarly, metal ions like magnesium (Mg^{+2}), zinc (Zn^{+2}), and mercury (Hg^{+2}) are found to reduce laccase yield [2]. Incubation time for maximum laccase yield varies species to species. For example, *Pseudomonas extremorientalis* BU118 [15] showed maximum laccase production in 24h, while *Bacillus tequilensis* SN4 [16] produced maximum laccase after 96h of incubation. Most of the bacterial species showed highest laccase yield between 30 to 45 °C, though thermophilic bacteria like *Geobacillus thermocatenulatus* MS5 requires 60 °C for production [17]. Studies showed different bacterial species produce maximum laccase at pH between 3.0 to 9.0. According to the previous reports, both solid-state fermentation (SSF) as well as submerged fermentation (SmF) are found to be effective in maximum laccase production. Moreover, statistical methods such as response surface method and the Plackett–Burman method are useful to achieve maximum laccase yield by optimizing each factor responsible for laccase production [14]. Cultural conditions and laccase production by various bacteria are summarized in Table 32.1.

4. Molecular Mechanism of Laccase

The mechanism at the molecular level of laccase involves the interplay of a complex series of interactions between copper ions and substrates, where, in addition to phenol, even non-phenolic compounds are oxidized and molecular oxygen gets reduced to water. Laccase contains four copper ions; these four copper ions are structured in specific sites such as T1, T2, and T3. The T1 site, serves as the primary electron transfer site, and is located near the enzyme's surface, where the substrate binds and undergoes oxidation [18]. Upon binding, laccase catalyzes the removal of a hydroxyl group electron from the of phenolic substrates, generating phenoxyl radicals. The degree of stability of the radical intermediate determines whether it proceeds through dimerization or polymerization or undergoes additional oxidative reactions accompanied by appropriate redox mediators. It starts with the T1 copper ion reduction, which is considered a rate-limiting step of laccase catalytic cycles. This decrease enables the transfer of electrons from the enzyme to the T2 and T3 sites, where molecular oxygen is converted to water. The redox potential of laccases varies significantly between different sources; for example, high-redox-potential laccases in fungi are very efficient in oxidizing a wide range of substrates, whereas laccases with low-redox-potential in plants and bacteria are more selective. Laccases can oxidize non-phenolic compounds, but this is usually dependent on the presence of small molecular weight mediators, including 2,2'-azinobis (3-ethylbenzthiazoline-6-sulfonate) or naturally occurring phenolic compounds, which enhance substrate oxidation by participating in radical-based reactions. Laccases are very important in lignin degradation, the oxidative ability of laccases makes them good for modifying lignin and other aromatic compounds effectively in processes like soil organic matter formation and plant defense mechanisms. In addition, laccases are involved in anabolic processes such as lignification and melanin biosynthesis where they

Table 32.1 Cultural condition and laccase production by various bacteria

Name of organism	Carbon source and fermented condition	Substrate use in enzyme assay	Temp. optimum of activity (°C)	Temp. stability (°C)	pH optima of activity	pH stability	Molecular weight of proteins (kDa)	Activator	Inhibitor	Reference
Anoxybacillusay-derensis SK3-4	LB/37 °C / SSF/16h	ABTS, SGZ	75	65	7.0	6.5-8.5	29.8	Cu^{2+} and Mg^{2+}	Zn^{2+} and Fe^{2+}	[39]
Proteus vulgaris ATCC 6896	LB/37 °C/ SF/ 5h	ABTS	60	45 - 60		5.0-8.0		Fe2+ , Cu2+	EDTA, sodium azide and sodium citrate	[40]
Lysinibacillusmac-roides LSO	LB/30°C/ SF/24h	DMP	30		7.0			$CuSO_4{\cdot}5H_2O$, $MnSO_4{\cdot}H_2O$		[41]
Pseudomonas spp.	Humic substances (HS) /15 °C/ SSF/14Days	ABTS	15							[42]
Bacillus sp. strain WT	NB/35 °C/ SF/7 Days	ABTS, syringaldazine	55		5.0		180	Na^+ and Ni^{2+},	$NaNO_3$ and NaCl	[43]
Bacillus sp. GZB	LB	ABTS	70	60–80	7.2	2.0–8.0	63	Cu^{2+}, Mg^{2+}, and Na^+,	Fe^{2+}, Ag^+, l-cysteine, dithiothreitol, and $NaNO_3$	[44]
Bacillus sp. CF96		Guaiacol, syringaldazine	60		8.0		63	Zn^{2+}, Mn^{2+} and Fe^2	SDS	[27]
Geobactermetal-lireducens GS-15	LB/ 37 °C	ABTS, syringaldazine, 2,6-DMP	75		6.0					[45]

facilitate the oxidative coupling of monolignols and other phenolic compounds into larger polymeric structures [19].

To gain a deeper knowledge of the molecular interactions between laccase and its substrates, lignin and ABTS, we performed molecular docking analysis. The 3D model of laccase protein from *Pseudomonas parafulva* (PDB ID-6VOX) was procured from the Protein Data Bank and the structures of phenolic compounds of ABTS and Lignin were retrieved from PubChem [20] and analysed by using PyMol and Discovery Studio [21].

The molecular docking analysis was performed by using AutoDockVina (version 1.1.2) [22]. A grid-based procedure was utilized with the following grid box parameters -44.467Å × -48.583 Å × -17.452Å with a spacing of 1 Å and center set at coordinates 82, 108, and 100 in x, y, and z axis, respectively to generate the affinity maps delimiting the protein binding site. In order to allow the ligand to bind in an unbiased binding pocket the grid size was kept at maximum, enveloping the whole surface of the protein. Among 2 phenolic compounds ABTS and lignin, lignin docked with laccase through ILE-370, ASN-331, ALA-371, PHE-381, PHE-441, and LEU-395 with -9.5 kcal/mol binding energy (Fig. 32.2A.). Likewise, ABTS interacted with laccase protein through GLU-192, GLY-197, TRP-232, ARG-423, THR-198, ALA-199, GLY-200, THR-231, ASN-196, THR-233, ARG-235, GLN-390, and TRP-264 with -7.3 kcal/mol binding energy (Fig. 32.2B.). Thus, laccase interacts to both the compounds ABTS and lignin with high binding affinity and changes the colorless ABTS to green and breaks lignin polymers to monomers [23].

5. Applications of Laccase

Bacterial laccases have attracted much attention with regard to their versatility in industrial and environmental applications, especially in bioremediation (Fig. 32.3). They catalyze the oxidation of non-phenolic and phenolic compounds for the efficient degradation of persistent organic pollutants like synthetic dyes, polychlorinated biphenyls (PCBs), and pesticides. The whole process is quite eco-friendly because it reduces effluent toxicity, which provides an alternative solution instead of the treatment involving harmful chemicals. Their broad substrate specificity and ability to handle diverse contaminants make them crucial in addressing pollution from industrial and agricultural sources [24].

5.1 Textile Industry

Laccases are being increasingly used is the textile industry for decolorization and bioremediation of dye-contaminated effluents. Textile industries produce enormous amounts of wastewater contaminated with synthetic dyes. Synthetic dyes are complex, toxic, and resistant to conventional treatments. They facilitate decolorization and detoxification through oxidation of phenolic groups in the dye molecule. This eco-friendly process greatly reduces effluent toxicity, thereby

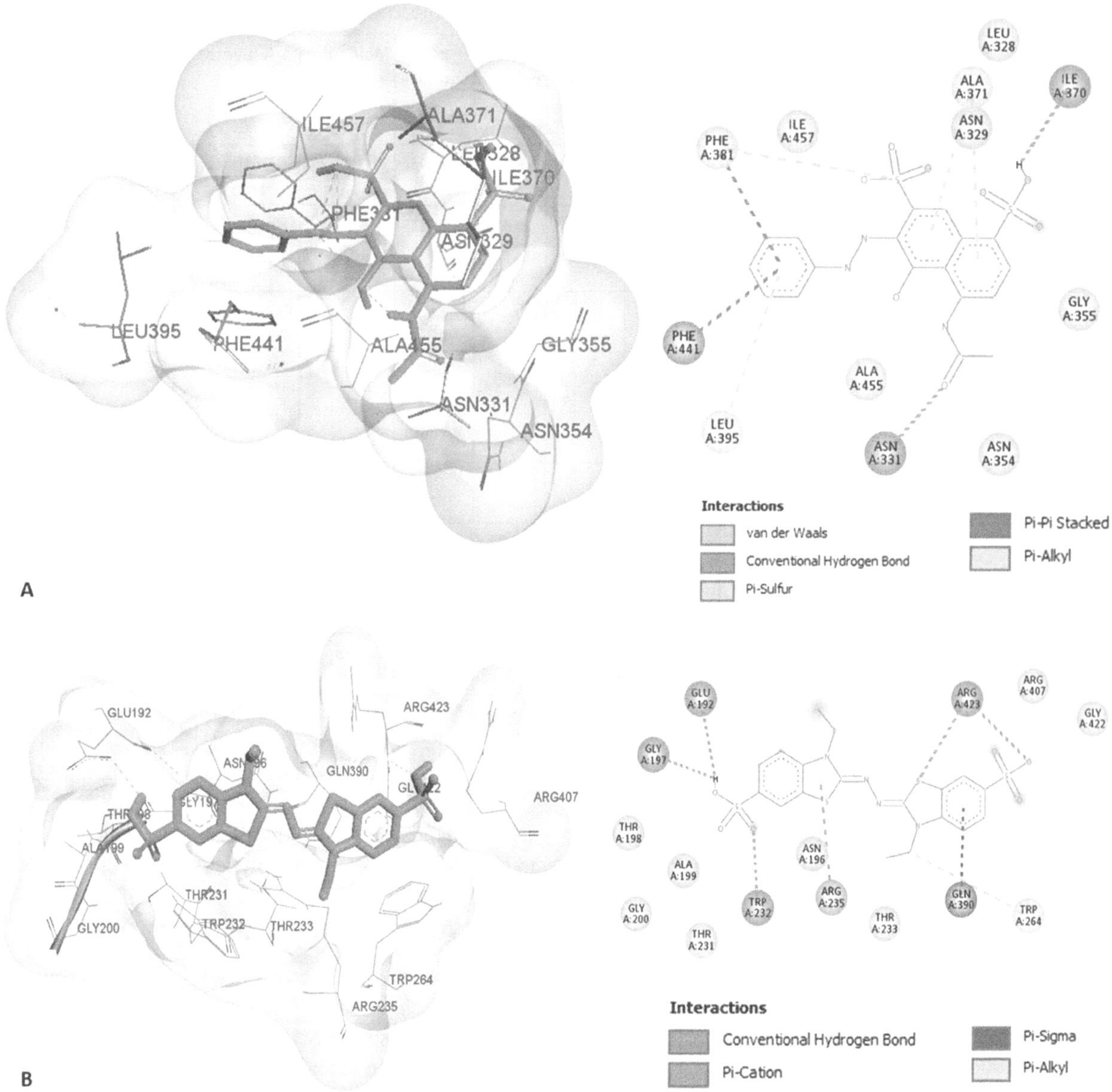

Fig. 32.2 Molecular docking of laccase with lignin (A) and ABTS (B)

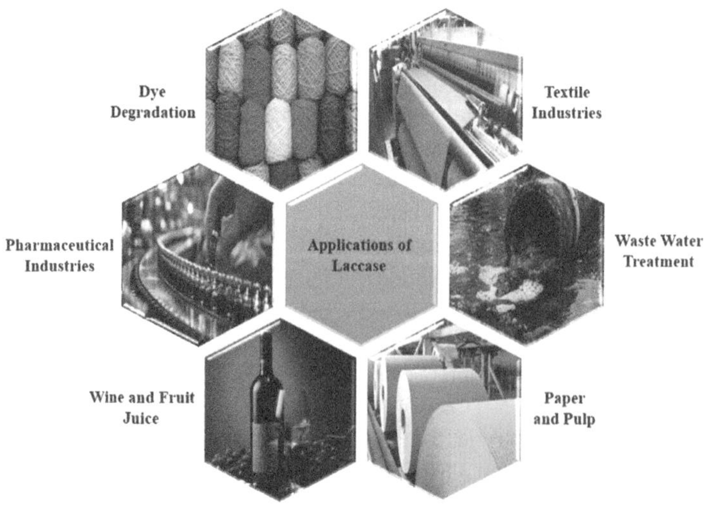

Fig. 32.3 Applications of laccase enzymes in various industries and wastewater treatment

presenting a sustainable alternative to chemical-intensive treatments [25]. Researchers have been using various unique strategies like bioengineering of microorganism, enzyme immobilization to enhance enzyme activity and increase its reusability. Till date, only a few studies have been reported about dye degradation by bacterial laccase. In a report, an engineered *Pseudomonas putida* cells with surface-immobilized bacterial laccases was developed with the capacity to decolorize a wide range of industrial synthetic dyes [26]. This innovation highlights the versatility and efficiency of laccases in textile waste treatment, showcasing their potential to address significant environmental concerns in this sector. In another study by [27], purified laccase from symbiotic bacterium *Bacillus* sp. CF96 showed a high effect on indigo dye with 90% bleaching capacity.

5.2 Paper and Pulp Industry

Bacterial laccases are involved in pulp and paper industry for the breakdown of lignin, a complex plant material polymer, to ensure better quality and strength of the paper, and to increase process efficiency. The catalytic action of lignin oxidation through laccases allows the removal of lignin and ensures environmental friendly bleaching instead of using hazardous chemicals. Laccases also eliminate lipophilic extractives such as pitch, making production more efficient and sustainable while ensuring higher quality paper products. These are substances that may cause the formation of deposits in papermaking machinery and thereby influence the efficiency of the production process. These wood-based extractives can lead to issues such as pipe and equipment blockages, downtime, and increased maintenance costs [28]. Laccases break down these substances that reduce the possibility of pitch deposition and thus enhance overall efficiency of paper production. Thus the enzyme can be used to improve the quality of products while decreasing industry's environmental footprint, hence contributing to more sustainable manufacturing practices. In summary, bacterial laccases are an effective weapon for environmental problems in both paper and pulp industries [29].

5.3 Pharmaceutical Industry

Bacterial laccases are currently being used in the pharmaceutical industry for drug development, transformation, and quality control because of their ability to oxidise a wide range of organic compounds. Laccases are currently used for synthesis of drug precursors and biotransformation of Active Pharmaceutical Ingredients (APIs). The controlled oxidative reactions catalyzed by laccases modify the chemical structure of substrates to create novel drug metabolites that exhibit enhanced pharmacological properties such as increased efficacy, bioavailability, and metabolic stability. They can also generate prodrug forms, which are biologically inactive molecules that become metabolized into active therapeutic agents within the body, thereby providing an avenue for fine-tuning the pharmacokinetics and pharmacodynamics of drugs. Another innovative use of bacterial laccases in pharmaceuticals involves the development of enzymatic biosensors for detection and quantification of pharmaceutical compounds. In these biosensors, catalytic activity of laccase catalyzes reaction with specific drug molecules to generate measurable outputs such as color, fluorescence, or electrical signals [30]. The laccase-based biosensors show high specificity, rapid analysis, and can detect the low concentration of pharmaceuticals, hence useful in monitoring drug levels in biological samples and optimizing dosage. In manufacturing, they guarantee quality control by checking the consistency and concentration of pharmaceutical compounds, thereby streamlining regulatory compliance. Bacterial laccases have great potentials for pharmaceutical applications, from drug synthesis and biotransformation to quality monitoring. With advanced researches, laccases would be potential candidates to play a pivotal role in drug discovery, development, and manufacturing, contributing to more efficient and cost-effective pharmaceutical processes [31].

5.4 Waste Water Treatment

Bacterial laccases have been used for wastewater treatment due to their ability to degrade various environmental pollutants, offering a sustainable and eco-friendly alternative to chemical methods. Laccases catalyze the oxidation of phenolic and non-phenolic compounds, efficiently by breaking down the complex organic contaminants like synthetic dyes, phenolic compounds, and other recalcitrant pollutants commonly found in industrial wastewater. Their inherent catalytic properties make them valuable for bioremediation, reducing the environmental and economic drawbacks of traditional chemical treatments. One of the significant applications of laccases from bacteria is the biodegradation of synthetic dyes and other phenolic toxic compounds, which are used on a large scale in agriculture, textiles, food, and pharmaceuticals. The dyes, which are otherwise resistant to regular treatment, are non-biodegradable and persist in water, inducing toxicity to aquatic organisms [32]. Laccases oxidize the phenolic groups and aromatic rings of dyes, breaking them down into smaller, less toxic compounds and reducing total water toxicity. Laccases further break down phenolic industrial effluent compounds, breaking them down into less toxic byproducts and diminishing their environmental impact. Laccase acts by transferring electrons to oxygen and producing reactive oxygen species (ROS) like hydrogen peroxide, which break down pollutants. This process may also lead to polymerization, producing less harmful aggregates that are easier to remove from water. Unlike chemical treatments, laccases operate under mild conditions, such as neutral pH and ambient temperatures, reducing energy costs and environmental harm. Bacterial laccases, produced via renewable biotechnological methods, can be immobilized on supports for reuse in continuous systems, enhancing cost-effectiveness. Their ability to detoxify pollutants through oxidation or polymerization positioning them as green, efficient tools for wastewater treatment, contributing to cleaner water and a safer ecosystem [33].

5.5 Other Applications

Laccase enzyme has been used immensely in textile, pulp and paper, pharmaceutical industries and bioremediation of waste water. Laccase enzymes are also used for other purposes such as, fruit juice clarification that contains many phenolic compound increases its turbidity. Moreover, laccase has been employed to stabilise fruit juice and wine colour [34]. It has also been applied to decrease bad odor from livestock farms and garbage disposals [35]. Recent study has shown the formation of novel bioactive phenazine compounds by laccase from benzoic and naphthalene amino derivatives [36].

6. Conclusion and Future Trends

Bacterial laccases have been brought into the limelight, mainly due to their multifarious applications in bioremediation, textile processes, and biosensors. However, only a few bacterial laccase has been reported though they are distributed over 20 bacterial phyla. Novel laccase with desirable characteristics such as stability at wide temperature, and pH range, salt tolerance etc. Difficulty in novel strain isolation, limited culture media, and low enzyme expression by native strain are primary reasons. One possible solution of these problem can be metagenomic isolation of laccase coding bacterial genes directly from environmental samples and clone them into suitable host using heterologous expression system. Bacterial members, such as *Escherichia coli* and *Bacillus subtilis*, offer several advantages, including high growth rates and potentially high-density fermentation [37]. Despite these advantages, some issues remain like optimization of codon usage for efficient expression, making cost-effective and scalable fermentation processes, and overcoming issues like enzyme solubility and stability. Large-scale production is still expensive since a specialized culture medium and special growth conditions are used. Research in this field still focuses on improving the expression systems by genetic engineering and better fermentation strategies along with improved enzyme recovery techniques. Moreover, sophisticated genetic engineering such as site-directed mutagenesis, direct evolution, engineering of promoter, and CRISPR-CAS9 system have been applied to improve enzyme stability, specific activity, and productivity [38]. Although recombinant expression systems are promising for optimizing bacterial laccase production, further progress is needed to achieve maximal yields at low costs for commercial use.

6.1 Statements and Declarations

Consent for publication: All authors read and approved the final manuscript.

Competing Interests: The authors declare that they have no competing interests

Authors' contribution: SG & KM - Writing original draft, conceptualization, data curation, formal analysis, **AJ, SP & SS** - Data collection, formal analysis, writing original draft, **SS &TJ** - writing original draft, data curation, **KCM** - Review, Final editing, Validation, Supervision & Conceptualization.

Acknowledgement

SG is thankful to the University Grant Commission (UGC), Government of India, for financial assistance. Authors are thankful to the Department of Biotechnology (DBT), India, for funding the Bioinformatics division (Project ID: BT/PR40176/BTIS/137/84/2023), Department of Microbiology, Vidyasagar University.

References

1. Mondal, S., Biswal, D., Pal, K., Rakshit, S., Halder, S. K., Mandavgane, S. A., ... & Mondal, K. C. (2022). Biodeinking of waste papers using combinatorial fungal enzymes and subsequent production of butanol from effluent. *Bioresource Technology*, *353*, 127078.
2. Janusz, G., Pawlik, A., Świderska-Burek, U., Polak, J., Sulej, J., Jarosz-Wilkołazka, A., & Paszczyński, A. (2020). Laccase properties, physiological functions, and evolution. *International journal of molecular sciences*, *21*(3), 966.
3. Mondal, S., Halder, S. K., & Mondal, K. C. (2019). Fungal enzymes for bioconversion of lignocellulosic biomass. *Recent Advancement in White Biotechnology Through Fungi: Volume 3: Perspective for Sustainable Environments*, 349–380.
4. Bhardwaj, N., Kumar, B., Agrawal, K., & Verma, P. (2021). Current perspective on production and applications of microbial cellulases: a review. *Bioresources and Bioprocessing*, *8*, 1–34.
5. Jana, A., Halder, S. K., Banerjee, A., Paul, T., Pati, B. R., Mondal, K. C., & Mohapatra, P. K. D. (2014). Biosynthesis, structural architecture and biotechnological potential of bacterial tannase: a molecular advancement. *Bioresource technology*, *157*, 327–340
6. Akram, F., Ashraf, S., Haq, I. U., Shah, F. I., &Aqeel, A. (2022). Eminent industrial and biotechnological applications of laccases from bacterial source: a current overview. *Applied Biochemistry and Biotechnology*, 1–21.
7. Mahuri, M., Paul, M., & Thatoi, H. (2023). A review of microbial laccase production and activity toward different biotechnological applications. *Systems Microbiology and Biomanufacturing*, *3*(4), 533–551.
8. Larkin, M. A., Blackshields, G., Brown, N. P., Chenna, R., McGettigan, P. A., McWilliam, H., ...& Higgins,

D. G. (2007). Clustal W and Clustal X version 2.0. *bioinformatics*, *23*(21), 2947–2948.

9. Zhang, D., Gao, F., Jakovlić, I., Zou, H., Zhang, J., Li, W. X., & Wang, G. T. (2020). PhyloSuite: An integrated and scalable desktop platform for streamlined molecular sequence data management and evolutionary phylogenetics studies. *Molecular ecology resources*, *20*(1), 348–355.
10. Letunic, I., & Bork, P. (2024). Interactive Tree of Life (iTOL) v6: recent updates to the phylogenetic tree display and annotation tool. *Nucleic acids research*, *52*(W1), W78–W82.
11. Wang, W., Ge, Q., Wen, J., Zhang, H., Guo, Y., Li, Z., ...& Xie, C. (2024). Horizontal gene transfer and symbiotic microorganisms regulate the adaptive evolution of intertidal algae, Porphyra sense lato. *Communications Biology*, *7*(1), 976.
12. Givaudan, A., Effosse, A., Faure, D., Potier, P., Bouillant, M. L., & Bally, R. (1993). Polyphenol oxidase in *Azospirillumlipoferum* isolated from rice rhizosphere: evidence for laccase activity in non-motile strains of *Azospirillumlipoferum*. *FEMS Microbiology Letters*, *108*(2), 205–210.
13. Chaudhary, S., Varma, A., Mandal, M., Prasad, R., & Porwal, S. (2023). Isolation and characterization of a novel laccase-producing bacteria *Bhargavaea beijingensis* from paper and pulp effluent-treated soil using in silico approaches. *Current Microbiology*, *80*(8), 241.
14. Durán-Sequeda, D., Suspes, D., Maestre, E., Alfaro, M., Perez, G., Ramírez, L., ...& Sierra, R. (2021). Effect of nutritional factors and copper on the regulation of laccase enzyme production in *Pleurotus ostreatus*. *Journal of Fungi*, *8*(1), 7.
15. Neifar, M., Chouchane, H., Mahjoubi, M., Jaouani, A., & Cherif, A. (2016). *Pseudomonas extremorientalis* BU118: a new salt-tolerant laccase-secreting bacterium with biotechnological potential in textile azo dye decolourization. *3 Biotech*, *6*, 1–9.
16. Sondhi, S., Sharma, P., Saini, S., Puri, N., & Gupta, N. (2014). Purification and characterization of an extracellular, thermo-alkali-stable, metal tolerant laccase from *Bacillus tequilensis* SN4. *PloS one*, *9*(5), e96951.
17. Verma, A., & Shirkot, P. (2014). Research Article Purification and Characterization of ThermostableLaccase from Thermophilic *Geobacillus thermocatenulatus* MS5 and its applications in removal of Textile Dyes. *Scholars Academic Journal of Biosciences*, *2*(8), 479–485.
18. Chaurasia, P. K., Yadav, R. S. S., & Yadava, S. (2013). A review on mechanism of laccase action. *Res Rev Biosci*, *7*(2), 66–71.
19. Pinto, P. A., Fraga, I., Bezerra, R. M., & Dias, A. A. (2020). Phenolic and non-phenolic substrates oxidation by laccase at variable oxygen concentrations: Selection of bisubstrate kinetic models from polarographic data. *Biochemical Engineering Journal*, *153*, 107423.
20. Kim, S., Thiessen, P. A., Bolton, E. E., Chen, J., Fu, G., Gindulyte, A., ...& Bryant, S. H. (2016). PubChem substance and compound databases. *Nucleic acids research*, *44*(D1), D1202–D1213.
21. Constans, A. (2002). Building an informatics bridge: Accelrys' Discovery Studio suite facilitates scientific collaboration. (Tools & Technology). *The Scientist*, *16*(20), 54–55.
22. Trott, O., & Olson, A. J. (2010). AutoDockVina: improving the speed and accuracy of docking with a new scoring function, efficient optimization, and multithreading. *Journal of computational chemistry*, *31*(2), 455–461.
23. Kumar, V. P., Sridhar, M., & Rao, R. G. (2022). Biological depolymerization of lignin using laccase harvested from the autochthonous fungus *Schizophyllum* commune employing various production methods and its efficacy in augmenting in vitro digestibility in ruminants. *Scientific Reports*, *12*(1), 11170.
24. Jana, A., Ghosh, D., Dasgupta, D., Das Mohapatra, P. K., & Mondal, K. C. (2017). Biopulping of lignocellulose. *Lignocellulosic biomass production and industrial applications. Beverly: Scrivener Publishing LLC*, 93–109..
25. Jana, T., Mondal, S., Pal, K., Mondal, K., Patra, S., Hilaluddin, ... & Mondal, K. C. (2024). Quality improvement of banana fiber through sequential enzymatic treatment. *Systems Microbiology and Biomanufacturing*, *4*(4), 1284–1297.
26. Wang, W., Zhang, Z., Ni, H., Yang, X., Li, Q., & Li, L. (2012). Decolorization of industrial synthetic dyes using engineered *Pseudomonas putida* cells with surface-immobilized bacterial laccase. *Microbial cell factories*, *11*, 1–14.
27. Javadzadeh, S. G., & Asoodeh, A. (2020). A novel textile dye degrading extracellular laccase from symbiotic bacterium of *Bacillus* sp. CF96 isolated from gut termite (Anacanthotermes). *International Journal of Biological Macromolecules*, *145*, 355–363.
28. Singh, G., & Arya, S. K. (2019). Utility of laccase in pulp and paper industry: A progressive step towards the green technology. *International journal of biological macromolecules*, *134*, 1070–1084.
29. Mondal, S., Mondal, K., Halder, S. K., Thakur, N., & Mondal, K. C. (2022). Microbial Amylase: Old but still at the forefront of all major industrial enzymes. *Biocatalysis and agricultural biotechnology*, *45*, 102509.
30. Upadhyay, P., Shrivastava, R., & Agrawal, P. K. (2016). Bioprospecting and biotechnological applications of fungal laccase. *3 Biotech*, *6*(1), 15.
31. Singh, D., & Gupta, N. (2020). Microbial Laccase: a robust enzyme and its industrial applications. *Biologia*, *75*(8), 1183–1193.
32. Jahangiri, E., Thomas, I., Schulze, A., Seiwert, B., Cabana, H., & Schlosser, D. (2018). Characterisation of electron beam irradiation-immobilised laccase for application in wastewater treatment. *Science of the Total Environment*, *624*, 309–322.
33. Das, A., Ghosh, P., Ghosh, U., & Mondal, K. C. (2020). Prospect of microbes for future fuel. In *Frontiers in soil and environmental microbiology* (pp. 159–166). CRC Press.
34. Minussi, R. C., Pastore, G. M., & Durán, N. (2002). Potential applications of laccase in the food industry. *Trends in Food Science & Technology*, *13*(6-7), 205–216.
35. Li, S., Sun, K., Latif, A., Si, Y., Gao, Y., & Huang, Q. (2022). Insights into the applications of extracellular laccase-aided humification in livestock manure composting. *Environmental Science & Technology*, *56*(12), 7412–7425.
36. Polak, J., Wlizło, K., Pogni, R., Petricci, E., Grąz, M., Szałapata, K., ... & Jarosz-Wilkołazka, A. (2020). Structure

and bioactive properties of novel textile dyes synthesised by fungal laccase. *International Journal of Molecular Sciences*, *21*(6), 2052.

37. Schumann, W. (2007). Production of recombinant proteins in Bacillus subtilis. *Advances in applied microbiology*, *62*, 137–189.
38. Boukid, F., Ganeshan, S., Wang, Y., Tülbek, M. Ç., & Nickerson, M. T. (2023). Bioengineered enzymes and precision fermentation in the food industry. *International journal of molecular sciences*, *24*(12), 10156.
39. Wang, J., Chang, F., Tang, X., Li, W., Yin, Q., Yang, Y., & Hu, Y. (2020). Bacterial laccase of *Anoxybacillus ayderensis* SK3-4 from hot springs showing potential for industrial dye decolorization. *Annals of Microbiology*, *70*, 1–9.
40. Britos, C. N., Gianolini, J. E., Portillo, H., &Trelles, J. A. (2018). Biodegradation of industrial dyes by a solvent, metal and surfactant-stable extracellular bacterial laccase. *Biocatalysis and Agricultural Biotechnology*, *14*, 221–227.
41. Abdelgalil, S. A., Soliman, N. A., Abo-Zaid, G. A., & Abdel-Fattah, Y. R. (2021). Bioprocessing strategies for cost-effective large-scale production of bacterial laccase from *Lysinibacillus macroides* LSO using bio-waste. *International Journal of Environmental Science and Technology*, 1–20.
42. Park, H. J., Lee, Y. M., Do, H., Lee, J. H., Kim, E., Lee, H., & Kim, D. (2021). Involvement of laccase-like enzymes in humic substance degradation by diverse polar soil bacteria. *Folia Microbiologica*, *66*, 331–340.
43. Siroosi, M., Amoozegar, M. A., & Khajeh, K. (2016). Purification and characterization of an alkaline chloride-tolerant laccase from a halotolerant bacterium, *Bacillus* sp. strain WT. *Journal of Molecular Catalysis B: Enzymatic*, *134*, 89–97.
44. Das, R., Li, G., Mai, B., & An, T. (2018). Spore cells from BPA degrading bacteria *Bacillus* sp. GZB displaying high laccase activity and stability for BPA degradation. *Science of the Total Environment*, *640*, 798–806.
45. Berini, F., Verce, M., Ausec, L., Rosini, E., Tonin, F., Pollegioni, L., & Mandić-Mulec, I. (2018). Isolation and characterization of a heterologously expressed bacterial laccase from the anaerobe *Geobacter metallireducens*. *Applied microbiology and biotechnology*, *102*, 2425–2439.

Note: All the figures and the table in this chapter were made by the authors.

Research and Innovations in Industrial and Marine Biotechnology: A Circular Economy 2024 – Prof. Hrudayanath Thatoi et al. (eds)

33 Contribution of Indian Scientist to Probiotics and Antimicrobial Proteins Journal: A Scientometric Analysis

Arindam Ganguly
Department of Microbiology, Bankura Sammilani College,
Bankura, W.B., India

Deep Kumar Kirtania*, Monishankar Chhetri
Central Library, Bankura Sammilani College,
Bankura, W.B., India

Sourav Chattaraj
Centre for Industrial Biotechnology Research,
School of Pharmaceutical Sciences,
Siksha 'O' Anusandhan, Deemed to be University,
Kalinga Nagar, Bhubaneswar, Odisha, India

Abstract: The present study conducts a scientometric analysis of contribution of Indian scientists to the journal *Probiotics and Antimicrobial Proteins*, revealing a steady and substantial growth in research output over the past fifteen years. India ranks second in contributions, accounting for 16.49% of the journal's publications, showcasing the country's expanding presence in probiotics and antimicrobial protein research. The analysis highlights significant international collaborations primarily with the US, South Korea, and Germany. Key scientometric indicators, including publication trends, authorship patterns, and citation impact, demonstrate India's strong research base and growing global relevance. This comprehensive assessment provides valuable insights into the role of Indian scientists in shaping global research trends in the context of probiotic study.

Keywords: Probiotics, Microbes, Scientometric assessment, Database, Citation impact

1. Introduction

Probiotics are beneficial viable microbes which when administered in sufficient quantities, confer health benefits to the host. They confer protection against virulent pathogens by regulating intestinal microbiome, and stimulating host defense mechanism [1]. They often secrete short-chain fatty acids, siderophores, bacteriocins, and antimicrobial peptides to combat fish pathogens [2]. They may also inhibit viral colonization [3]. They regulate the intestinal pH through the production of lactic acid, butyric acids and volatile fatty acids [4]. They are able to stimulate humoral and cell-mediated immune responses and thus act as a sustainable alternative to antibiotics [6]. A probiotic can retain its viability for prolonged period without any genetic alteration [7]. It can tolerate high bile and acid concentration in the digestive tract of host, display cell-surface adhesion to the intestinal wall [5]. Probiotics must not contain any antibiotic-resistant genes and should remain non-pathogenic, non-toxic to the host [8]. These beneficial microorganisms play a crucial role in promoting fecundity and feed digestibility of aquatic organisms [9, 10].

The concept of probiotics has a longstanding history that dates back more than a hundred years. It began with the pioneering work of Elie Metchnikoff who proposed that consuming fermented milk products have health

*Corresponding author: deep.kirto@gmail.com

DOI: 10.1201/9781003759003-33

benefits [11]. Probiotic was later defined as organisms and substances that help maintain the microbial balance of the intestine [12]. India has emerged as a significant contributor to the global probiotic research landscape. Recent advances in the field of fish nutrition and disease management has resulted significant growth in aquaculture sector [13, 14]. Bairagi et al. [15] isolated unique microbial enzymes from the gastrointestinal tract of *Clarias batrachus*. This finding has profound implications for the development of optimized feed formulations. The production of acyl homoserine lactone by *Lysinibacillus sphaericus*, *Bacillus amyloliquefaciens* and *Bacillus cereus* probiotics can effectively prevent the onset of motile aeromonad septicemia in *Clarias gariepinus* [16].

Probiotics and Antimicrobial Proteins stands as a major journal in the field of probiotic research. It is an interdisciplinary journal that focuses on application of probiotic organisms. The journal publishes diverse articles supporting both cutting-edge discoveries and practical advancements. With an Impact Factor of 4.4, *Probiotics and Antimicrobial Proteins* stands as a leading and influential publication in this rapidly evolving field. *Probiotics and Antimicrobial Proteins* plays a pivotal role in shaping the understanding and real-world utilization of probiotic organisms and antimicrobial agents. This study seeks to showcase India's profound influence on the progress of probiotic research through this pioneering journal.

2. Research Methodology

This study started by collecting research articles published in *Probiotic and Antimicrobial Proteins* journal, especially those by Indian scientists. The *Web of Science* database was used to retrieve the published articles from the publication source [17]. A search was conducted using the name of the specific journal to identify the relevant publications (total journal publication $n = 1431$). After filtering the results, the year 2025 was excluded and India was selected as the country. Finally, 236 publications published by Indian scientists in the journals were considered for the present scientometric analysis. Later, the articles were stored in Ms-Excel according to their bibliographic details, which were then presented in tabular form. In addition, data visualization was performed using the Bibliometrix package in R software (https://www.bibliometrix.org/home).

3. Results and Discussion

3.1 Journal Publication Growth

From 2009 to 2024, the number of publications in the journal *Probiotics and Antimicrobial Proteins* has shown a significant upward trend, with a total of 1,431 articles published during this period (Table 33.1). In the context of the present study, the publication trend can broadly be divided into three phases. In the initial growth phase (2009–2016), the annual number of articles ranged from 23 to 33, accounting for 15.79% of the total output. This was followed by an acceleration phase (2017–2019), during which the number of publications rose sharply compared to earlier years, reaching 170 articles in 2019. The most notable growth occurred in the maturity phase (2020–2024), which contributed 62.75% of the total publications, with the highest number of articles (230) published in 2024. This rapid increase in recent years may be attributed to the growing global interest in probiotics, antimicrobial resistance, and immunity.

Table 33.1 Year wise growth of journal publications

Publication Years	Publication Count	Percentage (%)
2009	23	1.61
2010	33	2.31
2011	26	1.82
2012	32	2.24
2013	31	2.17
2014	23	1.61
2015	32	2.24
2016	26	1.82
2017	54	3.77
2018	83	5.80
2019	170	11.88
2020	189	13.21
2021	149	10.41
2022	156	10.90
2023	174	12.16
2024	230	16.07
Total	**1431**	**100**

3.2 Top Contributing Country

An analysis of the country-specific contributions to the journal "*Probiotics and Antimicrobial Proteins*" shows that the research output is diverse worldwide, but the notable thing here is the dominance of Asian countries (Table 33.2). China occupies the top position with 249 publications (17.40%), followed by India in second place with 236 publications (16.49%), which contributes more than one-third of the total published articles in the journal. This statistical data highlights a strong presence from both developing and developed countries, reflecting the widespread global interest in probiotic and antimicrobial protein research.

3.3 Contribution of Indian Scientists

The contribution of Indian scientists to the journal *Probiotics and Antimicrobial Proteins* has shown a significant upward trend from 2010 to 2024. A total of 236 publications were published by Indian scientists

Table 33.2 Top 10 contributing counties in the journal

Countries/Regions	Publication Count	Percentage (%)
China	249	17.40
India	236	16.49
Iran	157	10.97
USA	141	9.85
Brazil	129	9.01
South Korea	92	6.43
Egypt	58	4.05
Canada	56	3.91
France	50	3.49
Russia	49	3.42

during the period, which is 16.49% of the journal's overall publications. In the initial phase (2010-2016), the number of publications was relatively low, with 3 to 12 articles published per year, which was only 22.88% of the total Indian publications. There has been a significant increase since 2017, which peaked in 2019 with 32 publications (13.56%). Between 2020 and 2024, Indian researchers have consistently published more than 24 articles annually, accounting for 56.36% of the country's total contributions during this five-year period. This data clearly indicates India's growing and strong role in probiotic and antimicrobial protein research, highlighting the recent transition from emerging interest to established scientific involvement (Fig. 33.1).

3.4 Major Collaborating Counties

Analyzing the pattern of international collaborations, it is found that Indian scientists are involved in research partnerships with several countries, along with publications (Table 33.3). Among international collaborators, the United States leads with 15 joint publications (1.05%), followed by South Korea (0.56%) and Germany (0.35%). Other notable collaborators include Brazil, New Zealand, Nigeria, Russia, Saudi Arabia, Japan, Malaysia, Norway, Portugal and South Africa. It indicates a growing trend towards global scientific engagement. These collaborations can help increase the visibility, quality and impact of Indian research in the field of *probiotics and antimicrobial proteins*. Figure 33.2 illustrates the country collaboration network of global publications.

Table 33.3 Major collaborating counties

Country Name	Publication Count	Percentage (%)
India	236	16.49
USA	15	1.05
South Korea	8	0.56
Germany	5	0.35
Brazil	4	0.28
Nigeria	3	0.21
Russia	3	0.21
Japan	2	0.14
Malaysia	2	0.14
New Zealand	2	0.14
Norway	2	0.14
Portugal	2	0.14
Saudi Arabia	2	0.14
South Africa	2	0.14

3.5 Keyword Analysis

The keyword distribution highlights a comprehensive research approach, aligning with the scope of the *Probiotics and Antimicrobial Proteins* journal (Fig. 33.3). The keywords with the highest co-occurrence frequency were "Lactic-acid bacteria," "strains," "identification," "bacteria," "*in-vitro*," "expression" and "probiotics". Scientometric analysis of research trends in *Probiotics and Antimicrobial Proteins* Journal revealed that research on probiotics in India had been increasingly focused on lactic-acid bacteria (54 occurrences). This aligns closely with the journal's scope, which often explores microbial strains with probiotic and antimicrobial functions. The term "strains" (31 occurrences) suggests a focus on the

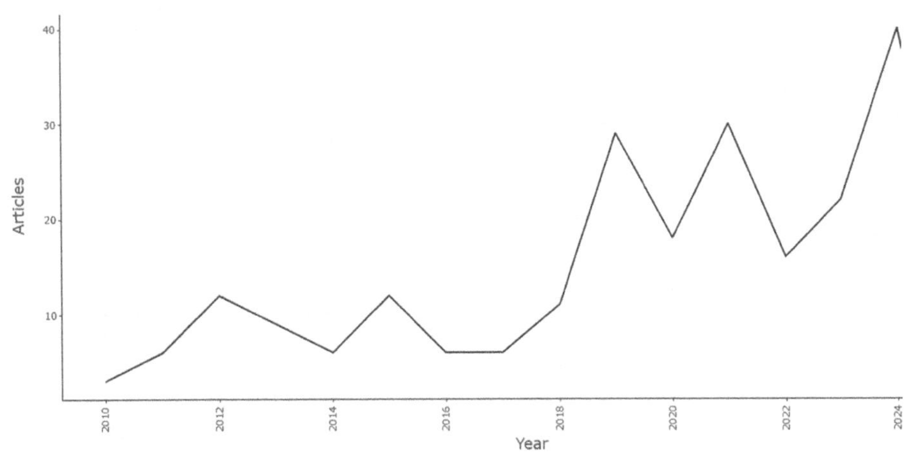

Fig. 33.1 Publication trend of Indian scientists

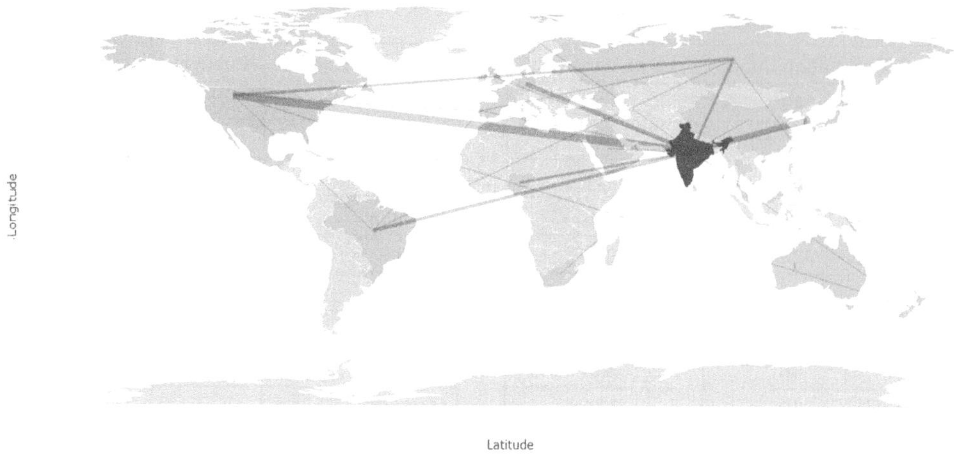

Fig. 33.2 Country collaboration network

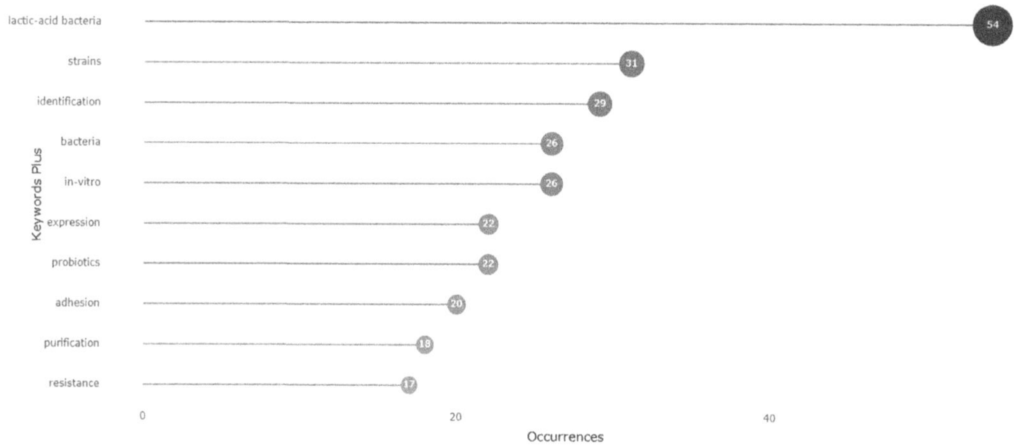

Fig. 33.3 Frequency of keywords

diversity and specific characteristics of bacterial isolates. The study thus reveals current research priorities and shape future investigations.

3.6 Trending Topics

Indian researchers have played a vital role in advancing probiotic research. The use of indigenous microbial strains in promoting gut health and developing functional foods was a key area of focus (Fig. 33.4). Research has focused on "gut microbiota," "probiotics," "prebiotics," and "*Lactobacillus*," indicating a shift toward holistic microbiome studies. Indian researchers are making significant strides in probiotic research, focusing on adhesion ability of beneficial bacteria to the intestinal lining. Additionally, application of indigenous probiotic cultures in dairy industry has also been widely studied. Advanced gene sequencing techniques are also being utilized for therapeutic and commercial applications.

3.7 Content Analysis of Top 10 Most Cited Papers

Several studies have explored the multifaceted health benefits and functional properties of probiotics. Venkataraman et al. [18] conducted a placebo-controlled, double-blind clinical trial to examine the effects of a multi-strain probiotic preparation on examination-related stress on eighty students aged 18 to 24 years. Yadav et al. [19] evaluated the hypocholesterolemic effects of *Lactobacillus fermentum* in male Wistar rats fed a cholesterol-enriched diet. Antioxidant enzyme activities were also being elevated. Giri et al. [20] isolated autochthonous probiotics from the gut of *Labeo rohita* [21] developed *Lactobacillus johnsonii* CPN23 which has shown increased acid, bile, phenol tolerance, enzymatic activity and cell-mediated immunity. It has also reduced ammonia, alongside. The results confirm the efficacy of canine-origin *L. johnsonii* CPN23 as a probiotic for pets. Hati et al. [22] studied the fermentation potential of *Lactobacillus* in skim and soy milk. *Streptococcus thermophilus* MD2 and *Lactobacillus helveticus* V3 showed superior acidification, growth, and proteolysis. Ahire et al. [23] characterized *L. plantarum* UBLP40 for its probiotic attributes. Singh et al. [24] isolated nine *Lactobacillus reuteri* strains from human infant feces that survived acidic, bile, and duodenal conditions. Despite their hydrophilic nature, they exhibited strong antagonistic activity and bile salt deconjugation.

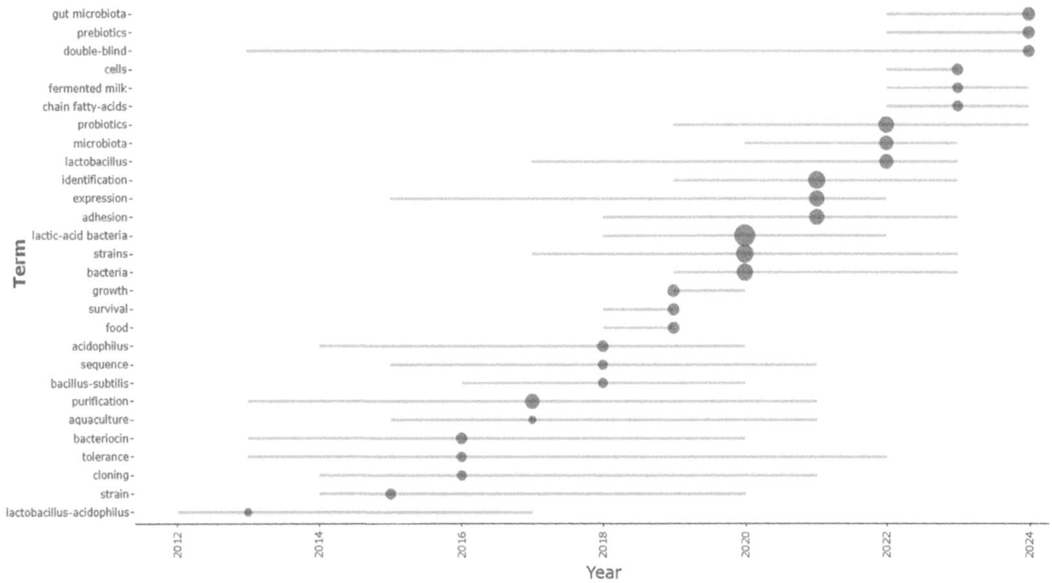

Fig. 33.4 Trending topics

Kumar et al. [25] focused on bile salt hydrolyzing activity among indigenous *Lactobacillus* strains. Garsa et al. [26] studied the thermal stability and antimicrobial activity of bacteriocins. Yoha et al. [27] emphasized the importance of encapsulation in enhancing probiotic stability, survivability, and targeted delivery. Various encapsulation techniques were discussed, noting their influence on probiotic efficacy and the ongoing challenges in commercialization and performance evaluation. Probiotics are essential for maintaining microbial ecosystem stability, while the bacterial consortia effectively enhance nutrient removal and provide significant economic and environmental benefits in wastewater valorization [28].

4. Conclusion

A scientometric evaluation of Indian contributions to *Probiotics and Antimicrobial Proteins* reveals significant growth, with India ranking second globally and contributing 16.49% of the journal's output. Collaborative research, especially with the U.S., South Korea, and Germany, reflects India's strong presence in this field. The study highlights the need for expanded international and interdisciplinary collaborations to enhance impact and calls for greater institutional support to sustain this momentum.

References

1. Chattaraj, S. and Das Mohapatra, P.K. (2024). Immunostimulatory and antagonistic potential of the methanolic extract of *Oedogonium intermedium* SCB in *Cirrhinus reba* challenged with *Aeromonas hydrophila*. *Aquac. Int.*, 32(3), 2523–2548.
2. Chattaraj, S., Behera, B.K. and Das Mohapatra, P.K. (2024). Effective valorization of *Chlorella* biomass and brewers' spent grain substituting fish meal and soybean meal in the diet of herbivorous fish *Cirrhinus reba* for higher growth, digestibility and sustainable cultivation. *J. Appl. Phycol.*, 36(1), 217–232.
3. Chattaraj, S., Ganguly, A., Mandal, A. and Das Mohapatra, P.K. (2022). A review of the role of probiotics for the control of viral diseases in aquaculture. *Aquac. Int.* https://doi.org/10.1007/s10499-022-00915-6
4. Markowiak-Kopeć, P. and Śliżewska, K. (2020). The effect of probiotics on the production of short-chain fatty acids by human intestinal microbiome. *Nutrients*, 12(4), 1107. https://doi.org/10.3390/nu12041107
5. Chattaraj, S., Mitra, D., Ganguly, A., Das Mohapatra, P.K. and Thatoi, H. (2024). 16S amplicon sequencing of the gastrointestinal microbiota of *Cirrhinus reba* and isolation of an autochthonous probiotic using culture-based approaches. *Syst. Microbiol. Biomanuf.* https://doi.org/10.1007/s43393-024-00285-5
6. Ganguly, A., Chattaraj, S., Ganguly, M., Chattaraj, M., Banerjee, A., Mandal, A., Khan, M.A., Sen, S.K. and Das Mohapatra, P.K. (2024). Effect of three probiotic *Bacillus* strains supplemented feeds on growth, carcass composition and blood parameters of *Clarias magur* (Hamilton). *J. Appl. Aquacult.* https://doi.org/10.1080/10454438.2024.2330499
7. Ganguly, A., Banerjee, A., Mandal, A. and Das Mohapatra, P.K. (2018). Probiotic-based cultivation of *Clarias batrachus*: Importance and future perspective. *Acta Biol. Szeged.*, **62**(2), 158–168. https://doi.org/10.14232/abs.2018.2.158-168
8. Ganguly, A., Banerjee, A., Mandal, A. and Das Mohapatra, P.K. (2018). Optimization of effective dose of a newly isolated probiotic bacteria for growth and disease resistance of *Clarias batrachus* (Linn.). *Res. J. Life Sci. Bioinform. Pharm. Chem. Sci.*, 4(4), 344–354.
9. Ganguly, A., Banerjee, A., Mandal, A., Khan, M.A. and Das Mohapatra, P.K. (2019). Isolation and characterization of bacteria from the intestine of *Clarias batrachus* for probiotic organism. *Proc. Zool. Soc.*, 72(4), 411–419. https://doi.org/10.1007/s12595-018-0283-x

10. Chattaraj, S., Mitra, D., Chattaraj, M., Ganguly, A., Thatoi, H. and Das Mohapatra, P.K. (2024). Brewers' spent grain as fish feed ingredient: Evaluation of bio-safety and analysis of its impact on gut bacteria of *Cirrhinus reba* by 16S metagenomic sequencing. *Curr. Res. Microb. Sci.*, 7, 100286
11. Mackowiak, P.A. (2013). Recycling Metchnikoff: Probiotics, the intestinal microbiome and the quest for long life. *Front. Public Health*, 1, 52. https://doi.org/10.3389/fpubh.2013.00052
12. Parker, R.B. (1974). Probiotics, the other half of the antibiotics story. *Anim. Nutr. Health*, 29, 4–8.
13. Chattaraj, S., Mitra, D., Ganguly, A., Thatoi, H. and Das Mohapatra, P.K. (2024). A critical review on the biotechnological potential of brewers' waste: Challenges and future alternatives. *Curr. Res. Microb. Sci.*, 27, 100228.
14. Chattaraj, S., & Das Mohapatra, P. K. (2024). Immunostimulatory and antagonistic potential of the methanolic extract of Oedogonium intermedium SCB in Cirrhinus reba challenged with Aeromonas hydrophila. *Aquaculture International*, *32*(3), 2523–2548.
15. Bairagi, A., Ghosh, K.S., Sen, S.K. and Ray, A.K. (2002). Enzyme producing bacterial flora isolated from fish digestive tracts. *Aquac. Int.*, **10**, 109–121. https://doi.org/10.1023/A:1021355406412
16. Novita, H., Rusmana, I., Yuhana, M. and Pasaribu, F.H. (2015). Potential of *Bacillus* sp., as a producer of AHL lactonase and its application as a probiotic for the prevention of MAS in catfish (*Clarias gariepinus*). *J. Fish. Aquat. Sci.*, 10(6), 464–476. https://doi.org/10.3923/jfas.2015.464.476
17. Ganguly, A., Kirtania, D. K., Chhetri, M., & Chattaraj, S. (2025). Sustainable development through probiotics: A scientometric analysis of Indian research and innovation. *Discover Sustainability, 6:*455. https://doi.org/10.1007/s43621-025-01263-0
18. Venkataraman, R., Madempudi, R.S., Neelamraju, J., Ahire, J.J., Vinay, H.R., Lal, A., Thomas, G. and Stephen, S. (2021). Effect of multi-strain probiotic formulation on students facing examination stress: A double-blind, placebo-controlled study. *Probiotics Antimicrob. Proteins*, 13(1), 12–18.
19. Yadav, R., Khan, S.H., Mada, S.B., Meena, S., Kapila, R. and Kapila, S. (2019). Consumption of probiotic *Lactobacillus fermentum* MTCC:5898-fermented milk attenuates dyslipidemia, oxidative stress, and inflammation in male rats fed on cholesterol-enriched diet. *Probiotics Antimicrob. Proteins*, 11, 509–518.
20. Giri, S.S., Sukumaran, V., Sen, S.S., Vinumonia, J., Banu, B.N. and Jena, P.K. (2011). Antagonistic activity of cellular components of potential probiotic bacteria, isolated from the gut of *Labeo rohita*, against *Aeromonas hydrophila*. *Probiotics Antimicrob. Proteins*, 3, 214–222.
21. Kumar, S., Pattanaik, A.K., Sharma, S., Jadhav, S.E., Dutta, N. and Kumar, A. (2017). Probiotic potential of a *Lactobacillus* bacterium of canine faecal-origin and its impact on select gut health indices and immune response of dogs. *Probiotics Antimicrob. Proteins*, 9, 262–277.
22. Hati, S., Patel, N. and Mandal, S. (2018). Comparative growth behaviour and biofunctionality of lactic acid bacteria during fermentation of soy milk and bovine milk. *Probiotics Antimicrob. Proteins*, 10, 277–283.
23. Ahire, J.J., Jakkamsetty, C., Kashikar, M.S., Lakshmi, S.G. and Madempudi, R.S. (2021). In vitro evaluation of probiotic properties of *Lactobacillus plantarum* UBLP40 isolated from traditional indigenous fermented food. *Probiotics Antimicrob. Proteins*, 13(5), 1413–1424.
24. Singh, T.P., Kaur, G., Malik, R.K., Schillinger, U., Guigas, C. and Kapila, S. (2012). Characterization of intestinal *Lactobacillus reuteri* strains as potential probiotics. *Probiotics Antimicrob. Proteins*, 4, 47–58.
25. Kumar, R., Grover, S. and Batish, V.K. (2012). Bile salt hydrolase (BSH) activity screening of lactobacilli: *In vitro* selection of indigenous *Lactobacillus* strains with potential bile salt hydrolyzing and cholesterol-lowering ability. *Probiotics Antimicrob. Proteins*, 4, 162–172.
26. Garsa, A.K., Kumariya, R., Sood, S.K., Kumar, A. and Kapila, S. (2014). Bacteriocin production and different strategies for their recovery and purification. *Probiotics Antimicrob. Proteins*, 6, 47–58.
27. Yoha, K.S., Nida, S., Dutta, S., Moses, J.A. and Anandharamakrishnan, C. (2022). Targeted delivery of probiotics: Perspectives on research and commercialization. *Probiotics Antimicrob. Proteins*, 1–34. https://doi.org/10.1007/s12602-022-09902-2
28. Chattaraj, S., Das, S., Ganguly, A., Thatoi, H., & Das Mohapatra, P. K. (2024). Valorization of wastewater by the application of probiotic, nitrifying, and denitrifying bacterial consortium. In *Application of microbial technology in wastewater treatment and bioenergy recovery* (pp. 133–156). Springer Nature. https://doi.org/10.1007/978-981-97-3458-0_6

Note: All the figures and tables in this chapter were made by the authors.

Research and Innovations in Industrial and Marine Biotechnology: A Circular Economy 2024 – Prof. Hrudayanath Thatoi et al. (eds)

34 Bioprospecting of Mahua Flowers into Biofuel and other Commodities

Aurodeepa Samantaray, Subhashree Rath, Ramesh Chandra Ray, Hrudayanath Thatoi*
Centre for Industrial Biotechnology Research,
Siksha 'O' Anusandhan Deemed to be University,
Bhubaneswar, Odisha

Abstract: Mahua is an indigenous tree of the Indian subcontinent, and has long been recognised for its ecological, cultural, and economic value, particularly among tribal people. The flowers of Mahua contain fermentable sugars, vitamins, amino acids, proteins, minerals, and numerous bioactive chemicals, which have enormous bioprospecting potential for high-value products. The important objective of this present review was to evaluate the biological and chemical properties of Mahua flowers, as well as their traditional and current use. Special attention was placed on their potential as a renewable feedstock for biofuel generation. Beyond biofuels, Mahua flowers are rapidly being used in nutraceuticals, medicines, and cosmetics due to their antioxidant, anti-inflammatory, and antibacterial characteristics. The integration of Mahua into commodities such as functional food, bioplastics, and personal care products demonstrates its adaptability in promoting a sustainable bioeconomy. By combining traditional knowledge with modern scientific ideas, this review highlighted the multiple utilities of Mahua flowers, which could be useful for their wider economic utilisation in a sustainable manner.

Keywords: Mahua, Economic value, Bioprospecting, Cosmetics, High-value products

1. Introduction

In recent years, global energy demand has been sharply rising, and by 2030, it is predicted to have increased by 53%. Fossil-based fuels (coal (30.5%), natural gas (24.4%), and petroleum fuels (33.7%) account for a significant portion of energy consumption (88.6%). However, fossil fuels are expected to run out soon because they are not renewable [1]. According to Ashraful et al. [1], coal deposits are predicted to last until 2088, while oil reserves are expected to run out by 2052 (at the current rate of consumption of 4 billion tons/ year). Consequently, bio-renewable energy platforms that use renewable biomass, like bioethanol, biobutanol, and biodiesel, are currently receiving more attention. [2]. Forest biomass is a very intriguing feedstock in this context because it can be used to make transportation-related biofuels. Forest biomass is used to create a variety of production methods, such as fermenting lignocellulose to produce ethanol or gasifying wood and other forest biomass to produce syngas that can be converted into diesel, methanol, methane, and other fuels [3].

The Indian subcontinent is home to the endemic mahua forest tree. It goes by several names, such as Mowarh (North) and Mahua. Its blossoms and tora seeds are highly valued, and it is a necessary tree for the poor. The tree has aesthetic and religious significance in tribal culture. Because they are tended to by forest dwellers, mahua trees have the best girth in the forest. Tribal and impoverished people use this in place of grains. While the dry husk can be used to make alcoholic beverages, the fruit pulp can be used to make sugar. Seeds contain a lot of oil [4]. Additionally, the flowers are used to make vinegar, cattle feed, portable spirits, and distilled spirits [5]. With Mahua flowers and seeds serving as examples of raw materials, this chapter examines the potential applications of forest biomass to produce bioethanol and biodiesel. For the

*Corresponding author: director.cibr@soa.ac.in

DOI: 10.1201/9781003759003-34

production of bioethanol, a variety of feedstocks have been used, including lignocellulose, sugar, and starch [3].

This review highlighted the inclusive scope of Mahua flower for its biological and chemical characteristics, its traditional and modern applications, and its valorisation into biofuels, nutraceuticals, pharmaceuticals, and cosmetic commodities. By identifying future potential, this review also explored the significance of Mahua as a useful bioresource in the emerging economy.

2. Biological and Chemical Profile of Mahua Flowers

With a maximum height of 1200 meters, this medium-to large deciduous tree can be found in India's verdant forests. Its thick, leathery leaves, many branches, and large, rounded crown are all short and holey. The bark is dark coloured, cracked, and milky with fleshy, greenish fruits. The corolla is tubular and aromatic [6]. This plant can be cultivated or self-sown. Flowering of mahua takes place annually in between March to April [7]. There are diverse groups of phytochemicals found in various parts of the mahua plant. One species of mahua, *i.e., M. longifolia,* reported to contain alkaloids, tannins, proteins, and carbohydrates, and has been shown to exhibit antioxidant, anti-ulcer activity, Hepatoprotective activity, and Anti-fertility activity [8-10] (Table 34.1). Another species, *Madhuca indica,* has been reported to contain various phytochemicals which is useful for activities such as antibacterial and analgesic activity [11,12] (Table 34.1.).

Table 34.1 Distribution and biological activities of *Madhuca* sp

Sl. no	Madhuca sp.	Distribution	Biological activity	Preparation	Remarks	References
1	*Madhuca longifolia*	South Asia, India (Andhra Pradesh, Telangana, Karnataka, Kerala, Maharashtra, and Odisha)	Antioxidant activity	Bark extract using 70 % ethanol	*In vitro* and *in vivo* experiments on rats for hepatic injury	[8]
3	*Madhuca indica*	Dry deciduous forests of India (Maharashtra, Madhya Pradesh, Odisha, Uttar Pradesh, Jharkhand, Gujarat, Karnataka, Andhra Pradesh, Bihar, Chhattisgarh, and West Bengal), Nepal, and Sri Lanka	Antibacterial activity	Extraction of flowers using water and methanol	Antibacterial activity (*Klebsiella pneumoniae* and *Bacillus subtilis*)	[11]
4	*M. longifolia*	South Asia, India (Andhra Pradesh, Telangana, Karnataka, Kerala, Maharashtra, and Odisha)	Anti-ulcer activity	Ethanol extract of the flower	Reducing the volume of gastric fluid, total acidity, and free acidity	[9,10]
5	*M. indica*	Dry deciduous forests of India (Maharashtra, MP, Odisha, UP, Jharkhand, Gujarat, West Bengal, Andhra Pradesh, Bihar, Chhattisgarh, and Karnataka), Nepal, and Sri Lanka	Analgesic activity	Extracts using methanol	Marginal analgesic ability	[12]
6	*M. longifolia*	South Asia, India (Andhra Pradesh, Telangana, Karnataka, Kerala, Maharashtra, and Odisha)	Wound healing activity	95% of the Ether-benzene and ethanol extracts of mahua leaves	Use for the treatment of wounds	[13]
7	*M. longifolia*	Nepal, Sri Lanka and Myanmar, India (Gujarat, Odisha, Chhattisgarh, Jharkhand, Bihar, and Uttar Pradesh)	Hepatoprotective activity	Extract of flowers using methanol	Induce hepatotoxicity in rats	[14]
8	*M. longifolia*	South Asia, India (Andhra Pradesh, Telangana, Karnataka, Kerala, Maharashtra, and Odisha)	Nephroprotective activity	Aqueous leaf extract	Positive effect against DFC-persuaded renal toxicity in female rats (Wistar albino)	[15]
9	*M. longifolia*	Nepal, Sri Lanka and Myanmar, India (Gujarat, Odisha, Chhattisgarh, Jharkhand, Bihar, and Uttar Pradesh)	Hepatoprotective activity	Aqueous extract of leaves	Stabilize the modifications initiated by DFC-induced toxicity in rats	[16]
10	*M. longifolia*	South Asia, India (Andhra Pradesh, Telangana, Karnataka, Kerala, Maharashtra, and Odisha)	Antioxidant activity	Leaf ethanolic extract (90%)	Toxicity brought on by acetaminophen	[17]
12	*M. longifolia*	Nepal, Sri Lanka, and Myanmar, India (Gujarat, Odisha, Chhattisgarh, Jharkhand, Bihar, and Uttar Pradesh)	Anti-fertility activity	Extracts of alcohol	Effects on male Swiss albino rats that inhibit fertility	[18]

3. Bioprospecting Mahua for Biofuel Production

The mahua (Madhuca indica) tree is becoming a valuable non-edible oilseed tree with enormous potential for producing biofuel. To create biodiesel, the seeds were used to extract 30–40% oil by solvent extraction or mechanical milling, then the pre-treated and trans-esterified (Fig. 34.1). Environmental compatibility and processing efficiency have been further enhanced by recent developments in enzymatic and heterogeneous catalysis [19,20]. Under ideal circumstances, Mahua oil can produce up to 95% biodiesel, making it a competitive substitute for traditional diesel. With the added benefit of Mahua's resilience and reduced input requirements, Mahua-based biodiesel performs similarly to other non-edible oils like Jatropha and Pongamia in terms of calorific value and combustion characteristics. It is environmentally sustainable because Mahua biofuel production uses underutilized forest resources, helps sequester carbon, and reduces land-use conflict with food crops. Overall, Mahua has a lot of potential in the bioprospecting landscape for the production of sustainable biofuels with careful investments in supply chain infrastructure, technology, and policy support [19,21].

4. Valorisation into Commodities: Diverse Applications

Mahua tree is one of the versatile tree species that is mostly cultivated or harvested for three main purposes such as food, fodder, and fuel [22]. It is a distinct plant among all NTFP plants as it is allied with the tribal life systems in diverse ways. It generates significant seasonal revenue, food, and other needs of tribal people. The tree produces a variety of useful items. It is appreciated in India because its flowers, fruits, and seeds are widely used [23]. The seeds of mahua contribute significantly to the rural agricultural economy since its contents have unique chemical qualities that make them appropriate for industrial usage in the production of soap and biofuels, as well as the supply of nutritional and functional products.

5. Nutraceuticals, Pharmaceuticals, Cosmetic and Personal Care Products from Mahua Flower

Mahua plants are a rich source of various proteins, fibre, amino acids, minerals, and bioactive compounds, making them a potential source for nutraceuticals and pharmaceuticals. Bioactive phytochemicals are responsible for a variety of pharmacological qualities, including antidiabetic, antibacterial, anticancer, and antiulcer actions [24]. The flowers of mahua contain numerous polysaccharides, proteins, fibre, amino acids, minerals (calcium (0.14-0.25%), phosphorus (0.13-0.14%), iron (0.015-0.03%), potassium (1.2%), sodium (0.02%), and magnesium (0.21%)), vitamins (Thiamine, riboflavin, niacin, folic acid, and ascorbic acid), enzymes (amylase, maltase, invertase, catalase, and oxidase), phytochemicals, and organic acids [25,26]. Mahua flowers could be utilised as a sugar substitute due to their high sugar content [25]. The flowers can also be used to alleviate coughs [27]. Mahua flowers have high nutritional value. As a result, mahua flowers are used to make a variety of value-added food products, including cake, cookies, jam, jelly, candy, and others, all with high nutraceutical value [28]. A large quantity of flowers is utilised in the manufacturing of distilled liquor. The fruit is also used to make jam, a traditional food made by tribal co-operatives in Maharashtra. In Bihar, sun-dried mahua plants are ground into flour and used in various breads [29]. Oil extracted from seeds can also be administered as ointment for the treatment of wounds, skin nourishment, and pain relief. Patel and Naik (2008) [30] reported that mature (fully grown) but unripe fruits

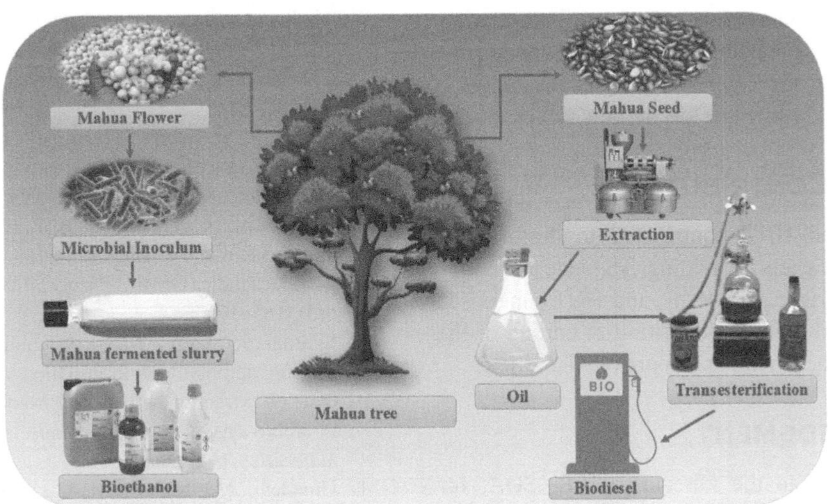

Fig. 34.1 Production of biofuel using mahua flower

are converted into jam with citric acid. The pulp is also processed into marmalade or syrup, which are used as food. Jelly can also be created from the pulp alone or blended with guava to change the astringent flavour. The pulp is also used for pickle formation. Furthermore, the mahua tree is also known as Indian butter nut trees as its seeds contain 33-61% of semi-solid fat, which is useful for the production of valuable mahua butter or mowrah butter. Mahua flower is also utilised in the production of bioplastics and biodegradable products. Oil derived from *Madhuca longifolia* seeds is a potential surfactant which is used in making bio-detergents as it contains a high amount of fatty acid. *Ocimum basilicum* leaves and plant *M. longifolia* seed oil work well together to enhance wash performance [31]. Mahua fruit seeds have 16.9% protein and 51.5% oil (oleic acid (46.3%), palmitic acid (17.8%), stearic acid (14.0%), and linoleic acid (17.9%), which is useful for producing cosmetics. According to different reports on mahua, seed cake and blossom pulp of mahua after fermentation can be used to offer nourishment to cattle. Use of Mahua in cosmetics has both ecological and socioeconomic benefits, making it a promising candidate for the production of advanced, greener cosmetics.

6. Conclusion

Despite the potential of the mahua flower, its commercialization and utilization on industrial scale face several challenges, such as geographically constrained availability and limited flowering period hampering its continuous supply chain, the absence of preservation techniques leads to microbial degradation and losses, a lack of standardized extraction of phytochemicals pose challenges in development of products, inadequate policy frame works affect the integration of mahua products into mainstream markets, lack of public awareness limited market exposure etc. Innovations in the production of nutraceuticals, cosmetics, and pharmaceuticals could be useful for the formulation of products from mahua. Plantation of the mahua tree through agroforestry could ensure a continuous supply and be useful in carbon sequestration. As the global focus intensifies on circular bioeconomy models, Mahua flowers offer a strategic advantage in bridging sustainability and socioeconomic development.

Authors Contribution

AS, SR, RCR, and HNT contributed to drafting the original review article and formatting. AS made and edited the figures of the article. SR, RCR, and HNT supervised the whole work and guided the writing & editing of the article. All authors have read and approved the article.

Acknowledgment

Authors are grateful to the Director, CIBR, SOA, for providing infrastructure facilities to conduct the writing of the review work. The authors are also thankful to the Director, CIBR, SOA, and SOA University for providing the facility to contribute a chapter to the Conference proceedings RIIMBCE-2024.

References

1. Ashraful, A. M., Masjuki, H. H., Kalam, M. A., Fattah, I. R., Imtenan, S., Shahir, S. A., & Mobarak, H. M. (2014). Production and comparison of fuel properties, engine performance, and emission characteristics of biodiesel from various non-edible vegetable oils: A review. Energy Convers. Manag. 80:202–228
2. Zhang, F., Johnson, D. M., & Sutherland, J. W. (2011). A GIS-based method for identifying the optimal location for a facility to convert forest biomass to biofuel. BIOMASS BIOENERG. 35(9):3951–3961.
3. Li, C., Sun, L., Simmons, B. A., & Singh, S. (2013). Comparing the recalcitrance of eucalyptus, pine, and switchgrass using ionic liquid and dilute acid pretreatments. Bioenergy Res. 6:14–23.
4. Singh, S., Singh, A. K., Apparao, W., Bagle, B. G., & Dhandar, D. G. (2005). Genetic divergence in Mahua (Bassia latifolia) under semi-arid ecosystem of Gujarat. *Indian Journal of Plant Genetic Resources*, *18*(03), 244–249.
5. Dwivedi, A., Priyadarshini, A., & Induar, S. (2022). Mahua (Madhuca longifolia) flower and its application in food industry: A review. *International Journal of Chemical Studies*, *10*(1), 80–84.
6. Bisht, V., Neeraj, V. K. S., & Dalal, N. (2018). Mahua an important Indian species: A review. *Journal of Pharmacognosy and Phytochemistry*, *7*(2), 3414–3418.
7. Behl, P. N., & Srivastava, G. (1993). *Herbs useful in dermatological therapy*. CBS Publishers & Distributors.
8. Odili, V. U., Akpe, A. I., Arigbe-Osula, M. E., & Igbinaduwa, P. O. (2010). Antioxidant and hepatoprotective activity of Madhuca longifolia (koenig) bark against CCl4-induced hepatic injury in rats: in vitro and in vivo studies.
9. Shrivastava, A. (2018). A study on promotion/branding of Mahua (Madhuca longifolia) in Chhattisgarh state. *JARIIT*, *103*, 332–336.
10. Patel, P. K., Janghel, V., Chandel, S. S., & Sahu, J. (2019). Madhuca indica (Mahua)-pharmaceutical, nutraceutical and economical importance for tribal people of Chhattisgarh state. *Int. J. Pharm. Phytopharm. Res*, *9*(3), 16–28.
11. Verma, K. S., Neerja Saxena, N. S., Rajshree Sinha, R. S., & Abha Agarwal, A. A. (2010). Phytochemical screening and therapeutic profiling of Madhuca indica JF Gmel.
12. Shekhawat, N., & Vijayvergia, R. (2010). Investigation of anti-inflammatory, analgesic and antipyretic properties of Madhuca indica GMEL. *European journal of inflammation*, *8*(3), 165–171.
13. Sharma, S., Sharma, M. C., & Kohli, D. V. (2010). Wound healing activity and formulation of ether-benzene-95% ethanol extract of herbal drug Madhuca longifolia leaves in albino rats. *Journal of optoelectronics and Biomedical materials*, *1*(1), 13–15.
14. Umadevi, M., Maheswari, C., Jothi, R., Paleti, S. K., Reddy, Y. S., & Narayanan, R. V. (2011). Hepatoprotective

Activity of Flowers of Madhuca longifolia (Koen.) Macbr. against paracetamol-induced hepatotoxicity. *Research Journal of Pharmacy and Technology*, *4*(2), 259–262.

15. Prince, S. E. (2018). Diclofenac-induced renal toxicity in female Wistar albino rats is protected by the pre-treatment of aqueous leaves extract of Madhuca longifolia through suppression of inflammation, oxidative stress and cytokine formation. *Biomedicine & Pharmacotherapy*, *98*, 45–51.
16. Simon, J. P., & Evan Prince, S. (2018). Aqueous leaves extract of Madhuca longifolia attenuate diclofenac-induced hepatotoxicity: Impact on oxidative stress, inflammation, and cytokines. *Journal of cellular biochemistry*, *119*(7), 6125–6135.
17. Palani, S., Raja, S., Karthi, S., Archana, S., & Kumar, B. S. (2010). In vivo analysis of nephro & hepato protective effects and antioxidant activity of Madhuca longifolia against acetaminophen-induced toxicity & oxidative stress. *Journal of Pharmacy research*, *3*(1), 9–16.
18. Das, U., Ray, R. C., & Hansdah, B. (2022). Ethnomedicinal and biological activities of tropical mahua (Madhuca species)–A comprehensive review. *Annals of Tropical Research*, *44*(2), 67–88.
19. Puhan, S., Vedaraman, N., Ram, B. V., Sankarnarayanan, G., & Jeychandran, K. (2005). Mahua oil (Madhuca Indica seed oil) methyl ester as biodiesel-preparation and emission characterstics. BIOMASS BIOENERG. *28*(1):87–93.
20. Ghadge, S. V., & Raheman, H. (2005). Biodiesel production from mahua (Madhuca indica) oil having high free fatty acids. BIOMASS BIOENERG. 28(6):601–605.
21. Thapa, S., Indrawan, N., & Bhoi, P. R. (2018). An overview on fuel properties and prospects of Jatropha biodiesel as fuel for engines. Environ. Technol. Innov. 9:210–219.
22. Patel, S., Patel, S., & Patel, V. (2011). Investigation into the mechanism of action of Madhuca longifolia for its anti-epileptic activity. Methods. 10(11).
23. Ramadan, M. F., Sharanabasappa, G., Parmjyothi, S., Seshagiri, M., & Moersel, J. T. (2006). Profile and levels of fatty acids and bioactive constituents in mahua butter from fruit-seeds of buttercup tree [Madhuca longifolia (Koenig)]. Eur. Food Res. Technol. 222:710–718
24. Dubey, I., Chhajed, M., Chourasiya, R., Chouhan, P. S., Walvekar, A., Bhandari, Y., & Verma, K. (2023). A Review of the Botanical, Conventional Applications, Phytochemical Constituents, and Pharmacology of Madhuca longifolia (Koenig) JF Macb. Phcog Rev. 17(34).
25. Mishra, A., & Poonia, A. (2019). Mahua (Madhuca longifolia) flowers: review on processing and biological properties. Food sci. nutr. (6):1153–1163.
26. Gopalan C, Rama Sastri BV and Balasubramanian SC, Nutritive value of Indian foods, National Institute of Nutrition, ICMR, Hyderabad, India, 2004
27. Mishra, A., Nandini, V., & Joglekar, A. (2021). Development of new product by mahua (Madhuca longifolia) flowers. *Kala Sarovar*, *24*(1):9–12.
28. Mishra, M., Pattnaik, S., Singh, H., & Naik, P. K. (2023). Exploring the role of Mahua as a functional food and its future perspectives. In Recent Frontiers of Phytochemicals (pp. 109–121). Elsevier
29. Mahapatra, H. Effects of Mahua in Skin Cancer. *NEW DELHI PUBLISHERS*, 310.
30. Patel, M., & Naik, S. N. (2008). Biochemical investigations of fresh mahua (Madhuca indica) flowers for nutraceutical (Doctoral dissertation, Indian Institute of Technology).
31. Suresh Kumar, S., Venkatesh Srinivasan, S. R., Venkadeswaran Karuppasamy, N. S., Padmapriya, B., & Sumitha, R. Green synthesis of bio-based detergent from Madhuca longifolia seed oil. *Research Journal of Chemical Sciences ISSN*, *2231*, 606X.

Note: The figures and the tables in this chapter were made by the authors.

Research and Innovations in Industrial and Marine Biotechnology: A Circular Economy 2024 – Prof. Hrudayanath Thatoi et al. (eds)
© 2026 Taylor & Francis Group, London, ISBN 978-1-041-28285-3

35 Exploration of Potential Termitomyces Species for their Health and Wellbeing: A Review

Jibanjyoti Panda[1], Debasis Nayak[2]
Bioresources and Traditional Knowledge Laboratory,
Department of Wildlife and Biodiversity Conservation,
Maharaja Sriram Chandra Bhanja Deo University, Sriram Chandra Vihar,
Takatpur, Baripada, India

Yugal Kishore Mohanta[3]
Nano-biotechnology and Translational Knowledge Laboratory,
Department of Applied Biology, School of Biological Sciences,
University of Science and Technology Meghalaya,
Techno City, 9th Mile, Baridua, India

Abstract: Wild edible mushrooms are well known for their potential applications in the emerging field of food and pharmaceuticals. There is a variety of wild edible mushrooms found around the globe, in which *Termitomyces* occupies a special importance due to its nutraceutical- and pharmaceutical- properties. The termites of the subfamily Macrotermitinae benefit from a symbiotic relationship with these mushrooms. The texture, flavour, nutritional content, and medicinal properties of all *Termitomyces* species give them a special place in the food industry. In addition to their scientific value, *Termitomyces* have been acknowledged for their ethnomedicinal value. Cancer, hyperlipidaemia, gastroduodenal illnesses, and Alzheimer's disease are just some of the human ailments that may be combated with *Termitomyces*' bioactive substances. In addition, *Termitomyces* also well recognised for its antioxidants, antibacterial, antiviral, anticancer and many health beneficial activities. Here, an effort has been made to discuss globally found five *Termitomyces* species (*Termitomyces clypeatus*, *T.* eurrhizus, *T.* heimii, *T.* medius, and *T. microcarpus*) and their potential health beneficial activities.

Keywords: *Termitomyces*, Antimicrobial, Antioxidant, Anticancer, Health and wellbeing

1. Introduction

Fungi are the most abundant, diverse, and widely distributed source of natural compound exhibiting positive impact on human health as well as environment [1]. Mushrooms refer to the fruiting bodies of fungi and are interconnected with insect, parasite, saprotrophs, and mycorrhizae, playing important roles in many ecosystems. Mushrooms are well recognised for their high protein, fibre, and antioxidants contain. Mushrooms are low in fat and calories while being rich in nutrients like iron, phosphorus, copper, potassium, riboflavin, tocopherol, selenium, ascorbic acid, thiamine, and cobalamin, calciferol [2]. The nutrient content of wild edible mushrooms includes 80–90% water, 2.67–7.39% protein, and 0.18–1.70% fat [3]. While most mushroom varieties require cooking before consumption; but *Laetiporus sulphureus* is consumed raw in Cameroon, which reveals, there may have therapeutic or nutritional benefits among indigenous peoples.

The fascinating thing about *Termitomyces* fungi is that they frequently coexist with termites. Aside from their obvious importance as a source of food for the local population, these also have potential as a nutritional supplement and in ethno-medicinal applications. It has long been held among the Yoruba people of Nigeria that

[1]jibanjyotipanda83@gmail.com, [2]deb63nayak@gmail.com, [3]ykmohanta@gmail.com

DOI: 10.1201/9781003759003-35

this particular genus of fungus is both edible and magical. Not as much research has been done on this species as compare to other wild edible mushrooms, therefore its potential taxonomic growth, nutritional prospects, medial value, and socio-economic relevance are all yet unknown [4]. However, there are a number of *Termitomyces* species are reported as well as consumed across India Some of the *Termitomyces* species such as *T. clypeatus, T. eurrhizus, T. heimii, T. medius*, and *T. microcarpus* are well known for their involvement in health and wellbeing [5, 6]. Efforts have been made to assemble extensive documentation of five wild *Termitomyces* species, including information on traditional value and potential applications in term of health and well-being.

2. Ethnomedicinal Value

Numerous communities worldwide rely heavily on their own systems of indigenous medicine. Though there are many sources of indigenous medicine, mushrooms also play an important role among them. Several species of *Termitomyces* have been discovered to have ethnomedical value (Table 35.1.). For example, *T. microcarpus*, which is widespread all over the world in places like Asia and Africa, has a wide range of potential ethnomedical activities. This species is used to treat gonorrhoea among the Yoruba people of Nigeria. Fever, cold, and fungal diseases are all treated with it in India. To promote vitality and strengthen the immune system, natives in Tanzania and Nepal consume it as a tonic [7]. Locals in Cameroon's Kilum-Ijim forest utilize this fungus to treat fever and strengthen their kids' bones. Nonetheless, Aryal and Budathoki, [8] described nineteen different species of the fungus that are employed by ethnic populations in Nepal for the prevention and treatment of illness.

3. Nutritional Aspect

Termitomyces species are known for its edibility as well as health beneficial activities. Numerous scientific research corroborates the protein, carbohydrate, vitamins, minerals, amino acid, and dietary fibre content of various *Termitomyces* species, which makes them a potential source of human nutrition. The presences of carbohydrate, protein, fats, fibre and ash contain in *T. clypeatus* found to be 27.67, 26.34, 7.90, 35.15 and 2.94 mg/100g of dry weight. Protein (29.40), fats (6.27), fibre (26.64) and ash (11.52) contain observed in *T.* eurrhizus. *T.* heimii recorded with a value of 47.66, 23.75, 3.58, 6.02 and 7.40 mg/100g (dry sample) for carbohydrate, protein, fats, fibre and ash contains respectively [16]. At the same time, *T. microcarpus* observed with carbohydrate 44.23mg, protein 30.69mg, fats 2.17mg, fibre 11.60mg and ash 11.30 mg per 100g of dry weight [17].

3.1 Bioactive Compounds for Health and Wellbeing

The main secondary metabolite of many mushrooms is phenolic compounds. Phenolic substances have aromatic rings replaced by hydroxyl groups. Most phenolic compounds are tannins, flavonoids, stilbenes, acids, and lignans. Phytochemicals regulate several biological processes, including antioxidant, anti-inflammatory, antimicrobial properties. *Termitomyces* species possess many phenolic compounds exhibiting verity of health promoting activities. The mushroom polysaccharide, which possesses mediating, nutritive, and antioxidant properties, is intriguing [18]. Cerebrosides, saponins, fatty acid amides, serine, ergostanes, and proteases are among the bioactive compounds found in *Termitomyces* species. However, cerebrosides have been demonstrated to treat

Table 35.1 Ethnomedicinal values of some *Termitomyces* species

Mushrooms	Uses	Sources
T. clypeatus	Pox treatment	[9]
	Treatment of measles and yellow fevers	[8]
	Recommended for gastric and constipation for adult as well as underweight children	[10]
T. eurrhizus	Recommended for rheumatism, high bp and diarrhea treatment	[6]
	With the combination of *Cynodon doctylon* used for skin disorders	[8]
	Treatment of measles and fevers	[11]
	Chicken pox treatment	[12]
T. heimii	Recommended for cold and fever, as well as fungal infections	[13]
	Used for clotting and wound healing	[14]
	Syrup is used to treat diarrhea and jaundice	[8]
T. microcarpus	Provide strength to bone of minor one and recovers from fever.	[15]
	Recommended for cold and fever, as well as fungal infections	[13]
	Used to treat gonorrhoea and enhance immunity	[7]
	Used as an energy-boosting tonic	[8]
	Adults use it for constipation and gastritis, and doctors recommend it for kids who are too skinny	[10]

certain life style diseases [19]. (Fig. 35.1.) exhibits potential health benefits associated with *Termitomyces* species.

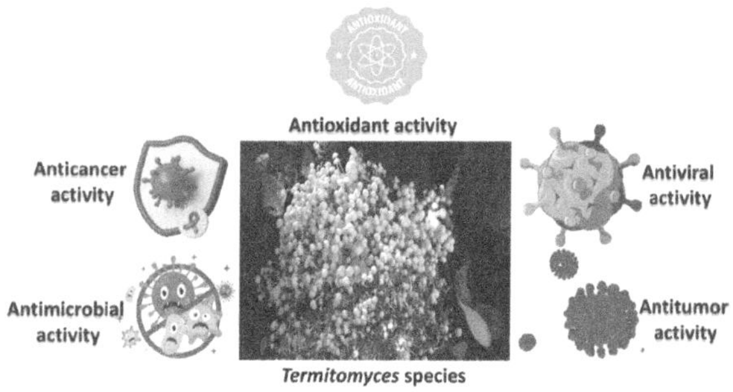

Fig. 35.1 Potential health benefits of *Termitomyces* species

Source: Authors

Cellular oxygen in animal cell can be converted into free radicals by physiological and metabolic processes and external sources. All living organisms fight free radical damage with antioxidant enzymes and substances. Free radical activity disturbing the antioxidant fortification system can cause many diseases [20]. The *T. medius* crud polysaccharides and *T. clypeatus* heteroglycan have exhibited antioxidant and ROS-reducing properties [21]. Ethanolic and water extract of *T. clypeatus* have been tested for antioxidant activity against ascorbic acid, curcumin, Butylated hydroxytoluene (BHT), catechin, EDTA, α-tocopherol, and Butylated hydroxyanisole (BHA). The extracts recorded with more antioxidant activity than compared to the standard antioxidants (Fig. 35.2.) [22].

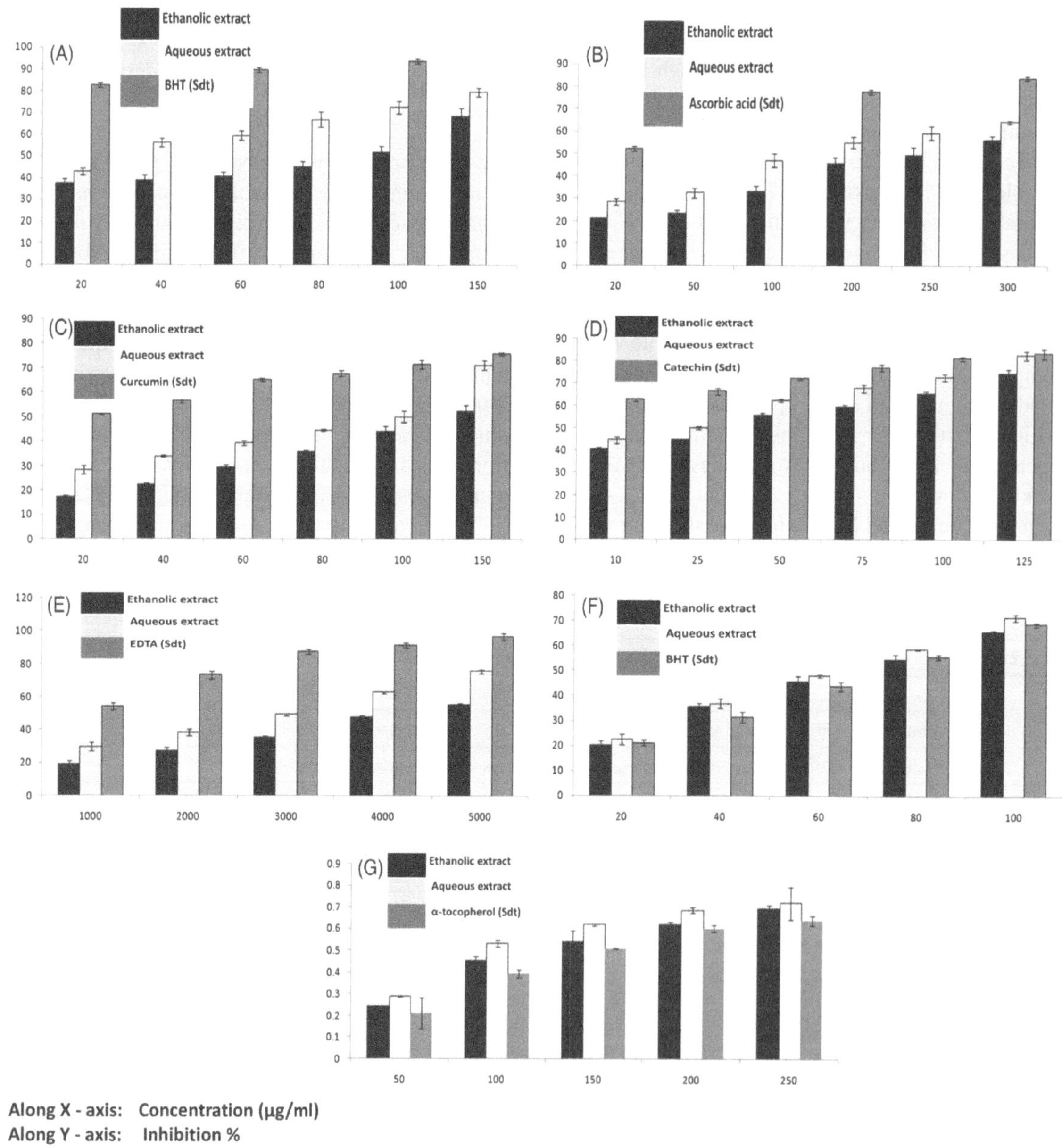

Fig. 35.2 Antioxidant scavenging activity of aqueous and ethanolic extract of *T. clypeatus:* DPPH (A), nitric acid (B), superoxide anion (C), hydroxyl (D), change in levels of chelating ability (E), total-antioxidant activity (F) and reducing activity (G) [22]

Now a days antibiotics are considered as threats for human society, due to the emerging multi drug resistance pathogenic bacteria. To fight drug-resistant bacteria and other dangerous diseases, the WHO emphasizes the necessity of finding and employing alternative therapies and agents [23]. Antibiotics found in nature are safe and effective for the treatments for microbial infections. Some compounds found in wild edible mushrooms have the potential to be employed as antibiotics. *Termitomyces* have shown potential activity against many human pathogenic bacteria and various fungal infections. Different extracts as well as polysaccharide from *T. clypeatus, T. eurrhizus*, and *T. heimii* has exhibited potential antimicrobial activity against a variety of pathogens [24]. The antimicrobial properties of *Tremitomyces* species are exhibited in (Table 35.2.) For the first time, antiviral activity of *T. clypeatus* at a concentration of 100µg/mL exhibited inhibition of 95.74 ± 4.01% and 87.13 ± 3.61% in virus CHIKV and SARS-CoV-2 respectively. The oral administration of mushroom extracts to BALB/c recorded with no cytotoxicity. Findings of the experiments provides a platform for potential and safe future utilization of *T. clypeatus* in term of functional food for the management of RNA viruses [25].

Mushrooms are a promising alternative source for strong cancer drugs without cytotoxicity Recent research indicates that mushrooms may have therapeutic potential as a cancer medication. Research on *Termitomyces*' potential as a cancer treatment is limited in comparison to that of other edible mushrooms [29]. 1, 2-dimethylhydrazine-induced hyperplasia of colon cancer in Swiss albino rats was reduced by crude polysaccharides of *T. heimii* [30]. Five types of ergostane and betulinic acid from *T. microcarpus* were found to be potential anticancer properties against a series of cancer cell, including the SR leukemia line, the T-47D breast cancer cell line, the LOX IMVI melanoma line, the colon cancer cell line, and some ovarian, prostate, and central nervous system cancer cell lines. *T. clypeatus* found to be effective against HL-60, OAW-42, HepG2, A549, MDA-MB-468, U937, U373MG, and Y-79 through aqueous extract. cytotoxicity. Result showed decrease in tumor size, increase in hemoglobin and RCB counts, and improvement in survival time [31]. Most promising cytotoxic activity reported against U937 cells. A new mycocompound, neoergosterol, derived from *T heimii*, exhibits selective and potent apoptosis in non-small cell of lung cancer cells while offering a chemoprotective barrier to normal cells, presenting significant potential for future medication development in lung cancer treatment [32]. In a study, anticancer activity of *T. clypeatus* was determined for a series of cancer cell line, and found cytotoxic effects, with a heightened activity observed against U937-histiocytic lymphoma cell line with IC_{50}25 ± 1.02µg/mL. Subjecting EAC-bearing mice to different dosages of aqueous extract resulted in a notable reduce tumour cell count as well as an improvement in RBC count, haemoglobin-content, tumour inhibition, mean survival time, and percentage increase in life-span (Fig. 35.3.) [22].

4. Conclusion and Future Aspects

The good health advantages associated with mushrooms have led to their natural components being used more frequently as dietary supplements. The abundance of secondary metabolites, vitamins, and micro-nutrients in the *Termitomyces* species gives them therapeutic and nutritional significance. This study presents the various health-promoting qualities of *Termitomyces*, including their antibacterial, anticancer, antioxidant, and many more uses. It suggests that *Termitomyces* could be a valuable resource for future therapeutic research. However, current and ongoing studies should focus on the commercialization of wild edible mushroom production. Currently, there are no viable methods for the artificial cultivation of wild edible mushrooms, particularly *Termitomyces*. Therefore, the development of artificial processes for the mass cultivation as well as production of these mushrooms is another focus of future research. Furthermore, research is necessary to assess wild edible mushrooms to underscore their potential for the identification of novel compounds for health and wellbeing as well as other applications.

Table 35.2 Different *Termitomyces* species with antimicrobial activities

Mushrooms	Extracts	Pathogenic microbes	Sources
T. clypeatus	Water	*Escherichia coli, Staphylococcus aureus, Enterobacter aerogenes, Candida albicans*, and *C. glabrata, Salmonella typhi*	[26]
	Methanol	*Pseudomonas aeruginosa*	[26]
T. eurhizus	Methanol	*E. coli, Proteus vulgaris* and *Vibrio cholera*	[27]
	Water	*Bacillus brevis* and *V. cholera*	[27]
	Ethanol	*B. brevis* and *V. cholera*	[27]
T. heimii	Water	*Pseudomonas sp., S. aureus, S. pyogenes, E. coli, Ralstonia sp., Salmonella sp., Streptococcus sp.* and *Klebsiella pneumoniae*	[24]
T. microcarpus	Methanol	*P. vulgaris* and *B. cereus*	[28]

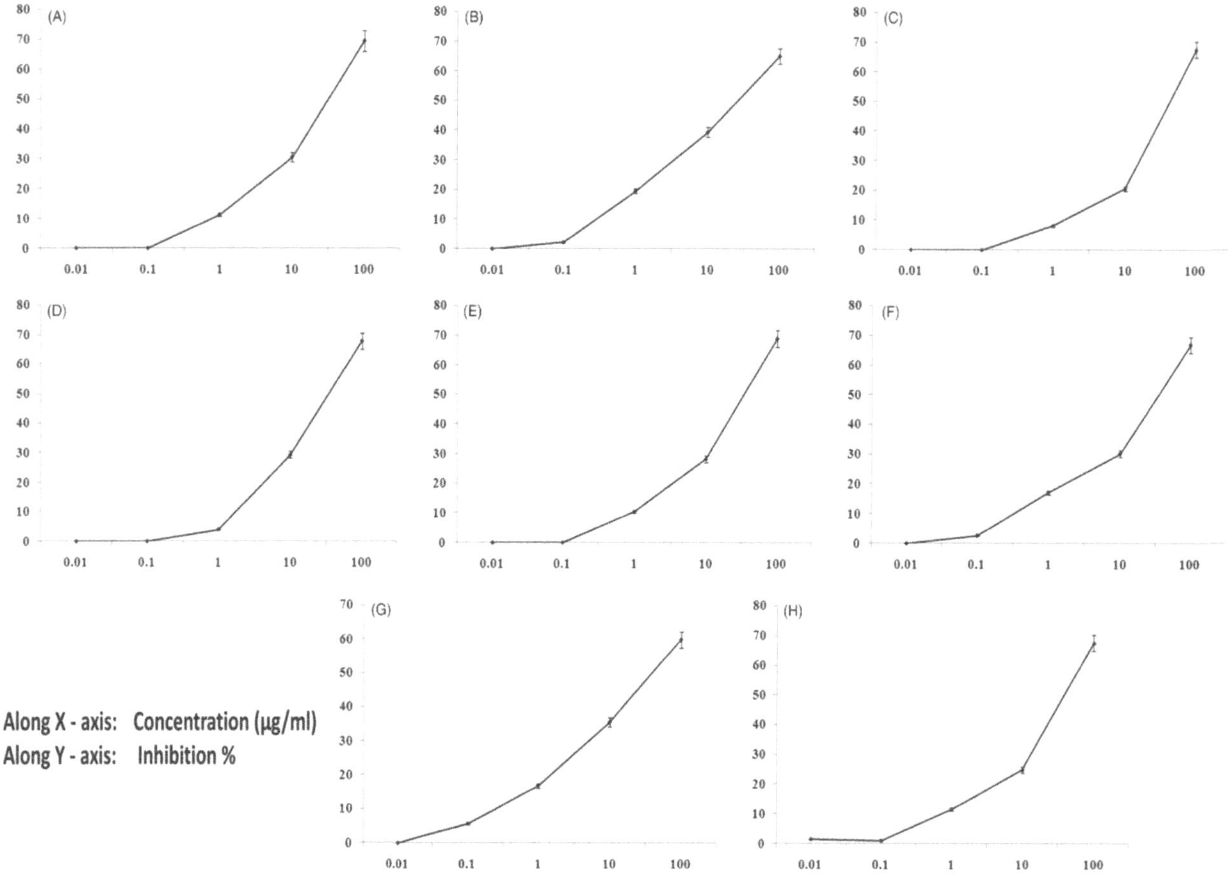

Fig. 35.3 Anticancer activity of *T. clypeatus* (aqueous extract): MAD-MB-468 (A), HL-60 (B), Hep G2 (C), A549 (D), U-937 (E), Y-79 (F), U-373MG (G) and OAW-42 (H) [22]

References

1. Shamim, M. Z., Mishra, A. K., Kausar, T., Mahanta, S., Sarma, B., Kumar, V., et al. (2023). Exploring Edible Mushrooms for Diabetes: Unveiling Their Role in Prevention and Treatment. *Molecules*, 28, 2837.
2. Nayak, D., Mishra, A. K., Malla, S., Swain, U., Panigrahi, K., Panda, J., et al. (2024). Eco-Friendly Mycogenic Synthesis of Iron Oxide Nanoparticles Using Volvariella volvacea and Unveiling its Potential as Antibiofilm and Anticancer Agents. *ECS J. Solid State Sci. Technol.*, 13, 087003.
3. Panda, J., Mishra, A. K., Nath, P. C., Mahanta, S., Sharma, M., Nayak, P. K., et al. (2024). Wild edible mushrooms to achieve sustainable development goals: Novel sources for food security, health, and well-being. *Food Biosci.*, 60, 104277.
4. Panda, J., and Gupta, N. (2022). Bioactive Potential of Different Solvent Extracts of Some Woody and Fleshy Mushrooms. *Mushroom Res.*, 30, 207–211.
5. Panda, M., Barik, K., Thatoi, H., and Tayung, K. (2018). Diversity of Wild Edible Mushrooms in Mayurbhanj District of Odisha, India. *Environ. Ecol.*, 6, 219–225.
6. Sachan, S. K. S., Patra, J. K., and Thatoi, H. N. (2013). Indigenous knowledge of ethnic tribes for utilization of wild mushrooms as food and medicine in similipal biosphere reserve, Odisha, India. *Int. J. Agric. Technol.*, 9, 335–348.
7. Tibuhwa, D. D. (2012). Termitomyces Species from Tanzania, Their Cultural Properties and Unequalled Basidiospores. *J. Biol. Life Sci.*, 3, 140–159.
8. Aryal, H. P., and Budathoki, U. (2016). Ethnomycology of Termitomyces R. Heim in Nepal. *J. Yeast Fungal Res.*, 7, 28–38.
9. Dutta, A. K., and Acharya, K. (2014). Traditional and ethno-medicinal knowledge of mushrooms in West Bengal, India. *Asian J. Pharm. Clin. Res.*, 7, 36–41.
10. Sitotaw, R., Lulekal, E., and Abate, D. (2020). Ethnomycological study of edible and medicinal mushrooms in Menge District, Asossa Zone, Benshangul Gumuz Region, Ethiopia. *J. Ethnobiol. Ethnomed.*, 16, 11.
11. Atri, N. S., and Mridu (2018). Mushrooms—Some ethnomycological and sociobiological aspect. *Kavaka*, 51, 11–19.
12. Manna, S., Ray, D., and Roy, A. (2014). Tribal relation to spatio-temporal variation of wild mushrooms in eastern lateritic part of India. *Ethnobot. Res. Appl.*, 12, 15–24.
13. Venkatachalapathi, A., and Paulsamy, S. (2016). Exploration of wild medicinal mushroom species in Walayar valley, the Southern Western Ghats of Coimbatore District Tamil Nadu. *Mycosphere*, 7, 118–130.
14. Chandrawati, P. S., and Narendra Kumar, N. N. T. (2014). Macrofungal Wealth of Kusumhi Forest of Gorakhpur UP, India. *Am. Int. J. Res. Form. Appl. Nat. Sci.*, 5, 71–75.
15. Teka, A., Asfaw, Z., Demissew, S., and Van Damme, P. (2020). Medicinal plant use practice in four ethnic

communities (Gurage, Mareqo, Qebena, and Silti), south central Ethiopia. *J. Ethnobiol. Ethnomed.*, 16.

16. Due, E., Koffi, D., and Digbeu, Y. (2016). Physicochemical and Functional Properties of Flour from the Wild Edible Mushroom *Termitomyces heimii* Natarajan Harvested in Côte d'Ivoire. *Turkish J. Agric. - Food Sci. Technol.*, 4, 651.
17. Ache, N. T., Manju, E. B., Lawrence, M. N., and Tonjock, R. K. (2021). Nutrient and mineral components of wild edible mushrooms from the Kilum-Ijim forest, Cameroon. *African J. Food Sci.*, 15, 152–161.
18. Paloi, S., Kumla, J., Paloi, B. P., Srinuanpan, S., Hoijang, S., Karunarathna, S. C., et al. (2023). Termite Mushrooms (Termitomyces), a Potential Source of Nutrients and Bioactive Compounds Exhibiting Human Health Benefits: A Review. *J. fungi*, 9, 112.
19. Elkhateeb, A. W. (2020). Termitomyces Marvel Medicinal Mushroom Having a Unique Life Cycle. *J. Pharm. Res.*, 4, 000197.
20. Tabibzadeh, F., Alvandi, H., Hatamian-Zarmi, A., Kalitukha, L., Aghajani, H., and Ebrahimi-Hosseinzadeh, B. (2024). Antioxidant activity and cytotoxicity of exopolysaccharide from mushroom Hericium coralloides in submerged fermentation. *Biomass Convers. Biorefinery*, 14, 26953–26963.
21. Mitra, P., Khatua, S., Mandal, N., and Acharya, K. (2021). Beneficial properties of crude polysaccharides from Termitomyces medius of West Bengal to scavenge free radicals as well as boost immunity: A new report. *Res. J. Pharm. Technol.*, 14, 1073–1078.
22. Mondal, A., Banerjee, D., Majumder, R., Maity, T. K., and Khowala, S. (2016). Evaluation of in vitro antioxidant, anticancer and in vivo antitumour activity of Termitomyces clypeatus MTCC 5091. *Pharm. Biol.*, 54, 2536–2546.
23. Kungwani, N. A., Panda, J., Mishra, A. K., Chavda, N., Shukla, S., Vikhe, K., et al. (2024). Combating bacterial biofilms and related drug resistance: Role of phyto-derived adjuvant and nanomaterials. *Microb. Pathog.*, 106874.
24. Ahmad, R., Sellathoroe, S., Ngadi, E., Tengku Saharuddin, T. S., Zakaria, I. I., Selvakumaran, S., et al. (2021). Isolation, identification, cultivation and determination of antimicrobial β-glucan from a wild-termite mushroom *Termitomyces heimii* RFES 230662. *Biocatal. Agric. Biotechnol.*, 37, 102187.
25. Khumlianlal, J., Rajkumari, J., Keshry, S. S., Jena, S., Chattopadhyay, S., Mukherjee, P. K., et al. (2024). Analysis of nutritional value, antiviral potential and in vivo toxicological evaluation of Termitomyces clypeatus R. Hiem mycelial extract, a wild edible mushroom. *Food Biosci.*, 61, 104817.
26. Mahamat, O., André-Ledoux, N., Chrisopher, T., Mbifu, A. A., and Albert, K. (2018). Assessment of antimicrobial and immunomodulatory activities of termite associated fungi, *Termitomyces clypeatus* R. Heim (Lyophyllaceae, Basidiomycota). *Clin. Phytoscience,* 4, 28.
27. Singdevsachan, S. K., Patra, J. K., Tayung, K., Sarangi, K., and Thatoi, HrudayanathEvaluation of nutritional and nutraceutical potentials of three wild edible mushrooms from Similipal Biosphere Reserve, Odisha, I. (2014). Evaluation of nutritional and nutraceutical potentials of three wild edible mushrooms from Similipal Biosphere Reserve, Odisha, India. *J. fur Verbraucherschutz und Leb.*, 9, 111–120.
28. Giri, S., Biswas, G., Pradhan, P., Mandal, S. C., and Acharya, K. (2012). Antimicrobial activities of basidiocarps of wild edible mushrooms of West Bengal, India. *Int. J. PharmTech Res.*, 4, 1554–1560.
29. Jeitler, M., Michalsen, A., Frings, D., Hübner, M., Fischer, M., Koppold-Liebscher, D. A., et al. (2020). Significance of Medicinal Mushrooms in Integrative Oncology: A Narrative Review. *Front. Pharmacol.* 11.
30. Gebreyohannes, G., Nyerere, A., Bii, C., and Sbhatu, D. B. (2020). Investigation of Antioxidant and Antimicrobial Activities of Different Extracts of Auricularia and Termitomyces Species of Mushrooms. *Sci. World J.*, 7357048.
31. Zhao, S., Gao, Q., Rong, C., Wang, S., Zhao, Z., Liu, Y., et al. (2020). Immunomodulatory effects of edible and medicinal mushrooms and their bioactive immunoregulatory products. *J. Fungi,* 6, 1–37.
32. Ray, R., Saha, S., Pyne, N., Pal, A., and Paul, S. (2024). Neoergosterol-rich mushroom extract, resourced from wild edible mushroom Termitomyces heimii Natarajan, induces robust apoptosis against lung cancer. *South African J. Bot.*, 170, 229–249.

36 A Review on Molecular Cloning of Microbial Xylanase Gene

Arpita Sarangi
Department of Biotechnology,
Maharaja Sriram Chandra Bhanjadeo University,
Takatpur, Baripada, Odisha, India

Subhashree Rath, Hrudayanath Thatoi*
Center for Industrial Biotechnology,
Sikha 'O' Anusandhan Deemed to be University,
Bhubanseswar, Odisha, India

Abstract: Xylan, the most common and fundamental kind of hemicellulose, is made up of β-D xylopyranosyl units connected by glycosidic linkages (1-4). Microorganisms produce xylanases, which can degrade xylan into xylose. The mechanism of microbial xylan breakdown by microorganisms and their enzymes requires more research since the enzyme system is essential to examine the potential applications of xylan. Recent genomics advancements have helped to overcomeissues such as substrate scope, operational stability and restricted enzyme supply. Genes encoding xylanases have been cloned in both heterologous and homologous hosts to increase enzyme production and modify their characteristics for commercial purposes. Furthermore, recent advancements in molecular cloning and heterologous expression of microbial xylanase genes are discussed, emphasizing strategies for enhanced enzyme production, genetic engineering techniques, host selection, and promoter optimization. Cloning of xylanase genes has facilitated structural-functional studies and enabled the development of recombinant strains with superior enzymatic properties. The integration of omics approaches and synthetic biology holds promising prospects for future biotechnological applications. This review aims to provide a comprehensive understanding of microbial xylanases and the molecular tools employed for their cloning and expression, thereby offering insights for future research and industrial exploitation.

Keywords: Glycosidic linkages, Recombinant DNA, Xylanolytic enzyme, Cloning, Lignocellulosic biomass

1. Introduction

Hemicellulose is a potential polysaccharides found abundantly in plant biomass. These have complex structure composed of hexoses, pentoses, and other chemical remnants [1]. Xylan is the major component of this hemicellulose (20-30%) and is composed of xylose residues linked together by beta-1,4 linkage. Xylanases are key hydrolytic enzymes that degrade the β-1,4-xylosidic linkages in xylan, converting it into xylo-oligosaccharides and xylose. These enzymes play a vital role in the bioconversion of lignocellulosic biomass into fermentable sugars, which is central to the development of eco-friendly biotechnological processes. Microorganisms, particularly bacteria and fungi, are prolific producers of xylanases. Their ease of cultivation, high enzyme productivity, and adaptability to diverse environmental conditions make them ideal candidates for industrial enzyme production. Microbial xylanases are extensively used in various sectors, including the pulp and paper industry (for biobleaching), animal feed (to improve digestibility), food and beverage (for clarification and baking), textiles, and

*Corresponding author: hnthatoi@gmail.com

DOI: 10.1201/9781003759003-36

biofuel production. Advancements in genetic engineering and molecular biology have opened new avenues for enhancing xylanase production through molecular cloning and recombinant DNA technologies. Cloning of microbial xylanase genes into suitable expression systems not only improves yield and stability but also allows for the engineering of enzymes with desired properties such as thermostability, alkali tolerance, and substrate specificity [2].

Recombinant DNA has helped build industrial-grade xylanolytic enzymes [3, 4]. Many industrially significant enzyme genes have been cloned and expressed to produce more enzymes, better use substrates, and achieve other economically beneficial traits [9]. A certain enzyme is hard to extract in pure form from a bacterial preparation. For this reason, recombinant DNA technology can be used more successfully [6]. The creation of xylanolytic systems devoid of cellulolytic enzymes and the introduction of xylanase and xylosidase genes to improve the fermentation properties of industrially significant organisms are the primary obstacles facing recombinant DNA technology in xylan bioconversion [5]. Genes for xylanases have been cloned in homologous and heterologous hosts to overproduce and alter the enzyme for commercial usage [7,8]. This review examines a variety of molecular techniques that are employed to enhance the physiological properties of xylanases for commercial use in industries, including site-directed mutagenesis, metagenomic approaches,TAIL-PCR, genome-walking PCRand StEP recombination.

2. Xylan and Xylanases

Xylan, a heteropolysaccharide, is replaced with monosaccharides like D-galactose, L-arabinose, and D-mannoses, as well as organic acids like ferulic acid, glucuronic acid and acetic acid. These are subsequently woven together to generate hemicelluloses via glycosidic and ester linkages [10]. It comprises 15-20% of hardwoods and 7-10% of softwood. Depolymerization of xylan is needed for efficient industrial applications. Xylanase, a group of enzymes, depolymerizes xylan into simple monosaccharides and xylooligosaccharides [11]. Microorganisms like bacteria, fungi, and actinomycetes are the primary producers of xylanases on an industrial scale [12]. In recent years, xylanase has been used in several sectors, including medicines, feed, food, paper,and pulp bleaching.Thus, to produce xylanase, powerful microorganisms must be chosen, and the components of the medium must then be optimized for maximum output. In this context, the discovery of sophisticated biotechnological methods, such as rDNA technology, has prompted several attempts to locate, separate, and clone the xylanase gene in an appropriate system. Using this method makes it easier to develop effective microorganisms with the required qualities for increased xylanase production.

3. Molecular Approaches for Xylanase Production

Computational design, molecular dynamics, and X-ray crystallographic data all offer information that confirms the structure-function link of xylanases and makes it easier to create the "ideal xylanase" that can survive the harsh conditions seen in commercial operations. As a result, great efforts are undertaken to increase the stability of xylanase at higher temperatures and alkaline pH. The rDNA technique allows for the rational design of proteins.This might improve the unique properties of current xylanases. Designing a suitable xylanase requires understanding its behavior, thermostabilizing domains, including catalytic areas, essential amino acids, substrate binding domains, and covalent and non-covalent interactions [13]. Recombinant xylanase synthesis has been reported from a variety of hosts, such as yeast and bacteria, in the past. The overproduction of the enzyme and the modification of its properties for commercial use have been facilitated by the cloning of xylanase-encoding genes in both heterologous and homologous hosts [14, 15]. The rapid growth of this host on inexpensive media, the simplicity of its transformation techniques, and the ease of protein isolation and purification are all factors contributing to its success as a recombinant expression platform.

4. Cloning Xylanase Gene using Metagenomic Approaches

Metagenomics is a powerful tool for bioprospection and discovering bioactive molecules from extreme ecosystems with unique features. Evolution has created diverse physiologies and molecular adaptations for microorganisms, useful in technical processes. However, most microorganisms cannot be cultured in the lab, leading to the use of culture-independent approaches. These methods involve cloning DNA from environmental samples, constructing genomic libraries, and analyzing them for novel genes or pathways. This approach maximizes the potential of naturally occurring microbial resources. It is necessary to use metagenomic technology to strengthen the future research for bacterial xylanases from uncultured microorganisms.A clone (TSDV-MX1) was detected in a screening library, displaying xylan hydrolysis. The xylanase gene was subcloned into a vector and expressed in *E. coli* BL21. The recombinant xylanase showed activity over various pH and temperature ranges, with optimal activity at pH 9.0 and 80°C [16]. In an effort to generate metagenomic DNA libraries for novel xylanases, a study was conducted that employed controlled decomposition and environmental enrichment. One enzyme, XYL40, demonstrated superior efficacy in the hydrolysis of wheat straw [17].Tengchong hot spring yielded a unique xylanase gene, xynDRTY1, which was then refined for use in biotechnological applications. 73.43% of the amino acid sequence matched that of a protein from the *Bryobacterales* bacterium. The gene showed activity with natural glycosides and was synthesized and overexpressed in *E. coli*. At 6.0 pH and 65 °C, it was thermostable, exhibiting 140% stability and 110% relative enzyme activity [18]. *B. sonorensis T6's* xylanase gene was cloned and expressed in *P. pastoris* (producing rXynT6-P) and *E. coli* (producing an enzyme known as rXynT6-E). It was discovered that the recombinant xylanases were most active between 47 and 55°C and pH 6.0 and 7.0. compared to that produced in *E. coli*, the recombinant xylanase expressed in *P. pastoris* has 40% greater heat stability. Recombinant xylanases maintained 100% activity after 10 hours in pH 3-11, 68% at pH 2.0, with ideal conditions rXynT6-E and rXynT6-P having 1030.2 and 873.8 U/mg, respectively [19]. *Thxyn11A, a xylanase gene cloned from Thermobifida halotolerans* YIM 90462 T strain, was produced using E. coli, with 80% of mature xylanase from Nocardiopsis dassonvillei DSM 43111 containing the same ORF.A GH11 domain-containing enzyme with a high isoelectric point (9.1), Thxyn11A is distinct from other xylanases due to its massive molecular mass. It can withstand extreme pH and temperature changes; at pH 9.0 and 70 °C, it is most active [20]. The xynA gene, encoding xylanase A of *Paenibacillus* sp. DG-22, was extracted using PCR amplification and screened for positive clones using Congo-red staining. The 630-bp open reading frame encodes a 210-amino acid protein with a 28-residue signal peptide. The cloned DNA fragment shares 76% identity with the transcriptional activator of *B. halodurans* C-125. The xynA e was subcloned into the pQE60 expression vector [21]. The KRICT PX1 gene, found in *Paenibacillus* sp. strain HPL-001, is highly active against birchwood xylan and has been cloned and expressed in *E. coli*, with optimal activity at pH 5.5 and 9.5 at 50 °C [22]. A 642 bp xylanase gene was isolated, cloned in *E. coli* BL21 cells, and optimal pH and temperature for enzyme activity were 60°C and 6.5°C [23]. The xylanase-encoding gene xyn1923, found in *Microbacterium imperiale* YD-01, is a 1352 amino acid protein that maintains over 85% of its initial activity after 16 hours of incubation at pH 9.0 [24]. *B. velezensis* and *S. rochei* produced two endo-xylanases, with SrocXyn10 showing the highest degree of identity at 77.22%. Its stability was exceptional at 45°C or pH 4.5-11.0, while rBvelXyn11-Ec was most active at pH 6.0 and 50°C. Both enzymes showed specific activity on wheat arabinoxylan [25]. The *B. amyloliquefaciens* xynA gene was amplified, cloned into the pCold vector, and expressed in *E. coli* to evaluate its thermostability. The pCold vector, with its unique characteristics, showed high temperature and pH resistance. The cloned xynA-pCold (rxynApC) produced the xynA gene, with a molecular weight of 27 kDa. The optimal temperature and pH for rxynApC activity were 70°C and 8.0°P, with 90% residual activity at pH 8.0. The thermogravimetric analysis revealed high stability of the cloned enzyme [26]. *Allostreptomyces psammosilenae* YIM DR4008 T provided the xylanase gene (576 bp), known as apxyn11a, which was cloned and produced heterologously in *E. coli* BL21 (DE3). Ni 2+-affinity chromatography was used to identify and purify the recombinant xylanase (ApXyn11A). The recombinant ApXyn11A has a molecular weight of 22.7 kDa. Its ideal pH was 5.6 and its ideal reaction temperature was 65°C. After being incubated for 120 minutes at 55°C, it retained over 95% relative activity, and after being incubated for 24 hours at pH 4.0–6.0, it retained over 80% residual activity [27]. The XyA gene, a deduced xylanase with a family 11 catalytic domain and signal peptide, was cloned in *E. coli* DH5α cells using the pUC19 vector after isolation from *B. velezensis* RB.IBE29 genomic DNA. The pColdII vector was used to express xyA in E. coli BL21-CodonPlus (DE3)-RIPL cells [28]. The cspA promoter's distinctive feature is that it produced a high yield of the alkali- and thermostable-property rxynApC enzyme in the surrogate host *E. coli*. Thus, considering its thermostability and

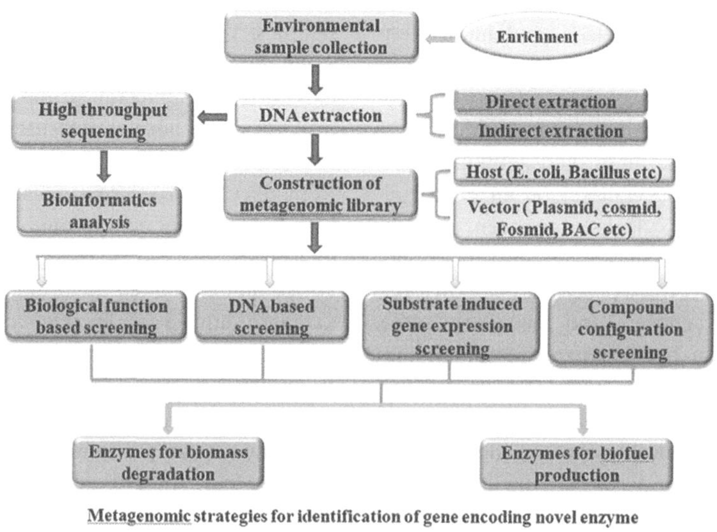

Fig. 36.1 Metagenomic strategies for identification of gene encoding novel enzyme

Table 36.1 Different approaches for xylanase production and their application in various industrial processes

Microbial source	Cloning strategy	Expression host	Vector	Optimal condition	Enzyme activity	Yield % after cloning	Industrial application	Reference
Bacillus sonorensis T6	PCR amplification and codon optimization	*E. coli, P, pastoris*	pET	pH 6.0 and 47 °C(E. coli) and pH 7.o and 55 °C (P. pastoris)	1030.2 and 873.8 U/mg	NA	**Biomass degradation, biofuel production**	[19]
Thermobifida halotolerans strain YIM 90462 T	PCR amplification of thxyn11A xylanase gene followed by expression	*E. coli*	pET-28a (+) vector	pH 7.0, **50-55°C**.	**2,500 U/mL**	NA	**Biofuel production, agricultural waste degradation, ligno-cellulosic biomass degradation**	[20]
Bacillus halodurans C-125	PCR amplification xylanase gene followed by expressionIn suitable vector	*E. coli*	pET-28a (+)	pH 7.0, **50-55°C**.	**4,800 U/mL**	NA	**Biofuel production, agriculture waste degradation, and paper and pulp industries.**	[21]
Paenibacillus sp. strain HPL-001 (KCTC11365BP)	PCR amplification of the KRICT PX1 gene followed by cloning into an expression vector	*E. coli*	NA	pH range of 5.0 to 11.0, **50 °C**.	NA	NA	**Lignocellulosic biomass degradation, biofuel production,**	[22]
Bacillus subtilis RTS	PCR amplification of xyn xylanase gene followed by cloning into the pET21c expression vector	*E. coli* BL21	pET21c	pH 6.5, 60 °C	NA	NA	**Biomass degradation, biofuel production**	[23]
Microbacterium imperiale YD-01	Full genome study led to the discovery of the xylanaseencoding gene **xyn1923.**	NA	NA	pH 7.0, **70°C**	NA	NA	**Biomass degrada-tion, biofuel produc-tion, and paper/pulp industries.**	[24]

increased enzyme activity, the recombinant xynA gene may be used to meet various industrial applications [26].

5. Next Generation Xylanase Production by CRISPR Cas

CRISPR-Cas technology also has huge prospects for enhancing production of enzymes such as xylanase, particularly in industrial applications such as the use of biofuels, paper manufacturing, and animal feeding. It is applicable for silencing, activation, knockout, and knockin for numerous genes, as well as complete metabolic routes. Due to its simplicity and efficiency, the CRISPR/Cas method has already been used in several filamentous fungal species for a range of applications, such as the production of secondary metabolites, pathogenicity research, and heterologous protein production, including the cellulases and hemicellulases [29]. CRISPR-Cas9 can be utilized to improve the production of xylanase in microorganisms such as *A. niger* and *T. reesei*. This includes gene knockouts

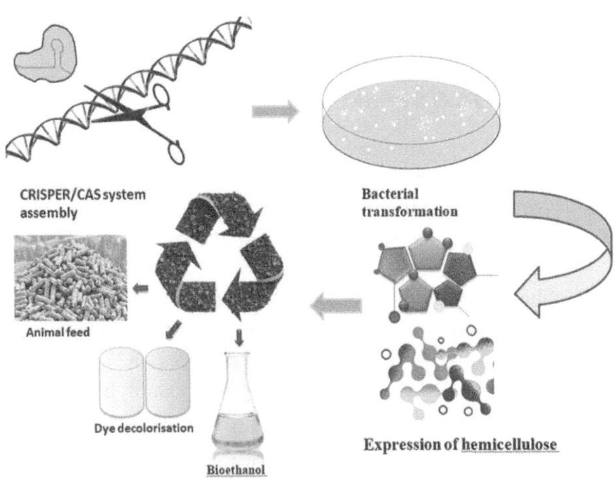

Fig. 36.2 CRISPER/CAS assembly system

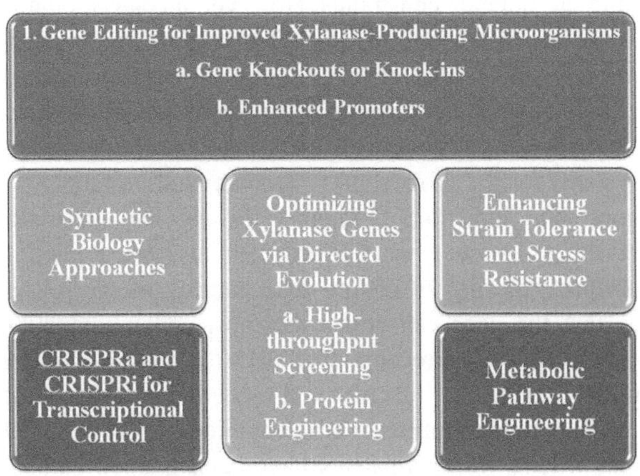

Fig. 36.3 Breakdown of how CRISPR-Cas could be used for next-generation xylanase production

or knock-ins, promoter improvement, and xylanase gene optimization by directed evolution. As β-xylosidase and endo-xylanase, the hemicellulases were introduced with a CRISPR-Cas9 system to enable the hydrolysis of xylan polymers and the XR/XDH pathway for *S. cerevisiae* to assimilate xylose monomers. The resulting strains grew on xylose-based medium and xylooligosaccharides, indicating that the β-xylosidase enzyme and the XR/XDH pathway were active [30].

Fig. 36.4 Challenges that can affect efficiency, scalability, and cost-effectiveness

6. Overcome the Limitation of the Traditional Xylanase Production Method by Advanced Cloning

Conventional methods involve cultivating microorganisms, which may face yield, stability, and time inefficiency constraints. However, advanced cloning methods involve isolating the xylanase gene from a source microorganism and cloning it into an appropriate host organism, like *E. coli*, yeast, or *Saccharomyces cerevisiae*. These approaches allow the identification ofeffective host systems for the production of recombinant proteins, with good and inducible promoters driving the expression of the xylanase gene. Cloning can also be applied to optimize the use of codons and stability of the mRNA so that the gene can utilize the most codon-compatible codons. Recently, recombinant DNA technology has been utilised to extract, identify, and clone the xylanase gene, enabling the generation of efficient microbes for increased output [31]. Various patents have been granted globally for genetic modification of microbial strains for xylanase production. Gram-positive bacteria [32] like *B. subtilis* and *Lactobacillus* species are used for expression of xylanase because they have the ability to N-glycosylate and secrete higher levels of protein [33]. These organisms are better adapted for heterologous expression of protein due to the fact that by virtue of being Generally Recognised as Safe (GRAS), they represent an attractive substitute for xylanase production [34].

7. Conclusion

Xylanases are essential enzymes in various industries due to their ability to degrade xylan, a key component of hemicellulose. Microbial sources offer a promising platform for sustainable xylanase production. However, traditional methods are limited by low yield, specificity, stability, and purification difficulties. Recent molecular approaches, such as recombinant DNA technology, have revolutionized enzyme biotechnology. Cloning and expression of xylanase genes in host systems has enhanced production and enabled functional modification. Metagenomic techniques and genome-editing tools are essential for optimizing xylanase expression and regulation. In summary, the future of xylanase production lies in harnessing modern molecular and computational tools to create robust, high-yielding microbial systems capable of producing highly efficient enzymes, thus paving the way for greener and more cost-effective bioprocessing technologies.

Authors' Contributions

AS and SR formatted and contributed to writing the original review. HT supervised the whole work, conceptualized the research, and guided the writing & editing of the manuscript.

Acknowledgements

The author expresses gratitude to Siksha 'O' Anusandhan Odisha, Director of the Centre for Industrial Biotechnology Research, for providing valuable knowledge and assistance in conducting the research work, and to DST for providing funds for the research.

References

1. Elgharbi, F., Hmida-Sayari, A., Zaafouri, Y., & Bejar, S. (2015). Expression of an Aspergillus niger xylanase in yeast: Application in breadmaking and in vitro digestion. *International journal of biological macromolecules, 79*, 103–109.
2. Sharma, N., & Sharma, N. (2017). Microbial xylanases and their industrial applications as well as future perspectives: a review. *Global J. Biol. Agric. Health Sci, 6*(3), 5–12.
3. Sunna, A., & Antranikian, G. (1997). Xylanolytic enzymes from fungi and bacteria. *Critical reviews in biotechnology, 17*(1), 39–67.
4. Beg, Q., Kapoor, M., Mahajan, L., & Hoondal, G. S. (2001). Microbial xylanases and their industrial applications:

a review. *Applied microbiology and biotechnology*, *56*, 326–338.

5. Biely, P. (1985). Microbial xylanolytic systems. *Trends in biotechnology*, *3*(11), 286–290.
6. Korona, B., Korona, D., & Bielecki, S. (2006). Efficient expression and secretion of two co-produced xylanases from Aspergillus niger in Pichia pastoris directed by their native signal peptides and the Saccharomyces cerevisiae α-mating factor. *Enzyme and microbial technology*, *39*(4), 683–689.
7. Baba, T., Shinke, R., & Nanmori, T. (1994). Identification and characterization of clustered genes for thermostable xylan-degrading enzymes, beta-xylosidase and xylanase, of Bacillus stearothermophilus 21. *Applied and environmental microbiology*, *60*(7), 2252–2258.
8. Jamil, A., Nairn, S., Ahmad, S., & Ashraf, M. (2005). Production of industrially important enzymes using molecular approaches with special reference to xylanases and cellulases. *Genetic resources and Biotechnology*, *2*, 143.
9. Sharma, P. K., & Chand, D. (2012). Purification and characterization of thermostable cellulase free xylanase from Pseudomonas Sp. XPB-6. *Advances in Microbiology*, *2*(1), 17–25.
10. Bhardwaj, N., Chanda, K., Kumar, B., Prasad, H. K., Sharma, G. D., & Verma, P. (2017). Statistical optimization of nutritional and physical parameters for xylanase production from newly isolated Aspergillus oryzae LC1 and its application in the hydrolysis of lignocellulosic agro-residues. *BioResources*, *12*(4), 8519–8538.
11. Walia, A., Guleria, S., Mehta, P., Chauhan, A., & Parkash, J. (2017). Microbial xylanases and their industrial application in pulp and paper biobleaching: a review. *3 Biotech*, *7*, 1–12.
12. Motta, F. L., Andrade, C. C. P., & Santana, M. H. A. (2013). A Review of Xylanase Production by the Fermentation of Xylan: classification. *Sustainable Degradation of Lignocellulosic Biomass: Techniques, Applications and Commercialization*, 251.
13. Verma, D., & Satyanarayana, T. (2012). Molecular approaches for ameliorating microbial xylanases. *Bioresource technology*, *117*, 360–367.
14. Kallel, F., Driss, D., Chaari, F., Zouari-Ellouzi, S., Chaabouni, M., Ghorbel, R., & Chaabouni, S. E. (2016). Statistical optimization of low-cost production of an acidic xylanase by Bacillus mojavensis UEB-FK: its potential applications. *Biocatalysis and Agricultural Biotechnology*, *5*, 1–10.
15. Thomas, L., Joseph, A., Singhania, R. R., Patel, A. K., & Pandey, A. (2017). Industrial enzymes: xylanases. In *Current developments in biotechnology and bioengineering* (pp. 127–148). Elsevier.
16. Verma, D., & Satyanarayana, T. (2013). Production of cellulase-free xylanase by the recombinant Bacillus subtilis and its applicability in paper pulp bleaching. *Biotechnology Progress*, *29*(6), 1441–1447.
17. Ellilä, S., Bromann, P., Nyyssönen, M., Itävaara, M., Koivula, A., Paulin, L., & Kruus, K. (2019). Cloning of novel bacterial xylanases from lignocellulose-enriched compost metagenomic libraries. *AMB Express*, *9*, 1–12.
18. Yin, Y. R., Li, L., Yang, R. F., Li, X. W., Liu, H. Y., Sang, P., & Yang, L. Q. (2024). Characterization of a metagenome-derived thermostable xylanase from Tengchong hot spring. *Biomass Conversion and Biorefinery*, *14*(9), 10027–10034.
19. Kiribayeva, A., Mukanov, B., Silayev, D., Akishev, Z., Ramankulov, Y., & Khassenov, B. (2022). Cloning, expression, and characterization of a recombinant xylanase from Bacillus sonorensis T6. *PLoS One*, *17*(3), e0265647.
20. Zhang, F., Chen, J. J., Ren, W. Z., Lin, L. B., Zhou, Y., Zhi, X. Y., Tang, S. K., & Li, W. J. (2012). Cloning, expression, and characterization of an alkaline thermostable GH11 xylanase from Thermobifida halotolerans YIM 90462T. *Journal of Industrial Microbiology and Biotechnology*, *39*(8), 1109–1116.
21. Lee, T. H., Lim, P. O., & Lee, Y. E. (2007). Cloning, characterization, and expression of xylanase A gene from Paenibacillus sp. DG-22 in Escherichia coli. *Journal of Microbiology and Biotechnology*, *17*(1), 29–36.
22. Hwang, I. T., Lim, H. K., Song, H. Y., Cho, S. J., Chang, J. S., & Park, N. J. (2010). Cloning and characterization of a xylanase, KRICT PX1 from the strain Paenibacillus sp. HPL-001. *Biotechnology advances*, *28*(5), 594–601.
23. Saleem, A., Waris, S., Ahmed, T., & Tabassum, R. (2021). Biochemical characterization and molecular docking of cloned xylanase gene from Bacillus subtilis RTS expressed in E. coli. *International Journal of Biological Macromolecules*, *168*, 310–321.
24. Tang, K., Cui, Y., Xiao, J., Ding, M., Chao, H., Wu, J., Han, Z., Liu, J., Li, X., & Yan, D. (2021). Molecular cloning and characterization of a novel xylanase from *Microbacterium imperiale* YD-01. *Journal of Food Biochemistry*, *45*(12), e13988.
25. Zhang, J., Qin, Y., Wang, Q., Liu, S., Zhou, J., He, B., Liang, X., Xian, L., & Wu, J. (2023). Gene cloning, expression, and characterization of two endo-xylanases from Bacillus velezensis and Streptomyces rochei, and their application in xylooligosaccharide production. *Frontiers in Microbiology*, *14*, 1292726.
26. Patel, D. K., & Dave, G. (2022). pCold-assisted expression of a thermostable xylanase from Bacillus amyloliquefaciens: cloning, expression and characterization. *3 Biotech*, *12*(10), 245.
27. Li, X.W., Zhu, D., Li, L., Yang, R.F., Fan, S.Y., Lv, Z.H., Rao, M.D., Song, R.H., Sang, P., Yin, Y.R. & Yang, L.Q. (2023). Cloning, heterologus expression and characterization of a thermophilic and salt tolerant GH11 xylanase from Allostreptomyces psammosilenae YIM DR4008 T.
28. Tran, D. M., Huynh, T. U., Nguyen, T. H., Do, T. O., & Nguyen, A. D. (2024). Data on gene cloning, expression, purification, and characterization of the glycoside hydrolase family 11 from Bacillus velezensis. *Data in Brief*, *52*, 109834.
29. Silva, F.F., Rabelo, N.G., Reis, K.C., Cassiano, C.S.S., de Melo, A.F., de Oliveira Lopes, D., de Souza, W.R., Rodrigues, M.Q.R. and Gonçalves, D.B. (2024). Foreshadowing an exponential market: A brief story, applications, and perspectives of CRISPR/Cas system for the production of (hemi-) cellulases in filamentous fungi. *Fungal Biology Reviews*, *49*, p.100366.

30. Lönnqvist, E. (2023). Development of xylan-and xylose assimilating Saccharomyces cerevisiae using CRISPR-Cas9 technology.
31. Bhardwaj, N., Kumar, B., & Verma, P. (2019). A detailed overview of xylanases: an emerging biomolecule for current and future prospective. *Bioresources and Bioprocessing*, *6*(1), 1–36.
32. Chang, S., Guo, Y., Wu, B., & He, B. (2017). Extracellular expression of alkali tolerant xylanase from Bacillus subtilis Lucky9 in E. coli and application for xylooligosaccharides production from agro-industrial waste. *International Journal of Biological Macromolecules*, *96*, 249–256.
33. Liu, Z., Dai, X., Zhang, J., Xu, J., Duan, S., Zheng, K., Feng, X., Cheng, L. and Shi, J. (2011). Screening of a xylanase high-producing strain and its rapid separation and purification. *Annals of microbiology*, *61*, pp.901–906.
34. Malhotra, G., & Chapadgaonkar, S. S. (2018). Production and applications of xylanases–an overview. *BioTechnologia. Journal of Biotechnology Computational Biology and Bionanotechnology*, *99*(1).

Note: All the figures and the table in this chapter were made by the authors.

Research and Innovations in Industrial and Marine Biotechnology: A Circular Economy 2024 – Prof. Hrudayanath Thatoi et al. (eds)

37 Recent Advancement and Application of Gallic Acid in Industrial, Pharmaceutical, and Agricultural Field

Sangram Basudev Mallik, Pratikshya Parhi, Bikash Ranjan Giri
Centre for Industrial Biotechnology Research, Siksha 'O' Anusandhan Deemed to be University, Kalinganagar, Odisha, India

Mehak Kanwar
Centre for Industrial Biotechnology Research, Siksha 'O' Anusandhan Deemed to be University, Kalinganagar, Odisha, India
Department of Physiology, Immunology Laboratory, University of Calcutta, University Colleges of Science and Technology, 92 APC Road, Kolkata, West Bengal, India

Pradeep Kumar Das Mohapatra
Department of Microbiology, Raiganj University, Raiganj, Uttar Dinajpur, West Bengal, India

Hrudayanath Thatoi, Amrita Banerjee*
Centre for Industrial Biotechnology Research, Siksha 'O' Anusandhan Deemed to be University, Kalinganagar, Odisha, India

Abstract: The naturally occurring tri-phenolic compound Gallic acid (GA) exists widely in plants and scientists study it extensively because of its various pharmaceutical properties and industrial uses. The review presents an overview of existing knowledge regarding GA's biochemical features together with its pharmacological effects and therapeutic applications. The review demonstrates how Gallic acid produces antioxidant and anti-inflammatory effects, anticancer, antidiabetic, neuroprotective and antimicrobial effects by modifying NF-κB, MAPK, PI3K/Akt and PPARγsignaling pathways. The pharmaceutical industry should consider GA because it shows potential to manage oxidative stress while blocking tumour growth and improving insulin sensitivity, protecting neural tissues. The bioactive compound Gallic acid functions as a multifunctional substance in food preservation, cosmetics and agriculture applications. Research into advanced delivery systems and sustainable applications continues to demonstrate the expanding importance of Gallic acid across different sectors.

Keywords: Gallic acid, Pharmacological activities, Anti-oxidant and anti-inflammatory effects, Therapeutic applications, Polyphenolic compound

1. Introduction

Plant metabolites known as polyphenolic compounds contain at least one aromatic ring structure together with multiple hydroxyl groups which serve vital functions in plant defence and human wellness [1]. The everyday foods contain these compounds which scientists divide into four subgroups including flavonoid stannins, phenolic acids and anthocyanins [2]. The therapeutic value of gallic acid (GA) stands out because it exists as a low molecular weight tri-phenolic acid which occurs widely in plants. The compound exists in nature as both free molecules and hydrolysable tannins called gallotannins [3]. The compound gallic acid exists naturally in tea leaves as well as in oak bark [4], galls [5], various fruits including apples, grapes, and berries [6]. The multiple beneficial properties of GA including antioxidant effects, anti-inflammatory, anticancer, antimicrobial and neuroprotective activities

*Corresponding author: amritabanerjee@soa.ac.in

DOI: 10.1201/9781003759003-37

have made it a promising bioactive compound for pharmaceutical, food and agricultural industries [7, 8]

2. Chemical Structure of Gallic Acid

The crystalline compound Gallic acid appears as yellowish-white crystals that possess the molecular formula $C_7H_6O_5$ with a molecular weight of 170.12 g/mol. A benzene ring structure exists within the compound while hydroxyl groups occupy positions 3, 4 and 5 and the compound features a carboxylic acid group at position 1. The antioxidant properties together with redox potential emerge from its particular molecular structure (Fig. 37.1.). The molecule adopts a planar shape which preserves its structural integrity [9] . Gallic acid appears in free form and as gallate esters and hydrolysable tannins within different plant tissues [10].

3. Pharmacological Properties of Gallic Acid

3.1 Antioxidant Activity

Gallic acid (GA) attains its antioxidant properties through the three hydroxyl groups which neutralize reactive oxygen species (ROS) and free radicals. The antioxidant mechanism of GA protects biomolecules from oxidative stress because this pathway serves as the main mechanism in aging cancer and neurodegenerative diseases [11]. The antioxidant properties of GA function through three different pathways to prevent lipid peroxidation while boosting antioxidant enzymes and performing resonance processes that stabilize free radicals [12]. GA functions by controlling natural defense systems to sustain redox equilibrium which positions it as a therapeutic candidate to treat disorders linked to oxidative stress (Fig. 37.2.) [7].

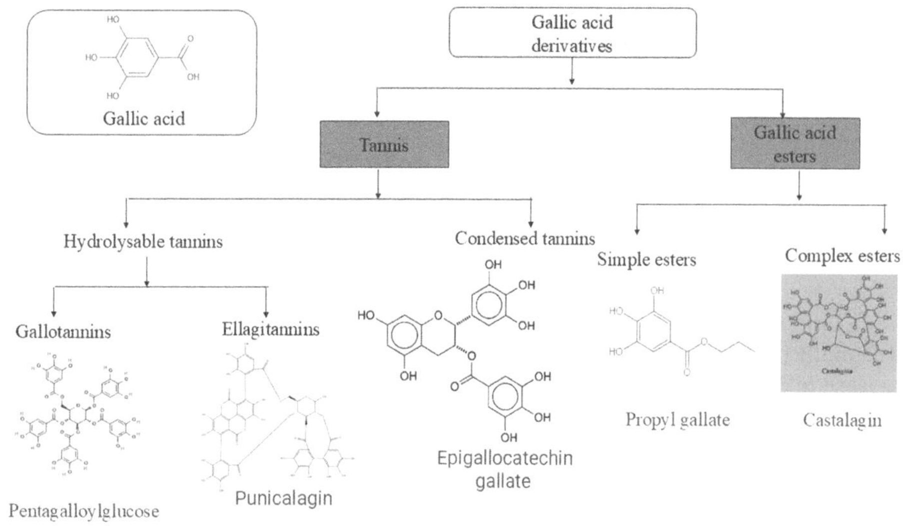

Fig. 37.1 General classification and main natural sources of GA and its derivatives

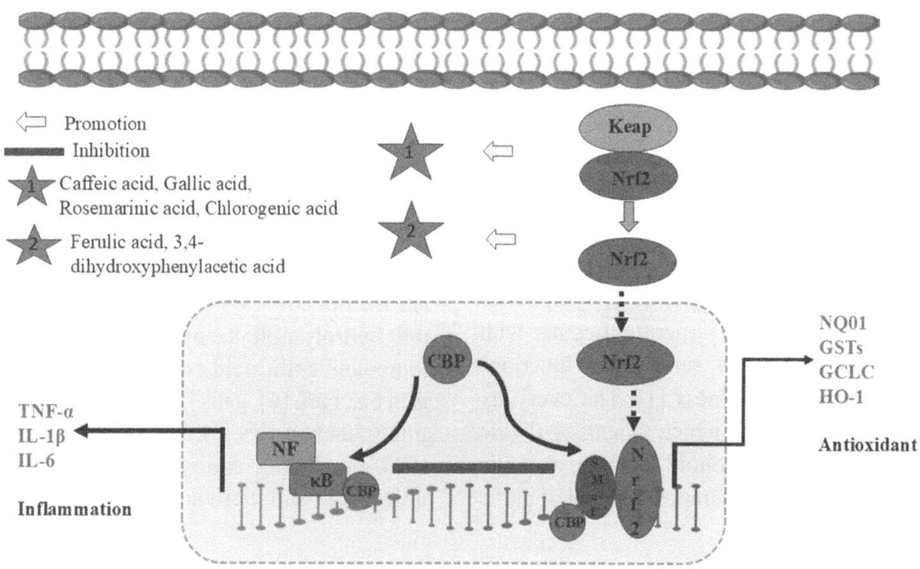

Fig. 37.2 Pathway showing antioxidant and anti-inflammatory activity

3.2 Anti-inflammatory Activity

The scientific community has extensively studied gallic acid for its anti-inflammatory properties which show promise in treating arthritis along with inflammatory bowel disease (IBD) and respiratory conditions [12]. The NF-kB and MAPK signaling pathways experience modifications through gallic acid treatment which results in the suppression of TNF-α, IL-6 and IL-1β pro-inflammatory cytokines [13]. The anti-inflammatory effects of GA remain significant throughout extended periods because of its ability to activate NF-kB and Nrf2 pathways both in laboratory tests and biological systems [14]. The NF-kB activation,signaling pathway suppression, inflammatory mRNA and protein expression suppression are the mechanisms by which GA exerts its anti-inflammatory action (Fig. 37.2.) [9].

3.3 Anti-Cancer Activity

Gallic acid (GA) demonstrates anticancer properties through its ability to trigger cancer cell death and prevent cancer cell movement and cell cycle advancement in different tumor cell lines. The compound triggers cancer cell death through p53, p38 MAPK and Wnt/β-catenin signaling pathway activation without affecting normal cells [15]. The compound enhances cancer cells' sensitivity to chemotherapy and radiotherapy treatments [7]. The compound attacks multiple pathways while maintaining low toxicity levels which makes it suitable as an additional cancer treatment (Fig. 37.3.).

3.4 Neuroprotective Activity

Gallic acid (GA) protects the brain through its mechanism of decreasing oxidative stress, blocking inflammation and protecting neurons (Fig. 37.2.). The compound protects against neurodegenerative diseases including Alzheimer's and Parkinson's through its ability to manage signalling pathways and inhibit pro-inflammatory cytokines [16]. The compound regulates brain-derived neurotrophic factor (BDNF) expression to promote neurogenesis and synaptic plasticity [17]. The blood-brain barrier permeability of GA is possible because of its antioxidant and anti-inflammatory properties which suggests therapeutic potential for neurodegenerative disease treatment (Fig. 37.4.).

3.5 Anti Diabetes Activity

Gallic acid (GA) demonstrates antidiabetic effects through two mechanisms which enhance insulin sensitivity and simultaneously lead to decrement of oxidative stress while preserving normal glucose metabolism. The PI3K/Akt and PPAR-γ pathways activated by GA lead to increased GLUT4 expression and improved insulin-dependent glucose uptake in insulin-responsive tissues [18]. The protective effects of GA on blood sugar regulation and pancreatic β-cell function emerge from its ability to decrease inflammatory cytokines and oxidative markers [9]. The dual antioxidant and anti-inflammatory properties of GA make it a promising therapeutic agent for diabetes management because these characteristics protect against neuropathy, nephropathy, and cardiovascular disease complications (Fig. 37.5.).

3.6 Anti-Obesity Activity

The weight loss properties of Gallic acid (GA) stem from its dual action on metabolic pathways and its ability to boost energy consumption and improve insulin sensitivity. The PI3K/Akt and AMPK signalling pathways become active when exposed to GA which results in increased expression of PPAR-γ and SIRT1/PGC1α leading to elevated mitochondrial biogenesis and adipose tissue browning [9]. The compound stops fat cell formation through reduced

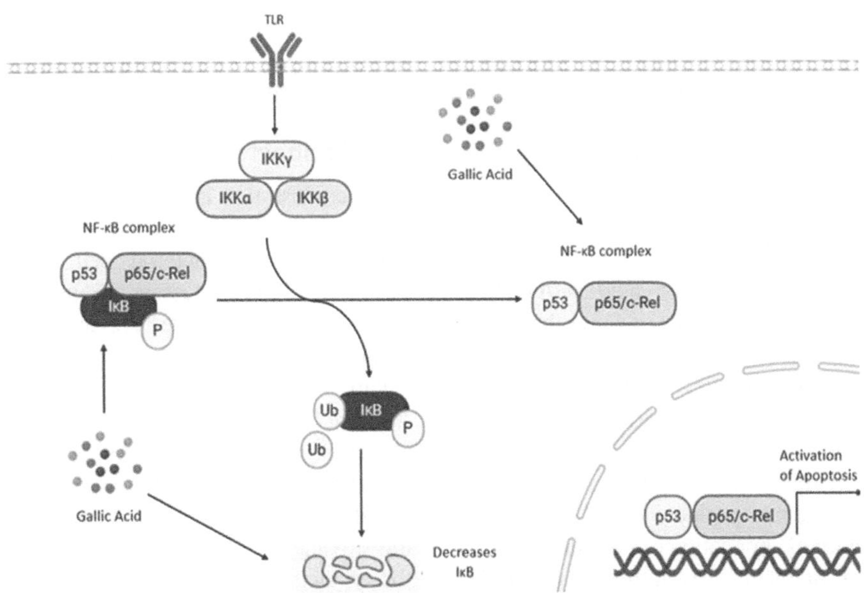

Fig. 37.3 Pathway showing anti-cancer activity

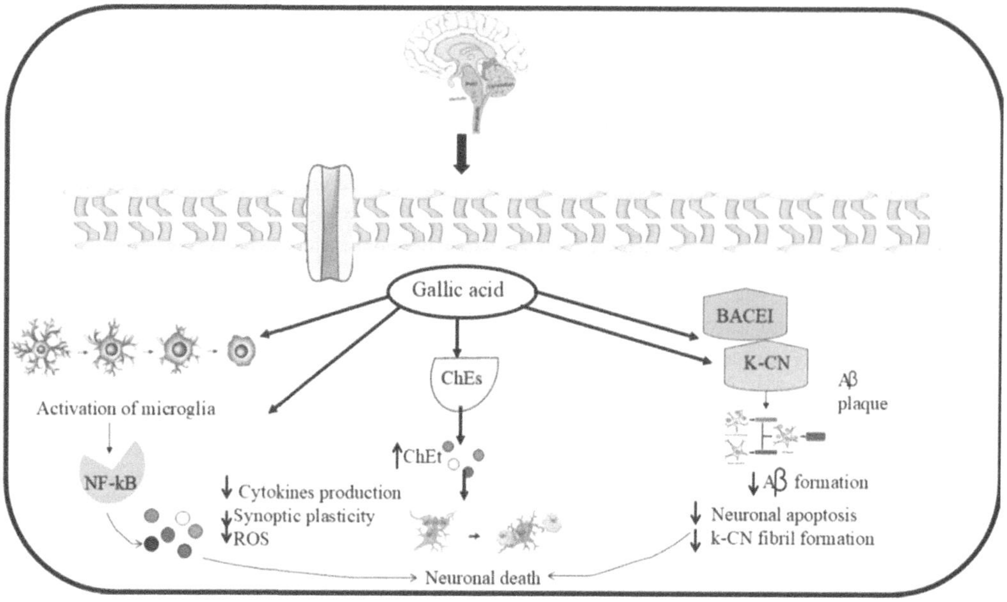

Fig. 37.4 Pathway showing neuroprotective activity

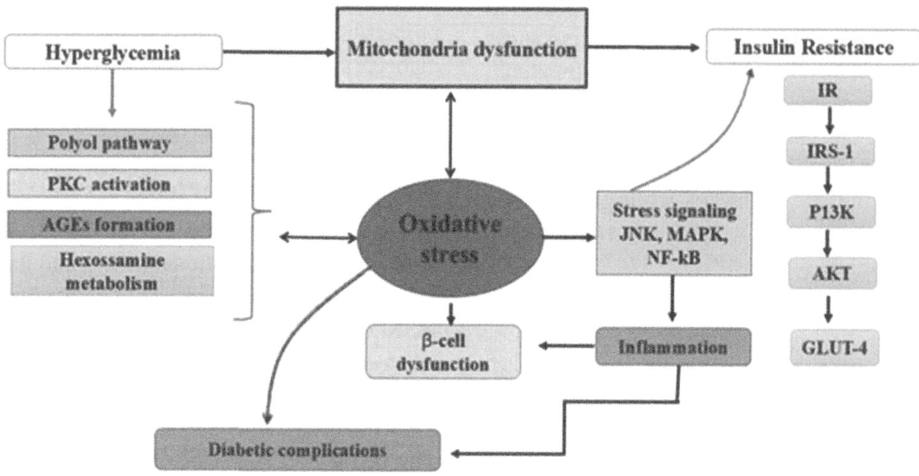

Fig. 37.5 Oxidative stress in diabetes

FAS, caspase activity and blocks cholesterol production by blocking HMG-CoA reductase. The multiple effects of GA lead to reduced fat storage and better metabolic health which makes it a promising natural therapeutic agent for obesity and related metabolic disorders.

3.7 Antifungal Properties

The antifungal properties of Gallic acid (GA) show effectiveness against multiple species of fungi that affect plants and humans. According to El-Nagar et al. [19] GA demonstrates antifungal properties by damaging fungal cell structures and blocking spore germination against *Fusarium solani* and *Alternaria solani*. GA protective phytochemical properties along with its derivatives prevent fungal colonization on plants and reduce fungal diseases. The agricultural application of GA demonstrates its value as a natural fungicide. The antifungal properties of GA together with its low toxicity make it suitable for developing environmentally friendly alternatives to synthetic antifungal agents

3.8 Antibacterial Activity

GA demonstrates antibacterial properties which affect numerous pathogenic bacteria. The research reveals that GA breaks bacterial cell membranes and halts essential cellular processes through its interference with dihydrofolate reductase enzymes [20]. GA exerts its antimicrobial action on both Gram-positive and Gram-negative bacteria which includes *Staphylococcus aureus, Escherichia coli, Listeria innocua* and *Pseudomonas sp.* GA exerts its antibacterial impact through modifications of pH levels and chelation of essential metal ions. The broad antibacterial properties of GA together with its low toxicity level make it a suitable natural substitute for synthetic antibiotics when used in food preservation, medical treatments and agricultural applications.

3.9 Anti-Viral Activity

The antiviral effects of gallic acid (GA) and its derivatives have proven effective against human rhinovirus, HIV-1 and HSV-1. Research indicates that GA prevents viral reproduction while interrupting host-virus connections which results in delayed viral progression [8]. The antiviral potency of GA246, MG247, and octyl gallate exceeds that of the parent compound. The dual functionality of GA and its low toxicity level make it an interesting option for developing wide-range antiviral pharmaceuticals. The demonstrated effectiveness against RNA viruses demonstrates its potential use for treating new viral diseases [7].

3.10 Gut Microbiota Modulation

Research studies have demonstrated that gallic acid functions as a gut microbiota regulator through its ability to enhance Lactobacillus and Bifidobacterium populations while suppressing opportunistic pathogens [21]. The gut microbiota breaks down gallic acid to produce phenolic compounds which produce systemic anti-inflammatory and antidiabetic effects. The two-way relationship between GA makes it an attractive candidate for developing gut-specific treatments and managing metabolic syndrome (Fig. 37.6.).

4. APPLICATIONS OF GALLIC ACID

4.1 Pharmaceutical Application

Pharmaceutical companies focus on gallic acid (GA) because this compound shows multiple therapeutic benefits that include antioxidant properties along with anti-inflammatory effects and anticancer, neuroprotective and antimicrobial activities. Researchers study gallic acid as a medical compound for treating chronic diseases and infections because of its bioactive properties. Scientists at present work to enhance GA bioavailability by developing nanocarrier-based systems, liposomes and hydrogels as advanced delivery systems [22]. The delivery methods provide better stability and performance of GA when patients receive it as a body treatment. Gallic acid stands as a promising pharmaceutical agent because it contains multiple therapeutic targets and natural origin properties that make it suitable for developing safe and effective pharmaceutical agents.

Current research investigates GA applications in bio-inspired materials development for tissue engineering and synthetic biology applications. Research teams have created antioxidant-rich hydrogels and bioadhesives for wound healing through GA fabrication. The scientists have incorporated GA into nanocarrier systems such as GA-conjugated gold nanoparticles and chitosan micelles for targeted delivery to tumors [22]. The applications of GA expand its conventional pharmacological role into the development of biomedical devices for future generations.

4.2 Industrial Application

The industries choose Gallic acid (GA) because it possesses antioxidant characteristics along with its natural stabilizing and preservative capabilities. The food industry utilizes GA to lengthen product shelf life by preventing oxidation-based spoilage while providing a natural

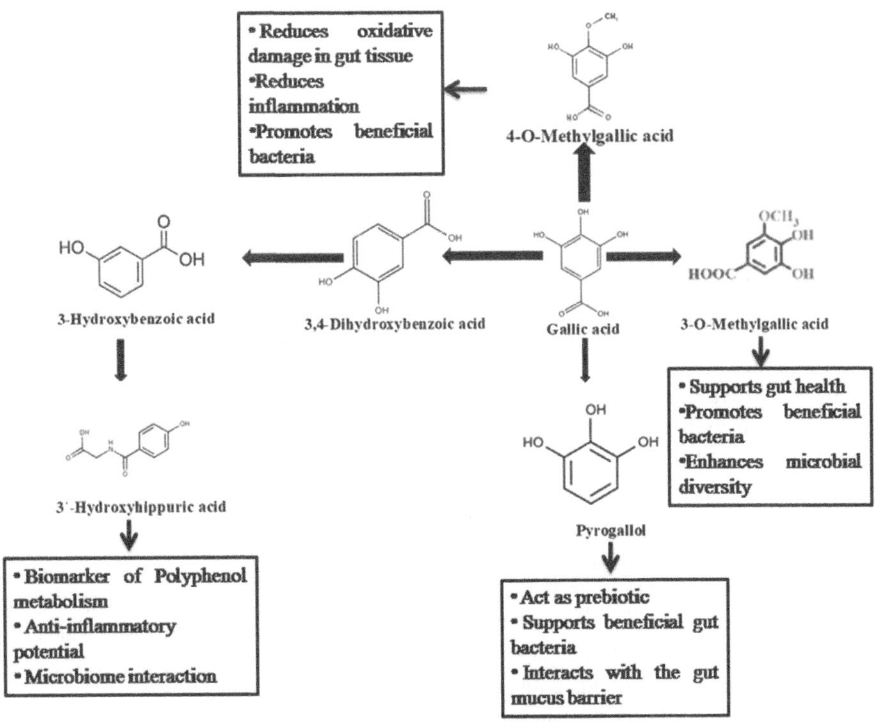

Fig. 37.6 Impact of gallic acid on gut health

alternative to artificial preservatives [7]. The cosmetic industry uses GA as both a protective agent for skin and an anti-aging treatment. The manufacturing process of inks, dyes, leather tanning agents, pharmaceutical and antioxidant formulations utilize GA. The growing consumer preference for environmentally friendly plant-based ingredients increases the market value of GA which benefits both food manufacturing, cosmetic and chemical manufacturing sectors.

4.3 Agricultural Application

Gallic acid (GA) serves sustainable agricultural purposes through its antifungal and antibacterial and plant-protective characteristics. The antifungal activity of GA kills *Alternaria solani* and *Fusarium solani* through structural damage that blocks spore germination [19]. The fungicidal and bactericidal properties of GA and its derivatives provide a potential replacement for synthetic agrochemicals through their natural characteristics. The biostimulant properties of GA increase plant defense capabilities while encouraging plant development. Integrated pest management and sustainable agricultural practices benefit from GA because it is biodegradable while having low toxicity and showing multiple beneficial bioactivities.

5. Challenges and Future Direction

The therapeutic and industrial use of gallic acid faces multiple challenges despite its wide pharmacological potential. The main barrier to medical use comes from GA's poor oral availability because of its low water solubility and rapid metabolic breakdown and limited absorption in the digestive tract. GA's instability during physiological conditions along with its short systemic half-life reduces its body effectiveness. The process of moving GA from laboratory testing to medical use encounters barriers because there is insufficient clinical data and no established formulation protocols. Some directions must be the focus of future research to address these limitations. (a) Research should develop drug delivery systems including nanoparticles, liposomes and hydrogels to enhance GA stability as well as targeted delivery and pharmacokinetic profiles. (b) Human population efficacy and safety validation needs in vivo studies together with clinical trials. (c) Medical studies should investigate how GA operates through distinct biological pathways in disease models to establish logical therapeutic uses. (d) The scientific community should develop gallic acid derivatives and conjugates which keep their biological activity intact and offer improved solubility and metabolic stability. (e) The research should examine how the combination of natural or synthetic compounds with gallic acid leads to better therapeutic results.(f) Agri-industrial scalability should be achieved through the adoption of green chemistry approaches that develop sustainable extraction and formulation methods. (g) A complete realization of gallic acid's biomedical and industrial potential requires addressing existing challenges.

6. Conclusion

The naturally occurring triphenolic compound gallic acid (GA) exhibits a wide range of pharmacological and industrial applications due to its antioxidant, anti-inflammatory, anticancer, antidiabetic, neuroprotective, antimicrobial, and antiviral properties. The combination of its multifunctionality, favourable safety profile, and natural origin makes GA a strong candidate for therapeutic development and integration into pharmaceuticals, nutraceuticals, food preservation, cosmetics, and sustainable agriculture. Advances in drug delivery systems, including nanocarriers and hydrogels, have improved its bioavailability and in vivo efficacy, thereby expanding its clinical potential. GA's role as a natural preservative and agrochemical substitute aligns with the global shift toward sustainable, eco-friendly solutions. Future research should focus on elucidating its molecular mechanisms, pharmacokinetics, and clinical validation to support translational application and commercial scalability. Collectively, GA represents a promising multifunctional agent with considerable potential for innovation across biomedical and industrial domains. Given its natural abundance and low environmental footprint, GA aligns with the principles of green chemistry. Its integration into climate-smart agriculture and biodegradable product formulations offers a sustainable alternative to petrochemical-derived agents.

References

1. Garavand, F., Jalai-Jivan, M., Assadpour, E., & Jafari, S. M. (2021). Encapsulation of phenolic compounds within nano/microemulsion systems: A review. *Food Chemistry, 364*, 130376.
2. Alara, O. R., Abdurahman, N. H., & Ukaegbu, C. I. (2021). Extraction of phenolic compounds: A review. *Current research in food science, 4*, 200–214.
3. Hagerman, A. E., & Butler, L. G. (1978). Protein precipitation method for the quantitative determination of tannins. *Journal of Agricultural and Food chemistry, 26*(4), 809–812.
4. Valencia-Avilés, E., García-Pérez, M. E., Garnica-Romo, M. G., Figueroa-Cárdenas, J. D. D., Meléndez-Herrera, E., Salgado-Garciglia, R., & Martínez-Flores, H. E. (2018). Antioxidant properties of polyphenolic extracts from Quercus laurina, Quercus crassifolia, and Quercus scytophylla bark. *Antioxidants, 7*(7), 81.
5. Rodríguez, H., De Las Rivas, B., Gómez-Cordovés, C., & Muñoz, R. (2008). Degradation of tannic acid by cell-free extracts of Lactobacillus plantarum. *Food Chemistry, 107*(2), 664–670.
6. Suleria, H. A., Barrow, C. J., &Dunshea, F. R. (2020). Screening and characterization of phenolic compounds and

their antioxidant capacity in different fruit peels. *Foods, 9*(9), 1206.

7. Badhani, B., Sharma, N., & Kakkar, R. (2015). Gallic acid: A versatile antioxidant with promising therapeutic and industrial applications. *Rsc Advances, 5*(35), 27540–27557.
8. Kratz, J. M., Andrighetti-Fröhner, C. R., Kolling, D. J., Leal, P. C., Cirne-Santos, C. C., Yunes, R. A., ... & Simões, C. M. O. (2008). Anti-HSV-1 and anti-HIV-1 activity of gallic acid and pentyl gallate. *Memórias do Instituto Oswaldo Cruz, 103*, 437–442.
9. Hadidi, M., Liñán-Atero, R., Tarahi, M., Christodoulou, M. C., &Aghababaei, F. (2024). The potential health benefits of gallic acid: Therapeutic and food applications. *Antioxidants, 13*(8), 1001.
10. Grundhöfer, P., Niemetz, R., Schilling, G., & Gross, G. G. (2001). Biosynthesis and subcellular distribution of hydrolyzable tannins. *Phytochemistry, 57*(6), 915–927.
11. Gao, J., Hu, J., Hu, D., & Yang, X. (2019). A role of gallic acid in oxidative damage diseases: A comprehensive review. *Natural Product Communications, 14*(8), 1934578X19874174.
12. Bai, J., Zhang, Y., Tang, C., Hou, Y., Ai, X., Chen, X., ... & Meng, X. (2021). Gallic acid: Pharmacological activities and molecular mechanisms involved in inflammation-related diseases. *Biomedicine & pharmacotherapy, 133*, 110985.
13. Kahkeshani, N., Farzaei, F., Fotouhi, M., Alavi, S. S., Bahramsoltani, R., Naseri, R., ... &Bishayee, A. (2019). Pharmacological effects of gallic acid in health and diseases: A mechanistic review. *Iranian journal of basic medical sciences, 22*(3), 225.
14. Li, K., Gong, Q., Lu, B., Huang, K., Tong, Y., Mutsvene, T. E., ... & Hu, L. (2023). Anti-inflammatory and antioxidative effects of gallic acid on experimental dry eye: in vitro and in vivo studies. *Eye and Vision, 10*(1), 17.
15. Liao, W., Wen, Y., Wang, J., Zhao, M., Chen, N., Li, Y., ... & Zeng, J. (2023). Gallic acid alleviates gastric precancerous lesions through inhibition of epithelial mesenchymal transition via Wnt/β-catenin signaling pathway. *Journal of Ethnopharmacology, 302*, 115885.
16. Bhuia, M. S., Rahaman, M. M., Islam, T., Bappi, M. H., Sikder, M. I., Hossain, K. N., ... & Sharifi-Rad, J. (2023). Neurobiological effects of gallic acid: Current perspectives. *Chinese medicine, 18*(1), 27.
17. Yang, K., Zhang, L., Liao, P., Xiao, Z., Zhang, F., Sindaye, D., ... & Deng, B. (2020). Impact of gallic acid on gut health: focus on the gut microbiome, immune response, and mechanisms of action. *Frontiers in immunology, 11*, 580208.
18. Variya, B. C., Bakrania, A. K., & Patel, S. S. (2020). Antidiabetic potential of gallic acid from Emblica officinalis: Improved glucose transporters and insulin sensitivity through PPAR-γ and Akt signaling. *Phytomedicine, 73*, 152906.
19. El-Nagar, A., Elzaawely, A. A., Taha, N. A., &Nehela, Y. (2020). The antifungal activity of gallic acid and its derivatives against Alternaria solani, the causal agent of tomato early blight. *Agronomy, 10*(9), 1402.
20. Tian, Q., Wei, S., Su, H., Zheng, S., Xu, S., Liu, M., ... & Li, J. (2022). Bactericidal activity of gallic acid against multi-drug resistance Escherichia coli. *Microbial Pathogenesis, 173*, 105824.
21. Chandrasekaran, P., Weiskirchen, S., & Weiskirchen, R. (2024). Effects of probiotics on gut microbiota: an overview. *International journal of molecular sciences, 25*(11), 6022.
22. Harwansh, R. K., Deshmukh, R., Shukla, V. P., Khunt, D., Prajapati, B. G., Rashid, S., ... & Kumar, A. (2024). Recent advancements in gallic acid-based drug delivery: applications, clinical trials, and future directions. *Pharmaceutics, 16*(9), 1202.

Note: All the figures in this chapter were made by the authors.

Research and Innovations in Industrial and Marine Biotechnology: A Circular Economy 2024 – Prof. Hrudayanath Thatoi et al. (eds)

38 Gamma-Aminobutyric Acid (GABA): Production by Human Gut Microbiome: Prevalence, Regulation, and Role in Acid Stress Tolerance

Sonali Mohapatra[1]
Department of Biological System Engineering,
University of Wisconsin, 1710 University Avenue,
Madison, Wisconsin, USA

Subhashree Rath, Hrudayanath Thatoi[2]
Centre for Industrial Biotechnology Research,
School of Pharmaceutical Sciences, Siksha 'O' Anusandhan,
Deemed to be University, Kalinga Nagar,
Bhubaneswar, Odisha, India

Abstract: Gamma-aminobutyric acid (GABA) is an important non-protein free amino acid, acts as a neurotransmitter in many different organisms. It regulates neuronal activity and maintains overall neurological function in the brain. It exists as a zwitterion, which allows it to interact with other molecules and engage in a variety of physiological activities. It also inhibits neurotransmission, which sends signals, reduces neuron excitability, and helps maintain the balance of excitation and inhibition in the brain. Bacteria having GABA-modulating potential have been found as essential participants in GABAergic gut systems, act as a critical interface between the gut and brain. Glutamate decarboxylase (GAD) gene expression can produce GABA. There are various bacterial strains known to produce GABA. On the other hand, strains that need GABA to develop have also been identified in the human gut microbiota. The abundance of GABA-producing species, regulatory mechanisms affecting microbial GABA production, and its developing function in gut physiology are the main topics of this review, which examines the manufacture of GABA by gut-resident microorganisms. The GAD pathway is highlighted as the primary mechanism of GABA production and its role in preserving pH homeostasis in the face of acid stress. The review also looks at how host activities, such as immunological regulation, gut-brain axis communication, and epithelial barrier integrity, are affected by GABA generated from microbes. Novel insights into gut health, microbial resilience, and new treatment approaches for neurological and gastrointestinal illnesses can be useful for the regulation and adaptation significance of microbial GABA synthesis.

Keywords: Gamma-aminobutyric acid, GAD gene, Neurotransmission, Neurotransmitter, Immunological

1. Introduction

GABA is a four-carbon non-protein free amino acid, gaining attention due to its abundant role in maintaining physiological potential and providing health benefits to humans and animals [1]. This molecule naturally in many plants and animals feed and food. GABA acts as a crucial inhibitory neurotransmitter in human neurological system, which aids in information transmission, mood, regulation of neuronal growth, and enhancement of sleep [2,3]. Moreover, it has antihypertensive, anti-diabetic, and anti-inflammatory qualities [4]. Due to its distribution in the central nervous system and the nerves surrounding different organs, GABA has a significant impact on a

[1]smohapatra4@wisc.edu, [2]director.cibr@soa.ac.in

DOI: 10.1201/9781003759003-38

wide range of illnesses. As a result, it regulates human functioning through a variety of receptors and nerve signal transmission [5]. Several gut-dwelling bacteria (*Lactobacillus, Lactococcus, Streptococcus* and *Bifidobacterium*) have the enzyme machinery, particularly glutamate decarboxylase (GAD), to produce GABA from glutamate. This microbial GABA synthesis has sparked widespread interest because of its potential applications in gut-brain communication, metabolic regulation, and stress responses [6]. Although these microbes can produce GABA in several ways, the putrescine and glutamic acid decarboxylase (GAD) pathways are the most common for the synthesis of GABA. The prevalence and diversity of GABA-producing bacteria vary by individual and are regulated by diet, age, health condition, and microbial community makeup. Microbial GABA production is regulated by both intrinsic genetic processes and external environmental signals, such as pH changes and substrate availability [7]. Nowadays, microbial fermentation [8] or chemical synthesis [9] are the primary methods used to manufacture GABA. Notably, because of the potential toxicity, chemically produced GABA is not permitted to be utilized as a food additive in the food industry. The food industry has expressed a strong interest in GABA-enriched foods, which facilitate the development of meals for specific health uses. In the market, various functional foods rich in GABA, such as rice, dairy products, and tea, are generally sought by consumers. This has encouraged growing attention in microbial fermentation-based approaches and the production of GABA-supplemented efficient foods, such as GABA-fortified rice, dairy products, and tea [10]. The natural foods contain very low levels of GABA [11]. Additionally, heat treatment above 105 °C may result the thermal breakdown, that lowers the concentration of GABA even though it has a high thermal stability [12].

This review investigates the production of GABA by the human gut microbiome, its distribution among microbial taxa, role of GABA in disorders, the regulatory networks that govern its synthesis, and its crucial role in microbial adaptation to acid stress. Understanding these relationships lays the groundwork for investigating microbiome-targeted therapies that modify GABA levels for therapeutic purposes.

2. The Function of GABA in Diseases

GABA is significant for the psychological conditions of humans and other animals. In the central nervous system (CNS), GABA serves as an inhibitory neurotransmitter, controlling the excitability of neurons [13]. It helps to regulate anxiety, mood, and stress responses.

2.1 Anxiety Disorders

GABA calms the brain and helps to reduce stress. People suffering from anxiety disorders such as social anxiety issues, generalized anxiety disorder (GAD), and panic disorder have been found to exhibit reduced functionality of GABA receptors. Studies reveal that GABAergic deficiencies may contribute to greater anxiety symptoms and increased neuronal excitation in anxiety-related brain circuits [14].

2.2 Depression

GABAergic dysfunction has also been linked to depression. According to research, decreased GABAergic activity may be connected with depressive symptoms and mood disturbances. Changes in GABAergic transmission, along with other neurotransmitter types, contribute to the complex neurobiology of depression [15].

2.3 Post-Traumatic Stress Disorder (PTSD)

This is a condition of mental health that can develop after experiencing a stressful mental condition. Altered GABAergic signalling may lead to dysregulation of fear responses, emotion control, and the initiation of PTSD symptoms [16].

2.4 GABA and its Executive Functions

GABA also helps to regulate executive processes in the brain. Executive functions are a set of cognitive processes that enable goal-directed activity. They include decision making, working memory, attention, concentration control, and inhibition. GABAergic neurotransmission regulates key executive processes. GABAergic neurotransmission influences decision-making processes by balancing reward seeking and inhibitory control. Research has demonstrated that GABA levels in specific brain regions, such as the prefrontal cortex and striatum, are related to decision-making ability and impulsivity [17]. The capacity to hold and mentally handle information for brief intervals is known as working memory. GABAergic transmission is involved in controlling neurons.

3. Effect of GABA in Modulating the Gut Bacteria

GABA may function as a fine-tuner/modulator or as a meal, altering important bacterial ecosystems to influence brain function. The GABA was first recognised as the primary inhibitory neurotransmitter. It is a rich carbon and nitrogen source which is widely found in plants. It was found in vertebrate brain and potato tubers from more than 70 years ago [18]. As a result, it is no surprise that GABA is an essential vitamin for the human microbiome. This implies that microbes producing GABA is useful for human health and consider as an intermediate inter-kingdom messenger, imparting a number of health benefits to both animals and humans [19]. GABA may potentially influence the prevalence and profusion of precise microbial populations via more targeted approaches. For example, there is substantial indication that plants employ GABA to counteract the biotic stress generated by plant pathogenic bacteria [18]. GABA play a crucial role in restricting the Ti plasmid's conjugation and amplification by protecting against pathogenic colonization through the suppression of specific quorum signalling molecules [20]. It is surprising that *A. tumefaciens* possesses a specific GABA-binding protein with amino acid residues that are highly conserved and are essential for the deactivation of the quorum signal involved in Ti plasmid activities. Consequently, there is a specific and essential mechanism that facilitates the protective effects of GABA against microbial infections, suggesting that a comparable process may be operational in the gastrointestinal systems of mammals [21].

4. Role of GABA in Bacterial GABA Receptors

GABA play significant role in altering bioelectrical properties of microbes in their environment. It is a dynamic aminoacid which can be used for a number of purposes and communication tactics. Two recent researched on GABA showed the use of this amino acid for the measurements of bacterial membrane potential, microbial population. In this process the fluorescent voltage-sensitive dyes were used that showed that the membrane depolarization of bacteria was linked with the growth of bacteria [22]. Furthermore, the concentrations of GABA in sub-micromolar can lessen the degree of depolarization of *Lactobacillus reuteri* and *Enterococcus foecalis*. The effect of GABA on bacterial growth has yet to be determined because the eventual effect of depolarization appears to be depending on whether the bacteria is stimulated or inhibited [22].

There are various pentameric ligand-gated channels act as potential molecular targets for the effect of GABA. The Erwinia ligand-gated ion channels (ELICs) from *Erwinia chrysanthemi* and Gloeobacter ligand-gated ion channels (GLICs) from *Gloeobacter violaceus* of the *Cyanobacteria* phylum are potential molecular targets of GABA effects. These receptor homologues respond to GABA (ELIC) and/or GABA-active ligands such neurosteroids, which has intriguing implications for human health [23].

5. Probiotic Interventions

The two genus of probiotic such as *Lactobacillus* and *Bifidobacterium* are the most commonly used probiotics in the food and beverage sector among the GABA-producing bacteria used in dietary treatments. Such GABA-based food and drink products have been linked to various health conditions, including improvement in mental health conditions like anxiety, depression, schizophrenia, and cognition, neurological conditions like epilepsy, and pain with heart conditions like cancer, hypertension and Here, we highlight the data supporting the potential advantages of GABA-based dietary therapies for mental health and talk about the developments needed to fully realize their translational potential. The positive effect of GABA-based foods in numerous illnesses is largely supported by studies conducted in animal models. Recent reviews on clinical studies on GABA also offer a favourable prognosis. Probiotics, especially the strains of *Lactobacilli* and *Bifidobacteria* that are known to produce GABA. Though these bacteria do not exclusively produce GABA, they may help to reduce psychological symptoms related to depression and possibly worry. Furthermore, compared to healthy cohorts, reduction of psychological symptoms is generally more consistently visible in clinical settings. Although these studies show promise, there is still a lack of clinical agreement about the use of probiotic dietary therapies in psychopathology. Confounding variables include the clinical trials' restricted scope and heterogeneity, which have made it more difficult to interpret the results. It is obvious that in order to make definitive conclusions about the fundamental association between the intervention and the measured clinical outcome, these limitations must be addressed in addition to Mendelian randomization.

6. Prebiotic Interventions

In particular, these prebiotics enhance traditional probiotics belonging to the Bifidobacterium and Lactobacillus genera. The human gut is home to numerous prebiotic-supported organisms, which, among their primary metabolic outputs, include SCFAs and GABA. The *Lactobacillus* and *Bifidobacterium* are the most researched and producers of GABA in the food industry. The prebiotic or mixtures of prebiotics may also boost the population of GABA-producing probiotic strains present in the human gut. Among these are the genera Eubacterium and Bacteroides. In fact, Bacteroides and *Eubacterium* include a large number of inulin-degrading species, and these strains may indirectly contribute to gut health (see below). Additionally, in a recent in vitro gut model, Humans treated with specific HMOs either by themselves or in different combination blends have been demonstrated to have higher levels of GABA in their feces, particularly in adults. In line with earlier research, HMOs significantly increased the production of GABA, most likely due to an increase in a variety of microbial species, particularly Bifidobacterium adolescentis. However, when fructans were utilized as prebiotics, a significant association between GABA and Bacteroides species was also observed in the same study, suggesting a selective effect of prebiotics on the gut microbiota composition. This research implies that some prebiotic combinations may increase GABA synthesis through particular bacterial species, hence achieving optimal health advantages. Additionally, a recent study that used an in vitro human model showed that supplementing with both 2′-fucosyllactose and oligofructose significantly increased the synthesis of GABA in the body. Polyphenols, or non-carbohydrate compounds, are another family of prebiotics that are of great interest. They are widely found in plants and have been connected to several health advantages, including improved mental wellness. These ligands could also be used to support GABA-producing species directly or indirectly through their enzymatic capacities in order to develop tailored GABA-based dietary treatments. For instance, bacteria use vitamin B6 to produce GABA. There is growing evidence that microorganisms in the human intestine consume GABA. Mutualistic interactions between gut bacteria are crucial for a robust and flexible gut ecology, and may indirectly support other microorganisms. As a result, GABA may have a significant and likely both directly and indirectly mediated effect on current evidence in the setting of a healthy brain gut microbiome. Better-designed randomised controlled trials on probiotic and prebiotic therapies are needed to reinforce the evidence that GABA-based dietary interventions can be useful for better brain function. There are not many studies with strict controls for: concurrent medication; the presence of dysbiosis; and the length of time and function of food before, throughout, and following the intervention. Additionally, more consistent analysis techniques are needed to increase agreement across various investigations. New developments will bring about in a new era in the development of beneficial brain-modulating dietary interferences, as well as identification of useful prebiotic and/or probiotics.

7. Conclusion and Future Prospects

GABA is currently emerging as a ubiquitous signaling chemical found in a variety of life forms, including bacteria, plants, and invertebrates. Its importance in bacterial communities, beyond host interactions, is becoming increasingly clear, impacting microbial characteristics like as quorum sensing and pathogenicity. Understanding GABA signaling in microbial communities is critical for determining the whole influence on human health via the gut-brain axis. Future study should focus on microbial GABA transmission systems and their systemic effects on the host. Advancing this knowledge will not only improve our understanding of microbial endocrinology, but will also open up new avenues for microbiome-targeted therapies, paving the way for novel interventions in neurodevelopmental, metabolic, and inflammatory disorders via microbial GABA pathway modulation.

References

1. Luo, H., Liu, Z., Xie, F., Bilal, M., Liu, L., Yang, R., & Wang, Z. (2021). Microbial production of gamma-aminobutyric acid: applications, state-of-the-art achievements, and future perspectives. Critical Reviews in Biotechnology, 41(4), 491–512.
2. Hepsomali, P., Groeger, J. A., Nishihira, J., & Scholey, A. (2020). Effects of oral gamma-aminobutyric acid (GABA) administration on stress and sleep in humans: A systematic review. *Frontiers in neuroscience*, *14*, 559962.
3. Siucinska, E. (2019). Γ-Aminobutyric acid in adult brain: an update. Behavioural brain research, 376, 112224.
4. Diez-Gutiérrez, L., San Vicente, L., Barrón, L. J. R., del Carmen Villarán, M., & Chávarri, M. (2020). Gamma-aminobutyric acid and probiotics: Multiple health benefits and their future in the global functional food and nutraceuticals market. Journal of Functional Foods, 64, 103669.
5. Mazzoli, R., & Pessione, E. (2016). The neuro-endocrinological role of microbial glutamate and GABA signaling. *Frontiers in microbiology*, *7*, 1934.
6. Icer, M. A., Sarikaya, B., Kocyigit, E., Atabilen, B., Çelik, M. N., Capasso, R., ... & Budán, F. (2024). Contributions of gamma-aminobutyric acid (GABA) produced by lactic acid bacteria on food quality and human health: Current applications and future prospects. *Foods*, *13*(15), 2437.
7. Cui, Y., Miao, K., Niyaphorn, S., & Qu, X. (2020). Production of gamma-aminobutyric acid from lactic acid bacteria: A systematic review. *International Journal of Molecular Sciences*, *21*(3), 995.
8. Zhu, L., Wang, Z., Gao, L., & Chen, X. (2024). Unraveling the Potential of γ-Aminobutyric Acid: Insights into Its Biosynthesis and Biotechnological Applications. Nutrients, 16(16), 2760.
9. Sahab, N. R., Subroto, E., Balia, R. L., & Utama, G. L. (2020). γ-Aminobutyric acid found in fermented foods and beverages: current trends. *Heliyon*, *6*(11).
10. Diana, M., Rafecas, M., Arco, C., & Quílez, J. (2014). Free amino acid profile of Spanish artisanal cheeses: Importance of gamma-aminobutyric acid (GABA) and ornithine content. Journal of food composition and analysis, 35(2), 94–100.
11. Toyoizumi, T., Kosugi, T., Toyama, Y., & Nakajima, T. (2021). Effects of high-temperature cooking on the gamma-aminobutyric acid content and antioxidant capacity of germinated brown rice (Oryza sativa L.). CyTA-Journal of Food, 19(1), 360–369.
12. Etkin, A., Prater, K. E., Schatzberg, A. F., Menon, V., & Greicius, M. D. (2009). Disrupted amygdalar subregion functional connectivity and evidence of a compensatory network in generalized anxiety disorder. Archives of general psychiatry, 66(12), 1361–1372.
13. Liberzon, I., & Abelson, J. L. (2016). Context processing and the neurobiology of post-traumatic stress disorder. *Neuron*, *92*(1), 14–30.
14. Gabbay, V., Mao, X., Klein, R. G., Ely, B. A., Babb, J. S., Panzer, A. M., ... & Shungu, D. C. (2012). Anterior cingulate cortexγ-aminobutyric acid in depressed adolescents: relationship to anhedonia. Archives of general psychiatry, 69(2), 139–149.
15. Fatemi, S. H., Reutiman, T. J., Folsom, T. D., & Thuras, P. D. (2009). GABA A receptor downregulation in brains of subjects with autism. Journal of autism and developmental disorders, 39, 223–230.
16. Clark, A. S., Costine, B. A., Jones, B. L., Kelton-Rehkopf, M. C., Meerts, S. H., Nutbrown-Greene, L. L., ... & Henderson, L. P. (2006). Sex-and age-specific effects of

anabolic androgenic steroids on reproductive behaviors and on GABAergic transmission in neuroendocrine control regions. *Brain research*, *1126*(1), 122–138.
17. Quillin, S. J., Tran, P., & Prindle, A. (2021). Potential roles for gamma-aminobutyric acid signaling in bacterial communities. *Bioelectricity*, *3*(2), 120–125.
18. Strandwitz, P., Kim, K. H., Terekhova, D., Liu, J. K., Sharma, A., Levering, J., ... & Lewis, K. (2019). GABA-modulating bacteria of the human gut microbiota. Nature microbiology, 4(3), 396–403.
19. Strandwitz, P., Kim, K. H., Terekhova, D., Liu, J. K., Sharma, A., Levering, J., ... & Lewis, K. (2019). GABA-modulating bacteria of the human gut microbiota. *Nature microbiology*, *4*(3), 396–403.
20. Lang, J., Gonzalez-Mula, A., Taconnat, L., Clement, G., & Faure, D. (2016). The plant GABA signaling downregulates horizontal transfer of the Agrobacterium tumefaciens virulence plasmid. *New Phytologist*, *210*(3), 974–983.
21. Planamente, S., Vigouroux, A., Mondy, S., Nicaise, M., Faure, D., & Moréra, S. (2010). A conserved mechanism of GABA binding and antagonism is revealed by structure-function analysis of the periplasmic binding protein Atu2422 in Agrobacterium tumefaciens. *Journal of Biological Chemistry*, *285*(39), 30294–30303.
22. Mazzoli, R., & Pessione, E. (2016). The neuro-endocrinological role of microbial glutamate and GABA signaling. *Frontiers in microbiology*, *7*, 1934.
23. Brams, M., Govaerts, C., Kambara, K., Price, K. L., Spurny, R., Gharpure, A., ... & Ulens, C. (2020). Modulation of the Erwinia ligand-gated ion channel (ELIC) and the 5-HT3 receptor via a common vestibule site. *Elife*, *9*, e51511.

Research and Innovations in Industrial and Marine Biotechnology: A Circular Economy 2024 – Prof. Hrudayanath Thatoi et al. (eds)

39 Microalgal Biotechnology – An Industrial Perspective Towards Circular and Sustainable Economy

Thajuddin Nooruddin*
B.S. Abdur Rahman Crescent Institute of Science & Technology,
(Deemed to be University,) Vandalur, Chennai

Abstract: Microalgae and cyanobacteria play a central role in making oxygen and sequestering carbon dioxide on Earth. With an increasing importance on sustainable development, these microorganisms have gained momentous position in biotechnology. Research highlights their several applications, including biofuel production, wastewater treatment, agriculture, pharmaceuticals, and nanotechnology. *Spirulina and Chlorella,* which are rich in proteins and essential nutrients, are particularly valuable as dietary supplements. Some strains of these microorganisms even produce bioactive compounds that possess antimicrobial and anticancer properties. Recent advancements in the field include large-scale cultivation techniques and the use of magnetic field stimulation to enhance lipid content. Cyanobacteria also contribute to rice field ecosystems by fixing nitrogen. India's national microalgal repositories reflect efforts to conserve biodiversity. Additionally, the ability of algae to thrive on non-arable land positions them as vital contributors in the fight against climate change and resource scarcity. By integrating algal biotechnology into various industries, we can promote economic growth while supporting environmental sustainability.

Keywords: Biofuel production, Microalgal biotechnology, Sustainable bioeconomy

1. Introduction

Microalgae and Cyanobacteria (formerly known as Blue-green algae), the tiniest plants on our planet, appeared on Earth billions of years ago and transformed the CO_2 atmosphere into an oxygen-rich atmosphere that enabled land plants and animals to evolve. Each day, they replenish 60% of the earth's oxygen, more than the contribution of all forests and fields combined. They efficiently sequester CO_2 and entwine the hydrogen with carbon to make energy-rich hydrocarbons and release oxygen into the atmosphere. They thrive in various aquatic habitats, including freshwater[1], marine environments[2]soils and agricultural fields [3], sewage and effluents [4]and even extreme conditions[5]. Not all species are safe to consume, as some produce toxins and contribute to water fouling.

Recent pioneering work has raised the status of these microbes, making them valued in biotechnological fields. They are considered an ideal biotechnological tool, and their importance in producing food, feed, fuel, fertilizer, fine chemicals, and pharmaceuticals is reflected in their role in pollution abatement [6]. To utilize these organisms for our needs, it is decisive to understand and preserve their biodiversity while also sightseeing their biotechnological applications.Many studies have been documented on marine and freshwater microalgae and cyanobacteria biodiversity using taxonomic tools: isolation, purification, and the establishment of national repositories, along with efforts to utilize these organisms for various needs.

2. Algae Innovations: From Bioactive Compounds to Circular Bioeconomy Solutions

2.1 Bioactive and Nutritional Potential

Microalgae and cyanobacteria exhibit a range of pharmacological activities, including antimicrobial, anticancer, immunostimulatory, and antioxidant

*Corresponding author: provc@crescent.education & nthaju2002@yahoo.com

DOI: 10.1201/9781003759003-39

effects[7]. Beyond their utility as biofertilizers and for bioremediation, these organisms are sources of various valuable biomolecules, such as enzymes, amino acids, lipids, and fatty acids, as well as sequence-specific endonucleases. Their market potential is enhanced by the comparatively low cost of biomass production, which is significantly more economical than that of traditional bacteria or fungi (Fig. 39.1). Notably, *Spirulina*, a prominent cyanobacterium, is valued as a dietary supplement due to its high protein content (60–71%) and its abundance of polysaccharides, essential amino acids, vitamins, and minerals. Its delicate cell wall also contributes to improved digestibility, making it an attractive option for nutrition.

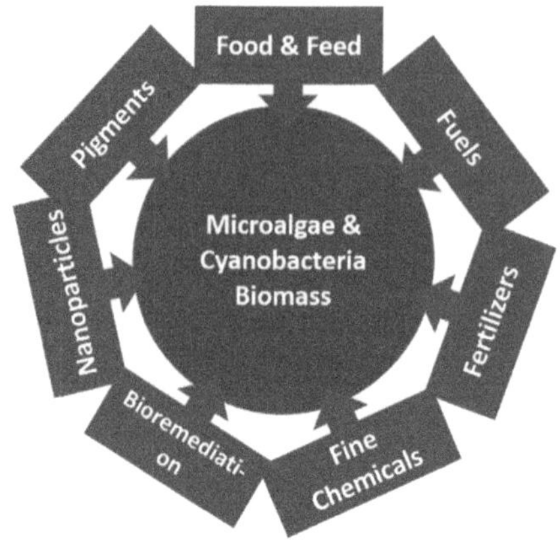

Fig. 39.1 Various applications of microalgal and cyanobacterial biomass

Source: Authors

2.2 Biofuel Production

Intensive research has been carried out on screening efficient microalgal strains for biodiesel production, optimizing a process for semi-continuous and continuous cultivation of selected isolates under outdoor open tanks and raceway ponds of 5KL and 35KL capacity and producing biodiesel from the harvested biomass (Fig. 39.2). For the first time, we reported the application of a pulsed magnetic field (PMF) in a 35KL raceway pond and reported a two-fold increase in the lipid content from the harvested *Chlorella* biomass [8]. Industry experts believe that algae are the most advantageous feedstock

Fig. 39.2 Microalgal biomass production process flow. (1) Collection of specimens from aquatic environment (2) Isolation & purification of microalgae using dilution & streak plate method (3) Scaling up the efficient microalgal strains in terms of high lipid content 250 ml (4) 5 litres (5) 20 litres (6) 500 litres (7) 5000 litres & 35,000 litres in raceway ponds (8) Harvesting of microalgal biomass using plankton net cloth (Filtration) (9) Drying the harvested biomass in the form of noodle like flakes (10 & 11) Weighing and powdering of dried microalgal biomass (Baldev et al., 2016)

for biofuels due to their versatility and efficiency. They can produce various fuel end products such as biodiesel, ethanol, butanol, methane, jet fuel, and even crude oil, through multiple processing pathways, making them a promising sustainable energy source [9; 10; 11; 12; 13; 14].

2.3 Cyanobacterial Extracts as Biostimulants in Agriculture

Cyanobacteria are crucial in rice field ecosystems since they act as biological nitrogen fixers, improving soil fertility and increasing crop productivity. They produce phytohormones, polypeptides, amino acids, and polysaccharides that promote plant growth. During their growth, cyanobacteria release ammonia and nitrogenous polypeptides vital for plant nutrition. Their decomposition also releases secondary metabolites that influence soil dynamics and plant interactions. We report that biomass wet extracts of several cyanobacterial strains, namely *Scytonemabohneri MBDU 104, Dolichospermum spiroides MBDU 903, Nostoc ellipsosporum, Dolichospermum flos-aquae, Oscillatoria acuminata, Anabaena variabilis* and *Nostoccalcicola*showed plant growth promotion in *Pisum sativum L, Gossypium hirsutum L, Zea mays, Sorghum bicolour, Paspalum scrobiculate and Vigna unguiculata* identified the presence of Indole-3-Acetic Acid (IAA), Indole-3-butyric acid (IBA), cinnamic acid and free fatty acids (FAs) volatiles as growth promoting molecular elicitors [15;16].

2.4 Algae Derived Bioactive targeting Resistant Pathogens

The rise of antibiotic resistance and decreasing antibiotic efficacy have prompted the search for new antimicrobial agents. Cyanobacteria and microalgae have shown promise as sources of bioactive compounds with pharmacological activities, potentially providing alternatives against resistant bacterial strains. An elaborate attempt has been made to screen and characterize cyanobacteria and microalgae in the search for novel bioactive compounds and effectively utilize them as antimicrobial and anti-cancerous compounds in human health [17; 18;19]. A detailed attempt has been made on the screening and characterization of cyanobacteria and microalgae for the development of novel bioactive compounds against pathogenic bacteria, fungi, Extended Spectrum β Lactamase (ESBL) producers and pathogenic biofilms and study their antioxidant and cytotoxic properties against cancer cells. We reported a novel cyanobacterium *Oscillatoria acuminata* and its purified fractions active against ESBL-producing pathogenic bacteria and identified the active fraction as MGDG-palmitoyl using sophisticated instruments and techniques [20].

2.5 Antibiofilm Activity

The methanolic extract of *Spirulina platensis* at a concentration of 100 ng mL^{-1} efficiently inhibited the biofilms of *Vibrio parahaemolyticus* (ATCC17802), *Chromobacterium violaceum* (ATCC 12742) and *Vibrio alginolyticus* (ATCC17749). Significant reduction in cell surface hydrophobicity (CSH), inhibition of extracellular polymeric substances (EPS) revealed the antibiofilm potential of *S. platensis* against a broad spectrum of both Gram-positive and Gram-negative bacteria [21]. In another study, the marine cyanobacterium *Oscillatoria subuliformis* was used against the biofilm and Quorum Sensing (QS) of *Pseudomonas aeruginosa.* Different concentration of *O. subuliformis* methanolic extract (OME) inhibited biofilm, EPS, CSH, pyocyanin, elastase activity and swarming motility in *P. aeruginosa*[22; 23; 24; 6].

2.6 Green Nanoparticle Synthesis

Synthesis of nanoparticles from microalgae and cyanobacteria is a cost-effective and eco-friendly alternative to traditional methods, offering non-toxic and sustainable production. The microalgae and cyanobacteria mediated synthesis of various types and shapes of nanoparticles such as silver, CdS nanoparticles, silicon- germanium (Si-Ge) oxide nanocomposite, gold nanoparticles of different shapes (spherical, triangular, hexagonal and cubical) and zinc oxide nanoparticles and their applications were reported [25;26;27; 10]

2.7 NRMC: A Resource Hub for Algal Taxonomy and Biotechnology

India is recognized for its rich diversity of algae and contributions to phycology. The advancement of algal biotechnology relies on well-maintained culture collections that provide authenticated biological materials. This has led to the establishment of two publicly accessible germplasm collections: the National Repository for Microalgae and Cyanobacteria - Marine (NRMC-M) and Freshwater (NRMC-F) at Bharathidasan University in Tamil Nadu, funded by the Department of Biotechnology, Government of India.These repositories are tasked with collecting, isolating, purifying, identifying, and maintaining microalgal and cyanobacterial cultures, offering live cultures upon request, and producing detailed catalogs with DNA barcoding for effective traceability and identification.

2.8 Algae-based Industries for a Circular Bioeconomy

In recent years, Algal Industries are started appearing in many countries especially the tropical and sub-tropical countries. Now there are several products coming from algae and using them in industries is really beneficial for the sustenance of our Universe. The advantages of using algae in industries particularly Microalgae/Cyanobacteria are listed below:

1. Algae can be cultivated using minimal land, water, nutrients, you need not have to add a big media supplement as in the case of heterotrophic bacterial and fungal cultures. They can grow in different types of environments including waste water, saline water etc.
2. They can be grown in non-arable land, use waste water or brackish water and they can minimize competition between agricultural resources.
3. They are capable of absorbing CO_2 much more efficiently than the land plants due to photosynthesis as a result of which they mitigate the greenhouse gas emission and they are able to combat climate change.
4. A number of products can be obtained from these algae, a number of renewable chemicals such as anti-oxidants, pigments, bioactive compounds and by getting them from these organisms, we reduce the need of petrochemical derived alternatives.
5. Algae biomass is a key source for biofuels, offering a sustainable alternate to fossil fuels. This shift reduces reliance on non-renewable energy and lowers greenhouse gas emissions, contributing to a more circular economy in fuel production.
6. Some algae, particularly *Spirulina* and *Chlorella*, offer a nutrient-dense option that can effectively contribute protein, Omega-3 fatty acids, vitamins, and minerals to the food and feed industries.
7. Bioplastics can be obtained from cyanobacterial polysaccharides there by making it a more sustainable materials economy. One of the very important features of these microalgae particularly is the ability to grow in waste waters, removing the pollutants and thereby utilize the treated water for irrigation and aquaculture.
8. Microalgae not only cleans the water, but it also generates biomass that can be utilized for different applications.

By establishing the different types of algal industries, we are also able to create a number of new job opportunities in research, cultivation and processing and product development. The algae based industries offer a versatile and sustainable solution to various challenges faced by conventional industries. By integrating algae into circular economy strategies, we can promote resource efficiency, reduce waste and contribute to a more environmentally friendly and resilient economic model.

3. Conclusion

Microalgae and cyanobacteria represent valuable resources for global health, energy, food security, and environmental sustainability. The ability of these organisms to thrive in a variety of environments, such as non-arable land and wastewater systems, positions them as economically viable alternatives for sustainable production. These microorganisms have applications in biofuel production, nanoparticle synthesis, and therapeutic development. *Spirulina* and *Chlorella* serve as nutrient supplements, while others show antimicrobial properties. National repositories in India emphasize conserving algal diversity. Integrating these organisms into industrial systems supports a circular bioeconomy while contributing to climate change mitigation. They are becoming central to a sustainable future.

References—

1. Narchonai, G.,Arutselvan, C., Lewis-Oscar, F. and Thajuddin, N. (2019). Deciphering the microalgal diversity and water quality assessment of two urban temple ponds in Pondicherry, India. Biocatal. Agric. Biotechnol. 22:101427.
2. Thajuddin, N., and Subramanian, G. (2019). Diversity and Utilization of Marine Cyanobacteria. In: Handbook of Algal Technologies and Phytochemicals. (Eds.) Gokare A. Ravishankar and Rangarao Ambati. CRC Press (Taylor & Francis Group). Chapter 14: 149–169.
3. Thajamanbi, M., Rout, J. and Thajuddin, N. (2016a). Blue Green Algae from Rice Fields of Karimganj District, Assam, North East India. International Journal of Life Sciences and Pharma Research. 6(4): 25–34.
4. Singh, S. M., Singh P. and Thajuddin, N. (2008). Biodiversity and distribution of Cyanobacteria at Dronning Maud Land, East Antarctica. Acta Botanica Malacitana. 33: 7–8.
5. Thajuddin, N., and Subramanian G. (2005). Cyanobacterial biodiversity and potential applications in biotechnology. Current Science, 89: 47–57.
6. Nagasathya, A. and N. Thajuddin (2008). Antioxidant property of *hypersaline cyanobacterium Phormidium tenue* (KMD 33) International Journal of Pharmacology. 4(2): 125–129.
7. Baldev, E., MubarakAli, D., Sivasubramanian, V., Pugazhendhi, A. and Thajuddin, N. (2021a). Unveiling the Induced Lipid Production in *Chlorella vulgaris* under Pulsed Magnetic Field Treatment. Chemosphere. 279: 130673.
8. Lewis-Oscar, F., Praveenkumar, R. and Thajuddin, N. (2015a). Bioethanol production using starch extracted from microalga *Stigeoclonium* sp. Kütz. BUM11007 cultivated in domestic wastewater. Research Journal of Environmental Sciences 9 (5): 216–224.
9. Thajuddin, N., Vinitha, G., MubarakAli, D., and Lewis-Oscar, F. (2016). Development and Application of Nanocatalyst for Algal Biofuel Production. In: Biocatalysts in Biomass and Bioproducts. (Eds.) K. Ramasamy, S.Karthikeyan and U. Sivakumar. Chapter 7, 121–134. Tamil Nadu Agricultural University Publications. Coimbatore.
10. Baldev, E., MubarakAli, D., Pugazhendhi, A and Thajuddin, N. (2021b). Wastewater as an economical and eco-friendly green medium for microalgal biofuel production. Fuel. 294: 120484.

11. Suresh, A., Soundararajan, S., Elavarasi, S., LewisOscar, F. and Thajuddin, N. (2019). Evaluation and characterization of the plant growth promoting potentials of two heterocystous cyanobacteria for improving food grains growth. Biocatal. Agric. Biotechnol. 17: 647–652
12. Suresh A., Praveenkumar, R., Thangaraj, R., Lewis-Oscar, F., Dhanasekaran, D. and N. Thajuddin. (2014). Microalgal fatty acid methyl ester a new source of bioactive compounds with anitimicrobial activity. Asian Pacific Journal of Tropical Disease. 4(2): S979–S984.
13. MubarakAli, D., PraveenKumar, R., Shenbagavalli, T., MariNivetha, T., ParveezAhamed, A., Al-Dhabi, N.A., and Thajuddin. N. (2012a). New reports on anti-bacterial and anti-candidal activities of fatty acid methyl esters (FAME) obtained from *Scenedesmus bijugatus* var. *bicellularis* biomass RSC Advances 2: 11552–11556
14. MubarakAli, D., Baldev, E., Thajuddin N., Lee, S.Y. and Kim, J.W. (2018). An evidence of C16 fatty acid methyl esters extracted from microalga for effective antimicrobial and antioxidant property. Microb. Pathogen. 115: 233–238.
15. ParveezAhamed, A., Rasheed, M.U., Noorani, K.P.M., Reehana, N., Santhoshkumar, S., Imran, M.Y.M., Naiyf, A.S., Arunachalam, C., SulaimanAli, A., Akbarsha, M.A. and Thajuddin, N. (2017). In vitro antibacterial activity of MGDG-Palmitoyl from *Oscillatoria acuminata* NTAPC05 against extended spectrum beta lactamase producers. The Journal of Antibiotics. 70(6): 754–762.
16. Lewis-Oscar, F., Nithya, C., Bakkiyaraj, D., Arunkumar, M., Alharbi, N.S. and Thajuddin, N. (2015b). Biofilm inhibitory effect of *Spirulina platensis* extracts on bacteria of clinical significance. PNAS Biological Sciences, 87 (2), 537–544.
17. Nithya, C., Lewis-Oscar, F., Kanaga, S., Kavitha, R., Bakkiyaraj, D., Arunkumar, M., Alharbi, N.S., Arunachalam, C., SulaimanAli A. and Thajuddin, N. (2014). Biofilm inhibitory potential of *Chlamydomonas* sp. extract against *Pseudomonas aeruginosa*. J. Algal. Biomass. Utln. 5(4): 74–81.
18. Santhakumari, S., Kannappan, A., Pandian, S. K., Thajuddin, N., BabuRajendran, R. and Veera Ravi, A. (2016). Inhibitory effect of marine cyanobacterial extract on biofilm formation and virulence factors production of bacterial pathogens causing vibriosis in aquaculture. J. Appl. Phycol. 28: 313–324.
19. Lewis-Oscar, F., Nithya, C., SulaimanAli, A., Naiyf, A.S., and Thajuddin, N. (2018). In vitro and in silico attenuation of quorum sensing mediated pathogenicity in *Pseudomonas aeruginosa* using *Spirulina platensis*. Microb. Pathogen. 116: 246–256.
20. MubarakAli, D., Gopinath, V., Rameshbabu, N. and Thajuddin, N. (2012b). Synthesis and characterization of CdS nanoparticles using c-phycoerythrin from the marine cyanobacteria. Materials letters 74: 8–11.
21. MubarakAli, D., Arunkumar, J., Harish Nag, K., Ishack, S.S.K.A., Baldev, E., Pandiaraj, D. and Thajuddin, N. (2013). Gold nanoparticles from Pro and eukaryotic photosynthetic microorganisms - Comparative studies on synthesis and its application on biolabelling. Colloids Surf., B. 103: 166–173.
22. MurpinKumar, P.S., MubarakAli, D., Saratale, R.G., Saratale, G.D., Pugazhendhi, A., Gopalakrishnan, K. and Thajuddin. N. (2017). Synthesis of nano-cubical gold particles for effective antimicrobial property against clinical human pathogens. Microb. Pathogen. 113: 68–73.
23. Baldev, E., MubarakAli, D and N. Thajuddin (2016). Microalgal Biomass Production: Lab-to-Land practices in Bharathidasan University, India. ENVIS Newsletter, 14 (3): 2–4.

Research and Innovations in Industrial and Marine Biotechnology: A Circular Economy 2024 – Prof. Hrudayanath Thatoi et al. (eds)

40 Enhanced Growth Performance, Non-Specific Immune Responses, and Enzymatic Activity in *Labeo Rohita* (Hamilton, 1822) via Oral Administration of Glycolipid Surfactant-Enriched Diets Derived from Marine Microbial Sources: A First Report

Sameer Ranjan Sahoo
Centre for Biotechnology,
Siksha 'O' Anusandhan (Deemed to be University),
Bhubaneswar, Odisha, India

Arabinda Jena
District Program Manager,
Fisheries, UNDP (Collaboration with Directorate Fisheries),
Cuttack, Odisha, India

Shakti Ketan Prusty
Faculty of Pharmaceutical Sciences,
Siksha 'O' Anusandhan (Deemed to be University),
Bhubaneswar, Odisha, India

Arun Kumar Pradhan*
Centre for Biotechnology,
Siksha 'O' Anusandhan (Deemed to be University),
Bhubaneswar, Odisha, India

Abstracts: Rhamnolipid, a biosurfactant from *Pseudomonas* sp. Kmka-114, was evaluated for its effects on juvenile *Labeo rohita*. Graded dietary supplementation enhanced growth, non-specific immunity (notably myeloperoxidase and respiratory burst activity), and enzyme responses without toxicity. Lactate dehydrogenase and alkaline phosphatase remained within normal ranges, and liver histology showed no damage at the highest dose (6X mg/kg). Post-withdrawal, physiological parameters remained stable, indicating sustained effects. These results support rhamnolipid's potential as a safe, bioactive feed additive, warranting further investigation into its mechanisms of action.

Keywords: Antioxidants, Biosurfactant, Growth performance, Immunity, *Labeo rohita*, Rhamnolipid

*Corresponding author: arunpradhan@soa.ac.in

DOI: 10.1201/9781003759003-40

1. Introduction

The intensification of aquaculture has led to increased disease outbreaks, underscoring the demand for natural and sustainable alternatives to antibiotics [1]. Biosurfactants, particularly rhamnolipids produced by *Pseudomonas* species, are surface-active molecules known for their antimicrobial and immunomodulatory properties. Despite their potential, limited studies have examined their use in aquaculture species [2]. This study investigates the effects of dietary rhamnolipid, extracted from *Pseudomonas* sp. Kmka-114 (Accession Number: PP474329), on the growth, haematological, immunological, and enzymatic profiles of *Labeo rohita*. Dietary doses of 0.05 (1X), 0.15 (3X), and 0.3 (6X) mg/kg followed by a 10-day withdrawal. Parameters assessed included immune response, enzyme activity, and liver histology. The results aim to support sustainable, antibiotic-free disease management in aquaculture, particularly relevant for South Asia, where rohu is economically and culturally important.

2. Material and Methods

2.1 Experimental Diet

Rhamnolipid was produced using *Pseudomonas* sp. Kmka-114 and purified following standard protocols [3]. Iso-nitrogenous (35% crude protein) and iso-caloric diets were formulated using locally sourced ingredients to include 0 (control), 0.05, 0.15, and 0.3 mg rhamnolipid/kg feed. All ingredients were thoroughly mixed, pelletized, and stored at 4 °C until use (Table 40.1.).

Table 40.1 Detailed nutrient breakdown of medicated and control feed (mg kg^{-1})

Composition of medicated feed and control feed (mg kg^{-1})				
Feed ingredients	Control	T1 (mg/kg)	T2 (mg/kg)	T3 (mg/kg)
Fish meal	50	50	50	50
Soya meal	280	280	280	280
GNOC	260	260	260	260
Rice bran	200	200	200	200
Corn flour	150	150	150	150
Oil mix(ml)	40	40	40	40
Vitamin and mineral mixture	20	19.95	19.85	19.7
Biosurfactant (BS)	0	0.05	0.15	0.3

2.2 Experimental Fish and Design

Healthy *L. rohita* fingerlings (18 ± 0.78 g) were obtained from hatchery and acclimatized for 15 days. Fish were randomly distributed into tanks (triplicates per treatment, 20 fish/tank) with continuous aeration and water exchange. Feeding was conducted twice daily at 3% body weight. For a 30 days trial, three groups received different surfactant doses: 0.050 mg kg^{-1}(T1), 0.15 mg kg^{-1}(T2), and 0.3 mgkg^{-1} (T3), followed by a 10-day withdrawal. Water quality was maintained per APHA guidelines [4]. This setup evaluated surfactant impacts on health and withdrawal dynamics.

2.3 Experimental Fish Sampling

On days 10, 20, 30, and 40 of the experiment, fish growth was assessed. Fish body weight during a one-day period of feed restriction was determined at the beginning and end of the study, and nutritional intake was noted. Feed conversion ratio (FCR), specific growth rate (SGR), weight gain ratio (WGR), Initial body weight (IBW), final body weight (FBW), daily feed intake (DFI), and survival rate (SR) were documented. (Table 40.2). To ensure equitable treatment, five fish each tank were chosen sedatedblood was collected from the caudal vein using heparinized syringes.Serum biochemical indices (total protein, albumin, globulin) were analyzed using commercial kits.

2.4 Assessment of Non-Specific Immune Parameters

Numerous antibacterial substances, including proteins and enzymes including lysozyme proteolytic enzymes, complement proteins immunoglobulins, lectins, and C-reactive proteins, are present in fish blood. Non-specific immunological measures such as serum lysozyme, myeloperoxidase (MPO) [5], nitroblue tetrazolium (NBT) assay [6], and lysozyme [7] were evaluated using spectrophotometer. Enzyme activities (ALP, LDH, and SOD) were measured using commercial kits and standard protocols. ALP [8] and LDH were assessed in serum, while SOD activity [9] was analyzed in liver homogenates. Liver tissues from control and treated groups were histologically examined post-experiment using hematoxylin-eosin staining for cellular alterations [10].

2.5 Hepatosomatic and Viscerosomatic Index

Fish liver and intestinal weights for each group were determined using the equation at the conclusion of the experiment.

$$\text{Hepatosomatic index (HSI)} = \frac{\text{Liver weight (g)} \times 100}{\text{Weight of the fish (g)}}$$

$$\text{Viscerosomatic index (VSI)} = \frac{\text{Intestine weight (g)} \times 100}{\text{Weight of the fish (g)}}$$

2.6 Total Erythrocyte (TE) and Total Leucocyte (TL) Count

20 µl of blood was mixed with 3980 µl of Hayem's or Turk's solution, shaken, and 30 µl loaded into a Neubauer hemocytometer. RBCs were counted in five small squares, WBCs in four large squares under 40× magnification. Cells/mm^3 were calculated using the standard formula.

$$Number\ of\ \frac{cells}{mm3} = \frac{[N \times dilution]}{[Areacounted \times Depthoffluid]}$$

*N : total number of cells counted.

2.7 Statistical Analysis

Analysis was followed using one-way analysis of variance (ANOVA) in SPSS (23.0 version, USA). The data were presented as the arithmetic mean ± standard error (SE). At $p < 0.05$, significance was taken into account. This thorough and exacting method of gathering and analyzing data guarantees the authenticity and dependability of the results in clarifying how biosurfactant infusion affects several physiological and immunological parameters in fish.

3. Results and Discussion

With a growing focus on bacterial secondary metabolites for disease control in aquaculture, this study examines biosurfactants (BS) from *Pseudomonas* sp. and their potential to boost immunity and growth in fish. Surprisingly, a literature survey reveals a dearth of evidence concerning metabolites isolated from *Pseudomonas* sp. in the Mangrove littoral region of Karnataka as fish feed supplements. A growing focus on bacterial secondary metabolites for disease control in aquaculture, this study examines biosurfactants (BS) from Pseudomonas and their potential to boost immunity and growth in fish. The study tested BS effectiveness by feeding fish different doses (50, 150, and 300 mg/kg) and maintained stable water conditions (7.0 ± 0.4 pH, dissolved oxygen 5.0 ± 0.83 ppm, total alkalinity at 103 ± 2 ppm, total hardness at 94 ± 1 ppm, ammonia at 1.6 ± 0.09 ppm, nitrite at 0.03 ± 0.003 ppm, nitrate at 0.3 ± 0.06 ppm and 28.0 ± 0.5°C) across all tanks. Growth analysis showed only 10% increase in mass difference between the control and T2, T3 (Table 40.2). Previous studies also found that BS concentrations between 12.5-100 mg/kg promoted growth in species like *Oreochromis niloticus*, [11] noted that a combination of 100 mg/kg NT-antimicrobial lipopeptides, including iturins and fengycins, along with surfactin, led to increased yields, though the mechanisms behind this growth effect remain unclear.Based on previous studies, it can be hypothesized this improved growth may be linked to the antimicrobial activity and the role of antimicrobial peptides as effective immune regulators [12]. Additionally, this effect may be influenced by unexamined factors related to water quality and host microbiomes, which were beyond the scope of this investigation.

The study primarily focused on immune parameters critical for pathogen resistance. Notably, myeloperoxidase, respiratory burst, and lysozyme activities increased significantly ($p < 0.05$) in treated fish but returned to baseline after a 10-day BS withdrawal period. Higher respiratory activity was noted in 3x and 6x treated groups, and myeloperoxidase activity remained elevated in T2 and T3 until day 30. Myeloperoxidase, an enzyme essential for microbial defense, aligns with studies on immunomodulatory effects of commercial antibiotics in other fish species. MPO is a crucial enzyme produced by neutrophils during the respiratory burst (RBT/NBT) (Fig. 40.1). It uses hydrogen peroxide generated in this process to create hypochlorous acid, which exhibits strong microbicidal properties[13]. This observation aligns with findings from other studies using commercial antibiotics on sea breams, emphasizing the immunomodulatory effects of the biosurfactant, contingent on dose, administration route, duration, and fish stage[14].

Activities of liver enzymes, particularly lactate dehydrogenase (LDH) and alkaline phosphatase (ALP), were also monitored as stress indicators. T2 and T3 showed slightly elevated ALP and LDH during the feeding period, but these values returned to control levels post-BS withdrawal, suggesting reversible physiological effects (Fig. 40.2). Histological analysis of liver samples showed no significant tissue damage (Fig. 40.2.a, b).The conversion of pyruvate into lactate, which raises the blood's lactic acid concentration, may be the cause of the observed increase in LDH activity in *Labeo rohita*. When injury occurs in tissues abundant in enzymes, several enzymes leak from damaged cells, leading to changes in plasma enzyme activities. Importantly, present study revealed no alarming outcomes, suggesting no evident harm to internal organs. During the withdrawal period, a

Table 40.2 Growth performance, survival, and feed efficiency indicators for *Labeo rohita*

0-40 days experiment				
Parameters	**Control**	**T1**	**T2**	**T3**
IBW(g)	18.81 ± 0.00425	18.68 ± 0.00925	18.80 ± 0.00925	18.83 ± 0.00175
FBW (g)	37.58 ± 0.01	37.09 ± 0.04	40.33 ± 0.05	42.57 ± 0.05
WG (%)	99.76 ± 0.004	98.47 ± 0.007	114.69 ± 0.0053	126.12 ± 0.009
SGR %	1.72 ± 9643	1.71 ± 376	1.90 ± 717	2.03 ± 9307
DFI	1.19 ± 394	1.22 ± 055	1.24 ± 881	1.30 ± 154
FCR	2.54 ± 4494	2.65 ± 269	2.32 ± 0587	2.19 ± 27
SR (%)	100	100	100	100

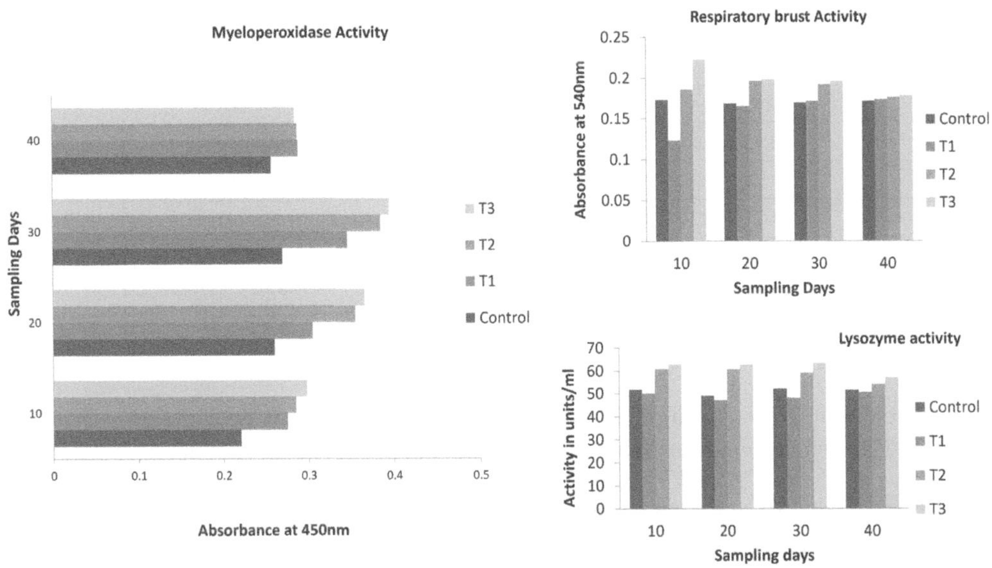

Fig. 40.1 Non-specific immune parameters (MPO, RBT and lysozyme activity) of *Labeo rohita* in control at each sampling day

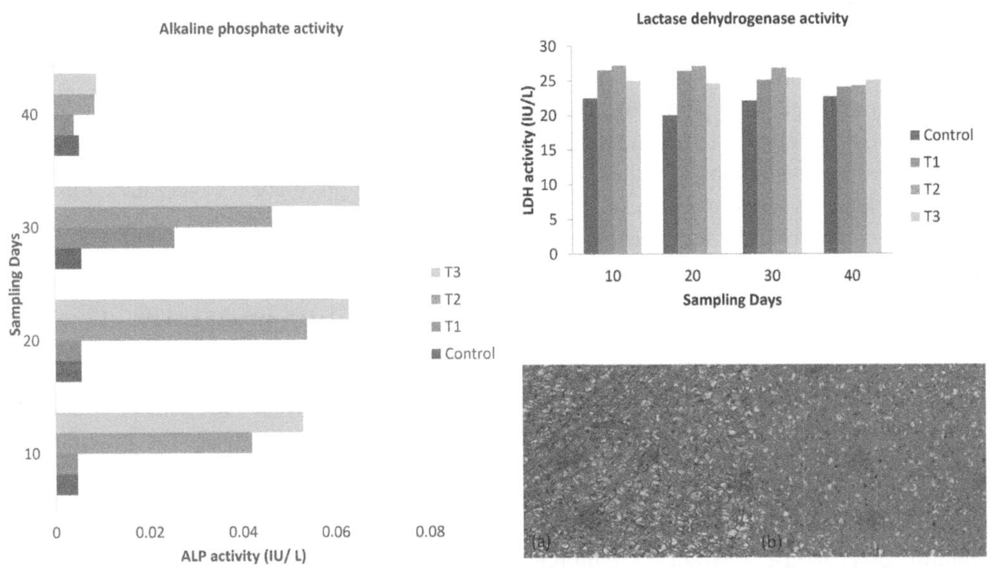

Fig. 40.2 Enzyme activity: Alkaline phosphatase activity, Lactate dehydrogenase, Histology of fish liver (a) Control (b) Biosurfactant

decline in enzyme levels indicated a reversible alteration in organs. Adhering strictly to administration protocols is essential, as higher doses may induce irreversible changes. Blood proteins, including albumin and globulin, were notably higher in T3 and T4 groups, and these levels persisted even after BS withdrawal (Table 40.3.).

Table 40.3 Serum biochemical parameters of *Labeo rohita* fingerlings under surfactant exposure: Protein, albumin, globulin, and glucose

30 days experiment				
	Serum protein (g/dl)	Serum albumin (g/dl)	Globulin (g/dl)	Serum glucose (mg/dl)
Control	2.15 ± 0.013	0.95 ± 0.005	1.2 ± 0.008	90.34 ± 0.487
T1	2.72 ± 0.031	1.07 ± 0.04	1.65 ± 0.009	95.78 ± 0.59
T2	2.91 ± 0.008	1.52 ± 0.005	1.39 ± 0.003	97.93 ± 0.926
T3	2.81 ± 0.002	1.77 ± 0.005	1.04 ± 0.007	87.20 ± 0.627

Table 40.4 Haematological markers, antioxidant enzyme activity (SOD), HIS, and VSI in experimental groups at 40 days

	After 40th day			
Parameters	**Control**	**T1**	**T2**	**T3**
Hb (g dl^{-1})	6.73 ± 0.34	8.01 ± 0.586	9.36 ± 0.31	9.22 ± 0.025
HIS Index	1.71 ± 005	1.77 ± 0.009	1.99 ± 0.003	1.97 ± 0.002
VSI Index	3.6 ± 0.003	4.26 ± 0.006	4.2 ± 0.05	4.06 ± 0.003
SOD of liver	180.4 ± 0.42	174.4 ± 0.34	150.8 ± 0.26	152.4 ± 0.18
TEC (106/mm^3)	1.48 ± 0.024	1.90 ± 0.05	2.40 ± 0.04	2.55 ± 0.13
TLC (10^6/mm^3)	0.26 ± 0.004	0.28 ± 0.006	0.35 ± 0.002	0.38 ± 0.012

Furthermore, hematological research showed that all treatment groups had greater hemoglobin (Hb) and red blood cell (RBC) levels, whereas T2 and T3 groups had higher white blood cell counts. The T3 and T4 groups had the lowest levels of hepatic superoxide dismutase (SOD) activity. There were substantial differences between the groups' HIS and VSI values (Table 40.4.).

This study found that biosurfactant supplementation had no adverse effects on fish behavior or liver health. Histological analysis of liver tissues from control and treated (T3) groups showed intact structures (Fig. 40.2.) with no vacuoles, haemorrhage, or hypertrophy, and only minimal nuclear pyknosis, likely due to normal blood cell maturation. Behavioural observations revealed normal swimming, with no lethargy or stress. These findings align with prior studies reporting the immunostimulatory and antiparasitic effects of biosurfactants from *Bacillus*, *Pseudomonas*, and *Staphylococcus* species in fish and shrimp without toxicity [15]. For instance, *Staphylococcus hominis* biosurfactants enhanced immunity in *Oreochromis mossambicus*, while biosurfactants showed antiparasitic activity in rainbow trout and increased pathogen resistance in *Litopenaeus vannamei* [16, 17]. Effective, non-toxic doses ranged between 10–100 µg/mL. Overall, the results support the safe use of biosurfactants in aquaculture to improve immunity and disease resistance, reinforcing their potential as sustainable alternatives to antibiotics.

The study observed improved hemato-immunological parameters in fish fed biosurfactant (BS)-supplemented diets, indicating enhanced health. Factors like age, species, and nutrition influence these markers [18]. A decrease in SOD activity suggests reduced oxidative stress, possibly due to the antioxidant properties of BS, which may aid ROS detoxification. These findings align with previous reports on probiotics reducing oxidative stress in *Megalobrama terminalis* [19], *Labeorohita*[20], and *Anguilla japonica* [21]. Immune-boosting agents like yeast RNA and β-glucan similarly elevate immunity in fish. No significant changes were seen in hepatosomatic (HSI) and viscerosomatic (VSI) indices, suggesting BS safety and suitability as a dietary additive. These indices reflect metabolic reserves [22] and can vary with nutrition or pollutant exposure [23]. Overall, rhamnolipid-based biosurfactants show potential as safe immunostimulants in aquaculture, strengthening non-specific immunity and enhancing disease resilience in fish without compromising metabolic health.

4. Conclusion

This study confirms the safety and potential of rhamnolipid as a non-toxic dietary immunostimulant in aquaculture, enhancing fish health without hepatic damage. As the first study from the Karnataka Mangrove region to investigate a naturally derived compound on fish, this research lays the groundwork for subsequent pharmacological and pharmacokinetic investigations in aquaculture and potentially in higher vertebrates. Findings support its broader application and call for further research on dosage, mechanisms, and cross-species use.

Acknowledgment

The authors wish to express sincere thanks to Dr. Manojranjan Nayak, President of S'O'A (Deemed to be University) Bhubaneswar, for providing the necessary facilities to carry out the investigation.

References

1. Seal, B.S., Lillehoj, H.S., Donovan, D.M., & Gay, C.G., (2013). Alternatives to antibiotics: A symposium on the challenges and solutions for animal production. Anim. Health Res. Rev., 14, 78–87.
2. Hruzová, K., Patel, A., Masák, J., Matátková, O., Rova, U., Christakopoulos., P., &Matsakas, L., (2020). A novel approach for the production of green biosurfactant from Pseudomonas aeruginosa using renewable forest biomass. *Sci. Total Environ.*, 711, 135099. Santa Anna, L. M., Sebastian, G.V., Pereira Jr., N., Alves, T.L.M., Menezes, E.P., & Freire, D.M.G., (2001). Production of biosurfactant from a new and promising stain of *Pseudomonas aeruginosa* PA1. *Appl. Biochem. Biotechno.l*, 91, 459–467.
3. APHA. (2012). Standard Methods for the Examination of Water and Waste Water. 22nd Edition, American Public Health Association, American Water Works Association, Water Environment Federation.
4. Quade, M. J., and Roth, J. A., (1997). A rapid, direct assay to measure degranulation of bovine neutrophil primary

granules. *Veterinary Immunology and Immunopathology.*, 58, 239–248.

5. Anderson, D. P., and Siwicki, A. K. (1994). Duration of protection against Aeromonas salmonicida in brook trout immunostimulatedimmunostimulated with glucan or chitosan by injection or immersion. *The Progressive Fish-Culturist.*, 56, 258–261.
6. Sankaran, K.,& Gurnani, S., (1972). On the variation in the catalytic activity of lysozyme in fishes, *Indian J. Biochem. Biophys.*, 9, 162.
7. Michell, R.H., Karnovsky, M.J., &Karnovsky, M.L., (1970). The distributions of some granule-associated enzymes in guinea-pig polymorphonuclear leucocytes. *Biochemical Journal.*, 116(2), 207.
8. Marklund, S., &Marklund, G.,(1974). Involvement of the superoxide anion radical in the autoxidation of pyrogallol and a convenient assay for superoxide dismutase. *FEBS J.*, 47(3), 469–474.
9. Ashish, K. M., and Banalata, M., (2008). Acute toxicity impacts of hexavalent chromium on behavior and histopathology of gill, kidney and liver of the freshwater fish, *Channa punctatus* (Bloch). *Environmental Toxicology and Pharmacology.*, 26, 136.
10. Shi, G., Sun, L.J., Wang, Y.L., Liu, H.M., Xu, D.F., Nie, F.H., Liu, Y. & Ye R.Y., (2014). Effects of NT-6 antimicrobial lipopeptide on growth performance of *Litopenaeusvannamei* and *Vibrio* number during breeding process. *Guangdong J Agric Sci.*, 12, 119.
11. Xiao, H., Shao, F.Y., Wu, M.M., Ren, W.K., Xiong, X., Tan, B. & Yin, Y.L., (2015). The application of antimicrobial peptides as growth and health promoters for swine. *J Anim Sci Biotechnol,*, 6, 19.
12. Dalmo, R.A., Ingebrightsen, K. &Bogwald, J., (1997). Non-specific defense mechanisms in fish, with particular reference to the reticuloendothelial system (RES). *J. Fish Dis.*, 20, 241.
13. Serezli, R., Çağirgan, H., Okumuş, İ., Akhan, S.,& Balta, F., (2005).The effect of oxytetracycline on non-specific immune response in sea bream (*Sparus aurata* L. 1758). *Turkish Journal of Veterinary andAnimal Sciences.*, 29, 31.
14. Serezli, R., Çağirgan, H., Okumuş, İ., Akhan, S.,& Balta, F., (2005).The effect of oxytetracycline on non-specific immune response in sea bream (*Sparus aurata* L. 1758). *Turkish Journal of Veterinary andAnimal Sciences.*, 29, 31.
15. Donio, M.B.S., Ronica, S.F.A., Thanga Viji, V., Velmurugan, S., Adlin Jenifer, J., Michaelbabu, M., &Citarasu, T. (2013). Isolation and characterization of halophilic *Bacillus sp.* BS3 able to produce pharmacologically important biosurfactants. *Asian Pac. J. Trop. Med.,* 6, 876–883.
16. Al-Jubury, A., Lu, C., Kania, P. W., Von Gersdor Jørgensen, L., Liu, Y., de Bruijn, I., Raaijmakers, J., and Buchmann, K. (2018). Impact of *Pseudomonas* H6 surfactant on all external life cycle stages of the fish parasitic ciliate *Ichthyophthiriusmultifiliis.J. Fish Dis.,* 41, 1147–1152.
17. Yan, M., Wang, W., Huang, X., Wang, X., & Wang, Y., (2020). Interactive effects of dietary cholesterol and phospholipids on the growth performance, expression of immune-related genes and resistance against Vibrio alginolyticus in white shrimp (*Litopenaeusvannamei*). *Fish Shellfish Immunol.*, 97, 100–107.
18. Kim, D.H., Subramanian, D., &Heo, M.S., (2017). Dietary effect of probiotic bacteria, Bacillus amyloliquefaciens-JFP2 on growth and innate immune response in rock bream Oplegnathus fasciatus, challenged with Streptococcus iniae. Isr. J. Aquac. 1354, 1–11.
19. Zhang, C.N., Li, X.F., Xu, W.N., Jiang, G.Z., Lu, K.L., Wang, L.N., &Liu, W.B., (2013). Combined effects of dietary fructo-oligosaccharide and Bacillus licheniformis on innate immunity, antioxidant capability and disease resistance of triangular bream (*Megalobrama terminalis*). *Fish. Shellfish. Immunol.*, 35, 1380–1386.
20. Giri, S.S., Sukumaran, V., Sen, S.S., &Jena, P.K., (2014). Effect of dietary supplementation of potential probiotic Bacillus subtilis VSG1 singularly or in combination with Lactobacillus plantarum VSG3 or/ and Pseudomonas aeruginosa VSG2 on the growth, immunity and disease resistance of Labeorohita. Aquac. Nutr., 20, 163–171.
21. Lee, S., Katya, K., Park, Y., Won, S., Seong, M., Hamidoghli, A., &Bai, S.C., (2017). Comparative evaluation of dietary probiotics Bacillus subtilis WB60 and Lactobacillus plantarum KCTC3928 on the growth performance, immunological parameters, gut morphology and disease resistance in Japanese eel, Anguilla japonica. *Fish. Shellfish. Immunol.*, 61, 201–210.
22. Larsen, D.A, Beckman, B.R., Dickhoff, WW.,(2001). The effect of low tempera ture and fasting during the winter on metabolic stores and endo crine physiology (insulin, insulin-like growth factor-I, and thyroxine) of coho salmon, Oncorhynchus kisutch. *Gen Comp Endocrinol.*, 123 (3),308–323.
23. Al-Ghais, S. M. (2013). Acetylcholinesterase, glutathione and hepatosomatic index as potential biomarkers of sewage pollution and depuration in fish. *Mar Poll Bull.*, 74(1),183–186.

Note: All the figures and tables in this chapter were made by the authors.

Research and Innovations in Industrial and Marine Biotechnology: A Circular Economy 2024 – Prof. Hrudayanath Thatoi et al. (eds)

41 Elucidation of Novel Therapeutic Producers from Marine Environments

Jyoti Srivastava[1]
School of Engineering, Ajeenkya D Y Patil University,
Pune, Maharashtra, India

Hrudayanath Thatoi[2]
Centre for Industrial Biotechnology Research,
Siksha O Anusandhan, Bhubaneswar,
Odisha, India

Mohammed Shabab*,
Nawneet Kurrey, S M Khade
School of Engineering, Ajeenkya D Y Patil University,
Pune, Maharashtra, India

Abstract: The present study delineates the exploitation of marine microbes' potential in producing a variety of antimicrobial compounds. Considering the increase in antimicrobial resistance globally, finding novel antimicrobial producers is the need of the hour. With using genome mining and metagenomics approach, the biosynthetic gene clusters (BGC's) to produce antimicrobial compounds can be identified. Marine microbes are the prolific source of novel antibiotics, offering unique bioactive compounds due to their adaptation to extreme environments like high salinity, pressure, and low temperatures. It has been observed that, many microbes have been identified to yield distinct secondary metabolites with potent antimicrobial properties, many of which show efficacy against multidrug-resistant pathogens. Key examples include Salinosporamide A, an anticancer agent with antibacterial properties, and Marinomycin, which targets resistant bacterial strains. However, harnessing these bioactive compounds presents challenges because of difficulty in culturing many marine microbes under laboratory conditions. Advanced cultivation techniques, including co-culturing and optimization of physico-chemical parameters, have facilitated the growth of these microbes, enabling the extraction of their metabolites. Moreover, genome mining and metagenomics study delineates to identify biosynthetic gene clusters associated with antibiotic production. The biotechnological production of marine-derived antibiotics involves optimizing yield and sustainability, often through bioreactors that replicate marine conditions or genetic engineering to enhance metabolite output. With the growing threat of antimicrobial resistance, antibiotics from marine microbes represent a valuable avenue for new drug discovery with potential pharmaceutical applications. Future research focuses on sustainable extraction methods, advanced microbial cultivation, and synthetic biology approaches to maximize the therapeutic potential of these marine-based compounds.

Keywords: Antibiotics, Genome mining, Marine isolates, Metagenomics, Multidrug resistance

1. Introduction

Antimicrobial resistance (AMR) is foremost attentive universal health challenges of the 21st century. It compromises the effectiveness of current antibiotics, resulting in prolonged illness, additional healthcare costs, and elevateddeath rates (World Health Organization, 2019). With the antibiotic pipeline drying up, the discovery

*Corresponding author: peptech@gmail.com

DOI: 10.1201/9781003759003-41

of new classes of antibiotics has become a priority. Marine ecosystems, which account for 70% of Earth's surface and 95% of its biosphere, are a promising yet underexplored source of microbial diversity [1]

Marine microbes have evolved unique survival strategies to thrive in extreme environments like high salinity, low temperatures, and intense pressure. These adaptations result in the secretion of secondary metabolites with unprecedented structural and functional diversity[2]. On the contrary to terrestrial microbes, marine-based compounds display distinctive chemical scaffolds that make them highly effective against multidrug-resistant (MDR) pathogens [3].

This chapter consists of a comprehensive overview of marine microbes as sources of novel antimicrobial agents. It discusses the key compounds discovered, challenges in culturing these microbes, advanced methodologies for their exploitation, and future perspectives in the fight against AMR.

2. Marine Microbes: A Unique Reservoir of Bioactive Compounds

2.1 Biodiversity of Marine Microbes

Marine ecosystems harbor an extensive range of microbial taxa, including bacteria (e.g., *Vibrio*, *Pseudoalteromonas*), actinomycetes (e.g., *Salinispora*, *Micromonospora*), and fungi (e.g., *Aspergillus*, *Penicillium*). These microorganisms account for a significant portion of Earth's genetic diversity and are a rich source of bioactive secondary metabolites[4].The extreme and dynamic conditions in marine habitats have driven the evolution of unique metabolic pathways, enabling the production of structurally complex and highly potent bioactive compounds. For example, halophilic bacteria produce antimicrobial peptides that inhibit the growth of multidrug-resistance(MDR) pathogens, while psychrophilic microbes from polar regions exhibit potent antifungal activity[5].

Key Bioactive Compounds

Several bioactive compounds derived from marine microbes have demonstrated remarkable antimicrobial activity:

Salinosporamide A

Salinosporamide A, also named as marizomib, is a naturallyoccurring compound with significant potential in the field of cancer therapy. It was first isolated from *Salinispora tropica*, a marine actinobacterium discovered in ocean sediments. This compound belongs to a class of natural products called β-lactone-γ-lactams and is notable for its potent activity as a proteasome inhibitor [6]. Recently Moore et al investigated the synthesis pathway of Salinosporamide A which is catalyzed by ketosynthase and SalC [7]. 20s proteosome is the central driving force to regulate the cellular proteins and hence becoming the promising target to control the cellular activities [8]. The inhibition of 20s, 26s proteosome is the underlying mechanism in regulating the cancer progression by salinosporamide A[9,10].In addition to anticancer agent, Salinosporamide A also exhibits to control the T cell proliferationby inhibiting the MAPK pathway and arresting the cell cycle and thereby serves in treating the autoimmune disorders and graft-versus-host disease[11]. MAPK pathway is critical for survival, spreading, and drug resistance of human cancer cells. Various filamentous Actinobacteria are known for the novel natural products producers which are indigenously present in marine environment. However, it is also observed that in many Actinobacteria the secondary metabolites producing biosynthetic gene clusters (BGCs) are silent or cryptic often referred to as orphan BGCs. However, co-culture technique is one of the most promising methods to stimulate the expression of orphan BGCs for many microorganisms[12,13].

Marinopyrrole A

A pyrrolyl derivative from *Streptomyces* species that disrupts bacterial cell membranes. Marinopyrrole A was primarily isolated from a marine-derived Streptomyces species. Streptomyces, a genus of actinobacteria, is well-acknowledged for its prolific ability to synthesize secondary metabolites with bioactive properties. The discovery of Marinopyrrole A emerged from efforts to explore marine microorganisms for novel drug leads. These microorganisms often thrive under extreme conditions, such as high pressure, low temperatures, or varying salinity, which drive the production of unique and structurally complex molecules.The potential and stability of Marinopyrrole A in human serum was increased by optimizing the structure by the chloro-derivative of Marinopyrrole A as [(4-chloro-2-hydroxyphenyl) (4,4′,5,5′-tetrachloro-2′-(2-hydroxybenzoyl)-1′H-1,3′-bipyrrole-2-yl)methanone] against methicillin-resistant *Staphylococcus aureus* bacteria with a Minimum Inhibitory Concentration (MIC) of 25-50 μM[14].These pathogens pose important challenges in healthcare because of their resistance to commonly used antibiotics. Marinopyrrole A's mechanism of action is believed to involve disruption of bacterial membranes and interference with vital enzymatic pathways. Beyond its antibacterial potential, Marinopyrrole A shows promise in cancer research [15]. The biosynthesis of Marinopyrrole A involves a highly specialized metabolic pathway encoded within the genome of the producing microorganism. The genes responsible for the biosynthesis of Marinopyrrole A are typically organized in a biosynthetic gene cluster (BGC). These clusters encode a variety of enzymes, including polyketide synthases (PKSs), non-ribosomal peptide synthetases (NRPSs), and tailoring enzymes such as halogenases and methyltransferases[16].

Table 41.1 Potential therapeutic molecule producers from marine isolates

Compounds	Source Organism	Mechanism of Action	Therapeutic Potential	Reference
Salinosporamide A	*Salinispora tropica*	Inhibits proteasome, leading to protein degradation	Treatment of resistant bacterial infections, cancer	[20,21]
Marinomycin A	*Streptomyces* sp.	Disrupts bacterial cell membranes integrity	Effective against Gram-positive resistant strains	[18,22]
Marinopyrrole A	*Streptomyces* sp.	Inhibits microtubule polymerization	Broad-spectrum antibacterial agent	[23]
Halichondrin B	*Halichondria* spp.	microtubule polymerization	Treatment of cancer, especially breast cancer	[24,25]
Aplysinopsin	*Aplysina fistularis*	Inhibits protein synthesis in microbial cells	Antifungal applications	[26]

Marinomycin A

Marinomycin A was firstly derived from a marine-based actinomycete, a member of the genus *Streptomyces*. Marinomycin A exhibits exceptional activity against Gram-positive bacteria, comprising multidrug-resistant strains like methicillin-resistant *Staphylococcus aureus* (MRSA) and vancomycin-resistant *Enterococci* (VRE) [17]. The heterologous expression of BGC's encoding Marinomycin A by transformation of *Streptomyces lividans* using the BGC construct were promising in increasing the production of Marinomycin A[18].In addition to its antibacterial effects, Marinomycin A shows promising cytotoxicity against various cancer cell lines. Studies have demonstrated its ability to induce apoptosis, particularly in highly aggressive and drug-resistant cancers [19]. These examples underscore the potential of marine microbes in addressing unmet medical needs.

3. Challenges in Harnessing Marine Microbial Potential

3.1 Cultivation Barriers

Despite their potential, the majority of marine microbes remain unculturable using conventional laboratory techniques. Factors such as oligotrophic growth requirements, dependency on symbiotic relationships, and the need for specific physico-chemical conditions hinder their cultivation[27]. Advanced cultivation strategies, such as the isolation chip (iChip), have enabled the growth of previously unculturable strains by simulating natural environments [28]. iChip is a device used to grow and isolate microorganisms in their natural environments. It is a membrane diffusion-based technology ability to carry out high-throughput cultivation of microorganisms. The device has been designed with a plate exhibiting the holes as microchambers to holdand grow one cell per chamber with two sealing membranes having 20-30nm pore size[29]. This strategy increased efficiency in 300-fold in isolating and culturing the microbes than the conventional platingmethod[30].

3.2 Metabolite Stability

The bioactivity of marine-derived metabolites can be compromised by their instability under non-marine conditions. The stability of bioactives can be studied by various approaches like environmental factors and formulation enhancements.For example, many polyketides degrade when exposed to atmospheric oxygen, limiting their practical applications[2]. The stability of metabolites can be increased by encapsulating liposomes or nanoparticles protecting from the environmental factors. *Shafaa et al* investigated the liposome encapsulation marine derived anticancer compound butylcycloheptylprodigiosin resulted in greater stability and effective cytotoxic activity [31].

3.3 Scalability Issues

Scaling up the production of marine-derived compounds remains challenging due to low metabolite yields and the high costs of marine media. Optimizing bioreactor designs and fermentation conditions is essential for sustainable production.

4. Advanced Techniques for Cultivation and Isolation

4.1 Co-Cultivation Strategies

Co-culturing marine microbes with symbiotic partners or competitors enhance the secretion of secondary metabolites. During the co-culturing the metabolites released from one microorganism stimulate the expressions of silent genes of another microbe stimulating the production of secondary metabolites. For instance, co-culturing *Streptomyces* with marine fungi stimulated the production of novel polyketides with potent antimicrobial properties[32].*Yu, Ding and Ma* (2016) co-cultured the marine isolates *Aspergillus flavipes* with the actinomycetes *Streptomyces* sp. and investigated the stimulation of cytochalasin production in many folds than the monoculture [33].

4.2 Bioreactor Systems

Marine bioreactors replicate the environmental conditions of the ocean, enabling the large-scale growth of marine microbes. Continuous culture systems, such as chemostats, offer a sustainable solution for metabolite production while minimizing environmental impacts.The actinomycin-D production from the estuarian isolate *Streptomyces* sp. MS 310 in the optimized physicochemical conditions that cultured in 25 L of Rotating Disk Bioreactor (RDBR) with

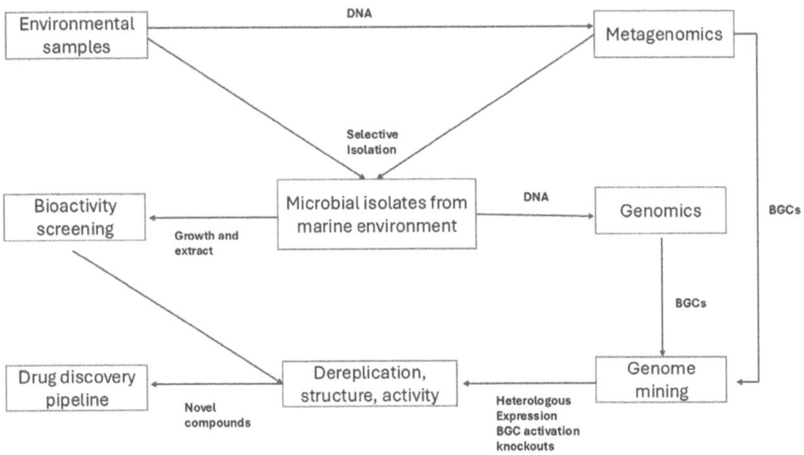

Fig. 41.1 Overview of the utilization of genome mining and metagenomic techniques to discover a therapeutic compound
Source: Authors

rotation speed of 1 revolution per day by half-submerging the disk and mimicking the intertidal conditions of estuarian niche. This mimicking estuarian conditions increased the aeration rate from 3 to 9 L/min resulted in increased actinomycin-D production by 33% [34].

5. Omics Approaches: Genome Mining and Metagenomics

5.1 Genome Mining for Biosynthetic Gene Clusters (BGCs)

Genome mining has revolutionized the identification of novel antimicrobial agents by pinpointing biosynthetic gene clusters responsible for secondary metabolite synthesis. Tools like antiSMASH and BiG-SCAPE analyze microbial genomes for clusters expressing non-ribosomal peptide synthetases (NRPS) and polyketide synthases (PKS)[35]. Mansson et al [36], have correlated the dithiolopyrrolone holomycin antibiotic in biomass extracts to that of the corresponding gene clusters by antiSMASH.

5.2 Metagenomics for Unculturable Microbes

Metagenomics involves sequencing environmental DNA to uncover genetic information from unculturable microbes. This approach has directed to the discovery of novel bioactive compounds, viz., teixobactin, a promising antibiotic active against Gram-positive pathogens.

6. Future Prospects of Marine-Derived Isolates

Marine microorganisms offer significant potential as sources of innovative antibiotics, antiviral compounds, and anticancer agents. These isolates are particularly valuable in addressing the growing challenge of antibiotic resistance. Recent progress in genome mining has uncovered hidden biosynthetic pathways, paving the way for the development of novel therapeutic drugs. Marine microorganisms are valuable for industrial applications due to their production of extremozymes, which are enzymes capable of maintaining functionality under harsh conditions like high salinity or pressure. These unique enzymes are increasingly utilized in the production of biofuels, the formulation of detergents, and the development of pharmaceuticals.

References

1. Frieri, M., Kumar, K., & Boutin, A. (2017). Antibiotic resistance. *Journal of infection and public health*, *10*(4), 369–378.
2. Fenical, W., & Jensen, P. R. (2006). Developing a new resource for drug discovery: marine actinomycete bacteria. *Nature chemical biology*, *2*(12), 666–673.
3. Lewis, K. (2020). The science of antibiotic discovery. *Cell*, *181*(1), 29–45.
4. Ziemert, N., Alanjary, M., & Weber, T. (2016). The evolution of genome mining in microbes–a review. *Natural product reports*, *33*(8), 988–1005.
5. Blunt, J. W., Copp, B. R., Munro, M. H., Northcote, P. T., & Prinsep, M. R. (2006). Marine natural products. *Natural product reports*, *23*(1), 26–78.
6. Feling, R. H., Buchanan, G. O., Mincer, T. J., Kauffman, C. A., Jensen, P. R., &Fenical, W. (2003). Salinosporamide A: a highly cytotoxic proteasome inhibitor from a novel microbial source, a marine bacterium of the new genus Salinospora. *AngewandteChemie International Edition*, *42*(3), 355–357.
7. Bauman, K. D., Shende, V. V., Chen, P. Y. T., Trivella, D. B., Gulder, T. A., Vellalath, S., ... & Moore, B. S. (2022). Enzymatic assembly of the salinosporamide γ-lactam-β-lactone anticancer warhead. *Nature chemical biology*, *18*(5), 538–546.
8. Serrano-Aparicio, N., Moliner, V., & Swiderek, K. (2021). Nature of Irreversible Inhibition of Human 20S Proteasome by Salinosporamide A. The Critical Role of Lys–Asp Dyad Revealed from Electrostatic Effects Analysis. *ACS catalysis*, *11*(6), 3575–3589.
9. Oh, K.-K., Yoon, S.-J., Song, S. H., Park, J. H., Kim, J. S., Kim, M. J., . . . Suk, K.-T. (2024). A scheme to underpin

key mediator (s) in Salinosporamide (s) against pan-tumor via systems biology concept. *Journal of Translational Medicine, 22*(1), 492.

10. Serrano-Aparicio, N., Moliner, V., & Swiderek, K. (2021). On the origin of the different reversible characters of salinosporamide A and homosalinosporamide A in the covalent inhibition of the human 20S proteasome. *ACS Catalysis, 11*(18), 11806–11819.
11. Lee, H. S., & Jeong, G. S. (2020). Salinosporamide A, a marine-derived proteasome inhibitor, inhibits T cell activation through regulating proliferation and the cell cycle. *Molecules, 25*(21), 5031.
12. Baker, K. V., Takano, E., & Breitling, R. (2018). The "three Cs" of novel antibiotic discovery and production through synthetic biology: Biosynthetic gene clusters, heterologous chassis, and synthetic microbial consortia. *Advanced Biosystems, 2*(11), 1800064.
13. Li, X., Xu, H., Li, Y., Liao, S., & Liu, Y. (2023). Exploring diverse bioactive secondary metabolites from marine microorganisms using co-culture strategy. *Molecules, 28*(17), 6371.
14. Liu, Y., Haste, N. M., Thienphrapa, W., Li, J., Nizet, V., Hensler, M., & Li, R. (2014). Marinopyrrole derivatives as potential antibiotic agents against methicillin-resistant Staphylococcus aureus (III). *Marine drugs, 12*(5), 2458–2470.
15. Coulter, D. W., Chhonker, Y. S., Kumar, D., Kesherwani, V., Aldhafiri, W. N., McIntyre, E. M., ... & Chaturvedi, N. K. (2024). Marinopyrrole derivative MP1 as a novel anti-cancer agent in group 3 MYC-amplified Medulloblastoma. *Journal of Experimental & Clinical Cancer Research, 43*(1), 18.
16. Agarwal, V., Miles, Z. D., Winter, J. M., Eustáquio, A. S., El Gamal, A. A., & Moore, B. S. (2017). Enzymatic halogenation and dehalogenation reactions: pervasive and mechanistically diverse. *Chemical reviews, 117*(8), 5619–5674.
17. Jensen, P. R., & Mafnas, C. (2006). Biogeography of the marine actinomycete Salinispora. *Environmental Microbiology, 8*(11), 1881–1888.
18. Abraham, E., Lawther, H. A., Wang, Y., Zarins-Tutt, J. S., Rivera, G. S., Wu, C., ... & Goss, R. J. (2024). The identification and heterologous expression of the biosynthetic gene cluster encoding the antibiotic and anticancer agent marinomycin. *Biomolecules, 14*(1), 117.
19. Friedrich, R. M., & Friestad, G. K. (2020). Inspirations from tetrafibricin and related polyketides: new methods and strategies for 1, 5-polyol synthesis. *Natural product reports, 37*(9), 1229–1261.
20. Kim, H., Kim, S., Kim, M., Lee, C., Yang, I., & Nam, S.-J. (2020). Bioactive natural products from the genus Salinospora: a review. *Archives of pharmacal research, 43*, 1230–1258.
21. Wang, E., Sorolla, M. A., Gopal Krishnan, P. D., & Sorolla, A. (2020). From seabed to bedside: A review on promising marine anticancer compounds. *Biomolecules, 10*(2), 248.
22. Ballaschk, F., Bensberg, K., Crone, B., Kirsch, S. F., & Menz, H. (2024). Synthesis of the monomeric counterpart of Marinomycin A and B. *Organic & Biomolecular Chemistry, 22*(25), 5127–5133.
23. Guo, F., Xiao, F., Song, H., Li, X., Xiao, Y., Qin, Y., & Lei, X. (2024). An Optimized Marinopyrrole A Derivative Targets 6-Phosphoglucosamine Synthetase to Inhibit Methicillin-Resistant Staphylococcus aureus. *ACS Central Science, 10*(11), 2090–2098.
24. Dissanayake, D. S., Nagahawatta, D. P., Lee, J. S., & Jeon, Y. J. (2024). Immunomodulatory effects of halichondrin isolated from marine sponges and its synthetic analogs in oncological applications. *Marine Drugs, 22*(9), 426.
25. Nicolaou, K. C., Pan, S., Shelke, Y., Rigol, S., Bao, R., Das, D., & Ye, Q. (2022). A unified strategy for the total syntheses of eribulin and a macrolactam analogue of halichondrin B. *Proceedings of the National Academy of Sciences, 119*(32), e2208938119.
26. El-Sawy, E. R., El-Shahid, Z. A., Soliman, A. A., Nassrallah, A., Abdelwahab, A. B., Kirsch, G., & Abdelmegeed, H. (2022). Synthetic Analogs of Marine Alkaloid Aplysinopsin Suppress Anti-Apoptotic Protein BCL2 in Prostate Cancer. *Molecules, 28*(1), 109.
27. Hugenholtz, P., Goebel, B. M., & Pace, N. R. (1998). Impact of culture-independent studies on the emerging phylogenetic view of bacterial diversity. *Journal of bacteriology, 180*(18), 4765–4774.
28. Nichols, D., Cahoon, N., Trakhtenberg, E. M., Pham, L., Mehta, A., Belanger, A., ... & Epstein, S. (2010). Use of ichip for high-throughput in situ cultivation of "uncultivable" microbial species. *Applied and environmental microbiology, 76*(8), 2445–2450.
29. Lewis, W. H., Tahon, G., Geesink, P., Sousa, D. Z., & Ettema, T. J. (2021). Innovations to culturing the uncultured microbial majority. *Nature Reviews Microbiology, 19*(4), 225–240.
30. Zhang, Z. F., Liu, F., Liu, L. R., Li, M., Cai, L., Liu, S., & Mao, J. (2024). Culturing the uncultured marine fungi in the omics age: Opportunities and challenges. *Fungal Biology Reviews, 48*, 100353.
31. Shafaa, M. W., Hassan, E. S., Faraag, A. H., Essawy, E., & Abdelfattah, M. S. (2022). Fabrication and characterization of pigmented secondary metabolites bound liposomes with improved cytotoxic activity against prostate and hepatic cancer. *International Nano Letters, 12*(4), 409–420.
32. Peng, X. Y., Wu, J. T., Shao, C. L., Li, Z. Y., Chen, M., & Wang, C. Y. (2021). Co-culture: stimulate the metabolic potential and explore the molecular diversity of natural products from microorganisms. Marine life science & technology, 1–12.
33. Yu, L., Ding, W., & Ma, Z. (2016). Induced production of cytochalasans in co-culture of marine fungus Aspergillus flavipes and actinomycete Streptomyces sp. *Natural Product Research, 30*(15), 1718–1723.
34. Sarkar, S., Mukherjee, J., & Roy, D. (2009). Antibiotic production by a marine isolate (MS 310) in an ultra-low-speed rotating disk bioreactor. *Biotechnology and bioprocess engineering, 14*, 775–780.
35. Medema, M. H., Blin, K., Cimermancic, P., De Jager, V., Zakrzewski, P., Fischbach, M. A., ... & Breitling, R. (2011). antiSMASH: rapid identification, annotation and analysis of secondary metabolite biosynthesis gene clusters in bacterial and fungal genome sequences. *Nucleic acids research, 39*(suppl_2), W339–W346.
36. Mansson, M., Gram, L., & Larsen, T. O. (2011). Production of bioactive secondary metabolites by marine Vibrionaceae. *Marine drugs, 9*(9), 1440–1468.

Research and Innovations in Industrial and Marine Biotechnology: A Circular Economy 2024 – Prof. Hrudayanath Thatoi et al. (eds)
© 2026 Taylor & Francis Group, London, ISBN 978-1-041-28285-3

42 Unveiling the Potential of Microalgae for Biofuel Production: A Review

D P Krishna Samal[1], Lala Behari Sukla[2]
Designation/Affiliation - Biofuels and Bioprocessing Research Center,
Institute of Technical Education and Research,
Siksha 'O' Anusandhan (Deemed to be University),
Bhubaneswar, India

Abstract: Fossil fuels continue to provide a substantial portion of the overall energy supply, but their limited availability and environmental impact are concerning. As a result, sustainable energy solutions become more relevant to the population in terms of remaining requirements by 2040. Because of their quick growth rates, small footprint, and carbon neutrality, microalgae are a promising source of third-generation biofuel. Micro-algal biofuels are very productive, with oil reaching 20-50% of dry biomass or more and axially increasing biomass more than three times in hours under perfect growth circumstances. *Chlorella*, *Botryococcusbraunii*, and *Scenedesmus obliquus* are preferred for biofuel production due to their high lipid content.This review explores the potential for microalgae-based biofuels, emphasizing its ability to meet the world's expanding energy demands.

Keywords: Biofuel, Microalgae, Algal fuel, Sustainable fuel

1. Introduction

Economic growth and population expansion will result in increased energy demands[1]. Since fossil fuels resources are already scarce it is imperative to look for renewable energy alternatives right away. Sustainable energy sources are under strain since world energy demand is predicted to rise significantly by 2040[2]. Biofuel is produced from renewable sources like vegetable oils, animal fats, microalgae and seaweeds will serve as a potential substitute for conventional fossil fuels [3]. Microalgae are considered fossil fuel alternatives because of their high growth rates and carbon neutrality. They absorb significant amounts of CO_2 during cultivation, reducing emissions from biofuel production and usage. Furthermore, microalgae may be grown on uncultivated land avoiding the usage of agricultural land for food production. These are renewable fuel consists primarily of esters created from the reaction of methanol or ethanol with long-chain fatty acids like palmitic, stearic, oleic, and linoleic acids. Therefore research on micro algal based biofuel production has garnered significant global interest in recent years.

Microalgae have faster growth, high oil content,cultivate easily and offering better oil yield than oilseed crops [4]. Their growth in aqueous environments alleviates water stress and environmental footprints. Microalgae have fast growth rates and some species have oil contents as high as 20-50% of dry biomass which triples their biomass in the course of an hour. In addition, they play a role in air quality improvement via CO_2 biofixation[5]. Nutrients for growth can be derived from wastewater, and leftover biomass/co-products can be used as raw materials or converted into bioethanol or biogas. *Chlorella*, *Botryococcusbraunii*, and *Scenedesmus obliquus* species are commonly used in biofuel synthesis [6]. This is owing to their high lipid content, which is easily turned into biofuels. This review paper delves deeply into microalgae-based biofuels, emphasizing its potential as a means of meeting global energy demands.

[1]dpkrishnasamal@soa.ac.in, [2]lalabeharisukla@soa.ac.in

DOI: 10.1201/9781003759003-42

2. Types of Biofuels

Biofuels are sustainable energy sources instead of fossil fuels. They exist in liquid, solid, and gaseous forms (Table 42.1). They derived from agriculture that use plants, wood, seeds, and biomass. Bioethanol manufacturing, a more fuel-efficient alternative to gasoline, dates back to the 1800s. The biggest producers are the United States and Brazil, which grow it from maize and sugarcane. Corn production, on the other hand, competes for land with food crops. Alternative feedstocks, such as straw, wood chips, and forestry waste, provide more sustainable possibilities; however their processing is typically complicated (Table 42.1). Advancements such as integrated bioprocessing are being investigated to lower manufacturing costs. Transesterification produces biodiesel by converting fatty acids in vegetable oils and animal fats to methyl esters [7]. Biogases are renewable energy source that has been utilized to generate electricity. Biogas is widely utilized in agriculturally intensive nations like India, China, and Brazil, and it has effective uses in sectors such as food processing, pulp and paper, and domestic waste treatment.

Table 42.1 Types of biofuels and their source and applications

States of Biofuels	Types of Biofuels	Derived sources	Applications
Liquid	Biodiesel, Bioethanol	sugarcane, vegetable oils	Power generation, fuel additives
Solid	Animal dung, Charcoal, Fuelwood	Agricultural products, non-fossil feedstocks	Heat and energy generation
Gaseous	Biogas, Biohydrogen	Biomass via pyrolysis and gasification	Electricity generation, heating, transportation fuel

3. Evolution of Biofuel Generations

The evolution of biofuel production is grouped into four generations (Fig. 42.1). The first-generation biofuel made from edible crops like corn, soybean, and sugarcanes [8]. It can be derived from anaerobic digestion, Pyrolysis etc. These were resource-intensive and affecting land and water availability. Second-generation biofuels use non-food biomass such as agricultural waste, wood, and other plant materials. The non-food sources lead to minimizing competition with food production. Third-generation biofuel capitalizes on the ability of microalgae and seaweeds to produce lipids (Fig. 42.1). Microalgae have an innate property to yield up to 70% lipids [9]. They are cultivated in water and thus not in competition with arable land and have short growth cycles. Their growth rate is higher and they consume CO_2 in the course of photosynthesis. Thus, considering micro-algae for biofuel generation increases its feasibility. Algal species such as *Chlorella* and *Spirulina* have now been subjected to a great deal of research. Algal biomass can converted in to biofuels by different processes like biochemical, thermochemical, and chemical methods [10].

4. Microalgae

Microalgae are photosynthetic microorganisms live in a wide range of habitats from aquatic to terrestrial[11]. They use photosynthesis to create chemical energy from light, and their complete development cycle lasts a few days. With proper condition microalgae grow rapidly and survive in diverse environments. They serve as feedstock for biodiesel, methane, hydrogen, and ethanol. Sulphur-free algae-based biodiesel performs similarly to petroleum diesel[12]. Prominent species includes for biofuel productions are *Chlorella vulgaris*, *Chlorella protothecoides*,

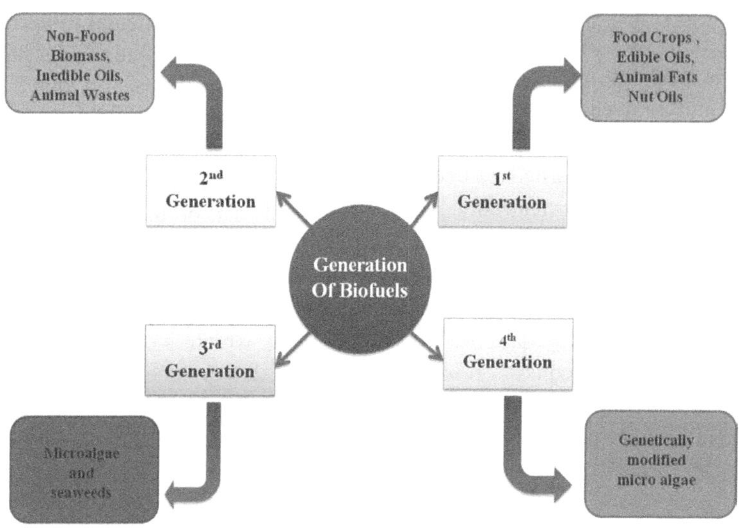

Fig. 42.1 Evolution of generation of biofuels with examples

Dunaliella salina, Scenedesmus obliquus, Nannochloropsisoculata, Botryococcusbraunii, Chlorellasorokiniana, Tetraselmissuecica, Haematococcuspluvialis, etc[13,14]. These species have variable lipid concentrations, ranging from 5% to more than 70%, as well as lipid and biomass productivities, making them viable candidates for biodiesel production (Table 42.2.).

Table 42.2 Diverse microalgal species and their lipid content

Name of the microalgae	Lipid content(%)
Ankistrodesmus sp.	24–31
Botryococcusbraunii	25–75
Chlorella vulgaris	5–58
Chlorococcum sp.	19.3
Nannochloropsis sp.	12-53
Nitzschiasp	16-47
Scenedesmus sp.	19.6-21.1
Dunaliella sp.	17.5-67
Ellipsoidion sp.	27.4

4.1 Microalgae: A Potential Source of Production of Biofuel

Microalgae are photosynthetic organisms ideal for sustainable biofuel production. Because of their fast uptake in rapid growth conditions found in various environments they are most promising options for biofuel production. Algae are an economically viable option for the future as an ecofriendly fuel source. Microalgae are unicellular and their biomass is rich in lipids, proteins, and carbohydrates. Macroalgae on the other hand gives higher yields for bioethanol. Thus, production of biofuels from algae is reducing GHG emissions in climate change mitigation [15]. Algae are carbon-neutral organisms and do not contribute to atmospheric carbon. Their growth and triglyceride content make microalgae essential in biofuel production.

Strain Selection and Algal Harvesting

The right strain of microalgae must be selected for biofuel production as different algae species differ in the amount of lipid accumulation. For biofuel production, rapid neutral lipid accumulation and high levels of neutral lipid content during growth stages are required. Alternatively, too much saturation of lipids may alter combustion which resulting in oxidized fuel injector lines. Selecting microalgal strains with balanced lipids enables efficient, sustainable biodiesel production.

Harvesting algae from massive quantities can turn out to be one of the most critical steps. Simple filtration methods lead to continuous back-mixing and recovery problems with dewatering [16]. Hence different methods are being used to recover biomass. Flocculation, flotation, centrifugation, and filtration are commonly used in algal harvesting. Using filtration and centrifugation together may improve the efficiency of separation [17].

5. Micro Algae Cultivation

5.1 Open Cultivation Systems

Open-cultivation systems were among the first used to cultivate microalgal species. It is frequently undertaken in small ponds and depends upon sunlight.Raceway ponds are the most common type of open systems (Fig. 42.2). A raceway pond system requires a large area of land. Some of these systems are economical and are made with concrete or plastic walls [18]. They depend on nutrients like nitrogen and phosphorus that come straight from water or sewage treatment plants.In general open systems are low-yielding and very sensitive to environmental factors. It has certain drawbacks as well including as rapid evaporation, temperature variations, and restricted gas transport, which raises concerns about environmental contamination.

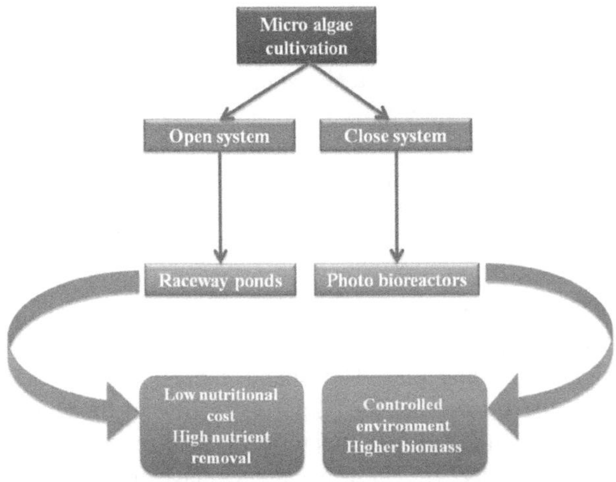

Fig. 42.2 Microalgae cultivation methods and their advantages

Closed Cultivation Systems

Closed cultivation systems operate in a controlled environment, eliminating contamination hazards and increasing biomass yield. While they are more expensive because to the numerous infrastructure investment possibilities, they produce higher biomass concentrations in shorter periods of time than open systems produce [10]. Tubular photobioreactors, which use transparent tubes to let sunlight into the suspension deeply and provide the best possible nutrient circulation, are particularly well-suited for commercial production out of all the closed systems (Fig. 42.2). These systems may also be utilized to efficiently treat industrial and agricultural wastewaters, making it easier to scale up operations and remove nutrients[19].

6. Production of Biofuel from Microalgae

The algae biofuel production process consists of several steps: algae cultivation, water removal or harvesting, lipid extraction and processing of algal oil, and its further conversion into biofuels [20]. Biofuel production begins by separating algal biomass from cultivated water. Centrifugation or filtration is a commonly used harvest method for the separation of algae. Various processes, such as membrane separation, flocculations are also there. After harvesting, algal biomass must be dried to attain a moisture percentage of 12-15%[21]. Solar drying, convection drying, spray drying, and freeze drying are mostly used for drying processes. Solar drying is a low-cost procedure, although it is time-consuming and can degrade biomass. Convective drying involves circulating hot air for around 12 hours. Spray drying produces nutrient rich green powder while freeze drying preserve cell contents without damaging the cell wall.

Algal cell walls are made up of polysaccharides and cellulose. For extraction of lipids, the cellulose and polysaccharide-based algal cell walls must be broken down [22].Various methods, such as bead beating, microwave treatment, and sonication, are employed for this. Cold pressing, solvent extraction, supercritical fluid extraction, and ultrasonic technology are popular ways for extracting oil from algal biomass. Cold-pressing is easy and large-scale, and the procedure takes a long period, yielding around 75% of the oil. Solvent extraction is the process of extracting oil from biomass. Commercially, hexane is the most extensively utilized and affordable solvent, resulting in a high oil production by rupturing algal cell walls [23]. Ultrasound extraction is quicker and offers larger yields. Lipid extraction methods like soxhlet extraction and supercritical fluid extraction are widely used [24]. These techniques have been used to isolate triglycerides. Supercritical extraction requires high pressure and temperature to burst cells and separate the oil, however certain samples may interact with one another, necessitating a longer extraction period. Supercritical fluid extraction methods gained prominence for their ability to produce high-quality oils without the use of harmful organic solvents. This method is a sustainable and an efficient alternative to algae-based biofuel production.

Environmental and operational parameters including pH, light, growth temperature, and growth medium composition affect microalgae cultivation. To maximize algal development, a pH range of 8.2 to 8.7 should be maintained [25]. CO_2 is introduced into the system in order to do this. Since various algae species have varying light needs, photoperiods and light intensity are also significant. Another crucial element is temperature, which will dictate the ideal location for growing. By controlling these variables, algae will be grown in open pond systems, photobioreactors, or hybrid systems.

7. Conclusion

Biofuel production from algal feedstocks is a long-term alternative to traditional petroleum fuels that has both environmental and economic benefits. Algae-based biofuels have the potential to transform the energy economy and play a critical role in combating greenhouse gas emissions.Large scale microalgae cultivation needs rigorous monitoring of light, nutrients, temperature, and CO_2 concentration. Furthermore, efficiency may be increased by adjusting harvesting processes, oil extraction procedures, and CO_2 supplies. Microalgal biofuels like bioethanol, biomethane, syngas and biohydrogen offer almost unlimited potential inside a sustainable energy future. Innovations in microalgal biofuels create scalable and green solutions to mankind. Future strategies entail the cultivation of lipid-rich genetically modified microalgae in marine and wastewater systems to provide an alternative to freshwater. Advances in pretreatment methods, genetic engineering and catalytic systems are some approaches to increasing production while cutting costs. To ensure the microalgae industry's long-term viability, efforts must be made to reduce production costs, employ low quality CO_2 sources and nutrient-rich effluent, and fine-tune culture systems. These advancements will not only minimize the environmental imprint, but will also allow for a broader range of applications in the microalgae sector, resulting in improved efficiency, sustainability, and competitiveness.

Declaration of Competing Interest

The authors declare that they have no known competing interests.

Acknowledgements

The authors are grateful to Prof. (Dr.) Manojranjan Nayak, President of Siksha 'O' Anusandhan University, for providing infrastructure and encouragement throughout the research process.

References

1. Samal, D. P. K., Sukla, L. B., Pattanaik, A., & Pradhan, D. (2020). Role of microalgae in treatment of acid mine drainage and recovery of valuable metals. *Materials Today: Proceedings*, 30(Part 2), 346–350.
2. Palaniappan, K. (2017). An overview of applications of nanotechnology in biofuel production. *World Applied Sciences Journal*, 35, 1305–1311.
3. Malik, K., Capareda, S. C., Kamboj, B. R., Malik, S., Singh, K., Arya, S., & Bishnoi, D. K. (2024). Biofuels production: A review on sustainable alternatives to traditional fuels and energy sources. *Fuels*, 5(2), 157–175.
4. Oves, M., Qari, H. A., & Ismail, I. M. (2022). Biofuel formation from microalgae: a renewable energy source for eco-sustainability. Current World Environment, 17(1), 4.Doi: http://dx.doi.org/10.12944/CWE.17.1.2.

5. Gaurav, K., Neeti, K., & Singh, R. (2024). Microalgae-based biodiesel production and its challenges and future opportunities: A review. *Green Technologies and Sustainability*, 2(1), 100060.
6. Chhandama, M. V. L., Ruatpuia, J. V., Ao, S., Chetia, A. C., Satyan, K. B., &Rokhum, S. L. (2023). Microalgae as a sustainable feedstock for biodiesel and other production industries: Prospects and challenges. Energy Nexus, 12, 100255.
7. Bardhan, P., Deka, A., Bhattacharya, S. S., Mandal, M., & Kataki, R. (2022). Economical aspect in biomass to biofuel production. In S. Yusup & N. A. Rashidi (Eds.), Value-Chain of Biofuels (pp. 395–427). *Elsevier.*
8. Sikarwal, V. S., Zhao, M., Fennell, P., Shah, N., & Anthony, E. J. (2017). Progress in biofuel production from gasification. *Progress in Energy and Combustion Science*, 61, 189–248.
9. Ahmed, S. F., Rafa, S. J., Mehjabin, A., Tasannum, N., Ahmed, S., Mofijur, M., Lichtfouse, E., Almomani, F., Badruddin, I. A., & Kamangar, S. (2023). Bio-oil from microalgae: Materials, production, technique, and future. *Energy Reports*, 10, 3297–3314.
10. Razzak, S. A., Lucky, R. A., Hossain, M. M., &deLasa, H. (2022). Valorization of microalgae biomass to biofuel production: A review. *Energy Nexus*, 7, 100139.
11. Thoré, E. S. J., Muylaert, K., Bertram, M. G., & Brodin, T. (2023). Microalgae. *Current Biology*, 33(3), R91–R95. doi: 10.1016/j.cub.2022.12.032. PMID: 36750029.
12. Abdullah, M., Ali, Z., Yasin, M. T., Amanat, K., Sarwar, F., Khan, J., & Ahmad, K. (2024). Advancements in sustainable production of biofuel by microalgae: Recent insights and future directions. *Environmental Research*, 262(Part 2), 119902.
13. Khoo, K. S., Ahmad, I., Chew, K. W., Iwamoto, K., Bhatnagar, A., & Show, P. L. (2023). Enhanced microalgal lipid production for biofuel using different strategies including genetic modification of microalgae: A review. *Progress in Energy and Combustion Science*, 96, 101071.
14. Siddiki, S. Y., Mofijur, M., Kumar, P., Ahmed, S., Inayat, A., Kusumo, F., ... & Mahlia, T. M. I. (2022). Microalgae biomass as a sustainable source for biofuel, biochemical, and biobased value-added products: An integrated biorefinery concept. *Fuel*, 307, 121782. 10.1016/j.fuel.2021.121782.
15. Sarwer, A., Hamed, S. M., Osman, A. I., Jamil, F., Al-Muhtaseb, A. A. H., Alhajeri, N. S., & Rooney, D. W. (2022). Algal biomass valorization for biofuel production and carbon sequestration: a review. Environmental Chemistry Letters, 20(5), 2797–2851.
16. Deepa, P., Sowndhararajan, K., & Kim, S. (2023). A review of the harvesting techniques of microalgae. *Water*, 15(17), 3074.
17. Vu, H. P., Nguyen, L. N., Emmerton, B., Wang, Q., Ralph, P. J., & Nghiem, L. D. (2021). Factors governing microalgae harvesting efficiency by flocculation using cationic polymers. *Bioresource Technology*, 340, 125669.
18. Matanguihan, A. E. D., Demafelis, R. B., Martinez-Goss, M., Nacorda, J. O. O., Torreta, N. K., Sanchez, D. E. S., ... & Dizon, L. S. H. (2020). Design, Fabrication, and Performance Evaluation of Open Raceway Ponds for the Cultivation of Chlorella vulgaris Beijerinck in the Philippines. *Philippine Journal of Science*, *149*(2).
19. Novoveská, L., Nielsen, S. L., Eroldoğan, O. T., et al. (2023). Overview and challenges of large-scale cultivation of photosynthetic microalgae and cyanobacteria. *Marine Drugs*, 21(8), 445.
20. Zewdie, D. T., & Ali, A. Y. (2020). Cultivation of microalgae for biofuel production: Coupling with sugarcane-processing factories. *Energy, Sustainability and Society*, 10, 27. Bilad, M. R., Arafat, H. A., &Vankelecom, I. F. J. (2014). Membrane technology in microalgae cultivation and harvesting: A review. *Biotechnology Advances*, 32(6), 1283–1300. doi: 10.1016/j.biotechadv.2014.07.008.
21. Ganesan, R., Manigandan, S., Samuel, M. S., Shanmuganathan, R., & Pugazhendhi, A. (2020). A review on prospective production of biofuel from microalgae. *Biotechnology Reports*, 27, e00509. Pôjo, V., Tavares, T., &Malcata, F. X. (2021). Processing methodologies of wet microalga biomass toward oil separation: An overview. *Molecules*, 26(3), 641.
22. Carreira-Casais, A., Otero, P., Garcia-Perez, P., et al. (2021). Benefits and drawbacks of ultrasound-assisted extraction for the recovery of bioactive compounds from marine algae. *International Journal of Environmental Research and Public Health*, 18(17), 9153. doi: 10.3390/ijerph18179153.
23. Dammak, I., Fersi, M., Hachicha, R., &Abdelkafi, S. (2023). Current insights into growing microalgae for municipal wastewater treatment and biomass generation. *Resources,* 12(10), 119.

Note: All the figures and tables in this chapter were made by the authors.

Research and Innovations in Industrial and Marine Biotechnology: A Circular Economy 2024 – Prof. Hrudayanath Thatoi et al. (eds)

43 Study of the Physico-Chemical Characters of Water of a Normal Habitat of *Cirrhinus Reba* at Monthly Interval

Sourav Chattaraj*
Centre for Industrial Biotechnology Research,
School of Pharmaceutical Sciences, Siksha 'O' Anusandhan Deemed to be University,
Kalinga Nagar, Bhubaneswar, Odisha, India

Arindam Ganguly
Department of Microbiology, Bankura Sammilani College,
Bankura, West Bengal, India

Bikash Ranjan Giri, Subhashree Rath
Centre for Industrial Biotechnology Research,
School of Pharmaceutical Science, Siksha 'O' Anusandhan University,
Kalinga Nagar, Bhubaneswar, Odisha, India

Manasi Chattaraj
Department of Geography, Bankura University,
Bankura, West Bengal, India

Debasis Mitra
Department of Microbiology, Graphic Era (Deemed to be University),
Dehradun, Uttarakhand, India

Hrudayanath Thatoi
Centre for Industrial Biotechnology Research,
School of Pharmaceutical Science, Siksha 'O' Anusandhan University,
Kalinga Nagar, Bhubaneswar, Odisha, India

Pradeep K. Das Mohapatra
Department of Microbiology, Raiganj University,
Raiganj, Uttar Dinajpur, West Bengal, India

Abstract: *Cirrhinus reba*, a valued table fish in the Indian subcontinent, faces threats from overharvesting, habitat degradation, and disease. This study examines the Kulik River near Bandar Ghat, Uttar Dinajpur, West Bengal, assessing monthly physico-chemical parameters to evaluate habitat suitability. Key findings include temperature variations from 17.67 °C (January) to 25.53 °C (June), pH peaks in April, and elevated ammonia, nitrate, and nitrite levels in July. Dissolved oxygen peaked in October, while CO_2 levels and bacterial loads were highest in July. Salinity was highest in May, and hardness, calcium, magnesium, and TDS peaked in January. These seasonal trends highlight the need for regular water quality monitoring to support *C. reba* survival and sustainable aquaculture. The study emphasizes the role of stable limnological conditions in optimizing yields, improving fish health, and conserving vulnerable fish populations. Promoting sustainable practices can enhance local livelihoods while contributing to ecological balance in the region.

Keywords: *Cirrhinus reba*, Limnological, Physico-chemical characters

*Corresponding author: souravchattaraj@soa.ac.in

DOI: 10.1201/9781003759003-43

1. Introduction

Cirrhinus reba, a popular table fish in India and Bangladesh, faces threats due to overharvesting, habitat loss, ecological changes, and disease, making it vulnerable in these regions [1,2]. Local fishermen report a higher availability of *C. reba* in the Kulik River near Bandar Ghat, Uttar Dinajpur, West Bengal, India[3]. The study focuses on assessing water quality parameters essential for aquaculture. Proper physicochemical conditions like temperature, pH, dissolved oxygen, and salinity are crucial for fish health and growth. Poor water quality can lead to stress, disease, and poor growth rates. Nutrient levels like nitrogen and phosphorus affect aquatic ecosystems and fish development, with high levels causing harmful algal blooms. Additionally, pollution from industrial effluents and agricultural chemicals further degrades water quality. A stable water environment is key to supporting fish development. There is a lack of global efforts to cultivate *C. reba* sustainably, particularly in economically disadvantaged areas like Uttar Dinajpur, where aquaculture could provide both ecological restoration and commercial benefits. This study investigates the hydrobiological parameters and bacterial flora of the region's natural *C. reba* habitat to promote sustainable cultivation and restore the species.

2. Materials and Methods

2.1 Assessment of Physico-Chemical Parameters of Water

In a sterile container, water samples were taken at random, in the morning, during the final week of each month, from a depth of 50 ± 10 cm below the water surface. Conventional BOD bottles were used for sampling to estimate the amount of dissolved oxygen (DO) in the water. Physicochemical characteristics were determined according to the recommended methodology (APHA, 2008).

Hydrogen Ion Concentration (pH)

A pencil pH meter (model no. B0096N8OWI/ LA-3THK-J5L5) was used to test the pH of the water samples, and a digital pH meter was used to confirm the results.

Total Dissolved Solid (TDS)

The TDS level in the water was determined using a digital TDS Meter (HM Digital AP-1 AquaPro).

Water Temperature

At the sampling location, the surface temperature of the water was assessed using a hydrothermometer with a 0.01-graduated centigrade scale.

Dissolved Oxygen (DO)

The Winkler technique was used to determine the amount of dissolved oxygen (Montegomery et al., 1964). The water sample (in a BOD container) was simultaneously mixed with 1 ml of manganous sulphate solution and 1 ml of alkaline iodide solution at the collecting site and was kept for ten minutes in darkness. The precipitate was then dissolved carefully by mixing with 1 ml of concentrated H_2SO_4. 50 ml of the sample was then transferred to a conical flask. Starch solution was incorporated (1-2 drops), and the solution was carefully titrated with N/40 thiosulphate to reach a colourless end point and DO was calculated by the following formulae:

$$\textit{Concentration of DO (ppm)} = \textit{Amount (ml) of thiosulphate required} \times 4$$

Free Carbon Dioxide (CO_2)

The free CO_2, pH, and bicarbonate equilibrium were interrelated. The test water (50 ml) was collected in a white porcelain container. It was then titrated against N/44 NaOH with three to four drops of phenolphthalein indicator and steadily swirled until a pink tint emerged at the endpoint. The following formula was used to determine the free CO_2:

$$\textit{Concentration of free } CO_2 \textit{ (ppm)} = \textit{ml of N/44 NaOH consumed} \times 20$$

Total Alkalinity

The titrimetric technique was used to calculate total alkalinity. In a conical flask containing 50 ml of water sample, a few drops of methyl orange indicator were added, and titrated with 0.02(N) H_2SO_4, which was indicated by a color shift from yellow to pink. Total alkalinity was determined using the following formula:

$$\textit{Total alkalinity (ppm)} = \textit{ml of } 0.02(N)\ H_2SO_4 \textit{ required} \times 20$$

Salinity

The amount of salt (including magnesium and calcium sulphates, bicarbonate, and sodium chloride) dissolved in the water is referred to as the salinity. To evaluate the level of chlorinity, a few drops of K_2CrO_4 indicator were first incorporated into a 25 ml of water sample and titrated against N/100 $AgNO_3$. The following formula was used to determine the salinity:

$$\textit{Salinity (ppm)} = \textit{Chlorinity (ppm)} \times 1.805 + 0.03$$

Dissolved Inorganic Nitrogen

Inorganic forms of nitrogen, such as ammonium (NH_4^+), nitrate (NO_3^-), and nitrite (NO_2^-) ions, are frequently dissolved in river water. Nitrogenous levels were determined using the Kjeldahl technique.

Ammonium and Nitrate

A Kjeldahl flask equipped with distillation equipment was used to sample 250 ml of water. The flask was then filled with 10 ml of 40% NaOH solution and 20 ml of a H_3BO_3

solution. The condenser was installed immediately. The distillation procedure was maintained until 40 ml of distillate was collected in the collecting flask. The distillate was titrated against 0.02 (N) H_2SO_4 until a reddish tint emerged. A second conical flask with 20 ml of 4% H_3BO_3 solution was placed beneath the condenser tip to measure the nitrate concentration. Davarda's alloy (0.5 g) was added to the water sample, and the distillation process was maintained until the water evaporated. The distillate was titrated until a reddish hue appeared. The following formula was used to calculate ammonium and nitrate concentrations:

$$N\,(ppm)\ in\ the\ form\ of\ ammonium\ (NH_4^+),\ nitrate\ (NO_3^-) = \frac{A}{V} \times 280$$

where A is the volume of 0.02 (N) H_2SO_4 used for titration, and V= Volume of water utilized.

Nitrite

Owing to the instability of nitrite, 90 ml of the obtained water samples were promptly treated with 2 ml 6 N HCl and 5 ml sulfanilamide solution. This was continued for further study. The treated samples were gently blended and allowed for settling. Ammonium sulfate (1 mL) was then introduced, followed by 3 min of waiting before adding 1 mL of napthylethylenediamine solution. Distilled water was used to bring the total volume to 100 ml. The absorbance of the solution was determined at 530 nm using UV-VIS Spectrophotometry (Lasany Li 2700). Different concentrations of the standard solutions were used to plot a standard curve. Nitrite concentration was computed using the following formula:

$$N\,(ppm)\ nitrite\ (NO_2^-) = A \times 1.11$$

where, A is the observed concentration of nitrite of water sample contrasted to the standard curve.

Calcium and Magnesium

Considerable attention has been paid to standardize EDTA. In a volumetric flask, 5 ml of a 0.01 N Ca solution was added, and the volume was increased to 25 ml by adding distilled water. It was subsequently given an orange-red color by adding 25 mg of the Murexide indicator and 5 ml of 4 N NaOH. The solution was then titrated until a purple tint appeared against 0.01 (N) EDTA.

Calcium

A volumetric flask containing 5 ml of water sample was filled with distilled water to a level of 25 ml. 25 mg of murexide indicator and 5 ml of 4 (N) NaOH were added to it to provide it an orange red coloration. It was then titrated until a purple tone appeared against 0.01 (N) EDTA.

Magnesium

In a volumetric flask, 5 ml of water sample was placed, and the volume was increased to 25 ml by adding distilled water. To get a wine-red coloration, 1 ml of the ammonium chloride-ammonium hydroxide buffer and few drops of EBT were added. It was then titrated until a blue shade appeared against 0.01 (N) EDTA. The following formula was used to determine the levels of calcium and magnesium:

$$Ca\,(ppm) = used\ EDTA\ (ml) \times F \times 40$$

$$Mg\,(ppm) = EDTA\ utilized\ (ml)\ for\ Ca + Mg - EDTA\ utilized\ (ml)\ for\ Ca) \times F \times 24$$

$$F = 5/V,\ V = \text{ml of EDTA utilized}$$

Total Hardness (TH)

Titration with standard ethylene diaminetetraacetic acid (EDTA) was used to calculate the total hardness. The calcium (ppm) in water was multiplied by 50.04/20.04 to obtain total calcium (as $CaCO_3$ equivalent). The magnesium (ppm) in water was multiplied by 50.04/12.16 to produce total magnesium (as $CaCO_3$ equivalent). The sum of these two values yielded the water's overall hardness.

Bacteriological Analysis

In a sterilized stopper container, water and sediment samples had been carefully collected from the sampling site. With double-distilled water, the samples were diluted in series (10^{-1} to 10^{-10}). By using the spread-plate method, the diluted samples (10^{-5} to 10^{-9}) were properly inoculated on nutrient agar plates and maintained at 37 °C for 24-48 h. The study was performed in triplicates. A digital colony counter was used to count the number of bacteria in the river sediment and water.

3. Results

3.1 Physico-Chemical Parameters of the Water

The physico-chemical parameters of the water of the fish sampling site have been shown in Table 43.1 and fluctuations were observed in the parameters assessed at monthly intervals. The water temperature reached a maximum of 25.53 °C during June and fell down to 17.67 °C during January. Highest pH was there in April and September experienced the lowest. The content of ammonia, nitrate, and nitrite in the water was the maximum in July. October revealed maximum dissolved oxygen content, while June had the lowest. Highest alkalinity was observed in January and September had the lowest. July had the highest CO_2 content and May revealed the maximum salinity. Total hardness, Ca^{2+}, Mg^{2+},and TDS reached the maximum in January. The bacterial load of river water and sediment was maximum at July and June respectively.

4. Discussion

The physico-chemical characteristics of river water exhibit seasonal fluctuations, influencing aquatic life

Table 43.1 Measurement of physico-chemical parameters and bacterial load of *C. reba* sampling pointof the river

Month	Temp. (°C)	pH	Ammonia (ppm)	Nitrate (ppm)	Nitrite (ppm)	DO (mg/l)	Alkalinity (mg/l)	CO_2	Salinity (mg/l)	TH (mg/l)	Ca2+ (mg/l)	Mg2+ (mg/l)	TDS (mg/l)	BLW (CFU/ml)	BLS (CFU/g)
Mar	21.47±0.31	7.17±0.06	0.13±0.03	0.03±0.02	0.02±0.01	6.1±0.1	24.26±0.23	23.3±0.26	105.6±1.24	193.3±1.53	77.51±0.52	103.7±1.74	251.7±1.15	8.2×10^3	8.7×10^4
Apr	22.4±0.3	7.37±0.06	0.18±0.06	0.08±0.03	0.02±0	5.87±0.06	25.27±0.15	26.9±0.2	111±1.17	184±2.65	75.33±0.34	92.39±0.97	246.6±0.58	2.9×10^4	7.8×10^4
May	24.57±0.47	6.97±0.12	0.22±0.03	0.12±0.03	0.02±0.01	5.56±0.12	22.36±0.19	27.3±0.1	116.6±1.66	179.6±1.53	76.3±0.22	89.94±0.45	233±2	6.1×10^5	5.6×10^5
Jun	25.53±0.67	7±0.1	0.27±0.02	0.17±0.02	0.02±0	5.37±0.12	23.23±0.09	28.5±0.46	110.7±1.24	174±2.65	73.6±0.4	86.47±1.24	226±1	7.4×10^5	8.1×10^6
Jul	23.07±0.45	6.77±0.06	0.32±0.03	0.2±0.05	0.03±0	5.77±0.06	22.18±0.15	29.47±0.12	99.3±0.99	164.67±3.21	71.53±0.3	82.3±0.83	233±1.73	7.6×10^5	6.6×10^6
Aug	23.2±0.56	6.7±0.1	0.23±0.03	0.09±0.05	0.01±0.01	5.96±0.05	21.42±0.06	28.33±0.25	84.7±1.04	173.3±2.31	75.51±0.24	86.74±0.97	229.3±0.58	8.2×10^4	7.4×10^5
Sep	22.5±0.66	6.67±0.06	0.22±0.02	0.03±0.02	0.01±0	6.2±0.1	21.02±0.05	26.53±0.23	88.31±1.06	163.7±1.53	69.48±0.14	81.2±0.61	233.7±2.31	9.7×10^4	5.2×10^5
Oct	21.37±0.42	6.93±0.15	0.12±0.03	0.01±0.01	0.01±0	6.27±0.06	23.4±0.19	23.43±0.25	79±0.79	183.3±2.08	76.5±0.25	92.13±1.18	242±1	8×10^4	5.5×10^5
Nov	19.77±0.45	7.23±0.06	0.08±0.02	0.02±0.01	0.01±0	6±0.1	23.46±0.06	21.07±0.15	74.65±1.27	189.3±1.53	79.15±0.52	95.93±0.78	246.3±0.58	7.9×10^3	6.3×10^5
Dec	18.43±0.15	7.3±0.0	0.17±0.03	0.01±0.00	0.01±0	5.93±0.06	24.74±0.1	19.33±0.21	86.68±1.81	206.3±1.53	78.3±0.13	109.3±1.74	257±2	3.1×10^3	5.9×10^5
Jan	17.67±0.45	7.33±0.15	0.15±0.05	0.07±0.01	0.01±0	6.1±0.1	26.24±0.08	17.33±0.35	95.14±0.78	238±3.61	85.26±0.33	116.5±0.95	271.67±1.15	1.6×10^3	6.4×10^4
Feb	20.03±0.7	7.23±0.06	0.13±0.02	0.04±0.03	0.01±0	6.2±0.1	25.26±0.08	18.3±0.1	88.14±0.8	220.3±3.06	81.59±0.22	112±1.54	262.3±2.52	2.2×10^3	4.4×10^4

Theresultsweregivenin (Mean ± S.E.)

BLW = Bacterial load ofriver water, BLS = Bacterial load of river sediment, TH = Total Hardness

Source: Authors

and aquaculture potential [4,5]. In summer, increased temperatures—due to clear skies, bright atmosphere, and reduced water levels—affect dissolved oxygen (DO), biomass, and fish yield. Temperature regulates metabolic processes in aquatic organisms [6] and impacts bacterial diversity [7]. Viable bacterial populations in water and sediment were lower in winter. pH, crucial for aquatic metabolism, remained within optimal aquaculture ranges [8]. Summer pH rose with increased aquatic activity and lower water levels, while rain runoff caused acidic pH during the monsoon. pH fluctuations influence bacterial diversity [9,10,11,12],and free CO_2 impacts summer pH. Alkalinity, the water's buffering capacity, was suitable for fish production, though excess may cause turbidity and growth retardation. Nitrogenous compounds—ammonia, nitrate, and nitrite—remained within safe levels [13], avoiding fish mortality. TDS levels were below 400 mg/l, supporting diversified fish culture. Summer DO levels dropped due to higher temperatures, limiting oxygen solubility. Low DO (<3.0 mg/l) impairs fish growth and metabolism. Morning sampling revealed elevated free CO_2, linked to DO-CO_2 diurnal dynamics and organic matter decomposition [14]. Summer salinity increased, while winter saw reductions; fish adapt through osmoregulation. River water was consistently hard [15], potentially due to anthropogenic activities. Idol immersions release calcium carbonate, increasing hardness, which buffers toxic metals and supports zooplankton [16]. Water hardness also reduces zinc toxicity [17]. This monthly monitoring offers insights into dynamic aquatic parameters, essential for effective resource management and *Cirrhinus reba* conservation.

References——

1. Gupta, S., & Banerjee, S. (2016). A review on feeding and reproductive biology of Cirrhinus reba (Hamilton, 1822), a threatened freshwater fish of Indian subcontinent with an emphasis on its conservation. *Fisheries and Aquaculture Journal*, *7*(2), 1–5.
2. Chattaraj S, Das Mohapatra PK. Immunostimulatory and antagonistic potential of the methanolic extract of Oedogonium intermedium SCB in Cirrhinus reba challenged with Aeromonas hydrophila. Aquaculture International. 2024. 32(3):2523–48.
3. Chattaraj, S., Chattaraj, M., Mitra, D., Ganguly, A., Thatoi, H., & Das Mohapatra, P. K. (2025). 16S amplicon sequencing of the gastrointestinal microbiota of Cirrhinus reba and isolation of an autochthonous probiotic using culture based approaches. *Systems Microbiology and Biomanufacturing*, *5*(1), 156–170.
4. Chattaraj, S., Ganguly, A., Mandal, A., & Das Mohapatra, P. K. (2022). A review of the role of probiotics for the control of viral diseases in aquaculture. *Aquaculture International*, *30*(5), 2513–2539.
5. Chattaraj, S., Ganguly, A., Mitra, D., Mitra, D., & Das Mohapatra, P. K. (2023). Study of intestinal bacteria of Cirrhinus reba and characterization of a new probiotic bacteria: an initiative to save the threatened species of Cirrhinus. *Applied Biochemistry and Microbiology*, *59*(6), 833–849.
6. Al-Deghayem, W. A., Al-Balawi, H. F., Kandeal, S. A., & Suliman, E. A. M. (2017). Gonadosomatic index and some hematological parameters in African catfish Clariasgariepinus (Burchell, 1822) as affected by feed type and temperature level. *Brazilian archives of biology and technology*, *60*(00), e17160157.
7. Bisht, A., Singh, U. P., & Pandey, N. N. (2014). Comparative study of seasonal variation in bacterial flora concomitant with farm raised fingerlings of Cyprinuscarpio at tarai region of Uttarakhand. *Journal of Environmental Biology*, *35*(2), 363.
8. Chattaraj, S., Mitra, D., Chattaraj, M., Ganguly, A., Thatoi, H., & Mohapatra, P. K. D. (2024). Brewers' spent grain as fish feed ingredient: evaluation of bio-safety and analysis of its impact on gut bacteria of Cirrhinus reba by 16S Metagenomic sequencing. *Current Research in Microbial Sciences*, *7*, 100286.
9. Maurer, L. M., Yohannes, E., Bondurant, S. S., Radmacher, M., &Slonczewski, J. L. (2005). pH regulates genes for flagellar motility, catabolism, and oxidative stress in Escherichia coli K-12. *Journal of bacteriology*, *187*(1), 304–319.
10. Chattaraj, S., Mitra, D., Chattaraj, A., Chattaraj, M., Kundu, M., Ganguly, A., & Mohapatra, P. K. D. (2023). Antioncogenic potential of probiotics: challenges and future prospective. *Indian J Microbiol Res*, *10*(1), 1–10.
11. Chattaraj, S., Behera, B. K., & Das Mohapatra, P. K. (2024). Effective valorization of Chlorella biomass and Brewers spent grain substituting fish meal and soybean meal in the diet of herbivorous fish Cirrhinus reba for higher growth, digestibility and sustainable cultivation. *Journal of Applied Phycology*, *36*(1), 217–232.
12. Chattaraj, S., Mitra, D., Ganguly, A., Thatoi, H., & Mohapatra, P. K. D. (2024). A critical review on the biotechnological potential of Brewers' waste: Challenges and future alternatives. *Current Research in Microbial Sciences*, 100228.
13. Bhatnagar, A., & Devi, P. (2013). Water quality guidelines for the management of pond fish culture. *International journal of environmental sciences*, *3*(6), 1980–2009.
14. Coello-Camba, A., Agustí, S., Holding, J., Arrieta, J. M., & Duarte, C. M. (2014). Interactive effect of temperature and CO2 increase in Arctic phytoplankton. *Frontiers in Marine Science*, *1*, 49.
15. Choi, C. Y., Li, Z., Song, J. A., & Park, Y. S. (2022). Water hardness can reduce the accumulation and oxidative stress of zinc in goldfish, Carassius auratus. Antioxidants, 11(4), 715.
16. Chiba, S., Batten, S., Martin, C. S., Ivory, S., Miloslavich, P., &Weatherdon, L. V. (2018). Zooplankton monitoring to contribute towards addressing global biodiversity conservation challenges. *Journal of plankton research*, *40*(5), 509–518.
17. Choi, C. Y., Li, Z., Song, J. A., & Park, Y. S. (2022). Water hardness can reduce the accumulation and oxidative stress of zinc in goldfish, Carassius auratus. *Antioxidants*, *11*(4), 715.

Research and Innovations in Industrial and Marine Biotechnology: A Circular Economy 2024 – Prof. Hrudayanath Thatoi et al. (eds)

44 Recent Advances in Probiotics for Controlling Microbial Disease in Aquaculture

Subhashree Subhasmita Sahoo,
Aurodeepa Samantaray, Subhashree Rath
Centre for Industrial Biotechnology Research,
School of Pharmaceutical Sciences, Siksha 'O' Anusandhan
Deemed to be University,
Kalinganagar, Bhubaneswar, Odisha, India

Swati Sonalika Rath,
Rashmi Ranjan Mishra
MITS School of Biotechnology(P), Infocity,
Patia, Chandaka Industrial Estate,
Bhubaneswar, Odisha, India

Hrudayanath Thatoi[1], Sourav Chattaraj[2]
Centre for Industrial Biotechnology Research,
School of Pharmaceutical Sciences, Siksha 'O' Anusandhan
Deemed to be University,
Kalinganagar, Bhubaneswar, Odisha, India

Abstract: Probiotics, which are live, beneficial microorganisms, when ingested through food and drink, improve the internal microbial balance in the gastrointestinal tract, hence promoting better health by improving internally. Probiotic bacteria inhibit the proliferation of hazardous pathogens through the secretion of siderophores, proteases, bacteriocins, hydrogen peroxide and lysozymes. In aquaculture, probiotics host of advantages including enhanced disease resistance growth performance, intestinal epithelial barrier integrity, immunity, gut microbiota, and the quality of water. Furthermore, by integrating the beneficial use of probiotics into aquaculture diets may lessen the antibiotic negative consequences. The possible mode of probiotics action in protecting against diseases includes strengthening the immune system, competing for binding sites, competition for nutrients and producing antibacterial substances. The review article investigated the potential of various probiotics to be utilized as protective agents against a variety of pathogens, mechanisms of action, and their applications against fish diseases. Nutritionists, researchers, agricultural engineers, scientists, pharmacists, veterinarians and pharmaceutical industries, are anticipated to discover these significantly useful.

Keywords: Probiotics, Mode of action, Beneficial aspects, Aquatic diseases controlled by probiotics, Fish nutrition health

1. Introduction

Aquaculture is the practice of growing aquatic organisms in both coastal and inland areas, by employing modifications in the raising process to heighten productivity. Over the last 70 years, the number of fish produced in Aquaculture has gone up tremendously, from less than a million tons in the early 1950s to 82 million tons in 2018, with a value of USD 250 billion [1]. Recently, governments and development organizations have focused more on fish

Corresponding author: [1]hnthatoi@gmail.com (H.N.T), [2]souravchattaraj@soa.ac.in (S.C)

DOI: 10.1201/9781003759003-44

farming, as aquaculture is considered the most feasible sector for fulfilling global food needs [2]. A variety of obstacles arise with the growing need for aquaculture production currently, such as maintaining water quality due to heightened commercialization, managing disease outbreaks, enhancing broodstock and domestication efforts, creating regulatory-compliant feed pellets and feeding systems, and innovating hatchery and rearing technologies [3].

The application of probiotics represents an emerging approach in aquaculture, but has not been thoroughly investigated, it demonstrates promise in improving growth, feed efficiency, immune function, and water quality [4]. Direct injection, incorporation into the water column, and usage in supplemented pellets are some of their application [5,6]. Aquaculture encounters several challenges with antimicrobial resistance, making it essential to implement efficient strategies to safeguard fish, aquaculture practices, and public health [7]. A significant amount of research has been conducted to develop safe and affordable feed additives, including phytogenic compounds, essential oils, prebiotics, and probiotics, for aquaculture [8]. This study examines probiotics, their mechanisms, health advantages, and their ability to minimize microbial diseases in fish farming.

2. Mode of Action of Probiotics

Probiotics may function through various modes such as competitive exclusion, chemicals, producing beneficial compounds or energy, nutrient competition, adhesion site competition, assisting in digestion, supplying macro- and micronutrients, and boosting immune response [8]. Beneficial isolates from freshwater and marine species' intestines have shown a negative effect against a range of diseases affecting fish and shellfish. The extracellular substances from five selected probiotics obtained from the common clown fish's stomach and intestine (*Amphiprion percula*) demonstrated a possible effect of inhibition against species like *A. salmonicida, A. hydrophila, V. anguillarum, V. damsela, V. alginolyticus, Carnobacterium piscicola* and *V. harveyi*. Several compounds have been shown to possess bacteriostatic or bactericidal qualities, include hydrogen peroxide, carbon dioxide, lysozymes, proteases, siderophores, and bacteriocins. Also, intestinal pH may be affected by the production of organic acids (lactic acid, propanoic acid and butyric acid) [8]. Probiotics might be able to outpace the growth of harmful opportunistic pathogenic microorganisms *in vivo*. Also, some probiotic can stop infections from growing on the lining of the gut by competing with them for readily available attachment sites. It was shown that LAB, includes *L. lactics, L. fermentum, L. plantarum,* prevent pathogens such as *V. anguillarum, A. hydrophila, A. salmonicida,* and *Y. ruckeri* from attaching to rainbow trout intestinal mucus in *in vitro* laboratory conditions. This inhibition of pathogen adhesion action could be attributed to the manufacturing of antimicrobial substances such as siderophores or antibiotic substances [9].

3. Advantages of Probiotics in Aquaculture

The effectiveness of probiotics in low-protein diets has been demonstrated effective results, which could reduce manufacturing expenses. Additionally, the effects of distinct probiotic attributes (high adherence and poor adhesion) on hybrid tilapia FCR and weight growth have varied [11]. The effectiveness of probiotics has been demonstrated in high-density stock and high-protein levels. The incorporation of freeze-dried, microencapsulated probiotic *S. cerevisiae* to the diet of striped catfish (Pangasianodon hypophthalmus) resulted in a considerable improvement in FCR and growth performance [11]. The growth and survival rates of bighead catfish (Clarias macrocephalus) were enhanced when the probiotic Acinetobacter KU011TH was added to their diet. The results support the use of Acinetobacter KU011TH as a food supplement in the aquaculture of catfish [13]. White leg prawns (*Litopenaeus vannamei*) were fed with a diet that contained many probiotic strains instead of just one, which enhanced the shrimp's development and general health and increased their odds of surviving [13]. According to reports, the prawns were given a variety of probiotic strains – S. cerevisiae P13, L. fermentum LW2, L. pentosus BD6 and B. subtilis E20over 56 days. The findings indicated considerable enhancements in health status, disease resistance and growth rate of the prawns [13] (Fig. 44.1.).

Microencapsulating probiotics is crucial for the determination of their effects in in vivo environments. In one study, rainbow trout (*Oncorhynchus mykiss*) were given probiotic *L. rhamnosus* ATCC 7469, which was microencapsulated using hi-maize starch and alginate, followed by a chitosan covering and (microencapsulated *L. rhamnosus*) to unencapsulated probiotics. The microencapsulated probiotic significantly enhanced the growth performance, health, and flesh quality of the fish [14]. A probiotic vaccine containing chitosan-alginate microcapsules expressing the G-protein of the Spring Viremia of carp virus (SVCV) produced a strong immune response and effectively protected carp against SVCV in two studies. Additionally, probiotic vaccines are advised for the widespread oral immunization of fish [15]. Bioaugmentation of *Bacillus spp.,* which is a probiotic bacterium, increases immunity, growth, and survival in biofloc systems. Biofloc systems boost survival, growth, and immunity of the Indian prawn (*Penaeus indicus*) by considerably increasing immune gene expression [16]. Probiotics have been linked to the myeloperoxidase's enzymatic release to produce hydrochloric acid, which kills harmful pathogens and direct effect on the lysis

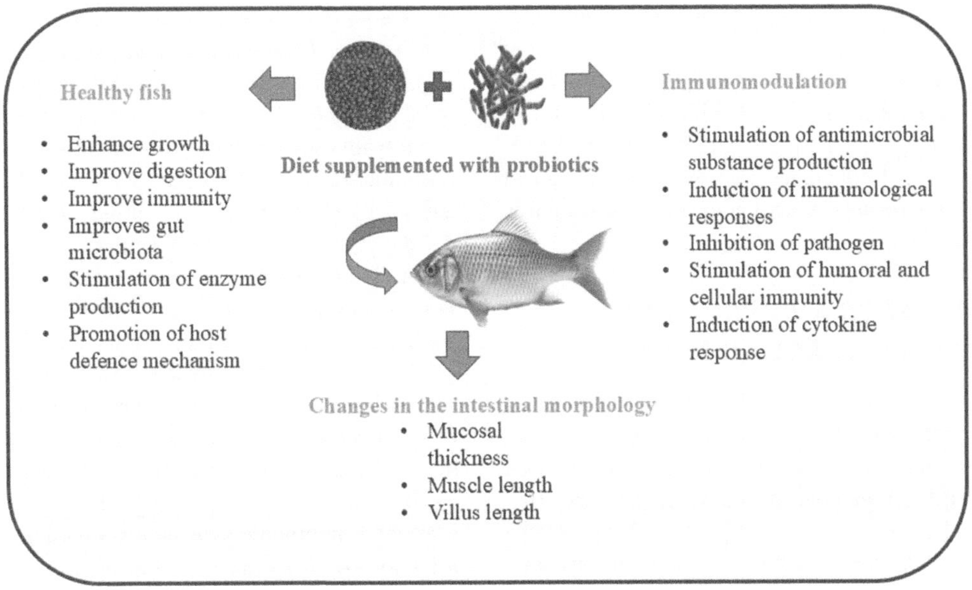

Fig. 44.1 Effects of probiotics on fish health and probiotics

Source: Authors

of the microbial cell [17]. Pathogenic bacteria, such as *Pseudomonas fluorescens* and *Aeromonas* sp., were more abundant in the control and probiotic groups. *Acinetobacter* spp., *Enterobacteriaceae*., *Serratia* sp., and *Cetobacterium* sp. were identified as the most common bacteria in probiotic groups and controls [18]. Probiotics with high adhesive capacity, such as Lactobacilli, can adhere bacteria to the tilapia's gastrointestinal tract for 10 days at rates more than 10^7 CFU/g diet [10]. Within the gastrointestinal system, epithelial cells and mucous membranes contribute to the innate immunity as they offer a prompt reaction to infections. Microbes can influence and alter various functions of the Gastrointestinal tract. The research could subsequently employ both light and electron microscopes to examine the histological alterations (mucous cells, epithelial layer thickness, microvilli cells, intra-epithelial leukocytes, and goblet cells). The influence of probiotics on intestinal histological changes was observed [19]. Researchers have proven that the probiotics can improve the thickness of the midgut epithelial layer and considerably improve the absorptive surface index [20]. Administering a high dose of probiotics can lead to an increase in intraepithelial leukocytes, absorptive surfaces, and find goblet cells [21]. Fish groups that are fed with probiotic had improved phagocytic capacity and less damage to the cells exposed to a pathogen in the intestine. As a result, histological alterations may be utilized to assist the efficacy of probiotics in fish health, immunity of gut immunity, and the growth rate of fish.

A yeast-based commercial probiotic, Aqualase®, has been proven to increase the production and health of rainbow trout in aquaculture. Two yeast species that make up Aqualase® are: *Saccharomyces elipsoedas* and *Saccharomyces cerevisiae*. According to the study's findings, adding the commercial probiotic Aqualase® (Thepax®) to the diet indicates to improve the cultured fish's development and general health. This yeast-based probiotic product offers multiple benefits, including altering immune responses, improving intestinal microbiota, particularly enhancing the ability of skin mucus to prevent fish pathogens, supporting intestinal enzymatic physiology, and ultimately promoting growth [22].

4. Probiotics in Controlling Microbial Diseases in Aquaculture

Probiotics offer several benefits to improve the health of aquatic organisms, including western king prawns, Japanese flounder, *Penaeus monodon*, black tiger prawns, and white leg prawns. Probiotics has been reported to impact natural killer (NK) cells, monocular phagocytes, polymorphonuclear leukocytes (neutrophils), monocytes and other elements of the non-specific immune system [23].

5. Probiotics and Viral Diseases in Aquaculture

Viral diseases are a major cause of mass death rates in the aquaculture sector. The absence of effective vaccines presents a critical challenge, potentially leading to substantial economic losses. Few studies have indicated the potential of probiotics to be applied as tool for infection using disease management. According to reports, using feed to shrimp culture environment with probiotics is an effective way to manage and prevent viral infections [24]. Strong antagonistic activity against hematopoietic necrosis virus (IHNV) and Oncorhynchus masou virus

(OMV) was shown by Vibrio species isolated from a tiger shrimp hatchery. Probiotic treatment and the assessment of its antiviral effects in diverse shrimp species [25]. When *Litopenaeus vannamei* is treated with 10^5 CFU mL-1 probiotic *Vibrio alginolyticus*, they are resistant to WSSV [26]. Son et al. [27] concluded that the potential use of probiotics (*L. plantarum*) in the diet to suppress iridovirus in *Epinephelus cooides*.

6. Probiotics and Parasitic Diseases in Aquaculture

There was limited evidence available on the usage of probiotics to treat parasitic diseases in shellfish and fish. Rainbow trout fed diets supplemented with *Aeromonas sobria* GC2 BA211 at concentrations of 10^8 and 10^{10} cells g^{-1} for 14 days demonstrated protection against the parasite *Ichthyophthirius multifiliis*. The mortality rate declined from 98%-0% [28]. *Lactobacillus plantarum* FNCC 226 is used to inhibit the parasitic growth of Saprolegnia parasitica A3 on catfish. Studies conducted both in vivo and in vitro showed that L. plantarum can inhibit S. parasitica and can be used to protect catfish from parasitic diseases [29].

7. Probiotics and Bacterial Diseases in Aquaculture

Arthrobacter XE-7 supplemented in the Shrimp diet, positively enhances the resistance to *V. parahaemolyticus and also* the immune system functions, gut microbiota [30]. Several studies have been carried out about the use of *Lactobacillus* species as a probiotic in fish culture. In *Nile tilapia*, *Lactobacillus acidophilus* had a favourable impact on resistance and immunity against *Streptococcus iniae* and *Pseudomonas fluorescens* [31]. Safari et al. [32] recently investigated the benefits of host-derived candidate probiotic, *E. casseliflavus*, in juvenile rainbow trout when administered in the diet, resulting in enhanced disease resistance and growth performance by *E. casseliflavus* when challenged with *S. iniae*. After 20 days of adding *Vagococcus fluvialis* (10^9cfu g^{-1}) to the sea bass diet, when challenged with *V.* anguillarum, the probiotic-treated *anguillarum*, probiotic-treated fish had a higher relative survival rate (42.3%) than the control group. The intestine of catla-catla contains Bacillus circulans PB7, which is then introduced to the fingerlings' food at a rate of 2×10^6, 2×10^5, and 2×10^4 cells per 100g. The injected fish showed improved immunological indicators and resistance to infection by *A. hydrophila* after 60days (Das Mohapatra and Bandyopadhyay, 2009). It has been reported that intraperitoneal treatment of components of the cell (Whole cell proteins and proteins found in cell walls) of *B. pumilus* and *Bacillus licheniformis* protects Rohu (*Rohita labeo*) against *A. hydrophila* infection by enhancing the immunological parameters [35] (Table 44.1).

8. Conclusion and Future Perspectives

Diseases drastically reduce aquaculture production. Traditionally, chemical compounds have been used to treat particular diseases. Alternative approaches are crucial to control these diseases. Probiotics provide a

Table 44.1 Overview of the probiotics' ability to inhibit harmful bacteria in fish

Sl no.	Disease/ Pathogen	Infected fish name	Effective probiotic culture	Dose/duration	Efficacy	References
1	*Streptococcus iniae* (Streptococcosis- bacterial diseases)	Nile tilapia	*Lactobacillus acidophilus*	1×10^7 cells/g feed; 8weeks	Challenge intraperitoneally; approximately 47% relative protection	[31]
2	*Lactococcus garvieae* (Lactococcosis-bacterial disease)	Rainbow trout (12gm)	*Bacillus* sp.	2×10^8cells/g; Feed; 14 days	Intraperitoneal test; complete safety	[6]
3	*Ichthyophthirius multifiliis* (White spot- Protozoan disease)	Rainbow trout (25gm)	*Aeromonas obria*	10^8 cells/gm; Feed; 14 days	100% survival in an immersion challenge	[28]
4	*Pseudomonas fluorescens* (Bacterial disease)	*Nile tilapia* (5gm)	*Bacillus subtilis*	1×10^7 cells/gm; Feed; 8 weeks	Approximately 43% survival in an intraperitoneal challenge	[31]
5	*Aeromonas hydrophila* (Bacterial disease)	Indian major carp (15gm)	*Bacillus subtilis*	1.5×10^7cfu/gm; Feed 2 weeks	87.5% survival rate increases; intraperitoneal challenge	[13]
6	*Aeromonas veronii* (Bacterial disease)	Snakehead (120gm)	*Bacteriovorux*sp.	1×10^4 PFU/mL; via tank water; immediately	RPS 75%; bath challenge	[35]

7	*Vibrio anguillarum* (Vibriosis-viral disease)	Atlantic salmon (21gm)	*Vibrio alginolyticus*	~10^8 cells/mL; via water; 10 min	Mortality decreases up to 47%; immersion challenges	[36]
8	*Aeromonas salmonicida Furunculosis-* (bacterial disease)	Atlantic salmon (21 gm)	*V. alginolyticus*	~108 cells/mL; via water; 10 min	Mortality rate decreases to 18%	[36]
9	ERM (Enteric red mouth disease): *Yersiniosis*	Rainbow trout (110 g)	*Bacillus mojavensis*	60 days; 1 × 10^8 cells/gm feed	Survival rate increases up to 99%	[37]
10	*Edwardsiella tarda* (Edwardsiellosis- bacterial diseases)	European eel (30 gm)	*Enterococcus faecium* (From Cernivet® LBC)	Spraying 1gm Cernivet® in 100mL over 1000gm of feed for two weeks	Survival rate is increases up to 73%	[38]
11	*Flavobacteriumpsychrophilum* (Chronic wasting disease)	Rainbow trout (5 gm)	*Enterobacter* sp.,	For 10 days 10^{6-8} cells/gm; feed	Mortality from subcutaneous challenge: mortality range decreases up to ~27-49%	[40]
12	*Aeromonas sobria*	Perch (10–15 gm)	*Pseudomonas chlororaphis*	Through rearing water 1 × 10^8 cfu/mL for 22 hours	Mortality decreases up to 16%	[40]
13	*Vibrio ordalii*	Atlantic salmon (21 g)	*Vibrio alginolyticus*	Approximately 10^8 cells/mL; in water; 10 min	Mortality decreases up to 74%	[36]
14	*Vibrio harveyi*	Rainbow trout (15 g)	*A. hydrophila A3-51*	109 cells/mL; 6 weeks; feeding	Intraperitoneal challenges; RPS 70%	[41]
15	Haemorrhagic septicaemia: *Aeromonas sp.*	Haemorrhagic septicaemia	*A. subtilis*	14 days; feed; 10^7 cells/ gm	Completely safety (100%)	[42]

variety of health benefits in aquaculture and are essential to improving resistance to various diseases, promoting beneficial microbiota in the gut, maintaining epithelial barrier integrity and improving water quality as well as immune system. As feed additives, probiotics help to ensure that the diet is properly digested and provide nutrients for increased growth and productivity. Also, probiotics have beneficial roles in aquaculture, may reduce the negative impacts of antibiotic use. Probiotics have been shown to enhance growth activity, immunity, blood chemistry, antioxidant and haematological functions, and gut microbiota in fish. Probiotics can also be given to fish meals to enhance immune responses. Further studies should focus on choosing the right probiotic strain in order to provide the fish with the best possible outcomes. Probiotics' effects on the immune system are currently unexplored, and further investigation is needed to elucidate and understand their modes of action, particularly the molecular mechanisms underlying their interaction with the host.

References—

1. Bauer, R. T. (2023). Fisheries and aquaculture. In *Shrimps: their diversity, intriguing adaptations and varied lifestyles* (pp. 583–655). Cham: Springer International Publishing.
2. Delgado, C. L., Wada, N., Rosegrant, M. W., Meijer, S., & Ahmed, M. (2003). *Outlook for fish to 2020: meeting global demand* (Vol. 15). Intl food policy res inst.
3. El-Saadony, M. T., Alagawany, M., Patra, A. K., Kar, I., Tiwari, R., Dawood, M. A., ... & Abdel-Latif, H. M. (2021). The functionality of probiotics in aquaculture: An overview. *Fish & shellfish immunology*, *117*, 36–52.
4. Amenyogbe, E., Chen, G., Wang, Z., Huang, J., Huang, B., & Li, H. (2020). The exploitation of probiotics, prebiotics and synbiotics in aquaculture: present study, limitations and future directions.: a review. *Aquaculture International*, *28*, 1017–1041.
5. El-Kady, A. A., Magouz, F. I., Mahmoud, S. A., & Abdel-Rahim, M. M. (2022). The effects of some commercial probiotics as water additive on water quality, fish performance, blood biochemical parameters, expression of growth and immune-related genes, and histology of Nile tilapia (Oreochromis niloticus). *Aquaculture*, *546*, 737249.
6. Hai, N. V. (2015). The use of probiotics in aquaculture. *Journal of applied microbiology*, *119*(4), 917–935.
7. Caputo, A., Bondad-Reantaso, M. G., Karunasagar, I., Hao, B., Gaunt, P., Verner-Jeffreys, D., ... & Dorado-Garcia, A. (2023). Antimicrobial resistance in aquaculture: A global analysis of literature and national action plans. *Reviews in Aquaculture*, *15*(2), 568–578.
8. El-Saadony, M. T., Alagawany, M., Patra, A. K., Kar, I., Tiwari, R., Dawood, M. A., ... & Abdel-Latif, H. M. (2021). The functionality of probiotics in aquaculture: An overview. *Fish & shellfish immunology*, *117*, 36–52.
9. Balcázar, J. L., Vendrell, D., de Blas, I., Ruiz-Zarzuela, I., Muzquiz, J. L., &Girones, O. (2008). Characterization of probiotic properties of lactic acid bacteria isolated from intestinal microbiota of fish. *Aquaculture*, *278*(1–4), 188–191.

10. Liu, W., Ren, P., He, S., Xu, L., Yang, Y., Gu, Z., & Zhou, Z. (2013). Comparison of adhesive gut bacteria composition, immunity, and disease resistance in juvenile hybrid tilapia fed two different Lactobacillus strains. *Fish & shellfish immunology*, *35*(1), 54–62.
11. Boonanuntanasarn, S., Ditthab, K., Jangprai, A., & Nakharuthai, C. (2019). Effects of microencapsulated Saccharomyces cerevisiae on growth, hematological indices, blood chemical, and immune parameters and intestinal morphology in striped catfish, Pangasianodonhypophthalmus. *Probiotics and Antimicrobial Proteins*, *11*, 427–437.
12. Bunnoy, A., Na-Nakorn, U., &Srisapoome, P. (2019). Probiotic effects of a novel strain, Acinetobacter KU011TH, on the growth performance, immune responses, and resistance against Aeromonashydrophila of bighead catfish (Clarias macrocephalus Günther, 1864). *Microorganisms*, *7*(12), 613.
13. Wang, Y. C., Hu, S. Y., Chiu, C. S., & Liu, C. H. (2019). Multiple-strain probiotics appear to be more effective in improving the growth performance and health status of white shrimp, Litopenaeusvannamei, than single probiotic strains. *Fish & shellfish immunology*, *84*, 1050–1058.
14. Hooshyar, Y., Abedian Kenari, A., Paknejad, H., &Gandomi, H. (2020). Effects of Lactobacillus rhamnosus ATCC 7469 on different parameters related to health status of rainbow trout (Oncorhynchus mykiss) and the protection against Yersinia ruckeri. *Probiotics and antimicrobial proteins*, *12*, 1370–1384.
15. Jia, S., Zhou, K., Pan, R., Wei, J., Liu, Z., & Xu, Y. (2020). Oral immunization of carps with chitosan–alginate microcapsule containing probiotic expressing spring viremia of carp virus (SVCV) G protein provides effective protection against SVCV infection. *Fish & Shellfish Immunology*, *105*, 327–329.
16. Panigrahi, A., Das, R. R., Sivakumar, M. R., Saravanan, A., Saranya, C., Sudheer, N. S., ... & Gopikrishna, G. (2020). Bio-augmentation of heterotrophic bacteria in biofloc system improves growth, survival, and immunity of Indian white shrimp Penaeus indicus. *Fish & shellfish immunology*, *98*, 477–487.
17. Wang, Y. B., Li, J. R., & Lin, J. (2008). Probiotics in aquaculture: challenges and outlook. *Aquaculture*, *281*(1–4), 1–4.
18. He, S., Zhang, Y., Xu, L., Yang, Y., Marubashi, T., Zhou, Z., & Yao, B. (2013). Effects of dietary Bacillus subtilis C-3102 on the production, intestinal cytokine expression and autochthonous bacteria of hybrid tilapia Oreochromis niloticus♀× Oreochromis aureus♂. *Aquaculture*, *412*, 125–130.
19. Nakandakare, I. B., Iwashita, M. K. P., Dias, D. D. C., Tachibana, L., Ranzani-Paiva, M. J. T., & Romagosa, E. (2013). Growth performance and intestinal histomorphology of Nile tilapia juveniles fed probiotics. *ActaScientiarum. Animal Sciences*, *35*, 365–370.
20. Standen, B. T., Rodiles, A., Peggs, D. L., Davies, S. J., Santos, G. A., & Merrifield, D. L. (2015). Modulation of the intestinal microbiota and morphology of tilapia, Oreochromis niloticus, following the application of a multi-species probiotic. *Applied microbiology and biotechnology*, *99*, 8403–8417.
21. Standen, B. T., Peggs, D. L., Rawling, M. D., Foey, A., Davies, S. J., Santos, G. A., & Merrifield, D. L. (2016). Dietary administration of a commercial mixed-species probiotic improves growth performance and modulates the intestinal immunity of tilapia, Oreochromis niloticus. *Fish & Shellfish Immunology*, *49*, 427–435.
22. Adel, M., Lazado, C. C., Safari, R., Yeganeh, S., &Zorriehzahra, M. J. (2017). Aqualase®, a yeast-based in-feed probiotic, modulates intestinal microbiota, immunity and growth of rainbow trout Oncorhynchus mykiss. *Aquaculture Research*, *48*(4), 1815–1826.
23. Hoseinifar, S. H., Sun, Y. Z., Wang, A., & Zhou, Z. (2018). Probiotics as means of diseases control in aquaculture, a review of current knowledge and future perspectives. *Frontiers in microbiology*, *9*, 2429.
24. Lakshmi, B., Viswanath, B., & Sai Gopal, D. V. R. (2013). Probiotics as antiviral agents in shrimp aquaculture. *Journal of pathogens*, *2013*(1), 424123.
25. Direkbusarakom, S., Yoshimizu, M., Ezura, Y., Ruangpan, L., &Danayadol, Y. (1998). Vibrio spp., the dominant flora in shrimp hatchery against some fish pathogenic viruses. *Journal of Marine Biotechnology*, *6*(4), 266–267.
26. Rodríguez, J., Espinosa, Y., Echeverría, F., Cárdenas, G., Román, R., & Stern, S. (2007). Exposure to probiotics and β-1, 3/1, 6-glucans in larviculture modifies the immune response of Penaeusvannamei juveniles and both the survival to White Spot Syndrome Virus challenge and pond culture. *Aquaculture*, *273*(4), 405–415.
27. Son, V. M., Chang, C. C., Wu, M. C., Guu, Y. K., Chiu, C. H., & Cheng, W. (2009). Dietary administration of the probiotic, Lactobacillus plantarum, enhanced the growth, innate immune responses, and disease resistance of the grouper Epinepheluscoioides. *Fish & Shellfish Immunology*, *26*(5), 691–698.
28. Pieters, N., Brunt, J., Austin, B., & Lyndon, A. R. (2008). Efficacy of in-feed probiotics against Aeromonasbestiarum and Ichthyophthiriusmultifiliis skin infections in rainbow trout (Oncorhynchus mykiss, Walbaum). *Journal of Applied Microbiology*, *105*(3), 723–732.
29. Nurhajati, J., Aryantha, I. N. P., & Indah, D. G. (2012). The curative action of Lactobacillus plantarum FNCC 226 to Saprolegnia parasitica A3 on catfish (PangasiushypophthalamusSauvage). *International Food Research Journal*, *19*(4).
30. Li, J., Tan, B., Mai, K., Ai, Q., Zhang, W., Liufu, Z., & Xu, W. (2008). Immune responses and resistance against Vibrio parahaemolyticus induced by probiotic bacterium Arthrobacter XE-7 in Pacific white shrimp, Litopenaeusvannamei. *Journal of the World Aquaculture Society*, *39*(4), 477–489.
31. Aly, S. M., Ahmed, Y. A. G., Ghareeb, A. A. A., & Mohamed, M. F. (2008). Studies on Bacillus subtilis and Lactobacillus acidophilus, as potential probiotics, on the immune response and resistance of Tilapia nilotica (Oreochromis niloticus) to challenge infections. *Fish & shellfish immunology*, *25*(1–2), 128–136.
32. Sameni, H. R., Ramhormozi, P., Bandegi, A. R., Taherian, A. A., Mirmohammadkhani, M., & Safari, M. (2016). Effects of ethanol extract of propolis on histopathological

changes and anti-oxidant defense of kidney in a rat model for type 1 diabetes mellitus. *Journal of diabetes investigation*, *7*(4), 506–513.
33. Sorroza, L., Padilla, D., Acosta, F., Román, L., Grasso, V., Vega, J., & Real, F. (2012). Characterization of the probiotic strain Vagococcusfluvialis in the protection of European sea bass (Dicentrarchuslabrax) against vibriosis by Vibrio anguillarum. *Veterinary microbiology*, *155*(2-4), 369–373.
34. Ramesh, D., Vinothkanna, A., Rai, A. K., & Vignesh, V. S. (2015). Isolation of potential probiotic Bacillus spp. and assessment of their subcellular components to induce immune responses in Labeorohita against Aeromonashydrophila. *Fish & shellfish immunology*, *45*(2), 268–276.
35. Cao, Y., Liang, Y., Tanaka, K., Nguyen, C. T., Jedrzejczak, R. P., Joachimiak, A., & Stacey, G. (2014). The kinase LYK5 is a major chitin receptor in Arabidopsis and forms a chitin-induced complex with related kinase CERK1. *elife*, *3*, e03766.
36. Austin, B., Stuckey, L. F., Robertson, P. A. W., Effendi, I., & Griffith, D. R. W. (1995). A probiotic strain of Vibrio alginolyticus effective in reducing diseases caused by Aeromonassalmonicida, Vibrio anguillarum and Vibrio ordalii. *Journal of fish diseases*, *18*(1).
37. Capkin, E., &Altinok, I. (2009). Effects of dietary probiotic supplementations on prevention/treatment of yersiniosis disease. *Journal of applied microbiology*, *106*(4), 1147–1153.
38. Chang, C. I., & Liu, W. Y. (2002). An evaluation of two probiotic bacterial strains, Enterococcus faecium SF68 and Bacillus toyoi, for reducing edwardsiellosis in cultured European eel, Anguilla anguilla L.
39. Burbank, D. R., Shah, D. H., LaPatra, S. E., Fornshell, G., & Cain, K. D. (2011). Enhanced resistance to coldwater disease following feeding of probiotic bacterial strains to rainbow trout (Oncorhynchus mykiss). *Aquaculture*, *321*(3-4), 185–190.
40. Gobeli, S., Goldschmidt-Clermont, E., Frey, J., & Burr, S. E. (2009). Pseudomonas chlororaphis strain JF3835 reduces mortality of juvenile perch, Perca fluviatilis L., caused by Aeromonassobria. *Journal of fish diseases*, *32*(7), 597–602.
41. Arijo, S., Brunt, J., Chabrillón, M., Díaz-Rosales, P., & Austin, B. (2008). Subcellular components of Vibrio harveyi and probiotics induce immune responses in rainbow trout, Oncorhynchus mykiss (Walbaum), against V. harveyi. *Journal of Fish Diseases*, *31*(8), 579–590.
42. Newaj-Fyzul, A., Adesiyun, A. A., Mutani, A., Ramsubhag, A., Brunt, J., & Austin, B. (2007). Bacillus subtilis AB1 controls Aeromonas infection in rainbow trout (Oncorhynchus mykiss, Walbaum). *Journal of applied microbiology*, *103*(5), 1699–1706.

Research and Innovations in Industrial and Marine Biotechnology: A Circular Economy 2024 – Prof. Hrudayanath Thatoi et al. (eds)

45 Assessing the LC_{50} Values of *Cinnamomum* Extracts for Larvicidal Activity Against *Culex quinquefasciatus*: Towards Sustainable Mosquito Control Strategies

Aditi Pal
Centre for Biotechnology,Siksha 'O' Anusandhan Deemed to be University,
Kalinganagar, Bhubaneswar, Odisha, India
Medical Entomology Division, ICMR-Regional Medical Research Centre,
Chandrasekharpur, Bhubaneswar, Odisha, India

Mahesh Chandra Sahu*
Medical Entomology Division,
ICMR-Regional Medical Research Centre, Chandrasekharpur,
Bhubaneswar, Odisha, India

Arun Kumar Pradhan
Centre for Biotechnology,
Siksha 'O' Anusandhan Deemed to be University, Kalinganagar,
Bhubaneswar, Odisha, India

Mitali Rath
Department of Pathology, IMS and SUM Hospital–II,
Phulnakhara, Cuttack, Odisha, India

Abstract: Mosquito-borne diseases, such as lymphatic filariasis and West Nile virus, present global health challenges, particularly through *Cx. quinquefasciatus*. With chemical insecticides facing resistance and environmental concerns, plant-based alternatives are gaining attention. This research examines the larvicidal effectiveness of aqueous extracts from *Cinnamomum cassia*, *Piper nigrum*, *Citrussinensis*, *Arachis*, and *Calotropis* species on *Cx. quinquefasciatus* larvae. Larvae were collected from rural and urban areas of Bhubaneswar, Odisha. They were exposed to plant extracts at concentrations of 1000 ppm, 500 ppm, 250 ppm, 125 ppm, and 62.5 ppm, prepared using n-hexane, aqueous, methanol, acetone, and ethanol solvents. Mortality was recorded at 24, 48, and 72 hours. Probit analysis determined lethal concentrations (LC_{10}, LC_{25}, LC_{50}, LC_{75}, LC_{90}), and histopathological studies assessed damage to larval tissues. The aqueous extract of *Cinnamomum cassia* demonstrated the greatest larvicidal effectiveness, with an LC_{50} value of 0.429 ppm and an LC_{90} of 552.055 ppm after 72 hours. Extracts from *Piper nigrum* and *Citrus sinensis* also displayed notable larvicidal effects, though less potent than *Cinnamomum cassia*. Histopathological analysis revealed significant damage in larvae exposed to higher concentrations of *Cinnamomum cassia*, including disarrayed muscle fibers and degenerated epithelial cells. Lower concentrations caused mild cellular disturbances, while control larvae exhibited normal tissue structure. The study demonstrates the strong larvicidal potential of *Cinnamomum cassia* aqueous extracts, suggesting their viability as eco-friendly alternatives to synthetic insecticides for mosquito control. Further research and field trials are recommended to integrate these plant-based solutions into mosquito management programs.

Keywords: *Cinnamomum* extract, Larvicide, Plant extracts, *Culex quinquefasciatus*, Probit value, LC_{50}

*Corresponding author: mchsahu@gmail.com

DOI: 10.1201/9781003759003-45

1. Introduction

Mosquito-borne diseasesare still prevalent and contribute significantly towards the global burden of diseases, especially in tropical and subtropical climates. In densely populated metropolitan areas, the *Culex quinquefasciatus* is a major contributor to Lymphatic filariasis and Japanese Encephalitis, along with being a representative vector of West Nile Virus [1]. Due to these diseases, high levels of morbidity and high economic wastage are experienced [2]. Due to the continuous use of synthetic insecticides to control mosquitos, resistance to effective insecticides has reached alarming degrees, alongside widespread environmental pollution and non-target toxicity [3]. This resistance to insecticides poses a threat to traditional intervention measures that target vectors; it also requires the immediate establishment of effective environmentally sound options [4]. Botanical insecticides, derived from plants with bioactive compounds, have gained attention as potential substitutes for conventional chemical pesticides [5, 6]. Plant-based larvicides are known for their biodegradability, minimal environmental impact, and safety for non-target organisms, including humans. Among these, extracts from plants such as *Cinnamomum cassia, Piper nigrum, Citrus sinensis,* and *Arachis hypogaea* have demonstrated promising insecticidal properties. For instance, *C. cassia* is rich in essential oils and phenolic compounds like cinnamaldehyde and eugenol, known for their antibacterial and larvicidal activities. Similarly, *P. nigrum* and *C. sinensis* exhibit bioactive components with toxic effects on mosquito larvae, making them strong candidates for eco-friendly mosquito control [7, 8]. Govindarajan et al. (2016) reported that essential oils derived from *Cinnamomum* exhibited significant larvicidal activity against *Aedes aegypti*, with LC_{50} values indicating high potency at low concentrations [9]. Similarly, some studies highlighted the strong larvicidal effects of *C.verum* essential oil against *Anopheles stephensi* larvae, attributing the observed mortality to the synergistic action of cinnamaldehyde and eugenol [10]. Despite this, *Cx. quinquefasciatus* has shown greater resilience to botanical insecticides compared to other mosquito vectors, emphasizing the need for targeted studies assessing the species-specific effectiveness of *Cinnamomum* extracts [10]. *Citrus* species, such as *C. sinensis* and *C. aurantifolia*, generate volatile chemicals that exhibit significant insecticidal properties, with *C. sinensis* demonstrating greater efficacy in research. Although they have potential, the larvicidal efficacy of these plant extracts against *Cx. quinquefasciatus* larvae remain underexplored [11, 12]. Moreover, the toxicological profiling of botanical larvicides, including the determination of LC_{50} values, is crucial for ensuring both efficacy and safety in large-scale mosquito control programs. Establishing these lethal concentration benchmarks enables precise dosing, minimizes environmental risks, and facilitates the integration of plant-based larvicides into broader vector management strategies [13]. Lately, emphasis has been given on plant based larvicides as they exhibit properties that make them economically viable and environmentally sound; and limit the chances of development for resistance, making them suitable potentials for integrated vector control management systems [9]. *Cinnamomum* spices are considered as one of the effective plant-based alternatives due to the presence of bioactive components such as eugenol, terpenoid, and cinnamaldehyde that have possible pesticidal and antimicrobial effects [14]. Recent studies have demonstrated the larvicidal potential of *Cinnamomum* extracts against *Aedes* and *Anopheles sp.*, but data on their efficacy against *Cx. quinquefasciatus* remain limited [15].

This study aims to address the existing knowledge gap by evaluating the larvicidal activity of *Cinnamomum* extracts against *Cx. quinquefasciatus*larvae and determining the LC_{50} values under controlled laboratory conditions. By contributing to the growing body of research on plant-based larvicides, this study supports the development of sustainable mosquito control strategies that align with global health initiatives to combat vector-borne diseases. Focusing on the larval stage, an aquatic and stationary phase, is essential for effective management. Investigating these natural substances may yield environmentally sustainable and precise methods to mitigate worldwide disease transmission [7, 8]. Furthermore, the research underscores the importance of leveraging indigenous plant resources to promote environmentally conscious solutions to vector control, thus reducing the dependency on synthetic chemical insecticides.

2. Materials and Methods

2.1 Study Sites

Mosquitoes are captured from different rural and urban locations, these sites were selected for mosquito collections using manual aspirators: Firikinali, Dalua, Patrasahi, Bhalunga, Mundulietc villages and NiladriVihar, Saliyasai urban areas.

2.2 Mosquito Collection and Morphological Identification

The collection of *Culex* mosquito (adult) was carried out inside of residences using manual aspirators in the morning (during the morning resting period). Morning resting collections were performed by using hand nets and aspirators. After collecting, we identified and recorded them. Collections were conducted from 5 to 8 a.m. All adult mosquitoes were placed into small cages. Field data was recorded (Table 45.1). The identification of adult mosquitoes was conducted using morphology-based methods according to the established identification keys [16].

Table 45.1 Indoor collection records of adult *Cx. quinquefasciatus* mosquito counted after morphological identification

Serial No.	Name of site	Types of species	Total mosquito	Male	Female
1.	Firikinali	*Cx. quinquefasciatus*	89	21	68
2.	Dalua	*Cx. quinquefasciatus*	40	17	23
3.	Patrasahi	*Cx. quinquefasciatus*	30	16	14
4.	Bhalunga	*Cx. quinquefasciatus*	42	9	33
5.	Munduli	*Cx. quinquefasciatus*	37	16	21
6.	Saliya sai	*Cx. quinquefasciatus*	39	5	34
7.	Niladri Vihar	*Cx. quinquefasciatus*	41	11	30
Grand Total			318	95	223

2.3 Colony Maintenance of Adult Mosquito and Larvae

The colony was kept at a temperature of 27°C ± 2°C, with relative humidity ranging from 75% to 85%, and maintained under a 14-hour light and 10-hour dark cycle. Adults were kept in cages and fed a 10% sucrose solution in a petriplate on a regular basis by soaking it with a cotton pad. The following day, the adults received a blood meal from a rabbit that had been kept in resting cages overnight for the females' blood-feeding. A bowl containing 50 mL of tap water, attached with filter paper, was placed in the cage to facilitate oviposition.

2.4 Selection and Procurement of Plants

Cinnamon bark stick of *C. cassia* sp. belongs to *Lauraceae* family, orange peel of *C.sinensis*. belongs to *Rutaceae*family, black peeper of *P.nigrum* belongs to *Piperaceae*family, and Peanut, a by-product of the leguminous plant *A.hypogaea L.,* belongs to the subfamily *Papilionaceae* within the *Fabaceae* family, were collected from a local area in Bhubaneswar, Khorda, Odisha.

2.5 Preparation of Plant Extract

The extraction of cinnamon bark powder was performed using aqueous solvents with dH_2O, applying the soxhlet extraction technique [17]. 100 gm of cinnamon bark powder was used for the extraction with 1000 ml of deionized water (dH_2O) as solvent at 8°C for 48 hrs. Following extraction, any peel particles were eliminated from the extract by passing it through Whatman No. 2 filter paper. The extracts were stored at room temperature until further use. The same process followed for all other aqueous extracts.

2.6 Larvicidal Bioassay

The 4th instar larvae of *Cx. quinquefasciatus* were used in independent toxicity tests for the crude extracts of leaves, peel, and shell. A stock solution (1000 ppm) was created by dissolving 10 ml of the stock solution in 90 ml of dH_2O. Different dilutions of 500 ppm, 250 ppm, 125 ppm, and 62.5 ppm were made in 200 ml of field-collected water within a 250 ml bowl, and total 25 no. of 4th instar larvae were introduced; mortality was reported after 24 hours. In a mosquito incubator, the larvae were exposed to 200 ml of water with 50 ml of dH_2O as a reference, and the conditions were maintained at 28°C-30°C, relative humidity about 70% to 80%, and 12-hours light and 12 hours dark cycles. Each treatment was duplicated five times [18].

2.7 Larval Susceptibility Tests

The larvae of *Cx. quinquefasciatus* in their 4th instar were inserted in each test solution to observe the larvicidal property using the following approach. Extract solutions were made with the same concentrations: 1000 ppm, 500 ppm, 250 ppm, 125 ppm, and 62.5 ppm. 25 larvae were introduced into 250 ml of the extract solution. Control trials devoid of extract were conducted concurrently. The mortality rate of larvae evaluated at 24, 48, and 72 hours respectively. Larvae exhibiting no movement or disturbance were classified as deceased and subsequently removed from the dishes to prevent degradation. The procedures were conducted in five replicates. The proportion of morality was calculated using Abbott's formula [19].

$$\% \text{ Mortality} = \frac{\text{Number of dead larvae}}{\text{Number of total larvae taken}} \times 100 \quad (1)$$

2.8 Histopathological Studies

Each larva was put in a separate container with 10 % neutral buffered formalin and labeled 1 through 6. All 6 larva samples were sent to the histology laboratory where each larva was wrapped in filter paper and put in a separate cassette. All the cassettes were put into an automatic tissue processor and a 12-hour program was started. The cassettes were retrieved from the final wax jar of the tissue processor. Each larva sample was then embedded in paraffin wax at the embedding station and wax blocks were prepared. After cooling, sections of the paraffin-embedded samples were cut on microtome at 4 µm ensuring that only a single layer of cells makes up the section. Selected sections were put into the water bath from where they were taken on albumenized labeled slide. After drying, these slides were stained with H & E stain [20, 21]. Probit analysis was applied to the lethality percentage data to determine LC_{10}, LC_{25}, LC_{50}, LC_{75}, and LC_{90} values.

3. Results

3.1 Mosquito Collection

Adult mosquitoes are collected from Firikinali, Dalua, Patrasahi, Bhalunga, Mundulietc villages. Mainly mosquitoes are collected from cattle sheds, goat sheds, human dwelling places, vegetation, etc. both indoors and outdoors (Fig. 45.1.).

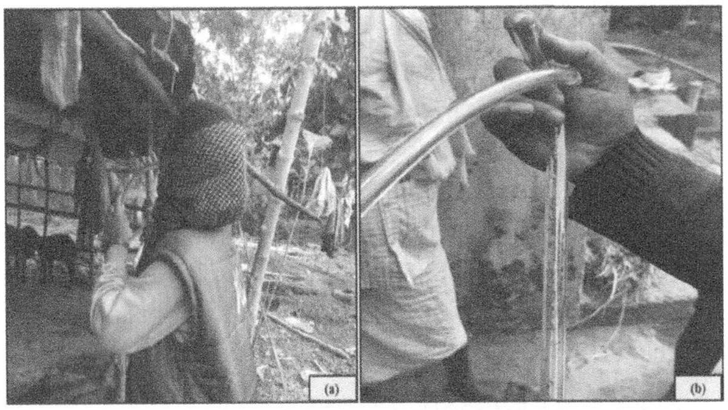

Fig. 45.1 Adult mosquito collection in different villages; (a) Adult mosquito collection using aspirator, (b) After collecting mosquito in aspirator

3.2 Colony Maintenance

Eggs are laid 3 to 7 days after blood feeding (Fig. 45.2.) by placing a transparent 250 ml cup, partially filled with dH_2O, as an oviposition dish in the mosquito cage overnight (Fig. 45.3.). A small amount (about 0.2 g) of ground larval food and 200 ml of dH_2O are added to a larval flat containing the egg rafts (Fig. 45.4.). The entire egg rafts were carefully lifted using a wooden brush and placed on the water surface of the larval flat, maintaining the same arrangement as in the oviposition cup. If the eggs have already hatched, transfer the contents of the oviposition dish directly into the larval flat immediately. Most eggs take 48 hours to develop into larvae. The larvae (Fig. 45.5.) were fed with a 3:1:1 mixture of dog biscuits, yeast powder, and algae that was obtained from ponds. Once we moved the pups from the trays to a dish filled with tap water, we kept them in our insectary cages, which are 45 x 45 x 40 cm, until they grew into adults.

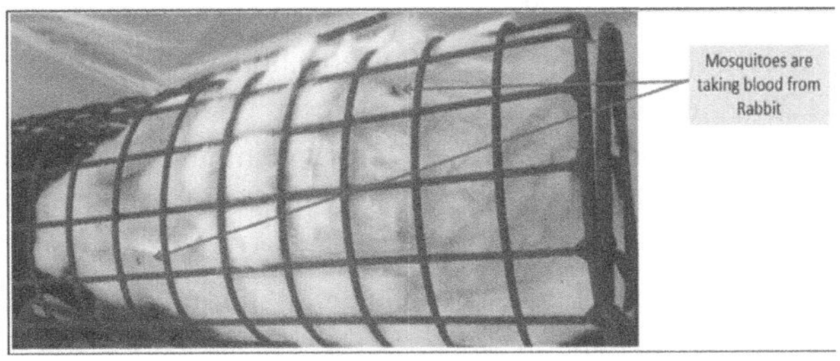

Fig. 45.2 Blood feeding of adult mosquito

3.3 Larvicidal Bioassay

Cinnamon Aqueous Extract

The study evaluated the relationship between the logarithmic concentration of extracts and probit values

Fig. 45.3 Colony maintenance of adult mosquito and larvae; (a) Adult mosquito maintenance in mosquito net, (b) Sucrose feeding, pupa to adult transformation, and oviposition bowel, (c) Larvae maintenance in enamel trays

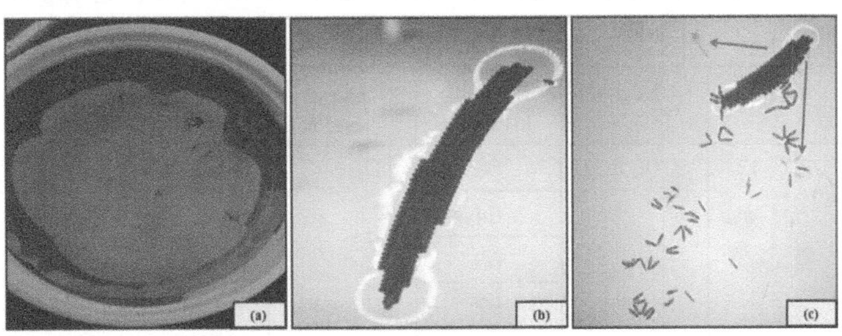

Fig. 45.4 *Culex* Eggs in raft form; (a) Culture image, (b) One whole raft under stereo microscope, (c) Hatched egg raft under stereo microscope

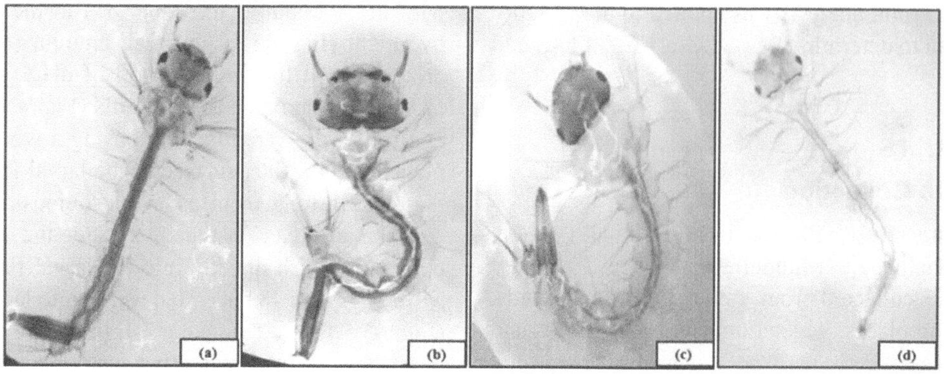

Fig. 45.5 *Culex* mosquito Larvae under stereo microscope; (a) 4th instar, (b) 3rd instar, (c) 2nd instar, and (d) 1st instar

for 4th instar larvae lethality over 24, 48, and 72 hours of incubation (Fig. 45.6.).

After 24 hours, the regression equation y = 1.1418x + 2.2047, demonstrated a strong linear relationship, with an R-squared value of 0.9778, explaining 97.78 % of variability (Table 45.2.) (Fig. 45.7.). At 48 hours, the equation y = 1.1291x + 2.4572, showed a slightly lower but significant linear relationship, with an R-squared value of 0.9088, accounting for 90.88 % variability (Table 45.2.) (Fig. 45.7.). By 72 hours, the equation y = 1.3535x + 2.4583, revealed a strong linear relationship with an R-squared value of 0.9209, explaining 92.09 % variability. In all cases, probit values consistently increased with higher log10 concentrations, indicating a robust dose-response relationship. These results highlight the effectiveness of the extracts in predicting lethality across different incubation periods, with all regression models showing a very good fit to the observed data (Table 45.2) (Fig. 45.7).

Orange Peel Aqueous Extract

The study evaluated the relationship between the logarithmic concentration of extracts and probit values

Fig. 45.6 Experiment on different concentration for all extracts; (a) 1000 ppm, (b) 500 ppm, (c) 250 ppm, (d) 125 ppm, (e) 62.5 ppm, (f) 0 ppm

Table 45.2 Probit transformation and computations of probit values of 24 hr, 48 hr, and 72 hr observed and expected partial lethal ranges for the aqueous *Cinnamomum* extract with 4th instar larvae of *Cx. quinquefasciatus*

Concen-tration (ppm)	24 hr			48 hr			72 hr		
	Percent lethality	LC_{50}	LC_{90}	Percent lethality	LC_{50}	LC_{90}	Percent lethality	LC_{50}	LC_{90}
1000	72	280.543	3706.807	80	178.648	2432.204	96	75.509	666.806
500	60			64			80		
250	52			60			72		
125	36			52			64		
62.5	20			24			48		

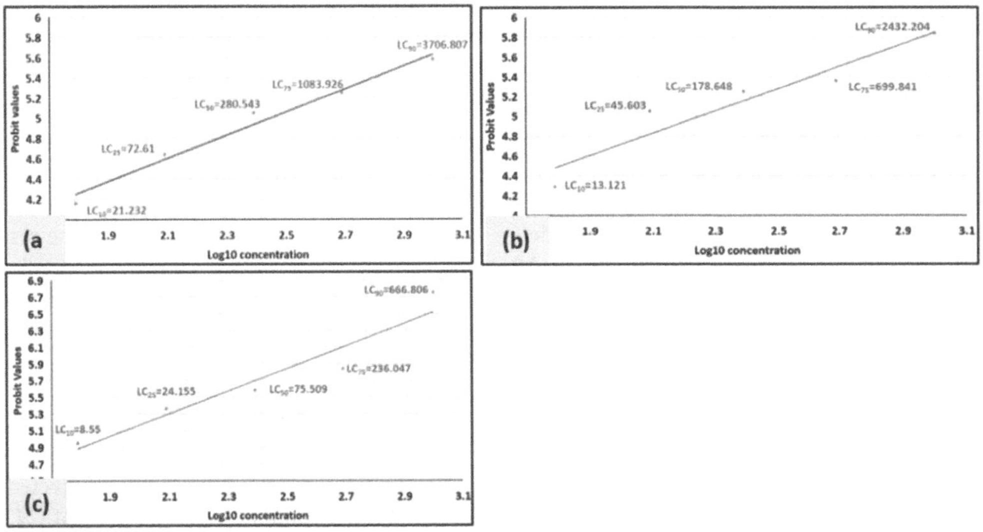

Fig. 45.7 Determination of lethal concentration (LC) Thresholds for the cinnamon extract against 4th instar larvae of *Cx. quinquefasciatus*: (a) 24 hrs, (b) 48 hrs, and (c) 72 hrs

for 4th instar larvae lethality over 24, 48, and 72 hours of incubation. After 24 hours, the regression equation $y = 1.075x + 1.9306$ demonstrated a strong linear relationship, with an R-squared value of 0.9724, explaining 97.24 % of variability (Table 45.3) (Fig. 45.8). At 48 hours, the equation $y = 1.036x + 2.2899$, showed a slightly lower but significant linear relationship, with an R-squared value of 0.9914, accounting for 99.14 % variability

Table 45.3 Probit transformation and computations of probit values of 24 hr, 48 hr, and 72 hr observed and expected partial lethal ranges for the aqueous orange peel extract with 4th instar larvae of *Cx. quinquefasciatus*

Concen-tration	24 hr			48 hr			72 hr		
	Percent lethality	LC_{50}	LC_{90}	Percent lethality	LC_{50}	LC_{90}	Percent lethality	LC_{50}	LC_{90}
1000	52	716.14	11117.00	64	413.05	7095.80	76	211.84	2582.30
500	48			56			68		
250	32			40			56		
125	20			28			40		
62.5	12			20			24		

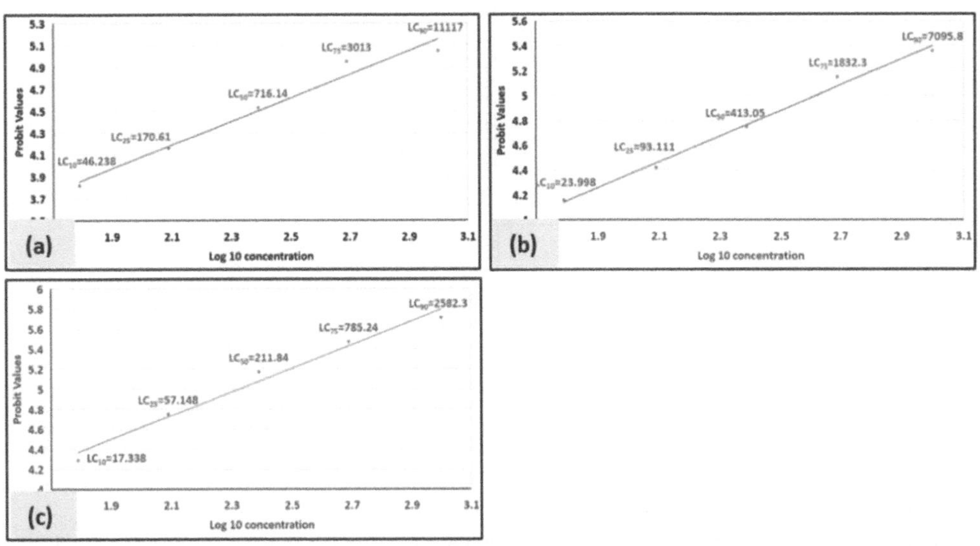

Fig. 45.8 Determination of lethal concentration (LC) thresholds for the orange peel aqueous extract against 4th instar larvae of *Cx. quinqifaciatus*: (a) 24 hrs, (b) 48 hrs, and (c) 72 hrs

(Table 45.3.)(Fig. 45.8.). By 72 hours, the equation y = 1.1779x + 2.2605, revealed a strong linear relationship with an R-squared value of 0.9809, explaining 98.09% variability. In all cases, probit values consistently increased with higher log10 concentrations, indicating a robust dose-response relationship. These results highlight the effectiveness of the extracts in predicting lethality across different incubation periods, with all regression models showing a very good fit to the observed data (Table 45.3.) (Fig. 45.8.).

Black Peeper Aqueous Extract

The study evaluated the relationship between the logarithmic concentration of extracts and probit values for 4th instar larvae lethality over 24, 48, and 72 hours of incubation. After 24 hours, the regression equation y=0.7782x+2.1864 demonstrated a strong linear relationship, with an R-squared value of 0.997, explaining 99.7 % of variability (Table 45.4.) (Fig. 45.9.). At 48 hours, the equation y=0.7965x+2.6947 showed a slightly lower but significant linear relationship, with an R-squared value of 0.8835, accounting for 88.35 % of variability (Table 45.4.) (Fig. 45.9.). By 72 hours, the equation y=0.9586x+2.9671 revealed a strong linear relationship with an R-squared value of 0.932, explaining 93.2 % variability. In all cases, probit values consistently increased with higher log10 concentrations, indicating a robust dose-response relationship. These results highlight the effectiveness of the extracts in predicting lethality across different incubation periods, with all regression models showing a very good fit to the observed data (Table 45.4.) (Fig. 45.9.).

Peanut Shell Aqueous Extract

The research examined the relationship between dosage and lethality in 4th instar larvae subjected to different extract concentrations over periods of 24, 48, and 72 hours. After 24 hours, a strong linear relationship was observed, represented by the regression equation y = 0.7782x + 2.1864, with an R-squared value of 0.997,

Table 45.4 Probit transformation and computations of probit values of 24 hr, 48 hr, and 72 hr observed and expected partial lethal ranges for the aqueous black peeper extract with 4th instar larvae of *Cx. quinquefasciatus*

Concentration	24 hr			48 hr			72 hr		
	Percent lethality	LC_{50}	LC_{90}	Percent lethality	LC_{50}	LC_{90}	Percent lethality	LC_{50}	LC_{90}
1000	32	4149.50	183231.44	60	783.429	31695.67	84	132.13	2857.59
500	28			36			64		
250	24			32			60		
125	20			28			48		
62.5	12			20			40		

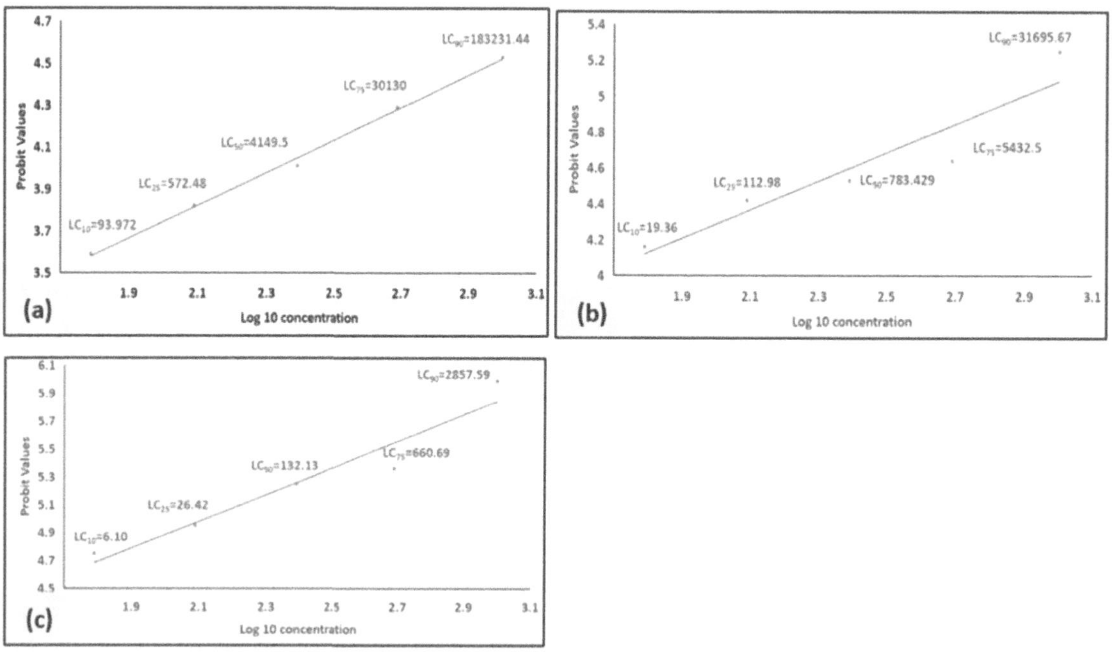

Fig. 45.9 Determination of lethal concentration (LC) thresholds for the black peeper aqueous extract against 4th instar larvae of *Cx. quinquefasciatus*: (a) 24 hrs, (b) 48 hrs, and (c) 72 hrs

indicating that 99.7 % of the variability was explained (Table 45.5.) (Fig. 45.10.). At 48 hours, the regression equation $y = 0.7103x + 2.667$ indicated a slightly lower yet significant linear relationship, with an R-squared value of 0.8868, which accounts for 88.68 % of the variability (Table 45.5.) (Fig. 45.10.). At 72 hours, the equation $y = 0.7729x+2.7052$ exhibited a robust linear relationship, characterized by an R-squared value of 0.9265, which accounts for 92.65 % of the variability. Probit values consistently increased with higher log10 concentrations of extracts, confirming a strong dose-response relationship. The results demonstrate a strong fit of the regression models, underscoring the extracts' effectiveness in predicting lethality over various time intervals (Table 45.5.) (Fig. 45.10.). The aqueous cinnamon extract was found to be most potent against both the 4th instar larvae of *Cx. quinquefasciatus* with LC_{50} and LC_{90} values of 75.509 ppm and 666.806 ppm respectively.

Histopathological Studies

In the control sample with a concentration of 0 ppm, the muscle fibers appear regularly and exhibit a dense pattern of staining (Fig. 45.11.). The epithelial cells appear normal, with a thick eosinophilic cytoplasm, a round nucleus, and a prominent nucleolus. At a dosage of 1000 ppm, muscle fibers exhibit degenerative alterations, whereas epithelial cells undergo total degeneration (Fig. 45.11.). At a concentration of 500 ppm, muscle fibers exhibit disarray and reduced staining, while epithelial cells display indications of degeneration characterized by cell enlargement and irregular nucleus (Fig. 45.11.). At a concentration of 250 ppm, muscle fibers exhibit disarray and reduced staining. They display degenerative alterations and uneven staining patterns (Fig. 45.11.). Epithelial cells appear enlarged with irregular cell boundaries and a rounded nucleus. At a concentration of 125 ppm, muscle fibers exhibit a consistent and compact staining pattern. Epithelial cells are slightly disturbed, displaying cytopathological changes such as cell enlargement and the presence of many cytoplasmic vacuoles (Fig. 45.11.). At a concentration of 62.5 ppm, muscle fibers exhibit a consistent and compact staining pattern. Epithelial cells appear flattened and are positioned on the basement membrane, displaying a dense eosinophilic cytoplasm,

Table 45.5 Probit transformation and computations of probit values of 24 hr, 48 hr, and 72 hr observed and expected partial lethal ranges for the aqueous peanut shell extract with 4th instar larvae of *Cx. quinquefasciatus*

Concen-tration	24 hr			48 hr			72 hr		
	Percent lethality	LC_{50}	LC_{90}	Percent lethality	LC_{50}	LC_{90}	Percent lethality	LC_{50}	LC_{90}
1000	32	4130.48	181970.09	48	1927.520	122179.970	56	931.11	42169.65
500	24			28			36		
250	16			24			32		
125	12			20			24		
62.5	8			16			20		

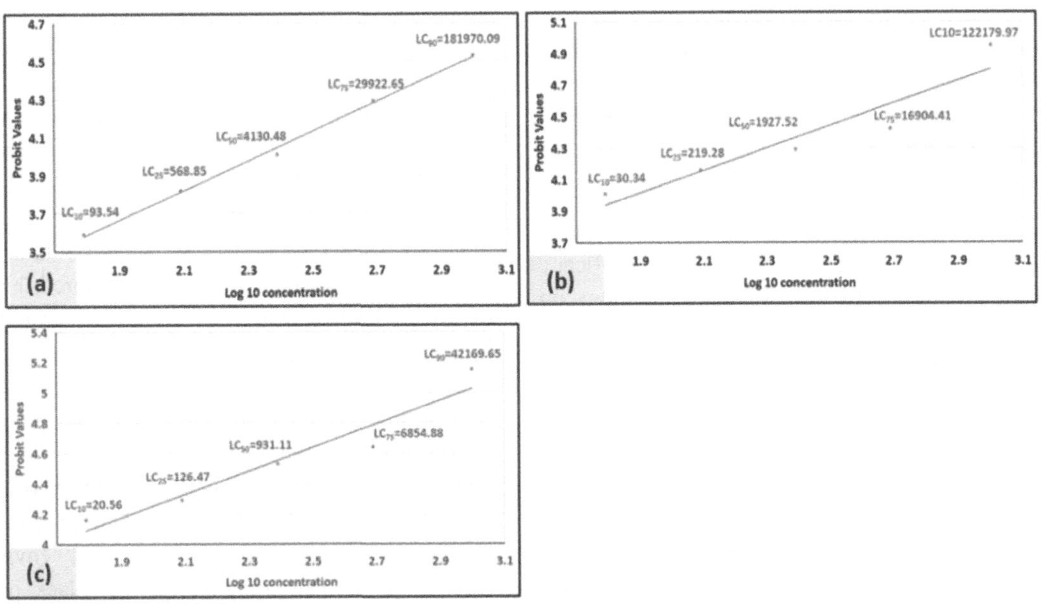

Fig. 45.10 Determination of lethal concentration (LC) thresholds for the peanut shell aqueous extract against 4th instar larvae of *Cx. quinqifaciatus*: (a) 24 hrs, (b) 48 hrs, and (c) 72 hrs

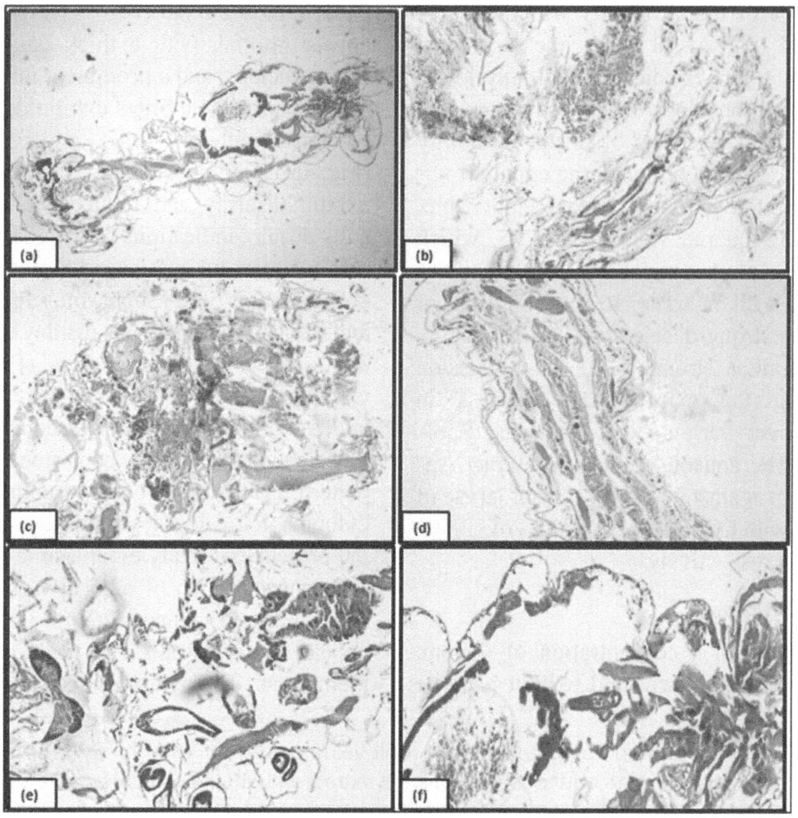

Fig. 45.11 (a) 0 ppm: Muscle fibers are regular and show dense pattern of staining, and epithelial cells looks normal with dense eosinophilic cytoplasm, round nucleus and prominent nucleolus, (b) 1000 ppm: Muscle fibers show degenerative changes, epithelial cells are completely degenerated, (c) 500 ppm: Muscle fibers are in disorder and under-stained, epithelial cells shows signs of degeneration with cell swelling and irregular nucleus, (d) 250 ppm: Muscle fibers show degenerative changes, irregular staining patterns, epithelial cells are swollen with irregular cell outlines and globular nucleus, (e) 125 ppm: Muscle fiber show regular and dense pattern of staining, Epithelial cells are mildly disrupted showing cytopathological alterations like cell swelling and numerous cytoplasmic vacuoles, and (f) 62.5 ppm: Muscle fibers show regular and dense pattern of staining, epithelial cells are flattened resting on basement membrane having dense eosinophilic cytoplasm, regular nucleus and brush borders at the apical surface

regular nucleus, and brush boundaries on the upper surface (Fig. 45.13.).

4. Discussion

The present study evaluated the larvicidal activity of *Cinnamomum, Arachis, Piper, and Citrus* plants against *Cx. quinquefasciatus* larvae, showing significant efficacy with low LC_{50} values, aligning with prior findings on the bioactive insecticidal compounds in *Cinnamomum* [22]. Studies have shown that botanical extracts like *C.verum* essential oils exhibit strong larvicidal activity against mosquitoes, such as *Ae. aegypti*, with LC_{50} values comparable to this study's findings [23]. Similarly, scientists reported the larvicidal efficacy of cinnamaldehyde against *Cx. quinquefasciatus* larvae, with an LC_{50}value of 68 ppm, indicating a comparable effectiveness to our results [24]. In another studies, researchers assessed the insecticidal effects of *C.zeylanicum* oil against *Alphitobiusdiaperinus* and observed significant mortality rates, which further supports the potential of *Cinnamomum*-derived compounds as effective insecticides [25, 26]. The insecticidal properties of botanical extracts are not limited to *Cinnamomum, Arachis, Piper* and *Citrus* species. For example, Scientists emphasized the potential of plant-derived compounds in sustainable pest management, noting their broad spectrum of activity and environmental safety [27, 28]. Additionally, researchers explored the potential of essential oils as inhibitors of odorant-binding proteins in mosquitoes, highlighting the diverse mechanisms through which botanical insecticides can exert their effects [29]. A study developed eco-friendly mosquito repellent dhoop from orange peel powder mixed with natural ingredients. The dhoop effectively repels mosquitoes for up to two hours, offering a safe alternative to chemical repellents while reducing health and environmental risks [30, 31]. The study shows that black pepper and piperine have strong larvicidal effects on insecticide-resistant and susceptible *Anopheles sp.*, highlighting their potential as natural alternatives for managing malaria vectors and combating insecticide resistance [32]. Histopathological studies in this research provided insights into the potential mechanisms underlying the larvicidal activity of *Cinnamomum* extracts. The observed degenerative changes in muscle fibers and epithelial cells, such as disarray, reduced staining, cell enlargement, and irregular nuclei, are indicative of significant physiological disruption caused by the extracts. Similar histopathological effects were reported by some scientists, who found that *Artemisia vulgaris* extract caused substantial damage to the midgut epithelial cells of *Ae. Aegypti larvae* [33].

The presence of cytoplasmic vacuoles and other cytopathological changes in the larvae further supports the larvicidal action of the extracts. These findings suggested that the bioactive compounds in *Cinnamomum* extracts may target the neuromuscular and cellular integrity of the larvae, leading to their mortality. This mode of action is consistent with the effects observed in studies on other botanical insecticides, such as the work by researchers, which highlighted the disruptive impact of *Chlorellasp.* extracts on mosquito larvae [34]. The use of botanical insecticides like *Cinnamomum* extracts presents a promising alternative to conventional synthetic insecticides, which are often associated with environmental pollution and the development of resistance in mosquito populations [35]. The biodegradability and low mammalian toxicity of botanical insecticides make them attractive candidates for integrated vector management programs. Furthermore, the varied mechanisms of action of these natural chemicals can assist in reducing the likelihood of resistance emergence [36].

The findings of this study contribute to the growing body of evidence supporting the efficacy of botanical insecticides. For example, some studies have emphasized the potential of plant-derived compounds in sustainable pest management, highlighting their broad spectrum of activity and environmental safety [37]. Moreover, numerous research has addressed the obstacles and progress in the development of botanical pesticides for sustainable agriculture as well as pest management [38].

5. Challenges and Future Research

Despite the promising results, several challenges need to be addressed to translate these findings into practical mosquito control strategies. The variability in the efficacy of different *Cinnamomum* species and plant parts suggests that further research is needed to optimize the extraction and formulation processes. Additionally, field trials are essential to assess the real-world effectiveness and environmental impact of these extracts. Future studies should explore the synergistic effects of combining *Cinnamomum* extracts with other botanical or synthetic agents to enhance their larvicidal activity and reduce the required concentration. Investigating the potential non-target effects on other aquatic organisms and ecosystems will be crucial for ensuring the environmental safety of these botanical insecticides.

6. Conclusion

In conclusion, the study demonstrated that *Cinnamomum* extracts possess more significant larvicidal activity in *Cx. quinquefasciatus* larvae, with a strong dose-response relationship and clear histopathological evidence of their mechanism of action compared to other extracts. These findings highlight the potential of *Cinnamomum* compounds as eco-friendly alternatives to synthetic insecticides, contributing to the formulation of sustainable strategies for mosquito control. Additional studies and field validation are necessary to fully harness the benefits of these botanical insecticides in public health programs.

Acknowledgement

This work is a part of Miss. Aditi Pal, PhD Research Scholar (Reg No: 2381611004) at Centre for Biotechnology, Siksha 'O' Anusandhan Deemed to be university, Bhubaneswar. Authors are thankful to Dean Research, SOA University and Director, ICMR-RMRC, Bhubaneswar for extending facility in research.

References

1. Duguma, D., Rueda, L. M., & Debboun, M. (2020). Mosquito-borne diseases. In *Mosquitoes, Communities, and Public Health in Texas* (pp. 319–337). Academic Press.
2. Rekha, R., Vaseeharan, B., Vijayakumar, S., Abinaya, M., Govindarajan, M., Alharbi, N. S., ...& Al-Anbr, M. N. (2019). Crustin-capped selenium nanowires against microbial pathogens and Japanese encephalitis mosquito vectors–Insights on their toxicity and internalization. *Journal of Trace Elements in Medicine and Biology*, *51*, 191–203.
3. Hemingway, J., Ranson, H., Magill, A., Kolaczinski, J., Fornadel, C., Gimnig, J., ...&Hamon, N. (2016). Averting a malaria disaster: will insecticide resistance derail malaria control?. *The Lancet*, *387*(10029), 1785–1788.
4. Zhang, Y., Wang, M., Huang, M., & Zhao, J. (2024). Innovative strategies and challenges mosquito-borne disease control amidst climate change. *Frontiers in Microbiology*, *15*, 1488106.
5. Ukoroije, R. B., &Otayor, R. A. (2020). Review on the bio-insecticidal properties of some plant secondary metabolites: types, formulations, modes of action, advantages and limitations. *Asian Journal of Research in Zoology*, *3*(4), 27–60.
6. Tyagi, B. K. (2016). Advances in vector mosquito control technologies, with particular reference to herbal products. *Herbal insecticides, repellents and biomedicines: effectiveness and commercialization*, 1–9.

7. Ragavendran, C., Mariappan, T., & Natarajan, D. (2017). Larvicidal, histopathological efficacy of Penicilliumdaleae against larvae of Culexquinquefasciatus and Aedesaegypti plus biotoxicity on Artemianauplii a non-target aquatic organism. *Frontiers in pharmacology*, *8*, 773.
8. Badalamenti, N., Ilardi, V., Bruno, M., Pavela, R., Boukouvala, M. C., Kavallieratos, N. G., ...& Benelli, G. (2021). Chemical composition and broad-spectrum insecticidal activity of the flower essential oil from an ancient Sicilian food plant, Ridolfiasegetum. *Agriculture*, *11*(4), 304.
9. Moungthipmalai, T., Puwanard, C., Aungtikun, J., Sittichok, S., &Soonwera, M. (2023). Ovicidal toxicity of plant essential oils and their major constituents against two mosquito vectors and their non-target aquatic predators. *Scientific Reports*, *13*(1), 2119.
10. Ameh, S., Ibekwe, N. N., Ambi, A. A., Abdulkareem, T., Toge, B. K., Ebeshi, B. U., ... & Garba, M. (2014). Diversity, utility, analytical methods and use implications of aroma-active compounds from select angiosperm families. *Eur J Med Plants*, *4*, 1046–1086.
11. S. Mann, R., & E. Kaufman, P. (2012). Natural product pesticides: their development, delivery and use against insect vectors. *Mini-reviews in organic chemistry*, *9*(2), 185–202.
12. Benelli, G., &Mehlhorn, H. (2016). Declining malaria, rising of dengue and Zika virus: insights for mosquito vector control. *Parasitology research*, *115*, 1747–1754.
13. Souto, A. L., Sylvestre, M., Tölke, E. D., Tavares, J. F., Barbosa-Filho, J. M., &Cebrián-Torrejón, G. (2021). Plant-derived pesticides as an alternative to pest management and sustainable agricultural production: Prospects, applications and challenges. *Molecules*, *26*(16), 4835.
14. Ghosh, A., Chowdhury, N., & Chandra, G. (2012). Plant extracts as potential mosquito larvicides. *Indian journal of medical research*, *135*(5), 581–598.
15. Jourdain, F., Picard, M., Sulesco, T., Haddad, N., Harrat, Z., Sawalha, S. S., ...& Robert, V. (2018). Identification of mosquitoes (Diptera: Culicidae): an external quality assessment of medical entomology laboratories in the MediLabSecure Network. *Parasites & vectors*, *11*, 1–7.
16. López-Bascón, M. A., & De Castro, M. L. (2020). Soxhlet extraction. In *Liquid-phase extraction* (pp. 327–354). Elsevier.
17. Sigamani, S., Chinnasamy, R., Dharmaraj, R. K., Ramamurthy, D., Devarajan, N., Narayanasamy, M., &Natarajan, H. (2020). Larvicidal potency of the extracts from Chlorella sp. against Aedesaegypti. *Biocatalysis and Agricultural Biotechnology*, *27*, 101663.
18. Imam, M. H., Riaz, Z., &Sofi, G. (2013). Evaluation of mosquito larvicidal effect of Nagarmotha (Cyperusrotundus) extracts against Aedesaegypti L. larvae. *International Journal of Green Pharmacy (IJGP)*, *7*(1).
19. Al-Mehmadi, R. M., & Al-Khalaf, A. A. (2010). Larvicidal and histological effects of Meliaazedarach extract on Culexquinquefasciatus Say larvae (Diptera: Culicidae). *Journal of King Saud University-Science*, *22*(2), 77–85.
20. FOUDA, M. A., HASSAN, M. I., EL-SHEIKH, T. M., ABD-ELGHAPHAR, A. E. A., & HASABALLAH, A. I. (2011). Histopathological effect of certain heavy metals on the mosquito vector CULEX pipiens L.(diptera: culicidae). *Al-Azhar Bulletin of Science*, *22*(1-C), 69–84.
21. Lim, H., Lee, S. Y., Ho, L. Y., & Sit, N. W. (2023). Mosquito larvicidal activity and cytotoxicity of the extracts of aromatic plants from Malaysia. *Insects*, *14*(6), 512.
22. M do AF Navarro, D., CB da Silva, P., FR da Silva, M., H Napoleao, T., & MG Paiva, P. (2013). Larvicidal activity of plant and algae extracts, essential oils and isolated chemical constituents against Aedesaegypti. *The Natural Products Journal*, *3*(4), 268–291.
23. Arena, J. S., Merlo, C., Defagó, M. T., &Zygadlo, J. A. (2020). Insecticidal and antibacterial effects of some essential oils against the poultry pest Alphitobiusdiaperinus and its associated microorganisms. *Journal of Pest Science*, *93*, 403–414.
24. Subekti, N., Cahyaningrum, S. H., &Maulana, S. (2022). Effective control of Alphitobiusdiaperinus using natural bioinsecticides: Effective control of Alphitobiusdiaperinus using natural bioinsecticides. *Journal of Tropical Life Science*, *12*(3), 289–297.
25. Hasan, W., Hussain, G. J., Doggalli, G., Alagumanian, S., Jena, N. K., Saravanan, A., ...&Saravanamoorthy, M. D. (2023). Plant-Based Products as Control Agents of Stored Product Insect Pests: Prospects, Applicationsand Challenges. *Int. J. Plant Soil Sci*, *35*(22), 866–873.
26. Quadros, D. G., Johnson, T. L., Whitney, T. R., Oliver, J. D., &Oliva Chávez, A. S. (2020). Plant-derived natural compounds for tick pest control in livestock and wildlife: Pragmatism or Utopia?. *Insects*, *11*(8), 490.
27. Gupta, I., Singh, R., Muthusamy, S., Sharma, M., Grewal, K., Singh, H. P., &Batish, D. R. (2023). Plant essential oils as biopesticides: Applications, mechanisms, innovations, and constraints. *Plants*, *12*(16), 2916.
28. Rahangdale, S., Deobhankar, K., &Phal, D. (2023). Larvicidal and repellent efficacy evaluation of Calotropisprocera against Aedesaegypti Linn and Culexquinquefasciatus (Diptera: Culicidae) mosquito species under laboratory condition.
29. Sahu, B., Dutta, S., Mishra, S. P., Khute, S., Kumar, L., Soni, A. G., &Dewangan, K. (2021). A brief review on dhoop and its properties. *Journal of Preventive Medicine and Holistic Health*, *7*(1), 3–9.
30. Marcião Vieira, A. C., Azevedo, S. G., Linhares, R. A., BrandãoJustiniano, S. C., Pontes, G. O., Lima, A. R., ... &Sanches, E. A. (2022). Biodefensive Based on Piper nigrum Essential Oil for Controlling of Anopheles aquasalis Larvae: Influence of Temperature (35° C) and Preservatives. *Biomolecules*, *12*(11), 1711.
31. Balasubramani, S., Sabapathi, G., Moola, A. K., Solomon, R. V., Venuvanalingam, P., & Bollipo Diana, R. K. (2018). Evaluation of the leaf essential oil from Artemisia vulgaris and its larvicidal and repellent activity against dengue fever vector Aedesaegypti—an experimental and molecular docking investigation. *ACS omega*, *3*(11), 15657–15665.
32. Câmara, J. S., Perestrelo, R., Ferreira, R., Berenguer, C. V., Pereira, J. A., & Castilho, P. C. (2024). Plant-derived terpenoids: A plethora of bioactive compounds with several health functions and industrial applications—A comprehensive overview. *Molecules*, *29*(16), 3861.
33. Ullah, H., Iqbal, T., Al-Mutairi, K. A., Shahjeer, K., Ullah, R., Ahmed, S., ...&Khater, H. F. (2022). Botanical

insecticides are a non-toxic alternative to conventional pesticides in the control of insects and pests. *Global decline of insects*, 103.
34. da Silva Sá, G. C., Bezerra, P. V. V., Da Silva, M. F. A., Da Silva, L. B., Barra, P. B., de FátimaFreire de MeloXimenes, M., & Uchôa, A. F. (2023). Arbovirus vectors insects: are botanical insecticides an alternative for its management?. *Journal of Pest Science*, *96*(1), 1–20.
35. Souto, A. L., Sylvestre, M., Tölke, E. D., Tavares, J. F., Barbosa-Filho, J. M., &Cebrián-Torrejón, G. (2021). Plant-derived pesticides as an alternative to pest management and sustainable agricultural production: Prospects, applications and challenges. *Molecules*, *26*(16), 4835.
36. Khursheed, A., Rather, M. A., Jain, V., Wani, A. R., Rasool, S., Nazir, R., ...&Majid, S. A. (2022). Plant based natural products as potential ecofriendly and safer biopesticides: A comprehensive overview of their advantages over conventional pesticides, limitations and regulatory aspects. *Microbial pathogenesis*, *173*, 105854.

Note: All the figures and tables in this chapter were made by the authors.

Research and Innovations in Industrial and Marine Biotechnology: A Circular Economy 2024 – Prof. Hrudayanath Thatoi et al. (eds)

46 Exploiting Microbial Amphiphiles as Anticancer Chemotherapeutics

Sumithra Bapatla*
Department of Biotechnology, Chaitanya Bharathi Institute of Technology, Gandipet, Hyderabad, Telangana, India

Jahanvi Madasu
Department of Biotechnology, Chaitanya Bharathi Institute of Technology, Gandipet, Hyderabad, Telangana, India
Biopharma, Vimta Labs Ltd., Shameerpet, Hyderabad, Telangana, India

Golla Sowmya
Department of Biotechnology, Chaitanya Bharathi Institute of Technology, Gandipet, Hyderabad, Telangana, India

Alisha Chunduri
Department of Biotechnology, Chaitanya Bharathi Institute of Technology, Gandipet, Hyderabad, Telangana, India
Department of Biotechnology Northeastern University, Boston, MA 02115, USA

Shibani Mohapatra
Centre for Biotechnology, Siksha 'O' Anusandhan (Deemed to be University), Bhubaneswar, Odisha, India
Centre for Industrial Biotechnology Research, Siksha 'O' Anusandhan (Deemed to be University), Bhubaneswar, Odisha, India

Bishwambhar Mishra, Sanjeeb Kumar Mandal
Department of Biotechnology, Chaitanya Bharathi Institute of Technology, Gandipet, Hyderabad, Telangana, India

Venkatramanan Varadharajan
Department of Biotechnology, PSG College of Technology, Peelamedu, Coimbatore, India

Abstract: The incidence and prevalence of cancers, the leading cause of mortality worldwide, are increasing substantially; and so the number of cases is expected to surge in the near future. Despite impressive breakthroughs in cancer therapeutics, there has been only a little progress in the survival rate of patients. Furthermore, the current standard of care has significant limitations, making this disease irremediable. Researchers from all across the world have made unremitting efforts in exploring various compounds that benefit the lives of patients. As a result, natural compounds, notably microbial amphiphiles, have emerged as possible anticancer chemotherapeutic agents in cancer prevention and treatment. The amphiphiles unique properties like lower toxicity, high efficacy and better biodegradability have made them intriguing new-generation anticancer chemotherapeutics. Additionally, these novel anticancer agents have

*Corresponding author:sumithra.das@gmail.com

DOI: 10.1201/9781003759003-46

shown to exhibit anticancer properties like cancer cell cytotoxicity, induction of apoptosis and inhibition of cancer cell proliferation. Their amphiphilic nature has not only made them a suitable anticancer drug candidate but also holds a great promise as vehicles for carrying anticancer drugs. The potent effect of these amphiphiles on malignant cells, several classes of amphiphiles like lipopeptides, and glycolipids, have been investigated for their mechanistic studies that contribute to their anticancer efficacy. Additionally, among lipopeptidessurfactins, iturins, and fengycins are most well studied as anticancer chemotherapeutic agents. As a result, this review will attempt to address the role of amphiphiles as anticancer chemotherapeutics against different cancers.

Keywords: Amphiphiles, Anticancer, Glycolipids, Lipopeptides, Nanotechnology

1. INTRODUCTION

Cancer is the second most prevalent cause of mortality, accounting for more than 14 million new cases each year. This is a multifactorial disease, with decades of in-depth research revealing the causative factors, which include an unhealthy lifestyle, an inadequate diet, heredity, and environmental exposure to carcinogens and other pollutants. To date, there is no curative for this disease; nevertheless, surgical resection, chemotherapy, and radiotherapy are current standards of care used to increase the survival rates of patients. [1]. However, these conventional therapies are associated with several downsides. Due to the inadequate removal of cancer cells, surgical resection has resulted in cancer recurrence. Because of the lack of specificity to cancer cells, radiotherapy and chemotherapy have always been toxic to normal cells, this results in a variety of side effects such as nausea, vomiting, exhaustion, hair loss, anaemia, and others. The late effects of chemotherapy include cardiovascular disorders, neurological disorders, infertility, second malignant neoplasm, psychological and psychosocial effects [2].

All these limitations have led to the necessity of developing anticancer chemotherapeutics that are less toxic, biodegradable and highly effective. Cancer treatment with the emergence of microbial therapy was first outlined in the 19th century which laid a path to the use of diverse microbes as therapeutic agents due to their relatively high growth rate, higher efficacy, biodegradability, and lower toxicity. Microbial amphiphiles, also known as biosurfactants, are surface-active compounds produced by microorganisms. They play a vital role across various sectors, including food, healthcare, and environmental applications.Most of the amphiphiles are extracellular secondary metabolites secreted by microbes and have tremendous biological activities such as antimicrobial, anti-viral, anti-fungal, immunomodulatory, etc. [3]. Types of amphiphiles include lipopeptides, glycolipids, phospholipids have been most commonly reported for their cytotoxicity on various cancer cell lines. These amphiphiles exhibit outstanding emulsifying exertions and enlarge the surface area at the interface by reducing the surface tension. These molecules interact with the tumor cell membrane and embody biological activities at the target site. It has been reported that biosurfactants agents were able to inhibit the proliferation of malignant tumor cells and impede DNA synthesis in tumor cells [4]. This review attempts to appraise the potential application of various microbial amphiphiles as anticancer chemotherapeutic agents

2. TYPES OF AMPHIPHILES AND THEIR EFFECT AS ANTICANCER DRUGS

2.1 Lipopeptides

Lipopeptides are lipids containing molecules connected by peptides. These molecules are known for their diverse biological functions ranging from antibacterial to antitumor. These are also the second-largest class of biosurfactants and are primarily derived from bacterial species. Surfactins, iturins, fengycin, lichenysins, viscosins, amphisins and putisolvins are the most well studied lipopeptides. As potential antibacterial, antiviral, antifungal, and anti-inflammatory agents, these lipopeptides are also being investigated for their anti-tumor activity. These lipopeptides are reported to be a potent anti-cancer agent against various cancer cell lines employing different mechanisms of action.

2.2 Surfactin

Surfactins, a cyclic lipoheptapeptide, is a secondary metabolite produced by Bacillus species. Due to its diverse structure and biochemical function, it is considered as an efficient antibacterial, antifungal, antimycoplasma, antiviral, and anti-inflammatory chemotherapeutic agent. A continual effort on exploring its bioactivity has resulted in its substantial cytotoxic effect on various cancer cell lines which includes MCF7 [5], T47D [6], Bcap-37 [7], HCT15 [3], HT29 [3], K562, HepG2 [8] and SW-1990 [6]. A recent research reported that surfactin produced by marine actinomyceteMicromonospora marina exhibited an cytotoxic effect on human breast cancer cell line, MCF-7 through increasing the production of reactive oxygen species (ROS) and cleaving mitochondrial membrane which thereby resulted in apoptosis of MCF7 cells [5]. Hong et al., recently revealed that five surfactin isomers generated during cheonggukjang fermentation of B. pumilus HY1 suppressed the proliferation of two cancer cell lines significantly, MCF-7 and Caco-2 [9].

2.3 Iturins

It has been demonstrated that the biosurfactantiturin, a nonribosomal cyclic lipopeptide generated by different strains of the *Bacillus* species, induces cytotoxicity against a variety of cancer types, including breast, cervical, colon, gastric, and liver cancer. Treatment with iturin can slow the spread of cancer by preventing growth, cell cycle progression, apoptosis, and metastasis. Many research has recently looked into the mechanisms underlying iturin's anticancer effects because of how powerfully it affects cancer cells. A study reported that iturin like lipopeptide extracted from *B. subtilis* was found to trigger apoptosis, paraoptosis in human epithelial colorectal adenocarcinoma (Caco-2) cell lines. Iturin was found to inhibit or downregulate the expression of bcl-2, upregulated expression of apoptotic genes bad and bax, and also stimulates the release of cytochrome-C from mitochondria into the cytoplasm, all of which are having an anticancer effect on Caco-2 cell line [10]. Additionally, *B. subtilis* lipopetideiturin was reported to induce apoptosis and inhibit autophagy in K562 cell lines at 100 μM concentration, and at IC50 of 65.76 μM. Moreover, this lipopeptide was found to enhance the production of ROS in K562 cell lines, which thereby inhibits Bcl-2 expression and promotes the release of cytochrome-C (Cyto-C), which further led to apoptosis [10]. Another study reported that bacillomycinLb obtained from new strain *Bacillus amyloliquefaciens*X030, exhibited a broad spectrum of antitumor activity in various cancer cell lines which includes SMMC-7721, B16, MDA-MB-231, CT26, MCF-7, 4T1 [11]. Moreover, bacillomycin D-C16, derived from the *Bacillus subtilis* strain fmbJ, has also been shown to trigger apoptosis in the Bgc-823 cell line via the PI3K/Akt and FoxO3a signalling pathways [12]. All these studies have depicted the significant antitumor property of iturin.

2.4 Other Lipopeptides

In addition to the aforementioned lipopeptides, several more have been discovered to have anticancer effectiveness. Fengycin, a cyclic lipopeptide complex, has shown a significant anticancer activity in breast, lung, gastric and colon cancer. Recent study reported that fengycin extracted from B. subtilis exhibited an antitumor activity in colon cancer HT29 cell line. Their mechanistic study revealed that this compound was found to inhibit the progression of colon cancer by targeting the Bax/Bcl-2 pathway. Somocystinamide A, extracted from Lyngbyamajuscula was shown to exhibit an antitumor property against a wide range of cancer cell lines which include Jurkatleukemia (at IC50 of 3 nM), CEM leukemia (at IC50 of14 nM), A549 lung carcinoma (at IC50 of 46 nM), Molt4 T leukemia (at IC50 of 60 nM), MCF-7 breast cancer (at IC50 of 210 nM), NB7 neuroblastoma (at IC50 of 810 nM), PC-3 prostate carcinoma (at IC50 of 970 nM), M21 melanoma (at IC50 of 1.3 μM), and U266 myeloma (at IC50 of 5.8 μM) (Rosário and Costa, 2015) [13]. Apratoxins, cyclic depsipeptides with significant cytotoxic effects, were discovered to block cotranslational translocation of secretory proteins, particularly receptor tyrosine kinases and their associated ligands. Analogues of apratoxins namely apratoxins S10, was recently reported to inhibit the release of VEGF-A and IL-6 from cancer cells by negatively regulating the vascular endothelial growth factor receptor 2 (VEGFR2). Additionally, it also suppressed cancer cell growth by inhibiting the

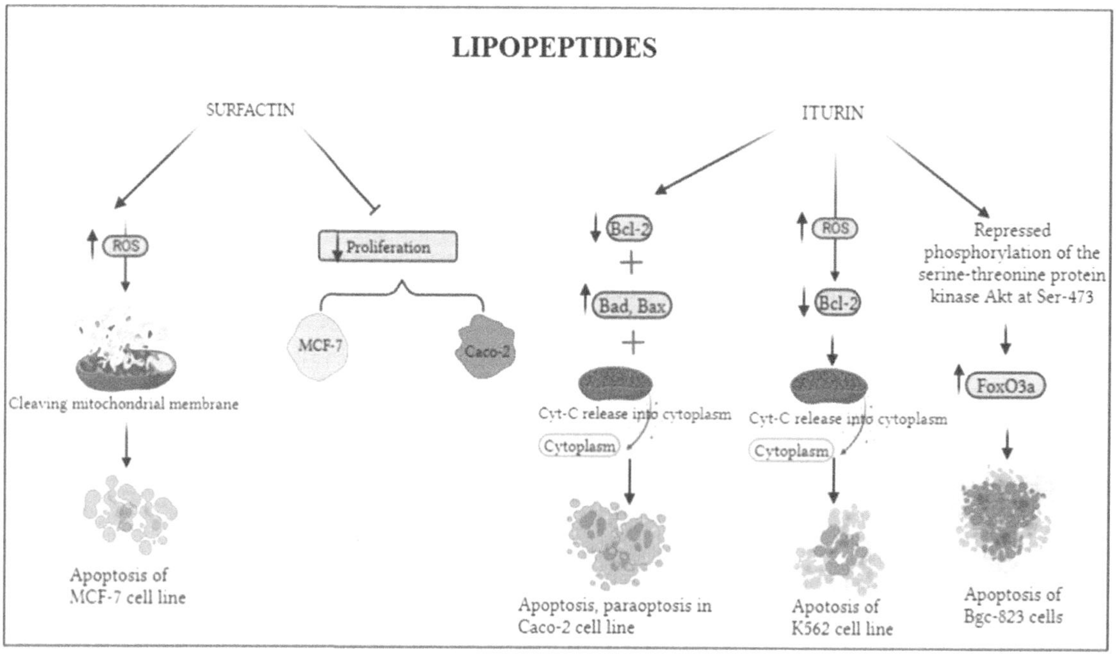

Fig. 46.1 Molecular mechanisms involved in the anticancer activity of Surfactin and Iturin against different cancer cell lines
Source: Author

expression of several receptor tyrosine kinases (RTKs), and thus reported that it outperformed already approved RTK inhibitors in both angiogenesis and cancer cell proliferation [14]. Many such lipopeptides are being studied for their anticancer potential in various cancer cell lines. Their distinct method of action has proven them to be a potential anticancer chemotherapy.

2.5 Glycolipids

Glycolipids are well-known biosurfactants with low molecular weight that are prominent in cancer treatment and have been explicitly implicated in the cell growth arrest and apoptosis of various tumor cells. Glycolipid as the name implies it embraces two parts: a carbohydrate moiety and fatty chain allied by a glycosidic bond. Based on sugar moiety glycolipids are further classified and the most copiously synthesized groups are rhamnolipids, sophorolipids, mannosylerythritol lipids, cellobiase lipids, xylo lipids, etc. Glycolipids have become a feasible proxy against chemical amphiphiles due to their unprecedented biological activities such as anti-cancerogenic, anti-microbial, immunomodulatory properties, etc. [15].

2.6 Rhamnolipids

Rhamnolipids are one of the most studied microbial glycolipid produced by bacteria namely Pseudomonas aeruginosa, Burkholderiathailandensis, Acinetobactercalcoaceticus, Enterobacter spp., pantoea spp., etc and proclaimed as "oily glycolipids". Rhamnolipids are biological molecules that are surface active and flaunt proficient emulsifying capabilities. They also lower surface tension and create microemulsions in an amalgam of immiscible organic and aqueous phases [16]. It has been proclaimed that Pseudomonas aeruginosa B189 brings about two homologs namely Rha-Rha-C10-C10 (mono-rhamnolipid) and Rha-Rha-C10-C12 (di-rhamnolipid). The homologs were tested for cytotoxicity against human breast cancer (MCF-7), human Non-small cell lung cancer (H460), herpes simplex virus, colon cancer (CaCo-2), liver cancer (HepG2), human malignant keratinocyte (SK-MEL-28), human urinary bladder cancer, promyelocyticleukemia cell lines and other cancer cell lines [17]. Rha-Rha-C10-C10 compounds laid out the hindrance of cancer cell proliferation of human breast cancer with 6.25 μg/ml minimum inhibitory concentration whereas Rha-Rha-C10-C12 could not exhibit any anti-tumor potential activity. Furthermore, at a concentration of 50 μg/ml (vero cell lines) both homologs did not influence growth of normal cell lines [18] In accordance to the report, the rhamnolipids trigger the cytotoxic activity by shrinking the surface tension rather than changing the molecule specificity, hence it has no selective cytotoxicity on discrete tumor cells. Mono-rhamnolipids have been reputed to be more cytotoxic against human tumor cell lines in contrast to di-rhamnolipids due to the structural modification of mono-rhamnolipids amenable for higher penetration in tumor cells routing to elevated depletion of tumor cell viability [19]. Rha-Rha-C10-C10 compounds beget variation in cancer cell lines such as blebbing of plasma membrane, chromatin condensation, nuclear rupture, etc escorting to cell apoptosis. These studies suggest that rhamnolipids might be effective chemotherapeutic agents for alleviating cancer [20].

2.7 Sophorolipids

Sophorolipids are microbial dawn glycolipid biosurfactants with immense biological activities namely anti-cancer, anti-bacterial, anti-viral, proinflammatory, immuno-modulator activities, etc. Sophorolipids are amphiphilic compounds consisting of a hydrophilic sophorose disaccharide moiety allied with a hydrophobic long chain fatty acid moiety [21]. These secondary metabolites are produced by a scope of non-pathogenic yeast including Starmerellabombicola, Candida batistae CBS 8550, Rhodotorulabogoriensis, Cryptococcus sp. VITGBN, Wickerhamielladomercqiae Y2A, Pichiaanomala, etc[22]. Sophorolipids have been proclaimed to manifest antitumor cytotoxicity against human liver (H7420), lung (A549), brain (HNCG-2), breast, cervical (HeLa), leukemia (HL60), melanoma (SK-MEL-28), esophageal (KYSE109), glioma cell lines (LN-229), etc [23; 24]. Based on anatomical variability sophorolipids are partitioned into lactonicsophorolipids (LSL) and acidic sophorolipids (ASL) where LSL is internally esterified with carboxy terminus while ASL is free, thus the cytotoxicity outcome of LSL is exceptional higher than the cytotoxicity of ASL. It has been outlined that LSL implicit inhibition of cancer cell proliferation, and aid in apoptosis of tumor. Calleghen evaluated the potential of LSL against esophageal and pancreatic cancer cell lines in a dose and time dependent approach which laid out the bioactive inhibitory properties of LSL [25] Over 85% of lung carcinoma are correlated to Non-small-cell lung cancer (NSCLC) which has acquired hindrance to chemotherapy and radiotherapy therapy as a result of the tumor's K-Ras mutations. In an in-vitro study [26] conducted on colorectal tumor induced mice feed orally 50mg/kg of ACL over 70 days in a dose dependent pattern resulted in elevated hematocrit levels, induced apoptosis, reduced colony formation and migration, along with decreased spleen size and red pulp area. These findings may suggest the potential use of sophorolipids as an anticancer therapeutic in human cancer cell lines due to their efficaciousness to tumor and lower toxicity to normal cell lines.

3. Conclusions and Future Perspective

Numerous studies have reported amphiphiles' anticancer activities. Their anticancer activity has mostly been reported to be associated with apoptosis, and inhibition of cancer cell proliferation. Given its amphiphilic nature,

Table 46.1 Anticancer activity of different microbial glycolipid biosurfactants against various human cancer cell lines

Microbial amphiphiles	Types of biosurfactants	Microbial source	Cytotoxic assay	Cancer cell lines	References
Rhamnolipids	Mono and Di-rhamolipids	Pseudomonas aeruginosa MR01, Pseudomonas spp.	MTT assay	Inhibits breast cancer cell lines (MCF-7), A549 lung cancer, HEPG2 liver cancer, HeLa cell lines.	[20]
	Rhizoleucinoside, RL amino alcohol hybrid amphiphiles	Lactobacillus casei, Bradyrhizobium spp. BRAil	MTT assay, cellTiter-Glo 2.0 assay	Suppresses HEp-2 cell lines of rat, Murine microglia.	[27; 28]
	MCTG107b (an amalgam of rhamnolipids congeners) , MCTG214 (analogues of di-rhamnolipids)	Marinobacter and Pseudomonas strains	Almar blue assay	Impedes Skin B16F10 HaCat keratinocytes cell lines, mice melanoma cell lines, THLE3 liver cancer.	[29]
Sophorolipids	Lactonicsophorolipids (LSL)	Starmerellabombicola, Candida batistae CBS 8850, Wickerhamielladomercqiae Y2A, etc.	MTT assay	Inhibits colorectal cancer cell lines, human malignant melanocyte (SK -MEL-28), 2 non transformed cell lines- colonic epithelium (CCD-81 CoN) and lung fibroblast(MRC-5).	[25]
	Acidic sophorolipids (ASL)	Starmerellabombicola, Wickerhamielladomercqiae Y2A, Cryptococcus spp., etc.	Chemotactic cell migration assay, animal cell lines	Obstructs mice colorectal cancer cell lines, human malignant melanocyte cell lines (SK-MEL-28) proliferation.	[26]
Other glycolipids	Glucolipds and dokdo lipids A, B, C	Candida bombicola, Actinoalloteichushymeniacidonis 179DD-027	MTT assay, sulforhodamine assay (SRB)	Breast cancer cell lines (MDA-MB-231)	[30]

these amphiphiles possess a great potential as a new generation anti-cancer chemotherapeutics. Their usage as nano-formulations, which have the ability to cause minimal toxicity to normal cells due to their specificity for cancer cells, might be a promising strategy for increasing microbial amphiphile's anticancer efficacy. Numerous synthetic amphiphiles have been developed and demonstrated to exhibit cytotoxic effects against various cancer cell lines. Furthermore, the use of advanced technologies such as metagenomics, proteomics, and bio-chemo-informatics can significantly enhance the discovery and development of novel natural amphiphiles from microorganisms.

References

1. Lewis-Oscar, F., Nithya, C., Bakkiyaraj, D., Arunkumar, M., Alharbi, N.S. and Thajuddin, N. (2015b). Biofilm inhibitory effect of *Spirulina platensis* extracts on bacteria of clinical significance. PNAS Biological Sciences, 87 (2), 537–544.
2. Ahmad, S. S., Reinius, M. A., Hatcher, H. M., and Ajithkumar, T. V. (2016). Anticancer chemotherapy in teenagers and young adults: managing long term side effects. BMJ (Clinical research ed.). 354, i4567.
3. Sivapathasekaran, C., Das, P., Mukherjee, S., Saravanakumar, J., Mandal, M., and Sen, R. (2010). Marine bacterium derived lipopeptides: characterization and cytotoxic activity against cancer cell lines. Int. J. Pept. Res. Ther. 16, 215–222.
4. Master, N.G., Markande, A.R. (2023). Importance of microbial amphiphiles: interaction potential of biosurfactants, amyloids, and other exo-polymeric-substances. World J MicrobiolBiotechnol 39, 320.
5. Ramalingam, V., Varunkumar, K., Ravikumar, V., and Rajaram, R. (2019). Production and structure elucidation of anticancer potential surfactin from marine actinomyceteMicromonospora marina. Process Biochem. 78, 169–177.
6. Duarte, C., Gudina, E. J., Lima, C. F., and Rodrigues, L. R. (2014). Effects of biosurfactants on the viability and proliferation of human breast cancer cells. AMB Express. 4, 40.
7. Liu, X., Tao, X., Zou, A., Yang, S., Zhang, L., and Mu, B. (2010). Effect of the microbial lipopeptide on tumor cell lines: apoptosis induced by disturbing the fatty acid composition of cell membrane. Protein Cell. 1, 584–594.
8. Wang, C. L., Liu, C., Niu, L. L., Wang, L. R., Hou, L. H., and Cao, X. H. (2013). Surfactin-induced apoptosis through ROS-ERS-Ca2+-ERK pathways in HepG2 cells. Cell Biochem. Biophys. 67, 1433–1439.
9. Hong, S. Y., Lee, D. H., Lee, J. H., Haque, M. A., and Cho, K. M. (2021). Five surfactin isomers produced during Cheonggukjang fermentation by Bacillus pumilus HY1 and their properties. Molecules. 26(15), 4478.
10. Zhao, H., Yan, L., Xu, X., Jiang, C., Shi, J., Zhang, Y., Liu, L., Lei, S., Shao, D. and Huang, Q. (2018). Potential of Bacillus subtilis lipopeptides in anti-cancer I: induction of apoptosis and paraptosis and inhibition of autophagy in K562 cells. Amb. Express. 8, 1–16.
11. Lu, J.Y., Zhou, K., Huang, W.T., Zhou, P., Yang, S., Zhao, X., Xie, J., Xia, L. and Ding, X. (2019). A comprehensive genomic and growth proteomic analysis of antitumor lipopeptidebacillomycinLb biosynthesis in Bacillus amyloliquefaciens X030. Appl. Microbiol. Biotechnol. 103(18), 7647–7662.
12. Lin, F., Yang, J., Muhammad, U., Sun, J., Huang, Z., Li, W., Lv, F. and Lu, Z. (2019). Bacillomycin D-C16 triggers apoptosis of gastric cancer cells through the PI3K/Akt and

FoxO3a signaling pathways. Anti-cancer drugs. 30(1), 46–55.
13. Cai, W., Chen, Q. Y., Dang, L. H., and Luesch, H. (2017). Apratoxin S10, a Dual Inhibitor of Angiogenesis and Cancer Cell Growth to Treat Highly Vascularized Tumors. ACS Med. Chem. Lett. 8(10), 1007–1012.
14. Kumar, A., Singh, S.K., Kant, C., Verma, H., Kumar, D., Singh, P.P., Modi, A., Droby, S., Kesawat, M.S., Alavilli, H. and Bhatia, S.K. (2021). Microbial biosurfactant: a new frontier for sustainable agriculture and pharmaceutical industries. Antioxidants. 10(9), 1472.
15. Varjani, S. J., and Upasani, V. N. (2017). Critical review on biosurfactant analysis, purification and characterization using rhamnolipid as a model biosurfactant. Bioresour. Technol. 232, 389–397.
16. Puyol McKenna P, Naughton PJ, Dooley JSG, Ternan NG, Lemoine P, Banat IM. Microbial Biosurfactants: Antimicrobial Activity and Potential Biomedical and Therapeutic Exploits. Pharmaceuticals (Basel). 2024 Jan 22;17(1):138.
17. Thakur, P., Saini, N. K., Thakur, V. K., Gupta, V. K., Saini, R. V., and Saini, A. K. (2021). Rhamnolipid the Glycolipid Biosurfactant: Emerging trends and promising strategies in the field of biotechnology and biomedicine. Microb. Cell Fact. 20(1), 1–15.
18. Rahimi, K., Lotfabad, T. B., Jabeen, F., and Ganji, S. M. (2019). Cytotoxic effects of mono-and di-rhamnolipids from Pseudomonas aeruginosa MR01 on MCF-7 human breast cancer cells. Colloids Surf. B: Biointerfaces. 181, 943–952.
19. Semkova, S., Antov, G., Iliev, I., Tsoneva, I., Lefterov, P., Christova, N., Nacheva, L., Stoineva, I., Kabaivanova, L., Staneva, G. and Nikolova, B. (2021). Rhamnolipid Biosurfactants—Possible Natural Anticancer Agents and Autophagy Inhibitors. Separations, 8(7), 92.
20. Wang, X., Xu, N., Li, Q., Chen, S., Cheng, H., Yang, M., Jiang, T., Chu, J., Ma, X. and Yin, D. (2021). Lactonicsophorolipid–induced apoptosis in human HepG2 cells through the Caspase-3 pathway. Appl. Microbiol. Biotechnol. 105(5), 2033–2042.
21. Roberto de Oliveira, M., Magri, A., Baldo, C., Camilios-Neto, D., Minucelli, T., Pedrine, M. A., and Celligoi, C. (2015). Review: Sophorolipids a promising biosurfactant and it's applications. Int. J. Adv. Biotechnol. Res. 6, 161–174.
22. Govindarajan, M. (2018). Amphiphilic glycoconjugates as potential anti-cancer chemotherapeutics. Eur. J. Med. Chem. 143, 1208–1253.
23. Adu, S. A., Twigg, M. S., Naughton, P. J., Marchant, R., and Banat, I. M. (2022). Biosurfactants as Anticancer Agents: Glycolipids Affect Skin Cells in a Differential Manner Dependent on Chemical Structure. Pharmaceutics. 14(2), 360.
24. Callaghan, B., Lydon, H., Roelants, S. L., Van Bogaert, I. N., Marchant, R., Banat, I. M., and Mitchell, C. A. (2016). LactonicSophorolipids increase tumor burden in Apcmin+/-mice. PloS one, 11(6), e0156845.
25. Callaghan, B., Twigg, M. S., Baccile, N., Van Bogaert, I. N., Marchant, R., Mitchell, C. A., and Banat, I. M. (2022). Microbial sophorolipids inhibit colorectal tumour cell growth in vitro and restore haematocrit in Apcmin+/– mice. Appl. Microbiol. Biotechnol. 1–14.
26. Chen, J., Sun, J., Deering, R. W., DaSilva, N., Seeram, N. P., Wang, H., and Rowley, D. C. (2016). Rhizoleucinoside, a Rhamnolipid–Amino Alcohol Hybrid from the RhizobialSymbiontBradyrhizobium sp. BTAi1. Org. Lett. 18(6), 1490–1493.
27. Merghni, A., Dallel, I., Noumi, E., Kadmi, Y., Hentati, H., Tobji, S., Amor, A.B. and Mastouri, M. (2017). Antioxidant and antiproliferative potential of biosurfactants isolated from Lactobacillus casei and their anti-biofilm effect in oral Staphylococcus aureus strains. Microb. Pathog. 104, 84–89.
28. Mishra, N., Rana, K., Seelam, S. D., Kumar, R., Pandey, V., Salimath, B. P., and Agsar, D. (2021). Characterization and Cytotoxicity of Pseudomonas Mediated Rhamnolipids Against Breast Cancer MDA-MB-231 Cell Line. Front. Bioeng. Biotechnol. 9.

Research and Innovations in Industrial and Marine Biotechnology: A Circular Economy 2024 – Prof. Hrudayanath Thatoi et al. (eds)

47 The Threat of ESKAPE Pathogens: A Closer Look through Clinical Surveillance in Hospital Settings

Poonamrani Mishra
Department of Microbiology, IMS and SUM Hospital,
Kalinganagar, Bhubaneswar, Odisha, India

Debasish Sahoo
Department of Microbiology, IMS and SUM Hospital,
Kalinganagar, Bhubaneswar, Odisha, India

Mahesh Chandra Sahu*
Department of Microbiology, ICMR-RMRC, Chandrasekharpur,
Bhubaneswar, Odisha, India

Abstract: ESKAPE pathogens are predominant in hospital and caused more morbidity and mortality. In this study, we have identified the ESKAPE pathogens from different clinical samples and determined their antibiotic sensitivity patterns. A total of 500 positive bacterial culture were collected between January to December 2023 from various clinical samples, including urine, blood, tracheal aspirate, wound swab, pus, vaginal swab and oral swabs. All bacteria were identified using conventional method and confirmed by VITEK 2. Antibiotic susceptibility testing was performed Kirby-Bauer *disk diffusion susceptibility test*. The majority of pathogens (90.2%) isolated in the clinical samples from a tertiary care hospital were from the ESKAPE group. The organisms most frequently isolated were *Klebsiellapneumoniae (28.8), Staphylococcus aureus (16.8), Pseudomonasaeruginosa (15.2%), Acinetobacterbaumannii (13.6%), Enterococcus faecium (8) and Enterobacter sp. (7.8%)*. A high resistance to carbapenems was detected for *Enterobacter Aerogenes (66-88%)* while 51% of *Staphylococcusaureus* isolates were confirmed to be methicillin resistant, among the *K. pneumonia* isolates, 73% were imipenem resistant. We detected 7.10% *E. faecium* and 11.50% *E. faecalis* vancomycin resistant isolates. Clinical surveillance in hospitals offers a crucial lens through which to scrutinize the threat posed by ESKAPE pathogens. Through meticulous monitoring, we unveil the intricate dynamics of antimicrobial resistance, emphasizing the urgent need for robust infection control measures and antimicrobial stewardship programs. As these pathogens continue to evolve and disseminate, their impact on patient outcomes, healthcare costs, and global public health cannot be overstated. By leveraging clinical surveillance data, healthcare stakeholders can strategize interventions to mitigate the spread of resistance, safeguarding the efficacy of antimicrobial agents and ensuring optimal patient care in the face of this escalating threat.

Keywords: ESKAPE, *Enterococcus faecium, Klebsiellapneumoniae, Staphylococcus aureus, Pseudomonas aeruginosa, Staphylococcus aureus, Enterobacterspecies*

1. Introduction

In the ever-evolving landscape of healthcare, the emergence and persistence of multidrug-resistant pathogens pose a formidable challenge to medical practitioners worldwide. Among these, the ESKAPE pathogens—*Enterococcus faecium*, *Staphylococcus aureus*, *Klebsiellapneumoniae*, *Acinetobacterbaumannii*, *Pseudomonas aeruginosa*, and *Enterobacter*species [1-6]. The term "ESKAPE" was coined to encapsulate the intrinsic ability of these

*Corresponding author: mchsahu@gmail.com

DOI: 10.1201/9781003759003-47

pathogens to escape the inhibitory effects of commonly used antimicrobial agents [7, 8]. Originally introduced by (Rice et al. in 2008), the ESKAPE pathogens have since become a focal point of research and concern within the global healthcare community [9, 10].

E. faecium, a member of the ESKAPE group, has evolved from a harmless commensal organism into a significant nosocomial pathogen, responsible for infections like urinary tract infections and bacteremia. The emergence of vancomycin resistance, driven by the acquisition of vanA and vanB genes, has rendered conventional treatments ineffective. This shift underscores the urgent need to explore the molecular mechanisms underlying its resistance to develop effective therapeutic strategies[9-10].

S. aureus, a key member of the ESKAPE group, is a major challenge in healthcare due to the rise of methicillin-resistant strains (MRSA). Renowned for its ability to form biofilms on medical devices and deploy numerous virulence factors, MRSA complicates treatment efforts. Its clinical impact spans a wide range of diseases, from skin and soft tissue infections to severe conditions like pneumonia and endocarditis, highlighting the urgent need for innovative therapeutic approaches[11-12].

K. pneumoniae, a Gram-negative ESKAPE pathogen, is a major contributor to the global antimicrobial resistance crisis. Its ability to produce extended-spectrum β-lactamases (ESBLs) and carbapenemases, including Klebsiellapneumoniaecarbapenemase (KPC), has led to a rise in multidrug-resistant infections, particularly in healthcare settings. This surge underscores the critical need for robust surveillance and effective infection control strategies[13-14].

A. baumannii, a formidable ESKAPE pathogen, is known for its intrinsic resistance and environmental resilience, enabling it to persist on surfaces and medical equipment, thus posing a significant nosocomial threat. Its proficiency in acquiring resistance genes through horizontal gene transfer exacerbates treatment challenges, highlighting the need for comprehensive insights into its epidemiology and resistance mechanisms [15-16].

P. aeruginosa, a highly adaptable Gram-negative bacterium, is a formidable nosocomial pathogen due to its intrinsic and acquired resistance mechanisms and ability to form biofilms. It poses a significant threat in hospital settings, particularly among immunocompromised and critically ill patients, as it is often linked to severe and hard-to-treat infections[17-18].

Enterobacter species are versatile and opportunistic pathogens responsible for a wide range of infections. The rise of extended-spectrum β-lactamase (ESBL) and carbapenemase-producing strains has significantly complicated treatment options, posing a serious challenge in clinical settings. Their ability to thrive in healthcare environments underscores the need for robust infection prevention and control measures to mitigate their spread and impact[19-20].

Amid the challenge of multidrug-resistant ESKAPE pathogens, clinical surveillance stands as a vital strategy in combating their impact. Hospitals, being hubs of healthcare, also serve as hotspots for the spread of these resilient organisms. Surveillance efforts, from routine antimicrobial resistance monitoring to advanced molecular techniques, provide critical insights into their epidemiology, resistance mechanisms, and transmission dynamics. By integrating clinical, microbiological, and genomic data, this study explores the prevalence, distribution, and genetic traits of ESKAPE pathogens in hospital settings. These findings aim to inform evidence-based interventions and enhance infection control measures to improve patient outcomes.

2. Materials and Methods

This observational study comprehensively investigated the prevalence, transmission dynamics and clinical impact of ESKAPE pathogens in hospital settings. The study conducted in tertiary care hospitals, to capture a broad spectrum of patient populations and clinical scenarios. The different clinical specimens from the admitted patients were cultured in blood agar, nutrient agar and MacConkey agar for growth of bacteria. We exclude the fungal growth in this study. All the bacteria were identified with conventional method and confirmed by (VITEK 2bioMérieux,Headquarters: Marcy-l'Étoile, France ,Founded: 1963 Website: bioMérieux Official Website) methods.

2.1 Sample Collection

From January to December 2023, a total of 500 positive bacterial cultures were obtained from various clinical specimens. The specimens included urine, blood, tracheal aspirate, wound swab, pus, vaginal swab, and oral swabs. Samples were collected from several wards, cabins, and the ICU, all under the observation of experienced nurses or technician. Following collection, the samples were quickly sent to the laboratory for further processing.

2.2 Antibiotic Susceptibility and Identifications Assays

Antibiotic susceptibility testing was performed using the Kirby-Bauer disk diffusion method, a standard technique for assessing bacterial susceptibility to various antibiotics, providing essential guidance for therapeutic treatment [11]. Following sample receipt in the microbiology department, cultures were grown on appropriate media, and subsequent biochemical tests were conducted for bacterial identification. The identification process combined interpretations of biochemical reactions with culture morphology of the isolated bacteria. All isolates

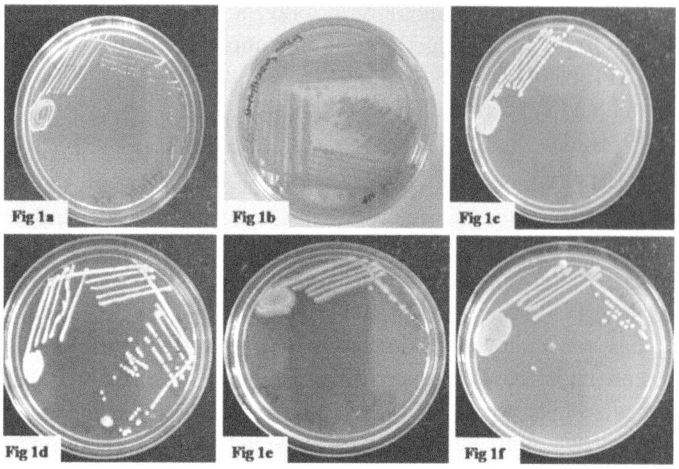

Fig. 47.1 Pure culture of ESKAPE bacteria on nutrient agar a: *Enterococcus faecium,* b: *Staphylococcus aureus,* c: *Klebsiellapneumoniae,* d: *Acinetobacterbaumannii,* e: *Pseudomonas aeruginosa,* f: *and Enterobacter* species

were identified using conventional methods and further validated with the VITEK 2 system to ensure the accuracy of species determination.

2.3 Identification of Bacteria

Bacterial identification was carried out methodically, with an emphasis on organisms from the ESKAPE group (*Enterococcus faecium, Staphylococcus aureus, Klebsiellapneumoniae, Acinetobacterbaumannii, Pseudomonas aeruginosa,* and *Enterobacter species*). Additionally, biochemical assays were used to better describe the isolates, allowing for more reliable identification (Fig. 47.1.).

Acinetobacterbaumannii

*A.baumannii*was identified basing on its colony characteristic on nutrient agar (NA), and MAC agar as well as from the results of biochemical procedures: it grew as colorless, smooth, raised colonies on NA, but as colourless, smooth, raised and non-lactose-fermenting (NLF) colonies on MAC agar. The colonies were non-pigmented when they grew on blood agar. It was positive to catalase, Voges-Proskauer (VP), citrate and motility tests, whereas was negative to oxidase, indole, methyl red (MR) and nitrate tests.

Enterobacter sp.

Enterobacter sp. produced white, convex with haemolytic colonies on BA, and lactose fermenting (LF), and mucoid colonies on MAC agar; *Enterobacter sp.* was positive to catalase, citrate, VP, nitrate, urease tests and motility tests, whereas was negative to oxidase, indole, MR test and a TSI slant, it produced acid in a slant and gas in the butt.

Staphylococcus Aureus

When a sample of Gram-positive cocciresponded positively to both catalase and coagulase test, it was confirmed to be *S.aureus.* It produces bubbles when hydrogen peroxide is added to the bacterial colony. Coagulase-positive strains of *S. aureus* can clot plasma.

Klebsiellapneumoniae

K.pneumoniae produced LF, pink-coloured, mucoid colonies on MAC agar. *K.pneumoniae* was positive to catalase, VP, citrate urease and nitrate tests, whereas it was negative to indole, MR, oxidase and motility tests. On TSI agar, *K.pneumoniae*strains produced acid in slant and along with gas production in the butt.

Pseudomonas Aeruginosa

*P.aeruginosa*produced large, irregular, opaque colonies with blue-green pigment on NA; it was positive to catalase, oxidase, urease, nitrate and motility tests, whereas negative to indole, MR and VP tests.

Enterococcus sp.

Bile-esculin producing colonies, negative to catalase test were taken as *Enterococcus sp.*This produced grayish, round, small colonies with haemolytic zones on blood agar.

2.4 Antibiotic Sensitivity Patterns

The identified protocols were followed in order to ascertain the antibiotic sensitivity patterns of the isolated microorganisms. This required determining each isolate's sensitivity to a variety of antibiotics often used in clinical settings. The sensitivity profiles that were produced provide important information on how well different antimicrobial drugs worked against the identified bacterial pathogens (Fig. 47.2.).

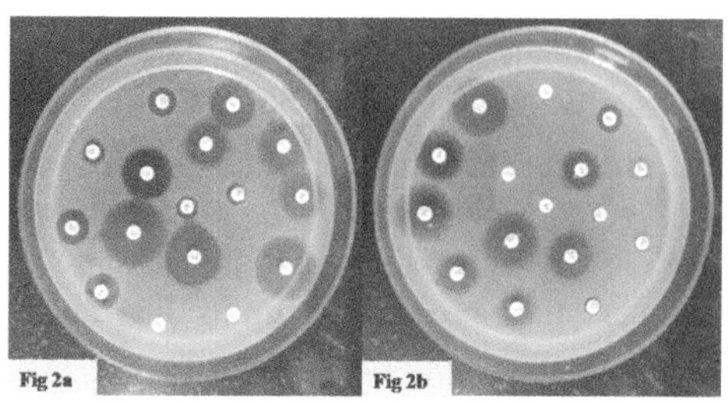

Fig. 47.2 Antibiotic sensitivity patterns of both gram positive and gram negative of ESKAPE bacteria

3. Result

In this prospective study, various clinical samples were collected from different areas of the hospital, including the ICU, ward, and cabins. These samples were cultured on specific mediums to facilitate bacterial growth. Following the growth of bacterial colonies, each colony was subjected to Gram staining to distinguish between Gram-positive and Gram-negative bacteria. Additionally, biochemical tests were conducted to further identify the bacteria.

A total of 500 bacteria were identified in the study, with 124 (24.8%) being Gram-positive and 376 (75.2%) being Gram-negative. Notably, among these bacteria, 454 (90.8%) were classified as ESKAPE pathogens, which are known for their ability to escape the effects of antibiotics and are often implicated in hospital-acquired infections. It was observed that ESKAPE pathogens were predominant among the hospitalized infectious bacteria, as indicated in Table 47.1.

Table 47.1 Percentage of isolated bacteria from different clinical samples

Organisms	Total	Percentage
Enterococcus faecium	40	8
Staphylococcus aureus	84	16.8
Klebsiellapneumoniae	144	28.8
Acinetobacterbaumannii	68	13.6
Pseudomonas aeruginosa	76	15.2
Enterobacter sp.	39	7.8
Salmonellasp.	3	0.6
Shigellasp.	1	0.2
Citrobactersp.	2	0.4
E. coli	43	8.6
500		100

Furthermore, all identified Gram-positive and Gram-negative bacteria underwent antibiotic sensitivity testing to assess their susceptibility to various classes of antibiotics. For Gram-negative bacteria, 13 classes of antibiotics were used, including cephalosporins, carbapenems, fluoroquinolones, monobactams, chloramphenicol, polymyxins, aminoglycosides, penicillins, quinolones, phosphonics, sulfonamides, and tetracyclines.

The results revealed high levels of antibiotic resistance among several bacterial species. For instance, *K.pneumoniae*exhibited high resistance to netilmicin (94%), cefepime (91%), and meropenem (90%). Similar patterns of resistance were observed in other bacteria such as *A.baumannii*, *P.aeruginosa*, *Enterobacter* sp., and *E. coli*, as detailed in Table 47.2.

Similarly, Gram-positive bacteria were also subjected to antibiotic sensitivity testing using 14 classes of antibiotics, including ansamycins, nitrofurans, glycopeptides, oxazolidinones, lipopeptides, lincomycin, macrolides, β-lactams, penicillins, aminoglycosides, quinolones, fluoroquinolones, tetracyclines, and sulfonamides, as outlined in Table 47.3.

The findings indicated varying levels of resistance among different bacterial species against these antibiotics. Notably, *E. faecium*exhibited high resistance to several antibiotics, such as rifampicin, nitrofurantoin, vancomycin, teicoplanin, benzylpenicillin, oxacillin, tigecycline, and sulfamethoxazole. Similar patterns of resistance were observed in other Gram-positive bacteria, including *S. aureus* and *E. faecalis*. These results underscore the growing challenge of antibiotic resistance among clinically significant bacteria, highlighting the importance of judicious antibiotic use and the development of novel therapeutic strategies to combat resistant infections.

4. Discussion

ESKAPE pathogens—comprising *E.faecium*, *S.aureus*, *K.pneumoniae*, *A.baumannii*, *P. aeruginosa*, and *Enterobacter* species—are leading causes of hospital-acquired infections (HAIs) and major contributors to the global rise in multidrug-resistant organisms (MDROs). Their high antimicrobial resistance (AMR), driven by mechanisms like biofilm formation, efflux pumps, and antibiotic-degrading enzymes (e.g., β-lactamases), severely limits treatment options and complicates patient care. This growing threat highlights the urgent need for enhanced clinical surveillance and targeted infection control measures to mitigate their impact[12].

Infections caused by ESKAPE pathogens are linked to prolonged hospital stays, higher morbidity and mortality rates, and increased healthcare costs. Co-infections involving multiple ESKAPE organisms, as highlighted in global studies, exacerbate these issues, often resulting in treatment failures and poor outcomes, particularly in critically ill patients [13].

This study highlights the critical threat of ESKAPE pathogens in hospital settings, with 454 out of 500 bacterial isolates identified as ESKAPE species, including both Gram-positive and Gram-negative bacteria. Their predominance among hospital-acquired infections (HAIs) aligns with global trends, underscoring their role in increasing antibiotic resistance and their ability to evade commonly used treatments [14].

The study found that 90.8% of the identified bacteria were ESKAPE pathogens, emphasizing their significant role in hospital-acquired infections (HAIs), particularly in intensive care units (ICUs) [25]. Their persistence in hospital settings and resistance to multiple antibiotics are consistent with global findings, highlighting their contribution to the HAI burden and the urgent need for robust infection control measures.

Table 47.2 Resistance patterns of gram-negative bacteria

Class of antibiotics	**cephalosporins**							**carbapenem**		**Fluoroquinolonew**	**Monobactams**	**Chloroamphenicol**	**polymyxin**		**aminoglycoside**	**Penicillin**			**Aminoglycoside**			**Quinolone**	**phosphonic**	**Sulfonamide**	**tetracycline**			
Antibiotic	**cefoxitin**	**ceftizoxime**	**ceftzidime**	**Cefuroxime**	**Ertapenem**	**Ceftriaxone**	**cefepime**	**Imipenem**	**meropenem**	**Levofloxacin**	**Aztreonam**	**Chloroamphenicol**	**colistin**	**polymyxine B**	**Netilmicin**	**Ampicillin**	**Amoxicillin**	**Tazobactam**	**Tobramycin**	**Amikacin**	**Gentamicin**	**ciproflaxcin**	**Fosfomycin**	**sulfamethoxazole**	**Tigecycline**	**Minocycline**	**Doxycycline**	**Tetracycline**
Symbol	**CFX**	**CFZX**	**CFZ**	**CFXI**	**ET**	**CFXO**	**CFP**	**IM**	**ME**	**LF**	**AZ**	**CHL**	**CL**	**POLY B**	**NE**	**AMP**	**AMX**	**TAZ**	**TOB**	**AK**	**G**	**CIP**	**FO**	**S**	**TGC**		**DOXY**	**TE**
Klebsiellapneumoniae	86	77%	81	86	75	77	91	73	90	81	86	68	25	53	94	80	81	89	81	49	70	79	44	73	53	50	75	72
Acinetobacterbaumannii	89	63	72	83	73	61	82	80	68	76	85	64	6	48	98	67	77	83	73	67	80	85	38	70	41	63	75	69
Pseudomonas aeruginosa	76	68	75	82	68	71	51	61	63	72	68	68	15	47	84	61	78	52	78	52	59	68	60	53	64	56	73	65
Enterobacter sp.	80	53	40	70	46	46	53	46	40	46	80	40	0	33	86	70	76	50	63	13	33	43	26	36	33	26	80	53
E.Coli	90	95	96	95	85	84	87	69	63	88	90	62	7.10	67	95	72	86	83	83	83	62	93	34	88	32	46	72	79
Enterobacteraerogenes	0	44	0	77	44	55	44	66	88	44	77	55	22	33	88	33	66	66	77	33	44	66	33	55	66	66	70	55
Salmonesallasp	5	36	5	6	11	10	5	50	0	30	0	0	0	30	4	10	60	40	20	10	2	30	5	5	5	5	5	5
Shigellasp	0	0	0	0	0	3	7	10	7	17	10	5	8	3	0	8	10	5	7	3	2	6	15	25	50	64	40	55

Table 47.3 Resistance patterns of gram-positive bacteria

Class of antibiotics	Antibiotic	Symbol	Enterococcus faecium	Staphylococcus aureus	Enterococcus faecalis
Ansamycins	Rifampicin	RMP	100%	12%	100%
Nitrofuran	Nitrofurantoin	NF	50%	2%	3.80%
Glycopeptide	Vancomycin	VA	7.10%	12%	11.50%
	Teicoplanin	TEI	7.10%	6%	3.80%
Oxazolidinones	Linezolid	LZ	9.10%	10%	8.30%
Lipopeptide	Daptomycin	DAP	0%	5%	8.70%
Lincomycin	Clindamycin	CL	0%	58%	33%
Macrolide	Erythromycin	ERY	63%	66%	52%
Β-lactam	Benzylpenicillin	BEN	71%	79%	48%
Penicillins	Oxacillin	OX	100%	51%	30%
Aminoglycoside	Gentamicin	GEN	23%	16%	28%
Quinolone	ciproflaxcin	CIP	69%	72%	69%
Fluoroquinolone	Levofloxacin	LF	71%	72%	65%
Tetracycline	Tigecycline	TGC	100%	5%	4.20%
Sulphonamide	Sulfamethoxazole	SF	100%	33%	37%

Antibiotic susceptibility testing revealed alarming resistance levels in both Gram-positive and Gram-negative bacteria. *K. pneumoniae* showed particularly high resistance to netilmicin (94%), cefepime (91%), and meropenem (90%), undermining last-resort treatments like carbapenems. Similarly, Gram-negative pathogens such as *A. baumannii* and *P.aeruginosa* exhibited significant resistance, posing critical challenges for infection management. Among Gram-positive bacteria, *E. faecium* demonstrated resistance to rifampicin, vancomycin, and tigecycline, with vancomycin-resistant *Enterococcus* (VRE) raising serious concerns due to limited treatment options. High resistance in *S. aureus* and *E. faecalis* further complicates therapy, necessitating alternative strategies [26,27].

The high levels of antibiotic resistance identified in this study have serious clinical implications, including prolonged hospital stays, increased healthcare costs, and heightened morbidity and mortality among patients[28]. These findings emphasize the urgent need for robust antimicrobial stewardship programs to optimize antibiotic use and curb resistance development. Continuous surveillance of resistance patterns is equally vital to inform empirical therapy and ensure treatment protocols remain effective, ultimately mitigating the impact of multidrug-resistant pathogens on patient outcomes[29].

The predominance of ESKAPE pathogens and their high resistance rates call for stringent infection control measures, including strict hand hygiene, PPE usage, and environmental decontamination, to curb their transmission [30]. Robust antibiotic stewardship programs are also essential to preserve antibiotic efficacy and combat resistance. In Indian hospitals, overcrowding, inadequate infection control, and overuse of broad-spectrum antibiotics exacerbate the problem, accelerating the emergence of drug-resistant strains [31]. Effective management requires tailored treatment strategies based on susceptibility testing and clinical surveillance, as a "one-size-fits-all" approach is no longer adequate for these diverse and resilient pathogens [32].

Surveillance is vital for identifying and controlling ESKAPE pathogen infections, as it enables healthcare providers to track prevalence and resistance patterns, anticipate outbreaks, and implement timely interventions. Effective surveillance has been shown to reduce infection rates by guiding policies on isolation, hygiene, and antibiotic use[33]. However, in resource-limited settings like India, inadequate infrastructure, overcrowding, poor sanitation, and insufficient sterilization practices exacerbate the spread of these pathogens. The absence of comprehensive national surveillance systems further impedes efforts to track resistance patterns and implement evidence-based strategies[34]. A major policy overhaul is needed to integrate global best practices into India's healthcare framework.

Strengthening infection prevention and control (IPC) measures is equally vital. Successful programs worldwide, particularly in high-income settings, emphasize the importance of hand hygiene, environmental cleaning, and contact precautions to minimize pathogen transmission. However, the effectiveness of these strategies in low-resource settings can be limited by poor compliance, lack of training, and insufficient resources. Addressing these gaps requires concerted efforts to improve hospital infrastructure and promote a culture of infection prevention among healthcare workers [15].

Indian hospitals must prioritize the adoption of antimicrobial stewardship programs (ASP) tailored to their specific needs. These programs should emphasize the judicious use of antibiotics, guided by diagnostic testing and local resistance data. Furthermore, expanding the role of IPC teams and fostering multidisciplinary collaboration among clinicians, microbiologists, and infection control specialists will be critical to controlling the spread of ESKAPE pathogens in healthcare facilities [16].

The findings from this study emphasize the need for ongoing research into novel therapeutic strategies, including the development of new antibiotics and alternative treatments such as bacteriophage therapy or immunotherapy [17]. In addition, the study advocates for the integration of rapid diagnostic tools to enable early detection and appropriate management of infections caused by resistant bacteria [18]. Collaboration between healthcare providers, researchers, and policymakers is crucial to developing comprehensive strategies to combat the growing threat of ESKAPE pathogens.

5. Conclusion

This study provides critical insights into the prevalence and resistance patterns of ESKAPE pathogens in a hospital setting, reinforcing their status as major contributors to HAIs. The high levels of antibiotic resistance observed among these pathogens present a significant challenge to healthcare management. To address this challenge, it is imperative to strengthen infection control measures, optimize antibiotic use through stewardship programs, and invest in research and development of novel therapeutic approaches.

Acknowledgements

This work is part of PhD in Medical Science thesis of Poonamrani Mishra at SOA University (PhD Reg. No 2281404006). The authors are grateful to HOD, Microbiology Department, IMS and SUM hospital and all staffs for their technical supports. The authors are thankful to the Dean, IMS and SUM Hospital and Director, ICMR-RMRC, Bhubaneswar for the extended facility in research

References

1. PH, S., Attavar, P. C., TR, R., Kotian, M. S., & NS, D. (2024). Emergence of High-Level Antibiotic Resistance in Klebsiellapneumoniae: A Narrative Review. *South Asian Journal of Research in Microbiology*, *18*(2), 1–8.
2. Alharbi, J., Qiraty, I. H., Alfaify, A., Huraysi, M. S., Huraysi, O., Mashragi, I. Q., ...& Hadi, M. A. A. A. (2023). The Next Chapter In Infection Prevention: A Systematic Exploration Of Contemporary Technologies And Strategies In Healthcare. *Journal of Namibian Studies: History Politics Culture*, *34*, 3147–3181.
3. Ramsamy, Y., Essack, S. Y., Sartorius, B., Patel, M., &Mlisana, K. P. (2018). Antibiotic resistance trends of ESKAPE pathogens in Kwazulu-Natal, South Africa: a five-year retrospective analysis. *African journal of laboratory medicine*, *7*(2), 1–8.
4. Dar, M. A., Gul, R., Karuppiah, P., Al-Dhabi, N. A., & Alfadda, A. A. (2022). Antibacterial activity of cerium oxide nanoparticles against ESKAPE pathogens. *Crystals*, *12*(2), 179.
5. Ma, Y. X., Wang, C. Y., Li, Y. Y., Li, J., Wan, Q. Q., Chen, J. H., ... &Niu, L. N. (2020). Considerations and caveats in combating ESKAPE pathogens against nosocomial infections. *Advanced Science*, *7*(1), 1901872.
6. Vale de Macedo, G. H. R., Costa, G. D. E., Oliveira, E. R., Damasceno, G. V., Mendonça, J. S. P., Silva, L. D. S., ... & Nascimento da Silva, L. C. (2021). Interplay between eskape pathogens and immunity in skin infections: An overview of the major determinants of virulence and antibiotic resistance. *Pathogens*, *10*(2), 148.
7. De Oliveira, D. M., Forde, B. M., Kidd, T. J., Harris, P. N., Schembri, M. A., Beatson, S. A., ... & Walker, M. J. (2020). Antimicrobial resistance in ESKAPE pathogens. *Clinical microbiology reviews*, *33*(3), 10–1128.
8. Pendleton, J. N., Gorman, S. P., & Gilmore, B. F. (2013). Clinical relevance of the ESKAPE pathogens. *Expert review of anti-infective therapy*, *11*(3), 297–308.
9. Hunashal, Y., Kumar, G. S., Choy, M. S., D'Andréa, É. D., Da Silva Santiago, A., Schoenle, M. V., ... & Peti, W. (2023). Molecular basis of β-lactam antibiotic resistance of ESKAPE bacterium E. faecium Penicillin Binding Protein PBP5. *Nature Communications*, *14*(1), 4268.
10. Sood, S., Malhotra, M., Das, B. K., &Kapil, A. (2008). Enterococcal infections & antimicrobial resistance. *Indian journal of medical research*, *128*(2), 111–121.
11. Denissen, J., Reyneke, B., Waso-Reyneke, M., Havenga, B., Barnard, T., Khan, S., & Khan, W. (2022). Prevalence of ESKAPE pathogens in the environment: Antibiotic resistance status, community-acquired infection and risk to human health. *International journal of hygiene and environmental health*, *244*, 114006.
12. Kline, K. A., & Lewis, A. L. (2017). Gram-positive uropathogens, polymicrobial urinary tract infection, and the emerging microbiota of the urinary tract. *Urinary tract infections: molecular pathogenesis and clinical management*, 459–502.
13. Khan, A., Miller, W. R., & Arias, C. A. (2018). Mechanisms of antimicrobial resistance among hospital-associated pathogens. *Expert Review of Anti-Infective Therapy*, *16*(4), 269–287.
14. Darby, E. M., Trampari, E., Siasat, P., Gaya, M. S., Alav, I., Webber, M. A., & Blair, J. M. (2023). Molecular mechanisms of antibiotic resistance revisited. *Nature Reviews Microbiology*, *21*(5), 280–295.
15. Lee, J. Y., & Howden, B. P. (2015). Vancomycin in the treatment of methicillin-resistant Staphylococcus aureus–a clinician's guide to the science informing current practice. *Expert Review of Anti-infective Therapy*, *13*(7), 855–869.
16. Stephen, J., Salam, F., Lekshmi, M., Kumar, S. H., & Varela, M. F. (2023). The major facilitator superfamily and antimicrobial resistance efflux pumps of the ESKAPEE pathogen Staphylococcus aureus. *Antibiotics*, *12*(2), 343.
17. Tigabu, A., &Getaneh, A. L. E. M. (2021). Staphylococcus aureus, ESKAPE Bacteria Challenging Current Health

Care and Community Settings: a Literature Review. *Clinical Laboratory*, (7).

18. Kwon, J., Mistry, T., Ren, J., Johnson, M. E., &Mehboob, S. (2018). A novel series of enoylreductase inhibitors targeting the ESKAPE pathogens, Staphylococcus aureus and Acinetobacterbaumannii. *Bioorganic & medicinal chemistry*, *26*(1), 65–76.
19. Dubey, D., Rath, S., Sahu, M. C., Pattnaik, L., Debata, N. K., & Padhy, R. N. (2013). Surveillance of infection status of drug resistant Staphylococcus aureus in an Indian teaching hospital. *Asian Pacific journal of tropical disease*, *3*(2), 133–142.
20. Dubey, D., Rath, S., Sahu, M. C., Rout, S., Debata, N. K., &Padhy, R. N. (2013). A report on infection dynamics of inducible clindamycin resistance of Staphylococcus aureus isolated from a teaching hospital in India. *Asian Pacific Journal of Tropical Biomedicine*, *3*(2), 148–153.
21. Beargie, R. A., Bracken, E. C., & Riley Jr, H. D. (1965). Micromethod (spot-plate) determination of in vitro antibiotic susceptibility. *Applied Microbiology*, *13*(2), 279–280.
22. Isticato, R., & Ricca, E. (2016). Spore surface display. *The bacterial spore: from molecules to systems*, 349–366.
23. Gauba, A., &Rahman, K. M. (2023). Evaluation of antibiotic resistance mechanisms in gram-negative bacteria. *Antibiotics*, *12*(11), 1590.
24. Haque, M., McKimm, J., Sartelli, M., Dhingra, S., Labricciosa, F. M., Islam, S., ... &Charan, J. (2020). Strategies to prevent healthcare-associated infections: a narrative overview. *Risk management and healthcare policy*, 1765–1780.
25. Migliara, G., Di Paolo, C., Barbato, D., Baccolini, V., Salerno, C., Nardi, A., ... &Villari, P. (2019). Multimodal surveillance of healthcare associated infections in an intensive care unit of a large teaching hospital. *Annali Di IgieneMedicinaPreventiva e Di Comunità*, *31*(5), 399–413.
26. Okeah, B. O., Morrison, V., & Huws, J. C. (2021). Antimicrobial stewardship and infection prevention interventions targeting healthcare-associated Clostridioidesdifficile and carbapenem-resistant Klebsiellapneumoniae infections: a scoping review. *BMJ open*, *11*(8), e051983.
27. Vrancianu, C. O., Pelcaru, C. F., Alistar, A., Gheorghe, I., Marutescu, L., Popa, M., ... & Chifiriuc, M. C. (2021). EscapingfromESKAPE. Clinical significance and antibiotic resistance mechanisms in acinetobacterbaumannii: a review. *Biointerface Res Appl Chem*, *11*(1), 8190–8203.
28. Ayoub Moubareck, C., & Hammoudi Halat, D. (2020). Insights into Acinetobacterbaumannii: a review of microbiological, virulence, and resistance traits in a threatening nosocomial pathogen. *Antibiotics*, *9*(3), 119.
29. Aldali, J. A. (2023). Acinetobacterbaumannii: A multidrug-resistant pathogen, has emerged in Saudi Arabia. *Saudi Medical Journal*, *44*(8), 732.
30. Labrador Herrera, G. (2020). Integration of omics and bioinformatics to identify new therapeutic targets for Acinetobacterbaumannii. Virulence role of CarO in Acinetobacterbaumannii infections.
31. Gedefie, A., Demsis, W., Ashagrie, M., Kassa, Y., Tesfaye, M., Tilahun, M., ...&Sahle, Z. (2021). Acinetobacterbaumannii biofilm formation and its role in disease pathogenesis: a review. *Infection and drug resistance*, 3711–3719.
32. Ravi, K., & Singh, B. (2024). ESKAPE: Navigating the Global Battlefield for Antimicrobial Resistance and Defense in Hospitals. *Bacteria*, *3*(2), 76–98.
33. Sahu, M. C., Swain, S. K., &Kar, S. K. (2019). Genetically diversity of Pseudomonas aeruginosa isolated from chronic suppurative otitis media with respect to their antibiotic sensitivity pattern. *Indian Journal of Otolaryngology and Head & Neck Surgery*, *71*, 1300–1308.
34. Loyola-Cruz, M. Á., Durán-Manuel, E. M., Cruz-Cruz, C., Márquez-Valdelamar, L. M., Bravata-Alcántara, J. C., Cortés-Ortíz, I. A., ...& Bello-López, J. M. (2023). ESKAPE bacteria characterization reveals the presence of Acinetobacterbaumannii and Pseudomonas aeruginosa outbreaks in COVID-19/VAP patients. *American journal of infection control*, *51*(7), 729–737.
35. Mesquita, C. S., Soares-Castro, P., Santos, P. M., & Mendez-Vilas, A. (2013). Pseudomonas aeruginosa: phenotypic flexibility and antimicrobial resistance. *Microbial pathogens and strategies for combating them: science, technology and education*, *1*, 650–665.
36. Verdial, C., Serrano, I., Tavares, L., Gil, S., & Oliveira, M. (2023). Mechanisms of antibiotic and biocide resistance that contribute to Pseudomonas aeruginosa persistence in the hospital environment. *Biomedicines*, *11*(4), 1221.
37. Verdial, C., Serrano, I., Tavares, L., Gil, S., & Oliveira, M. (2023). Mechanisms of antibiotic and biocide resistance that contribute to Pseudomonas aeruginosa persistence in the hospital environment. *Biomedicines*, *11*(4), 1221.
38. Arbune, M., Gurau, G., Niculet, E., Iancu, A. V., Lupasteanu, G., Fotea, S., ... & Tatu, A. L. (2021). Prevalence of antibiotic resistance of ESKAPE pathogens over five years in an infectious diseases hospital from South-East of Romania. *Infection and drug resistance*, 2369–2378.

Note: All the figures and tables in this chapter were made by the authors.

Research and Innovations in Industrial and Marine Biotechnology: A Circular Economy 2024 – Prof. Hrudayanath Thatoi et al. (eds)

48 Emerging Antimicrobial Resistance in Burn Wound Infections: Analysis from a Burn ICU in a Tertiary Care Hospital

Swikrutee Rout[1]
School of Pharmaceutical Sciences,
Sum Hospital, Siksha'O'Anusandhan Deemed to be University,
Bhubaneswar, Odisha, India

Rahul Kumar[2]
Amity Institute of Biotechnology, Amity University Jharkhand,
Ranchi, Jharkhand, India

Kundan Kumar Sahu[3]
Microbiology, Institute of Medical Science and Sum Hospital,
Siksha 'O'Anusandhn Adeemed to be University,
Bhubaneswar, Odisha, India

Abstract: The rise in antimicrobial resistance among bacterial pathogens in burn patients over recent years has significantly complicated treatment efforts, increasing the risk of severe infections and impacting patient outcomes. This retrospective study aimed to recognize the bacterial isolates from burn wounds and examine their antimicrobial susceptibility patterns over four years (2019–2022) in the Burn ICU at SUM Hospital, Bhubaneswar, Odisha. A total of 120 bacterial isolates were recovered from burn wounds of 105 patients. The most frequently identified organisms were *Acinetobacterbaumannii* (23.6%), *Pseudomonas aeruginosa* (12%), *Staphylococcus aureus* (11.2%), and *Escherichia coli* (10%). Alarmingly, high levels of multidrug resistance were observed, especially in *A. baumannii*, for which tigecycline and colistin were the most effective treatments. For other gram-negative bacteria, carbapenems and amikacin showed the highest efficacy, while linezolid and vancomycin were effective against gram-positive isolates. These results highlight the critical importance of implementing stringent infection control protocols to curb the spread of multidrug-resistant bacteria within burn care units.

Keywords: *Acinetobacterbaumannii*, Antibiotic susceptibility, Antimicrobial resistance, Burn ICU, Burn wound infections, *Escherichia coli*, Infection control, Multidrug-resistant bacteria, *Pseudomonas aeruginosa, Staphylococcusaureus*

1. Introduction

Burn injuries are between the mejority severe forms of trauma, posing a critical global health concern due to their high levels of morbidity, mortality, and potential for long-term disability. The extensive tissue damage in burn injuries compromises the skin's natural barrier, leaving patients especially vulnerable to infections, which are common in the course of burn care. This barrier disruption creates an avascular, nutrient-rich environment that favors microbial colonization and growth [1]Moreover, burn injuries impair immune function, limiting the host's ability to clear pathogens and increasing the risk of invasive infections.

As a result, infections are amongst the most important complications in burn patients, with sepsis accounting for over 73% of early deaths following severe burn injuries. The risk of infection in burn patients is influenced by

[1]routfunny5@gmail.com, [2]rhlkmr104@gmail.com, [3]kundansahu@soa.ac.in

DOI: 10.1201/9781003759003-48

a combination of patient-related factors (such as age, extent, and depth of injury) and microbial factors (such as species, quantity, enzyme production, and motility of pathogens)[2][3]. Burn wound infections are often caused by gram-positive pathogens like *Staphylococcus aureus*, *Enterococcus* spp., and coagulase-negative staphylococci, as well as gram-negative organisms such as *Pseudomonas aeruginosa*, *Escherichia coli*, *Klebsiellapneumoniae*, and *Acinetobacter* spp. In particular, *Acinetobacterbaumannii* has been increasingly reported as a primary pathogen in burn units, particularly in tropical climates where it can be introduced through patient admission or environmental sources[4].

In recent years, a rise in antimicrobial resistance among burn wound pathogens has created additional challenges in managing infections effectively. Resistant organisms, including multidrug-resistant *A. baumannii*, *P. aeruginosa*, and methicillin-resistant *S. aureus* (MRSA), limit the available treatment options and necessitate stronger infection control measures[5][6]. Antimicrobial resistance is a significant concern, especially as broad-spectrum antibiotic use in burn units can further promote the selection of resistant strains. In many cases, burn units struggle with the recurrent emergence of highly resistant pathogens capable of surviving in hospital environments and transmitting between patients, making burn infections a source of high morbidity and mortality[7].

This invesigation was conducted at the Burn ICU of SUM Hospital, Bhubaneswar, Odisha, to examine the bacterial isolates from burn wounds and assess their antimicrobial resistance profiles over a four-year period[8]. Identifying the spectrum of bacterial pathogens and their resistance patterns provides valuable insights into the specific challenges of burn care and the need for tailored infection control practices. Additionally, findings from this study are expected to contribute to developing more effective therapeutic strategies, ultimately improving patient outcomes and reducing infection-related mortality among burn patients[9,10].By focusing on patterns unique to this center, this research also adds to the global understanding of burn wound infections and the broader issue of antimicrobial resistance in burn care settings[11].This study examines the bacterial isolates and antimicrobial resistance patterns in the Burn ICU of SUM Hospital, Bhubaneswar, Odisha. Burn injuries make an environment conducive to bacterial colonization, increasing the risk of infections and sepsis.

The study focuses on enhancing infection control measures and optimizing treatment protocols. In our burn unit, the practice of early burn excision with skin grafting is key interventions, and we limit the use of broad-spectrum antibiotics to reduce resistance. Topical fusidic acid is selectively applied to deep excisions. Bacterial identification was performed using standard microbiological techniques and the Phoenix Automated Microbiology System. Specimens were cultured on 5% sheep blood agar and Eosin Methylene Blue agar, and resistance was evaluated according to CLSI standards, where multidrug resistance was defined as resistance against three or more classes of antimicrobials. Data were analyzed using SPSS 17.0. The study aims to improve patient outcomes by refining treatment and infection control strategies[12]13][14].

A significant research gap exists due to the limited local pathogen variability data, which affects the ability to tailor interventions for specific regions or hospitals. Furthermore, many studies offer inadequate molecular characterization, often omitting key factors like virulence genes or resistance mechanisms. Finally, short-term surveillance snapshots are common, but there is a critical need for ongoing, long-term monitoring to track pathogen evolution and resistance trends. Addressing these gaps would enhance infection control and treatment strategies[15][16][17]. The novelty in this investigation lies in its broad examination of antimicrobial resistance patterns in burn wound infections over a four-year period in a single burn ICU at SUM Hospital, Bhubaneswar, Odisha. The study highlights the predominance of multidrug-resistant *Acinetobacterbaumannii* and other gram-negative pathogens, offering insights into local microbial trends and resistance profiles. Unlike many studies that rely heavily on systemic antibiotic use, this research emphasizes the use of a minimalist antimicrobial protocol, including selective application of fusidic acid, which may offer a more sustainable approach to managing infections while minimizing resistance. Furthermore, the study underscores the urgent need for stringent infection control measures in burn units to prevent the spread of resistant organisms, contributing to both global and regional understanding of antimicrobial resistance in burn care settings.

2. Materials and Method

2.1 Data Collection

Burn injuries pose a main global wellbeing challenge due to their high risk of infection and potential for lasting complications. The compromised skin barrier in burn patients creates an ideal environment for bacterial colonization and growth, increasing susceptibility to severe infections and sepsis, which accounts for a significant portion of early mortality in these patients[12]. Rising antibiotic resistance among pathogens further complicates treatment, limiting effective therapeutic options. This study examines the bacterial isolates and their antimicrobial resistance patterns in the Burn ICU of SUM Hospital, Bhubaneswar, Odisha, aiming to enhance infection control measures and treatment protocols for burn patients[13].

2.2 Integrated Approaches of Innovative Wound Dressing Techniques and their Efficacy in Burn Wound Healing: Comprehensive Strategies for Improved Outcomes

In our burn unit, we adopt a streamlined approach to burn management, focusing on early burn excision and skin grafting as primary interventions. Unlike conventional burn care protocols, we do not routinely administer standard systemic or topical antimicrobials like mafenide or silver sulfadiazine. This approach minimizes patient exposure to broad-spectrum antimicrobials, potentially reducing the risk of antimicrobial resistance[14]. Topical fusidic acid is applied selectively, limited to cases involving deep excisions where additional infection control support is essential. This minimalist antimicrobial protocol emphasizes targeted care, reducing drug-related costs and possible adverse reactions, while maintaining effective infection control through precise, case-specific application. Early excision combined with this focused strategy supports rapid recovery, potentially leading to better outcomes and shorter hospital stays for patients[15].

2.3 Microbial Identification and Antibiotic Sensitivity Testing

Samples were cultured overnight at 37°C on 5% sheep blood agar and Eosin Methylene Blue agar, with bacterial isolates identified through standard microbiological and biochemical techniques. The Phoenix Automated Microbiology System provided specific identification and antimicrobial susceptibility rates[15]. Spare isolates were excluded, distinct as multiple isolates of the similar bacterial species with identical susceptibility profiles from the same patient. *Pseudomonas aeruginosa* and *Acinetobacter*spp. viewing resistance to 3 or more antimicrobial groups were classified as multidrug-resistant. Antimicrobial susceptibilities followed CLSI guidelines. Data was analyzed using SPSS 17.0 to assess antibiotic resistance patterns for each bacterial isolate[16][17].

3. Results

Over a four-year period, a whole of 120 bacterial isolates were identified from wound swabs collected from 105 patients. The predominant isolate was *Acinetobacterbaumannii*, accounting for 23.6% of the total, followed by coagulase-negative staphylococci at 13.6%, *Pseudomonas aeruginosa* at 12%, *Staphylococcus aureus* at 11.2%, and *Escherichia coli* at 10%. A complete breakdown of these isolates is presented in Table 48.1.

Table 48.1 Identification and management of common burn wound pathogens

Micro-organisms	Number	Percentage
Acinetobacterboumannii	32	25.2
Coagulase negative *Staphylococci*	14	11.5
Pseudomonas aeruginosa	12	13.0
Staphylococcus aureus	14	10.7
Escherichia coli	11	11.3
Enterococcus spp.	12	7.9
Klebsiellapneumoniae	8	8.9
Other *Enterobacteriaceae spp.**	13	11.5
Others**	4	2.3
Total	120	100

The susceptibility patterns of the bacterial isolates to various antibiotics varied significantly. All *Acinetobacter*spp. isolates (n=37) were found to be sensitive to tigecycline and colistin (n=43); however, a high rate of multidrug resistance was observed, with 55 isolates (93%) classified as multidrug-resistant. Among the *Pseudomonas aeruginosa* isolates, 13 (43%) were identified as multidrug-resistant. The antibiotics most effective against *P. aeruginosa* included meropenem, amikacin, ciprofloxacin, and cefepime. All tested *Escherichia coli* isolates exhibited susceptibility to amikacin (n=17), imipenem (n=19), and meropenem (n=21). Additionally, gentamicin demonstrated in vitro effectiveness against *Klebsiellapneumoniae* and other Enterobacteriaceae species.. Notably, extended-spectrum beta-lactamases (ESBL) were detected in 13 out of 25 (52%) *E. coli* isolates and in 7 out of 18 (39%) *K. pneumoniae*isolates. In the burn center, 19% of the *Staphylococcus aureus* isolates were recognized as methicillin-resistant *S. aureus* (MRSA). The most useful antimicrobial agents next to these *S. aureus* isolates were vancomycin and linezolid. Importantly, all tested *Enterococcus* spp. showed complete susceptibility to vancomycin, with no resistance detected. The susceptibility profiles of gram-positive organisms are summarized in Table 48.2.

Table 48.2 Assessment of antimicrobial susceptibility in gram-positive bacterial isolates from burn wound infections

	S.aureus		*Enterococcus* spp.	
Antibiotics	n-28	R(%)	n-22	R(%)
Penisilin	27	26 (95)	8	2 (12)
Trimetoprim-Sulfametoksazol	26	1 (8)	nt	no
Klindamisin	24	2 (5)	no	no
V ancomisin	21	-(-)	21	-(-)
Linezolid	18	-(-)	23	-(-)
Daptomisin	12	-(-)	7	2(16)
Ampisilin	no	no	21	-(-)

4. Discussion

The study highlights the major occurrence of multidrug-resistant (MDR) pathogens in burn wound infections, emphasizing the growing challenges faced in burn care management. Burn patients are particularly vulnerable to infections because of disruption of skin barriers, extended hospital stays, and exposure to enveloping procedures. These factors create an ideal environment for colonization and infection by opportunistic pathogens, many of which exhibit resistance to multiple antibiotic classes[18] [19]. Among the identified pathogens, *Acinetobacterbaumannii* was the most frequently isolated organism, reflecting its prominence as a major nosocomial pathogen in burn units, especially in tropical regions. The warm and humid conditions in these settings likely contribute to the survival and spread of *A. baumannii*, making it a persistent threat in healthcare environments. This finding aligns with global trends that have increasingly recognized *A. baumannii* as a key MDR pathogen. Interestingly, *Pseudomonas aeruginosa*, another notorious burn wound pathogen, showed a lower prevalence in this study compared to global reports[20][21][22]. This discrepancy suggests potential regional or environmental variations influencing the microbial landscape in burn care settings. Despite its lower prevalence, the MDR rates in *P. aeruginosa* remain a significant concern, with resistance noted against key antibiotics, including imipenem and ceftazidime. Such resistance patterns severely limit treatment options and underscore the need for targeted interventions to curb its spread[23].

The findings also highlight a considerable burden of MRSA and ESBL-producing Enterobacteriaceae, organisms that significantly hinder effective management of burn wound infections. MRSA is a well-known reason of nosocomial infections and poses significant treatment challenges due to its resistance to beta-lactam antibiotics. In this study, vancomycin and linezolid were found to be effective against MRSA, reaffirming their role as critical agents in the conduct of gram-positive infections. For ESBL-producing Enterobacteriaceae, carbapenems such as imipenem and meropenem demonstrated efficacy, making them essential options in the management of these infections[24]. However, the increasing reliance on carbapenems raises concerns about the potential emergence of carbapenem-resistant strains, which could further limit therapeutic options. This highlights the urgent need for antimicrobial stewardship programs to conserve the efficiency of these critical antibiotics. The findings of this study underline the significance of implementing robust contamination control actions to address the high prevalence of MDR pathogens in burn units[25]. Strategies such as strict hand hygiene practices, routine surveillance of resistance patterns, isolation of infected or colonized patients, and environmental disinfection are crucial in preventing the spread of MDR pathogens. Additionally, burn care teams should adopt evidence-based guidelines for the empirical and targeted use of antibiotics to reduce the development of resistance[26].

Although the study offers important contributions, certain limitations must be noted. The retrospective design limits causal inference and the identification of temporal trends in resistance. Additionally, conducting the study at a single burn center narrows the applicability of the results to broader healthcare contexts, particularly those with diverse patient populations or distinct environmental conditions. Additionally, the lack of molecular testing to identify specific resistance mechanisms represents a significant gap, as such analyses could provide deeper insights into the genetic basis of antimicrobial resistance[27,28]. The relatively small sample size of this study may also have limited its ability to capture the full spectrum of microbial diversity and resistance patterns in burn wound infections. Larger, multi-center studies would be better equipped to provide a more comprehensive understanding of the epidemiology of MDR pathogens in burn units. Incorporating molecular diagnostic tools, such as whole-genome sequencing or polymerase chain reaction (PCR) assays, could further enhance the detection of resistance genes and elucidate the mechanisms driving antimicrobial resistance in burn care settings.

The study findings have important implications for the management of burn wound infections[29][30]. The emergence of MDR pathogens, particularly *Acinetobacterbaumannii, Pseudomonas aeruginosa*, MRSA, and ESBL-producing Enterobacteriaceae, underscores the urgent need for coordinated efforts to address antimicrobial resistance in burn units. Furthur study should prioritize multi-center or area analyses to better understand the distribution and resistance patterns of these pathogens across diverse settings. Such studies could help identify common trends and inform the development of standardized protocols for infection prevention and treatment.In conclusion, the study highlights the critical challenges posed by MDR pathogens in burn wound infections, emphasizing the need for a multi-faceted approach to their management. Stringent infection control measures, judicious use of antibiotics, continuous surveillance of resistance patterns, and the incorporation of molecular diagnostic tools are essential to mitigating the impact of antimicrobial resistance in burn care[31][32][33]. Addressing these challenges through collaborative research and innovative strategies will be crucial to improving outcomes for burn patients and combating the growing threat of antimicrobial resistance in healthcare settings. These findings reinforce the need for enhanced infection control strategies and the optimization of antimicrobial therapy in burn units. By addressing the gaps identified in this study, future efforts can offer a extra inclusive sympathetic of resistance patterns and improve the management of burn wound infections, ultimately leading to better outcomes for burn patients globally[34][35][36].

Because this study was conducted in a single burn center with a limited sample size, its findings may not fully represent the wider population of burn patients, particularly with respect to regional variations in antimicrobial resistance. Patients included in the study were admitted to SUM Hospital following burn accidents, either domestic or industrial, with no specific selection criteria. Both male and female patients of varying age groups were represented, ensuring diverse demographic coverage. However, the single-center nature of the research restricts its ability to provide insights into broader resistance trends. Future studies should consider multi-center or area analyses to offer a more inclusive accepting of burn wound infections and microbial resistance patterns. Expanding the scope could also enhance the generalizability of findings[37][38].

5. Conclusion

It is highlights a significant prevalence of multidrug-resistant pathogens, particularly *Acinetobacterbaumannii* and *Pseudomonas aeruginosa*, in burn unit infections. The high resistance rates to key antibiotics underscore the need for diligent infection control practices to limit the spread of these pathogens. The appearance of MRSA and ESBL-producing strains further complicates treatment options in burn care. Continued monitoring of antimicrobial resistance patterns and stricter protocols are crucial. Further studies should explore preventive strategies and the impact of antibiotic use on resistance trends in burn units.

Acknowledgements

The authors sincerely thank the hospital laboratory technical staff for their valuable assistance in carrying out the investigations.

Author Contributions

SR led the data analysis and manuscript drafting, *critically revising* the manuscript and providing final approval, ensuring the integrity and accuracy of all aspects of the work. RK and KS were involved in the conception and design of the study, performed data analysis and interpretation, and contributed to drafting the manuscript.

Funding

This work received self-sponsorship from SUM Hospital and Siksha 'O'Anusandhan University, Bhubaneswar, Odisha, India.

Declarations

Informed consent was obtained from all participants and their legal guardians prior to enrollment, and the study protocols were reviewed and approved by the Institutional Ethics Committee.

Ethical Consideration

Here was no direct participation of any individual or animalmodel in this investigation.Organization Ethical Committee authorization number is Ref.no/ICE/IMS.SH/SOA/2024/892.

References

1. Khumalo, B. (2021). *Prevalence of clinically relevant acanthamoeba and bacteria in a South African paediatric burns unit*. University of Johannesburg (South Africa).
2. Azizian, K., Alikhani, M. Y., Mashouf, R. Y., Gholizadeh, P., &Noshak, M. A. (2019). Antibiotic resistance patterns and frequency of metallo-beta-lactamases in Klebsiella pneumoniae in Hamadan, Iran. *Journal of Contemporary Clinical Practice*, *5*(1), 10–7.
3. Samie, S. A., Rizk, Y. E., Al-Husseini, N. F., & Ibrahim, D. A. (2020). Biofilm genes among drug resistant Pseudomonas aeruginosa. *Benha Journal of Applied Sciences*, *5*(8 part (1)-(2)), 211–223.
4. Lompo P, Heroes AS, Agbobli E, Kühne V, Tinto H, Affolabi D, Jacobs J. Bacterial Contamination of Antiseptics, Disinfectants and Hand Hygiene Products in Healthcare Facilities in High-Income Countries: A Scoping Review. Hygiene. 2023 Apr 19;3(2):136–75.
5. Jacobs, S. E., & Walsh, T. J. (2023). Non-Aspergillus hyaline molds: a host-based perspective of emerging pathogenic fungi causing sinopulmonary diseases. *Journal of Fungi*, *9*(2), 212.
6. Noël, K. C. (2019). *Antibiotic use in hospitalized children: current practices and the impact of virus diagnostic testing on antibiotic-related decisions*. McGill University (Canada).
7. Morrison, L., & Zembower, T. R. (2020). Antimicrobial resistance. *Gastrointestinal Endoscopy Clinics*, *30*(4), 619–635.
8. Gajic, I., Kabic, J., Kekic, D., Jovicevic, M., Milenkovic, M., Mitic Culafic, D., ... &Opavski, N. (2022). Antimicrobial susceptibility testing: a comprehensive review of currently used methods. *Antibiotics*, *11*(4), 427.
9. Vasala, A., Hytönen, V. P., & Laitinen, O. H. (2020). Modern tools for rapid diagnostics of antimicrobial resistance. *Frontiers in cellular and infection microbiology*, *10*, 308.
10. Khan, Z. A., Siddiqui, M. F., & Park, S. (2019). Current and emerging methods of antibiotic susceptibility testing. *Diagnostics*, *9*(2), 49.
11. Gupta, M., Naik, A. K., & Singh, S. K. (2019). Bacteriological profile and antimicrobial resistance patterns of burn wound infections in a tertiary care hospital. *Heliyon*, *5*(12).
12. Hubab, M., Maab, H., Hayat, A., & Ur Rehman, M. (2020). Burn wound microbiology and the antibiotic susceptibility patterns of bacterial isolates in three burn units of Abbottabad, Pakistan. *Journal of Burn Care & Research*, *41*(6), 1207-1211.
13. Chaudhary, N. A., Munawar, M. D., Khan, M. T., Rehan, K., Sadiq, A., Bhatti, H. W., & Rizvi, Z. A. (2019). Epidemiology, bacteriological profile, and antibiotic

sensitivity pattern of burn wounds in the burn unit of a tertiary care hospital. *Cureus*, *11*(6).

14. Haghighifar, E., & Kamali Dolatabadi, R. (2020). Bacterial infections and antimicrobial resistance patterns of burn wound infections: A one year study from burn Hospital, Isfahan, Iran. *Journal of Advances in Medical and Biomedical Research*, *28*(128), 144–150.
15. Emami, A., Pirbonyeh, N., Keshavarzi, A., Javanmardi, F., Moradi Ghermezi, S., & Ghadimi, T. (2020). Three year study of infection profile and antimicrobial resistance pattern from burn patients in southwest Iran. *Infection and drug resistance*, 1499–1506.
16. Sisay, M., Worku, T., & Edessa, D. (2019). Microbial epidemiology and antimicrobial resistance patterns of wound infection in Ethiopia: a meta-analysis of laboratory-based cross-sectional studies. *BMC Pharmacology and Toxicology*, *20*, 1–19.
17. Vinaik, R., Barayan, D., Shahrokhi, S., & Jeschke, M. G. (2019). Management and prevention of drug resistant infections in burn patients. *Expert review of anti-infective therapy*, *17*(8), 607–619.
18. Hosny, A. E. D. M., Rasmy, S. A., Aboul-Magd, D. S., Kashef, M. T., & El-Bazza, Z. E. (2019). The increasing threat of silver-resistance in clinical isolates from wounds and burns. *Infection and drug resistance*, 1985-2001.
19. Bramardipa, A. A. B., Sukrama, I. D. M., & Budayanti, N. N. S. (2019). Bacterial pattern and its susceptibility toward antibiotic on burn infection in Burn Unit Sanglah General Hospital. *Bali Medical Journal*, *8*(1), 328–333.
20. Mahmoudi, H., Pourhajibagher, M., Chiniforush, N., Soltanian, A. R., Alikhani, M. Y., & Bahador, A. (2019). Biofilm formation and antibiotic resistance in meticillin-resistant and meticillin-sensitive Staphylococcus aureus isolated from burns. *Journal of wound care*, *28*(2), 66–73.
21. Ranjbar, R., & Farahani, A. (2019). Study of genetic diversity, biofilm formation, and detection of Carbapenemase, MBL, ESBL, and tetracycline resistance genes in multidrug-resistant Acinetobacter baumannii isolated from burn wound infections in Iran. *Antimicrobial Resistance & Infection Control*, *8*, 1–11.
22. Guan, H., Dong, W., Lu, Y., Jiang, M., Zhang, D., Aobuliaximu, Y., ... & Lu, S. (2021). Distribution and antibiotic resistance patterns of pathogenic bacteria in patients with chronic cutaneous wounds in China. *Frontiers in medicine*, *8*, 609584.
23. Ladhani, H. A., Yowler, C. J., & Claridge, J. A. (2021). Burn wound colonization, infection, and sepsis. *Surgical infections*, *22*(1), 44–48.
24. Sedaghat, A., Khadem-Rezaiyan, M., Ahmadabadi, A., Abbaspour, H., Youssefi, M., Shirzad, M. M., ... & Ramezani, M. (2019). Antibacterial resistance pattern of Acinetobacter baumannii in burn patients in Northeast of Iran. *Jundishapur Journal of Microbiology*, *12*(10), 1–8.
25. Atef, N. M., Shanab, S. M., Negm, S. I., & Abbas, Y. A. (2019). Evaluation of antimicrobial activity of some plant extracts against antibiotic susceptible and resistant bacterial strains causing wound infection. *Bulletin of the National Research Centre*, *43*(1), 1–11.
26. Khalil, M. A., El Maghraby, G. M., Sonbol, F. I., Allam, N. G., Ateya, P. S., & Ali, S. S. (2021). Enhanced efficacy of some antibiotics in presence of silver nanoparticles against multidrug resistant Pseudomonas aeruginosa recovered from burn wound infections. *Frontiers in microbiology*, *12*, 648560.
27. Ijaz, M., Siddique, A. B., Rasool, M. H., & Shafique, M. (2019). Frequency of multi drug resistant Pseudomonas aeruginosa in different wound types of hospitalized patients. *Pakistan journal of pharmaceutical sciences*, *32*.
28. Qader, A. R., & Muhamad, J. A. (2010). Nosocomial infection in sulaimani burn hospital, IRAQ. *Annals of burns and fire disasters*, *23*(4), 177.
29. Ahuja, R. B., Gupta, A., & Gur, R. (2009). A prospective double-blinded comparative analysis of framycetin and silver sulphadiazine as topical agents for burns: a pilot study. *Burns*, *35*(5), 672–676.
30. Church, D., Elsayed, S., Reid, O., Winston, B., & Lindsay, R. (2006). Burn wound infections. *Clinical microbiology reviews*, *19*(2), 403–434.
31. Avni, T., Levcovich, A., Ad-El, D. D., Leibovici, L., & Paul, M. (2010). Prophylactic antibiotics for burns patients: systematic review and meta-analysis. *Bmj*, *340*.
32. Richcane, A., Samuel, C. T., Pius, A., Enoch, F., & Poku, O. S. P. (2017). Bacteriological profile of burn wound isolates in a burns center of a tertiary hospital. *Journal of acute disease*, *6*(4), 181–186.
33. Chim, H., Tan, B. H., & Song, C. (2007). Five-year review of infections in a burn intensive care unit: High incidence of Acinetobacter baumannii in a tropical climate. *Burns*, *33*(8), 1008–1014.
34. Fournier, P. E., Richet, H., & Weinstein, R. A. (2006). The epidemiology and control of Acinetobacter baumannii in health care facilities. *Clinical infectious diseases*, *42*(5), 692–699.
35. Gupta, A. K., Uppal, S., Garg, R., Gupta, A., & Pal, R. (2011). A clinico-epidemiologic study of 892 patients with burn injuries at a tertiary care hospital in Punjab, India. *Journal of Emergencies, Trauma, and Shock*, *4*(1), 7–11.
36. Rezaei, E., Safari, H., Naderinasab, M., &Aliakbarian, H. (2011). Common pathogens in burn wound and changes in their drug sensitivity. *Burns*, *37*(5), 805–807.
37. Sharma, B. R. (2007). Infection in patients with severe burns: causes and prevention thereof. *Infectious disease clinics of North America*, *21*(3), 745–759.
38. Huan, J. N., & Tang, J. J. (2011). Drug-resistance Acinetobacter baumannii infection in burn patients: current situation and countermeasure. *Zhonghua Shao Shang za zhi = Zhonghua Shaoshang Zazhi = Chinese Journal of Burns*, *27*(2), 84–87.

Note: All the tables in this chapter were made by the authors.

Research and Innovations in Industrial and Marine Biotechnology: A Circular Economy 2024 – Prof. Hrudayanath Thatoi et al. (eds)

49 Evaluating the Potential of *Microchiritahamosa* for Targeted Therapy in Periodontitis

Pratikshya Mohanty, Kalpita Bhatta*
Department of Botany, School of Applied Sciences,
Centurion University of Technology and Management,
Bhubaneswar, India, Odisha

Himansu Bhusan Samal
Department of Pharmaceutics,
School of Pharmacy and Life Sciences,
Centurion University of Technology and Management,
Bhubaneswar, India, Odisha

Ashish Panigrahi
Department of Botany, School of Applied Sciences,
Centurion University of Technology and Management,
Bhubaneswar, India, Odisha

Abstract: The present investigation explores the therapeutic efficacy of secondary metabolite present in *Microchiritahamosa* for treating periodontal disease. *Microchiritahamosa* belongs to the family Gesneriaceae. This family has high pharmacological efficacy and above 300 phyto-compounds. However, the genus *Microchirata* is less explored and documented. The potential of the bioactive compound can be well validated and elaborated by studying antimicrobial and molecular docking. Compared to Methanol and Chloroform, the ethanolic leaf extract showed exceptional bacterial activity against S. aureus and P. aeruginosa. A higher inhibition zone against *S. aureus* (12-13mm) and a lower zone of inhibition against *P. aeruginosa* (9-10mm) was detected. A docking between MMP2 and phytocompound compounds such as (PubChem, CID-656506, CID-75581, and CID-535560) from GC-MS analysis was performed. CID-656506 shows a good docking score (-8.4kcal/mol) as compared to others. *Microchiritahamosa* bioactive compound can be well tailored for designing novel therapeutic drugs for periodontal disease and treating a wide array of other diseases increasing its therapeutic value it.

Keywords: Antibacterial, Docking, Ethanolic extract, *Microchiritahamosa*, Periodontal, Zone of inhibition

1. Introduction

Maintaining oral care is vital for overall good physical condition and fitness, as well as supporting constitutive day-to-day activities. When amplified on existing explanations, dental care can be viewed as a complex concept that encompasses physical, psychological, emotional, and social dimensions, all of which are essential to an individual's total wellness [1,2]. Oral health issues rank among the most prevalent diseases globally and have promptly increased, a significant global pandemic in recent years [3]. As of 2022, the WHO evaluated that dental infection impact nearly 3.5 billion individuals globally. Periodontitis is a widespread chronic inflammatory condition which damages the gums, alveolar bone and periodontal ligament which have determinable effect on the tissues supporting the teeth [4]. A range of diseases and conditions, such as

*Corresponding author: kalpita.bhatta@cutm.ac.in

DOI: 10.1201/9781003759003-49

congenital anomalies, craniofacial disorders, injuries, and diseases, impact both the ligaments and muscle tissues in the oral cavity [3]. These issues encompass erosion, caries, attrition, abscesses, and periodontitis. These issues encompass dental caries, abscesses, erosion, and attrition, and periodontal diseases. Denticle decay is a complex, variable disease negotiates by biofilms that leads to periodic desalination and decalcification of the calcified tissues of the teeth [5]. Caries can affect both the crown of the tooth and exposed root surfaces later in life and can occur at any age in both primary and permanent teeth [6]. Various factors, including the patient's overall care, socioeconomic status, way of lifestyle, gender, age, ethnic background, genetic predispositions, climatic influences, and favoured system response, affect the progression of the disease, alongside local factors such as plaque and calculus [7]. If periodontal disease remains untreated, individuals may face an increased risk of developing other systemic conditions. These include Alzheimer's disease, respiratory infections, cardiovascular issues, oral and colorectal cancers, insulin resistance, adverse pregnancy outcomes, digestive disorders, and diabetes [7]. Consequently, the different chemical and synthetic substances used for oral hygiene demonstrate varying methods for preventing and treating these oral issues. Unfortunately, they also come with several disadvantages, such as altering the dental microflora and staining teeth, Therefore, it is crucial to explore substitute remedial and neutralizing strategies for maintaining oral hygiene [8]. For centuries, herbal therapy has served as a trusted treatment option for various disorders in regions like India, China, and Indonesia, valued for its notable advantages over synthetic medications. These advantages include a significantly lower risk of adverse drug reactions and a reputation for being both safe and gentle [9,10]. In light of the increasing prevalence of multidrug-resistant pathogens, there is a pressing need for affordable, safe, and effective alternative oral care products derived from natural sources. This demand has fuelled a flourishing number of people preferred in plant-based health products, especially among patients with non-communicable diseases [11]. *Microchiritahamosa* (R. Br) Yin Z. Wang is a member of the Gesneriaceae family (Yunnan and W. & S. Guangxi) with its more diverse flora in Indo-China. This species is an annual plant that primarily thrives in subtropical environments. *Microchiritahamosa*is a remarkable plant species known for its pharmacological benefits, and potent anti-inflammatory, antioxidant, and antimicrobial properties. Research into various species within the *Microchirita* genus has revealed a wealth of bioactive compounds- such as flavonoids, alkaloids, and phenolics- that can modulate inflammatory responses and combat microbial growth [12].

As drug discovery and designing is time-consuming and has many challenges, the use of innovative methods such as molecular docking reduces the period and eventually makes the procedure easy. An approach such as virtual screening of compounds hit identification and validation has a major role to play in drug designing [13-15]. This paper tries to explore the curative values of *Microchirata*, a less-known genera and its pharmacological value with a pragmatic approach.

2. Material and Methods

2.1 Identification and Collection

The herb was collected from the mountain region of Dhenkanal District Odisha and using the herbarium at Regional Plant Research Centre Bhubaneswar and then identified and verified. After a proper wash, the whole part of the herb undergoes drying under suitable conditions, which are dark and dry. Once the plants were dried, they were ground into powder for extraction purposes.

2.2 Preparation of Ethanol Extract from Herbs

The percolation method and 70° ethanol were employed in this investigation. Consequently, a decanter filled with 50g of powdered herbal sample with 250 ml of 70° ethanol was assessed it step-by-step. We heated it first before pouring it into the decanter to add the ethanol. We kept adding ethanol until the herbs in the decanter were fully soaked and some ethanol was visible on the sample surface. An hour later, we switched on the decanter faucet to allow the solvent to escape, and then we put it back in the decanter and did it three times. Depending on the type of organ (root, leaves, or flower), the entire extraction process took 24 to 72 hours. Using a rotary and vacuum distillation technique, the solvent(ethanol) was extracted and separated from the extract [16].

2.3 Antimicrobial Activity Studies

Strains of Bacteria

Recently, *S.aureus* (MTCC 96), and *P. aeruginosa* (MTCC424),were obtained from Microbial Type Culture Collection and Gene Bank (MTCC), Chandigarh to determine the antibacterial activity of *M. hamosa*. On an agar slants, an axenic culture of microflora was kept at 4 °C. All the biochemical tests were performed to validate this bacterial isolates.

Antimicrobial Activity

The bactericidal activeness of leaves ethanol extract was evaluated excluding clinical isolates by the agar-well diffusion method as described byUddin etal [17]. Bacterial strains freshly prepared in broth form were used for antimicrobial determinations. A cork borer with a 6 mm diameter was employed to create uniform wells in the agar plates. Subsequently, a sterile glass spreader uniformly distributed an aliquot of 100 µl inoculum for each bacterial strain across the pre-punched nutrient agar surface. A sterilized cotton swab was then used to ensure even application, and the plates were left to settle at ambient temperature. 100 μg/ml concentration of ethanol extract was added to the well. Gentamicin was used as a positive control. Distilled water was employed as the negative control in the study. The plates were initially maintained at a temperature range of 2–8 °C in a refrigerator to allow the diffusion of the extracts into the agar matrix. They were incubated at 37 °C for 24 hours to facilitate microbial proliferation. The diameters of the inhibition zones were meticulously recorded to the nearest millimetre.A clear inhibition zone measuring ≥7 mm in diameter was deemed to be a significant indicator of microbial susceptibility to the extract. The outcomes were benchmarked against those of a standard antibiotic disc. All procedures were executed under strict aseptic conditions to uphold the reliability and integrity of the results.

2.4 In-Silico Activity

A docking approach was used to study the molecular interactions between the small molecules (Ligands) and protein of interest.Which permits us to identify the behaviour of small molecule in the binding site of target protein and also to illuminate fundamental biochemical process. The binding of small molecules on the active site infer a lot of data regarding their interactions which can pave way for screening of the best small molecule for future studies.

Molecular docking process was fulfilled with AutoDock 4.2.

The compound details were obtained from the PubChem database and its 3D structure was downloaded in SDF format and converted into PDB format using the Pymol tool. Here, the target protein is MMP2 and The RCSB Proteins Database Library was employed to obtain certain proteins' X-ray crystallography shapes (www.pdb.org) with PDB ID 1CK7 respectively. By usage of auto docktools polar and nonpolar hydrogen were added which in large prepares the protein for docking.. The pdb files of the proteins were converted to pdbqt files after adding Kollmancharge using Auto Dock MGL Tools1.5.6. The position of the ligand on the binding site of the protein is determined by Auto grid by organizing the grid coordinates (x,yandz) which were discovered by PrankWeb. Ligand tethering of the protein is carried out by controlling the Lamarckian genetic algorithm parameter, using 10 runs of GA capital. The run with lowest binding energy was noted from its rmsd cluster table and then the final docking complex was produced and was saved for visualization and analysis using PyMol.

3. Results and Discussions

3.1 Antimicrobial Activity

We have taken *Staphylococcus aureus* and *Pseudomonas aeruginosa* which contains antimicrobial activity against ethanol leaf extract. In one plate we contain the *Staphylococcus aureus* Strain where gentamicin has positive control and water has negative control. At the same time, we have taken *Pseudomonas aeruginosa* Strain against ethanol leaf extract, with gentamicin as positive control, and water as negative control. The Zone of Inhibition is shown in Table 49.1. Ethanol leaf extract contains a good zone of Inhibition (12 mm) as compared with Gentamicin against *Staphylococcus aureus* Strain whereas *Pseudomonas aeruginosa* Contains a lower zone of Inhibition (9mm) as compared to *Staphylococcus aureus* Strain (Fig. 49.1)

Table 49.1 The table shows a comparative study of the zone of inhibition between the two bacterial strains

Sl. no.	Bacterial strain	Ethanol Leaf extract (in mm)	Positive Control (Gentamicin) mm)	Negative Control (Water)
1	*Staphylococcus aureus*	12	10	0
2	*Pseudomonas aeruginosa*	9	0	0

[Note: *=Gram positive Bacteria]

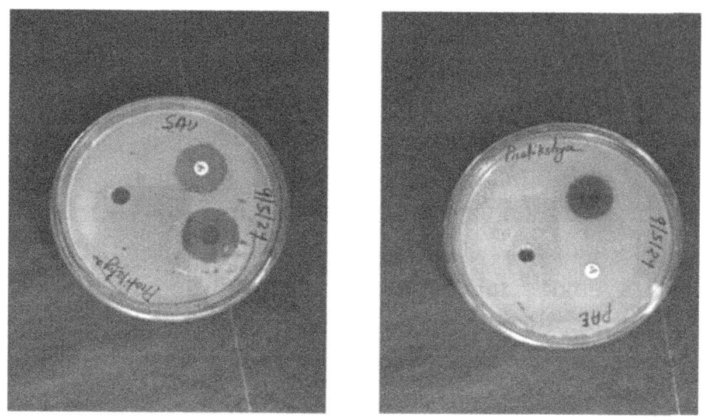

(a) (b)

Fig. 49.1 Antibacterial activity of Ethanol leaf extract showing inhibition zone against (a): *Staphylococcus aureus*, (b) *Pseudomonas aeruginosa*

3.2 In-Silico Activity

A docking between MMP2, an enzyme that plays an essential role in developing periodontitis, and phytocompound from GC-MS analysis was performed. The 3D structures of the ligands were downloaded from PubChem in .sdfformat. They were then converted into .pdb format using PyMOL software. The result showed binding energies of -8.4kcal/mol, -7.0kcal/mol, and -6.9kcal/mol, respectively (Table 49.2). CID-656506 (Glucobrassicin) shows a good docking score (-8.4kcal/mol) as compared to others.

Microchiratahamosa belongs to the Gesneriaceae family has a long history *of* therapeutic properties as it is widely seen in Didymocarpus [18]. C.B Clarke has reported the

Table 49.2 Depicting the receptor-ligand interactions with binding energy

Protein	Ligand	Pub-Chem ID	Binding Energy (Kcal/mol)
MMP2	Glucobrassicin	CID- 656506	-8.4
	1H-Indene, 1-methylene-	CID- 75581	-7.0
	2-Myristynoyl pantetheine	CID- 535560	-6.9

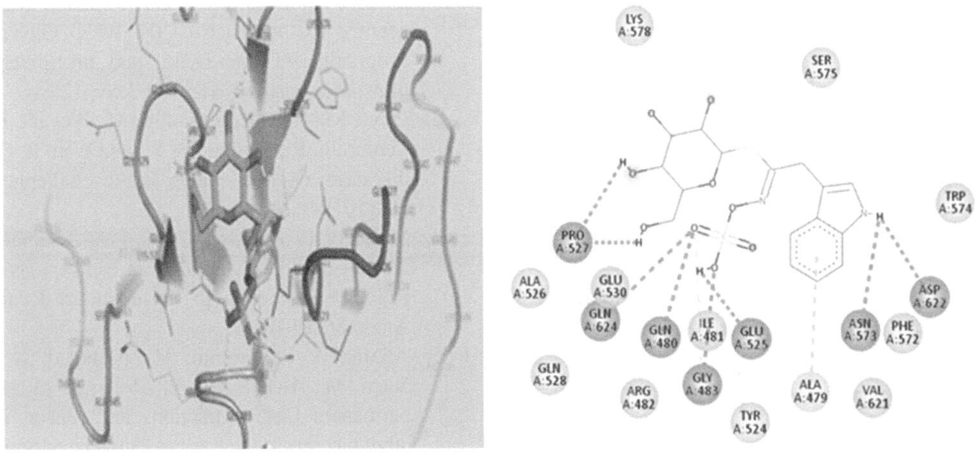

(a)

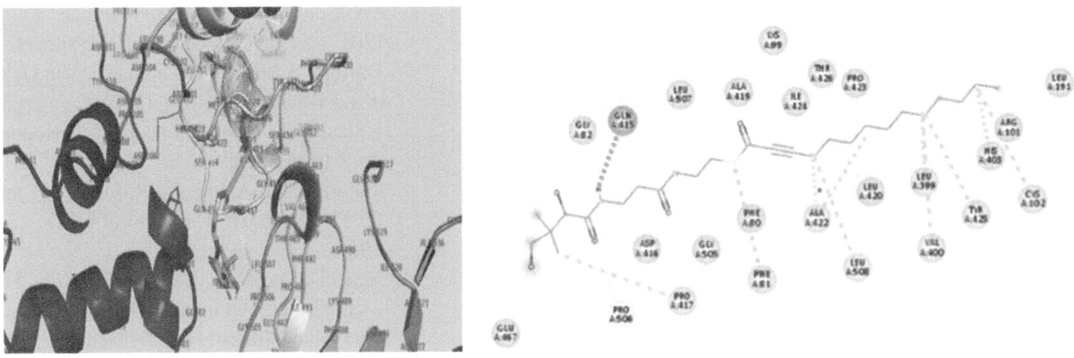

(b)

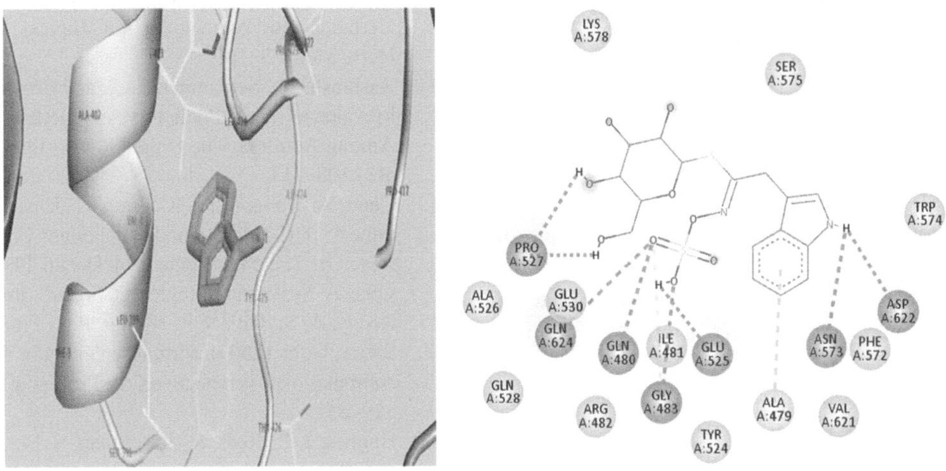

(c)

Fig. 49.2 Protein-ligand interaction and its 2D diagram: (a) MMP2 protein with glucobrassicin, (b) MMP2 protein with 1H-Indene, 1-methylene, (c) MMP2 protein with 2-Myristynoyl pantetheine use of whole plant of *Didymocarpusalbicalyx* as herbal medicine in veterinary uses among the Tamang people in central Nepal [19,20] revealing the fact plant from Gesneriaceae family is widely used for pharmacological efficacy. This is equally observed in *Microchiritahamosa* showing 12mm and 9mm in *Staphylococcus aureus* and *Pseudomonas aeruginosa*. Although biological activity of this genera is less explored. Work could be done to establish the efficacy of the genera. Koyyaimutu and Sathyavathi *etal* have documented that *Didymocarpustomentosus* Wight., a herb has been widely used in treatment of inflammation [21,22] which is quite evident in the docking studies where a good result is well observed with protein MMP2 and Ligand such as Glicobarsin,1H-Indene,1-methylene and 2-Myristynoyl pantetheine. Future comparisons with other studies on natural products should encompass a wider array of pathogens and the potential synergistic effects with existing periodontal treatment.

4. Conclusion and Future Prospective

M. hamosa is expected to contain compounds with potent antimicrobial properties that can inhibit the growth of periodontal pathogens. This antimicrobial potential, if validated, would be especially valuable as it offers a natural, plant-based alternative to synthetic antibiotics, reducing the likelihood of resistance development and allowing for a more sustainable treatment approach. *M. hamosa* is hypothesized to possess high antioxidant activity due to the presence of flavonoids and phenolic compounds, which could play a role in scavenging free radicals in periodontal tissues, thus reducing tissue destruction and supporting regeneration. Utilizing in silico methods to screen and predict the binding of bioactive compounds from *M. hamosa* to key protein targets involved in inflammation and bacterial pathogenesis will help to identify specific molecular mechanisms of action. So also, all the Gesneriaceae, still unexplored have an array of pharmacological properties which need to be investigated. The results of this research pave the way for exciting future explorations and advancements in the treatment of periodontal disease using *Microchiritahamosa*, specifically through the isolation and characterization of active compounds, mechanistic studies, *in-vivo* validation, synergistic studies, formulation development, molecular docking, and dynamic simulations, as well as clinical trials.

Acknowledgement

We are indebted to Department of Botany, Centurion University of Technology and Management, School of Applied Sciences for giving us the opportunity to use the laboratory facilities.

References

1. Glick, M., Williams, D. M., Kleinman, D. V., Vujicic, M., Watt, R. G., and Weyant, R. J. (2016). A new definition for oral health developed by the FDI World Dental Federation opens the door to a universal definition of oral health. Brit. Dent. Jour., 221(12):792–793.
2. Poul Erik Petersen (2003). The World Oral Health Report 2003: continuous improvement of oral health in the 21st century–the approach of the WHO Global Oral Health Programme. Comm.Denti. and orl.Epidem., 31: 3–24. https://doi.org/10.1046/j..2003.com122.x
3. Peres, M. A., Macpherson, L. M., Weyant, R. J., Daly, B., Venturelli, R., Mathur, M. R., and Watt, R. G. (2019). Oral diseases: a global public health challenge. The Lancet, 394(10194):249–260.
4. Mohanty, P., Bhatta, K., Das, I. J., &Samal, H. B. (2024) Advances in Periodontal Drug Delivery Systems and The Role of Probiotics in Periodontitis Treatment.Jour. of Angio.8(3):1–12
5. Aljafar, A., Alibrahim, H., Alahmed, A., AbuAli, A., Nazir, M., Alakel, A., and Almas, K. (2021).Reasons for permanent teeth extractions and related factors among adult patients in the Eastern Province of Saudi Arabia. The Scientific World Journal, 2021(1): 5534455.
6. Pitts, N. B., Zero, D. T., Marsh, P. D., Ekstrand, K., Weintraub, J. A., Ramos-Gomez, F., ...and Ismail, A. (2017). Dent.Cari. Nat Rev Dis Primers.,3: 17030.
7. Bartold, P. Mark, and Thomas E. Van Dyke. "Periodontitis: a host-mediated disruption of microbial homeostasis. Unlearning learned concepts." Periodontology 2000 62, no. 1 (2013): 203–217.
8. Taheri, J. B., Azimi, S., Rafieian, N., and Zanjani, H. A. (2011). Herbs in dentistry.Interna.Dent. Jour., 61(6):287–296.
9. Rezaei-Tazangi, F., Mirhosseini, A. F., Fathi, A., Roghani-Shahraki, H., Arefnezhad, R., and Vasei, F. (2024). Herbal And Nano-Based Herbal Medicine: New Insights into Their Therapeutic Aspects Against Periodontitis. Avice. Jour. of Phytomed., 14(4): 430.
10. Khogta, S., Patel, J., Barve, K., and Londhe, V. (2020). Herbal Nano-Formulations for Topical Delivery.Jour.Of Herb. Med., 20:100300.
11. Rashrash, M., Schommer, J. C., and Brown, L. M. (2017). Prevalence And Predictors of Herbal Medicine Use Among Adults in The United States. Jour. Of Pati.Exper., 4(3):108–113.
12. Chen, Y., Wong, R. W., Mcgrath, C., Hagg, U., and Seneviratne, C. J. (2014). Natural Compounds Containing Mouth-rinses in The Management of Dental Plaque and Gingivitis: A Systematic Review. Clin.Orl. Invest., 18: 1–16.
13. Reddy, A. S., Pati, S. P., Kumar, P. P., Pradeep, H. N., and Sastry, G. N. (2007). Virtual screening in drug discovery-a computational perspective.Curr.Prot. and Pept. Sci., 8(4): 329–351.
14. Hughes, J. P., Rees, S., Kalindjian, S. B., and Philpott, K. L. (2011). Principles of early drug discovery. Brit. Jour. of pharma., 162(6): 1239–1249.
15. Cui, W., Aouidate, A., Wang, S., Yu, Q., Li, Y., and Yuan, S. (2020). Discovering anti-cancer drugs via computational methods. Front. inpharma., 11: 733.

16. Koohsari, H., Ghaemi, E. A., Sheshpoli, M. S., Jahedi, M., and Zahiri, M. (2015). The Investigation of Antibacterial Activity of Selected Native Plants from North of Iran.Jour. of Med. and Life., 8(2): 38.
17. Uddin, B., Hossan, T., Paul, S., Ahmed, T., Nahar, T., and Ahmed, S. (2010). Antibacterial Activity of The Ethanol Extracts of Hibiscus Rosa-Sinensis Leaves and Flowers Against Clinical Isolates of Bacteria. Bangl. J. Life Sci., 22(2): 65–73.
18. Lama, Y. C., Ghimire, S. K., and Aumeeruddy-Thomas, Y. (2001). Medicinal plants of Dolpo. Amchis' knowledge and conservation. WWF Nepal Program, Katmandu.
19. Luitel, D. R., Rokaya, M. B., Timsina, B., and Münzbergová, Z. (2014). Medicinal plants are used by the Tamang community in the Catawampus district of central Nepal. Jour. of Ethno.andethnomed., 10:1–11.
20. Li, H. B., and Chen, F. (2005). Isolation and purification of baicalein, wogonin, and Oroxylum A from the medicinal plant Scutellariabaicalensis by high-speed counter-current chromatography.Jour. of Chromatogr. A, 1074(1-2): 107–110.
21. Kottaimuthu, R. "Ethnobotany of the Valaiyans of Karandamalai, Dindigul District, Tamil Nadu, India." Ethnobotanical Leaflets 2008, no. 1 (2008): 24.
22. Sathyavathi, R., and K. J. Janardhanan. "Folklore medicinal practices of Badaga community in Nilgiri biosphere reserve, Tamilnadu, India." Int J Pharm Res Dev 3 (2011): 50–63.

Note: All the figures and tables in this chapter were made by the authors.

Research and Innovations in Industrial and Marine Biotechnology: A Circular Economy 2024 – Prof. Hrudayanath Thatoi et al. (eds)

50 Sustainable Therapeutic Potentials of Medicinal Mushrooms

Rusmita Buragohain, Akashi Bora
Nano-biotechnology and Translational Knowledge Laboratory,
Department of Applied Biology, School of Biological Sciences,
University of Science and Technology Meghalaya,
Techno City, 9th Mile, Baridua, India

Hrudayanath Thatoi
Center for Industrial Biotechnology Research,
Siksha 'O' Anusandhan (Deemed to be University),
Bhubaneswar, Odisha, India

Yugal Kishore Mohanta*
Nano-biotechnology and Translational Knowledge Laboratory,
Department of Applied Biology, School of Biological Sciences,
University of Science and Technology Meghalaya,
Techno City, 9th Mile, Baridua, India

Abstract: Medicinal mushrooms offer a promising and sustainable source of bioactive compounds with diverse therapeutic potentials Due to rich in various bioactive compounds, medicinal mushrooms are considered as promising candidates for therapeutics development. Numerous pharmacological activities, including antioxidant, antibacterial, antiviral, hepatoprotective, antidiabetic, and nephroprotective effects, are supported by their phytochemical richness. Consequently, mushrooms are becoming more well-known in both conventional and alternative medicine. Their therapeutic potential is still being discovered through ongoing research in both controlled and natural environments. For long-term applications on health, future research must concentrate on finding new species of medicinal mushrooms and comprehending the pharmacological characteristics of their bioactive compounds.

Keywords: Medicinal mushrooms, Health benefits, Therapeutic compounds

1. Introduction

Medicinal mushrooms exhibit substantial health-promoting characteristics, now evaluated through the medicinal effectiveness of their identified bioactive components and employed in healthcare for addressing small ailments to pandemic illnesses [1]. The primary phytoconstituent in mushroom fruiting bodies is polysaccharide, supplemented by substantial amounts of terpenoids, proteins, fibres, and other saccharides. Medicinal mushrooms also rich in verity of minerals, vitamins and amino acids [2]. Furthermore, secondary metabolites in medicinal mushrooms enhance various therapeutic properties, such as antimicrobial, anticancer, antioxidant, antihyperlipidemic, anti-inflammatory, immunoregulatory, cardioprotective activity and many more. Medicinal mushroom species have the potential to treat and cure many lifestyle disorders [3,4].

Ethnopharmacological studies have recorded the traditional utilization of mushrooms, providing a basis for the formulation of novel medications derived from the insights gained in that research[5]. Isolation, identification as well as characterization of mushroom-based

*Corresponding author: ykmohanta@gmail.com

DOI: 10.1201/9781003759003-50

polysaccharides is a significant area of research.Human clinical trial for anticancer as well as immunostimulant activity of these purified compounds have been also performed[6]. Therapeutic potential of these medicinal mushrooms, highlights the imperative for improved production. Bioactive compounds of these mushrooms including flavonoids, phenols carotenoids, and vitamins are responsible for notable antioxidant activity, which ultimatelyplay a vital role in the prevention of wide range of diseases related to free radicals[4]. Therefore, an extensive understanding of the many functional and therapeutic properties of medicinal mushrooms would serve as a crucialresource for researchers and scientists in the field of healthcare. Currently, there has been a notable increase in research dedicated to mushrooms for the targeted extraction of bioactive compounds that may activate and improve human immune cell responses[7]. Furthermore, other medicinal mushroom species known for their distinct potential characteristics have been discovered. This review clarifies the therapeutic and pharmacological characteristics of many researched medicinal mushrooms.

2. Potential Applications of Medicinal Mushrooms

Medicinal mushrooms are employed to alter human immune responses, encompassing antibacterial, anticancer, and antioxidant properties. These mushrooms comprise substantial constituents includes polysaccharides, terpenoids, polyphenols and alkaloids play a major role for the treatment of various human illnesses [1]. Moreover, this makes new avenue to unvail their implications in addressing human diseases, especially neurodegenerative disorders (e.g., Huntington's disease, Alzheimer's disease, prion disease, multiple sclerosis, Parkinson's disease, and motor neuron disease) [8]. The applications of medicinal mushrooms in wide range of therapeutic actions are depicted in Fig. 50.1.

2.2 Antimicrobial Activity

The antibacterial properties of mushrooms may protect against Gram-positive and Gram-negative bacteria[9]. Grifolin, an *Albatrellus dispansus* derived compound, inhibits harmful fungus. It performed better than *Oudeman siellacanarii*, *A. bisporus*, and *Candida species*[10]. A protein from *Cordyceps militaris* that can kill cancer cells also killed a harmful fungus in patients with breast and bladder cancer [11]. *In vitro* and *in vivo* animal studies showed *Ganoderma* mushrooms' antibacterial and antiviral capabilities. *G. lucidum* polysaccharides can greatly reduce the amount of hepatitis B viral DNA and HbeAg in animal studies [12]. Research has shown that medicinal fungus such as *L. edodes, P. ostreatus, G. lucidum,* and *G. colossus* can inhibit the growth of HIV [13]. It has been found that *A. brasiliensis* and *G. lucidum* have antiviral properties against Herpes simplex virus (HSV) [14]. In addition, phenolic extracts from *Inonotus hispidus*, sesquiterpenes from *Phellinu signiarius*, and hispidin from *Phellinus baumii* have all shown potential against the H5N1 influenza virus [15]. Bioactive components of certain medicinal mushroom target hepatitis B and C viruses (HBV, HCV). For example, *Antrodia camphorata* contains polysaccharides for HBV, *G. lucidum* contains ganoderic acid, *L. edodes* contains a mycelial solid culture extract for HCV, and *P. ostreatus* contains a lectin for HBV. Bioactive substances derived from mushrooms, such as ergosterol, polysaccharides, and colossolactones, have recently been proposed as potential treatments for COVID-19 [15,16].

2.3 Antioxidant Activity

Mushrooms are rich in antioxidants such ascorbic acid, tocopherols, flavonoids, and carotenoids. The antioxidant mechanisms of mushroom species extract are based on its bioactive properties to donate hydrogen, chelate metals, and scavenge free radicals and superoxide [17]. Phenolic compounds are the main antioxidants in Boletus

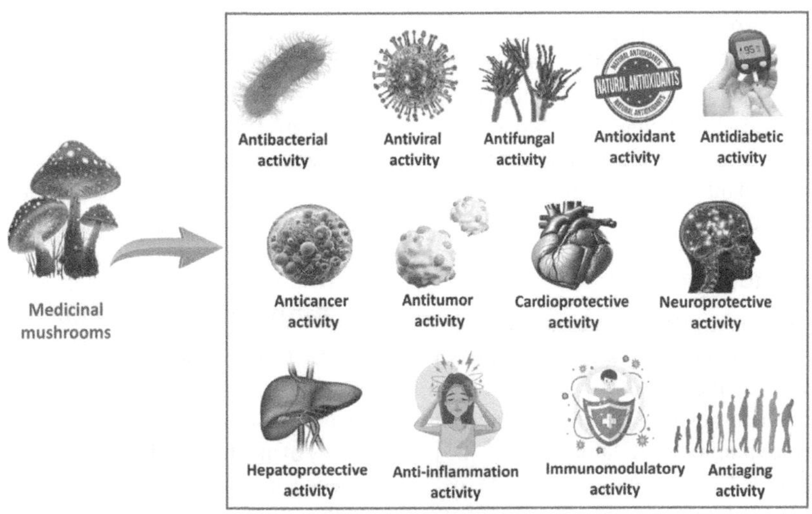

Fig. 50.1 Potential therapeutic application of medicinal mushrooms

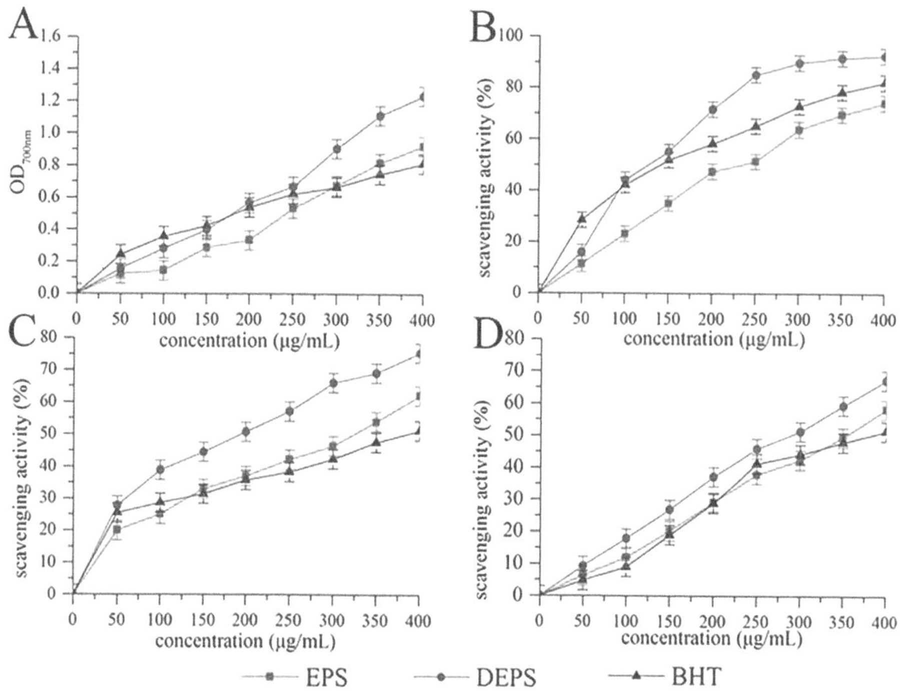

Fig. 50.2 *In-vitro* antioxidant activity of *Termitomyces albuminosus* EPS and DEPS; (A) reducing sugar, (B) DPPH activity, (C) hydroxyl radicals, and (D) superoxide anion radicals. Figure is adopted from [19] under CC-BY licence

mushrooms, according to a study. *Boletus* is a natural antioxidant source due to its high phenolic component content and antioxidant capabilities [18]. Depolymerized exopolysaccharide (DEPS) was isolated from the exopolysaccharide (EPS) of *Termitomyces albuminosus. In vitro* antioxidant activity of both DEPS and EPS were evaluated [Fig. 50.2(A-D)][19].

2.4 Anti-Inflammation and Anti-Aging Activity

Arteriosclerosis, diabetes, neurological disorders, and cancer are incurable inflammation-related diseases. Due to the nutritional value and therapeutic characteristics, mushrooms have been used to relieve inflammation for thousands of years [3]. G. lucidum mycelium extracted with ethanol reduced mouse skin inflammation [20]. The extracts reduced chronic inflammatory paw-edema caused by carrageenan by 56% and formalin by 60%. Mushrooms are rich in antioxidants ergothioneine and glutathione, which enhance health and slow aging [21]. Mushrooms contain polysaccharides that have the potential to slow down the aging process exhibiting anti-aging properties caused by harmful chemicals [22].

2.5 Immunomodulatory Activity

Polysaccharide-protein complexes conjugated by mushrooms boost the immune system. Splenocyte proliferation showed that the water-soluble polysaccharide-protein combination from *G. lucidum* spores had considerable immunomodulatory effects [23]. This combination inhibited Lewis lung carcinoma cell growth. Immunosuppressed mice received an aqueous extract of *Inonotus obliquus* to test its immunomodulatory properties. Oral extract increased serum IL-6 [24].

2.6 Hepatoprotective Activity

Hepatic diseases and abnormalities have traditionally been treated with mushrooms. *G. lucidum*, with its beneficial hepatoprotective qualities, is unquestionably the most commonly considered species among the many mushrooms under study for the treatment of liver diseases. The therapy of hepatocellular injury with moderate dosages of *G. lucidum*[12]. To assess *Morchella esculenta* mushroom's hepatoprotective properties against ethanol-induced chronic hepatotoxicity, antioxidant levels and liver function marker enzymes were measured. The mushroom extract lowered serum levels and restored liver antioxidant levels after ethanol exposure, demonstrating its hepatoprotective properties[12,25]. Pharmacological effects of residual *Cordyceps militaris* polysaccharides on oxidative stress and lipid metabolism were examined. The residual carbohydrate decreased glycosaccharide, arabinose, and mannose and enhanced glutamate pyruvate transaminase. Histopathological annotations confirmed *C. militaris*' hepatoprotective effects.

2.7 Antitumour and Anticancer Activity

In order to show their anticancer capabilities, mushrooms stimulate lymphocytes, which are immune cells that fight cancer. The molecular mechanisms behind the anticancer activity of mushrooms have been illuminated by the verified presence of their pharmacologically active compounds, which are used in cancer treatment [26]. In recent years, mushrooms have found use as immunomodulators and anticancer medications. Research has demonstrated the safety of mushroom (*G. lucidum, Agaricus blazei* and *Grifola frondosus*) consumption known for their antitumor and anticancer properties by analyzing phase I clinical trials that included human patients [27]. A dose-dependent response was observed in the cancer cells when they were exposed to *Hericium coralloides* EPS for 24 or 48 hours; but when compared to MKN-45, EPS was far more hazardous to the AGS cell line[28].

2.8 Cardioprotective and Neuroprotective Activity

Cardiovascular disease is a leading cause of death and a major health issue. Mushroom bioactive substances lower cholesterol, fatty acids, lipoproteins, and triacylglycerols, reducing cardiovascular disease risk[29]. Mushrooms can lower cardiovascular disease risk by affecting metabolic indicators like homocysteine and LDL/HDL[30]. *G. lucidum* extract was tested for cardio protection in perfused rat hearts after 45 minutes of global ischemia and 30 minutes of reperfusion. The antioxidant capabilities of mushroom extract reduced cardiomyocyte necrosis and reperfusion contracture, proving its cardioprotective effects[31]. Various medicinal mushrooms have antihypertensive and cardioprotective qualities, which suggests they could be used to treat cardiovascular diseases and related ailments. Wild or farmed mushrooms prevent several age-related brain illnesses. Basidiomycetes mushrooms have several physiologically active chemicals with strong therapeutic effects, according to a study. Immunological, anticancer, neuroprotective, and nephroprotective characteristics are found in compounds like this[21].

2.9 Antidiabetic Activity

Several edible and medicinal mushrooms decrease cholesterol and triglycerides. *Ganoderma, Agaricus, Grifola, Lentinus, Hericium, Pleurotus, Pholiota*. Alternative diabetes adjuvants were produced using *G. lucidum* proteoglycans, triterpenoids, polysaccharides, and proteins. Mice had lower plasma glucose and greater insulin levels, indicating a stronger hypoglycaemic impact [3]. *A. bisporus* was tested for its antidiabetic properties in streptozotocin-induced T2D in male Sprague-Dawley rats. Rats fed mushroom-enriched chow had lower triglyceride (TG) levels and higher antioxidant, dietary fibre, vitamin C, D, and B12 levels. These nutrients lowered diabetes by controlling insulin[32].

3. Conclusion

Mushrooms are rich in medicinal ingredients and may affect health. Numerous *in vitro* and *in vivo* studies have shown that medicinal mushrooms' polysaccharides, vitamins, minerals, amino acids, fatty acids, and phenolic compounds have many medicinal and pharmacological properties. These components follow complicated routes to illustrate biological and functional functions alone or together. These compounds may have antioxidant, anti-aging, antidiabetic, anticancer, antibacterial, anti-inflammatory, anti-obesity, and immunomodulatory properties. Medicinal mushrooms protect the heart, liver, kidneys, and neurons with phenolic and terpenoids. Anticancer and antitumour activity of medicinal mushrooms' bioactive substances shows their promise as natural medicines. More research is needed to determine the medicinal potential, bioactive ingredients, and health benefits of mushrooms in fostering a healthy lifestyle.

References

1. Phillips, J. M., Ooi, S. L., and Pak, S. C. (2022). Health-Promoting Properties of Medicinal Mushrooms and Their Bioactive Compounds for the COVID-19 Era-An Appraisal: Do the Pro-Health Claims Measure Up? *Molecules,* 27, 2302.
2. Sharma, E., Bairwa, R., Lal, P., Pattanayak, S., Chakrapani, K., Poorvasandhya, R., et al. (2024). Edible mushrooms trending in food: Nutrigenomics, bibliometric, from bench to valuable applications. *Heliyon,* 10, e36963.
3. Shamim, M. Z., Mishra, A. K., Kausar, T., Mahanta, S., Sarma, B., Kumar, V., et al. (2023). Exploring Edible Mushrooms for Diabetes: Unveiling Their Role in Prevention and Treatment. *Molecules*, 28, 2837.
4. Panda, J., Mishra, A. K., Nath, P. C., Mahanta, S., Sharma, M., Nayak, P. K., et al. (2024). Wild edible mushrooms to achieve sustainable development goals: Novel sources for food security, health, and well-being. *Food Biosci*., 60, 104277.
5. Hayat, S. A., Yaseen, T., AhsanAbbasi, B., Iqbal, J., Ijaz, S., Noreen, S., et al. (2024). Ethnobotanical diversity, phytochemical screening and biological evaluation of selected medicinal mushrooms species.*J. King Saud Univ. - Sci.*, 36, 103428.
6. Sivanesan, I., Muthu, M., Gopal, J., and Oh, J.-W. (2022). Mushroom Polysaccharide-Assisted Anticarcinogenic Mycotherapy: Reviewing Its Clinical Trials. *Molecules*, 27, 4090.
7. Fogarasi, M., Nemeş, S. A., Fărcaş, A., Socaciu, C., Semeniuc, C. A., Socaciu, M. I., et al. (2024). Bioactive secondary metabolites in mushrooms: A focus on polyphenols, their health benefits and applications. *Food Biosci.*,62, 105166.
8. Ito, T., Kobayashi, T., Egusa, C., Maeda, T., Abe, N., Okubo, Y., et al. (2020). A case of food allergy due to three different mushroom species.Allergol.Int. Off. J. Japanese Soc. *Allergol.,* 69, 152–153.
9. Panda, J., and Gupta, N. (2022). Bioactive Potential of Different Solvent Extracts of Some Woody and Fleshy Mushrooms. *Mushroom Res.*, 30, 207–211.
10. Alves, M., Ferreira, I. F. R., Dias, J., Teixeira, V., Martins, A., and Pintado, M. (2012). A review on antimicrobial activity of mushroom (basidiomycetes) extracts and isolated compounds.*Planta Med.*, 78, 1707–1718.
11. Park, B. T., Na, K. H., Jung, E. C., Park, J. W., and Kim, H. H. (2009). Antifungal and Anticancer Activities of a

Protein from the Mushroom Cordycepsmilitaris. Korean J. Physiol. Pharmacol. Off. J. Korean Physiol. Soc. Korean Soc. *Pharmacol.*, 13, 49–54.
12. Ahmad, M. F., Ahmad, F. A., Zeyaullah, M., Alsayegh, A. A., Mahmood, S. E., AlShahrani, A. M., et al. (2023). Ganodermalucidum: Novel Insight into Hepatoprotective Potential with Mechanisms of Action. *Nutrients*, 15, 1874.
13. Choengpanya, K., Ratanabunyong, S., Seetaha, S., Tabtimmai, L., and Choowongkomon, K. (2021). Anti-HIV-1 reverse transcriptase property of some edible mushrooms in Asia.*Saudi J. Biol. Sci.*, 28, 2807–2815.
14. Arunachalam, K., Sasidharan, S. P., and Yang, X. (2022). A concise review of mushrooms antiviral and immunomodulatory properties that may combat against COVID-19.*Food Chem. Adv.*, 1, 100023.
15. El-Ramady, H., Abdalla, N., Badgar, K., Llanaj, X., Törős, G., Hajdú, P., et al. (2022). Edible Mushrooms for Sustainable and Healthy Human Food: Nutritional and Medicinal Attributes. *Sustainability*, 14, 4941.
16. Baruah, P., Patra, A., Barge, S., Khan, M. R., and Mukherjee, A. K. (2023). Therapeutic Potential of Bioactive Compounds from Edible Mushrooms to Attenuate SARS-CoV-2 Infection and Some Complications of Coronavirus Disease (COVID-19).*J. fungi*, 9, 897.
17. Chun, S., Gopal, J., and Muthu, M. (2021). Antioxidant activity of mushroom extracts/polysaccharides—Their antiviral properties and plausible antiCOVID-19 properties. *Antioxidants*, 10, 1899.
18. Paloi, S., Kumla, J., Paloi, B. P., Srinuanpan, S., Hoijang, S., Karunarathna, S. C., et al. (2023). Termite Mushrooms (Termitomyces), a Potential Source of Nutrients and Bioactive Compounds Exhibiting Human Health Benefits: A Review. *J. fungi*, 9, 112.
19. Zhao, H., Li, J., Zhang, J., Wang, X., Liu, M., Zhang, C., et al. (2017). Hepatoprotective and in vitro antioxidant effects of native depolymerised-exopolysaccharides derived from *Termitomycesalbuminosus. Sci. Rep.*, 7, 3910.
20. Lakshmi, B., Ajith, T. A., Sheena, N., Gunapalan, N., and Janardhanan, K. K. (2003). Antiperoxidative, anti-inflammatory, and antimutagenic activities of ethanol extract of the mycelium of Ganodermalucidum occurring in South India. *Teratog.Carcinog.Mutagen.Suppl*, 1, 85–97.
21. Liuzzi, G. M., Petraglia, T., Latronico, T., Crescenzi, A., and Rossano, R. (2023). Antioxidant Compounds from Edible Mushrooms as Potential Candidates for Treating Age-Related Neurodegenerative Diseases. *Nutrients*, 15, 1913.
22. Luo, J., Ganesan, K., and Xu, B. (2024). Unlocking the Power: New Insights into the Anti-Aging Properties of Mushrooms. *J. Fungi*, 10, 215.
23. Wang, M., and Yu, F. (2022). Research Progress on the Anticancer Activities and Mechanisms of Polysaccharides FromGanoderma. *Front. Pharmacol.*, 13, 891171.
24. Shen, D., Feng, Y., Zhang, X., Liu, J., Gong, L., Liao, H., et al. (2022). In Vitro Immunomodulatory Effects of *Inonotusobliquus* Extracts on Resting M0 Macrophages and LPS-Induced M1 Macrophages. Evidence-Based Complement.*Altern.Med.* 2022, 8251344.
25. Soares, A. A., De Sá-Nakanishi, A. B., Bracht, A., Da Costa, S. M., Koehnlein, E. A., De Souza, C. G., et al. (2013). Hepatoprotective Effects of Mushrooms.*Molecules*, 18, 7609–7630.
26. Park, H.-J. (2022). Current Uses of Mushrooms in Cancer Treatment and Their Anticancer Mechanisms.*Int. J. Mol. Sci.*, 23, 10502.
27. Arshadi, N., Nouri, H., and Moghimi, H. (2023). Increasing the production of the bioactive compounds in medicinal mushrooms: an omics perspective. *Microb. Cell Fact.*, 22, 11.
28. Tabibzadeh, F., Alvandi, H., Hatamian-Zarmi, A., Kalitukha, L., Aghajani, H., and Ebrahimi-Hosseinzadeh, B. (2024).Antioxidant activity and cytotoxicity of exopolysaccharide from mushroom Hericiumcoralloides in submerged fermentation.*Biomass Convers.Biorefinery*, 14, 26953–26963.
29. Uffelman, C. N., Chan, N. I., Davis, E. M., Wang, Y., McGowan, B. S., and Campbell, W. W. (2023). An Assessment of Mushroom Consumption on Cardiometabolic Disease Risk Factors and Morbidities in Humans: A Systematic Review. *Nutrients*, 15, 1079.
30. Krittanawong, C., Isath, A., Hahn, J., Wang, Z., Fogg, S. E., Bandyopadhyay, D., et al. (2021). Mushroom Consumption and Cardiovascular Health: A Systematic Review. *Am. J. Med.*, 134, 637–642.e2.
31. Anusiya, G., Gowthama Prabu, U., Yamini, N. V, Sivarajasekar, N., Rambabu, K., Bharath, G., et al. (2021). A review of the therapeutic and biological effects of edible and wild mushrooms. *Bioengineered*, 12, 11239–11268.
32. Hashemi Yusefabad, H., Hosseini, S. A., Zakerkish, M., Cheraghian, B., and Alipour, M. (2022). The effects of hot air-dried white button mushroom powder on glycemic indices, lipid profile, inflammatory biomarkers and total antioxidant capacity in patients with type-2 diabetes mellitus: A randomized controlled trial. *J. Res. Med. Sci. Off. J. Isfahan Univ. Med. Sci.*, 27, 49.

Note: All the figures in this chapter were made by the authors.

Research and Innovations in Industrial and Marine Biotechnology: A Circular Economy 2024 – Prof. Hrudayanath Thatoi et al. (eds)

51 The Emerging Threat of Nipah Virus: Challenges and Solutions

Arindam Ganguly,
Saptarshi Mahapatra, Shibsankar Ray,
Sayantan Chattopadhyay, Md. Jabiul Islam, Sathi Garai
Department of Microbiology, Bankura Sammilani College,
Bankura, W.B., India

Sourav Chattaraj*
Centre for Industrial Biotechnology Research, School of Pharmaceutical Sciences,
Siksha O Anusandhan Deemed to be University,
Bhubaneswar, Odisha, India

Tapas Kumar Dutta[3]
Department of Zoology, Bankura Sammilani College,
Bankura, W.B., India

Abstract: Nipah virus, a zoonotic pathogen of global concern, features a distinctive structural and genetic profile, encoding a range of proteins that enable key processes such as host cell attachment, replication, and transmission. The virus has been detected in Indian subcontinent, carried by fruit bats. The World Health Organization classified Nipah virus as a priority pathogen. This study aims to summarize the advance understanding of Nipah virus epidemiology, clinical features, and transmission dynamics, highlighting the challenges in outbreak management and the need for coordinated global action.

Keywords: Nipah virus, Outbreaks, Fatality, Transmission, Prevention, Vaccine

1. Introduction

Infectious particle like Nipah virus (NiV) poses global health threat, requiring early detection, continuous vigilance, and innovative strategies [1-4]. NiV was initially identified in 1998-1999 during an epidemic in Malaysia [5], followed by cases in Singapore [6], and recurring outbreaks in Bangladesh and India from 2001 [7]. Bangladesh has experienced the highest fatality rates, particularly in winter [8]. In India, the virus resurfaced in Kerala in 2018 [9]. Human transmission heightens the potential of widespread outbreaks [10], and the virus has an estimated fatality rate of 40–75% [11]. Fruit bats (*Pteropus* spp.) are natural reservoirs, transmitting the virus via contaminated date palm sap or direct contact [10,12]. NiV causes symptoms ranging from asymptomatic infection to fatal encephalitis and respiratory distress. Currently, no licensed vaccines or antiviral treatments exist; only supportive care is available. The WHO prioritizes NiV research due to its outbreak potential, zoonotic nature, and adaptability in humans.

2. Structural Organization

NiV features a pleomorphic, lipid-bound envelope derived from host cell membranes, which is adorned with two critical glycoproteins that play critical roles in its structure, function, and infectivity (Fig. 51.1). Glycoprotein (G) facilitates attachment to host cells by binding to cell surface receptors, initiating a cellular invasion process

*Corresponding author: souravchattaraj@soa.ac.in

DOI: 10.1201/9781003759003-51

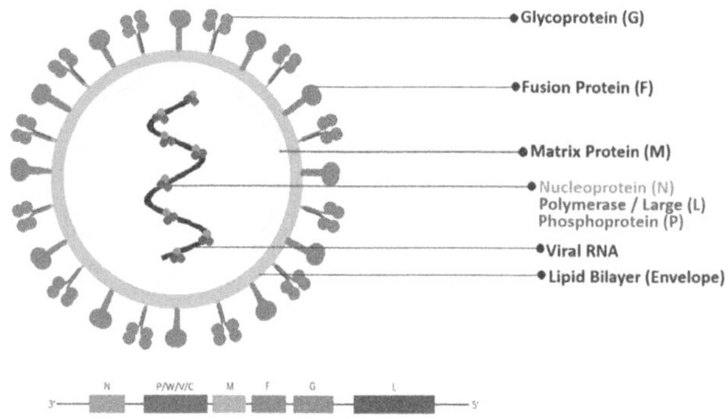

Fig. 51.1 Structural organization of NiV

Source: Authors

[13]. Fusion protein (F) mediates pH-independent membrane fusion, bypassing endosomal requirements (Aguilar et al., 2006) and ensuring direct cytoplasmic entry. Matrix protein (M) serves as a scaffold, linking the internal nucleocapsid to the viral membrane and stabilizing the envelope. The genomic part Nucleoprotein (N) forms a helical ribonucleoprotein complex, encapsidating viral RNA and protecting genetic material. Phosphoprotein (P) and Large polymerase (L) collaborate to enable RNA synthesis. Phosphoprotein acts as a cofactor, while large polymerase drives replication-transcription processes.The NiV genome is optimized for replicative efficiency. Its coding sequence follows a strategic organization: 3′–N–P–M–F–G–L–5′ [14]. Each gene plays a distinct role in the life cycle of virus. The N gene encodes the nucleocapsid, safeguarding viral RNA. The P gene employs RNA editing to produce non-structural proteins (V, W, C) that evade host immunity [15]. The M, F, and G genes facilitate virion assembly, membrane fusion, and receptor binding. The L gene contains the RNA-dependent RNA polymerase, driving viral replication. NiV's structural and genomic organization underlies its zoonotic potential. Receptor plasticity (ephrin-B2/B3 binding) enables cross-species spillover. Immune evasion (P gene products) dismantles interferon defences. Direct membrane fusion (F protein) accelerates cell-to-cell spread.

3. Epidemiology of NiV

Fruit bats serve as perfect reservoir for Nipah virus, carrying the pathogen without getting infected by the virus [16,17]. These flying mammals, with their tooth for nectar and fruit, often live near human farms and orchards, creating an invisible bridge for the virus to cross into other species [16]. Their global presence across tropical regions from Asia to Africa explains why NiV outbreaks occur in these areas [16,17]. Theinfected bats expel the virus through their body fluids[17,18]. Scientists have found evidence of NiV exposure in bat populations from Southeast Asia to West Africa, showing how widely this hidden threat has spread. In human, the risk of contracting the Nipah virus arises primarily through three key transmission routes: touching surfaces contaminated with bat fluids, eating virus-laden fruit, or caring for infected people [10]. The silent transmission of the NiVfrom seemingly healthy bats to unsuspecting humans is the most serious concerns in the natural environment.

4. Transmission of NiV

NiVmay also get transmitted by infected pigs [19]. The virus was introduced to pigs when they consumed fruits that had been contaminated by infected bats [20]. Human infection occurred through direct exposure to infected pigs, while human -to-human transmission was possible through close contact, aerosols, and by contaminated surfaces. Abattoir workers faced heightened risks due to their frequent exposure to body fluids and raw meat pigs. Since infected pigs developed severe respiratory symptoms, NiV also spread through aerosols, making respiratory transmission a significant concern [21] (Nor et al., 2000). NiV further spread to Singapore through imported pigs from Malaysia, leading to infections among residents living near pig farms.

5. Replication

NiVattaches to cell surface receptors(e.g., ephrin-B2 and ephrin-B3) on host cells through its glycoprotein G, facilitating viral entry through the action of its fusion (F) protein[13,22]. This entry also involves a pH-independent endocytic pathway using structural changes in F protein [23]. Inside the host cell, the viral RNA-dependent RNA polymerase (L protein) transcribes the negative-sense RNA genome into positive-sense mRNAs, which are translated into structural and non-structural proteins. These include the nucleocapsid (N), phosphoprotein (P), matrix (M), glycoproteins (G and F), and the L polymerase itself. Viral replication proceeds via synthesis of a full-length antigenome, serving as a template for new genomic RNA, with the N protein encapsidating the RNA into ribonucleoprotein (RNP) complexes [24]. Assembly occurs at the plasma membrane where the M protein coordinates incorporation of RNPs and glycoproteins into budding virions[25]. NiV evades host immunity through P, V, and W proteins that inhibit interferon responses by blocking STAT1 activation [26]. Additionally, NiV induces cytoskeletal changes and syncytia formation, enhancing viral spread within the host.

6. Pathogenesis and Clinical Symptoms

Nipah virus (NiV) infection presents symptoms ranging from mild to fatal, typically within two weeks but with possible incubation up to two months [28]. Early signs include fever, headache, vomiting, and myalgia [29]. In severe cases, cytokine storms (IL-6, IL-8, G-CSF, CXCL10) and lung endothelial infiltration lead to ARDS [29]. NiV targets bronchial epithelium and type II pneumocytes via ephrin-B2/B3 receptors [30], spreading systemically and affecting organs like the spleen, kidneys, and brain [31]. It invades the CNS, compromising the BBB and triggering IL-1β, TNF-α–driven neurological damage [16, 29], resulting in seizures, encephalitis, and coma [32]. Survivors may suffer chronic fatigue and cognitive impairment [33]. Risks include septicemia, renal failure, and gastrointestinal bleeding [27]. In pigs, NiV causes porcine respiratory and encephalitis syndrome (PRES), mainly affecting piglets with respiratory distress [32]. Infected dogs and cats develop lung inflammation, renal necrosis, and vascular pathology [27]. Experimental models (hamsters, guinea pigs, African green monkeys) show CNS and vascular damage [27].

7. Diagnosis

Proper diagnosis is crucial for controlling disease outbreaks[34]. To achieve this, various diagnostic methods have been established, each with its own rationale and limitations. Molecular diagnostics play a vital role, with techniques such as Reverse Transcription-Polymerase Chain Reaction [6], and Loop-Mediated Isothermal Amplification (LAMP) [35] being particularly important. In addition to molecular diagnostics, serological testing methods, including ELISA, Virus Neutralization Test (VNT), and Viral Isolation, are also employed for the diagnosis of NiV.

8. Prophylaxis

Preventing Nipah virus (NiV) transmission involves using personal protective equipment (PPE), disinfection, and avoiding contact with infected body fluids, especially in healthcare settings [20]. Livestock infection control is essential in regions where animals act as intermediate hosts[36]. Both phytomedicines [37, 38] and probiotics have been increasingly investigated for their potential to boost immune responses[39, 40].Avoiding contact with pigs, farm animals, and raw date palm sap, along with planting bat-roosting trees away from farms, reduces infection risks [41]. Surveillance and understanding of bat-to-human transmission are crucial in preventing zoonotic spillover [27]. Patients are often advised to take rest, drink fluids and electrolytes. Pharmacological interventions are still under research. Ribavirin has shown a 36% mortality reduction. The monoclonal antibody m102.4 offers passive immunity, and Favipiravir, an RdRp inhibitor used against influenza, has protected animals from lethal infection [41, 42]. Progress in vaccine development is promising. Vectored and subunit vaccines, such as recombinant measles virus and recombinant VSV vectored vaccines, have shown protective efficacy in animal models. Virus-like particle (NiV-VLP) vaccines and peptide-based vaccines developed via immunoinformatics also show potential [43]. Notably, Oxford University's ChAdOx1 NipahB vaccine has entered first-in-human clinical trials (https://cepi.net/nipah-virus-deadly-illness-without-vaccine).

References

1. Ganguly, A., Banerjee, A., Mandal, A., Khan, M.A. and Das Mohapatra, P.K. (2019). Isolation and characterization of bacteria from the intestine of *Clariasbatrachus* for probiotic organism. *Proc. Zool. Soc.* 72(4):411–419. https://doi.org/10.1007/s12595-018-0283-x
2. Ganguly, A., Konar, U., Kundu, A., Ghosh, S., Chatterjee, I., Nad, S., Chatterjee, S., Nandi, S., Singha, S. and Kali, S. (2020). The prevalence, preventive measures, and economic impact of pandemic COVID-19 in India: The initial phase. *Acta Biol. Szeged.* 64(1):43–61. https://doi.org/10.14232/abs.2020.1.43-61
3. Chattaraj, S., Ganguly, A., Mandal, A. and Das Mohapatra, P.K. (2022). A review of the role of probiotics for the control of viral diseases in aquaculture. *Aquac. Int.* 30(5):2513–2539. https://doi.org/10.1007/s10499-022-00915-6
4. Mitra, D., Nachhmin, B., Ganguly, A., & Das Mohapatra, P. K. (2022). Computational approach to assess Mucormycosis: A systematic review. In *Computational intelligence in healthcare applications* (pp. 71–85). Academic Press. https://doi.org/10.1016/B978-0-323-99031-8.00004-1
5. Bhowmik, A., Hasan, M., Redoy, M.M.H. and Saha, G. (2024). Nipah virus outbreak trends in Bangladesh during the period 2001 to 2024: A brief review. *Sustain. One Health.* 1(0):100103. https://doi.org/10.1016/j.soh.2024.100103
6. Chua, K.B., Bellini, W.J., Rota, P.A. et al. (2000). Nipah virus: A recently emergent deadly paramyxovirus. *Science.* 288(5470):1432–1435. https://doi.org/10.1126/science.288.5470.1432
7. Harcourt, B.H., Tamin, A., Ksiazek, T.G., Rollin, P.E., Anderson, L.J. and Bellini, W.J. (2000). Molecular characterization of Nipah virus, a newly emergent paramyxovirus. *Virology.* 271(2):334–349. https://doi.org/10.1006/viro.2000.0340
8. Chan, X.H.S. et al. (2025). Therapeutics for Nipah virus disease: A systematic review to support prioritisation of drug candidates for clinical trials. *Lancet Microbe.* 0(0):101002. https://doi.org/10.1016/j.lanmicro.2025.101002
9. Banerjee, S., Gupta, N., Kodan, P., Mittal, A., Ray, Y., Nischal, N., Soneja, M., Biswas, A. and Wig, N. (2019). Nipah virus disease: A rare and intractable disease. *Intractable Rare Dis. Res.* 8(1):1–8. https://doi.org/10.5582/irdr.2018.01130
10. Luby, S.P., Hossain, M.J., Gurley, E.S. et al. (2009). Recurrent zoonotic transmission of Nipah virus into humans, Bangladesh, 2001–2007. *Emerg. Infect. Dis.* 15(8):1229–1235. https://doi.org/10.3201/eid1508.081237
11. World Health Organization. (2023). 2023 annual review of diseases prioritized under the Research and Development Blueprint. https://www.who.int/activities/prioritizing-diseases-for-research-and-development-in-emergency-contexts
12. Pulliam, J.R.C., Epstein, J.H., Dushoff, J. et al. (2012). Agricultural intensification, priming for persistence, and

the emergence of Nipah virus: A lethal bat-borne zoonosis. *J. R. Soc. Interface.* 9(66):89–101. https://doi.org/10.1098/rsif.2011.0223

13. Negrete, O.A., Levroney, E.L., Aguilar, H.C., Bertolotti-Ciarlet, A., Nazarian, R., Tajyar, S. and Lee, B. (2005). EphrinB2 is the entry receptor for Nipah virus, an emergent deadly paramyxovirus. *Nature.* 436(7049):401–405. https://doi.org/10.1038/nature03838
14. Chan, Y.P., Chua, K.B., Koh, C.L., Lim, M.E. and Lam, S.K. (2001). Complete nucleotide sequences of Nipah virus isolates from Malaysia. *J. Gen. Virol.* 82(9):2151–2155. https://doi.org/10.1099/0022-1317-82-9-2151
15. Ganguly, A., Mahapatra, S., Ray, S. et al. (2025). The rising threat of Nipah virus: a highly contagious and deadly zoonotic pathogen. *Virol. J.* 22:139. https://doi.org/10.1186/s12985-025-02728-4
16. Epstein, J.H., Field, H.E., Luby, S., Pulliam, J.R. and Daszak, P. (2006). Nipah virus: impact, origins, and causes of emergence. *Curr. Infect. Dis. Rep.* 8(1):59–65. https://doi.org/10.1007/s11908-006-0036-2
17. Halpin, K., Hyatt, A.D., Fogarty, R., Middleton, D., Bingham, J., Epstein, J.H. et al. (2011). Pteropid bats are confirmed as the reservoir hosts of henipaviruses: a comprehensive experimental study of virus transmission. *Am. J. Trop. Med. Hyg.* 85(5):946.
18. Chattu, V.K., Kumar, R., Kumary, S., Kajal, F. and David, J.K. (2018). Nipah virus epidemic in southern India and emphasizing "One Health" approach to ensure global health security. *J. Fam. Med. Prim. Care.* 7(2):275–283.
19. Looi, L.M. and Chua, K.B. (2007). Lessons from the Nipah virus outbreak in Malaysia. *Malays. J. Pathol.* 29(2): 63–67.
20. Luby, S.P. (2013). The pandemic potential of Nipah virus. *Antiviral Res.* 100(1):38–43. https://doi.org/10.1016/j.antiviral.2013.07.011
21. Nor, M., Gan, C.H. and Ong, B.L. (2000). Nipah virus infection of pigs in peninsular Malaysia. *Rev. Sci. Tech. Off. Int. Epiz.* 19(1):160–165.
22. Bonaparte, M.I., Dimitrov, A.S., Bossart, K.N., Crameri, G., Mungall, B.A., Bishop, K.A. and Broder, C.C. (2005). Ephrin-B2 ligand is a functional receptor for Hendra virus and Nipah virus. *Proc. Natl. Acad. Sci. U.S.A.* 102(30):10652–10657. https://doi.org/10.1073/pnas.0504887102
23. Aguilar, H.C., Matreyek, K.A., Filone, C.M., Hashimi, S.T., Levroney, E.L., Negrete, O.A., Bertolotti-Ciarlet, A., Choi, D.Y., McHardy, I., Fulcher, J.A., Su, S.V., Wolf, M.C., Kohatsu, L., Baum, L.G. and Lee, B. (2006). A novel receptor-induced activation site in the Nipah virus attachment glycoprotein (G) involved in triggering the fusion glycoprotein (F). *J. Virol.* 80(16):7906–7916. https://doi.org/10.1128/JVI.00762-06
24. Halpin, K., Bankamp, B., Harcourt, B.H., Bellini, W.J. and Rota, P.A. (2004). Nipah virus conforms to the rule of six in a minigenome replication assay. *J. Gen. Virol.* 85(3):701–707. https://doi.org/10.1099/vir.0.19685-0
25. Ciancanelli, M.J., Volchkova, V.A., Shaw, M.L., Volchkov, V.E. and Basler, C.F. (2009). Nipah virus sequesters inactive STAT1 in the nucleus via a P gene-encoded mechanism. *J. Virol.* 83(16):7828–7841. https://doi.org/10.1128/JVI.02610-08
26. Shaw, M.L., Cardenas, W.B., Zamarin, D., Palese, P. and Basler, C.F. (2004). Nuclear localization of the Nipah virus W protein allows for inhibition of both virus- and toll-like receptor 3-triggered signaling pathways. *J. Virol.* 78(22):12015–12021. https://doi.org/10.1128/JVI.79.10.6078-6088.2005
27. Singh, R.K., Dhama, K., Chakraborty, S., Tiwari, R., Natesan, S., Khandia, R. et al. (2019). Nipah virus: epidemiology, pathology, immunobiology and advances in diagnosis, vaccine designing and control strategies – a comprehensive review. *Vet. Q.* 39(1):26–55.
28. Bruno, L., Nappo, M.A., Ferrari, L., Di Lecce, R., Guarnieri, C., Cantoni, A.M. et al. (2022). Nipah virus disease: epidemiological, clinical, diagnostic and legislative aspects of this unpredictable emerging zoonosis. *Animals.* 13(1).
29. Rockx, B., Bossart, K.N., Feldmann, F., Geisbert, J.B., Hickey, A.C., Brining, D., Callison, J., Safronetz, D., Marzi, A., Kercher, L. et al. (2010). A novel model of lethal Hendra virus infection in African green monkeys and the effectiveness of ribavirin treatment. *J. Virol.* 84(19):9831–9839. https://doi.org/10.1128/JVI.01163-10
30. Escudero-Pérez, B., Lawrence, P. and Castillo-Olivares, J. (2023). Immune correlates of protection for SARS-CoV-2, Ebola and Nipah virus infection. *Front. Immunol.* 14.
31. Rathish, B. and Vaishnani, K. (2024). Nipah virus. StatPearls. Treasure Island (FL).
32. Giangaspero, M. (2013). Nipah virus. *Trop. Med. Surg.* 1:4. http://dx.doi.org/10.4172/2329-9088.1000129
33. Verma, A., Anand, A., Khatib, M.N., Zahiruddin, Q.S., Gaidhane, A.M., Kukreti, N. et al. (2024). Beyond neurology: unravelling Nipah virus's cardiovascular conundrum – an editorial. *Ann. Med. Surg. (Lond.)* 86(6):3204–3205.
34. Das, S., Sinha, D., Chatterji, S., Ganguly, A., De, A., Majgaonkar, A., Kazi, Z., Maurya, A. K., Sohail, M., & Bhat, N. (2025). The role of marine bacteria-derived bioactive compounds in COVID-19 management. In *Anti-coronavirus marine bioactive compounds* (Chapter 7, pp. 185–224). Apple Academic Press.
35. Ma, L., Chen, Z., Guan, W., Chen, Q. and Liu, D. (2019). Rapid and specific detection of all known Nipah virus strains' sequences with reverse transcription-loop-mediated isothermal amplification. *Front. Microbiol.* 10:418. https://doi.org/10.3389/fmicb.2019.00418
36. Pal, S., Mitra, P., Dey, S., Ganguly, A. and Mandal, A. (2024). Appraisal of ethno-veterinary practices used for different livestock ailments in rural and periurban areas of PurbaBardhaman, West Bengal, India. Ethnobot. Res. Appl., 27, 30. https://doi.org/10.32859/era.27.30.1-21
37. Sinha, D., Kazi, Z., Muherjee, R., Ganguly, A., Banerjee, S., Maurya, A.K., Chowdhury, A.A., Majgaonkar, A. and Dutta, S. (2024). Integrated molecular strategies for enhanced production of medicinal plant-derived flavonoids. In: *Biotechnology, Multiple Omics, and Precision Breeding in Medicinal Plants*. Springer Nature. https://doi.org/10.1201/9781003475491-23
38. Chattaraj, S., Behera, B. K., & Das Mohapatra, P. K. (2024). Effective valorization of Chlorella biomass and Brewers spent grain substituting fish meal and soybean meal in the diet of herbivorous fish *Cirrhinusreba* for higher growth,

digestibility and sustainable cultivation. Journal of Applied Phycology, 36(1), 217-232.

39. Chattaraj, S., Mitra, D., Chattaraj, A., Chattaraj, M., Kundu, M., Ganguly, A. and Das Mohapatra, P.K. (2023). Anti-oncogenic potential of probiotics: Challenges and future prospects. Indian J. Microbiol. Res., 10(1), 1–10. https://doi.org/10.18231/j.ijmr.2023.001
40. Ganguly, A., Kirtania, D. K., Chhetri, M., &Chattaraj, S. (2025). Sustainable development through probiotics: A scientometric analysis of Indian research and innovation. *Discover Sustainability, 6*, Article 455. https://doi.org/10.1007/s43621-025-01263-0
41. Aditi and Shariff, M. (2019). Nipah virus infection: a review. *Epidemiol. Infect.* 147:e95. https://doi.org/10.1017/S09502688190000
42. Dawes, B.E., Kalveram, B., Ikegami, T., Juelich, T., Smith, J.K., Zhang, L., Park, A., Lee, B., Komeno, T., Furuta, Y. and Freiberg, A.N. (2018). Favipiravir (T-705) protects against Nipah virus infection in the hamster model. *Sci. Rep.* 8:7604. https://doi.org/10.1038/s41598-018-25914-x
43. Singh, R.K., Dhama, K., Malik, Y.S., Ramakrishnan, M.A., Karthik, K., Khandia, R., Tiwari, R., Munjal, A., Saminathan, M., Sachan, S. et al. (2017). Ebola virus – epidemiology, diagnosis, and control: threat to humans, lessons learnt, and preparedness plans – an update on its 40 year's journey. *Vet. Q.* 37(1):98–135. https://doi.org/10.1080/01652176.2017.1309474

Research and Innovations in Industrial and Marine Biotechnology: A Circular Economy 2024 – Prof. Hrudayanath Thatoi et al. (eds)

52 Functional Evolution and Therapeutic Application of Superoxide Dismutase and Catalase: A Critical Review

Saptarshi Mukherjee
Department of Microbiology, Vidyasagar University, Midnapore, West Bengal, India

Mehak Kanwar
Centre for Industrial Biotechnology Research,
Siksha 'O' Anusandhan Deemed to be University, Kalinganagar, Odisha, India
Department of Physiology, Immunology Laboratory, University of Calcutta,
University Colleges of Science and Technology, 92 APC Road, Kolkata, West Bengal, India

Pradeep Kumar Das Mohapatra
Department of Microbiology, Raiganj University, Raiganj,
Uttar Dinajpur, West Bengal, India

Hrudayanath Thatoi, Amrita Banerjee*
Centre for Industrial Biotechnology Research,
Siksha 'O' Anusandhan Deemed to be University, Campus-2, Bhubaneswar, Odisha, India

Abstract: The cellular antioxidant defense system depends on superoxide dismutase (SOD) and catalase to counter oxidative stress caused by reactive oxygen species (ROS). SOD converts superoxide radicals into hydrogen peroxide, which catalase then decomposes into water and oxygen. They work together to preserve redox balance and defend cellular structures including lipids, proteins and DNA from oxidative destruction. These enzymes are vital across all forms of life—from cyanobacteria managing photosynthesis-derived ROS to humans mitigating oxidative stress. Their evolutionary development reflects adaptation to changing oxygen levels, resulting in functional specialization. In medicine and biotechnology, SOD and catalase serve as essential biomarkers, therapeutic agents, and drug development tools. Their extensive industrial applications further underscore their importance in mitigating ROS-induced cellular damage.

Keywords: SOD, CATALASE, ROS system, Enzyme

1. Introduction

The antioxidant defense system depends on superoxide dismutase (SOD) and catalase to maintain cellular homeostasis by reducing oxidative stress. The metabolic byproducts superoxide radicals and hydrogen peroxide function as reactive oxygen species (ROS) which cause damage to lipids proteins and DNA. SOD transforms superoxide radicals into hydrogen peroxide which catalase decomposes into water and oxygen to stop the formation of dangerous hydroxyl radicals.

The enzymes have developed across different life forms to operate under different oxygen concentrations starting from cyanobacteria protecting photosystems to humans controlling oxidative stress in mitochondria and peroxisomes. SOD and catalase enzymes in cell cultures protect viability by eliminating ROS produced by toxins and drugs. Their activity functions as a biomarker to

*Corresponding author: amritabanerjee@soa.ac.in

DOI: 10.1201/9781003759003-52

evaluate oxidative status and drug-induced cytotoxicity. The measurement of these enzymes helps determine appropriate drug dosages and monitor therapeutic outcomes thus making them crucial tools for biomedical research and drug development [1].

2. Function of Superoxide Dismutase (SOD)

Superoxide Dismutase (SOD) is an enzyme that is crucial in protecting cells from oxidative stress by converting superoxide radicals (O_2^{-}•) into hydrogen peroxide (H_2O_2) and molecular oxygen (O_2) [2]. By neutralizing these highly reactive metabolic byproducts, SOD prevents oxidative damage to lipids, proteins, and nucleic acids, thereby maintaining redox homeostasis.

2.1 Mechanism of Action

SOD functions as the first line of defense against reactive oxygen species (ROS) [3]. It facilitates the conversion of superoxide radicals into H_2O_2, which is further detoxified by catalase or glutathione peroxidase. This two-step mechanism limits ROS accumulation and protects cellular structures (Fig. 52.1.).

2.2 Isoforms and Localization

SOD exists in three isoforms:

- SOD1 (Cu/Zn-SOD): Cytoplasmic and nuclear localization [4].
- SOD2 (Mn-SOD): Mitochondrial matrix, where ROS are generated during respiration.
- SOD3 (EC-SOD): Extracellular compartments, protecting tissues from circulating ROS.

2.3 Physiological and Pathophysiological Roles

Beyond antioxidant defense, SOD regulates redox signaling, inflammation, cell proliferation, and apoptosis. Dysregulation of SOD activity is implicated in numerous diseases. Mutations in SOD1 are causative in amyotrophic lateral sclerosis (ALS), while altered expression influences tumor progression, cardiovascular disease, and neurodegeneration.

2.4 Applications in Research and Medicine

SOD serves as a key biomarker for oxidative stress and is used to monitor cellular responses to drugs and disease states. Therapeutic strategies enhancing SOD activity are under investigation for conditions such as ischemia-reperfusion injury, inflammation, and age-related disorders. Its role in maintaining oxidative balance makes SOD indispensable for cellular function and disease prevention.

3. Function of Catalase

Catalase serves as an essential antioxidant enzyme [5] which decomposes hydrogen peroxide (H_2O_2) into water and oxygen to protect cells from oxidative damage. Catalase acts as an enzyme which decomposes H_2O_2 to prevent the dangerous accumulation of highly toxic hydroxyl radicals and thus protects both redox stability and cell structure.

3.1 Mechanism of Action

The enzyme catalase displays outstanding catalytic speed because it breaks down thousands of H_2O_2 molecules per second without any need for external cofactors. The

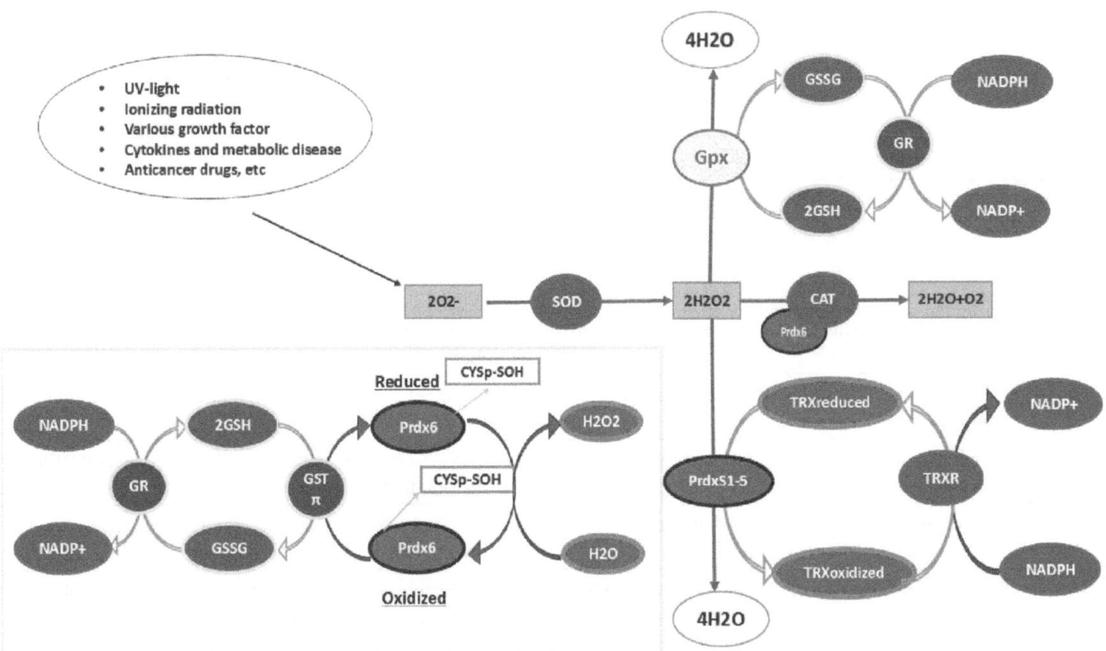

Fig. 52.1 Function of SOD in release of oxidative stress

heme prosthetic group functions as a crucial element for redox catalysis [6]. The primary defense enzyme catalase operates to detoxify both naturally occurring and externally introduced H_2O_2 thus reducing oxidative stress in its production areas.

3.2 Localization and Isoforms

Catalase exists mainly in peroxisomes to detoxify H_2O_2 produced during fatty acid β-oxidation and xenobiotic metabolism. Some organisms and tissues express catalase in their cytoplasm and mitochondria to provide localized ROS regulation.

3.3 Physiological Roles

The roles played by catalase are listed below.

- Hydrogen Peroxide Detoxification: Prevents oxidative injury by eliminating H_2O_2.
- Peroxisomal Homeostasis: Supports lipid metabolism and detoxification of metabolic intermediates.
- Redox Regulation: Acts in concert with glutathione peroxidase and other antioxidants to maintain ROS equilibrium [7].
- Aging and Longevity: Higher catalase activity is associated with decreased oxidative damage and delayed cellular aging.

3.4 Pathophysiological Implications

The lack of proper catalase function leads to multiple disease states:

- Acatalasia: A rare genetic disorder marked by the absence of catalase activity, resulting in H_2O_2 accumulation.
- Neurodegenerative and Cardiovascular Diseases: Inadequate detoxification of H_2O_2 exacerbates oxidative stress in conditions such as Alzheimer's, Parkinson's, and atherosclerosis [8].
- Diabetes Mellitus: The activity of catalase is reduced in diabetic patients which leads to increased oxidative stress and tissue damage.

3.5 Applications in Research and Medicine

Catalase functions as a biomarker to measure oxidative stress levels in medical diagnostics and research investigations. Exogenous catalase treatment is used in cell cultures to protect against ROS-induced damage. Medical researchers study catalase as a potential therapeutic agent to treat diseases connected to ROS such as ischemia-reperfusion injury and chronic inflammation and aging. The enzyme activity functions as an analytical tool for monitoring drug doses and evaluating cytotoxic effects in addition to screening processes.

The enzyme catalase continues to be essential for cellular defense while maintaining its central position in biomedical research and therapeutic development .

4. Evolutionary Dynamics of SOD and Catalase

Early Earth history saw the simultaneous development of superoxide dismutase (SOD) and catalase enzymes because atmospheric oxygen levels increased while oxidative stress became the primary force of natural selection [9]. The enzymes developed as essential antioxidant defense components through natural selection processes and environmental ROS pressures while life evolved in complexity (Table 52.1.) [10].

4.1 Superoxide Dismutase (SOD)

Genetic Adaptations

SOD genes show strong conservation across all domains of life while they adapt to specific cellular needs. Different species have adapted their metal cofactor usage (Cu, Zn, Mn, Fe) based on their environmental redox states and

Table 52.1 Functional evolution of SOD and catalase

Organism Type	SOD Evolution	Catalase Evolution
Bacteria	Primitive Fe-SOD and Mn-SOD neutralize superoxide radicals ($2O_2^- + 2H^+ \rightarrow H_2O_2 + O_2$)	Basic catalase activity protects against hydrogen peroxide ($2H_2O_2 \rightarrow 2H_2O + O_2$) generated during metabolism.
	Essential for survival in oxygenated environments.	Vital for defence against oxidative stress and immune responses like phagocytosis.
Fungi	Emergence of Cu/Zn-SOD in cytosol alongside Mn-SOD in mitochondria.	Enhanced catalase activity for oxidative stress during filamentous growth and metabolic shifts.
Plants	Diversification into Cu/Zn-SOD (cytosol), Mn-SOD (mitochondria), Fe- SOD (chloroplasts).	Catalase localizes to peroxisomes for ROS detoxification in photorespiration and fatty acid metabolism.
Invertebrates	Cu/Zn-SOD protects cytosolic compartments, Mn-SOD safeguards mitochondria.	Catalase regulates ROS during immune responses, such as oxidative bursts in phagocytosis.
Humans	Specialized isoforms: Cu/Zn-SOD (cytosol), Mn-SOD (mitochondria), EC- SOD (extracellular).	Highly efficient peroxisomal catalase works with glutathione peroxidase to maintain ROS balance.
	Plays key roles in disease prevention, including neurodegeneration and cancer protection.	Mutations linked to conditions like acatalasemia highlight its critical function in oxidative stress defence.

their metabolic requirements as well as the available oxygen levels.

Molecular Evolution

Research on genomic comparisons shows how SOD isoforms from plants, animals, fungi and bacteria develop both similar and dissimilar evolutionary traits [11]. SOD types have evolved separately to perform best in the cytosol and mitochondria and extracellular space.

4.2 Catalase

Genetic Evolution

Catalase genes display major genetic differences between different species. The evolution of different isoforms of catalase resulted in their localization throughout peroxisomes, mitochondria and cytoplasm to detoxify hydrogen peroxide within different cellular areas. Most organisms possess multiple catalase isoforms to perform specialized oxidative stress responses.

Evolutionary Adaptations

Catalase developed in aerobic environments to decompose hydrogen peroxide while it works in conjunction with SOD. The existence of catalase-peroxidases in specific prokaryotic organisms shows how these organisms developed specialized ROS detoxification capabilities for survival in particular ecological settings .

4.3 Coevolution and Functional Integration

Complementary Functions

The enzyme SOD generates hydrogen peroxide from superoxide radicals which catalase subsequently breaks down into water and oxygen. The coordinated functions represent how the antioxidant defense system evolved as a unified system.

Complexity in Multicellular Organisms

Higher organisms use SOD and catalase to build complex redox regulatory systems which include peroxiredoxins, glutathione peroxidases and the NRF2 pathway as their oxidative stress responses evolve [12].

Convergent Evolution

Plants and animals developed equally efficient SOD and catalase systems through independent evolutionary processes to address their common oxidative stress problems.

4.4 Natural Selection and Molecular Adaptation

Adaptive Evolution

The enzymes remain under strong purifying and positive selection to protect their efficiency while their protective function becomes enhanced. Mutations which affect the enzyme's catalytic function or metal binding properties demonstrate adaptive mechanisms.

Gene Duplication and Divergence

The process of gene duplication led to the creation of isoforms which perform specialized functions across various cell regions and tissues for precise ROS regulation.

Adaptation to Extreme Environments

Extremophiles developed special SOD and catalase variants which gained thermostability in thermophiles and halotolerance in marine species to survive in harsh oxidative conditions.

5. Functional Evolution of Superoxide Dismutase (SOD) and Catalase Across Organisms

The roles of superoxide dismutase (SOD) and catalase have been conserved and specialized throughout evolution, from cyanobacteria to humans, reflecting increasing organismal complexity and adaptation to oxidative stress.

5.1 Cyanobacteria

Cyanobacteria as early oxygenic photosynthetic organisms played a major role in oxygenating the atmosphere. SOD converts superoxide radicals, generated during photosynthesis, into hydrogen peroxide, which catalase further decomposes into water and oxygen. The enzymatic system protects cellular components from oxidative damage and reduces photodamage under high oxygen and light conditions.

5.2 Algae and Plants

SOD and catalase in algae and higher plants operate in chloroplasts, mitochondria, and peroxisomes to handle reactive oxygen species (ROS) produced by photosynthesis, photorespiration, and respiration. SOD removes superoxide radicals produced by the chloroplast electron transport chain and catalase breaks down hydrogen peroxide in peroxisomes during photorespiration to protect energy metabolism and photosynthetic efficiency.

5.3 Invertebrates

SOD and catalase in invertebrates work to eliminate ROS produced by aerobic metabolism and environmental stress to maintain cellular homeostasis and oxidative resilience.

5.4 Vertebrates

The three SOD isoforms in vertebrates including humans are located in different compartments: Mn-SOD in mitochondria, Cu/Zn-SOD in the cytoplasm, and EC-SOD in extracellular spaces. The enzyme catalase located in peroxisomes breaks down hydrogen peroxide that results from metabolic processes. These enzymes work together to protect against ROS-related diseases including cancer and neurodegeneration and cardiovascular disorders while enabling redox signalling and inflammation control and cellular longevity [13].

6. Application of SOD and Catalase in Cell Culture and Others

Superoxide dismutase (SOD) along with catalase exhibit strong antioxidant properties which make them vital components in cell culture systems and clinical applications and biotechnology and industrial processes.

6.1 In Cell Culture

Protection Against Oxidative Stress

The cells benefit from protection against oxidative damage when SOD and catalase eliminate reactive oxygen species (ROS) that originate from metabolic processes as well as external factors like UV radiation and xenobiotics.

Enhanced Cell Viability

These enzymes support cell survival and proliferation while enhancing functionality of ROS-sensitive cells such as neurons and hepatocytes and stem cells.

Redox Stability in Media

These enzymes preserve experimental reproducibility and cellular integrity by preventing ROS accumulation in culture media.

6.2 In Medicine

Therapeutic Applications

SOD serves as an investigated therapeutic agent for treating conditions linked to oxidative stress including inflammation and ischemia-reperfusion injury as well as neurodegenerative disorders such as amyotrophic lateral sclerosis (ALS).

Researchers study catalase-based therapies to address diabetic wound healing as well as radiation-induced damage and oxidative tissue injuries [14].

Dermatological and Cosmetic Uses

The skincare and cosmetic industry utilizes SOD and catalase to combat UV radiation and environmental pollutant-induced oxidative damage which helps create anti-aging effects and dermal repair.

6.3 In the Food and Beverage Industry

Preservation and Quality Control

The food industry uses SOD and catalase enzymes in packaging materials and formulations to protect products from oxidative spoilage which lengthens shelf life and preserves nutritional value and sensory quality.

Protection Against Oxidative Degradation

These enzymes protect food products by preventing color changes and degradation of oils and juices and dairy products.

6.4 In Biotechnology and Industrial Applications

Bioremediation

Industrial effluent detoxification uses SOD and catalase enzymes to neutralize superoxide and hydrogen peroxide which decreases oxidative toxicity in wastewater.

Biofuel Production

The production of bioethanol and biodiesel employs catalase enzymes to remove hydrogen peroxide which forms during fermentation processes.

Enzyme Stabilization

The enzymes enhance both the oxidative stability and shelf life of industrial bioprocess enzyme formulations.

6.5 In Research

SOD and catalase serve as essential research tools for studying redox biology and oxidative damage together with ROS-mediated signalling pathways.

The enzymes serve dual functions in antioxidant screening tests as well as therapeutic development processes that target ROS-associated diseases.

7. Effect of Drugs on Cell Cultures: Evaluation using SOD and Catalase

The evaluation of drug effects on cell cultures requires monitoring superoxide dismutase (SOD) and catalase activities because these enzymes function as primary antioxidants that neutralize reactive oxygen species (ROS). The disruption of redox homeostasis through drug-induced oxidative stress leads cells to express SOD and catalase as biomarkers which indicate oxidative responses and potential cytotoxicity.

7.1 Effect of Drugs on SOD and Catalase

1. **Induction of Oxidative Stress:** The intracellular ROS levels increase when cells are exposed to chemotherapeutic agents doxorubicin and cisplatin as well as environmental toxins which results in oxidative stress. Cells respond to oxidative stress by increasing their production of SOD and catalase enzymes to neutralize superoxide radicals and hydrogen peroxide [15].
2. **Suppression of Antioxidant Defences:** impairment of endogenous antioxidant systems by certain drugs results in reduced SOD and catalase activity levels. The decrease in redox regulation indicates cells become more susceptible to oxidative damage.
3. **Transcriptional Regulation:** The expression of antioxidant enzymes changes through drug treatment because drugs modify both SOD and catalase mRNA and protein production levels. The transcriptional and post-transcriptional modifications indicate how

specific drugs affect oxidative stress pathways and cellular adaptation mechanisms.

7.2 Measurement Techniques

Enzyme Activity Assays

SOD Activity: Measured using colorimetric or spectrophotometric assays, such as the inhibition of nitro blue tetrazolium (NBT) reduction or WST-1 assays, which quantify superoxide scavenging activity [16].

Catalase Activity: Assessed by monitoring the decomposition of hydrogen peroxide, typically using spectrophotometry or the ammonium molybdate method.

Gene and Protein Expression Analysis

qPCR: Quantifies mRNA levels of SOD and catalase to evaluate transcriptional changes induced by drugs.

Western Blotting/ELISA: Measures protein levels of SOD and catalase to determine post-transcriptional effects.

Oxidative Stress Markers

Drug effects are indirectly assessed by measuring ROS levels or oxidative damage biomarkers (e.g., malondialdehyde or 8-oxo-dG) alongside SOD and catalase activities [17].

Cell Viability Correlation

The activities of SOD and catalase are often correlated with cell viability assays (e.g., MTT, LDH release) to determine if oxidative stress contributes to cytotoxic effects.

8. Dose Ditermination of Drugs using SOD and Catalase

Dose determination using SOD and catalase assesses drug-induced oxidative stress . Many drugs, like doxorubicin and cisplatin, generate ROS, affecting SOD and catalase activity. Measuring these enzyme levels at different drug doses identifies concentrations inducing manageable oxidative stress without overwhelming cellular defences. For example, doxorubicin increases SOD at sub-lethal doses, while excessive doses reduce activity. Cisplatin also shows dose-dependent effects. These assays, combined with cytotoxicity measurements, refine therapeutic doses to balance efficacy and safety.

9. Conclusion

Superoxide dismutase (SOD) and catalase are crucial for cellular antioxidant defence, mitigating oxidative stress from reactive oxygen species. Their mechanistic functions and evolution highlight their vital roles across life forms. These enzymes have vast biomedical and industrial applications, from disease management to drug development, enhancing health and combating oxidative damage.

References

1. Apel, K., & Hirt, H. (2004). Reactive oxygen species: metabolism, oxidative stress, and signal transduction. *Annu. Rev. Plant Biol.*, *55*(1), 373–399.
2. Fridovich, I. (1981). Superoxide radical and superoxide dismutases. *Oxygen and Living Processes: An Interdisciplinary Approach*, 250–272.
3. Imlay, J. A. (2003). Pathways of oxidative damage. *Annual Reviews in Microbiology*, *57*(1), 395–418.
4. Fukai, T., & Ushio-Fukai, M. (2011). Superoxide dismutases: role in redox signaling, vascular function, and diseases. *Antioxidants & redox signaling*, *15*(6), 1583–1606.
5. Chelikani, P., Fita, I., & Loewen, P. C. (2004). Diversity of structures and properties among catalases. *Cellular and Molecular Life Sciences CMLS*, *61*, 192–208.
6. Carrasco, S., & Mérida, I. (2007). Diacylglycerol, when simplicity becomes complex. *Trends in biochemical sciences*, *32*(1), 27–36.
7. Lubos, E., Loscalzo, J., & Handy, D. E. (2011). Glutathione peroxidase-1 in health and disease: from molecular mechanisms to therapeutic opportunities. *Antioxidants & redox signaling*, *15*(7).
8. Jomova, K., & Valko, M. (2011). Advances in metal-induced oxidative stress and human disease. *Toxicology*, *283*(2-3), 65–87.
9. Lushchak, V. I. (2011). Adaptive response to oxidative stress: Bacteria, fungi, plants and animals. *Comparative Biochemistry and Physiology Part C: Toxicology & Pharmacology*, *153*(2), 175–190.
10. Pigeolet, E., Corbisier, P., Houbion, A., Lambert, D., Michiels, C., Raes, M., ... & Remacle, J. (1990). Glutathione peroxidase, superoxide dismutase, and catalase inactivation by peroxides and oxygen derived free radicals. *Mechanisms of ageing and development*, *51*(3), 283–297.
11. Radi, R. (2018). Oxygen radicals, nitric oxide, and peroxynitrite: Redox pathways in molecular medicine. *Proceedings of the National Academy of Sciences*, *115*(23), 5839–5848.
12. Yang, J. C., Lu, M. C., Lee, C. L., Chen, G. Y., Lin, Y. Y., Chang, F. R., & Wu, Y. C. (2011). Selective targeting of breast cancer cells through ROS-mediated mechanisms potentiates the lethality of paclitaxel by a novel diterpene, gelomulide K. *Free Radical Biology and Medicine*, *51*(3), 641–657.
13. Valko, M., Leibfritz, D., Moncol, J., Cronin, M. T., Mazur, M., & Telser, J. (2007). Free radicals and antioxidants in normal physiological functions and human disease. *The international journal of biochemistry & cell biology*, *39*(1), 44–84.
14. Anwar, S., Alrumaihi, F., Sarwar, T., Babiker, A. Y., Khan, A. A., Prabhu, S. V., & Rahmani, A. H. (2024). Exploring therapeutic potential of catalase: Strategies in disease prevention and management. *Biomolecules*, *14*(6), 697.
15. Contestabile A. (2001). Oxidative stress in neurodegeneration: mechanisms and therapeutic perspectives. *Current topics in medicinal chemistry*, *1*(6), 553–568. https://doi.org/10.2174/1568026013394723
16. Weydert, C. J., & Cullen, J. J. (2010). Measurement of superoxide dismutase, catalase and glutathione peroxidase in cultured cells and tissue. *Nature protocols*, *5*(1), 51–66.
17. Park, S. Y., Yun, Y. H., Park, B. J., Seo, H. I., & Chung, I. (2021). Fabrication and biological activities of plasmid DNA gene carrier nanoparticles based on biodegradable L-tyrosine polyurethane. *Pharmaceuticals*, *15*(1), 17.

Note: The figures and the tables in this chapter were made by the authors.

Research and Innovations in Industrial and Marine Biotechnology: A Circular Economy 2024 – Prof. Hrudayanath Thatoi et al. (eds)

53 Baseline Assessment of Oral Polymorphonuclear Neutrophils in Healthy and Compared it with Periodontitis, and Oral Cancer Cases: A Cross-Sectional Study

Sudhansubala Lenka
Department of Medical Research,
IMS and SUM Hospital, Siksha 'O' Anusandhan (deemed to be) University,
Bhubaneswar, Odisha, India

Rajeshkumar Bhola
Department of Pathology, IMS and SUM Hospital,
Siksha 'O' Anusandhan (deemed to be) University,
Bhubaneswar, Odisha, India

Sanat Kumar Bhuyan
Department of Oral Medicine and Radiology,
Institute of Dental Science, Siksha 'O' Anusandhan (deemed to be) University,
Bhubaneswar, Odisha, India

Nihar Ranjan Panda
Department of Medical Research,
IMS and SUM Hospital, Siksha 'O' Anusandhan (deemed to be) University,
Bhubaneswar, Odisha, India

Ruchi Bhuyan*
Department of Oral Pathology and Microbiology,
Institute of Dental Science, Siksha 'O' Anusandhan (deemed to be) University,
Bhubaneswar, Odisha, India

Abstract: Oral polymorphonuclear neutrophils (oPMNs) are abundant white blood cells in the oral cavity; however, their role in oral squamous cell carcinoma is not well understood. This study aimed to quantify oPMNs and establish its load across health conditions, including oral cancer. Ninety individuals were enrolled and allocated equally into three groups: healthy controls, periodontitis, and oral cancer (30 participants each). Flow cytometry was used to analyze stained samples and determine oral neutrophil percentages. Results showed significant differences in oPMN levels among the groups, with oral cancer patients exhibiting the lowest mean percentage compared to those with periodontitis and healthy controls. Collectively, these findings suggest that oPMN levels could be employed as a non-invasive biomarker for OSCC prognosis and aid in assessing the severity of oral inflammatory diseases.

Keywords: Oral neutrophil, Oral cancer, Periodontitis, Saliva

*Corresponding author: ruchibhuyan@soa.ac.in

DOI: 10.1201/9781003759003-53

1. Introduction

Circulating PMNs are the most abundant kind of WBC, which constitutes about 50-70% of total WBC. It is the primary innate immune cell that forms the body's initial protective barrier against infection [1]. On the same line, oral neutrophils in the oral cavity maintain oral health equilibrium. Interestingly, every minute, about 30,000 PMNs are thought to pass through periodontal tissues [2]. Periodontitis is characterized as a prolonged inflammatory condition targeting the tissues surrounding and supporting the teeth and is linked to alterations in the oral microbiota [3] and immune response, including changes in oPMN levels [4]. According to a previous study, it is established that the increased periodontal inflamed surface area correlates with elevated oPMN levels in periodontitis [4]. Additionally, periodontitis is linked with various systemic diseases like cancer. Furthermore, it was obtained from a study that the oral neutrophil number remains constant in the follow-up patients [5]. So, we speculate that a change in oPMN number from its normal range in the oral cavity could be a diagnostic factor. Furthermore, the oral neutrophil load has been found to positively correlate with the severity of periodontal disease, as indicated by increased pocket depth and higher gingival index scores [6]. Since periodontitis is connected to various systemic diseases, including oral cancer [7], understanding the differences in oral neutrophil load between periodontitis and oral cancer is crucial. Thus, this study aims to establish a baseline comparison between healthy controls, individuals with periodontitis, and those with oral cancer. This is our initial effort to explore these differences.

Our objective is to find out any possible correlations between oPMNs levels and oral health status, as well as the potential use of oPMNs as prognostic indicators in the case of oral cancer, by quantifying and comparing their levels among different groups. This may help in the early diagnosis and treatment of oral inflammatory illnesses as well as the development of innovative diagnostic and treatment approaches for oral cancer.

2. Materials and Methods

This cross-sectional study was approved by the Institutional Ethics Committee of IMS and SUM Hospital (IEC/IMS.SH/SOA/2023/486; 17 Feb 2023) and conducted in accordance with the Declaration of Helsinki. Prior to enrollment, each participant was fully briefed on the study objectives and provided written informed consent.

2.1 Study Participants

A total of 90 participants were recruited from May 2023 until April 2024 at IMS and Sum Hospital and IDS. These 90 participants were divided into three groups: healthy controls, periodontitis, and oral cancer cases, each comprising 30 participants.

Healthy Controls

Healthy controls were selected from individuals visiting the hospital for routine health assessments. Specifically, individuals with a healthy oral health profile, characterized by a greater number of natural teeth and an absence of orthodontic braces, were selected. Their oral cavities underwent thorough examination by experienced dentists. Only participants who gave informed and willing consent were enrolled in the study.

Periodontitis

At the Institute of Dental Sciences, patients with untreated periodontitis underwent a selection process guided by several clinical markers. This included the identification of radiographic evidence indicating bone loss and the observation of plaque accumulation, assessed by experienced dentists. By utilizing this approach, individuals with untreated periodontitis were accurately identified.

OSCC

Patients diagnosed with OSCC were included. Patients with other systemic diseases were excluded from the study.

Oral Rinse Assay

Participants rinsed the oral cavity using 10 ml of 0.9% saline solution [4] and waited 30 minutes. After 30 minutes, 10 ml of the sample was again given to the patients to rinse the mouth, and the oral rinse specimens were collected in 50 ml sterile tubes. The same procedure was repeated three times with an interval of 3 to 4 minutes, and at the end, 30 ml of the sample was collected. The collected 30 ml sample was evenly distributed into two 15 ml centrifuge tubes. One of these tubes was promptly stored at -80°C to facilitate further analysis. Simultaneously, the second tube underwent centrifugation at 500 revolutions per minute (RFC) for a duration of 5 minutes at room temperature. Following centrifugation and washed in PBS. oPMNs were incubated with CD45 and CD15 stains for 30 minutes in the dark, after which flow cytometric acquisition and analysis were performed using a FACS-Calibur flow cytometer (BD Biosciences, USA) and CytExpert software (Beckman Coulter, version 2.0.1).

Figure 53.1 presents a schematic representation of the gating strategy. The live population of oPMNs was identified using forward scatter (FSC) and sideward scatter (SSC), which correspond to the distribution of cells according to size and intracellular composition, respectively.

2.2 Statistical Analysis

All statistical analyses were carried out with SPSS version 28. The results for continuous parameters are reported as mean values with standard deviations, while categorical parameters are given as numbers and percentages. To

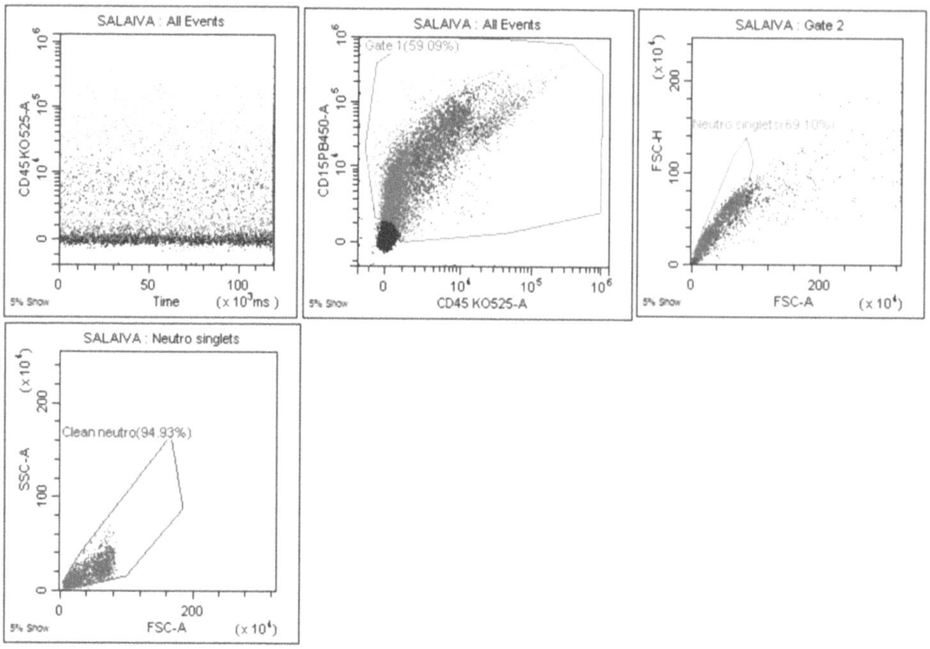

Fig. 53.1 Parental population of oPMN

compare groups, one-way ANOVA was employed, followed by Tukey's test for pairwise comparisons. Box plots and histograms were generated to illustrate the distribution of oPMNs across the study groups (Fig. 53.2).

3. Results

Gender distribution differed significantly among the groups ($p = 0.01$), indicating that gender was unevenly distributed across the different disease statuses. Additionally, age did not differ significantly between the study groups ($p = 0.431$).

Table 53.1

	Gender			
Disease status	**F**	**M**	**Total**	**P**
Cancer	5(14.7)	25(44.6)	30(33.3)	0.01
Control	16(47.1)	14(25)	30(33.3)	
Periodontitis	13(38.2)	17(30.2)	30(33.3)	
Age	46.2 ± 16.9	48.7 ± 12.4	47.7 ± 14.2	0.431

To assess which group had the highest population of oPMNs, the mean percentages across the group which had the highest population were assessed, and found that participants in the periodontitis group exhibited the highest mean oPMN percentage. A statistically significant difference was observed ($p < 0.001$), highlighting a clear variation in oPMN levels across the three groups.

To identify which two groups differed significantly, we conducted pair-wise comparisons of the mean differences in oPMN percentages among the cancer, control, and periodontitis groups. The cancer group, compared to the control group, exhibited a statistically significant mean difference of -3.56 ($t(87) = -3.21$, $p = 0.005$). Similarly, the difference between the cancer and periodontitis groups was even greater, with a mean difference of -4.84, which was highly significant ($t(87) = -4.36$, $p < 0.001$). However, the comparison between the control and periodontitis groups did not yield a statistically significant difference, with a mean difference of –1.28 ($t(87) = -1.15$, $p = 0.486$).

Table 53.2 Mean percentage of oPMN population

	Disease status	N	Mean	p
oPMN %parent	Cancer	30	92.6 ± 6.73	
	Control	30	96.1 ± 2.43	
	Periodontitis	30	97.4 ± 2.11	<0.001

Table 53.3 Pairwise comparisons of the mean differences in oPMN percentages

Disease status	Disease status	Mean Difference	df	t	p_{tukey}
Cancer	Control	-3.56	87	-3.21	**0.005**
	Periodontitis	-4.84	87	-4.36	**<.001**
Control	Periodontitis	-1.28	87	-1.15	0.486

3.1 Effects of Habits on oPMN Population

To assess the impact of various habits on oPMN%, we analyzed the duration of these habits among patients and calculated the mean oPMN percentage for each habit. The habits studied included betel leaf (pan) consumption, gutkha, khaini, smoking, and alcohol use. We found that, participants who did not consume pan, gutkhaand alcohol had a significantly higher mean oPMN percentage compared to those who consumed. For khaini use, there was no significant difference in oPMN percentage between non-users (95.4 ± 4.68) and users (94.6 ± 6.49). Likewise, smoking did not significantly affect oPMN levels; non-smokers had a mean oPMN percentage of 95.4 ± 4.84 and smokers had 94.6 ± 3.26 ($p = 0.643$) (Table 53.4).

Table 53.4 Impact of various habits on oPMN

	Habbit	Group	N	Mean ± SD	P Value
oPMN %parent	Pan	No	56	96.7 ± 2.43	
		Yes	34	93.1 ± 6.5	<0.001
oPMN %parent	Gutkha	No	76	96.2 ± 3.53	
		Yes	14	90.8 ± 7.41	<0.001
oPMN %parent	Khaini	No	86	95.4 ± 4.68	
		Yes	4	94.6 ± 6.49	0.731
oPMN %parent	Smoking	No	83	95.4 ± 4.84	
		Yes	7	94.6 ± 3.26	0.643
oPMN %parent	Alcohol	No	76	96.1 ± 3.61	
		Yes	14	91.1 ± 7.41	<0.001

Figure 53.2 illustrates the distribution of oPMN% among the three disease status groups: cancer, control, and periodontitis. The box plot shows the interquartile range (25%–75%) for each group, with the median represented by the bold line and the mean by the small square within each box. The whiskers represent within 1.5 times the IQR range, and outliers are depicted as diamonds. The Cancer group exhibits the lowest oPMN%, with a median of approximately 93 and a wider distribution, including outliers as low as 75. The control group shows a higher median oPMN% of around 96, with a narrower range compared to the cancer group. The periodontitis group has a median similar to the control group, around 97, with a comparable range. Statistical comparisons between the groups indicate significant differences.

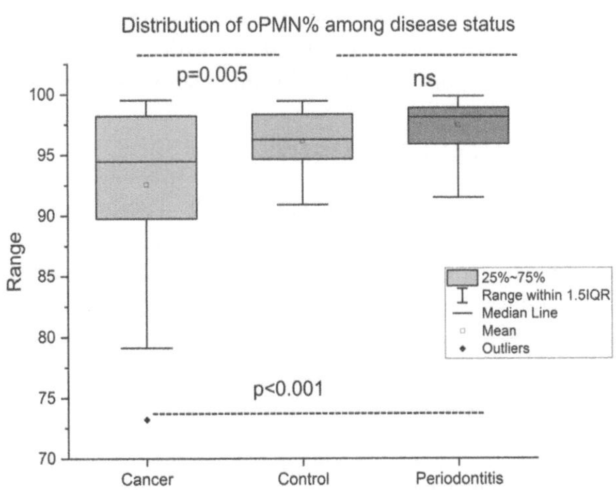

Fig. 53.2 Distribution of oPMN% among disease status

The green line represents the ROC curve, while the red dot marks the optimal cut-off point, determined using

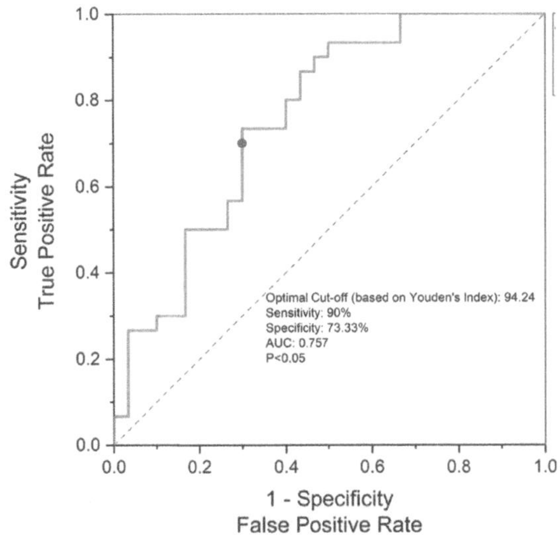

Fig. 53.3 Displays ROC curve for the oPMN%

Youden's Index. The optimal cut-off for oPMN% was identified at 94.24, which provides a sensitivity of 90% and a specificity of 73.33%. The AUC is 0.757, indicating a fair level of diagnostic accuracy. The AUC is statistically significant ($p < 0.05$), suggesting that oPMN% has a meaningful ability to distinguish between the groups under study.

3.2 Correlation of Duration of Habits with oPMN%

There is a negative correlation between the duration of habits and oPMN%. This suggests that as the increase in duration of habits decreases the percentage of oPMN%

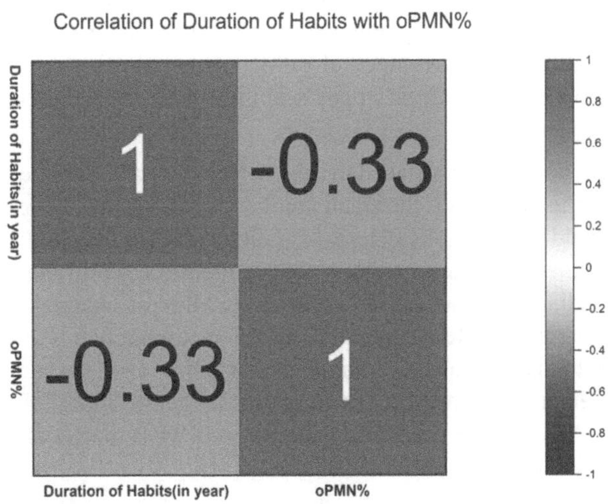

Fig. 53.4 The correlation between the duration of habits and oPMN%

4. Discussion

oPMNs act as important first-line defenders within the oral cavity. However, their functional capabilities may become limited or depleted in the presence of conditions such as cancer and periodontitis. Our study revealed that oral cancer patients exhibited a markedly reduced oPMN load compared to those with periodontitis and healthy controls. Moreover,

Previous research has shown that the quantity of oral neutrophils increases with the severity of periodontitis [4]. One study reported that oral neutrophil levels are 4.5 times higher in periodontitis cases than in healthy controls [8]. They also mentioned that the oPMN number is associated with inflamed areas of periodontitis. Parallel to these findings, in our study, we found that in the periodontitis case, the PMN% is increased than the control group. However, yet oPMN% was not established in oral cancer cases. In contrast, our findings indicate that the percentage of oPMNs is highest in periodontitis cases, surpassing both oral cancer and control groups. The lower oPMN% in cancer patients suggests its potential utility in monitoring disease progression, early diagnosis, and intervention in oral cancer, as well as in other inflammatory oral diseases. Furthermore, our analysis showed that individuals with longer durations of habitual use, such as betel leaf, khaini, gutka, and alcohol, tended to have lower oPMN percentages, while those who did not engage in these habits exhibited higher mean oPMN levels. Combined, these results indicate that both individuals with long-term habits and oral cancer patients tend to have lower oPMN levels. In the same line, another study [9] revealed that oPMN load is lower in smokers than in non-smokers. According to a study by [10] (2020), neutrophils in patients who consume excessive alcohol become less reactive and less effective in responding to inflammatory signals and infections. Thus, these findings suggest that prolonged engagement in such harmful habits may lead to decreased reactivity and activity of neutrophils, resulting in a reduced percentage of oPMN. This reduction could ultimately impair the body's ability to manage disease dependence.

Certain limitations need to be considered. A key limitation of this research is the small number of participants, which could influence the external validity of the results. Future studies with larger cohorts are required to confirm these findings and assess the role of oPMNs as diagnostic markers in different populations. Another limitation is that potential confounding variables, including disease stage, were not considered. These variables could impact the oPMN and the functional capacity of oPMNs, potentially affecting the study's outcomes.

Despite these limitations, the study lays the groundwork for future research and highlights the potential of oral neutrophils as a biomarker in oral disease diagnostics and monitoring.

5. Conclusion

The oral neutrophil percentage in oral cancer patients is lower compared to control and periodontitis cases. Thus, assessing oral neutrophil load could become a valuable method for monitoring the progression of oral cancer. Furthermore, these findings could assist oncologists and dentists in screening for oral infections and assessing the stage of oral cancer in the future. However, this percentage needs to be evaluated in larger populations and across different stages of oral cancer to validate its clinical significance.

6. Abbreviations

OSCC- Oral squamous cell carcinoma

oPMNs- Oral polymorphonuclear neutrophils

ROC- Receiver operating characteristic

AUC- Area under the curve

IQR- Interquartile range

7. Compliance with Ethical Standards

Conflict of Interest: The authors declare that they have no conflict of interest

Informed consent: All participants provided written informed consent before their inclusion in the study.

Funding information: None

Ethical approval: The investigation was performed in line with the Declaration of Helsinki, and ethical permission was obtained from the Institutional Ethics Committee, IMS and SUM Hospital (Approval No: IEC/IMS.SH/SOA/2023/486; 17/02/2023).

Consent for publication: Not applicable

8. Authors' Contributions

RB, RKB, and SKB designed the research. SL did the experiment and drafted the manuscript. NRP analyzed the data. Revisions were carried out with input from all authors, and approved the final version before submission.

Acknowledgment

We express our sincere thanks to Mr. Pabitra Mohan Mohanty for supporting our lab work. The authors wish to express their gratitude to the President of Siksha 'O' Anusandhan (Deemed to be University), India, for supporting this study by providing the necessary facilities.

References

1. Rosales, C. (2020). Neutrophils at the crossroads of innate and adaptive immunity. *Journal of Leucocyte Biology, 108*(1), 377–396.
2. Moonen, C. G., Hirschfeld, J., Cheng, L., Chapple, I. L., Loos, B. G., & Nicu, E. A. (2019). Oral neutrophils characterized: chemotactic, phagocytic, and neutrophil

extracellular trap (NET) formation properties. *Frontiers in immunology*, *10*, 635.

3. Tanwar, H., Gnanasekaran, J. M., Allison, D., Chuang, L. S., He, X., Aimetti, M., ...& Thumbigere-Math, V. (2023). Unraveling the link between periodontitis and inflammatory bowel disease: challenges and outlook. *ArXiv*.
4. Dlima, J. P., Paul, J., Thomas, S., Thomas, P., & Antony, J. (2023). Quantification of oral neutrophil counts in periodontal health and disease utilising a standardised oral rinse. *Journal of Oral and Maxillofacial Pathology*, *27*(4), 776.
5. Bui, F. Q., Almeida-da-Silva, C. L. C., Huynh, B., Trinh, A., Liu, J., Woodward, J., ...& Ojcius, D. M. (2019). Association between periodontal pathogens and systemic disease. *Biomedical journal*, *42*(1), 27–35.
6. Bender, J. S., Thang, H., & Glogauer, M. (2006). Novel rinse assay for the quantification of oral neutrophils and the monitoring of chronic periodontal disease. *Journal of periodontal research*, *41*(3), 214–220.
7. Ma, Y., Tuerxun, N., & Maimaitili, G. (2024). Periodontitis and the risk of oral cancer: a meta-analysis of case-control studies. *Acta Odontologica Scandinavica*, *83*, 40478.
8. Nicu, E. A., Rijkschroeff, P., Wartewig, E., Nazmi, K., & Loos, B. G. (2018). Characterization of oral polymorphonuclear neutrophils in periodontitis patients: a case-control study. *BMC Oral Health*, *18*, 1–9.
9. Do, H. T., Nguyen, T. T., Vo, T. L., Huynh, N. C., & Nguyen, A. T. K. (2023). The influence of smoking on oral neutrophils and matrix metalloproteinase-8 in periodontitis patients before and after nonsurgical treatment.Journal of oral biology and craniofacial research, 13(3), 442–447. https://doi.org/10.1016/j.jobcr.2023.05.
10. Malacco, N. L. S. O., Souza, J. A. M., Martins, F. R. B., Rachid, M. A., Simplicio, J. A., Tirapelli, C. R., Sabino, A. P., Queiroz-Junior, C. M., Goes, G. R., Vieira, L. Q., Souza, D. G., Pinho, V., Teixeira, M. M., &Soriani, F. M. (2020). Chronic ethanol consumption compromises neutrophil function in acute pulmonary Aspergillusfumigatus infection. eLife, 9, e58855. https://doi.org/10.7554/eLife.58855

Note: All the figures and tables in this chapter were made by the authors.

Research and Innovations in Industrial and Marine Biotechnology: A Circular Economy 2024 – Prof. Hrudayanath Thatoi et al. (eds)

54 Anther-Specific ß-1, 3-Glucanases in Plant Male Sterility: Insights and Applications

Milan Kumar Samanta*
Department of Human Genetics,
University of Michigan Medical School,
Ann Arbor, MI 48109-5618, USA

Amrita Banerjee
Centre for Industrial Biotechnology Research,
Siksha 'O' Anusandhan Deemed to be University, Campus-2,
Kalinganagar, Bhubaneswar, Odisha, India

Saikat Chakraborty
Department of Otolaryngology—Head and Neck Surgery,
Kresge Hearing Research Institute, University of Michigan,
Ann Arbor, MI 48109, USA

Abstract: Generating hybrid seeds in essential crop plants is of prime importance in modern agriculture, as it offers multiple advantages, including heterosis, uniformity, disease resistance, improved quality, and enhanced control and management. Male sterility is useful for producing hybrid seeds, especially in self-pollinated crop species. This review examines anther-specific genes, particularly *β-1,3-glucanase*, and various molecular strategies for inducing male sterility in self-pollinated crops. It also outlines how the anther tapetum-specific *β-1,3-glucanase* and its upstream regulatory element could induce artificial male sterility in self-pollinated crop species, shedding light on this important aspect of plant breeding.

Keywords: *β-1,3-glucanase*, Male sterility, Hybrid seed

1. Introduction

Crop productivity could be increased through heterosis or hybrid vigor. Heterosis offers several advantages, including higher yields, improved disease resistance, and crop uniformity compared to the parents. On average, 10- 30% more yield could be produced than in pure inbred lines [1], facilitating improved crop management. However, hybrid seed production in self-pollinated crops is more challenging due to the necessity of preventing self-pollination. While physical methods are commonly used, they are labor-intensive and limit the number of crosses [2]. The chemical method also harms fertility and the environment.

In contrast, the male sterility system offers a more desirable solution since no additional pollination steps are required. The genetic factor responsible for Cytoplasmic male sterility (CMS) remains unknown in some self-pollinated crops like sesame, although CMS has been successful in several crops. Consequently, nuclear male sterility (NMS) emerges as a promising alternative for generating male sterile lines in self-pollinated crop species, intending to produce hybrid vigor.

Several genetically engineered pollen killer systems have been successfully applied to generate NMS plants in various crops by altering the normal pollen development process that involves dividing diploid sporogenous cells into microspores within the anther locule, supported by

*Corresponding author: msamanta@umich.edu

DOI: 10.1201/9781003759003-54

non-reproductive cells like the tapetum, which supplies essential nutrients and enzymes [3,4]. Tapetum also secretes β-1, 3-glucanase (callase) enzyme, whose precise timing of expression and activity is vital for developing mature microspores [5,3]. Disrupting tapetum function by expression of callase prematurely inhibits normal pollen development, which causes male sterility [6]. Male sterility can be achieved artificially by targeting tapetum function with engineered genetic elements to control *β-1, 3-glucanase* expression prematurely or belatedly [7,8,9], making this a promising strategy for inducing nuclear male sterility. Thus, carefully controlling *β-1, 3-glucanase specific to the anther tapetum* strategically could help to induce male sterility. This review explicitly focuses on anther/tapetum-specific genetic elements, *β-1,3-glucanases*, and their application by different approaches in inducing artificial male sterility.

2. Major β-1,3-Glucanases Found in Plants

A variety of plant species express β-1,3-glucanases in almost all tissues. It plays many important roles in plants, including response to pathogen infection, response to wounding, environmental stress like cold, UV, microsporogenesis, anther development, pollen maturation, fruit ripening, and seed germination. This enzyme's expression and activity are controlled in a highly regulated manner. Multiple types of β-1,3-glucanases have been identified, and they are categorized according to their structural features, cellular localization, isoelectric points, and expression profile [10]. Each class is involved in specific roles in plants (Table 54.1.).

3. Pollen Development and Anther Tapetal-Specific β-1,3-Glucanases

The male reproductive process in flowering plants involves pollen formation within the stamen, specifically in the anther [11]. Diploid sporogenic cells within the anther locule are encased by a callose layer composed of β-1, 3-glucan. After meiosis I division, these cells result in two immature haploid microspores. After meiosis II, four haploid microspores are formed and remain enclosed in a callose-rich structure known as a tetrad, which is crucial for microsporogenesis. Following after, β-1, 3-glucanase (callase) is secreted from the tapetal cell, breaks down the callose layer, and releases free microspores (Fig. 54.1) [12,13,4].

Callase activity is strictly developmentally regulated and is not linked to plant defense [14]. This enzyme accumulates in various floral tissues, though its function remains unclear except in the anther, which is crucial for microspore release. Callase expression peaks during tetrad dissolution [3,5] and is pH-dependent, with optimal activity at pH 4.8. The locule pH rises to 5.9-6.2, triggering callase activity [6]. In summary, the tapetum and callase are vital for pollen grain production in flowering plants. This understanding opens avenues for inducing male sterility through genetic manipulation of the tapetal layer or callase function.

4. Genetic Engineering Approaches to Generate Male Sterility in Plants

Different molecular approaches have been adopted to generate NMS by disrupting pollen production. Among

Table 54.1 Different types of β-1,3-glucanases in plants

Class	Family member	Localization	Isoelectric point (pl)	Properties and functions
Class I (PR protein)	PR-2e	Vacuole	basic	Basic protein, induced by infections with pathogens
Class II	PR-2a PR-2b PR-2c	Extracellular	Acidic, secreted	Acidic isoform, secreted into the extracellular space
	Sp41a Sp41b	style	Acidic, secreted	unclear
Class III	PR-2d	PR-Q	Acidic, secreted	Acidic secreted, induced by viroid infection
Class IV	Tag1	Anther/tapetum	Acidic, secreted	Acidic-secreted pollen development

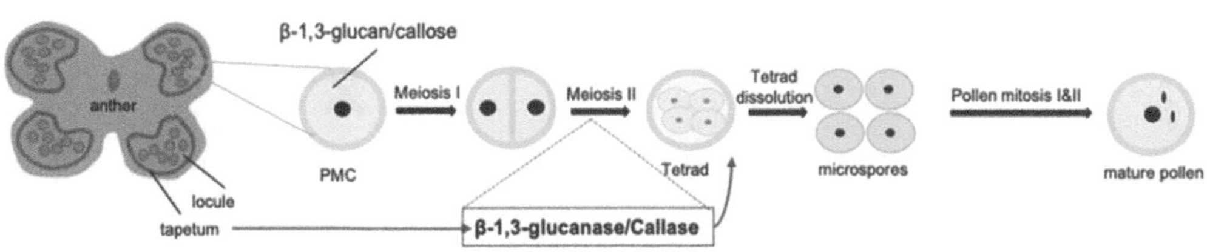

Fig. 54.1 Schematic representation of pollen development stages. Anther cross-section is adopted from Goldberg et al., 1993. Callase is expressed at the meiosis II stage and is active during the tetrad dissolution stage. PMC, pollen mother cell

them, the most widely used genetic approach is the barnase-barstar molecular system, which efficiently and successfully induces male sterility and restores fertility in plants [15]. This approach uses tapetum-specific promoters for the expression of the transgene. However, when *barnase* is expressed in other sporophytic tissues, it may also cause male sterility [16,17]. Moreover, in addition to *barnase*, several other cytotoxic genes such as *RNase T1*, bacterial toxin DTx-A, and ribosome-inactivating protein (RIP) have been tested, and results inducing male sterility [15,18]. Many other cytotoxic proteins, such as nucleases, proteases, lipases, DNA methylases, and poisonous proteins like actinidin and avidin, could similarly be approached to induce male sterility [4,19,20]. However, inducing male sterility by expressing such a cytotoxic gene in male gametophytes may not always be favorable for hybrid seed production practically because of its limitations, such as lack of specificity, early lethality, off-target effects, and restoration challenges.

Male sterility is achieved by hormonal engineering. For example, altering indole acetic acid (IAA) and gibberellin levels by expressing role B/rol C genes causes defective anther development that results in male sterility [21]. Antisense RNA strategies against essential genes associated with pollen development, like CCaMK, Bcp1, MYB103, and pigment biosynthesis genes, have been successfully implemented [22-25]. Additionally, induction of programmed cell death (PCD) in tapetum cells is another approach that has been effective in inducing male sterility [26-28].

Changing the normal timing of *β-1, 3-glucanase* expression can also lead to male sterility [4,6,29]. For instance, early expression of a modified vacuolar basic β-1,3-glucanase under a tapetum-specific promoter in transgenic plants can disrupt normal pollen development and cause male sterility [7,30-33]. Recently, male sterility in some key crop plants has been induced by targeting nuclear-origin genes related to microsporogenesis and microgametogenesis using a precise genome editing CRISPR/Cas-based tool [34-40]. The CRISPR/Cas9 tool effectively controls the reproductive traits in various plants by inducing male sterility.

5. Anther/Tapetum β-1,3-Glucanases- A Key Genetic Target for Inducing Male Sterility

Tapetum-specific β-1,3-glucanases are crucial for microspore release from the tetrad by dissolution of callose surrounding the developing microspores. Researchers can disrupt this process by manipulating the expression of β-1,3-glucanases within the tapetum. In past decades, modified β-1,3-glucanase was used to induce male sterility in anthers, which is naturally suppressed. However, tapetum β-1,3-glucanase (callase) is advantageous in male sterility induction, as it is naturally supported and non-cytotoxic to non-targeted cells [30]. Additionally, *callase* is different from other glucanases and more efficient for male sterility applications due to its transcriptional and post-transcriptional regulationalong with the qualities of natural occurrence and non-cytotoxic interaction beyond the target cell [30]. The schematic diagram to induce male sterility with tapetal-specific β-1,3-glucanase is shown in Fig. 54.2.

Different isoforms of tapetum-specific callase exist in some plants [41]. Therefore, isolation and characterization of different callase isoforms, determining their temporal and spatial regulation, and separation of the particular isoform, essential for tetrad disintegration, is important. Nowadays, researchers are introducing a number of techniques to find genes, important for anther/tapetum-specificity that are differently expressed, such as cDNA subtraction and CRISPR-based anther libraries [42, 43]. These approaches are useful for identifying and determining which callase isoform to use as a potential genetic weapon to induce male sterility.

6. Conclusive Remarks

In modern agricultural technique, hybrid seeds generation through male sterility induction plays avitalrolenow a days. The process includes various genetic engineering techniques with different pros and cons. As an illustration,

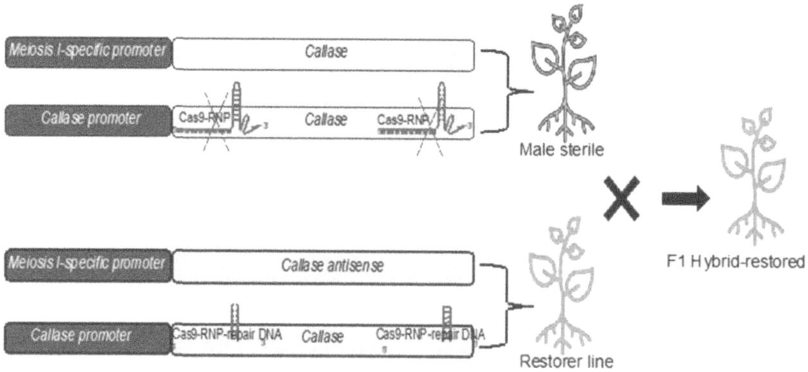

Fig. 54.2 Anther-tapetum-specific β-1,3-glucanase (*callase*) gene is utilized in a schematic representation of a genetically engineered system for male sterility and fertility restoration

the barnase-barstar system effeciently regulates male sterility and restores fertility; nevertheless, bacterial genes are used in this process, which challenges about the purity of the genetically modified organisms in light of unwanted gene flow and the adoption. Pollen forming gene silencing using RNA interference (RNAi) and securing male sterility, also gained importance globally. Higher specificity and reversibility are basic features of this approach. Reversibility, depends on the application of inducer and other regulatory systems to temporarily expressed RNAi construct. However, silencing effectiveness and stability might differ, and transgenic techniques encounter societal and regulatory challenges, just like the barnase-barstar system. Targeted gene disruption applying latest advanced technologies like CRISPR/Cas9, enables the knockout of pollen developing critical genes. Though, with the application of CRISPR/Cas9, off-target impacts and regulatory barriers in developing GMOs brings difficulties. Every one of these tactics has benefits and drawbacks. Therefore, the choice of strategy, depends upon the type of crop, production scale, environmental factors, and regulatory limitations. For better consistency and successive versatility, combination of several methods could provide more when it comes to producing male sterility in plants. This review has given how quickly genetic engineering is developing, further research and development should produce even more sophisticated methods of managing crop male fertility.

References——

1. Mayo, H. (1980). *The theory of plant breeding*. Clarendon Press.
2. Acquaah, G. (2007). *Principles of plant genetics and breeding*. Wiley-Blackwell.
3. Stieglitz, H., & Stern, H. (1973). Regulation of β-1,3-glucanase activity in developing anthers of *Lilium*. *Developmental Biology, 34*, 169–173.
4. Goldberg, R. B., Beals, T. P., & Sanders, P. M. (1993). Anther development: Basic principles and practical applications. *The Plant Cell, 5*, 1217–1229.
5. Frankel, R., Izhar, S., &Nitsan, J. (1969). Timing of callase activity and cytoplasmic male sterility in petunia. *Biochemical Genetics, 3*, 451–455.
6. Izhar, S., & Frankel, R. (1971). Mechanism of male sterility in petunia: The relationship between pH, callase activity in the anthers, and the breakdown of the microsporogenesis. *Theoretical and Applied Genetics, 41*, 104–108.
7. Worrall, D., Hird, D., Hodge, R., Wyatt, P., Draper, J., & Scott, R. (1992). Premature dissolution of the microsporocyte callose wall causes male sterility in transgenic tobacco. *The Plant Cell, 4*, 759–771.
8. Tsuchiya, T., Toriyama, K., Yoshikawa, M., Ejiri, S., &Hinata, K. (1995). Tapetum-specific expression of the gene for an endo-β-1,3-glucanase causes male sterility in transgenic tobacco. *Plant Cell Physiology, 36*, 487–494.
9. Scott, R. J., Draper, J., & Paul, W. (1999). Callase-related DNAs and their use in male sterility (U.S. Patent No. 5,955,653). United States Patent and Trademark Office.
10. Antoniw, J. F., Ritter, C. E., Pierpoint, W. S., & van Loon, L. C. (1980). Comparison of three pathogenesis-related proteins from plants of two cultivars of tobacco infected with TMV. *Journal of General Virology, 47*, 79–87.
11. Goldberg, R. B. (1988). Plants: Novel developmental processes. *Science, 240*, 1460–1467.
12. Pacini, E., Franchi, G. G., & Hesse, M. (1985). The tapetum: Its form, function, and possible phylogeny in fimbriophyta. *Plant Systematics and Evolution, 149*, 155–185.
13. Bedinger, P. (1992). The remarkable biology of pollen. *The Plant Cell, 4*, 879–887.
14. Lotan, T., Ori, N., &Fluhr, R. (1989). Pathogenesis-related proteins are developmentally regulated in tobacco flowers. *The Plant Cell, 1*, 881–887.
15. Mariani, C., De Beuckeleer, M., Treuttner, J., Leemans, J., & Goldberg, R. B. (1990). Induction of male sterility in plants by a chimeric ribonuclease gene. *Nature, 347*, 737–741.
16. Gomez, M. D., Beltran, J. P., & Canas, L. A. (2004). The pea END1 promoter drives anther-specific gene expression in different plant species. *Planta, 219*, 967–981.
17. Roque, E., Gomez, M. D., Ellul, P., Wallbraun, M., Madueno, F., Beltran, J., & Canas, L. A. (2007). The PsEND1 promoter: A novel tool to produce genetically engineered male-sterile plants by early anther ablation. *Plant Cell Reports, 26*, 313–325.
18. Cho, H. J., Kim, S., Kim, M., & Kim, B. D. (2001). Production of transgenic male sterile tobacco plants with the cDNA encoding a ribosome-inactivating protein in *Dianthus sinensis* L. *Molecules and Cells, 11*, 326–333.
19. Williams, M. E. (1995). Genetic engineering for pollination control. *Trends in Biotechnology, 13*, 344–349.
20. Prez-Prat, E., & Van LookerenCampagne, M. M. (2002). Hybrid seed production and the challenge of propagating male-sterile plants. *Trends in Plant Science, 7*, 199–203.
21. Spena, A., Estruch, J. J., Prensen, E., Nacken, W., Van Onckelen, H., &Sommer, H. (1992). Anther-specific expression of the rol6 gene of *Agrobacterium rhizogenes* increases IAA content in anthers and alters anther development in whole flower growth. *Theoretical and Applied Genetics, 84*, 520–527.
22. Xu, H., Knox, R. B., Taylor, P. E., & Singh, M. B. (1995). Bcp1, a gene required for male fertility in *Arabidopsis*. *Proceedings of the National Academy of Sciences, 92*, 2106–2110.
23. Fabijanski, S. F., Albani, D., Robert, L. S., &Arnison, P. G. (2000). Molecular methods of hybrid seed production (U.S. Patent No. 6,013,859). United States Patent and Trademark Office.
24. Higginson, T., Li, S. F., & Parish, R. W. (2003). AtMYB103 regulates tapetum and trichome development in *Arabidopsis thaliana*. *The Plant Journal, 35*, 177–192.
25. Li, S. F., Iacuone, S., & Parish, R. W. (2007). Suppression and restoration of male fertility using a transcription factor. *Plant Biotechnology Journal, 5*, 297–312.
26. Singh, S. P., Pandey, T., Srivastava, R., Verma, P. C., Singh, P. K., Tuli, R., & Sawant, S. V. (2010). BECLIN1 from *Arabidopsis thaliana* under the control of regulated expression systems, a strategy for developing male sterile plants. *Plant Biotechnology Journal, 8*, 1005–1022.

27. Singh, S. P., Singh, S. P., Pandey, T., Singh, R. R., & Sawant, S. V. (2015). A novel male sterility-fertility restoration system in plants for hybrid seed production. *Scientific Reports, 5*, 11274. https://doi.org/10.1038/srep11274
28. Kawanabe, T., Ariizumi, T., Kawai-Yamada, M., Uchimiya, H., &Toriyama, K. (2006). Abolition of the tapetum suicide program ruins microsporogenesis. *Plant and Cell Physiology, 47*, 784–787.
29. McCormick, S. (1993). Male gametophyte development. *The Plant Cell, 5*, 1265–1275.
30. Scott, R., Dagless, E., Hodge, R., Paul, W., Soufleris, I., & Draper, J. (1991). Patterns of gene expression in developing anthers of *Brassica napus*. *Plant Molecular Biology, 17*, 195–207.
31. Paul, W., Hodge, R., Smartt, S., Draper, J., & Scott, R. (1992). The isolation and characterization of the tapetum-specific *Arabidopsis thaliana* A9 gene. *Plant Molecular Biology, 19*, 611–622.
32. Takeuchi, Y., Yoshikawa, M., Takeba, G., Tanaka, K., Shibata, D., &Horino, O. (1990). Molecular cloning and ethylene induction of mRNA coding a phytoalexin elicitor-releasing factor, β-1,3-endoglucanase, in soybean. *Plant Physiology, 93*, 673–682.
33. Tsuchiya, T., Toriyama, K., Ejiri, S., & Hinata, K. (1994). Molecular characterization of rice genes specifically expressed in the anther tapetum. *Plant Molecular Biology, 26*, 1737–1746.
34. Jung, Y. J., Kim, D. H., Lee, H. J., Nam, K. H., Bae, S., Nou, I. S., et al. (2020). Knockout of the SlMS10 gene (Solyc02g079810) encoding a bHLH transcription factor using the CRISPR/Cas9 system confers a male sterility phenotype in tomato. *Plants, 9*(9), 1198. https://doi.org/10.3390/plants9091189
35. Bao, H., Ding, Y., Yang, F., Zhang, J., Xie, J., Zhao, C., Zhang, Y., Liu, H., Wang, L., &Xu, M. (2022). Gene silencing, knockout, and over-expression of a transcription factor aborted microspores (SlAMS) strongly affect pollen viability in tomato (*Solanumlycopersicum*). *BMC Genomics, 23*, 346. https://doi.org/10.1186/s12864-022-08549-x
36. Gökdemir, G., Seçgin, Z., Uluisik, S., & Kavas, M. (2022). CRISPR/Cas9 knockout of the SlPHD_MS1 (Solyc04g008420) gene results in complete male sterility in tomato. *Plant Growth Regulation, 98*, 329–341. https://doi.org/10.1007/s10725-022-00869-y
37. Pechar, G. S., Donaire, L., Gosalvez, B., Garcia-Almodovar, C., Sanchez-Pina, M. A., Truniger, V., et al. (2022). Editing melon eIF4E is associated with virus resistance and male sterility. *Plant Biotechnology Journal, 20*, 2006–2022. https://doi.org/10.1111/pbi.13885
38. Li, J., Wang, Z., He, G., Ma, L., & Deng, X. W. (2020). CRISPR/Cas9-mediated disruption of TaNP1 genes results in complete male sterility in bread wheat. *Journal of Genetics and Genomics, 47*, 263–272. https://doi.org/10.1016/j.jgg.2020.05.004
39. Okada, A., Arndell, T., Borisjuk, N., Sharma, N., Watson-Haigh, N. S., Tucker, E. J., et al. (2019). CRISPR/Cas9-mediated knockout of Ms1 enables the rapid generation of male-sterile hexaploid wheat lines for hybrid seed production. *Plant Biotechnology Journal, 17*, 1905–1913. https://doi.org/10.1111/pbi.13106
40. Chen, R., Xu, Q., Liu, Y., Zhang, J., Ren, D., Wang, G., et al. (2018). Generation of transgene-free maize male sterile lines using the CRISPR/Cas9 system. *Frontiers in Plant Science, 9*, 1180. https://doi.org/10.3389/fpls.2018.01180
41. Winiarczyk, K., Jaroszuk-Ściseł, J., &Kupisz, K. (2012). Characterization of callase (β-1,3-D-glucanase) activity during microsporogenesis in the sterile anthers of *Allium sativum* L. and the fertile anthers of *A. atropurpureum*. *Sexual Plant Reproduction, 25*(2), 123–131. https://doi.org/10.1007/s00497-012-0184-5
42. Parveen, S., Mazumder, M., & Bhattacharya, A. (2018). Identification of anther-specific genes from sesame and functional assessment of the upstream region of a tapetum-specific β-1,3-glucanase gene. *Plant Molecular Biology Reporter, 36*, 149–161.
43. Ma, K., Han, J., Hao, Y., Yang, Z., Chen, J., Liu, Y. G., Zhu, Q., & Chen, L. (2019). An effective strategy to establish a male sterility mutant mini-library by CRISPR/Cas9-mediated knockout of anther-specific genes in rice. *Journal of Genetics and Genomics, 46*(5), 273–275. https://doi.org/10.1016/j.jgg.2019.03.005

Note: All the figures and table in this chapter were made by the authors.

Research and Innovations in Industrial and Marine Biotechnology: A Circular Economy 2024 – Prof. Hrudayanath Thatoi et al. (eds)

55 Post-COVID Complications and Treatment: A Critical and Urgent Focus of Modern Healthcare

Pallabi Maity
Department of Microbiology, Raiganj University,
Raiganj, Uttar Dinajpur, West Bengal, India

Arindam Ganguly[1],
Kankana Acharya, Rahul Nandi
Department of Microbiology, Bankura Sammilani College,
Bankura, West Bengal, India

Mousumi Ganguly
Department of Nutrition, Bankura Sammilani College,
Bankura, West Bengal, India

Debasis Mitra
Department of Microbiology, Graphic Era (Deemed to be University),
Dehradun, Uttarakhand, India

Subhashree Rath
Centre for Industrial Biotechnology Research,
School of Pharmaceutical Sciences, Siksha 'O' Anusandhan,
Deemed to be University, Kalinga Nagar,
Bhubaneswar, Odisha, India

Pradeep Kumar Das Mohapatra
Department of Microbiology, Raiganj University, Raiganj,
Uttar Dinajpur, West Bengal, India

Sourav Chattaraj[2]
Centre for Industrial Biotechnology Research,
School of Pharmaceutical Sciences, Siksha 'O' Anusandhan,
Deemed to be University, Kalinga Nagar,
Bhubaneswar, Odisha, India

Abstract: The COVID pandemic has caused severe health, societal, and economic disruptions, exacerbated by the emergence of post-COVID complications, commonly termed long COVID. This heterogeneous condition mimics a chronic disease state, with symptoms such as fatigue, muscle weakness, cognitive dysfunction, and increased susceptibility to diabetes, cerebro-vascular events, and autoimmune disorders. The absence of specific diagnostic biomarkers presents a clinical challenge, while pre-existing chronic conditions, particularly cardiac, pulmonary, and renal diseases further deteriorates the condition. Persistent inflammation and immune system dysregulation play a critical role in the pathogenesis of long COVID, leading to cardiovascular and hepatic complications, including myocardial fibrosis, arrhythmias, hepatic fibrosis, and cirrhosis. Mortality rate was found to be higher among older adults and comorbid patients. These findings highlight the importance of implementing targeted healthcare strategies and optimizing resource allocation to address the specific needs of affected populations. This study employs a

Corresponding author: [1]arindam_ganguly@yahoo.com, [2]souravchattaraj@soa.ac.in

DOI: 10.1201/9781003759003-55

scientometric analysis to evaluate global research trends on post-COVID complications, identifying gaps in current knowledge and potential treatment pathways. The findings emphasize the necessity for further research, clinical trials, and policy interventions to address long COVID, ensuring improved patient outcomes and long-term healthcare sustainability.

Keywords: Post-COVID burden, Persistent inflammation, Scientometric insights, Treatment

1. INTRODUCTION

The COVID-19 pandemic has led to major health, societal, and economic impacts, compounded by post-acute COVID syndrome[1]. The long COVID often results fatigue, myalgia, cognitive dysfunction, diabetes and even autoimmune disorders[2]. Long COVID diagnosis remains challenging due to the absence of specific biomarkers. Risk factors, particularly pre-existing chronic conditions, increase susceptibility to post-COVID complications, including cardiovascular and hepatic conditions, with tissue damage linked to dysregulated immune responses [3]. A study of post-COVID mortality in the USA revealed higher mortality in males and older adults, highlighting the importance of targeted healthcare strategies for these vulnerable groups. Research gaps in post-COVID complications highlight the need for clinical trials and innovative treatment strategies to address the long-term consequences of COVID-19 [4]. A scientometric analysis aims to explore global research trends and gaps, informing future therapeutic approaches.

1.1 Systemic and Inflammatory Impact of SARS-CoV-2

Research on COVID has revealed the virus triggers systemic inflammation, affecting immune responses and causing severe complications beyond respiratory illness [5]. Elevated pro-inflammatory cytokines like IL-6, IL-1, and TNF-α contribute to pulmonary fibrosis, hypoxia, and death. Comorbidities increase mortality risk, and altered coagulation promotes thromboembolic risks and cardiac complications [5]. The virus spreads via the ACE2 receptor, exacerbating vascular inflammation and activating immune pathways like NF-kβ, worsening lung inflammation and prognosis. This dysregulated immune response creates an oxidative environment, worsening COVID-19 severity and potentially leading to fatal outcomes [5-7].

1.2 Molecular Mechanisms of the Complications in Different Organ Systems of Human Body

Post-COVID complications result from persistent inflammation, immune dysregulation, endothelial damage, and thromboembolic events, leading to chronic organ dysfunction [5]. Long COVID involves immune dysregulation, endothelial dysfunction, and viral persistence, affecting multiple organs. It leads to inflammation, cognitive dysfunction, cardiovascular, pulmonary, renal, gastrointestinal, and hematological complications. SARS-CoV-2 infection disrupts the cardiovascular system through endothelial invasion, coagulation activation, and platelet aggregation, leading to heart failure and arrhythmias [8]. Neurological issues arise from neuroinflammation and hypoxia, causing cognitive deficits and strokes [9]. Gastrointestinal, hepatic, and renal systems suffer from ACE2-mediated damage and gut dysbiosis[10]. Hematological complications include hypercoagulability, leading to thromboembolic events [8]. Musculoskeletal symptoms, such as fatigue and muscle pain, are attributed to immune-mediated inflammation and viral persistence [10]. Mental health issues like depression and PTSD result from chronic inflammation and HPA axis dysregulation[9]. These complications highlight the need for targeted interventions across various systems and long-term mental health monitoring.

1.3 Global Incidence of Post COVID Complications

Post COVID-19 condition (PCC), or long COVID, affects around 6% of COVID-19 patients, with symptoms lasting over two months and impacting multiple organ systems. While cases have declined, PCC remains a major global health concern. Risk factors include older age, female gender, excessive smoking, obesity, and severe COVID-19. Symptoms range from fatigue and cognitive issues to heart disease and mental health disorders. Long-term effects may include POTS and ME/CFS. Treatment mainly focuses on symptom management and rehabilitation, with no definitive cure. The WHO is conducting research and developing global guidelines to improve diagnosis and treatment. Future studies should address diagnostic gaps, ensure inclusivity, and focus on clinical trials to better understand and treat long COVID [11,12].

1.4 Therapeutic Approaches for COVID-19 and Post-COVID Complications

Since its emergence in December 2020, COVID-19 has significantly impacted global socio-economic conditions, prompting efforts to develop effective treatments, including drug repurposing. While some repurposed drugs, like remdesivir, favipiravir, and molnupiravir, offer antiviral effects, many have shown limited efficacy due to viral mutations. New drug molecules and biologics are in various stages of clinical trials, with some receiving emergency use approval. However, vaccines' limited protection against emerging variants highlights the need for more effective therapies. Treatment strategies for COVID-19 and post-COVID complications now include antiviral drugs, monoclonal antibodies, immunomodulators, and supportive therapies [13]. Phytomedicines [14] and probiotics are also being explored for their potential to enhance immunity [15-18].

Monoclonal antibodies such as bamlanivimab and sotrovimab target SARS-CoV-2's spike protein, preventing viral entry [6]. Immunomodulators like corticosteroids and anti-inflammatory agents help reduce excessive immune responses [7]. Anticoagulants such as apixaban and rivaroxaban are used for thromboembolic events, while ECMO assists severe respiratory failure cases [7]. Antibiotics are prescribed for secondary bacterial infections but raise concerns about antimicrobial resistance [19]. Antibody therapies neutralize the virus and reduce severity, with engineered antibodies like sotrovimab showing increased efficacy against variants [20, 21]. The rapid approval of monoclonal antibodies sets a precedent for accelerated biopharmaceutical innovations in infectious disease treatments, with future strategies focusing on improving stability and developing pan-coronavirus neutralizing antibodies [22,23].

2. Scientometric Analysis

The scientometric study of post-COVID complications is globally significant as it provides insights into research trends, key contributors, and emerging areas of study. By analyzing publication outputs, citation

Table 55.1 Multisystem complications of Post-COVID syndrome: A comprehensive overview of affected organs, pathophysiology, symptoms, and treatment strategies

Complication	Organ Affected	Mechanism of Infection	Symptoms	Treatment/Management	References
Pulmonary Fibrosis	Lungs	Persistent inflammation, cytokine storm, endothelial damage	Chronic cough, breathlessness, fatigue, dyspnea	Oxygen therapy, anti-fibrosis drugs (Nintedanib, Pirfenidone), ECMO for severe cases	[24,6,7]
Myocarditis	Heart	Direct viral invasion, systemic inflammation	Chest pain, palpitations, heart failure	Standard cardiac support, ACEi/ARB evaluation, ECMO for heart failure	[24,6,7]
Neurological Disorders	Brain, Nervous System	Neuroinflammation, ACE2 receptor invasion	Memory loss, headaches, dizziness, neuropathy	Antihypertensive drugs (ACEi/ARB), symptomatic neuroprotection	[25,6,7]
Thromboembolism	Blood Vessels	Endothelial dysfunction, hypercoagulability	Deep vein thrombosis, pulmonary embolism	Anticoagulation therapy, ECMO for severe cases	[26,6,7]
Liver Dysfunction	Liver	Inflammation, immune response, viral invasion	Jaundice, elevated liver enzymes, fatigue	Liver-protective drugs (glycyrrhizic acid, vitamin E), nutritional support	[24,6,7]
Chronic Fatigue	Muscles, Immune System	Mitochondrial dysfunction, persistent immune activation	Extreme tiredness, muscle pain, cognitive issues	Rehabilitation, physical therapy, nutritional support	[10,6,7]
Gastrointestinal Issues	Stomach, Intestines	Gut microbiotadysbiosis, direct viral invasion	Diarrhea, nausea, abdominal pain	Probiotics, enteral nutrition, ACE2 inhibitors	[24,6,7]
Kidney Injury	Kidneys	Inflammatory cytokines, endothelial damage	Reduced kidney function, swelling, fatigue	Continuous renal replacement therapy (CRRT), anticoagulation therapy	[26,6,7]
Urinary Disorders	Kidneys, Bladder	Viral invasion, immune response, cytokine storm	Proteinuria, hematuria, acute kidney injury	Monitoring renal function, CRRT, anticoagulation therapy	[6,7]
Mental Health Issues	Brain	Neuroinflammation, stress response dysregulation	Anxiety, depression, PTSD, sleep disturbances	Cognitive therapy, antidepres-sants, psychiatric support	[9,6,7]
Multisystem Inflammatory Syndrome (MIS)	Multiple organs	Hyperimmune response, cytokine storm	High fever, abdominal pain, cardiovascular dysfunction	Anti-inflammatory therapy, immune modulation	[26,6,7]
Guillain-Barré Syndrome (GBS)	Nervous System	Autoimmune reaction triggered by viral infection	Weakness, paralysis, neuropathy	Immunoglobulin therapy, physiotherapy	[25,6,7]
Sleep Disorders	Brain	Dysregulation of circadian rhythm, neuroinflammation	Insomnia, daytime sleepiness, fatigue	Sleep hygiene, cognitive behavioral therapy	[9,6,7]
Psychiatric Disorders	Brain	Prolonged stress response, neurotransmitter imbalance	Anxiety, depression, psychosis, PTSD	Psychiatric therapy, pharmacological support	[9,6,7]

impacts, and interdisciplinary collaborations, this study helps policymakers, researchers, and healthcare professionals identify gaps and prioritize future research [27]. It highlights the global burden of long COVID, guiding resource allocation for medical interventions, rehabilitation strategies, and socio-economic policies. Additionally, understanding regional disparities in research output fosters international collaboration, ensuring equitable access to healthcare solutions. This study ultimately aids in mitigating the long-term effects of COVID-19 and enhancing global public health resilience. Figure 55.1 provides a scientometric analysis of post-COVID complications based on various bibliometric indicators.

2.1 Geographical Distribution

The highest number of research contributions on post-COVID complications originates from the United States (5,056), followed by the United Kingdom (2,080), China (1,347), India (957), and other countries. This highlights the dominant role of high-income nations in post-COVID research.

2.2 Key Research Themes

The most prominent research areas include disease (8,325), pathology (4,387), pandemic (3,753), and intensive care medicine (3,843). Virology (2,969), immunology (3,493), and surgery (4,175) are other notable fields. Additionally, disciplines like psychiatry (2,464), pediatrics (2,646), computer science (1,808), and public health (1,387) indicate an interdisciplinary research approach. The presence of economics (1,794) and political science (1,674) suggests the socio-economic impact of post-COVID conditions is also being studied.

2.3 Publication Sources

The highest numbers of publications are from Scientific Reports, followed by Trials, BMC Public Health, Cureus, and other journals related to surgery, infectious diseases, and intensive care. This demonstrates the multidisciplinary nature of post-COVID research.

2.4 Citation Trends

The temporal distribution of publications and citations shows a peak in research activity between mid-2020 and

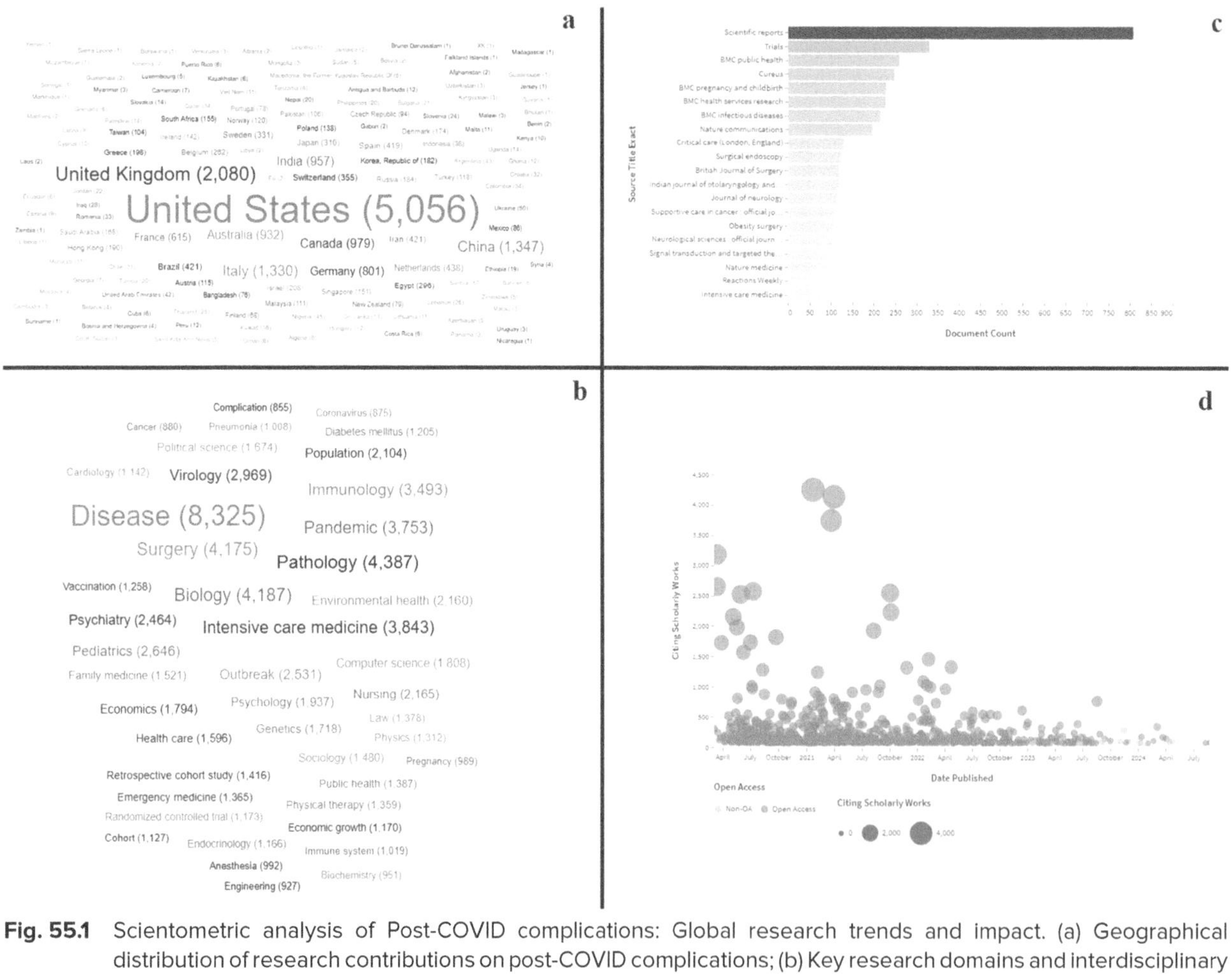

Fig. 55.1 Scientometric analysis of Post-COVID complications: Global research trends and impact. (a) Geographical distribution of research contributions on post-COVID complications; (b) Key research domains and interdisciplinary focus areas; (c) Leading journals publishing research on post-COVID complications; (d) Citation impact and publishing trends over time

Source: Author

2021, with a significant decline in 2022 and beyond. The larger circles represent studies with a high citation impact, suggesting that early pandemic research was highly influential. Open-access articles (light blue) dominate, reflecting the global demand for accessible COVID-19 research.

Socio-economic conditions also have a significant impact on the health of individuals [13]. Overall, the analysis highlights the rapid surge of research on post-COVID complications, with a strong focus on clinical, biological, and socio-economic aspects. However, the declining trend in publications post-2022 suggests a need for sustained research efforts to address long-term COVID-19 complications.

3. Conclusions

Post-COVID complications represent a major global health challenge, with long-term effects ranging from fatigue to severe cardiovascular and hepatic conditions. The absence of specific biomarkers complicates diagnosis, while pre-existing chronic diseases increase vulnerability. Mortality trends indicate a significant burden on healthcare systems, necessitating targeted interventions for high-risk groups. Scientometric analysis of research trends highlights existing gaps and the urgent need for innovative treatment strategies. Addressing long COVID requires a multidisciplinary approach, integrating clinical research, healthcare policies, and therapeutic advancements. Future studies must focus on biomarker discovery, risk stratification, and personalized treatment strategies to mitigate the long-term impact of COVID-19.

References

1. Mitra, D., Nachhmin, B., Ganguly, A., & Das Mohapatra, P. K. (2022). Computational approach to assess Mucormycosis: A systematic review. In *Computational intelligence in healthcare applications* (pp. 71–85). Academic Press. https://doi.org/10.1016/B978-0-323-99031-8.00004-1
2. Das, S., Sinha, D., Chatterji, S., Ganguly, A., De, A., Majgaonkar, A., Kazi, Z., Maurya, A. K., Sohail, M., & Bhat, N. (2025). The role of marine bacteria-derived bioactive compounds in COVID-19 management. In *Anti-coronavirus marine bioactive compounds* (Chapter 7, pp. 185–224). Apple Academic Press.
3. Lippi, G. and Sanchis-Gomar, F. (2025). Mortality of Post-COVID-19 Condition: 2025 Update. COVID, 5(1), 11.
4. Rizzi, M. and Sainaghi, P.P. (2025). COVID-19: Lessons Learned from Molecular and Clinical Research. Int. J. Mol. Sci., 26(2), 616.
5. Ganguly, A., Konar, U., Kundu, A., Ghosh, S., Chatterjee, I., Nad, S., Chatterjee, S., Nandi, S., Singha, S. and Kali, S. (2020). The prevalence, preventive measures and economic impact of pandemic COVID-19 in India: The initial phase. Acta Biol. Szeged., 64(1), 43–61. https://doi.org/10.14232/abs.2020.1.43-61
6. Wang, Y., et al. (2021). Treatment of COVID-19 complications. Front. Med., 8, 757605.
7. Basu, D., Chavda, V.P. and Mehta, A.A. (2022). Therapeutics for COVID-19 and post COVID-19 complications: An update. Curr. Res. Pharmacol. Drug Discov., 3, 100086.
8. Aul, R., Gates, J., Draper, A., Dunleavy, A., Ruickbie, S., Meredith, H., Walters, N., van Zeller, C., Taylor, V., Bridgett, M., Dunwoody, R., Grubnic, S., Jacob, T. and Ong, Y.E. (2021). Complications after discharge with COVID-19 infection and risk factors associated with development of post-COVID pulmonary fibrosis. Respir. Med., 188, 106602.
9. Zawilska, J.B. and Kuczyńska, K. (2022). Psychiatric and neurological complications of long COVID. J. Psychiatr. Res., 156, 349–360.
10. Shanbehzadeh, S., Tavahomi, M., Zanjari, N., Ebrahimi-Takamjani, I. and Amiri-arimi, S. (2021). Physical and mental health complications post-COVID-19: Scoping review. J. Psychosom. Res., 147, 110525.
11. World Health Organization. (2025). Post-COVID-19 condition. https://www.who.int/news-room/fact-sheets/detail/post-covid-19-condition. Last accessed on 26.03.2025.
12. Davis, H.E., McCorkell, L., Vogel, J.M. and Topol, E.J. (2023). Long COVID: major findings, mechanisms and recommendations. Nat. Rev. Microbiol., 21(3), 133–146
13. Ganguly, A., Banerjee, A., Mandal, A., Khan, M.A. and Das Mohapatra, P.K. (2019). Isolation and characterization of bacteria from the intestine of *Clariasbatrachus* for probiotic organism. Proc. Zool. Soc., 72(4), 411–419. https://doi.org/10.1007/s12595-018-0283-x
14. Sinha, D., Kazi, Z., Muherjee, R., Ganguly, A., Banerjee, S., Maurya, A.K., Chowdhury, A.A., Majgaonkar, A. and Dutta, S. (2024). Integrated molecular strategies for enhanced production of medicinal plant-derived flavonoids. In: *Biotechnology, Multiple Omics, and Precision Breeding in Medicinal Plants*. Springer Nature. https://doi.org/10.1201/9781003475491-23
15. Chattaraj, S., Ganguly, A., Mandal, A. and Das Mohapatra, P.K. (2022). A review of the role of probiotics for the control of viral diseases in aquaculture. Aquac. Int. https://doi.org/10.1007/s10499-022-00915-6
16. Chattaraj, S., Mitra, D., Chattaraj, A., Chattaraj, M., Kundu, M., Ganguly, A. and Das Mohapatra, P.K. (2023). Anti-oncogenic potential of probiotics: Challenges and future prospects. Indian J. Microbiol. Res., 10(1), 1–10. https://doi.org/10.18231/j.ijmr.2023.001
17. Ganguly, A., Mahapatra, S., Ray, S. et al. (2025). The rising threat of Nipah virus: a highly contagious and deadly zoonotic pathogen. *Virol. J.* 22:139. https://doi.org/10.1186/s12985-025-02728-4
18. Nad, S., Mandal, A., Das Mohapatra, P. K., & Ganguly, A. (2021). Herbal drug: A natural bioactive formulation & its scope against viral diseases. In *Handbook of Agriculture & Plant Sciences* (pp. 187–230). ABS Books.
19. Chedid, M., Waked, R., Haddad, E., Chetata, N., Saliba, G. and Choucair, J. (2021). Antibiotics in treatment of COVID-19 complications: a review of frequency, indications, and efficacy. J. Infect. Public Health, 14(5), 570–576.

20. Chen, J., Gao, K., Wang, R., Nguyen, D.D. and Wei, G.W. (2021). Review of COVID-19 antibody therapies. Annu. Rev. Biophys., 50(1), 1–30.
21. Kumar, G.V., Jeyanthi, V. and Ramakrishnan, S. (2020). A short review on antibody therapy for COVID-19. New Microbes New Infect., 35, 100682.
22. Kelley, B., De Moor, P., Douglas, K., Renshaw, T. and Traviglia, S. (2022). Monoclonal antibody therapies for COVID-19: lessons learned and implications for the development of future products. Curr. Opin. Biotechnol., 78, 102798.
23. Abraham, J. (2020). Passive antibody therapy in COVID-19. Nat. Rev. Immunol., 20(7), 401–403.
24. Silva Andrade, B., Siqueira, S., de AssisSoares, W. R., de Souza Rangel, F., Santos, N. O., dos Santos Freitas, A., ... &Barh, D. (2021). Long-COVID and post-COVID health complications: an up-to-date review on clinical conditions and their possible molecular mechanisms. *Viruses*, *13*(4), 700.
25. Ahmed, J.O., Ahmad, S.A., Hassan, M.N., Kakamad, F.H., Salih, R.Q., Abdulla, B.A., Fattah, F.H.R., Mohammed, S.H., Ali, R.K. and Salih, A.M. (2022). Post COVID-19 neurological complications: a meta-analysis. Ann. Med. Surg., 76, 103440.
26. Esendağlı, D., Yılmaz, A., Akçay, M.Ş. and Özlü, T. (2021). Post-COVID syndrome: pulmonary complications. Turk. J. Med. Sci., 51(7), 3359–3371.
27. Ganguly, A., Kirtania, D. K., Chhetri, M., &Chattaraj, S. (2025). Sustainable development through probiotics: A scientometric analysis of Indian research and innovation. *Discover Sustainability, 6*, Article 455. https://doi.org/10.1007/s43621-025-01263-0

Research and Innovations in Industrial and Marine Biotechnology: A Circular Economy 2024 – Prof. Hrudayanath Thatoi et al. (eds)
© 2026 Taylor & Francis Group, London, ISBN 978-1-041-28285-3

56 A Cross-Sectional Study on Knowledge, Attitudes, and Practices (KAP) Regarding Menstruation Among the Adolescent Girls in Bankura, West Bengal

Mousumi Ganguly
Department of Anthropology, Vidyasagar University,
Midnapore, West Bengal, India

Arindam Ganguly
Department of Microbiology, Bankura Sammilani College,
Bankura, West Bengal, India

Manasi Chattaraj
Department of Geography, Bankura University,
Bankura, West Bengal, India

Sourav Chattaraj
Centre for Industrial Biotechnology Research,
School of Pharmaceutical Sciences,
Siksha 'O' Anusandhan, Kalinga Nagar,
Bhubaneswar, Odisha, India

Dipak K. Midya*
Department of Anthropology, Vidyasagar University,
Midnapore, West Bengal, India

Abstract: This study investigates the demographic characteristics, menstrual health knowledge, practices, and perceptions among adolescents, highlighting the influence of socio-economic and familial factors on menstrual hygiene management. Data collection was conducted utilizing a pre-validated, structured questionnaire, followed by statistical analysis. A cross-sectional survey of 1014 adolescents in rural parts of Bankura revealed significant gaps in menstrual health knowledge, with 42.21% lacking prior knowledge about menstruation. Widespread misconceptions about menstruation's source and culturally influenced beliefs were prevalent. Sanitary pads were the most commonly used menstrual product, but 13.61% relied on cloth, with inadequate hygiene practices identified. The study underscores the need for targeted interventions to improve menstrual health education, enhance sanitary product access, and address socio-economic disparities.

Keywords: Menstrual hygiene, Sanitary napkins, Reproductive health, Participants, Taboo

1. Introduction

Reproductive age begins with menstruation, a normal physiological process, starting in adolescence [1,2]. However, many girls aged 10 to 19 yrs. enter puberty unprepared due to insufficient knowledge [3]. Social stigma and misinformation contribute to their discomfort discussing periods, reinforcing harmful beliefs [4,5]. These issues can negatively impact mental, emotional, and physical health, school attendance, and academic

*Corresponding author: dkmidya@gmail.com

DOI: 10.1201/9781003759003-56

performance [6]. Societal attitudes heavily influence menstrual hygiene practices, with knowledge linked to better hygiene maintenance [7]. Poor menstrual hygiene can lead to infections, reproductive issues, and lower self-esteem [8]. Many adolescent girls, particularly from low-income households, lack proper menstrual hygiene understanding and engage in risky practices [9,10]. The integration of menstrual health into healthcare systems and education programs is crucial to addressing these issues [11]. This study on college girls in Bankura district aims to assess menstrual hygiene knowledge and behaviors, providing essential insights for policy and further research development.

2. Materials and Methods

This study was a cross-sectional investigation conducted among adolescent females enrolled in schools from the VIth to XIIth grades, as well as first-year college students in the rural areas of Bankura district in West Bengal. The research took place between March 2023 and Feb 2024, involving a total of 1,014 adolescent girls aged 10 to 19 years.

Ethical approval was duly taken (VU/IHEC-4/9-23). Relevant stakeholders were formally approached through official letters and permissions were obtained at all levels. The study details were communicated to the participants. Given that a significant portion of the respondents were below the age of 18 yr., verbal consent was obtained from the parents/guardians of the children through telephonic communication. After coordinating with the parents, written consent was subsequently obtained from the teachers of the schools prior to conducting interviews. Once they approved to conduct the research, the researcher fixed dates for the collection of data at their convenience. Questionnaires were then distributed, and any doubts or queries were addressed. The collected data were analyzed using descriptive statistics after being imported into Microsoft Excel and SPSS IBM version 25.

3. Results

The demographic profile of the respondents (n=1014) has been thoroughly studied (Table 56.1). It outlines key characteristics of the participants. A majority of the participants (65%) were aged between 12 and 15 years, whereas the remaining 35% fell within the 16 to 19 yrs. age group. In terms of family type, the majority of participants (58.98%) came from nuclear families. Regarding maternal education, the highest percentage of mothers (61.74%) had completed primary or secondary education, followed by 21.69% of mothers who had attained higher secondary education. Furthermore, economic inequality exacerbates the issue, as it limits access to private sanitary facilities, thereby increasing the risk of infection (Table 56.1). The majority of the families (58.98%) reported an income of less than ₹10,000, while 30.57% had a monthly income ranging from ₹10,001 to ₹15,000. Only 10.45% of families reported a monthly income greater than ₹15,000. These demographic trends reflect the age distribution, family structure, maternal educational background, and economic conditions of the study sample.

Table 56.1 Demographic profile of the participants

Variable (n = 1014)	Frequency	Percentage (%)
Age (Years)		
12-15	659	65
16-19	355	35
Family Type		
Nuclear	598	58.98
Joint	416	41.02
Mother's education		
Illiterate	124	12.23
Primary/ Secondary	626	61.74
Higher secondary	220	21.69
Degree and above	44	4.34
Monthly family income		
<₹10000	598	58.98
₹10001- ₹15000	310	30.57
>₹15000	106	10.45

The study findings on menarche and perceptions about menstruation among the participants revealed significant insights (Table 56.2). The majority (88.95%) reported experiencing menarche between 10-13 years, while 11.05% had their first menstruation between 13-15 years. About 42.21% lack prior knowledge about menstruation. Notably, 38.07% were unaware about the source of menstrual bleeding, and misconceptions prevailed, with 30.77% identifying the vagina, 19.72% the bladder, and 11.44% the uterus. Emotional and discomfort reactions to first menstruation were reported by 51.88% and 48.12%,, respectively. A majority of participants attributed menstruation to disease (47.14%) or God's curse (36.59%). Various restrictions during menstruation were reported, including worship of God (23.49%), outdoor activities (17.67%), and consuming sour foods (12.29%). Interestingly, only 0.33% reported no restrictions. These findings highlight the need for improved menstrual health education, addressing misconceptions and cultural practices that impact menstrual health.

The majority of participants (86.39%) used sanitary pads, while 13.61% used cloth. Among cloth users, 65.22% cleaned the menstrual cloth with soap and water, and 34.78% used only water. Most participants (83.82%) dried their menstrual products in a hidden place. The frequency of changing absorbent material varied, with 67.06% changing once a day, and only 5.13% three times or more. The most common disposal method was

Table 56.2 Information about menarche and perception about menstruation

Single-response variable (n=1014)	Frequency	Percentage (%)
Age at menarche (Years)		
10-13	902	88.95
>13- 15	112	11.05
Awareness about menstruation prior menarche		
Yes	586	57.79
No	428	42.21
Sources of bleeding		
Uterus	116	11.44
Bladder	200	19.72
Vagina	312	30.77
Don't have idea	386	38.07
Reaction to first menstruation		
Emotional	526	51.88
Discomfort	488	48.12
Causes of menses		
Curse of God	371	36.59
Hormonal	165	16.27
Disease	478	47.14
Multi--response variables (n = 4257)		
Restrictions during menstruation		
Touching a person	467	10.97
Social gathering	350	8.22
Outdoor activity	752	17.67
Taking sour foods	523	12.29
Entering temple/ mosque	1000	23.49
Taking bath	78	1.83
Allowed in kitchen	450	10.57
Physical activity	623	14.63
No restriction	14	0.33

wrapping the product in paper and throwing it in a dustbin (50.69%), followed by burying in soil (25.25%), throwing in an open place (13.41%), and burning (9.47%). These findings highlight the need for education on hygienic menstrual product management and sustainable disposal methods, particularly given the reliance on dustbins and the use of cloth by a significant portion of the population (Table 56.3).

4. Discussion

The demographic characteristics of the study population provide valuable insights into the socio-economic and familial factors that may influence the health and well-being of adolescents. The age distribution revealed a significant concentration of participants in the 12-15 yrs. age group (65%), corresponding to a critical

Table 56.3 Disposal of menstrual product

Single-response variable (n=1014)	Frequency	Percentage (%)
Use of absorbent material during menstruation		
Cloth	138	13.61
Sanitary pads	876	86.39
Cleaning of menstrual cloth (n=138)		
Only with water	48	34.78
With soap and water	90	65.22
Place of drying menstrual material (n=1014)		
Hidden	850	83.82
Normal	164	16.18
Frequency of changing absorbent (n=1014)		
One time	680	67.06
Two time	282	27.81
Three times and more	52	5.13
Disposal method (n=1014)		
Wrap in paper and throw dustbin	514	50.69
Bury in soil	256	25.25
Throw open place	136	13.41
Flush in toilet	12	1.18
Burn	96	9.47

developmental stage during adolescence when menstrual health education and access to sanitation are paramount. Khanna et al. [12] reported a mean age of menarche of 13.2 years. The predominance of nuclear families (58.98%) is noteworthy, as family structure can impact resource availability and social support systems for adolescents, particularly in the context of health education and menstrual hygiene management. Nuclear families may face specific challenges, such as limited financial support, which could affect adolescent well-being, especially when access to sanitary products and proper menstrual health education is insufficient. Maternal knowledge is crucial in influencing the health outcomes of daughters. About 21.69% of mothers attained higher secondary education suggesting that those percentages of adolescents may have access to better education and health literacy. However, a large section of participants faced barriers in accessing accurate information regarding menstrual health and hygiene.

Socio-economic condition is often linked with sanitation and hygienic practices [13]. The economic conditions of the study population further complicate the situation. This can result inadequate access to water, sanitation and hygiene (WASH) facilities, elevating the risk of urinary tract infections and long-term health complications.

The interplay between family structure, maternal education, and economic conditions contributes significantly to adolescent health. The combination of low family income, limited maternal education, and inadequate sanitation facilities exacerbates menstrual health challenges. Targeted interventions including improved access to affordable sanitary products, menstrual health education and community-based awareness programs are necessary to mitigate these risks.

The majority of participants reported experiencing menarche between 10-13 years. However, 42.21% lacked prior knowledge about menstruation, highlighting a critical gap in health education. Misconceptions, social taboos and stigma about menstruation were prevalent among the adolescents, with 38.07% unaware of the source of menstrual bleeding. They have dearth of knowledge regarding the source of menstrual blood.

The emotional and physical responses to menarche were observed among the participants. This suggests that the first experience of menstruation can be both physically challenging and emotionally significant. Culturally influenced beliefs about menstruation were prevalent, with 47.14% attributing menstruation to disease and 36.59% considering it a curse from God. These misconceptions reflect the persistence of cultural taboos and stigmas surrounding menstruation, hindering open discussions about menstrual health and well-being. A range of restrictions during menstruation was reported.

The predominant use of sanitary pads (86.39%) suggests relatively high access to modern menstrual products. However, the notable reliance on cloth (13.61%) indicates barriers in accessing sanitary pads, likely due to economic constraints or limited availability. Among cloth users, 65.22% employed soap and water for cleaning, while 34.78% used only water. The use of soap and water is a more hygienic practice, reducing infection risk. However, the reliance on water alone by nearly one-third of cloth users suggests a need for education on soap use to prevent bacterial contamination. About 83.82% of participants dried menstrual products in hidden places, often due to cultural taboos. This practice can lead to inadequate drying, promoting bacterial growth and infection risk. Therefore, awareness of hygienic practices and the importance of air-drying menstrual products in well-ventilated areas are crucial. The frequency of changing absorbent materials varied, with 67.06% changing once a day. In terms of disposal methods, wrapping used products in paper and discarding in a dustbin was the most common practice (50.69%). This method raises environmental sustainability concerns due to increased disposable product use. Burying used menstrual products in soil (25.25%) is more environmentally sustainable but may not be feasible or hygienic in urban settings. Other disposal methods including throwing products in open places or putting in toilet chamber pose environmental contamination and health risks.

The data presented in this study highlights the urgent need for health-education policies, improved educational opportunities for women, financial support for low-income families and enhanced access to sanitary facilities. Adolescent girls may be advised to consume probiotic-enriched foods and indigenous fish [14-16]. They not only provide beneficial bioactive substances [17,18] or neutraceuticals [19,20] but also develop gut eubiosis [21,22]. The development of sanitary infrastructure is crucial when combined with health education and reproductive health programs [23,24,25].

5. Conclusion

This study emphasizes the need for comprehensive measures to improve menstrual health among adolescents, addressing socio-economic, cultural, and educational factors. Economic challenges, limited access to products, and social stigma exacerbate the issue. Educational programs, distribution of affordable menstrual products, and addressing harmful cultural practices are essential. Ensuring access to hygienic products and proper menstrual education will improve health, well-being, and dignity, empowering adolescent girls to manage their menstrual health confidently.

References

1. Ganguly, M., Ganguly, A., Chattaraj, S., & Midya, D. K. (2025a). A review on menstrual health in adolescent girls emphasizing multi-omics and machine learning strategies for preventing reproductive tract infections. Discov. Public Health, 22, 105. https://doi.org/10.1186/s12982-025-00485-x
2. Ganguly, M., Jana, S., Ganguly, A., Chattaraj, S., Banerjee, A., & Midya, D. K. (2025b). Menstrual hygiene management among the rural school-going adolescent girls with special emphasis to the Kora tribe in West Bengal, India. Discover Public Health, 22, 265. https://doi.org/10.1186/s12982-025-00663-x
3. Dasgupta, A., & Sarkar, M. (2008). Menstrual hygiene: How hygienic is the adolescent girl? Indian J. Community Med., 33(2), 77–80. https://doi.org/10.4103/0970-0218.40872
4. Sommer, M., Ackatia-Armah, N., Connolly, S., & Smiles, D. (2015). A comparison of the menstruation and education experiences of girls in Tanzania, Ghana, Cambodia, and Ethiopia. Compare: A Journal of Comparative and International Education, 45(4), 589–609. https://doi.org/10.1080/03057925.2013.871399
5. Ganguly, M., & Midya, D. K. (2023). Menstrual hygiene among school-going early adolescent girls (10–14 years): A socio-cultural study in Bankura District, West Bengal, India. Acta Biol. Szeged., 67(1), 103–110. https://doi.org/10.14232/abs.2023.1.103-110
6. Goel, M. K., & Kundan, M. (2011). Psycho-social behaviour of urban Indian adolescent girls during menstruation. Australas. Med. J., 4(1), 49. https://doi.org/10.4066/AMJ.2011.464
7. Adewuya, A., Loto, O., & Adewumi, T. (2008). Premenstrual dysphoric disorder amongst Nigerian university students: Prevalence, comorbid conditions,

and correlates. Arch. WomensMent. Health, 11(1), 13–18. https://doi.org/10.1007/s00737-008-0210-2
8. Omu, F. E., Al-Marzouk, R., Delles, H., Oranye, N. O., & Omu, A. E. (2011). Premenstrual dysphoric disorder: Prevalence and effects on nursing students' academic performance and clinical training in Kuwait. Journal of Clinical Nursing, 20(19–20), 2915–2923. https://doi.org/10.1111/j.1365-2702.2010.03574.x
9. Tegegne, T. K., & Sisay, M. M. (2014). Menstrual hygiene management and school absenteeism among female adolescent students in Northeast Ethiopia. BMC Public Health, 14(1), 1118. https://doi.org/10.1186/1471-2458-14-1118
10. Fakhri, M., Hamzehgardeshi, Z., Golchin, N. A. H., & Komili, A. (2012). Promoting menstrual health among Persian adolescent girls from low socioeconomic backgrounds: A quasi-experimental study. BMC Public Health, 12(1), 193. https://doi.org/10.1186/1471-2458-12-193
11. Poureslami, M., & Osati-Ashtiani, F. (2002). Assessing knowledge, attitudes, and behavior of adolescent girls in suburban districts of Tehran about dysmenorrhea and menstrual hygiene. Journal of International Women's Studies, 3(2), 51–61.
12. Khanna, A., Goyal, R. S., &Bhawsar, R. (2005). Menstrual practices and reproductive problems: A study of adolescent girls in Rajasthan. J. Health Manag., 7(1), 91–97.
13. Ganguly, M., & Ganguly, A. (2015). A study on anthropometric measurement, socio-economic conditions, and occupational health problems of Baluchari sari weavers of Bishnupur. Int. J. Curr. Res., 7(7), 17722–17729.
14. Ganguly, A., Chattaraj, S., Ganguly, M., Chattaraj, M., Banerjee, A., Mandal, A., Khan, M. A., Sen, S. K., & Das Mohapatra, P. K. (2024a). Effect of three probiotic Bacillus strains supplemented feeds on growth, carcass composition and blood parameters of *Clarias magur* (Hamilton). J. Appl. Aquacult. https://doi.org/10.1080/10454438.2024.2330499
15. Ganguly, A., Banerjee, A., Mandal, A., & Das Mohapatra, P. K. (2018a). Study of indigenous freshwater fish diversity of Bankura (West Bengal), India with special reference to *Clarias batrachus*. J. Appl. Nat. Sci., 10, 1162–1172. https://doi.org/10.31018/jans.v10i4.1892
16. Chattaraj, S., Behera, B. K., & Das Mohapatra, P. K. (2024). Effective valorization of Chlorella biomass and Brewers spent grain substituting fish meal and soybean meal in the diet of herbivorous fish Cirrhinusreba for higher growth, digestibility and sustainable cultivation. Journal of Applied Phycology, 36(1), 217–232.
17. Chattaraj, S., Mitra, D., Chattaraj, A., Chattaraj, M., Kundu, M., Ganguly, A., & Das Mohapatra, P.K. (2023a). Anti-oncogenic potential of probiotics: Challenges and future prospects. Indian J. Microbiol. Res., 10(1), 1–10. https://doi.org/10.18231/j.ijmr.2023.001
18. Ganguly, A., Kirtania, D. K., Chhetri, M., & Chattaraj, S. (2025c). Sustainable development through probiotics: A scientometric analysis of Indian research and innovation. *Discover Sustainability, 6*, 455. https://doi.org/10.1007/s43621-025-01263-0
19. Ganguly, A., Banerjee, A., Mandal, A., Khan, M. A., & Das Mohapatra, P. K. (2019). Isolation and characterization of bacteria from the intestine of *Clarias batrachus* for probiotic organism. Proc. Zool. Soc., 72(4), 411–419. https://doi.org/10.1007/s12595-018-0283-x
20. Chattaraj, S., Ganguly, A., Mitra, D., & Das Mohapatra, P.K. (2023b). Study of intestinal bacteria of *Cirrhinus reba* and characterization of a new probiotic bacteria: An initiative to save the threatened species of Cirrhinus. Appl. Biochem. Microbiol., 59(6), 833–849. https://doi.org/10.1134/S0003683823060248
21. Chattaraj, S., Ganguly, A., Mandal, A., & Das Mohapatra, P.K. (2022). A review of the role of probiotics for the control of viral diseases in aquaculture. Aquac. Int. https://doi.org/10.1007/s10499-022-00915-6
22. Ganguly, A., Banerjee, A., Mandal, A., & Das Mohapatra, P. K. (2018b). Probiotic-based cultivation of *Clarias batrachus*: Importance and future perspective. Acta Biol. Szeged., 62(2), 158–168. https://doi.org/10.14232/abs.2018.2.158-168
23. Ganguly, M., Jana, S., Ganguly, A., & Midya, D. K. (2024b). Menstruation in adolescent girls: Myths & taboos. Acta Biol. Slov., 67(2), 67. https://doi.org/10.14720/abs.67.2.18725
24. Ganguly, A., Konar, R., Kirtania, D. K., Ganguly, M., Chattaraj, M., Mitra, D., & Chattaraj, S. (2025). *Employing technological innovation for eco-friendly waste disposal at a global scale*. In *AI technologies for enhancing recycling processes* (pp. 135–152). IGI Global. https://doi.org/10.4018/979-8-3693-7282-1.ch008
25. Chattaraj, M., Goswami, A., Ganguly, A., & Chattaraj, S. (2025). *Considerations of policy and morality in waste management*. In *AI technologies for enhancing recycling processes* (pp. 233–266). IGI Global. https://doi.org/10.4018/979-8-3693-7282-1.ch012

Note: All the tables in this chapter were made by the authors.

Research and Innovations in Industrial and Marine Biotechnology: A Circular Economy 2024 – Prof. Hrudayanath Thatoi et al. (eds)
© 2026 Taylor & Francis Group, London, ISBN 978-1-041-28285-3

57 Patterns and Evolutionary Dynamics of Codon Usage Bias

Mehak Kanwar
Centre for Industrial Biotechnology Research,
Siksha 'O' Anusandhan Deemed to be University, Kalinganagar, Odisha, India
Department of Physiology, Immunology Laboratory, University of Calcutta,
University Colleges of Science and Technology, 92 APC Road,
Kolkata, West Bengal, India

Hrudayanath Thatoi
Director, Centre for Industrial Biotechnology Research,
Siksha 'O' Anusandhan Deemed to be University, Bhubaneswar, Odisha, India

Amrita Banerjee*
Assistant Professor (Research), Centre for Industrial Biotechnology Research,
Siksha 'O' Anusandhan Deemed to be University,
Bhubaneswar, Odisha, India

Abstract: The phenomenon of Codon Usage Bias (CUB) appears in various organisms through the preferred selection of specific synonymous codons for particular amino acids. Scientists first viewed CUB as an unimportant occurrence until they discovered it results from biological mechanisms which include mRNA stability, translation efficiency and cellular adaptability. The review examines the main determinants of codon usage patterns through mutational pressure, natural selection, genetic drift and tRNA availability while discussing interspecies differences. The review examines how codon bias affects proteome amino acid composition because it influences protein folding accuracy and synthesis speed and drives evolutionary processes.

Keywords: Translational efficiency, Synonymous codons, tRNA abundance, Protein folding, Codon usage bias

1. Introduction

The genetic code redundancy enables multiple synonymous codons to encode identical amino acids which leads to codon usage bias (CUB) where particular codons appear more frequently than others. The first explanation of codon usage bias as a result of neutral evolutionary mechanisms such as mutational drift [1] has evolved into an understanding that this phenomenon emerges from multiple evolutionary forces including natural selection, mutational bias, tRNA gene copy number and effective population size [2,3]. Selection forces in organisms with large populations and highly expressed genes choose codons that match abundant tRNAs to enhance translation efficiency, accuracy and mRNA stability [4,5]. The influence of genetic drift and mutational bias on codon preferences becomes more pronounced in genes with low expression levels and small effective population sizes of organisms [6]. Research using ribosome profiling and proteogenomic analysis shows that the selection of synonymous codons affects translation speed and protein folding during translation as well as the final protein functions [7,8]. The study of codon usage bias enables scientists to understand evolutionary mechanisms and produces practical benefits for gene expression control, vaccine design and synthetic biology applications. This

*Corresponding author: amritabanerjee@soa.ac.in

DOI: 10.1201/9781003759003-57

review explores the scientific foundation of codon usage patterns and their evolutionary processes and practical applications.

2. Determinants of CUB

Genomes choose synonymous codons non-randomly because evolutionary pressure along with molecular systems create Codon usage bias (CUB). Mutational pressure functions as the main cause of bias because it represents the unequal rates of nucleotide substitutions that match the genomic base composition. The nucleotide composition of genomes determines which codons containing G or C will be favored by high GC content genomes and which codons ending in A or T will be preferred by AT-rich genomes [1]. The genetic makeup of *Mycobacterium tuberculosis* and *Plasmodium falciparum* shows evidence of following nucleotide composition-based codon preferences [6]. The low strength of natural selection on genes with low expression levels results in more prominent mutation-driven codon bias.

Natural selection takes precedence as the dominant mechanism which determines codon preferences in highly expressed genes to enhance both translation accuracy and efficiency. The fast-growing bacteria *E. coli* and yeast *Saccharomyces cerevisiae* select codons that correspond to their available tRNA pool to achieve maximum translation speed with minimal errors [3,4]. Scientists created two quantitative assessment methods named tRNA Adaptation Index (tAI) and Codon Adaptation Index (CAI) to measure codon optimization levels [5].

The effectiveness of genetic drift in shaping codon usage patterns increases with decreasing effective population sizes in multicellular species. Human codon bias remains weaker than *Drosophila species* so the fixation of suboptimal codons becomes more likely [2]. The presence of tRNA molecules together with translational selection systems drives the evolutionary process of codon usage. The number of tRNA genes along with their expression levels in organisms functions to maximize translation speed but also prevent ribosomal delays. *E. coli* implements a translation mechanism which selects codons from highly expressed genes that correspond to its abundant tRNA population to enhance translation speed [3,9]. Gene expression and organismal adaptation emerges from the combination of mutational biases and selection pressures and genetic drift and translational demands which regulate the evolutionary development of codon usage patterns. (Fig. 57.1.)(Table 57.1.).

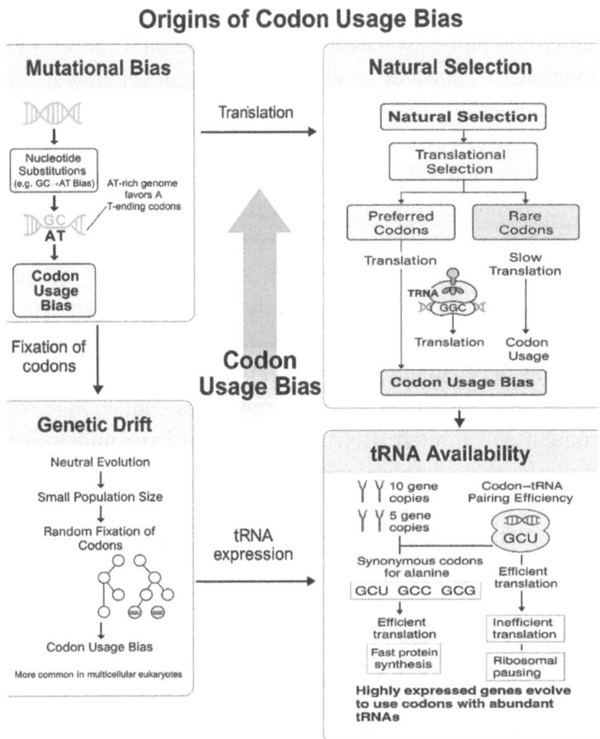

Fig. 57.1 Mechanisms driving CUB

3. Patterns of Codon Usage Across Organisms

The three main factors that drive codon usage pattern evolution are translational selection and mutational pressure and genomic composition in different organisms. Fast-growing prokaryotes including *Escherichia coli* select codons that match abundant tRNA molecules such as AAA

Table 57.1 Key factors that influence codon usage bias together with their mechanisms, dominant contexts and their effects on translation and genome evolution

Factor	Underlying Mechanism	Prominent in	Impact on CUB
Mutational Pressure	Base substitution tendencies linked to GC or AT content	Lowly expressed genes; genomes with extreme GC/AT bias	Establishes fundamental codon patterns reflecting nucleotide composition
Selective Pressure	Enhances translation speed, accuracy, and efficiency	Highly expressed microbial genes	Promotes preferred codons aligned with abundant tRNAs, boosting translation
Genetic Drift	Random allele fixation due to small effective population size	Complex multicellular organisms (e.g., mammals)	Reduces selection impact, leading to weaker or less consistent codon preferences
tRNA pool Composition	Variability in tRNA gene count and expression	Prokaryotes, yeast, fast-growing cells	Affects translation efficiency by favoring codons with matching abundant tRNAs

(Lys), GAA (Glu) and CAA (Gln) to enhance translation efficiency [4]. The GC content of species determines their codon usage because high-GC organisms such as Streptomyces select G/C-ending codons but low-GC organisms including *Bacillus* select A/T-ending codons. The codon preferences of *Saccharomyces cerevisiae* genes depend on tRNA abundance for highly expressed genes but low-expression genes show stronger effects from mutation and genetic drift [10]. Organisms adapt their codon usage patterns when they encounter environmental stress and changes in nutrient availability. The development of codon bias in multicellular eukaryotes results from the combined effects of gene expression levels and tissue specificity and splicing enhancers and mRNA secondary structure and chromatin organization [11]. Viruses select codons that match their host's preferences to boost their translation and replication speed. Scientists employ codon deoptimization techniques to develop attenuated viral vaccines for medical purposes [12]. The codon usage patterns of organelle genomes including mitochondria and chloroplasts differ because these genomes contain high AT content and limited tRNA diversity and have undergone evolutionary genome simplification [13].

4. Functional Implications of CUB

The various stages of gene expression and protein biosynthesis experience substantial effects from Codon usage bias (CUB). The use of optimal codons which match abundant cellular tRNAs leads to fast and precise translation that results in better protein production efficiency. The translation process becomes delayed because of rare codons which causes ribosomes to stall and triggers mRNA surveillance mechanisms that lead to degradation [14]. The placement of codons within coding sequences determines how proteins fold during co-translational processes. The strategic placement of slowly translated codons within coding sequences allows time for nascent polypeptides to fold properly, reducing the likelihood of misfolding and aggregation [15]. The selection of codons affects the stability of mRNA structure. The stability of mRNA secondary structures depends on specific codons which extend transcript longevity, but rare codons lead to decreased mRNA stability [16]. The arrangement of codons throughout an mRNA transcript controls how ribosomes move through the sequence. The arrangement of optimal codons enables ribosomes to move along mRNA transcripts in a continuous and uniform pattern. The translation process becomes disrupted when rare codons cluster together because ribosomes collide which affects protein output [17]. The selection of synonymous codons plays a crucial role in determining both transcript and protein-level results.

5. Amino Acid Composition and CUB

During translation, the selection of codons determines which amino acids enter a developing polypeptide chain and affects the final amino acid distribution throughout the proteome. In highly expressed genes the usage of tRNA codons in abundance leads to increased incorporation of alanine and glycine amino acids in translated proteins [18]. The codon-driven selection represents a resource-efficient strategy that allows cells to select amino acids with lower biosynthetic costs. The translational preference in *Escherichia coli* shows that codons which translate into inexpensive amino acids are used [19]. The non-random usage of synonymous codons leads to changes in amino acid frequencies throughout the proteome especially when genes face strong translational selection. Evolution establishes a synchronized connection between codon usage patterns and amino acid sequences to maximize both translation performance and protein functionality. The computational models ASUMDE and ROC-SEMPPR demonstrate how natural selection modifies codon usage patterns to achieve equilibrium between translation speed and efficiency and accuracy. The structure of proteins determines how codons are preferred in their sequences. The optimization of codon usage in structured

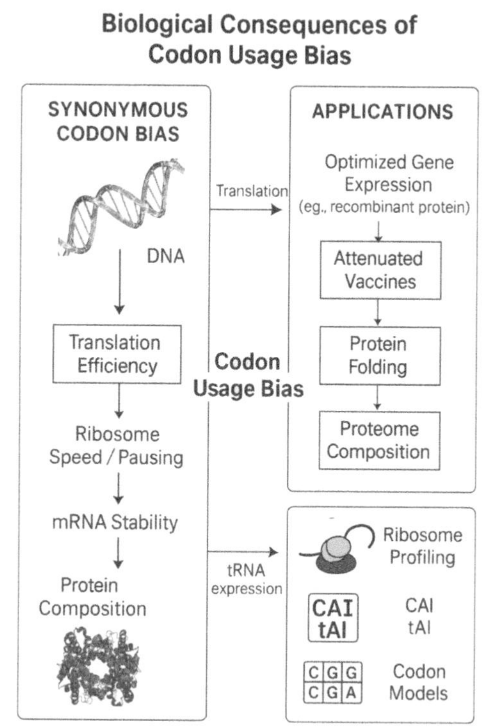

Fig. 57.2 Biological consequences of CUB. The translation process together with mRNA stability and protein folding are affected by CUB which also affects gene expression and enables applications in synthetic biology and vaccine design. The tools used are ribosome profiling, CAI, tAI, and codon models

domains promotes proper protein folding but intrinsically disordered regions accept a wider variety of codons [20]. The functional integrity, structural complexity and total amino acid composition of an organism's proteome directly depend on codon usage bias.

6. Mechanistic Insights and Molecular Interactions

The translational mechanisms show strong dependence on codon usage bias because of its effects on tRNA pools and ribosomes and mRNA structural elements. The regulation of tRNA gene copy numbers by organisms leads to improved translational efficiency because it matches codon usage patterns in highly expressed genes of *Escherichia coli* and *Saccharomyces cerevisiae* [3,9]. The presence of duplicate tRNA genes serves as a protective mechanism which maintains efficient translation during stressful conditions and times of rapid protein synthesis. The strategic placement of rare codons within protein domains enables ribosomal pausing which leads to correct co-translational folding [15]. The incorrect incorporation of amino acids at error-prone codons results in dysfunctional or toxic proteins thus natural selection works against these codons to maintain translational fidelity. The recognition between codons and anticodons depends on Watson–Crick base pairing and wobble rules which produce stronger interactions between G/C-ending codons and improve translation accuracy. The selection of codons affects mRNA secondary structure because stable stem-loops block ribosomal scanning, but unstructured regions promote initiation [7]. The patterns of codons influence mRNA stability through their impact on RNA-binding protein and decay complex interactions which establishes a connection between codon bias and post-transcriptional regulation [16].

7. Evolutionary Models Linking Amino Acid and Codon Bias

The codon usage evolution results from the combined actions of mutation, genetic drift and natural selection. The ASUMDE model demonstrates that large populations select optimal codons to boost translation efficiency, but small populations develop suboptimal codons because of genetic drift [18]. Genomes with elevated GC content tend to use alanine codons more frequently because of both natural mutation patterns and evolutionary selection forces. The ROC-SEMPPR Bayesian model predicts codon usage patterns through its analysis of gene expression levels and tRNA availability and mutation rates to determine translation efficiency and fidelity and energy costs [20]. Models that focus on specific contexts show that structured protein regions need stronger codon optimization to achieve proper folding and functional stability.

8. Experimental Evidence Supporting Codon Bias Effects

The results of synonymous mutagenesis studies demonstrate that modifying codon usage leads to significant changes in gene expression while maintaining protein sequence identity through the example of *E. coli* GFP expression which varies by more than 250-fold [7]. The translation analysis method called ribosome profiling shows that optimal codons create denser ribosome distribution which leads to better protein production [14]. E. coli cells in long-term evolution experiments under nutrient-rich conditions select optimal codons which leads to better protein folding and faster cellular growth [21].

9. Applications and Biotechnological Significance

The optimization of codons leads to better heterologous protein expression through the matching of codon usage with host tRNA availability and GC content. The tools GeneOptimizer and DNAWorks modify coding sequences to boost protein production levels without affecting regulatory elements or splicing signals or protein folding. The process of codon deoptimization leads to the development of attenuated vaccines through reduced viral replication as shown in polio and influenza. The use of host-optimized codon sequences in cancer therapy enables viral replication to occur specifically in tumor cells. Industrial biotechnology uses codon engineering to enhance enzyme yield and stability and activity. The engineered microbes that express optimized cellulase genes demonstrate better biomass degradation capabilities for biofuel production and pharmaceutical synthesis and food processing.

10. Future Directions and Research Gaps

The scientific community continues to face multiple essential questions regarding codon usage bias (CUB) despite recent advancements. The scientific community lacks comprehensive understanding about how CUB affects non-coding RNAs, how it regulates translation during extreme environmental conditions and how N6-methyladenosine (m6A) epitranscriptomic modifications affect codon-mediated translation. The combination of single-cell transcriptomics with cryo-electron microscopy and machine learning technologies provides researchers with new ways to study gene expression at the codon level. Research findings demonstrate that synonymous codons which were previously considered neutral influence translation speed and protein folding during translation and lead to cancer and neurodegenerative disease phenotypes.

The findings validate the sequence-based regulatory model of CUB which functions similarly to epigenetic modifications to shape proteome composition and cellular stress responses and evolutionary adaptability.

11. Conclusion

Non-random codon usage patterns are demonstrated by genetic codes because mutational pressure, natural selection, tRNA abundance and population have all influenced its evolution. The translation efficiency, mRNA stability and protein folding are influenced by codon usage bias (CUB) without any evident changes to the coded amino acid sequence. The variations in CUB across different species and genes and expression levels demonstrate both adaptive evolution and functional constraints. Ribosome profiling and computational analyses have shown that synonymous codons have a significant impact on gene expression and protein functionality. CUB is recognized as a regulatory element and plays a vital role in genome evolution, synthetic biology, and vaccine design. The continued exploration of CUB is essential for understanding molecular evolution and enhancing biotechnological applications.

References

1. Sueoka, N. (1962). On the genetic basis of variation and heterogeneity of DNA base composition. *Proceedings of the National Academy of Sciences*, *48*(4), 582–592.
2. Bulmer, M. (1991). The selection-mutation-drift theory of synonymous codon usage. *Genetics*, *129*(3), 897–907
3. Ikemura, T. (1981). Correlation between the abundance of Escherichia coli transfer RNAs and the occurrence of the respective codons in its protein genes: a proposal for a synonymous codon choice that is optimal for the E. coli translational system. *Journal of molecular biology*, *151*(3), 389–409.
4. Sharp, P. M., & Li, W. H. (1987). The codon adaptation index-a measure of directional synonymous codon usage bias, and its potential applications. *Nucleic acids research*, *15*(3), 1281–1295.
5. Reis, M. D., Savva, R., &Wernisch, L. (2004). Solving the riddle of codon usage preferences: a test for translational selection. *Nucleic acids research*, *32*(17), 5036–5044.
6. Chen, S. L., Lee, W., Hottes, A. K., Shapiro, L., & McAdams, H. H. (2004). Codon usage between genomes is constrained by genome-wide mutational processes. *Proceedings of the National Academy of Sciences*, *101*(10), 3480–3485.
7. Kudla, G., Murray, A. W., Tollervey, D., & Plotkin, J. B. (2009). Coding-sequence determinants of gene expression in Escherichia coli. *science*, *324*(5924), 255–258.
8. Plotkin, J. B., & Kudla, G. (2011). Synonymous but not the same: the causes and consequences of codon bias. *Nature Reviews Genetics*, *12*(1), 32–42.
9. Dong, H., Nilsson, L., & Kurland, C. G. (1996). Co-variation of trna abundance and codon usage inescherichia coliat different growth rates. *Journal of molecular biology*, *260*(5), 649–663.
10. Duret, L., &Mouchiroud, D. (1999). Expression pattern and, surprisingly, gene length shape codon usage in Caenorhabditis, Drosophila, and Arabidopsis. *Proceedings of the National Academy of Sciences*, *96*(8), 4482–4487.
11. Waldman, Y. Y., Tuller, T., Shlomi, T., Sharan, R., &Ruppin, E. (2010). Translation efficiency in humans: tissue specificity, global optimization and differences between developmental stages. *Nucleic acids research*, *38*(9), 2964–2974.
12. Mueller, S., Papamichail, D., Coleman, J. R., Skiena, S., & Wimmer, E. (2006). Reduction of the rate of poliovirus protein synthesis through large-scale codon deoptimization causes attenuation of viral virulence by lowering specific infectivity. *Journal of virology*, *80*(19), 9687–9696.
13. Smith, D. R., & Keeling, P. J. (2015). Mitochondrial and plastid genome architecture: reoccurring themes, but significant differences at the extremes. *Proceedings of the National Academy of Sciences*, *112*(33), 10177–10184.
14. Ingolia, N. T., Ghaemmaghami, S., Newman, J. R., & Weissman, J. S. (2009). Genome-wide analysis in vivo of translation with nucleotide resolution using ribosome profiling. *science*, *324*(5924), 218–223.
15. Buhr, F., Jha, S., Thommen, M., Mittelstaet, J., Kutz, F., Schwalbe, H., ... & Komar, A. A. (2016). Synonymous codons direct cotranslational folding toward different protein conformations. *Molecular cell*, *61*(3), 341–351.
16. Presnyak, V., Alhusaini, N., Chen, Y. H., Martin, S., Morris, N., Kline, N., ... & Coller, J. (2015). Codon optimality is a major determinant of mRNA stability. *Cell*, *160*(6), 1111–1124.
17. Tuller, T., Waldman, Y. Y., Kupiec, M., &Ruppin, E. (2010). Translation efficiency is determined by both codon bias and folding energy. *Proceedings of the national academy of sciences*, *107*(8), 3645–3650.
18. Gilchrist, M. A., Chen, W. C., Shah, P., Landerer, C. L., &Zaretzki, R. (2015). Estimating gene expression and codon-specific translational efficiencies, mutation biases, and selection coefficients from genomic data alone. *Genome biology and evolution*, *7*(6), 1559–1579.
19. Akashi, H., &Gojobori, T. (2002). Metabolic efficiency and amino acid composition in the proteomes of Escherichia coli and Bacillus subtilis. *Proceedings of the National Academy of Sciences*, *99*(6), 3695–3700.
20. Cope, A. L., Gilchrist, M. A., Shah, P., & Wallace, E. (2024). Evolutionary principles underpinning codon usage bias: patterns, functions, and mechanisms.
21. Barrick, J. E., Yu, D. S., Yoon, S. H., Jeong, H., Oh, T. K., Schneider, D., ... & Kim, J. F. (2009). Genome evolution and adaptation in a long-term experiment with Escherichia coli. *Nature*, *461*(7268), 1243–1247.

Note: All the figures and table in this chapter were made by the authors.

Research and Innovations in Industrial and Marine Biotechnology: A Circular Economy 2024 – Prof. Hrudayanath Thatoi et al. (eds)

58 Enhancement of Thermo-Oxidative Stability of Mustard Oil by Mangrove Plant Extract

Swagat Kumar Das*, Rojali Samantray
Department of Biotechnology, Odisha University of Technology and Research, Bhubaneswar, Odisha, India

Abstract: This study evaluated the oxidative resistance of mustard oil supplemented with extract of *Bruguiera sexangula* (BS) bark extracted using ethanol during accelerated storing and frying condition. The results revealed that BS possessed high total phenolic compound (119 mg CE/g extract) and total flavonoid compound (7 mg QE/ g extract). The IC_{50} values of antioxidant capacities of BS calculated were 74.43 µg/ml and 122.56 µg/ml respectively for DPPH and H_2O_2 study. BS at 0.5 % w/v could reduce the peroxide value (PV) during accelerated storage condition. Similarly, the BS could reduce the PV, carbonyl value (CV)and iodine value (IV) of the mustard oil during frying process. The result suggested that *B. sexangula* ethanol extract could be useful in prevention the mustard oil from oxidation under accelerated storage and frying condition.

Keywords: *Bruguiera sexangula*, Mustard oil, Rancidity, Accelerated storage, Frying

1. Introduction

Oil deterioration also known as oil rancidification involves either complete or partial auto-oxidation or hydrolysis of fats and oils upon contact with air, light, heat, moisture or bacteria. This led to unpleasant taste and odour. Therefore, heating of cooking of oil under high temperature in presence of moist air led to several chemical reactions e.g., thermal oxidation, fission, hydrolysis, and polymerization [1]. This causes decomposition of oil and generation of volatile compounds, monomers, polymers, reactive oxygen species, that are associated to inflammation, carcinogenesis and cardiovascular diseases[2].Therefore, numerous strategies are being carried out to enhance the oxidation resistance of storage oil and processing viz., changing the oil extraction conditions, dodging light, oxygen, avoiding high temperatures, and addition of antioxidant compounds. However, synthetic antioxidants that frequently used in oil like butylated hydroxy toluene (BHT), tertiary butylhydroquinone, butylated hydroxy anisole (BHA), and propyl gallate are only effective at low temperatures but ineffective during frying of oil at about 180°C and may not be safe for consumption [3]. Therefore, screening of antioxidants of natural origin *viz.*, phytochemical origin and essential oils, can be considered useful.

The mustard oil widely used for cooking contains about 81% of unsaturated fatty acids out of which 60 % are monounsaturated fatty acids (MUFA) and 21% are polyunsaturated fats (PUFA) whereas the saturated fatty acids accounts for 12 %[4].The major types of fatty acids were reported in mustard oil such as palmitic (16 carbon chain), stearic (18 carbon chain), oleic (18 carbon atom and single double bond), linoleic (18 carbon atom and two double bond), linolenic (18 carbon atom and 3 double bond), eicosanoic (22 carbon chain), and erucic (22 carbon chain with one double bond) acids [5]. The PUFA rich vegetable oils are more susceptible to degradation by the action of oxygen. Therefore, delaying lipid oxidation of oil would be of great value from both industry as well as health prospective.

Antioxidants obtained from different natural sources including plants, spices and herbs possess phytochemicals with enormous antioxidant potential that can slow down oxidation of lipid. *Bruguiera sexangula* a medicinal

*Corresponding author: das.swagat@gmail.com

DOI: 10.1201/9781003759003-58

mangrove plant growing in tropical intertidal zone and sub-tropical region has been documented for its enormous antioxidant properties. *B. sexangula* extract antioxidant potential is attributed to presence of different phytochemicals viz., phenols, flavonoids, dammarane triterpenes, pimaren diterpenes [6]. In the present study, bark extract of *Bruguiera sexangular* was evaluated for its potential to prevent rancidification of oil during frying and storage.

2. Materials and Method

2.1 Sample Materials and Chemicals

Mustard oil used for the study was procured from local markets of Bhubaneswar, Odisha, India. 2,2′-diphenyl-1-picrylhydrazyl (DPPH) reagent, butylatedhydroxytoluene (BHT), hydrogen peroxidewas obtained from SRL, India.

2.2 Preparation of Plant Extract

Bruguierasexangula plant extract was collected from Mahakalapada region of Kendrapara District, Odisha. The bark was dried under the shade and upon drying was pulverized to coarsely powdered form. About 10 g of pulverized bark powder was added with 150 ml of 90% ethanol solvent and was kept for 3 days under continuous agitation at room temperature. Then Whatman No. 1 chromatograph filter paper was used to filter the solution, and the filtrate was evaporated under 37 °C and the dried extract was stored at 4°C for further use.

2.3 Phytochemical Characterization

Qualitative Analysis

The ethanolic bark extract of *B.sexangula* plants were analyzed the presence of bioactive secondary metabolites like phenols, terpenoids, flavonoids, tannins, glycosides, saponins etc. [7].

Quantitative Analysis

The total phenol content (TPC) and total flavonoid content (TFC) of the bark extract of *B.sexangula* plant was evaluated using standard procedure [7].

2.4 Antioxidant Study

DPPH Scavenging Activity

The DPPH radical-scavenging test was carried out as per the described method with minor modifications [8]. *B.sexangula* ethanolic bark extract (BS) at 50,100 and 150 μg/ml concentrations were evaluated at 517 nm. BHT served as positive control.

H_2O_2 Scavenging Activity

The hydrogen peroxide (H_2O_2) scavenging potential was studied as per the standard method of [9] with minor modifications. The scavenging potential of bark sample was evaluated at 50, 100 and 150 μg/ml concentrations. BHT was used as positive control.

2.5 Mixture Preparation

B.sexangula ethanolic bark extract (BS), and synthetic antioxidant (BHT) were mixed thoroughly with mustard oil at 0.5 % w/v concentration using a shaking bath for 8 h at 150 rpm. A control sample was prepared devoid of any antioxidants.

2.6 Accelerated Storage Study

The Schaal oven test was used to examine the extract's potential to prevent oxidative degradation of oil during storage [10]. Oil samples were taken in uncapped vials and kept at 65°C under dark condition. At 24 h interval, samples were collected in separate vials and inspected for 7 days. The peroxide value (PV) was used to assess the oxidative stability of the oil sample. The extract's efficacy was compared against BHT, that served as a positive control.

2.7 Frying of Oil

The heating of oils was modified from the method of [11]. Pure oil, pure oil with BHT (BHT + Oil) and pure oil with *B. sexangula* bark extract (BS + Oil) were heated at 150°C intermittently for five rounds of 20 min in each round. The oils were allowed to cool for at least 5 h after each round. Oil samples were analyzed for PV value.

2.8 Analysis of Oil

Peroxide Value (PV)

The PV value (expressed as milliequivalents of active oxygen per kg of oil, meqO_2/kg) of the oil sample was determined by standard method (12).

Carbonyl Value (CV)

The CV value of the oil sample was determined by standard procedure[12]. The CV was expressed as meq/kg.

Iodine Value (IV)

The IV value of the oil sample was determined by standard procedure[12].

2.9 Statistical Study

The results were expressed as mean ± standard deviation.

3. Result and Discussion

3.1 Phytochemical Characterization

The ethanolic bark extract of *B.sexangula* (BS) demonstrated presence of different phytochemicals viz., phenols, flavonoids, terpenoids, tannins, glycosides, saponins (Table 58.1.). The TPC and TFC contents of the BS extract were 119 mg catechol eq/ g DW and 7.0 mg Quercetineq/g DW respectively (Table 58.2.).

Antioxidant Capacity

The analysis of the present study showed that ethanolic bark extract of *B.sexangula* could scavenge the DPPH

Table 58.1 Qualitative phytochemical analysis

Phytochemicals	Test	Result
Phenol	Extract + $FeCl_3$	Present
Flavonoids	Shinoda Test	Present
Terpenoids	Salkowski Test	Absent
Tannins	Gelatin test	Present
Glycosides	Borntrager's Test	Present
Saponins	Foam Test	Absent

Table 58.2 Quantitative phytochemical content

Phytochemicals	Content
TPC	119 ± 0.01 mg catechol eq/ g DW
TFC	7.0 ± 0.16 mg quercetineq/g DW

radicals at the different concentration (50-150 μg/ml). The BS extracts could scavenge the DPPH free radicals with IC_{50} value of 74.43 μg/ml. In the similar condition the standard antioxidant compound BHT could scavenge the DPPH radicals with IC_{50} value of 47.56 μg/ml. Similarly, the H_2O_2scavenging assay demonstrated that the BS extract could scavenge hydrogen peroxide in a concentration-dependent manner with IC_{50} value of 122.56 μg/ml. Under similar condition, BHT could scavenge hydrogen peroxide with IC_{50} value of 334.32 μg/ml (Table 58.3.).

Table 58.3 IC_{50} values obtained from DPPH assay and hydrogen peroxide (H_2O_2) assay

Sample	DPPH scavenging	H_2O_2 scavenging
BS	74.43 μg/ml	122.56 μg/ml
BHT	47.56 μg/ml	334.32 μg/ml

Accelerated Storage

The mustard oil after treatment with BS and was analyzed with Schaal oven test at 62 °C for seven days by measuring their PV. It was found that the PV values increased continuously in all the three samples on subsequent days of thermostatting during 7days study. The PV value for pure oil varies between 0.203 to 0.809 mEq O_2/kg, whereas for Oil +BHT and Oil+ BS the values varied between 0.116 to 0.726 mEq O_2/kg and 0.037 to 0.668 mEqO_2/kg respectively (Fig. 58.1). This showed clearly that supplementation with BS extract could lower the oxidation of mustard oil during 7-day accelerated storage study. Lower PV value further implicated lesser fatty acid composition changes in the mustard oil supplemented with BS extract. In a similar study, the ethanolic rosemary extract could effectively delay the oxidation of palm oil during the condition of accelerated storage [13].

Frying Oil-Thermal Oxidation Test

In presence of moisture and air and increased temperature of 150 °C to 190 °C, the cooking oil may undergo several chemical changes. Several chemical reactions including oxidation, hydrolysis, polymerization and fission led to decomposition of oil generating volatile compounds, monomers and polymers along undesirable oxidized product [14]. In the present study, the oxidation stability of mustard oil was studied by evaluating the PV value, iodine value and carbonyl value for seven consecutive days.

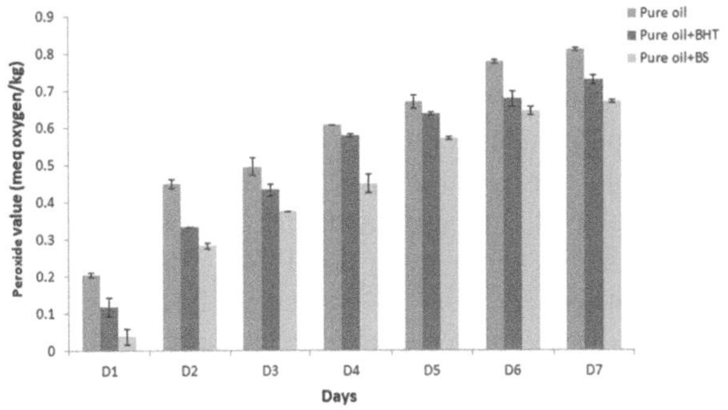

Fig. 58.1 Peroxide value for Schaal oven test

Peroxide Value

Higher peroxide values were observed with the growing frequency of heating during the seven consecutive days of study. The PV value raised increased from 0.095 to 1.286 mEq O_2/kg. However, during the same period, the Oil+BS showed increase in PV value from 0.037 to 0.385 mEq O_2/kg and that of Oil+BHT showed increase in value from 0.058 to 0.531 mEq O_2/kg (Fig. 58.2). The study clearly showed the potential of BS extractin inhibiting the rancidity of oil as the PV value in 7th day of frying decreased by 70%. The continuous increase in PV value indicated increased lipid peroxidation byproduct content in oil during heating process as number of frying increases the extent of oxidation. The results corroborated with the earlier reports [15] which demonstrated that the peanut skin extract offered better protection against oxidation of soyabean and mustard oil.

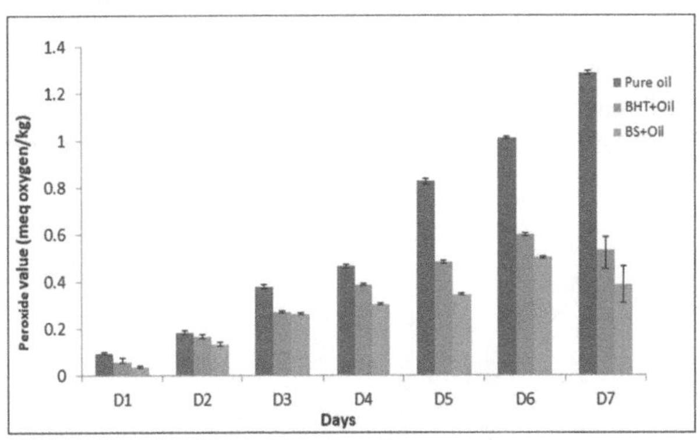

Fig. 58.2 Peroxide value for fried oil

Carbonyl Value (CV)

The CV value of pure mustard oil, Oil+ BHT and Oil + BS increased steadily with increase in frying in subsequent days. This is quite obvious since CV value which is an indicative of oxidative decomposition increases with increase in number of frying at high temperature. The CV value of pure mustard oil varies between 2.442 to 5.575 micro-mol/g during the seven-day study period. However, the CV value of Oil + BHT and Oil + BS varied between 1.353 to 4.791 micro-mol/g and 0.569 to 4.287 micro-mol/g respectively (Fig. 58.3). The study demonstrated reduction in CV values during frying upon addition of BHT or BS extract indicating the potency of BS extract in retardation of deterioration of frying oil. Earlier study conducted with ethanol extract of *Chuanminshen violaceum* also demonstrated retardation of the oxidative degradation of soyabean, rapeseed and palm oil during frying of oil by decreasing the CV value [16].

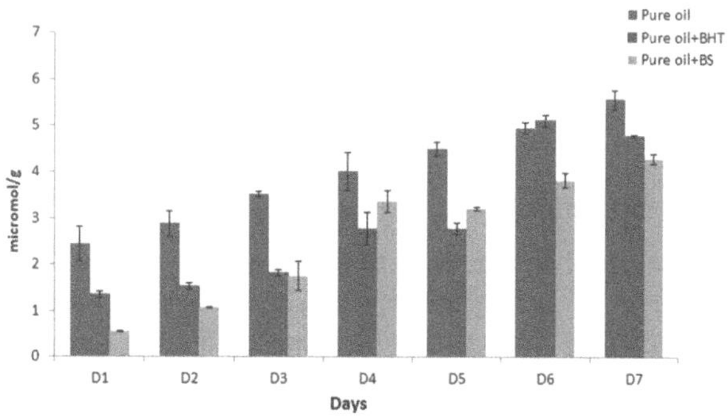

Fig. 58.3 Carbonyl value for fried oil

Iodine Value

Degree of unsaturation or the average number of double bonds present in fats and oils is represented by iodine value or iodine number or iodine index [17]. The oxidation of the oil is indicated by decrease in number of double bonds along with decrease in iodine value. The present study indicated that the iodine value decreased during the frying process from Day1 to Day7 indicating the increase in lipid oxidation during the frying process. The iodine values of all treated samples decreased continuously from day 1 to day 7 during the frying process (Fig. 58.4). However, the control and tested samples showed no significant difference. The present study corroborated with the earlier study of [13] that showed no obvious difference in Iodine values between control and samples with supplemented with antioxidants.

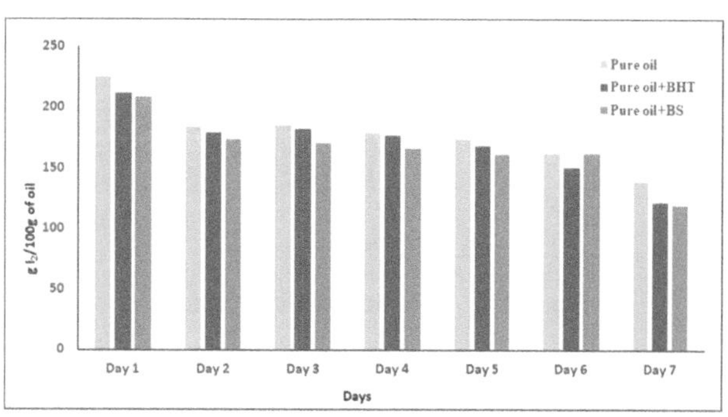

Fig. 58.4 Iodine number for fried oil

3.2 Influence of *B.sexangula* Extract on Stability of Mustard Oil Under Storage and Heating Condition

Earlier studies have revealed that degradation of cooking oil is more pronounced under high temperatures. This may be due to increase in the rate of hydrolytic and oxidative reactions along with thermal inactivation of the naturally antioxidants preset in the cooking oil. Use of natural antioxidants for prevention of thermal deterioration of cooking oils has been described in previous works [18,19].

The DPPH scavenging and H_2O_2 scavenging assay clearly demonstrated the antioxidant potential of phytoconstituents of BS extract. The results carried out in the present study indicates ethanolic bark extract of *B.sexangula* protect the oxidative damage of mustard oil under accelerated storage and frying condition. This effect is attributed to the presence of thermos-resistant antioxidant compounds of *B.sexangula* extract. The enhanced thermo-oxidative potential of oil using *B.sexangula* extract was reported for the first time in the present study. This is in corroboration with earlier study carried out on mangrove apple fruit extract of *Sonneratia apetala* (MAFE) which could lower peroxide, *p*-anisidine and TOTOX values (total oxidation value) beside conjugated dienes and trienes in Palmolein oil supplemented with MAFE (100 ppm) during 24 days of storage [3]. The present study clearly indicated the phytoconstituents in *B. sexangula* can be exploited and can serve as a good substitute to artificial antioxidants for enhancing the oxidative stability of mustard oil during frying and accelerated storage.

4. Conclusion

The ethanolic bark extract of *B.sexangula* was evaluated for its ability to enhance the oxidative resistance of mustard oil during cooking at elevated temperature and frying. The *B.sexangula* extract at the concentration of 0.5 %w/v exhibited antioxidant effect in the Schaal test by decreasing the peroxide value effectively. This study demonstrated the phytochemicals in *B.sexangula* could serve as an alternate natural antioxidant against a synthetic antioxidant like BHT during accelerated storage and frying of oil.

References

1. Choe, E. and Min, D.B. (2007). Chemistry of Deep-Fat Frying Oils. *J. Food Sci.*, 72(5), R77–86.
2. Grootveld, M., Percival, B.C., Leenders, J. and Wilson, P.B. (2020) Potential Adverse Public Health Effects Afforded by the Ingestion of Dietary Lipid Oxidation Product Toxins: Significance of Fried Food Sources. Vol. 12, Nutrients.

3. Yoong, M.H. and Tengku Rozaina, T.M. (2021). Effects of mangrove apple (Sonneratia caseolaris) fruit extract on oxidative stability of palm olein under accelerated storage. *Food Res.,* 5(1), 461–470.
4. Chowdhury, K., Banu, L., Khan, S. and Latif, A. (1970). Studies on the Fatty Acid Composition of Edible Oil. *Bangladesh J. Sci. Ind. Res.,* 42(3), 311–316.
5. Sovero, M. (1993). Rapeseed, a new oilseed crop for the United States. New crops. Wiley, New York; 302–307.
6. Nabeelah, Bibi, Fawzi, Gokhan, Rajesh, Nadeem, Kannan R.R., et al. (2019). Ethnopharmacology, Phytochemistry, and Global Distribution of Mangroves—A Comprehensive Review. *Mar. Drugs* 17(4), 231.
7. Harborne, J.B. (1984). Phytochemical Methods. Dordrecht: Springer Netherlands.
8. Brand-Williams, W., Cuvelier, M.E. and Berset, C. (1995). Use of a free radical method to evaluate antioxidant activity. *LWT - Food Sci. Technol.,* 28(1), 25–30.
9. Rath, S., Patra, J.K., Mohapatra, N., Mohanty, G., Dutta, S. and Thatoi, H. (2011). In Vitro Antibacterial and Antioxidant Studies of Croton roxburghii L., from Similipal Biosphere Reserve. *Indian J. Microbiol.,* 51,363–368.
10. Aladedunye, F. and Matthäus, B. (2014). Phenolic extracts from *Sorbus aucuparia* (L.) and *Malus baccata* (L.) berries: Antioxidant activity and performance in rapeseed oil during frying and storage. *Food Chem.,* 159, 273–281.
11. Owu, D.U., Osim. E.E. and Ebong, P.E. (1998). Serum liver enzymes profile of Wistar rats following chronic consumption of fresh or oxidized palm oil diets. *Acta Trop.,*69(1), 65–73.
12. Reboredo-Rodríguez, P., Figueiredo-González, M., Gonzalez-Barreiro, C., Simal-Gandara, J., Salvador, M. and Cancho-Grande, B. (2017). State of the Art on Functional Virgin Olive Oils Enriched with Bioactive Compounds and Their Properties. *Int. J. Mol. Sci.,* 18, 668.
13. Guo, Q., Gao, S., Sun, Y., Gao, Y., Wang, X. and Zhang, Z. (2016). Antioxidant efficacy of rosemary ethanol extract in palm oil during frying and accelerated storage. *Ind. Crops Prod.,*94, 82–88.
14. Yogesh, K., Jha, S.N. and Yadav, D.N. (2012). Antioxidant Activities of Murraya koenigii (L.) Spreng Berry Extract: Application in Refrigerated (4 ± 1 °C) Stored Meat Homogenates. *Agric. Res.* 1(2), 183–189.
15. Kumar, Y. (2014). Antioxidant activity of Peanut (Arachis Hypogaea L.) Skin Extract: Application in Soybean and Mustard Oil. *Int. J. Food Process Technol.,* 1, 26–31.
16. Zhang, Q., Wan, C., Tian, J., Qi, D., Liu, S. and Wu, D. (2020). Use of ethanol extract of Chuanminshen Violaceum to inhibit the deterioration of frying oil. *Ind. Crops Prod.,* 155,112808.
17. Kanner, J., Gorelik, S., Roman, S. and Kohen, R. (2012). Protection by Polyphenols of Postprandial Human Plasma and Low-Density Lipoprotein Modification: The Stomach as a Bioreactor. *J. Agric. Food Chem.,* 60(36), 8790–8796.
18. Sahasrabudhe, S.N., Rodriguez-Martinez, V., O'Meara, M. and Farkas, B.E. (2017). Density, viscosity, and surface tension of five vegetable oils at elevated temperatures: Measurement and modeling. *Int. J. Food Prop.,* 29, 1–17.
19. Neves, M., Miranda, A., Lemos, M.F.L., Silva, S. and Tecelao, C. (2020). Enhancing oxidative stability of sunflower oil by supplementation with prickled broom (*Pterospartum tridentatum*) ethanolic extract. *J. Food Sci.,* 85(9), 2812–2821.

Note: All the figures and tables in this chapter were made by the authors.

Research and Innovations in Industrial and Marine Biotechnology: A Circular Economy 2024 – Prof. Hrudayanath Thatoi et al. (eds)

59 Diagnostic Stewardship in Infectious Diseases is a Progressive Approach that Complements Antimicrobial Stewardship to Combat Antimicrobial Resistance

Rahul Kumar, Divya Gunsola
Department of Microbiology, Graphic Era
(Deemed to be University), 566/6, Clement Town,
Dehradun, Uttarakhand, India

Sourav Chattaraj
Centre for Industrial Biotechnology Research,
School of Pharmaceutical Sciences,
Siksha 'O' Anusandhan University, Kalinga Nagar,
Bhubaneswar, Odisha, India

Pankaj Gautam[1], Debasis Mitra[2]
Department of Microbiology, Graphic Era
(Deemed to be University), 566/6, Clement Town,
Dehradun, Uttarakhand, India

Abstract: The unacceptable use of diagnostic procedures and extreme antibiotic recommendation has intensified antimicrobial resistance, presenting an urgent warning to global healthiness. Antimicrobial and diagnostic stewardship involve ordering suitable tests and advocate for thoughtful use of prompt molecular diagnostics to guide antibiotic therapy and prevent broad-spectrum antibiotic overuse avoiding overdiagnosis and high costs. While numerous diagnostic kits are available, they face limitations in cost, accessibility, and user familiarity. Effective diagnostic stewardship requires assessment of clinical symptoms with epidemiological data for accurate microbiological interpretation. Multidisciplinary teams of trained clinicians should collaborate to advance diagnostic stewardship. Key challenges include resource limitations, inadequate personnel training, and lack of awareness about medical microbiology diagnostics' impact on antibiotic use.

Keywords: Antimicrobial resistance, Antimicrobial stewardship, Diagnostic stewardship, Infectious diseases

1. Introduction

Anti-microbial stewardship programs (ASPs) are proposed to focus anti-microbial resistance (AMR) by safeguarding timely and proper treatment while minimizing hostile drug events, abuse, and costs (Centers for Disease Control and Prevention (CDC) [1]. Diagnostic stewardship enhances ASPs by encouraging the correct use of diagnostics, facilitating early antibiotic termination, and modifying AMR risks [2, 3, 4]. This approach is critical in preventing over-testing and pointless antibiotic use, particularly among strictly ill or immunocompromised patients. Although diagnostic stewardship is fixed in high-income countries, its residue underutilized in clinical training and is inhibited by awareness gaps and the high cost of equipment in resource-limited

Corresponding author: [1]pankajgautam.bt@geu.ac.in, [2]debasismitra3@gmail.com

DOI: 10.1201/9781003759003-59

situations [5]. Interdisciplinary collaboration, particularly involving medical microbiologists, is crucial for efficient stewardship, contributing to compact antibiotic use and resistance [6,7]. Emerging tools for molecular and point-of-care diagnostics can backing stewardship energies, though their accessibility and cost continue to pose challenges. This review highlights the significance of diagnostic stewardship in enhancing infection management and examines its role in common infections with a focus on microbiological qualities.

2. Diagnostic Pathway, and Reliable Diagnostic Stewardship

Diagnostic approaches involve pre-analytical, analytical, and post-analytical steps, with diagnostic stewardship (DS) being crucial during. Clinicians should follow guidelines for judicious test use, reflecting accuracy, cost, and clinical importance [8]. Testing decisions should be based on pre-test possibility to prevent pointless testing [9]. Perfect specimen collection is must for diagnostic accuracy [2]. Laboratories should reject unacceptable samples and confine tests to relevant clinical setups [8]. Rapid and selective reporting promotes narrow-spectrum antibiotic use [10]. Modified laboratory reports indicating colonization reduce overtreatment [11]. Microbiologists guide treatment decisions and help discontinue unnecessary therapies [12].

3. Including Cutting-Edge Diagnostic Equipment in the Diagnostic Process

Interruptions in the administration of correct antibiotic treatment have been consistently linked with increased mortality rates [13]. Clinicians often face challenges in determining whether to employ broad-spectrum empirical treatment to address a range of infections, account for bacterial resistance, or narrow the spectrum to prevent the development of future resistance. For example, if empirical therapy fails to effectively target resistant species, the prognosis for patients with bloodstream infections affected by MRSA or *Pseudomonas aeruginosa* may be significantly compromised. Quick pathogen identification and susceptibility testing can reduce the time required to initiate the correct antibiotic treatment (RAT) and subsequently decrease mortality (Table 59.1).

4. Diagnosis by MALDI-TOF MS

Represent of MALDI-TOF MS a quick and cost-effective investigative technique capable of identifying pathogens, including fungi and mycobacteria, with turnaround times of less than one hour, thereby reducing identification time by up to 48 hours compared to traditional methods [14]. Nevertheless, it necessitates initial culturing and demonstrates suboptimal performance with polymicrobial samples. Its limited availability in low- and middle-income countries (LMICs) further constrains its widespread application. When use AST and real-time AMS, it markedly decreases identification (from 36.6 hours to 11 hours), susceptibility testing (from 47.1 hours to 24.4 hours), and therapy adjustment time (from 75 hours to 29 hours), thereby enhancing outcomes and reducing costs [15]. However, in the absence of AMS, the benefits in therapy optimization remain restricted [15] (Table 59.2).

4.1 PCR-Polymerase Chain Reaction

Molecular diagnostics show exceptional sensitivity and specificity for infections with low microbial loads. MRSA/MSSA assays from blood or wound samples show sensitivity of 98.3-100% and specificity of 98.6-99.4%; Xpert MRSA RT-PCR identifies mecA mutations

Table 59.1 Best analysis of pre-analytical phases for sampling and their preparation, transportation [2]

Common sense considerations	To ensure accurate antibiotic treatment, use samples from qualified experts with patient information labels. Provide clinical details while traveling and use innovative diagnostics for patient safety.
Cultures of urine	The recommendation is to educate patients on clean capture to reduce contamination and to use quick transportation or refrigeration to prevent the spread of pollutants.
Culturing of blood	The recommendation is to prefer sampling from peripheral venipunctures over core lines and to attempt to collect two samples.
Culturing for respiratory	To enhance sampling yield, swab pharynx and nostrils, provide sputum culture guidance, and consider BAL or mini-BAL procedures to boost diagnostic.
Pharynxinfections	Keep away throat cultures when the clinical history suggests an acute viral infection rather than a bacterial infection.
PCR, stool culture, and clostridium difficile toxin	Gather in an immaculate container and transport at room temperature within two hours of sampling.
PCR, STD, and Genital culture	To enhance *Neisseria gonorrhoea* detection in cultures, inoculate into growing medium near patients and facilitate quick transport.
Wound swab	Use needle aspiration from tissue cultures or wound margins after surgical debridement to ensure deep wound culturing and avoid contamination.

Table 59.2 New diagnostic methods for identifying the germs that cause bloodstream infections

Method	Found pathogens	Resistance indicators	Reaction time
MALDI-TOF FilmArray (BCID)	• *Mycobacteria,* Gram +ve and -ve bacteria **Gram (+ve) bacteria:** • *S. aureus Staphylococci, Enterococcus* spp. *L. monocytogenes, Streptococcus* spp. **Gram (-ve) bacteria** • *Acinetobacter baumannii* • *Haemophilus influenzae* • *Escherichia coli* • *Neisseria meningitidis* • *Enterobacter cloacae complex* • *K. pneumonia* and *K. oxytoca* • *Proteus* spp. • *Pseudomonas aeruginosa* • *Serratia marcescens*	Various genes (*van*A, *mec*A, *van*B) CTX-M, OXA-48-like, KPC, IMP, NDM, VIM, mcr-1	Between 10 to 30 minutes and 1 hour
Verigene Gram (+ve)	• *Escherichia coli* • *Shigella sp.* • *Klebsiella pneumoniae* and *Klebsiellaoxytoca* • *Pseudomonas aeruginosa* • *Citrobacter* spp. • *Serratia marcescens* • *Proteus* spp. • *Acinetobacter* spp. • *Enterobacter* spp.	KPC, NDM, CTX-M, VIM, IMP, and OXA	2h
Gene Xpert MRSA Verigene Gram (-ve)	• *Staphylococcus aureus* • *S. aureus & coagulase* (-ve) • *Staphylococci* • *Streptococcus species* • *Enterococcus faecalis* and *faecium* • *Listeria* spp.	*mec*A, *van*A, *van*B	< 1 hr 2.5 h
Quick FISH	**Gram positive** • *S. aureus & coagulase* (-ve) • *Enterococcus faecalis* • *Staphylococci* • Other *enterococci* **Gram negative** • *P. aureus* • *E. coli* • *K. pneumoniae*	NA	Less than 30 minutes
Peptide Nucleic Acid Fluorescence *In-Situ* Hybridization (PNA-FISH)	**Gram-positive bacteria** • *S. aureus & coagulase* (-ve) • *Staphylococci* • *Enterococcus faecalis & other enterococci* **Gram-negative bacteria** • *K. pneumoniae* • *E. coli* • *P. aeruginosa*	No	Between 1.5 to 3 hours

Source: Author

with 98.1% sensitivity and 99.6% specificity [16]. These diagnostics support antimicrobial stewardship (AMS) by reducing rapid antimicrobial therapy (RAT), length of stay (LOS), and costs. An RCT showed AMS with antimicrobial susceptibility testing (AST) improved de-escalation and reduced broad-spectrum antibiotic use [12]. Verigene multiplex PCR detected pathogens and resistance genes, though with 43% false-positive rate for *Streptococcus pneumoniae* [17]. Phenotypic testing remains essential for polymicrobial samples [18]. FilmArray BCID panel reduces identification time by 21 hours, improving de-escalation [17]. For respiratory infections, multiplex PCR panels aid therapeutic decisions but need careful interpretation with low pretest probability [18].

4.2 mNGS for Metagenomic Data

Compared to traditional methodologies, metagenomic next-generation sequencing offers rapid and precise identification of multiple infections and their resistance genes without necessitating culture [19, 20]. In clinical applications, mNGS has demonstrated a high level of diagnostic efficacy for infectious diseases, as evidenced by a meta-analysis of the technology. However, its presentation may be less efficient for RNA viruses, fungi, and intracellular bacteria [21]. Out-of-date culture methods experience an important reduction in diagnostic yield ensuing antibiotic management whereas mNGS can continue to detect pathogenic organism's post-antibiotic beginning thereby possibly enhancing the efficacy of antibiotic treatments. Nonetheless, mNGS is vulnerable to DNA contamination and cannot separate between colonization and infection [21].

5. Responses of Diagnosis

Host response-based diagnostics which apply gene expression signatures present confirming approaches for recognizing between infectious and non-infectious diseases particularly viral and bacterial infections [22]. For example, a board comprising three peptides (TRAIL, CRP, IP-10) has been shown to differentiate between viral and bacterial respiratory infections [23]. Gene representation analysis successfully identified non-infectious diseases in 74.1% of participants, thereby reducing overdiagnosis and useless treatment compared to the control group (33.3%). This approach determined greater precision than procalcitonin (71.5%) and clinical judgment (76.3%) in diagnostic decision-making [23]. Further research is justified to determine whether these findings explain into improved patient outcomes.

6. Challenges Stewardship Diagnostic

Diagnostic stewardship (DS) in ICUs challenges due to late antimicrobial therapy. Reducing avoidable testing can prevent but may delay illness detection. Research on AMS in LMICs is crucial. Biomarkers like IL-1 and IL-8 can support AMS with non-invasive testing [24]. Endotracheal aspirate (ETA) and invasive processes presented similar outcomes [25]. Modified sputum culture reporting increased de-escalation and reduced drug use [26]. Gram-stain-guided therapy reduced broad-spectrum antibiotic use. Clinical decision tools cut unnecessary blood cultures by 85% [27], and training improved positive rates [28]. Post-antibiotic BCs showed 20% lower positivity [29]. Two-step urinalysis reduced antibiotics without raising mortality, and microbiologist consultation improved asymptomatic bacteriuria treatment [28]. Reflex urine testing lowered catheter-associated urinary tract infection rates [30]. CSF microarray testing improved yield in immunocompetent patients [27]. EMR reminders and clinical criteria reduced *Clostridioides difficile* tests by 60% without affecting outcomes [31].

7. Conclusions

Diagnostic stewardship plays a crucial role in ensuring appropriate test selection and timing, enhancing patient outcomes and reducing unnecessary procedures. Despite increasing recognition, diagnostic stewardship remains insufficiently developed globally. To optimize effect on patient attention and costs, institutions must engage clinical microbiologists, uphold clinical judgment, and invest in research, particularly in resource-limited settings.

References

1. Centers for Disease Control and Prevention (CDC), 2019. *Core Elements of Hospital Antibiotic Stewardship Programs | Antibiotic Use*. CDC. Available at: https://www.cdc.gov/antibiotic-use/core-elements/hospital.html [Accessed 14 Dec. 2022].
2. World Health Organization, 2016. *Diagnostic stewardship: a guide to implementation in antimicrobial resistance surveillance sites*. Geneva: WHO.
3. Chattaraj, S., Ganguly, A., Mandal, A., & Das Mohapatra, P. K. (2022). A review of the role of probiotics for the control of viral diseases in aquaculture. *Aquaculture International*, *30*(5), 2513–2539. https://doi.org/10.1007/s10499-022-00915-6
4. Chattaraj, S., Mitra, D., Chattaraj, A., Chattaraj, M., Kundu, M., Ganguly, A., & Mohapatra, P. K. D. (2023). Antioncogenic potential of probiotics: challenges and future prospective. *Indian J Microbiol Res*, *10*(1), 1–10. https://doi.org/10.18231/j.ijmr.2023.001
5. Rolfe, R., Kwobah, C., Muro, F., Ruwanpathirana, A., Lyamuya, F., Bodinayake, C., ... &Tillekeratne, L. G. (2021). Barriers to implementing antimicrobial stewardship programs in three low-and middle-income country tertiary care settings: findings from a multi-site qualitative study. *Antimicrobial Resistance & Infection Control*, *10*, 1–11. doi:10.1186/s13756-021-00929-4.
6. Iskandar, K., Molinier, L., Hallit, S., Sartelli, M., Hardcastle, T. C., Haque, M., ... & Roques, C. (2021). Surveillance of antimicrobial resistance in low-and middle-income countries: a scattered picture. *Antimicrobial Resistance & Infection Control*, *10*, 1–19.doi:10.1186/s13756-021-00931-w.
7. Kumar, R., Kamboj, N., Kumar, V., Kumar, S., Kumar, N., & Gautam, P. (2025). Assessing the Contamination Risk of Salmonella enterica subsp. in Green Leafy Vegetables. Journal of Pure & Applied Microbiology, 19(1). https://doi.org/10.22207/JPAM.19.1.36
8. Caliendo, A. M., Gilbert, D. N., Ginocchio, C. C., Hanson, K. E., May, L., Quinn, T. C., ... & Infectious Diseases Society of America (IDSA). (2013). Better tests, better care: improved diagnostics for infectious diseases. *Clinical Infectious Diseases*, *57*(suppl_3), S139–S170. doi:10.1093/cid/cit578.
9. Daley, P., Garcia, D., Inayatullah, R., Penney, C., & Boyd, S. (2018). Modified reporting of positive urine cultures to reduce inappropriate treatment of asymptomatic bacteriuria among nonpregnant, noncatheterized inpatients: a randomized controlled trial. *infection control & hospital epidemiology*, *39*(7), 814–819. doi:10.1017/ice.2018.100.
10. Patel, R., & Fang, F. C. (2018). Diagnostic stewardship: opportunity for a laboratory–infectious diseases partnership. *Clinical infectious diseases*, *67*(5), 799–801. doi:10.1093/cid/ciy077.
11. Kenaa, B., Richert, M. E., Claeys, K. C., Shipper, A., Sullivan, K. V., Schrank, G. M., ... & Leekha, S. (2019). Ventilator-associated pneumonia: diagnostic test stewardship

and relevance of culturing practices. *Current Infectious Disease Reports*, *21*, 1–9.doi:10.1007/s11908-019-0708-3.
12. Banerjee, R., Özenci, V., & Patel, R. (2016). Individualized approaches are needed for optimized blood cultures. *Clinical Infectious Diseases*, *63*(10), 1332–1339. doi:10.1093/cid/ciw573
13. Vlieghe, E. R., Phe, T., De Smet, B., ChhunVeng, H., Kham, C., Lim, K., ... & Jacobs, J. A. (2013). Bloodstream infection among adults in Phnom Penh, Cambodia: key pathogens and resistance patterns. *PLoS One*, *8*(3), e59775. doi:10.1371/journal.pone.0059775.
14. Paolucci, M., Landini, M. P., &Sambri, V. (2010). Conventional and molecular techniques for the early diagnosis of bacteraemia. *International journal of antimicrobial agents*, *36*, S6–S16. doi:10.1016/j.ijantimicag.2010.11.010.
15. Perez, K. K., Olsen, R. J., Musick, W. L., Cernoch, P. L., Davis, J. R., Land, G. A., ... & Musser, J. M. (2013). Integrating rapid pathogen identification and antimicrobial stewardship significantly decreases hospital costs. *Archives of Pathology and Laboratory Medicine*, *137*(9), 1247–1254.doi:10.5858/arpa.2012-0651-OA.
16. Buchan, B. W., Allen, S., Burnham, C. A. D., McElvaniaTeKippe, E., Davis, T., Levi, M., ... &Ledeboer, N. A. (2015). Comparison of the next-generation Xpert MRSA/SA BC assay and the GeneOhmStaphSR assay to routine culture for identification of Staphylococcus aureus and methicillin-resistant S. aureus in positive-blood-culture broths. *Journal of clinical microbiology*, *53*(3), 804–809.doi:10.1128/JCM.03108-14.
17. Banerjee, R., Teng, C. B., Cunningham, S. A., Ihde, S. M., Steckelberg, J. M., Moriarty, J. P., ... & Patel, R. (2015). Randomized trial of rapid multiplex polymerase chain reaction–based blood culture identification and susceptibility testing. *Clinical Infectious Diseases*, *61*(7), 1071–1080.doi:10.1093/cid/civ447.
18. Huang, H. S., Tsai, C. L., Chang, J., Hsu, T. C., Lin, S., & Lee, C. C. (2018). Multiplex PCR system for the rapid diagnosis of respiratory virus infection: systematic review and meta-analysis. *Clinical Microbiology and Infection*, *24*(10), 1055–1063.doi:10.1016/j.cmi.2017.11.018.
19. Chattaraj, S., Chattaraj, M., Mitra, D., Ganguly, A., Thatoi, H., & Das Mohapatra, P. K. (2025). 16S amplicon sequencing of the gastrointestinal microbiota of Cirrhinusreba and isolation of an autochthonous probiotic using culture based approaches. *Systems Microbiology and Biomanufacturing*, *5*(1), 156–170. https://doi.org/10.1007/s43393-024-00285-5
20. Chattaraj, S., Mitra, D., Chattaraj, M., Ganguly, A., Thatoi, H., & Mohapatra, P. K. D. (2024). Brewers' spent grain as fish feed ingredient: evaluation of bio-safety and analysis of its impact on gut bacteria of Cirrhinusreba by 16S Metagenomic sequencing. *Current Research in Microbial Sciences*, *7*, 100286. https://doi.org/10.1016/j.crmicr.2024.100286
21. Liu, J., Zhang, Q., Dong, Y. Q., Yin, J., & Qiu, Y. Q. (2022). Diagnostic accuracy of metagenomic next-generation sequencing in diagnosing infectious diseases: a meta-analysis. *Scientific reports*, *12*(1), 21032. doi:10.1038/s41598-022-25314-y.
22. Tsalik, E. L., Henao, R., Nichols, M., Burke, T., Ko, E. R., McClain, M. T., ... & Woods, C. W. (2016). Host gene expression classifiers diagnose acute respiratory illness etiology. *Science translational medicine*, *8*(322), 322ra11–322ra11. doi:10.1126/scitranslmed.aad6873.
23. Jaffe, I. S., Jaehne, A. K., Quackenbush, E., Ko, E. R., Rivers, E. P., McClain, M. T., ... &Tsalik, E. L. (2021, December). Comparing the diagnostic accuracy of clinician judgment to a novel host response diagnostic for acute respiratory illness. In *Open forum infectious diseases* (Vol. 8, No. 12, p. ofab564). US: Oxford University Press. doi:10.1093/ofid/ofab564.
24. Hellyer, T. P., McAuley, D. F., Walsh, T. S., Anderson, N., Morris, A. C., Singh, S., ... & Simpson, A. J. (2020). Biomarker-guided antibiotic stewardship in suspected ventilator-associated pneumonia (VAPrapid2): a randomised controlled trial and process evaluation. *The Lancet Respiratory Medicine*, *8*(2), 182–191.doi:10.1016/S2213-2600(19)30367-4.
25. Berton, D. C., Kalil, A. C., & Teixeira, P. J. Z. (2012). Quantitative versus qualitative cultures of respiratory secretions for clinical outcomes in patients with ventilator-associated pneumonia. *Cochrane Database of Systematic Reviews*, (1).doi:10.1002/14651858.CD006482.pub4.
26. Musgrove, M. A., Kenney, R. M., Kendall, R. E., Peters, M., Tibbetts, R., Samuel, L., & Davis, S. L. (2018, July). Microbiology comment nudge improves pneumonia prescribing. In *Open forum infectious diseases* (Vol. 5, No. 7, p. ofy162). US: Oxford University Press. doi:10.1093/ofid/ofy162.
27. Copeland-Halperin, L. R., Emery, E., Collins, D., Liu, C., & Dort, J. (2018). Dogma without data: a clinical decision-making tool for postoperative blood cultures. *The American Surgeon*, *84*(8), 1339–1344. https://doi.org/10.1177/000313481808400849
28. Fabre, V., Klein, E., Salinas, A. B., Jones, G., Carroll, K. C., Milstone, A. M., ... & Cosgrove, S. E. (2020). A diagnostic stewardship intervention to improve blood culture use among adult nonneutropenic inpatients: the DISTRIBUTE study. *Journal of clinical microbiology*, *58*(10), 10–1128. doi:10.1128/JCM.01053-20.
29. Scheer, C. S., Fuchs, C., Gründling, M., Vollmer, M., Bast, J., Bohnert, J. A., ... & Kuhn, S. O. (2019). Impact of antibiotic administration on blood culture positivity at the beginning of sepsis: a prospective clinical cohort study. *Clinical Microbiology and Infection*, *25*(3), 326–331. doi:10.1016/j.cmi.2018.05.016.
30. Epstein, L., Edwards, J. R., Halpin, A. L., Preas, M. A., Blythe, D., Harris, A. D., ... & Leekha, S. (2016). Evaluation of a novel intervention to reduce unnecessary urine cultures in intensive care units at a tertiary care hospital in Maryland, 2011–2014. *infection control & hospital epidemiology*, *37*(5), 606–609.doi:10.1017/ice.2016.9.
31. Broadhurst, M. J., Dujari, S., Budvytiene, I., Pinsky, B. A., Gold, C. A., & Banaei, N. (2020). Utilization, yield, and accuracy of the FilmArray meningitis/encephalitis panel with diagnostic stewardship and testing algorithm. *Journal of clinical microbiology*, *58*(9), 10–1128.doi:10.1128/JCM.00311-20.

Research and Innovations in Industrial and Marine Biotechnology: A Circular Economy 2024 – Prof. Hrudayanath Thatoi et al. (eds)

60 Exploring Biodiversity: An Ethnographic Study of Medicinal Plants in Joypur Forest, West Bengal, India

Arindam Ganguly[1],
Susmita Dutta, Sima Satpathi
Department of Microbiology, Bankura Sammilani College,
Bankura, W.B., India

Somen Dey, Pritish Mitra,
Suvendu Pal, Asish Mandal
P.G.Department of Botany, Ramananda College, Bishnupur,
Bankura, West Bengal, India

Ritwick Konar
Institute of Health Sciences, Presidency University,
Kolkata, West Bengal. India

Manasi Chattaraj
Department of Geography, Bankura University,
Bankura, West Bengal, India

Sourav Chattaraj[2]
Centre for Industrial Biotechnology Research,
School of Pharmaceutical Sciences, Siksha 'O' Anusandhan
Deemed to be University, Kalinga Nagar,
Bhubaneswar, Odisha, India

Abstract: The rapid rise of multidrug-resistant bacterial pathogens has created a life-threatening situation in healthcare, significantly increasing mortality rates, particularly among immune-compromised individuals. The escalating issue of antimicrobial resistance necessitates alternative approaches to pharmacotherapy. Ethnobotanical studies offer a promising solution, uncovering therapeutic potentials of medicinal plants while promoting environmental preservation. Herbal drugs are crude or purified natural products extracted from raw plant materials, containing therapeutically active ingredients. The present study investigated the ecological distribution and diversity of medicinal plants in Joypur forest (Lat. 23.054562° Long 87.430324°), WB, India. The study identified a total of 21 species with potential health benefits. The dominant species include Gheṭu (*Clerodendrum infortunatum* L.), Kurci (*Holarrhenapubescens Wall. ex G.Don*), Anantamul (*Hemidesmus indicus* (L.) R. Br.), Bayara (*Terminaliabellirica* (Gaertn) Roxb), Nayantara (*Catharanthusroseus* (L) G. Don), Ban ochra (*Urenalobata* L.), Isarmul (*Aristolochiaindica* L.), Bel (*Aeglemarmelos* (L.) Correa), Kalmegh (*Andrographis paniculata* Burm.f.Ness), and Akasmani (*Acacia auriculiformis* A. Cunn. ex Benth). Plants including *Cassythafiliformis* L (Love Vine), *Ipomoea obscura* (L.) Ker Gawl.(Lotano Kalami), *Codariocalyxmotorius* (Houtt.) H. Ohashi (Ban Chandal), *Gymnemasylvestre* (Retz) R. Br. ex Sm. (Gurmar), *Dolichos lablab* L. (Ban Sim), *Azadirachta indica* A. Juss.(Neem), and *Smilax ovalifolia* Roxb.ex D. Don (Kumarica) have also been found. This kind of ethno-medicinal study has significant value to discover contemporary drugs from indigenous plant resources. It may opens up new possibilities regarding the exploration and utilization of wild herbal plant resources.

Keywords: Antimicrobial resistance, ethnobotany, *Hemidesmusindicus*, Joypur forest, *Terminaliabellirica*, traditional medicine

Corresponding author: [1]arindam_ganguly@yahoo.com, [2]souravchattaraj@soa.ac.in

DOI: 10.1201/9781003759003-60

1. Introduction

Ethnobotany explores the relationship between plants and cultures, focusing on their uses in medicine, rituals, cosmetics, and other aspects of daily life [1, 2]. Coined by Dr. John Harshberger in 1895, it was later refined to the study of plants' impact on life [3]. Ancient Indian texts like the Rig Veda and Mahabharata mention plants' uses in worship, medicine, and agriculture [4]. Ethnobotanical research in India has focused on documenting traditional healing practices, with figures like Hughes (1968) coining "ethnomedicine" for indigenous disease-related practices. West Bengal has a rich history of ethnobotanical research, especially in districts like Bankura, home to a significant tribal population and forest cover. Research in Bankura has documented several medicinal plants, though studies remain limited [5]. Previous works by Ghosh [6], Acharya and Mukherjee [7], and Mandal et al. (2014) recorded plants used for treating various ailments. Traditional phytoremedies have been employed for centuries to alleviate various menstrual disorders Ganguly et al [8]; Ganguly et al [9], providing natural relief for symptoms associated with menstrual health [10]. This study aims to systematically document ethnobotanical plants in Joypur Forest, West Bengal, contributing to the preservation of traditional knowledge and its integration into modern medicine while promoting cultural and biodiversity conservation.

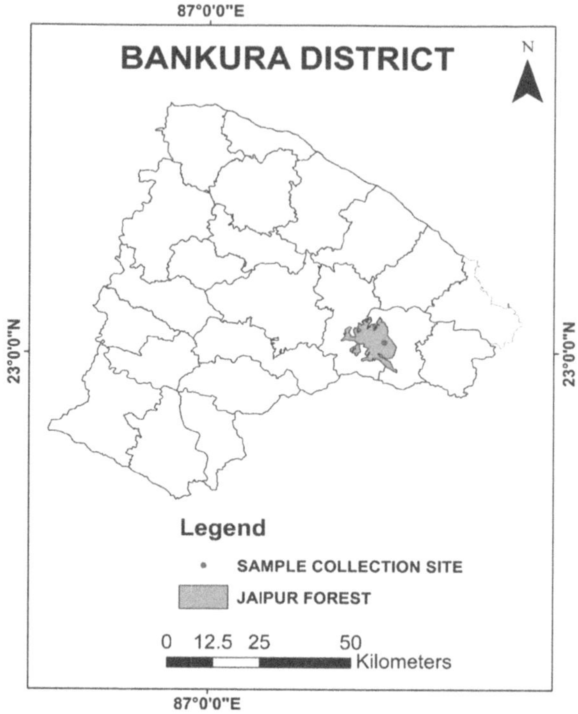

Fig. 60.1 Study area

2. Materials and Methods

2.1 Study Area

Joypur Forest(23.0474°N 87.4467°E), situated in the southeastern corner of Bankura district, West Bengal, is a vibrant exemplar of the region's ecological richness and cultural heritage (Fig. 60.1). This dense mixed forest boasts an impressive altitudinal range of 250-650 meters above sea level, fostering ecological diversity [9]. Dominated by Sal (*Shorearobusta C.F.Gaertn.*) trees, Joypur Forest is characterized by fertile, low-lying alluvial plains [10]. The forest's climate varies, with drier western uplands and more humid eastern regions, receiving approximately 1400 mm (55 inches) of annual rainfall, primarily during the June-September monsoon season. Temperatures fluctuate, reaching 45°C in May and dropping below 10°C in winter. Local villagers rely on iron-rich underground water sources, which are susceptible to microbial contamination, leading to waterborne diseases like jaundice. Joypur Forest plays a crucial role in biodiversity conservation, with its rich and diverse flora and fauna. This natural treasure trove is further enriched by the traditional knowledge of local communities, passed down through generations. Approximately 90.06% of the population resides in rural areas, whereas only 8.94% live in urban region.

2.2 Collection of Samples

In the verdant heart of Joypur Forest, our study explores the symbiotic bond between nature and tradition, uncovering the secrets of ethnomedicine and the resilient heritage of the region's healing arts. A simple random survey was conducted in Joypur village from May 2022 to May 2023 to gather data through interviews. Primary data was collected from local residents and medical practitioners.

To assess the abundance and distribution of medicinal plant species in Joypur Forest, the quadrat method was employed. This involved strategically placing 1m × 1m grid quadrats at random locations throughout the forest, ensuring representative sampling of the diverse forest ecosystem. This quadrat study transcends mere documentation of forest vegetation; it unlocks the landscape's influence on ethnomedicinal practices, providing an understanding of the interconnectedness between environment, culture, and traditional healing. Plant specimens (bark, flowers, fruits, and root) were collected and preserved following standard taxonomic procedures to ensure accurate identification and verification (Fig. 60.2).

3. Results and Discussion

A total of twenty-one ethnomedicinally significant plant species were collected from the study area. They have traditional importance. The subsequent data (Table 60.1) provides an in-depth summary of these observed plants (Fig. 60.3), illuminating their customary applications within the Santal community. Microbes play a substantial role in causing numerous diseases affecting humans, animals, and aquatic life (Ganguly et al., 2025c; Chattaraj et al., 2023; Ganguly et al., 2018b; Ganguly et al., 2019; Ganguly et al., 2024b; Mitra et al., 2022; Chattaraj & Das Mohapatra, 2024). In response, local villagers rely on

Fig. 60.2 Survey: (A) Collection and identification of medicinalplants;(B)Studyofplantdistributionthrough quadrat method

traditional medicinal plants to treat a range of ailments. They were also been effective in treating respiratory infections (Ganguly et al., 2020).

This study extensively surveys the ethno-medicinal plants in the Joypur forest, where 21 plants, including Ghețu (*Clerodendrum infortunatum* L), Kurci (*Holarrhenapubescens Wall. ex G.Don*), Anantamul (*Hemidesmusindicus* (L)R.Br.), Bayara (*Terminaliabellirica* (Gaertn) Roxb), Nayantara (*Catharanthusroseus* (L) G.Don), Ban ochra (Urenalobata L), Isarmul (*Aristolochiaindica* L), Bel (*Aeglemarmelos* (L)Correa), Kalmegh (*Andrographispaniculata* Burm.f.Ness), Akasmani (*Acacia auriculiformis* A.Cunn .ex. Benth), have dominated the population. Additionally, plants like Love vine (Cassytha Filiformis L), Lotanokalami (*Ipomoea aquatic* Forssk.), Ban Chandal (*Codariocalyxmotorius* (Houtt.) *H.Ohashi*), Gurmar (*Gymnema Sylvestre* (Retz) R.Br.ex Schult.), Ban sim (*Dolichos lablab* L), Nim (*Azadirachtaindica* A.Juss.), Kumarica (*Smilax ovalifolia Roxb.*exD.Don) and their parts are utilized as herbs.

The pie chart serves as a visual representation of the intricate plant species distribution within the surveyed quadrat in Joypur Forest (Fig. 60.4). Each segment

Table 60.1 Distribution and significance of herbal medicine

Sl. No	Vernacular Name	Scientific Name	Family	Parts Used	Medicinal Uses
1	Akashmoni	*Acacia auriculiformis*	Fabaceae	Bark, Leaves	Respiratory infections, skin disorders, gastrointestinal issues
2	Anatamul	*Hemidesmusindicus*	Apocynaceae	Roots	Blood purification, skin disorders
3	Arjun	*Terminalia arjuna*	Combretaceae	Bark	Cardiovascular issues, cholesterol management
4	Bel	*Aeglemarmelos*	Rutaceae	Fruits, Leaves	Digestive disorders, respiratory issues, diabetes
5	Joypal	*Croton bonplandianusbaill*	Euphorbiaceae	Leaves	Skin infections, gastrointestinal issues
6	Banchandal	*Codariocalyxmotorius*	Fabaceae	Fruits, Leaves	Diabetes, digestive issues, skin disorders
7	Boyra	*Terminaliabellirica*	Combretaceae	Bark, Fruits	Digestive ailments, respiratory problems, skin disorders
8	Caesarweed	*Urena lobata*	Malvaceae	Roots, Leaves	Urinary tract infections, respiratory ailments
9	ChupriAlu	*Smilax rotundifolia*	Smilacaceae	Rhizomes, Roots	Rheumatism, skin disorders, urinary issues.
10	Eswarimool	*Aristolochiaindica*	Aristolochiaceae	Roots	Gastrointestinal issues, respiratory problems
11	Ghetu	*Clerodendruminfortunatum*	Lamiaceae	Leaves	Fever, rheumatism, skin diseases.
12	Gurmar	*Gymnemasylvestre*	Apocynaceae	Leaves	Diabetes, weight management
13	Kalmegh	*Andrographis paniculata*	Acanthaceae	Whole plant	Immune system support, digestive disorders
14	Kurchi	*Holarrhenapubescens*	Apocynaceae	Bark	Diarrhea, dysentery, digestive issues
15	Love-vine	*Cassythafiliformis*	Lauraceae	Whole plant	Rheumatic disorders, digestive issues, respiratory ailments
16	Bon sim	*Dolichos lablab*	Fabaceae	Seed, Green leaves	Fever, skin infections, gastrointestinal problems
17	Lotanokalmi	*Ipomoea aquatica*	Convolvulaceae	Leaves	Fever, skin infections, gastrointestinal problems
18	Nayantara	*Catharanthus roseus*	Apocynaceae	Whole plant	Cancer, diabetes, hypertension
19	Neem	*Azadirachtaindica*	Meliaceae	Leaves, Bark	Skin infections, digestive disorders, diabetes
20	Petari	*Abutilon indicum*	Malvaceae	Leaves	Respiratory issues, urinary tract infections
21	Tassel-berry	*Antidesma venosum*	Phyllanthaceae	Fruits	Digestive ailments, skin infections

Fig. 60.3 Plant species obtained from study area: (A) Terminalia arjuna; (B) Urena lobata; (C) Clerodendrum infortunatum; (D) Croton bonplandionus boill; (E) Smilax rotundifolia; (F) Ipomoea aquatica; (G) Gymnema sylvestre; (H) Cassytha filiformis

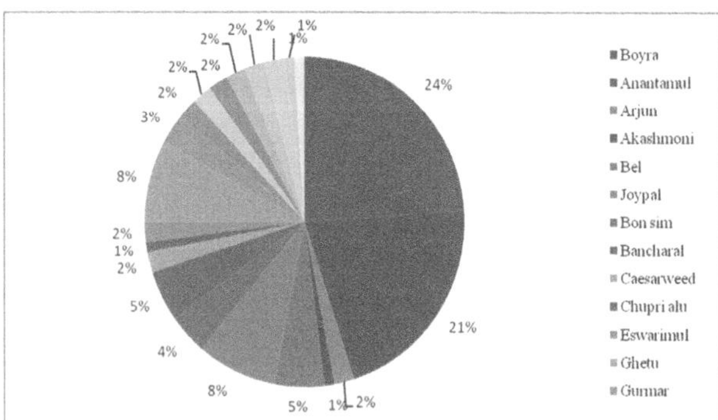

Fig. 60.4 Distribution of plant species in joypur forest

elegantly delineates the proportional abundance of distinct plant species, offering a snapshot of the botanical diversity present in this specific sampling area. This visual aid enhances our comprehension of the ecological dynamics, emphasizing the prevalence of the medicinal plants. The chart stands as a key reference in unravelling the nuanced interplay of flora within the surveyed ecosystem.

The prevalence of certain plant families and the utilization of specific plant parts provide valuable insights into the local traditional knowledge. The villagers, primarily from the Santal community, have developed a unique understanding of phytomedicines, employing indigenous plants to manage everyday health issues. The village economy is intricately tied to the Joypur forest, relying heavily on its resources and products. Indigenous knowledge, such as the traditional uses of forest plants, plays a crucial role in sustaining rural livelihoods and contributing to the local economy [14-18] Comparing our results with existing literature reveals similarities with studies conducted in neighboring regions. Sustainable agriculture is crucial for addressing the pressing global issues of food security and environmental degradation [4,31,35]. Microbe-based soil inoculants present a viable solution for sustainable agriculture [7,8]. Xylan, a complexcarbohydrate present in plant cell walls, holds significant potential for industrial applications [9]. However, unique characteristics in the distribution of plant families highlight the distinct ethnomedicinal landscape of Joypur forest. While this study sheds light on the current state of ethnomedicinal plant usage, further research is warranted. Future investigations could delve into the specific medicinal properties of these plants, their cultural significance, and potential ecological implications. The identified patterns and trends contribute valuable insights to the broader field of ethnobotany and provide a basis for more in-depth exploration in future research endeavors.

4. Conclusion

The study meticulously catalogues the distribution of ethano-medicinal plant data within the forest area of Joypur. It documents 21 ethnomedicinally significant plant species in Joypur forest, highlighting their traditional importance and customary applications within the Santal community. The study's findings have significant implications for the discovery of contemporary drugs from indigenous plant resources. The Joypur forest is home to 19 villages, predominantly inhabited by the Santal community, who possess a wealth of traditional knowledge. This study explores and documents the community's rich ethnobotanical heritage, investigating how their traditional knowledge is interpreted, transmitted, and valued. Preserving traditional knowledge for future generations is crucial. Documenting and sharing this knowledge with younger generations, researchers, and healthcare professionals ensures its survival and potential applications.

References

1. Acharya, J., & Mukherjee, A. (2010). Herbal therapy for urinary ailments as documented from Bankura district (West Bengal). *Indian Journal of Scientific Research, 1*(1), 67–69.

2. Archana Banerjee, A. B. (1999). Ethnobotany of some trees in the Santhal villages of Birbhum, West Bengal.
3. Bhatia, H., Sharma, Y. P., Manhas, R. K., & Kumar, K. (2015). Traditional phytoremedies for the treatment of menstrual disorders in district Udhampur, J&K, India. Journal of ethnopharmacology, 160, 202–210.
4. Ganguly, A., & Mandal, A. (2024). Production and optimization of xylanase enzyme from Bacillus cereus BSA1 by submerged fermentation. Int Res J Basic Appl Sci, 9(1), 13–20.
5. Chattaraj, S., & Das Mohapatra, P. K. (2024). Immunostimulatory and antagonistic potential of the methanolic extract of Oedogonium intermedium SCB in Cirrhinusreba challenged with Aeromonashydrophila. Aquaculture International, 32(3), 2523–2548.
6. Chattaraj, S., & Das Mohapatra, P. K. (2024). Immunostimulatory and antagonistic potential of the methanolic extract of Oedogonium intermedium SCB in Cirrhinusreba challenged with Aeromonashydrophila. Aquaculture International, 32(3), 2523–2548.
7. CHATTARAJ, S., MITRA, D., GANGULY, A., MOHAPATRA, P. K. D., & THATOI, H. (2025). Harnessing microbe-based soil inoculums, strigolactones, and nanotechnology for sustainable agriculture: Mechanisms, innovations, and challenges. Pedosphere.
8. Chattaraj, S., Samantaray, A., Ganguly, A., & Thatoi, H. (2025). Employing plant growth-promoting rhizobacteria for abiotic stress mitigation in plants: with a focus on drought stress. Discover Applied Sciences, 7(1), 68.
9. Ganguly, A., & Mandal, A. (2024). Production and optimization of xylanase enzyme from Bacillus cereus BSA1 by submerged fermentation. Int Res J Basic Appl Sci, 9(1), 13–20.
10. Ganguly, A., Banerjee, A., Mandal, A., Dutta, T. K., & Mohapatra, P. K. D. (2018). Study of indigenous freshwater fish diversity of Bankura (West Bengal), India with special reference to Clariasbatrachus. Journal of Applied and Natural Science, 10(4), 1162.
11. Ganguly, A., Banerjee, A., Mandal, A., & Mohapatra, P. K. D. (2018). Probiotic-based cultivation of Clariasbatrachus: importance and future perspective. ActaBiologicaSzegediensis, 62(2), 158–168.
12. Ganguly, A., Banerjee, A., Mandal, A., Khan, M. A., & Mohapatra, P. K. D. (2019, December). Isolation and characterization of bacteria from the intestine of Clariasbatrachus for probiotic organism. In Proceedings of the Zoological Society (Vol. 72, pp. 411–419). Springer India.
13. Ganguly, A., Chattaraj, S., Ganguly, M., Chattaraj, M., Banerjee, A., Mandal, A., ...& Das Mohapatra, P. K. (2025). Effect of three probiotic Bacillus strains supplemented feeds on growth, carcass composition and blood parameters of Clariasmagur (Hamilton). Journal of Applied Aquaculture, 37(1), 19–44.
14. Ganguly, A., Ganguly, M., Chowdhury, P., & Kumar, M. An Assessment of Nutritional status, Socio-economic Conditions and Occupational Health Hazards of Terracotta artisans of Bishnupur, West Bengal, India.
15. Ganguly, A., Konar, U., Kundu, A., Ghosh, S., Chatterjee, I., Nad, S., ...& Kali, S. (2020). The prevalence, preventive measures and economic impact of pandemic COVID-19 in India: the initial phase. ActaBiologicaSzegediensis, 64(1), 43–62.
16. Ganguly, A., Mahapatra, S., Ray, S., Chattopadhyay, S., Islam, M. J., Garai, S., ...& Chattaraj, S. (2025). The rising threat of Nipah virus: a highly contagious and deadly zoonotic pathogen. Virology Journal, 22(1), 1–11.
17. Ganguly, A., Nad, S., Singha, K., Pathak, R., Hazra, P., Singha, P., ...& Mandal, A. (2021). Diversity and distribution of wild mushrooms in different forest areas of Bankura district, WB, India. ActaBiologicaSzegediensis, 65(2), 185–198.
18. Ganguly, M., & Ganguly, A. (2015). A study on anthropometric measurement, socio-economic conditions & occupational health problems of Baluchari Shari weavers of Bishnupur. International Journal of Current Research, 7(7), 17722–17729.
19. Ganguly, A., Ganguly, M., Chowdhury, P., & Kumar, M. An Assessment of Nutritional status, Socio-economic Conditions and Occupational Health Hazards of Terracotta artisans of Bishnupur, West Bengal, India.
20. Ganguly, M., Ganguly, A., Chattaraj, S., & Midya, D. K. (2025). A review on menstrual health in adolescent girls emphasizing multi-omics and machine learning strategies for preventing reproductive tract infections. Discover Public Health, 22(1), 105.
21. Ganguly, M., Jana, S., Ganguly, A., & Midya, D. K. (2024). Menstruation in adolescent girls: myths and taboos. ActaBiologicaSlovenica, 67(2).
22. Ganguly, M., Jana, S., Ganguly, A., Chattaraj, M., & Midya, D. K. (2025). Menstrual hygiene management among the rural school-going adolescent girls with special emphasis to the Kora tribe in West Bengal, India. Discover Public Health, 22(1), 1–16.
23. Ganguly, M., Patsa, M.K., Chowdhury, P. and Ganguly, A. (2016b). Assessment of nutritional status and socio-economic conditions of terracotta artisans of Panchmura, West Bengal. *Int. J. Dev. Res.*, 6(5), 7741–7747.
24. Ganguly, M., Patsa, M. K., Ghosh, A., & Ganguly, A. (2016). An insight to the bell metal industry of Bankura, West Bengal, India. Int. J. Life Sci, 5(2), 105–111.
25. Ghosh, A. (2003). Herbal folk remedies of Bankura and Medinipur districts, West Bengal.
26. Manasi Mandal, M. M., Subhajit Paul, S. P., & Dey, S. (2014). Ethno-medicobotany of some tribal communities of Bankura district, West Bengal, India.
27. Matthew, K. M. (2004). William Roxburgh's plants of the coast of coromandel: An enumeration of species. Blumea-Biodiversity, Evolution and Biogeography of Plants, 49(2-3), 367–405.
28. Mitra, D., Nachhmin, B., Ganguly, A., & Mohapatra, P. (2022). Computational approach to assess mucormycosis: A systematic review. Computational Intelligence in Healthcare Applications, 71–85.
29. Morse, J. M. (1998). Charles Campbell Hughes, 1929–1997.
30. Mukhopadhyay, P., Ganguly, A., Ghanta, R., Mallick, S. K., Mandal, A., & Mukherjee, S. K. (2024). A detailed survey on fungal distribution and characterization under Bankura District, West Bengal, India. ActaBiologicaSlovenica, 67(2), 44.
31. Nad, S., Konar, U., Chattaraj, S., & Ganguly, A. (2024). Valorization of feather waste by microbial enzymatic

activity: bioconversion, production and application. In Agro-waste to Microbe Assisted Value Added Product: Challenges and Future Prospects: Recent Developments in Agro-waste Valorization Research (pp. 337–363). Cham: Springer Nature Switzerland.
32. Namhata, D., & Mukherjee, A. (1988). Ethnomedicine in Bankura District, West Bengal.
33. Pal, S., Mitra, P., Dey, S., Ganguly, A., & Mandal, A. (2024). Appraisal of Ethno-veterinary practices used for different livestock ailments in rural and peri-urban areas of PurbaBardhaman, West Bengal, India. Ethnobotany Research and Applications, 27, 1–21.
34. Robbins, W. W., Harrington, J. P., & Freire-Marreco, B. W. (1916). ... Ethnobotany of the Tewa Indians (Vol. 55). US Government Printing Office.
35. Samantaray, A., Chattaraj, S., Mitra, D., Ganguly, A., Kumar, R., Gaur, A., ...& Thatoi, H. (2024). Advances in microbial based bio-inoculum for amelioration of soil health and sustainable crop production. Current Research in Microbial Sciences, 100251.
36. Sinha, D., Kazi, Z., Muherjee, R., Ganguly, A., Banerjee, S., Maurya, A. K., ...& Dutta, S. Integrated Molecular Strategies for Enhanced Production of Medicinal Plant-Derived Flavonoids. In *Biotechnology, Multiple Omics, and Precision Breeding in Medicinal Plants* (pp. 314–332). CRC Press.

Note: All figures and tables have been prepared by the authors based on the analyzed data and findings of the present study.

Research and Innovations in Industrial and Marine Biotechnology: A Circular Economy 2024 – Prof. Hrudayanath Thatoi et al. (eds)
© 2026 Taylor & Francis Group, London, ISBN 978-1-041-28285-3

61 Ethnomedicinal Knowledge and Application of Plant Resources by the *Moyra* Community in West Bengal, India

Arindam Ganguly*,
Susmita Dutta, Chitra Kundu,
Pampa Maji, Puja Mondal
Department of Microbiology, Bankura Sammilani College,
Bankura, W.B., India

Mousumi Ganguly
Department of Nutrition, Bankura Sammilani College,
Bankura, West Bengal, India

Saptarshi Roy
Department of English, Bankura Sammilani College,
Bankura, W.B., India

Sourav Chattaraj
Centre for Industrial Biotechnology Research,
School of Pharmaceutical Science,
Siksha 'O' Anusandhan University, Kalinga Nagar,
Bhubaneswar, Odisha, India

Manasi Chattaraj
Department of Geography, Bankura University,
Bankura, West Bengal, India

Asish Mandal
Department of Botany, Ramananda College, Bishnupur,
Bankura, West Bengal, India

Abstract: Human-plant interactions have historically met essential human needs, including medicine. Ethnobotany, the study of these relationships, is crucial for preserving traditional knowledge. This study, conducted in Moyra village of Bankura district, West Bengal, documents indigenous medicinal practices of local Vaidhyas. It identifies 18 plant species used to treat various ailments using plant parts like leaves, roots, fruits, bark, and stems. Common preparation methods include decoction, poultice, and infusion. These treatments rely on local natural resources and are deeply tied to the cultural identity of rural and indigenous communities. The study emphasizes the significance of preserving this ethnobiological knowledge, much of which remains undocumented and risks being lost due to environmental changes and modernization. Highlighting unknown treatments in the south-eastern part of Bankura, the research underlines the need for sustainable use of biological resources and urgent documentation of local medicinal knowledge for future generations and scientific exploration.

Keywords: Antimicrobial resistance, Diseases, Ethnobotany, Moyra, Traditional medicine

*Corresponding author: arindam_ganguly@yahoo.com

DOI: 10.1201/9781003759003-61

1. INTRODUCTION

Human-plant interaction forms the cornerstone of survival, with plants providing food, medicine, fuel, and shelter [1]. Traditional knowledge of medicinal plant use has long been passed down orally and documented in ancient systems like Ayurveda, Siddha, and Unani [2,3]. Even amid modern allopathic medicine, herbal remedies continue to be practiced, though many remain unexplored. Ethnobotany, the study of human-plant relationships, has gained importance for conserving this knowledge [4]. Indigenous communities possess intricate ecological knowledge, which ethnobiologists aim to preserve and ethically integrate into modern research frameworks [5]. The urgency of documenting and revitalizing this knowledge stems from risks of genetic erosion and cultural loss. Ethnomedicine, a subdiscipline coined by Hughes in 1968 [6], focuses on traditional healing practices and plant-based treatments. India, with its rich cultural and floral diversity, has a long history of plant-based medicine, documented in texts like the Rigveda and Charak Samhita. Bankura district in West Bengal, home to tribal communities and forest resources, serves as an ethnobotanical hotspot. Studies here are limited, though notable works include Namhata and Mukherjee [7], Ghosh [8], Acharya and Mukherjee [9], and Mandal et al. [11], documenting various plant uses. This current study seeks to expand on that work by exploring the indigenous knowledge of Vaidhyas and locals in southeastern Bankura, focusing on their use of wild plants for traditional medicine and other purposes.

2. MATERIALS AND METHODS

Bankura district (Fig. 61.1) is impregnated over a vast area of about 6,882 km^2, lies between 22°38′ to 23°38′ N latitude and 86°36′ to 87°46′ E longitude. Moyra village is a remote place, at least five-six km away from any urban locality. Situated 4-5 km from Panchmura (famous for his pottery all over the world), Moyra is a village that roughly houses 300-400 households. It is surrounded by deep forest where only a few hundred people live. The unique combination of tropical climatic conditions and red laterite soil in this region creates an ideal environment for lush floral growth [11]. Although it is a remote place, it is not unknown to the outside world, especially those who come here from distant places to get some proper treatment of their long continuing diseases. People even come here not only from other districts but also from neighboring states. A simple random survey was conducted in the Moyra village for acquisition of data on interview basis during the period of July to September, 2024. The primary data was retrieved from the medical practitioners (Vaidya), workers and patients and captured through photography with a Nikon D5300 camera. The plant specimen was collected using standard taxonomical procedures.

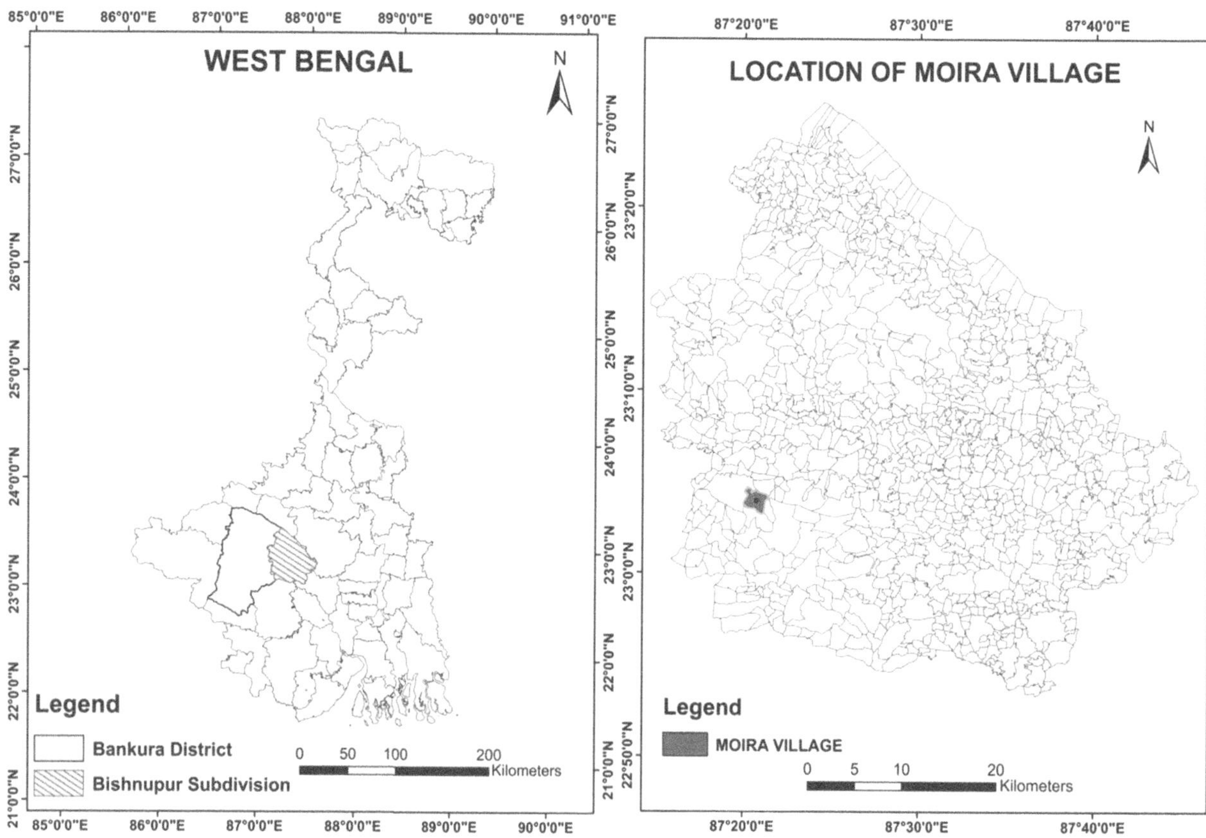

Fig. 61.1 Study area

3. Results and Discussion

Microorganisms are a significant etiological factor in various human, veterinary, and aquatic diseases [12-17]. The villagers utilize various medicinal plants to treat a range of illnesses. Although many are familiar with some of these remedies, they typically seek advice from *Vaidhyas* for diagnosis and treatment. This traditional knowledge of medicinal plants and healing practices has been transmitted orally across generations.

The present work focuses on different kinds of herbal plants used by the medical practitioners of Moyra village to treat patients (Table 61.1). The study also includes their binomial names and traditional uses. Eighteen different herbal plat species (e.g. Helencha, Peepal, Neem, Garlic, black pepper etc.) were identified during the study. Detailed records were kept regarding the plant parts used for treatment, the types of diseases they addressed, appropriate dosages, and methods of administration. Leaves and roots are the most commonly used plant

Table 61.1 Tribal plants used for medical purposes

Sl. No.	Name	Scientific Name	Uses
1	BAEL ROOT	*Aegle marmelos L*	Root bark is used in remission of intermittent fevers fever, fish poison, heart palpitation, melancholia. It is also used in the treatment of dog bite, digestive problems, cardiovascular disorders, amoebic infections and rheumatism.
2	HELENCHA	*Enhydra fluctuans*	It is useful in skin diseases, prickly heat treatment, anorexia, acidity, liver disorder, sleeplessness, neurological disorder, obesity, indigestion, laxative bronchitis, leucoderma, biliousness and small pox.
3	CAMPHOR	*Cinnamomum camphora*	It is used in the treatment of pain, warts, cold sores, hemorrhoids, and osteoarthritis. Additionally, it serves as an anti-itch agent, counterirritant, and is used to enhance local blood circulation.
4	RED SANDALWOOD	*Pterocarpus santalinus*	It is used for treating indigestion, fluid retention, and cough.
5	WHITE SANDALWOOD	*Santalum album*	It is used to cure common cold, cough, bronchitis, fever, headache. It is also used to treat gastric irritability, urinary tract infections, liver problems, cardiovascular discomfort, gonorrhea, and conditions of the heart and blood vessels.
6	PIGEON PEAS LEAF	*Cajanus cajan*	It is used as treatment of coughs, bronchitis, diarrhea, hemorrhages, sores and wounds.
7	KEBAB/CUBEB	*Euphorbia clava*	It is used in treatment of asthma, bronchitis, and chest congestion
8	PEEPAL	*Ficus religiosa*	It is used in amoebiasis, dysentery, small pox, mouth ulcers, night fall, asthma, abdominal pain, burning sensation, disease of the heart, contraceptive, constipation, chronic disease, dental care, diarrhea, diabetes, eye pain epistaxis, gastro intestinal disorder, nose bleed, hemorrhages, jaundice, ulcers, syphilis, piles, ring worm, throat ache, vaginal discharges, uterine tonic, leucorrhoea.
9	YESTHIMADHU	*Glycyrrhiza glabra*	It is used to treat in wasting disorder, blood vomiting, heart disorder, epilepsy, acid reflux, throat infection, urinary tract infection, body paralysis, respiratory tract infection and also applied in burning sensation.
10	NUTMEG	*Myristica fragrans*	It is used in increasing immune system function, prevention of leukemia, detoxify the body, reduce insomnia, alleviate oral condition strengthen cognitive function, improve blood circulation.
11	BLACK PEPPER	*Piper nigrum*	It is used to cure vitiligo, relieves cold cough improves dental health used as anti-depressant.
12	ATAP RICE	*Oryza sativa*	It is used to treat urinary dysfunctions, excessive lactation, poor appetite, and indigestion
13	RAW TURMERIC	*Curcuma longa*	It is used to boost digestion .It is used as antiseptic, blood purifier, pain removal & also used to treat osteoarthritis, itching.
15	LEMON JUICE	*Citrusx limon*	It is used to treat scurvy, common cold, flu, swine flu, tinnitus, abdominal discomfort, kidney stones, and pregnancy-related vomiting.
16	GARLIC	*Allium sativum*	It is used to reduce blood pressure ,combat sickness , common cold, improve cholesterols levels and reducing the risk of heart ailments, neurodegenerative disorder.
17	ASHWAGANDHA	*Withania somnifera*	It can reduce stress, anxiety, depression, infertility. It can boost testosterone in men and develop brain function.
18	CHINA ROSE	*Hibiscus rosasinensis*	Its leaves have anodyne, antidotal, demulcent, expectorant and refrigerant properties. It is also treat burns, pectoral and pulmonary complaints, swellings and other skin problems.

parts in the preparation of herbal medicines. Other plant parts like seeds, tubers, bulbs, sap and stem or the whole plant were also being used to treat certain diseases and health problems. Ong et al. [18] documented traditional knowledge of medicinal plants in Kampung Tanjung Sabtu, Terengganu, Malaysia, revealing 52 plant species used by Malay villagers. Negi et al. [19] investigated conventional healthcare practices in Rawain Valley, Uttarkashi, Uttarakhand, India, documenting 63 plant species with therapeutic significance.

The patient-oriented data were recorded (Fig. 61.2). Some of them came from distant part of the state and country. It was really surprising that patients suffering from different chronic ailments including cancer, high diabetes, and kidney failure were being satisfactorily treated. Most of them have previously gone through sustained allopathic medications and treatment. Phytomedicines, derived from plants, have shown promise in managing various health conditions [20, 21]. Traditional phytoremedies have been employed for centuries to alleviate various menstrual disorders, providing natural relief for symptoms associated with menstrual health [22-25]. They were also being effective in treating lung infections [26,27]

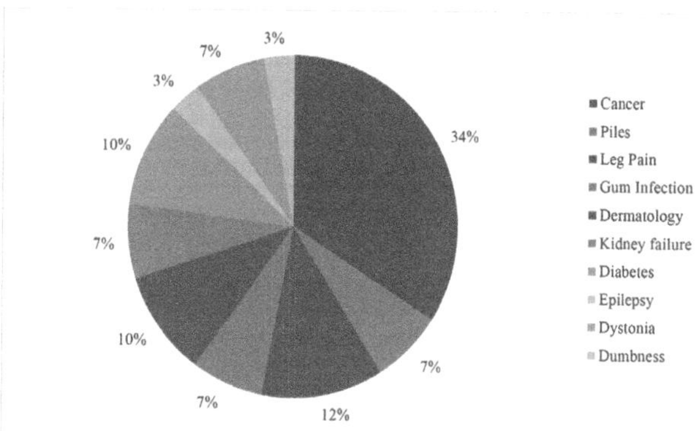

Fig. 61.2 Distribution of patients traveling to Moyra village for phyto-medicine treatment

Sustainable agricultural practices are increasingly essential for addressing the intertwined global challenges of food security and environmental degradation [28-29]. The villagers take part in harvesting various medicinal plants, arranging raw materials, and preparing several herbal medicines. Thus, the economy of this village is very much controlled by this Ayurvedic center. On the otherhand, indigenous knowledge on herbal plants, ethno-medicines and their uses also get developed.

The researcher found it really interesting and amazing that a few patients from a small Himalayan country visit this place on regular basis. Some of these patients have come here for the first time. They already had various treatments in their own country as well as in India. So it is very clear that these patients were not benefited either by herbal or by allopathic medicines in their country. It can also be said that many of them who are suffering so long, have finally found a cure.

The village people also take part in harvesting various medicinal plants, arranging raw materials and preparing several herbal medicines. The economy of this village is very much controlled by this Ayurvedic center. This kind of indigenous knowledge often plays vital role in rural economy and livelihood [30-35]. Nearly a hundred visitors come here every day to find some relief from their diseases. Medicines here vary from handmade tablets to pastes which are usually given for a span of 1 month, generally.

4. Conclusion

The study reveals that plant parts used in Moyra herbal medicine, mainly for general health, skin issues, and chronic diseases are significantly benefiting the rural economy. Folk medicine, deeply rooted in indigenous culture, offers affordable alternatives to modern drugs. However, globalization and environmental changes threaten this knowledge. Documenting and transmitting this knowledge to younger generations, as well as to researchers and health practitioners, ensures its survival and potential for future use. In a rapidly changing world, where traditional knowledge systems are under threat, it is essential to recognize the value of folk medicine not only as a tool for healing but also as a critical part of our global heritage. By safeguarding this knowledge and promoting its sustainable use, we can honor the wisdom of past generations, enrich modern medicine, and contribute to the well-being of future generations.

References

1. Sinha, D., Kazi, Z., Muherjee, R., Ganguly, A., Banerjee, S., Maurya, A.K., Chowdhury, A.A., Majgaonkar, A. and Dutta, S. (2024). Integrated molecular strategies for enhanced production of medicinal plant-derived flavonoids. In: *Biotechnology, Multiple Omics, and Precision Breeding in Medicinal Plants*. Springer Nature. https://doi.org/10.1201/9781003475491-23
2. Nad, S., Mandal, A., Das Mohapatra, P.K. and Ganguly, A. (2021). Herbal drug: A natural bioactive formulation and its scope against viral diseases. In: Sinha, D. (Ed.), *Handbook of Agriculture & Plant Sciences*, 187–230. ABS Books.
3. Bhatia, H., Sharma, Y.P., Manhas, R.K. and Kumar, K. (2015). Traditional phytoremedies for the treatment of menstrual disorders in district Udhampur, J&K, India. *J. Ethnopharmacol.*, 160, 202–210. https://doi.org/10.1016/j.jep.2014.11.041
4. Mukhopadhyay, P., Ganguly, A., Ghanta, R., Mallick, S.K., Mandal, A. and Mukherjee, S.K. (2024). A detailed survey on fungal distribution and characterization under Bankura District, West Bengal, India. *Acta Biol. Slov.*, 67(2). https://doi.org/10.14720/abs.67.2.18621

5. Pal, S., Mitra, P., Dey, S., Ganguly, A. and Mandal, A. (2024). Appraisal of ethno-veterinary practices used for different livestock ailments in rural and periurban areas of Purba Bardhaman, West Bengal, India. *Ethnobot. Res. Appl.*, 27, 30. https://doi.org/10.32859/era.27.30.1-21
6. Morse, J.M. (1998). Charles Campbell Hughes, 1929–1997. *Qual. Health Res.*, 8(2), 270–274. https://doi.org/10.1177/104973239800800209
7. Namhata, D. and Mukherjee, A. (1988). Ethnomedicine in Bankura District, West Bengal. *Indian J. Appl. Pure Biol.*, 3(2), 53–55.
8. Ghosh, A. (2003). Herbal folk remedies of Bankura, Medinipur districts, West Bengal. *Indian J. Tradit. Knowl.*, 2, 393–396.
9. Acharya, J. and Mukherjee, A. (2010). Herbal therapy for urinary ailments as documented from Bankura district (West Bengal). *Indian J. Sci. Res.*, 1(1), 67–69.
10. Mandal, M., Paul, S. and Dey, S. (2014). Ethno-medicobotany of some tribal communities of Bankura district, West Bengal, India. *Explor. Anim. Med. Res.*, 4(1), 64–80.
11. Ganguly, A., Banerjee, A., Mandal, A. and Das Mohapatra, P.K. (2018). Study of indigenous freshwater fish diversity of Bankura (West Bengal), India with special reference to *Clarias batrachus*. *J. Appl. Nat. Sci.*, 10, 1162–1172. https://doi.org/10.31018/jans.v10i4.1892
12. Ganguly, A., Mahapatra, S., Ray, S. *et al.* (2025). The rising threat of Nipah virus: a highly contagious and deadly zoonotic pathogen. *Virol. J.*, 22, 139. https://doi.org/10.1186/s12985-025-02728-4
13. Ganguly, A., Chattaraj, S., Ganguly, M., Chattaraj, M., Banerjee, A., Mandal, A., Khan, M.A., Sen, S.K. and Das Mohapatra, P.K. (2024). Effect of three probiotic *Bacillus* strains supplemented feeds on growth, carcass composition and blood parameters of *Clarias magur* (Hamilton). *J. Appl. Aquacult.* https://doi.org/10.1080/10454438.2024.2330499
14. Chattaraj, S., Ganguly, A. and Das Mohapatra, P.K. (2023). Study of intestinal bacteria of *Cirrhinus reba* and characterization of a new probiotic bacteria: An initiative to save the threatened species of *Cirrhinus*. *Appl. Biochem. Microbiol.*, 59(6), 833–849. https://doi.org/10.1134/S0003683823060248
15. Ganguly, A., Banerjee, A., Mandal, A., Khan, M.A. and Das Mohapatra, P.K. (2019). Isolation and characterization of bacteria from the intestine of *Clarias batrachus* for probiotic organism. *Proc. Zool. Soc.*, 72(4), 411–419. https://doi.org/10.1007/s12595-018-0283-x
16. Ganguly, A., Banerjee, A., Mandal, A. and Das Mohapatra, P.K. (2018). Probiotic-based cultivation of *Clarias batrachus*: Importance and future perspective. *Acta Biol. Szeged.*, 62(2), 158–168. https://doi.org/10.14232/abs.2018.2.158-168
17. Chattaraj, S., & Das Mohapatra, P. K. (2024). Immunostimulatory and antagonistic potential of the methanolic extract of Oedogonium intermedium SCB in Cirrhinus reba challenged with Aeromonas hydrophila. Aquaculture International, 32(3), 2523–2548.
18. Ong, H.C., Ruzalila, B.N. and Milow, P. (2011). Traditional knowledge of medicinal plants among the Malay villagers in Kampung Tanjung Sabtu, Terengganu, Malaysia. *Indian J. Tradit. Knowl.*, 10(3), 460–465.
19. Negi, V.S., Maikhuri, R.K. and Vashishtha, D.P. (2011). Traditional healthcare practices among the villages of Rawain valley, Uttarkashi, Uttarakhand, India. *Indian J. Tradit. Knowl.*, 10(3), 533–537.
20. Ganguly, A., Nad, S., Singha, K., Pathak, R., Hazra, P., Singha, P., Dhua, P., Mahapatra, P.K. and Mandal, A. (2021). Diversity and distribution of wild mushrooms in different forest areas of Bankura district, WB, India. *Acta Biol. Szeged.*, 65(2), 185–198. https://doi.org/10.14232/abs.2021.2
21. Mitra, D., Nachhmin, B., Ganguly, A., & Das Mohapatra, P. K. (2022). Computational approach to assess Mucormycosis: A systematic review. In *Computational Intelligence in Healthcare Applications* (pp. 71–85). Academic Press. https://doi.org/10.1016/B978-0-323-99031-8.00004-1
22. Ganguly, M., Jana, S., Ganguly, A., et al. (2025). Menstrual hygiene management among the rural school-going adolescent girls with special emphasis to the Kora tribe in West Bengal, India. *Discov. Public Health*, 22, 265. https://doi.org/10.1186/s12982-025-00663-x
23. Ganguly, M., Jana, S., Ganguly, A. and Midya, D.K. (2024). Menstruation in adolescent girls: Myths & taboos. *Acta Biol. Slov.*, 67(2), 67. https://doi.org/10.14720/abs.67.2.18725
24. Ganguly, M. and Midya, D.K. (2023). Menstrual hygiene among school-going early adolescent girls (10–14 years): A socio-cultural study in Bankura District, West Bengal, India. *Acta Biol. Szeged.*, 67(1), 103–110. https://doi.org/10.14232/abs.2023.1.103-110
25. Ganguly, A., Dutta, T.K., Ganguly, M. and Roy, S. (2016). School sanitation and hygiene: A glimpse of contemporary India. In *Health, Nutrition and Hygiene: The Dynamics of Social Ecology in India*, 197–207.
26. Ganguly, A., Konar, U., Kundu, A., Ghosh, S., Chatterjee, I., Nad, S., Chatterjee, S., Nandi, S., Singha, S. and Kali, S. (2020). The prevalence, preventive measures and economic impact of pandemic COVID-19 in India: The initial phase. *Acta Biol. Szeged.*, 64(1), 43–61. https://doi.org/10.14232/abs.2020.1.43-61
27. Das, S., Sinha, D., Chatterji, S., Ganguly, A., De, A., Majgaonkar, A., Kazi, Z., Maurya, A. K., Sohail, M., & Bhat, N. (2025). The role of marine bacteria-derived bioactive compounds in COVID-19 management. In *Anti-coronavirus marine bioactive compounds* (Chapter 7, pp. 185–224). Apple Academic Press.
28. Samantaray, A., Chattaraj, S., Mitra, D., Ganguly, A., Kumar, R., Gaur, A., Das Mohapatra, P.K., de los Santos-Villalobos, S., Rani, A. and Thatoi, H. (2024). Advances in microbial-based bio-inoculum for amelioration of soil health and sustainable crop production. *Curr. Res. Microb. Sci.*https://doi.org/10.1016/j.crmicr.2024.100251
29. Ganguly, A. and Mandal, A. (2024). Production and optimization of xylanase enzyme from *Bacillus cereus* BSA1 by submerged fermentation. *Int. Res. J. Basic Appl. Sci.*, 9, 13–20.
30. Nad, S., Konar, U., Chattaraj, S. and Ganguly, A. (2024). Valorization of feather waste by microbial enzymatic

activity: Bioconversion, production, and application. In *Agro-waste to Microbe Assisted Value Added Product: Challenges and Future Prospects*, 337–363. Springer Nature. https://doi.org/10.1007/978-3-031-58025-3_15

31. Ganguly, M., Patsa, M.K., Chowdhury, P. and Ganguly, A. (2016). Assessment of nutritional status and socio-economic conditions of terracotta artisans of Panchmura, West Bengal. *Int. J. Dev. Res.*, 6(5), 7741–7747.
32. Ganguly, M., Daripa, A., Patsa, M.K. and Ganguly, A. (2016). Assessment of nutritional status, socio-economic conditions, and occupational health hazards of conch shell workers of Bankura. *Int. J. Curr. Res.*, 8(3), 28530–28536.
33. Ganguly, M., Patsa, M.K., Ghosh, A. and Ganguly, A. (2016). An insight into the bell metal industry of Bankura, West Bengal, India. *Int. J. Life Sci.*, 5(2), 105–111.
34. Ganguly, A., Ganguly, M., Chowdhury, P. and Patsa, M.K. (2016). Assessment of nutritional status, socio-economic conditions, and occupational health hazards of terracotta artisans of Bishnupur, West Bengal, India. *Int. J. Life Sci.*, 5(2), 129–135.
35. Ganguly, M. and Ganguly, A. (2015). A study on anthropometric measurement, socio-economic conditions, and occupational health problems of Baluchari sari weavers of Bishnupur. *Int. J. Curr. Res.*, 7(7), 17722–17729.

Note: All figures and tables have been prepared by the authors based on the analyzed data and findings of the present study.

Research and Innovations in Industrial and Marine Biotechnology: A Circular Economy 2024 – Prof. Hrudayanath Thatoi et al. (eds)

62 Kyasanur Forest Disease Virus Research in India: A Scientometric Profile of an Emerging Tropical Disease

Deep Kumar Kirtania,
Monishankar Chhetri
Central Library, Bankura Sammilani College,
Bankura, W.B., India
Arindam Ganguly[1]
Department of Microbiology, Bankura Sammilani College,
Bankura, W.B., India
Sourav Chattaraj[2]
Centre for Industrial Biotechnology Research,
School of Pharmaceutical Sciences, Siksha 'O' Anusandhan University,
Odisha, India

Abstract: Kyasanur Forest Disease Virus is a tropical zoonotic pathogen which has become a major cause of concern for the last six decades. The objective of this study is to provide a scientometric analysis of Kyasanur Forest Disease Virus based on Web of Science data. The present work evaluates some key scientometric indicators such as authorship patterns, top contributing countries, prolific authors, key themes and most productive journals during 1989 to 2024. The findings reveal a positive growth in the number of publications as well as citation. This study also finds that, these research papers were published in leading scientific journals such as Indian Journal of Medical Research, International Journal of Infectious Diseases, PLOS Neglected Tropical Diseases.

Keywords: Kyasanur forest disease, KFD, KFDV, India, Scientometric analysis

1. Introduction

Outbreak of infectious diseases poses a significant threat [1-3]. Kyasanur Forest Disease Virus (KFDV) is a tropical zoonotic virus endemic to India, primarily in Maharashtra, Karnataka and Tamil Nadu. Transmitted by the *Haemaphysalis spinigera* tick, KFDV affects humans and various animals, including small mammals and non-human primates [4]. KFDV's expansion beyond Karnataka to states like Kerala, Goa, and Maharashtra highlights the risk of further spread [5]. Emerging viruses pose a substantial risk to global health, characterized by their rapid transmission, unpredictable behavior, and unclear patterns of transmission [6-7]. Although 80% of cases are asymptomatic, severe cases can cause hemorrhagic or neurological symptoms [4]. Initially isolated in 1957 [8], KFDV research has significantly advanced through key studies by Work and Trapido [9] and Trapido et al. [10]. Subsequent studies, including genomic analysis by Dodd et al. [11] and phylogenetic analysis by Yadav et al. [12], have provided deeper insights into the virus's evolution and transmission. A vaccine trial conducted by Bhatia et al. [13] evaluated a single-dose vaccine's potential.

KFDV is thus a neglected tropical disease with a growing impact on public health in India. Despite its immense significance, the scientific landscape of KFDV research remains unclear. This scientometric investigation aims

Corresponding author: [1]arindam.microbiology@gmail.com, [2]souravchattaraj@soa.ac.in

DOI: 10.1201/9781003759003-62

to explore the structural and dynamic aspects of KFDV research, examining the publication patterns, authorship networks, and thematic evolution of the field. Although many scientometrics studies have been already conducted on these types of related viruses, no such study have been found on Kyasanur Forest Disease Virus in the lens of scientometrics analysis. Hence the present study has tried to fulfill this present research gap.

2. Research Methodology

The Web of Science was chosen as the main data source for conducting the present study [14]. Relevant publications on probiotic research were retrieved using a structured search query [Kyasanur Forest disease (Topic) or *Haemaphysalis spinigera*]. It was observed that a total of one hundred ninety-six research papers on this topic have been published globally. The retrieved results were filtered by year (exclude 2025), which shows 195 research publication, has been selected for final analysis. The cut-off date of data collection for the present work is kept as 06.12.2024. Bibliographic information was systematically recorded in MS Excel to facilitate subsequent analysis and interpretation. The R software was employed for data visualization and analysis. The entire process is illustrated in detail through a flowchart (Fig. 62.1).

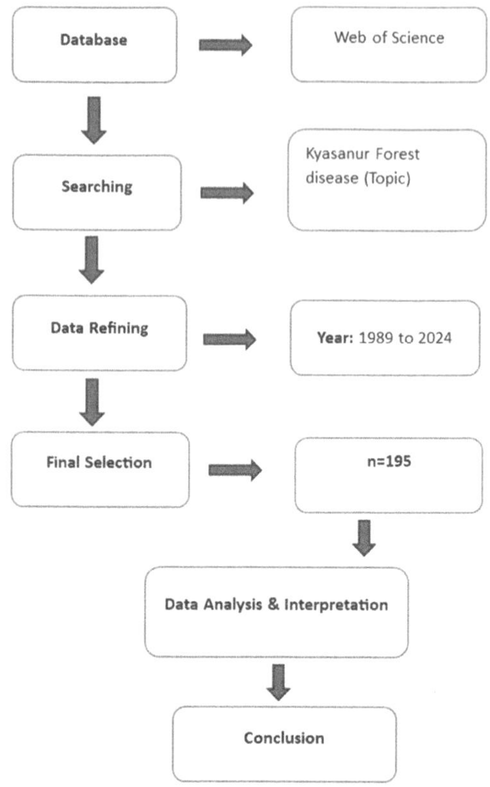

Fig. 62.1 Data analysis and interpretation

3. Literature Growth

Figure 62.2 highlights the year-wise growth of publication on Kyasanur Forest Disease Virus. From 1989 to 2003 only one or two papers were published per year, indicating limited interest in the topic. In the next ten to twelve years the number of writings increased gradually. The two years 2020 and 2021 have seen a significant increase in research output (42 papers, 21.54%). During this period, i.e. during COVID-19[15] research on new vaccine discovery or research on other emerging virus diseases may be published more in line with the progress. In recent times, several notable numbers of papers have been published in 2023 and 2024, with 19 each. It should be mentioned here that the publication data of 2024 till 06.12.2024 has been considered for this present study. The growth of literature over the years shows that many works have been published on this topic over a long period of time and a positive trend has been observed here.

4. Most Productive Journals

The top ten publishing journals were identified (Table 62.1). The Indian Journal of Medical Research led the list with

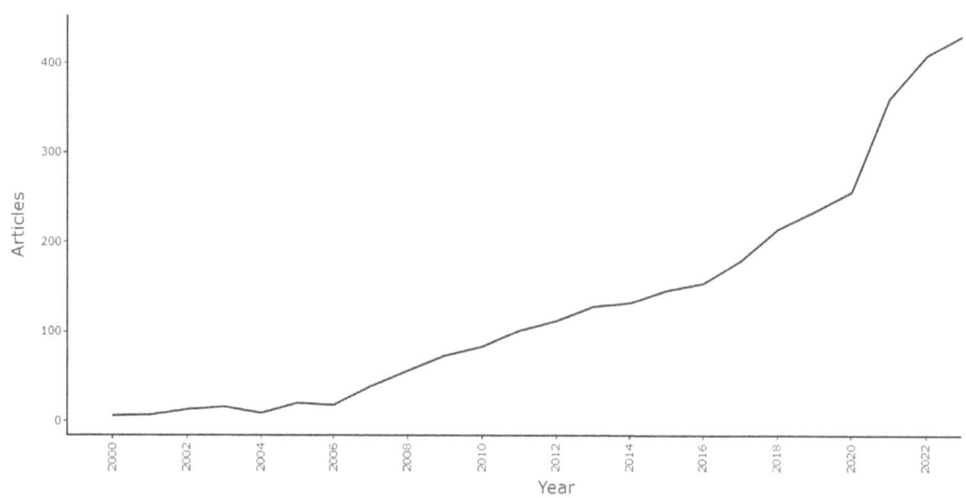

Fig. 62.2 Year wise distribution of publications

Table 62.1 Top ten publishing journals

Journal Titles	Publication	Publisher	Impact Factor	ISSN
Indian Journal of Medical Research	11	*Indian council of medical research*	2.7	0971-5916
International Journal of Infectious Diseases	10	*International society for infectious disease*	14.8	1201-9712
PLOS Neglected Tropical Diseases	10	*POLS*	3.4	1935-2727
Journal of Vector Borne Diseases	9	*Indian Council of Medical research*	0.8	0972-9062
Emerging Infectious Diseases	8	*Centers for disease control and prevention*	7.2	1080-6059
Ticks and Tick Borne Diseases	7	*Elsevier*	3.2	1877-9603
Antiviral Research	6	*International society for antiviral research*	4.5	0166-3542
Scientific Reports	6	*Nature*	3.8	2045-2322
Vector Borne and Zoonotic Diseases	5	*Mary Ann Liebert*	1.8	1557-7759
PLOS One	4	*POLS*	2.9	1932-6203

eleven publications (5.6%), indicating significant regional or national focus i.e. based on Indian context. Later there are several globally famous journals (e.g., *International Journal of Infectious Diseases*, *PLOS Neglected Tropical Diseases*). These journals have substantial relevance to infectious diseases and tropical medicine, providing a solid platform for substantial research on KFDV. In terms of impact factor, these journals range from 1 to 15, which is significant in terms of quality of publication.

5. Prolific Authors

Table 62.2 highlights the most prolific authors in KFDV research, with top contributors largely from the ICMR-National Institute of Virology (NIV), underscoring its pivotal role in KFDV studies. Regional institutions like the State Institute of Health & Family Welfare are also prominent, reflecting Karnataka's role as the virus's hotspot. The table lists researchers, their institutions, paper count, and h-index. While other influential researchers are acknowledged, the study focuses on the top five due to limitations.

Table 62.2 Most prolific authors

Researcher Profiles	Count	Institute	H index
Yadav, Pragya	30	ICMR - National Institute of Virology	36
Mourya, Devendra T.	24		32
Anita Shete- Aich	12		28
Kiran, S. K.	9	State Institute of Health & Family Welfare, Karnataka	6
Dr. Rima Rakesh kumar Sahay	7	ICMR - National Institute of Virology	20

6. Productive Counties

India has contributed 56.92% (111 papers) of the total research output on the subject, reflecting its dominance in KFDV research (Table 62.3). Countries such as USA (22.56%), England (10.77%), Australia (6.15%), and France (5.64%) have revealed themselves as one of the major contributors on this topic which indicates that they have shown positive interest in researching such diseases. Besides, among other countries, Saudi Arabia, Canada, Germany, China and Russia have contributed significantly to this disease. By seeing the names of so many countries, it is easy to understand that this disease is mainly based in India, but researchers from all over the world have shown their academic interest in this area. Research collaborations between these countries are shown through data visualization (Fig. 62.3).

Table 62.3 Most productive counties

Countries	Count	Percentage
India	111	56.92
USA	44	22.56
England	21	10.77
Australia	12	6.15
France	11	5.64
Saudi Arabia	9	4.62
Canada	8	4.10
Germany	8	4.10
China	7	3.59
Russia	7	3.59

7. Authorship Pattern

Under single authorship 12 papers have been published, which indicates a relatively low prevalence of single-authored papers in this area (Fig. 62.4). In terms of joint or collaborative authorship, 183 papers were published during the study period. This overwhelming percentage highlights a strong trend toward collaboration among researchers and their peer group. It reflected the cooperative nature of modern scientific endeavours and the interdisciplinary needs of this field.

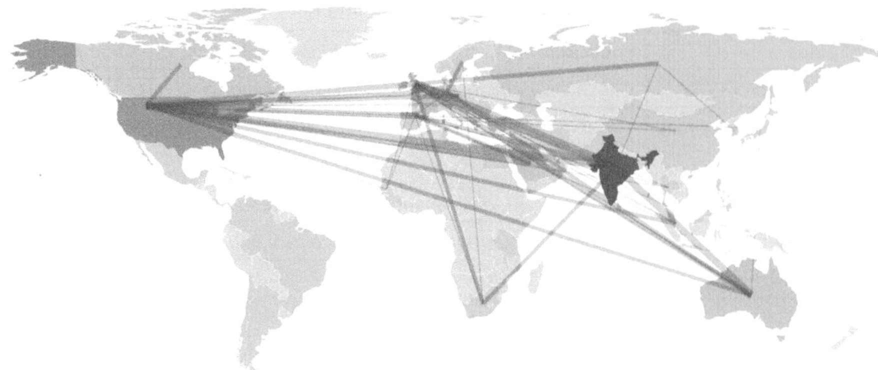

Fig. 62.3 Countries' collaboration network

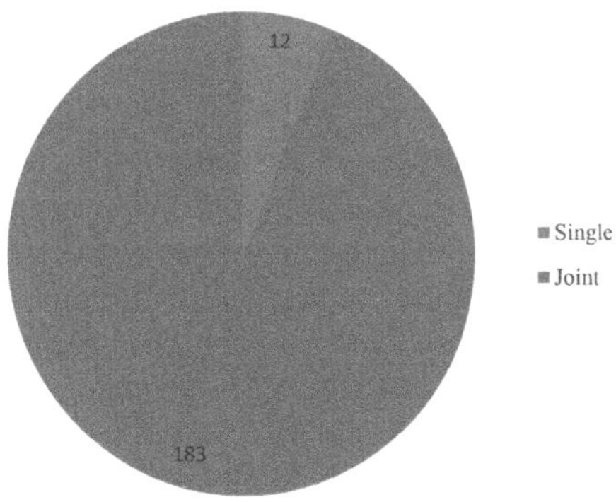

Fig. 62.4 Authorship pattern

8. CITATION STATUS

30 publications (27.03%) have no citations, which were published very recently (Table 62.4). Most citations came from 94 publications that were cited more than 10 times and collectively contributed 5,757 citations. From these aspects it is easy to understand that most of the research papers on this topic have been cited and created a strong research network.

Table 62.4 Citation status

Times cited	Total number of publications	Total
0	30	0
1	10	10
2	12	24
3	14	42
4	10	40
5	1	5
6	5	30
7	11	77
8	2	16
9	6	54
10	0	0
>10	94	5757
Total	195	6055

9. PUBLICATION TYPE

With 136 publications (69.74%), articles are the main form of publication in this topic, which focuses on primary research and empirical findings. Review articles (21.03%) indicate substantial efforts to synthesize existing scientific literatures, which may help others, guide future research and policy-making. Besides, Meeting Abstracts (4.10%), Letters (3.59%), Book Chapters, Editorial among other type of documents have been published by the researchers (Fig. 62.5).

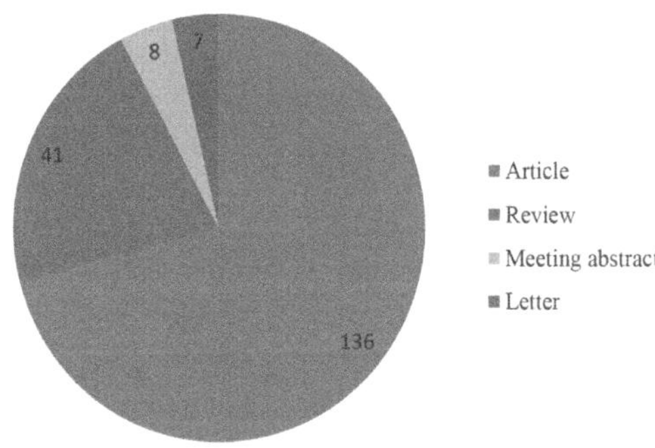

Fig. 62.5 Type of publications

10. KEYWORD ANALYSIS

The most frequently co-occurring keywords were "Kyasanur-forest-disease", "Outbreak", "India", "Virus", "Infection", and "Transmission" (Fig. 62.6). A scientometric analysis of research trends indicates a growing focus on disease outbreaks in India, with particular emphasis on affected zones and viral infections. Specifically, the analysis revealed 30 occurrences of "disease outbreak", 28 occurrences of "India", and 16 occurrences of "viral infection". These findings provide valuable insights into research priorities and may inform future research directions.

The current research trend on Kyasanur Forest Disease (KFD) is focused on understanding the disease transmission dynamics, prevalence zones, host-virus interactions, and vector ecology (Fig. 62.7). The modes of KFD

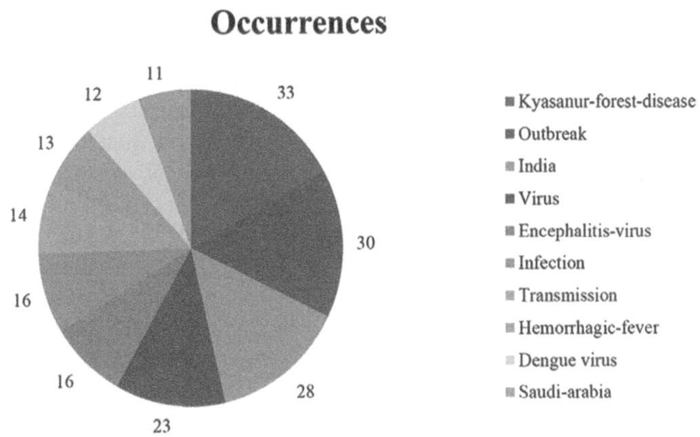

Fig. 62.6 Frequency analysis of cited papers

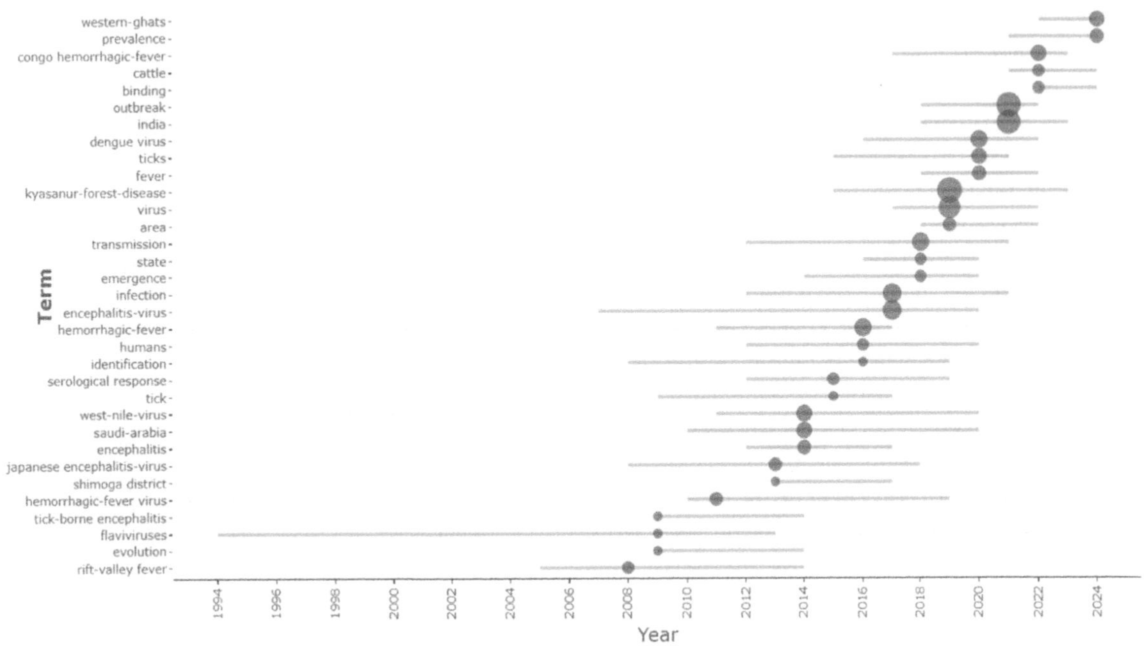

Fig. 62.7 Trending topics

transmission and its prevalence in the South-Indian Forest regions, particularly the Kyasanur Forest, have emerged as key research priorities. Furthermore, the scientific community is also investigating the characteristics of the virus and its closely related family of viruses. Researchers are exploring the efficacy of various drugs in alleviating KFD symptoms, along with the role of tick-borne viruses in the disease's transmission.

11. Major Research Area

The major research areas (Fig. 62.8) in the field of flaviviruses have been identified, with a clear focus on understanding the biology, transmission, and impact health. The most trusted research areas include Infectious Diseases (70), Parasitology (40), Immunology (34), Virology (31), and Tropical Medicine (30). Other notable research areas include Microbiology (27), Public, Environmental, and Occupational Health (21), General Internal Medicine (16), Research and Experimental Medicine (16), and Biochemistry and Molecular Biology (13). These research areas collectively contribute to a comprehensive understanding of flaviviruses. It also helps in developing effective control strategies.

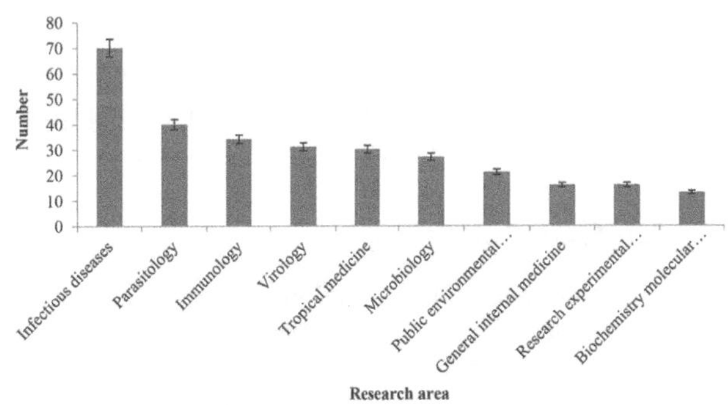

Fig. 62.8 Major research area

ƆNTENT ANALYSIS OF TOP TEN MOST REFERENCED PAPERS

The top ten most cited papers in the field of flaviviruses have been identified. The paper by Gould and Solomon [16] published in The Lancet holds the highest citation count with 548 citations in the WoS Core database. Following closely is the article by Gritsun et al. [17] in Antiviral Research with 419 citations. Other notable papers include those by Grard et al. [18] with 191 citations in Virology, Lasala and Holbrook[19] with 175 citations in Clinical Laboratory Medicine, and Kuhn et al. [20] with 158 citations in Archives of Virology. The list also includes papers by Mackenzie and Williams [21] with 144 citations in Zoonoses and Public Health, Hubálek et al. [22] with 141 citations in Advances in Virus Research, Pattnaik [23] with 130 citations in Reviews in Medical Virology, Mansfield et al. [24] with 112 citations in Frontiers in Cellular and Infection Microbiology, and Dobler [25] with 111 citations in Veterinary Microbiology.

Research on Flaviviruses has been gaining momentum in the last twenty years, with a significant increase in the incidence of tick-borne flaviviral diseases. The top ten most referenced papers in this field focus on understanding the genetic makeup, transmission patterns, and diseases caused by these viruses. Additionally, studies have concentrated on providing comprehensive reviews of arboviruses that impact warm-blooded animals.

Recent findings have also shed light on the emergence of new variants, such as Alkhurmahemorrhagic fever virus (AHFV), which shares 89% sequence homology with Kyasanur Forest disease virus. Furthermore, homology modeling of the KFDV envelope protein suggests a common mechanism of virus-cell fusion shared with other flaviviruses. However, despite the routine use of vaccines, cases of KFD have risen in Karnataka state from 1999 to 2005, indicating that the vaccine's efficacy may be insufficient. Overall, the trend of research on Flaviviruses highlights the need for continued surveillance, improved vaccine development, and increased awareness.

13. CONCLUSION

This scientometric investigation reveals significant growth in Kyasanur Forest Disease Virus (KFDV) research since the early 2000s, with increased focus during the COVID-19 pandemic. India leads research, with contributions from the Indian Journal of Medical Research and ICMR-NIV. The research spans infectious diseases, virology, parasitology, and immunology, highlighting global collaboration. Citation analysis shows key studies' impact, with emerging viruses like Chittor, Monkeypox, Zika, and Nipah expected to be further analyzed through scientometrics and bibliometrics.

References

1. Ganguly, A., Banerjee, A., Mandal, A., Khan, M.A. and Das Mohapatra, P.K. (2019). Isolation and characterization of bacteria from the intestine of *Clarias batrachus* for probiotic organism. Proc. Zool. Soc., 72(4), 411–419. https://doi.org/10.1007/s12595-018-0283-x
2. Chattaraj, S., Ganguly, A., Mandal, A. and Das Mohapatra, P.K. (2022). A review of the role of probiotics for the control of viral diseases in aquaculture. Aquac. Int. https://doi.org/10.1007/s10499-022-00915-6
3. Das, S., Sinha, D., Chatterji, S., Ganguly, A., De, A., Majgaonkar, A., Kazi, Z., Maurya, A. K., Sohail, M., & Bhat, N. (2025). The role of marine bacteria-derived bioactive compounds in COVID-19 management. In *Anti-coronavirus marine bioactive compounds* (Chapter 7, pp. 185–224). Apple Academic Press.
4. Rastogi, M. and Singh, S.K. (2017). Kyasanur Forest Disease. In: Singh, S.K. (ed.) *Emerging and Re-emerging Infectious Diseases of Livestock*, 373–386. Springer. https://doi.org/10.1007/978-3-319-68493-2_12
5. Mehla, R., Kumar, S.R., Yadav, P., Barde, P.V., Yergolkar, P.N., Erickson, B.R., Carroll, S.A., Mishra, A.C., Nichol, S.T. and Mourya, D.T. (2009). Recent ancestry of Kyasanur Forest disease virus. *Emerg. Infect. Dis.*, 15(9), 1431–1437. https://doi.org/10.3201/eid1509.080759
6. Ganguly, A., Mahapatra, S., Ray, S. et al. (2025). The rising threat of Nipah virus: a highly contagious and deadly zoonotic pathogen. *Virol. J.*, 22, 139. https://doi.org/10.1186/s12985-025-02728-4
7. Ganguly, A., Konar, U., Kundu, A., Ghosh, S., Chatterjee, I., Nad, S., Chatterjee, S., Nandi, S., Singha, S. and Kali, S. (2020). The prevalence, preventive measures, and economic impact of pandemic COVID-19 in India: The initial phase. *Acta Biol. Szeged.*, 64(1), 43–61. https://doi.org/10.14232/abs.2020.1.43-61
8. Holbrook, M.R. (2012). Kyasanur forest disease. *Antiviral Res.*, 96(3), 353–362. https://doi.org/10.1016/j.antiviral.2012.10.005
9. Work, T.H. and Trapido, H. (1957). Kyasanur Forest disease. A new virus disease in India. Summary of preliminary report of investigations of the virus research centre on an epidemic disease affecting forest villagers and wild monkeys of Shimoga District, Mysore. *Indian J. Med. Sci.*, 11(5), 341–342.
10. Trapido, H., Rajagopalan, P.K., Work, T.H. and Varma, M.G. (1959). Kyasanur Forest disease. VIII. Isolation of Kyasanur Forest disease virus from naturally infected ticks of the genus *Haemaphysalis*. *Indian J. Med. Res.*, 47(2), 133–138. PMID: 13653739
11. Dodd, K.A., Bird, B.H., Khristova, M.L., Albariño, C.G., Carroll, S.A., et al. (2011). Ancient ancestry of KFDV and AHFV revealed by complete genome analyses of viruses isolated from ticks and mammalian hosts. *PLoSNegl. Trop. Dis.*, 5(10), e1352. https://doi.org/10.1371/journal.pntd.0001352
12. Yadav, P.D., Patil, S., Jadhav, S.M., et al. (2020). Phylogeography of Kyasanur Forest Disease virus in India (1957–2017) reveals evolution and spread in the Western Ghats region. *Sci. Rep.*, 10, 1966. https://doi.org/10.1038/s41598-020-58242-w

13. Bhatia, B., Tang-Huau, T.L., Feldmann, F., Hanley, P.W., Rosenke, R., Shaia, C., Marzi, A. and Feldmann, H. (2023). Single-dose VSV-based vaccine protects against Kyasanur Forest disease in nonhuman primates. *Sci. Adv.*, 9(36), eadj1428. https://doi.org/10.1126/sciadv.adj1428
14. Ganguly, A., Kirtania, D. K., Chhetri, M., & Chattaraj, S. (2025). Sustainable development through probiotics: A scientometric analysis of Indian research and innovation. *Discover Sustainability, 6*, Article 455. https://doi.org/10.1007/s43621-025-01263-0
15. Mitra, D., Nachhmin, B., Ganguly, A. and Das Mohapatra, P.K. (2022). Computational approach to assess mucormycosis: A systematic review. In *Computational Intelligence in Healthcare Applications*, 71–85. Academic Press. https://doi.org/10.1016/B978-0-323-99031-8.00004-1
16. Gould, E.A. and Solomon, T. (2008). Pathogenic flaviviruses. *Lancet*, 371(9611), 500–509. https://doi.org/10.1016/S0140-6736(08)60238-X
17. Gritsun, T.S., Lashkevich, V.A. and Gould, E.A. (2003). Tick-borne encephalitis. *Antiviral Res.*, 57(1–2), 129–146. https://doi.org/10.1016/s0166-3542(02)00206-1
18. Grard, G., Moureau, G., Charrel, R.N., Lemasson, J.J., Gonzalez, J.P., Gallian, P., Gritsun, T.S., Holmes, E.C., Gould, E.A. and de Lamballerie, X. (2007). Genetic characterization of tick-borne flaviviruses: new insights into evolution, pathogenetic determinants and taxonomy. *Virology*, 361(1), 80–92. https://doi.org/10.1016/j.virol.2006.09.015
19. Lasala, P.R. and Holbrook, M. (2010). Tick-borne flaviviruses. *Clin. Lab. Med.*, 30(1), 221–235. https://doi.org/10.1016/j.cll.2010.01.002
20. Kuhn, J.H., Adkins, S., Alioto, D., Alkhovsky, S.V., Amarasinghe, G.K., Anthony, S.J., Avšič-Županc, T., Ayllón, M.A., Bahl, J., Balkema-Buschmann, A., et al. (2020). 2020 taxonomic update for phylum Negarnaviricota (Riboviria: Orthornavirae), including the large orders Bunyavirales and Mononegavirales. *Arch. Virol.*, 165(12), 3023–3072. https://doi.org/10.1007/s00705-020-04731-2
21. Mackenzie, J.S. and Williams, D.T. (2009). The zoonotic flaviviruses of southern, south-eastern and eastern Asia, and Australasia: the potential for emergent viruses. *Zoonoses Public Health*, 56(6–7), 338–356. https://doi.org/10.1111/j.1863-2378.2008.01208.x
22. Hubálek, Z., Rudolf, I. and Nowotny, N. (2014). Arboviruses pathogenic for domestic and wild animals. *Adv. Virus Res.*, 89, 201–275. https://doi.org/10.1016/B978-0-12-800172-1.00005-7
23. Pattnaik, P. (2006). Kyasanur forest disease: an epidemiological view in India. *Rev. Med. Virol.*, 16(3), 151–165. https://doi.org/10.1002/rmv.495
24. Mansfield, K.L., Jizhou, L., Phipps, L.P. and Johnson, N. (2017). Emerging tick-borne viruses in the twenty-first century. *Front. Cell. Infect. Microbiol.*, 7, 298. https://doi.org/10.3389/fcimb.2017.00298
25. Dobler, G. (2010). Zoonotic tick-borne flaviviruses. *Vet. Microbiol.*, 140(3–4), 221–228. https://doi.org/10.1016/j.vetmic.2009.08.024

Note: All figures and tables have been prepared by the authors based on the analyzed data and findings of the present study.

For Product Safety Concerns and Information please contact our EU representative GPSR@taylorandfrancis.com Taylor & Francis Verlag GmbH, Kaufingerstraße 24, 80331 München, Germany